American Government and Politics Today

The Essentials
2011–2012 Edition

Barbara A. Bardes
Mack C. Shelley II
Steffen W. Schmidt
William Earl Maxwell
Ernest Crain
Adolfo Santos
Albert C. Waite

Central Texas College Edition

Australia • Brazil • Japan • Korea • Mexico • Singapore • Spain • United Kingdom • United States

American Government and Politics Today
THE ESSENTIALS Central Texas College Edition
2011–2012

**Bardes • Shelley • Schmidt •
Maxwell • Crain • Santos • Waite**

Publisher: Suzanne Jeans

Executive Editor: Carolyn Merrill

Associate Development Editor: Katherine Hayes

Assistant Editor: Laura Ross

Editorial Assistant: Angela Hodge

Marketing Manager: Lydia LeStar

Marketing Communications Manager: Heather Baxley

Senior Content Production Manager: Ann Borman

Print Buyer: Fola Orekoya

Photo Research: Ann Hoffman, Anne Sheroff

Copy Editor: Mary Berry

Proofreader: Judy Kiviat

Indexer: Terry Casey

Art Director: Linda Helcher

Interior Design: IRDG

Cover Design: PHodepohl Design

Compositor: Parkwood Composition Service

Library of Congress Control Number: 2011928095

Student Edition ISBN-13: 978-1-111-83626-9
Student Edition ISBN-10: 1-111-83626-4

Wadsworth Political Science
25 Thomson Place
Boston, MA 02210

Cengage Learning products are represented in Canada by
Nelson Education, Ltd.

For your course and learning solutions, visit **academic.cengage.com**.
Purchase any of our products at your local college store or at our preferred online store at **www.ichapters.com**.

Printed in the United States of America

1 2 3 4 5 6 7 15 14 13 12 11

CONTENTS IN BRIEF

CONTENTS

Part I: The American System

AP Photo/Chuck Burton

(Jean Léon Gerome Ferris/The Granger Collection)

Part II: Civil Rights and Liberties

Part III: People and Politics

(AP Photo/Seth Perlman)

CHAPTER 9 Campaigns, Elections, and the Media 284

(AP Photo/The Temple Daily Telegram, Rusty Schramm)

Part IV: Political Institutions

CHAPTER 10 The Congress 332

CHAPTER 11 The President 368

(AP Photo/Pat Wellenbach)

(Larry Downing/Reuters/Landov)

(Alex Wong/Getty Images)

Part VI: Texas Politics

(Al Braden 2007)

(AP Photo/Corpus Christi Caller-Times, Todd Yates)

CHAPTER 20 Voting and Elections in Texas 638

(AP Photo/Houston Chronicle, Brett Coomer)

Chapter 21 The Texas Legislature 674

(AP Photo/LM Otero)

CHAPTER 22 The Texas Executive Branch 704

Chapter 23 The Texas Judiciary, Law, and Due Process 730

(AP Photo/Tony Gutierrez)

PREFACE

We are pleased to present the 2011–2012 Central Texas College edition of *American Government and Politics Today: The Essentials.* 2009 and 2010 were historic years—they were the first two years when the United States had its first African American president. They were marked by the ongoing Great Recession. They were years during which a major sector in our economy—health care—was transformed in ways that we are still trying to assess. During these two years, the nation also saw an expansion in the federal government in scope, size, and regulation the likes of which had not been seen since the administration of Franklin D. Roosevelt in the 1930s and 1940s.

Finally, these years concluded with one of the most dramatic and consequential midterm elections ever. The Democrats in the House of Representatives lost more seats than any party since 1938. Losses in the Senate were less severe, but the Democrats were still down six senators (and six governors). We analyze in depth the causes of this political turnaround, considering the impact of high unemployment and the perception that the Democrats expanded the role of government to an excessive degree.

2010 ELECTION RESULTS INCLUDED AND ANALYZED

Because we have learned that students respond to up-to-date information about political events, we have included results of the November 2010 elections. We have updated all of the text to reflect these results and have analyzed how the results will affect political processes at all levels of government. In each *Elections 2010* feature, we place the election results in the context of the chapter's subject matter.

THE TEXAS CHAPTERS

As with previous editions of *American Government and Politics Today, Central Texas College Edition,* the Texas chapters cover the major historical, institutional, and cultural factors which continue to shape our state's unique political landscape. As will become evident to users of previous editions, we have made an effort to streamline the Texas chapters to better meet the needs of instructors who must meet the requirements of the state's mandated curriculum.

Toward this end, we have edited the Texas chapters with the following goals in mind: First, the chapters should compliment but not duplicate material from the national government chapters. Second, political analysis and editorial comments have been reduced in favor of a straight description of actors, issues, and institutions. Finally, coverage of some material has been reduced to balance the overall text. This last point is particularly noticeable in the coverage of the Texas governor and the presiding officers of the Texas legislature.

We sincerely hope that this editorial effort has in no way diminished the spirit of the wonderful text the authors have created. *American Government and Politics Today, Central Texas College Edition* 2011-2012 remains a scholarly yet approachable work with a new and refreshing layout. We hope that students will enjoy this effort.—The Editors

THE INTERACTIVE FOCUS OF THIS TEXT–PARTICIPATION

Whether the topic is voter turnout, terrorism, or the problems that face the president, we constantly strive to involve the student in the analysis. We make sure that the student comes to understand that politics is not an abstract process but a very human enterprise. We emphasize how different outcomes can affect students' civil rights and liberties, employment opportunities, and economic welfare.

EMPHASIS ON CRITICAL THINKING

Throughout the text, we encourage the student to think critically. Almost all of the features end with questions designed to engage the student's critical-thinking and analytical skills. A feature titled *Which Side Are You On?* challenges the student to find a connection between controversial issues facing the nation and the student's personal positions on these issues.

END-OF-CHAPTER QUESTIONS FOR DISCUSSION AND ANALYSIS

We continue our tradition of engaging your students with a section titled "Questions for Discussion and Analysis," which appears at the end of each chapter. This section consists of a series of five questions, each of which asks the student to explore a particular issue relating to a topic covered in the chapter.

OTHER INTERACTIVE FEATURES

We further encourage interaction with the political system by ending each chapter with a feature titled *Why Should You Care?,* along with a subsection called *How You Can Make a Difference.* These features show students how to become politically involved and why it is important that they do so.

SPECIAL PEDAGOGY AND FEATURES

The 2011–2012 Central Texas College edition of *American Government and Politics Today: The Essentials* contains many pedagogical aids and high-interest features to assist both students and instructors. The following list summarizes the special elements that can be found in each chapter:

- **The Politics of Boom and Bust**—The nation continues to face severe economic difficulties, so we have provided this feature to show how our government and our citizens have responded to the problems.
- **What If . . .**—A chapter-opening feature that discusses a hypothetical situation concerning a topic covered in the chapter.
- **Margin Definitions**—For all important terms.
- **Did You Know . . . ?**—Margin features presenting various facts and figures that add interest to the learning process.
- **Which Side Are You On?**—A feature designed to challenge students to take a stand on controversial issues.
- **Politics and . . .**—A feature that examines the influence of politics on a variety of issues. Topics range from *Politics and Ideology,* to *Politics and Privacy,* to *Politics and Social Networking.*
- **Beyond Our Borders**—A feature that provides a context for American institutions by looking at the experiences of other countries.
- **Why Should You Care?**—A chapter-ending feature that gives the student some specific reasons why he or she should care about the topics covered in the chapter and provides ways in which she or he can become actively involved in American politics.
- **Questions for Discussion and Analysis**—A series of questions at the end of each chapter that are designed to promote in-class discussions.
- **Key Terms**—A chapter-ending list, with page numbers, of all terms in the chapter that are **boldfaced** in the text and defined in the margins.
- **Chapter Summary**—A point-by-point summary of the chapter text.
- **Selected Print and Media Resources**—An annotated list of suggested scholarly readings as well as popular books, films, and documentaries relevant to chapter topics.
- **E-mocracy**—A feature that discusses politics and the Internet and that offers Web sites and Internet activities related to the chapter's topics.

APPENDICES

Because we know that this book serves as a reference, we have included important documents for the student of American government to have close at hand. A fully annotated copy of the U.S. Constitution appears at the end of Chapter 2, as an appendix to that chapter. In addition, we have included the following appendices:

- The Declaration of Independence.
- How to Read Case Citations and Find Court Decisions.
- *Federalist Papers* Nos. 10, 51, and 78.
- Justices of the United States Supreme Court since 1900.
- Party Control of Congress since 1900.

Useful material is also located immediately inside the front and back covers of this text. Inside the front cover, you will find a pictorial diagram of the Capitol of the United States. Inside the back cover, you will find a cartogram that distorts the size of the various states to indicate their relative weight in the Electoral College.

A COMPREHENSIVE SUPPLEMENTS PACKAGE

We are proud to be the authors of a text that has the most comprehensive, accessible, and fully integrated supplements package on the market. Together, the text and the supplements listed below constitute a total teaching and learning package for you and your students.

At **CengageBrain.com,** students will be able to save up to 60 percent on their course materials through our full spectrum of options. Students will have the option to rent their textbooks or purchase print textbooks, e-textbooks, or individual e-chapters and audio books, all at substantial savings over average retail prices. CengageBrain.com also includes access to Cengage Learning's broad range of homework and study tools, including the student resources discussed here. Follow the URL below or search "Bardes" to access the book-specific resources.

For further information on any of these supplements, contact your Wadsworth, Cengage Learning sales representative.

POLITICAL THEATRE DVD 2.0

Bring politics home to students with Political Theatre 2.0, up to date through the 2008 election season. This is the second edition of this three-DVD series and includes real video clips that show American political thought throughout the public sector. Clips include both classic and contemporary political advertisements, speeches, interviews, and more. Available to adopters of Cengage textbooks, version 2.0 provides lots of added functionality with this updated edition.

JOININ™ ON TURNING POINT® FOR POLITICAL THEATRE

For even more interaction, combine Political Theatre with the innovative teaching tool of a classroom response system through JoinIn™. Poll your students with questions created for you or create your own questions. Built within the Microsoft® PowerPoint® software, it's easy to integrate into your current lectures in conjunction with the "clicker" hardware of your choice.

THE WADSWORTH NEWS VIDEOS FOR AMERICAN GOVERNMENT 2012 DVD

This collection of three- to six-minute video clips on relevant political issues serves as a great lecture or discussion launcher.

GREAT SPEECHES COLLECTION

Throughout the ages, great orators have stepped up to the podium and used their communication skills to persuade, inform, and inspire their audiences. Studying these speeches can provide tremendous insight into historical, political, and cultural events. The Great Speeches Collection includes the full text of more than sixty memorable orations for you to incorporate into your course. Speeches can be collated in a printed reader to supplement your existing course materials or bound into a core textbook.

ABC VIDEO: SPEECHES BY PRESIDENT BARACK OBAMA

This DVD presents nine famous speeches by President Barack Obama, from 2004 through his inauguration, including his speech at the 2004 Democratic National Convention; his 2008 speech on race, "A More Perfect Union"; and his 2009 inaugural address. Speeches are divided into short video segments for easy, time-efficient viewing. This instructor supplement also features critical-thinking questions and answers for each speech, designed to spark classroom discussion.

ELECTION 2010: AN AMERICAN GOVERNMENT SUPPLEMENT

Written by John Clark and Brian Schaffner, this booklet addresses the 2010 congressional and gubernatorial races, with both real-time analysis and references.

AMERICAN GOVERNMENT COURSEREADER: POLITICS IN CONTEXT

American Government CourseReader: Politics in Context will enable instructors to create a customized reader. Using a database of hundreds of documents, readings, and videos, instructors can search by various criteria or browse the collection, to preview and then select a customized collection to assign their students. The sources will be edited to an appropriate length and include pedagogical support—a headnote describing the document and critical-thinking and multiple-choice questions to verify that the student has read and understood the selection. Students will be able to take notes, highlight, and print content. CourseReader allows the instructor to select exactly what students will be assigned with an easy-to-use interface and also provides an easily used assessment tool. The sources can be delivered online or in print format.

THE OBAMA PRESIDENCY–YEAR ONE SUPPLEMENT

Much happens in the first year of a presidency, especially a historic one like that of Barack Obama. This full-color sixteen-page supplement by Kenneth Janda, Jeffrey Berry, and Jerry Goldman analyzes such issues as health care, the economy and the stimulus package, changes in the United States Supreme Court, and the effects Obama's policies have had on global affairs.

FOR USERS OF THE PREVIOUS EDITION

We thank you for your past support of our work. We have made numerous changes to this volume for the 2011–2012 edition, many of which we list below. We have rewritten the text as necessary, added many new features, and updated the book to reflect the events of the past two years.

- **Chapter 1 (The Democratic Republic)**—All the features in this chapter are new. The pervasiveness of government is demonstrated in a new section. We have revised the section on "big government" based on recent developments, including the Tea Party movement. A new *Politics of Boom and Bust* feature provides additional Tea Party coverage. Definitions of liberalism and conservatism are updated and use attitudes toward health-care reform as examples. A final section describes the current political scene—disillusionment with the parties, and at the same time, extreme partisanship.

- **Chapter 2 (The Constitution)**—The chapter-opening *What If . . .* feature examines possible alternatives to the Electoral College. Another new feature asks: *Just How Christian Were the Founders?* Recent United States Supreme Court rulings on firearms are described in a *Which Side Are You On?* feature. Throughout the text, the *Beyond Our Borders* feature is shorter but now appears in almost all chapters. In this chapter, it provides a basic description of the parliamentary system.
- **Chapter 3 (Federalism)**—*The Politics of Boom and Bust* feature describes the procyclical nature of state spending in a recession. In the text, we take note of how the National Guard is now used in wartime. *A Politics and . . . Education* feature looks at the No Child Left Behind legislation. Finally, a new *E-mocracy* feature explains how to find court cases online.
- **Chapter 4 (Civil Liberties)**—New sections describe the issues of religious displays on public property and the tax treatment of religious organizations. The death penalty section now covers methods of execution. The material on abortion is updated. The *Beyond Our Borders* feature looks at Britain's egregious libel laws.
- **Chapter 5 (Civil Rights)**—Native Americans receive new coverage in the feature *The Politics of . . . History: Were Native Americans Victims of Genocide?* Sections on the political participation of minority group members and women are updated, as is the material on same-sex marriage. We note recent developments concerning the Americans with Disabilities Act.
- **Chapter 6 (Public Opinion and Political Socialization)**—Public reaction to the AIG bailout is the new example of the power of popular opinion. The text adds substantial information on new media, including talk radio, cable television, blogs, and social networking sites such as Facebook. Material on the influence of demographic variables is updated. The section on the limits of relying on polling data when making policy now uses the health-care reform legislation as an example.
- **Chapter 7 (Interest Groups)**—We describe *Citizens United v. Federal Election Commission,* the U.S. Supreme Court ruling that independent expenditures by corporations and other organizations is constitutionally protected free speech. The text also looks at the policies of the Obama administration toward lobbyists.
- **Chapter 8 (Political Parties)**—The text now describes the recent loss of support by the Democratic Party and also updates earlier material on the loss of support by the Republicans through 2008. We examine how the Republican Party has changed under the Obama administration and consider the impact of the Tea Party movement. The *Which Side Are You On?* feature asks: *Are the Parties Becoming Too Radical?* We include new content on political polarization and on independents. For a look at the reality behind recent political rhetoric, we include the feature *Beyond Our Borders: The Real Socialists.*
- **Chapter 9 (Campaigns, Elections, and the Media)**—A feature now asks: *What If . . . There Were No Newspapers?* We provide more detail on *Citizens United v. Federal Election Commission.* The description of types of primary elections is more thorough. The media section provides more material on the troubles of the traditional press, and also more on how candidates have made use of the Internet. The section on press bias is updated and expanded.
- **Chapter 10 (The Congress)**—We have added substantial material on the Senate filibuster, including a description of how the practice affected the health-care legislative process. In addition to a *Which Side Are You On?* feature on the filibuster, we provide international context with *Beyond Our Borders: The Exceptional Power of the U.S. Senate.* New language explains how budgets are handled in presidential election years. The *Politics of Boom and Bust* feature focuses on the issue of federal budget deficits.
- **Chapter 11 (The President)**—Our account of signing statements is now based on the most recent research. *Politics and . . . Terrorism: George W. Obama* examines the surprising continuity between the current administration and its predecessor. We look

at Obama's views on domestic reform in *The Politics of Boom and Bust: The Audacity of Barack Obama.* The sections on presidential popularity and on the president's use of social networking media are updated.

- **Chapter 12 (The Bureaucracy)**—*The Politics of Boom and Bust* provides a look at Keynesianism and its critics, so this important topic is addressed well before the domestic policy chapter. We include new language on regulation, and the feature *Politics and . . . National Security* observes that *Bureaucrats Can't Protect Us from Every Threat.* New sections describe government-owned or -backed corporations in much greater detail.
- **Chapter 13 (The Courts)**—The sections that describe recent rulings by the Supreme Court are completely revised. A new section provides more ample coverage of *habeas corpus* and the Guantánamo prison issue. We discuss more completely the troubles that presidents have had in getting their judicial appointments through the Senate. New features of interest include *Which Side Are You On? Should State Judges Be Elected? and The Politics of Boom and Bust: The Constitutionality of Obamacare.*
- **Chapter 14 (Domestic and Economic Policy)**—This chapter is almost entirely rewritten, and now focuses on issues in dispute during the Obama years. The policymaking process uses the bank bailout bill of 2008 as an example. A matching feature is *The Politics of Boom and Bust: Bailouts and the Danger of Moral Hazard.* The extensive section on health-care reform is now thoroughly up to date. We have also updated the material on immigration. A new section, "Energy and the Environment," examines our dependence on foreign oil, the global warming debate, proposed energy legislation, and the BP oil spill in the Gulf of Mexico. The economics sections contain more information on unemployment, inflation, and monetary policy during recessions.
- **Chapter 15 (Foreign Policy)**—The section on terrorism is updated based on recent research. The material on Afghanistan is expanded and updated, and the Iraq section describes the American withdrawal. *Politics and . . . Social Networking: Tipping Off the Troops* provides an interesting glimpse of our men and women in uniform. We update coverage of U.S. relations with Iran, North Korea, China, and Russia. The section on the Israeli–Palestinian dispute is up to date. A new section on U.S. humanitarian efforts abroad uses the earthquake in Haiti as an example.
- **Chapter 16 (Texas History and Culture)**—Significant new coverage of the Texas civil rights movements complements the discussion of diversity, including Latino and African American participation in Texas politics.
- **Chapter 17 (The Texas Constitution)**—Includes updates to data showing how Texas's constitution compares to other states and new decisions about the constitutional right to keep and bear arms and the gun control debate.
- **Chapter 18 (Texas Interest Groups)**—Incorporates new discussions on selective incentives; conflicts of interest, using the HPV vaccine debate as an example; and a new list from the National Institute on Money in State Politics identifying the major industries in Texas by the amount of money they contribute.
- **Chapter 19 (Political Parties in Texas)**—Fresh sections describe the changes and significance of the Texas presidential primaries and the problems of the Texas Democratic caucuses.
- **Chapter 20 (Voting and Elections in Texas)**—The chapter includes new data on elections and campaign spending and incorporates recent changes in election law.
- **Chapter 21 (The Texas Legislature)**—Offers an expanded look at the role of race and gender in the membership of the Texas legislature. A new discussion about Tom Craddick as Speaker of the House is included, and two new tables help clarify the different types of committees and list the substantive and procedural standing committees in the Texas legislature.

- **Chapter 22 (The Texas Executive Branch)**—Contains a new discussion of the executive branch's quasi-judicial and quasi-legislative functions and revised discussions of the attorney general's role and the iron Texas star.
- **Chapter 23 (The Texas Judiciary, Law, and Due Process)**—A revised "What If . . . Texas Abolished the Death Penalty?" box includes the latest developments in the debate about capital punishment.
- **Chapter 24 (Texas Public Policy)**—A new "What If . . . Texas Required Individuals to Have Health Insurance?" box presents some of the most significant issues in the raging health-care debate. Recent data on Texas's regressive tax structure helps students understand their tax burdens. An expanded section about the history and recent trends in public education acquaints students with current developments in state schools.
- **Chapter 25 (Local Government)**—Includes an updated look at population trends and a strengthened discussion of how issues of national importance are also highly relevant to local governments, with new examples from a wide range of municipalities, counties, and special districts. An interesting discussion about the Democratic primary and caucuses in 2008 between Senators Obama and Clinton is also included.

In preparing this Texas edition of *American Government and Politics Today,* we were the beneficiaries of the expert guidance of a skilled and dedicated team of publishers and editors. We would like, first of all, to thank Publisher, Suzanne Jeans, for the support she has shown for this project. We have benefited greatly from the supervision and encouragement given by Carolyn Merrill, executive editor; Katherine Hayes, Associate Development Editor, and Laura Ross, Assistant Editor.

We are very grateful to Professor Rebecca Deen of the University of Texas at Arlington for her thoughtful suggestions and for her substantial contributions to this edition. Rebecca Green, our developmental editors also deserves our thanks for managing many details of project development. We are also indebted to editorial assistant Angela Hodge for her contributions to this project.

We are grateful to our content production managers Ann Borman and Ann Hoffman for making it possible to get the text out on time. In addition, our gratitude goes to all of those who worked on the various supplements offered with this text, especially Laura Hildebrand, who coordinates the Web site. We would also like to thank Lydia LeStar, marketing manager, for her tremendous efforts in marketing the text.

Any errors remain our own. We welcome comments from instructors and students alike. Suggestions that we have received in the past have helped us to improve this text and to adapt it to the changing needs of instructors and students.

STEFFEN SCHMIDT • MACK SHELLEY • BARBARA BARDES •
WILLIAM EARL MAXWELL • ERNEST CRAIN • ADOLFO SANTOS •
ALBERT C. WAITE

ABOUT THE AUTHORS

BARBARA A. BARDES

Barbara A. Bardes is a professor of political science at the University of Cincinnati. She received her bachelor of arts degree and master of arts degree from Kent State University. After completing her Ph.D. at the University of Cincinnati, she held faculty positions at Mississippi State University and Loyola University in Chicago. She returned to the University of Cincinnati as dean of one of its colleges. She has also worked as a political consultant and directed polling for a research center.

MACK C. SHELLEY II

Mack C. Shelley II is professor of political science, professor of statistics, and director of the Research Institute for Studies in Education at Iowa State University. After receiving his bachelor's degree from American University in Washington, D.C., he completed graduate studies at the University of Wisconsin at Madison, where he received a master's degree in economics and a Ph.D. in political science. He taught for two years at Mississippi State University before arriving at Iowa State in 1979.

STEFFEN W. SCHMIDT

Steffen W. Schmidt is a professor of political science at Iowa State University. He grew up in Colombia, South America, and studied in Colombia, Switzerland, and France. He obtained his Ph.D. from Columbia University, New York, in public law and government.

WILLIAM EARL MAXWELL

William Earl Maxwell is a professor emeritus at San Antonio College, where he has taught courses in U.S. and Texas government since 1971. San Antonio College is a teaching institution, and throughout his career Maxwell has focused on innovative teaching techniques and improving the teaching and learning environments for the students at the college.

ERNEST CRAIN

Ernest Crain has been in the political science department at San Antonio College for 35 years. He received his B.A. and M.A. degrees from the University of Texas at Austin. His specializations are political party competition, comparative state politics, and Texas public policy.

ADOLFO SANTOS

Adolfo Santos is the chair of the Department of Social Sciences at the University of Houston-Downtown and Associate Professor of Political Science. Dr. Santos received a Ph.D. from the University of Houston in 1998. He is the author of *Do Members of Congress Reward Their Future Employers? Evaluating the Revolving Door Syndrome.* He also writes about Hispanic representation in the U.S. Congress and the Texas legislature.

ALBERT C. WALTE

Albert C. Waite is a professor of political and social science at Central Texas College in Killeen Texas. He received his M.A. degree in history from Niagara University and has completed post-graduate work in government at the University of Texas at Austin. Waite is also a graduate of the Defense Language Institute in Monterrey, California and worked at the National Security Agency while serving in the Army Security Agency from 1968–1978. He was a recipient of the Central Texas Education Network Excellence in Higher Education Award (1998), was a Minnie Stevens Piper Professor nominee (1997–98) and was awarded the CTC Faculty Senate Professional Development Award (1994–95).

OTHER MEMBERS OF THE TEXAS TEAM

Elizabeth N. Flores is a professor of political science at Del Mar College in Corpus Christi. She received her M.A. degree from the University of Michigan. Flores has served as a director of the Corpus Christi Regional Transit Authority, written on politics for the Corpus Christi *Caller-Times,* and co-hosted a public affairs show on PBS.

Joseph Ignagni is a professor of political science at the University of Texas at Arlington, where he has received four teaching awards and served as an associate dean. Ignagni received a Ph.D. from Michigan State University. He has published articles in the *American Journal of Political Science, Political Research Quarterly, American Politics Quarterly, and Judicature.*

Cynthia Opheim is a professor of political science at Texas State University-San Marcos. Opheim received a Ph.D. from the University of Texas at Austin. She has published in the *Legislative Studies Quarterly, State and Local Government Review,* and *Public Administration Review.* She co-authored *State and Local Politics: The Individual and the Governments.* In 2003, she became president of the Southwestern Political Science Association (SWPSA).

Christopher Wlezien is a professor of political science at Temple University in Philadelphia and received a Ph.D. from the University of Iowa. Wlezien has published in the *American Journal of Political Science, British Journal of Political Science, Journal of Politics, Political Analysis,* and *Public Opinion Quarterly.* He is co-editor of the *Journal of Elections, Public Opinion and Parties,* and of the "Polls" section of *Public Opinion Quarterly,* and has edited the books *The Future of Election Studies* and *Britain Votes.* In 2004, he became president of the SWPSA.

chapter
1

The Democratic Republic

chapter contents

Politics and Government

Government Is Everywhere

Why Is Government Necessary?

Democracy and Other Forms of Government

What Kind of Democracy Do We Have?

Fundamental Values

Political Ideologies

One Nation, Divided

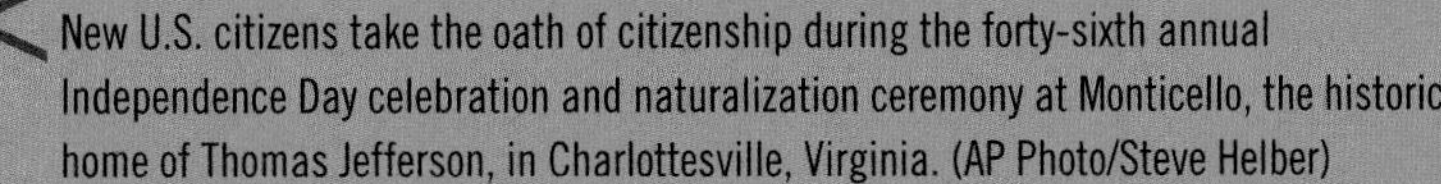

New U.S. citizens take the oath of citizenship during the forty-sixth annual Independence Day celebration and naturalization ceremony at Monticello, the historic home of Thomas Jefferson, in Charlottesville, Virginia. (AP Photo/Steve Helber)

WHAT IF... ...national laws were put to a popular vote?

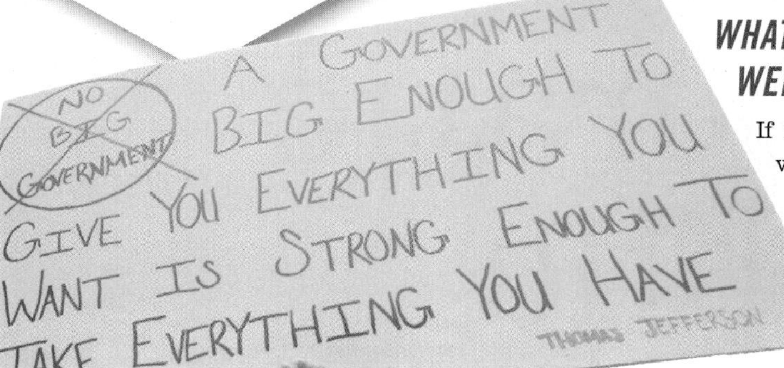

Protesters often express their views outside meetings of political groups, as shown here in Indianapolis, Indiana. What is this person protesting? (AP Photo/ Tom Strickland)

BACKGROUND

The United States is a democratic republic, or a *representative democracy.* In a representative democracy, the people elect representatives who make the laws. Governors and presidents are elected to carry out these laws. Representative democracy is not the only possible democratic system. An alternative is *direct democracy,* in which the people, rather than their representatives, make decisions. In ancient Greece, in the city of Athens, the citizens of the entire city gathered together in an assembly to make laws, to declare war, and to decide important issues.

Such an assembly is clearly not possible in a large country. But what if citizens could cast votes in elections on issues of national policy? After all, such votes are common at the state level. Depending on state law, citizens can vote for new laws in a number of ways. In a *referendum,* the legislature submits an issue to the voters. In an *initiative,* the voters themselves put an issue on the ballot by collecting a specified number of signatures. Some states, in addition, allow *recall elections,* in which the voters can remove elected officials before their terms of office expire.

WHAT IF NATIONAL LAWS WERE PUT TO A POPULAR VOTE?

If national laws were put to a popular vote, citizens would have a much more direct voice in government. Today, for example, public opinion polls indicate that a sizable number of Americans support the use of marijuana for medical purposes. If voters approved such use in a national initiative or referendum, medical marijuana would be legal in all states.

Under current law, the United States Supreme Court would surely hold that such national votes violate the U.S. Constitution, but the Constitution could be amended to allow them.

A LACK OF DELIBERATION

Giving voters more say on legislation could lead to some serious problems. For one thing, voters might not explore fully the consequences of their decisions. Before passing legislation, Congress normally looks at the possible ramifications. Congress often consults with federal agencies that have expertise in the relevant area. In contrast, few voters could take the time or would have the resources to assess the trade-offs involved in a particular issue.

If a spending proposal were put to a referendum, the voters would not be able to evaluate the impact of the proposal on the overall federal budget. Furthermore, the national government does not have to balance its budget as most state governments are required to by their constitutions. Voters in a national referendum could thus authorize new spending without raising taxes (or cut taxes without reducing spending), pushing the federal government further into debt.

Even under current conditions, members of Congress who refuse to approve tax increases face off against other members who refuse to accept cuts in spending. As a result, taxes don't rise, spending never drops, and the federal government's long-term budget outlook gets gloomier and gloomier. Many believe that if voters had the power to set national tax levels and spending on federal programs, future U.S. budget deficits would be even larger than they are now.

FOR CRITICAL ANALYSIS

1. If Congress could refer issues to a vote of the people, what kinds of issues do you think it might put to a vote?
2. If the people instead of Congress decided an issue, how might the people vote differently than Congress?

Politics, for many people, is the "great game"—better than soccer, better than chess. Scores may only be tallied every two years, at elections, but the play continues at all times. The game, furthermore, is played for high stakes. Politics can affect what you spend. It can determine what you can legally do in your spare time. In worst-case circumstances, it can even threaten your life. Few topics are so entertaining—and so important. How did the great game turn out in the elections held on November 2, 2010? We address that question in the *Elections 2010* feature on the following page.

In our democratic republic, ordinary citizens have an important role to play by voting and by participating in other ways. In many states, voters not only choose elected officials to make laws and administer the government, but they can also vote directly on state laws. Would it be a good idea if the people could vote directly on laws at the national level? We examined that question in the *What If . . .* feature that opened this chapter.

Although voting is extremely important, it is only one of the ways that citizens can exercise their political influence. Americans can also join a political organization or interest group, stage a protest, or donate funds to a political campaign or cause. There are countless ways to become involved. Informed participation begins with knowledge, however, and this text aims to provide you with a strong foundation in American government and politics. We hope that this book helps introduce you to a lifetime of political awareness and activity.

did you know?

That the Greek philosopher Aristotle favored enlightened authoritarianism over democracy, which to him meant mob rule.

Politics and Government

What is politics? **Politics** can be understood as the process of resolving conflicts and deciding, as political scientist Harold Lasswell put it in his classic definition, "who gets what, when, and how."[1] More specifically, politics is the struggle over power or influence within organizations or informal groups that can grant or withhold benefits or privileges.

We can identify many such groups and organizations. In families, all members may meet to decide on values, priorities, and actions. Wherever there is a community that makes decisions through formal or informal rules, politics exists. For example, when a church decides to construct a new building or hire a new minister, the decision may be made politically. Politics can be found in schools, social groups, and any other organized collection of people. Of all the organizations that are controlled by political activity, however, the most important is the government.

What is the government? Certainly, it is an **institution**—that is, an ongoing organization that performs certain functions for society. An institution has a life separate from the lives of the individuals who are part of it at any given moment in time. The **government** can be defined as an institution in which decisions are made that resolve conflicts or allocate benefits and privileges. The government is also the preeminent institution within society. It is unique because it has the ultimate authority for making decisions and establishing political values.

Politics
The process of resolving conflicts and deciding "who gets what, when, and how." More specifically, politics is the struggle over power or influence within organizations or informal groups that can grant or withhold benefits or privileges.

Institution
An ongoing organization that performs certain functions for society.

Government
The preeminent institution within society in which decisions are made that resolve conflicts or allocate benefits and privileges. It is unique because it has the ultimate authority for making decisions and establishing political values.

Government Is Everywhere

The government is even more important than politics. Many people largely ignore politics, but it is impossible to ignore government. It is everywhere, like the water you drink and the air you breathe. Both the air and water, by the way, are subject to government pollution standards. The food you eat comes from an agricultural industry that is heavily regulated and

1. Harold Lasswell, *Politics: Who Gets What, When, and How* (New York: McGraw-Hill, 1936).

subsidized by the government. Step outside your residence, and almost immediately you will walk down a government-owned street or drive on a government-owned highway.

From Your Birth

The county government records your birth. Your toys, crib, and baby food must meet government safety standards. After a few years, you'll start school, and 89 percent of all children attend public—which is to say, government—schools. Some children attend private schools or are home schooled, but their education must also meet government standards. Public school students spend many hours in an environment designed and managed by teachers and other government employees. If you get into trouble, you'll meet government employees you'd rather not see: the police, court employees, or even jail staff.

Through Your Life

Most young people look forward eagerly to receiving their government-issued driver's license. Many join the military on graduating from high school, and for those who do, every minute of the next several years will be 100 percent government issue. (That's why we call soldiers *GIs.*) A majority of young adults attend college at some point, and if you are reading this textbook, you are probably one of them. Many private colleges and universities exist, but 74 percent of all college students attend public institutions. Even most private universities are heavily dependent on government support.

In nearly all states, you began paying sales taxes from the moment you had your own funds to spend. Some of those funds are made up of currency issued by the government. When you enter the workforce, you'll begin paying substantial payroll and income taxes to the government. If, like most people, you are an employee, government regulations will set many of your working conditions. You might even work for the government itself—17 percent of employees do. If you are unfortunate enough to lose a job or fall into poverty, government programs will lend you a hand.

ELECTIONS 2010

REPUBLICAN RESURGENCE

For months, pundits had predicted that 2010 would be a Republican year. In November, these predictions came true. A provisional net total of sixty-four seats in the House of Representatives switched from the Democrats to the Republicans. Through 2010, the Democrats enjoyed a 255-to-180 majority. As of 2011, the Republican majority was 243 to 192. In the Senate, six seats switched parties, reducing the Democratic majority from fifty-nine to fifty-three. The Democrats also lost a net total of six governorships and a large number of state legislatures. Indeed, Republicans picked up at least a record 680 state legislative seats, exceeding the previous record of 628 seats picked up by Democrats in 1974. In at least five states, Republicans took the majority in both legislative chambers. Voter turnout among Republicans was way up, though it was also slightly above average among Democrats. Experts considered it inevitable that the Democrats would lose seats because the party in power is almost always punished when the economy is depressed and unemployment is high. In addition, unlike 2008, Democratic candidates were not able to "hold onto the coat-tails" of a popular presidential candidate. According to models developed by political scientists, those factors alone would have won the Republicans at least forty seats in the House.

Exit polls confirmed that independents, in particular, also turned against the Democrats because they believed that the party was doing too much and expanding the size of government. Given that much of what the Democrats had done—leaving aside health care—had been aimed at combating the effects of the recession, party leaders felt that they were in something of a double-bind. For the voters, however, such arguments did not matter.

To Your Death

Later in life, you may have health problems. One way or another, the government provides 50 percent of all health-care spending, and that is even without President Barack Obama's new health-care plan. Much of that spending comes from the federal Medicare program, which funds health care for almost everyone over the age of sixty-five. At that point in your life, you'll probably receive Social Security, the national government's pension plan that covers most employees. Eventually, the county government will record your death, and a government judge will oversee the distribution of your assets to your heirs.

Why Is Government Necessary?

Perhaps the best way to assess the need for government is to examine circumstances in which government, as we normally understand it, does not exist. What happens when multiple groups compete with each other for power within a society? There are places around the world where such circumstances exist. A current example is the African nation of Somalia. Since 1991, Somalia has not had a central government capable of controlling the country. The regions of the country are divided among various warlords and factions, each controlling a block of territory. When Somali warlords compete for control of a particular locality, the result is war, widespread devastation, and famine. In general, multiple armed forces compete by fighting, and the absence of a unified government is equivalent to ongoing civil war.

Order
A state of peace and security. Maintaining order by protecting members of society from violence and criminal activity is the oldest purpose of government.

The Need for Security

As the example of Somalia shows, one of the original purposes of government is the maintenance of security, or **order.** By keeping the peace, the government protects the people from violence at the hands of private or foreign armies. It dispenses justice and protects the people against the violence of criminals. If order is not present, it is not possible for the government to provide any of the other benefits that people expect from it.

Consider the situation in Afghanistan. The former rulers of that country, known as the Taliban, were allied with the al Qaeda network, which organized the terrorist attacks of September 11, 2001, from bases in Afghanistan.[2] Soon after the attacks, the United States, Britain, and other nations intervened to overthrow the Taliban regime by providing air support and special operations assistance to the Northern Alliance, an Afghan faction at war with the Taliban. The Northern Alliance soon occupied Kabul, the capital of the nation.

This Afghan soldier stands guard, holding a rocket launcher. He is reacting to an ambush by Taliban militants on a police patrol in a providence south of Kabul, Afghanistan. How does this conflict show that government is necessary? (AP Photo/Allauddin Khan)

Unfortunately, the new Afghan government never gained full control of its territory. The Taliban regrouped, and soon made it impossible for the government to undertake reconstruction efforts. Taliban units killed humanitarian workers, blew up newly constructed wells, and burned schools. The government, afflicted by massive corruption, survived only because the United States and its allies moved substantial ground forces into the country.

Today, millions of Afghan citizens still do not enjoy the benefits of personal security, pinned as they are between the Taliban and the government's international allies. Afghanistan has the highest infant mortality rate in the world. It has been rated as the nation with the world's second most serious corruption problem (after Somalia). A third of the economy is based on the production of illegal

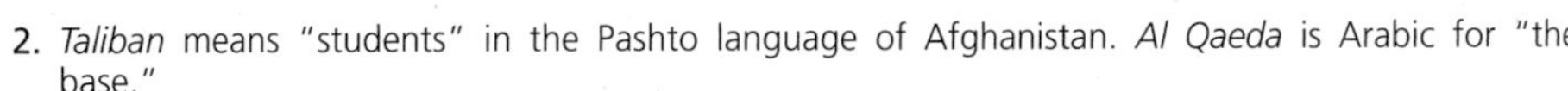

2. *Taliban* means "students" in the Pashto language of Afghanistan. *Al Qaeda* is Arabic for "the base."

drugs. Clearly, Afghanistan has a considerable distance to go before order is restored. (Order is a political value to which we will return later in this chapter.)

Limiting Government Power

A complete collapse of order and security, as seen in Somalia and parts of Afghanistan, is actually an uncommon event. Much more common is the reverse—too much government control. In 2010, the human rights organization Freedom House judged that forty-seven of the world's countries were "not free." These nations contain 34 percent of the world's population. Such countries may be controlled by individual dictators—Iraq's Saddam Hussein was one obvious example. Others include Libya's Muammar Qaddafi and Hosni Mubarak of Egypt. Alternatively, a political party, such as the Communist Party of China, may monopolize all the levers of power. The military may rule, as in Myanmar (formerly Burma).

In all of these examples, the individual or group running the country cannot be removed by legal means. Freedom of speech and the right to a fair trial are typically absent. Dictatorial governments often torture or execute their opponents. Such regimes may also suppress freedom of religion.

In short, protection from the violence of domestic criminals or foreign armies is not enough. Citizens also need protection from abuses of power by the government. To protect the liberties of the people, it is necessary to limit the powers of the government.

Liberty—the greatest freedom of the individual consistent with the freedom of other individuals—is a second major political value, along with order. We further discuss this value later in this chapter.

Liberty
The greatest freedom of the individual that is consistent with the freedom of other individuals in the society.

Authority
The right and power of a government or other entity to enforce its decisions and compel obedience.

Legitimacy
Popular acceptance of the right and power of a government or other entity to exercise authority.

Authority and Legitimacy

Every government must have **authority**—that is, the right and power to enforce its decisions. Ultimately, the government's authority rests on its control of the armed forces and the police. Almost no one in the United States, however, bases his or her day-to-day activities on fear of the government's enforcement powers. Most people, most of the time, obey the law because this is what they have always done. Also, if they did not obey the law, they would face the disapproval of friends and family. Consider an example: Do you avoid injuring your friends or stealing their possessions because you are afraid of the police—or because if you did these things, you would no longer have friends?

Under normal circumstances, the government's authority has broad popular support. People accept the government's right to establish rules and laws. When authority is broadly accepted, we say that it has **legitimacy.** Authority without legitimacy is a recipe for trouble.

Events in the nation of Iraq during recent years serve as an example. After the end of Saddam Hussein's regime, many Iraqis, especially Sunni Arabs (the former politically dominant group in Iraq), did not accept the legitimacy of the U.S.-led Coalition Provisional Authority or the elected Iraqi government that followed it. For many years, terrorists were able to organize attacks on coalition troops or even on innocent civilians, knowing that their neighbors would not report their activities. Although the government of Iraq has since gained a greater degree of legitimacy, terrorism remains a problem.

Democracy and Other Forms of Government

The different types of government can be classified according to which person or group of people controls society through the government.

Types of Government

At one extreme is a society governed by a **totalitarian regime.** In such a political system, a small group of leaders or a single individual—a dictator—makes all decisions for the society. Every aspect of political, social, and economic life is controlled by the government. The power of the ruler is total (thus, the term *totalitarianism*).

A second type of system is authoritarian government. **Authoritarianism** differs from totalitarianism in that only the government itself is fully controlled by the ruler. Social and economic institutions exist that are not under the government's control.

Many of our terms for describing the distribution of political power are derived from the ancient Greeks, who were the first Western people to study politics systematically. One form of rule was known to the Greeks as **aristocracy,** literally meaning "rule by the best." In practice, this meant rule by leading members of wealthy families. Another term from the Greeks is **theocracy,** which literally means "rule by God" (or the gods). In practice, theocracy means rule by self-appointed religious leaders. Iran is a rare example of a country in which supreme power is in the hands of a religious leader, the grand ayatollah Ali Khamenei. One of the most straightforward Greek terms is **oligarchy,** which simply means "rule by a few."

Anarchy is a term derived from a Greek word meaning the absence of government. Advocates of anarchy envision a world in which each individual makes his or her own rules for behavior. In reality, the absence of government typically results in rule by competing armed factions, many of which are indistinguishable from gangsters. This is the state of affairs in Somalia, which we described earlier.

Finally, the Greek term for rule by the people was **democracy.** Within the limits of their culture, some of the Greek city-states operated as democracies. Today, in much (but not all) of the world, the people will not grant legitimacy to a government unless it is based on democracy.

Direct Democracy as a Model

The system of government in the ancient Greek city-state of Athens is usually considered the purest model of **direct democracy** because the citizens of that community debated and voted directly on all laws, even those put forward by the ruling council of the city. The most important feature of Athenian democracy was that the **legislature** was composed of all of the citizens. Women, resident foreigners, and slaves, however, were excluded because they were not citizens. This form of government required a high level of participation from every citizen. That participation was seen as benefiting the individual and the city-state. The Athenians believed that although a high level of participation might lead to instability in government, citizens, if informed about the issues, could be trusted to make wise decisions.

Direct democracy has also been practiced at the local level in Switzerland and, in the United States, in New England town meetings. At these town meetings, which can include all of the voters who live in the town, important decisions—such as levying taxes, hiring city officials, and deciding local ordinances—are made by majority vote. Some states provide a modern adaptation of direct democracy for their citizens. In these states, representative democracy is supplemented by the **initiative** or the **referendum**—processes by which the people may vote directly on laws or constitutional amendments. The **recall** process, which is available in many states, allows the people to vote to remove an official from state office.

The Dangers of Direct Democracy

Although they were aware of the Athenian model, the framers of the U.S. Constitution were opposed to such a system. They regarded democracy as a dangerous idea that could lead to instability. Nevertheless, in the 1700s and 1800s, the idea of government based on

Totalitarian Regime
A form of government that controls all aspects of the political and social life of a nation.

Authoritarianism
A type of regime in which only the government itself is fully controlled by the ruler. Social and economic institutions exist that are not under the government's control.

Aristocracy
Rule by the "best"; in reality, rule by an upper class.

Theocracy
Literally, rule by God or the gods; in practice, rule by religious leaders, typically self-appointed.

Oligarchy
Rule by a few.

Anarchy
The condition of no government.

Democracy
A system of government in which political authority is vested in the people. The term is derived from the Greek words *demos* ("the people") and *kratos* ("authority").

Direct Democracy
A system of government in which political decisions are made by the people directly, rather than by their elected representatives; probably attained most easily in small political communities.

Legislature
A governmental body primarily responsible for the making of laws.

Initiative
A procedure by which voters can propose a law or a constitutional amendment.

Referendum
An electoral device whereby legislative or constitutional measures are referred by the legislature to the voters for approval or disapproval.

Recall
A procedure allowing the people to vote to dismiss an elected official from state office before his or her term has expired.

These Woodbury, Vermont, residents cast their ballots after a town meeting. They voted on the school budget and sales taxes. What type of political system does the town meeting best represent? (AP Photo/Toby Talbot)

the **consent of the people** gained increasing popularity. Such a government was the main aspiration of the American Revolution in 1775, the French Revolution in 1789, and many subsequent revolutions. At the time of the American Revolution, however, the masses were still considered to be too uneducated to govern themselves, too prone to the influence of demagogues (political leaders who manipulate popular prejudices), and too likely to subordinate minority rights to the tyranny of the majority.

James Madison, while defending the new scheme of government set forth in the U.S. Constitution, warned of the problems inherent in a "pure democracy":

> *A common passion or interest will, in almost every case, be felt by a majority of the whole . . . and there is nothing to check the inducements to sacrifice the weaker party or an obnoxious individual. Hence it is that such democracies have ever been spectacles of turbulence and contention, and have ever been found incompatible with personal security or the rights of property; and have in general been as short in their lives as they have been violent in their deaths.*[3]

Like other politicians of his time, Madison feared that pure, or direct, democracy would deteriorate into mob rule. What would keep the majority of the people, if given direct decision-making power, from abusing the rights of those in the minority?

A Democratic Republic

The framers of the U.S. Constitution chose to craft a **republic,** meaning a government in which sovereign power rests with the people, rather than with a king or a monarch. A republic is based on **popular sovereignty.** To Americans of the 1700s, the idea of a republic also meant a government based on common beliefs and virtues that would be fostered within small communities. The rulers were to be amateurs—good citizens who would take turns representing their fellow citizens.

The U.S. Constitution created a form of republican government that we now call a **democratic republic.** The people hold the ultimate power over the government through the election process, but all national policy decisions are made by elected officials. For the founders, even this distance between the people and the government was not sufficient. The Constitution made sure that the Senate and the president would be selected by political elites rather than by the people, although later changes to the Constitution allowed the voters to elect members of the Senate directly.

Despite these limits, the new American system was unique in the amount of power it granted to the ordinary citizen. Over the course of the following two centuries, democratic values became more and more popular, at first in Western nations and then throughout the rest of the world. The spread of democratic principles gave rise to another name for our system of government—**representative democracy.** The term *representative democracy* has almost the same meaning as *democratic republic,* with one exception. In a republic, not only are the people sovereign, but there is no king. What if a nation develops into a democracy but preserves the monarchy as a largely ceremonial institution? This is exactly what happened in Britain. Not surprisingly, the British found the term *democratic*

Consent of the People
The idea that governments and laws derive their legitimacy from the consent of the governed.

Republic
A form of government in which sovereign power rests with the people, rather than with a king or a monarch.

Popular Sovereignty
The concept that ultimate political authority is based on the will of the people.

Democratic Republic
A republic in which representatives elected by the people make and enforce laws and policies.

Representative Democracy
A form of government in which representatives elected by the people make and enforce laws and policies; may retain the monarchy in a ceremonial role.

3. James Madison, in Alexander Hamilton, James Madison, and John Jay, *The Federalist Papers,* No. 10 (New York: Mentor Books, 1964), p. 81. See Appendix C of this textbook.

republic to be unacceptable, and they described their system as a representative democracy instead.

Principles of Democratic Government. All representative democracies rest on the rule of the people as expressed through the election of government officials. In the 1790s in the United States, only free white males were able to vote, and in some states they had to be property owners as well. Women in many states did not receive the right to vote in national elections until 1920, and the right to vote was not secured in all states by African Americans until the 1960s. Today, **universal suffrage** is the rule.

Because everyone's vote counts equally, the only way to make fair decisions is by some form of **majority** will. But to ensure that **majority rule** does not become oppressive, modern democracies also provide guarantees of minority rights. If political minorities were not protected, the majority might violate the fundamental rights of members of certain groups—especially groups that are unpopular or that differ from the majority population, such as racial minorities.

To guarantee the continued existence of a representative democracy, there must be free, competitive elections. Thus, the opposition always has the opportunity to win elective office. For such elections to be totally open, freedom of the press and speech must be preserved so that opposition candidates may present their criticisms of the government.

The U.S. Constitution allows the people to hold the ultimate power over the government through the election process. This process does not work well, however, unless a large percentage of eligible Americans not only register to vote, but vote. This campaign worker at Davidson College in Davidson, North Carolina, explains the voter-registration process to a student. What do we call the form of republican government created by the U.S. Constitution for this country? (AP Photo/Chuck Burton)

Constitutional Democracy. Yet another key feature of Western representative democracy is that it is based on the principle of **limited government.** Not only is the government dependent on popular sovereignty, but the powers of the government are also clearly limited, either through a written document or through widely shared beliefs. The U.S. Constitution sets down the fundamental structure of the government and the limits to its activities. Such limits are intended to prevent political decisions based on the whims or ambitions of individuals in government rather than on constitutional principles.

Universal Suffrage
The right of all adults to vote for their representatives.

Majority
More than 50 percent.

Majority Rule
A basic principle of democracy asserting that the greatest number of citizens in any political unit should select officials and determine policies.

Limited Government
A government with powers that are limited either through a written document or through widely shared beliefs.

Majoritarianism
A political theory holding that in a democracy, the government ought to do what the majority of the people want.

What Kind of Democracy Do We Have?

Political scientists have developed a number of theories about American democracy, including *majoritarian* theory, *elite* theory, and theories of *pluralism.* Advocates of these theories use them to describe American democracy either as it actually is or as they believe it should be.

Some scholars argue that none of these three theories, which we discuss next, fully describes the workings of American democracy. These experts say that each theory captures a part of the true reality but that we need all three theories to gain a full understanding of American politics.

Democracy for Everyone

Many people believe that in a democracy, the government ought to do what the majority of the people want. This simple proposition is the heart of majoritarian theory. As a theory of what democracy should be like, **majoritarianism** is popular among both political scientists and ordinary citizens. Many scholars, however, consider majoritarianism to be a surprisingly poor description of how U.S. democracy actually works. In particular, they point to the low level of turnout for elections. Polling data have shown that many Americans are neither particularly interested in politics nor well informed. Few are able to name the persons running for Congress in their districts, and even fewer can discuss the candidates' positions.

Democracy for the Few

If ordinary citizens are not really making policy decisions with their votes, who is? One theory suggests that elites really govern the United States. This **elite theory** holds that society is ruled by a small number of people who exercise power to further their self-interest. American government, in other words, is a sham democracy. Elite theory is usually used simply to describe the American system. Few people today believe it is a good idea for the country to be run by a privileged minority. In the past, however, many people believed that it was appropriate for the country to be run by an elite. Consider the words of Alexander Hamilton, one of the framers of the Constitution:

did you know?

That there are more than 500,000 elected officials in the United States, which is more than all the bank tellers in the country.

> *All communities divide themselves into the few and the many. The first are the rich and the wellborn, the other the mass of the people. . . . The people are turbulent and changing; they seldom judge or determine right. Give therefore to the first class a distinct, permanent share in the government. They will check the unsteadiness of the second, and as they cannot receive any advantage by a change, they therefore will ever maintain good government.*[4]

Some versions of elite theory posit a small, cohesive elite class that makes almost all the important decisions for the nation,[5] whereas others suggest that voters choose among competing elites. New members of the elite are recruited through the educational system so that the brightest children of the masses allegedly have the opportunity to join the elite stratum.

Democracy for Groups

Elite Theory
A perspective holding that society is ruled by a small number of people who exercise power to further their self-interest.

Pluralism
A theory that views politics as a conflict among interest groups. Political decision making is characterized by compromise and accommodation.

A different school of thought holds that our form of democracy is based on group interests. Even if the average citizen cannot keep up with political issues or cast a deciding vote in any election, the individual's interests will be protected by groups that represent her or him.

Theorists who subscribe to **pluralism** see politics as a struggle among groups to gain benefits for their members. Given the structures of the American political system, group conflicts tend to be settled by compromise and accommodation. Because there are a multitude of interests, no one group can dominate the political process. Furthermore, because most individuals have more than one interest, conflict among groups need not divide the nation into hostile camps.

Many political scientists believe that pluralism works very well as a descriptive theory. As a theory of how democracy *should* function, however, pluralism has problems. Poor citizens are rarely represented by interest groups. At the same time, rich citizens are often overrepresented. As political scientist E. E. Schattschneider once observed, "The flaw in the pluralist heaven is that the heavenly chorus sings with a strong upper-class accent."[6]

---

4. Alexander Hamilton, "Speech in the Constitutional Convention on a Plan of Government," in Joanne B. Freeman, ed., *Writings* (New York: Library of America, 2001).
5. Michael Parenti, *Democracy for the Few,* 9th ed. (Belmont, Calif.: Wadsworth Publishing, 2010).
6. E. E. Schattschneider, *The Semi-Sovereign People* (Hinsdale, Ill.: The Dryden Press, 1975; originally published in 1960).

There are also serious doubts as to whether group decision making always reflects the best interests of the nation.

Indeed, critics see a danger that groups may grow so powerful that all policies become compromises crafted to satisfy the interests of the largest groups. The interests of the public as a whole, then, are not considered. Critics of pluralism have suggested that a democratic system can be close to paralyzed by the struggle among interest groups. We discuss interest groups at greater length in Chapter 7.

Political Culture
A patterned set of ideas, values, and ways of thinking about government and politics.

Political Socialization
The process by which political beliefs and values are transmitted to new immigrants and to our children. The family and the educational system are two of the most important forces in the political socialization process.

Civil Liberties
Those personal freedoms, including freedom of religion and freedom of speech, that are protected for all individuals. The civil liberties set forth in the U.S. Constitution, as amended, restrain the government from taking certain actions against individuals.

Bill of Rights
The first ten amendments to the U.S. Constitution.

Fundamental Values

The writers of the American Constitution believed that the structures they had created would provide for both popular sovereignty and a stable political system. They also believed that the nation would be sustained by its **political culture**—a concept defined as a patterned set of ideas, values, and ways of thinking about government and politics.

Even today, there is considerable consensus among American citizens about certain concepts—including the rights to liberty, equality, and property—that are deemed to be basic to the U.S. political system. Given that the vast majority of Americans are descendants of immigrants having diverse cultural and political backgrounds, how can we account for this consensus? Primarily, it is the result of **political socialization**—the process by which political beliefs and values are transmitted to new immigrants and to our children. The two most important sources of political socialization are the family and the educational system. (See Chapter 6 for a more detailed discussion of the political socialization process.)

The most fundamental concepts of the American political culture are those of the dominant culture. The term *dominant culture* refers to the values, customs, and language established by the group or groups that traditionally have controlled politics and government in a society. The dominant culture in the United States has its roots in Western European civilization. From that civilization, American politics has inherited a bias toward individualism, private property, and Judeo-Christian ethics.

Liberty versus Order

In the United States, our **civil liberties** include religious freedom—both the right to practice whatever religion we choose and freedom from any state-imposed religion. Our civil liberties also include freedom of speech—the right to express our opinions freely on all matters, including government actions. Freedom of speech is perhaps one of our most prized liberties, because a democracy could not endure without it. These and many other basic guarantees of liberty are found in the **Bill of Rights,** the first ten amendments to the Constitution. Americans are often more protective of their civil liberties than citizens of other democratic countries, a point that we discuss in this chapter's *Beyond Our Borders* feature on the following page.

Liberty, however, is not the only value widely held by Americans. A substantial portion of the American electorate believes that certain kinds of liberty threaten the traditional social order. The right to privacy is a particularly controversial liberty. The United States Supreme Court has held that the right to privacy can be derived from other rights that are explicitly stated in the Bill of Rights. The Supreme Court has also held that under the right to privacy, the government cannot

One of the most fundamental rights Americans have is the right to vote. Here, African Americans in Camden, Alabama, vote for the first time after passage of the 1965 Voting Rights Act. Does voting affect political socialization? (Bob Adelman/Corbis)

did you know?

That the phrase "In God We Trust" was made the national motto on July 30, 1956, but had appeared on U.S. coins as early as 1864.

ban either abortion[7] or private homosexual behavior by consenting adults.[8] Some Americans believe that such rights threaten the sanctity of the family and the general cultural commitment to moral behavior. Of course, others disagree with this point of view.

Security is another issue that follows from the principle of order. When Americans have felt particularly fearful or vulnerable, the government has emphasized national security over civil liberties. Following the terrorist attacks on the World Trade Center and the Pentagon on September 11, 2001, Congress passed legislation designed to provide greater security at the expense of some civil liberties. In particular, the USA Patriot Act gave law enforcement and intelligence-gathering agencies greater latitude to search out and investigate suspected terrorists. Many Americans objected to the Patriot Act, pointing out that it compromised numerous civil liberties, such as protection from unreasonable searches and seizures.

Equality versus Liberty

Equality
As a political value, the idea that all people are of equal worth.

The Declaration of Independence states, "All men are created equal." The proper meaning of equality, however, has been disputed by Americans since the Revolution.[9] Much of American history—and indeed, world history—is the story of how the value of **equality**—

7. *Roe v. Wade*, 410 U.S. 113 (1973).
8. *Lawrence v. Texas*, 539 U.S. 558 (2003).
9. Gary B. Nash, *The Unknown American Revolution: The Unruly Birth of Democracy and the Struggle to Create America* (New York: Viking, 2005); and Alfred F. Young, ed., *Beyond the American Revolution: Explorations in the History of American Radicalism* (DeKalb, Ill.: Northern Illinois University Press, 1993).

BEYOND OUR BORDERS

RESTRICTIONS ON CIVIL LIBERTIES IN OTHER DEMOCRATIC COUNTRIES

Americans value civil freedoms more than the people of most other democratic countries. Americans in particular prize freedom of speech. Not all democratic countries value it so highly. In Germany, for example, it is illegal to display the swastika, the emblem adopted by the Nazis. Swastikas cannot be affixed to plastic models of World War II–era aircraft. It is even a crime to give a Nazi-style straight-arm salute. Recently, a German sculptor got into serious trouble by crafting a satirical statue of a garden gnome giving such a salute. The German constitution gives the government the power to ban organizations that threaten the democratic order. Finally, if you are on German soil and you want—even for historical purposes—to purchase a copy of Hitler's autobiography and political statement, *Mein Kampf (My Struggle)*, you'll have to get it from another country via the Internet. The German state of Bavaria, which owns the rights to the book, has blocked reprints of *Mein Kampf* in Germany.

Most Americans are concerned about crime. Many Americans, however, would be even more concerned about possible injustices if they learned that 99.8 percent of all criminal prosecutions resulted in a conviction. Yet that is exactly what happens in democratic Japan. In that country, suspects can be held for up to twenty-three days before they are charged. The high conviction rate in Japan stems from a high confession rate. Those who are detained have no access to defense lawyers and no idea how long interrogation sessions will last. The Japanese constitution guarantees detainees the right to remain silent, but almost no Japanese citizens who are arrested are able to take advantage of that right. In several recent cases, innocent people have been browbeaten into making false confessions that are almost impossible to retract.

FOR CRITICAL ANALYSIS

Why would Germany continue to criminalize Nazi symbols more than sixty years after the end of World War II?

the idea that all people are of equal worth—has been extended and elaborated.

First, the right to vote was granted to all adult white males regardless of whether they owned property. The Civil War resulted in the end of slavery and established that, in principle at least, all citizens were equal before the law. The civil rights movement of the 1950s and 1960s sought to make that promise of equality a reality for African Americans. Other movements have sought equality for other racial and ethnic groups, for women, for persons with disabilities, and for gay men and lesbians. We discuss these movements in Chapter 5.

Although many people believe that we have a ways yet to go in obtaining full equality for all of these groups, we clearly have come a long way already. No American in the nineteenth century could have imagined that the 2008 Democratic presidential primary elections would be closely fought contests between an African American man (Illinois senator Barack Obama) and a white woman (New York senator Hillary Rodham Clinton). The idea that same-sex marriage could even be open to debate would have been mind-boggling as well.

To promote equality, it is often necessary to place limits on the desire by some to treat people unequally. In this sense, equality and liberty are conflicting values. Today, the right to deny equal treatment to members of a particular race has very few defenders. As recently as sixty years ago, though, such denial was a cultural norm.

When Barack Obama and Hillary Clinton became the front-runners for the Democratic presidential candidacy, history was made. At least on some level, equality had become more real in the United States. What inequalities still remain? (AP Photo/John Raoux)

Economic Equality. Equal treatment regardless of race, religion, gender, or other characteristics is a popular value today. Equal opportunity for individuals to develop their talents and skills is another value with substantial support. Equality of economic status, however, is a controversial value.

For much of history, few people even contemplated the idea that the government could do something about the division of society between rich and poor. Most people assumed that such an effort was either impossible or undesirable. This assumption began to lose its force in the 1800s. As a result of the growing wealth of the Western world and a visible increase in the ability of government to take on large projects, some people began to advocate the value of universal equality. Some radicals dreamed of a revolutionary transformation of society that would establish an *egalitarian system*—that is, a system in which wealth and power would be redistributed more equally.

Many others rejected this vision but still came to endorse the values of eliminating poverty and at least reducing the degree of economic inequality in society. Antipoverty advocates believed then and believe now that such a program could alleviate much suffering. In addition, they believed that reducing economic inequality would promote fairness and enhance the moral tone of society generally.

Property Rights and Capitalism. The value of reducing economic inequality is in conflict with the right to **property.** This is because reducing economic inequality typically involves the transfer of property (usually in the form of tax dollars) from some people to others. For many people, liberty and property are closely entwined. Our capitalist system is based on private property rights. Under **capitalism,** property consists not only of personal possessions but also of wealth-creating assets such as farms and factories. The investor-owned corporation is in many ways the preeminent capitalist institution.

Property
Anything that is or may be subject to ownership. As conceived by the political philosopher John Locke, the right to property is a natural right superior to human law (laws made by government).

Capitalism
An economic system characterized by the private ownership of wealth-creating assets, free markets, and freedom of contract.

The funds invested by the owners of a corporation are known as *capital*—hence, the very name of the system. Capitalism is also typically characterized by considerable freedom to make binding contracts and by relatively unconstrained markets for goods, services, and investments.

Property—especially wealth-creating property—can be seen as giving its owner political power and the liberty to do whatever he or she wants. At the same time, the ownership of property immediately creates inequality in society. The desire to own property, however, is so widespread among all classes of Americans that radical egalitarian movements have had a difficult time securing a wide following here.

The Proper Size of Government

Opposition to "big government" has been a constant theme in American politics. Indeed, the belief that government is overreaching its power dates back to the years before the American Revolution. Tensions over the size and scope of government have plagued Americans ever since. American citizens often express contradictory opinions on the size of government and the role that it should play in their lives. Those who complain about the amount of taxes that they pay each year may also worry over the lack of funds for more teachers in the local schools. Individuals who fear future terrorist attacks may react with outrage at the thought of a government official snooping through their e-mail correspondence.

The bank bailouts in 2008 and 2009 were not universally popular. Critics maintained that the taxpayer-provided funds were used to bail out bankers rather than to save or create jobs. Why did the federal government act? (AP Photo/ Jason DeCrow)

Big Government in Times of Crisis. Americans are most likely to call for the benefits of big government when they are reacting to a crisis. After the terrorist attacks of 9/11, the George W. Bush administration substantially increased the scope of federal authority, and government spending went up as well. Likewise, other recent crises have resulted in demands for an active government. Many Americans criticized the Obama administration for responding too slowly to the oil spill caused by the explosion on the BP Deepwater Horizon oil rig in the Gulf of Mexico in 2010. Certainly, the government's reaction to the Great Recession that began in December 2007 sparked intense disputes over the proper size of government.

Popular Reaction to Bank Bailouts. The federal government's first responses to the recession took place early in 2008, the last full year of the Bush administration. In February, Bush obtained from Congress $152 billion in tax rebates aimed at stimulating the economy. In March, the investment bank Bear Stearns collapsed, and the government intervened to supervise its demise. These steps met with some opposition, but far more controversial actions were to follow. After the collapse of the Lehman Brothers bank on September 15, the recession entered a new, dangerous phase. Fearing a complete collapse of the financial system, Treasury secretary Henry Paulson asked Congress for a $700 billion bank bailout package. Senators and representatives were deluged with hostile phone calls and messages. Protests were organized in more than a hundred cities. The House rejected the proposal. The next day, the Dow Jones Industrial Average, a measure of the value of stocks, dropped more than 777 points, its largest single-day point drop ever. Congress then adopted a revised bailout package.

Although the loudest public voices were opposed to the bailout, public opinion polls suggested that popular reaction was mixed. Approval or opposition to the measure depended heavily on how the question was worded. In November, the voters chose Democrat Barack Obama to be the new president, and Obama promised a far more activist government than his Republican opponent, Arizona senator John McCain.

Obama and Big Government. Americans expected that Obama would do something about the collapsing economy and the soaring unemployment rates, and he did, asking Congress for a $787 billion stimulus package in February 2009. Opposition to Paulson's bank bailout had crossed party lines, but this time, not a single Republican in the House supported the stimulus bill. Nevertheless, it passed. It was followed by measures to steer automakers General Motors and Chrysler through bankruptcy, which resulted in the government taking an ownership stake in both companies. Congress then turned to discussing a massive reorganization of the nation's health-insurance system.

By the middle of 2009, these ambitious measures had touched off a wave of conservative organizing that became known as the *Tea Party movement.* More ominously for the Democrats, large numbers of independent voters appeared to be losing faith in the administration's efforts. Some voters were alarmed at the increase in the size of government. Others were upset that, despite the stimulus act and other measures, the rate of unemployment was still above 10 percent. Had the government done too much—or not enough? Or the wrong things? Americans were seriously divided on this issue.

Political Ideologies

A political **ideology** is a closely linked set of beliefs about politics. The concept of *ideology* is often misunderstood. Many people think that only those whose beliefs lie well out on one or the other end of the political spectrum have an ideology. In other words, people with moderate positions are not ideological. Actually, almost everyone who has political opinions can be said to have an ideology. Some people may have difficulty in explaining the principles that underlie their opinions, but the principles are there nonetheless. To give one example: a belief in moderation itself is an ideological principle.

Political ideologies offer people well-organized theories that propose goals for the society and the means by which those goals can be achieved. At the core of every political ideology is a set of guiding values. The two ideologies most commonly referred to in discussions of American politics are *conservatism* and *liberalism.*

Ideology
A comprehensive set of beliefs about the nature of people and about the role of an institution or government.

Conservatism
A set of beliefs that includes a limited role for the national government in helping individuals, support for traditional values and lifestyles, and a cautious response to change.

Liberalism
A set of beliefs that includes the advocacy of positive government action to improve the welfare of individuals, support for civil rights, and tolerance for political and social change.

Conservatism versus Liberalism

Those who favor the set of beliefs called **conservatism** generally place a high value on the principle of order. This includes support for patriotism and traditional values. As a result, conservatives typically oppose such social innovations as same-sex marriage. Conservatives place a high value on liberty, but generally define it as freedom from government support of nontraditional values or from government interference in business. Conservatives believe that the private sector probably can outperform the government in almost any activity. Therefore, they usually oppose initiatives that would increase the role of the government in the economy, such as Obama's health-care reform. Conservatives place a relatively low value on equality. Believing that individuals and families are primarily responsible for their own well-being, conservatives typically oppose high levels of antipoverty spending and government expenditures to stimulate the economy. They usually favor tax rate cuts instead. Conservatives occupy a dominant position in the Republican Party.

Those who favor **liberalism**, in contrast, place a high value on social and economic equality. Liberals have championed the rights of minority group members and favor substantial antipoverty spending. In the recent health-care policy debates, liberals strongly endorsed the principle that all citizens should have access to affordable insurance. In contrast to conservatives, liberals are often willing to support government intervention in the economy. They believe that capitalism works best when the government curbs its excesses through regulation. Like conservatives, liberals place a high value on liberty, but they tend to view it as the freedom to live one's life according to one's own lights. Liberals, therefore, usually support gay rights, often including the right to marry. Liberals are an influential force within the Democratic Party.

In recent years, people traditionally known as *liberals* have, in large numbers, switched to an alternative label—*progressives.* We discuss the terminology change in this chapter's *Politics and Labels* feature on the facing page.

The Traditional Political Spectrum

A traditional method of comparing political ideologies is to array them on a continuum from left to right, based primarily on how much power the government should exercise to promote economic equality. Table 1–1 below shows how ideologies can be arrayed in a traditional political spectrum. In addition to liberalism and conservatism, the table includes the ideologies of socialism and libertarianism.

did you know?

That about 14 percent of all legal immigrants to the United States plan to live in the Los Angeles/Long Beach, California, area.

Socialism falls on the left side of the spectrum.[10] Socialists play a minor role in the American political arena, although socialist parties and movements have been important in other countries around the world. In the past, socialists typically advocated replacing investor ownership of major businesses with either government ownership or ownership by employee cooperatives. Socialists believed that such steps would break the power of the very rich and lead to an egalitarian society. In more recent times, socialists in Western Europe have advocated more limited programs that redistribute income.

On the right side of the spectrum is **libertarianism,** a philosophy of skepticism toward most government activities. Libertarians strongly support property rights and typically oppose regulation of the economy and redistribution of income. Libertarians support *laissez-faire* capitalism. (*Laissez faire* is French for "let it be.") Libertarians also tend to oppose government attempts to regulate personal behavior and promote moral values.

Socialism
A political ideology based on strong support for economic and social equality. Socialists traditionally envisioned a society in which major businesses were taken over by the government or by employee cooperatives.

Libertarianism
A political ideology based on skepticism or opposition toward most government activities.

Problems with the Traditional Political Spectrum

Many political scientists believe that the traditional left-to-right spectrum does not reflect the complexities of today's political ideologies. Take the example of libertarians. In Table 1–1 below, libertarians are placed to the right of conservatives. If the only question is how much power the government should have over the economy, this is where they belong. Libertarians,

10. The terms *left* and *right* in the traditional political spectrum originated during the French Revolution, when revolutionary deputies to the Legislative Assembly sat to the left of the assembly president and conservative deputies sat to the right.

TABLE 1–1 The Traditional Political Spectrum

	Socialism	Liberalism	Conservatism	Libertarianism
How much power should the government have over the economy?	Active government control over major economic sectors.	Positive government action in the economy.	Positive government action to support capitalism.	Almost no regulation over the economy.
What should the government promote?	Economic equality, community.	Economic security, equal opportunity, social liberty.	Economic liberty, morality, social order.	Total economic and social liberty.

POLITICS AND... labels

LIBERALS—OR PROGRESSIVES?

In January 2009, Illinois senator Barack Obama, a Democrat, was sworn in as president of the United States. Obama's politics have been widely described as liberal. Obama, however, does not use this label. Like most elected Democrats, he calls himself a *progressive*.

THE ORIGINS OF LIBERALISM

Those on the political left have long complained about conservatives' ability to make the word *liberal* an embarrassment. Indeed, most Americans today associate liberalism with big government, which is not a popular concept. A hundred years ago, however, a *liberal* was a person who believed in limited government and who opposed religion in politics, a philosophy that in some ways resembles modern-day libertarianism. For that reason, many libertarians today refer to themselves as *classical liberals.*

Theodore Roosevelt is shown here campaigning for president. When he ran against Woodrow Wilson in 1912, why did both candidates call themselves progressives? Does anyone use this term today? (© Bettmann/Corbis)

How did the meaning of the word *liberal* change? In the 1800s, the Democratic Party was seen as the more liberal of the two parties. Democrats opposed big-government Republican projects such as building roads, freeing the slaves, and prohibiting the sale of alcoholic beverages. Over time, however, the Democrats' economic policies began to change. By the time of President Franklin Delano Roosevelt (1933–1945), the Democrats stood for positive government action to help the economy. Roosevelt's policies were new, but he kept the old language—as Democrats had long done, he called himself a *liberal*. Outside the United States and Canada, the meaning of the word *liberal* never changed. European liberals continue to support free market, small-government policies.

THE ORIGINS OF THE PROGRESSIVE LABEL

Progressivism, as an American political label, came into fashion in the early twentieth century to describe a growing belief—in both of the major political parties—that a strong government was essential to curb the excesses of big business. In the presidential elections of 1912, both leading candidates, Woodrow Wilson and Theodore Roosevelt, called themselves *progressives*. By the end of the 1940s, however, members of the radical left had hijacked the label, and Democrats avoided it. Today, few people remember or care who called themselves progressive in the distant past, and the label is once again usable by the Democrats.

THE RETURN OF PROGRESSIVISM

If the word *liberal* has sunk beneath the weight of accumulated historical baggage, *progressive* is still going strong. A research organization called the Center for American Progress recently asked Americans not whether they were liberal or conservative, as is usually done, but whether they were liberal, progressive, conservative, or libertarian. The label *conservative* has long been far more popular than the label *liberal,* but when *progressive* is tossed into the mix, everything changes. Counting both strong and weak supporters, 47 percent of Americans identified themselves as liberal or progressive, and 48 percent as conservative or libertarian. It is no wonder that *progressive* has become the Democrats' label of choice.

FOR CRITICAL ANALYSIS

Are the labels with which politicians identify their philosophies and their desired political programs truly important? Why or why not?

however, advocate the most complete freedom possible in social matters. They oppose government action to promote traditional moral values, although such action is often favored by other groups on the political right. Libertarians' strong support for cultural freedoms seems to align them more closely with modern liberals than with conservatives.

Liberalism is often described as an ideology that supports "big government." If the objective is to promote equality, the description has some validity. In the moral sphere, however, conservatives tend to support more government regulation of social values and moral decisions than do liberals. Thus, conservatives tend to oppose gay rights legislation and propose stronger curbs on pornography. Liberals usually show greater tolerance for alternative lifestyle choices and oppose government attempts to regulate personal behavior and morals.

A Four-Cornered Ideological Grid

For a more sophisticated breakdown of American popular ideologies, many scholars use a four-cornered grid, as shown in Figure 1–1 below. The grid provides four possible ideologies. Each quadrant contains a substantial portion of the American electorate. Individual voters may fall anywhere on the grid, depending on the strength of their beliefs about economic and cultural issues.

did you know?

That a poll of New York University students revealed that one-fifth of them would give up their vote in the next election for an iPod and that half of them would renounce their vote permanently for $1 million.

Note that there is no generally accepted term for persons in the lower-left position, which we have labeled "economic liberals, cultural conservatives." Some scholars have used terms such as *populist* to describe this point of view, but such terms can be misleading. *Populism* more accurately refers to a hostility toward political, economic, or cultural elites, and it can be combined with a variety of political positions. We look at recent populist tendencies in American politics in this chapter's *The Politics of Boom and Bust* feature on the facing page.

Individuals who are economic liberals and cultural conservatives tend to support government action both to promote the values of economic equality and fairness and to defend traditional values, such as the family and marriage. These individuals may describe themselves as conservative or moderate. They may vote for a Republican candidate due to their conservative values. Alternatively, they may be Democrats due to their support for economic liberalism. Many of these Democrats are African Americans or members of other minority groups.

FIGURE 1–1 A Four-Cornered Ideological Grid

In this grid, the colored squares represent four different political ideologies. The vertical choices range from cultural order to cultural liberty. The horizontal choices range from economic equality to economic liberty.

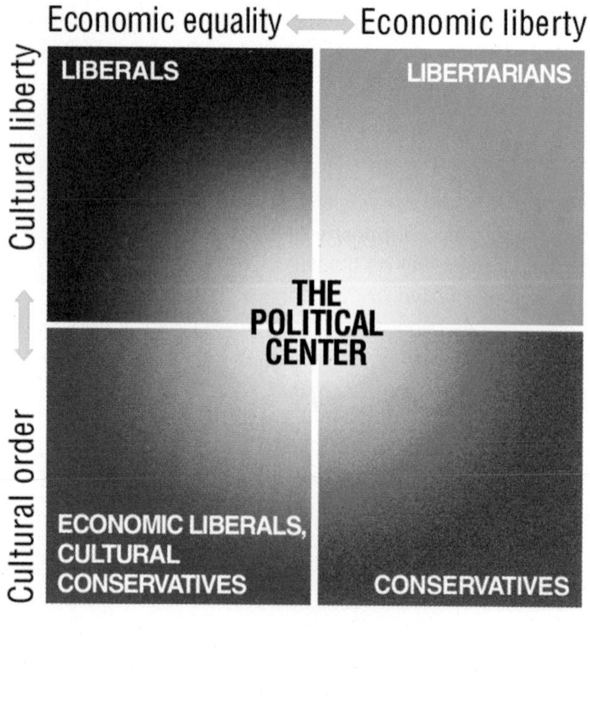

Economic equality ⟷ Economic liberty
Cultural liberty ⟷ Cultural order
LIBERALS
LIBERTARIANS
THE POLITICAL CENTER
ECONOMIC LIBERALS, CULTURAL CONSERVATIVES
CONSERVATIVES

Libertarian, as a position on our four-way grid, does not refer to the small Libertarian Party, which has only a minor role in the American political arena. Rather, libertarians more typically support the Republican Party. Economically successful individuals are more likely than members of other groups to hold libertarian opinions.

Classifying the Voters. If the traditional political spectrum held, most voters would fall into the liberal or conservative quarter of our ideological grid. Actually, there are a substantial number of voters in each quadrant. Asking whether the government should guarantee everyone a job, for example, divides the electorate roughly in half on the economic dimension. A question about abortion also divides the electorate roughly in half on the social dimension. Knowing how a voter answered one of these questions, however, does not tell us how he or she answered the other one. Many people would give a "liberal" answer to the jobs question but a "conservative" answer to the abortion question; also, many people would give a "conservative" answer to the jobs question and a "liberal" answer on abortion.

Conservative Popularity. Even though all four ideologies are popular, it does not follow that the various labels we have used in the four-cornered grid are equally favored. Voters are much more likely to describe themselves as conservative than as liberal. There are a variety

THE POLITICS OF BOOM AND BUST

THE LATEST BUST AND THE NEW POPULISM

Beginning in late 2006, the several-year-old housing boom turned into a housing bust. By early 2008, the Great Recession—as it is now called—was well under way. By 2009, the economy had started to grow again, but the unemployment rate was still as high as 10 percent. By the time you read this, the unemployment rate may have fallen or economic conditions might even have gotten worse in what policymakers call a *double-dip recession*. Either way, the new populism, born during the financial panic of 2008, will still be with us.

WHAT IS THE NEW POPULISM?

Populism has taken many forms, but it is always a matter of "them" against "us." Only the definition of *them* changes. In years past, *they* have been the heads of giant corporations that exploit their workers. *They* have been Harvard intellectuals who think they know everything. *They* have even been Hollywood types who corrupt the public morals through the movies. Today, of course, *they* are the bankers and Wall Street fat cats who wrecked the economy and were bailed out by the government. *We* are ordinary people—people on Main Street, who work in "real" jobs just to make ends meet. Populists, in short, see themselves as the *people* versus the *elites*.

Populism provides politicians and citizens alike with a simple way to think about the world. The latest recession may have had many causes, but it's easy just to put the blame on investment bankers. Did you borrow too much, hoping to make a quick profit in real estate—and get burned? It's really someone else's fault.

TEA PARTY POPULISM

The Tea Party movement, which began in the summer of 2009, is generally characterized as populist. Tea Party supporters see elites in government—the president and leaders in Congress—as the cause of our current economic problems. While not entirely unified in its politics, the Tea Party movement generally opposes higher tax rates, federal budget deficits, and increased government regulation. (The Boston Tea Party in 1773, which you'll read about in the next chapter, was a protest against a British tax imposed on tea.) For Tea Partiers, the people are ranged against government officials, elected or appointed, who are committed to a more active government.

THE ADMINISTRATION BORROWS POPULIST RHETORIC

As a graduate of Columbia who went on to lead his class at Harvard Law School, Barack Obama is not a natural populist. He has been widely criticized, from both the political right and the left, as too cozy with Wall Street. Still, the president is not about to pass up the chance to score political points through populist appeals. In his 2010 budget statement, Obama blamed our economic troubles on a "trend toward rising inequality." He spoke of "an era of profound irresponsibility that engulfed both private and public institutions . . . a disproportionate share of the nation's wealth has been accumulated by the wealthy." Obama believes that the government has a responsibility to reduce economic inequality. To that end, the administration has introduced such policies as a multibillion-dollar tax on banks, a $122 billion tax on overseas business profits, and an increase in tax rates on the nation's highest-earning individuals.

FOR CRITICAL ANALYSIS

From the founding of our republic until today, politicians have found populism to be a successful campaign theme. Why?

of reasons for this, but one is that *liberal* has come to imply "radical" to many people, whereas *conservative* often implies "moderate." Because most Americans value moderation, the conservative label has an advantage. The designation *libertarian* has an even more radical flavor than *liberal,* and the number of voters with obvious libertarian tendencies far exceeds the number who are willing to adopt the label. We will look further at popular ideologies in Chapter 6.

One Nation, Divided

When Barack Obama was inaugurated as president of the United States in January 2009, he was riding a wave of popular hope and support. According to a public opinion poll taken by the Gallup organization, 68 percent of the public approved of the way Obama was handling his job as president, and only 12 percent disapproved. By the middle of 2010, Obama's approval rating was down to about 45 percent, and his disapproval rating fluctuated around 45 percent as well. Clearly, the wave of popular support for the new president had crested.

Disenchantment with the Republicans

Obama, and the enhanced Democratic majorities in the U.S. House and Senate, took office at a time when the public was seriously disenchanted with the Republicans, who had run the government for most of the previous eight years. When Republican president George W. Bush was inaugurated in 2001, 56 percent of those questioned were satisfied with the way things were going in the country. By the end of 2008, that figure was down to 10 percent, a record low. It is not surprising that the public hoped that the new president would do better than the old.

The Bush administration received high marks from voters for its handling of terrorism following the attacks of September 11, 2001, although some contended that President Bush had done considerable damage to the nation's civil liberties in the process. It was the war in Iraq, however, which began in March 2003, that really damaged the popularity of Bush and his fellow Republicans. A major reason for going to war was weapons of mass destruction supposedly held by Iraq. They turned out not to exist. What was billed as a cheap and easy victory became a grinding and seemingly endless guerrilla war against insurgents who often employed terrorist methods. Prospects in Iraq remained grim until 2007, when the Iraqi people finally began to turn against the insurgents. This was too late for the Republicans—in 2006 they lost their majorities in the U.S. House and Senate.

Worse was to come. In December 2007, the nation entered an economic downturn, which by September 2008 had become the Great Recession, the worst economic crisis in more than seventy-five years. Few now remember that in early September 2008, Republican presidential candidate John McCain had drawn ahead of Obama in many opinion polls. After the beginning of the financial crisis on September 15, it was all downhill for the Republicans.

Disillusionment with the Democrats

Why, then, did the Democrats lose support so quickly during Obama's first year in office? In part the loss was inevitable. Much of the initial approval of the president came from Republicans, and that support was certain to evaporate as soon as the new administration began to make actual decisions. It became apparent that the Democrats were in a policy bind. The measures they undertook in an attempt to combat the recession involved large doses of government spending and government action. Yet Americans have always feared an over-mighty government—and despite the Democratic measures, record levels of unemployment continued to damage the lives of millions. With some justice, the Democrats could argue that if they had not acted, the economy would be much worse off. Yet many members of the public were not buying such arguments. The Democrats, in other words, were suffering both from the condition of the economy and the steps they took to right it.

One major Democratic policy initiative was not obviously directed at the recession, however, and that was health-care reform. To be sure, the Democrats had called for such reform during the 2008 elections, and they were carrying out a campaign promise. By spending the entire second half of 2009 and part of 2010 working on this one issue, however, Democrats in Congress gave the appearance of neglecting the nation's number-one issue, which was unemployment.

Division and Polarization

After George W. Bush's election as president in 2000, his chief political operative, Karl Rove, openly speculated that the Republicans might become so politically dominant that the Democrats would be shut out of power for many years. After the elections of 2008, some Democrats had the same aspiration for their party. The hopes of neither would be fulfilled. Americans remain closely divided in politics, as they have been for many decades. Current events may give the Republicans or the Democrats a temporary edge, but not a permanent one. Independents, who are more than a third of the electorate, continue to decide elections as they have in the past.

If one thing has changed in American politics in recent years, it may be the growth in political polarization. In Congress, the two major parties have never been more disciplined. Republicans, and to a lesser extent Democrats, have become used to voting as a monolithic block. Neither progressives nor conservatives trust the intentions of the other camp. In bookstores, among political bloggers on the Web, and on radio and television, rhetoric is more furious than it has been in a long time. The other side is not just wrong. It is evil.

In time, passions may cool. One point is clear, however. The decisions made today—by voters and leaders alike—are important, and they will shape the United States for many years to come.

How might tough economic times increase the polarization within Congress? (AP Photo/*The Canadian Press*/Andrew Vaughan)

WHY SHOULD YOU CARE ABOUT... OUR DEMOCRACY?

(© spxChrome/istockphotos.com)

Americans, for the most part, take our democracy for granted. We assume that our leaders, including the president, will uphold our democratic traditions. Nonetheless, the history of other nations has shown that even elected leaders can become overbearing and move a country away from its democratic underpinnings. In America, however, because most of us take democracy for granted, many of us do not even bother to vote.

In any democracy, citizens must, nonetheless, remain vigilant. A lot is at stake—our way of life in particular. How does an individual stay vigilant? One way is to stay informed about what's going on in government. Staying informed is a lot easier today than it was, say, a hundred years ago. Newspapers and news magazines are everywhere. Perhaps more importantly, the Internet allows you to stay in constant touch with what your government is doing. There are blogs galore of all political stripes created by Democrats, Republicans, independents, libertarians, and socialists.

OUR DEMOCRACY AND YOUR LIFE

Consider local legislative bodies. They can have a direct impact on your life. For example, city councils or county commissions typically oversee the police or the sheriff's department, and the behavior of the police is a matter of interest even if you live on campus. If you live off campus, local authorities are responsible for an even greater number of issues that affect you directly. Are there items that your local sanitation department refuses to pick up? You might be able to change its policies by lobbying your councilperson.

Even if there are no local issues that concern you, there are still benefits from observing a local legislative session. You may discover that local government works differently from what you expected. You might learn, for example, that the representatives of your political party do not serve your interests as well as you thought—or that the other party is much more sensible than you had presumed.

HOW YOU CAN MAKE A DIFFERENCE

If you want to affect our democracy, you have to learn firsthand how a democratic government works. The easiest way is to attend a session of a local legislative body. To do so, look up the phone number of the city hall or county building on the Internet. Call the clerk of your local council or city commission. Find out when the next city council or county board meeting is. If you live in a state capital such as Baton Rouge, Louisiana, or Santa Fe, New Mexico, you can view a meeting of the state legislature instead. In many communities, city council meetings and county board meetings can be seen on public-access TV channels.

Before attending a business session of the local council or commission, try to find out how the members are elected. Are the members chosen by the "at-large" method of election, so that each member represents the whole community? Or are they chosen by specific geographic districts or wards? What are the responsibilities of this body?

When you visit, keep in mind the theory of representative democracy. The commissioners or council members are elected to represent their constituents. Observe how often the members refer to their constituents or to the special needs of their communities. Listen for sources of conflict. If, for example, there is a debate over a zoning proposal that involves the issue of land use, try to figure out why some members oppose the proposal.

If you want to follow up on your visit, try to get a brief interview with one of the members of the council or board. In general, legislators are very willing to talk to students, particularly students who also are voters. Ask the member how he or she sees the job of representative. How can the wishes of constituents be identified? How does the representative balance the needs of the particular ward or district that she or he represents with the good of the entire community? You can also write to many legislators via e-mail.

questions for discussion and analysis

1. How well does the elite theory work as a description of American democracy? Can you provide evidence that suggests elites truly do rule on their own behalf? Is there evidence that contradicts the theory?
2. In Australia and Belgium, citizens are legally required to vote in elections. Would such a requirement be a good idea in the United States? What changes might take place if such a rule were in effect?
3. In your own life, what factors have contributed to your political socialization? To what extent were your political values shaped by your family, by school experiences, by friends, and by the media?
4. Following the terrorist attacks of September 11, 2001, the U.S. government imposed various restrictions, notably on airline passengers, in the belief that these measures would enhance our national security. How effective do you think these measures have been? In general, what limits on liberty should we accept as the price of security?
5. We have discussed various fundamental political values in this chapter—liberty, order or security, equality, and property. How were these values reflected in the attempts by the George W. Bush and Obama administrations to bail out the banking industry? How were they reflected in the Obama administration's health-care proposals?

key terms

anarchy 9
aristocracy 9
authoritarianism 9
authority 8
Bill of Rights 13
capitalism 15
civil liberties 13
consent of the people 10
conservatism 17
democracy 9
democratic republic 10
direct democracy 9
elite theory 12
equality 14
government 5
ideology 17
initiative 9
institution 5
legislature 9
legitimacy 8
liberalism 17
libertarianism 18
liberty 8
limited government 11
majoritarianism 11
majority 11
majority rule 11
oligarchy 9
order 7
pluralism 12
political culture 13
political socialization 13
politics 5
popular sovereignty 10
property 15
recall 9
referendum 9
representative democracy 10
republic 10
socialism 18
theocracy 9
totalitarian regime 9
universal suffrage 11

chapter summary

1. Politics is the process by which people decide which members of society get certain benefits or privileges and which members do not. It is the struggle over power or influence within institutions and organizations that can grant benefits or privileges. Government is the institution within which decisions are made that resolve conflicts or allocate benefits and privileges. It is unique because it has the ultimate authority within society.
2. Two fundamental political values are order, which includes security against violence, and liberty, the greatest freedom of the individual consistent with the freedom of other individuals. Liberty can be both promoted by government and invoked against government. To be effective, government authority must be backed by legitimacy.
3. Many of our terms for describing forms of government came from the ancient Greeks. In a direct democracy, such as ancient Athens, the people themselves make the important political decisions. The United States is a democratic republic, also called a representative democracy, in which the people elect representatives to make the decisions.
4. Theories of American democracy include majoritarianism, in which the government does what the majority wants; elite theory, in which the real power lies with one or more elites; and pluralist theory, in which organized interest groups contest for power.
5. Fundamental American values include liberty, order, equality, and property. Not all of these values are fully

compatible. The value of order often competes with civil liberties, and economic equality competes with property rights.

6. Popular political ideologies can be arrayed from left (liberal) to right (conservative). We can also analyze economic liberalism and conservatism separately from cultural liberalism and conservatism.

selected print & media resources

SUGGESTED READINGS

Fineman, Howard. ***The Thirteen American Arguments: Enduring Debates That Define and Inspire Our Country.*** New York: Random House Trade Paperbacks, 2009. Fineman, the senior Washington correspondent for *Newsweek,* describes questions that have divided Americans since the Revolution. Examples include: "Who Is an American," "The Role of Faith," and "America in the World." The book has won praise from Republicans and Democrats alike.

Hodgson, Godfrey. ***The Myth of American Exceptionalism.*** New Haven, Conn.: Yale University Press, 2009. A respected British commentator, Hodgson argues that America's history and political philosophy have always been more heavily influenced by the Old World than we have been willing to acknowledge.

Lasswell, Harold. ***Politics: Who Gets What, When and How.*** New York: McGraw-Hill, 1936. This classic work defines the nature of politics.

Obama, Barack. ***Dreams from My Father: A Story of Race and Inheritance.*** New York: Three Rivers Press, 2004. Obama's best-selling autobiography ends before his political career begins. He describes the sense of isolation resulting from his unusual background, and how he came to identify with the African American community. Obama's account provides fascinating insights into the many-sided American experience.

Riley-Smith, Tristram. ***The Cracked Bell: America and the Afflictions of Liberty.*** New York: Skyhorse Publishing, 2010. Riley-Smith, an English anthropologist, examines how the concepts of liberty and free markets have shaped America in the twenty-first century.

Stiglitz, Joseph E. ***Freefall: America, Free Markets, and the Sinking of the World Economy.*** New York: W. W. Norton & Co., 2010. A Nobel Prize–winning economist analyzes the Great Recession. From a liberal viewpoint, Stiglitz criticizes the bank bailouts sponsored by the Bush and Obama administrations.

Tocqueville, Alexis de. ***Democracy in America.*** Edited by Phillips Bradley. New York: Vintage Books, 1945. Life in the United States is described by a French writer who traveled through the nation in the 1820s.

MEDIA RESOURCES

All Things Considered—A daily broadcast of National Public Radio that provides extensive coverage of political, economic, and social news stories.

The Conservatives—A program that shows the rise of the conservative movement in America from the 1940s, through the presidential candidacy of Barry Goldwater, to the presidency of Ronald Reagan. In addition to Goldwater and Reagan, leaders interviewed include William F. Buckley, Jr., Norman Podhoretz, and Milton Friedman.

Liberalism vs. Conservatism—A 2001 film from Teacher's Video that focuses on two contrasting views of the role of government in society.

Mr. Smith Goes to Washington—A classic movie, produced in 1939, starring Jimmy Stewart as the honest citizen who goes to Congress trying to represent his fellow citizens. The movie dramatizes the clash between representing principles and representing corrupt interests.

The Values Issue and American Politics: Values Matter Most—Ben Wattenberg travels around the country in this 1995 program speaking to a broad range of ordinary Americans. He examines what he calls the "values issue"—the issues of crime, welfare, race, discipline, drugs, and prayer in the schools. Wattenberg believes that candidates who can best address these issues will win elections.

e-mocracy

CONNECTING TO AMERICAN GOVERNMENT AND POLITICS

The Web has become a virtual library, a telephone directory, a contact source, and a vehicle to improve your understanding of American government and politics today.

Increasingly, governments at all levels are using the Web to do business and communicate with citizens. In some states, individuals filing for unemployment compensation do so entirely online. Other states are using the Web to post public notices that in the past were published in newspapers.

To help you become familiar with Web resources, we conclude each chapter in this book with an *E-mocracy* feature. The *Logging On* section in each of these features includes Internet addresses, or uniform resource locators (URLs), that will take you to Web sites focusing on topics or issues discussed in the chapter. Realize that Web sites come and go continually, so some of the Web sites that we include in the *Logging On* section may not exist by the time you read this book.

A word of caution about Internet use: Many students surf the Web for political resources. When doing so, you need to remember to approach these sources with care. For one thing, you should be very careful when giving out information about yourself. You also need to use good judgment, because the reliability or intent of any given Web site is often unknown. Some sites are more concerned with accuracy than others, and some sites are updated to include current information while others are not.

LOGGING ON

You may want to visit the home page of Dr. Politics—offered by Steffen Schmidt, one of the authors of this book—for some interesting ideas and activities relating to American government and politics. Go to
www.public.iastate.edu/~sws/homepage.html

Information about the rules and requirements for immigration and citizenship can be found at the Web site of the U.S. Citizenship and Immigration Services:
www.uscis.gov/portal/site/uscis

For a basic "front door" to almost all U.S. government Web sites, click onto the very useful site maintained by the University of Michigan:
www.lib.umich.edu/government-documents-center/explore

For access to federal government offices and agencies, go to the U.S. government's official Web site at
www.usa.gov

The Web is a good place to learn about political science as a profession. The URL for the American Political Science Association is
www.apsanet.org

You can find the Web site of the International Political Science Association at
www.ipsa.org

chapter 2

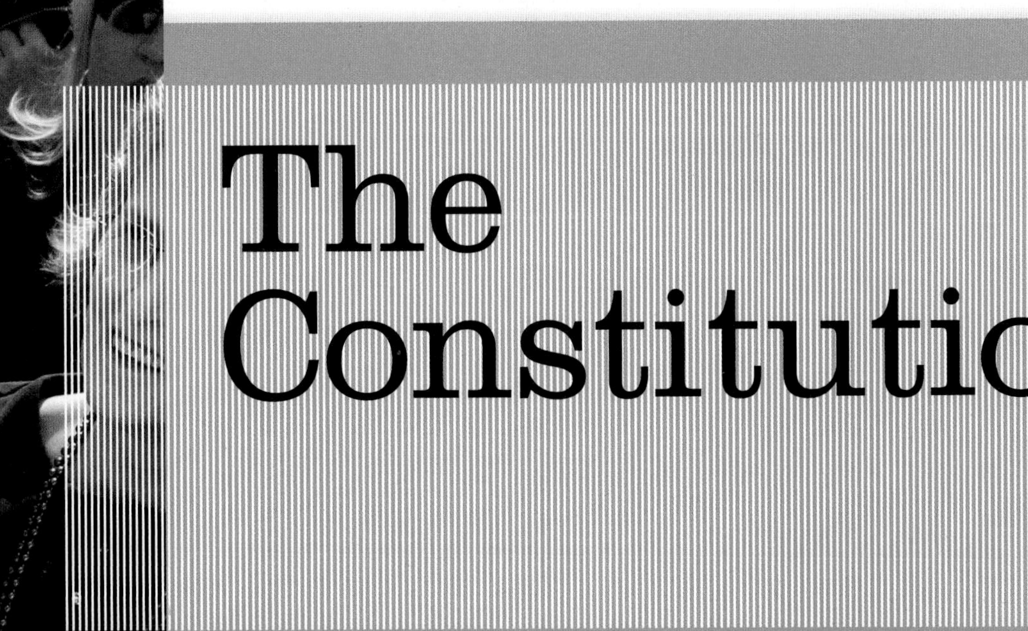

The Constitution

chapter contents

The Tea Party Express capped a cross-country bus tour with a rally in Washington, D.C., on Tax Day, April 15, 2010. (Mark Peterson/Redux)

WHAT IF... ...we elected the president by popular vote?

George W. Bush won the 2000 presidential elections although he received 540,000 fewer votes than Al Gore (right). (AP Photo/J. Scott Applewhite)

BACKGROUND

When you vote for president, the names of the candidates appear before you on the ballot. You don't, however, choose one of these candidates directly. You vote for a slate of *electors* who are pledged to support a particular candidate. There are 538 electors, one for each member of Congress plus three for the District of Columbia. Although the electors never gather together in one place, they are known collectively as the *electoral college*. This body was created by the founders in the hopes that the people would delegate the choice of president to a group of notables. The plan did not survive contact with reality. Electors publicly pledged themselves to candidates almost from the start, and so voters knew who they were choosing for president.

While the electoral college system has not prevented the people from choosing the president, it does have one side effect. A presidential candidate can win a majority of the popular votes but lose the election. This has happened. In 2000, Democrat Al Gore received 540,000 more votes than George W. Bush, the Republican. Still, Bush won enough electoral college votes to become president. Some citizens believe that the existing electoral college system should be abolished.

WHAT IF WE ELECTED THE PRESIDENT BY POPULAR VOTE?

Under the current system, in all but two small states, the winner of the state's popular vote takes all of the state's electoral votes. This winner-take-all provision is called the *unit rule*. As you might guess, presidential candidates have little reason to campaign in states where they are certain either to win or to lose by a large margin. During the last presidential elections, major campaigns took place in only ten key states, such as Florida, Pennsylvania, and Virginia. Partway through the campaign, Republican John McCain was forced to pull out of Michigan because he could not afford to run there, and Barack Obama was forced to close his operations in Georgia. These two states thus joined the "spectator" states, which included some of the nation's most populous—California, Illinois, New York, and Texas. If presidential candidates had to win a majority of the popular vote, they would be forced to campaign in every state.

Some believe, however, that without the electoral college and the unit rule, small states would be ignored. Also, the current system typically encourages certainty in elections by exaggerating the winner's margin of victory. Finally, under the existing system if the election is close and votes must be recounted, the recounts will take place in only a few jurisdictions. If the popular vote determined the winner, votes might have to be recounted in every corner of the country.

HOW A POPULAR VOTE SYSTEM COULD BE ESTABLISHED

Abolishing the electoral college would mean amending the Constitution, and that is very difficult. The unit rule could be abolished more easily, but political scientists have calculated that such a change might make it even less likely that the popular vote winner would carry the election. As an alternative, some people have proposed an interstate compact that would allow presidents to be elected by popular vote. Under the proposal, participating states would award their electoral votes to the candidate who wins the national popular vote. The plan would go into effect when enough states joined to control the electoral college. So far, five states have joined.

FOR CRITICAL ANALYSIS

1. Defenders of the existing system argue that it reduces voter fraud. How might that reduction happen?
2. Critics of the system argue that it prevents us from ever electing a third-party presidential candidate. Do you agree? Why or why not? And is this really a problem?

We the People of the United States, in Order to form a more perfect Union, establish Justice, insure domestic Tranquility, provide for the common defence, promote the general Welfare, and secure the Blessings of Liberty to ourselves and our Posterity, do ordain and establish this Constitution for the United States of America.

Every schoolchild in America has at one time or another been exposed to these famous words from the Preamble to the U.S. Constitution. The document itself is remarkable. The U.S. Constitution, compared with others in the fifty states and in the world, is relatively short. Because amending it is difficult, it also has relatively few amendments. The Constitution has remained largely intact for over two hundred years. To a great extent, this is because the principles set forth in the Constitution are sufficiently broad that they can be adapted to meet the needs of a changing society. (Sometimes questions arise over whether and how the Constitution should be adapted, as you read in this chapter's opening *What If . . .* feature.)

did you know?

That the first English claim to territory in North America was made by John Cabot, on behalf of King Henry VII, on June 24, 1497.

How and why the U.S. Constitution was created is a story that has been told and retold. It is worth repeating, because knowing the historical and political context in which this country's governmental machinery was formed is essential to understanding American government and politics today. The Constitution did not result just from creative thinking. Many of its provisions were grounded in the political philosophy of the time. The delegates to the Constitutional Convention in 1787 brought with them two important sets of influences: their political culture and their political experience. In the years between the first settlements in the New World and the writing of the Constitution, Americans had developed a political philosophy about how people should be governed and had tried out several forms of government. These experiences gave the founders the tools with which they constructed the Constitution.

The Colonial Background

In 1607, a company chartered by the English government sent a group of farmers to establish a trading post, Jamestown, in what is now Virginia. Jamestown was the first permanent English colony in the Americas. The king of England gave the backers of this colony a charter granting them "full power and authority" to make laws "for the good and welfare" of the settlement. The colonists at Jamestown instituted a **representative assembly,** a legislature composed of individuals who represent the population, thus setting a precedent in government that was to be observed in later colonial adventures.

Representative Assembly
A legislature composed of individuals who represent the population.

Separatists, the *Mayflower,* and the Compact

The first New England colony was established in 1620. A group made up in large part of extreme Separatists, who wished to break with the Church of England, came over on the ship *Mayflower* to the New World, landing at Plymouth (Massachusetts). Before going onshore, the adult males—women were not considered to have any political status—drew up the Mayflower Compact, which was signed by forty-one of the forty-four men aboard the ship on November 21, 1620. The reason for the compact was obvious. This group was outside the jurisdiction of the Virginia Company of London, which had chartered its settlement in Virginia, not Massachusetts. The Separatist leaders feared that some of the *Mayflower* passengers might conclude that they were no longer under any obligations of civil obedience. Therefore, some form of public authority was imperative. As William Bradford (one of the Separatist leaders) recalled in his accounts, there were "discontented

The signing of the compact aboard the *Mayflower.* In 1620, the Mayflower Compact was signed by almost all of the men aboard the *Mayflower* just before they disembarked at Plymouth, Massachusetts. It stated, "We . . . covenant and combine ourselves togeather into a civil body politick . . . ; and by vertue hearof to enacte, constitute, and frame such just and equal laws . . . as shall be thought [necessary] for the generall good of the Colonie." (The Granger Collection)

and mutinous speeches that some of the strangers [non-Separatists] amongst them had let fall from them in the ship; That when they came ashore they would use their owne libertie; for none had power to command them."[1]

The compact was not a constitution. It was a political statement in which the signers agreed to create and submit to the authority of a government, pending the receipt of a royal charter. The Mayflower Compact's historical and political significance is twofold: it depended on the consent of the affected individuals, and it served as a prototype for similar compacts in American history. By the time of the American Revolution, the compact was well on its way toward mythic status. In 1802, John Quincy Adams, son of the second American president, spoke these words at a founders' day celebration in Plymouth: "This is perhaps the only instance in human history of that positive, original social compact, which speculative philosophers have imagined as the only legitimate source of government."[2]

Although the Plymouth settlers committed themselves to self-government, in other ways their political ideas were not those that are prevalent today. The new community was a religious colony. Separation of church and state and most of our modern civil liberties were alien to the settlers' thinking. By the time the U.S. Constitution was written, the nation's leaders had a very different vision of the relationship between religion and government. We look at some of the founders' beliefs in this chapter's *Politics and Religion* feature on the facing page.

More Colonies, More Government

Another outpost in New England was set up by the Massachusetts Bay Colony in 1630. Then followed Rhode Island, Connecticut, New Hampshire, and others. By 1732, the last of the thirteen colonies, Georgia, was established. During the colonial period, Americans developed a concept of limited government, which followed from the establishment of the first colonies under Crown charters. Theoretically, London governed the colonies. In practice, owing partly to the colonies' distance from London, the colonists exercised a large measure of self-government. The colonists were able to make their own laws, as in the Fundamental Orders of Connecticut in 1639. The Massachusetts Body of Liberties in 1641 supported the protection of individual rights and was made a part of colonial law. In 1682, the Pennsylvania Frame of Government was passed. Along with the Pennsylvania Charter of Privileges of 1701, it foreshadowed our modern Constitution and Bill of Rights. All of this legislation enabled the colonists to acquire crucial political experience. After independence was declared in 1776, the states quickly set up their own new constitutions.

---

1. John Camp, *Out of the Wilderness: The Emergence of an American Identity in Colonial New England* (Middleton, Conn.: Wesleyan University Press, 1990).
2. Nathaniel Philbrick, *Mayflower: A Story of Courage, Community, and War* (New York: Penguin, 2007), p. 352. Today, the Mayflower Separatists are frequently referred to as the Pilgrims, but that name did not come into common use until two centuries after the colony was founded.

POLITICS AND... religion

JUST HOW CHRISTIAN WERE THE FOUNDERS?

Christianity utterly permeated the world of the first English settlers. The oldest colonial documents are filled with endorsements of Christianity. Regular church attendance was often mandatory. Nine of the colonies had churches that were established by law.

The Declaration of Independence, however, makes no reference to Christ. The word *God* does not appear in the Constitution. By 1790, established churches were found only in Connecticut and Massachusetts, and the Congregational Church in Massachusetts had drifted so far from its Puritan origins that many of its members no longer accepted the divinity of Jesus. They belonged to *Unitarian* congregations. One result of this development was that in the national elections of 1796 and 1800, neither major party fielded a presidential candidate who was, by modern definition, a Christian. John Adams, Unitarian, squared off against Thomas Jefferson, freethinker.

These developments raise the question: Just how Christian were the founders? More pointedly, did the founders intend the United States to be a "Christian nation"?

BY AND LARGE, THE FOUNDERS WERE DEVOUT CHRISTIANS . . .

In a recent public opinion poll, 65 percent of respondents agreed that "the nation's founders intended the United States to be a Christian nation," and 55 percent said they believed the Constitution established the country as a Christian nation. In recent years, a number of Christian conservatives have sought to have these propositions taught in the public schools.

The arguments of the Christian conservatives are not baseless. Plenty of American leaders throughout history have characterized the country as a Christian nation, beginning with John Jay, the first chief justice of the United States Supreme Court. Many of the revolutionaries of 1776 viewed the struggle in religious terms. Many believed that God had a special plan for America to serve as an example to the world. The overwhelming majority of the colonists considered themselves Christians. Today, 78 percent of Americans identify themselves as such. If "Christian nation" merely identifies the beliefs of the majority, it is undeniably an accurate label.

The Christian conservatives, however, mean much more. They argue that American law is based on the laws of Moses as set down in the Bible. They also believe that America's divine mission is not just an opinion held by many people—it should be taught in the schools as literal truth. Finally, according to this group, the separation of church and state is a liberal myth. The language of the First Amendment means only that the national government should not prefer one Protestant denomination over the others.

. . . WHO OPPOSED MIXING CHURCH AND STATE

Mainstream scholars disagree with these arguments, often vehemently. For example, Steven K. Green, a professor at Willamette University in Oregon, searched for American court cases that reference the laws of Moses. He found none.

Ultimately, to say that the founders were not serious about the separation of church and state is to ignore the plain language of the Constitution. True, most of the founders were Christians, but they were also steeped in Enlightenment rationalism that rejected "enthusiasm" in religion. *Enthusiasm* meant the spirit that allowed Protestant and Catholic Europeans to kill each other in the name of God over a period of two centuries. For the founders, mixing church and government was a recipe for trouble.

FOR CRITICAL ANALYSIS

Today, candidates for president clearly benefit when they use religious language and when they are comfortable discussing their faith. Is this at all troubling? Why or why not?

King George III
(1738–1820) was king of Great Britain and Ireland from 1760 until his death in 1820. Under George III, the British Parliament attempted to tax the American colonies. Ultimately, the colonies, exasperated at repeated attempts at taxation, proclaimed their independence on July 4, 1776. Why would Britain attempt to tax the colonists? (Painting by William Robinson/The Crown Estate/The Bridgeman Art Library International)

British Restrictions and Colonial Grievances

The conflict between Britain and the American colonies, which ultimately led to the Revolutionary War, began in the 1760s when the British government decided to raise revenues by imposing taxes on the American colonies. Policy advisers to Britain's King George III, who ascended the throne in 1760, decided that it was only logical to require the American colonists to help pay the costs of Britain's defending them during the French and Indian War (1756–1763). The colonists, who had grown accustomed to a large degree of self-government and independence from the British Crown, viewed the matter differently.

In 1764, the British Parliament passed the Sugar Act. Many colonists were unwilling to pay the tax imposed by the act. Further regulatory legislation was to come. In 1765, Parliament passed the Stamp Act, providing for internal taxation of legal documents and even newspapers—or, as the colonists' Stamp Act Congress, assembled in 1765, called it, "taxation without representation." The colonists boycotted the purchase of English commodities in return. The success of the boycott (the Stamp Act was repealed a year later) generated a feeling of unity within the colonies. The British, however, continued to try to raise revenues in the colonies. When Parliament passed duties on glass, lead, paint, and other items in 1767, the colonists again boycotted British goods. The colonists' fury over taxation climaxed in the Boston Tea Party: colonists dressed as Mohawk Indians dumped close to 350 chests of British tea into Boston Harbor as a gesture of tax protest. In retaliation, Parliament passed the Coercive Acts (the "Intolerable Acts") in 1774, which closed Boston Harbor and placed the government of Massachusetts under direct British control. The colonists were outraged—and they responded.

The Colonial Response: The Continental Congresses

New York, Pennsylvania, and Rhode Island proposed the convening of a colonial congress. The Massachusetts House of Representatives requested that all colonies hold conventions to select delegates to be sent to Philadelphia for such a congress.

The First Continental Congress

The First Continental Congress was held at Carpenter's Hall in Philadelphia on September 5, 1774. It was a gathering of delegates from twelve of the thirteen colonies (delegates from Georgia did not attend until 1775). At that meeting, there was little talk of independence. The congress passed a resolution requesting that the colonies send a petition to King George III expressing their grievances. Resolutions were also passed requiring that the colonies raise their own troops and boycott British trade. The British government condemned the congress's actions, treating them as open acts of rebellion.

did you know?

The celebration of King George III's birthday on June 4 gave rise to the custom of summer fireworks, and that after 1776, the celebration was rebranded and moved to the 4th of July.

The Second Continental Congress

By the time the Second Continental Congress met in May 1775 (this time all of the colonies were represented), fighting already had broken out between the British and the colonists. One of the main actions of the Second Congress was to establish an army. It did this by declaring the militia that had gathered around Boston an army and naming George Washington as commander in chief. The participants in that congress still attempted to reach a peaceful settlement with the British Parliament. One declaration of the congress stated explicitly that "we have not raised armies with ambitious designs of separating from Great Britain, and establishing independent states." But by the beginning of 1776, military encounters had become increasingly frequent.

Public debate was acrimonious. Then Thomas Paine's *Common Sense* appeared in Philadelphia bookstores. The pamphlet was a colonial best seller. (To do relatively as well today, a book would have to sell between 9 million and 11 million copies in its first year of publication.) Many agreed that Paine did make common sense when he argued that

> *a government of our own is our natural right: and when a man seriously reflects on the precariousness [instability, unpredictability] of human affairs, he will become convinced, that it is infinitely wiser and safer, to form a constitution of our own in a cool and deliberate manner, while we have it in our power, than to trust such an interesting event to time and chance.*[3]

Paine further argued that "nothing can settle our affairs so expeditiously as an open and determined declaration for Independence."[4]

Students of Paine's pamphlet point out that his arguments were not new—they were common in tavern debates throughout the land. Rather, it was the near poetry of his words—which were at the same time as plain as the alphabet—that struck his readers.

Declaring Independence

On April 6, 1776, the Second Continental Congress voted for free trade at all American ports with all countries except Britain. This act could be interpreted as an implicit declaration of independence. The next month, the congress suggested that each of the colonies establish state governments unconnected to Britain. Finally, in July, the colonists declared their independence from Britain.

The Resolution of Independence

On July 2, the Resolution of Independence was adopted by the Second Continental Congress:

> *RESOLVED, That these United Colonies are, and of right ought to be, free and independent States, that they are absolved from allegiance to the British Crown, and that all political connection between them and the state of Great Britain is, and ought to be, totally dissolved.*

Already by June 1776, Thomas Jefferson was writing drafts of the Declaration of Independence in the second-floor parlor of a bricklayer's house in Philadelphia. On adoption of the Resolution of Independence, Jefferson argued that a declaration clearly putting forth the causes that compelled the colonies to separate from Britain was necessary. The Second Congress assigned the task to him.

Milestones in Early U.S. Political History

1607	Jamestown established; Virginia Company lands settlers.
1620	Mayflower Compact signed.
1630	Massachusetts Bay Colony set up.
1639	Fundamental Orders of Connecticut adopted.
1641	Massachusetts Body of Liberties adopted.
1682	Pennsylvania Frame of Government passed.
1701	Pennsylvania Charter of Privileges written.
1732	Last of the thirteen colonies (Georgia) established.
1756	French and Indian War declared.
1765	Stamp Act; Stamp Act Congress meets.
1774	First Continental Congress.
1775	Second Continental Congress; Revolutionary War begins.
1776	Declaration of Independence signed.
1777	Articles of Confederation drafted.
1781	Last state (Maryland) signs Articles of Confederation.
1783	"Critical period" in U.S. history begins; weak national government until 1789.
1786	Shays' Rebellion.
1787	Constitutional Convention.
1788	Ratification of Constitution.
1791	Ratification of Bill of Rights.

3. *The Political Writings of Thomas Paine*, Vol. 1 (Boston: J. P. Mendum Investigator Office, 1870), p. 46.
4. *Ibid.*, p. 54.

July 4, 1776—The Declaration of Independence

Jefferson's version of the declaration was amended to gain unanimous acceptance (for example, his condemnation of the slave trade was eliminated to satisfy Georgia and North Carolina), but the bulk of it was passed intact on July 4, 1776. On July 19, the modified draft became "the unanimous declaration of the thirteen United States of America." On August 2, it was signed by the members of the Second Continental Congress.

Universal Truths. The Declaration of Independence has become one of the world's most famous and significant documents. The words opening the second paragraph of the Declaration are known most widely:

> *We hold these Truths to be self-evident, that all Men are created equal, that they are endowed by their Creator with certain unalienable Rights, that among these are Life, Liberty, and the Pursuit of Happiness—That to secure these Rights, Governments are instituted among Men, deriving their just Powers from the Consent of the Governed, that whenever any Form of Government becomes destructive of these Ends, it is the Right of the People to alter or abolish it, and to institute new Government.*

Natural Rights
Rights held to be inherent in natural law, not dependent on governments. John Locke stated that natural law, being superior to human law, specifies certain rights of "life, liberty, and property." These rights, altered to become "life, liberty, and the pursuit of happiness," are asserted in the Declaration of Independence.

Social Contract
A voluntary agreement among individuals to secure their rights and welfare by creating a government and abiding by its rules.

Natural Rights and a Social Contract. The statement that "all Men are created equal" and have **natural rights** ("unalienable Rights"), including the rights to "Life, Liberty, and the Pursuit of Happiness," was revolutionary at that time. Its use by Jefferson reveals the influence of the English philosopher John Locke (1632–1704), whose writings were familiar to educated American colonists, including Jefferson. In his *Two Treatises on Government,* published in 1690, Locke had argued that all people possess certain natural rights, including the rights to life, liberty, and property.

This claim was not inconsistent with English legal traditions. Locke went on, however, to argue that the primary purpose of government was to protect these rights. Furthermore, government was established by the people through a **social contract**—an agreement among the people to form a government and abide by its rules. As you read earlier, such contracts, or compacts, were not new to Americans. The Mayflower Compact was the first of several documents that established governments or governing rules based on the consent of the governed. In citing the "pursuit of happiness" instead of "property" as a right, Jefferson clearly meant to go beyond Locke's thinking.

Benjamin Franklin (left) sits with John Adams while Thomas Jefferson looks on during a meeting outside the Second Continental Congress. What important document came out of that congress? (Jean Léon Gerome Ferris/The Granger Collection)

After setting forth these basic principles of government, the Declaration of Independence goes on to justify the colonists' revolt against Britain. Much of the remainder of the document is a list of what "He" (King George III) had done to deprive the colonists of their rights. This indictment bore strong resemblances to an earlier British document: the English Bill of Rights, which Parliament drafted in 1689 to justify the ouster of James II. The earlier document formed a natural template for denunciations of a later monarch. (See Appendix A at the end of this book for the complete text of the Declaration of Independence.)

The Significance of the Declaration. The concepts of equality, natural rights, and government established by a social contract expressed in the Declaration of Independence were to have a lasting impact on American life. The Declaration set forth ideals that have since become a fundamental part of our national identity. The Declaration of Independence also became a model for use by other nations around the world.

Certainly, most Americans are familiar with the beginning words of the Declaration. Yet, as Harvard historian David Armitage noted in his study of the Declaration of Independence in the international context,[5] few Americans ponder the obvious question: What did these assertions in the Declaration have to do with independence? Clearly, independence could have been declared without these words. Even as late as 1857, Abraham Lincoln admitted, "The assertion that 'all men are created equal' was of no practical use in effecting our separation from Great Britain; and it was placed in the Declaration, not for that, but for future use."[6]

Essentially, the immediate significance of the Declaration of Independence, in 1776, was that it established the legitimacy of the new nation in the eyes of foreign governments, as well as in the eyes of the colonists themselves. What the new nation needed most were supplies for its armies and a commitment of foreign military aid. Unless it appeared to the world as a political entity separate and independent from Britain, no foreign government would enter into an agreement with its leaders. Once the Declaration had fulfilled its purpose of legitimizing the American Revolution, the document suffered relative neglect for many years. The lasting significance of the Declaration—as a founding document setting forth American ideals—came later.

The Rise of Republicanism

Although the colonists had formally declared independence from Britain, the fight to gain actual independence continued for five more years, until the British general Cornwallis surrendered at Yorktown in 1781. In 1783, after Britain formally recognized the independent status of the United States in the Treaty of Paris, Washington disbanded the army. During these years of military struggles, the states faced the additional challenge of creating a system of self-government for an independent United States.

Some colonists had demanded that independence be preceded by the formation of a strong central government. But others, who called themselves Republicans, were against a strong central government. They opposed monarchy, executive authority, and almost any form of restraint on the power of local groups.

From 1776 to 1780, all of the states adopted written constitutions. Eleven of the constitutions were completely new. Two of them—those of Connecticut and Rhode Island—were old royal charters with minor modifications. Republican sentiment led to increased power for the legislatures. In Georgia and Pennsylvania, **unicameral** (one-body) **legislatures** were unchecked by executive or judicial authority. Basically, the Republicans attempted to maintain the politics of 1776. In almost all states, the legislature was predominant.

Unicameral Legislature
A legislature with only one legislative chamber, as opposed to a bicameral (two-chamber) legislature, such as the U.S. Congress. Today, Nebraska is the only state in the Union with a unicameral legislature.

Confederation
A political system in which states or regional governments retain ultimate authority except for those powers they expressly delegate to a central government; a voluntary association of independent states, in which the member states agree to limited restraints on their freedom of action.

State
A group of people occupying a specific area and organized under one government; may be either a nation or a subunit of a nation.

The Articles of Confederation: Our First Form of Government

The fear of a powerful central government led to the passage of the Articles of Confederation, which created a weak central government. The term **confederation** is important; it means a voluntary association of independent **states,** in which the member states agree to only limited restraints on their freedom of action. As a result, confederations seldom have an effective executive authority.

5. David Armitage, *The Declaration of Independence: A Global History* (Cambridge, Mass.: Harvard University Press, 2007).
6. As cited in Armitage, *The Declaration of Independence,* p. 26.

did you know?

That the Articles of Confederation specified that Canada could be admitted to the Confederation if it ever wished to join.

In June 1776, the Second Continental Congress began the process of drafting what would become the Articles of Confederation. The final form of the Articles was achieved by November 15, 1777. It was not until March 1, 1781, however, that the last state, Maryland, agreed to ratify what was called the Articles of Confederation and Perpetual Union. Well before the final ratification of the Articles, however, many of them were implemented: the Continental Congress and the thirteen states conducted American military, economic, and political affairs according to the standards and the form specified by the Articles.[7]

The Articles Establish a Government

Under the Articles, the thirteen original colonies, now states, established on March 1, 1781, a government of the states—the Congress of the Confederation. The Congress was a unicameral assembly of so-called ambassadors from each state, with each state possessing a single vote. Each year, the Congress would choose one of its members as its president (that is, presiding officer), but the Articles did not provide for a president of the United States.

The Congress was authorized in Article X to appoint an executive committee of the states "to execute in the recess of Congress, such of the powers of Congress as the United States, in Congress assembled, by the consent of nine [of the thirteen] states, shall from time to time think expedient to vest with them." The Congress was also allowed to appoint other committees and civil officers necessary for managing the general affairs of the United States. In addition, the Congress could regulate foreign affairs and establish coinage and weights and measures. But it lacked an independent source of revenue and the necessary executive machinery to enforce its decisions throughout the land. Article II of the Articles of Confederation guaranteed that each state would retain its sovereignty. Figure 2–1 alongside illustrates the structure of the government under the Articles of Confederation; Table 2–1 on the facing page summarizes the powers—and the lack of powers—of Congress under the Articles of Confederation.

FIGURE 2–1 The Confederal Government Structure under the Articles of Confederation

Congress
Congress had one house. Each state had two to seven members, but only one vote. The exercise of most powers required approval of at least nine states. Amendments to the Articles required the consent of all the states.

↓

Committee of the States
A committee of representatives from all the states was empowered to act in the name of Congress between sessions.

↓

Officers
Congress appointed officers to do some of the executive work.

↓

The States

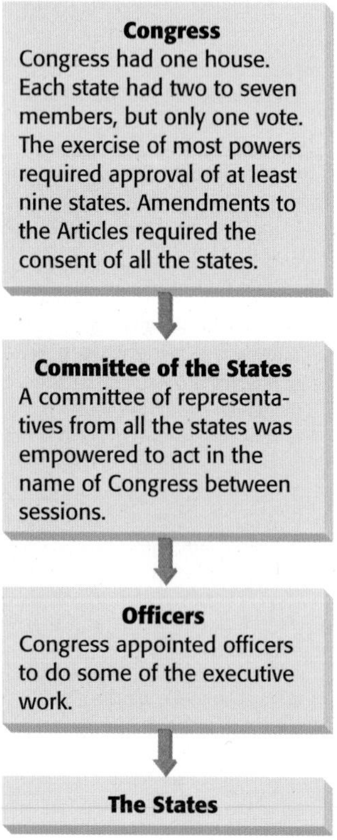

Accomplishments under the Articles

The new government had some accomplishments during its eight years of existence under the Articles of Confederation. Certain states' claims to western lands were settled. Maryland had objected to the claims of the Carolinas, Connecticut, Georgia, Massachusetts, New York, and Virginia. It was only after these states consented to give up their land claims to the United States as a whole that Maryland signed the Articles of Confederation. Another accomplishment under the Articles was the passage of the Northwest Ordinance of 1787, which established a basic pattern of government for new territories north of the Ohio River. All in all, the Articles represented the first real pooling of resources by the American states.

Weaknesses of the Articles

In spite of these accomplishments, the Articles of Confederation had many defects. Although Congress had the legal right to declare war and to conduct foreign policy, it did not have the right to demand revenues from the states. It could only ask for them. Additionally, the actions of Congress required the consent of nine states. Any amendments to the Articles required the unanimous consent of the Congress and confirmation by every state legislature. Furthermore, the Articles did not create a national system of courts.

7. Keith L. Dougherty, *Collective Action under the Articles of Confederation* (New York: Cambridge University Press, 2006).

TABLE 2–1 Powers of the Congress of the Confederation

Congress Had Power to	Congress Lacked Power to
• Declare war and make peace. • Enter into treaties and alliances. • Establish and control armed forces. • Requisition men and revenues from states. • Regulate coinage. • Borrow funds and issue bills of credit. • Fix uniform standards of weight and measurement. • Create admiralty courts. • Create a postal system. • Regulate Indian affairs. • Guarantee citizens of each state the rights and privileges of citizens in the several states when in another state. • Adjudicate disputes between states on state petition.	• Provide for effective treaty-making power and control foreign relations; it could not compel states to respect treaties. • Compel states to meet military quotas; it could not draft soldiers. • Regulate interstate and foreign commerce; it left each state free to set up its own tariff system. • Collect taxes directly from the people; it had to rely on states to collect and forward taxes. • Compel states to pay their share of government costs. • Provide and maintain a sound monetary system or issue paper money; this was left up to the states, and monies in circulation differed tremendously in value.

Basically, the functioning of the government under the Articles depended on the goodwill of the states. Article III of the Articles simply established a "league of friendship" among the states—no national government was intended.

Probably the most fundamental weakness of the Articles, and the most basic cause of their eventual replacement by the Constitution, was the lack of power to raise funds for the militia. The Articles contained no language giving Congress coercive power to raise revenues (by levying taxes) to provide adequate support for the military forces controlled by Congress. When states refused to send revenues to support the government (not one state met the financial requests made by Congress under the Articles), Congress resorted to selling off western lands to speculators or issuing bonds that sold for less than their face value. Due to a lack of resources, the Continental Congress was forced to disband the army after the Revolutionary War, even in the face of serious Spanish and British military threats.

Shays' Rebellion and the Need for Revision of the Articles

Because of the weaknesses of the Articles of Confederation, the central government could do little to maintain peace and order in the new nation. The states bickered among themselves and increasingly taxed each other's goods. At times they prevented trade altogether. By 1784, the country faced a serious economic depression. Banks were calling in old loans and refusing to make new ones. People who could not pay their debts were often thrown into prison.

By 1786, in Concord, Massachusetts, the scene of one of the first battles of the Revolution, there were three times as many people in prison for debt as there were for all other crimes combined. In Worcester County, Massachusetts, the ratio was even higher—twenty to one. Most of the prisoners were small farmers who could not pay their debts because of the disorganized state of the economy.

In August 1786, mobs of musket-bearing farmers led by former revolutionary captain Daniel Shays seized county courthouses and disrupted the trials of debtors in Springfield, Massachusetts. Shays and his men then launched an attack on the federal arsenal at Springfield, but they were

Tempers flared starting in 1784 when economic times became tough. This fight broke out during Shays' Rebellion in 1786. Who was Daniel Shays? (© Bettmann/Corbis)

repulsed. Shays' Rebellion demonstrated that the central government could not protect the citizenry from armed rebellion or provide adequately for the public welfare. The rebellion spurred the nation's political leaders to action. As John Jay wrote to Thomas Jefferson,

> *Changes are Necessary, but what they ought to be, what they will be, and how and when to be produced, are arduous Questions. I feel for the Cause of Liberty. . . . If it should not take Root in this Soil[,] Little Pains will be taken to cultivate it in any other.*[8]

Drafting the Constitution

The Virginia legislature called for a meeting of all the states to be held at Annapolis, Maryland, on September 11, 1786—ostensibly to discuss commercial problems only. It was evident to those in attendance (including Alexander Hamilton and James Madison) that the national government had serious weaknesses that had to be addressed if it was to survive. Among the important problems to be solved were the relationship between the states and the central government, the powers of the national legislature, the need for executive leadership, and the establishment of policies for economic stability.

The result of this meeting was a petition to the Continental Congress for a general convention to meet in Philadelphia in May 1787 "to consider the exigencies of the union." Congress approved the convention in February 1787. When those who favored a weak central government realized that the Philadelphia meeting would in fact take place, they endorsed the convention. They made sure, however, that the convention would be summoned "for the sole and express purpose of revising the Articles of Confederation." Those in favor of a stronger national government had different ideas.

The designated date for the opening of the convention at Philadelphia, now known as the Constitutional Convention, was May 14, 1787. Because few of the delegates had actually arrived in Philadelphia by that time, however, the convention was not formally opened in the East Room of the Pennsylvania State House until May 25.[9] Fifty-five of the seventy-four delegates chosen for the convention actually attended. (Of those fifty-five, only about forty played active roles at the convention.) Rhode Island was the only state that refused to send delegates.

Who Were the Delegates?

Who were the fifty-five delegates to the Constitutional Convention? They certainly did not represent a cross section of American society in the 1700s. Indeed, most were members of the upper class. Consider the following facts:

1. Thirty-three were members of the legal profession.
2. Three were physicians.
3. Almost 50 percent were college graduates.
4. Seven were former chief executives of their respective states.
5. Six were owners of large plantations.
6. Eight were important businesspersons.

They were also relatively young by today's standards: James Madison was thirty-six, Alexander Hamilton was only thirty-two, and Jonathan Dayton of New Jersey was twenty-six. The venerable Benjamin Franklin, however, was eighty-one and had to be carried in on

---

8. Excerpt from a letter from John Jay to Thomas Jefferson written in October 1786, as reproduced in Winthrop D. Jordan *et al., The United States,* combined ed., 6th ed. (Englewood Cliffs, N.J.: Prentice Hall, 1987), p. 135.
9. The State House was later named Independence Hall. This was the same room in which the Declaration of Independence had been signed eleven years earlier.

a portable chair borne by four prisoners from a local jail. Not counting Franklin, the average age was just over forty-two.

The Working Environment

The conditions under which the delegates worked for 115 days were far from ideal and were made even worse by the necessity of maintaining total secrecy. The framers of the Constitution believed that if public debate took place on particular positions, delegates would have a more difficult time compromising or backing down to reach agreement. Consequently, the windows were usually shut in the East Room of the State House. Summer quickly arrived, and the air became heavy, humid, and hot by noon of each day. Also, when the windows were open, flies swarmed into the room. The delegates did, however, have a nearby tavern and inn to which they retired each evening—the Indian Queen. It became the informal headquarters of the delegates.

did you know?

That James Madison was the only delegate to attend every meeting of the Constitutional Convention.

Factions among the Delegates

We know much about the proceedings at the convention because James Madison kept a daily, detailed personal journal. A majority of the delegates were strong nationalists—they wanted a central government with real power, unlike the central government under the Articles of Confederation. George Washington and Benjamin Franklin were among those who sought a stronger government. A few advocates of a strong central government, led by Gouverneur Morris of Pennsylvania and John Rutledge of South Carolina, distrusted the ability of the common people to engage in self-government.

Among the nationalists, several went so far as to support monarchy. This group included Alexander Hamilton, who was chiefly responsible for the Annapolis Convention's call for the Constitutional Convention. In a long speech on June 18, he presented his views: "I have no scruple in declaring . . . that the British government is the best in the world and that I doubt much whether anything short of it will do in America."

Another important group of nationalists were of a more democratic stripe. Led by James Madison of Virginia and James Wilson of Pennsylvania, these democratic nationalists wanted a central government founded on popular support.

Still another faction consisted of nationalists who were less democratic in nature and who would support a central government only if it was founded on very narrowly defined republican principles. This group was made up of a relatively small number of delegates, including Edmund Randolph and George Mason of Virginia, Elbridge Gerry of Massachusetts, and Luther Martin and John Francis Mercer of Maryland.

Many of the other delegates from Connecticut, Delaware, Maryland, New Hampshire, and New Jersey were concerned about only one thing—claims to western lands. As long as those lands became the common property of all of the states, these delegates were willing to support a central government.

Finally, there was a group of delegates who were totally against a national authority. Two of the three delegates from New York quit the convention when they saw the nationalist direction of its proceedings.

Elbridge Gerry (1744–1814), from Massachusetts, was a patriot during the Revolution. He was a signer of the Declaration of Independence and later became governor of Massachusetts (1810–1812). He became James Madison's vice president when Madison was reelected in December 1812. (Library of Congress)

Politicking and Compromises

The debates at the convention started on the first day. James Madison had spent months reviewing European political theory. When his Virginia delegation arrived ahead of most of the others, it got to work immediately. By the time George Washington opened the convention, Governor Edmund Randolph of

did you know?

That the word *democracy* does not appear once in the Constitution.

Virginia was prepared to present fifteen resolutions. In retrospect, this was a masterful stroke on the part of the Virginia delegation. It set the agenda for the remainder of the convention—even though, in principle, the delegates had been sent to Philadelphia for the sole purpose of amending the Articles of Confederation. They had not been sent to write a new constitution.

The Virginia Plan. Randolph's fifteen resolutions proposed an entirely new national government under a constitution. It was, however, a plan that favored the large states, including Virginia. Basically, it called for the following:

1. A **bicameral** (two-chamber) **legislature,** with the lower chamber chosen by the people and the smaller upper chamber chosen by the lower chamber from nominees selected by state legislatures. The number of representatives would be proportional to a state's population, thus favoring the large states. The legislature could void any state laws.
2. The creation of an unspecified national executive, elected by the legislature.
3. The creation of a national judiciary, appointed by the legislature.

It did not take long for the smaller states to realize they would fare poorly under the Virginia Plan, which would enable Massachusetts, Pennsylvania, and Virginia to form a majority in the national legislature. The debate on the plan dragged on for a number of weeks. It was time for the small states to come up with their own plan.

The New Jersey Plan. On June 15, lawyer William Paterson of New Jersey offered an alternative plan. After all, argued Paterson, under the Articles of Confederation all states had equality; therefore, the convention had no power to change this arrangement. He proposed the following:

1. The fundamental principle of the Articles of Confederation—one state, one vote—would be retained.
2. Congress would be able to regulate trade and impose taxes.
3. All acts of Congress would be the supreme law of the land.
4. Several people would be elected by Congress to form an executive office.
5. The executive office would appoint a Supreme Court.

Basically, the New Jersey Plan was simply an amendment of the Articles of Confederation. Its only notable feature was its reference to the **supremacy doctrine,** which was later included in the Constitution.

Bicameral Legislature
A legislature made up of two parts, called chambers. The U.S. Congress, composed of the House of Representatives and the Senate, is a bicameral legislature.

Supremacy Doctrine
A doctrine that asserts the priority of national law over state laws. This principle is rooted in Article VI of the Constitution, which provides that the Constitution, the laws passed by the national government under its constitutional powers, and all treaties constitute the supreme law of the land.

Great Compromise
The compromise between the New Jersey and Virginia Plans that created one chamber of the Congress based on population and one chamber representing each state equally; also called the Connecticut Compromise.

The "Great Compromise." The delegates were at an impasse. Most wanted a strong national government and were unwilling even to consider the New Jersey Plan. But when the Virginia Plan was brought up again, the small states threatened to leave. It was not until July 16 that a compromise was achieved. Roger Sherman of Connecticut proposed the following:

1. A bicameral legislature in which the lower chamber, the House of Representatives, would be apportioned according to the number of free inhabitants in each state, plus three-fifths of the slaves.
2. An upper chamber, the Senate, which would have two members from each state elected by the state legislatures.

This plan, known as the **Great Compromise** (it is also called the Connecticut Compromise because of the role of the Connecticut delegates in the proposal), broke the deadlock. It did exact a political price, however, because it permitted each state to have equal representation in the Senate. Having two senators represent each state in effect diluted the voting power of citizens living in more heavily populated states and gave the smaller states disproportionate political powers. But the Connecticut Compromise resolved the large-state/small-state controversy. In addition, the Senate could be expected to act as a check on the House, which many feared would be dominated by, and responsive to, the masses.

George Washington presided over the Constitutional Convention of 1787. (Stearns/ © Bettmann/Corbis)

The Three-Fifths Compromise. The Great Compromise also settled another major issue—how to deal with slaves in the representational scheme. Slavery was still legal in many northern states, but it was concentrated in the South. Many delegates were opposed to slavery and wanted it banned entirely in the United States. Charles Pinckney of South Carolina led strong southern opposition to a ban on slavery. Furthermore, the South wanted slaves to be counted along with free persons in determining representation in Congress. Delegates from the northern states objected. Sherman's three-fifths proposal was a compromise between northerners who did not want the slaves counted at all and southerners who wanted them counted in the same way as free whites. Actually, Sherman's Connecticut Plan spoke of three-fifths of "all other persons" (and that is the language of the Constitution itself). It is not hard to figure out, though, who those other persons were.

The three-fifths compromise illustrates the power of the southern states at the convention.[10] The three-fifths rule meant that the House of Representatives and the electoral college would be apportioned in part on the basis of *property*—specifically, property in slaves. Modern commentators have referred to the three-fifths rule as valuing African Americans only three-fifths as much as whites. Actually, the additional southern representatives elected because of the three-fifths rule did not represent the slaves at all. Rather, these extra representatives were a gift to the slave owners—the additional representatives enhanced the power of the South in Congress.

The Slave Trade and the Future of Slavery. The three-fifths compromise did not completely settle the slavery issue. There was also the question of the slave trade. Eventually, the delegates agreed that Congress could not ban the importation of slaves until after 1808.

did you know?

That during the four centuries of slave trading, an estimated 10 million to 11 million Africans were transported to North and South America—and that only 6 percent of those slaves were imported into the United States.

The compromise meant that the matter of slavery itself was never addressed directly. The South won twenty years of unrestricted slave trade and a requirement that escaped slaves in free states be returned to their owners in slave states.

Clearly, many delegates, including slave owners such as George Washington and James Madison, had serious objections to slavery. Why, then, did they allow slavery to continue? Historians have long maintained that the framers had no choice—that without a slavery compromise, the delegates from the South would have abandoned the convention. Indeed, this was the fear of a number of the antislavery delegates to the convention. Madison, for example, said, "Great as the evil is, a dismemberment of the Union would be even worse."[11]

10. See Garry Wills, *"Negro President": Jefferson and the Slave Power* (New York: Houghton Mifflin, 2003).
11. Speech before the Virginia ratifying convention on June 17, 1788, as cited in Bruno Leone, ed., *The Creation of the Constitution* (San Diego: Greenhaven Press, 1995), p. 159.

did you know?

That the U.S. Constitution, at 4,400 words without its amendments, is the shortest written constitution of any major nation.

Other scholars, however, contend that not only would it have been possible for the founders to ban slavery, but by doing so they would have achieved greater unity for the new nation.[12]

Other Issues. The South also worried that the northern majority in Congress would pass legislation unfavorable to its economic interests. Because the South depended on agricultural exports, it feared the imposition of export taxes. In return for acceding to the northern demand that Congress be able to regulate commerce among the states and with other nations, the South obtained a promise that export taxes would not be imposed. As a result, the United States is among the few countries that do not tax their exports.

There were other disagreements. The delegates could not decide whether to establish only a Supreme Court or to create lower courts as well. They deferred the issue by mandating a Supreme Court and allowing Congress to establish lower courts. They also disagreed over whether the president or the Senate would choose the Supreme Court justices. A compromise was reached with the agreement that the president would nominate the justices and the Senate would confirm the nominations.

These compromises, as well as others, resulted from the recognition that if one group of states refused to ratify the Constitution, it was doomed.

Working toward Final Agreement

The Connecticut Compromise was reached by mid-July. The makeup of the executive branch and the judiciary, however, was left unsettled. The remaining work of the convention was turned over to a five-man Committee of Detail, which presented a rough draft of the Constitution on August 6. It made the executive and judicial branches subordinate to the legislative branch.

Separation of Powers
The principle of dividing governmental powers among different branches of government.

Madisonian Model
A structure of government proposed by James Madison in which the powers of the government are separated into three branches: executive, legislative, and judicial.

Checks and Balances
A major principle of the American system of government whereby each branch of the government can check the actions of the others.

The Madisonian Model—Separation of Powers. The major issue of **separation of powers** had not yet been resolved. The delegates were concerned with structuring the government to prevent the imposition of tyranny—either by the majority or by a minority. It was Madison who proposed a governmental scheme—sometimes called the **Madisonian model**—to achieve this: the executive, legislative, and judicial powers of government were to be separated so that no one branch had enough power to dominate the others. The separation of powers was by function, as well as by personnel, with Congress passing laws, the president enforcing and administering laws, and the courts interpreting laws in individual circumstances.

Each of the three branches of government would be independent of the others, but they would have to cooperate to govern. According to Madison, in *Federalist Paper* No. 51 (see Appendix C), "the great security against a gradual concentration of the several powers in the same department consists in giving to those who administer each department the necessary constitutional means and personal motives to resist encroachments of the others."

The Madisonian Model—Checks and Balances. The "constitutional means" Madison referred to is a system of **checks and balances** through which each branch of the government can check the actions of the others. For example, Congress can enact laws, but the president has veto power over congressional acts. The Supreme Court has the power to declare acts of Congress and of the executive unconstitutional, but the president appoints the justices of the Supreme Court, with the advice and consent of the

12. See, for example, Paul Finkelman, *Slavery and the Founders: Race and Liberty in the Age of Jefferson*, 2d ed. (Armonk, N.Y.: M. E. Sharpe, 2001); and Gary B. Nash, *The Forgotten Fifth: African Americans in the Age of Revolution* (Cambridge, Mass.: Harvard University Press, 2006).

Senate. (The Supreme Court's power to declare acts unconstitutional was not mentioned in the Constitution, although arguably the framers assumed that the Court would have this power—see the discussion of *judicial review* later in this chapter.) Figure 2–2 below outlines these checks and balances.

Madison's ideas of separation of powers and checks and balances were not new. Indeed, the influential French political thinker Baron de Montesquieu (1689–1755) had explored these concepts in his book *The Spirit of the Laws,* published in 1748. Montesquieu not only discussed the "three sorts of powers" (executive, legislative, and judicial) that were necessarily exercised by any government but also gave examples of how, in some nations, certain checks on these powers had arisen and had been effective in preventing tyranny.

Even though separation of powers is central to the American political system, the principle was not widely adopted when representative democracy began to spread across the world. In a majority of democratic countries, the nation's chief executive is also the leader of the largest party (or coalition of parties) in the legislature, and so the legislative and executive powers are united. This alternative institutional arrangement, called the parliamentary system, originated in Britain, and we describe it in the *Beyond Our Borders* feature on page 47.

The Development of the Madisonian Model. In the years since the Constitution was ratified, the checks and balances built into it have evolved into a sometimes complex give-and-take among the branches of government. Generally, for nearly every check that one branch has over another, the branch that has been checked has found a way of getting around it. For example, suppose that the president checks Congress by vetoing a bill.

FIGURE 2–2 Checks and Balances

The major checks and balances among the three branches are illustrated here. The U.S. Constitution does not mention some of these checks, such as judicial review—the power of the courts to declare federal or state acts unconstitutional—and the president's ability to refuse to enforce judicial decisions or congressional legislation. Checks and balances can be thought of as a confrontation of powers or responsibilities. Each branch checks the actions of another; two branches in conflict have powers that can result in balances or stalemates, requiring one branch to give in or both to reach a compromise.

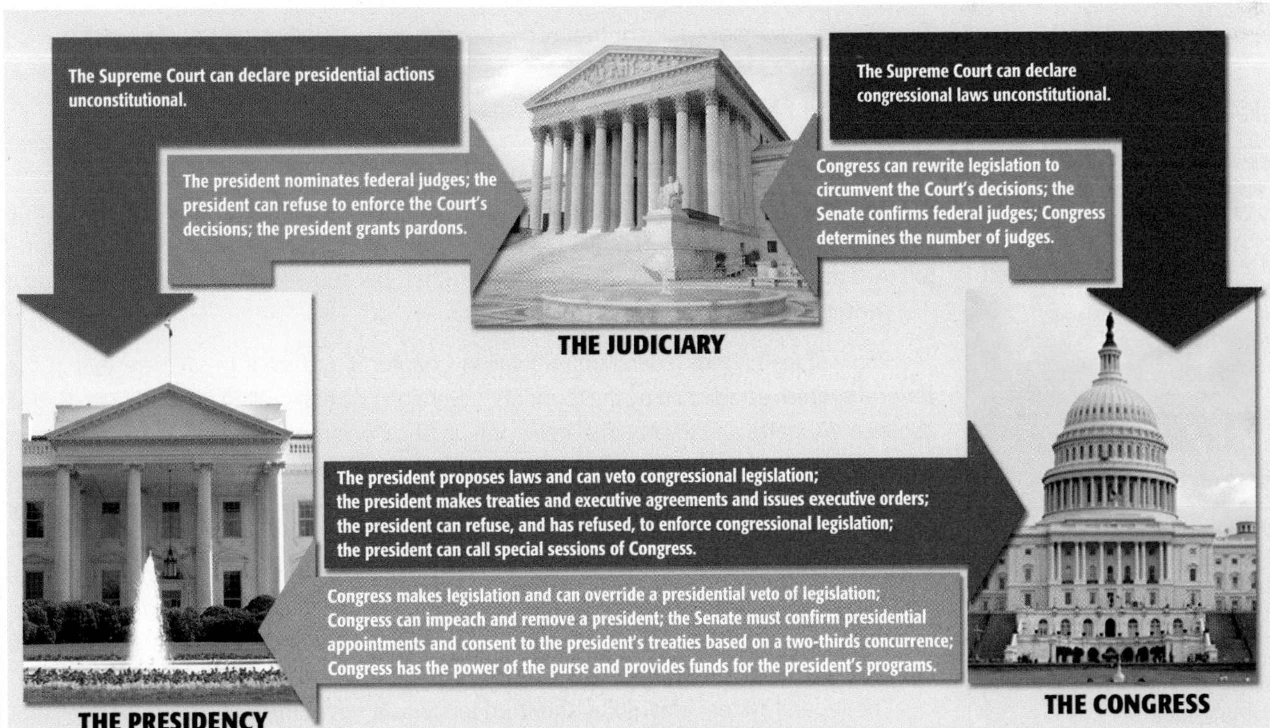

(Creative Commons)

James Madison (1751–1836) earned the title "master builder of the Constitution" because of his persuasive logic during the Constitutional Convention. His contributions to the *Federalist Papers* showed him to be a brilliant political thinker and writer. (© Bettmann/Corbis)

Congress can override the presidential veto by a two-thirds vote. Additionally, Congress holds the "power of the purse." If it disagrees with a program endorsed by the executive branch, it can simply refuse to appropriate the funds necessary to operate that program. Similarly, the president can impose a countercheck on Congress if the Senate refuses to confirm a presidential appointment, such as a judicial appointment. The president can simply wait until Congress is in recess and then make what is called a "recess appointment," which does not require the Senate's approval.

The Executive. Some delegates favored a plural executive made up of representatives from the various regions. This was abandoned in favor of a single chief executive. Some argued that Congress should choose the executive. To make the presidency completely independent of the proposed Congress, however, an **electoral college** was adopted. To be sure, the electoral college created a cumbersome presidential election process (see Chapter 9). The process even made it possible for a candidate who comes in second in the popular vote to become president by being the top vote getter in the electoral college, as we explained in this chapter's opening *What If* . . . feature. The electoral college insulated the president, however, from direct popular control. The seven-year single term that some of the delegates had proposed was replaced by a four-year term and the possibility of reelection.

The Final Document

On September 17, 1787, the Constitution was approved by thirty-nine delegates. Of the fifty-five who had attended originally, only forty-two remained. Three delegates refused to sign the Constitution. Others disapproved of at least parts of it but signed anyway to begin the ratification debate.

The Constitution that was to be ratified established the following fundamental principles:

1. Popular sovereignty, or control by the people.
2. A republican government in which the people choose representatives to make decisions for them.
3. Limited government with written laws, in contrast to the powerful British government against which the colonists had rebelled.
4. Separation of powers, with checks and balances among branches to prevent any one branch from gaining too much power.
5. A federal system that allows for states' rights, because the states feared too much centralized control.

You will read about federalism in detail in Chapter 3. Suffice it to say here that in the **federal system** established by the founders, sovereign powers—ruling powers—are divided between the states and the national government. The Constitution expressly granted certain powers to the national government. For example, the national government was given the power to regulate commerce among the states. The Constitution also declared that the president is the nation's chief executive and the commander in chief of the armed forces. Additionally, the Constitution made it clear that laws made by the national government take priority over conflicting state laws. At the same time, the Constitution provided for extensive states' rights, including the right to control commerce within state borders and to exercise those governing powers that were not delegated to the national government.

The federal system created by the founders was a novel form of government at that time—no other country in the world had such a system. It was invented by the founders

Electoral College
A group of persons called *electors* selected by the voters in each state and the District of Columbia (D.C.); this group officially elects the president and vice president of the United States. The number of electors in each state is equal to the number of each state's representatives in both chambers of Congress. The Twenty-third Amendment to the Constitution grants D.C. as many electors as the state with the smallest population.

Federal System
A system of government in which power is divided between a central government and regional, or subdivisional, governments. Each level must have some domain in which its policies are dominant and some genuine political or constitutional guarantee of its authority.

as a compromise solution to the controversy over whether the states or the central government should have ultimate sovereignty. As you will read in Chapter 3, the debate over where the line should be drawn between states' rights and the powers of the national government has characterized American politics ever since. The founders did not go into detail about where this line should be drawn, thus leaving it up to scholars and court judges to divine the founders' intentions.

did you know?

That Alexander Hamilton wanted the American president to hold office for life and to have absolute veto power over the legislature.

The Difficult Road to Ratification

The founders knew that **ratification** of the Constitution was far from certain. Indeed, because it was almost guaranteed that many state legislatures would not ratify it, the delegates agreed that each state should hold a special convention. Elected delegates to these conventions would discuss and vote on the Constitution. Further departing from the Articles of Confederation, the delegates agreed that as soon as nine states (rather than all thirteen) approved the Constitution, it would take effect, and Congress could begin to organize the new government.

Ratification
Formal approval.

Federalist
The name given to one who was in favor of the adoption of the U.S. Constitution and the creation of a federal union with a strong central government.

Anti-Federalist
An individual who opposed the ratification of the new Constitution in 1787. The Anti-Federalists were opposed to a strong central government.

The Federalists Push for Ratification

The two opposing forces in the battle over ratification were the Federalists and the Anti-Federalists. The **Federalists**—those in favor of a strong central government and the new Constitution—had an advantage over their opponents, called the **Anti-Federalists,** who wanted to prevent the Constitution as drafted from being ratified. In the first place, the

BEYOND OUR BORDERS

THE PARLIAMENTARY ALTERNATIVE

In contrast to the American political system, in many democratic countries the legislature, or Parliament, chooses the *head of government.* In Britain, the lower house of Parliament, the House of Commons, effectively chooses the head of government. (An upper house exists—the House of Lords—but it has few powers.) Australia, Canada, India, Ireland, Israel, and Japan use the parliamentary system. Most nations on the European continent also have parliamentary systems that resemble the British model.

In a parliamentary system, the *head of state* is either a monarch or an elected president with very limited responsibilities. Real authority is exercised by the head of government, who represents a majority (or a plurality) of the national legislature. In most countries, the head of government is called the *prime minister.*

After an election in a parliamentary system, the head of state formally asks the leader of the largest party in the lower house of Parliament to "form a government." The prime minister—the leader of the largest party or coalition of parties—then names various people, usually current members of Parliament, to cabinet positions. These cabinet members, called ministers, must support the policy of the government in power.

FOR CRITICAL ANALYSIS

Would you feel comfortable with a head of government for whom you did not have a chance to vote? Why or why not?

Federalists had assumed a positive name, leaving their opposition the negative label of *Anti*-Federalist.[13] More important, the Federalists had attended the Constitutional Convention and knew of all the deliberations that had taken place. Their opponents had no such knowledge, because those deliberations had not been open to the public. Thus, the Anti-Federalists were at a disadvantage in terms of information about the document. The Federalists also had time, power, and wealth on their side. Communications were slow. Those who had access to the best communications were Federalists—mostly wealthy bankers, lawyers, plantation owners, and merchants living in urban areas, where communications were better. The Federalist campaign was organized relatively quickly and effectively to elect Federalists as delegates to the state ratifying conventions.

The Anti-Federalists, however, had at least one strong point in their favor: they stood for the status quo. In general, the greater burden is always placed on those advocating change.

The *Federalist Papers*. In New York, opponents of the Constitution were quick to attack it. Alexander Hamilton answered their attacks in newspaper columns over the signature "Caesar." When the Caesar letters had little effect, Hamilton switched to the pseudonym Publius and secured two collaborators—John Jay and James Madison. In a very short time, those three political figures wrote a series of eighty-five essays in defense of the Constitution and of a republican form of government.

These widely read essays, called the *Federalist Papers,* appeared in New York newspapers from October 1787 to August 1788 and were reprinted in the newspapers of other states. Although we do not know for certain who wrote every one, it is apparent that Hamilton was responsible for about two-thirds of the essays. These included the most important ones interpreting the Constitution, explaining the various powers of the three branches, and presenting a theory of *judicial review*—to be discussed later in this chapter. Madison's *Federalist Paper* No. 10 (see Appendix C), however, is considered a classic in political theory; it deals with the nature of groups—or factions, as he called them. We discuss the ways in which groups influence our government in Chapter 7. In spite of the rapidity with which the *Federalist Papers* were written, they are considered by many to be perhaps the best example of political theorizing ever produced in the United States.[14]

Patrick Henry in the First Continental Congress. Painting by Clyde Osmer Deland. (© Bettmann/Corbis)

The Anti-Federalist Response. The Anti-Federalists used such pseudonyms as Montezuma and Philadelphiensis in their replies. Many of their attacks on the Constitution were also brilliant. The Anti-Federalists claimed that the Constitution was written by aristocrats and would lead to aristocratic tyranny. More important, the Anti-Federalists believed that the Constitution would create an overbearing and overburdening central government hostile to personal liberty. (The Constitution said nothing about freedom of the press, freedom of religion, or any other individual liberty.) They wanted to include a list of guaranteed liberties, or a bill of rights. Finally, the Anti-Federalists decried the weakened power of the states.[15]

---

13. There is some irony here. At the Constitutional Convention, those opposed to a strong central government pushed for a federal system because such a system would allow the states to retain some of their sovereign rights (see Chapter 3). The label *Anti-Federalists* thus contradicted their essential views.
14. Some scholars believe that the *Federalist Papers* played only a minor role in securing ratification of the Constitution. Even if this is true, they still have lasting value as an authoritative explanation of the Constitution.
15. Herbert J. Storing edited seven volumes of Anti-Federalist writings and released them in 1981 as *The Anti-Federalist.* Political science professor Murray Dry has prepared a more manageable, one-volume version of this collection: Herbert J. Storing, ed., *The Anti-Federalist: An Abridgment of the Complete Anti-Federalist* (Chicago: University of Chicago Press, 2006).

The Anti-Federalists cannot be dismissed as unpatriotic extremists. They included such patriots as Patrick Henry and Samuel Adams. They were arguing what had been the most prevalent view in that era. This view derived from the French political philosopher Montesquieu, who, as mentioned earlier, was an influential political theorist. Montesquieu believed that a republic was possible only in relatively small societies governed by direct democracy or by a large legislature with small districts. The Madisonian view favoring a large republic, particularly expressed in *Federalist Papers* No. 10 and No. 51 (see Appendix C), was actually an exceptional view at the time. Madison was probably convincing because citizens were already persuaded that a strong national government was necessary to combat foreign enemies and to prevent domestic insurrections. Still, some researchers believe it was mainly the bitter experiences with the Articles of Confederation, rather than Madison's arguments, that persuaded the state conventions to ratify the Constitution.

The March to the Finish

The struggle for ratification continued. Strong majorities were procured in Connecticut, Delaware, Georgia, New Jersey, and Pennsylvania. After a bitter struggle in Massachusetts, that state ratified the Constitution by a narrow margin on February 6, 1788. By the spring, Maryland and South Carolina had ratified by sizable majorities. Then on June 21 of that year, New Hampshire became the ninth state to ratify the Constitution. Although the Constitution was formally in effect, this meant little without Virginia and New York—the latter did not ratify for another month (see Table 2–2 below).

Did the Majority of Americans Support the Constitution?

In 1913, historian Charles Beard published *An Economic Interpretation of the Constitution of the United States.*[16] This book launched a debate that has continued ever since—the debate over whether the Constitution was supported by a majority of Americans.

16. Charles A. Beard, *An Economic Interpretation of the Constitution of the United States* (New York: Macmillan, 1913; New York: Free Press, 1986).

TABLE 2–2 Ratification of the Constitution

State	Date	Vote For–Against
Delaware	Dec. 7, 1787	30–0
Pennsylvania	Dec. 12, 1787	43–23
New Jersey	Dec. 18, 1787	38–0
Georgia	Jan. 2, 1788	26–0
Connecticut	Jan. 9, 1788	128–40
Massachusetts	Feb. 6, 1788	187–168
Maryland	Apr. 28, 1788	63–11
South Carolina	May 23, 1788	149–73
New Hampshire	June 21, 1788	57–46
Virginia	June 25, 1788	89–79
New York	July 26, 1788	30–27
North Carolina	Nov. 21, 1789*	194–77
Rhode Island	May 29, 1790	34–32

*Ratification was initially defeated on August 4, 1788, by a vote of 84–184.

did you know?

That 64 percent of Americans believe that the Constitution declared English to be the national language of the United States.

Beard's Thesis. Beard's central thesis was that the Constitution had been produced primarily by wealthy property owners who desired a stronger government able to protect their property rights. Beard also claimed that the Constitution had been imposed by undemocratic methods to prevent democratic majorities from exercising real power. He pointed out that there was never any popular vote on whether to hold a constitutional convention in the first place.

Furthermore, even if such a vote had been taken, state laws generally restricted voting rights to property-owning white males, meaning that most people in the country (white males without property, women, Native Americans, and slaves) were not eligible to vote. Finally, Beard pointed out that even the word *democracy* was distasteful to the founders. The term was often used by conservatives to smear their opponents.

State Ratifying Conventions. As for the various state ratifying conventions, the delegates had been selected by only 150,000 of the approximately 4 million citizens. That does not seem very democratic—at least not by today's standards. Some historians have suggested that if a Gallup poll could have been taken at that time, the Anti-Federalists would probably have outnumbered the Federalists.[17]

Certainly, some of the delegates to state ratifying conventions from poor, agrarian areas feared that an elite group of Federalists would run the country just as oppressively as the British had governed the colonies. Amos Singletary, a delegate to the Massachusetts ratifying convention, contended that those who urged the adoption of the Constitution "expect to get all the power and all the money into their own hands, and then they will swallow up all us little folks . . . just as the whale swallowed Jonah."[18] Others who were similarly situated, though, felt differently. Jonathan Smith, who was also a delegate to the Massachusetts ratifying convention, regarded a strong national government as a "cure for disorder"—referring to the disorder caused by the rebellion of Daniel Shays and his followers.[19]

Support Was Probably Widespread. Much has also been made of the various machinations used by the Federalists to ensure the Constitution's ratification (and they did resort to a variety of devious tactics, including purchasing at least one printing press to prevent the publication of Anti-Federalist sentiments). Yet the perception that a strong central government was necessary to keep order and protect the public welfare appears to have been fairly pervasive among all classes—rich and poor alike.

Further, although the need for strong government was a major argument in favor of adopting the Constitution, even the Federalists sought to craft a limited government. Compared with constitutions adopted by other nations in later years, the U.S. Constitution, through its checks and balances, favors limited government over "energetic" government to a marked degree.

The Bill of Rights

The U.S. Constitution would not have been ratified in several important states if the Federalists had not assured the states that amendments to the Constitution would be passed to protect individual liberties against incursions by the national government. Many

17. Jim Powell, "James Madison—Checks and Balances to Limit Government Power," *The Freeman,* March 1996, p. 178.
18. As quoted in Leone, ed., *The Creation of the Constitution,* p. 215.
19. *Ibid.,* p. 217.

of the recommendations of the state ratifying conventions included specific rights that were considered later by James Madison as he labored to draft what became the Bill of Rights.

"Remember, gentlemen, we aren't here just to draft a constitution. We're here to draft the best damned constitution in the world."
(© The New Yorker Collection, 1982. Peter Steiner, from cartoonbank.com. All Rights Reserved.)

A "Bill of Limits"

Although called the Bill of Rights, essentially the first ten amendments to the Constitution were a "bill of limits," because the amendments limited the powers of the national government over the rights and liberties of individuals.

Ironically, a year earlier Madison had told Jefferson, "I have never thought the omission [of the Bill of Rights] a material defect" of the Constitution. Madison was not the only founder who believed a bill of rights to be unnecessary. We discuss the reasons for this in the *Politics and . . . liberty* feature on the next page. Jefferson's enthusiasm for a bill of rights apparently influenced Madison, however, as did Madison's desire to gain popular support for his election to Congress. Madison promised in his campaign letter to voters that once elected, he would force Congress to "prepare and recommend to the states for ratification, the most satisfactory provisions for all essential rights."

Madison had to cull through more than two hundred state recommendations. It was no small task, and in retrospect he chose remarkably well. One of the rights appropriate for constitutional protection that he left out was equal protection under the laws—but that was not commonly regarded as a basic right at that time. Not until 1868 did the states ratify an amendment guaranteeing that no state shall deny equal protection to any person.

The final number of amendments that Madison and a specially appointed committee came up with was seventeen. Congress tightened the language somewhat and eliminated five of the amendments. Of the remaining twelve, two—dealing with the apportionment of representatives and the compensation of the members of Congress—were not ratified immediately by the states. Eventually, Supreme Court decisions led to reform of the apportionment process. The amendment on the compensation of members of Congress was ratified 203 years later—in 1992![20]

Adoption of the Bill of Rights

On December 15, 1791, the national Bill of Rights was adopted when Virginia agreed to ratify the ten amendments. On ratification, the Bill of Rights became part of the U.S. Constitution. The basic structure of American government had already been established. Now the fundamental rights and liberties of individuals were protected, at least in theory, at the national level. The proposed amendment that Madison characterized as "the most valuable amendment in the whole lot"—which would have prohibited the states from infringing on the freedoms of conscience, press, and jury trial—had been eliminated by the Senate. Thus, the Bill of Rights as adopted did not limit state power, and individual citizens had to rely on the guarantees contained in a particular state constitution or state bill of rights. The country had to wait until the violence of the Civil War before significant limitations on state power in the form of the Fourteenth Amendment became part of the national Constitution.

---

20. For perspectives on these events, see Richard E. Labunski, *James Madison and the Struggle for the Bill of Rights* (New York: Oxford University Press, 2008); and Steven Waldman, *Founding Faith: How Our Founding Fathers Forged a Radical New Approach to Religious Liberty* (New York: Random House Trade Paperbacks, 2009).

One of the great themes of American history has been the expansion of our civil liberties over time. In the most recent extension of these liberties, the United States Supreme Court has ruled that the right to bear arms is an individual, not just a collective, right. We discuss the issue in this chapter's *Which Side Are You On?* feature on page 54.

Altering the Constitution: The Formal Amendment Process

As amended, the U.S. Constitution consists of 7,000 words. It is shorter than any state constitution except that of Vermont, which has 6,880 words. One of the reasons the federal Constitution is short is that the founders intended it to be only a framework for the new government, to be interpreted by succeeding generations. One of the reasons it has remained short is that the formal amending procedure does not allow for changes to be made easily. Article V of the Constitution outlines the ways in which amendments may be proposed and ratified (see Figure 2–3 on the facing page).

POLITICS AND... liberty

WHY DIDN'T THE FOUNDERS THINK THAT A BILL OF RIGHTS WAS NECESSARY?

All Americans know about our rights to freedom of speech, freedom of the press, freedom of religion, and other freedoms. Indeed, we take these freedoms for granted. In the original Constitution, however, the framers did not include any of these rights. How could they have left them out?

RIGHTS IN THE MAIN BODY OF THE CONSTITUTION

Many of the framers felt that specific guarantees of fundamental rights were unnecessary because the Constitution already included certain prohibitions. Article 1, Section 9, for example, prohibits so-called *bills of attainder.* These are acts of the legislature that allow punishment for accused criminals without normal judicial proceedings. In that same section of the Constitution, there is a prohibition against *ex post facto* laws, which are laws passed after the commission of an act that retroactively make that act illegal.

In Article 1, Section 9, the framers included a prohibition against government detention of individuals without due process of law. They did so by allowing a judge (via a writ of *habeas corpus*) to inquire of an arresting officer or jailer about a person who is in custody. When no proper explanation is given, the judge can order the person's release. Finally, Article 3, Section 2, imposes a requirement of a trial by jury in federal criminal cases.

In other words, the framers had already created a number of guarantees of civil liberties. The founders believed that these guarantees were sufficient.

SPECIFIC LIMITATIONS VIEWED AS DANGEROUS

Many framers also had something else in mind when they did not include a bill of rights in the original Constitution. They believed that there was a danger in enumerating specific civil liberties. The danger lay in the possibility that future governments might assume that rights that were not listed in a bill of rights did not exist. The framers wanted to avoid a view of the federal government under which it could do anything that wasn't explicitly prohibited.

FOR CRITICAL ANALYSIS

If there were no Bill of Rights, would that necessarily mean that residents of this country would not enjoy freedom of speech or freedom of the press? Why or why not?

FIGURE 2–3 The Formal Constitutional Amending Procedure

There are two ways of proposing amendments to the U.S. Constitution and two ways of ratifying proposed amendments. Among the four possibilities, the usual route has been proposal by Congress and ratification by state legislatures.

PROPOSING AMENDMENTS

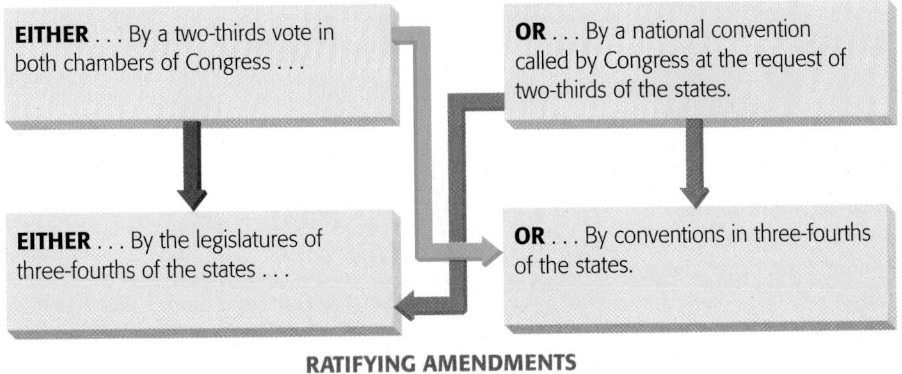

Typical (used for all except one amendment)
Used only once (Twenty-first Amendment)
Never used

Two formal methods of proposing an amendment to the Constitution are available: (1) a two-thirds vote in each chamber of Congress or (2) a national convention that is called by Congress at the request of two-thirds of the state legislatures (the second method has never been used).

Ratification can occur by one of two methods: (1) by a positive vote in three-fourths of the legislatures of the various states or (2) by special conventions called in the states and a positive vote in three-fourths of them. The second method has been used only once, to repeal Prohibition (the ban on the production and sale of alcoholic beverages). That situation was exceptional because it involved an amendment (the Twenty-first) to repeal another amendment (the Eighteenth, which had created Prohibition). State conventions were necessary for repeal of the Eighteenth Amendment because the "pro-dry" legislatures in the most conservative states would never have passed the repeal. (Note that Congress determines the method of ratification to be used by all states for each proposed constitutional amendment.)

did you know?

That the Constitution explicitly says that no amendment can alter the equal representation of the states in the Senate, and that this is the only such "entrenched" provision in the document.

Many Amendments Proposed, Few Accepted

Congress has considered more than eleven thousand amendments to the Constitution. Many proposed amendments have been advanced to address highly specific problems. An argument against such "narrow" amendments has been that amendments ought to embody broad principles, in the way that the existing Constitution does. For that reason, many people have opposed such narrow amendments as one to protect the American flag.

Only thirty-three amendments have been submitted to the states after having been approved by the required two-thirds vote in each chamber of Congress, and only twenty-seven have been ratified—see Table 2–3 on page 55. (The full, annotated text of the U.S. Constitution, including its amendments, is presented in a special appendix at the end of this chapter.) It should be clear that the amendment process is much more difficult than a graphic depiction such as Figure 2–3 above can indicate. Because of competing social and economic interests, the requirement that two-thirds of both the House and the Senate approve the amendments is hard to achieve. Thirty-four senators, representing only seventeen sparsely populated states, could block any amendment. For example, the Republican-controlled

WHICH SIDE ARE YOU ON?

IS THE SUPREME COURT RIGHT ABOUT GUNS?

The Second Amendment to the U.S. Constitution states: "A well regulated Militia, being necessary to the security of a free State, the right of the people to keep and bear Arms, shall not be infringed." This is ambiguous. Why does the amendment speak of a "well regulated Militia"? The other amendments that make up the Bill of Rights do not come with such preambles. Two interpretations of the amendment are in circulation. According to one, Congress may pass no law infringing the right of individuals to possess firearms. According to the other, the right to bear arms is constitutionally protected only when individuals function as part of a state militia. The right to bear arms, in other words, is guaranteed to the National Guard, not to individual citizens.

On the one hand, gun owners are a large, well-organized constituency. On the other hand, about 30,000 Americans are killed each year by guns. For decades, Americans have engaged in highly charged policy fights over gun control. Yet surprisingly, the Supreme Court has rarely ruled on Second Amendment issues. Before 2008, the only significant Supreme Court case was heard in 1939. At that time, the Court found that the constitutional right to bear arms was limited to state militias.[a] In 2008, however, the Court ruled that individuals have this right. The ruling only limited the actions of the federal government, however, not those of the states. Therefore, it was effective only in the District of Columbia, a federal jurisdiction.[b]

The Court then took up the question of whether the Second Amendment limits the powers of state and local governments. The issue was raised by a Chicago law that banned almost all handguns. In June 2010, the Court found that state and local governments were required to recognize an individual right to possess firearms. As in the earlier District of Columbia decision, the Court also observed that laws to prohibit possession of guns by felons and the mentally ill were acceptable, and so were laws banning guns from schools or government buildings and laws regulating gun sales.[c]

a. *United States v. Miller,* 307 U.S. 174 (1939). For information on how to look up court cases online, see the *E-mocracy* feature at the end of Chapter 3.
b. *District of Columbia v. Dick Anthony Heller,* 128 S.Ct. 2783 (2008).
c. *McDonald v. Chicago,* 130 S.Ct. 1317 (2010).

YOU CAN'T IGNORE WHAT THE CONSTITUTION SAYS

Those who believe that the Supreme Court has ruled correctly in the recent gun control cases argue that when the Second Amendment was ratified, the "militia" in any locality was the entire body of free adult males. The militia was not limited to a selective body such as today's National Guard. Therefore, the right to bear arms is granted to all individuals. The "people" mentioned in the Second Amendment are exactly the same "people" who enjoy the right to free speech and all of the other liberties contained in the Bill of Rights.

Gun rights advocates also contend that in states that allow concealed weapons, murder and armed robbery rates are lower. Why? The reason supposedly is that criminals fear an armed citizenry. Self-defense in the home is a legitimate right, and therefore a universal ban on handguns in the home has to be unconstitutional.

THE SUPREME COURT CAN BE WRONG

Others argue that if the founders had wanted the Second Amendment to apply to individuals, they would have expressly so stated and not included the "militia" wording. Cities, states, and the federal government not only have the right but the obligation to regulate gun ownership, and that can include banning handguns. Gun rights advocates will use the latest Supreme Court decisions as a legal tool in their attempts to strike down gun control laws. America will become a more dangerous place, and our standing in the world will drop even further.

In any event, constitutional rights are not absolute. In spite of the First Amendment guarantee of free speech, many restrictions on speech have been deemed constitutional. Thus, even assuming that the Second Amendment applies to individuals, every state and city should have broad rights to restrict gun ownership and use.

TABLE 2–3 Amendments to the Constitution

Amendment	Subject	Year Adopted	Time Required for Ratification
1st–10th	The Bill of Rights	1791	2 years, 2 months, 20 days
11th	Immunity of states from certain suits	1795	11 months, 3 days
12th	Changes in electoral college procedure	1804	6 months, 3 days
13th	Prohibition of slavery	1865	10 months, 3 days
14th	Citizenship, due process, and equal protection	1868	2 years, 26 days
15th	No denial of vote because of race, color, or previous condition of servitude	1870	11 months, 8 days
16th	Power of Congress to tax income	1913	3 years, 6 months, 22 days
17th	Direct election of U.S. senators	1913	10 months, 26 days
18th	National (liquor) prohibition	1919	1 year, 29 days
19th	Women's right to vote	1920	1 year, 2 months, 14 days
20th	Change of dates for congressional and presidential terms	1933	10 months, 21 days
21st	Repeal of the Eighteenth Amendment	1933	9 months, 15 days
22d	Limit on presidential tenure	1951	3 years, 11 months, 3 days
23d	District of Columbia electoral vote	1961	9 months, 13 days
24th	Prohibition of tax payment as a qualification to vote in federal elections	1964	1 year, 4 months, 9 days
25th	Procedures for determining presidential disability and presidential succession and for filling a vice-presidential vacancy	1967	1 year, 7 months, 4 days
26th	Prohibition of setting the minimum voting age above eighteen in any election	1971	3 months, 7 days
27th	Prohibition of Congress's voting itself a raise that takes effect before the next election	1992	203 years

House approved the Balanced Budget Amendment within the first one hundred days of the 104th Congress in 1995, but it was defeated in the Senate by one vote.

After an amendment has been approved by Congress, the process becomes even more arduous. Three-fourths of the state legislatures must approve the amendment. Only those amendments that have wide popular support across parties and in all regions of the country are likely to be approved.

Why was the amendment process made so difficult? The framers feared that a simple amendment process could lead to a tyranny of the majority, which could pass amendments to oppress disfavored individuals and groups. The cumbersome amendment process does not seem to stem the number of amendments that are proposed each year in Congress, however, particularly in recent years.

Limits on Ratification

A reading of Article V of the U.S. Constitution reveals that the framers of the Constitution specified no time limit on the ratification process. The Supreme Court has held that Congress can specify a time for ratification as long as it is "reasonable." Since 1919, most proposed amendments have included a requirement that ratification be obtained within seven years. This was the case with the proposed Equal Rights Amendment, which sought to guarantee equal rights for women. When three-fourths of the states had not ratified in the allotted seven years, however, Congress extended the limit by an additional three years and three months. That extension expired on June 30, 1982, and the amendment still had not been ratified. Another proposed amendment, which would have guaranteed congressional representation for the District of Columbia, fell far short of the thirty-eight state ratifications needed before its August 22, 1985, deadline.

On May 7, 1992, Michigan became the thirty-eighth state to ratify the Twenty-seventh Amendment (on congressional compensation)—one of the two "lost" amendments of the twelve that originally were sent to the states in 1789. Because most of the amendments proposed in recent years have been given a time limit of only seven years by Congress, it was questionable for a time whether the amendment would take effect even if the necessary number of states ratified it. Is 203 years too long a lapse of time between the proposal and the final ratification of an amendment? It apparently was not, because the amendment was certified as legitimate by archivist Don Wilson of the National Archives on May 18, 1992.

The U.S. Constitution is silent on laws relating to marriage. Consequently, the states govern in this area. This recent demonstration outside the Massachusetts State House in Boston involves the question of marriage. Present were those who were in favor of legalizing same-sex marriages as well as those who were against it. Why do states and not the federal government decide whether to legalize same-sex marriages? (Brian Snyder/Reuters/Landov)

The National Convention Provision

The Constitution provides that a national convention requested by the legislatures of two-thirds of the states can propose a constitutional amendment. Congress has received approximately 400 convention applications since the Constitution was ratified; every state has applied at least once. Fewer than 20 applications were submitted during the Constitution's first hundred years, but more than 150 have been filed in the last two decades. No national convention has been held since 1787, and many national political and judicial leaders are uneasy about the prospect of convening a body that conceivably could do as the Constitutional Convention did—create a new form of government. The state legislative bodies that originate national convention applications, however, do not appear to be uncomfortable with such a constitutional modification process; more than 230 state constitutional conventions have been held.

Informal Methods of Constitutional Change

Formal amendments are one way of changing our Constitution, and, as is obvious from their small number, they have been resorted to infrequently. If we discount the first ten amendments (the Bill of Rights), which were adopted soon after the ratification of the Constitution, there have been only seventeen formal alterations of the Constitution in the more than two hundred years of its existence.

But looking at the sparse number of formal constitutional amendments gives us an incomplete view of constitutional change. The brevity and ambiguity of the original document have permitted great alterations in the Constitution by way of varying interpretations over time. As the United States grew, both in population and in territory, new social and political realities emerged. Congress, presidents, and the courts found it necessary to interpret the Constitution's provisions in light of these new realities. The Constitution has proved to be a remarkably flexible document, adapting itself time and again to new events and concerns.

Congressional Legislation

The Constitution gives Congress broad powers to carry out its duties as the nation's legislative body. For example, Article I, Section 8, of the Constitution gives Congress the power to regulate foreign and interstate commerce. Although there is no clear definition of foreign commerce or interstate commerce in the Constitution, Congress has cited the *commerce clause* as the basis for passing thousands of laws that regulate foreign and interstate commerce.

Similarly, Article III, Section 1, states that the national judiciary shall consist of one supreme court and "such inferior courts, as Congress may from time to time ordain and establish." Through a series of acts, Congress has used this broad provision to establish the federal court system of today.

In addition, Congress has frequently delegated to federal agencies the legislative power to write regulations. These regulations become law unless challenged in the court system. Nowhere does the Constitution outline this delegation of legislative authority.

did you know?

That the states have still not ratified an amendment (introduced by Congress in 1810) barring U.S. citizens from accepting titles of nobility from foreign governments.

Presidential Actions

Even though the Constitution does not expressly authorize the president to propose bills or even budgets to Congress,[21] presidents since the time of Woodrow Wilson (1913–1921) have proposed hundreds of bills to Congress each year. Presidents have also relied on their Article II authority as commander in chief of the nation's armed forces to send American troops abroad into combat, although the Constitution provides that Congress has the power to declare war.

The president's powers in wartime have waxed and waned through the course of American history. President George W. Bush significantly expanded presidential power in the wake of the terrorist attacks of 2001. Until then, there had been a period of decline in the latitude given to presidents since the Vietnam War ended in 1975.

Presidents have also conducted foreign affairs by the use of **executive agreements,** which are legally binding documents made between the president and a foreign head of state. The Constitution does not mention such agreements.

Executive Agreement
An international agreement between chiefs of state that does not require legislative approval.

Judicial Review
The power of the Supreme Court and other courts to declare unconstitutional federal or state laws and other acts of government.

Judicial Review

Another way of changing the Constitution—or of making it more flexible—is through the power of judicial review. **Judicial review** refers to the power of U.S. courts to examine the constitutionality of actions undertaken by the legislative and executive branches of government. A state court, for example, may rule that a statute enacted by the state legislature violates the state constitution. Federal courts (and ultimately, the United States Supreme Court) may rule unconstitutional not only acts of Congress and decisions of the national executive branch but also state statutes, state executive actions, and even provisions of state constitutions.

Not a Novel Concept. The Constitution does not specifically mention the power of judicial review. Those in attendance at the Constitutional Convention, however, probably expected that the courts would have some authority to review the legality of acts by the executive and legislative branches, because, under the common law tradition inherited from England, courts exercised this authority. Indeed, Alexander Hamilton, in *Federalist Paper* No. 78 (see Appendix C), explicitly outlined the concept of judicial review. Whether the power of judicial review can be justified constitutionally is a question that has been subject to some debate, particularly in recent years. For now, suffice it to say that in 1803, the Supreme Court claimed this power for itself in *Marbury v. Madison,*[22] in which the Court ruled that a particular provision of an act of Congress was unconstitutional.

Allows Court to Adapt the Constitution. Through the process of judicial review, the Supreme Court adapts the Constitution to modern situations. Electronic technology, for example, did not exist when the Constitution was ratified. Nonetheless, the Court has used

21. Note, though, that the Constitution, in Article II, Section 3, does state that the president "shall from time to time . . . recommend to [Congress's] Consideration such Measures as he shall judge necessary and expedient." Some scholars interpret this phrase to mean that the president has the constitutional authority to propose bills and budgets to Congress for consideration.
22. 5 U.S. 137 (1803). See Chapter 13 for a further discussion of the *Marbury v. Madison* case.

U.S. Supreme Court
Justices gather for an official picture at the Supreme Court in Washington, D.C., October 8, 2010. They are (1st row, L-R) Justice Clarence Thomas, Justice Antonin Scalia, Chief Justice John Roberts, Justice Anthony M. Kennedy, Justice Ruth Bader Ginsburg, (2nd row, L-R), Justice Sonia Sotomayor, Justice Stephen G. Breyer, Justice Samuel Alito, Justice Elena Kagan. (AP Photo/Pablo Martinez Monsivais)

the Fourth Amendment guarantees against unreasonable searches and seizures to place limits on the use of wiretapping and other electronic eavesdropping methods. The Court has had to decide whether antiterrorism laws passed by Congress or state legislatures, or measures instituted by the president, violate the Fourth Amendment or other constitutional provisions. Additionally, the Court has changed its interpretation of the Constitution in accordance with changing values. It ruled in 1896 that "separate-but-equal" public facilities for African Americans were constitutional; but by 1954 the times had changed, and the Court reversed that decision.[23] Woodrow Wilson summarized the Court's work when he described it as "a constitutional convention in continuous session." Basically, the law is what the Supreme Court says it is at any point in time.

Interpretation, Custom, and Usage

The Constitution has also been changed through interpretation by both Congress and the president. Originally, the president had a staff consisting of personal secretaries and a few others. Today, because Congress delegates specific tasks to the president and the chief executive assumes political leadership, the executive office staff alone has increased to several thousand persons. The executive branch provides legislative leadership far beyond the expectations of the founders.

Executive Order
A rule or regulation issued by the president that has the effect of law. Executive orders can implement and give administrative effect to provisions in the U.S. Constitution, treaties, or statutes.

One of the ways in which presidents have expanded their powers is through **executive orders.** (Executive orders will be discussed in Chapter 11, in the context of the presidency.) Executive orders have the force of legislation and allow presidents to significantly affect the political landscape. Consider, for example, that affirmative action programs have their origin in executive orders.

Changes in the ways of doing political business have also altered the Constitution. The Constitution does not mention political parties, yet these informal, "extraconstitutional" organizations make the nominations for offices, run the campaigns, organize the members of Congress, and in fact change the election system from time to time. Perhaps most striking, the Constitution has been adapted from serving the needs of a small, rural republic to providing a framework of government for an industrial giant with vast geographic, natural, and human resources.

---

23. *Brown v. Board of Education of Topeka,* 347 U.S. 483 (1954).

WHY SHOULD YOU CARE ABOUT... THE CONSTITUTION?

The U.S. Constitution is an enduring document that has survived more than two hundred years of turbulent history. It is also a changing document, however. Twenty-seven amendments have been added to the original Constitution. Why should you, as an individual, care about the Constitution?

THE CONSTITUTION AND YOUR LIFE

The laws of the nation have a direct impact on your life, and none more so than the Constitution—the supreme law of the land. The most important issues in society are often settled by the Constitution. For example, for the first seventy-five years of the republic, the Constitution implicitly protected the institution of slavery. If the Constitution had never been changed by an amendment, the process of abolishing slavery would have been much different and might have involved revolutionary measures.

Since the passage of the Fourteenth Amendment in 1868, the Constitution has defined who is a citizen and who is entitled to the protections the Constitution provides. Constitutional provisions define our liberties. The First Amendment protects our freedom of speech more thoroughly than do the laws of many other nations. Few other countries have constitutional provisions governing the right to own firearms (the Second Amendment). Disputes involving these rights are among the most fundamental issues we face.

(AP Photo/Joe Marquette)

HOW YOU CAN MAKE A DIFFERENCE

Consider how one person decided to affect the Constitution. Shirley Breeze, head of the Missouri Women's Network, decided to bring the Equal Rights Amendment (ERA) back to life after its "death" in 1982. She spearheaded a movement that has gained significant support. Today, bills to ratify the ERA have been introduced not only in Missouri but also in other states that did not ratify it earlier, including Illinois, Oklahoma, and Virginia.

At the time of this writing, national coalitions of interest groups are supporting or opposing a number of proposed amendments. One hotly debated proposed amendment concerns abortion. If you are interested in this issue and would like to make a difference, you can contact one of several groups.

An organization whose primary goal is to secure the passage of the Human Life Amendment is

American Life League
P.O. Box 1350
Stafford, VA 22555
540-659-4171
www.all.org

The Human Life Amendment would recognize in law the "personhood" of the unborn, secure human rights protections for an unborn child from the time of fertilization, and prohibit abortion under any circumstances.

A political action and information organization working on behalf of "pro-choice" issues—that is, the right of women to have control over reproduction—is

NARAL Pro-Choice America (formerly the National Abortion and Reproductive Rights Action League)
1156 15th St., Suite 700
Washington, DC 20005
202-973-3000
www.naral.org

There is also another way that you can affect the Constitution—by protecting your existing rights and liberties under it. In the wake of the September 11, 2001, terrorist attacks, a number of new laws have been enacted that many believe go too far in curbing our constitutional rights. If you agree and want to join with others who are concerned about this issue, a good starting point is the Web site of the American Civil Liberties Union (ACLU) at

www.aclu.org

questions for discussion and analysis

1. Naturalized citizens—immigrants—have almost all of the rights of natural-born citizens, but under the Constitution they cannot be elected president. If the Constitution were changed to allow an immigrant to become president, do you think that today's voters would be reluctant to vote for such an individual? Why might a naturalized leader be more nationalistic than a natural-born one?

2. As you have learned, historian Charles Beard argued that the Constitution was produced primarily by wealthy property owners who wanted a stronger government that could protect their property rights. Do you see any provisions in the text of the Constitution that would support Beard's argument? Even if Beard is right, is this in any way a problem?

3. Consider what might have happened if Georgia and the Carolinas had stayed out of the Union because of a desire to protect slavery. What would subsequent American history have been like? Would the eventual freedom of the slaves have been delayed—or advanced?

4. A result of the Great Compromise is that representation in the Senate dramatically departs from the one-person, one-vote rule. The 38 million people who live in California elect two senators, as do the half-million people living in Wyoming. What political results might occur when the citizens of small states are much better represented than the citizens of large ones? Do you see any signs that your predictions have actually come true?

key terms

Anti-Federalist 47
bicameral legislature 42
checks and balances 44
confederation 37
electoral college 46
executive agreement 57
executive order 58
federal system 46
Federalist 47
Great Compromise 42
judicial review 57
Madisonian model 44
natural rights 36
ratification 47
representative assembly 31
separation of powers 44
social contract 36
state 37
supremacy doctrine 42
unicameral legislature 37

chapter summary

1. The first permanent English colonies were established at Jamestown in 1607 and Plymouth in 1620. The Mayflower Compact created the first formal government in New England.

2. In the 1760s, the British began to impose a series of taxes and legislative acts on their increasingly independent-minded colonies. The colonists responded with protests and boycotts of British products. Representatives of the colonies formed the First Continental Congress in 1774. The Second Continental Congress established an army in 1775 to defend the colonists against attacks by British soldiers.

3. On July 4, 1776, the Second Continental Congress approved the Declaration of Independence. Perhaps the most revolutionary aspects of the Declaration were its statements that people have natural rights to life, liberty, and the pursuit of happiness; that governments derive their power from the consent of the governed; and that people have a right to overthrow oppressive governments. During the Revolutionary War, the states signed the Articles of Confederation, creating a weak central government with few powers. The Articles proved to be unworkable because the national government had no way to ensure compliance by the states with such measures as securing tax revenues.

4. Dissatisfaction with the Articles of Confederation prompted the call for a convention at Philadelphia in 1787. Delegates focused on creating a constitution for a new form of government. The Virginia Plan, which favored the larger states, and the New Jersey Plan, which favored smaller ones, did not garner sufficient support. A compromise offered by Connecticut providing for a bicameral legislature resolved the large-state/small-state dispute. The final version of the Constitution provided for the separation of powers, checks and balances, and a federal form of government.

5. Fears of a strong central government prompted the addition of the Bill of Rights to the Constitution. The Bill of

Rights, which includes the freedoms of religion, speech, and assembly, was initially applied only to the federal government, but amendments to the Constitution following the Civil War were interpreted to ensure that the Bill of Rights would apply to the states as well.

6. An amendment to the Constitution may be proposed either by a two-thirds vote in each chamber of Congress or by a national convention called by Congress at the request of two-thirds of the state legislatures. Ratification can occur either by the approval of three-fourths of the legislatures of the states or by special conventions called in the states for the purpose of ratifying the amendment and approval by three-fourths of these conventions. Informal methods of constitutional change include reinterpretation through congressional legislation, presidential actions, and judicial review.

selected print & media resources

SUGGESTED READINGS

Daniel, Marcus. ***Scandal and Civility: Journalism and the Birth of American Democracy.*** **New York: Oxford University Press, 2009. The American Revolution led to a new breed of journalists who were partisan, irreverent, and satirical—and who ignited debates over the very nature of the country. Daniel gives us a fuller view of the times through the careers of these journalists, who were quite different from the often straightlaced founders.**

Ferling, John. ***The Ascent of George Washington: The Hidden Political Genius of an American Icon.*** **New York: Bloomsbury Press, 2009. Ferling's argument is hard to dispute, once you think about it: George Washington was a brilliant politician who took the greatest pains concerning his presentation and reputation.**

Kasper, Eric T. ***To Secure the Liberty of the People: James Madison's Bill of Rights and the Supreme Court's Interpretation.*** **Dekalb: Northern Illinois University Press, 2010. Kasper discusses Madison's work on the Bill of Rights in the context of his view of the world and the writers who influenced him. The work also examines how members of the United States Supreme Court have interpreted Madison's thinking.**

McCullough, David. ***1776.*** **New York: Simon and Schuster, 2006. McCullough, an esteemed historian, covers the military side of the nation's first year, when the fate of the independence movement hung in the balance. McCullough provides unusually sharp portraits of both George Washington and Britain's King George III.**

MEDIA RESOURCES

In the Beginning—**A 1987 Bill Moyers program that features discussions with three prominent historians about the roots of the Constitution and its impact on our society.**

John Adams—**A widely admired 2008 HBO miniseries on founder John Adams and his wife, Abigail Adams, and other prominent Americans of the revolutionary period. The series is largely based on David McCullough's book** ***John Adams.***

John Locke—**A 1994 video exploring the character and principal views of John Locke.**

Thomas Jefferson—**A 1996 documentary by acclaimed director Ken Burns. The film covers Jefferson's entire life, including his writing of the Declaration of Independence, his presidency, and his later years in Virginia. Historians and writers interviewed include Daniel Boorstin, Garry Wills, Gore Vidal, and John Hope Franklin.**

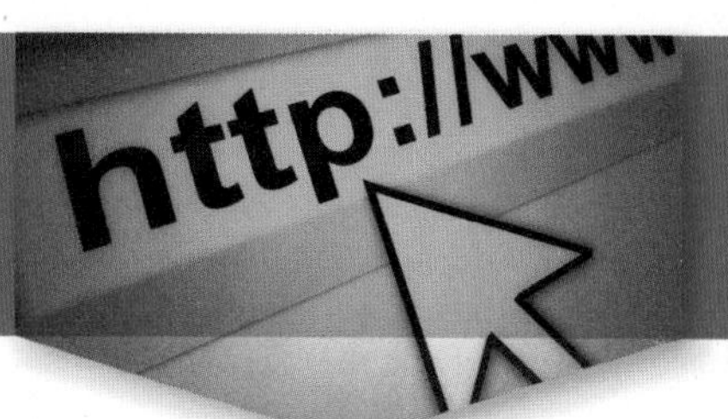

e-mocracy

THE INTERNET AND OUR CONSTITUTION

Today, you can find online many important documents from the founding period, including descriptions of events leading up to the American Revolution, the Articles of Confederation, notes on the Constitutional Convention, the Federalists' writings, and the Anti-Federalists' responses.

You are able to access the Internet and explore a variety of opinions on every topic imaginable because you enjoy the freedoms—including freedom of speech—guaranteed by our Constitution. Even today, more than two hundred years after the U.S. Bill of Rights was ratified, citizens in some countries do not enjoy the right to free speech. Nor can they surf the Web freely, as U.S. citizens do.

For example, the Chinese government employs a number of methods to control Internet use. One method is to use filtering software to block electronic pathways to objectionable sites, including the sites of Western news organizations. Another technique is to prohibit Internet users from sending or discussing information that has not been publicly released by the government. Still another practice is to monitor the online activities of Internet users. None of these methods is foolproof, however. Indeed, some observers claim that the Internet, by exposing citizens in politically oppressive nations to a variety of views on politics and culture, will eventually transform those nations.

We should note that such restrictions also can exist in the United States. For example, there have been persistent efforts by Congress and many courts to limit access to Web sites deemed pornographic. Free speech advocates have attacked these restrictions as unconstitutional, as you will read in Chapter 4.

LOGGING ON

For U.S. founding documents, including the Declaration of Independence, scanned originals of the U.S. Constitution, and the *Federalist Papers,* go to Emory University School of Law's Web site at
library.law.emory.edu

The University of Oklahoma Law Center has a number of U.S. historical documents online, including many of those discussed in this chapter. Go to
www.law.ou.edu/hist

The National Constitution Center provides information on the Constitution—including its history, current debates over constitutional provisions, and news articles—at
www.constitutioncenter.org

To look at state constitutions, go to
www.findlaw.com/casecode/state.html

APPENDIX TO CHAPTER 2

THE CONSTITUTION OF THE UNITED STATES*

The Preamble

We the People of the United States, in Order to form a more perfect Union, establish Justice, insure domestic Tranquility, provide for the common defence, promote the general Welfare, and secure the Blessings of Liberty to ourselves and our Posterity, do ordain and establish this Constitution for the United States of America.

The Preamble declares that "We the People" are the authority for the Constitution (unlike the Articles of Confederation, which derived their authority from the states). The Preamble also sets out the purposes of the Constitution.

ARTICLE I. (Legislative Branch)

The first part of the Constitution, Article I, deals with the organization and powers of the lawmaking branch of the national government, the Congress.

Section 1. Legislative Powers

All legislative Powers herein granted shall be vested in a Congress of the United States, which shall consist of a Senate and House of Representatives.

Section 2. House of Representatives

Clause 1: Composition and Election of Members. The House of Representatives shall be composed of Members chosen every second Year by the People of the several States, and the Electors in each State shall have the Qualifications requisite for Electors of the most numerous Branch of the State Legislature.

Each state has the power to decide who may vote for members of Congress. Within each state, those who may vote for state legislators may also vote for members of the House of Representatives (and, under the Seventeenth Amendment, for U.S. senators). When the Constitution was written, nearly all states limited voting rights to white male property owners or taxpayers at least twenty-one years old. Subsequent amendments granted voting power to African American men, all women, and everyone at least eighteen years old.

Clause 2: Qualifications. No Person shall be a Representative who shall not have attained to the Age of twenty five Years, and been seven Years a Citizen of the United States, and who shall not, when elected, be an Inhabitant of that State in which he shall be chosen.

Each member of the House must be at least twenty-five years old, a citizen of the United States for at least seven years, and a resident of the state in which she or he is elected.

Clause 3: Apportionment of Representatives and Direct Taxes. Representatives [and direct Taxes][1] shall be apportioned among the several States which may be included within this Union, according to their respective Numbers [which shall be determined by adding to the whole Number of free Persons, including those bound to Service for a Term of Years, and excluding Indians not taxed, three fifths of all other Persons].[2] The actual Enumeration shall be made within three Years after the first Meeting of the Congress of the United States, and within every subsequent Term of ten Years, in such Manner as they shall by Law direct. The Number of Representatives shall not exceed one for every thirty Thousand, but each State shall have at Least one Representative; and until such enumeration shall be made, the State of New Hampshire shall be entitled to chuse three, Massachusetts eight, Rhode Island and Providence Plantations one, Connecticut five, New York six, New Jersey four, Pennsylvania eight, Delaware one, Maryland six, Virginia ten, North Carolina five, South Carolina five, and Georgia three.

A state's representation in the House is based on the size of its population. Population is counted in each decade's census, after which Congress reapportions House seats. Since early in the twentieth century, the number of seats has been limited to 435.

Clause 4: Vacancies. When vacancies happen in the Representation from any State, the Executive Authority thereof shall issue Writs of Election to fill such Vacancies.

The "Executive Authority" is the state's governor. When a vacancy occurs in the House, the governor calls a special election to fill it.

Clause 5: Officers and Impeachment. The House of Representatives shall chuse their Speaker and other Officers; and shall have the sole Power of Impeachment.

The power to impeach is the power to accuse. In this case, it is the power to accuse members of the executive or judicial branch of wrongdoing or abuse of power. Once a bill of impeachment is issued, the Senate holds the trial.

Section 3. The Senate

Clause 1: Term and Number of Members. The Senate of the United States shall be composed of two Senators from each State [chosen by the Legislature thereof],[3] for six Years; and each Senator shall have one Vote.

Every state has two senators, each of whom serves for six years and has one vote in the upper chamber. Since the Seventeenth Amendment was passed in 1913, all

* The spelling, capitalization, and punctuation of the original have been retained here. Brackets indicate passages that have been altered by amendments to the Constitution. We have added article titles (in parentheses), section titles, and clause designations. We have also inserted annotations in blue italic type.

1. Modified by the Sixteenth Amendment.
2. Modified by the Fourteenth Amendment.
3. Repealed by the Seventeenth Amendment.

senators have been elected directly by voters of the state during the regular election.

Clause 2: Classification of Senators. Immediately after they shall be assembled in Consequence of the first Election, they shall be divided as equally as may be into three Classes. The Seats of the Senators of the first Class shall be vacated at the Expiration of the second Year, of the second Class at the Expiration of the fourth Year, and of the third Class at the Expiration of the sixth Year, so that one third may be chosen every second Year; [and if Vacancies happen by Resignation, or otherwise, during the Recess of the Legislature of any State, the Executive thereof may make temporary Appointments until the next Meeting of the Legislature, which shall then fill such Vacancies].[4]

One-third of the Senate's seats are open to election every two years (in contrast, all members of the House are elected simultaneously).

Clause 3: Qualifications. No Person shall be a Senator who shall not have attained to the Age of thirty Years, and been nine Years a Citizen of the United States, and who shall not, when elected, be an Inhabitant of that State for which he shall be chosen.

Every senator must be at least thirty years old, a citizen of the United States for a minimum of nine years, and a resident of the state in which he or she is elected.

Clause 4: The Role of the Vice President. The Vice President of the United States shall be President of the Senate, but shall have no Vote, unless they be equally divided.

The vice president presides over meetings of the Senate but cannot vote unless there is a tie. The Constitution gives no other official duties to the vice president.

Clause 5: Other Officers. The Senate shall chuse their other Officers, and also a President pro tempore, in the Absence of the Vice President, or when he shall exercise the Office of President of the United States.

The Senate votes for one of its members to preside when the vice president is absent. This person is usually called the president pro tempore because of the temporary nature of the position.

Clause 6: Impeachment Trials. The Senate shall have the sole Power to try all Impeachments. When sitting for that Purpose, they shall be on Oath or Affirmation. When the President of the United States is tried, the Chief Justice shall preside: And no Person shall be convicted without the Concurrence of two thirds of the Members present.

The Senate conducts trials of officials that the House impeaches. The Senate sits as a jury, with the vice president presiding if the president is not on trial.

Clause 7: Penalties for Conviction. Judgment in Cases of Impeachment shall not extend further than to removal from Office, and disqualification to hold and enjoy any Office of honor, Trust, or Profit under the United States: but the Party convicted shall nevertheless be liable and subject to Indictment, Trial, Judgment, and Punishment, according to Law.

On conviction of impeachment charges, the Senate can only force an official to leave office and prevent him or her from holding another office in the federal government. The individual, however, can still be tried in a regular court.

Section 4. Congressional Elections: Times, Manner, and Places

Clause 1: Elections. The Times, Places and Manner of holding Elections for Senators and Representatives, shall be prescribed in each State by the Legislature thereof; but the Congress may at any time by Law make or alter such Regulations, except as to the Places of chusing Senators.

Congress set the Tuesday after the first Monday in November in even-numbered years as the date for congressional elections. In states with more than one seat in the House, Congress requires that representatives be elected from districts within each state. Under the Seventeenth Amendment, senators are elected at the same places as other officials.

Clause 2: Sessions of Congress. [The Congress shall assemble at least once in every Year, and such Meeting shall be on the first Monday in December, unless they shall by Law appoint a different Day.][5]

Congress has to meet every year at least once. The regular session now begins at noon on January 3 of each year, subsequent to the Twentieth Amendment, unless Congress passes a law to fix a different date. Congress stays in session until its members vote to adjourn. Additionally, the president may call a special session.

Section 5. Powers and Duties of the Houses

Clause 1: Admitting Members and Quorum. Each House shall be the Judge of the Elections, Returns, and Qualifications of its own Members, and a Majority of each shall constitute a Quorum to do Business; but a smaller Number may adjourn from day to day, and may be authorized to compel the Attendance of absent Members, in such Manner, and under such Penalties as each House may provide.

Each chamber may exclude or refuse to seat a member-elect.

The quorum rule requires that 218 members of the House and 51 members of the Senate be present to conduct business. This rule normally is not enforced in the handling of routine matters.

Clause 2: Rules and Discipline of Members. Each House may determine the Rules of its Proceedings, punish

4. Modified by the Seventeenth Amendment.

5. Changed by the Twentieth Amendment.

its Members for disorderly Behaviour, and, with the Concurrence of two thirds, expel a Member.

The House and the Senate may adopt their own rules to guide their proceedings. Each may also discipline its members for conduct that is deemed unacceptable. No member may be expelled without a two-thirds majority vote in favor of expulsion.

Clause 3: Keeping a Record. Each House shall keep a Journal of its Proceedings, and from time to time publish the same, excepting such Parts as may in their Judgment require Secrecy; and the Yeas and Nays of the Members of either House on any question shall, at the Desire of one fifth of those Present, be entered on the Journal.

The journals of the two chambers are published at the end of each session of Congress.

Clause 4: Adjournment. Neither House, during the Session of Congress, shall, without the Consent of the other, adjourn for more than three days, nor to any other Place than that in which the two Houses shall be sitting.

Congress has the power to determine when and where to meet, provided, however, that both chambers meet in the same city. Neither chamber may recess for more than three days without the consent of the other.

Section 6. Rights of Members

Clause 1: Compensation and Privileges. The Senators and Representatives shall receive a Compensation for their services, to be ascertained by Law, and paid out of the Treasury of the United States. They shall in all Cases, except Treason, Felony and Breach of the Peace, be privileged from Arrest during their Attendance at the Session of their respective Houses, and in going to and returning from the same; and for any Speech or Debate in either House, they shall not be questioned in any other Place.

Congressional salaries are to be paid by the U.S. Treasury rather than by the members' respective states. The original salaries were $6 per day; in 1857 they were $3,000 per year. Both representatives and senators were paid $174,000 in 2010.

Treason is defined in Article III, Section 3. A felony is any serious crime. A breach of the peace is any indictable offense less than treason or a felony. Members cannot be arrested for things they say during speeches and debates in Congress. This immunity applies to the Capitol Building itself and not to their private lives.

Clause 2: Restrictions. No Senator or Representative shall, during the Time for which he was elected, be appointed to any civil Office under the Authority of the United States, which shall have been created, or the Emoluments whereof shall have been encreased during such time; and no Person holding any Office under the United States, shall be a Member of either House during his Continuance in Office.

During the term for which a member was elected, he or she cannot concurrently accept another federal government position.

Section 7. Legislative Powers: Bills and Resolutions

Clause 1: Revenue Bills. All Bills for raising Revenue shall originate in the House of Representatives; but the Senate may propose or concur with Amendments as on other Bills.

All tax and appropriation bills for raising money have to originate in the House of Representatives. The Senate, though, often amends such bills and may even substitute an entirely different bill.

Clause 2: The Presidential Veto. Every Bill which shall have passed the House of Representatives and the Senate, shall, before it becomes a Law, be presented to the President of the United States; If he approve he shall sign it, but if not he shall return it, with his Objections to the House in which it shall have originated, who shall enter the Objections at large on their Journal, and proceed to reconsider it. If after such Reconsideration two thirds of that House shall agree to pass the Bill, it shall be sent together with the Objections, to the other House, by which it shall likewise be reconsidered, and if approved by two thirds of that House, it shall become a Law. But in all such Cases the Votes of both Houses shall be determined by Yeas and Nays, and the Names of the Persons voting for and against the Bill shall be entered on the Journal of each House respectively. If any Bill shall not be returned by the President within ten Days (Sundays excepted) after it shall have been presented to him, the Same shall be a Law, in like Manner as if he had signed it, unless the Congress by their Adjournment prevent its Return in which Case it shall not be a Law.

When Congress sends the president a bill, he or she can sign it (in which case it becomes law) or send it back to the chamber in which it originated. If it is sent back, a two-thirds majority of each chamber must pass it again for it to become law. If the president neither signs it nor sends it back within ten days, it becomes law anyway, unless Congress adjourns in the meantime.

Clause 3: Actions on Other Matters. Every Order, Resolution, or Vote to which the Concurrence of the Senate and House of Representatives may be necessary (except on a question of Adjournment) shall be presented to the President of the United States; and before the Same shall take Effect, shall be approved by him, or being disapproved by him, shall be repassed by two thirds of the Senate and House of Representatives, according to the Rules and Limitations prescribed in the Case of a Bill.

The president must have the opportunity to either sign or veto everything that Congress passes, except votes to adjourn and resolutions not having the force of law.

Section 8. The Powers of Congress

Clause 1: Taxing. The Congress shall have Power to lay and collect Taxes, Duties, Imposts and Excises, to pay the Debts and provide for the common Defence and general Welfare of the United States; but all Duties, Imposts and Excises shall be uniform throughout the United States;

Duties are taxes on imports and exports. Impost is a generic term for tax. Excises are taxes on the manufacture, sale, or use of goods.

Clause 2: Borrowing. To borrow Money on the credit of the United States;

Congress has the power to borrow money, which is normally carried out through the sale of U.S. Treasury bonds on which interest is paid. Note that the Constitution places no limit on the amount of government borrowing.

Clause 3: Regulation of Commerce. To regulate Commerce with foreign Nations, and among the several States, and with the Indian Tribes;

This is the commerce clause, *which gives to Congress the power to regulate interstate and foreign trade. Much of the activity of Congress is based on this clause.*

Clause 4: Naturalization and Bankruptcy. To establish an uniform Rule of Naturalization, and uniform Laws on the subject of Bankruptcies throughout the United States;

Only Congress may determine how aliens can become citizens of the United States. Congress may make laws with respect to bankruptcy.

Clause 5: Money and Standards. To coin Money, regulate the Value thereof, and of foreign Coin, and fix the Standard of Weights and Measures;

Congress mints coins and prints and circulates paper money. Congress can establish uniform measures of time, distance, weight, and the like. In 1838, Congress adopted the English system of weights and measurements as our national standard.

Clause 6: Punishing Counterfeiters. To provide for the Punishment of counterfeiting the Securities and current Coin of the United States;

Congress has the power to punish those who copy American currency and pass it off as real. Currently, the penalty may be imprisonment for up to fifteen years plus fines.

Clause 7: Roads and Post Offices. To establish Post Offices and post Roads;

Post roads include all routes over which mail is carried—highways, railways, waterways, and airways.

Clause 8: Patents and Copyrights. To promote the Progress of Science and useful Arts, by securing for limited Times to Authors and Inventors the exclusive Right to their respective Writings and Discoveries;

Authors' and composers' works are protected by copyrights established by copyright law, which currently is the Copyright Act of 1976, as amended. Copyrights are valid for the life of the author or composer plus seventy years. Inventors' works are protected by patents, which vary in length of protection from fourteen to twenty years. A patent gives a person the exclusive right to control the manufacture or sale of her or his invention.

Clause 9: Lower Courts. To constitute Tribunals inferior to the supreme Court;

Congress has the authority to set up all federal courts, except the Supreme Court, and to decide what cases those courts will hear.

Clause 10: Punishment for Piracy. To define and punish Piracies and Felonies committed on the high Seas, and Offences against the Law of Nations;

Congress has the authority to prohibit the commission of certain acts outside U.S. territory and to punish certain violations of international law.

Clause 11: Declaration of War. To declare War, grant Letters of Marque and Reprisal, and make Rules concerning Captures on Land and Water;

Only Congress can declare war, although the president, as commander in chief, can make war without Congress's formal declaration. Letters of marque and reprisal authorized private parties to capture and destroy enemy ships in wartime. Since the middle of the nineteenth century, international law has prohibited letters of marque and reprisal, and the United States has honored the ban.

Clause 12: The Army. To raise and support Armies, but no Appropriation of Money to that Use shall be for a longer Term than two Years;

Congress has the power to create an army; the funds used to pay for it must be appropriated for no more than two-year intervals. This latter restriction gives ultimate control of the army to civilians.

Clause 13: Creation of a Navy. To provide and maintain a Navy;

This clause allows for the maintenance of a navy. In 1947, Congress created the U.S. Air Force.

Clause 14: Regulation of the Armed Forces. To make Rules for the Government and Regulation of the land and naval Forces;

Congress sets the rules for the military mainly by way of the Uniform Code of Military Justice, which was enacted in 1950 by Congress.

Clause 15: The Militia. To provide for calling forth the Militia to execute the Laws of the Union, suppress Insurrections and repel Invasions;

The militia is known today as the National Guard. *Both Congress and the president have the authority to call the National Guard into federal service.*

Clause 16: How the Militia Is Organized. To provide for organizing, arming, and disciplining the Militia, and for governing such Part of them as may be employed in the Service of the United States, reserving to the States respectively, the Appointment of the Officers, and the Authority of training the Militia according to the discipline prescribed by Congress;

This clause gives Congress the power to "federalize" state militia (National Guard). When called into such service, the National Guard is subject to the same rules that Congress has set forth for the regular armed services.

Clause 17: Creation of the District of Columbia. To exercise exclusive Legislation in all Cases whatsoever, over such District (not exceeding ten Miles square) as may, by Cession of particular States, and the Acceptance of Congress, become the Seat of the Government of the United States, and to exercise like Authority over all Places purchased by the Consent of the Legislature of the State in which the Same shall be, for the Erection of Forts, Magazines, Arsenals, dock-Yards, and other needful Buildings;—And

Congress established the District of Columbia as the national capital in 1791. Virginia and Maryland had granted land for the District, but Virginia's grant was returned because it was believed it would not be needed. Today, the District covers sixty-nine square miles.

Clause 18: The Elastic Clause. To make all Laws which shall be necessary and proper for carrying into Execution the foregoing Powers, and all other Powers vested by this Constitution in the Government of the United States, or in any Department or Officer thereof.

This clause—the necessary and proper clause, *or the* elastic clause*—grants no specific powers, and thus it can be stretched to fit different circumstances. It has allowed Congress to adapt the government to changing needs and times.*

Section 9. The Powers Denied to Congress

Clause 1: Question of Slavery. The Migration or Importation of such Persons as any of the States now existing shall think proper to admit, shall not be prohibited by the Congress prior to the Year one thousand eight hundred and eight, but a Tax or duty may be imposed on such Importation, not exceeding ten dollars for each Person.

"Persons" referred to slaves. Congress outlawed the slave trade in 1808.

Clause 2: Habeas Corpus. The privilege of the Writ of Habeas Corpus shall not be suspended, unless when in Cases of Rebellion or Invasion the public Safety may require it.

A writ of habeas corpus *is a court order directing a sheriff or other public officer who is detaining another person to "produce the body" of the detainee so the court can assess the legality of the detention.*

Clause 3: Special Bills. No Bill of Attainder or ex post facto Law shall be passed.

A bill of attainder *is a law that inflicts punishment without a trial. An* ex post facto law *is a law that inflicts punishment for an act that was not illegal when it was committed.*

Clause 4: Direct Taxes. [No Capitation, or other direct, Tax shall be laid, unless in Proportion to the Census or Enumeration herein before directed to be taken.][6]

A capitation *is a tax on a person. A* direct tax *is a tax paid directly to the government, such as a property tax. This clause was intended to prevent Congress from levying a tax on slaves per person and thereby taxing slavery out of existence.*

Clause 5: Export Taxes. No Tax or Duty shall be laid on Articles exported from any State.

Congress may not tax any goods sold from one state to another or from one state to a foreign country. (Congress does have the power to tax goods that are bought from other countries, however.)

Clause 6: Interstate Commerce. No Preference shall be given by any Regulation of Commerce or Revenue to the Ports of one State over those of another: nor shall Vessels bound to, or from, one State, be obliged to enter, clear, or pay Duties in another.

Congress may not treat different ports within the United States differently in terms of taxing and commerce powers. Congress may not give one state's port a legal advantage over the ports of another state.

Clause 7: Treasury Withdrawals. No Money shall be drawn from the Treasury, but in Consequence of Appropriations made by Law; and a regular Statement and Account of the Receipts and Expenditures of all public Money shall be published from time to time.

Federal funds can be spent only as Congress authorizes. This is a significant check on the president's power.

Clause 8: Titles of Nobility. No Title of Nobility shall be granted by the United States: And no Person holding any Office of Profit or Trust under them, shall, without the Consent of the Congress, accept of any present, Emolument, Office, or Title, of any kind whatever, from any King, Prince, or foreign State.

No person in the United States may hold a title of nobility, such as duke or duchess. This clause also discourages bribery of American officials by foreign governments.

Section 10. Those Powers Denied to the States

Clause 1: Treaties and Coinage. No State shall enter into any Treaty, Alliance, or Confederation; grant Letters of Marque and Reprisal; coin Money; emit Bills of Credit; make any Thing but gold and silver Coin a Tender in Payment of Debts; pass any Bill of Attainder, ex post facto Law, or Law impairing the Obligation of Contracts, or grant any Title of Nobility.

6. Modified by the Sixteenth Amendment.

Prohibiting state laws "impairing the Obligation of Contracts" was intended to protect creditors. (Shays' Rebellion—an attempt to prevent courts from giving effect to creditors' legal actions against debtors—occurred only one year before the Constitution was written.)

Clause 2: Duties and Imposts. No State shall, without the Consent of the Congress, lay any Imposts or Duties on Imports or Exports, except what may be absolutely necessary for executing its inspection Laws; and the net Produce of all Duties and Imposts, laid by any State on Imports or Exports, shall be for the Use of the Treasury of the United States; and all such Laws shall be subject to the Revision and Controul of the Congress.

Only Congress can tax imports. Further, the states cannot tax exports.

Clause 3: War. No State shall, without the Consent of Congress, lay any Duty of Tonnage, keep Troops, or Ships of War in time of Peace, enter into any Agreement or Compact with another State, or with a foreign Power or engage in War, unless actually invaded, or in such imminent Danger as will not admit of delay.

A duty of tonnage *is a tax on ships according to their cargo capacity. No states may tax ships according to their cargo unless Congress agrees. Additionally, this clause forbids any state to keep troops or warships during peacetime or to make a compact with another state or foreign nation unless Congress so agrees. A state, in contrast, can maintain a militia, but its use has to be limited to disorders that occur within the state—unless, of course, the militia is called into federal service.*

ARTICLE II. (Executive Branch)

Section 1. The Nature and Scope of Presidential Power

Clause 1: Four-Year Term. The executive Power shall be vested in a President of the United States of America. He shall hold his Office during the Term of four Years, and, together with the Vice President, chosen for the same Term, be elected, as follows.

The president has the power to carry out laws made by Congress, called the executive power. *He or she serves in office for a four-year term after election. The Twenty-second Amendment limits the number of times a person may be elected president.*

Clause 2: Choosing Electors from Each State. Each State shall appoint, in such Manner as the Legislature thereof may direct, a Number of Electors, equal to the whole Number of Senators and Representatives to which the State may be entitled in the Congress; but no Senator or Representative, or Person holding an Office of Trust or Profit under the United States, shall be appointed an Elector.

The "Electors" are known more commonly as the "electoral college." The president is elected by electors—that is, representatives chosen by the people—rather than by the people directly.

Clause 3: The Former System of Elections. [The Electors shall meet in their respective States, and vote by Ballot for two Persons, of whom one at least shall not be an Inhabitant of the same State with themselves. And they shall make a List of all the Persons voted for, and of the Number of Votes for each; which List they shall sign and certify, and transmit sealed to the Seat of the Government of the United States, directed to the President of the Senate. The President of the Senate shall, in the Presence of the Senate and House of Representatives, open all the Certificates, and the Votes shall then be counted. The Person having the greatest Number of Votes shall be the President, if such Number be a Majority of the whole Number of Electors appointed; and if there be more than one who have such Majority, and have an equal Number of Votes, then the House of Representatives shall immediately chuse by Ballot one of them for President; and if no Person have a Majority, then from the five highest on the List the said House shall in like Manner chuse the President. But in chusing the President, the Votes shall be taken by States, the Representation from each State having one Vote; A quorum for this Purpose shall consist of a Member or Members from two thirds of the States, and a Majority of all the States shall be necessary to a Choice. In every Case, after the Choice of the President, the Person having the greater Number of Votes of the Electors shall be the Vice President. But if there should remain two or more who have equal Votes, the Senate shall chuse from them by Ballot the Vice President.][7]

The original method of selecting the president and vice president was replaced by the Twelfth Amendment. Apparently, the framers did not anticipate the rise of political parties and the development of primaries and conventions.

Clause 4: The Time of Elections. The Congress may determine the Time of chusing the Electors, and the Day on which they shall give their Votes; which Day shall be the same throughout the United States.

Congress set the Tuesday after the first Monday in November every fourth year as the date for choosing electors. The electors cast their votes on the Monday after the second Wednesday in December of that year.

Clause 5: Qualifications for President. No person except a natural born Citizen, or a Citizen of the United States, at the time of the Adoption of this Constitution, shall be eligible to the Office of President; neither shall any Person be eligible to that Office who shall not have attained to the Age of thirty five Years, and been fourteen Years a Resident within the United States.

The president must be a natural-born citizen, be at least thirty-five years of age when taking office, and have been a resident within the United States for at least fourteen years.

Clause 6: Succession of the Vice President. [In Case of the Removal of the President from Office, or of his Death,

7. Changed by the Twelfth Amendment.

Resignation or Inability to discharge the Powers and Duties of the said Office, the same shall devolve on the Vice President, and the Congress may by Law provide for the Case of Removal, Death, Resignation or Inability, both of the President and Vice President, declaring what Officer shall then act as President, and such Officer shall act accordingly, until the Disability be removed, or a President shall be elected.][8]

This section provided for the method by which the vice president was to succeed to the presidency, but its wording is ambiguous. It was replaced by the Twenty-fifth Amendment.

Clause 7: The President's Salary. The President shall, at stated Times, receive for his Services, a Compensation, which shall neither be encreased nor diminished during the Period for which he shall have been elected, and he shall not receive within that Period any other Emolument from the United States, or any of them.

The president maintains the same salary during each four-year term. Moreover, she or he may not receive additional cash payments from the government. Originally set at $25,000 per year, the salary is currently $400,000 a year plus $169,000 in various expense accounts.

Clause 8: The Oath of Office. Before he enter on the Execution of his Office, he shall take the following Oath or Affirmation: "I do solemnly swear (or affirm) that I will faithfully execute the Office of President of the United States, and will to the best of my Ability, preserve, protect and defend the Constitution of the United States."

The president is "sworn in" prior to beginning the duties of the office. The taking of the oath of office occurs on January 20, following the November election. The ceremony is called the inauguration. *The oath of office is administered by the chief justice of the United States Supreme Court.*

Section 2. Powers of the President

Clause 1: Commander in Chief. The President shall be Commander in Chief of the Army and Navy of the United States, and of the Militia of the several States, when called into the actual Service of the United States; he may require the Opinion, in writing, of the principal Officer in each of the executive Departments, upon any Subject relating to the Duties of their respective Offices, and he shall have Power to grant Reprieves and Pardons for Offences against the United States, except in Cases of Impeachment.

The armed forces are placed under civilian control because the president is a civilian but still commander in chief of the military. The president may ask for the help of the head of each of the executive departments (thereby creating the cabinet). The cabinet members are chosen by the president with the consent of the Senate, but they can be removed without Senate approval.

The president's clemency powers extend only to federal cases. In those cases, he or she may grant a full or conditional pardon, or reduce a prison term or fine.

Clause 2: Treaties and Appointment. He shall have Power, by and with the Advice and Consent of the Senate, to make Treaties, provided two thirds of the Senators present concur; and he shall nominate, and by and with the Advice and Consent of the Senate, shall appoint Ambassadors, other public Ministers and Consuls, Judges of the supreme Court, and all other Officers of the United States, whose Appointments are not herein otherwise provided for, and which shall be established by Law; but the Congress may by Law vest the Appointment of such inferior Officers, as they think proper, in the President alone, in the Courts of Law, or in the Heads of Departments.

Many of the major powers of the president are identified in this clause, including the power to make treaties with foreign governments (with the approval of the Senate by a two-thirds vote) and the power to appoint ambassadors, Supreme Court justices, and other government officials. Most such appointments require Senate approval.

Clause 3: Vacancies. The President shall have Power to fill up all Vacancies that may happen during the Recess of the Senate, by granting Commissions which shall expire at the end of their next Session.

The president has the power to appoint temporary officials to fill vacant federal offices without Senate approval if the Congress is not in session. Such appointments expire automatically at the end of Congress's next term.

Section 3. Duties of the President

He shall from time to time give to the Congress Information of the State of the Union, and recommend to their Consideration such Measures as he shall judge necessary and expedient; he may, on extraordinary Occasions, convene both Houses, or either of them, and in Case of Disagreement between them, with Respect to the Time of Adjournment, he may adjourn them to such Time as he shall think proper; he shall receive Ambassadors and other public Ministers; he shall take Care that the Laws be faithfully executed, and shall Commission all the Officers of the United States.

Annually, the president reports on the state of the union to Congress, recommends legislative measures, and proposes a federal budget. The State of the Union speech is a statement not only to Congress but also to the American people. After it is given, the president proposes a federal budget and presents an economic report. At any time, the president may send special messages to Congress while it is in session. The president has the power to call special sessions, to adjourn Congress when its two chambers do not agree on when to adjourn, to receive diplomatic representatives of other governments, and to ensure the proper execution of all federal laws. The president further has the ability to empower federal officers to hold their positions and to perform their duties.

Section 4. Impeachment

The President, Vice President and all civil Officers of the United States, shall be removed from Office on Impeachment for, and Conviction of, Treason, Bribery, or other high Crimes and Misdemeanors.

8. Modified by the Twenty-fifth Amendment.

Treason *denotes giving aid to the nation's enemies. The phrase* high crimes and misdemeanors *is usually considered to mean serious abuses of political power. In either case, the president or vice president may be accused by the House (called an* impeachment*) and then removed from office if convicted by the Senate. (Note that impeachment does not mean removal but rather refers to an accusation of treason or high crimes and misdemeanors.)*

ARTICLE III. (Judicial Branch)

Section 1. Judicial Powers, Courts, and Judges

The judicial Power of the United States, shall be vested in one supreme Court, and in such inferior Courts as the Congress may from time to time ordain and establish. The Judges, both of the supreme and inferior Courts, shall hold their Offices during good Behaviour, and shall, at stated Times, receive for their Services a Compensation, which shall not be diminished during their Continuance in Office.

The Supreme Court is vested with judicial power, as are the lower federal courts that Congress creates. Federal judges serve in their offices for life unless they are impeached and convicted by Congress. The payment of federal judges may not be reduced during their time in office.

Section 2. Jurisdiction

Clause 1: Cases under Federal Jurisdiction. The judicial Power shall extend to all Cases, in Law and Equity, arising under this Constitution, the Laws of the United States, and Treaties made, or which shall be made, under their Authority;–to all Cases affecting Ambassadors, other public Ministers and Consuls;–to all Cases of admiralty and maritime Jurisdiction;–to Controversies to which the United States shall be a Party;–to Controversies between two or more States; [–between a State and Citizens of another State;–][9] between Citizens of different States;–between Citizens of the same State claiming Lands under Grants of different States, [and between a State, or the Citizens thereof, and foreign States, Citizens or Subjects.][10]

The federal courts take on cases that concern the meaning of the U.S. Constitution, all federal laws, and treaties. They also can take on cases involving citizens of different states and citizens of foreign nations.

Clause 2: Cases for the Supreme Court. In all Cases affecting Ambassadors, other public Ministers and Consuls, and those in which a State shall be a Party, the supreme Court shall have original Jurisdiction. In all the other Cases before mentioned, the supreme Court shall have appellate Jurisdiction, both as to Law and Fact, with such Exceptions, and under such Regulations as the Congress shall make.

In a limited number of situations, the Supreme Court acts as a trial court and has original jurisdiction. These cases involve a representative from another country or involve a state. In all other situations, the cases must first be tried in the lower courts and then can be appealed to the Supreme Court. Congress may, however, make exceptions. Today, the Supreme Court acts as a trial court of first instance on rare occasions.

Clause 3: The Conduct of Trials. The Trial of all Crimes, except in Cases of Impeachment, shall be by Jury; and such Trial shall be held in the State where the said Crimes shall have been committed; but when not committed within any State, the Trial shall be at such Place or Places as the Congress may by Law have directed.

Any person accused of a federal crime is granted the right to a trial by jury in a federal court in that state in which the crime was committed. Trials of impeachment are an exception.

Section 3. Treason

Clause 1: The Definition of Treason. Treason against the United States, shall consist only in levying War against them, or, in adhering to their Enemies, giving them Aid and Comfort. No Person shall be convicted of Treason unless on the Testimony of two Witnesses to the same overt Act, or on Confession in open Court.

Treason *is the making of war against the United States or giving aid to its enemies.*

Clause 2: Punishment. The Congress shall have Power to declare the Punishment of Treason, but no Attainder of Treason shall work Corruption of Blood, or Forfeiture except during the Life of the Person attainted.

Congress has provided that the punishment for treason ranges from a minimum of five years in prison and/or a $10,000 fine to a maximum of death. "No Attainder of Treason shall work Corruption of Blood" prohibits punishment of the traitor's heirs.

ARTICLE IV. (Relations among the States)

Section 1. Full Faith and Credit

Full Faith and Credit shall be given in each State to the public Acts, Records, and judicial Proceedings of every other State. And the Congress may by general Laws prescribe the Manner in which such Acts, Records and Proceedings shall be proved, and the Effect thereof.

All states are required to respect one another's laws, records, and lawful decisions. There are exceptions, however. A state does not have to enforce another state's criminal code. Nor does it have to recognize another state's grant of a divorce if the person obtaining the divorce did not establish legal residence in the state in which it was given.

Section 2. Treatment of Citizens

Clause 1: Privileges and Immunities. The Citizens of each State shall be entitled to all Privileges and Immunities of Citizens in the several States.

A citizen of a state has the same rights and privileges as the citizens of another state in which he or she happens to be.

9. Modified by the Eleventh Amendment.
10. Modified by the Eleventh Amendment.

Clause 2: Extradition. A Person charged in any State with Treason, Felony, or other Crime, who shall flee from Justice, and be found in another State, shall on Demand of the executive Authority of the State from which he fled, be delivered up, to be removed to the State having Jurisdiction of the Crime.

Any person accused of a crime who flees to another state must be returned to the state in which the crime occurred.

Clause 3: Fugitive Slaves. [No Person held to Service or Labour in one State, under the Laws thereof, escaping into another, shall, in Consequence of any Law or Regulation therein, be discharged from such Service or Labour, but shall be delivered up on Claim of the Party to whom such Service or Labour may be due.][11]

This clause was struck down by the Thirteenth Amendment, which abolished slavery in 1865.

Section 3. Admission of States

Clause 1: The Process. New States may be admitted by the Congress into this Union; but no new State shall be formed or erected within the Jurisdiction of any other State; nor any State be formed by the Junction of two or more States, or Parts of States, without the Consent of the Legislatures of the States concerned as well as of the Congress.

Only Congress has the power to admit new states to the union. No state may be created by taking territory from an existing state unless the state's legislature so consents.

Clause 2: Public Land. The Congress shall have Power to dispose of and make all needful Rules and Regulations respecting the Territory or other Property belonging to the United States; and nothing in this Constitution shall be so construed as to Prejudice any Claims of the United States, or of any particular State.

The federal government has the exclusive right to administer federal government public lands.

Section 4. Republican Form of Government

The United States shall guarantee to every State in this Union a Republican Form of Government, and shall protect each of them against Invasion; and on Application of the Legislature, or of the Executive (when the Legislature cannot be convened) against domestic Violence.

Each state is promised a republican form of government—that is, one in which the people elect their representatives. The federal government is bound to protect states against any attack by foreigners or during times of trouble within a state.

ARTICLE V. (Methods of Amendment)

The Congress, whenever two thirds of both Houses shall deem it necessary, shall propose Amendments to this Constitution, or on the Application of the Legislatures of two thirds of the several States, shall call a Convention for proposing Amendments, which, in either Case, shall be valid to all Intents and Purposes, as Part of this Constitution, when ratified by the Legislatures of three fourths of the several States, or by Conventions in three fourths thereof, as the one or the other Mode of Ratification may be proposed by the Congress; Provided that no Amendment which may be made prior to the Year One thousand eight hundred and eight shall in any Manner affect the first and fourth Clauses in the Ninth Section of the First Article; and that no State. without its Consent, shall be deprived of its equal Suffrage in the Senate.

Amendments may be proposed in either of two ways: by a two-thirds vote of each chamber (Congress) or at the request of two-thirds of the states. Ratification of amendments may be carried out in two ways: by the legislatures of three-fourths of the states or by the voters in three-fourths of the states. No state may be denied equal representation in the Senate.

ARTICLE VI. (National Supremacy)

Clause 1: Existing Obligations. All Debts contracted and Engagements entered into, before the Adoption of this Constitution shall be as valid against the United States under this Constitution, as under the Confederation.

During the Revolutionary War and the years of the Confederation, Congress borrowed large sums. This clause pledged that the new federal government would assume those financial obligations.

Clause 2: Supreme Law of the Land. This Constitution, and the Laws of the United States which shall be made in Pursuance thereof; and all Treaties made, or which shall be made, under the Authority of the United States, shall be the supreme Law of the Land; and the Judges in every State shall be bound thereby, any Thing in the Constitution or Laws of any State to the Contrary notwithstanding.

This is typically called the supremacy clause; *it declares that federal law takes precedence over all forms of state law. No government at the local or state level may make or enforce any law that conflicts with any provision of the Constitution, acts of Congress, treaties, or other rules and regulations issued by the president and his or her subordinates in the executive branch of the federal government.*

Clause 3: Oath of Office. The Senators and Representatives before mentioned, and the Members of the several State Legislatures, and all executive and judicial Officers, both of the United States and of the several States, shall be bound by Oath or Affirmation, to support this Constitution; but no religious Test shall ever be required as a Qualification to any Office or public Trust under the United States.

Every federal and state official must take an oath of office promising to support the U.S. Constitution. Religion may not be used as a qualification to serve in any federal office.

11. Repealed by the Thirteenth Amendment.

ARTICLE VII. (Ratification)

The Ratification of the Conventions of nine States shall be sufficient for the Establishment of this Constitution between the States so ratifying the Same.

Nine states were required to ratify the Constitution. Delaware was the first and New Hampshire the ninth.

Done in Convention by the Unanimous Consent of the States present the Seventeenth Day of September in the Year of our Lord one thousand seven hundred and Eighty seven and of the Independence of the United States of America the Twelfth. In witness whereof we have hereunto subscribed our Names,

Go. WASHINGTON
Presid't.
and deputy from Virginia

Attest William Jackson Secretary

DELAWARE: Geo. Read, Gunning Bedford jun, John Dickinson, Richard Bassett, Jaco. Broom

MARYLAND: James McHenry, Dan of St. Thos. Jenifer, Danl. Carroll

VIRGINIA: John Blair, James Madison Jr.

NORTH CAROLINA: Wm. Blount, Richd. Dobbs Spaight, Hu. Williamson

SOUTH CAROLINA: J. Rutledge, Charles Cotesworth Pinckney, Charles Pinckney, Pierce Butler

GEORGIA: William Few, Abr. Baldwin

NEW HAMPSHIRE: John Langdon, Nicholas Gilman

MASSACHUSETTS: Nathaniel Gorham, Rufus King

CONNECTICUT: Wm. Saml. Johnson, Roger Sherman

NEW YORK: Alexander Hamilton

NEW JERSEY: Wh. Livingston, David Brearley, Wm. Paterson, Jona. Dayton

PENNSYLVANIA: B. Franklin, Thomas Mifflin, Robt. Morris, Geo. Clymer, Thos. FitzSimons, Jared Ingersoll, James Wilson, Gouv. Morris

AMENDMENTS TO THE CONSTITUTION OF THE UNITED STATES[12]

Articles in addition to, and amendment of, the Constitution of the United States of America, proposed by Congress and ratified by the Legislatures of the several states, pursuant to the Fifth Article of the original Constitution.

AMENDMENT I.

(Religion, Speech, Assembly, and Petition)

Congress shall make no law respecting an establishment of religion, or prohibiting the free exercise thereof; or abridging the freedom of speech, or of the press; or the right of the people peaceably to assemble, and to petition the Government for a redress of grievances.

Congress may not create an official church or enact laws limiting the freedom of religion, speech, the press, assembly, and petition. These guarantees, like the others in the Bill of Rights (the first ten amendments), are not absolute–each may be exercised only with regard to the rights of other persons.

AMENDMENT II.

(Militia and the Right to Bear Arms)

A well regulated Militia, being necessary to the security of a free State, the right of the people to keep and bear Arms, shall not be infringed.

To protect itself, each state has the right to maintain a volunteer armed force. States and the federal government regulate the possession and use of firearms by individuals.

AMENDMENT III.

(The Quartering of Soldiers)

No Soldier shall, in time of peace be quartered in any house, without the consent of the Owner, nor in time of war, but in a manner to be prescribed by law.

Before the Revolutionary War, it had been common British practice to quarter soldiers in colonists' homes. Military troops do not have the power to take over private houses during peacetime.

AMENDMENT IV.

(Searches and Seizures)

The right of the people to be secure in their persons, houses, papers, and effects, against unreasonable searches and seizures, shall not be violated, and no Warrants shall issue, but upon probable cause, supported by Oath or affirmation, and particularly describing the place to be searched, and the persons or things to be seized.

Here the word warrant *means "justification" and refers to a document issued by a magistrate or judge indicating the name, address, and possible offense committed. Anyone asking for the warrant, such as a police officer, must be able to convince the magistrate or judge that an offense probably has been committed.*

AMENDMENT V.

(Grand Juries, Self-Incrimination, Double Jeopardy, Due Process, and Eminent Domain)

No person shall be held to answer for a capital, or otherwise infamous crime, unless on a presentment or indictment of a Grand Jury, except in cases arising in the land or naval forces, or in the Militia, when in actual service in time of War or public danger; nor shall any person be subject for the same offence to be twice put in jeopardy of life or limb; nor shall be compelled in any criminal case to be a witness against himself, nor be deprived of life, liberty, or property, without due process of law; nor shall private property be taken for public use, without just compensation.

There are two types of juries. A grand jury *considers physical evidence and the testimony of witnesses and decides whether there is sufficient reason to bring a case to trial. A* petit jury *hears the case at trial and decides it. "For the same offence to be twice put in jeopardy of life or limb" means to be tried twice for the same crime. A person may not be tried for the same crime twice or forced to give evidence against herself or himself. No person's right to life, liberty, or property may be taken away except by lawful means, called the* due process of law. *Private property taken for public use must be paid for by the government.*

AMENDMENT VI.

(Criminal Court Procedures)

In all criminal prosecutions, the accused shall enjoy the right to a speedy and public trial, by an impartial jury of the State and district wherein the crime shall have been committed, which district shall have been previously ascertained by law, and to be informed of the nature and cause of the accusation; to be confronted with the witnesses against him; to have compulsory process for obtaining witnesses in his favor, and to have the Assistance of Counsel for his defence.

Any person accused of a crime has the right to a fair and public trial by a jury in the state in which the crime took place. The charges against that person must be indicated. Any accused person has the right to a lawyer to defend him or her and to question those who testify against him or her, as well as the right to call people to speak in his or her favor at trial.

AMENDMENT VII.

(Trial by Jury in Civil Cases)

In Suits at common law, where the value in controversy shall exceed twenty dollars, the right of trial by jury shall be preserved, and no fact tried by jury, shall be otherwise re-examined in any Court of the United States, than according to the rules of the common law.

12. On September 25, 1789, Congress transmitted to the state legislatures twelve proposed amendments, two of which, having to do with congressional representation and congressional pay, were not adopted. The remaining ten amendments became the Bill of Rights. In 1992, the amendment concerning congressional pay was adopted as the Twenty-seventh Amendment.

A jury trial may be requested by either party in a dispute in any case involving more than $20. If both parties agree to a trial by a judge without a jury, the right to a jury trial may be put aside.

AMENDMENT VIII.
(Bail, Cruel and Unusual Punishment)

Excessive bail shall not be required, nor excessive fines imposed, nor cruel and unusual punishments inflicted.

Bail *is an amount of money that a person accused of a crime may be required to deposit with the court as a guaranty that she or he will appear in court when requested. The amount of bail required or the fine imposed as punishment for a crime must be reasonable compared with the seriousness of the crime involved. Any punishment judged to be too harsh or too severe for a crime is prohibited.*

AMENDMENT IX.
(The Rights Retained by the People)

The enumeration in the Constitution, of certain rights, shall not be construed to deny or disparage others retained by the people.

Many civil rights that are not explicitly enumerated in the Constitution are still held by the people.

AMENDMENT X.
(Reserved Powers of the States)

The powers not delegated to the United States by the Constitution, nor prohibited by it to the States, are reserved to the States respectively, or to the people.

Those powers not delegated by the Constitution to the federal government or expressly denied to the states belong to the states and to the people. This amendment in essence allows the states to pass laws under their "police powers."

AMENDMENT XI.
(Ratified on February 7, 1795—
Suits against States)

The Judicial power of the United States shall not be construed to extend to any suit in law or equity, commenced or prosecuted against one of the United States by Citizens of another State, or by Citizens or Subjects of any Foreign State.

This amendment has been interpreted to mean that a state cannot be sued in federal court by one of its own citizens, by a citizen of another state, or by a foreign country.

AMENDMENT XII.
(Ratified on June 15, 1804—
Election of the President)

The Electors shall meet in their respective states, and vote by ballot for President and Vice-President, one of whom, at least, shall not be an inhabitant of the same State with themselves; they shall name in their ballots the person voted for as President, and in distinct ballots the person voted for as Vice-President, and they shall make distinct lists of all persons voted for as President, and of all persons voted for as Vice-President, and of the number of votes for each, which lists they shall sign and certify, and transmit sealed to the seat of the government of the United States, directed to the President of the Senate;—The President of the Senate shall, in the presence of the Senate and House of Representatives, open all the certificates and the votes shall then be counted;—The person having the greatest number of votes for President, shall be the President, if such number be a majority of the whole number of Electors appointed; and if no person have such majority, then from the persons having the highest numbers not exceeding three on the list of those voted for as President, the House of Representatives shall choose immediately, by ballot, the President. But in choosing the President, the votes shall be taken by States, the representation from each State having one vote; a quorum for this purpose shall consist of a member or members from two-thirds of the States, and a majority of all States shall be necessary to a choice. [And if the House of Representatives shall not choose a President whenever the right of choice shall devolve upon them, before the fourth day of March next following, then the Vice-President shall act as President, as in the case of the death or other constitutional disability of the President.][13]—The person having the greatest number of votes as Vice-President, shall be the Vice-President, if such number be a majority of the whole number of Electors appointed, and if no person have a majority, then from the two highest numbers on the list, the Senate shall choose the Vice-President; a quorum for the purpose shall consist of two-thirds of the whole number of Senators, and a majority of the whole number shall be necessary to a choice. But no person constitutionally ineligible to the office of President shall be eligible to that of Vice-President of the United States.

The original procedure set out for the election of president and vice president in Article II, Section 1, resulted in a tie in 1800 between Thomas Jefferson and Aaron Burr. It was not until the next year that the House of Representatives chose Jefferson to be president. This amendment changed the procedure by providing for separate ballots for president and vice president.

AMENDMENT XIII.
(Ratified on December 6, 1865—
Prohibition of Slavery)

Section 1.

Neither slavery nor involuntary servitude, except as a punishment for crime whereof the party shall have been duly convicted, shall exist within the United States, or any place subject to their jurisdiction.

Some slaves had been freed during the Civil War. This amendment freed the others and abolished slavery.

Section 2.

Congress shall have power to enforce this article by appropriate legislation.

13. Changed by the Twentieth Amendment.

AMENDMENT XIV.
**(Ratified on July 9, 1868—
Citizenship, Due Process, and
Equal Protection of the Laws)**

Section 1.

All persons born or naturalized in the United States, and subject to the jurisdiction thereof, are citizens of the United States and of the State wherein they reside. No State shall make or enforce any law which shall abridge the privileges or immunities of citizens of the United States; nor shall any State deprive any person of life, liberty, or property, without due process of law; nor deny to any person within its jurisdiction the equal protection of the laws.

Under this provision, states cannot make or enforce laws that take away rights given to all citizens by the federal government. States cannot act unfairly or arbitrarily toward, or discriminate against, any person.

Section 2.

Representatives shall be apportioned among the several States according to their respective numbers, counting the whole number of persons in each State, excluding Indians not taxed. But when the right to vote at any election for the choice of electors for President and Vice President of the United States, Representatives in Congress, the Executive and Judicial officers of a State, or the members of the Legislature thereof, is denied to any of the male inhabitants of such State, being [twenty-one][14] years of age, and citizens of the United States, or in any way abridged, except for participation in rebellion, or other crime, the basis of representation therein shall be reduced in the proportion which the number of such male citizens shall bear to the whole number of male citizens twenty-one years of age in such State.

Section 3.

No person shall be a Senator or Representative in Congress, or elector of President and Vice President, or hold any office, civil or military, under the United States, or under any State, who having previously taken an oath, as a member of Congress, or as an officer of the United States, or as a member of any State legislature, or as an executive or judicial officer of any State, to support the Constitution of the United States, shall have engaged in insurrection or rebellion against the same, or given aid or comfort to the enemies thereof. But Congress may by a vote of two-thirds of each House, remove such disability.

This provision forbade former state or federal government officials who had acted in support of the Confederacy during the Civil War to hold office again. It limited the president's power to pardon those persons. Congress removed this "disability" in 1898.

Section 4.

The validity of the public debt of the United States, authorized by law, including debts incurred for payment of pensions and bounties for services in suppressing insurrection or rebellion, shall not be questioned. But neither the United States nor any State shall assume or pay any debt or obligation incurred in aid of insurrection or rebellion against the United States, or any claim for the loss or emancipation of any slave, but all such debts, obligations and claims shall be held illegal and void.

Section 5.

The Congress shall have power to enforce, by appropriate legislation, the provisions of this article.

AMENDMENT XV.
**(Ratified on February 3, 1870—
The Right to Vote)**

Section 1.

The right of citizens of the United States to vote shall not be denied or abridged by the United States or by any State on account of race, color, or previous condition of servitude.

No citizen can be refused the right to vote simply because of race or color or because that person was once a slave.

Section 2.

The Congress shall have power to enforce this article by appropriate legislation.

AMENDMENT XVI.
**(Ratified on February 3, 1913—
Income Taxes)**

The Congress shall have power to lay and collect taxes on incomes, from whatever source derived, without apportionment among the several States, and without regard to any census or enumeration.

This amendment allows Congress to tax income without sharing the revenue so obtained with the states according to their population.

AMENDMENT XVII.
**(Ratified on April 8, 1913—
The Popular Election of Senators)**

Section 1.

The Senate of the United States shall be composed of two Senators from each State, elected by the people thereof, for six years; and each Senator shall have one vote. The electors in each State shall have the qualifications requisite for electors of the most numerous branch of the State legislatures.

Section 2.

When vacancies happen in the representation of any State in the Senate, the executive authority of such State shall issue writs of election to fill such vacancies: *Provided,* That the legislature of any State may empower the executive thereof to make temporary appointments until the people fill the vacancies by election as the legislature may direct.

Section 3.

This amendment shall not be so construed as to affect the election or term of any Senator chosen before it becomes valid as part of the Constitution.

14. Changed by the Twenty-sixth Amendment.

This amendment modified portions of Article I, Section 3, that related to election of senators. Senators are now elected by the voters in each state directly. When a vacancy occurs, either the state may fill the vacancy by a special election, or the governor of the state involved may appoint someone to fill the seat until the next election.

AMENDMENT XVIII.
(Ratified on January 16, 1919— Prohibition)

Section 1.
After one year from the ratification of this article the manufacture, sale, or transportation of intoxicating liquors within, the importation thereof into, or the exportation thereof from the United States and all territory subject to the jurisdiction thereof for beverage purposes is hereby prohibited.

Section 2.
The Congress and the several States shall have concurrent power to enforce this article by appropriate legislation.

Section 3.
This article shall be inoperative unless it shall have been ratified as an amendment to the Constitution by the legislatures of the several States, as provided in the Constitution, within seven years from the date of the submission hereof to the States by the Congress.[15]

This amendment made it illegal to manufacture, sell, and transport alcoholic beverages in the United States. It was repealed by the Twenty-first Amendment.

AMENDMENT XIX.
(Ratified on August 18, 1920— Women's Right to Vote)

Section 1.
The right of citizens of the United States to vote shall not be denied or abridged by the United States or by any State on account of sex.

Section 2.
Congress shall have power to enforce this article by appropriate legislation.

Women were given the right to vote by this amendment, and Congress was given the power to enforce this right.

AMENDMENT XX.
(Ratified on January 23, 1933— The Lame Duck Amendment)

Section 1.
The terms of the President and Vice President shall end at noon on the 20th day of January, and the terms of Senators and Representatives at noon on the 3d day of January, of the years in which such terms would have ended if this article had not been ratified; and the terms of their successors shall then begin.

This amendment modified Article I, Section 4, Clause 2, and other provisions relating to the president in the Twelfth Amendment. The taking of the oath of office was moved from March 4 to January 20.

Section 2.
The Congress shall assemble at least once in every year, and such meeting shall begin at noon on the 3d day of January, unless they shall by law appoint a different day.

Congress changed the beginning of its term to January 3. The reason the Twentieth Amendment is called the Lame Duck Amendment is that it shortens the time between when a member of Congress is defeated for reelection and when he or she leaves office.

Section 3.
If, at the time fixed for the beginning of the term of the President, the President elect shall have died, the Vice President elect shall become President. If a President shall not have been chosen before the time fixed for the beginning of his term, or if the President elect shall have failed to qualify, then the Vice President elect shall act as President until a President shall have qualified; and the Congress may by law provide for the case wherein neither a President elect nor a Vice President elect shall have qualified, declaring who shall then act as President, or the manner in which one who is to act shall be selected, and such person shall act accordingly until a President or Vice President shall have qualified.

This part of the amendment deals with problem areas left ambiguous by Article II and the Twelfth Amendment. If the president dies before January 20 or fails to qualify for office, the presidency is to be filled as described in this section.

Section 4.
The Congress may by law provide for the case of the death of any of the persons from whom the House of Representatives may choose a President whenever the right of choice shall have devolved upon them, and for the case of the death of any of the persons from whom the Senate may choose a Vice President whenever the right of choice shall have devolved upon them.

Congress has never created legislation pursuant to this section.

Section 5.
Sections 1 and 2 shall take effect on the 15th day of October following the ratification of this article.

Section 6.
This article shall be inoperative unless it shall have been ratified as an amendment to the Constitution by the legislatures of three-fourths of the several States within seven years from the date of its submission.

AMENDMENT XXI.
(Ratified on December 5, 1933— The Repeal of Prohibition)

Section 1.
The eighteenth article of amendment to the Constitution of the United States is hereby repealed.

15. The Eighteenth Amendment was repealed by the Twenty-first Amendment.

Section 2.
The transportation or importation into any State, Territory, or possession of the United States for delivery or use therein of intoxicating liquors, in violation of the laws thereof, is hereby prohibited.

Section 3.
This article shall be inoperative unless it shall have been ratified as an amendment to the Constitution by conventions in the several States, as provided in the Constitution, within seven years from the date of the submission hereof to the States by the Congress.

The amendment repealed the Eighteenth Amendment but did not make alcoholic beverages legal everywhere. Rather, they remained illegal in any state that so designated them. Many such "dry" states existed for a number of years after 1933. Today, there are still "dry" counties within the United States, in which the sale of alcoholic beverages is illegal.

AMENDMENT XXII.
(Ratified on February 27, 1951— Limitation of Presidential Terms)

Section 1.
No person shall be elected to the office of the President more than twice, and no person who has held the office of President, or acted as President, for more than two years of a term to which some other person was elected President shall be elected to the office of President more than once. But this Article shall not apply to any person holding the office of President when this Article was proposed by the Congress, and shall not prevent any person who may be holding the office of President, or acting as President, during the term within which this Article becomes operative from holding the office of President or acting as President during the remainder of such term.

Section 2.
This article shall be inoperative unless it shall have been ratified as an amendment to the Constitution by the legislatures of three-fourths of the several States within seven years from the date of its submission to the States by the Congress.

No president may serve more than two elected terms. If, however, a president has succeeded to the office after the halfway point of a term in which another president was originally elected, then that president may serve for more than eight years, but not to exceed ten years.

AMENDMENT XXIII.
(Ratified on March 29, 1961— Presidential Electors for the District of Columbia)

Section 1.
The District constituting the seat of Government of the United States shall appoint in such manner as the Congress may direct:

A number of electors of President and Vice President equal to the whole number of Senators and Representatives in Congress to which the District would be entitled if it were a State, but in no event more than the least populous State; they shall be in addition to those appointed by the States, but they shall be considered, for the purposes of the election of President and Vice President, to be electors appointed by a State; and they shall meet in the District and perform such duties as provided by the twelfth article of amendment.

Section 2.
The Congress shall have power to enforce this article by appropriate legislation.

Citizens living in the District of Columbia have the right to vote in elections for president and vice president. The District of Columbia has three presidential electors, whereas before this amendment it had none.

AMENDMENT XXIV.
(Ratified on January 23, 1964— The Anti–Poll Tax Amendment)

Section 1.
The right of citizens of the United States to vote in any primary or other election for President or Vice President, for electors for President or Vice President, or for Senator or Representative in Congress, shall not be denied or abridged by the United States, or any State by reason of failure to pay any poll tax or other tax.

Section 2.
The Congress shall have power to enforce this article by appropriate legislation.

No government shall require a person to pay a poll tax to vote in any federal election.

AMENDMENT XXV.
(Ratified on February 10, 1967— Presidential Disability and Vice-Presidential Vacancies)

Section 1.
In case of the removal of the President from office or of his death or resignation, the Vice President shall become President.

Whenever a president dies or resigns from office, the vice president becomes president.

Section 2.

Whenever there is a vacancy in the office of the Vice President, the President shall nominate a Vice President who shall take office upon confirmation by a majority vote of both Houses of Congress.

Whenever the office of the vice presidency becomes vacant, the president may appoint someone to fill this office, provided Congress consents.

Section 3.
Whenever the President transmits to the President pro tempore of the Senate and the Speaker of the House of Representatives his written declaration that he is unable to discharge the powers and duties of his office, and until

he transmits to them a written declaration to the contrary, such powers and duties shall be discharged by the Vice President as Acting President.

Whenever the president believes she or he is unable to carry out the duties of the office, she or he shall so indicate to Congress in writing. The vice president then acts as president until the president declares that she or he is again able to carry out the duties of the office.

Section 4.

Whenever the Vice President and a majority of either the principal officers of the executive departments or of such other body as Congress may by law provide, transmit to the President pro tempore of the Senate and the Speaker of the House of Representatives their written declaration that the President is unable to discharge the powers and duties of his office, the Vice President shall immediately assume the powers and duties of the office as Acting President.

Thereafter, when the President transmits to the President pro tempore of the Senate and the Speaker of the House of Representatives his written declaration that no inability exists, he shall resume the powers and duties of his office unless the Vice President and a majority of either the principal officers of the executive department or of such other body as Congress may by law provide, transmit within four days to the President pro tempore of the Senate and the Speaker of the House of Representatives their written declaration that the President is unable to discharge the powers and duties of his office. Thereupon Congress shall decide the issue, assembling within forty-eight hours for that purpose if not in session. If the Congress, within twenty-one days after receipt of the latter written declaration, or, if Congress is not in session, within twenty-one days after Congress is required to assemble, determines by two-thirds vote of both Houses that the President is unable to discharge the powers and duties of his office, the Vice President shall continue to discharge the same as Acting President; otherwise, the President shall resume the powers and duties of his office.

Whenever the vice president and a majority of the members of the cabinet believe that the president cannot carry out her or his duties, they shall so indicate in writing to Congress. The vice president shall then act as president. When the president believes that she or he is able to carry out her or his duties again, she or he shall so indicate to the Congress. However, if the vice president and a majority of the cabinet do not agree, Congress must decide by a two-thirds vote within three weeks who shall act as president.

AMENDMENT XXVI.

(Ratified on July 1, 1971—
The Eighteen-Year-Old Vote)

Section 1.

The right of citizens of the United States, who are eighteen years of age or older, to vote shall not be denied or abridged by the United States or by any State on account of age.

No one over eighteen years of age can be denied the right to vote in federal or state elections by virtue of age.

Section 2.

The Congress shall have power to enforce this article by appropriate legislation.

AMENDMENT XXVII.

(Ratified on May 7, 1992—
Congressional Pay)

No law, varying the compensation for the services of the Senators and Representatives, shall take effect, until an election of representatives shall have intervened.

This amendment allows the voters to have some control over increases in salaries for congressional members. Originally submitted to the states for ratification in 1789, it was not ratified until 203 years later, in 1992.

chapter

3

Federalism

chapter contents

A helicopter lands on Highway 610 in 2005 after searching for Hurricane Katrina survivors stranded on rooftops because of the floodwater that surrounded their neighborhoods. (© Larry W. Smith/epa/Corbis)

WHAT IF... ...one state's same-sex marriages had to be recognized nationwide?

This replica of President Abraham Lincoln was used at a protest rally in favor of legally recognizing same-sex marriages. Why are same-sex marriages a political lightning rod? (Frederic Larson/Corbis/*San Francisco Chronicle*)

BACKGROUND

In November 2003, the Massachusetts Supreme Judicial Court ruled that same-sex couples have a right to civil marriage under the state constitution.[a] The California Supreme Court legalized same-sex marriages in May 2008, but California voters overturned the ruling in November by amending the state constitution.[b] By 2010, however, Connecticut, the District of Columbia, Iowa, New Hampshire, and Vermont had all accepted same-sex marriage.

As you will learn in this chapter, the U.S. Constitution requires that each state give full faith and credit to every other state's public acts. If a man and woman are married under the laws of Nevada, the other forty-nine states must recognize that marriage. But what if one state recognizes same-sex marriages? Does that mean that all other states must recognize such marriages and give each partner to the marriage the benefits accorded to partners in opposite-sex marriages?

In 1996, Congress attempted to prevent such a result through the Defense of Marriage Act, which allows state governments to ignore same-sex marriages performed in other states. But what would happen if the United States Supreme Court ruled that the Defense of Marriage Act is unconstitutional? If this happened, then all of the state laws that refuse to recognize same-sex marriages performed in another state would be unconstitutional as well.

WHAT IF ONE STATE'S SAME-SEX MARRIAGES HAD TO BE RECOGNIZED NATIONWIDE?

If same-sex marriages were recognized nationwide, then same-sex relationships would be much more conspicuous. Marriage is an issue in many contexts—from registering at a hotel to applying for a line of credit. Hotel clerks or bankers who would prefer not to deal with same-sex couples would be forced to confront the reality of these relationships.

The national government has traditionally left marriage laws to the states. In the past, the Internal Revenue Service and other federal agencies recognized marriages when, and only when, the states recognized them. Under the Defense of Marriage Act, however, federal agencies do not recognize same-sex marriages no matter what the states do. In July 2010, however, a federal district court judge in Massachusetts ruled that it was unconstitutional for the federal government to deny benefits to same-sex couples married under state laws. The judge did not require states to recognize other states' same-sex marriages, however. This ruling is certain to be appealed all the way to the Supreme Court.

ENFORCING THE LAW

A majority of the American public is opposed to same-sex marriages. In November 2009, for example, voters in Maine repealed a state law that would have allowed same-sex couples to marry. Either by statute or by constitutional amendment, thirty states ban same-sex marriages, and these marriages remain illegal in an additional fourteen states. If same-sex marriages were legal nationwide, officials in conservative states might refuse to recognize such marriages, regardless of the law. It could take a long campaign of lawsuits to enforce widespread compliance.

FOR CRITICAL ANALYSIS

1. Conservatives have proposed an amendment to the U.S. Constitution to ban same-sex marriage. What difficulties do the advocates of this amendment face in getting it adopted?
2. What impact might widespread same-sex marriage have on American culture generally?

---

a. *Goodridge v. Department of Public Health,* 798 N.E.2d 941 (Mass. 2003).

b. *In re Marriage Cases,* 183 P.3d 384 (Cal. 2008). California continues to recognize same-sex marriages performed between May and November 2008. Maryland and New York recognize same-sex marriages performed in other states.

In the United States, rights and powers are reserved to the states by the Tenth Amendment. It may appear that since the terrorist attacks of September 11, 2001, the federal government, sometimes called the national or central government, predominates. Nevertheless, that might be a temporary exaggeration, for there are 88,576 separate governmental units in this nation, as you can see in Table 3–1 alongside.

Visitors from countries such as France or Spain are often awestruck by the complexity of our system of government. Consider that a criminal action can be defined by state law, by national law, or by both. Thus, a criminal suspect can be prosecuted in the state court system or in the federal court system (or both). Often, economic regulation covering exactly the same issues exists at the local level, the state level, and the national level—generating multiple forms to be completed, multiple procedures to be followed, and multiple laws to be obeyed. Many programs are funded by the national government but administered by state and local governments.

Relations between central governments and local units are structured in various ways. *Federalism* is one of these ways. Understanding federalism and how it differs from other forms of government is important in understanding the American political system. Indeed, many political issues today would be substantially different if we did not have a federal form of government in which governmental authority is divided between the central government and various subunits. States, for example, might not have the right to set their own marriage laws, as we discussed in this chapter's opening *What If . . .* feature.

TABLE 3–1

Governmental Units in the United States

With almost 89,000 separate governmental units in the United States today, it is no wonder that intergovernmental relations in the United States are so complicated. Actually, the number of school districts has decreased over time, but the number of special districts created for single purposes, such as flood control, has increased from only about 8,000 during World War II to more than 36,000 today.

Federal government	**1**
State governments	**50**
Local governments	**88,525**
Counties	**3,034**
Municipalities (mainly cities or towns)	**19,429**
Townships (less extensive powers)	**16,504**
Special districts (water, sewer, and the like)	**36,052**
School districts	**13,506**
TOTAL	**88,576**

Source: U.S. Census Bureau.

Three Systems of Government

There are nearly two hundred independent nations in the world today. Each of these nations has its own system of government. Generally, though, we can describe how nations structure relations between central governments and local units in terms of three models: (1) the unitary system, (2) the confederal system, and (3) the federal system. The most popular, both historically and today, is the unitary system.

A Unitary System

A **unitary system** of government is the easiest to define. Unitary systems place ultimate governmental authority in the hands of the national, or central, government. Consider a typical unitary system—France. There are regions, departments, and municipalities (communes) in France. The regions, departments, and communes have elected and appointed officials. So far, the French system appears to be very similar to the U.S. system, but the similarity is only superficial. Under the unitary French system, the decisions of the lower levels of government can be overruled by the national government. The national government also can cut off the funding of many local government activities. Moreover, in a unitary system such as that in France, all questions of education, police, the use of land, and welfare are handled by the national government. Britain, Egypt, Ghana, Israel, Japan, the Philippines, and Sweden—in fact, most countries today—have unitary systems of government.[1]

Unitary System
A centralized governmental system in which ultimate governmental authority rests in the hands of the national, or central, government.

Confederal System
A system consisting of a league of independent states, each having essentially sovereign powers. The central government created by such a league has only limited powers over the states.

A Confederal System

You were introduced to the elements of a **confederal system** of government in Chapter 2, when we examined the Articles of Confederation. A *confederation* is the opposite of a unitary governing system. It is a league of independent states, each having essentially sovereign powers. In a confederation, a central government or administration handles only those

1. Recent legislation has altered somewhat the unitary character of the French political system. In Britain, the unitary nature of the government has been modified by the creation of the Scottish Parliament.

This member of the 304th Air Reserve Squadron from Portland, Oregon, was part of the Air Force rescue team that saved many lives after Hurricane Katrina hit the mainland in the fall of 2005. How does the federal government work with the states during emergencies? (© US Air Force—digital version c/Science Faction/Corbis)

matters of common concern expressly delegated to it by the member states. The central government has no ability to make laws directly applicable to member states unless the members explicitly support such laws. The United States under the Articles of Confederation was a confederal system.

Few, if any, confederations of this kind exist. One possible exception is the European Union (EU), a league of countries that has developed a large body of Europe-wide laws that all members must observe. Many members even share a common currency, the euro. Recent problems in the Eurozone, which we describe in this chapter's *Beyond Our Borders* feature on the following page, demonstrate the limits of a confederal system.

A Federal System

The federal system lies between the unitary and confederal forms of government. As mentioned in Chapter 2, in a *federal system,* authority is divided, usually by a written constitution, between a central government and regional, or subdivisional, governments (often called *constituent governments*). The central government and the constituent governments both act directly on the people through laws and through the actions of elected and appointed governmental officials. Within each government's sphere of authority, each is supreme, in theory. Thus, a federal system differs sharply from a unitary one, in which the central government is supreme and the constituent governments derive their authority from it. In addition to the United States, Australia, Brazil, Canada, Germany, India, and Mexico are examples of nations with federal systems. See Figure 3–1 on page 86 for a comparison of the three governmental systems.

Why Federalism?

Why did the United States develop in a federal direction? We look here at that question, as well as at some of the arguments for and against a federal form of government.

A Practical Solution

As you saw in Chapter 2, the historical basis of our federal system was laid down in Philadelphia at the Constitutional Convention, where advocates of a strong national government opposed states' rights advocates. This dichotomy continued through to the ratifying conventions in the several states. The resulting federal system was a compromise. The supporters of the new Constitution were political pragmatists—they realized that without a federal arrangement, the new Constitution would not be ratified. The appeal of federalism was that it retained state traditions and local power while establishing a strong national government capable of handling common problems.

Even if the founders had agreed on the desirability of a unitary system, size and regional isolation would have made such a system difficult operationally. At the time of the Constitutional Convention, the thirteen states taken together were much larger geographically than England or France. Slow travel and communication, combined with geographic spread, contributed to the isolation of many regions within the states. It could take several weeks for all of the states to be informed about a particular political decision.

did you know?

That under Article I, Section 10, of the Constitution, no state is allowed to enter into any treaty, alliance, or confederation.

Other Arguments for Federalism

The arguments for federalism in the United States and elsewhere involve a complex set of factors, some of which we have already noted. First, for big countries, such as Canada, India, and the United States, federalism allows many functions to be "farmed out" by the central government to the states or provinces. The lower levels of government that accept these responsibilities thereby can become the focus of political dissatisfaction rather than the national authorities. Second, even with modern transportation and communications systems, the large area or population of some nations makes it impractical to locate all political authority in one place. Finally, federalism brings government closer to the people. It allows more direct access to, and influence on, government agencies and policies, rather than leaving the population restive and dissatisfied with a remote, faceless, all-powerful central authority.

BEYOND OUR BORDERS

EUROPE FACES THE PERILS OF CONFEDERALISM

Until recently, the world has marveled at the success of the largest confederal arrangement on earth—the European Union (EU). The EU consists of twenty-seven countries linked by a set of treaties. Central governing bodies meet in Brussels, Belgium, and in Strasbourg, France. The EU member countries' finance ministers gather every month. A European Commission has generated more than a million rules and regulations that establish Europe-wide standards for food safety, manufacturing processes, and product specifications. Of the twenty-seven member countries, in 2010 sixteen shared a common currency—the euro.

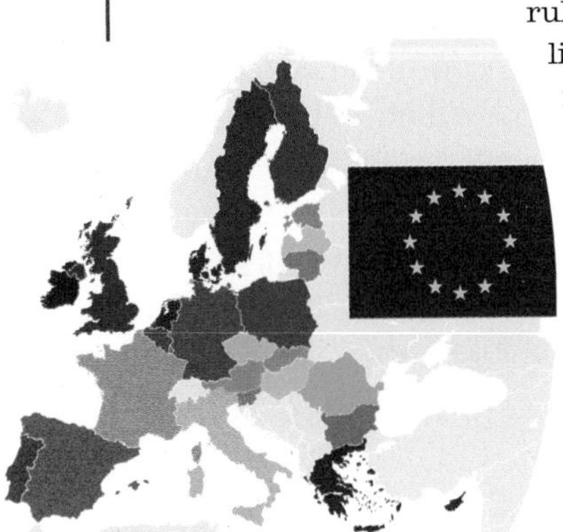

(Kaligraph/iStockphoto)

CRISIS IN THE EUROZONE

When the euro was created in 1999, each of the eleven nations adopting the new currency agreed to keep its budget deficit below 3 percent. The five who joined later accepted the same obligation. Few nations actually held to this pledge, however, and some of them violated it spectacularly. Greece is a case in point. In 2010, the Greek government was on the verge of bankruptcy due to years of budget deficits caused by, among other things, the 2004 Olympics and bloated government payrolls (over a third of the Greek labor force works for the government). It seemed possible that the Greek government might lose the ability to borrow more funds and would therefore be forced to default on its existing debt.

In the days before the euro, the foreign exchange markets would have reacted by driving down the value of the Greek currency (the drachma). To the extent that the government owed debt in drachmas, the value of this debt would fall. Greek exports would also be cheaper, and the country could try to earn its way out of danger through exports. With the euro, however, such adjustments are impossible. When the crisis threatened to spread to other nations, such as Ireland, Portugal, and Spain, the governments of Germany and France hinted that they might help bail out Greece, perhaps by guaranteeing its borrowing. German citizens, however, reacted with a storm of anger to the idea of a bailout. Angela Merkel, Germany's leader, even spoke of expelling Greece from the Eurozone. In fact, there was no practical way to make Greece stop using the euro, even if its government were to default on its debts. In the end, Eurozone members were forced to create an enormous bailout package.

FOR CRITICAL ANALYSIS

Many U.S. state governments have experienced massive budget crises and have been forced to cut spending, raise taxes, or both. Yet no one has ever suggested that a state should stop using the dollar. What does that say about the differences between this country and the EU?

FIGURE 3–1 The Flow of Power in Three Systems of Government

In a unitary system, power flows from the central government to the local and state governments. In a confederal system, power flows in the opposite direction—from the state governments to the central government. In a federal system, the flow of power, in principle, goes both ways.

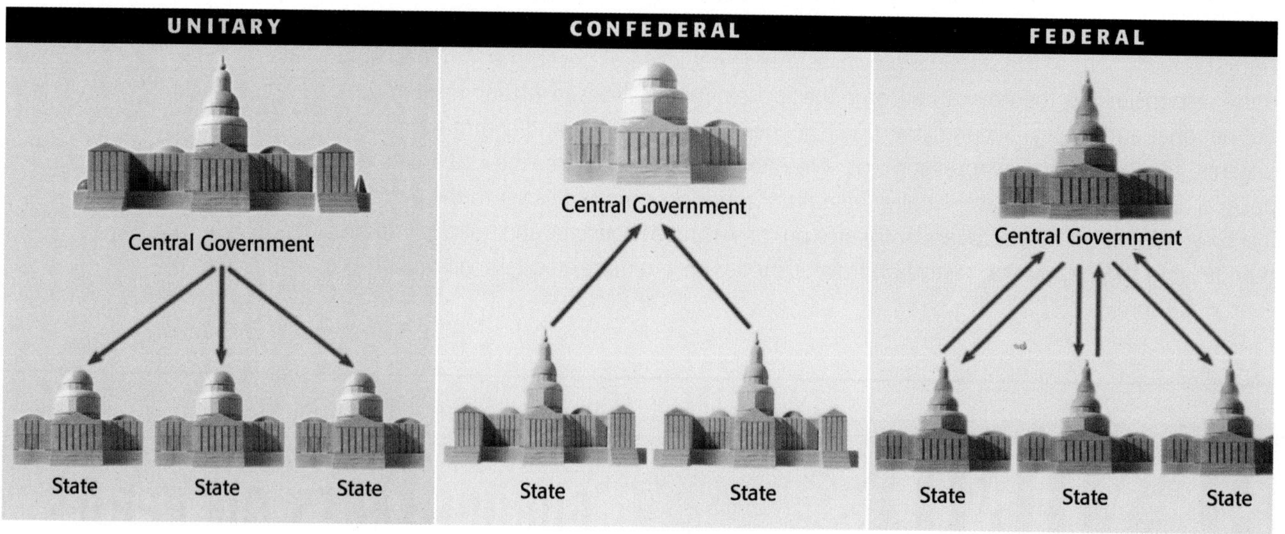

Benefits for the United States. In the United States, federalism historically has yielded many benefits. State governments long have been a training ground for future national leaders. Many presidents made their political mark as state governors. The states themselves have been testing grounds for new government initiatives. As United States Supreme Court justice Louis Brandeis once observed:

> *It is one of the happy incidents of the federal system that a single courageous state may, if its citizens choose, serve as a laboratory and try novel social and economic experiments without risk to the rest of the country.*[2]

did you know?

That state governments in the United States are unitary governments and, as a result, most local governments are mere creatures of the states.

Examples of programs pioneered at the state level include unemployment compensation, which began in Wisconsin, and air-pollution control, which was initiated in California. Today, states are experimenting with policies ranging from education reform to homeland security defense strategies. Since the passage of the 1996 welfare reform legislation—which gave more control over welfare programs to state governments—states also have been experimenting with different methods of delivering welfare assistance. One example of how the federal government has recently deferred to the states is a 2007 law allowing state governors to decide when the flag should be lowered, even at federal facilities.

Allowance for Many Political Subcultures. The American way of life always has been characterized by a number of political subcultures, which divide along the lines of race and ethnic origin, region, wealth, education, and, more recently, degree of religious devoutness and sexual preference. The existence of diverse political subcultures would appear to be incompatible with a political authority concentrated solely in a central government. Had the United States developed into a unitary system, various political subcultures certainly would be less able to influence government behavior than they have been, and continue to be, in our federal system.

---

2. *New State Ice Co. v. Liebmann*, 285 U.S. 262 (1932). See the *E-mocracy* feature at the end of this chapter for information on how to look up court cases online.

Do the states pay for all freeways, such as these in Los Angeles? If not, why? (© moodboard/Corbis)

Arguments against Federalism

Not everyone thinks federalism is such a good idea. Some see it as a way for powerful state and local interests to block progress and impede national plans. Smaller political units are more likely to be dominated by a single political group. (This was essentially the argument that James Madison put forth in *Federalist Paper* No. 10, which you can read in Appendix C of this text.) The dominant groups in some cities and states have resisted implementing equal rights for minority groups. Some argue, however, that the dominant factions in other states have been more progressive than the national government in many areas, such as the environment.

Critics of federalism also argue that too many Americans suffer as a result of the inequalities across the states. Individual states differ markedly in educational spending and achievement, crime and crime prevention, and even the safety of their buildings. Not surprisingly, these critics argue for increased federal legislation and oversight. This might involve creating national standards for education and building codes, national expenditure minimums for crime control, and similar measures.

Others see dangers in the expansion of national powers at the expense of the states. President Ronald Reagan (1981–1989) said, "The Founding Fathers saw the federalist system as constructed something like a masonry wall. The States are the bricks, the national government is the mortar. . . . Unfortunately, over the years, many people have increasingly come to believe that Washington is the whole wall."[3]

The Constitutional Basis for American Federalism

The term *federal system* cannot be found in the U.S. Constitution. Nor is it possible to find a systematic division of governmental authority between the national and state governments in that document. Rather, the Constitution sets out different types of powers. These powers can be classified as (1) the powers of the national government, (2) the powers of the states, and (3) prohibited powers. The Constitution also makes it clear that if a state or local law conflicts with a national law, the national law will prevail.

Powers of the National Government

The powers delegated to the national government include both expressed and implied powers, as well as the special category of inherent powers. Most of the powers expressly delegated to the national government are found in the first seventeen clauses of Article I, Section 8, of the Constitution. These **enumerated powers,** also called *expressed powers,* include coining money, setting standards for weights and measures, making uniform naturalization laws, admitting new states, establishing post offices, and declaring war. Another important enumerated power is the power to regulate commerce among the states—a topic we deal with later in this chapter.

Enumerated Powers
Powers specifically granted to the national government by the Constitution. The first seventeen clauses of Article I, Section 8, specify most of the enumerated powers of the national government.

3. Text of the address by the president to the National Conference of State Legislatures, Atlanta, Georgia (Washington, D.C.: The White House, Office of the Press Secretary, July 30, 1981), as quoted in Edward Millican, *One United People: The Federalist Papers and the National Idea* (Lexington, Ky.: The University Press of Kentucky, 1990).

The Necessary and Proper Clause. The implied powers of the national government are also based on Article I, Section 8, which states that Congress shall have the power

> *to make all Laws which shall be necessary and proper for carrying into Execution the foregoing Powers, and all other Powers vested by this Constitution in the Government of the United States, or in any Department or Officer thereof.*

Elastic Clause, or Necessary and Proper Clause
The clause in Article I, Section 8, that grants Congress the power to do whatever is necessary to execute its specifically delegated powers.

Police Power
The authority to legislate for the protection of the health, morals, safety, and welfare of the people. In the United States, most police power is reserved to the states.

This clause is sometimes called the **elastic clause,** or the **necessary and proper clause,** because it provides flexibility to the U.S. constitutional system. It gives Congress the power to do whatever is necessary to execute its specifically designated powers. The clause was first used in the Supreme Court decision of *McCulloch v. Maryland*[4] (discussed later in this chapter) to develop the concept of implied powers. Through this concept, the national government has succeeded in strengthening the scope of its authority to meet the many problems that the framers of the Constitution did not, and could not, anticipate.

Inherent Powers. A special category of national powers that is not implied by the necessary and proper clause consists of what have been labeled the *inherent powers* of the national government. These powers derive from the fact that the United States is a sovereign power among nations, and so its national government must be the only government that deals with other nations. Under international law, it is assumed that all nation-states, regardless of their size or power, have an inherent right to ensure their own survival. To do this, each nation must have the ability to act in its own interest among and with the community of nations—by, for instance, making treaties, waging war, seeking trade, and acquiring territory.

Note that no specific clause in the Constitution says anything about the acquisition of additional land. Nonetheless, through the federal government's inherent powers, we made the Louisiana Purchase in 1803 and then went on to acquire Florida, Texas, Oregon, Alaska, Hawaii, and other lands. The United States grew from a mere thirteen states to fifty states, plus several territories.

The national government has these inherent powers whether or not they have been enumerated in the Constitution. Some constitutional scholars categorize inherent powers as a third type of power, completely distinct from the delegated powers (both expressed and implied) of the national government.

Powers of the State Governments

"They have very strict anti-pollution laws in this state." (© Mischa Richter/ www.cartoonbank.com)

The Tenth Amendment states that the powers not delegated to the United States by the Constitution, nor prohibited by it to the states, are reserved to the states, or to the people. These are the reserved powers that the national government cannot deny to the states. Because these powers are not expressly listed, there is sometimes a question as to whether a certain power is delegated to the national government or reserved to the states.

State powers have been held to include each state's right to regulate commerce within its borders and to provide for a state militia. States also have the reserved power to make laws on all matters not prohibited to the states by the U.S. Constitution or state constitutions and not expressly, or by implication, delegated to the national government. Furthermore, the states have **police power**—the authority to legislate for the protection of the health, morals, safety, and welfare of the people. Their police power enables states to pass laws governing such activities as crimes, marriage, contracts, education, intrastate transportation, and land use.

4. 17 U.S. 316 (1819).

The ambiguity of the Tenth Amendment has allowed the reserved powers of the states to be defined differently at different times in our history. When there is widespread support for increased regulation by the national government, the Tenth Amendment tends to recede into the background. When the tide turns the other way (in favor of states' rights), the Tenth Amendment is resurrected to justify arguments supporting increased states' rights.

Concurrent Powers

In certain areas, the states share **concurrent powers** with the national government. Most concurrent powers are not specifically listed in the Constitution; they are only implied. An example of a concurrent power is the power to tax. The types of taxation are divided between the levels of government. For example, states may not levy a tariff (a set of taxes on imported goods); only the national government may do this. Neither government may tax the facilities of the other. If the state governments did not have the power to tax, they would not be able to function other than on a ceremonial basis. Additional concurrent powers include the power to borrow funds, to establish courts, and to charter banks and corporations. To a limited extent, the national government exercises police power, and to the extent that it does, police power is also a concurrent power. Concurrent powers exercised by the states are normally limited to the geographic area of each state and to those functions not granted by the Constitution exclusively to the national government (such exclusively national functions include the coinage of money and the negotiation of treaties).

Concurrent Powers
Powers held jointly by the national and state governments.

Supremacy Clause
The constitutional provision that makes the Constitution and federal laws superior to all conflicting state and local laws.

Prohibited Powers

The Constitution prohibits, or denies, a number of powers to the national government. For example, the national government expressly has been denied the power to impose taxes on goods sold to other countries (exports). Moreover, any power not granted expressly or implicitly to the federal government by the Constitution is prohibited to it. For example, many legal experts believe that the national government could not create a national divorce law system without a constitutional amendment. The states are also denied certain powers. For example, no state is allowed to enter into a treaty on its own with another country.

The Supremacy Clause

The supremacy of the national constitution over subnational laws and actions is established in the **supremacy clause** of the Constitution. The supremacy clause (Article VI, Clause 2) states the following:

> *This Constitution, and the Laws of the United States which shall be made in Pursuance thereof; and all Treaties made . . . under the Authority of the United States, shall be the supreme Law of the Land; and the Judges in every State shall be bound thereby, any Thing in the Constitution or Laws of any State to the Contrary notwithstanding.*

In other words, states cannot use their reserved or concurrent powers to thwart national policies. All national and state officers, including judges, must be bound by oath to support the Constitution. Hence, any legitimate exercise of national governmental power supersedes any conflicting state action. Of course, deciding whether a conflict actually exists is a judicial matter, as you will see when we discuss the case of *McCulloch v. Maryland.*

The National Guard can serve as an example of how federal power supersedes that of the states. Normally, the National Guard functions as a state militia under the command of the governor. It is frequently called out to assist with recovery efforts from natural disasters such as hurricanes, floods, and earthquakes. The president, however, can assume command of any National Guard unit at any time. President Bush repeatedly "federalized" such units so that he could deploy them in Iraq. As a result, by 2005 National Guard members and reservists made up a larger percentage of the forces in actual combat duty than in any previous war in U.S. history (about 43 percent in Iraq and 55 percent in Afghanistan). By 2008, Guard deployments were down to 7 percent of the troops in Iraq and 15 percent of those in Afghanistan. By 2010, however, the Guard's share was back up to about a third of those deployed.

National government legislation in a concurrent area is said to *preempt* (take precedence over) conflicting state or local laws or regulations in that area. One of the ways in which the national government has extended its powers, particularly during the twentieth century, is through the preemption of state and local laws by national legislation. In the first decade of the twentieth century, fewer than twenty national laws preempted laws and regulations issued by state and local governments. By the beginning of the twenty-first century, the number had grown into the hundreds.

Some political scientists believe that national supremacy is critical for the longevity and smooth functioning of a federal system. Nonetheless, the application of this principle has been a continuous source of conflict. As you will see, the most extreme example of this conflict was the Civil War.

Vertical Checks and Balances

Recall from Chapter 2 that one of the concerns of the founders was to prevent the national government from becoming too powerful. For that reason, they divided the government into three branches—legislative, executive, and judicial. They also created a system of checks and balances that allowed each branch to check the actions of the others. The federal form of government created by the founders also involves checks and balances. These are sometimes called *vertical checks and balances* because they involve relationships between the states and the national government. They can be contrasted with *horizontal checks and balances,* in which the branches of government that are on the same level—either state or national—can check one another.

For example, the reserved powers of the states act as a check on the national government. Additionally, the states' interests are represented in the national legislature (Congress), and the citizens of the various states determine who will head the executive branch (the presidency). The founders also made it impossible for the central government to change the Constitution without the states' consent, as you read in Chapter 2. Finally, many national programs and policies are administered by the states, which gives the states considerable control over the ultimate shape of those programs and policies.

The national government, in turn, can check state policies by exercising its constitutional powers under the clauses just discussed, as well as under the commerce clause (to be examined later). Furthermore, the national government can influence state policies indirectly through federal grants, as you will learn later in this chapter.

Interstate Relations

So far we have examined only the relationship between central and state governmental units. The states, however, have constant commercial, social, and other dealings among themselves. The national Constitution imposes certain "rules of the road" on interstate relations. These rules have had the effect of preventing any one state from setting itself apart from the other states. The three most important clauses governing interstate relations in the Constitution, all taken from the Articles of Confederation, require each state to do the following:

1. Give full faith and credit to every other state's public acts, records, and judicial proceedings (Article IV, Section 1).

2. Extend to every other state's citizens the privileges and immunities of its own citizens (Article IV, Section 2).
3. Agree to return persons who are fleeing from justice in another state back to their home state when requested to do so (Article IV, Section 2).

Additionally, states may enter into agreements called **interstate compacts**—if consented to by Congress. In reality, congressional consent is necessary only if such a compact increases the power of the contracting states relative to other states (or to the national government). Typical examples of interstate compacts are the establishment of the Port Authority of New York and New Jersey by a compact between those two states in 1921 and the regulation of the production of crude oil and natural gas by the Interstate Oil and Gas Compact of 1935.

Interstate Compact
An agreement between two or more states. Agreements on minor matters are made without congressional consent, but any compact that tends to increase the power of the contracting states relative to other states or relative to the national government generally requires the consent of Congress.

Defining Constitutional Powers—The Early Years

Recall from Chapter 2 that constitutional language, to be effective and to endure, must have some degree of ambiguity. Certainly, the powers delegated to the national government and the powers reserved to the states contain elements of ambiguity, thus leaving the door open for different interpretations of federalism. Disputes over the boundaries of national versus state powers have characterized this nation from the beginning. In the early 1800s, the most significant disputes arose over differing interpretations of the implied powers of the national government under the necessary and proper clause and over the respective powers of the national government and the states to regulate commerce.

Although political bodies at all levels of government play important roles in the process of settling such disputes, ultimately it is the Supreme Court that casts the final vote. As might be expected, the character of the referee will have an impact on the ultimate outcome of any dispute. From 1801 to 1835, the Supreme Court was headed by Chief Justice John Marshall, a Federalist who advocated a strong central government. We look here at two cases decided by the Marshall Court: *McCulloch v. Maryland*[5] and *Gibbons v. Ogden*.[6] Both cases are considered milestones in the movement toward national government supremacy.

This new train car replaces older cars on the Port Authority Trans-Hudson (PATH) rapid transit line, which is run by the Port Authority of New York and New Jersey. These new PATH cars are equipped with television screens showing news, weather, and sports. What political device did the governments of New York and New Jersey use in order to create the Port Authority? (AP Photo/ Mike Derer)

McCulloch v. Maryland (1819)

The U.S. Constitution says nothing about establishing a national bank. Nonetheless, at different times Congress chartered two banks—the First and Second Banks of the United States—and provided part of their initial capital; thus, they were national banks. The government of Maryland imposed a tax on the Second Bank's Baltimore branch in an attempt to put that branch out of business. The branch's cashier, James William McCulloch, refused to pay the Maryland tax. When Maryland took McCulloch to its state court, the state of Maryland won. The national government appealed the case to the Supreme Court.

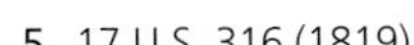

5. 17 U.S. 316 (1819).
6. 22 U.S. 1 (1824).

One of the issues before the Court was whether the national government had the implied power, under the necessary and proper clause, to charter a bank and contribute capital to it. The other important question before the Court was the following: If the bank was constitutional, could a state tax it? In other words, was a state action that conflicted with a national government action invalid under the supremacy clause?

Chief Justice Marshall held that if establishing such a national bank aided the national government in the exercise of its designated powers, then the authority to set up such a bank could be implied. Having established this doctrine of implied powers, Marshall then answered the other important question before the Court and established the doctrine of national supremacy. Marshall ruled that no state could use its taxing power to tax an arm of the national government. If it could, "the declaration that the Constitution . . . shall be the supreme law of the land, is [an] empty and unmeaning [statement]."

Marshall's decision enabled the national government to grow and to meet problems that the Constitution's framers were unable to foresee. Today, practically every expressed power of the national government has been expanded in one way or another by use of the necessary and proper clause.

Gibbons v. Ogden (1824)

One of the most important parts of the Constitution included in Article I, Section 8, is the so-called **commerce clause,** in which Congress is given the power "to regulate Commerce with foreign Nations, and among the several States, and with the Indian Tribes." The meaning of this clause was at issue in *Gibbons v. Ogden.*

Commerce Clause
The section of the Constitution in which Congress is given the power to regulate trade among the states and with foreign countries.

The Background of the Case. Robert Fulton and Robert Livingston secured a monopoly on steam navigation on the waters in New York State from the New York legislature in 1803. They licensed Aaron Ogden to operate steam-powered ferryboats between New York and New Jersey. Thomas Gibbons, who had obtained a license from the U.S. government to operate boats in interstate waters, decided to compete with Ogden, but he did so without New York's permission. Ogden sued Gibbons. New York's state courts prohibited Gibbons from operating in New York waters. Gibbons appealed to the Supreme Court.

did you know?

That the Liberty Bell cracked when it was rung at the funeral of John Marshall in 1835.

There were actually several issues before the Court in this case. The first issue was how the term *commerce* should be defined. New York's highest court had defined the term narrowly to mean only the shipment of goods or the interchange of commodities, *not* navigation or the transport of people. The second issue was whether the national government's power to regulate interstate commerce extended to commerce within a state (*intra*state commerce) or was limited strictly to commerce among the states (*inter*state commerce). The third issue was whether the power to regulate interstate commerce was a concurrent power (as the New York court had concluded) or an exclusive national power.

Marshall's Ruling. Marshall defined *commerce* as all commercial intercourse—all business dealings—including navigation and the transport of people. Marshall also held that the commerce power of the national government could be exercised in state jurisdictions, even though it cannot reach *solely* intrastate commerce. Finally, Marshall emphasized that the power to regulate interstate commerce was an *exclusive* national power. Marshall held that because Gibbons was duly authorized by the national government to navigate in interstate waters, he could not be prohibited from doing so by a state court.

Marshall's expansive interpretation of the commerce clause in *Gibbons v. Ogden* allowed the national government to exercise increasing authority over all areas of economic affairs throughout the land. Congress did not immediately exploit this broad grant of power. In the 1930s and subsequent decades, however, the commerce clause became the primary constitutional basis for national government regulation—as you will read later in this chapter.

When John Marshall (1755–1835), was chief justice of the United States Supreme Court, he championed the power of the federal government. What are the most famous cases that the Marshall court decided? (© Corbis)

States' Rights and the Resort to Civil War

The controversy over slavery that led to the Civil War took the form of a dispute over national government supremacy versus the rights of the separate states. Essentially, the Civil War brought to an ultimate and violent climax the ideological debate that had been outlined by the Federalist and Anti-Federalist parties even before the Constitution was ratified.

The Shift Back to States' Rights

As we have seen, while John Marshall was chief justice of the Supreme Court, he did much to increase the power of the national government and to reduce that of the states. During the Jacksonian era (1829–1837), however, a shift back to states' rights began. The question of the regulation of commerce became one of the major issues in federal-state relations. When Congress passed a tariff in 1828, the state of South Carolina unsuccessfully attempted to nullify the tariff (render it void), claiming that in cases of conflict between a state and the national government, the state should have the ultimate authority over its citizens.

During the next three decades, the North and South became even more sharply divided—over tariffs that mostly benefited northern industries and over the slavery issue. On December 20, 1860, South Carolina formally repealed its ratification of the Constitution and withdrew from the Union. On February 4, 1861, representatives from six southern states met at Montgomery, Alabama, to form a new government called the Confederate States of America.

War and the Growth of the National Government

The ultimate defeat of the South in 1865 permanently ended any idea that a state could successfully claim the right to secede, or withdraw, from the Union. Ironically, the Civil War—brought about in large part because of the South's desire for increased states' rights—resulted in the opposite: an increase in the political power of the national government.

The War Effort. Thousands of new employees were hired to run the Union war effort and to deal with the social and economic problems that had to be handled in the aftermath of war. A billion-dollar ($1.3 billion, which is more than $17 billion in today's dollars) national government budget was passed for the first time in 1865 to cover the increased government expenditures. The first (temporary) income tax was imposed on citizens to help pay for the war. This tax and the increased national government spending were precursors to the expanded future role of the national government in the American federal system. Civil liberties were curtailed in the Union and in the Confederacy in the name of the wartime emergency. The distribution of pensions and widows' benefits also boosted the national government's social role. Many scholars contend that the North's victory set the nation on the path to a modern industrial economy and society.

did you know?

That only after the Civil War did people commonly refer to the United States as "it" instead of "they."

President Lincoln meets with some of his generals and other troops on October 3, 1862. While the Civil War was fought over the issue of slavery, it was also a battle over the supremacy of the national government. Once the North won the war, what happened to the size and power of our national government? (Library of Congress)

The Civil War Amendments. The expansion of the national government's authority during the Civil War was reflected in the passage of the Civil War amendments to the Constitution. Before the war, it was a bedrock constitutional principle that the national government should not interfere with slavery in the states. The Thirteenth Amendment, ratified in 1865, did more than interfere with slavery—it abolished the institution altogether. By abolishing slavery, the amendment also in effect abolished the rule by which three-fifths of the slaves were counted when apportioning seats in the House of Representatives (see Chapter 2). African Americans were now counted in full.

The Fourteenth Amendment, ratified in 1868, defined who was a citizen of each state. It sought to guarantee equal rights under state law, stating that

> *[no] State [shall] deprive any person of life, liberty, or property, without due process of law; nor deny to any person within its jurisdiction the equal protection of the laws.*

In time, the courts interpreted these words to mean that the national Bill of Rights applied to state governments, a development that we will examine in Chapter 4. The Fourteenth Amendment also confirmed the abolition of the three-fifths rule. Finally, the Fifteenth Amendment (1870) gave African Americans the right to vote in all elections, including state elections—although a century would pass before that right was enforced in all states.

The Continuing Dispute over the Division of Power

Although the outcome of the Civil War firmly established the supremacy of the national government and put to rest the idea that a state could secede from the Union, the war by no means ended the debate over the division of powers between the national government and the states. The debate over the division of powers in our federal system can be viewed as progressing through at least two general stages since the Civil War: dual federalism and cooperative federalism.

Dual Federalism and the Retreat of National Authority

Dual Federalism
A model of federalism in which the states and the national government each remain supreme within their own spheres. The doctrine looks on nation and state as co-equal sovereign powers. Neither the state government nor the national government should interfere in the other's sphere.

During the decades following the Civil War, the prevailing model was what political scientists have called **dual federalism**—a doctrine that emphasizes a distinction between federal and state spheres of government authority. The doctrine looks on nation and state as co-equal sovereign powers. Neither the state government nor the national government should interfere in the other's sphere.

Various images have been used to describe different configurations of federalism over time. Dual federalism is commonly depicted as a layer cake, because the state governments and the national government are viewed as separate entities, like separate layers in a cake. The national government is the top layer of the cake; the state government is the bottom layer. The two layers are physically separate. They do not mix. For the most part, advocates of dual federalism believed that the state and national governments should not exercise authority in the same areas.

A Return to Normal Conditions. The doctrine of dual federalism represented a revival of states' rights following the expansion of national authority during the Civil War. Dual federalism, after all, was a fairly accurate model of the prewar consensus on state-national relations. For many people, it therefore represented a return to normal. The national income tax, used to fund the war effort and the reconstruction of the South, was ended in 1872. The most significant step to reverse the wartime expansion of national power took place in 1877, when President Rutherford B. Hayes withdrew the last federal troops from the South. This meant that the national government was no longer in a position to regulate state actions that affected African Americans. Although the black population was no longer enslaved, it was again subject to the authority of southern whites.

The Role of the Supreme Court. The Civil War crisis drastically reduced the influence of the United States Supreme Court. In the prewar *Dred Scott* decision,[7] the Court had attempted to abolish the power of the national government to restrict slavery in the territories. In so doing, the Court placed itself on the losing side of the impending conflict. After the war, Congress took the unprecedented step of exempting the entire process of southern reconstruction from judicial review. The Court had little choice but to acquiesce.

In time, the Supreme Court reestablished itself as the legitimate constitutional umpire. Its decisions tended to support dual federalism, defend states' rights, and limit the powers of the national government. In 1895, for example, the Court ruled that a national income tax was unconstitutional.[8] In subsequent years, the Court gradually backed away from this decision and eventually might have overturned it. In 1913, however, the Sixteenth Amendment explicitly authorized a national income tax.

For the Court, dual federalism meant that the national government could intervene in state activities through grants and subsidies, but for the most part, it was barred from regulating matters that the Court considered to be purely local. The Court generally limited the exercise of police power to the states. For example, in 1918, the Court ruled that a 1916 national law banning child labor was unconstitutional because it attempted to regulate a local problem.[9] In effect, the Court placed severe limits on the ability of Congress to legislate under the commerce clause of the Constitution.

Child labor was still common in the early 1900s. Why didn't the federal government simply ban it then? (AP Photo)

The New Deal and Cooperative Federalism

The doctrine of dual federalism receded into the background in the 1930s as the nation attempted to deal with the Great Depression. Franklin D. Roosevelt was inaugurated on March 4, 1933, as the thirty-second president of the United States. In the previous year, nearly 1,500 banks had failed (and 4,000 more would fail in 1933). Thirty-two thousand businesses had closed down, and almost one-fourth of the labor force was unemployed. The public expected the national government to do something

7. *Dred Scott v. Sandford,* 60 U.S. 393 (1856).
8. *Pollock v. Farmers' Loan & Trust Co.,* 157 U.S. 429 (1895); *Pollock v. Farmers' Loan & Trust Co.,* 158 U.S. 601 (1895).
9. *Hammer v. Dagenhart,* 247 U.S. 251 (1918). This decision was overruled in *United States v. Darby,* 312 U.S. 100 (1940).

President Franklin Delano Roosevelt (1933–1945). Roosevelt's national approach to addressing the effects of the Great Depression was overwhelmingly popular, although many of his specific initiatives were controversial. How did the Great Depression change the political beliefs of many ordinary Americans? (© Bettmann/Corbis)

about the disastrous state of the economy. But for the first three years of the Great Depression (1930–1932), the national government had done very little.

The "New Deal." President Herbert Hoover (1929–1933) clung to the doctrine of dual federalism and insisted that unemployment and poverty were local issues. The states, not the national government, had the sole responsibility for combating the effects of unemployment and providing relief to the poor. Roosevelt, however, did not feel bound by this doctrine, and his new Democratic administration energetically intervened in the economy. Roosevelt's "New Deal" included large-scale emergency antipoverty programs. In addition, the New Deal introduced major new laws regulating economic activity, such as the National Industrial Recovery Act of 1933, which established the National Recovery Administration (NRA). The NRA, initially the centerpiece of the New Deal, provided codes for every industry to restrict competition and regulate labor relations.

The End of Dual Federalism. Roosevelt's expansion of national authority was challenged by the Supreme Court, which continued to adhere to the doctrine of dual federalism. In 1935, the Court ruled that the NRA program was unconstitutional.[10] The NRA had turned out to be largely unworkable and was unpopular. The Court, however, rejected the program on the ground that it regulated intrastate, not interstate, commerce. This position appeared to rule out any alternative recovery plans that might be better designed. Subsequently, the Court struck down the Agricultural Adjustment Act, the Bituminous Coal Act, a railroad retirement plan, legislation to protect farm mortgages, and a municipal bankruptcy act.

In 1937, Roosevelt proposed legislation that would allow him to add up to six new justices to the Supreme Court. Presumably, the new justices would be more friendly to the exercise of national power than the existing members were. Roosevelt's move was widely seen as an assault on the Constitution. Congressional Democrats refused to support the measure, and it failed. Nevertheless, the "court-packing scheme" had its intended effect. Although the membership of the Court did not change, after 1937 the Court ceased its attempts to limit the national government's powers under the commerce clause. For the next fifty years, the commerce clause would provide Congress with an essentially unlimited justification for regulating the economic life of the country.

Cooperative Federalism
A model of federalism in which the states and the national government cooperate in solving problems.

Cooperative Federalism. Some political scientists have described the era since 1937 as characterized by **cooperative federalism,** in which the states and the national government cooperate in solving complex common problems. Roosevelt's New Deal programs, for example, often involved joint action between the national government and the states. The pattern of national-state relationships during these years gave rise to a new metaphor for federalism—that of a marble cake. Unlike a layer cake, in a marble cake the two types of cake are intermingled, and any bite contains cake of both flavors.

10. *Schechter Poultry Corp. v. United States,* 295 U.S. 495 (1935).

As an example of how national and state governments work together under the cooperative federalism model, consider Aid to Families with Dependent Children (AFDC), a welfare program that was established during the New Deal. (In 1996, AFDC was replaced by Temporary Assistance to Needy Families—TANF.) Under the AFDC program, the national government provided most of the funding, but state governments established benefit levels and eligibility requirements for recipients. Local welfare offices were staffed by state, not national, employees. In return for national funding, the states had to conform to a series of regulations on how the program was to be carried out. These regulations tended to become more elaborate over time.

The 1960s and 1970s were a time of even greater expansion of the national government's role in domestic policy. The evolving pattern of national-state-local government relationships during those decades gave rise to yet another metaphor—**picket-fence federalism,** a concept devised by political scientist Terry Sanford. The horizontal boards in the fence represent the different levels of government (national, state, and local), while the vertical pickets represent the various programs and policies in which each level of government is involved. Officials at each level of government work together to promote and develop the policy represented by each picket.

These women are working at the Newport Canning Project, which was a small part of the Works Progress Administration (WPA) program implemented by President Franklin Roosevelt during the Great Depression. Why do you think that the federal government created the WPA? (AP Photo/Works Progress Administration)

Methods of Implementing Cooperative Federalism

Even before the Constitution was adopted, the national government gave grants to the states in the form of land to finance education. The national government also provided land grants for canals, railroads, and roads. In the twentieth century, federal grants increased significantly, especially during Roosevelt's administration throughout the Great Depression and again in the 1960s, when the dollar amount of grants quadrupled. These funds were used for improvements in education, pollution control, recreation, and highways. With this increase in grants, however, came a bewildering number of restrictions and regulations.

Picket-Fence Federalism
A model of federalism in which specific programs and policies (depicted as vertical pickets in a picket fence) involve all levels of government—national, state, and local (depicted by the horizontal boards in the picket fence).

Categorical Grants
Federal grants to states or local governments that are for specific programs or projects.

Categorical Grants. By 1985, **categorical grants** amounted to more than $100 billion a year. They were spread out across four hundred separate programs, but the five largest accounted for more than 50 percent of the revenues spent. These five programs were Medicaid (health care for the poor), highway construction, unemployment benefits, housing assistance, and welfare programs to assist mothers with dependent children and people with disabilities. For fiscal year 2009, the national government gave $538 billion to the states. In President Obama's proposed 2011 budget, the 2010 figure was estimated to be $654 billion. The estimate for fiscal year 2011 was $646 billion. The shift toward a greater role for the central government in the United States can be seen in Figure 3–2 on the next page, which shows the increase in central government spending as a percentage of total government spending.

Before the 1960s, most categorical grants by the national government were *formula grants.* These grants take their name from the method used to allocate funds. They fund state programs using a formula based on such variables as the state's needs, population, or willingness to come up with matching funds. Beginning in the 1960s, the national government began increasingly to offer *program grants.* This funding requires states to apply for grants for specific programs. The applications are evaluated by the national government, and the applications may compete with one another. Program grants give the

FIGURE 3–2 The Shift toward Central Government Spending

In the years before the Great Depression, local governments accounted for close to three-fifths of all government spending, and the federal government accounted for only about 30 percent. After Franklin D. Roosevelt's New Deal, federal spending began to rival state and local spending combined. The federal share is still about 46 percent today, not counting transfers to state and local governments. The size of the pies reflects total spending.

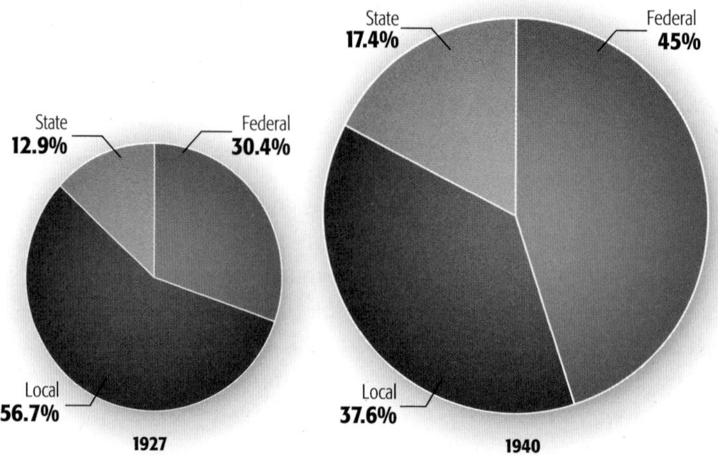

Sources: *Historical Statistics of the United States,* Bureau of the Census, and authors' calculations.

national government a much greater degree of control over state activities than do formula grants.

Federal grants to the states have increased significantly, as shown in Figure 3–3 on page 100. One reason for this increase is that Congress has decided to offload some programs to the states and provide a major part of the funding for them. Also, Congress continues to use grants to persuade states and cities to operate programs devised by the federal government. Finally, states often are happy to apply for grants because they are relatively "free," requiring only that the state match a small portion of each grant. States can still face criticism for accepting the grants, because their matching funds may be diverted from other state projects.

The Great Recession of the late 2000s had a devastating impact on state budgets, and in response the federal government substantially increased the amount of funding available to the states in 2009 and 2010. Much of this support came through President Obama's stimulus plan, passed by Congress in February 2009. The new federal funds, however, did not fully compensate the states for the lost revenue and increased expenses resulting from the recession. We look at state spending in this chapter's *The Politics of Boom and Bust* feature on the facing page.

Feeling the Pressure—The Strings Attached to Federal Grants. No dollars sent to the states are completely free of "strings"; all funds come with requirements that must be met by the states. Often, through the use of grants, the national government has been able to exercise substantial control over matters that traditionally have been under the purview of state governments. When the federal government gives federal funds for highway improvements, for example, it may condition the funds on the state's cooperation with a federal policy. This is exactly what the federal government did in the 1980s and 1990s to force the states to raise their minimum drinking age to twenty-one.

Such carrot-and-stick tactics have been used as a form of coercion in recent years as well. In 2002, for example, President George W. Bush signed the No Child Left Behind (NCLB) Act into law. Under the NCLB, Bush promised billions of dollars to the states to bolster their education budgets. The funds would only be delivered, however, if states agreed to hold schools accountable on standardized tests. Education traditionally had been under state control, and the conditions for receiving NCLB funds effectively stripped the states of some autonomy in creating standards for public schools. We take a closer look at the No Child Left Behind program in this chapter's *Politics and Education* feature on page 101.

Block Grants
Federal programs that provide funds to state and local governments for broad functional areas, such as criminal justice or mental-health programs.

Block Grants. **Block grants** lessen the restrictions on federal grants given to state and local governments by grouping a number of categorical grants under one broad heading.

THE POLITICS OF BOOM AND BUST: STATE SPENDING IN A RECESSION

During the boom years in the mid-2000s, many state governments experienced a substantial increase in revenue from taxes and other sources. Quite a few states responded with increased spending. Employment at state colleges and universities, for example, increased 14 percent from 2000 to 2007. After the Great Recession began in December 2007, high-spending states soon found themselves in big trouble. So great was the impact of the financial calamity, however, that even the most responsible state governments experienced serious difficulties.

DECLINING STATE AND LOCAL REVENUES

Some states and municipalities have traditionally relied on high-income individuals and businesses to fund a large share of their activities. For example, before the Great Recession, California collected about 50 percent of the state's personal income taxes from the top 1 percent of the state's income earners. New York City was in a similar situation.

In a recession, however, the incomes of the rich actually fall faster than the incomes of ordinary people. Much of this income, after all, comes from business profits and Wall Street stocks. In bad years, these sources of income can decline spectacularly. States that relied on taxing the rich saw their revenues decline spectacularly as well. In 2009, California made headlines for weeks because it was on the verge of a fiscal collapse. Other states faced similar scenarios. By 2010, the state of Illinois had a deficit equal to more than one-third of its entire budget. In that same year, the states, taken together, faced $180 billion in additional budget deficits for fiscal year 2011.

THE STATES' REACTIONS

Unlike the federal government, most states have a balanced budget requirement written into their constitutions. As a result, there are limits to how much they can borrow, and for how long. Some state and local governments have reacted to their budget deficits with dramatic steps, such as closing schools or libraries. Others have furloughed or permanently laid off many government employees. In fiscal year 2009, state general fund spending fell by 3.4 percent, and in fiscal year 2010 spending declined by an additional 5.4 percent. The last time there was an annual decline in state spending was in 1983. On the revenue side, as to be expected, states and municipalities have enacted tax and fee increases. For fiscal year 2010, those increases added more than $20 billion in additional revenues. Some believe that state spending cuts and tax increases caused by the recession have the effect of making the recession even worse.

THE FEDERAL GOVERNMENT STEPS IN

One of the biggest sources of stopgap financing for the states has come from the federal government. The 2009 stimulus bill allotted more than $100 billion for state governments. In 2010, as the stimulus aid began to run out, governors were lobbying Washington, D.C., for yet additional federal dollars. California asked for $6.9 billion. Illinois hinted it wanted even more. The federal government is facing its own huge deficits, however. Unless policies change, the cumulative deficit over the next ten years could exceed $10 trillion—that's $10,000 billion.

FOR CRITICAL ANALYSIS

Is the federal government under any obligation to aid state governments that find themselves in financial difficulty? Why or why not?

FIGURE 3–3 The Rise in Federal Transfers to State and Local Governments

The chart shows the percentage of the nation's state and local revenues supplied by the federal government. The federal government has gained leverage over state and local governments by supplying an increasing share of their revenues. The drop in federal transfers from 1980 to 1990 took place during the presidency of Ronald Reagan, as we explain in "The 'New Federalism'" on pages 102 and 103.

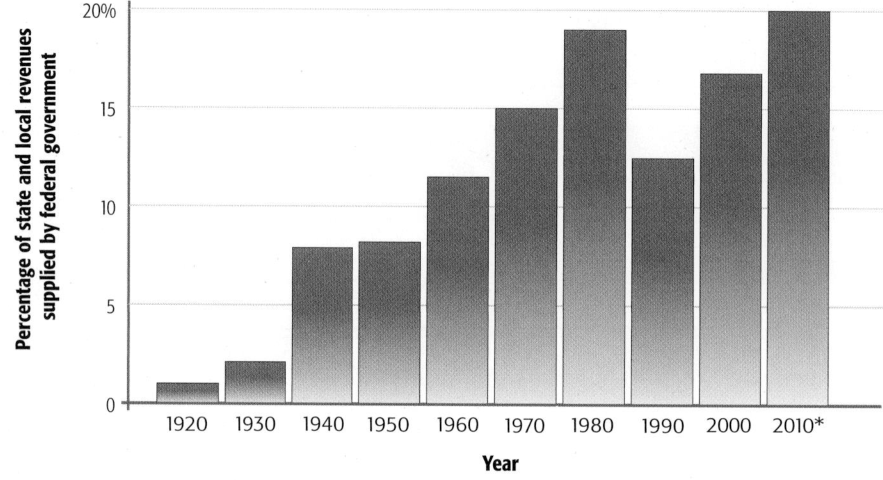

*The figure for 2010 is an estimate.

Sources: *Historical Statistics of the United States; Statistical Abstract of the United States, 2008;* and *Budget of the United States Government, FY 2009 and FY 2011.*

Governors and mayors generally prefer block grants because such grants give the states more flexibility in how the funds are spent.

One major set of block grants provides aid to state welfare programs. The Personal Responsibility and Work Opportunity Reconciliation Act of 1996 ended the AFDC program. The TANF program that replaced AFDC provided a welfare block grant to each state. Each grant has an annual cap. According to some, this is one of the most successful block grant programs. Although state governments prefer block grants, Congress generally favors categorical grants because the expenditures can be targeted according to congressional priorities.

Federal Mandates. For years, the federal government has passed legislation requiring that states improve environmental conditions and the civil rights of certain groups. Since the 1970s, the national government has enacted many hundreds of **federal mandates** requiring the states to take some action in areas ranging from the way voters are registered, to ocean-dumping restrictions, to the education of people with disabilities. The Unfunded Mandates Reform Act of 1995 requires the Congressional Budget Office to identify mandates that cost state and local governments more than $50 million to implement. Nonetheless, the federal government routinely continues to pass mandates for state and local governments that cost more than that to implement.

Federal Mandate
A requirement in federal legislation that forces states and municipalities to comply with certain rules.

did you know?
That part of the $4.2 million federal block grants received by four Native American tribes since 1997 has gone toward the building of "smoke shops"—stores that sell discounted cigarettes and pipe tobacco.

For example, the National Conference of State Legislatures has identified federal mandates to the states in transportation, health care, education, environment, homeland security, election laws, and other areas with a total cost of $29 billion per year. Water-quality mandates appear to be particularly expensive.

One way in which the national government has moderated the burden of federal mandates is by granting *waivers,* which allow individual states to try out innovative approaches to carrying out the mandates. For example, Oregon

POLITICS AND... education

CAN "NO CHILD LEFT BEHIND" BE FIXED?

For most of our nation's history, public education has been the responsibility of local and state governments. In recent years, however, the national government has become more involved. The No Child Left Behind (NCLB) Act, passed in 2002, was a major step toward setting educational policy at the national level.

PROBLEMS WITH THE NO CHILD LEFT BEHIND ACT

Some lauded the passage of the NCLB as a step in the direction of national standards. Others believe the act is an example of the problems that national standards can create. Some NCLB standards may well be impossible to meet. By 2014, all students in all schools are expected to pass state tests. If a *single student* fails a test, the student's school will be "in need of improvement." Any school that remains in need of improvement for more than five years must be "restructured," which may involve replacing staff or turning school operations over to a private firm or the state education agency.

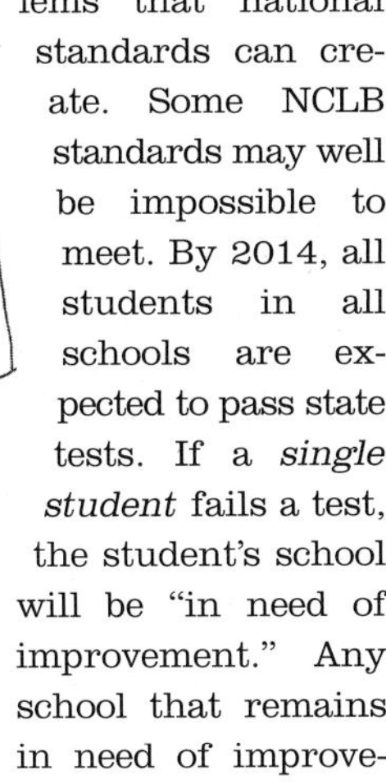

"The Feds have authorized me to leave your child behind." (© The New Yorker Collection, 2004. Michael Shaw, from cartoonbank.com. All Rights Reserved.)

Many states responded to the NCLB by "dumbing down" the state tests so that more students would pass them. Teachers responded to the act by "teaching to the test," which often meant spending less time on subjects that were not tested, such as science, social studies, and Spanish.

A final complaint is that the NCLB is just another unfunded mandate. For example, New Hampshire estimated its cost of implementing the act as almost $500 per student per year.

OBAMA AND EDUCATION REFORM

In 2010, the Obama administration revealed its plan for reforming the NCLB. Under the proposal, only the lowest-performing schools—5 percent of the total—would be subject to radical intervention, including firing the principal and many of the teachers. The next-lowest 5 percent would be placed on a watch list. Mid-ranking schools would be left alone, and highfliers would be rewarded. Rather than judging schools by how well they reach or exceed math and reading standards, schools would be encouraged to produce "college-ready and career-ready" students. Even if these changes are passed, however, they will take many years to implement.

CAN THESE REFORMS WORK?

Not everyone is elated about further reform of federal education policy. Some simply oppose making policy in Washington, D.C. We are a diverse nation, these people say, and ought to have diverse, locally oriented education systems.

Others ask whether current policies are headed in the right direction. To an overwhelming extent, the one variable that has a real effect on educational outcomes is simply the identity of the teacher. Some teachers are just a lot better than others, and that makes all the difference. A common response to this is "Fire the bad teachers and replace them." Obama's proposals contain an element of that.

This idea, however, has problems. Although firing the very worst teachers might be desirable, there are millions of teachers. We cannot possibly replace hundreds of thousands of them. We wouldn't be able to get all the new teachers we would need, nor would we be able to ensure they would be any better. Is it possible to make existing teachers more effective? Education expert Elizabeth Green argues that astonishingly little practical work has been done on that. She maintains that we might be able to make real improvements in education through teacher training based on studying the methods of known good teachers.[a]

FOR CRITICAL ANALYSIS

Why do you think that federal legislation has not focused on teacher training?

a. Elizabeth Green, "Can Good Teaching Be Learned?" *The New York Times Magazine,* March 7, 2010, p. 30.

received a waiver to experiment with a new method of rationing health-care services under the federally mandated Medicaid program.

The Politics of Federalism

As we have observed, the allocation of powers between the national and state governments continues to be a major issue. We look here at some further aspects of the ongoing conflict between national authority and states' rights in our federal system.

What Has National Authority Accomplished?

Why is it that conservatives have favored the states and liberals have favored the national government? One answer is that throughout American history, the expansion of national authority typically has been an engine of social change. Far more than the states, the national government has been willing to alter the status quo. The expansion of national authority during the Civil War freed the slaves—a major social revolution. During the New Deal, the expansion of national authority meant unprecedented levels of government intervention in the economy. In both the Civil War and New Deal eras, support for states' rights was a method of opposing these changes and supporting the status quo.

Another example of the use of national power to change society was the presidency of Lyndon B. Johnson (1963–1969). Johnson oversaw the greatest expansion of national authority since the New Deal. Under Johnson, a series of civil rights acts forced the states to grant African Americans equal treatment under the law. Crucially, these acts included the abolition of all measures designed to prevent African Americans from voting. Johnson's Great Society and War on Poverty programs resulted in major increases in spending by the national government. As before, states' rights were invoked to support the status quo—states' rights meant no action on civil rights and no increase in antipoverty spending.

Why Should the States Want to Limit National Authority?

When state governments have authority in a particular field, there may be great variations from state to state in how the issues are handled. Inevitably, some states will be more conservative than others. Therefore, bringing national authority to bear on a particular issue may have the effect of imposing national standards on states that, for whatever reason, have not adopted such standards. One example is the voting rights legislation passed under President Johnson. By the 1960s, there was a national consensus that all citizens, regardless of race, should have the right to vote. A majority of the white electorate in certain states, however, did not share this view. National legislation was deemed necessary to impose the national consensus on the recalcitrant states.

Another factor that may make the states more receptive to limited government, especially on economic issues, is competition among the states. It is widely believed that major corporations are more likely to establish new operations in states with a "favorable business climate." National legislation regulating business activities within all states will make it more difficult for an individual state to create a more favorable business climate within its borders relative to other states.

The "New Federalism"

Devolution
The transfer of powers from a national or central government to a state or local government.

In the years after 1968, the **devolution** of power from the national government to the states became a major ideological theme for the Republican Party. Republican president Richard Nixon (1969–1974) advocated what he called a "New Federalism" that would devolve authority from the national government to the states. In part, the New Federalism involved the conversion of categorical grants into block grants, thereby giving state governments greater flexibility in spending. A second part of Nixon's New Federalism was *revenue sharing.* Under the revenue-sharing plan, the national government provided direct, unconditional financial support to state and local governments.

Nixon was able to obtain only a limited number of block grants from Congress. The block grants he did obtain, plus revenue sharing, substantially increased financial support to state governments. Republican president Ronald Reagan (1981–1989) was also a strong advocate of federalism, but some of his policies withdrew certain financial support from the states. Reagan was more successful than Nixon in obtaining block grants, but Reagan's block grants, unlike Nixon's, were less generous to the states than the categorical grants they replaced. Under Reagan, revenue sharing was eliminated. You can see the results of these actions in Figure 3–3 on page 100.

Sometimes states use federal funds to create programs to help underachieving grade school students. This is an example of what type of federalism? (AP Photo/Marcio Jose Sanchez)

Federalism Today

In recent years, it has not been clear whether competing theories of federalism divide the Republicans from the Democrats at all, at least in practice. Consider that the passage of welfare reform legislation in 1996, which involved transferring significant control over welfare programs to the states, took place under Democratic president Bill Clinton (1993–2001). In contrast, under Republican president George W. Bush, Congress enacted the No Child Left Behind Act of 2001, which was signed into law in 2002. This act increased federal control over education and educational funding, which had traditionally been under the purview of state governments.

Beginning in 2009, however, conservative activists began to rediscover states' rights. One reason may be that in that year the Democrats added the presidency to their control of the U.S. House and Senate. Republicans were shut out at the national level. The ambitious program of the Obama administration also alarmed conservatives. Obama's initiatives generally involved greater federal control of the private sector, not of state and local governments. Still, many conservatives hoped that the states could be a counterweight to the newly active national government.

Federalism and Today's Supreme Court

The United States Supreme Court, which normally has the final say on constitutional issues, necessarily plays a significant role in determining where the line is drawn between federal and state powers. Consider the decisions rendered by Chief Justice John Marshall in the cases discussed earlier in this chapter. Since the 1930s, Marshall's broad interpretation of the commerce clause has made it possible for the national government to justify its regulation of almost any activity, even when an activity would appear to be purely local in character. In the 1990s and 2000s, however, the Court has evidenced a willingness to impose some limits on the national government's authority under the commerce clause and other constitutional provisions. As a result, it is difficult to predict how today's Court might rule on a particular case involving federalism.

The Trend toward States' Rights

Since the mid-1990s, the Supreme Court has tended to give greater weight to states' rights than it did during previous decades. In a widely publicized 1995 case, *United States v. Lopez,*[11] the Supreme Court held that Congress had exceeded its constitutional authority under the commerce clause when it passed the Gun-Free School Zones Act in 1990. The Court stated that the act, which banned the possession of guns within one thousand feet of any school, was unconstitutional because it attempted to regulate an area that had "nothing to do with commerce, or any sort of economic enterprise." This marked the first time in sixty years that the Supreme Court had placed a limit on the national government's authority under the commerce clause. The Court subsequently invalidated portions of another law on the ground that Congress had exceeded its authority under the commerce clause.[12]

In 1999 and the early 2000s, the Court also issued decisions that bolstered the authority of state governments under the Eleventh Amendment to the Constitution. The cases involved employees and others who sought redress for state-government violations of federal laws regulating employment. The Court held that the Eleventh Amendment, in most circumstances, precludes lawsuits against state governments for violations of rights established by federal laws unless the states consent to be sued.[13] Additionally, the Court supported states' rights under the Tenth Amendment when it invalidated, in 1997, provisions of a federal law that required state employees to check the backgrounds of prospective handgun purchasers.[14]

California governor Arnold Schwarzenegger is shown signing a state executive order that established low-carbon fuel standards. California has often led the nation in environmental rules and legislation. Could new federal laws and regulations preempt California's? (AP Photo/Rich Pedroncelli)

The Court Sends Mixed Messages

Although the Court has tended to favor states' rights in many decisions, in other decisions it has backed the federal government's position. For example, in two cases decided in 2003 and 2004, the Court, in contrast to its earlier rulings involving the Eleventh Amendment, ruled that the amendment could not shield states from suits by individuals complaining of discrimination based on gender and disability, respectively.[15] Also, in 2005 the Court held that the federal government's power to seize and destroy illegal drugs trumped California's law legalizing the use of marijuana for medical treatment.[16] Yet less than a year later, the Court favored states' rights when it upheld Oregon's controversial "death with dignity" law, which allows patients with terminal illnesses to choose to end their lives early and thus alleviate suffering.[17]

---

11. 514 U.S. 549 (1995).
12. *United States v. Morrison,* 529 U.S. 598 (2000).
13. See, for example, *Alden v. Maine,* 527 U.S. 706 (1999); and *Kimel v. Florida Board of Regents,* 528 U.S. 62 (2000).
14. *Printz v. United States,* 521 U.S. 898 (1997).
15. *Nevada v. Hibbs,* 538 U.S. 721 (2003); and *Tennessee v. Lane,* 541 U.S. 509 (2004).
16. *Gonzales v. Raich,* 545 U.S. 1 (2005).
17. *Gonzales v. Oregon,* 546 U.S. 243 (2006).

The Supreme Court also supported state claims in a 2007 case, *Massachusetts v. EPA*.[18] This case, which many have since hailed as the most significant decision on environmental law for decades, was brought against the Environmental Protection Agency (EPA) by Massachusetts and several other states, as well as various cities and environmental groups. The groups claimed that the EPA, which administers the Clean Air Act and other laws regulating the environment, had the authority to—and should—regulate carbon dioxide and other greenhouse gases. The EPA maintained that it lacked the authority to do so, arguing that members of Congress, when passing the Clean Air Act, had not envisioned a massive greenhouse-gas control program. The Court, however, held that the EPA *did* have such regulatory authority. The Court stated that the EPA could choose not to regulate auto emissions and other heat-trapping gases, but only if it could provide a scientific basis for its refusal.

In 2008, Massachusetts and the other states were back in federal court, suing the EPA for dragging its feet on issuing a carbon dioxide recommendation. The Obama administration's attitude toward greenhouse gases, however, was quite different from that of the George W. Bush team. In April 2009, the EPA ceased resisting the Supreme Court order and provisionally declared carbon dioxide and five other heat-trapping gases to be pollutants that endanger public health and welfare. In December 2009, it confirmed this finding. This step raises the possibility that the EPA could take measures to control the emission of gases suspected of causing global warming even if Congress fails to act.

In a further gesture toward the states, the EPA granted California, thirteen other states, and the District of Columbia a waiver in June 2009 that allows them to impose tougher tailpipe emissions standards than those in effect nationally. The Bush administration had denied the waiver request.

---

18. 549 U.S. 497 (2007).

These environmentalists celebrate the Global Day of Climate Action in Racine, Wisconsin. The number "350" in the foreground represents 350 parts per million, which some believe is the upper limit of carbon dioxide in the atmosphere. Is there any way to determine what the optimal amount of carbon dioxide is? (AP Photo/Journal Times, Mark Hertzberg)

WHY SHOULD YOU CARE ABOUT... THE FEDERAL SYSTEM?

Why should you, personally, care about the federal system? The system encourages debate over whether a particular issue should be a national, state, or local question. Because many questions are, in fact, state or local ones, it is easier for you to make a significant contribution to the discussion on these issues. Even in the largest states, there are many fewer people to persuade than in the nation as a whole. Attempts to influence your fellow citizens can therefore be more effective.

THE FEDERAL SYSTEM AND YOUR LIFE

In this chapter, we have described a variety of issues arising from our federal system that may concern you directly. Although the national government provides aid to educational programs, education is still primarily a state and local responsibility. The total amount of money spent on education is determined by state and local governments. Therefore, you can address this issue at the state or local level. Gambling laws are another state responsibility. Do you enjoy gambling—or do you believe that the effects of gambling make it a social disaster? State law—or state negotiations with American Indian tribes—determines the availability of gambling.

(© Liv Friis-Larsen, 2008. Used under license from Shutterstock.com.)

HOW YOU CAN MAKE A DIFFERENCE

In our modern era, the number of ways in which you can communicate your opinion is vast. You can post a response on any of thousands of blogs. You could develop your own mini-video and post it on YouTube. Politicians use Facebook and MySpace to organize their supporters and often have thousands of online "friends." This can provide you with the opportunity to make your views known to someone who might be able to act on them.

If you want to effect policy change at the state or local level, however, the local newspaper, in both its paper and online formats, continues to be essential. Blogs, YouTube, and other new venues tend to be nationally and even internationally oriented. Most newspapers, however, are resolutely local and are the natural hub for discussions of local issues. Most papers allow blog responses on their sites, and you can make a point by contributing in that fashion. Nothing, however, will win you a wider audience than an old-fashioned letter to the editor. Use the following rules to compose an effective communication:

1. Use a computer, and double-space the lines. Use a spelling checker and grammar checker.
2. Include a lead topic sentence that is short, to the point, and powerful.
3. Keep your thoughts on target—choose only one topic to discuss. Make sure it is newsworthy and timely.
4. Make sure your communication is concise; never let it exceed a page and a half in length (double-spaced).
5. If you know that facts were misstated or left out in current news stories about your topic, supply the facts. The public wants to know.
6. Don't be afraid to express moral judgments. You can go a long way by appealing to readers' sense of justice.
7. Personalize the communication by bringing in your own experiences, if possible.
8. If you are writing a letter, sign it and give your address (including your e-mail address) and your telephone number. Blog entries and other communications may have their own rules on identifying yourself; follow them.
9. If writing a letter, send or e-mail it to the editorial office of the newspaper of your choice. Almost all publications now have e-mail addresses. Their Web sites usually give information on where you can send mail.

questions for discussion and analysis

1. While federal funding of primary and secondary education and federal influence on local schools have both grown considerably in recent years, K–12 education is still largely under the control of state and local governments. How might U.S. public schools be different if, like France, we had a unitary system of government?
2. The United States Supreme Court has interpreted the Fourteenth Amendment to the Constitution, adopted after the Civil War, to mean that most provisions of the Bill of Rights apply to state governments. If the First Amendment, with its guarantees of freedom of speech and religion, did not apply to the states, might some states seek to abridge these rights? If so, how might they do this?
3. Traditionally, conservatives have favored states' rights and liberals have favored national authority. Can you think of modern-day issues in which these long-standing preferences might be reversed, with conservatives favoring national authority and liberals favoring states' rights? Explain.
4. Sometimes, state and local governments take action in areas that are normally considered to be the responsibility of the national government. Immigration is one example. A few localities, such as San Francisco and New Haven, Connecticut, have taken measures to protect unauthorized immigrants (also known as illegal immigrants or undocumented workers). A greater number have taken a more negative approach. Arizona, for example, has passed laws that severely penalize employers who hire undocumented workers. Critics of such laws argue that they generate discrimination against Hispanics who are citizens or legal residents. How might this happen?

key terms

block grants 99
categorical grants 97
commerce clause 92
concurrent powers 89
confederal system 83
cooperative federalism 96
devolution 102
dual federalism 94
elastic clause, or necessary and proper clause 88
enumerated powers 87
federal mandate 100
interstate compact 91
picket-fence federalism 97
police power 88
supremacy clause 89
unitary system 83

chapter summary

1. There are three basic models for ordering relations between central governments and local units: (a) a unitary system (in which ultimate power is held by the national government), (b) a confederal system (in which ultimate power is retained by the states), and (c) a federal system (in which governmental powers are divided between the national government and the states).
2. The Constitution expressly delegated certain powers to the national government in Article I, Section 8. In addition to these enumerated powers, the national government has implied and inherent powers. Implied powers are those that are reasonably necessary to carry out the powers expressly delegated to the national government. Inherent powers are those held by the national government by virtue of its being a sovereign state with the right to preserve itself.
3. The Tenth Amendment to the Constitution states that powers not delegated to the United States by the Constitution, nor prohibited by it to the states, are reserved to the states, or to the people. In certain areas, the Constitution provides for concurrent powers (such as the power to tax), which are powers that are held jointly by the national and state governments. The Constitution also denies certain powers to both the national government and the states.
4. The supremacy clause of the Constitution states that the Constitution, congressional laws, and national treaties are the supreme law of the land. States cannot use their reserved or concurrent powers to override national policies.
5. Chief Justice John Marshall's expansive interpretation of the necessary and proper clause of the Constitution in *McCulloch v. Maryland* (1819), and his affirmation of the

supremacy clause, enhanced the power of the national government. Marshall's broad interpretation of the commerce clause in *Gibbons v. Ogden* (1824) further extended the powers of the national government.

6. The controversy over slavery that led to the Civil War took the form of a fight over national government supremacy versus the rights of the separate states. Since the Civil War, federalism has evolved through at least two general phases: dual federalism and cooperative federalism. In dual federalism, each of the states and the federal government remain supreme within their own spheres. The era since the Great Depression has sometimes been labeled one of cooperative federalism, in which states and the national government cooperate in solving complex common problems.

7. Categorical grants from the federal government to state governments help finance many projects. By attaching special conditions to federal grants, the national government can effect policy changes in areas typically governed by the states. Block grants usually have fewer strings attached, thus giving state and local governments more flexibility in using funds. Federal mandates—laws requiring states to implement certain policies—have generated controversy.

8. Traditionally, conservatives have favored states' rights, and liberals have favored national authority. In part, this is because the national government has historically been an engine of change.

selected print & media resources

SUGGESTED READINGS

Hamilton, Alexander, *et al.* ***The Federalist: The Famous Papers on the Principles of American Government.*** **Benjamin F. Wright, ed. New York: Friedman/Fairfax Publishing, 2002. These essays remain an authoritative exposition of the founders' views on federalism.**

King, Preston. ***Federalism and Federation.*** **London: Frank Cass & Co., 2008. This analysis of federalism and federation distinguishes these two forms of government and examines the different types of federalism now in existence.**

Ravitch, Diane. ***The Death and Life of the Great American School System: How Testing and Choice Are Undermining Education.*** **New York: Basic Books, 2010. Ravitch, a historian of education at New York University, served in the Department of Education under both Republican and Democratic presidents. She was formerly an advocate of market-driven accountability and school choice, but she has changed her mind based on her evaluation of the events of the past decade. In particular, Ravitch believes that No Child Left Behind has been a disaster that imposed perverse incentives on the public schools.**

Simon, Scott. ***Windy City: A Novel of Politics.*** **New York: Random House Trade Paperbacks, 2009. The mayor of Chicago is dead, face down in a pizza, and Alderman Sundaran "Sunny" Roopini, the interim mayor, has more than one problem on his hands. Simon's comic novel portrays the gritty urban politics that Barack Obama emerged from as an Illinois state senator.**

MEDIA RESOURCES

Can the States Do It Better?—**A 1996 film in which various experts discuss how much power the national government should have. The film uses documentary footage and other resources to illustrate this debate.**

The Civil War—**The PBS documentary series that made director Ken Burns famous. *The Civil War,* first shown in 1990, marked a revolution in documentary technique. Photographs, letters, eyewitness memoirs, and music are used to bring the war to life. The DVD version was released in 2002.**

Last Man Standing: Politics, Texas Style—**A hilarious look at two Texas races, one for a legislative seat and one for governor. The winning Republican gubernatorial candidate is none other than George W. Bush. Paul Stekler's 2004 film includes enlightening interviews with Bush adviser Karl Rove and the late Molly Ivins, a much-beloved liberal commentator.**

McCulloch v. Maryland and *Gibbons v. Ogden*—**These programs are part of the series *Equal Justice under Law: Landmark Cases in Supreme Court History.* They provide more details on cases that defined our federal system.**

Street Fight—**A 2005 documentary by Marshall Curry, this film chronicles the unsuccessful attempt by young City Council member Cory Booker to unseat long-time Newark mayor Sharpe James in 2002. Curry captures on film James's abuse of police and code enforcement officers to sabotage Booker's campaign. In 2006, the voters elected Booker mayor of Newark. In 2008, James was sentenced to twenty-seven months in prison on corruption charges.**

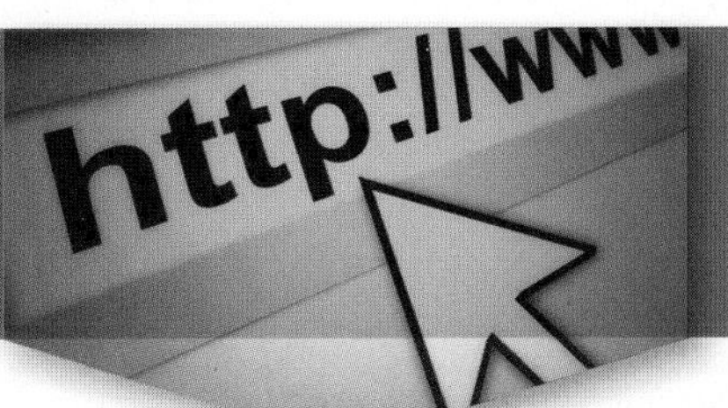

e-mocracy

HOW TO FIND COURT CASES ONLINE

As you have learned in this chapter, the federal courts have a major impact on how federalism has been interpreted and implemented in the United States. Beginning with this chapter and continuing through the rest of the text, you will find many references to court cases, typically ones decided by the United States Supreme Court. An excellent way to find out more about the role of the courts in the American system is to learn about key cases.

You'll notice in the footnotes that refer to cases that there is a standard format for citing them. Consider *New State Ice Co. v. Liebmann,* which is cited on page 86. In addition to the name of the case, the citation includes the rather mysterious term "285 U.S. 262 (1932)." This case was decided by the United States Supreme Court in 1932, and "U.S." is an abbreviation for *United States Reports,* the official edition of the decisions of the Supreme Court; "285" is the volume number, and "262" is the page number on which the decision begins.

There's no need for you to track down these large, dusty volumes when you want to investigate cases, however. Important cases are easy to find on the Web. Most of the time, you won't need to bother with anything other than the name of the case. That's because the cases referred to in this text are almost always famous, and you can find dozens of reports on them simply by typing the name of the case into a search engine such as Google.

Two kinds of results are likely to appear when you employ a search engine. One is the text of the Court's decision. Dozens of sites carry the text of an important case. If you want to read the text, you might find that Findlaw.com does a good job of formatting cases so that they are easy to read. In addition, the search engine will toss up articles describing the case and its importance. Wikipedia, for example, has articles on most important cases. You might find it useful to read one or more of these articles first—and then if you want to delve deeper, you can read the Court's decision.

Sometimes, the name of the case is not enough to locate it. What if the name is *United States v. Johnson*? Twelve cases by that name are important enough to merit articles in Wikipedia. If you are searching for such a case, you'll want to enter the full citation into the search engine, for example, "*United States v. Johnson* 457 U.S. 537 (1982)."

LOGGING ON

Federalism is an important aspect of our democracy. To learn more about the establishment of our federal form of government and about current issues relating to federalism, visit the Web sites listed in the remainder of this section.

To learn the founders' views on federalism, you can access the *Federalist Papers* online at
thomas.loc.gov/home/histdox/fedpapers.html

The University of Richmond offers links to the constitutions of many nations around the globe through its Web site. Go to
confinder.richmond.edu

The Council of State Governments is a good source for information on state responses to federalism issues. Go to
www.csg.org

Another good source of information on issues facing state governments and federal-state relations is the National Governors Association's Web site at
www.nga.org

The Brookings Institution's policy analyses and recommendations on a variety of issues, including federalism, can be accessed at
www.brookings.edu

For a libertarian approach to issues relating to federalism, go to the Cato Institute's Web page at
www.cato.org

chapter 4

Civil Liberties

chapter contents

Prior to the passage of Arizona's tough 2010 anti-immigration law, protesters prayed in front of the state capitol. (© Rick D'Elia/Corbis)

WHAT IF... ...*Roe v. Wade* were overturned?

Tempers flare in Washington, D.C., when the abortion issue comes to the fore. Both sides of the controversy are represented by the many signs here. What are the arguments used by each side? (© Susan Steinkamp/Corbis)

BACKGROUND

The Bill of Rights and other provisions of the U.S. Constitution are the ultimate protections of our civil rights and liberties. But how do these rights work out in practice? How do we determine what our rights are in any given situation? One way is through *judicial review,* the power of the United States Supreme Court or other courts to declare laws and other acts of government unconstitutional.

Supreme Court cases are often hotly contested, and the decision in the 1973 case *Roe v. Wade* is one of the most contentious ever handed down. In the *Roe v. Wade* case, the Court declared that a woman's constitutionally protected right to privacy includes the right to have an abortion. The Court concluded that the states cannot restrict a woman's right to an abortion during the first three months of pregnancy. More than thirty-five years later, however, the debate over the legality of abortion still rages in the United States. Most recently, members of Congress have debated whether President Obama's health-care reform would involve the federal government in the business of funding abortions.

WHAT IF ROE V. WADE *WERE OVERTURNED?*

If the Supreme Court overturned *Roe v. Wade,* the authority to regulate abortion would fall again to the states. Before the *Roe v. Wade* case, each state decided whether abortion would be legal within its borders. State legislatures made the laws that covered abortion. Some critics of *Roe v. Wade*'s constitutional merits have argued that allowing the Supreme Court to decide the legality of abortion nationwide is undemocratic because the justices are not elected officials. In contrast, if state legislatures regained the power to create abortion policy, the resulting laws would reflect the majority opinion of each state's voters.

Simply overturning *Roe v. Wade* would not make abortion in the United States illegal overnight. In many states, abortion rights are very popular, and the legislatures in those states would not consider measures to ban abortion or to further restrict access to abortion. Some states have laws that would protect abortion rights even if *Roe v. Wade* were overturned. Access to abortions would likely continue in the West Coast states and in much of the Northeast. In most of the South and parts of the Midwest, however, abortion could be seriously restricted or even banned. Some states have "trigger laws" that would immediately outlaw abortion if *Roe v. Wade* were overturned.

Women living in conservative states such as the Dakotas, Kentucky, and Mississippi already face serious difficulties in obtaining an abortion. In each of these states, 98 percent of the counties do not have an abortion clinic. Many women desiring the procedure already have to travel long distances. If abortion were banned, these women could still cross state lines to obtain an abortion. If twenty-one of the most conservative states banned abortion, only 170 providers would be affected—less than 10 percent of the national total.

FOR CRITICAL ANALYSIS

1. Why do you think that abortion remains a contentious topic more than thirty-five years after the *Roe v. Wade* decision? Should that decision be revisited? Why or why not?
2. How significant a role should the courts play in deciding constitutional questions about abortion? Do you feel that individual states should have a say in the legality of abortion within their own borders? Why or why not?

"The land of the free." When asked what makes the United States distinctive, Americans commonly say that it is a free country. Americans have long believed that limits on the power of government are an essential part of what makes this country free. Recall from Chapter 1 that restraints on the actions of government against individuals are generally referred to as *civil liberties.* The first ten amendments to the U.S. Constitution—the Bill of Rights—place such restraints on the national government. Of these amendments, none is more famous than the First Amendment, which guarantees freedom of religion, speech, and the press, as well as other rights.

Most other democratic nations have laws to protect these and other civil liberties, but none of the laws is quite like the First Amendment. Take the issue of "hate speech." What if someone makes statements that stir up hatred toward a particular race or other group of people? In Germany, where memories of Nazi anti-Semitism remain alive, such speech is unquestionably illegal. In the United States, the issue is not so clear. The courts have often extended constitutional protection to this kind of speech.

In this chapter, we describe the civil liberties provided by the Bill of Rights and some of the controversies that surround them. We look first at the First Amendment, including the establishment clause. We also discuss the right to privacy, which is at the heart of the abortion issue introduced in the *What If . . .* feature that opened this chapter. We also examine the rights of defendants in criminal cases.

The Bill of Rights

As you read through this chapter, bear in mind that the Bill of Rights, like the rest of the Constitution, is relatively brief. The framers set forth broad guidelines, leaving it up to the courts to interpret these constitutional mandates and apply them to specific situations. Thus, judicial interpretations shape the true nature of the civil liberties and rights that we possess. Because judicial interpretations change over time, so do our liberties and rights. As you will read in the following pages, there have been many conflicts over the meaning of such simple phrases as *freedom of religion* and *freedom of the press.*

To understand what freedoms we actually have, we need to examine how the courts—and particularly the United States Supreme Court—have resolved some of those conflicts. One important conflict was over the issue of whether the Bill of Rights in the federal Constitution limited the powers of state governments as well as those of the national government.

These people who are in favor of school vouchers show their support in Austin, Texas, in front of the state capital. Which groups might be against such vouchers and why? (AP Photo/LM Otero)

Extending the Bill of Rights to State Governments

Many citizens do not realize that, as originally intended, the Bill of Rights limited only the powers of the national government. At the time the Bill of Rights was ratified, there was little concern over the potential of state governments to curb civil liberties. For one thing, state governments were closer to home and easier to control. For another, most state constitutions already had bills of rights. Rather, the fear was of the potential tyranny of the national government. The Bill of Rights begins with the words, "Congress shall make no law . . . ." It says nothing about *states* making laws that might abridge citizens' civil liberties. In 1833, in *Barron v. Baltimore,*[1] the United States Supreme Court held that the Bill of Rights did not apply to state laws.

We mentioned that most states had bills of rights. These bills of rights were similar to the national one, but there were some differences. Furthermore, each

1. 32 U.S. 243 (1833).

did you know?

That in a recent survey, nearly one-fourth of the respondents could not name any First Amendment rights.

state's judicial system interpreted the rights differently. Citizens in different states, therefore, effectively had different sets of civil liberties. It was not until after the Fourteenth Amendment was ratified in 1868 that civil liberties guaranteed by the national Constitution began to be applied to the states. Section 1 of that amendment provides, in part, as follows:

No State shall . . . deprive any person of life, liberty, or property, without due process of law.

Incorporation of the Fourteenth Amendment

There was no question that the Fourteenth Amendment applied to state governments. For decades, however, the courts were reluctant to define the liberties spelled out in the national Bill of Rights as constituting "due process of law," which was protected under the Fourteenth Amendment. Not until 1925, in *Gitlow v. New York,*[2] did the United States Supreme Court hold that the Fourteenth Amendment protected the freedom of speech guaranteed by the First Amendment to the Constitution.

Incorporation Theory The view that most of the protections of the Bill of Rights apply to state governments through the Fourteenth Amendment's due process clause.

Only gradually did the Supreme Court accept the **incorporation theory**—the view that most of the protections of the Bill of Rights are incorporated into the Fourteenth Amendment's protection against state government actions. Table 4–1 below shows the rights that the Court has incorporated into the Fourteenth Amendment and the case in which it first applied each protection. As you can see in that table, in the fifteen years following the *Gitlow* decision, the Supreme Court incorporated into the Fourteenth Amendment the other basic freedoms (of the press, assembly, the right to petition, and

2. 268 U.S. 652 (1925).

TABLE 4–1 Incorporating the Bill of Rights into the Fourteenth Amendment

Year	Issue	Amendment Involved	Court Case
1925	Freedom of speech	I	*Gitlow v. New York,* 268 U.S. 652.
1931	Freedom of the press	I	*Near v. Minnesota,* 283 U.S. 697.
1932	Right to a lawyer in capital punishment cases	VI	*Powell v. Alabama,* 287 U.S. 45.
1937	Freedom of assembly and right to petition	I	*De Jonge v. Oregon,* 299 U.S. 353.
1940	Freedom of religion	I	*Cantwell v. Connecticut,* 310 U.S. 296.
1947	Separation of church and state	I	*Everson v. Board of Education,* 330 U.S. 1.
1948	Right to a public trial	VI	*In re Oliver,* 333 U.S. 257.
1949	No unreasonable searches and seizures	IV	*Wolf v. Colorado,* 338 U.S. 25.
1961	Exclusionary rule	IV	*Mapp v. Ohio,* 367 U.S. 643.
1962	No cruel and unusual punishment	VIII	*Robinson v. California,* 370 U.S. 660.
1963	Right to a lawyer in all criminal felony cases	VI	*Gideon v. Wainwright,* 372 U.S. 335.
1964	No compulsory self-incrimination	V	*Malloy v. Hogan,* 378 U.S. 1.
1965	Right to privacy	I, III, IV, V, IX	*Griswold v. Connecticut,* 381 U.S. 479.
1966	Right to an impartial jury	VI	*Parker v. Gladden,* 385 U.S. 363.
1967	Right to a speedy trial	VI	*Klopfer v. North Carolina,* 386 U.S. 213.
1969	No double jeopardy	V	*Benton v. Maryland,* 395 U.S. 784.
2010	Right to bear arms	II	*McDonald v. Chicago,* 561 U.S. ___.

religion) guaranteed by the First Amendment. These and the later Supreme Court decisions listed in Table 4–1 have bound the fifty states to accept for their citizens most of the rights and freedoms that are set forth in the U.S. Bill of Rights. We now look at some of those rights and freedoms, beginning with freedom of religion.

Freedom of Religion

In the United States, freedom of religion consists of two main principles as they are presented in the First Amendment. The **establishment clause** prohibits the establishment of a church that is officially supported by the national government, thus guaranteeing a division between church and state. The **free exercise clause** constrains the national government from prohibiting individuals from practicing the religion of their choice. These two precepts can inherently be in tension with each other, however. For example, would prohibiting a group of students from holding prayer meetings in a public school classroom infringe on the students' right to free exercise of religion? Or would allowing the meetings amount to unconstitutional government support for religion? You will read about a number of difficult freedom of religion issues in the following discussion.

Establishment Clause
The part of the First Amendment prohibiting the establishment of a church officially supported by the national government. It is applied to questions of the legality of giving state and local government aid to religious organizations and schools, allowing or requiring school prayers, and teaching evolution versus intelligent design.

Free Exercise Clause
The provision of the First Amendment guaranteeing the free exercise of religion. The provision constrains the national government from prohibiting individuals from practicing the religion of their choice.

The Separation of Church and State—The Establishment Clause

The First Amendment to the Constitution states, in part, that "Congress shall make no law respecting an establishment of religion." In the words of Thomas Jefferson, the *establishment clause* was designed to create a "wall of separation between Church and State." Perhaps Jefferson was thinking about the religious intolerance that characterized the first colonies. Many of the American colonies were founded by groups that were in pursuit of religious freedom. Nonetheless, the early colonists were quite intolerant of religious beliefs that did not conform to those held by the majority of citizens within their own communities. Jefferson undoubtedly was also aware that state churches were formerly the rule; among the original thirteen American colonies, nine had official churches.

did you know?
That on the eve of the American Revolution, fewer than 20 percent of American adults adhered to a church in any significant way, compared with the 55 percent that do so today.

As interpreted by the United States Supreme Court, the establishment clause in the First Amendment means at least the following:

> *Neither a state nor the federal government can set up a church. Neither can pass laws which aid one religion, aid all religions, or prefer one religion over another. Neither can force nor influence a person to go to or to remain away from church against his will or force him to profess a belief or disbelief in any religion. No person can be punished for entertaining or professing religious beliefs or disbeliefs, for church attendance or nonattendance. No tax in any amount, large or small, can be levied to support any religious activities or institutions, whatever they may be called, or whatever form they may adopt to teach or practice religion. Neither a state nor the federal government can, openly or secretly, participate in the affairs of any religious organizations or groups and vice versa.*[3]

The establishment clause covers all conflicts about such matters as the legality of giving state and local government aid to religious organizations and schools, allowing or requiring school prayers, teaching evolution versus intelligent design, placing religious displays in schools or public places, and discriminating against religious groups in publicly operated institutions. The establishment clause's mandate that government can neither promote nor discriminate against religious beliefs raises particularly knotty questions at times.

3. *Everson v. Board of Education,* 330 U.S. 1 (1947).

I'm taking my voucher and going to circus school. (© The New Yorker Collection, 2002. Charles Barsotti, from cartoonbank.com. All rights reserved.)

Aid to Church-Related Schools. In the United States, almost 11 percent of school-age children attend private schools, of which about 80 percent have religious affiliations. The United States Supreme Court has tried to draw a fine line between permissible public aid to students in these schools and impermissible public aid to religion. These issues have arisen most often at the elementary and secondary levels.

In 1971, in *Lemon v. Kurtzman,*[4] the Court ruled that direct state aid could not be used to subsidize religious instruction. The Court in the *Lemon* case gave its most general statement on the constitutionality of government aid to religious schools, stating that the aid had to be secular (nonreligious) in aim, that it could not have the primary effect of advancing or inhibiting religion, and that the government must avoid "an excessive government entanglement with religion." All laws under the establishment clause are now subject to the three-part *Lemon* test. How the test is applied, however, has varied over the years.

In a number of cases, the Supreme Court has held that state programs helping church-related schools are unconstitutional. The Court also has denied state reimbursements to religious schools for field trips and for developing achievement tests. In a series of other cases, however, the Supreme Court has allowed states to use tax funds for lunches, textbooks, diagnostic services for speech and hearing problems, standardized tests, computers, and transportation for students attending church-operated elementary and secondary schools, as well as for special educational services for disadvantaged students attending religious schools.

School Vouchers. An ongoing controversial issue concerning the establishment clause has to do with school vouchers. One solution to the problem of poor educational performance has been for state and local governments to issue school vouchers (representing state-issued funds) that can be used to "purchase" education at any school, public or private. At issue is whether voucher programs violate the establishment clause.

In 2002, the United States Supreme Court held that a voucher program in Cleveland, Ohio, did not violate the establishment clause. The Court concluded that because the vouchers could be used for public as well as private schools, the program did not unconstitutionally entangle church and state.[5] The Court's 2002 decision was encouraging to those who support school choice, whether it takes the form of school vouchers or tuition tax credits to offset educational expenses in private schools.

Today, ten states allow public funds to be used for private education. Four states have small-scale voucher programs for a limited number of students, and seven states offer tuition tax-subsidy programs. At the national level, President George W. Bush strongly supported the use of public funds for private education, but with little success. Indeed, voucher programs have been eliminated in several jurisdictions. In 2005, the Florida Supreme Court ruled that vouchers violated the Florida state constitution. In 2007, Utah voters rejected a voucher plan that was created earlier that year by the state legislature. In March 2009, the U.S. Congress voted to halt a voucher program in the District of Columbia. President Barack Obama has opposed voucher systems, and new ones are unlikely to be established in the immediate future

The Issue of School Prayer—*Engel v. Vitale.* Do the states have the right to promote religion in general, without making any attempt to establish a particular religion? That is the question raised by school prayer and was the precise issue presented in 1962

4. 403 U.S. 602 (1971).
5. *Zelman v. Simmons-Harris,* 536 U.S. 639 (2002).

in *Engel v. Vitale,*[6] the so-called Regents' Prayer case in New York. The State Board of Regents of New York had suggested that a prayer be spoken aloud in the public schools at the beginning of each day. The recommended prayer was as follows:

> *Almighty God, we acknowledge our dependence upon Thee,*
> *And we beg Thy blessings upon us, our parents, our teachers,*
> *and our Country.*

Such a prayer was implemented in many New York public schools.

The parents of a number of students challenged the action of the regents, maintaining that it violated the establishment clause of the First Amendment. At trial, the parents lost. On appeal, however, the Supreme Court ruled that the regents' action was unconstitutional because "the constitutional prohibition against laws respecting an establishment of a religion must mean at least that in this country it is no part of the business of government to compose official prayers for any group of the American people to recite as part of a religious program carried on by any government." The Court's conclusion was based in part on the "historical fact that governmentally established religions and religious persecutions go hand in hand." In *Abington School District v. Schempp,*[7] the Supreme Court outlawed officially sponsored daily readings of the Bible and recitation of the Lord's Prayer in public schools.

did you know?

That in 1657, more than a century before the First Amendment, thirty Dutch citizens on Long Island in what was then a Netherlands colony signed the Flushing Remonstrance, a document that called for religious tolerance.

The Debate over School Prayer Continues. Although the Supreme Court has ruled repeatedly against officially sponsored prayer and Bible-reading sessions in public schools, other means for bringing some form of religious expression into public education have been attempted. In *Wallace v. Jaffree,*[8] the Supreme Court struck down as unconstitutional an Alabama law authorizing one minute of silence for prayer or meditation in all public schools. The Court concluded that the law violated the establishment clause because it was "an endorsement of religion lacking any clearly secular purpose."

Since then, the lower courts have interpreted the Supreme Court's decision to mean that states can require a moment of silence in the schools as long as they make it clear that the purpose of the law is secular, not religious.

These students pray around the flagpole before classes at Lufkin High School in Texas. Are such actions constitutional? (AP Photo/*The Lufkin Daily News,* Joel Andrews)

Forbidding the Teaching of Evolution. For many decades, certain religious groups have opposed the teaching of evolution in the schools. To these groups, evolutionary theory directly counters their religious belief that human beings did not evolve but were created fully formed, as described in the biblical story of the creation. State and local attempts to forbid the teaching of evolution, however, have not passed constitutional muster in the eyes of the United States Supreme Court. For example, in 1968 the Supreme Court held, in *Epperson v. Arkansas,*[9] that an Arkansas law prohibiting the teaching of evolution violated the establishment clause, because it imposed religious beliefs on students. The Louisiana legislature passed a law requiring the teaching of the biblical story of the creation alongside the

6. 370 U.S. 421 (1962).
7. 374 U.S. 203 (1963).
8. 472 U.S. 38 (1985).
9. 393 U.S. 97 (1968).

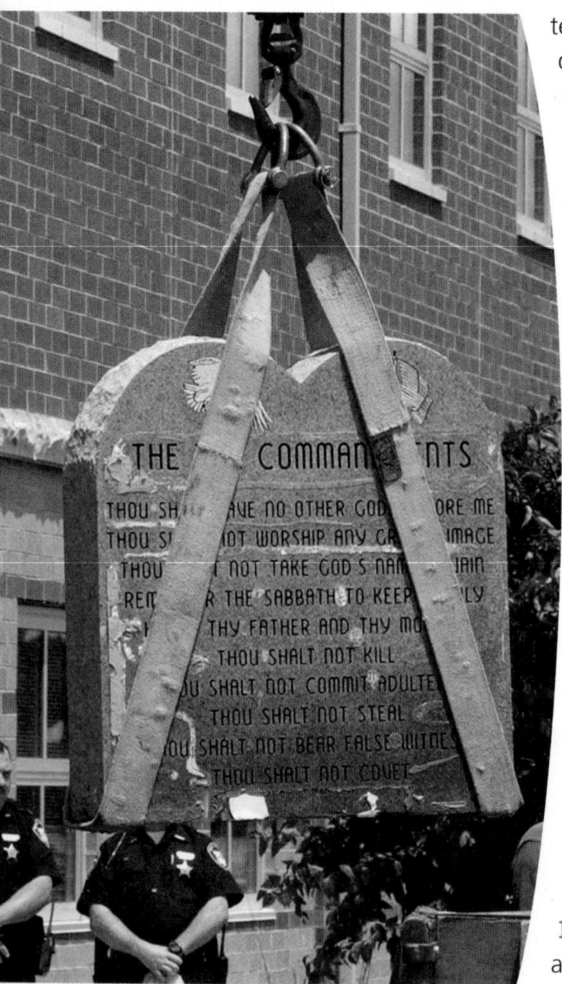

A Ten Commandments monument is removed from a high school in West Union, Ohio. Why have federal judges ordered the removal of such monuments from public schools and county courthouses? (AP Photo/ Al Behrman)

teaching of evolution. In 1987, in *Edwards v. Aguillard,*[10] the Supreme Court declared that this law was unconstitutional, in part because it had as its primary purpose the promotion of a particular religious belief.

Nonetheless, state and local groups around the country continue their efforts against the teaching of evolution. Some school districts have considered teaching "intelligent design" as an alternative explanation of the origin of life. Proponents of intelligent design contend that evolutionary theory has "gaps" that can be explained only by the existence of an intelligent creative force (God).

The federal courts took up the issue of intelligent design in 2005. The previous year, the Dover Area Board of Education in Pennsylvania had voted to require the presentation of intelligent design as an explanation of the origin of life. In December 2005, a U.S. district court ruled that the Dover mandate was unconstitutional. Judge John E. Jones III, appointed in 2002 by President George W. Bush, issued a 139-page decision that criticized the intelligent design theory in depth.[11] All of the school board members who endorsed intelligent design were voted out of office, and the new school board declined to appeal the decision.

Some school officials who oppose the theory of evolution have avoided lawsuits by employing ambiguous language. For example, until 2009, the statewide Texas Board of Education required public school students to discuss the "strengths and weaknesses" of evolution. Biology teachers who believed there were no "weaknesses" largely ignored this requirement. As of 2009, the board encourages students to examine "all sides" of scientific explanations, an even more ambiguous standard.

Religious Displays on Public Property. On a regular basis, the courts are asked to determine whether religious symbols placed on public property violate the establishment clause. A frequent source of controversy is the placement of a crèche, or nativity scene, on public property during the Christmas season. The Supreme Court has allowed some displays but prohibited others. In general, a nativity scene is acceptable if it is part of a broader display that contains secular objects such as lights, Christmas trees, Santa Claus figures, and reindeer. A stand-alone crèche is not acceptable.[12] A related issue is whether the Ten Commandments may be displayed on public property. As with nativity displays, acceptability turns on whether the Ten Commandments are part of a larger secular display or whether the context is overtly religious.

In a new twist on the Ten Commandments controversy, the Supreme Court ruled in 2009 that the city of Pleasant Grove, Utah, was not required to accept a monument from Summum, a small religious group, and place it in a city park. The proposed monument would have listed Summum's principles. A variety of donated monuments were already installed in the park, including one that displayed the Ten Commandments. Summum based its argument on freedom of speech grounds, not the establishment clause. In response, the Court ruled that by accepting or not accepting monuments, the city was exercising its own freedom of speech, rather than regulating the speech of others. When New York accepted the Statue of Liberty from France, it was under no obligation also to accept a "statue of autocracy" from somewhere else.[13]

---

10. 482 U.S. 578 (1987).
11. *Kitzmiller v. Dover Area School District,* 400 F.Supp.2d 707 (M.D.Pa. 2005).
12. *Lynch v. Donnelly,* 465 U.S. 668 (1984).
13. *Pleasant Grove City v. Summum,* 129 S.Ct. 1125 (2009).

The Free Exercise Clause

The First Amendment constrains Congress from prohibiting the free exercise of religion. Does this *free exercise clause* mean that no type of religious practice can be prohibited or restricted by government? Certainly, a person can hold any religious belief that he or she wants, or a person can have no religious belief. When, however, religious *practices* work against public policy and the public welfare, the government can act. For example, regardless of a child's or parent's religious beliefs, the government can require certain types of vaccinations. Additionally, public school students can be required to study from textbooks chosen by school authorities.

This scientist who studies human evolution is surrounded by different human skulls, some dating back many thousands of years. Why is the theory of evolution often attacked?(© Marc Charuel/Sygma/Corbis)

Tax Treatment of Religious Organizations. Churches and other religious organizations are tax-exempt bodies, and as a result they are not allowed to endorse candidates for office or make contributions to candidates' campaigns. Churches are allowed to take positions on ballot proposals, however, and may even contribute to referendum campaigns. For example, both the Church of Jesus Christ of Latter-day Saints (the Mormons) and the Roman Catholic Church were able to fund the campaign for California's 2008 Proposition 8, a measure to ban same-sex marriage.

The Internal Revenue Service (IRS) rarely bothers to threaten the tax-exempt status of a church based on simple candidate endorsements, however. For example, in September 2008, thirty-three ministers collectively endorsed Republican presidential candidate John McCain in a deliberate challenge to the 1954 law that prohibits such endorsements. So far, the IRS has not responded. In 1995, however, the IRS did revoke the tax-exempt status of Branch Ministries, Inc., and in 2000 a federal district court supported the revocation.[14] Branch Ministries went far beyond simply endorsing a candidate from the pulpit. The church had used tax-exempt income to buy newspaper advertisements denouncing Democratic presidential candidate Bill Clinton.

A fascinating recent issue involving the accommodation of religion is to what extent public colleges and universities ought to accommodate the religious practices of Muslim students. We look at this controversial topic in the *Which Side Are You On?* feature on the following page.

Freedom of Expression

Perhaps the most frequently invoked freedom that Americans have is the right to free speech and a free press without government interference. Each of us has the right to have our say, and all of us have the right to hear what others say. For the most part, Americans can criticize public officials and their actions without fear of reprisal by any branch of government.

---

14. *Branch Ministries v. Rossetti,* 211 F.3d 137 (D.C.Cir. 2000).

WHICH SIDE ARE YOU ON?

SHOULD MUSLIMS' RELIGIOUS NEEDS BE ACCOMMODATED ON CAMPUS?

The United States is known as a land of religious tolerance. Americans practice many minority religions in addition to the major faiths. So long as religious practices do not interfere with the rights of others, they are legally acceptable. The courts have drawn the line, though, when religious practices involve illegal activities, such as leaving beheaded animals on the side of the road or using prohibited drugs.

Recently, college campuses have been asked to accommodate the religious needs of Muslim students. Observant Muslims seek to wash their feet before they pray. Should universities build footbaths that Muslim students can then use? The Dearborn campus of the University of Michigan, where 16 percent of the students are Muslim, decided to do just that, in part to keep students from washing their feet in the restroom sinks. The university spent more than $25,000 to install foot-washing stations in a number of restrooms.

And what about separate prayer rooms for Muslim students in public schools? There is also the issue of whether food in cafeterias conforms to Muslims' religious requirements. Finally, what about religious holidays? School calendars already accommodate Christians with vacations around Easter and Christmas. Why not also Muslim holidays?

CAMPUS OFFICIALS SHOULD BE TOLERANT

While providing footbaths for Muslims on college campuses may seem strange, that is only because most students are not used to having Muslims around them. Just because America is basically a nation whose major religions are based on Judeo-Christian doctrines does not mean that we can't accommodate a growing alternative religion. One of the fastest-growing religions in the United States is indeed Islam. We should consider most Muslim student requests for accommodation on campuses as simply part of those students' right to practice their religion.

Campus authorities are going to have to face the issue of accommodating Muslim religious practices sooner or later anyway. In addition to the University of Michigan, at least fifteen other universities have installed footbaths in new buildings. The footbaths can be used by anyone, including sweaty athletes and janitors who fill buckets. They are not for the exclusive use of Muslim students. Such footbaths have no symbolic value; they are not stylized in a religious manner.

WHAT ABOUT SEPARATION OF CHURCH AND STATE?

Those who oppose religious accommodation for Muslims argue that, at least on public college campuses, the funding of such actions necessarily violates the constitutionally mandated separation of church and state. Footbaths are essentially structures for a particular religious tradition. The Constitution prohibits the government from endorsing any particular religion. On college campuses, the footbaths are being financed out of building-maintenance fees paid by students. Students aren't given any voice in the decision, and that is wrong. Many colleges no longer sponsor Christmas music on campus, so why would those universities behave any differently when it comes to accommodating Muslims? The Constitution should be our guide.

These members of the Johns Hopkins University Student Muslim Association gather for prayer during one of their weekly meetings. To what extent should universities accommodate the needs of devout Muslim students? When does such accommodation violate the separation of church and state? (AP Photo/John Gillis)

No Prior Restraint

Restraining an activity before that activity has actually occurred is called **prior restraint.** When expression is involved, prior restraint means censorship, as opposed to subsequent punishment. Prior restraint of expression would require, for example, that a permit be obtained before a speech could be made, a newspaper published, or a movie or TV show exhibited. Most, if not all, Supreme Court justices have been very critical of any governmental action that imposes prior restraint on expression. The Court clearly displayed this attitude in *Nebraska Press Association v. Stuart,*[15] a case decided in 1976:

> *A prior restraint on expression comes to this Court with a "heavy presumption" against its constitutionality. . . . The government thus carries a heavy burden of showing justification for the enforcement of such a restraint.*

Prior Restraint
Restraining an activity before it has actually occurred. When expression is involved, this means censorship.

Symbolic Speech
Expression made through articles of clothing, gestures, movements, and other forms of nonverbal conduct. Symbolic speech is given substantial protection by the courts.

One of the most famous cases concerning prior restraint was *New York Times v. United States,*[16] the so-called Pentagon Papers case. In 1971, the *Times* and the *Washington Post* were about to publish the Pentagon Papers, an elaborate secret history of the U.S. government's involvement in the Vietnam War (1964–1975). The secret documents had been obtained illegally by a disillusioned former Pentagon official. The government wanted a court order to bar publication of the documents, arguing that national security was threatened and that the documents had been stolen. The newspapers argued that the public had a right to know the information contained in the papers and that the press had the right to inform the public. The Supreme Court ruled six to three in favor of the newspapers' right to publish the information. This case affirmed the no-prior-restraint doctrine.

The Protection of Symbolic Speech

Not all expression is in words or in writing. Articles of clothing, gestures, movements, and other forms of nonverbal expressive conduct are considered **symbolic speech.** Such speech is given substantial protection today by our courts. For example, in a landmark decision issued in 1969, *Tinker v. Des Moines School District,*[17] the United States Supreme Court held that the wearing of black armbands by students in protest against the Vietnam War was a form of speech protected by the First Amendment.

In 1989, in *Texas v. Johnson,*[18] the Supreme Court ruled that state laws that prohibited the burning of the American flag as part of a peaceful protest also violated the freedom of expression protected by the First Amendment. Congress responded by passing the Flag Protection Act of 1989, which was ruled unconstitutional by the Supreme Court in June 1990.[19] Congress and President George H. W. Bush immediately pledged to work for a constitutional amendment to "protect our flag"—an effort that has yet to be successful.

In 2003, however, the Supreme Court concluded in a Virginia case that a state, consistent with the First Amendment, may ban cross burnings carried out with the intent to intimidate. The Court reasoned that historically, cross burning was a sign of impending violence, and a state has the right to ban threats of violence. The Court also ruled, however, that the state must prove intimidation, and cannot

William F. Hornsby Jr., of Euclid, Ohio sits at home reading a schoolbook after being suspended in 1965 for six school days from Euclid High School. Hornsby wore a black arm band to classes in mourning for the American and Vietnamese dead in the Vietnam War. School officials said they were not against Hornsby taking a position, but thought that outward display of his feelings would disrupt classes. Do high school students have the same free speech rights as adults? (AP Photo)

---

15. 427 U.S. 539 (1976). See also *Near v. Minnesota,* 283 U.S. 697 (1931).
16. 403 U.S. 713 (1971).
17. 393 U.S. 503 (1969).
18. 488 U.S. 884 (1989).
19. *United States v. Eichman,* 496 U.S. 310 (1990).

infer it from the cross burnings themselves. In an impassioned dissent, Justice Clarence Thomas, who is African American and usually one of the Court's most conservative members, argued that cross burnings should be automatic evidence of intent to intimidate.[20]

Commercial Speech
Advertising statements, which increasingly have been given First Amendment protection.

Clear and Present Danger Test
The test proposed by Justice Oliver Wendell Holmes for determining when government may restrict free speech. Restrictions are permissible, he argued, only when speech creates a *clear and present danger* to the public order.

The Protection of Commercial Speech

Commercial speech usually is defined as advertising statements. Can advertisers use their First Amendment rights to prevent restrictions on the content of commercial advertising? Until the 1970s, the Supreme Court held that such speech was not protected at all by the First Amendment. By the mid-1970s, however, more and more commercial speech had been brought under First Amendment protection. According to Justice Harry A. Blackmun, "Advertising, however tasteless and excessive it sometimes may seem, is nonetheless dissemination of information as to who is producing and selling what product for what reason and at what price."[21] Nevertheless, the Supreme Court will consider a restriction on commercial speech valid as long as it (1) seeks to implement a substantial government interest, (2) directly advances that interest, and (3) goes no further than necessary to accomplish its objective. In particular, a business engaging in commercial speech can be subject to liability for factual inaccuracies in ways that do not apply to noncommercial speech.

Permitted Restrictions on Expression

At various times, restrictions on expression have been permitted. A description of several such restrictions follows.

Clear and Present Danger. When a person's remarks create a clear and present danger to the peace or public order, they can be curtailed constitutionally. Justice Oliver Wendell Holmes used this reasoning in 1919 when examining the case of a socialist who had been convicted for violating the Espionage Act by distributing a leaflet that opposed the military draft. Holmes stated:

> *The question in every case is whether the words are used in such circumstances and are of such a nature as to create a* clear and present danger *that they will bring about the substantive evils that Congress has a right to prevent. It is a question of proximity and degree.*[22] [Emphasis added.]

According to the **clear and present danger test,** then, expression may be restricted if evidence exists that such expression would cause a dangerous condition, actual or imminent, that Congress has the power to prevent.

Modifications to the Clear and Present Danger Rule. Over the course of the twentieth century, the United States Supreme Court modified the clear and present danger rule, limiting the constitutional protection of free speech in 1925 and 1951, and then broadening it substantially in 1969. In *Gitlow v. New York,*[23] the Court reintroduced the earlier *bad tendency rule,* which placed greater restrictions on speech than Justice Holmes's formulation. According to this rule, speech or other First Amendment freedoms may be curtailed if there is a possibility that such expression might lead to some "evil." In the *Gitlow* case, a member of a left-wing group was convicted of violating New York State's criminal anarchy statute when he published and distributed a pamphlet urging the violent overthrow of the U.S. government. In its majority opinion, the Supreme Court held that

20. *Virginia v. Black,* 538 U.S. 343 (2003).
21. *Virginia State Board of Pharmacy v. Virginia Citizens Consumer Council, Inc.,* 425 U.S. 748 (1976).
22. *Schenck v. United States,* 249 U.S. 47 (1919).
23. 268 U.S. 652 (1925).

the First Amendment afforded protection against state incursions on freedom of expression—the first time that the First Amendment was ever invoked against a state government (see the discussion of incorporation on page 114). Nevertheless, Gitlow could be punished legally in this particular instance because his expression would tend to bring about evils that the state had a right to prevent.

Some claim that the United States did not achieve true freedom of political speech until 1969. In that year, in *Brandenburg v. Ohio*,[24] the Supreme Court overturned the conviction of a Ku Klux Klan leader for violating a state statute. The statute prohibited anyone from advocating "the duty, necessity, or propriety of sabotage, violence, or unlawful methods of terrorism as a means of accomplishing industrial or political reform." The Court held that the guarantee of free speech does not permit a state "to forbid or proscribe [disallow] advocacy of the use of force or of law violation except where such advocacy is directed to inciting or producing imminent lawless actions and is likely to incite or produce such action." The incitement test enunciated by the Court in this case is a difficult one for prosecutors to meet. As a result, the Court's decision significantly broadened the protection given to advocacy speech.

Unprotected Speech: Obscenity

A large number of state and federal statutes make it a crime to disseminate obscene materials. Generally, the courts have not been willing to extend constitutional protections of free speech to what they consider obscene materials. But what is obscenity? Justice Potter Stewart once stated that even though he could not define *obscenity,* "I know it when I see it." The problem, of course, is that even if it were agreed on, the definition of *obscenity* changes with the times. Victorians deeply disapproved of the "loose" morals of the Elizabethan Age. The works of Mark Twain and Edgar Rice Burroughs at times have been considered obscene (after all, Tarzan and Jane were not legally wedded).

Definitional Problems. The Supreme Court has grappled from time to time with the difficulty of specifying an operationally effective definition of **obscenity.** In 1973, in *Miller v. California*,[25] Chief Justice Warren Burger created a formal list of requirements that must be met for material to be legally obscene. Material is obscene if (1) the average person finds that it violates contemporary community standards; (2) the work taken as a whole appeals to a prurient interest in sex; (3) the work shows patently offensive sexual conduct; and (4) the work lacks serious redeeming literary, artistic, political, or scientific merit. The problem, of course, is that one person's prurient interest is another person's medical interest or artistic pleasure. The Court went on to state that the definition of *prurient interest* would be determined by the community's standards. The Court avoided presenting a definition of *obscenity,* leaving this determination to local and state authorities. Consequently, the *Miller* case has been applied in a widely inconsistent manner.

Obscenity
Sexually offensive material. Obscenity can be illegal if it is found to violate a four-part test established by the United States Supreme Court.

Protecting Children. The Supreme Court has upheld state laws making it illegal to sell materials showing sexual performances by minors. In 1990, in *Osborne v. Ohio*,[26] the Court ruled that states can outlaw the possession of child pornography in the home. The Court reasoned that the ban on private possession is justified because owning the material perpetuates commercial demand for it and for the exploitation of the children involved. At the federal level, the Child Protection Act of 1984 made it a crime to receive knowingly through the mail sexually explicit depictions of children. In 2008, the Court upheld the legality of a 2003 federal law that made it a crime to offer child pornography, even if the pornography

24. 395 U.S. 444 (1969).
25. 413 U.S. 5 (1973).
26. 495 U.S. 103 (1990).

First Assistant U.S. Attorney Marc Haws discusses the formation of a statewide Idaho Internet Crimes Against Children Task Force during a press conference in January 2008. What has the federal government done in an attempt to prevent online crimes against children, such as child pornography? (AP Photo/*Idaho Press-Tribune*/Mike Vogt)

in question does not actually exist.[27] The Court also, however, has invalidated a 1996 law banning virtual pornography, which involves only digitally rendered images and no actual children. The Court concluded that the law was overbroad and thus unconstitutional.[28]

Pornography on the Internet. A significant problem facing Americans and their lawmakers today is how to prevent young children from exposure to pornography that is disseminated by way of the Internet. In 1996, Congress first attempted to protect minors from pornographic materials on the Internet by passing the Communications Decency Act (CDA). The act made it a crime to make available to minors online any "obscene or indecent" message that "depicts or describes, in terms patently offensive as measured by contemporary community standards, sexual or excretory activities or organs." The act was immediately challenged in court as an unconstitutional infringement on free speech. The Supreme Court held that the act imposed unconstitutional restraints on free speech and was therefore invalid.[29] In the eyes of the Court, the terms *indecent* and *patently offensive* covered large amounts of nonpornographic material with serious educational or other value.

A second attempt to protect children from online obscenity, the Child Online Protection Act (COPA) of 1998, met with a similar fate. Although the COPA was more narrowly tailored than its predecessor, the CDA, it still used "contemporary community standards" to define which material was obscene and harmful to minors. Ultimately, in 2004 the Supreme Court concluded that it was likely that the COPA did violate the right to free speech, and the Court prevented enforcement of the act.[30]

In 2000, Congress enacted the Children's Internet Protection Act (CIPA), which requires public schools and libraries to install filtering software to prevent children from viewing Web sites with "adult" content. The CIPA was also challenged on constitutional grounds, but in 2003 the Supreme Court held that the act did not violate the First Amendment. The Court concluded that because libraries can disable the filters for any patrons who ask, the system does not burden free speech to an unconstitutional extent.[31]

Unprotected Speech: Slander

Defamation of Character
Wrongfully hurting a person's good reputation. The law imposes a general duty on all persons to refrain from making false, defamatory statements about others.

Can you say anything you want about someone else? Not really. Individuals are protected from **defamation of character,** which is defined as wrongfully hurting a person's good reputation. The law imposes a general duty on all persons to refrain from making false, defamatory statements about others. Breaching this duty orally is the wrongdoing called *slander.* Breaching it in writing is the wrongdoing called *libel,* which we discuss later. The government itself does not bring charges of slander or libel. Rather, the defamed person may bring a civil suit for damages.

27. *United States v. Williams,* 553 U.S. 285 (2008).
28. *Ashcroft v. Free Speech Coalition,* 535 U.S. 234 (2002).
29. *Reno v. American Civil Liberties Union,* 521 U.S. 844 (1997).
30. *American Civil Liberties Union v. Ashcroft,* 542 U.S. 646 (2004).
31. *United States v. American Library Association,* 539 U.S. 194 (2003).

Legally, **slander** is the public uttering of a false statement that harms the good reputation of another. Slanderous public uttering means that the defamatory statements are made to, or within the hearing of, persons other than the defamed party. If one person calls another dishonest, manipulative, and incompetent to his or her face when no one else is around, that does not constitute slander. The message is not communicated to a third party. If, however, a third party accidentally overhears defamatory statements, the courts have generally held that this constitutes a public uttering and therefore slander, which is prohibited.

Slander
The public uttering of a false statement that harms the good reputation of another. The statement must be made to, or within the hearing of, persons other than the defamed party.

Student Speech

In recent years, high school and university students at public institutions have faced a variety of free speech challenges. Court rulings on these issues have varied by the level of school involved. Elementary schools, in particular, have great latitude in determining what kinds of speech are appropriate for their students. High school students have more free speech rights, and college students have the most rights of all.

Rights of Public School Students. High schools can impose speech restrictions that would not be allowed in a college setting or in the general society. For example, high school officials may censor publications such as newspapers and yearbooks produced by the school's students. Courts have argued that a school newspaper is an extension of the school's educational mission, and thus subject to control by the school administration. One of the most striking rulings to illustrate the power of school officials was handed down by the United States Supreme Court in 2007. An Alaska high school student had displayed a banner reading "Bong Hits 4 Jesus" on private property across from the school as students on the school grounds watched the Winter Olympics torch relay. The school principal crossed the street, seized the banner, and suspended the student from school. The Supreme Court later held that the school had an "important—indeed, perhaps compelling—interest" in combating drug use that allowed it to suppress the banner.[32] The Court's decision was widely criticized.

This University of Arizona student demonstrates in favor of what he calls intellectual diversity in the classroom. Some college students believe that their grades will suffer if they are vocal in challenging their professors' political views. Do you believe that this is a serious problem on campus? (AP Photo/*The Arizona Daily Wildcat,* Roxana Vasquez)

College Student Activity Fees. Should a college student have to subsidize, through student activity fees, organizations that promote causes that the student finds objectionable? In 2000, this question came before the Supreme Court in a case brought by several University of Wisconsin students. The students argued that their mandatory student activity fees—which helped to fund liberal causes with which they disagreed, including gay rights—violated their First Amendment rights of free speech, free association, and free exercise of religion. They contended that they should have the right to choose whether to fund organizations that promoted political and ideological views that were offensive to their personal beliefs.

To the surprise of many, the Supreme Court rejected the students' claim and ruled in favor of the university. The Court stated that "the university may determine that its mission is well served if students have the means to engage in dynamic discussions of philosophical, religious, scientific, social and political subjects in their extracurricular life. If the university reaches this conclusion, it is entitled to impose a mandatory fee to sustain an open dialogue to these ends."[33]

Campus Speech and Behavior Codes. Another free speech issue is the legitimacy of campus speech and behavior codes. Some state universities have established codes that challenge the boundaries of the protection of free speech provided by the

32. *Morse v. Frederick,* 551 U.S. 393 (2007).
33. *Board of Regents of the University of Wisconsin System v. Southworth,* 529 U.S. 217 (2000).

First Amendment. These codes are designed to prohibit so-called hate speech—abusive speech attacking persons on the basis of their ethnicity, race, or other criteria. For example, a University of Michigan code banned "any behavior, verbal or physical, that stigmatizes or victimizes an individual on the basis of race, ethnicity, religion, sex, sexual orientation, creed, national origin, ancestry, age, marital status, handicap," or Vietnam-veteran status. A federal court found that the code violated students' First Amendment rights.[34]

Although the courts generally have held, as in the University of Michigan case, that campus speech codes are unconstitutional restrictions on the right to free speech, such codes continue to exist. Defenders of campus speech codes argue that they are necessary not only to prevent violence but also to promote equality among different cultural, ethnic, and racial groups on campus and greater sensitivity to the needs and feelings of others. Most educators acknowledge that a certain degree of civility is required for productive campus discourse. Moreover, some hostile speech can rise to the level of illegal threats or illegal forms of harassment. A number of students also support restraints on campus hate speech. In 2002, for example, the student assembly at Wesleyan University passed a resolution declaring that the "right to speech comes with implicit responsibilities to respect community standards."

Hate Speech on the Internet

Extreme hate speech appears on the Internet, including racist materials and denials of the Holocaust (the murder of millions of Jews by the Nazis during World War II). Can the federal government restrict this type of speech? Should it? Consider that even if Congress succeeded in passing a law prohibiting particular speech on the Internet, an army of "Internet watchers" would be needed to enforce it. Also, what if other countries attempt to impose on U.S. Web sites their laws that restrict speech? This is not a theoretical issue. In 2000, a French court found Yahoo in violation of French laws banning the display of Nazi memorabilia. In 2001, however, a U.S. district court held that this ruling could not be enforced against Yahoo in the United States.[35]

Freedom of the Press

Freedom of the press can be regarded as a special instance of freedom of speech. Of course, at the time of the framing of the Constitution, the press meant only newspapers, magazines, and books. As technology has modified the ways in which we disseminate information, the laws touching on freedom of the press have been modified. What can and cannot be printed still occupies an important place in constitutional law, however.

Defamation in Writing

Libel
A written defamation of a person's character, reputation, business, or property rights.

Libel is defamation in writing (or in pictures, signs, films, or any other communication that has the potentially harmful qualities of written or printed words). As with slander, libel occurs only if the defamatory statements are observed by a third party. If one person writes a private letter to another wrongfully accusing him or her of embezzling funds, that does not constitute libel. It is interesting that the courts have generally held that dictating a letter to a secretary constitutes communication of the letter's contents to a third party, and therefore, if defamation has occurred, the wrongdoer can be sued.

A 1964 case, *New York Times Co. v. Sullivan,*[36] explored an important question regarding libelous statements made about public officials. The Supreme Court held that only

---

34. *Doe v. University of Michigan,* 721 F. Supp. 852 (1989).
35. *Yahoo!, Inc. v. La Ligue Contre le Racisme et l'Antisémitisme,* 169 F.Supp.2d 1181 (N.D.Cal. 2001).
36. 376 U.S. 254 (1964).

when a statement against a public official was made with **actual malice**—that is, with either knowledge of its falsity or a reckless disregard for the truth—could damages be obtained.

The standard set by the Court in the *New York Times* case has since been applied to **public figures** generally. Public figures include not only public officials but also public employees who exercise substantial governmental power and any persons, such as movie stars, who are generally in the public limelight. Statements made about public figures, especially when they are made through a public medium, usually are related to matters of general public interest. They are made about people who substantially affect all of us. Furthermore, public figures generally have some access to a public medium for answering disparaging falsehoods about themselves, whereas private individuals do not. For these reasons, public figures have a greater burden of proof in defamation cases than do private individuals; they must prove that the statements were made with actual malice.

Generally, libel is more difficult to prove in the United States than in many other countries. The person who claims that he or she was libeled bears the burden of proving his or her case in court. British courts, in contrast, place the burden of proof on the accused. We take a brief look at British libel law in this chapter's *Beyond Our Borders* feature on the following page.

Actual Malice
Either knowledge of a defamatory statement's falsity or a reckless disregard for the truth.

Public Figure
A public official, a public employee who exercises substantial governmental power, or any other person, such as a movie star, known to the public because of his or her position or activities.

Gag Order
An order issued by a judge restricting the publication of news about a trial or a pretrial hearing to protect the accused's right to a fair trial.

A Free Press versus a Fair Trial: Gag Orders

Another major issue relating to freedom of the press concerns media coverage of criminal trials. The Sixth Amendment to the Constitution guarantees the right of criminal suspects to a fair trial. In other words, the accused have rights. The First Amendment guarantees freedom of the press. What if the two rights appear to be in conflict? Which one prevails?

Jurors certainly may be influenced by reading news stories about the trial in which they are participating. In the 1970s, judges increasingly issued **gag orders,** orders that restricted the publication of news about a trial in progress or even a pretrial hearing to protect the accused's right to a fair trial. In a landmark 1976 case, *Nebraska Press Association v. Stuart,*[37] the Supreme Court unanimously ruled that a Nebraska judge's gag order had violated the First Amendment's guarantee of freedom of the press. Chief Justice Warren Burger indicated that even pervasive adverse pretrial publicity did not necessarily lead to an unfair trial and that prior restraints on publication were not justified. Despite the *Nebraska Press Association* ruling, the Court has upheld gag orders when it believed that publicity was likely to harm a defendant's right to a fair trial.

Films, Radio, and TV

As we have noted, in only a few cases has the Supreme Court upheld prior restraint of published materials. The Court's reluctance to accept prior restraint is less evident with respect to motion pictures. In the first half of the twentieth century, films were routinely submitted to local censorship boards. In 1968, the Supreme Court ruled that a film can be banned only under a law that provides for a prompt hearing at which the film is shown to be obscene. Today, few local censorship boards exist. Instead, the film industry regulates itself primarily through the industry's rating system.

Radio and television broadcasting has the least First Amendment protection. Broadcasting initially received less protection than the printed media because, at that time, the number of airwave frequencies was limited. In

This student in West Virginia shows two popular books written by Pat Conroy that were banned from use in English classes in Nitro High School in Charleston, West Virginia. The ban occurred after several parents of students complained about the author's depiction of violence, suicide, and sexual assault. Should high school English teachers be able to use any works of fiction they wish to in their classes? (AP Photo/Jeff Gentner)

37. 427 U.S. 539 (1976).

1934, the national government established the Federal Communications Commission (FCC) to regulate electromagnetic wave frequencies. No one has a right to use the airwaves without a license granted by the FCC. The FCC grants licenses for limited periods and imposes a variety of regulations on broadcasting. For example, the FCC can impose sanctions on radio or TV stations that broadcast "filthy words," even if the words are not legally obscene.

The Right to Privacy

No explicit reference is made anywhere in the Constitution to a person's right to privacy. Until the second half of the 1900s, the courts did not take a very positive approach toward the right to privacy. For example, during Prohibition, suspected bootleggers' telephones were tapped routinely, and the information obtained was used as a legal basis for prosecution. In *Olmstead v. United States*[38] in 1928, the Supreme Court upheld such an invasion of privacy. Justice Louis Brandeis, a champion of personal freedoms, strongly dissented

---

38. 277 U.S. 438 (1928). This decision was overruled later in *Katz v. United States,* 389 U.S. 347 (1967).

BEYOND OUR BORDERS

THE TROUBLE WITH BRITISH LIBEL LAW

Because Americans value free speech highly, it is not easy to sue someone for libel successfully. Britain, in contrast, has a much lower standard for proving libel.

THE DIFFERENCE BETWEEN U.S. AND BRITISH LAWS

To succeed in a libel suit in the United States, the *plaintiff,* the person who is suing, has to prove that the offending speech was false and published with reckless disregard for the truth. In contrast, British law assumes that any offending speech is false. It is the writer or author who must prove that it is in fact true in order to prevail against a libel charge.

Britain also has been willing to hear cases in which the alleged libel took place in another country. As a result, during the past decade, Britain has become the international destination of choice for those who wish to file libel suits. For example, a Tunisian businessperson sued Al Arabiya, a satellite television network based in Dubai and broadcasting in Arabic, in London. The Tunisian disputed allegations that he had ties to terrorist groups. Why London? The Al Arabiya program was available by satellite in Britain. A court awarded the plaintiff $325,000.

A further problem is that defending oneself against a libel suit in Britain is very expensive. A wealthy plaintiff can wind up bankrupting a defendant even if the plaintiff's case is weak.

SOME STATES AND CITIES IN THE UNITED STATES FIGHT BACK

In reaction to easy libel lawsuits in Britain, some states and cities in the United States have adopted laws to protect their citizens. An example is New York State's Libel Terrorism Protection Act. It protects New York–based publishers and writers from the enforcement of most foreign libel judgments. California, Florida, and Illinois have passed similar laws.

FOR CRITICAL ANALYSIS

British lawmakers are considering reforming their nation's libel laws. Why might they do this?

from the majority decision in this case, though. He argued that the framers of the Constitution gave every citizen the right to be left alone. He called such a right "the most comprehensive of rights and the right most valued by civilized men."

In the 1960s, the highest court began to modify the majority view. In 1965, in *Griswold v. Connecticut,*[39] the Supreme Court overturned a Connecticut law that effectively prohibited the use of contraceptives, holding that the law violated the right to privacy. Justice William O. Douglas formulated a unique way of reading this right into the Bill of Rights. He claimed that the First, Third, Fourth, Fifth, and Ninth Amendments created "penumbras [shadows], formed by emanations [things sent out] from those guarantees that help give them life and substance," and he went on to describe zones of privacy that are guaranteed by these rights. When we read the Ninth Amendment, we can see the foundation for his reasoning: "The enumeration in the Constitution, of certain rights, shall not be construed to deny or disparage [belittle] others retained by the people." In other words, just because the Constitution, including its amendments, does not specifically talk about the right to privacy does not mean that this right is denied to the people.

Some of today's most controversial issues relate to privacy rights. One issue involves the erosion of privacy rights in an information age, as computers make it easier to compile and distribute personal information. Other issues concern abortion and the "right to die."

Privacy Rights in an Information Age

An important privacy issue, created in part by new technology, is the amassing of information on individuals by government agencies and private businesses such as marketing firms. Personal information on the average American citizen is filed away in dozens of agencies—such as the Social Security Administration and the Internal Revenue Service. Because of the threat of indiscriminate use of private information by unauthorized individuals, Congress passed the Privacy Act in 1974. This was the first law regulating the use of federal government information about private individuals. Under the Privacy Act, every citizen has the right to obtain copies of personal records collected by federal agencies and to correct inaccuracies in such records.

The ease with which personal information can be obtained by using the Internet for marketing and other purposes has led to unique privacy issues. Some fear that privacy rights in personal information may soon be a thing of the past. Whether privacy rights can survive in an information age is a question that Americans continue to confront.

Privacy Rights and Abortion

Historically, abortion was not a criminal offense before the "quickening" of the fetus (the first movement of the fetus in the uterus, usually between the sixteenth and eighteenth weeks of pregnancy). During the last half of the nineteenth century, however, state laws became more severe. By 1973, performing an abortion at any time during pregnancy was a criminal offense in a majority of the states.

Roe v. Wade. In 1973, in *Roe v. Wade,*[40] the United States Supreme Court accepted the argument that the laws against abortion violated "Jane Roe's" right to privacy under the Constitution. The Court held that during the first trimester (three months) of pregnancy, abortion was an issue solely between a woman and her physician. The state could not limit abortions except to require that they be performed by licensed physicians. During the second trimester, to protect the health of the mother, the state was allowed to specify the conditions under which an abortion could be performed. During the final trimester,

---

39. 381 U.S. 479 (1965).
40. 410 U.S. 113 (1973). Jane Roe was not the real name of the woman in this case. It is a common legal pseudonym used to protect a person's privacy.

the state could regulate or even outlaw abortions except when necessary to preserve the life or health of the mother.

After the *Roe* case, the Supreme Court issued decisions in a number of cases defining and redefining the boundaries of state regulation of abortion. During the 1980s, the Court twice struck down laws that required a woman who wished to have an abortion to undergo counseling designed to discourage abortions. In the late 1980s and early 1990s, however, the Court took a more conservative approach. For example, in *Webster v. Reproductive Health Services*[41] in 1989, the Court upheld a Missouri statute that, among other things, banned the use of public hospitals or other taxpayer-supported facilities for performing abortions. And, in *Planned Parenthood v. Casey*[42] in 1992, the Court upheld a Pennsylvania law that required pre-abortion counseling, a waiting period of twenty-four hours, and, for girls under the age of eighteen, parental or judicial permission. As a result, abortions are now more difficult to obtain in some states than others.

This protester stands in front of the Planned Parenthood center in Aurora, Illinois. What limits are placed on anti-abortion protesters? (AP Photo/ Stacie Freudenberg)

Protests at Abortion Clinics. Because of several episodes of violence attending protests at abortion clinics, in 1994 Congress passed the Freedom of Access to Clinic Entrances Act. The act prohibits protesters from blocking entrances to such clinics. The Supreme Court ruled in 1993 that such protesters can be prosecuted under laws governing racketeering, and in 1998 a federal court in Illinois convicted right-to-life protesters under these laws. In 2006, however, the Supreme Court unanimously reversed its earlier decision that right-to-life protesters could be prosecuted under laws governing racketeering.[43]

In 1997, the Supreme Court upheld the constitutionality of prohibiting protesters from entering a fifteen-foot "buffer zone" around abortion clinics and from giving unwanted counseling to those entering the clinics.[44] In a 2000 decision, the Court upheld a Colorado law requiring demonstrators to stay at least eight feet away from people entering and leaving clinics unless people consented to be approached. The Court concluded that the law's restrictions on speech-related conduct did not violate the free speech rights of abortion protesters.[45]

Partial-Birth Abortion. Another issue in the abortion controversy concerns "partial-birth" abortion. A partial-birth abortion, which physicians call intact dilation and extraction, is a procedure that can be used during the second trimester of pregnancy. Abortion rights advocates claim that in limited circumstances the procedure is the safest way to perform an abortion and that the government should never outlaw specific medical procedures. Opponents argue that the procedure has no medical merit and that it ends the life of a fetus that might be able to live outside the womb.

In 2000, the Supreme Court addressed this issue when it reviewed a Nebraska law banning partial-birth abortions. Similar laws had been passed by at least twenty-seven states. The Court invalidated the Nebraska law on the ground that, as written, the law could be used to ban other abortion procedures and contained no provisions for protecting the health of the pregnant woman.[46]

---

41. 492 U.S. 490 (1989).
42. 505 U.S. 833 (1992).
43. *Scheidler v. National Organization for Women,* 547 U.S. 9 (2006).
44. *Schenck v. ProChoice Network,* 519 U.S. 357 (1997).
45. *Hill v. Colorado,* 530 U.S. 703 (2000).
46. *Stenberg v. Carhart,* 530 U.S. 914 (2000).

In 2003, legislation similar to the Nebraska statute was passed by the U.S. Congress and signed into law by President George W. Bush. In 2007, the Supreme Court, with several changes in membership since the 2000 ruling, upheld the federal law in a five-to-four vote, effectively reversing its position on partial-birth abortion.[47] Furthermore, said the Court, "government has a legitimate and substantial interest in preserving and promoting fetal life." The Court also noted that there was an alternative (though less safe, according to the act's opponents) abortion procedure that could be used in the second trimester. The Court emphasized that the law allowed partial-birth abortion to be performed when a woman's life was in jeopardy. In her dissent to the majority opinion, Justice Ruth Bader Ginsburg said that the ruling "cannot be understood as anything other than an effort to chip away at a right declared again and again by this Court"—that right being a woman's right to choose.

The Controversy Continues. Abortion continues to be a divisive issue. Right-to-life forces continue to push for laws banning abortion, to endorse political candidates who support their views, and to organize protests. In recent years, abortion opponents have concentrated on state ballot proposals that could lay the groundwork for an eventual challenge to *Roe.* They have not been very successful, however. In 2008, Colorado voters rejected a measure that would have granted full constitutional rights to a fertilized egg. The Colorado proposal failed by a margin of almost three to one. Also in 2008, South Dakota voters refused to ban most abortions in that state. Two years earlier, in 2006, South Dakotans had rejected a measure that would have banned all abortions, even in cases of incest, rape, or danger to the mother's life or health.

Privacy Rights and the "Right to Die"

A 1976 case involving Karen Ann Quinlan was one of the first publicized "right-to-die" cases.[48] The parents of Quinlan, a young woman who had been in a coma for nearly a year and who had been kept alive during that time by a respirator, wanted her respirator removed. In 1976, the New Jersey Supreme Court ruled that the right to privacy includes the right of a patient to refuse treatment and that patients unable to speak can exercise that right through a family member or guardian. In 1990, the Supreme Court took up the issue. In *Cruzan v. Director, Missouri Department of Health,*[49] the Court stated that a patient's life-sustaining treatment can be withdrawn at the request of a family member only if there is "clear and convincing evidence" that the patient did not want such treatment.

What If There Is No Living Will? Since the 1976 *Quinlan* decision, most states have enacted laws permitting people to designate their wishes concerning life-sustaining procedures in "living wills" or durable health-care powers of attorney. These laws and the Supreme Court's *Cruzan* decision have resolved the right-to-die controversy for situations in which the patient has drafted a living will. Disputes are still possible if there is no living will. An example is the case of Terri Schiavo. The husband of the Florida woman who had been in a persistent vegetative state for more than a decade sought to have her feeding tube removed on the basis of oral statements that she would not want her life prolonged in such circumstances. Schiavo's parents fought this move in court but lost on the ground that a spouse, not a parent, is the appropriate legal guardian for a married person. Although the Florida legislature passed a law allowing Governor Jeb Bush to overrule the courts, the state supreme court held that the law violated the state constitution.[50]

---

47. *Gonzales v. Carhart,* 550 U.S. 124 (2007).
48. *In re Quinlan,* 70 N.J. 10 (1976).
49. 497 U.S. 261 (1990).
50. *Bush v. Schiavo,* 885 So.2d 321 (Fla. 2004).

Physician-assisted suicide continues to be an emotional issue for many Americans. Only three states allow such action by physicians. Does the Constitution give any guidelines about the "right-to-die" controversy? (AP Photo/ Charles Dharapak)

In March 2005, the U.S. Congress intervened and passed a law allowing Schiavo's case to be heard in the federal court system. The federal courts, however, essentially agreed with the Florida state courts and refused to order the reconnection of the feeding tube, which had been disconnected a few days earlier. After twice appealing to the United States Supreme Court without success, the parents gave up hope, and Schiavo died shortly thereafter.

Physician-Assisted Suicide. In the 1990s, another issue surfaced: Do privacy rights include the right of terminally ill people to end their lives through physician-assisted suicide? Until 1996, the courts consistently upheld state laws that prohibited this practice, either through specific statutes or under their general homicide statutes. In 1996, after two federal appellate courts ruled that state laws banning assisted suicide (in Washington and New York) were unconstitutional, the issue reached the United States Supreme Court. In 1997, in *Washington v. Glucksberg,*[51] the Court stated that the liberty interest protected by the Constitution does not include a right to commit suicide, with or without assistance. In effect, the Supreme Court left the decision to the states. Since then, assisted suicide has been allowed in only three states—Montana, Oregon, and Washington. In 2006, the Supreme Court upheld Oregon's physician-assisted suicide law against a challenge from the Bush administration.[52]

Civil Liberties versus Security Issues

As former Supreme Court justice Thurgood Marshall once said, "Grave threats to liberty often come in times of urgency, when constitutional rights seem too extravagant to endure." Not surprisingly, antiterrorist legislation since the attacks on September 11, 2001, has eroded certain basic rights, in particular the Fourth Amendment protections against unreasonable searches and seizures.

Roving Wiretaps

One Fourth Amendment issue involves legislation that allows the government to conduct "roving" wiretaps. Previously, only specific telephone numbers, cell phone numbers, or computers could be tapped. Now a person under suspicion can be monitored electronically no matter what form of electronic communication he or she uses. Such roving wiretaps contravene the Supreme Court's interpretation of the Fourth Amendment, which requires a judicial warrant to describe the place to be searched, not just the person. One of the goals of the framers was to avoid general searches. Further, once a judge approves an application for a roving wiretap, when, how, and where the monitoring occurs is left to the discretion of law enforcement agents. As an unavoidable result, a third party may have access to the conversations and e-mails of hundreds of people who falsely believe them to be private.

---

51. 521 U.S. 702 (1997).
52. *Gonzales v. Oregon,* 546 U.S. 243 (2006).

The USA Patriot Act

Much of the government's failure to anticipate the terrorist attacks of September 11, 2001, has been attributed to a lack of cooperation among government agencies. At that time, barriers prevented information sharing between the law enforcement and intelligence arms of the government. Lawmakers claimed that the USA Patriot Act of 2001 would improve lines of communication between agencies such as the Federal Bureau of Investigation (FBI) and the Central Intelligence Agency (CIA), allowing the government to better anticipate terrorist plots.

The Patriot Act also eased restrictions on the government's ability to investigate and arrest suspected terrorists. Because of the secretive nature of terrorist groups, supporters of the Patriot Act argue that the government must have greater latitude in pursuing leads on potential terrorist activity. The act authorizes law enforcement officials to secretly search a suspected terrorist's home. It also allows the government to monitor a suspect's Internet activities, phone conversations, financial records, and book purchases. For the first time in American history, the government can even open a suspect's mail. Under the Patriot Act, FBI agents are required to certify the need for search warrants to the court, but the court cannot, in fact, reject the request for a warrant.

National Security Letters. The Patriot Act also authorized National Security Letters (NSLs), which are subpoenas issued by the FBI itself and which do not require probable cause or judicial oversight. In addition, an individual or financial institution that is served with such a warrant cannot speak about the government's investigation to anyone. Thus, many argue that this provision of the Patriot Act contradicts the First Amendment by making free speech a crime. In addition to First Amendment issues, this provision raises the concern that no one would be allowed to blow the whistle on abuses of the government's powers. As a result of these concerns, a U.S. district court found the NSL provisions of the Patriot Act to be unconstitutional in 2004 and again in 2007.[53] Finally, if the government decides to take a suspected terrorist into custody, the suspect can be summarily denied bail—a breach of the Eighth Amendment.

Civil Liberties and the Patriot Act. Proponents of the Patriot Act insist that ordinary, law-abiding citizens have nothing to fear from the government's increased search and surveillance powers. Groups such as the American Civil Liberties Union have objected to the Patriot Act, however, arguing that it poses a grave threat to constitutionally guaranteed rights and liberties. Opponents of the Patriot Act fear that these expanded powers of investigation might be used to silence government critics or to threaten members of interest groups who oppose government policies today or in the future.

Congress debated all of these issues in 2005 and then renewed most of the provisions of the act in 2006. It is certainly true that the government has used the Patriot Act to develop cases that have nothing at all to do with terrorism, as we show in this chapter's *Politics and Privacy* feature on the next page.

National Security Agency Surveillance

Shortly after 9/11, President George W. Bush issued an executive order authorizing the National Security Agency (NSA) to conduct secret surveillance. The NSA was ordered to monitor, without obtaining warrants, phone calls and other communications between

---

53. *Doe v. Ashcroft,* 334 F.Supp.2d 471 (S.D.N.Y. 2004); and *Doe v. Gonzales,* 500 F.Supp.2d 379 (S.D.N.Y. 2007).

foreign parties and persons within the United States when one of the parties had suspected links to a terrorist organization. When the American public learned of this secret program in December 2005, the news led to intense criticism by civil liberties groups. These groups and other Americans called for the immediate termination of the allegedly illegal surveillance.

In 2007, Congress passed a law to authorize the warrantless NSA wiretaps. The law expired in 2008, however, and its reauthorization was held up by a dispute between Congress and the Bush administration as to whether telephone companies should receive blanket immunity from lawsuits stemming from their past cooperation with the wiretaps. When it finally passed, the reauthorization protected the telephone companies, as Bush

POLITICS AND... privacy

SOME UNINTENDED CONSEQUENCES OF THE PATRIOT ACT

"Client 9" had arranged to meet a prostitute named "Kristen" in room 871 of the Mayflower Hotel in Washington, D.C. Kristen reported back to her employer that Client 9 had paid her $4,300 (part of this amount was offered as a "down payment" for the next encounter). Not too long afterward, federal investigators informed the governor of New York, Eliot Spitzer, that they knew he was Client 9. Spitzer eventually resigned in one of the most high-profile sex scandals in his state's history. Less widely known is the fact that it was the USA Patriot Act that caused him to be snagged by the federal government.

AFTER THE 9/11 ATTACKS, CONGRESS PASSED THE PATRIOT ACT

Most law enforcement agencies hailed the Patriot Act as a powerful tool that would allow them to track down the accomplices of Osama bin Laden, the mastermind behind the suicide attacks against the World Trade Center Towers in New York City and the Pentagon in Washington, D.C. The Patriot Act gave the Federal Bureau of Investigation (FBI) increased authority to snoop on unsuspecting terrorists.

In the fine print of that act, the Treasury Department was authorized to demand more information from banks about financial transactions. The goal was to seek out terrorists who were laundering money through the U.S. banking system. Banks are now required to report any unusual transactions by submitting Suspicious Activity Reports (SARs). Banks spent tens of millions of dollars to develop sophisticated software to do just that. In 2001, they submitted 200,000 SARs, and that number has jumped to about 1.5 million today. These data are stored in an Internal Revenue Service (IRS) building in Detroit and are accessible by law enforcement agencies throughout the country.

THE NET CLOSES AROUND ELIOT SPITZER

In the summer of 2007, New York's North Fork Bank filed a SAR about money transfers that Governor Spitzer had made. Spitzer had asked the bank to transfer funds in someone else's name. Federal authorities became curious enough to follow the money trail. They ultimately discovered that New York's governor had wired $80,000 to various accounts that looked suspicious. The authorities then learned that the accounts were owned by an Internet prostitution service. The rest is now part of New York's colorful history.

In the end, Spitzer was not prosecuted because he did not use public funds to pay for his trysts. Since then, he has become a columnist for Slate.com specializing in the financial crisis, appears on MSNBC, and has made regular public appearances in an attempt to rehabilitate his reputation.

FOR CRITICAL ANALYSIS

Why do you think banks in this country cooperate so completely with the federal government?

had wanted. The law was supported by, among others, the then Illinois senator Barack Obama, who received criticism from fellow Democrats for his vote.

The Great Balancing Act: The Rights of the Accused versus the Rights of Society

The United States has one of the highest murder rates in the industrialized world. It is not surprising, therefore, that many citizens have extremely strong opinions about the rights of those accused of violent crimes. When an accused person, especially one who has confessed to some criminal act, is set free because of an apparent legal "technicality," many people believe that the rights of the accused are being given more weight than the rights of society and of potential or actual victims. Why, then, give criminal suspects rights? The answer is partly to avoid convicting innocent people, but mostly because due process of law and fair treatment benefit everyone who comes in contact with law enforcement or the courts.

The courts and the police must constantly engage in a balancing act of competing rights. At the basis of all discussions about the appropriate balance is, of course, the U.S. Bill of Rights. The Fourth, Fifth, Sixth, and Eighth Amendments deal specifically with the rights of criminal defendants. (You will learn about some of your rights under the Fourth Amendment in the *Why Should You Care about Civil Liberties?* feature at the end of this chapter.)

Rights of the Accused

The basic rights of criminal defendants are outlined next. When appropriate, the specific constitutional provision or amendment on which a right is based is also given.

Limits on the Conduct of Police Officers and Prosecutors

- No unreasonable or unwarranted searches and seizures (Amend. IV).
- No arrest except on probable cause (Amend. IV).
- No coerced confessions or illegal interrogation (Amend. V).
- No entrapment.
- On questioning, a suspect must be informed of her or his rights.

Defendant's Pretrial Rights

- **Writ of *habeas corpus*** (Article I, Section 9).
- Prompt **arraignment** (Amend. VI).
- Legal counsel (Amend. VI).
- Reasonable bail (Amend. VIII).
- To be informed of charges (Amend. VI).
- To remain silent (Amend. V).

Writ of *Habeas Corpus*
Habeas corpus means, literally, "you have the body." A writ of *habeas corpus* is an order that requires jailers to bring a prisoner before a court or a judge and explain why the person is being held.

Arraignment
The first act in a criminal proceeding, in which the defendant is brought before a court to hear the charges against him or her and enter a plea of guilty or not guilty.

Trial Rights

- Speedy and public trial before a jury (Amend. VI).
- Impartial jury selected from a cross section of the community (Amend. VI).
- Trial atmosphere free of prejudice, fear, and outside interference.
- No compulsory self-incrimination (Amend. V).
- Adequate counsel (Amend. VI).
- No cruel and unusual punishment (Amend. VIII).
- Appeal of convictions.
- No double jeopardy (Amend. V).

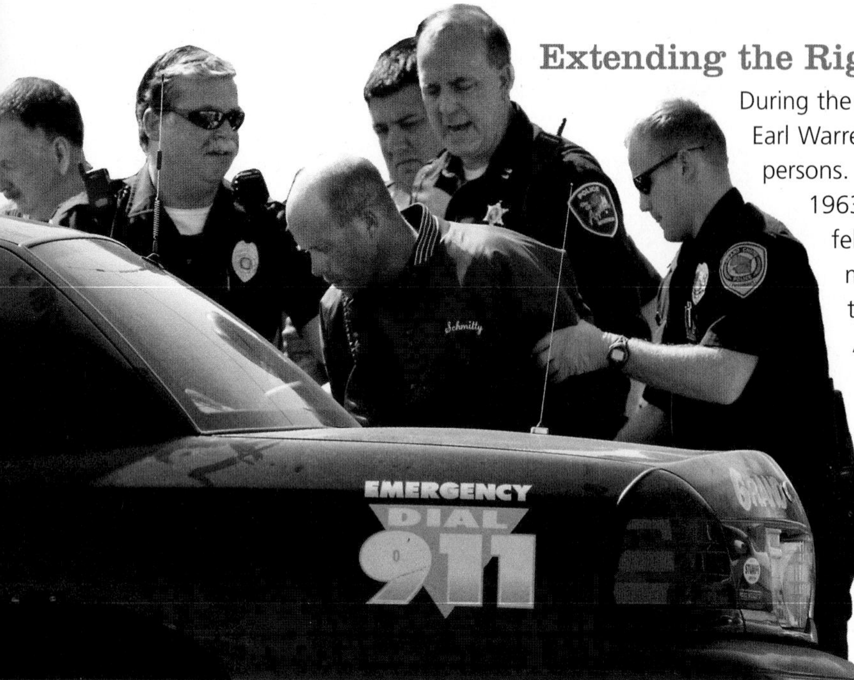

These Grand Chute, Wisconsin, police officers are arresting Scott E. Schmidt after he killed his wife and his mother-in-law. What rights did Schmidt have after his arrest? (AP Photo/ Post-Crescent, Sharon Cekada)

Extending the Rights of the Accused

During the 1960s, the Supreme Court, under Chief Justice Earl Warren, significantly expanded the rights of accused persons. In *Gideon v. Wainwright,*[54] a case decided in 1963, the Court held that if a person is accused of a felony and cannot afford an attorney, an attorney must be made available to the accused person at the government's expense. Although the Sixth Amendment to the Constitution provides for the right to counsel, the Court had previously held that only criminal defendants in capital (death penalty) cases automatically had a right to legal counsel.

Miranda v. Arizona. In 1966, the Court issued its decision in *Miranda v. Arizona.*[55] The case involved Ernesto Miranda, who was arrested and charged with the kidnapping and rape of a young woman. After two hours of questioning, Miranda confessed and was later convicted. Miranda's lawyer appealed his conviction, arguing that the police had never informed Miranda that he had a right to remain silent and a right to be represented by counsel. The Court, in ruling in Miranda's favor, enunciated the *Miranda* rights that are now familiar to almost all Americans:

> *Prior to any questioning, the person must be warned that he has a right to remain silent, that any statement he does make may be used against him, and that he has a right to the presence of an attorney, either retained or appointed.*

Exceptions to the *Miranda* Rule. As part of a continuing attempt to balance the rights of accused persons against the rights of society, the Supreme Court has made a number of exceptions to the *Miranda* rule. In 1984, for example, the Court recognized a "public-safety" exception to the rule. The need to protect the public warranted the admissibility of statements made by the defendant (in this case, indicating where he had placed a gun) as evidence in a trial, even though the defendant had not been informed of his *Miranda* rights.

In 1985, the Court further held that a confession need not be excluded even though the police failed to inform a suspect in custody that his attorney had tried to reach him by telephone. In an important 1991 decision, the Court stated that a suspect's conviction will not be automatically overturned if the suspect was coerced into making a confession. If the other evidence admitted at trial is strong enough to justify the conviction without the confession, then the fact that the confession was obtained illegally in effect can be ignored.[56] In yet another case, in 1994, the Supreme Court ruled that suspects must unequivocally and assertively state their right to counsel in order to stop police questioning. Saying, "Maybe I should talk to a lawyer" during an interrogation after being taken into custody is not enough. The Court held that police officers are not required to decipher the suspect's intentions in such situations.[57]

---

54. 372 U.S. 335 (1963).
55. 384 U.S. 436 (1966).
56. *Arizona v. Fulminante,* 499 U.S. 279 (1991).
57. *Davis v. United States,* 512 U.S. 452 (1994).

Video Recording of Interrogations. In view of the numerous exceptions, there are no guarantees that the *Miranda* rule will survive indefinitely. Increasingly, though, law enforcement personnel are using digital movie cameras to record interrogations. According to some scholars, the recording of *all* custodial interrogations would satisfy the Fifth Amendment's prohibition against coercion and in the process render the *Miranda* warnings unnecessary. Others argue, however, that recorded interrogations can be misleading.

The Exclusionary Rule

At least since 1914, judicial policy has prohibited the admission of illegally seized evidence at trials in federal courts. This is the so-called **exclusionary rule.** Improperly obtained evidence, no matter how telling, cannot be used by prosecutors. This includes evidence obtained by police in violation of a suspect's *Miranda* rights or of the Fourth Amendment. The Fourth Amendment protects against unreasonable searches and seizures and provides that a judge may issue a search warrant to a police officer only on *probable cause* (a demonstration of facts that permit a reasonable belief that a crime has been committed). The courts must determine what constitutes an "unreasonable" search and seizure.

Exclusionary Rule
A judicial policy prohibiting the admission at trial of illegally seized evidence.

The reasoning behind the exclusionary rule is that it forces police officers to gather evidence properly, in which case their due diligence will be rewarded by a conviction. Nevertheless, the exclusionary rule has always had critics who argue that it permits guilty persons to be freed because of innocent errors.

This rule was first extended to state court proceedings in a 1961 United States Supreme Court decision, *Mapp v. Ohio.*[58] In this case, the Court overturned the conviction of Dollree Mapp for the possession of obscene materials. Police found pornographic books in her apartment after searching it without a search warrant and despite her refusal to let them in.

During the past several decades, the Supreme Court has diminished the scope of the exclusionary rule by creating some exceptions to its applicability. For example, in 1984 the Court held that illegally obtained evidence could be admitted at trial if law enforcement personnel could prove that they would have obtained the evidence legally anyway. In another case decided in the same year, the Court held that a police officer who used a technically incorrect search warrant form to obtain evidence had acted in good faith and therefore the evidence was admissible at trial. The Court thus created the "good faith" exception to the exclusionary rule. In 2009, for example, the Court found that the good faith exception applies when an officer makes an arrest based on an outstanding warrant in another jurisdiction, even if the warrant in question was based on a clerical error.[59]

Under the Fourth Amendment, search warrants must describe the persons or things to be seized. In addition, however, officers are entitled to seize items not mentioned in the search warrant if the materials are in "plain view" and reasonably appear to be contraband or evidence of a crime.[60]

The Death Penalty

Capital punishment remains one of the most debated aspects of our criminal justice system. Those in favor of the death penalty maintain that it serves as a deterrent to serious crime and satisfies society's need for justice and fair play. Those opposed to the death penalty do not believe

did you know?
That in eighteenth-century England, pocket picking and similar crimes were punishable by the death penalty.

---

58. 367 U.S. 643 (1961).
59. *Herring v. United States,* 555 U.S. ___ (2009).
60. *Texas v. Brown,* 460 U.S. 730 (1983); and *Horton v. California,* 496 U.S. 128 (1990).

it has any deterrent value and hold that it constitutes a barbaric act in an otherwise civilized society.

Capital punishment elicits strong sentiment by those who are for or against this criminal penalty. Is the death penalty a "cruel and unusual" punishment and therefore prohibited by the Eighth Amendment? (AP Photo/Charles Smith)

Cruel and Unusual Punishment?

The Eighth Amendment prohibits cruel and unusual punishment. Throughout history, "cruel and unusual" referred to punishments that were more serious than the crimes—the phrase referred to torture and to executions that prolonged the agony of dying. The Supreme Court has never interpreted "cruel and unusual" as prohibiting all forms of capital punishment in all circumstances. Indeed, a number of states have imposed the death penalty for a variety of crimes and allowed juries to decide when the condemned could be sentenced to death. Many people came to believe, however, that the imposition of the death penalty was random and arbitrary, and in 1972 the Supreme Court agreed, in *Furman v. Georgia.*[61]

The Supreme Court's 1972 decision stated that the death penalty, as then applied, violated the Eighth and Fourteenth Amendments. The Court ruled that capital punishment is not necessarily cruel and unusual if the criminal has killed or attempted to kill someone. In its opinion, the Court invited the states to enact more precise laws so that the death penalty would be applied more consistently. By 1976, twenty-five states had adopted a two-stage, or *bifurcated,* procedure for capital cases. In the first stage, a jury determines the guilt or innocence of the defendant for a crime that has been determined by statute to be punishable by death. If the defendant is found guilty, the jury reconvenes in the second stage and considers all relevant evidence to decide whether the death sentence is, in fact, warranted.

In 1976, in *Gregg v. Georgia,*[62] the Supreme Court ruled in favor of Georgia's bifurcated process, holding that the state's legislative guidelines had removed the ability of a jury to "wantonly and freakishly impose the death penalty." The Court upheld similar procedures in Texas and Florida, establishing a "road map" for all states to follow that would assure them protection from lawsuits based on Eighth Amendment grounds.

The Death Penalty Today

Today, thirty-five states (see Figure 4–1 on the facing page) and the federal government have capital punishment laws based on the guidelines established by the *Gregg* case. State governments are responsible for almost all executions in this country. At this time, there are about 3,280 prisoners on death row across the nation.

The number of executions per year reached a high in 1998 at ninety-eight and then began to fall. Some believe that the declining number of executions reflects the waning support among Americans for the imposition of the death penalty. In 1994, polls indicated that 80 percent of Americans supported the death penalty in cases involving murder. Recent polls, however, suggest that this number has dropped to about 65 percent.

The decline in the number of executions may be due in part to the Supreme Court's 2002 ruling in *Ring v. Arizona.*[63] The Court held that only juries, not judges, could impose the death penalty, thus invalidating the laws of five states that allowed judges to make this decision. The ruling meant that the death sentences of 168 death row inmates would have to be reconsidered by the relevant courts. The sentences of many of these inmates have been commuted to life in prison.

---

61. 408 U.S. 238 (1972).
62. 428 U.S. 153 (1976).
63. 536 U.S. 548 (2002).

Time Limits for Death Row Appeals

In 1996, Congress passed the Anti-Terrorism and Effective Death Penalty Act. The law limits access to the federal courts for defendants convicted in state courts. It also imposes a severe time limit on death row appeals. The law requires federal judges to hear these appeals and issue their opinions within a specified time period. Many are concerned that the shortened appeals process increases the possibility that innocent persons may be put to death. Recently, DNA testing has shown that some innocent people may have been convicted unjustly of murder. Since 1973, more than one hundred prisoners have been freed from death row after new evidence suggested that they were convicted wrongfully. On average, it takes about seven years to exonerate someone on death row. Currently, however, the time between conviction and execution has been shortened from an average of ten to twelve years to an average of six to eight years.

Methods of Execution

The most recent controversy concerning the death penalty is whether execution by injecting the condemned prisoner with lethal drugs is a cruel and unusual punishment. Lethal injection is currently used in almost all executions. Evidence exists that when performed incompetently, death by lethal injection can be extremely painful. Some death penalty opponents have claimed that the procedure is painful in so many instances that it constitutes cruel and unusual punishment. The United States Supreme Court took up this matter in a Kentucky case in 2007. In 2008, it ruled by a seven-to-two margin that Kentucky's method of execution by lethal injection was constitutional.[64]

64. *Baze v. Rees,* 553 U.S. 35 (2008).

FIGURE 4–1 The States and the Death Penalty: Executions since 1976 and the Death Row Population

Today, as shown in this figure, fifteen states have abolished the death penalty. The most recent state to act was New Mexico, which abolished the penalty in 2009. The District of Columbia, Puerto Rico, Guam, and the U.S. Virgin Islands also have no death penalty. Kansas, New Hampshire and the U.S. military have inmates on death row but have not actually executed anyone since 1972.

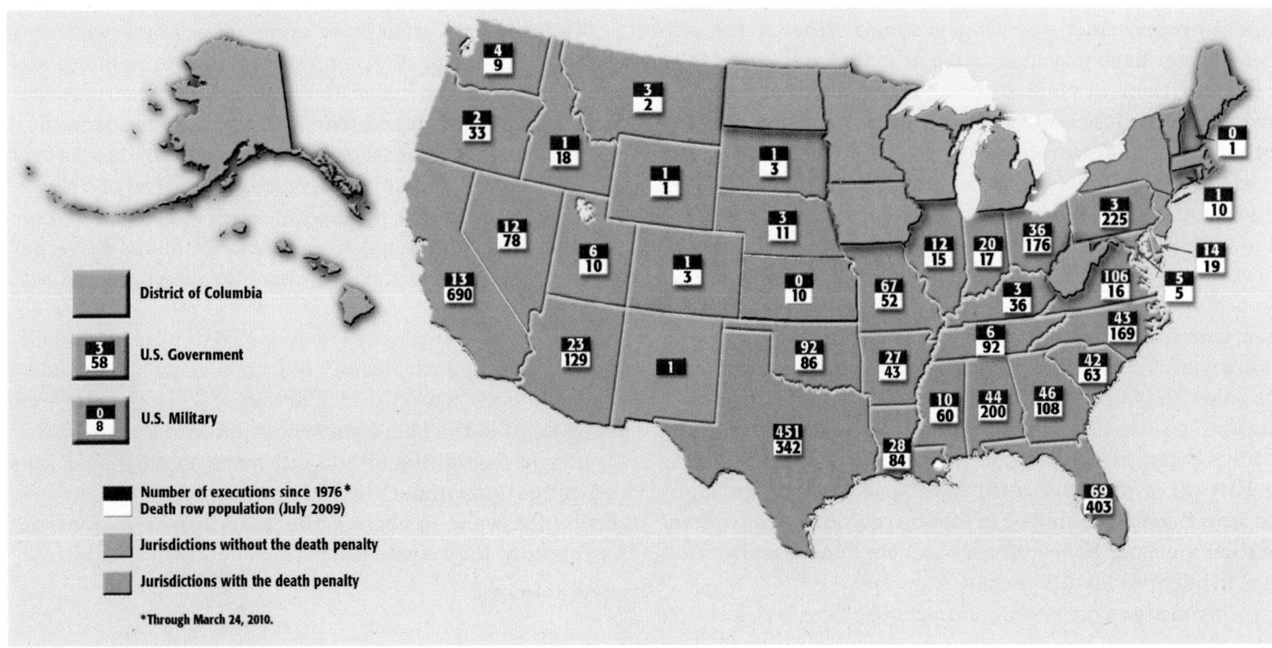

Source: Bureau of Justice Statistics.

WHY SHOULD YOU CARE ABOUT... CIVIL LIBERTIES?

The Bill of Rights includes numerous provisions that protect persons who are suspected of criminal activity. Among these are limits on how the police can conduct searches and seizures.

CIVIL LIBERTIES AND YOUR LIFE

You may be the most law-abiding person in the world, but that will not guarantee that you will never be stopped, arrested, or searched by the police. Sooner or later, the great majority of all citizens will have some kind of interaction with the police. People who do not understand their rights or how to behave toward law enforcement officers can find themselves in serious trouble. The words of advice in this feature actually provide you with key survival skills for life in the modern world.

HOW YOU CAN MAKE A DIFFERENCE

How should you behave if you are stopped by police officers? Your civil liberties protect you from having to provide information other than your name and address. Normally, even if you have not been placed under arrest, the officers have the right to frisk you for weapons, and you must let them proceed. The officers cannot, however, check your person or your clothing further if, in their judgment, no weaponlike object is produced.

The officers may search you only if they have a search warrant or probable cause to believe that a search will likely produce incriminating evidence. What if the officers do not have probable cause or a warrant? Physically resisting their attempt to search you can lead to disastrous results. It is best simply to refuse orally to give permission for the search, preferably in the presence of a witness. Being polite is better than acting out of anger and making the officers irritable. It is usually advisable to limit what you say to the officers. If you are arrested, it is best to keep quiet until you can speak with a lawyer.

If you are in your car and are stopped by the police, the same fundamental rules apply. Always be ready to show your driver's license and car registration. You may be asked to get out of the car. The officers may use a flashlight to peer inside if it is too dark to see otherwise. None of this constitutes a search. A true search requires either a warrant or probable cause. No officer has the legal right to search your car simply to find out if you may have committed a crime. Police officers can conduct searches that are incident to lawful arrests, however.

If you are in your home and a police officer with a search warrant appears, you can ask to examine the warrant before granting entry. A warrant that is correctly made out will state the place or persons to be searched, the object sought, and the date of the warrant (which should be no more than ten days old); and it will bear the signature of a judge or magistrate. If the warrant is in order, you need not make any statement. If you believe the warrant to be invalid, or if no warrant is produced, you should make it clear orally that you have not consented to the search, preferably in the presence of a witness. If the search later is proved to be unlawful, normally any evidence obtained cannot be used in court.

Officers who attempt to enter your home without a search warrant can do so only if they are pursuing a suspected felon into the house. Rarely is it advisable to give permission for a warrantless search. You, as the resident, must be the one to give permission if any evidence obtained is to be considered legal. The landlord, manager, or head of a college dormitory cannot give legal permission. A roommate, however, can give permission for a search of his or her room, which may allow the police to search areas where you have belongings.

If you are a guest in a place that is being legally searched, you may be legally searched as well. But unless you have been placed under arrest, you cannot be compelled to go to the police station or get into a squad car.

If you would like to find out more about your rights and obligations under the laws of searches and seizures, you might want to contact the American Civil Liberties Association. Its Website is at:

www.aclu.org

questions for discussion and analysis

1. Review the *Which Side Are You On?* feature on page 120. To what extent should college campuses accommodate the religious needs of students? Does installing footbaths that especially benefit Muslims (although the footbaths can be used by anyone) go too far? Why or why not?
2. If freedom of speech were not a constitutional right, but merely a matter of tradition and custom, in what ways might the government be tempted to limit it?
3. The courts have never held that the provision of military chaplains by the armed forces is unconstitutional, despite the fact that chaplains are religious leaders who are employed by and under the authority of the U.S. government. What arguments might the courts use to defend the military chaplain system?
4. The courts have banned the teaching of the theory of creation by intelligent design in public school biology classes, arguing that the theory is based on religion, not science. Indeed, it is not hard to detect a religious basis in the classroom materials recently disseminated by the intelligent design movement. Is it possible to make an argument in favor of intelligent design that would not promote a religious belief?
5. In a surprisingly large number of cases, arrested individuals do not choose to exercise their right to remain silent. Why might a person not exercise his or her *Miranda* rights?

key terms

actual malice 127
arraignment 135
clear and present danger test 122
commercial speech 122
defamation of character 124
establishment clause 115
exclusionary rule 137
free exercise clause 115
gag order 127
incorporation theory 114
libel 126
obscenity 123
prior restraint 121
public figure 127
slander 125
symbolic speech 121
writ of *habeas corpus* 135

chapter summary

1. Originally, the Bill of Rights limited only the power of the national government, not that of the states. Gradually and selectively, however, the Supreme Court accepted the incorporation theory, under which no state can violate most provisions of the Bill of Rights.
2. The First Amendment protects against government interference with freedom of religion by requiring a separation of church and state (under the establishment clause) and by guaranteeing the free exercise of religion. Controversial issues that arise under the establishment clause include: aid to church-related schools, school prayer, the teaching of evolution versus intelligent design, school vouchers, the placement of religious displays on public property, and discrimination against religious speech. The government can interfere with the free exercise of religion only when religious practices work against public policy or the public welfare.
3. The First Amendment protects against government interference with freedom of speech, which includes symbolic speech (expressive conduct). The Supreme Court has been especially critical of government actions that impose prior restraint on expression. Commercial speech (advertising) by businesses has received limited First Amendment protection. Restrictions on expression are permitted when the expression may incite immediate lawless action. Other speech that has not received First Amendment protection includes expression judged to be obscene or slanderous.
4. The First Amendment protects against government interference with the freedom of the press, which can be regarded as a special instance of freedom of speech. Speech by the press that does not receive protection includes libelous statements. Publication of news about a criminal trial may be restricted by a gag order in some circumstances.

5. Under the Ninth Amendment, rights not specifically mentioned in the Constitution are not necessarily denied to the people. Among these unspecified rights protected by the courts is a right to privacy, which has been inferred from the First, Third, Fourth, Fifth, and Ninth Amendments. A major privacy issue today is how best to protect privacy rights in cyberspace. Whether an individual's privacy rights include a right to an abortion or a "right to die" continues to provoke controversy. Another major challenge concerns the extent to which Americans must forfeit civil liberties to control terrorism.

6. The Constitution includes protections for the rights of persons accused of crimes. Under the Fourth Amendment, no one may be subject to an unreasonable search or seizure or be arrested except on probable cause. Under the Fifth Amendment, an accused person has the right to remain silent. Under the Sixth Amendment, an accused person must be informed of the reason for his or her arrest. The accused also has the right to adequate counsel, even if he or she cannot afford an attorney, and the right to a prompt arraignment and a speedy and public trial before an impartial jury selected from a cross section of the community.

7. In *Miranda v. Arizona* (1966), the Supreme Court held that criminal suspects, before interrogation by law enforcement personnel, must be informed of the right to remain silent and the right to be represented by counsel.

8. The exclusionary rule forbids the admission in court of illegally seized evidence. There is a "good faith exception" to the exclusionary rule: evidence need not be thrown out owing to, for example, a clerical error in a database. Under the Eighth Amendment, cruel and unusual punishment is prohibited. Whether the death penalty is cruel and unusual punishment continues to be debated.

selected print & media resources

SUGGESTED READINGS

Davis, Darren W. ***Negative Liberty: Public Opinion and the Terrorist Attacks on America.*** **New York: Russell Sage Foundation Publications, 2009. The attacks of September 11, 2001, generated considerable tension between the principles of liberty and security. Davis shows how Americans, initially willing to cede some of their rights in the cause of fighting terrorism, soon reverted to their traditional support for civil liberties.**

Kitcher, Philip. ***Living with Darwin: Evolution, Design, and the Future of Faith.*** **New York: Oxford University Press, 2007. This brief book looks at the history of the controversy over evolution as part of a larger conflict between religious faith and the discoveries of modern science.**

Krimsky, Sheldon, and Tania Simoncelli. ***Genetic Justice: DNA Data Banks, Criminal Investigations, and Civil Liberties.*** **New York: Columbia University Press, 2010. National DNA databanks were originally established to help identify violent criminals and sex offenders. Have these databanks become a threat to the liberties of ordinary citizens? Krimsky and Simoncelli believe that the answer is "yes."**

Mayer, Jane. ***The Dark Side: The Inside Story of How the War on Terror Turned into a War on American Ideals.*** **New York: Doubleday, 2008. Mayer, a staff writer for the *New Yorker*, provides a dramatic account in which she alleges that torture became an unofficial policy of the George W. Bush administration. Mayer contends that up to half of the mistreated individuals were in fact imprisoned by mistake.**

MEDIA RESOURCES

The Abortion War: Thirty Years after Roe v. Wade—**An ABC News program released in 2003 that examines the abortion issue.**

The End of America: Director's Cut—**Naomi Wolf, who acts in this 2008 documentary, is a well-known author of best-selling feminist books. Wolf, along with directors Ricki Stern and Annie Sundberg, believes that President George W. Bush and his administration had a disastrous impact on our civil liberties.**

Gideon's Trumpet—**An excellent 1980 movie about the *Gideon v. Wainwright* case. Henry Fonda plays the role of the convicted petty thief Clarence Earl Gideon.**

God's Christian Warriors—**A controversial 2007 CNN special on how evangelical Christians seek to influence American politics and society. Reported by CNN chief international correspondent Christiane Amanpour, the two-hour show is part of a broader series that includes *God's Jewish Warriors* and *God's Muslim Warriors.***

May It Please the Court: The First Amendment—**A set of audiocassette recordings and written transcripts of** the oral arguments made before the Supreme Court in sixteen key First Amendment cases. Participants in the recordings include nationally known attorneys and several Supreme Court justices.

Taxi to the Dark Side—Winner of the 2008 Academy Award for best documentary. Director Alex Gibney focuses on an Afghan taxi driver named Dilawar who was apparently beaten to death by U.S. soldiers at Bagram Air Base. The film goes on to examine America's policy on torture and interrogation in general.

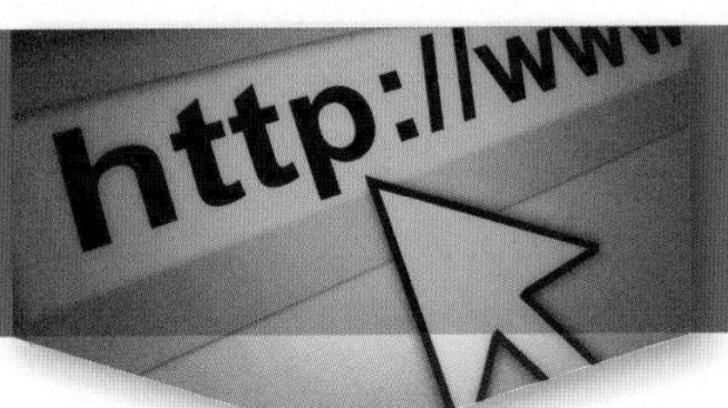

e-mocracy

UNDERSTANDING YOUR CIVIL LIBERTIES

Today, the online world offers opportunities for Americans to easily access information concerning the nature of their civil liberties, how they originated, and how they may be threatened by various government actions. Several of the Web sites in the *Logging On* section of Chapter 2 present documents that set forth and explain the civil liberties guaranteed by the Constitution. In the *Logging On* section that follows, we list other Web sites you can visit to gain insights into the nature of these liberties.

LOGGING ON

The American Civil Liberties Union (ACLU), the nation's leading civil liberties organization, provides an extensive array of information and links concerning civil rights issues at
www.aclu.org

The Liberty Counsel describes itself as "a nonprofit religious civil liberties education and legal defense organization established to preserve religious freedom." The URL for the Web site of this conservative group is
www.lc.org

Summaries and the full text of Supreme Court decisions concerning constitutional law, plus a virtual tour of the Supreme Court, are available at
www.oyez.org

If you want to read historic Supreme Court decisions, you can search for them at
supct.law.cornell.edu/supct/search

The Center for Democracy and Technology (CDT) focuses on how developments in communications technology are affecting the constitutional liberties of Americans. You can access the CDT's site at
www.cdt.org

The American Library Association's Web site provides information on free speech issues, especially issues of free speech on the Internet. Go to
www.ala.org/ala/issuesadvocacy

You can find current information on Internet privacy issues at the Electronic Privacy Information Center's Web site. Go to
www.epic.org/privacy

chapter 5

Civil Rights

chapter contents

<< Immigration reform is one of today's hot-button issues. These demonstrators are standing in front of a government building in Phoenix, Arizona. (Monica Almeida/*The New York Times*/Redux)

WHAT IF... ...unauthorized immigrants were granted citizenship?

These Mexicans were caught trying to enter the United States at the border and are being held in a detention center. What drives foreigners to enter this country illegally? (© J. Emilio Flores/Corbis)

BACKGROUND

By common estimates, there may be as many as 12 million unauthorized immigrants living in the United States. The majority of these people, who are also called illegal immigrants, illegal aliens, or undocumented workers, came to the United States from Latin American countries, with more than half coming from Mexico. In 2006, many unauthorized immigrants and their advocates took to the streets to protest legislation that would have raised penalties for illegal immigration and classified as felons all unauthorized immigrants and anyone who helped them. (The legislation did not pass.) The protesters also voiced an overriding request: allow illegal immigrants to obtain U.S. citizenship.

WHAT IF UNAUTHORIZED IMMIGRANTS WERE GRANTED CITIZENSHIP?

Granting citizenship to unauthorized immigrants now living in the United States would have significant repercussions. The immigrants' sheer numbers would command attention from both political parties. The already important "Hispanic vote" would take on even greater significance. In recent years, voter participation within the Hispanic, or Latino, community has increased. Latinos have become more politically active and outspoken. A growing number of individuals of Hispanic descent hold public office as mayors of major cities, governors, and members of Congress.

EMPLOYMENT AND TAXES

Most illegal immigrants come to the United States to work. Many of them send part of their earnings in America back to relatives in their home countries. The wages sent home to family members by individuals working in the United States (both legally and illegally) are the second-largest source of foreign income in Mexico.

The Internal Revenue Service has had difficulty collecting taxes on the wages that unauthorized immigrants earn, however. Some employers who knowingly hire undocumented workers simply pay those workers in cash "under the table" to avoid a paper trail. If unauthorized immigrants were granted citizenship, most employers would no longer be able to engage in such tax-evasion schemes, and tax revenues would increase.

Employers sometimes use illegal immigrants as employees because the latter often accept lower wages than American citizens would. Some employers break the law by hiring unauthorized immigrants to get around paying state or federal minimum wages. If citizenship were granted to unauthorized immigrants, employers would have to reconsider their practices.

U.S. IMMIGRATION POLICY

Obviously, unauthorized immigrants violate U.S. immigration laws. Anyone seeking to enter the United States legally faces a lengthy application process and annual quota limitations that depend on national origin.

Granting citizenship to all unauthorized immigrants now living in the United States could be considered unfair to all those who are waiting for legal entry. It is worth noting that the number of applications for legal immigration from countries such as Mexico has held up right through the Great Recession. The number of new illegal immigrants, however, has plummeted, at least for now.

FOR CRITICAL ANALYSIS

1. In 2010, senators Charles Schumer (D., N.Y.) and Lindsey Graham (R., S.C.) made a new proposal to reform the nation's immigration laws by creating ways in which unauthorized immigrants could regularize their status, by making it harder to employ undocumented workers, and by allowing more legal immigration. Do you think that Congress is likely to adopt such measures any time before the 2012 elections? Why or why not?
2. Do you think immigration would significantly increase if the United States unveiled some type of policy to grant citizenship to unauthorized immigrants? Why or why not?

In spite of the words set forth in the Declaration of Independence that "all Men are created equal," the concept of equal treatment under the law was a distant dream in our nation's early years. In fact, the majority of the population had few rights at that time. As you learned in Chapter 2, the framers of the Constitution permitted slavery to continue. Slaves thus were excluded from the political process. Women also were excluded for the most part, as were Native Americans, African Americans who were not slaves, and even white men who did not own property.

Today, in contrast, we have numerous civil rights. Equality is at the heart of the concept of civil rights. Generally, the term **civil rights** refers to the rights of all Americans to equal protection under the law, as provided for by the Fourteenth Amendment to the Constitution. Although the terms *civil rights* and *civil liberties* are sometimes used interchangeably, scholars make a distinction between the two. As discussed in Chapter 4, civil liberties are basically limitations on government; they specify what the government *cannot* do. Civil rights, in contrast, specify what the government *must* do—to ensure equal protection and freedom from discrimination.

Civil Rights
Generally, all rights rooted in the Fourteenth Amendment's guarantee of equal protection under the law.

The history of civil rights in America is the story of the struggle of various groups to be free from discriminatory treatment. In this chapter, we first look at two movements that had significant consequences for the history of civil rights in America: the civil rights movement of the 1950s and 1960s and the women's movement, which began in the mid-1800s and continues today. Each of these movements resulted in legislation that secured important basic rights for all Americans—the right to vote and the right to equal protection under the laws.

did you know?

That at the time of the American Revolution, African Americans made up 21 percent of the American population of about 2.5 million.

As you read in the chapter-opening *What If . . .* feature, the Hispanic American population has grown rapidly during the past two decades. In this chapter, we look at some of the issues related to Hispanic Americans and immigration. Note that most minorities in this nation have suffered—and some continue to suffer—from discrimination. Native Americans, Asian Americans, and Arab Americans all have had to struggle for equal treatment, as have people from other countries and older Americans. The fact that these groups are not singled out for special attention in the following pages should not be construed to mean that their struggle for equality is any less significant than the struggles of those groups that we do discuss. We take a special look at the catastrophic historical experience of Native Americans in the *Politics and . . . History* feature on the following page.

First Lady Michelle Obama was present at the unveiling of a bust of Sojourner Truth in the Emancipation Hall of the U.S. Capitol. Truth is the first African American to be so honored in the Capitol. (AP Photo/Manuel Balce Ceneta)

African Americans and the Consequences of Slavery in the United States

Before 1863, the Constitution protected slavery and made equality impossible in the sense in which we use the word today. African American leader Frederick Douglass pointed out that "Liberty and Slavery—opposite as Heaven and Hell—are both in the Constitution." As Abraham Lincoln stated sarcastically, "All men are created equal, except Negroes."

The constitutionality of slavery was confirmed just a few years before the outbreak of the Civil War in the famous *Dred Scott v. Sandford*[1] case of 1857. The Supreme Court held that

1. 60 U.S. 393 (1857).

slaves were not citizens of the United States, nor were they entitled to the rights and privileges of citizenship. The Court also ruled that the Missouri Compromise, which banned slavery in the territories north of 36°30′ latitude (the southern border of Missouri), was unconstitutional. The *Dred Scott* decision had grave consequences. Many observers contend that the ruling contributed to making the Civil War inevitable.

POLITICS AND... history

WERE NATIVE AMERICANS VICTIMS OF GENOCIDE?

By the end of the nineteenth century, the Native American population was much smaller than it had been four hundred years earlier. Is this because Native Americans living in what is now the United States were victims of genocide? Genocide has been defined as a crime committed with the intent to destroy a national, racial, ethnic, or religious group. Were the indigenous peoples of America the victims of a "Euro-American genocidal war" as historian David Stannard contends?

HOW MANY NATIVE AMERICANS LIVED BEFORE COLUMBUS?

In 1894, the U.S. Census Bureau estimated that before Christopher Columbus's discovery of America, there were fewer than 500,000 indigenous people in what is now the United States. In dramatic contrast, anthropologist Henry Dobyns argued in 1966 that the true figure was between 10 and 12 million. A recent consensus estimate puts the sum at a more moderate 3.8 million. Still, any number must come with a vast margin of error. In *Numbers from Nowhere*, historian David Henige wrote: "If I had to pick the most unanswerable question in the world to get into heaven, that would be a good choice. It is impossible to answer. Yet, people have written tens of thousands of pages on it." What we do know for certain is that the American Indian population bottomed out at 250,000 at the end of the nineteenth century, before recovering to 3.2 million today.

WHY DID THEY DIE?

Did millions of Native Americans die in the years immediately after Columbus discovered America? Yes, of that we are certain. The Europeans brought with them Old World diseases to which American Indians had no immunity. The indigenous population was hit with several diseases at once—including smallpox, cholera, malaria, mumps, yellow fever, influenza, and measles. A person who resisted one disease might die from another. It is probable that 90 percent of the population died, far exceeding the mortality caused by the Black Death in medieval Europe (up to a third of the population). To be sure, the Spanish conquistadores were brutal and many Native Americans died at their hands. Most of those who perished, however, did so without ever seeing a white man. For their part, the Europeans had no conception of what caused diseases, no intention of infecting the indigenous peoples, and in truth did not even understand what was happening.

The continued decrease in the American Indian population straight through the nineteenth century—a time when the European American and African American populations were experiencing explosive growth—is more of a problem for the nation's conscience. This decrease was largely due to the concentration of Native Americans onto ever-smaller territories. Depriving a people of territory in such a way that their numbers drop is a violation of modern antigenocide treaties. It is not, however, what most people mean when they use the word *genocide*.

FOR CRITICAL ANALYSIS

Is there any way that European Americans would have allowed the indigenous tribes to keep more of their lands? Why or why not?

Ending Servitude

With the emancipation of the slaves by President Lincoln's Emancipation Proclamation in 1863 and the passage of the Thirteenth, Fourteenth, and Fifteenth Amendments during the Reconstruction period following the Civil War, constitutional inequality was ended.

The Thirteenth Amendment (1865) states that neither slavery nor involuntary servitude shall exist within the United States. The Fourteenth Amendment (1868) tells us that *all* persons born or naturalized in the United States are citizens of the United States. It states, furthermore, that "no State shall make or enforce any law which shall abridge the privileges or immunities of citizens of the United States; nor shall any State deprive any person of life, liberty, or property, without due process of law; nor deny to any person within its jurisdiction the equal protection of the laws." Note the use of the terms *citizen* and *person* in this amendment. *Citizens* have political rights, such as the right to vote and run for political office. Citizens also have certain privileges or immunities (see Chapter 3). All *persons,* however, including noncitizen immigrants, have a right to due process of law and equal protection under the law.

The Fifteenth Amendment (1870) reads as follows: "The right of citizens of the United States to vote shall not be denied or abridged by the United States or by any State on account of race, color, or previous condition of servitude."

did you know?

That slaves in several states, including Arkansas, Louisiana, Oklahoma, and Texas, did not learn about the Emancipation Proclamation until more than two years after it had taken effect in 1863.

The Civil Rights Acts of 1865 to 1875

In 1865, southern state legislatures responded to the freeing of the slaves by enacting "Black Codes" to regulate the African American freedmen. The codes were so severe that they almost amounted to a new form of slavery. Typically, African Americans were required to enter into annual labor contracts and were subject to close regulation by their employers. Corporal punishment was permitted. In 1866, however, the U.S. Congress placed all the rebellious states except Tennessee under military rule, and the Black Codes were revoked.

From 1865 to 1875, Congress passed a series of civil rights acts to negate the Black Codes and enforce the Thirteenth, Fourteenth, and Fifteenth Amendments. The Civil Rights Act of 1866 extended citizenship to anyone born in the United States and gave African Americans full equality before the law. The act further authorized the president to enforce the law with national armed forces. The Enforcement Act of 1870 set out specific criminal sanctions for interfering with the right to vote as protected by the Fifteenth Amendment and by the Civil Rights Act of 1866. Equally important was the Civil Rights Act of 1872, known as the Anti–Ku Klux Klan Act. This act made it a federal crime for anyone to use law or custom to deprive an individual of rights, privileges, and immunities secured by the Constitution or by any federal law. The Second Civil Rights Act, passed in 1875, declared that everyone is entitled to full and equal enjoyment of public accommodations, theaters, and other places of public amusement, and it imposed penalties on violators.

Abraham Lincoln reads a draft of the Emancipation Proclamation to his cabinet in July 1862. The Proclamation did not abolish slavery (that was done by the Thirteenth Amendment, in 1865), but it ensured that slavery would be abolished when the North won the Civil War. After the Battle of Antietam on September 17, 1862, Lincoln publicly announced the Emancipation Proclamation, which declared that all slaves living in states that were still in rebellion on January 1, 1863, would be freed once those states came under the control of the Union Army. (Library of Congress)

did you know?

That Justice John Marshall Harlan, who wrote the only dissent to *Plessy v. Ferguson*, stated in that very dissent, just a few paragraphs after his now-famous words that our Constitution is "color-blind," that Chinese people are members of "a race so different from our own" that it is permissible to deny them citizenship rights.

The Ineffectiveness of the Civil Rights Laws

The Reconstruction statutes, or civil rights acts, ultimately did little to secure equality for African Americans. Both the *Civil Rights Cases* and the case of *Plessy v. Ferguson* (discussed below) effectively nullified these acts. Additionally, various barriers were erected that prevented African Americans from exercising their right to vote.

The *Civil Rights Cases*. The United States Supreme Court invalidated the 1875 Civil Rights Act when it held, in the *Civil Rights Cases*[2] of 1883, that the enforcement clause of the Fourteenth Amendment (which states that "no State shall make or enforce any law which shall abridge the privileges or immunities of citizens") was limited to correcting actions by states in their *official* acts; thus, the discriminatory acts of *private* citizens were not illegal. ("Individual invasion of individual rights is not the subject matter of the Amendment.") The 1883 Supreme Court decision met with widespread approval throughout most of the United States.

Twenty years after the Civil War, the white majority was all too willing to forget about the three Civil War amendments and the civil rights legislation of the 1860s and 1870s. The other civil rights laws that the Court did not specifically invalidate became dead letters in the statute books, although they were never repealed by Congress. At the same time, many former proslavery secessionists had regained political power in the southern states.

Separate-but-Equal Doctrine
The doctrine holding that separate-but-equal facilities do not violate the equal protection clause of the Fourteenth Amendment to the U.S. Constitution.

***Plessy v. Ferguson*: Separate but Equal.** A key decision during this period concerned Homer Plessy, a Louisiana resident who was one-eighth African American. In 1892, he boarded a train in New Orleans. The conductor made him leave the car, which was restricted to whites, and directed him to a car for nonwhites. At that time, Louisiana had a statute providing for separate railway cars for whites and African Americans.

Segregated drinking fountains were common in southern states in the late 1800s and during the first half of the twentieth century. What landmark Supreme Court case made such segregated facilities legal? (© Bettmann/Corbis)

Plessy went to court, claiming that such a statute was contrary to the Fourteenth Amendment's equal protection clause. In 1896, the United States Supreme Court rejected Plessy's contention. The Court concluded that the Fourteenth Amendment "could not have been intended to abolish distinctions based upon color, or to enforce social . . . equality." The Court stated that segregation alone did not violate the Constitution: "Laws permitting, and even requiring, their separation in places where they are liable to be brought into contact do not necessarily imply the inferiority of either race to the other."[3] So was born the **separate-but-equal doctrine.**

Plessy v. Ferguson became the judicial cornerstone of racial discrimination throughout the United States. Even though the *Plessy* decision upheld segregated facilities in railway cars only, it was assumed that the Supreme Court was upholding segregation everywhere as long as the separate facilities were equal. The result was a system of racial segregation, particularly in the South—supported by laws collectively known as Jim Crow laws—that required separate drinking fountains; separate seats

2. 109 U.S. 3 (1883).
3. *Plessy v. Ferguson*, 163 U.S. 537 (1896).

in theaters, restaurants, and hotels; separate public toilets; and separate waiting rooms for the two races. "Separate" was indeed the rule, but "equal" was never enforced, nor was it a reality.

Voting Barriers. The brief voting enfranchisement of African Americans ended after 1877, when the federal troops that occupied the South during the Reconstruction era were withdrawn. Southern politicians regained control of state governments and, using everything except race as a formal criterion, passed laws that effectively deprived African Americans of the right to vote. By using the ruse that political parties were private bodies, the Democratic Party was allowed to keep black voters from its primaries. The **white primary** was upheld by the United States Supreme Court until 1944 when, in *Smith v. Allwright,*[4] the Court ruled that it violated the Fifteenth Amendment.

Another barrier to African American voting was the **grandfather clause,** which restricted voting to those who could prove that their grandfathers had voted before 1867. **Poll taxes** required the payment of a fee to vote. Thus, poor African Americans—as well as poor whites—who could not afford to pay the tax were excluded from voting. Not until the Twenty-fourth Amendment to the Constitution was ratified in 1964 was the poll tax eliminated as a precondition to voting. **Literacy tests** were also used to deny the vote to African Americans. Such tests asked potential voters to read, recite, or interpret complicated texts, such as a section of the state constitution, to the satisfaction of local registrars—who were, of course, never satisfied with the responses of African Americans.

White Primary
A state primary election that restricts voting to whites only; outlawed by the Supreme Court in 1944.

Grandfather Clause
A device used by southern states to disenfranchise African Americans. It restricted voting to those whose grandfathers had voted before 1867.

Poll Tax
A special tax that must be paid as a qualification for voting. In 1964, the Twenty-fourth Amendment to the Constitution outlawed the poll tax in national elections, and in 1966 the Supreme Court declared it unconstitutional in state elections as well.

Literacy Test
A test administered as a precondition for voting, often used to prevent African Americans from exercising their right to vote.

Extralegal Methods of Enforcing White Supremacy. The second-class status of African Americans was also a matter of social custom, especially in the South. In their interactions with southern whites, African Americans were expected to observe an informal but detailed code of behavior that confirmed their inferiority. The most serious violation of the informal code was "familiarity" toward a white woman by an African American man or boy. The code was backed up by the common practice of *lynching*—mob action to murder an accused individual, usually by hanging and sometimes accompanied by torture. Lynching was a common response to an accusation of "familiarity." Of course, lynching was illegal, but southern authorities rarely prosecuted these cases, and white juries would not convict.[5]

did you know?

That the original Constitution failed to describe the status of *citizen* or how this status could be acquired.

African Americans outside the South were subject to a second kind of violence—race riots. In the early twentieth century, race riots were typically initiated by whites. Frequently, the riots were caused by competition for employment. For example, there were a number of serious riots during World War II (1939–1945), when labor shortages forced northern employers to hire more black workers.

The End of the Separate-but-Equal Doctrine

As early as the 1930s, several court rulings began to chip away at the separate-but-equal doctrine. The United States Supreme Court did not explicitly overturn *Plessy v. Ferguson* until 1954, however, when it issued one of the most famous judicial decisions in U.S. history.

In 1951, Oliver Brown decided that his eight-year-old daughter, Linda Carol Brown, should not have to go to an all-nonwhite elementary school twenty-one blocks from her home, when there was a white school only seven blocks away.

Linda Carol Brown was only eight years old when her father started a lawsuit to allow her to attend a nearby white grammar school. The result was the landmark decision *Brown v. Board of Education of Topeka,* rendered in 1954. What was the impact of this Supreme Court decision? (AP Photo)

4. 321 U.S. 649 (1944).
5. One of the most notorious organizations enforcing white supremacy was the Ku Klux Klan, which made its first appearance in 1866.

The National Association for the Advancement of Colored People (NAACP), formed in 1909, decided to support Oliver Brown. The outcome would have a monumental impact on American society.

Brown v. Board of Education of Topeka. The 1954 unanimous decision of the United States Supreme Court in *Brown v. Board of Education of Topeka*[6] established that the segregation of races in the public schools violates the equal protection clause of the Fourteenth Amendment. Chief Justice Earl Warren said that separation implied inferiority, whereas the majority opinion in *Plessy v. Ferguson* had said the opposite.

"With All Deliberate Speed." The following year, in *Brown v. Board of Education*[7] (sometimes called the second *Brown* decision), the Court declared that the lower courts needed to ensure that African Americans would be admitted to schools on a nondiscriminatory basis "with all deliberate speed." The district courts were to consider devices in their desegregation orders that might include "the school transportation system, personnel, [and] revision of school districts and attendance areas into compact units to achieve a system of determining admission to the public schools on a nonracial basis."

James Meredith, the first African American student to enroll at the University of Mississippi, holds a newspaper as he attempts to register at the university. Why were Meredith's actions so important to the civil rights movement? (© Bettmann/Corbis)

Reactions to School Integration

The white South did not let the Supreme Court ruling go unchallenged. Governor Orval Faubus of Arkansas used the state's National Guard to block the integration of Central High School in Little Rock in September 1957. The federal court demanded that the troops be withdrawn. Finally, President Dwight Eisenhower had to federalize the Arkansas National Guard and send in the Army's 101st Airborne Division to quell the violence. Central High became integrated.

Universities in the South, however, remained segregated. When James Meredith, an African American student, attempted to enroll at the University of Mississippi in Oxford in 1962, violence flared there, as it had in Little Rock. The white riot at Oxford was so intense that President John Kennedy was forced to send in 30,000 U.S. combat troops, a larger force than the one then stationed in Korea. There were 375 military and civilian injuries, many from gunfire, and two bystanders were killed. Ultimately, peace was restored, and Meredith began attending classes.[8]

De Facto Segregation
Racial segregation that occurs because of past social and economic conditions and residential racial patterns.

De Jure Segregation
Racial segregation that occurs because of laws or administrative decisions by public agencies.

An Integrationist Attempt at a Cure: Busing

In most parts of the United States, residential concentrations by race have made it difficult to achieve racial balance in schools. Although it is true that a number of school boards in northern districts created segregated schools by drawing school district lines arbitrarily, the residential concentration of African Americans and other minorities in well-defined geographic locations has contributed to the difficulty of achieving racial balance. This concentration results in ***de facto* segregation,** as distinct from ***de jure* segregation,** which results from laws or administrative decisions.

Court-Ordered Busing. The obvious solution to both *de facto* and *de jure* segregation seemed to be transporting some African American schoolchildren to white schools

6. 347 U.S. 483 (1954).
7. 349 U.S. 294 (1955).
8. William Doyle, *An American Insurrection: James Meredith and the Battle of Oxford, Mississippi, 1962* (New York: Anchor, 2003).

and some white schoolchildren to African American schools. Increasingly, the courts ordered school districts to engage in such **busing** across neighborhoods. Busing led to violence in some northern cities, such as in south Boston, where African American students were bused into blue-collar Irish Catholic neighborhoods. Indeed, busing was unpopular with many groups. In the mid-1970s, almost 50 percent of African Americans interviewed were opposed to busing, and approximately three-fourths of the whites interviewed held the same opinion. Nonetheless, through the next decade, the United States Supreme Court fairly consistently upheld busing plans in the cases it decided.

Busing
In the context of civil rights, the transportation of public school students from areas where they live to schools in other areas to eliminate school segregation based on residential patterns.

The End of Integration? During the 1980s and the early 1990s, the Supreme Court tended to back away from its earlier commitment to busing and other methods of desegregation. By the late 1990s and early 2000s, the federal courts were increasingly unwilling to uphold race-conscious policies designed to further school integration and diversity. For example, in 2001, a federal appellate court held that the Charlotte-Mecklenburg school district in North Carolina had achieved the goal of integration,[9] meaning that race-based admission quotas could no longer be imposed constitutionally. Indeed, today, school admissions policies that favor minority applicants in any way may end up being challenged on equal protection grounds. (For a further discussion of this issue, see the section on affirmative action later in this chapter.)

did you know?

That during the Mississippi Summer Project in 1964, organized by students to register African American voters, 1,000 students and voters were arrested, 80 were beaten, 35 were shot, and 6 were murdered; 30 buildings were bombed; and 25 churches were burned.

The Resurgence of Minority Schools. Today, many schools around the country are effectively segregated, in large part because of *de facto* segregation. The rapid decline in the relative proportion of whites who live in large cities and high birthrates of some minority groups have increased the minority presence in those urban areas. One out of every three African American and Latino students goes to a school with more than 90 percent minority enrollment. In the largest U.S. cities, fifteen out of sixteen African American and Hispanic students go to schools with almost no non-Hispanic whites.

Generally, Americans are now taking another look at what desegregation means. The goal of racially balanced schools envisioned in the 1954 *Brown v. Board of Education of Topeka* decision is giving way to the goal of better education for children, even if that means educating them in schools in which students are of the same race or in which race is not considered.

The Civil Rights Movement

The *Brown* decision applied only to public schools. Not much else in the structure of existing segregation was affected. In December 1955, a forty-three-year-old African American woman, Rosa Parks, boarded a public bus in Montgomery, Alabama. When the bus became crowded and several white people stepped aboard, Parks was asked to move to the rear of the bus (the "colored" section). She refused, was arrested, and was fined $10; but that was not the end of the matter. For an entire year, African Americans boycotted the Montgomery bus line. The protest was headed by a twenty-seven-year-old Baptist minister, Dr. Martin Luther King, Jr. In the face of overwhelming odds, the protesters won. In 1956,

This Montgomery, Alabama, sheriff's department booking photo of Rosa Parks shows her after she was arrested for refusing to give up her seat on a bus and move to the "colored" section in 1955. What happened after her arrest? (AP Photo/ Montgomery County Sheriff's Office)

9. *Belk v. Charlotte-Mecklenburg Board of Education*, 269 F.3d 305 (4th Cir. 2001).

a federal district court issued an injunction prohibiting the segregation of buses in Montgomery. The era of civil rights protests had begun.

King's Philosophy of Nonviolence

Civil Disobedience
A nonviolent, public refusal to obey allegedly unjust laws.

The following year, in 1957, King formed the Southern Christian Leadership Conference (SCLC). King advocated nonviolent **civil disobedience** as a means to achieve racial justice. King's philosophy of civil disobedience was influenced, in part, by the life and teachings of Mahatma Gandhi (1869–1948). Gandhi had led resistance to the British colonial system in India from 1919 to 1947. He used tactics such as demonstrations and marches, as well as nonviolent, public disobedience of unjust laws. King's followers successfully used these methods to gain wider public acceptance of their cause.

did you know?
That by September 1961, more than 3,600 students had been arrested for participating in civil rights demonstrations and that 141 students and 58 faculty members had been expelled by colleges and universities for their part in civil rights protests.

Nonviolent Demonstrations. For the next decade, African Americans and sympathetic whites engaged in sit-ins, freedom rides, and freedom marches. In the beginning, such demonstrations were often met with violence, and the contrasting image of nonviolent African Americans and violent, hostile whites created strong public support for the civil rights movement. When African Americans in Greensboro, North Carolina, were refused service at a Woolworth's lunch counter, they organized a sit-in that was aided day after day by other African Americans and by sympathetic whites. Enraged customers threw ketchup on the protesters. Some spat in their faces. The sit-in movement continued to grow, however. Within six months of the first sit-in at the Greensboro Woolworth's, hundreds of lunch counters throughout the South were serving African Americans.

The sit-in technique also was successfully used to integrate interstate buses and their terminals, as well as railroads engaged in interstate transportation. Although buses and railroads engaged in interstate transportation were prohibited by law from segregating African Americans from whites, they stopped doing so only after the sit-in protests.

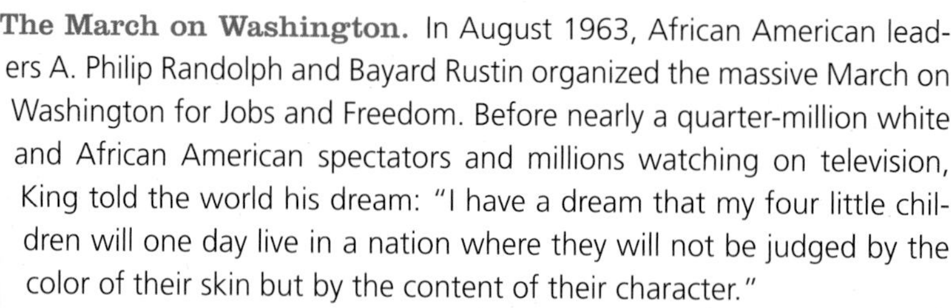

The March on Washington. In August 1963, African American leaders A. Philip Randolph and Bayard Rustin organized the massive March on Washington for Jobs and Freedom. Before nearly a quarter-million white and African American spectators and millions watching on television, King told the world his dream: "I have a dream that my four little children will one day live in a nation where they will not be judged by the color of their skin but by the content of their character."

In August 1963, a quarter of a million whites and blacks descended on Washington, D.C., for a massive March for Jobs and Freedom. Who was the most important speaker at that event? (AP Photo)

Another Approach—Black Power

Not all African Americans agreed with King's philosophy of nonviolence. Black Muslims and other African American separatists advocated a more militant stance and argued that desegregation should not result in cultural assimilation. During the 1950s and 1960s, when King was spearheading nonviolent protests and demonstrations to achieve civil rights for African Americans, black power leaders insisted that African Americans should "fight back" instead of turning the other cheek. Indeed, some would argue that without the fear generated by black militants, a "moderate" such as King would not have garnered such widespread support from white America.

Malcolm Little (who became Malcolm X when he joined the Black Muslims in 1952) and other leaders in the black power movement believed that African Americans fell into two groups: the "Uncle Toms," who peaceably accommodated the white establishment, and the "New Negroes," who took pride in their color and culture and who preferred and demanded racial separation as well as power. Malcolm X was assassinated in 1965, but he became an important reference point for a new generation of African Americans and a symbol of African American identity.

Martin Luther King in a quiet moment as he prepared to speak in Montgomery, Alabama. What type of resistance against segregation did King advocate? (© Bob Adelman/Corbis)

The Climax of the Civil Rights Movement

Attacks on demonstrators by police dogs, cattle prods, high-pressure water hoses, beatings, and bombings—plus the March on Washington—all led to an environment in which Congress felt compelled to act on behalf of African Americans. The second era of civil rights acts, sometimes referred to as the second Reconstruction period, was under way.

Civil Rights Legislation

As the civil rights movement mounted in intensity, equality before the law came to be "an idea whose time has come," in the words of then Republican Senate minority leader Everett Dirksen.

The Civil Rights Act of 1964. The Civil Rights Act of 1964, the most far-reaching bill on civil rights in modern times, forbids discrimination on the basis of race, color, religion, gender, or national origin. The major provisions of the act are as follows:

1. It outlawed arbitrary discrimination in voter registration.
2. It barred discrimination in public accommodations, such as hotels and restaurants, which have operations that affect interstate commerce.
3. It authorized the federal government to bring suits to desegregate public schools and facilities.
4. It expanded the power of the Civil Rights Commission and extended its life.
5. It provided for the withholding of federal funds from programs administered in a discriminatory manner.
6. It established the right to equality of opportunity in employment.

Title VII of the Civil Rights Act of 1964 is the cornerstone of our employment-discrimination laws. It prohibits discrimination in employment based on race, color, religion, gender, or national origin. Under Title VII, executive orders were issued that banned employment discrimination by firms that received any federal funding. The 1964 Civil Rights Act created a five-member commission, the Equal Employment Opportunity Commission (EEOC), to administer Title VII.

At its inception, the EEOC relied on conciliation, education, outreach, and technical assistance, because that was all that the law permitted. In 1972, however, Congress gave the EEOC the right to sue employers, unions, and employment agencies, and litigation became a focal point for the agency. Congress also expanded Title VII to cover federal, state, and local governments, as well as schools and colleges.

The Voting Rights Act of 1965. As late as 1960, only 29.1 percent of African Americans of voting age were registered in the southern states, in stark contrast to 61.1 percent of whites. The Voting Rights Act of 1965 addressed this issue. The act had two major provisions. The first outlawed discriminatory voter-registration tests. The second authorized federal registration of voters and federally administered voting procedures in any political subdivision or state that discriminated electorally against a particular group. The act also provided that certain political subdivisions could not change their voting procedures and election laws without federal approval. The act targeted counties, mostly in the South, in which fewer than 50 percent of the eligible population were registered to vote. Federal voter registrars were sent to these areas to register African Americans who had been kept from voting by local registrars. Within one week after the act was passed, forty-five federal examiners were sent to the South. A massive voter-registration drive covered the country.

Urban Riots. Even as the civil rights movement was experiencing its greatest victories, a series of riots swept through African American inner-city neighborhoods. These urban riots were different in character from the race riots described earlier in this chapter. The riots in the first half of the twentieth century were street battles between whites and blacks. The urban riots of the late 1960s and early 1970s, however, were not directed against individual whites—in some instances, lower-class whites actually participated in small numbers. The riots were primarily civil insurrections, although these disorders were accompanied by large-scale looting of stores. Inhabitants of the affected neighborhoods attributed the riots to racial discrimination.[10] The riots dissipated much of the goodwill toward the civil rights movement that had been built up earlier in the decade among northern whites. Together with widespread student demonstrations against the Vietnam War (1964–1975), the riots pushed many Americans toward conservatism.

President Lyndon Johnson is shown signing the Civil Rights Act of 1968. What are some of the provisions of that far-reaching law? (© Bettmann/Corbis)

The Civil Rights Act of 1968 and Other Housing Reform Legislation. Martin Luther King, Jr., was assassinated on April 4, 1968. Despite King's message of peace, his death was followed by the most widespread rioting to date. Nine days after King's death, President Johnson signed the Civil Rights Act of 1968, which forbade discrimination in most housing and provided penalties for those attempting to interfere with individual civil rights (giving protection to civil rights workers, among others). Subsequent legislation added enforcement provisions to the federal government's rules against discriminatory mortgage-lending practices. Today, all lenders must report to the federal government the race, gender, and income of all mortgage-loan seekers, along with the final decision on their loan applications.

Consequences of Civil Rights Legislation

As a result of the Voting Rights Act of 1965 and its amendments, and the large-scale voter-registration drives in the South, the number of African Americans registered to vote climbed dramatically. By 1980,

10. Angus Campbell and Howard Schuman, *ICPSR 3500: Racial Attitudes in Fifteen American Cities, 1968* (Ann Arbor, Mich.: Inter-University Consortium for Political and Social Research, 1997). Campbell and Schuman's survey documented both white participation and the attitudes of the inhabitants of affected neighborhoods.

55.8 percent of African Americans of voting age in the South were registered. Some of the provisions in the Voting Rights Act of 1965 were due to "sunset" (expire) in 2007. In July 2006, however, President George W. Bush signed a twenty-five-year extension of these provisions following heated congressional debate. In recent national elections, turnout by African American voters has come very close to the white turnout. In 2008, with an African American on the presidential ballot, African American turnout exceeded that of whites for the first time in history.[11]

Hispanic
Someone who can claim a heritage from a Spanish-speaking country. The term is used only in the United States or other countries that receive immigrants—Spanish-speaking persons living in Spanish-speaking countries normally do not apply the term to themselves.

Latino
An alternative to the term *Hispanic* that is preferred by many.

Political Participation by African Americans. Today, there are more than ten thousand African American elected officials in the United States. The movement of African American citizens into high elected office has been sure, if exceedingly slow. Notably, recent polling data show that most Americans do not consider race a significant factor in choosing a president. In 1958, when a Gallup poll first asked whether respondents would be willing to vote for an African American as president, only 38 percent of the public said yes. By 2008, this number had reached 94 percent. This high figure may have been attained, at least in part, because of the emergence of several African Americans of presidential caliber. Of course, Illinois senator Barack Obama was elected president in 2008 on the Democratic ticket. Two Republican African Americans have also been mentioned in the past as presidential possibilities: Colin Powell, formerly chair of the Joint Chiefs of Staff and later secretary of state under President George W. Bush; and Condoleezza Rice, who succeeded Powell at the State Department.

Political Participation by Other Minorities. The civil rights movement focused primarily on the rights of African Americans. Yet the legislation resulting from the movement ultimately benefited nearly all minority groups. The Civil Rights Act of 1964, for example, prohibits discrimination against any person because of race, color, or national origin. Subsequent amendments to the Voting Rights Act of 1965 extended its protections to other minorities, including **Hispanic** Americans (or **Latinos**), Asian Americans, Native Americans, and Native Alaskans. To further protect the voting rights of minorities, the law

11. One widely reported study claimed that African American turnout did not quite match that of whites, but this conclusion was based on an overestimate of the number of African Americans eligible to vote.

Half a century ago, not even 40 percent of Americans said they would vote for an African American for president. Since then, many African Americans have emerged as high government officials, including Colin Powell, secretary of state, and Condoleezza Rice, who succeeded him in that office during the Bush administration. Today America has its first African American president. What does Barack Obama's victory in the 2008 presidential elections tell you about changing racial attitudes in this country? (From left to right, Charles Haynes/Creative Commons, AP Photo/J. J. Guillen, and AP Photo/Jae C. Hong)

now provides that states must make bilingual ballots available in counties where 5 percent or more of the population speaks a language other than English.

The political participation of non–African American minority groups has increased in recent years. Hispanics, for example, have gained political power in several states. Hispanics do not vote at the same rate as African Americans, in large part because many Hispanics are immigrants who are not yet citizens. Still, there are now about five thousand Hispanic elected officials in the United States. In 2004, Hispanics were 8 percent of the voters in Colorado, 10 percent in Nevada, and 32 percent in New Mexico. In 2008, these figures were 13 percent, 15 percent, and 41 percent, respectively. Election analysts have concluded that the Hispanic vote in these three states would have tipped them to Obama—and handed him the presidency—even if Republican presidential candidate John McCain had a 1 percent lead in the national polls. The impact of immigration will be discussed in greater detail later in this chapter.

Lingering Social and Economic Disparities. According to recent census data, social and economic disparities between whites and blacks (and other minorities) persist. Data released by the U.S. Census Bureau for 2008 (the latest data available) showed that mean incomes in non-Hispanic white households were 62 percent higher than in black households and 111 percent higher than in Hispanic households. White adults were also more likely than black and Hispanic adults to have college degrees and to own their own homes. Whites are also less likely to live in poverty. Consider that the poverty rate for non-Hispanic white families was 6.1 percent, compared with a poverty rate of 21.2 percent for blacks and 18.9 percent for Hispanics.

Finally, even today, race consciousness continues to divide African Americans and white Americans. Whether we are talking about college attendance, media stereotyping, racial profiling, or academic achievement, the black experience is different from the white one. As a result, African Americans view the nation and many specific issues differently than their white counterparts do. In survey after survey, when blacks are asked whether they have achieved racial equality, few believe that they have. In contrast, whites are much more likely than blacks to believe that racial equality has been achieved. In spite of the civil rights movement and civil rights legislation, African Americans continue to feel a sense of

ELECTIONS 2010

MINORITY PARTICIPATION

African Americans and members of other minority groups tend to support the Democratic Party, and when they run for office they usually do so as Democrats. It might follow that a Republican "wave" election such as the one we saw in 2010 would trim the number of minority group members in Congress. As it happened, it did not. True, The U.S. Senate no longer contained an African American member. Still, the House of Representatives had forty-one African Americans, down only one from the previous Congress. One reason that African American representation remained stable was the large number of black Republicans who ran in 2010, doubtless encouraged by the example of Barack Obama. Two of these candidates were successful.

A record eight Hispanic Republicans were elected, bringing total Latino representation on Capitol Hill to a near-record twenty-seven. Asian American representation was stable at thirteen members of Congress. Minority group members also made significant progress in winning governorships. In particular, Hispanic Republicans triumphed in gubernatorial races in Nevada and New Mexico, and a Republican woman of Indian-American origin became governor of South Carolina.

injustice in matters of race, and this feeling is often not apparent to, or appreciated by, the majority of white Americans.

One response to lingering social and economic disparities that has garnered considerable attention is to focus on differences of socioeconomic class, regardless of race. The resulting programs would attempt to lift up poor and lower-class families regardless of whether they were white, black, Hispanic, Native American, or Asian. For example, some cities have attempted to integrate their school systems based on economic class, rather than race. Indeed, the 2005 National Assessment of Educational Progress appeared to show that low-income students attending more affluent schools scored almost two grade levels higher than low-income students attending schools in high-poverty neighborhoods. A number of leaders have proposed class-based programs in education, such as admitting the best students from every high school to the state university. (Such a move benefits both students from minority high schools *and* low-income rural whites.)

Women's Struggle for Equal Rights

Like African Americans and other minorities, women also have had to struggle for equality. During the first phase of this struggle, the primary goal of women was to obtain the right to vote. Some women had hoped that the founders would provide such a right in the Constitution. The Constitution did not include a provision guaranteeing women the right to vote, but neither did it deny to women—or to any others—this right. Rather, the founders left it up to the states to decide such issues, and, as mentioned earlier, by and large, the states limited the franchise to adult white males who owned property.

Early Women's Political Movements

Suffrage
The right to vote; the franchise.

The first political cause in which women became actively engaged was the movement to abolish slavery. Yet male abolitionists felt that women should not take an active role in public. When the World Antislavery Convention was held in London in 1840, women delegates were barred from active participation. Partly in response to this rebuff, two American delegates, Lucretia Mott and Elizabeth Cady Stanton, returned from that meeting with plans to work for women's rights in the United States.

In 1848, Mott and Stanton organized the first women's rights convention in Seneca Falls, New York. The three hundred people who attended approved a Declaration of Sentiments: "We hold these truths to be self-evident: that all men and women are created equal." In the following twelve years, groups that supported women's rights held seven conventions in different cities in the Midwest and East. With the outbreak of the Civil War, however, advocates of women's rights were urged to put their support behind the war effort, and most agreed to do so.

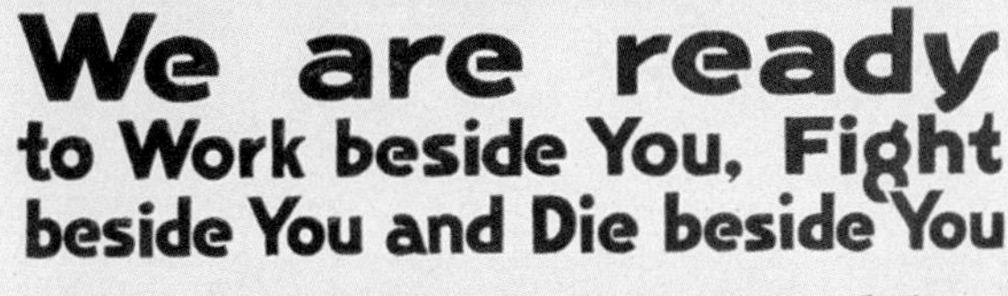

Women did not get the right to vote throughout the United States until 1920. Prior to that, though, there was a strong women's suffrage movement. This cardboard poster is asking voters to support candidates who favor women's right to vote. (© David J. & Janice L. Frent Collection/Corbis)

Women's Suffrage Associations

Susan B. Anthony and Elizabeth Cady Stanton formed the National Woman Suffrage Association in 1869, after the war. In their view, women's **suffrage**—the right to vote—was a means to achieve major improvements in the economic and social situation of women in the United States. In other words, the vote was to be used to seek broader goals. Nowadays, we commonly see the women's rights movement as a liberal cause, but many of the broader goals of the suffrage advocates would not be regarded as liberal today. An example was the prohibition of alcoholic beverages, which received widespread support among women in general and women's rights activists in particular. It should be noted that many women considered prohibition to be a method of combating domestic violence.

did you know?

That in 1916, four years before the Nineteenth Amendment gave women the right to vote, Jeannette Rankin became the first woman to be elected to the U.S. House of Representatives.

Unlike Anthony and Stanton, Lucy Stone, a key founder of the rival American Woman Suffrage Association, believed that the vote was the only major issue. Members of the American Woman Suffrage Association traveled to each state; addressed state legislatures; and wrote, published, and argued their convictions. They achieved only limited success. In 1880, the two organizations joined force. The resulting National American Woman Suffrage Association had only one goal—the enfranchisement of women—but it made little progress.

The Congressional Union, founded in the early 1900s by Alice Paul, rejected the state-by-state approach. Instead, the Union adopted a national strategy of obtaining an amendment to the U.S. Constitution. The Union also employed militant tactics. It sponsored large-scale marches and civil disobedience—which resulted in hunger strikes, arrests, and jailings. Finally, in 1920, the Nineteenth Amendment was passed: "The right of citizens of the United States to vote shall not be denied or abridged by the United States or by any State on account of sex." (Today, the word *gender* is typically used instead of *sex*.) Although it may seem that the United States was slow to give women the vote, it was really not too far behind the rest of the world (see Table 5–1 below).

The Modern Women's Movement

Feminism
The movement that supports political, economic, and social equality for women.

Historian Nancy Cott contends that the word *feminism* first began to be used around 1910. At that time, **feminism** meant, as it does today, political, social, and economic equality for women—a radical notion that gained little support among members of the suffrage movement.

After gaining the right to vote in 1920, women engaged in little independent political activity until the 1960s. The civil rights movement of that decade resulted in a growing awareness of rights for all groups, including women. Increased participation in the workforce gave many women greater self-confidence. Additionally, the publication of Betty Friedan's *The Feminine Mystique* in 1963 focused national attention on the unequal status of women in American life.

In 1966, Friedan and others who were dissatisfied with existing women's organizations, and especially with the failure of the Equal Employment Opportunity Commission to address discrimination against women, formed the National Organization for Women (NOW). Many observers consider the founding of NOW to be the beginning of the modern women's movement—the feminist movement.

TABLE 5–1 Years, by Country, in Which Women Gained the Right to Vote

1893: New Zealand	**1919:** Germany	**1945:** Italy	**1953:** Mexico
1902: Australia	**1920:** United States	**1945:** Japan	**1956:** Egypt
1913: Norway	**1930:** South Africa	**1947:** Argentina	**1963:** Kenya
1918: Britain	**1932:** Brazil	**1950:** India	**1971:** Switzerland
1918: Canada	**1944:** France	**1952:** Greece	**1984:** Yemen

Source: Center for the American Woman and Politics.

Feminism gained additional impetus from young women who entered politics to support the civil rights movement or to oppose the Vietnam War. Many of them found that despite the egalitarian principles of these movements, women remained in second-class positions. These young women sought their own movement. In the late 1960s, "women's liberation" organizations began to spring up on college campuses. Women also began organizing independent "consciousness-raising groups" in which they discussed how gender issues affected their lives. The new women's movement experienced explosive growth, and by 1970 it had emerged as a major social force.

Betty Friedan, feminist spokeswoman shown in 1974. (AP Photo)

The Equal Rights Amendment. The initial focus of the modern women's movement was to eradicate gender inequality through a constitutional amendment. The proposed Equal Rights Amendment (ERA), which was first introduced in Congress in 1923 by leaders of the National Women's Party (a successor to the Congressional Union), states as follows: "Equality of rights under the law shall not be denied or abridged by the United States or by any state on account of sex." For years the amendment was not even given a hearing in Congress, but finally it was approved by both chambers and sent to the state legislatures for ratification in 1972.

As noted in Chapter 2, any constitutional amendment must be ratified by the legislatures (or conventions) in three-fourths of the states before it can become law. Since the early 1900s, most proposed amendments have required that ratification occur within seven years of Congress's adoption of the amendment. The necessary thirty-eight states failed to ratify the ERA within the seven-year period specified by Congress, even though it was supported by numerous national party platforms, six presidents, and both chambers of Congress. To date, efforts to reintroduce the amendment have not succeeded.

did you know?

That in 1922, at age eighty-seven, Rebecca Latimer Felton was the first and oldest woman to serve in the U.S. Senate—although she was appointed as a token gesture and was allowed to serve only one day.

During the national debate over the ratification of the ERA, a women's countermovement emerged. Some women perceived the goals pursued by NOW and other liberal women's organizations as a threat to their way of life. One leader of the countermovement was Republican Phyllis Schlafly. The "Stop ERA" campaign of her conservative organization, Eagle Forum, found significant support among fundamentalist religious groups and various other conservative organizations.

Additional Women's Issues. While NOW concentrated on the ERA, a large number of other women's groups, many of them entirely local, addressed a spectrum of added issues. One of these was the issue of *domestic violence*—that is, assaults within the family. Typically, this meant husbands or boyfriends assaulting their wives or girlfriends. During the 1970s, feminists across the country began opening *battered women's shelters* to house victims of abuse.

Abortion soon emerged as a key concern. Almost the entire organized women's movement united behind the "freedom-of-choice" position, at the cost of alienating potential women's rights supporters who favored the "right-to-life" position instead. Because abortion was a national issue, the campaign was led by national organizations such as NARAL Pro-Choice America, formerly the National Abortion and Reproductive Rights Action League. (For information about organizations on both sides of this debate, see the *Why Should You Care about the Constitution?* feature on page 59 in Chapter 2.)

Phyllis Schlafly appears at a Senate Labor and Human Resources Committee hearing in 1981 to argue that sexual harassment is not an important problem. (AP Photo/Harrity)

did you know?

That a Gallup poll taken in early 2000 found that 15 percent of the women polled described themselves as homemakers, but not one man described himself as such.

Another issue—pornography—tended to divide the women's movement rather than unite it. While a majority of feminists found pornography demeaning to women, many were also strong supporters of free speech. Others, notably activists Andrea Dworkin and Catharine Mackinnon, believed that pornography was so central to the subjugation of women that First Amendment protections should not apply. In some ways, the campaign against pornography was reminiscent of some of the campaigns waged by the suffrage movement, such as support for prohibition.

Gender Discrimination
Any practice, policy, or procedure that denies equality of treatment to an individual or to a group because of gender.

Challenging Gender Discrimination in the Courts. When the ERA failed to be ratified, women's rights organizations began a campaign to win national and state laws that would guarantee the equality of women. This more limited campaign met with much success. Women's rights organizations also challenged discriminatory statutes and policies in the federal courts, contending that **gender discrimination** violated the Fourteenth Amendment's equal protection clause. Since the 1970s, the United States Supreme Court has tended to scrutinize gender classifications closely and has invalidated a number of such statutes and policies. For example, in 1977 the Court held that police and firefighting units cannot establish arbitrary rules, such as height and weight requirements, that tend to keep women from joining those occupations.[12] In 1983, the Court ruled that life insurance companies cannot charge different rates for women and men.[13]

Congress sought to guarantee equality of treatment in education by passing Title IX of the Education Amendments of 1972, which states: "No person in the United States shall, on the basis of sex, be excluded from participation in, be denied the benefits of, or be subjected to discrimination under any education program or activity receiving Federal financial assistance." Title IX's best known and most controversial impact has been on high school and collegiate athletics, although the original statute made no reference to athletics.

More women are joining the U.S. Marines today. Are women in the military allowed to participate in on-the-ground combat? (Dermot Tatlow/laif/Redux)

A question that the Supreme Court has not ruled on is whether women should be allowed to participate in military combat. Generally, the Court has left this decision up to Congress and the Department of Defense. Recently, women have been allowed to serve as combat pilots and on naval warships. To date, however, they have not been allowed to join infantry direct-combat units, although they are now permitted to serve in combat-support units. In 1996, the Supreme Court held that the state-financed Virginia Military Institute's policy of accepting only males violated the equal protection clause.[14]

Women in Politics Today

The efforts of women's rights advocates have helped to increase the number of women holding political offices at all levels of government. In 2008, eight women served as state governors, and women made up almost a quarter of the nation's state legislators.

Women in Congress. Although a men's club atmosphere still prevails in Congress, the number of women holding congressional seats has increased significantly in recent years. Elections during the 1990s brought more women to Congress than either the Senate or the House had seen before. In 2001, for the first time, a woman was

12. *Dothard v. Rawlinson,* 433 U.S. 321 (1977).
13. *Arizona v. Norris,* 463 U.S. 1073 (1983).
14. *United States v. Virginia,* 518 U.S. 515 (1996).

elected to a leadership post in Congress—Nancy Pelosi of California became the Democrats' minority whip in the House of Representatives. In 2002, she was elected minority leader, and in 2006, she was chosen to be the first woman Speaker of the House in the history of the United States. In all, 154 women ran for the House or Senate in 2010 on major-party tickets. In 2011, the House contained 72 women. Following the 2010 elections, the Senate included 17 women, the same as before.

Hillary Clinton was appointed secretary of state by President Obama. She is the third female to hold that office. Clinton almost became the Democratic presidential candidate in the 2008 elections. Are women fully represented in our Congress? (AP Photo/J. Scott Applewhite)

Women in the Executive and Judicial Branches. In 1984, for the first time, a woman, Geraldine Ferraro, became the Democratic nominee for vice president. Another woman, Elizabeth Dole, made a serious run for the Republican presidential nomination in the 2000 campaigns. In 2008, Hillary Clinton mounted a major campaign for the Democratic presidential nomination, and Sarah Palin became the Republican nominee for vice president. Recent Gallup polls show that close to 90 percent of Americans say they would vote for a qualified woman for president if she was nominated by their party.

Increasing numbers of women are also being appointed to cabinet posts. President George W. Bush appointed several women to cabinet positions, including Condoleezza Rice as his secretary of state in 2005. President Barack Obama named his former rival Hillary Clinton to be secretary of state and added six other women to his cabinet.

Increasing numbers of women are sitting on federal judicial benches as well. President Ronald Reagan (1981–1989) was credited with a historic first when he appointed Sandra Day O'Connor to the United States Supreme Court in 1981. President Clinton appointed a second woman, Ruth Bader Ginsburg, to the Court. O'Connor retired from the Court in 2006. In 2009, President Obama named Sonia Sotomayor to the Court. She became the third woman and first Hispanic to serve. In 2010, Obama appointed Elena Kagan to the Court, bringing the number of women on the Court to three.

Continuing Disproportionate Leadership. For all the achievements of women in the political arena, the number of them holding political offices remains disproportionately low compared with their participation as voters, and the number of women holding elective office may have leveled off in the last few years. In recent elections, the turnout of female voters nationally has been slightly higher than that of male voters.

ELECTIONS 2010

POLITICAL LEADERSHIP BY WOMEN

As was true of racial and ethnic minorities, a substantial number of women ran as Republicans in 2010. Some of the fiercest advocates of the Tea Party cause were women. Sarah Palin, the former Republican vice-presidential candidate, described them as her "mama grizzlies." Winning Republicans included Nikki Haley, who became governor of South Carolina, Susana Martinez, elected governor of New Mexico, and Kelly Ayotte, who won the Senate race in New Hampshire. In the end, women won an estimated seventy-two house seats, down one. Their representation in the Senate remained steady at seventeen. Seven women were governors.

Not all Republican women were victorious, of course. California saw two Republican women of great personal wealth running for the top positions—Meg Whitman for governor and Carly Fiorina for the Senate. Both were unsuccessful, even though Whitman dropped $140 million of her own funds into her campaign. Two other Republican women who became famous through losing were Sharron Angle, who ran against Senate Democratic leader Harry Reid in Nevada, and Christine O'Donnell, the Republican candidate for the Senate in Delaware. Angle and O'Donnell were so radical in their Tea Party beliefs that they may have handed both Senate seats to the Democrats.

Gender-Based Discrimination in the Workplace

Traditional cultural beliefs concerning the proper role of women in society continue to be evident not only in the political arena but also in the workplace. Since the 1960s, however, women have gained substantial protection against discrimination through laws mandating equal employment opportunities and equal pay.

Title VII of the Civil Rights Act of 1964

Title VII of the Civil Rights Act of 1964 prohibits gender discrimination in employment and has been used to strike down employment policies that discriminate against employees on the basis of gender. Even so-called protective policies have been held to violate Title VII if they have a discriminatory effect. In 1991, for example, the United States Supreme Court held that a fetal protection policy established by Johnson Controls, Inc., the country's largest producer of automobile batteries, violated Title VII. The policy required all women of childbearing age working in jobs that entailed periodic exposure to lead or other hazardous materials to prove that they were infertile or to transfer to other positions. Women who agreed to transfer often had to accept cuts in pay and reduced job responsibilities. The Court concluded that women who are "as capable of doing their jobs as their male counterparts may not be forced to choose between having a child and having a job."[15]

In 1978, Congress amended Title VII to expand the definition of gender discrimination to include discrimination based on pregnancy. Pregnancy and related conditions must be treated—for all employment-related purposes, including the receipt of benefits under employee benefit programs—the same as any other health issue.

Sexual Harassment

Sexual Harassment
Unwanted physical or verbal conduct or abuse of a sexual nature that interferes with a recipient's job performance, creates a hostile work environment, or carries with it an implicit or explicit threat of adverse employment consequences.

The United States Supreme Court has also held that Title VII's prohibition of gender-based discrimination extends to **sexual harassment** in the workplace. Sexual harassment occurs when job opportunities, promotions, salary increases, and the like are given in return for sexual favors. A special form of sexual harassment, called hostile-environment harassment, occurs when an employee is subjected to sexual conduct or comments that interfere with the employee's job performance or are so pervasive or severe as to create an intimidating, hostile, or offensive environment.

In two 1998 cases, the Supreme Court clarified the responsibilities of employers in preventing sexual harassment. In *Faragher v. City of Boca Raton,* the question was the following: Should an employer be held liable for a supervisor's sexual harassment of an employee even though the employer was unaware of the harassment? The Court ruled that the employer in this case was liable but stated that the employer might have avoided such liability if it had taken reasonable care to prevent harassing behavior—which the employer had not done. In the second case, *Burlington Industries v. Ellerth,* the Court made a similar finding.[16]

In another 1998 case, *Oncale v. Sundowner Offshore Services, Inc.,*[17] the Supreme Court addressed a further issue: Should Title VII protection be extended to cover situations in which individuals are harassed by members of the same gender? The Court answered this question in the affirmative.

---

15. *United Automobile Workers v. Johnson Controls, Inc.,* 499 U.S. 187 (1991).
16. 524 U.S. 775 (1998); and 524 U.S. 742 (1998).
17. 523 U.S. 75 (1998).

Wage Discrimination

As of 2010, women constituted a majority of U.S. workers. Although Title VII and other legislation since the 1960s have mandated equal employment opportunities for men and women, women continue to earn less, on average, than men do.

Pay equity was the subject of Lilly Ledbetter's speech at the Democratic National Convention in 2008. When she sued her employer, Goodyear Tire, for back pay and lost, Congress responded with the Lilly Ledbetter Fair Pay Act of 2009. Why is equal pay for men and women still a subject of concern in the United States? (AP Photo/Charlie Neibergall)

The Equal Pay Act of 1963. The issue of wage discrimination was first addressed during World War II (1939–1945), when the War Labor Board issued an "equal pay for women" policy. In implementing the policy, the board often evaluated jobs for their comparability and required equal pay for comparable jobs. The board's authority ended with the war. Although it was supported by the next three presidential administrations, the Equal Pay Act was not enacted until 1963 as an amendment to the Fair Labor Standards Act of 1938.

Basically, the Equal Pay Act requires employers to provide equal pay for substantially equal work. In other words, males cannot legally be paid more than females who perform essentially the same job. The Equal Pay Act did not address the fact that certain types of jobs traditionally held by women pay lower wages than the jobs usually held by men. For example, more women than men are salesclerks and nurses, whereas more men than women are construction workers and truck drivers. Even if all clerks performing substantially similar jobs for a company earned the same salaries, they typically would still be earning less than the company's truck drivers.

When Congress passed the Equal Pay Act in 1963, a woman, on average, made 59 cents for every dollar earned by a man. By the mid-1990s, this amount had risen to 75 cents. Figures recently released by the U.S. Department of Labor indicate, though, that since then there has been little change. By 2009, women were still earning, on average, 80 cents for every dollar earned by men. While women continued to earn less than men through the Great Recession, they at least suffered less from unemployment, as we explain in this chapter's *The Politics of Boom and Bust* feature on the following page.

The Glass Ceiling. Although greater numbers of women are holding jobs in professions or business enterprises that were once dominated by men, few women hold top positions in their firms. Women now hold fewer than 16 percent of the top corporate officer positions in Fortune 500 companies—the nation's leading corporations. Although this percentage has grown from 8.7 percent in 1995, women continue to face barriers to advancement in the corporate world. Because these barriers are subtle and not easily pinpointed, they have been referred to as the "glass ceiling."

Immigration, Latinos, and Civil Rights

Immigration, and in particular unauthorized immigration, has become one of the hottest political issues under debate. Issues include whether we should create a path toward citizenship for unauthorized immigrants, as discussed in the *What If . . .* feature at the beginning of this chapter, or whether such a move amounts to an unacceptable amnesty for lawbreakers. A second major issue is how to limit unauthorized immigration in the first place. Closely allied to these issues are those affecting legal immigrants. Are we admitting too many legal immigrants—or not enough? Are laws restricting the rights of immigrants appropriate—or too tough? We examine immigration issues in detail in Chapter 14.

A century ago, most immigrants to the United States came from Europe. Today, however, most come from Latin America and Asia. Tables 5–2, 5–3, and 5–4 on pages 167 and 168 show the top countries of origin for immigrants, both legal and unauthorized, entering the United States. Note the large number of immigrants from Spanish-speaking countries, or "Hispanic" countries, which are marked in red on the tables.

The large number of new immigrants from Spanish-speaking countries increases the Hispanic proportion of the U.S. population. The number of persons who identify themselves as *multiracial* is also growing due to interracial marriages. Those who consider themselves as multiracial may have one parent of Chinese descent and another of Mexican descent, for example.

Hispanic versus *Latino*

To the U.S. Census Bureau, Hispanics are those who identify themselves by that term. Hispanics can be of any race. Hispanics can be new immigrants or the descendants of families that have lived in the United States for centuries. Hispanics may come from any of about twenty

THE POLITICS OF BOOM AND BUST

THE MALE RECESSION

Back in the halcyon days of the mid-2000s, the unemployment rate hovered around 5 percent. It even dropped to 4.6 percent in 2006 and 2007. By Christmas Eve 2009, it was 10 percent. The Great Recession had taken its toll.

HIGHER UNEMPLOYMENT AMONG MEN

Since 2008, men twenty years of age and older have suffered higher rates of unemployment than women in the same age brackets. Throughout 2009, the male unemployment rate was more than two percentage points greater than the female rate. That two-percentage-point gap continued into 2010.

WHY THE MALE RECESSION?

Several factors explain why two and a half million more men than women were out of work. One has to do with the nature of the latest recession. The crisis first struck the housing sector. After the crash in that market, construction plummeted. Men make up 88 percent of all workers in construction, and many of them lost their jobs. Thereafter, manufacturing began to plummet. Men make up 70 percent of manufacturing employment. The financial industry also imploded. Men make up a majority of the employees in that sector, too.

Not all sectors declined during the Great Recession. Which two sectors were hurt the least? Education and health care. Women make up 77 percent of the employees in those two sectors. Consequently, many of them were able to keep their jobs. There was an additional consideration: because women traditionally have been paid less than men, some employers may have chosen to lay off more of their expensive male workers.

MEN ARE ALSO LAGGING IN EDUCATIONAL ACHIEVEMENT

Since 1981, women have earned 135 bachelor's degrees for every 100 received by men. In recent years, the ratio has risen to an astonishing 185 to 100. Women are also receiving 150 master's degrees for every 100 earned by men. During any recession, the unemployment rate among college graduates is relatively low. In the latest recession, it was less than half the rate experienced by those with only a high school degree.

As one result, nearly 20 percent of men between ages twenty-five and fifty-four did not have jobs at the beginning of 2010. This is the highest figure reported since the government began collecting these data in 1948.

FOR CRITICAL ANALYSIS

Why are more women than men earning college degrees?

primarily Spanish-speaking countries,[18] and they differ among themselves in many ways. Hispanic Americans, as a result, are a highly diverse population. The three largest Hispanic groups are Mexican Americans, at 65.7 percent of all Hispanics; Puerto Ricans (all of whom are U.S. citizens), at 8.9 percent of the total; and Cuban Americans, at 3.5 percent.

The term *Hispanic* itself, although used by the government, is not particularly popular among Hispanic Americans. Many prefer the term *Latino,* and for that reason we frequently use that term throughout this text. When possible, Latinos prefer a name that identifies their heritage more specifically—for example, many Mexican Americans would rather be called that than *Latino* or *Hispanic.* Some Mexican Americans prefer the term *Chicano.*

TABLE 5–2 Top Ten Countries of Origin for the Foreign-Born Population

Hispanic countries are marked in red.

Country	Number
Mexico	11,451,299
Philippines	1,685,102
India	1,626,906
China	1,339,131
Vietnam	1,154,667
El Salvador	1,078,319
Korea	1,034,719
Cuba	987,772
Canada	824,347
Dominican Republic	779,249
ALL COUNTRIES	38,016,102

Source: Pew Hispanic Center. Figures are for 2008.

The Changing Face of America

As a result of immigration, the ethnic makeup of the United States is changing. The percentage of Latinos and Asian Americans in the population is growing rapidly. At the same time, the percentage of African Americans is staying relatively constant and the percentage of European Americans is dropping, though both groups continue to grow in absolute numbers.

Immigration is not the only factor contributing to changes in the American ethnic mosaic. Another factor is ethnic differences in the *fertility rate.* The **fertility rate** measures the average number of children that women in a given group are expected to have over the course of a lifetime. A fertility rate of 2.1 is the "long-term replacement rate." In other words, if a nation or group maintains a fertility rate of 2.1, its population will eventually stabilize. This can take many years, however. Because of past growth, the median age of the population may be younger than it would otherwise be. This means that there are more potential mothers and fathers. Only after its residents age will the population of a group or country stabilize.

Fertility Rate
A statistic that measures the average number of children that women in a given group are expected to have over the course of a lifetime.

Today, the United States actually has a fertility rate of 2.1 children per woman. Hispanic Americans, however, have a current fertility rate of 2.9. (The fertility rate in Mexico itself is only 2.3.) African Americans have a fertility rate of 2.1. Non-Hispanic white Americans have a fertility rate of 1.84. Figure 5–1 on the following page shows the projected changes in the U.S. ethnic distribution in future years.

TABLE 5–3 Top Ten Countries of Birth for Unauthorized Immigrants

Also referred to as "illegal" or "undocumented" immigrants. Of necessity, these figures are rough estimates. Hispanic countries are marked in red.

Country	Number
Mexico	7,030,000
El Salvador	570,000
Guatemala	430,000
Philippines	300,000
Honduras	300,000
Korea	240,000
China	220,000
Brazil*	180,000
Ecuador	170,000
India	160,000
ALL COUNTRIES	11,600,000

*Although Brazil is located in South America, its language is Portuguese, and the Bureau of the Census does not consider it a Hispanic country.

Source: U.S. Department of Homeland Security. Figures are for 2008.

The Civil Rights of Immigrants

Citizens who are Hispanic Americans have the same rights as all other Americans. Further, the law recognizes that in years past, Latinos have been subjected to many of the same forms of ill treatment as African Americans, so Latinos are usually grouped with African Americans and American Indians (Native Americans) in laws and programs that seek to protect minorities from discrimination or to address the results of past discrimination. Such programs often cover Asian Americans as well.

Immigrants who are not yet citizens, however, possess fewer civil rights than any other identifiable group in the United States. The rights of unauthorized immigrants are fewer still. As one example, even most legal immigrants are not eligible for various federal antipoverty programs such as food stamps. The terrorist attacks on September 11, 2001, reinforced the belief that the rights of noncitizens should be limited. Among the most obvious characteristics of the terrorists who perpetrated the 9/11 attacks is that they were all foreign citizens.

18. According to the census definition, *Hispanic* includes the relatively small number of Americans whose ancestors came directly from Spain itself. Few of these people are likely to check the "Hispanic" box on a census form, however.

TABLE 5–4 Top Ten Countries of Origin for Legal Immigrants

The following figures are for a single year only. Legal immigrants are persons obtaining official permanent resident status in that year. Hispanic countries are marked in red.

Country	Immigrants
Mexico	164,067
China	60,896
Philippines	58,107
India	54,360
Dominican Republic	49,381
Cuba	38,111
Vietnam	28,397
Colombia	27,221
Korea	25,582
Haiti	23,994
ALL COUNTRIES	1,130,818

Source: U.S. Department of Homeland Security. Figures are for 2009.

The Constitutional Rights of Noncitizens. Immigrants who are not citizens have rights. The Bill of Rights contains no language that limits its protections to citizens. The Fourteenth Amendment specifies that all *persons* (as opposed to *citizens*) shall enjoy "due process of law." In decisions spanning more than a century, the United States Supreme Court has ruled that there are constitutional guarantees that apply to every person within our borders, including "aliens whose presence in this country is unlawful."

Immigrants who are not here legally are subject to deportation. In 1903, however, the Supreme Court ruled that the government could not deport someone without a hearing that meets constitutional due process standards.[19] Today, most people facing deportation are entitled to a hearing before an immigration judge, to representation by a lawyer, and to the right to see the evidence presented against them. The government must prove that its grounds for deportation are valid.

Limits to the Rights of Deportees: Due Process. Despite the language of the Fourteenth Amendment, the courts have often deferred to government assertions that noncitizens cannot make constitutional claims. The Supreme Court has stated, "In exercise of its broad power over naturalization and immigration, Congress may make rules as to aliens that would be unacceptable if applied to citizens."[20] Immigration and antiterrorism laws passed by Congress in 1996 were especially restrictive. The government was given the right to deport noncitizens in cases of alleged terrorism without any federal court review of the deportation order. Further, the government is now allowed to deport noncitizens based on secret evidence that the deportee is not permitted to see.

19. *Yamataya v. Fisher,* 189 U.S. 86 (1903).
20. See, for example, *Demore v. Hyung Joon Kim,* 538 U.S. 510 (2003).

FIGURE 5–1 Projected Changes in U.S. Ethnic Distribution

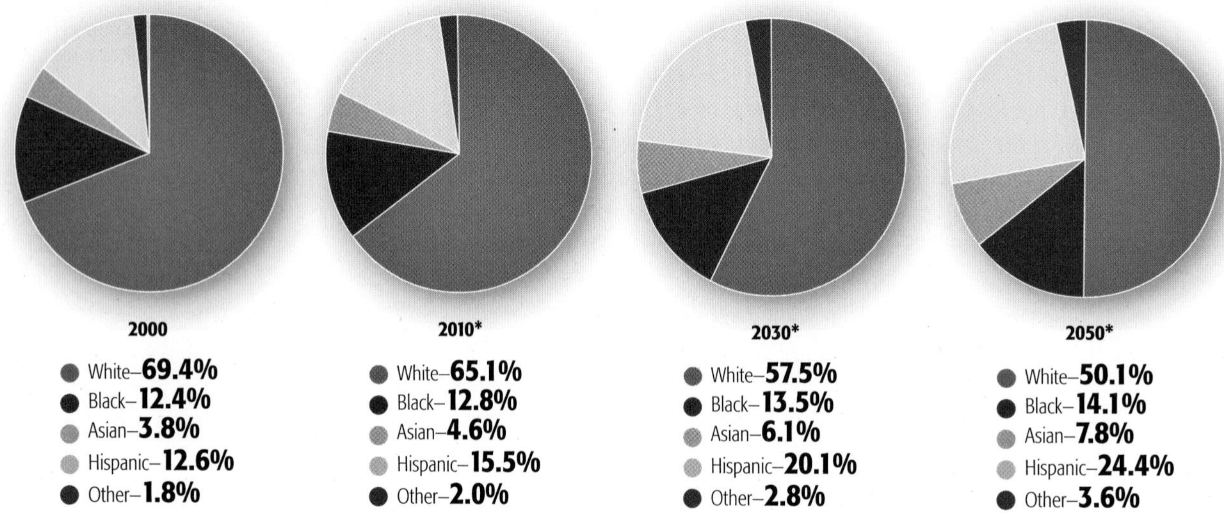

*Data for 2010, 2030, and 2050 are projections.
Hispanics may be of any race. The chart categories *White, Black, Asian,* and *Other* are limited to non-Hispanics.
Other consists of the following non-Hispanic groups: *American Indian, Native Alaskan, Native Hawaiian, Other Pacific Islander,* and *Two or more races.*

Source: U.S. Bureau of the Census and authors' calculations.

Immediately after 9/11, the government arrested more than 1,200 foreign citizens on suspicion of terrorism. These persons were cleared of terrorism, but most were deported for violating immigration rules. The deportation hearings were secret—a reversal of past procedure. Even the names of the persons held were not released. In June 2003, a federal appellate court ruled that the government was within its rights to maintain such secrecy.[21] The Supreme Court refused to review the issue. As a result, the public will never know how these cases were handled.

These immigrants swear their allegiance to the United States during citizenship ceremonies on Ellis Island. Why are immigrants and their children changing the makeup of the U.S. population? (© Michael S. Yamashita/Corbis)

Limits to the Rights of Deportees: Freedom of Speech. A case in 1999 involved a group of noncitizens associated with the Popular Front for the Liberation of Palestine (PFLP). The PFLP had carried out terrorist acts in Israel, but there was no evidence of criminal conduct by the group arrested in the United States. In *Reno v. American-Arab Anti-Discrimination Committee*,[22] the Supreme Court ruled that aliens have no First Amendment rights to object to deportation, even if the deportation is based on their political associations. This ruling also covers permanent residents—noncitizens with "green cards" that allow them to live and work in the United States on a long-term basis.

Affirmative Action
A policy in educational admissions or job hiring that gives special attention or compensatory treatment to traditionally disadvantaged groups in an effort to overcome present effects of past discrimination.

Limits to the Rights of Deportees: *Ex Post Facto* Laws. Article I, Section 9, of the Constitution prohibits *ex post facto* laws—laws that inflict punishments for acts that were not illegal when they were committed. This provision may not apply to deportation cases, however. The 1996 immigration and antiterrorism laws mentioned earlier provide mandatory deportation for noncitizens convicted of an aggravated felony, even if the crime took place before 1996. The term *aggravated felony* sounds serious, but under immigration law it can include misdemeanors. Until recently, mere possession of marijuana was usually considered an aggravated felony. Under the 1996 laws, permanent residents have been deported to nations that they left when they were small children. In some cases, deported persons did not even speak the language of the country to which they were deported.

Affirmative Action

As noted earlier in this chapter, the Civil Rights Act of 1964 prohibited discrimination against any person on the basis of race, color, national origin, religion, or gender. The act also established the right to equal opportunity in employment. A basic problem remained, however: minority groups and women, because of past discrimination, often lacked the education and skills to compete effectively in the marketplace. In 1965, the federal government attempted to remedy this problem by implementing the concept of affirmative action. **Affirmative action** policies attempt to "level the playing field" by giving special preferences in educational admissions and employment decisions to groups that have been discriminated against in the past.

This U.S. Border Patrol employee checks the health of a captured illegal immigrant because such individuals may be a source of tuberculosis. (© Karen Kasmauski/Science Faction/Corbis)

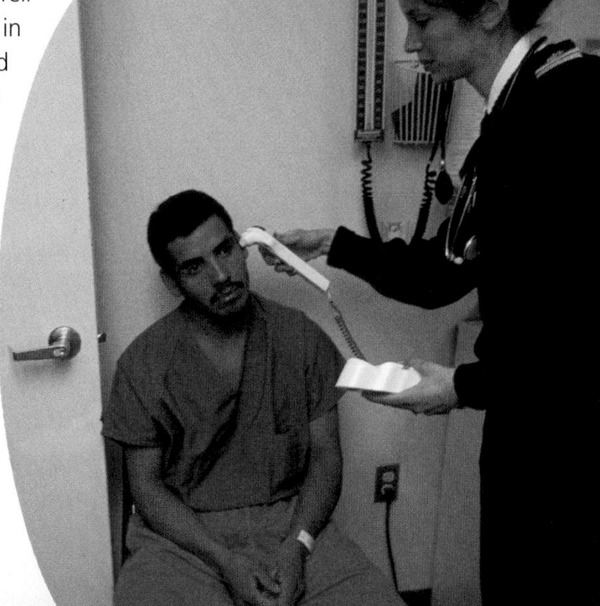

21. *Center for National Security Studies v. U.S. Department of Justice*, 331 F.3d 918 (D.C.Cir. 2003).
22. 525 U.S. 471 (1999).

(Walt Handelsman/*Newsday*)

In 1965, President Lyndon Johnson issued Executive Order 11246, which mandated affirmative action policies to remedy the effects of past discrimination. All government agencies, including those of state and local governments, were required to implement such policies. Additionally, affirmative action requirements were imposed on companies that sell goods or services to the federal government and on institutions that receive federal funds. Affirmative action policies were also required whenever an employer had been ordered to develop such a plan by a court or by the Equal Employment Opportunity Commission because of evidence of past discrimination. Finally, labor unions that had been found to discriminate against women or minorities in the past were required to establish and follow affirmative action plans.

Affirmative action programs have been controversial because they allegedly result in discrimination against majority groups, such as white males (or discrimination against other minority groups that may not be given preferential treatment under a particular affirmative action program). At issue in the current debate over affirmative action programs is whether such programs, because of their discriminatory nature, violate the equal protection clause of the Fourteenth Amendment to the Constitution.

While the term *affirmative action* was coined in the United States, other countries, such as India, Malaysia, and South Africa, have attempted to implement similar policies. We look at India's program of affirmative action for the lower castes in its society in this chapter's *Beyond Our Borders* feature on the facing page.

The *Bakke* Case

The first United States Supreme Court case addressing the constitutionality of affirmative action examined a program implemented by the University of California at Davis. Allan Bakke, a white student who had been turned down for medical school at the Davis campus, discovered that his academic record was better than those of some of the minority applicants who had been admitted to the program. He sued the University of California regents, alleging **reverse discrimination.** The UC-Davis Medical School had held sixteen places out of one hundred for educationally "disadvantaged students" each year, and the administrators at that campus admitted to using race as a criterion for admission for these particular minority slots. At trial in 1974, Bakke said that his exclusion from medical school violated his rights under the Fourteenth Amendment's provision for equal protection of the laws. The trial court agreed. On appeal, the California Supreme Court agreed also. Finally, the regents of the university appealed to the United States Supreme Court.

Reverse Discrimination
The situation in which an affirmative action program discriminates against those who do not have minority status.

In 1978, the Supreme Court handed down its decision in *Regents of the University of California v. Bakke.*[23] The Court did not rule against affirmative action programs. Rather, it held that Bakke must be admitted to the medical school because its admissions policy had used race as the sole criterion for the sixteen "minority" positions. Justice Lewis Powell, speaking for the Court, indicated that while race can be considered "as a factor" among others in admissions (and presumably hiring) decisions, race cannot be the sole factor. So affirmative action programs, but not quota systems, were upheld as constitutional.

---

23. 438 U.S. 265 (1978).

Further Limits on Affirmative Action

A number of cases decided during the 1980s and 1990s placed further limits on affirmative action programs. In a landmark decision in 1995, *Adarand Constructors, Inc. v. Peña,*[24] the Supreme Court held that any federal, state, or local affirmative action program that uses racial or ethnic classifications as the basis for making decisions is subject to "strict scrutiny" by the courts. Under a strict-scrutiny standard, to be constitutional, a discriminatory law or action must be narrowly tailored to meet a *compelling* government interest. In effect, the Court's opinion in the *Adarand* case means that an affirmative action program cannot make use of quotas or preferences for unqualified persons. Furthermore, once the program has succeeded in achieving its purpose, it must be changed or dropped.

24. 515 U.S. 200 (1995).

BEYOND OUR BORDERS

HIRING QUOTAS IN INDIA

Americans have become used to affirmative action programs designed to eradicate discrimination in the workplace. In the past, such programs sometimes involved actual quotas for hiring members of racial minorities or admitting them into college. Over the years, the courts have struck down programs that established outright quotas, while permitting plans that consider race as one factor among many. Some states have passed laws prohibiting any consideration of race in admissions to public universities.

In India, the world's most populous democracy with more than a billion inhabitants, however, quotas for hiring and college admissions are widespread. Preferences are based not on minority status, as in the United States, but rather on Hinduism's caste system.

India's traditional caste system is bound up with its dominant religion. For millennia, Hindu teachings have endorsed a rigid social hierarchy. Today, the caste system is strongest in India's rural villages, but its effects are felt throughout the country. Members of the upper castes get the larger share of good jobs. The untouchables—the *Dalits*—get few.

QUOTAS IN THE PUBLIC SECTOR

Today, almost 25 percent of public sector jobs and university admissions are reserved for Dalits and for members of tribes that fall outside the caste system. In 1993, another 25 percent of university admissions and public sector jobs were reserved for "other backward classes," low-ranking subcastes that nonetheless have higher status than the Dalits. Not everyone is happy about such quotas. There have been riots by those in India who have lost out because they are not designated as either untouchables or part of "other backward classes."

EXTENDING QUOTAS TO THE PRIVATE SECTOR

Recently, some members of India's government have argued that quotas should be applied to private companies. One Dalit leader has said that he believes that 30 percent of company jobs should be reserved for Dalits, members of "other backward classes," and the Muslim poor. Indian businesses argue against such preferences. They contend that those employees who are given a right to a job tend not to work very hard. Some enterprises, however, have responded to these arguments by setting up affirmative action programs for Dalits that are not based on quotas.

India has not seen the kind of reverse discrimination cases that have come before U.S. courts over the last twenty years. Nonetheless, some Indian attorneys are starting to prepare their arguments.

FOR CRITICAL ANALYSIS

Given that any quota system means that someone loses out on university admission or employment because of that system, is there any procedure that can be used to reduce the frictions among affected groups?

In 1996, a federal appellate court went even further. In *Hopwood v. State of Texas,*[25] two white law school applicants sued the University of Texas School of Law in Austin, alleging that they had been denied admission because of the school's affirmative action program. The program allowed admissions officials to take race and other factors into consideration. The federal appellate court held that the program violated the equal protection clause because it discriminated in favor of minority applicants. Significantly, the court directly challenged the *Bakke* decision by stating that the use of race even as a means of achieving diversity on college campuses "undercuts the Fourteenth Amendment."

In 2003, however, in two cases involving the University of Michigan, the Supreme Court indicated that limited affirmative action programs continue to be acceptable and that diversity is a legitimate goal. The Court struck down the affirmative action plan used for undergraduate admissions at the university, which automatically awarded a substantial number of points to applicants based on minority status.[26] At the same time, it approved the admissions plan used by the law school, which took race into consideration as part of a complete examination of each applicant's background.[27]

These concerned Seattle residents listen to a news conference that discussed the Supreme Court's 2000 decision concerning the voluntary integration plans for school districts in Seattle. The Court ruled that race could not be the deciding factor in denying admission to a particular school. How does the Fourteenth Amendment to the Constitution enter into this discussion? (AP Photo/Joe Nicholson)

The End of Affirmative Action?

Although in 2003 the United States Supreme Court upheld the admissions plan used by the University of Michigan Law School, a Michigan ballot initiative passed in 2006 prohibited affirmative action programs in all public universities and state government positions. In addition to Michigan, other states, including California, Florida, Nebraska, and Washington, have banned all state-sponsored affirmative action programs. In 2008, however, Colorado voters rejected such a ban.

In 2007, the United States Supreme Court heard a case involving voluntary integration plans in school districts in Seattle, Washington, and in Louisville, Kentucky. The schools' racial-integration guidelines permitted race to be a deciding factor if, say, two persons sought to be admitted to the school and there was space for only one. The schools' policies were challenged by parents of students, most of them white, who were denied admission because of their race. In a close (five-to-four) decision, the Court ruled that the schools' policies violated the Constitution's equal protection clause. (The Court did not, however, go so far as to invalidate the use of race as a factor in admissions policies.)[28]

Securing Rights for Persons with Disabilities

Persons with disabilities did not fall under the protective umbrella of the Civil Rights Act of 1964. In 1973, however, Congress passed the Rehabilitation Act, which prohibited discrimination against persons with disabilities in programs receiving federal aid. A 1978 amendment to the act established the Architectural and Transportation Barriers Compliance

25. 84 F.3d 720 (5th Cir. 1996).
26. *Gratz v. Bollinger,* 539 U.S. 244 (2003).
27. *Grutter v. Bollinger,* 539 U.S. 306 (2003).
28. *Parents Involved in Community Schools v. Seattle School District No. 1,* 551 U.S. 701 (2007).

Board. Regulations for ramps, elevators, and the like in all federal buildings were implemented. Congress passed the Education for All Handicapped Children Act in 1975. It guarantees that all children with disabilities will receive an "appropriate" education. The most significant federal legislation to protect the rights of persons with disabilities, however, is the Americans with Disabilities Act (ADA), which Congress passed in 1990.

The Americans with Disabilities Act of 1990

The ADA requires that all public buildings and public services be accessible to persons with disabilities. The act also mandates that employers must reasonably accommodate the needs of workers or potential workers with disabilities. Physical access means ramps; handrails; wheelchair-accessible restrooms, counters, drinking fountains, telephones, and doorways; and easily accessible mass transit. In addition, other steps must be taken to comply with the act. Car rental companies must provide cars with hand controls for disabled drivers. Telephone companies are required to have operators to pass on messages from speech-impaired persons who use telephones with keyboards.

The ADA requires employers to "reasonably accommodate" the needs of persons with disabilities unless to do so would cause the employer to suffer an "undue hardship." The ADA defines persons with disabilities as persons who have physical or mental impairments that "substantially limit" their everyday activities. Health conditions that have been considered disabilities under federal law include blindness, a history of alcoholism, heart disease, cancer, muscular dystrophy, cerebral palsy, paraplegia, diabetes, acquired immune deficiency syndrome (AIDS), and infection with the human immunodeficiency virus (HIV) that causes AIDS.

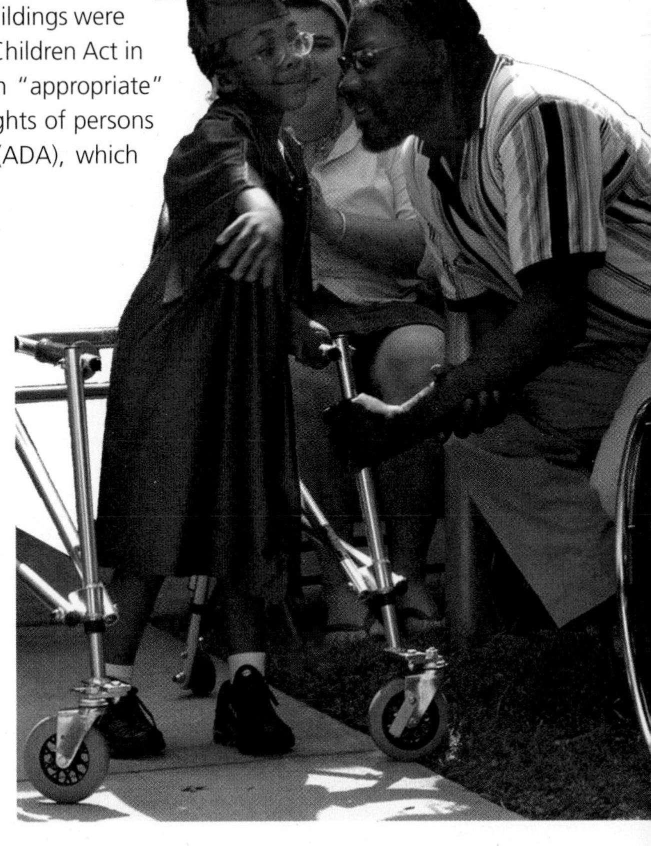

This child, who uses a walker for mobility assistance, is a beneficiary of the Education for All Handicapped Children Act of 1975. What other federal legislation was passed to help persons with disabilities in the United States? (Realistic Reflections)

The ADA does not require that *unqualified* applicants with disabilities be hired or retained. If a job applicant or an employee with a disability, with reasonable accommodation, can perform essential job functions, however, then the employer must make the accommodation. Required accommodations may include installing ramps for a wheelchair, establishing more flexible working hours, creating or modifying job assignments, and creating or improving training materials and procedures.

Limiting the Scope and Applicability of the ADA

Beginning in 1999, the United States Supreme Court issued a series of decisions that effectively limited the scope of the ADA. In 1999, for example, the Court held in *Sutton v. United Airlines, Inc.,*[29] that a condition (in this case, severe nearsightedness) that can be corrected with medication or a corrective device (in this case, eyeglasses) is not considered a disability under the ADA. In other words, the determination of whether a person is substantially limited in a major life activity is based on how the person functions when taking medication or using corrective devices, not on how the person functions without these measures. Thereafter, the courts held that plaintiffs with bipolar disorder, epilepsy, diabetes, and other conditions do not fall under the ADA's protections if the conditions can be corrected with medication or corrective devices—even if the plaintiffs were discriminated against because of their conditions.

---

29. 527 U.S. 471 (1999).

In September 2008, President George W. Bush signed into law the ADA Amendments Act. This legislation overturned limits that the Supreme Court had placed on the ADA. With the exception of eyeglasses, the courts are no longer allowed to consider how a person functions when using "mitigating measures," but must assess whether a person is disabled without such assistance. The new law also struck down a Supreme Court decision that seriously restricted the meaning of "major life activities." In this case, the Court refused to consider carpal tunnel syndrome as a disability because the manual tasks that sufferers were unable to perform did not qualify as a major life activity.[30]

The Supreme Court has also limited the applicability of the ADA by holding that lawsuits under the ADA cannot be brought against state government employers.[31] In a 2001 case, the Court concluded that states, as sovereigns, are immune from lawsuits brought against them by private parties under the federal ADA.

The Rights and Status of Gay Males and Lesbians

On June 27, 1969, patrons of the Stonewall Inn, a New York City bar popular with gay men and lesbians, responded to a police raid by throwing beer cans and bottles because they were angry at what they felt was unrelenting police harassment. In the ensuing riot, which lasted two nights, hundreds of gay men and lesbians fought with police. Before Stonewall, the stigma attached to homosexuality and the resulting fear of exposure had tended to keep most gay men and lesbians quiescent. In the months immediately after Stonewall, however, "gay power" graffiti began to appear in New York City. The Gay Liberation Front and the Gay Activist Alliance were formed, and similar groups sprang up in other parts of the country.

Growth in the Gay Male and Lesbian Rights Movement

The Stonewall incident marked the beginning of the movement for gay and lesbian rights. Since then, gay men and lesbians have formed thousands of organizations to exert pressure on legislatures, the media, schools, churches, and other organizations to recognize their right to equal treatment.

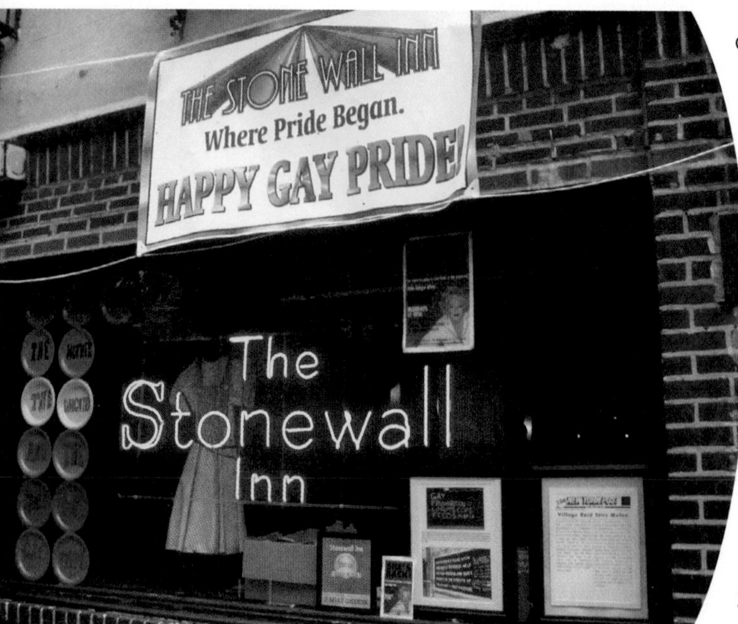

In the summer of 1969, gay men and lesbians who frequented a New York City bar called the Stonewall Inn had had enough. They were tired of unrelenting police harassment. For two nights, they fought with police. Out of these riots came a "gay power" movement. ("DoctorWho," Creative Commons)

To a great extent, lesbian and gay groups have succeeded in changing public opinion—and state and local laws—that pertain to their status and rights. Nevertheless, they continue to struggle against age-old biases against homosexuality, often rooted in deeply held religious beliefs, and the rights of gay men and lesbians remain an extremely divisive issue in American society.

State and Local Laws Targeting Gay Men and Lesbians

Before the Stonewall incident, forty-nine states had sodomy laws that made various kinds of sexual acts, including homosexual acts, illegal (Illinois, which had repealed its sodomy law in 1962, was the only excep-

30. *Toyota Manufacturing, Kentucky, Inc. v. Williams,* 534 U.S. 184 (2002).
31. *Board of Trustees of the University of Alabama v. Garrett,* 531 U.S. 356 (2001).

tion). During the 1970s and 1980s, more than half of these laws were either repealed or struck down by the courts.

The trend toward repealing state antigay laws was suspended in 1986 with the Supreme Court's decision in *Bowers v. Hardwick.*[32] In that case, the Court upheld, by a five-to-four vote, a Georgia law that made homosexual conduct between two adults a crime. In 2003, the Court reversed its earlier position on sodomy with its decision in *Lawrence v. Texas.*[33] In this case, the Court held that laws against sodomy violate the due process clause of the Fourteenth Amendment. The Court stated: "The liberty protected by the Constitution allows homosexual persons the right to choose to enter upon relationships in the confines of their homes and their own private lives and still retain their dignity as free persons." The result of *Lawrence v. Texas* was to invalidate all remaining sodomy laws throughout the country.

did you know?

That Albert Einstein was among six thousand persons in Germany in 1903 who signed a petition to repeal a portion of the German penal code that made homosexuality illegal.

Today, twenty-five states, the District of Columbia, and more than 180 cities and counties have enacted laws protecting lesbians and gay men from discrimination in employment in at least some workplaces. Many of these laws also ban discrimination in housing, in public accommodation, and in other contexts. At one point, Colorado adopted a constitutional amendment to invalidate all state and local laws protecting homosexuals from discrimination. Ultimately, however, the Supreme Court, in *Romer v. Evans,*[34] invalidated the amendment, ruling that it violated the equal protection clause of the U.S. Constitution because it denied to homosexuals in Colorado—but to no other Colorado residents—"the right to seek specific protection of the law." Several laws at the national level have also been changed over the past two decades. Among other things, the government has lifted a ban on hiring gay men and lesbians and voided a 1952 law prohibiting gay men and lesbians from immigrating to the United States.

The Gay Community and Politics

Politicians at the national level have not overlooked the potential significance of homosexual issues in American politics. While conservative politicians generally have been critical of efforts to secure gay and lesbian rights, liberals, by and large, have been speaking out for gay rights in the last thirty years. In 1980, the Democratic platform included a gay plank for the first time.

President Bill Clinton was the first sitting president to address a gay rights organization. In 1997, in a speech intentionally reminiscent of Harry Truman's 1947 speech to an African American civil rights group, Clinton pledged his support for equal rights for gay and lesbian Americans at a fund-raiser sponsored by the Human Rights Campaign Fund. In 2000, George W. Bush became the first Republican presidential candidate to meet with a large group of openly gay leaders to discuss their issues. Although Bush asserted that he would continue to oppose gay marriage and adoption, he also said that being openly gay would not disqualify a person from serving in a prominent position in his administration.

To date, thirteen openly gay men and lesbians have been elected to the House of Representatives, and four were seated in 2011.[35] None has succeeded yet in gaining a seat in the Senate. Gay rights groups continue to work for increased political representation in Congress.

Army National Guard Lieutenant Dan Choi was dismissed subsequent to the Army's "don't ask, don't tell" policy with respect to gay men in the military. What are the issues in this debate? (AP Photo/Damian Dovarganes, File)

---

32. 478 U.S. 186 (1986).
33. 539 U.S. 558 (2003).
34. 517 U.S. 620 (1996).
35. Tammy Baldwin (D., Wisc.), David Cicilline (D., R.I.), Barney Frank (D., Mass.), and Jared Polis (D., Colo.).

Gay Men and Lesbians in the Military

The U.S. Department of Defense traditionally has viewed homosexuality as incompatible with military service. Supporters of gay and lesbian rights have attacked this policy in recent years, and in 1993 the policy was modified. In that year, President Clinton announced that a new policy, generally characterized as "don't ask, don't tell," would be in effect. Enlistees would not be asked about their sexual orientation, and gay men and lesbians would be allowed to serve in the military so long as they did not declare that they were gay or lesbian or commit homosexual acts. Military officials endorsed the new policy, after opposing it initially, but supporters of gay rights were not enthusiastic. Clinton had promised during his presidential campaign to repeal outright the long-standing ban.

Several gay men and lesbians who have been discharged from military service have protested their discharges by bringing suit against the Defense Department. Recent polling data show that military personnel may be more accepting of gay men and lesbians today than they were in years past. For example, in one poll of more than five hundred service members returning from Afghanistan and Iraq, 75 percent of those responding said that they would be comfortable interacting with gay people.[36] The Obama administration has stated that it intends to allow gay men and lesbians to serve openly in the armed forces, and it is preparing plans to implement this policy. The administration has been criticized by gay and lesbian activists, however, who believe that it is moving too slowly on this issue. In October 2010, a federal district court judge ruled that the military could not enforce "don't ask, don't tell." An appeal is certain.

Same-sex marriages have traditionally not been legal throughout the United States, but are currently performed in five states. The circumstances in California are unique. Same-sex marriage became legal in June 2008 but was then banned in November of that year. Still, the state continues to recognize marriages performed from June through November. Do all states have to recognize same-sex marriages from states where they are legal? Why or why not? (Redux/Peter DaSilva/ *The New York Times*)

Same-Sex Marriage

Perhaps one of the hottest political issues concerning the rights of gay and lesbian couples is whether they should be allowed to marry.

Defense of Marriage Act. The controversy over this issue in the United States began in 1993 when the Hawaii Supreme Court ruled that denying marriage licenses to gay couples might violate the equal protection clause of the Hawaii Constitution.[37] In the wake of this event, other states began to worry about whether they might have to treat gay men or lesbians who were legally married in another state as married couples in their state as well. Opponents of gay rights pushed for state laws banning same-sex marriages, and a number of states enacted such laws. At the federal level, Congress passed the Defense of Marriage Act of 1996, which bans federal recognition of lesbian and gay couples and allows state governments to ignore same-sex marriages performed in other states. (Chapter 3's *What If . . .* feature discussed the Defense of Marriage Act in greater depth—see page 82.)

In 1999, the Vermont Supreme Court ruled that gay couples are entitled to the same benefits of marriage as opposite-sex couples.[38] Subsequently, in April 2000, the Vermont legislature passed a law permitting gay and lesbian couples to form "civil unions." The law entitled partners forming civil unions to receive some three hundred state benefits available to married couples, including the rights to inherit a partner's property and to decide on medical treatment for an incapacitated partner. It did not, however, entitle those partners to receive any benefits allowed to married couples under federal law, such as spousal

36. As cited in John M. Shalikashvili, "Second Thoughts on Gays in the Military," *The New York Times,* January 2, 2007.
37. *Baehr v. Lewin,* 852 P.2d 44 (Hawaii 1993).
38. *Baker v. Vermont,* 744 A.2d 864 (Vt. 1999).

Social Security benefits. As of 2010, ten states have approved some system of rights for same-sex couples, not counting the five states (and the District of Columbia) that fully recognize same-sex marriages.[39]

State Recognition of Gay Marriages. In November 2003, the Massachusetts Supreme Judicial Court ruled that same-sex couples have a right to civil marriage under the Massachusetts state constitution.[40] In November 2008, the Connecticut Supreme Court legalized same-sex marriage, and the Iowa Supreme Court issued a similar ruling in April 2009. New Hampshire became the first state to legalize the marriages through an act of the legislature, passed in June 2009. The Vermont legislature followed in September of that year, as did the Council of the District of Columbia in December. New York and Maryland do not perform same-sex marriages, but recognize them when they are performed in other jurisdictions.

Two states have abolished existing same-sex marriage rights through referenda. In November 2008, California voters approved Proposition 8, which overturned a June 2008 California Supreme Court ruling. Uniquely, same-sex couples married in California from June through November retain their marriage rights, but no more such marriages may be performed. In Maine, the voters rejected a same-sex marriage law in November 2009 before it could take effect. Twenty-nine states now have constitutional amendments explicitly barring the recognition of same-sex marriage. Same-sex marriage is accepted nationwide in Canada and several other countries.

In July 2010, a U.S. district court judge in Massachusetts ruled that the provisions of the Defense of Marriage Act under which the federal government refuses to recognize same-sex marriages performed by the states are unconstitutional, in part, because their sole purpose is to penalize a specific class of persons. If the ruling stands, the U.S. government will have to provide a wide range of benefits to same-sex married persons. The ruling is certain to be appealed all the way to the United States Supreme Court.

A second ruling by a District Court judge in August 2010 was also certain to be appealed. In this case, a judge in San Francisco held that California's vote to withdraw marriage rights from same-sex couples—Proposition 8—violated the due process and equal protection clauses of the Fourteenth Amendment. If this ruling were to be endorsed by the Supreme Court, same-sex marriage would immediately become legal in every state.

Child Custody and Adoption

Gay men and lesbians have also faced difficulties in obtaining child-custody and adoption rights. Courts around the country, when deciding which of two parents should have custody, have wrestled with how much weight, if any, should be given to a parent's sexual orientation. For some time, the courts were split fairly evenly on this issue. In about half the states, courts held that a parent's sexual orientation should not be a significant factor in determining child custody. Courts in other states, however, tended to give more weight to sexual orientation. In one case, a court even went so far as to award

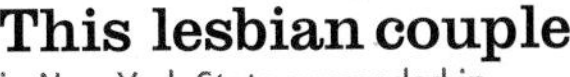

This lesbian couple in New York State succeeded in adopting a child, whom they brought to New York's Gay Pride Parade in June 2008. Why aren't such adoptions common in some states? (AP Photo/ Tina Fineberg)

39. California, Colorado, Hawaii, Maine, Maryland, Nevada, New Jersey, Oregon, Washington, and Wisconsin. The five states that allow same-sex marriage are Conneticut, Iowa, Massachusetts, New Hampshire, and Vermont.
40. *Goodridge v. Department of Public Health,* 798 N.E.2d 941 (Mass. 2003).

Since 1971, those over the age of eighteen have been allowed to vote. Students on many college campuses, such as those pictured here at the University of Pennsylvania, volunteer to "get out the vote." They are helping a university employee fill out his voter-registration form. Which amendment to the Constitution gave eighteen-year-olds the right to vote? (AP Photo/Manuel Balce Ceneta, File)

custody to a father because the child's mother was a lesbian, even though the father had served eight years in prison for killing his first wife. Today, however, courts in the majority of states no longer deny custody or visitation rights to persons solely on the basis of their sexual orientation.

The last decade has also seen a sharp climb in the number of gay men and lesbians who are adopting children. Today, nearly half the states allow lesbians and gay men to adopt children through state-operated or private adoption agencies. Single-parent adoptions by gay men or lesbians are now legal in every state but Florida.

The Rights and Status of Juveniles

Approximately 75 million Americans—about 24 percent of the total population—are under eighteen years of age. The definition of *children* ranges from persons under age sixteen to persons under age twenty-one. However defined, children in the United States have fewer rights and protections than adults.

The reason for this lack of rights is the presumption of society that children basically are protected by their parents. This is not to say that children are the exclusive property of the parents. Rather, an overwhelming case in favor of *not* allowing parents to control the actions of their children must be presented before children can be given authorization to act without parental consent (or before the state can be authorized to act on children's behalf without regard to their parents' wishes).

did you know?

That the United Nations Convention on the Rights of the Child calls for the provision of effective legal assistance for children so that their interests can be "heard directly."

Supreme Court decisions affecting children's rights began a process of slow evolution with *Brown v. Board of Education of Topeka,* the landmark civil rights case of 1954 discussed earlier in this chapter. In the *Brown* case, the Court granted children the status of rights-bearing persons. In the 1967 case *In re Gault,*[41] the Court expressly held that children have a constitutional right to be represented by counsel at the government's expense in a criminal action. Five years later, the Court acknowledged that "children are 'persons' within the meaning of the Bill of Rights. We have held so over and over again."[42]

---

41. 387 U.S. 1 (1967).
42. *Wisconsin v. Yoder,* 406 U.S. 205 (1972).

Voting Rights and the Young

The Twenty-sixth Amendment to the Constitution, ratified on July 1, 1971, reads as follows:

> *The right of citizens of the United States, who are eighteen years of age or older, to vote shall not be denied or abridged by the United States or by any State on account of age.*

Before this amendment was ratified, the age at which citizens could vote was twenty-one in most states. One of the arguments used for granting suffrage to eighteen-year-olds was that, because they could be drafted to fight in the country's wars, they had a stake in public policy. At the time, the example of the Vietnam War (1964–1975) was paramount.

In 1972, immediately after the passage of the Twenty-sixth Amendment, 58 percent of eighteen- to twenty-year-olds were registered to vote, and 48.4 percent reported that they had voted. But by the 2004 presidential elections, among U.S. residents in the eighteen-to-twenty age bracket, just 50.7 percent were registered, and only 41 percent reported that they had voted. In contrast, voter turnout among Americans ages sixty-five or older is very high, usually between 60 and 70 percent.

The Rights of Children in Civil and Criminal Proceedings

Children today have limited rights in civil and criminal proceedings in our judicial system. Different procedural rules and judicial safeguards apply under civil and criminal laws. **Civil law** relates to such matters as contracts among private individuals, domestic relations, and business transactions between private parties. **Criminal law** relates to crimes against society that are defined by society acting through its legislatures and prosecuted by a public official, such as a district attorney.

Civil Law
The law regulating conduct between private persons over noncriminal matters, including contracts, domestic relations, and business interactions.

Criminal Law
The law that defines crimes and provides punishment for violations. In criminal cases, the government is the prosecutor.

Majority
The age at which a person is entitled by law to the right to manage her or his own affairs.

Necessaries
Things necessary for existence. In contract law, necessaries include whatever is reasonably necessary for suitable subsistence as measured by age, state, condition in life, and the like.

Common Law
Judge-made law that originated in England from decisions shaped according to prevailing customs. Decisions were applied to similar situations and thus gradually became common to the nation.

Civil Rights of Juveniles. The civil rights of children are defined exclusively by state laws. The legal definition of **majority**—the age at which a person is entitled by law to the right to manage his or her own affairs—varies from eighteen to twenty-one years of age, depending on the state. As a rule, an individual who is legally a minor cannot be held responsible for contracts that he or she forms with others. In most states, only contracts entered into for so-called **necessaries** (things necessary for subsistence, as determined by the courts) can be enforced against minors. Also, when minors engage in negligent behavior, typically their parents are liable. If, for example, a minor destroys a neighbor's fence, the neighbor may bring a suit against the child's parent but not against the child.

Civil law also encompasses the area of child custody. Child-custody rulings traditionally have given little weight to the wishes of the child. Courts have maintained the right to act on behalf of the child's "best interests" but have sometimes been constrained from doing so by the "greater" rights possessed by adults. For instance, a widely publicized Michigan Supreme Court ruling awarded legal custody of a two-and-a-half-year-old Michigan resident to an Iowa couple, the child's biological parents. A Michigan couple, who had cared for the child since shortly after her birth and who had petitioned to adopt the child, lost out in the custody battle. The court said that the law had allowed it to consider only the parents' rights and not the child's best interests.

did you know?
That the first juvenile court in the United States opened in Chicago on July 3, 1899.

Children's rights and their ability to articulate their rights for themselves in custody matters were strengthened, however, by several well-publicized rulings involving older children. In one case, for example, an eleven-year-old Florida boy filed suit in his own name, assisted by his own privately retained legal counsel, to terminate his relationship with his biological parents and to have the court affirm his right to be adopted by foster parents. The court granted his request, although it did not agree procedurally with the method by which the boy initiated the suit.[43]

did you know?

That the number of juveniles sent to adult prisons for violent offenses in the United States has tripled since 1985.

Criminal Rights of Juveniles. One of the main requirements for an act to be criminal is intent. The law has given children certain defenses against criminal prosecution because of their presumed inability to have criminal intent. Under the **common law,** children up to seven years of age were considered incapable of committing a crime because they did not have the moral sense to understand that they were doing wrong. Children between the ages of seven and fourteen were also presumed to be incapable of committing a crime, but this presumption could be challenged by showing that the child understood the wrongful nature of the act. Today, states vary in their approaches. Most states retain the common law approach, although age limits vary from state to state. Other states have simply set a minimum age for criminal responsibility.

All states have juvenile court systems that handle children below the age of criminal responsibility who commit delinquent acts. The aim of juvenile courts is allegedly to reform rather than to punish. In states that retain the common law approach, children who are above the minimum age but are still juveniles can be turned over to the criminal courts if the juvenile court determines that they should be treated as adults. Children sent to juvenile court do not have the right to trial by jury or to post bail. Also, in most states parents can commit their minor children to state mental institutions without allowing the child a hearing.

Although minors usually do not have the full rights of adults in criminal proceedings, they have certain advantages. In felony, manslaughter, murder, armed robbery, and assault cases, traditionally juveniles were not tried as adults. They were often sentenced to probation or "reform" school for a relatively short term regardless of the seriousness of their crimes. Today, however, most states allow juveniles to be tried as adults (often at the discretion of the judge) for certain crimes, such as murder. When they are tried as adults, they are given due process of law and tried for the crime, rather than being given the paternalistic treatment reserved for the juvenile delinquent. Juveniles who are tried as adults may also face adult penalties. These used to include the death penalty. In 2005, however, the United States Supreme Court ruled that executing persons who were under the age of eighteen when they committed their crimes would constitute cruel and unusual punishment. The Court opined that sixteen- and seventeen-year-olds do not have a fully developed sense of right and wrong, nor do they necessarily understand the full gravity of their misdeeds.[44] In May 2010, the Court also ruled that juveniles who commit crimes in which no one is killed may not be sentenced to life in prison without the possibility of parole.[45]

A sheriff's officer leads sixteen-year-old Shahid Baskerville out of the county courthouse in Newark, New Jersey, in April 2008. Baskerville and another youth were charged with the murder of three college students in a Newark schoolyard the previous summer. Are there any advantages to being prosecuted as an adult, rather than as a juvenile, in criminal proceedings? (AP Photo/Mike Derer)

43. *Kingsley v. Kingsley,* 623 So.2d 780 (Fla.App. 1993).
44. *Roper v. Simmons,* 543 U.S. 551 (2005).
45. *Graham v. Florida,* 560 U.S. ___ (2010).

WHY SHOULD YOU CARE ABOUT... CIVIL RIGHTS?

Why should you, as an individual, care about civil rights? Some people may think that discrimination is only a problem for members of racial or ethnic minorities. Actually, almost everyone can be affected. Consider that in some instances, white men have actually experienced "reverse discrimination"—and have obtained redress for it. Also, discrimination against women is common, and women constitute half the population. Even if you are male, you probably have female friends whose well-being is of interest to you. Therefore, the knowledge of how to proceed when you suspect discrimination is another useful tool to have when living in the modern world.

(AP Photo/Javier Galeano)

HOW YOU CAN MAKE A DIFFERENCE

Anyone applying for a job may be subjected to a variety of possibly discriminatory practices based on race, color, gender, religion, age, sexual preference, or disability. There may be tests, some of which could have a discriminatory effect. At both the state and federal levels, the government continues to examine the fairness and validity of criteria used in screening job applicants. As a result, there are ways of addressing the problem of discrimination.

If you believe that you have been discriminated against by a potential employer, consider the following steps:

1. Evaluate your own capabilities, and determine if you are truly qualified for the position.
2. Analyze the reasons why you were turned down. Would others agree with you that you have been the object of discrimination, or would they uphold the employer's claim?
3. If you still believe that you have been treated unfairly, you have recourse to several agencies and services.

You should first speak to the personnel director of the company and explain politely that you believe you have not been evaluated adequately. If asked, explain your concerns clearly. If necessary, go into explicit detail, and indicate that you may have been discriminated against.

If a second evaluation is not forthcoming, contact your local state employment agency. If you still do not obtain adequate help, contact one or more of the following state agencies, usually listed in your telephone directory under "State Government":

1. If a government entity is involved, a state ombudsperson or citizen aide may be available to mediate.
2. You can contact the state civil rights commission, which at least will give you advice even if it does not wish to take up your case.
3. The state attorney general's office normally has a division dealing with discrimination and civil rights.
4. There may be a special commission or department specifically set up to help you, such as a women's status commission or a commission on Hispanics or Asian Americans. If you are a woman or a member of such a minority group, contact these commissions.

Finally, at the national level, you can contact:

American Civil Liberties Union
125 Broad St., 18th Floor
New York, NY 10004-2400
212-549-2500
www.aclu.org

You can also contact the most appropriate federal agency:

Equal Employment Opportunity Commission
131 M St. NE
Washington, DC 20507
202-663-4900
www.eeoc.gov

questions for discussion and analysis

1. Not all African Americans agreed with the philosophy of nonviolence espoused by Dr. Martin Luther King, Jr. Advocates of black power called for a more militant approach. Can militancy make a movement more effective (possibly by making a more moderate approach seem like a reasonable compromise), or is it typically counterproductive? Either way, why?
2. Women in the military are currently barred from assignments that are likely to place them in active combat. (Of course, the nature of war is such that support units sometimes find themselves in combat, regardless of assignment.) Such barriers can keep female officers from advancing to the highest levels within the armed services. Are these barriers appropriate? Why or why not?
3. While polls of military personnel suggest that rank-and-file soldiers are more accepting of gay men and lesbians than in years past, the current policy, known as "don't ask, don't tell," continues to result in the discharge of large numbers of military personnel on the basis of their sexual orientation. Is the current policy appropriate, or should it be liberalized? Either way, why? If a different policy were adopted, what should it be?
4. The prevention of terrorist acts committed by adherents of radical Islamism is a major policy objective today. Can we defend ourselves against such acts without abridging the civil rights and liberties of American Muslims and immigrants from predominantly Muslim countries? What measures that might be undertaken by the authorities are legitimate? Which are not?

key terms

affirmative action 169
busing 153
civil disobedience 154
civil law 179
civil rights 147
common law 179
criminal law 179
***de facto* segregation 152**
***de jure* segregation 152**
feminism 160
fertility rate 167
gender discrimination 162
grandfather clause 151
Hispanic 157
Latino 157
literacy test 151
majority 179
necessaries 179
poll tax 151
reverse discrimination 170
separate-but-equal doctrine 150
sexual harassment 164
suffrage 159
white primary 151

chapter summary

1. Before the Civil War, most African Americans were slaves, and slavery was protected by the Constitution. Constitutional amendments after the Civil War ended slavery, and African Americans gained citizenship, the right to vote, and other rights. This protection was largely a dead letter by the 1880s, however, and African American inequality continued.
2. Segregation was declared unconstitutional by the Supreme Court in *Brown v. Board of Education of Topeka* (1954), in which the Court stated that separation implied inferiority. In 1955, the modern civil rights movement began with a boycott of segregated public transportation in Montgomery, Alabama. The Civil Rights Act of 1964 bans discrimination on the basis of race, color, religion, gender, or national origin in employment and public accommodations.
3. The Voting Rights Act of 1965 outlawed discriminatory voter-registration tests and authorized federal voter registration. The Voting Rights Act and other protective legislation apply not only to African Americans but to other ethnic groups. Minorities have been increasingly represented in national and state politics, although they have yet to gain representation proportionate to their numbers. Lingering social and economic disparities continue to exist.
4. In the early history of the United States, women had no political rights. After the first women's rights convention in 1848, the women's movement gained momentum. Not until 1920, however, when the Nineteenth Amendment was ratified, did women obtain the right to vote nationwide. The modern women's movement began in the 1960s in the wake of the civil rights and anti–Vietnam War

movements. Efforts to secure the ratification of the Equal Rights Amendment failed, but the women's movement has been successful in obtaining new laws, changes in social customs, and increased political representation for women.

5. The number of women in Congress and in other government bodies increased significantly in the 1990s and 2000s. Federal government efforts to eliminate gender discrimination in the workplace include Title VII of the Civil Rights Act of 1964, which prohibits gender-based discrimination, including sexual harassment on the job. Wage discrimination continues to be a problem for women.

6. Today, most immigrants come from Asia and Latin America, especially Mexico. Many are unauthorized immigrants (also called illegal aliens or undocumented workers). The large number of Spanish-speaking immigrants means that the percentage of Latinos, or Hispanic Americans, in the population is growing rapidly. This population is also growing because Hispanic families have more children than other Americans. By 2050, non-Hispanic whites will make up only half of the nation's residents. While Latinos who are citizens benefit from the same antidiscrimination measures as African Americans, immigrants who are not citizens have few civil rights.

7. Affirmative action programs have been controversial because they may lead to reverse discrimination against majority groups or even other minority groups. United States Supreme Court decisions have limited affirmative action programs, and several states now ban state-sponsored affirmative action.

8. The Americans with Disabilities Act of 1990 prohibits job discrimination against persons with physical and mental disabilities, requiring that positive steps be taken to comply with the act. The act also requires expanded access to public facilities, including transportation, and to services offered by such private concerns as car rental and telephone companies. The courts have limited the impact of this law, however.

9. Gay and lesbian rights groups became commonplace after 1969. During the 1970s and 1980s, sodomy laws that criminalized specific sexual practices were repealed or struck down by the courts in nearly half of the states. In 2003, a United States Supreme Court decision effectively invalidated all remaining sodomy laws nationwide. Twenty-five states and more than 180 cities and counties now have laws prohibiting at least some types of discrimination based on sexual orientation. The military's "don't ask, don't tell" policy has fueled extensive controversy, as have same-sex marriages and child-custody issues.

10. Children have few rights and protections, in part because it is presumed that their parents protect them. The Twenty-sixth Amendment grants the right to vote to those ages eighteen or older. In nearly all states, most contracts entered into by minors cannot be enforced. When minors engage in negligent acts, their parents may be held liable. Minors have some defense against criminal prosecution because of their presumed inability to have criminal intent below certain ages. For those under the age of criminal responsibility, there are state juvenile courts. When minors are tried as adults, they are entitled to the procedural protections afforded to adults and are sometimes subject to adult penalties.

selected print & media resources

SUGGESTED READINGS

Baldwin, Lewis. ***The Voice of Conscience: The Church in the Mind of Martin Luther King, Jr.*** **New York: Oxford University Press, 2010. King, the great civil rights leader, was unquestionably a man of the church. Lewis examines King's theology and his prophetic Christianity.**

Friedan, Betty. ***The Feminine Mystique.*** **New York: W. W. Norton, 2001. Betty Friedan's work is the feminist classic that helped launch the modern women's movement in the United States. This edition contains an up-to-date introduction by columnist Anna Quindlen.**

Gilmore, Glenda Elizabeth. ***Defying Dixie: The Radical Roots of Civil Rights, 1919–1950.*** **New York: W. W. Norton, 2008. Gilmore, an award-winning history professor at Yale, looks at the radicalism of those who sought to overthrow Jim Crow laws before the time of the civil rights movement. In 2002, Gilmore gained national attention for strongly opposing the war in Iraq before it had even begun.**

Litwack, Leon F. ***How Free Is Free? The Southern Black Experience.*** **Cambridge, Mass.: Harvard University Press, 2009. The African American struggle for freedom and dignity has lasted for generations and continues today. Litwack, a prizewinning University of California history professor, confronts a painful history in a series of inspiring lectures.**

Riley, Glenda. ***Inventing the American Woman: An Inclusive History,*** **4th ed. Wheeling, Ill.: Harlan Davidson, 2007. This updated edition covers a wide range of women's** experiences in the United States from colonial times to the present.

MEDIA RESOURCES

Eyes on the Prize: America's Civil Rights Years 1954–1965—This three-DVD collection, released in 2010, contains episodes that have won Emmys, an International Documentary Award, and a Television Critics Association Award. It tells the story of the civil rights era from the perspective of the ordinary people who participated in it.

Iron Jawed Angels—This 2004 HBO movie, starring Hilary Swank, Margo Martindale, and Anjelica Huston, depicts the struggles of the women's suffrage movement. It is a stirring film and excellent history, even if the sound track is a bit too modern.

Malcolm X—This 1992 film, directed by Spike Lee and starring Denzel Washington, depicts the life of Malcolm X, the controversial "black power" leader. Malcolm X, who was assassinated on February 21, 1965, clearly had a different vision from that of Martin Luther King, Jr., regarding how to achieve civil rights, respect, and equality for black Americans.

Martin Luther King, Jr.: The Essential Box Set: The Landmark Speeches and Sermons of Dr. Martin Luther King, Jr.—Released in 2009, this CD contains twenty of King's most important speeches and sermons. Hearing King's oratory live is definitely more compelling than just reading it. The advantage of audio over film is that many important talks were recorded, but never filmed.

The Ring—Popular culture provides few depictions of Mexican American life in East Los Angeles in the 1950s. This 1952 black-and-white oldie is one of the few. It's an excellent choice for those who want to learn about discrimination—or boxing.

Tying the Knot—A film festival favorite, this 2003 documentary argues in favor of same-sex marriage and shows some of the disasters that can befall lesbian or gay male couples when they lack marriage rights.

e-mocracy

CIVIL RIGHTS INFORMATION ONLINE

Today, thanks to the Internet, information on civil rights issues is literally at your fingertips. By simply accessing the American Civil Liberties Union's Web site (the URL for this organization is given below, in the *Logging On* section), you can learn about the major civil rights issues facing Americans today. A host of other Web sites offer data on the extent to which groups discussed in this chapter are protected under state and federal laws. You can also find many advocacy sites that describe what you can do to help promote the rights of a certain group.

LOGGING ON

For information on, and arguments in support of, affirmative action and the rights of the groups discussed in this chapter, a good source is the American Civil Liberties Union's Web site. Go to
www.aclu.org

The National Organization for Women (NOW) offers online information and updates on the status of women's rights, including affirmative action cases involving women. Go to
www.now.org

An excellent source of information on issues facing African Americans is the Web site of the National Association for the Advancement of Colored People at
www.naacp.org

You can find information on the Americans with Disabilities Act (ADA) of 1990, including the act's text, at
askjan.org/links/adalinks.htm

You can access the Web site of the Human Rights Campaign Fund, the nation's largest gay and lesbian political organization, at
www.hrc.org

If you are interested in children's rights and welfare, a good starting place is the Web site of the Child Welfare Institute. Go to
www.gocwi.org

chapter 6

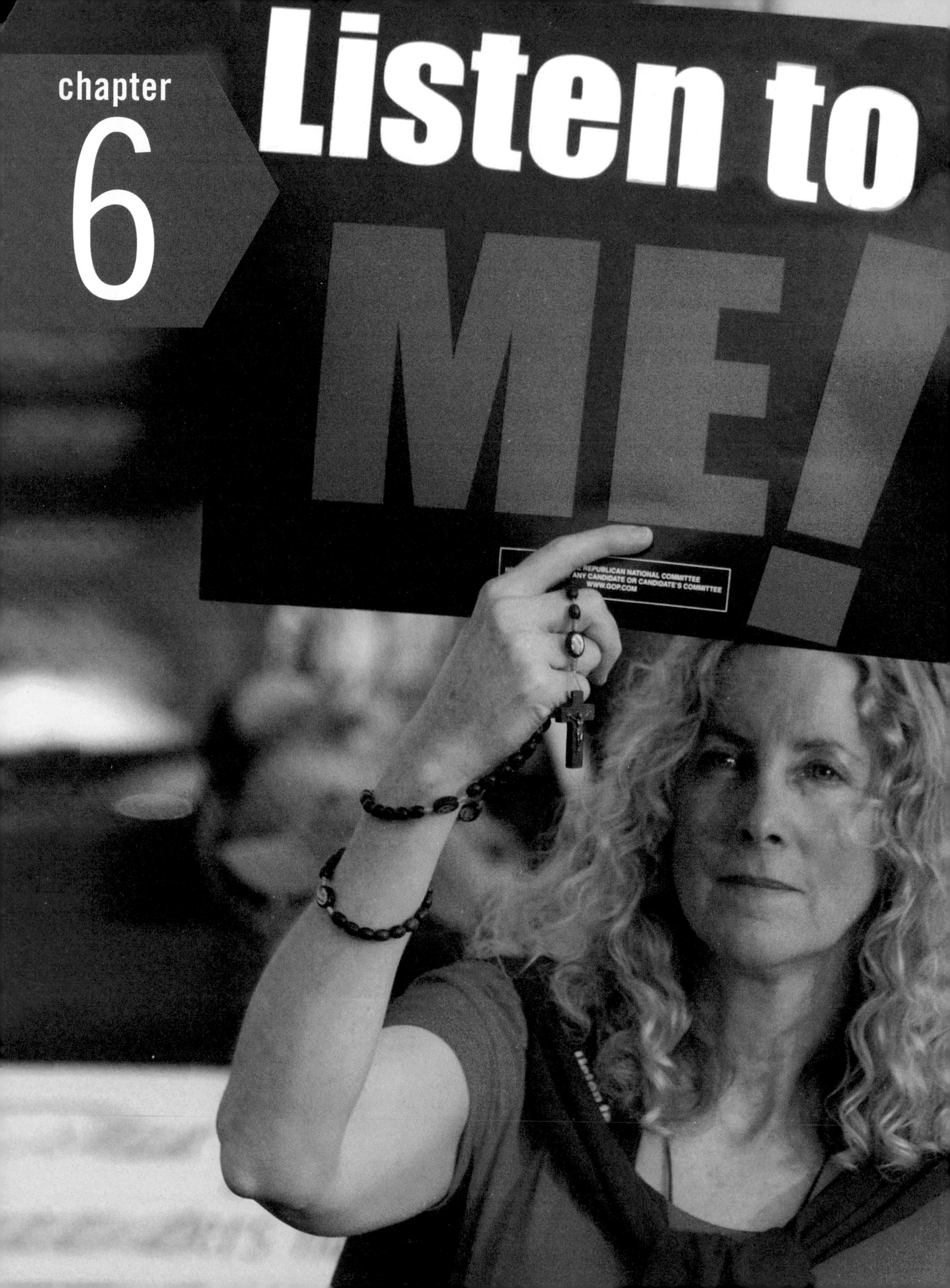

Listen to ME!

Public Opinion and Political Socialization

chapter contents

<< This Tea Party demonstrator stands at the foot of the Washington Monument on April 15, 2010—the day when Americans must pay their income taxes. She was not only expressing her opinions, but she was also trying to influence the opinions of others. (Sipa via AP Images)

WHAT IF... ...scientific opinion polling had never been invented?

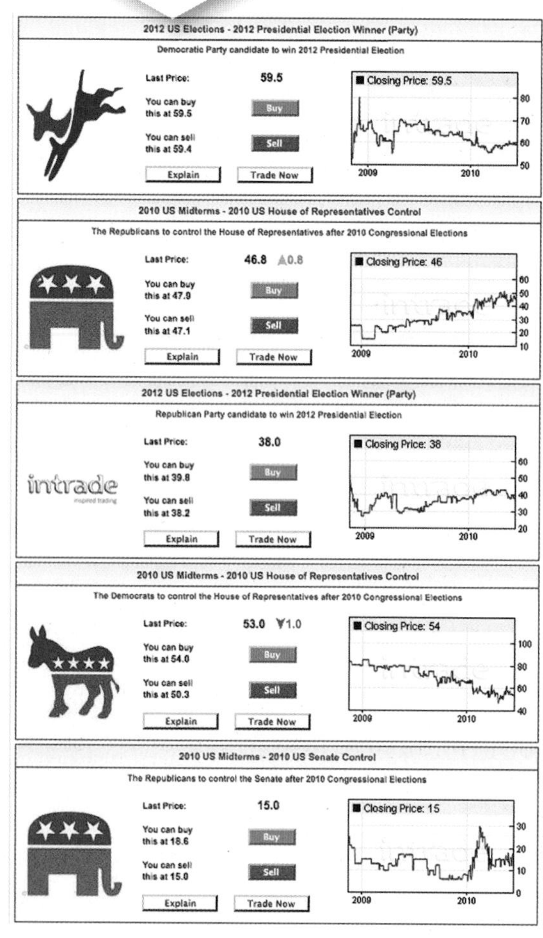

(Courtesy of www.intrade.com)

Not a day goes by, especially during an election year, without the results of yet another opinion poll being proudly announced in the media. One presidential candidate is pulling away from the other. Or perhaps the candidates are now neck and neck. Or maybe the Republicans might take forty additional seats in the U.S. House of Representatives. As you will learn in this chapter, opinion polls use random, representative sampling in an effort to make accurate predictions. Scientific opinion polling was invented in the 1930s and refined in the 1940s and 1950s.

WHAT IF SCIENTIFIC OPINION POLLING HAD NEVER BEEN INVENTED?

Before the development of scientific polling, newspapers frequently carried predictions about who would be elected president. Those predictions were often based on the latest betting odds. In the 1916 presidential elections, for example, more than $150,000 (measured in 2011 dollars) was wagered on the election outcome. That sum constituted twice the amount spent on the election campaign itself. At that time, a variety of firms were in the business of receiving and placing bets on election outcomes. Newspapers routinely showed the odds on the two presidential candidates, Woodrow Wilson and Charles Evans Hughes. The betting favored Wilson by a slight margin, and indeed he won. When various state and federal gambling laws were instituted later in the twentieth century, however, betting on political events became illegal. In the United States today, online gambling is illegal under most circumstances.

ENTER THE IOWA ELECTRONIC MARKETS

In 1993, a group of researchers at the University of Iowa obtained permission from the federal government to establish an experimental academic program that allows betting on elections. The bets are limited to a maximum of $500. The program, called Iowa Electronic Markets (**www.biz.uiowa.edu/iem**), claims that since 1993, its results have been more accurate than the opinion polls 75 percent of the time. Intrade (**www.intrade.com**), based in Dublin, Ireland, where gambling is legal, reports that its betting operation predicted the results correctly in forty-eight states in the 2008 presidential elections.

THE DIFFERENCE BETWEEN OPINION POLLS AND BETTING

Well-crafted opinion polling requires, as stated above, not only a representative sample but truthful responses by those interviewed. Election prediction markets, in contrast, require neither. When a person can win or lose a $500 bet by predicting who will be the next president and what the margin will be, a lot more care goes into that prediction than might go into the answer to a polling question. The old saying "Put your money where your mouth is" turns out to result in good political predictions. Unfortunately, the Iowa Electronic Markets is the only legal market in the country for betting on elections.

FOR CRITICAL ANALYSIS

1. Is there any difference between "placing a bet" on the future value of a stock by buying it in the stock market and placing a bet on who will become president? Explain.
2. Economist Robin Hanson has suggested that after voters decide on national goals, betting markets could be used to determine optimum policies to reach those goals: "Betting markets are our best known institution for aggregating information." Does his suggestion make any sense? Why or why not?

In a democracy, the ability of the people to freely express their opinions is fundamental. Americans can express their opinions in many ways. They can write letters to newspapers. They can share their ideas in online forums. They can organize politically. They can vote. They can respond to opinion polls. Public opinion clearly plays an important role in our political system, just as it does in any democracy.

President Barack Obama and his administration found out how important public opinion was in March 2009 when the giant insurance corporation AIG announced bonuses for executives in its financial unit amounting to $450 million. Only days before, AIG admitted that it lost $61.7 billion in the final three months of 2008, the largest corporate loss in world history. The losses were due almost entirely to bad judgment by AIG's financial unit, the very same group receiving $450 million in bonuses. In 2008 and 2009, the federal government pumped $170 billion into AIG out of a fear that its collapse would bring down the rest of the financial system. The obvious conclusion: AIG was using taxpayer funds to reward the very people who had caused the catastrophe.

Public Opinion
The aggregate of individual attitudes or beliefs shared by some portion of the adult population.

Consensus
General agreement among the citizenry on an issue.

Divided Opinion
Public opinion that is polarized between two quite different positions.

The resulting public outrage was severe. Senator Chuck Grassley (R., Iowa) actually suggested that AIG executives consider Japanese-style ritual suicide. The House quickly passed a measure to tax the bonuses out of existence (which the Senate quietly ignored). In the wake of this scandal, it was almost impossible for the Obama administration to push through Congress any more bailouts for financial institutions. Treasury secretary Timothy Geithner was left scrambling to find ways to prop up troubled banks that did not involve congressional action.

There is no doubt that public opinion can be powerful. The extent to which public opinion affects policymaking is not always so clear, however. For example, suppose that public opinion strongly supports a certain policy. If political leaders adopt that position, is it because they are responding to public opinion or because they share the public's beliefs? Also, political leaders themselves can shape public opinion to a degree. For these and other reasons, scholars must deal with many uncertainties when analyzing the impact of public opinion on policymaking.

This person expresses her feelings about a variety of subjects during a Take America Back rally in Washington, D.C. Why is she wearing the American flag? (© Mark Peterson/Redux)

Defining Public Opinion

There is no single public opinion, because there are many different "publics." In a nation of more than 310 million people, there may be innumerable gradations of opinion on an issue. What we do is describe the distribution of opinions among the members of the public about a particular question. Thus, we define **public opinion** as the aggregate of individual attitudes or beliefs shared by some portion of the adult population.

Typically, public opinion is distributed among several different positions, and the distribution of opinion can tell us how divided the public is on an issue and whether compromise is possible. When polls show that a large proportion of the American public appears to express the same view on an issue, we say that a **consensus** exists, at least at the moment the poll was taken. Figure 6–1 on the next page shows a pattern of opinion that might be called consensual. Issues on which the public holds widely differing attitudes result in **divided opinion** (see Figure 6–2 on the next page). Sometimes, a poll shows a distribution of opinion indicating that most Americans either have no information about the issue or are not interested enough in the issue to formulate a position. Politicians may believe that the public's lack of knowledge about an issue gives them more room to maneuver, or they may be wary of taking any action for fear that opinion will crystallize after a crisis.

FIGURE 6–1 Consensus Opinion

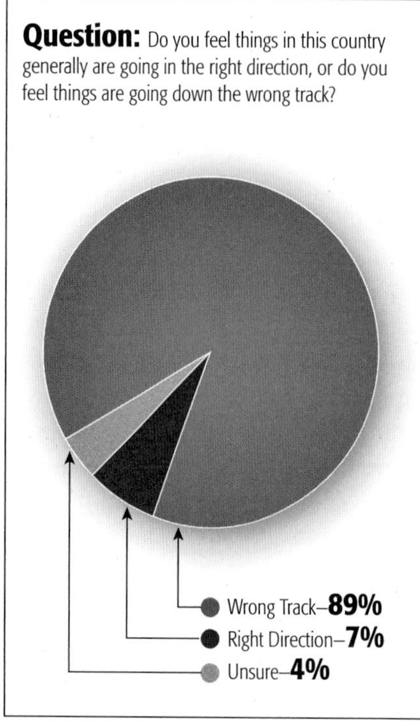

Source: CBS News/*New York Times* Poll, October 10–13, 2008.

FIGURE 6–2 Divided Opinion

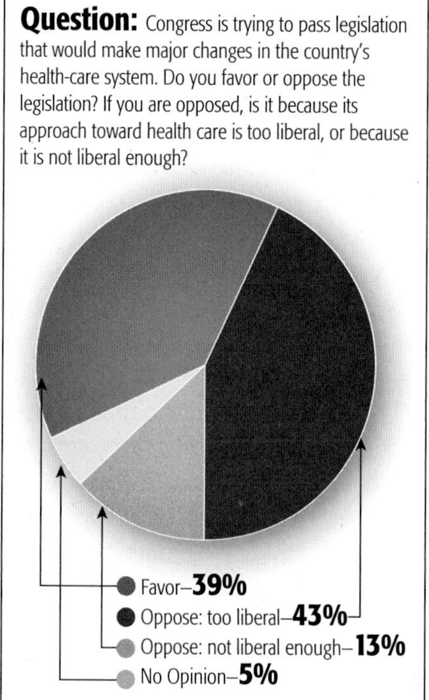

Source: CNN Opinion Research Poll, March 19–21, 2010.

An interesting question arises as to when private opinion becomes public opinion. Everyone probably has a private opinion about the competence of the president, as well as private opinions about more personal concerns, such as the state of a neighbor's lawn. We say that private opinion becomes public opinion when the opinion is publicly expressed and concerns public issues. When someone's private opinion becomes so strong that the individual is willing to take action, then the opinion becomes public opinion. Many kinds of action are possible. An individual may go to the polls to vote for or against a candidate or an issue, participate in a demonstration, discuss the issue at work, speak out online, or participate in the political process in any one of a dozen other ways.

How Public Opinion Is Formed: Political Socialization

Most Americans are willing to express opinions on political issues when asked. How do people acquire these opinions and attitudes? Typically, views that are expressed as political opinions are acquired through the process of **political socialization.** By this we mean that people acquire their political beliefs and values, often including their party identification, through relationships with their families, friends, and co-workers.

Political Socialization The process by which people acquire political beliefs and values.

Models of Political Socialization

The most important early sources of political socialization are the family and the schools. Individuals' basic political orientations are formed in the family if other family members hold strong views. When the adults in a family view politics as relatively unimportant and describe themselves as independent voters or disaffected from the political system, children may receive very little political socialization.

In the past few decades, more and more sources of information about politics have become available to all Americans, and especially to young people. Although their basic outlook on the political system still may be formed by early family influences, young people are now exposed to many other sources of information about issues and values. This greater access to information may explain why young Americans are often more liberal than their parents on many social issues, such as gay rights. We look at one major source of online information that is popular among younger people in this chapter's *Politics and . . . the Web* feature on the following page.

The Family and the Social Environment

Not only do our parents' political beliefs, values, and actions affect our opinions, but the family also links us to other factors that affect opinion, such as race, social class, educational environment, and religious beliefs. How do parents transmit their political values to their offspring?

Studies suggest that the influence of parents is due to two factors: communication and receptivity. Parents communicate their feelings and preferences to children constantly. Because children have such a strong need for parental approval, they are very receptive to their parents' views.

Children are less likely to influence their parents, because parents expect deference from their children.[1] Nevertheless, other studies show that if children are exposed to political ideas at school and in the media, they will share these ideas with their parents, giving the parents what some scholars call a "second chance" at political socialization.[2]

These students attend Oscar de La Hoya Amino Charter School in Los Angeles. Are their teachers' political views important? (© David Butow/Corbis)

Education as a Source of Political Socialization. From the early days of the republic, schools were perceived to be important transmitters of political information and attitudes. Children in the primary grades learn about their country mostly in patriotic ways. They learn about the Pilgrims, the flag, and some of the nation's presidents. They also learn to celebrate national holidays. In the middle grades, children learn additional historical facts and come to understand the structure of government and the functions of the president, judges, and Congress. By high school, students have a more complex understanding of the political system, may identify with a political party, and may take positions on issues.

Generally, education is closely linked to political participation. The more education a person receives, the more likely that person will be interested in politics, be confident in his or her ability to understand political issues, and be an active participant in the political process.

Peers and Peer Group Influence. Once a child enters school, the child's friends become an important influence on behavior and attitudes. For children and for adults, friendships and associations in **peer groups** affect political attitudes. We must, however, separate the effects of peer group pressure on opinions and attitudes in general from the

Peer Group
A group consisting of members sharing common social characteristics. These groups play an important part in the socialization process, helping to shape attitudes and beliefs.

---

1. Barbara A. Bardes and Robert W. Oldendick, *Public Opinion: Measuring the American Mind,* 3d ed. (Belmont, Calif.: Wadsworth Publishing Co., 2006), p. 73.
2. Michael McDevitt and Steven H. Chaffee, "Second Chance Political Socialization: 'Trickle-up' Effects of Children on Parents," in Thomas J. Johnson *et al.*, eds., *Engaging the Public: How Government and the Media Can Reinvigorate American Democracy* (Lanham, Md.: Rowman & Littlefield Publishers, 1998), pp. 57–66.

effects of peer group pressure on political opinions. For the most part, associations among peers are nonpolitical. Political attitudes are more likely to be shaped by peer groups when the peer groups are involved directly in political activities.

Individuals who join interest groups based on ethnic identity may find, for example, a common political bond through working for the group's civil liberties and rights. African American activist groups may consist of individuals who join together to support government programs that will aid the African American population. Members of a labor union may be strongly influenced to support certain pro-labor candidates.

POLITICS AND...the web

THE YOUTUBE/ FACEBOOK GENERATION ROCKS THE VOTE

During the last election cycle, the new medium that drew the most attention was YouTube. With more than 75 million users watching as many as 2.5 billion online videos a month, YouTube had a major impact on the elections. Candidates eagerly posted videos that promoted their candidacy. Many candidates also learned the dangers of the new medium. For example, clips posted online of allegedly anti-American sermons by Barack Obama's former pastor, the Reverend Jeremiah Wright, forced Obama to disassociate himself completely from Wright and to defend his decision to remain a member of Wright's church for more than twenty years.

(Courtesy of www.facebook.com)

THE RISE OF FACEBOOK

Social networking sites, notably MySpace and Facebook, have been around for a while. With 500 million members, Facebook has pulled away from MySpace to become the clear winner as the leading social networking site. It is now also the site with the second-highest traffic volume, after Google. Social networking sites work because they create a sense of connection between people who use them to link to their many online "friends." Many young people access Facebook every day.

Politicians have come to realize that they too need a lot of "friends" on social networking sites. By September 2010, Barack Obama had 13.1 million friends on Facebook. Sarah Palin was in second place with 2.2 million friends. What started as a college networking system for students has ended up as a networking system for politicians as well.

Facebook's first major political venture was in January 2008, when 1 million Facebook users participated in presidential primary debates cosponsored by the site. Participants took part in debate groups and submitted questions to the candidates. Facebook also played a major role during the heated debates leading up to the passage of the health-care system overhaul in March 2010. Friendly chitchat sometimes turned into passionate arguments for or against the health-care bill.

FACEBOOK AND THE 2010 ELECTIONS

Facebook activity may have provided an early glimpse of the outcome of the 2010 elections. Most, but not all, members of Congress had Facebook accounts. By May 2010, Republicans in Congress were adding new Facebook friends at a faster clip than the Democrats. By August 2010, Republicans had twice as many fans as Democrats.

FOR CRITICAL ANALYSIS

Does it matter from where students obtain their political information? Why or why not?

Opinion Leaders' Influence. We are all influenced by those whom we are closely associated with or whom we hold in high regard—friends at school, family members and other relatives, and teachers. In a sense, these people are **opinion leaders,** but on an *informal* level; that is, their influence on our political views is not necessarily intentional or deliberate. We are also influenced by *formal* opinion leaders, such as presidents, lobbyists, congresspersons, news commentators, and religious leaders, who have as part of their jobs the task of swaying people's views.

Opinion Leader
One who is able to influence the opinions of others because of position, expertise, or personality.

Media
The channels of mass communication.

Agenda Setting
Determining which public-policy questions will be debated or considered.

Fairness Doctrine
A Federal Communications Commission rule enforced between 1949 and 1987 that required radio and television to present controversial issues in a manner that was (in the commission's view) honest, equitable, and balanced.

The Impact of the Media

Clearly, the **media**—newspapers, television, radio, and Internet sources—strongly influence public opinion. This is because the media inform the public about the issues and events of our times and thus have an **agenda-setting** effect. In other words, to borrow from Bernard Cohen's classic statement about the media and public opinion, the media may not be successful in telling people what to think, but they are "stunningly successful in telling their audience what to think about."[3] The media's influence will be discussed in more detail in Chapter 9.

Popularity of the Media. Today, many contend that the media's influence on public opinion has grown to equal that of the family. For example, in her analysis of the role played by the media in American politics,[4] media scholar Doris A. Graber points out that high school students, when asked where they obtain the information on which they base their attitudes, mention the mass media far more than they mention their families, friends, and teachers. This trend may significantly alter the nature of the media's influence on public debate in the future.

The Impact of the New Media. The extent to which new forms of media have supplanted older ones—such as newspapers and the major broadcast networks—has been a major topic of discussion for several years. New forms include the World Wide Web, but also talk radio and cable television. Talk radio would seem to be a very old kind of medium, given that radio first became important early in the twentieth century. Between 1949 and 1987, however, the Federal Communications Commission enforced the **Fairness Doctrine,** which required radio and television to present controversial issues in a manner that was (in the commission's view) honest, equitable, and balanced. Modern conservative talk radio took off only after the Fairness Doctrine was abolished.

The impacts of the various forms of new media appear to vary considerably. Talk radio and cable networks such as Fox News have given conservatives new methods for promoting their views and socializing their audiences. It is probable, however, that such media mostly strengthen the beliefs of those who are already conservative, rather than recruiting new members to the political right. A similar observation is often made about political blogs on the Internet, although in this medium liberals are at least as well represented as conservatives. Blogs appear to radicalize their readers, rather than turning conservatives into liberals or vice versa. Indeed, cable news, talk radio, and political blogs are widely blamed for the increased polarization that has characterized American politics in recent years.

did you know?
That CNN reaches more than 1.5 billion people in more than 200 countries.

The impact of social networking sites such as Facebook is more ambiguous. Facebook does have strongly political "pages" that in effect are political blogs. Many interactions on Facebook, however, are between members of peer groups, such as students who attend

3. *The Press and Foreign Policy* (Princeton, N.J.: Princeton University Press, 1963), p. 81.
4. Doris A. Graber, *Mass Media and American Politics,* 8th ed. (Chicago: University of Chicago Press, 2009).

Markos Moulitsas Zuniga founded the progressive blogging site called The Daily Kos. "Kos" was his nickname while in the U.S. Army. What qualifications are necessary to create and run a political opinion Web site? (AP Photo/J. Kamp)

a particular school or individuals who work in the same profession. Such groups are more likely to contain a variety of views than ones explicitly organized around a political viewpoint. Facebook, in other words, may enhance peer group influence and even serve as a force for political moderation as well.

The Influence of Political Events

Generally, older Americans tend to be somewhat more conservative than younger Americans, particularly on social issues but also, to some extent, on economic issues. This effect is known as the **lifestyle effect.** It probably occurs because older adults are likely to retain the social values that they learned at a younger age. The experience of marriage and raising a family also has a measurable conservatizing effect. Young people, especially today, are more liberal than their grandparents on social issues, such as the rights of gay men and lesbians and racial and gender equality. Nevertheless, a more important factor than a person's age is the impact of significant political events that shape the political attitudes of an entire generation. When events produce such a long-lasting result, we refer to it as a **generational effect** (also called a *cohort effect*).

Voters who grew up in the 1930s during the Great Depression were likely to form lifelong attachments to the Democratic Party, the party of Franklin D. Roosevelt. In the 1960s and 1970s, the war in Vietnam and the **Watergate break-in** and the subsequent presidential cover-up fostered widespread cynicism toward government. There is evidence that the years of economic prosperity under President Ronald Reagan during the 1980s led many young people to identify with the Republican Party. The high levels of support that younger voters gave to Barack Obama during his presidential campaign may be good news for the Democratic Party in future years, even if it had little effect in 2010.

Lifestyle Effect
A phenomenon in which certain attitudes occur at certain chronological ages.

Generational Effect
A long-lasting effect of the events of a particular time on the political opinions of those who came of political age at that time.

Watergate Break-In
The 1972 illegal entry into the Democratic National Committee offices by participants in President Richard Nixon's reelection campaign.

Socioeconomic Status
The value assigned to a person due to occupation or income. An upper-class person, for example, has high socioeconomic status.

Political Preferences and Voting Behavior

A major indicator of voting behavior is, of course, party identification. In addition, however, there are a variety of socioeconomic and demographic factors that also appear to influence political preferences. These factors include education, income and **socioeconomic status,** religion, race, gender, geographic region, and similar traits. People who share the same religion, occupation, or any other demographic trait are likely to influence one another and may also have common political concerns that follow from the common characteristic. Other factors, such as perception of the candidates and issue preferences, are closely connected to the electoral process itself. Table 6–1 on the facing page illustrates the impact of some of these variables on voting behavior.

Because of the relationship between various characteristics and voting behavior, campaign managers often target particular groups when creating campaign advertising. Today, campaign managers and consultants are going even further in this attempt to "sell" their candidate to very specific groups by using "microtargeting".

Party Identification and Demographic Influences

With the possible exception of race, party identification has been the most important determinant of voting behavior in national elections. Party affiliation is influenced by family and peer groups, by generational effects, by the media, and by the voter's assessment of candidates and issues.

TABLE 6–1 Votes by Groups in Presidential Elections, 1992–2008 (in Percentages)

	1992			1996		2000		2004		2008	
	Clinton (Dem.)	Bush (Rep.)	Perot (Ref.)	Clinton (Dem.)	Dole (Rep.)	Gore (Dem.)	Bush (Rep.)	Kerry (Dem.)	Bush (Rep.)	Obama (Dem.)	McCain (Rep.)
Total Vote	43	38	19	49	41	48	48	48	51	53	46
Gender											
Men	41	38	21	43	44	42	53	44	55	49	48
Women	46	37	17	54	38	54	43	51	48	56	43
Race											
White	39	41	20	43	46	42	54	41	58	43	55
Black	82	11	7	84	12	90	8	88	11	95	4
Hispanic	62	25	14	72	21	67	31	58	40	67	31
Educational Attainment											
Not a high school graduate	55	28	17	59	28	59	39	50	50	63	35
High school graduate	43	36	20	51	35	48	49	47	52	52	46
College graduate	40	41	19	44	46	45	51	46	52	50	48
Postgraduate education	49	36	15	52	40	52	44	54	45	58	40
Religion											
White Protestant	33	46	21	36	53	34	63	32	68	34	65
Catholic	44	36	20	53	37	49	47	47	52	54	45
Jewish	78	12	10	78	16	79	19	75	24	78	21
White evangelical	23	61	15	NA	NA	NA	NA	21	79	24	74
Union Status											
Union household	55	24	21	59	30	59	37	59	40	59	39
Family Income											
Under $15,000	59	23	18	59	28	57	37	63	37	73	25
$15,000–29,000	45	35	20	53	36	54	41	57	41	60	37
$30,000–49,000	41	38	21	48	40	49	48	50	49	55	43
Over $50,000	40	42	18	44	48	45	52	43	56	49	49
Size of Place of Residence											
Population over 500,000	58	28	13	68	25	71	26	60	40	70	28
Population 50,000 to 500,000	50	33	16	50	39	57	40	50	50	59	39
Population 10,000 to 50,000	39	42	20	48	41	38	59	48	51	45	53
Rural	39	40	20	44	46	37	59	39	60	45	53

NA = Not asked.

Sources: Excerpted and adapted from *The New York Times;* Voter News Service; CBS News; and the National Election Pool.

In the middle to late 1960s, party attachment began to weaken. Whereas independent voters were only a little more than 20 percent of the eligible electorate during the 1950s, they constituted more than 30 percent of all voters by the mid-1990s, and their numbers have grown since that time. New voters are likely to identify themselves as independent voters, although they may be more ready to identify with one of the major parties by their mid-thirties. There is considerable debate among political scientists over whether those who call themselves independents are truly so: when asked, a majority say that they are "leaning" toward one party or the other. (For further discussion of party affiliation, see Chapter 8.)

Demographic influences reflect the individual's personal background and place in society. Some factors have to do with the family into which a person was born: race and (for most people) religion. Others may be the result of choices made throughout an individual's life: place of residence, educational achievement, and profession. It is also clear that many of these factors are interrelated. People who have more education are likely to have higher incomes and to hold professional jobs. Similarly, children born into wealthier families are far more likely to complete college than children from poor families.

Education. In the past, having a college education tended to be associated with voting for Republicans. In recent years, however, this correlation has become weaker. In particular, individuals with a postgraduate education—more than a bachelor's degree—have voted predominantly Democratic. Many people with postgraduate degrees are professionals, such as physicians, attorneys, and college instructors. Typically, a postgraduate degree is an occupational requirement for professionals.

Despite the recent popularity of the master of business administration (MBA) degree, businesspersons are more likely to have only a bachelor's degree or no degree at all. They are also much more likely to vote Republican.

Also, a higher percentage of voters with only a high school education voted Republican in the 2000, 2004, and 2008 presidential elections, compared with the pattern in previous elections, in which that group of voters tended to favor Democrats. Today, the voting behavior of this group is quite close to the behavior of the electorate as a whole.

The Influence of Economic Status. Family income is a strong predictor of economic liberalism or conservatism. Those with low incomes tend to favor government action to benefit the poor or to promote economic equality. Those with high incomes tend to oppose government intervention in the economy or to support it only when it benefits business. On political issues, therefore, the traditional political spectrum described in Chapter 1 on page 18 is a useful tool. The rich tend toward the right; the poor tend toward the left.

If we examine cultural as well as economic issues, however, the four-cornered ideological grid discussed in Chapter 1 on page 20 becomes important. It happens that upper-class voters are more likely to endorse cultural liberalism and lower-class individuals are more likely to favor cultural conservatism. Support for the right to have an abortion, for example, rises with income. It follows that libertarians—those who oppose government action on both economic and social issues—are concentrated among the wealthier members of the population. (Libertarians constitute the upper-right-hand corner of the grid in Figure 1–1 in Chapter 1.) Those who favor government action both to promote traditional moral values and to promote economic equality—economic liberals, cultural conservatives—are concentrated among groups that are less well off. (This group fills up the lower-left-hand corner of the grid.)

Normally, the higher a person's income, the more likely the person will be to vote Republican. Manual laborers, factory workers, and especially union members are more likely to vote Democratic. There are no hard-and-fast rules, however. Some very poor individuals are devoted Republicans, just as some extremely wealthy people support the Democratic Party.

Religious Influence: Denomination. Traditionally, scholars have examined the impact of religion on political attitudes by dividing the population into such categories as Protestant, Catholic, and Jewish. In recent decades, however, such a breakdown has become less valuable as a means of predicting someone's political preferences. It is true that, as they were in the past, Jewish voters are notably more liberal than members of other groups, on both economic and cultural issues. Persons reporting no religion are very liberal on social issues but have mixed economic views. Protestants and Catholics, however, have grown closer to each other politically in recent years. This represents something of a change—in the late 1800s and early 1900s, northern Protestants were distinctly more likely to vote Republican, and northern Catholics were more likely to vote Democratic. Even today, in a few parts of the country, Protestants and Catholics tend to line up against each other when choosing a political party.

Religious Influence: Commitment and Beliefs. Today, two factors turn out to be major predictors of political attitudes among members of the various Christian denominations. One is the degree of religious commitment, as measured by such actions as regular churchgoing. The other is the degree to which the voter adheres to religious beliefs that (depending on the denomination) can be called conservative, evangelical, or fundamentalist. High scores on either factor are associated with cultural conservatism on political issues—that is, with beliefs that place a high value on social order. (See Chapter 1 for a discussion of the contrasting values of order and liberty.)

Voters who are more devout, regardless of their church affiliation, tend to vote Republican, while voters who are less devout are more often Democrats. In the 2008 presidential elections, for example, Protestants who regularly attended church gave 67 percent of their votes to Republican candidate John McCain, compared with 54 percent of those who attended church less often. Among Catholics, there was a similar pattern: a majority of Catholics who attended church regularly voted Republican, while a slim majority of Catholics who were not regular churchgoers voted for Democratic candidate Barack Obama. Exit polls following the 2006 congressional elections showed the same pattern. There is an exception to this trend: African Americans of all religions have been strongly supportive of Democrats.

Do Jewish voters tend to vote for liberal or for conservative candidates? (© Leland Bobbé/Corbis)

The politics of Protestant Americans who can be identified as holding evangelical or fundamentalist beliefs deserves special attention. Actually, a majority of American Protestants can be characterized as evangelical. Not all are politically conservative. Some are politically liberal, such as former Democratic presidents Jimmy Carter and Bill Clinton. Fundamentalists are a subset of evangelicals who believe in a number of doctrines not held by all evangelicals. In particular, fundamentalists believe in biblical inerrancy—that is, that every word of the Bible is literally true. In politics, fundamentalists are notably more conservative than other evangelicals. Liberal fundamentalists are rare indeed.[5]

The Influence of Race and Ethnicity. Although African Americans are, on average, somewhat conservative on certain cultural issues, such as same-sex marriage and abortion, they tend to be more liberal than whites on social-welfare matters, civil liberties, and even foreign policy. African Americans voted principally for Republicans until Democrat Franklin Roosevelt's New Deal in the 1930s. Since then, they have largely identified with the Democratic Party. Indeed, Democratic presidential candidates have received, on average,

5. George M. Marsden, *Understanding Fundamentalism and Evangelicalism* (Grand Rapids, Mich.: Eerdmans Publishing Co., 1991); and Karen Armstrong, *The Battle for God* (New York: Ballantine Books, 2001).

These Hispanic protesters at the capitol in Jackson, Mississippi, are shown supporting immigration reform. Why did the Hispanic vote turn against the Republican Party? (AP Photo/ Rogelio Solis)

more than 80 percent of the African American vote since 1956. Of course, Barack Obama's support among African Americans was overwhelming.

Most Asian American groups lean toward the Democrats, although Vietnamese Americans are strongly Republican. Most Vietnamese Americans left Vietnam because of the Communist victory in the Vietnam War, and their strong anticommunism translates into conservative politics.

Muslim American immigrants and their descendants are an interesting category.[6] In 2000, a strong majority of Muslim Americans of Middle Eastern ancestry voted for Republican George W. Bush because they shared his cultural conservatism. By 2010, the issue of Muslim civil liberties had turned Islamic voters into one of the nation's most Democratic blocs.

The Hispanic Vote. The diversity among Hispanic Americans has resulted in differing political behavior. The majority of Hispanic Americans vote Democratic. Cuban Americans, however, are usually Republican. Most Cuban Americans left Cuba because of Fidel Castro's Communist regime. As in the example of the Vietnamese, anticommunism leads to political conservatism.

In 2000, Republican presidential candidate George W. Bush received 31 percent of the Hispanic vote. In 2004, Bush's Hispanic support may have approached 40 percent. (A widely quoted survey put Bush's support at 44 percent, but that figure was almost certainly erroneous.) Since his days as Texas governor, Bush had envisioned creating a stronger long-term Republican coalition by adding Hispanics. Indeed, Hispanic voters appeared to show considerable sympathy for Bush's campaign appeals based on religious and family values and patriotism.

In 2006, however, Hispanics favored Democratic candidates over Republicans by 73 percent to 26 percent. In 2008, Barack Obama won more than two-thirds of the Hispanic vote. Why did Hispanic support for the Republicans fall so greatly? In a word: immigration. Bush favored a comprehensive immigration reform that would have granted unauthorized immigrants (also known as illegal or undocumented immigrants) a path to citizenship. Most Republicans in Congress refused to support Bush on this issue, and instead called for a hard line against unauthorized immigration. Although many Hispanics are also concerned about unauthorized immigration, the harsh rhetoric of some Republicans on this issue convinced many Hispanics that the Republicans were hostile to Hispanic interests.

Gender Gap
The difference between the percentage of women who vote for a particular candidate and the percentage of men who vote for the candidate.

The Gender Gap. Until the 1980s, there was little evidence that men's and women's political attitudes were different. Following the election of Ronald Reagan in 1980, however, scholars began to detect a **gender gap.** A May 1983 Gallup poll revealed that men were more likely than women to approve of Reagan's job performance. The gender gap has reappeared in subsequent elections, with women being more likely than men to support the Democratic candidate (see Figure 6–3 on the facing page). The gender gap narrowed somewhat in 2004, when only 51 percent of women voted for Democrat John F. Kerry, as opposed to 44 percent of men. The gap stayed at about 7 percent in 2008, when 56 percent of women voted for Democrat Barack Obama, compared with 49 percent of men. (Due to third-party candidates, Obama's 49 percent was still enough to carry the male vote.)

6. At least one-third of U.S. Muslims actually are African Americans whose ancestors have been in this country for a long time. In terms of political preferences, African American Muslims are more likely to resemble other African Americans than to resemble Muslim immigrants from the Middle East.

Women also appear to hold different attitudes from their male counterparts on a range of issues other than presidential preferences. They are much more likely than men to oppose capital punishment and the use of force abroad. Studies also have shown that women are more concerned about risks to the environment, more supportive of social welfare, and more in agreement with extending civil rights to gay men and lesbians than are men. Notably, women were also more concerned than men about the security issues raised by the terrorist attacks of September 11, 2001. This last fact may have pushed women in a more conservative direction for a time.

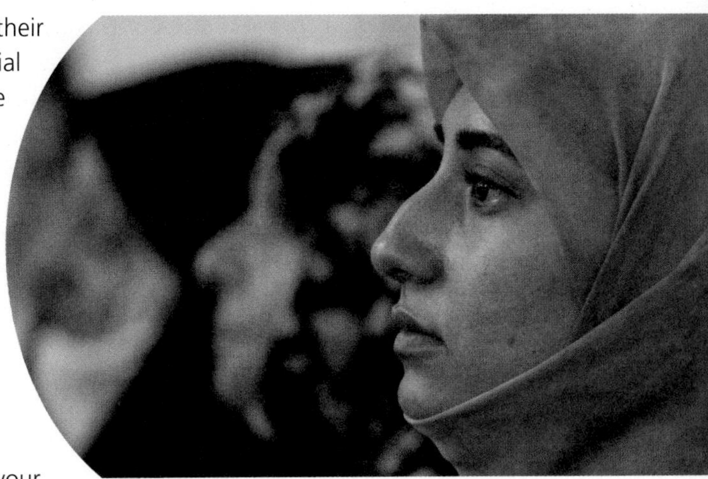

Today, Muslim American immigrants of Middle Eastern ancestry tend to favor Democratic candidates. Why? (AP Photo/M. Spencer Green)

Geographic Region. Finally, where you live can influence your political attitudes. The former solid Democratic South has now become the solid Republican South. Only 42 percent of the votes from the southern states went to Democrat John Kerry in 2004, while 58 percent went to Republican George W. Bush. Barack Obama did better than Kerry, but Obama still won only 45 percent of the southern vote.

There is a tendency today, at least in national elections, for the South, the Great Plains, and several of the Rocky Mountain states to favor the Republicans and for the West Coast and the Northeast to favor the Democrats. Perhaps more important than region is residence—urban, suburban, or rural. People in large cities tend to be liberal and Democratic. Those who live in smaller communities tend to be conservative and Republican.

did you know?

That Britain had a major gender gap for much of the twentieth century—because women were much more likely than men to support the Conservative Party rather than the more left-wing Labour Party.

Election-Specific Factors

Factors such as perception of the candidates and issue preferences may have an effect on how people vote in particular elections. Candidates and issues can change greatly, and voting behavior can therefore change as well.

FIGURE 6–3 Gender Gap in Presidential Elections, 1984–2008

A gender gap in voting is apparent in the percentage of women and the percentage of men voting in the last seven presidential elections. Even when women and men favor the same candidate, they do so by different margins, resulting in a gender gap.

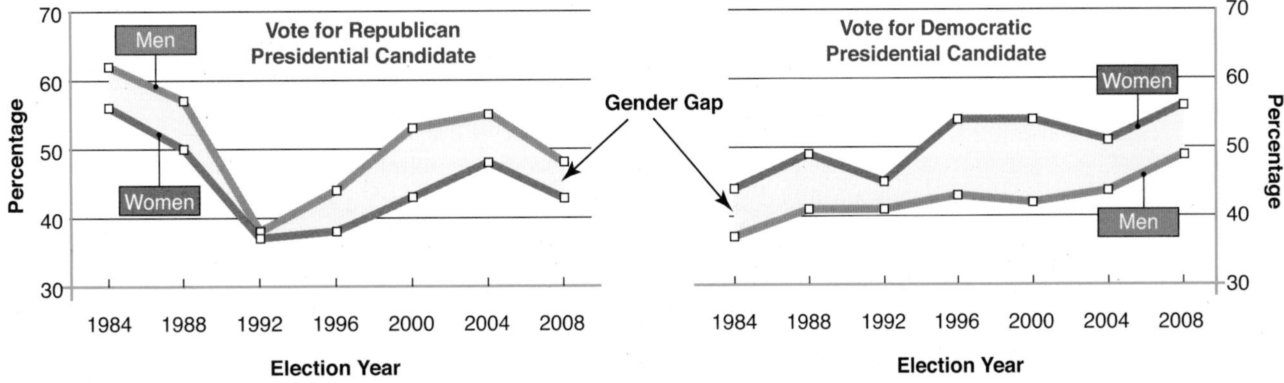

Note: Data in the chart include votes for Republican and Democratic candidates only. The effect of third-party candidates on the gender gap was nominal except in 1992, when H. Ross Perot received 17 percent of the vote among women and 21 percent among men. Perot's impact, if factored into the data, would widen the gap pictured in the chart for 1992. To a lesser extent, it would also widen the gap shown for 1996, when his candidacy drew fewer votes.

Sources: Adapted from Center for American Women and Politics (CAWP); Eagleton Institute of Politics; and Rutgers University.

Perception of the Candidates. The image of the candidate seems to be important in a voter's choice, especially for a presidential candidate. To some extent, voter attitudes toward candidates are based on emotions (such as trust) rather than on any judgment about experience or policy. In some years, voters have been attracted to a candidate who appeared to share their concerns and worries. In other years, voters have sought a candidate who appeared to have high integrity and honesty. Voters have been especially attracted to these candidates in elections that follow a major scandal, such as Richard Nixon's Watergate scandal (1972–1974) or Bill Clinton's sex scandal (1998–1999).

Issue Preferences. Issues make a difference in presidential and congressional elections. Although personality or image factors may be very persuasive, most voters have some notion of how the candidates differ on basic issues or at least know which candidates want a change in the direction of government policy.

Historically, economic concerns have been among the most powerful influences on public opinion. When the economy is doing well, it is very difficult for a challenger, especially at the presidential level, to defeat the incumbent. In contrast, inflation, unemployment, or high interest rates are likely to work to the disadvantage of the incumbent.

The 2008 Presidential Elections. Economic issues, in particular the collapse of the financial markets in September and the full onset of the Great Recession, guaranteed Barack Obama the presidency in 2008. Obama's personality also helped. Obama's steady temperament seemed well suited to chaotic times—his own staff members frequently referred to him as "no-drama Obama." John McCain's more volatile character, expressed in his frequent changes to his campaign, was not as reassuring to many voters. In 2010, however, continued high unemployment hurt the Democrats.

Measuring Public Opinion

In a democracy, people express their opinions in a variety of ways, as mentioned in this chapter's introduction. One of the most common means of gathering and measuring public opinion on specific issues is, of course, through the use of **opinion polls.**

Opinion Poll
A method of systematically questioning a small, selected sample of respondents who are deemed representative of the total population.

The History of Opinion Polls

During the 1800s, certain American newspapers and magazines spiced up their political coverage by doing face-to-face straw polls (unofficial polls indicating the trend of political opinion) or mail surveys of their readers' opinions. In the early twentieth century, the magazine *Literary Digest* further developed the technique of opinion polling by mailing large numbers of questionnaires to individuals, many of whom were its own subscribers, to determine their political opinions. From 1916 to 1932, more than 70 percent of the magazine's election predictions were accurate.

Literary Digest's polling activities suffered a setback in 1936, however, when the magazine predicted, based on more than 2 million returned questionnaires, that Republican candidate Alfred Landon would win over Democratic candidate Franklin D. Roosevelt. Landon won in only two states. A major problem with the *Digest*'s polling technique was its use of nonrepresentative respondents. In 1936, several years into the Great Depression, the magazine's subscribers were, for one thing, considerably more affluent than the average American. In other words, they did not accurately represent all of the voters in the U.S. population.

did you know?
That 30 percent of people asked to participate in an opinion poll refuse.

Several newcomers to the public opinion poll industry accurately predicted Roosevelt's landslide victory. These newcomers are still active in the poll-taking industry today: the Gallup poll of George Gallup and the Roper poll founded by Elmo Roper. Gallup and Roper, along with

Archibald Crossley, developed the modern polling techniques of market research. Using personal interviews with small samples of selected voters (fewer than two thousand), they showed that they could predict with accuracy the behavior of the total voting population.

By the 1950s, improved methods of sampling and a whole new science of survey research had been developed. Survey research centers sprang up throughout the United States, particularly at universities. Some of these survey groups are the American Institute of Public Opinion at Princeton, in New Jersey; the National Opinion Research Center at the University of Chicago; and the Survey Research Center at the University of Michigan.

Sampling Techniques

How can interviewing fewer than two thousand voters tell us what tens of millions of voters will do? Clearly, it is necessary that the sample of individuals be representative of all voters in the population. Consider an analogy. Let's say we have a large jar containing ten thousand pennies of various dates, and we want to know how many pennies were minted within certain decades (1960–1969, 1970–1979, and so on).

Representative Sampling. One way to estimate the distribution of the dates on the pennies—without examining all ten thousand—is to take a representative sample. This sample would be obtained by mixing the pennies up well and then removing a handful of them—perhaps one hundred pennies. The distribution of dates might be as follows:

- *1960–1969: 5 percent*
- *1970–1979: 5 percent*
- *1980–1989: 20 percent*
- *1990–1999: 30 percent*
- *2000–present: 40 percent*

If the pennies are very well mixed within the jar, and if you take a large enough sample, the resulting distribution will probably approach the actual distribution of the dates of all ten thousand coins.

The Principle of Randomness. The most important principle in sampling, or poll taking, is randomness. Every penny or every person should have a known chance, and especially an *equal chance,* of being sampled. If this happens, then a small sample should be representative of the whole group, both in demographic characteristics (age, religion, race, region, and the like) and in opinions. The ideal way to sample the voting population of the United States would be to put all voter names into a jar—or a computer—and randomly sample, say, two thousand of them. Because this is too costly and inefficient, pollsters have developed other ways to obtain good samples. One technique is simply to choose a random selection of telephone numbers and interview the respective households. This technique produces a relatively accurate sample at a low cost.

To ensure that the random samples include respondents from relevant segments of the population—rural, urban, northeastern, southern, and the like—most survey organizations randomly choose, say, urban areas that they will consider as representative of all urban areas. Then they randomly select their

When public opinion research centers gather information, they typically do so over the phone. How do such research centers decide whom to call? (AP Photo/Jim McKnight)

respondents within those areas. A generally less accurate technique is known as *quota sampling*. Here, survey researchers decide how many persons of certain types they need in the survey—such as minorities, women, or farmers—and then send out interviewers to find the necessary number of each type. Not only is this method often less accurate, but it also may be biased if, say, the interviewer refuses to go into certain neighborhoods or will not interview after dark.

The Importance of Accuracy

Generally, the national survey organizations take great care to select their samples randomly, because their reputations rest on the accuracy of their results. The Gallup and Roper polls usually interview about 1,500 individuals, and their results have a very high probability of being correct—within a margin of 3 percentage points. The accuracy with which the Gallup poll has predicted presidential election results is shown in Figure 6–4 below.

Polling organizations have also had some notable successes in accurately predicting the results of midterm elections. Certainly, the 2006 election forecasts were mostly on the mark. Indeed, pollsters were publicly ecstatic about how closely their preelection forecasts matched the results. Two pollsters, Mark Blumenthal and John McIntyre, took the average of five polls conducted by major organizations (including Harris, Roper, and Gallup) on each of the last five days before the elections. The averaged forecasts were correct for every candidate. In addition, the average of polls had Democrats picking up six Senate seats, which they did. According to Blumenthal, "The reason polls continue to do reasonably well is that people who actually vote are people who take the trouble to be interviewed."

Problems with Polls

Public opinion polls are snapshots of the opinions and preferences of the people at a specific moment in time and as expressed in response to a specific question. Given that definition, it is fairly easy to understand situations in which the polls are wrong. For example, opinion polls leading up to the 1980 presidential elections showed President Jimmy Carter defeating challenger Ronald Reagan. Only a few analysts noted the large number of "undecided" respondents a week before the elections. Those voters shifted massively to Reagan at the last minute, and Reagan won the elections.

The famous photo, on the facing page, of Harry Truman showing the front page of the newspaper that declared his defeat in the 1948 presidential elections is another tribute to the weakness of polling. Again, the poll that predicted his defeat was taken more than a week before Election Day. Truman won the election with 49.9 percent of the vote.

FIGURE 6–4 Gallup Poll Accuracy Record

This chart compares the percentage of the vote received by the winning presidential candidate with Gallup's final prediction.

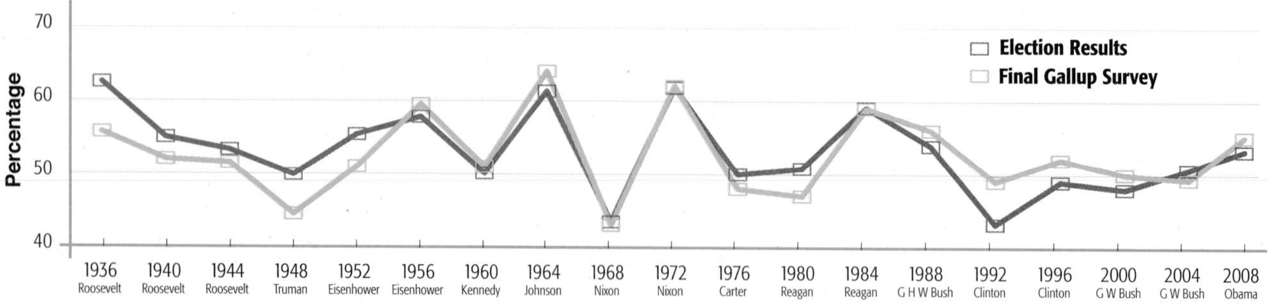

Sources: *The Gallup Poll Monthly*, November 1992; *Time*, November 21, 1994; *The Wall Street Journal*, November 6, 1996; and authors' updates.

ELECTIONS 2010

THE ACCURACY OF THE 2010 POLLS

In 2010, many polling experts were seriously concerned whether the polls would be as accurate as in past years. It was becoming more difficult to persuade Americans to participate in surveys. Additionally, not all polling organizations were prepared to undertake the extra expense involved in contacting voters who use cell phones exclusively. In the end, however, the polls proved to be largely accurate. Pollsters had become very proficient in weighing their samples to compensate for bias resulting from the difficulty in reaching various types of voters. Analyst Nate Silver surveyed the entire field of polling data from multiple firms. He predicted that the most likely election result would be that the Democrats would lose fifty-three seats in the House and seven or eight in the Senate. The actual losses were sixty-four in the House and six in the Senate, well within anyone's margin of error.

Some problems did emerge, however. Robo-polling firms were not as accurate as pollsters who used human interviewers. The importance of sophisticated weighting schemes meant that a firm with a bad model could end up with egg on its face. This happened to the venerable Gallup organization, which seriously underestimated Democratic turnout. Finally, most pollsters underestimated the Hispanic vote because they did not employ Spanish-speaking interviewers. This problem was noticeable in California, Colorado, and Nevada, where the Democrats did better than expected. It had little impact on the national totals, however.

Sampling Errors. Polls may also report erroneous results because the pool of respondents was not chosen in a scientific manner. **Sampling error** is the difference between the sample result and the true result if the entire population had been interviewed. Sampling error can generally be controlled by taking a large enough random sample, although the cost of doing so may be prohibitive. Other forms of sampling bias are possible. A sample would be biased, for example, if the poll interviewed people by telephone and did not correct for the fact that more women than men answer the telephone and that some populations (college students and very poor individuals, for example) cannot be found so easily by telephone.

Sampling Error
The difference between a sample's results and the true result if the entire population had been interviewed.

As poll takers get close to Election Day, they become even more concerned about their sample of respondents. Some pollsters continue to interview eligible voters, meaning those over age eighteen and registered to vote. Many others use a series of questions in the poll and other methods to try to identify "likely voters" so that they can be more accurate in their election-eve predictions. When a poll changes its method from reporting the views of eligible voters to reporting those of likely voters, the results tend to change dramatically.

President Harry Truman holds up the front page of the *Chicago Daily Tribune* issue that predicted his defeat on the basis of a Gallup poll. The poll had indicated that Truman would lose the 1948 contest for his reelection by a margin of 55.5 to 44.5 percent. The Gallup poll was completed more than a week before the election, so it missed a shift by undecided voters to Truman. (AP Photo/Byron Rollins)

"Is 'oblivious' the same as 'undecided'?"
(© The New Yorker Collection, 2008. Michael Shaw, from cartoonbank.com. All Rights Reserved.)

False Precision. Often, surveys report very detailed results with percentages carried out to one or even two decimal places. For example, you may read about two candidates being within, say, 3.2 percentage points of each other. But if the survey has a margin of error of plus or minus 4 percentage points, then the difference between the candidates could be as much as 7 points or as little as zero. This is not a very comforting result if you are trying to make predictions about who will win.

Most national polling organizations will take an election sample of one thousand or so potential voters and state that the sampling error is plus or minus 3 percentage points for each candidate. So what does that tell you? If two candidates are evenly matched in the polls, it means that the final result could be 47 percent for one and 53 for the other.

Poll Questions. It makes sense to expect that the results of a poll will depend on the questions that are asked. Depending on what question is asked, voters could be said either to support a particular proposal or to oppose it. One of the problems with many polls is the yes/no answer format. For example, suppose the poll question asks, "Do you favor or oppose the war in Afghanistan?" Respondents might wish to answer that they favored the war at the beginning but not as it is currently being waged, or that they favor fighting terrorism but not a military occupation. They have no way of indicating their true position with a yes or no answer. Respondents also are sometimes swayed by the inclusion of certain words in a question: more of the respondents will answer in the affirmative if the question asks, "Do you favor or oppose the war in Afghanistan as a means of fighting terrorism?"

How a question is phrased can change the polling outcome dramatically. The Roper polling organization once asked a double-negative question that was very hard to understand: "Does it seem possible or does it seem impossible to you that the Nazi extermination of the Jews never happened?" The survey results showed that 20 percent of Americans seemed to doubt that the Holocaust ever occurred. When the Roper organization rephrased the question more clearly, the percentage of doubters dropped to less than 1 percent.

Polling outcomes can also be affected if the participants do not fully grasp the meaning of various terms used in the questions. A *trillion,* for example, is a hard quantity for most people to grasp. We provide help in this chapter's *Politics of Boom and Bust* feature on the facing page.

Respondents' answers are also influenced by the order in which questions are asked, by the possible answers from which they are allowed to choose, and, in some cases, by their interaction with the interviewer. To a certain extent, people try to please the interviewer. They answer questions about which they have no information and avoid some answers to try to measure up to the interviewer's expectations.

Unscientific and Fraudulent Polls. A perennial issue is the promotion of surveys that are unscientific or even fraudulent. All too often, a magazine or Web site asks its readers to respond to a question—and then publishes the answers as if they were based on a scientifically chosen random sample. Other news media may then publicize the survey as if it were a poll taken by such reliable teams as Gallup or the *New York Times*/CBS. Critical consumers should watch out for surveys with self-selected respondents and other types of skewed samples. These so-called polls may be used to deliberately mislead the public.

THE POLITICS OF BOOM AND BUST

JUST WHAT IS A TRILLION DOLLARS, ANYWAY?

"A billion here, a billion there, pretty soon, you're talking real money." This remark has been attributed to Everett Dirksen, who represented Illinois in the U.S. Senate from 1950 to 1969. If Dirksen were alive today, he might quip instead: "A trillion dollars here, a trillion dollars there . . . ." Since the beginning of the latest economic crisis, references to trillions of dollars have been tossed around in the press, by the president, and certainly by Congress. People's opinions about political developments—and the answers they give to poll takers—depend on their understanding key terms such as *$1 trillion*.

A TRILLION IS BIG, BUT HOW BIG?

Even trained economists have a hard time "getting their arms around" a trillion dollars. The sum is far out of the range of ordinary experience. Consider the following ways of viewing $1 trillion: If you lay a trillion one-dollar bills end to end, you'll have a chain that stretches from the earth to the moon and back about 200 times. It would take a jet flying at the speed of sound, reeling out a roll of dollar bills behind it, 14 years to reel out a trillion dollars.

Can you imagine what a trillion dollars looks like? (Shutterstock)

More to the point, the total cost of the various stimulus packages and bailouts approved by the U.S. Congress in 2008 and 2009 easily exceeded $1 trillion. Total government spending at all levels exceeded $6 trillion in fiscal year 2010. The federal budget deficit (spending in excess of revenues) has been estimated as $1.56 trillion for 2010 and $1.27 trillion for 2011. The value of the U.S. Treasury notes owned openly by the government of China is about $0.85 trillion, and other types of Chinese holdings almost certainly push that total well above $1 trillion.

RELATING $1 TRILLION TO THE ECONOMY

One way to make sense of $1 trillion is to divide it among every man, woman, and child in the United States. Each person would get about $3,225. The total annual income of the entire nation (called gross domestic product, or GDP) is around $14 trillion, so $1 trillion is just over 7 percent of that. How long would it take $14 trillion in national income to increase by $1 trillion if the economy grew at a healthy rate of 3 percent a year? About two and one-third years. From the beginning of the current recession in December 2007 through March 2009, stock values on Wall Street dropped by more than $11 trillion, so $1 trillion is less than 10 percent of what investors lost in the economic crisis.

WHAT DO TRILLIONS IN GOVERNMENT SPENDING MEAN TO YOU?

Even if $1 trillion seems abstract, the consequences of $1 trillion in additional government spending, whether on stimulus projects or bank bailouts, does affect you. We cannot fund government expenditures with resources that come from Mars. Rather, additional government spending must eventually be paid back either through future taxes or through inflation. You may think that your share of additional taxes will be small, but don't be so sure. As of December 2010, the average family's share of the federal government's debt was about $150,000. As the saying goes, someday we all must pay the piper.

FOR CRITICAL ANALYSIS

The economic stimulus bill passed by Congress in February 2009 has recently been recalculated to amount to $814 billion. In the future, the total cost could grow to $1 trillion. With future interest charges, the total cost of this bill alone may exceed $1 trillion. How could you determine whether that additional federal spending is good or bad for you? For the nation? For the world economy?

did you know?

That a straw poll conducted by patrons of Harry's New York Bar in Paris has an almost unbroken record of predicting the outcomes of U.S. presidential contests.

Push Polls. Some campaigns have used "push polls," in which the respondents are given misleading information in the questions asked to persuade them to vote against a candidate. Indeed, the practice has spread throughout all levels of U.S. politics—local, state, and federal. In 1996, in a random survey of forty-five candidates, researchers found that thirty-five of them claimed to have been victimized by negative push-polling techniques used by their opponents.[7] Now even advocacy groups, as well as candidates for political offices, are using push polls. Push polling was prevalent during the campaigns in 2004, the congressional campaigns in 2006 and 2010, and the 2008 presidential and congressional campaigns. Its use was widespread in campaigns for governorships and other state offices.

Technology and Opinion Polls

Public opinion polling is based on scientific principles, particularly the principle of randomness. Today, technological advances allow polls to be taken over the Internet, but serious questions have been raised about the ability of pollsters to obtain truly random samples using this medium. The same was said not long ago when another technological breakthrough changed public opinion polling—the telephone.

The Advent of Telephone Polling

During the 1970s, telephone polling began to predominate over in-person polling. Obviously, telephone polling is less expensive than sending interviewers to poll respondents in their homes. Additionally, telephone interviewers do not have to worry about safety problems, which is particularly important for interviewers working in high-crime areas. Finally, telephone interviews can be conducted relatively quickly. They allow politicians or the media to poll one evening and report the results the next day.

Telephone Polling Problems. Somewhat ironically, the success of telephone polling has created major problems for the technique. The telemarketing industry in general has become so pervasive that people increasingly refuse to respond to telephone polls. More than 40 percent of households now use either caller ID or some other form of call screening. Calls may be automatically rejected, or the respondent may not pick up the call. This has greatly reduced the number of households that polling organizations can reach.

For most telephone polls, the nonresponse rate has increased to as high as 80 percent. Such a high nonresponse rate undercuts confidence in the survey results. In most cases, polling only 20 percent of those on the list cannot lead to a random sample. Even more important for politicians is the fact that polling organizations are not required to report their response rates.

The Cell Phone Problem. An additional problem for telephone polling is the popularity of cell phones. Cellular telephone numbers are not always included in random-digit dialing programs and are not listed in telephone directories. Furthermore, individuals with cell phones may be located anywhere in the United States or the world, thus confounding attempts to reach people in a particular area. As more people, and especially younger Americans, choose to use only a cell phone and do not have a landline at all, polling accuracy is further reduced because these individuals are ignored by many polls.

7. Karl T. Feld, "When Push Comes to Shove: A Polling Industry Call to Arms," *Public Perspective*, September/October 2001, p. 38.

Enter Internet Polling

Obviously, Internet polling is not done on a one-on-one basis, because there is no voice communication. In spite of the potential problems, the Harris poll, a widely respected national polling organization, conducted online polls during the 1998 elections. Its election predictions were accurate in many states. Nonetheless, it made a serious error in one southern gubernatorial election. The Harris group subsequently refined its techniques and continues to conduct online polls. This organization believes that proper weighting of the results will achieve the equivalent of a random-sampled poll.

Public opinion experts, however, argue that the Harris poll procedure violates the mathematical basis of random sampling. Even so, the Internet population is looking more like the rest of America: just as many women go online as men (74 percent for both genders), 70 percent of African American adults are online, and so are 64 percent of Hispanics (compared with 76 percent of non-Hispanic whites).[8]

did you know?

That when Americans were asked if they thought race relations were good or bad in the United States, 68 percent said that they were "bad," but when asked about race relations in their own communities, 75 percent said that they were "good."

"Nonpolls" on the Internet. Even if organizations such as the Harris poll succeed in obtaining the equivalent of a random sample when polling on the Internet, another problem will remain: the proliferation of "nonpolls" on the Internet. Every media outlet that maintains a Web site allows users to submit their opinions. A variety of organizations and for-profit companies send so-called polls to individuals through e-mail. Mister Poll (**www.misterpoll.com**) bills itself as the Internet's largest online polling database. Mister Poll allows you to create your own polls just for fun and to include them on your home page. Mister Poll, like many other polling sites, asks questions on various issues and solicits answers from those who log on to its Web site. Although the Mister Poll site states, "None of these polls is scientific," sites such as this one undercut the efforts of legitimate pollsters to use the Internet scientifically.

Does Internet Polling Devalue Polling Results? Although nonpolls certainly existed before the Internet, the ease with which they can be conducted and disseminated is accelerating another trend: the indiscriminate use of polling. Though Americans may not want to be bothered by telemarketers or unwanted telephone polls, they seem to continue to want reports of polling results during presidential elections and news stories about the president's approval ratings and similar topics. When asked, a majority of Americans say that polling results are interesting to them. Yet the proliferation of polls, often on the Internet, conducted with little effort to ensure the accuracy of the results presents a major threat to the science of polling.

This freshman at Franklin & Marshall College in Lancaster, Pennsylvania, is accessing the Internet in preparation for an online debate after the presidential elections. How representative would this student's opinion be if she had been polled on the Internet prior to the elections? (AP Photo/Daniel Shanken)

Public Opinion and the Political Process

Public opinion affects the political process in many ways. Politicians, whether in office or in the midst of a campaign, see public opinion as important to their careers. The president, members of Congress, governors, and other elected officials realize that strong support by the public as expressed in opinion polls is a source of power in dealing with other politicians. It is far more difficult for a senator to

8. Pew Internet and American Life Project, *Nov.–Dec. 2009 Tracking Survey.*

say no to the president if the president is immensely popular and if polls show approval of the president's policies. Public opinion also helps political candidates identify the most important concerns among the people and may help them shape their campaigns successfully.

Political Culture and Public Opinion

Americans are divided into a multitude of ethnic, religious, regional, and political subgroups. Given the diversity of American society and the wide range of opinions contained within it, how is it that the political process continues to function without being stalemated by conflict and dissension? One explanation is rooted in the concept of the American political culture, which can be described as a set of attitudes and ideas about the nation and the government. As discussed in Chapter 1, our political culture is widely shared by Americans of many different backgrounds. To some extent, it consists of symbols, such as the American flag, the Liberty Bell, and the Statue of Liberty. The elements of our political culture also include certain shared beliefs about the most important values in the American political system, including liberty, equality, and property.

Political Culture and Support for Our Political System. The political culture provides a general environment of support for the political system. If the people share certain beliefs about the system and a reservoir of good feeling exists toward the institutions of government, the nation will be better able to weather periods of crisis. Such was the case after the 2000 presidential elections when, for several weeks, it was not certain who the next president would be and how that determination would be made. At the time, some contended that the nation was facing a true constitutional crisis. Certainly, in many nations this would have been true. In fact, however, the broad majority of Americans did not believe that the uncertain outcome of the elections had created a constitutional crisis. Polls taken during this time found that, on the contrary, most Americans were confident in our political system's ability to decide the issue peaceably and in a lawful manner.[9]

Political Trust
The degree to which individuals express trust in the government and political institutions, usually measured through a specific series of survey questions.

Political Trust. The political culture also helps Americans evaluate their government's performance. **Political trust,** the degree to which individuals express trust in political institutions, has been measured by a variety of polling questions. One of these is whether the respondent is satisfied with "the way things are going in the United States." Figure 6–5 below shows the responses to this question over time, which correspond to

9. As reported in *Public Perspective,* March/April 2002, p. 11, summarizing the results of Gallup/CNN/*USA Today* polls conducted between November 11 and December 10, 2000.

FIGURE 6–5 Political Satisfaction Trend

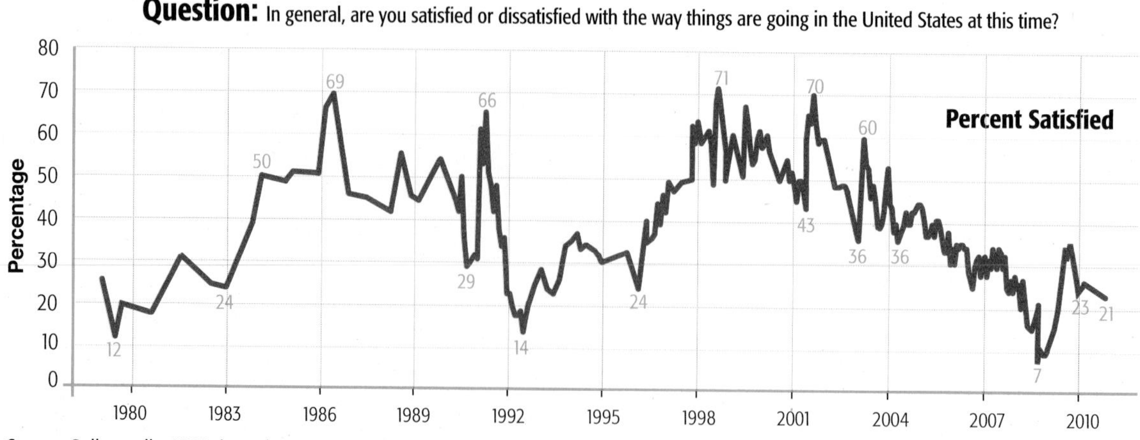

Source: Gallup polls, 1979 through 2010.

political developments. During the presidency of Republican Ronald Reagan (1981–1989), satisfaction levels rose. Republican George H. W. Bush (1989–1993) enjoyed relatively high levels of satisfaction until 1992, when economic problems and other difficulties handed the presidency to Democrat Bill Clinton (1993–2001). Polling suggests that Clinton's two terms were largely successful. Under Republican George W. Bush (2001–2009), however, satisfaction levels fell. In October 2008, at the height of the crisis in the financial industry, satisfaction fell to an unprecedented 7 percent. The subsequent recovery was very modest.

Public Opinion about Government

A vital component of public opinion in the United States is the considerable ambivalence with which the public regards many major national institutions. Figure 6–6 below shows trends from 1989 to 2010 in opinion polls asking respondents how much confidence they had in the institutions listed. Over the years, military and religious organizations have ranked highest. Note, however, the decline in confidence in churches in 2002 following a substantial number of sex-abuse allegations against Catholic priests. The public has consistently had more confidence in the military than in any of the other institutions shown in Figure 6–6. In 2002 and 2003, confidence in the military soared even higher, most likely because Americans recognized the central role being played by the military in the war on terrorism. From 2004 to 2008, this confidence waned due to difficulties experienced during the war in Iraq. As the Iraqi situation improved, confidence in the military returned to a high level in 2009.

The United States Supreme Court and the banking industry have scored well over time, although banking took big hits in 2009 and 2010 due to the financial crisis and the resulting bailouts. Less confidence is expressed in newspapers, television, big business,

FIGURE 6–6 Confidence in Institutions Trend

Question: I am going to read a list of institutions in American society. Please tell me how much confidence you, yourself, have in each one: a great deal, quite a lot, some, or very little?

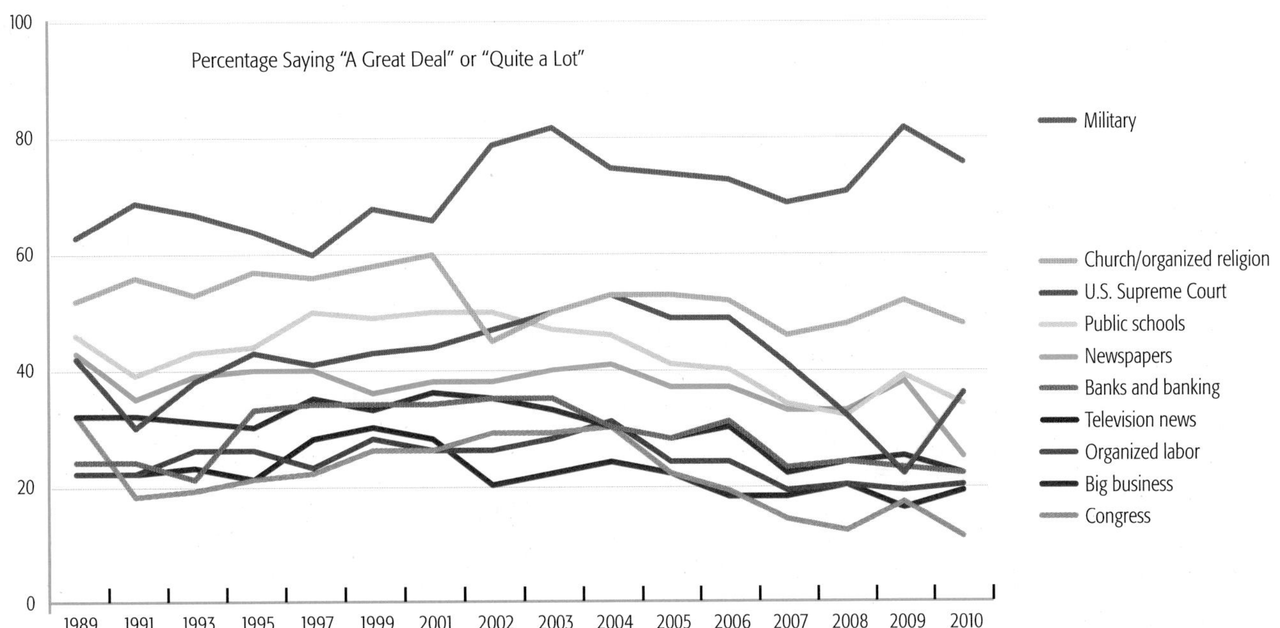

NA = Not asked.

Sources: Gallup polls over time.

did you know?

That in its "Cess Poll," an Iowa radio station assesses voters' preferences for presidential primary candidates by reading a candidate's name over the air, asking supporters of that candidate to flush their toilets, and measuring the resulting drop in water pressure.

and organized labor. In 1991, following a scandal involving congressional banking practices, confidence in Congress fell to 18 percent, but then recovered. From 2007 on, however, confidence in Congress almost disappeared. By 2010, the figure was down to 11 percent, an all-time low.

At times, popular confidence in all institutions may rise or fall, reflecting optimism or pessimism about the general state of the nation. For example, a 2008 Gallup poll showed that the level of national satisfaction with the state of the nation had dropped to 14 percent—the lowest rating since 1992. This general dissatisfaction is reflected in Figure 6–6.

Although people may not have much confidence in government institutions, they nonetheless turn to government to solve what they perceive to be the major problems facing the country. Table 6–2 below, which is based on Gallup polls conducted from the years 1981 to 2010, shows that the leading problems have changed over time. The public tends to emphasize problems that are immediate and that have been the subject of many stories in the media. When coverage of a particular problem increases suddenly, the public is more likely to see that as the most important problem. Thus, the fluctuations in the "most important problem" cited in Table 6–2 may, at times, be attributed to media agenda setting. In other years, however, the nation's leading problem has been so obvious that media attention is a minor factor. The Great Recession, which began in December 2007, is one example.

Public opinion is not limited to the United States. Our nation's foreign policy can be affected by the attitudes of people in other countries toward our government. We look at recent trends in foreign attitudes toward America in this chapter's *Beyond Our Borders* feature on the facing page.

Public Opinion and Policymaking

If public opinion is important for democracy, are policymakers really responsive to public opinion? A classic study by political scientists Benjamin I. Page and Robert Y. Shapiro in the early 1990s suggested that in fact the national government is very responsive to the public's

TABLE 6–2 Most Important Problem Trend, 1981 to Present

Year	Problem	Year	Problem
1981	High cost of living, unemployment	1996	Budget deficit
1982	Unemployment, high cost of living	1997	Crime, violence
1983	Unemployment, high cost of living	1998	Crime, violence
1984	Unemployment, fear of war	1999	Crime, violence
1985	Fear of war, unemployment	2000	Morals, family decline
1986	Unemployment, budget deficit	2001	Economy, education
1987	Unemployment, economy	2002	Terrorism, economy
1988	Economy, budget deficit	2003	Terrorism, economy
1989	War on drugs	2004	War in Iraq, economy
1990	War in Middle East	2005	War in Iraq
1991	Economy	2006	War in Iraq, terrorism
1992	Unemployment, budget deficit	2007	War in Iraq, health care
1993	Health care, budget deficit	2008	Economy, war in Iraq
1994	Crime, violence, health care	2009	Economy
1995	Crime, violence	2010	Economy, unemployment

Sources: *New York Times*/CBS News poll, January 1996; and Gallup polls, 1981 through 2010.

demands for action.[10] In looking at changes in public opinion poll results over time, Page and Shapiro showed that when the public supports a policy change, the following occurs: policy changes in a direction consistent with the change in public opinion 43 percent of the time, policy changes in a direction opposite to the change in opinion 22 percent of the time, and policy does not change at all 33 percent of the time. Page and Shapiro also showed, as should be no surprise, that when public opinion changes dramatically—say, by 20 percentage points rather than by just 6 or 7 percentage points—government policy is much more likely to follow changing public attitudes.

Setting Limits on Government Action. Although opinion polls cannot give exact guidance on what the government should do in a specific instance, the opinions measured in polls may set an informal limit on government action. For example, consider the highly controversial issue of abortion. Most Americans are moderates on this issue; they do not approve of abortion as a means of birth control, but they do feel that it should be available under certain circumstances. Yet sizable groups of people express very intense feelings both for and against legalized abortion. Many politicians also hold polarized

10. Benjamin I. Page and Robert Y. Shapiro, *The Rational Public: Fifty Years of Trends in Americans' Policy Preferences* (Chicago: University of Chicago Press, 1992).

BEYOND OUR BORDERS

WHAT THE WORLD THINKS OF AMERICA

One of Barack Obama's arguments during the 2008 elections was that Republican president George W. Bush had damaged our standing in the world. As president, Obama claimed, he could restore America's reputation more effectively than his Republican opponent, John McCain. Fast-forward to June 2010. Did anti-Americanism decrease? Data from the Pew Global Attitudes Project suggested that the answer was yes.

During the Bush years, the greatest decline in U.S. favorability ratings occurred in Europe, particularly in France, Germany, and Spain. By the end of the Bush administration, positive ratings had fallen to 42 percent, 31 percent, and 33 percent, respectively. After Obama's first eighteen months in office, positive ratings increased to 73 percent in France, 63 percent in Germany, and 61 percent in Spain. America's reputation seemed to be making a recovery.

Confidence in the United States rose in other parts of the world, including China, Japan, Russia, and many countries of Latin America. A major exception was Mexico, where favorability ratings dropped sharply after Arizona passed a strict new immigration law. Opinions of America in Eastern Europe, India, and sub-Saharan Africa were relatively high in the Bush years and remained so under Obama.

MOST MUSLIM COUNTRIES, IN CONTRAST, REMAIN ANTI-AMERICAN

Although Western Europe and several other regions may now view the United States in a better light, the same cannot be said for most countries in the Middle East and for many Muslim countries elsewhere. For example, according to Pew, U.S. favorability ratings in Egypt and Jordan were only 17 amd 21 percent, respectively. In the Palestinian Territories, the rating was 15 percent. These figures show no improvement at all. In Pakistan, the U.S. favorability rating actually dropped somewhat after Obama's election, to 17 percent. This may be due to Obama's increased engagement in the Afghanistan war and his use of unmanned aircraft to kill al Qaeda and Taliban leaders living in Pakistan's border regions.

FOR CRITICAL ANALYSIS

Why does America's image abroad matter?

Speaker of the House Nancy Pelosi (D., Calif.) speaks at a news conference concerning proposed additional health insurance for American children. To what extent do you think that public opinion about this important topic influenced what Congress did? (AP Photo/Caleb Jones)

beliefs on the topic of abortion. Political party platforms take firm positions on abortion, and members of Congress regularly make impassioned speeches on behalf of the right-to-life or freedom-of-choice positions. The strong words, however, are not matched with strong actions. Abortion policies have been roughly stable for years. Politicians know that radical changes to abortion policies would offend the opinions of the moderate majority. In this example, as in many others, *public opinion does not make public policy; rather, it restrains officials from taking truly unpopular actions.* If officials do act in the face of public opposition, the consequences will be determined at the ballot box.

To what degree should public opinion influence policymaking? It would appear that members of the public view this issue differently than policy leaders do. Polls indicate that whereas a majority of the public feel that public opinion should have a great deal of influence on policy, a majority of policy leaders hold the opposite position. Why would a majority of policy leaders not want to be strongly influenced by public opinion? One answer to this question is that public opinion polls can provide only a limited amount of guidance to policymakers.

The Limits of Polling. Policymakers cannot always be guided by opinion polls. In the end, politicians must make their own choices. When they do so, their choices necessarily involve trade-offs. If politicians vote for increased spending to improve education, for example, by necessity fewer resources are available for other worthy projects. Moreover, to make an informed policy choice requires an understanding not only of the policy area but also of the consequences of any given choice. Almost no public opinion polls make sure that those polled have such information.

Finally, government decisions cannot be made simply by adding up individual desires. Politicians engage in a type of "horse trading" with each other. Politicians also know that they cannot satisfy every desire of every constituent. Therefore, each politician attempts to maximize the net benefits to his or her constituents, while keeping within whatever the politician believes the government can afford.

Health-Care Reform as an Example. We can examine the limits of public opinion polling as an influence on policymaking through the health-care reform bills adopted by Congress in March 2010. Republicans argued that at least one reason to reject the reforms was that they were massively unpopular. "We have failed to listen to America," said House Republican Leader John Boehner. Why did the Democrats press ahead with reforms that were so controversial? If politicians always responded to public opinion, the Democrats would not have passed a package that was opposed by a majority of the voters in most polls.

One reason to proceed was that health-care reform did not poll as badly as the Republicans claimed. Republicans implied that the public held consensus opinion on this issue, as illustrated in Figure 6–1 on page 190. Actually, health care was an excellent example of divided opinion, as shown in Figure 6–2 on the same page. Note that in Figure 6–2, 13 percent of respondents opposed the reforms *from the political left.* True, the sample in this poll opposed the legislation by 56 percent to 39 percent, but it also rejected the Republican position—that the reforms were too liberal—by 52 percent to 43 percent. Other polls revealed that most individual elements of the package had majority support, which suggested that many people were misinformed about what the legislation actually contained.

Representative John Lewis, left, (D., Ga.) greets voters as he arrives to cast his vote, on November 4, 2008, at Westlake High School in Atlanta. (AP Photo/Gregory Smith)

Health-Care Consequences. As noted above, polls cannot reflect necessary trade-offs or the consequences of decisions. For example, polls reported that the idea of incremental change in health care was popular, and that many people distrusted large, comprehensive programs. Senate Republican Leader Mitch McConnell argued that Congress should have adopted simple measures that abolished the preexisting condition rule and made other limited changes. Unfortunately, abolishing the preexisting condition rule, in the absence of other changes, would destroy the market for private health insurance. The rule was not put in place because insurance companies are evil. Rather, it was established to force individuals to take out insurance while they were still healthy, before they required expensive treatments. If people bought insurance only when they needed to file costly claims, companies would lose money on most of their customers. Companies would be forced to stop writing these kinds of policies.

Without the preexisting condition rule, some other way had to be found to compel healthy people to buy insurance—hence the highly controversial "individual mandate." If everyone must buy insurance, however, the problem arises that many people cannot afford it and therefore need subsidies. At this point, you have a package with a distinct family resemblance to Obamacare. Needless to say, no polling firm tried to explain these complications to its respondents.

Every politician has different sets of constituents. For example, Representative Keith Ellison (D., Minn.), third from right, is shown with constituents from his home district in Minneapolis. The group shown is the Amyotrophic Lateral Sclerosis Association. How does a member of Congress react to the varying demands of different groups of constituents? (Courtesy of Keith Ellison, Creative Commons)

WHY SHOULD YOU CARE ABOUT... POLLS AND PUBLIC OPINION?

Why should you, as an individual, care about public opinion and opinion polls? Americans are inundated with the results of public opinion polls. The polls purport to tell us a variety of things: whether the president's popularity is up or down, whether gun rights are more in favor now than previously, or who is leading the pack for the next presidential nomination. What must be kept in mind with this blizzard of information is that poll results are not equally good or equally believable.

(Courtesy www.pollster.com)

OPINION POLLS AND YOUR LIFE

As a critical consumer, you need to be aware of what makes one set of public opinion poll results valid and other results useless or even dangerously misleading. Knowing what makes a poll accurate is especially important if you plan to participate actively in politics. Successful participation depends on accurate information, and that includes knowing what your fellow citizens are thinking. If large numbers of other people really agree with you that a particular policy needs to be changed, there may be a good chance that the policy can actually be altered. If almost no one agrees with you on a particular issue, there may be no point in trying to change policy immediately; the best you can do is to try to sway the opinions of others, in the hope that someday enough people will agree with you to make policy changes possible.

HOW YOU CAN MAKE A DIFFERENCE

Pay attention only to opinion polls that are based on scientific, or random, samples. In these so-called *probability samples,* a known probability is used to select each person interviewed. Do not give credence to the results of opinion polls that consist of shopping-mall interviews or the like. The main problem with this kind of opinion taking is that not everyone has an equal chance of being in the mall when the interview takes place. Also, it is almost certain that the people in the mall are not a reasonable cross section of a community's entire population.

Probability samples are useful because you can calculate the range within which the results would have fallen if everybody had been interviewed. Well-designed probability samples will allow the pollster to say, for example, that he or she is 95 percent sure that in February 2009, 58 percent of the public, plus or minus 3 percentage points, opposed giving aid to U.S. automakers that were in danger of going bankrupt. It turns out that if you want to be twice as precise about a poll result, you need to collect a sample four times as large. This tends to make accurate polls expensive and difficult to conduct.

Pay attention as well to how people were contacted for the poll—by mail, by telephone, in person in their homes, or in some other way (such as through the Internet). Because of its lower cost, polling firms have turned more and more to telephone interviewing. This method can produce accurate results; however, it has its disadvantages, as discussed on page 206. Another disadvantage is that telephone interviews typically need to be short and to deal with questions that are fairly easy to answer. Interviews in person are better for getting useful information about why a particular response was given. They take much longer to complete, however. Results from mailed questionnaires should be taken with a grain of salt. Usually, only a small percentage of people send them back.

When viewers or listeners of television or radio shows are encouraged to call in their opinions to an 800 telephone number, the polling results are meaningless. Users of the Internet also have an easy way to make their views known. Only people who own computers and are interested in the topic will take the trouble to respond, however, and that group may not be representative of the general public.

questions for discussion and analysis

1. Years ago, people with postgraduate degrees were more likely to vote for Republican than Democratic candidates, but in recent years, highly educated voters have been trending Democratic. Why might physicians and lawyers be more likely to vote Democratic than in the past? For what reasons might college professors tilt to the Democrats?

2. In recent years, more and more Americans have begun refusing to talk to poll takers. Also, many people now rely on cell phones, which have numbers that are not available to telephone pollsters. What problems could these two developments pose for polling organizations? How might these developments bias polling results?

3. Some political scientists claim that individual polls are relatively meaningless but that a number of polls averaged together can be fairly accurate. Why would a number of polls averaged together have more predictive power?

4. Why do you think the American people express a relatively high degree of confidence in the military as an institution? Why do people express less confidence in Congress than in other major institutions? Could people be holding various institutions to different standards, and if so, what might these standards be?

key terms

agenda setting 193
consensus 189
divided opinion 189
Fairness Doctrine 193
gender gap 198
generational effect 194
lifestyle effect 194
media 193
opinion leader 193
opinion poll 200
peer group 191
political socialization 190
political trust 208
public opinion 189
sampling error 203
socioeconomic status 194
Watergate break-in 194

chapter summary

1. Public opinion is the aggregate of individual attitudes or beliefs shared by some portion of the adult population. A consensus exists when a large proportion of the public appears to express the same view on an issue. Divided opinion exists when the public holds widely different attitudes on an issue. Sometimes, a poll shows a distribution of opinion indicating that most people either have no information about an issue or are not interested enough in the issue to form a position on it.

2. People's opinions are formed through the political socialization process. Important factors in this process are the family, educational experiences, peer groups, opinion leaders, the media, and political events. The influence of the media as a socialization factor may be growing relative to the influence of the family. Party identification is one of the most important indicators of voting behavior. Voting behavior is also influenced by demographic factors, such as education, economic status, religion, race and ethnicity, gender, and region. Finally, voting behavior is influenced by election-specific factors, such as perception of the candidates and issue preferences.

3. Most descriptions of public opinion are based on the results of opinion polls. The accuracy of polls depends on sampling techniques. An accurate poll includes a representative sample of the population being polled and ensures randomness in the selection of respondents.

4. Problems with polls include sampling errors (which may occur when the pool of respondents is not chosen in a scientific manner), the difficulty of knowing the degree to which responses are influenced by the type and order of questions asked, the use of a yes/no format for answers to the questions, and the interviewer's techniques. Many people are concerned about the use of "push polls" (in which the questions "push" the respondent toward a particular candidate). "Polls" that rely on self-selected respondents are inherently inaccurate and should be discounted.

5. Advances in technology have changed polling techniques over the years. During the 1970s, telephone polling came to be widely used. Today, largely because of extensive telemarketing, people often refuse to answer calls, and nonresponse rates in telephone polling have skyrocketed. Due to

the difficulty of obtaining a random sample in the online environment, Internet polls are often "nonpolls." Whether Internet polls can overcome this problem remains to be seen.

6. Public opinion affects the political process in many ways. The political culture provides a general environment of support for the political system, allowing the nation to weather periods of crisis. The political culture also helps Americans to evaluate their government's performance. At times, the level of trust in government has been relatively high; at other times, the level of trust has declined steeply. Similarly, Americans' confidence in government institutions varies over time, depending on a number of circumstances. Generally, though, Americans turn to government to solve what they perceive to be the major problems facing the country. In 2010, Americans ranked the economy and unemployment as the two most significant problems facing the nation.

7. Public opinion also plays an important role in policymaking. Although polling data show that a majority of Americans would like policy leaders to be influenced to a great extent by public opinion, politicians cannot always be guided by opinion polls. This is because the respondents often do not understand the costs and consequences of policy decisions or the trade-offs involved in making such decisions. An important function of public opinion is to set limits on government action through public pressure.

selected print & media resources

SUGGESTED READINGS

Asher, Herbert. *Polling and the Public: What Every Citizen Should Know.* Washington, D.C.: CQ Press, 2004. This clearly written and often entertaining book explains what polls are, how they are conducted and interpreted, and how the wording and ordering of survey questions, as well as the interviewer's techniques, can significantly affect the respondents' answers.

Bishop, Bill. *The Big Sort: Why the Clustering of Like-Minded America Is Tearing Us Apart.* New York: Houghton Mifflin, 2008. Jam-packed with polling data, Bishop's book argues that we have clustered into like-minded communities as never before. Results include political polarization and an inability to understand Americans of different backgrounds or beliefs.

Fiorina, Morris P., with Samuel J. Adams and Jeremy C. Pope. *Culture War? The Myth of a Polarized America,* 3d ed. New York: Longman, 2010. Fiorina and his colleagues use polling data to argue that most Americans are politically moderate, even though our political leaders are highly polarized. Topics include abortion, same-sex marriage, school prayer, and gun control. A new chapter in this edition analyzes the 2008 elections.

Grabe, Maria Elizabeth, and Erik Page Bucy. *Image Bite Politics: News and the Visual Framing of Elections.* New York: Oxford University Press, 2009. Grabe and Bucy examine the visual presentation of presidential candidates in news reports and connect these images to shifts in public opinion. They argue that "image bites" can be more influential than "sound bites."

Lewis-Beck, Michael S., Helmut Norpoth, William G. Jacoby, and Herbert F. Weisberg. *The American Voter Revisited.* Ann Arbor: University of Michigan Press, 2008. Four political scientists have re-created the 1960 classic *The American Voter* with up-to-date data and analysis. They find that voter behavior has been remarkably consistent, even over half a century.

MEDIA RESOURCES

Faith and Politics: The Christian Right—A 1995 documentary hosted by Dan Rather and produced by CBS News. It focuses on the efforts of the Christian conservative movement to affect educational curricula and public policy. Members of the Christian right who are interviewed include Ralph Reed and Gary Bauer. Critics of the Christian right who are interviewed include Senator Arlen Specter.

Vox Populi: Democracy in Crisis—A PBS special focusing on why public confidence in government, which has plummeted during recent decades, still has not recovered.

Wag the Dog—A 1997 film that provides a very cynical look at the importance of public opinion. The film, which features Dustin Hoffman and Robert De Niro, follows the efforts of a presidential political consultant who stages a foreign policy crisis to divert public opinion from a sex scandal in the White House.

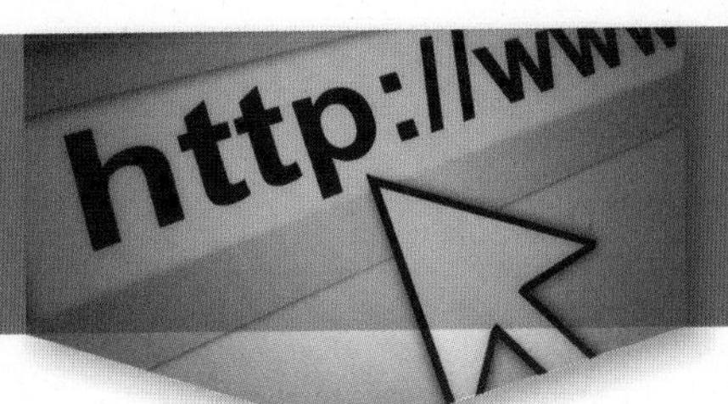

e-mocracy

ONLINE POLLING AND POLL DATA

News organizations, interest groups, not-for-profit groups, and online e-zines are now using online polling to gather the opinions of their readers and viewers. All the user has to do is log on to the Web site and click on the box indicating the preferred response. People can respond to online polls more easily than to call-in polls, and in most cases, online polls are free to the user. Realize, though, that online polls are totally nonscientific because the respondents are all self-selected. Essentially, Internet polls are nonpolls because only those who choose to do so respond, making the polls much more likely to be biased and based on an unrepresentative sample.

At the same time, the Internet is an excellent source for finding reliable polling reports and data. All of the major polling organizations have Web sites that include news releases about polls they have conducted. Some sites make the polling data available for free to users; others require that a user pay a subscription fee before accessing the polling archives on the site.

LOGGING ON

The Polling Report Web site offers polls and their results organized by topic. It is up to date and easy to use. Go to
www.pollingreport.com

The Gallup organization's Web site offers not only polling data (although a user must pay a subscription fee to obtain access to many polling reports) but also information on how polls are constructed, conducted, and interpreted. Go to
www.gallup.com

The Pew Research Center, a major public opinion research group, sponsors projects on journalism, the Internet, religion, Hispanics, global attitudes, and other topics. Its sites include
pewresearch.org, **people-press.org**, **www.journalism.org**, **pewinternet.org**, **pewforum.org** (religion), **pewhispanic.org**, **pewglobal.org**, **and pewsocialtrends.org**

Real Clear Politics is known for its "poll of polls," which aggregates results from leading pollsters in the run-up to elections. The site also aggregates polls on the president's job approval rating and other indicators. Although the site is run by conservatives, it offers opinion pieces from multiple media sources on its home page. See it at
www.realclearpolitics.com

In recent years, Nate Silver has won a reputation as one of the Web's sharpest students of polling data. Follow his analyses and those of his colleagues at
www.fivethirtyeight.com

chapter 7

Interest Groups

chapter contents

These campaign volunteers in Levittown, Pennsylvania, are shown preparing for a neighborhood drive to register more voters. (Mark Peterson/Redux)

WHAT IF... ...lobbying were abolished?

These three lobbyists are shown outside the White House. What would happen if lobbying were eliminated? (© Stephen Crowley/*The New York Times*/Redux)

BACKGROUND

Lobbyists—persons hired in an attempt to influence members of Congress (and state legislatures, too)—have been around for a long time. In America, lobbying goes back to colonial times. The Reverend Increase Mather lobbied in London for a new charter for Massachusetts. Benjamin Franklin served as a lobbyist for Pennsylvania and other colonies.

Today, lobbyists are deeply unpopular. Lobbying is often seen as an essentially corrupt activity. All presidential candidates in recent years have promised to stand up against "special interests" and the lobbyists they employ. Congress—the main target of lobbying—has devised many rules and regulations in an attempt to regulate lobbyists. None have had much effect.

Lobbying is protected by the First Amendment to the Constitution, which states that Congress shall make no law abridging the right of the people "to petition the Government for a redress of grievances." Let us assume, however, that the Constitution has been amended in such a way that lobbying could be abolished.

WHAT IF LOBBYING WERE ABOLISHED?

If lobbying were abolished, about 35,000 lobbyists who swarm Capitol Hill in Washington, D.C., would be out of work. Currently, corporate America spends $6 million a day or more on lobbying. The abolition of lobbying would free up these funds. Yet just because these dollars would no longer go to lobbyists does not mean they would go to stockholders, customers, or employees. Doubtless, if lobbying were abolished, big business would spend more on media campaigns to "educate" voters about what kinds of politicians would be best for America. Other interest groups would also spend more to sway the public to vote for favored candidates who would then in turn vote the "right" way on pending legislation.

NO LOBBYING COULD LEAD TO LESS DEMOCRACY, NOT MORE

As you learned in the previous chapter, the "will of the people" in a complex nation such as ours is hard to define. Students of public opinion believe that there are many different "publics" in a country of more than 310 million people. Lobbying improves the public debate by providing an outlet for more constituencies. In this way, lobbying is an expression of democracy. Without lobbyists, Congress might ignore many of the various interests with which Americans identify. In fact, lobbyist Nick Allard has argued for more lobbyists, not fewer. He believes that we need lobbyists for the poor, the young, and all of the people who are not adequately represented today.

LOBBYISTS AND CONGRESSIONAL STAFF

Lobbying provides lawmakers with information—lobbyists try to woo lawmakers with facts, not just campaign donations. Without lobbyists, Congress would have to hire more staff members to research the multitude of issues facing government. Congress would have more staff specializing in energy, health care, education, and other topics. Ultimately, taxpayers would foot the bill for additional staff members, who might be responsive to the political parties instead of interest groups.

FOR CRITICAL ANALYSIS

1. Why has *lobbying* become a dirty word?
2. The American Cancer Society spends $3 million a year on lobbyists and AARP (representing seniors) spends $15 million. Are such lobbying activities open for criticism? Explain.

The structure of American government invites the participation of **interest groups** at various stages of the policymaking process. For example, Americans can form groups in their neighborhoods or cities and lobby the city council or their state government. They can join statewide groups or national groups and try to influence government policy through Congress or through one of the executive agencies or cabinet departments. Representatives of large corporations may seek to influence the president personally at social events or fund-raisers. When attempts to influence government through the executive and legislative branches fail, interest groups can turn to the courts, filing suit in state or federal court to achieve their political objectives.

Interest Group
An organized group of individuals sharing common objectives who actively attempt to influence policymakers.

The many "pressure points" for interest group activity in American government help to explain why there are so many—more than one hundred thousand—interest groups at work in our society. Another reason is that the right to join a group is protected by the First Amendment to the U.S. Constitution (see Chapter 4). Not only are all people guaranteed the right "peaceably to assemble," but they are also guaranteed the right "to petition the Government for a redress of grievances." This constitutional provision encourages Americans to form groups and to express their opinions to the government or to their elected representatives as members of a group. Group membership makes the individual's opinions appear more powerful and strongly conveys the group's ability to vote for or against a representative. The constitutional protection of groups is one reason that it would be very difficult to satisfy the occasional demand that *lobbyists*—persons hired to represent interest groups to the government—be abolished. As noted in the chapter-opening *What If . . .* feature, such a change would require a constitutional amendment.

Interest groups play a significant role in American government at all levels. As you will read later in this chapter and in Chapter 9, one of the ways in which interest groups attempt to influence government policies is through campaign contributions to members of Congress who intend to run for reelection. It is the interplay between campaign financial assistance and legislation favorable to specific interests that has caused some observers to claim that Congress has been sold to the highest bidder. Certainly, devising a system in which campaigns can be financed *without* jeopardizing objectivity on the part of members of Congress is a major challenge for our nation today. Recall from Chapter 1, however, that in our pluralist society, the competition by interest groups for access to lawmakers automatically checks the extent to which any one particular group can influence Congress.

Former South Dakota senator Tom Daschle, who became a lobbyist, was nominated as secretary of health and human services in the new Obama administration. Ultimately, revelations about unpaid taxes forced him out of contention. Why are former lobbyists closely scrutinized during confirmation hearings? (AP Photo/Susan Walsh)

Interest Groups: A Natural Phenomenon

Alexis de Tocqueville observed in the early 1830s that "in no country of the world has the principle of association been more successfully used or applied to a greater multitude of objectives than in America."[1] The French traveler was amazed at the degree to which Americans formed groups to solve civic problems, establish social relationships, and speak for their economic or political interests. Perhaps James Madison, when he wrote *Federalist Paper* No. 10 (see Appendix C), had already judged the character of his country's citizens similarly. He supported the creation of a large republic with many states to encourage the formation of multiple interests. The multitude of interests, in Madison's view, would work to discourage the formation of an oppressive majority interest.

Poll data show that more than two-thirds of all Americans belong to at least one group or association. Although the majority of these affiliations could not be classified as "interest groups" in the political sense, Americans certainly understand the principles of working in groups.

1. Alexis de Tocqueville, *Democracy in America,* Vol. 1 [1835], ed. Phillips Bradley (New York: Knopf, 1980), p. 191.

did you know?

That at least half of all lobbyists in Washington, D.C., are women.

Today, interest groups range from the elementary school parent-teacher association and the local "Stop the Sewer Plant Association" to the statewide association of insurance agents. They include small groups such as local environmental organizations and national groups such as the Boy Scouts of America, the American Civil Liberties Union, the National Education Association, and the American League of Lobbyists.

These women want Congress to give them the right to vote. Did they have much support then? (© Hulton-Deutsch Collection/Corbis)

Interest Groups and Social Movements

Interest groups are often spawned by mass **social movements.** Such movements represent demands by a large segment of the population for change in the political, economic, or social system. Social movements are often the first expression of latent discontent with the existing system. They may be the authentic voice of weaker or oppressed groups in society that do not have the means or standing to organize as interest groups. For example, most mainstream political and social leaders disapproved of the women's movement of the 1800s. Because women were unable to vote or take an active part in the political system, it was difficult for women who desired greater freedom to organize formal groups. After the Civil War, when more women became active in professional life, organizations seeking to win women the right to vote came into being.

African Americans found themselves in an even more disadvantaged situation after the end of the Reconstruction period (1865–1877). They were unable to exercise political rights in many southern and border states, and their participation in any form of organization could lead to economic ruin, physical harassment, or even death. The civil rights movement of the 1950s and 1960s was clearly a social movement. To be sure, the movement received support from several formal organizations—including the Southern Christian Leadership Conference, the National Association for the Advancement of Colored People, and the Urban League. Yet only a social movement could generate the kinds of civil disobedience that took place in hundreds of towns and cities across the country.

Social movements are often precursors of interest groups. They may generate interest groups with specific goals that successfully recruit members by offering certain incentives. In the example of the women's movement of the 1960s, the National Organization for Women was formed in part out of a demand to end gender-segregated job advertising in newspapers.

Why Do Americans Join Interest Groups?

Social Movement
A movement that represents the demands of a large segment of the public for political, economic, or social change.

Latent Interests
Public-policy interests that are not recognized or addressed by a group at a particular time.

One puzzle that has fascinated political scientists is why some people join interest groups, while many others do not. Everyone has some interest that could benefit from government action. For many individuals, however, those concerns remain unorganized interests, or **latent interests.**

According to political theorist Mancur Olson,[2] it simply may not be rational for individuals to join most groups. In his classic work on this topic, Olson introduced the idea of the "collective good." This concept refers to any public benefit that, if available to any

2. Mancur Olson, *The Logic of Collective Action* (Cambridge, Mass.: Harvard University Press, 1965).

member of the community, cannot be denied to any other member, whether or not he or she participated in the effort to gain the good.

Although collective benefits are usually thought of as coming from such public goods as clean air and national defense, benefits are also bestowed by the government on subsets of the public. Price subsidies to dairy farmers and loans to college students are examples. Olson used economic theory to propose that it is not rational for interested individuals to join groups that work for *group* benefits. In fact, it is often more rational for the individual to wait for others to procure the benefits and then share them. How many community college students, for example, join the American Association of Community Colleges, an organization that lobbies the government for increased financial aid to students? The difficulty interest groups face in recruiting members when the benefits can be obtained without joining the groups is referred to as the **free rider problem.**

Free Rider Problem
The difficulty interest groups face in recruiting members when the benefits they achieve can be gained without joining the group.

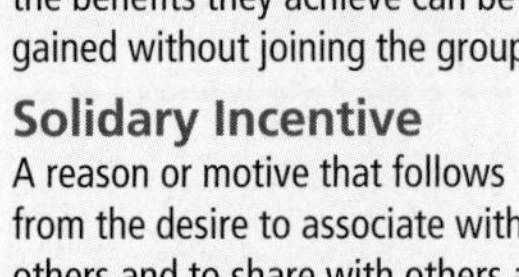

Solidary Incentive
A reason or motive that follows from the desire to associate with others and to share with others a particular interest or hobby.

Material Incentive
A reason or motive based on the desire to enjoy certain economic benefits or opportunities.

If so little incentive exists for individuals to join together, why are there thousands of interest groups lobbying in Washington? According to the logic of collective action, if the contribution of an individual *will* make a difference to the effort, then it is worth it to the individual to join. Thus, smaller groups, which seek benefits for only a small proportion of the population, are more likely to enroll members who will give time and funds to the cause. Larger groups, which represent general public interests (the women's movement or the American Civil Liberties Union, for example), will find it relatively more difficult to get individuals to join. People need an incentive—material or otherwise—to participate.

Solidary Incentives

Interest groups offer **solidary incentives** for their members. Solidary benefits include companionship, a sense of belonging, and the pleasure of associating with others. Although the National Audubon Society was originally founded to save the snowy egret from extinction, today most members join to learn more about birds and to meet and share their pleasure with other individuals who enjoy bird-watching as a hobby. Even though the incentive might be solidary for many members, this organization nonetheless also pursues an active political agenda, working to preserve the environment and to protect endangered species. Still, most members may not play any part in working toward larger, more national goals unless the organization can convince them to take political action or unless some local environmental issue arises.

Material Incentives

For other individuals, interest groups offer direct **material incentives.** A case in point is AARP (formerly the American Association of Retired Persons), which provides discounts, insurance plans, and organized travel opportunities for its members. Because of its exceptionally low dues ($16 annually) and the benefits gained through membership, AARP has become the largest—and a very powerful—interest group in the United States. AARP can claim to represent the interests of millions of senior citizens and can show that they actually have joined the group. For most seniors, the material incentives outweigh the membership costs. Another example of such an interest group is the American Automobile Association (AAA). Most people who join this organization do so for its

(Courtesy of http://www.aarp.org)

Purposive Incentive
A reason for supporting or participating in the activities of a group that is based on agreement with the goals of the group. For example, someone with a strong interest in human rights might have a purposive incentive to join Amnesty International.

emergency roadside assistance and trip planning. Many members may not realize that the AAA is also a significant interest group seeking to shape laws that affect drivers.

Many other interest groups offer indirect material incentives for their members. Such groups as the American Dairy Association and the National Association of Automobile Dealers do not give discounts or "freebies" to their members, but they do offer indirect benefits and rewards by, for example, protecting the material interests of their members from government policymaking that is injurious to their industry or business.

Purposive Incentives

Interest groups also offer the opportunity for individuals to pursue political, economic, or social goals through joint action. **Purposive incentives** offer individuals the satisfaction of taking action when the goals of a group correspond to their beliefs or principles. The individuals who belong to a group focusing on the abortion issue or gun control, for example, do so because they feel strongly enough about the issues to support the group's work with money and time.

did you know?
That the activities of interest groups at the state level have been growing faster than in the nation's capital, with more than 45,000 registered state lobbyists in 2009.

Some scholars have argued that many people join interest groups simply for the discounts, magazine subscriptions, and other tangible benefits and are not really interested in the political positions taken by the groups. According to William P. Browne, however, research shows that people really do care about the policy stance of an interest group. Representatives of a group seek people who share the group's views and then ask them to join. As one group leader put it, "Getting members is about scaring the hell out of people."[3] People join the group and then feel that they are doing something about a cause that is important to them.

Types of Interest Groups

Thousands of groups exist to influence government. Among the major types of interest groups are those that represent the main sectors of the economy. In addition, a number of "public-interest" organizations have been formed to represent the needs of the general citizenry. These include many "single-issue" groups. The interests of foreign governments and foreign businesses are represented in the American political arena as well. The names and Web addresses of some major interest groups are shown in Table 7–1 on the facing page.

This farmer in central Illinois may support lobbying efforts to continue taxpayer subsidies for agriculture. How might he benefit? (AP Photo/Seth Perlman)

Economic Interest Groups

More interest groups are formed to represent economic interests than any other set of interests. The variety of economic interest groups mirrors the complexity of the American economy. The major sectors that seek influence in Washington, D.C., include business, agriculture, labor unions, government workers, and professionals.

Business Interest Groups. Thousands of business groups and trade associations work to influence government policies that affect their respective industries. "Umbrella groups" represent collections of businesses or other entities. The U.S. Chamber of Commerce, for example, is an umbrella group that represents a wide variety of businesses, while the

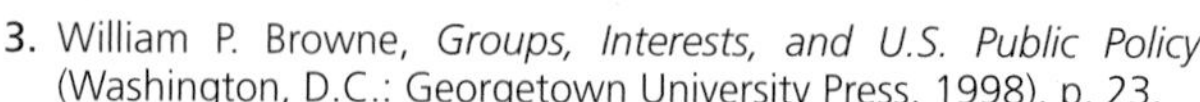

3. William P. Browne, *Groups, Interests, and U.S. Public Policy* (Washington, D.C.: Georgetown University Press, 1998), p. 23.

TABLE 7–1 A List of Effective Interest Groups

BUSINESS
American Bankers Association: **www.aba.com**
American Farm Bureau Federation (representing farmers): **www.fb.org**
American Hospital Association: **www.aha.org**
America's Health Insurance Plans: **www.ahip.org**
Business Roundtable: **www.businessroundtable.org**
Chamber of Commerce of the United States: **www.uschamber.org**
National Association of Home Builders: **www.nahb.org**
National Association of Manufacturers (NAM): **www.nam.org**
Pharmaceutical Research and Manufacturers of America: **www.phrma.org**

LABOR
American Federation of Labor—Congress of Industrial Organizations (AFL-CIO): **www.aflcio.org**
American Federation of State, County, and Municipal Employees (AFSCME): **www.afscme.org**
Change to Win (a federation of labor unions): **www.changetowin.org**
International Brotherhood of Teamsters: **www.teamster.org**
National Education Association (NEA—representing teachers): **www.nea.org**
Service Employees International Union: **www.seiu.org**

PROFESSIONAL
American Association for Justice (formerly the Association of Trial Lawyers of America): **www.justice.org**
American Medical Association (AMA—representing physicians): **www.ama-assn.org**
National Association of Realtors: **www.realtor.org**

IDENTITY
League of United Latin American Citizens (LULAC): **www.lulac.org**
National Association for the Advancement of Colored People (the NAACP—represents African Americans): **www.naacp.org**
National Organization for Women (NOW): **www.now.org**

ENVIRONMENTAL
National Audubon Society (an environmentalist group): **www.audubon.org**
National Wildlife Federation: **www.nwf.org**
Nature Conservancy: **www.nature.org**
Sierra Club: **www.sierraclub.org**

OTHER
AARP (formerly the American Association of Retired Persons): **www.aarp.org**
American Civil Liberties Union (ACLU): **www.aclu.org**
American Israel Public Affairs Committee (AIPAC—pro-Israel): **www.aipac.org**
American Legion (veterans): **www.legion.org**
American Society for the Prevention of Cruelty to Animals (ASPCA): **www.aspca.org**
Amnesty International USA (human rights): **www.amnesty.org**
Handgun Control, Inc. (favors gun control): **www.bradycampaign.org**
Mothers Against Drunk Driving (MADD): **www.madd.org**
NARAL Pro-Choice America (formerly the National Abortion and Reproductive Rights Action League—favors legalized abortion): **www.naral.org**
National Rifle Association (NRA): **home.nra.org**
National Right to Life Committee (opposed to legalized abortion): **www.nrlc.org**

National Association of Manufacturers is an umbrella group that represents only manufacturing concerns. The American Pet Products Manufacturers Association works for the good of manufacturers of pet food, pet toys, and other pet products, as well as for pet shops. This group strongly opposes increased regulation of stores that sell animals and restrictions on importing pets. Other major organizations that represent business interests, such as the Better Business Bureaus, take positions on policies but do not actually lobby in Washington, D.C.

Some business groups are decidedly more powerful than others. The U.S. Chamber of Commerce, which represents more than 3 million businesses, can bring constituent influence to bear on every member of Congress. Another powerful lobbying organization is the National Association of Manufacturers. With a staff of about 150 people in Washington, D.C., the organization can mobilize dozens of well-educated, articulate **lobbyists** to work the corridors of Congress on issues of concern to its members.

Lobbyist
An organization or individual who attempts to influence legislation and the administrative decisions of government.

did you know?

That the names of many interest groups suggest goals opposite from the organization's true objectives—for example, the Palm Oil Truth Foundation does not seek to expose the dangers of palm oil use, but to expand the use of palm oil in food and oppose action against global warming.

Agricultural Interest Groups. American farmers and their employees represent less than 1 percent of the U.S. population. Nevertheless, farmers' influence on legislation beneficial to their interests has been significant. Farmers have succeeded in their aims because they have very strong interest groups. They are geographically dispersed and therefore have many representatives and senators to speak for them.

The American Farm Bureau Federation, established in 1919, represents more than 6 million families (a majority of whom are not actually farm families) and is usually seen as conservative. It was instrumental in getting government guarantees of "fair" prices during the Great Depression in the 1930s.[4] Another important agricultural interest organization is the National Farmers' Union (NFU), which is considered more liberal. As farms have become larger and "agribusiness" has become a way of life, single-issue farm groups have emerged. The American Dairy Association, the Peanut Growers Group, and the National Soybean Association, for example, work to support their respective farmers and associated businesses. In recent years, agricultural interest groups have become active on many new issues. Among other things, they have opposed immigration restrictions and are very involved in international trade matters as they seek new markets. One of the newest agricultural groups is the American Farmland Trust, which supports policies to conserve farmland and protect natural resources.

Labor Movement
Generally, the economic and political expression of working-class interests; politically, the organization of working-class interests.

Agricultural interest groups have probably been more successful than any other groups in obtaining subsidies from American taxpayers. U.S. farm subsidies cost taxpayers at least $20 billion a year directly, and another $12 billion a year in higher food prices. Republicans and Democrats alike have supported agricultural subsidy legislation, showing the success of agricultural lobbying groups. The latest legislation, passed in 2008, created the most expensive agricultural subsidy program ever.

The farm bill was passed over the president's veto. It had a price tag of about $100 billion over a five-year period, not counting food stamps and other food aid. The bill included tax breaks for racehorse owners, marketing subsidies for fruit and vegetable growers, research funding for organic farmers, and increased price supports for domestic sugar producers. At the last minute, the salmon industry obtained $170 million. Although 2008 saw some of the highest prices for agricultural products ever recorded, the bill provided for permanent disaster assistance for corn, wheat, cotton, rice, and soybean growers.

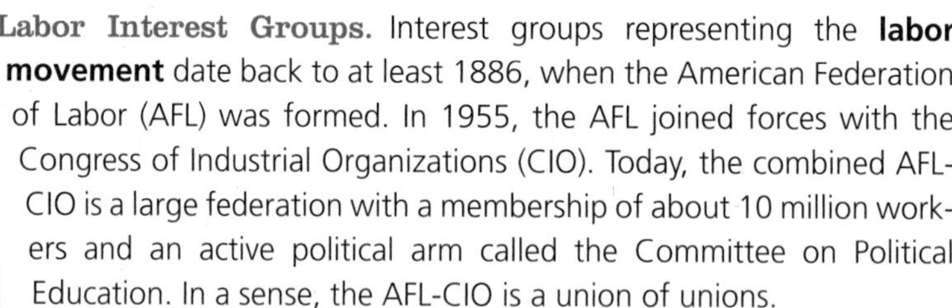

This Goodyear Tire & Rubber Company union employee supports a strike against his employer. Are labor unions still a major lobbying force in the United States? (AP Photo/ Tony Dejak)

Labor Interest Groups. Interest groups representing the **labor movement** date back to at least 1886, when the American Federation of Labor (AFL) was formed. In 1955, the AFL joined forces with the Congress of Industrial Organizations (CIO). Today, the combined AFL-CIO is a large federation with a membership of about 10 million workers and an active political arm called the Committee on Political Education. In a sense, the AFL-CIO is a union of unions.

The AFL-CIO remained the predominant labor union organization for fifty years. The AFL-CIO experienced discord within its ranks during 2005, however, as four key unions left the federation and formed the Change to Win Coalition. Today, the Change to Win Coalition has a membership of about 6 million workers. Many labor advocates fear that the split will reduce organized labor's influence, and in 2009 leaders of the two federations met to discuss the possibility of reunification.

4. The Agricultural Adjustment Act of 1933 (declared unconstitutional) was replaced by the 1938 Agricultural Adjustment Act and later changed and amended several times.

Indeed, the role of unions in American society has declined in recent years, as witnessed by the decrease in union membership (see Figure 7–1 below). In the age of automation and with the rise of the **service sector,** blue-collar workers in basic industries (autos, steel, and the like) represent a smaller and smaller percentage of the total working population.

Service Sector
The sector of the economy that provides services—such as health care, banking, and education—in contrast to the sector that produces goods.

Because of this decline in the industrial sector of the economy, national unions are looking to nontraditional areas for their membership, including migrant farmworkers, service workers, and especially public employees—such as police officers, firefighting personnel, and teachers, including college professors and even graduate assistants. Indeed, public-sector unions are the fastest-growing labor organizations.

Although the proportion of the workforce that belongs to a union has declined over the years, American labor unions have not given up their efforts to support sympathetic candidates for Congress or for state office. Currently, the AFL-CIO, under the leadership of coal miner Richard Trumka, has a large political budget, which it uses to help Democratic candidates nationwide. Labor offers a candidate (such as Democratic presidential candidate Barack Obama in 2008) a corps of volunteers in addition to campaign contributions. A massive turnout by labor union members in critical elections can significantly increase the final vote totals for Democratic candidates. Recently, labor unions have pushed members of Congress to pass legislation that would make it easier for employees to join unions—and thus boost union membership. For a discussion of the controversy surrounding this effort, see this chapter's feature *Which Side Are You On? Should Workers Forgo Secret Ballots When Trying to Organize a Union?* on the following page.

Public Employee Unions. The degree of unionization in the private sector has declined over the past fifty years, but this has been partially offset by growth in the unionization of public employees. Figure 7–1 below displays the growth in public-sector unionization. With a total membership of almost 8 million, public-sector unions are likely to continue expanding.

Both the American Federation of State, County, and Municipal Employees and the American Federation of Teachers are members of the AFL-CIO's Public Employee

FIGURE 7–1 Decline in Union Membership, 1948 to Present

The percentage of the total workforce that consists of labor union members has declined precipitously during the last forty or so years. In contrast, the percentage of government workers who are union members increased significantly in the 1960s and 1970s and has remained stable since.

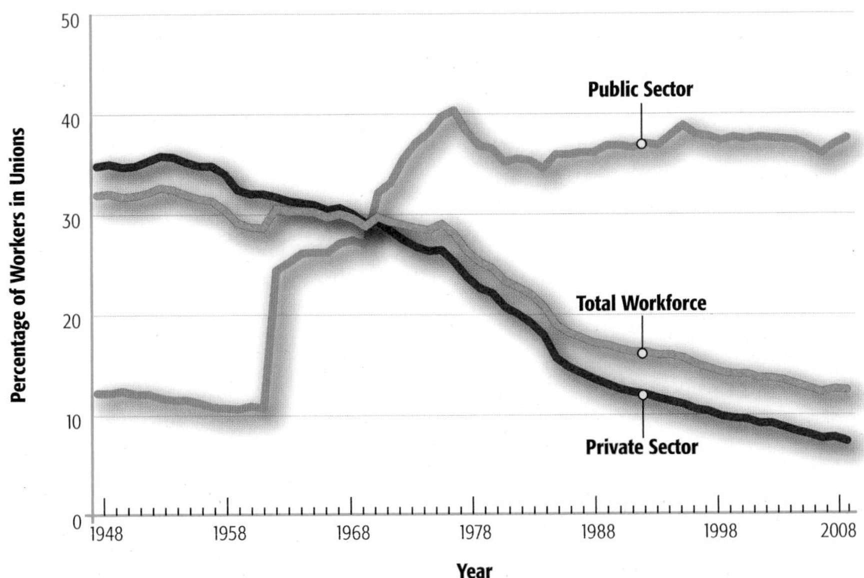

Source: Bureau of Labor Statistics.

Department. Over the years, public employee unions have become quite militant and are often involved in strikes. Most of these strikes are illegal, because almost no public employees have the right to strike.

A powerful interest group lobbying on behalf of its public employees is the National Education Association (NEA), a nationwide organization of about 3.2 million teachers and others connected with education. Most NEA locals function as labor unions. The NEA lobbies intensively for increased public funding of education.

WHICH SIDE ARE YOU ON? SHOULD WORKERS FORGO SECRET BALLOTS WHEN TRYING TO ORGANIZE A UNION?

Several years ago, with union membership waning, union leaders began putting pressure on Congress to pass legislation that would help promote new membership. That legislation would allow for "card checks," which would permit a union to become the bargaining agent for a workplace if a majority of the workers signed cards indicating their support. Currently, companies do not have to recognize a union unless workers vote by a secret ballot in favor of union representation. Under existing law, companies can voluntarily agree to a card check, but they are not required to do so, and the method is rarely used. Under the new law, unions would be the ones to decide whether to employ a card check or a secret ballot, and they would probably choose the card-check system in most instances. Whenever America has a Democratic president and Democratic control of Congress, we are likely to see serious attempts to pass legislation that allows card checks to replace secret ballots.

MAKING THE ENVIRONMENT MORE PROUNION

Those who have supported card-check legislation, such as the late Senator Ted Kennedy (D., Mass.), claim that this legislation would level the playing field between union members and management. It would do so by removing "large loopholes" in today's labor laws that purportedly allow employers to intimidate workers in the period leading up to a secret-ballot election.

Moreover, say proponents of the card-check bill, the decline of unionism does not bode well for the status of workers. Workers in general should do everything possible to strengthen their negotiating positions and to expand the choices available to them. When unions are strong, even nonunion workers benefit, because companies will improve wages and working conditions to avoid unionization. Former Democratic vice-presidential candidate John Edwards said: "If you can join the Republican Party by just signing a card, you should be able to join a union by just signing a card."

SECRET BALLOTS ARE THE BACKBONE OF DEMOCRACY

In 2006, the Opinion Research Corporation surveyed a variety of Americans and found that 75 percent chose secret-ballot elections as the most democratic method of unionization. In 1991, the District of Columbia Circuit Court stated that "freedom of choice is a matter at the very center of our national labor relations policy, and a secret election is the preferred method of gauging choice." Back in 2001, many members of Congress, including Representatives Barney Frank (D., Mass.), George Miller (D., Calif.), and Bernie Sanders (Ind., Vt.), wrote to Mexican officials stating that "we are writing to encourage you to use the secret ballot in all union recognition elections. . . . We feel that the secret ballot is absolutely necessary in order to ensure that workers are not intimidated into voting for a union they might not otherwise choose."

In accord with all these views, opponents of the card-check bill claim that secret ballots are the only path to true democracy. Furthermore, they argue, even assuming that companies do intimidate workers before union elections, there is no guarantee that union organizers won't intimidate workers in attempts to convince them to sign union cards.

FOR CRITICAL ANALYSIS

Under what circumstances, if any, would a simple card-check system to establish union representation be legitimate? Do you see any essential differences between union representation contests and elections to choose public officials?

Interest Groups of Professionals. Numerous professional organizations exist, including the American Bar Association, the Association of General Contractors of America, the Institute of Electrical and Electronics Engineers, and others. Some professional groups, such as those representing lawyers and physicians, are more influential than others because of their social status. Lawyers have a unique advantage—a large number of members of Congress share their profession. In terms of funds spent on lobbying, however, one professional organization stands head and shoulders above the rest—the American Medical Association (AMA). Founded in 1847, it is affiliated with more than 1,000 local and state medical societies and has a total membership of about 240,000.

The Unorganized Poor. Some have argued that the system of interest group politics leaves out poor Americans and U.S. residents who are not citizens and cannot vote. Americans who are disadvantaged economically cannot afford to join interest groups. If they are members of the working poor, they may hold two or more jobs just to survive, leaving them no time to participate in interest groups. Other groups in the population—including non-English-speaking groups, resident aliens, single parents, Americans with disabilities, and younger voters—may not have the time or expertise even to find out what group might represent them. Consequently, some scholars suggest that interest groups and lobbyists are the privilege of upper-middle-class Americans and those who belong to unions or other special groups.

R. Allen Hays examines the plight of poor Americans in his book *Who Speaks for the Poor?*[5] Hays studied groups and individuals who have lobbied for public housing and other issues related to the poor and concluded that the poor depend largely on indirect representation. Most efforts on behalf of the poor come from a policy network of groups—including public housing officials, welfare workers and officials, religious groups, public-interest groups, and some liberal general interest groups—that speak loudly and persistently for the poor. Poor Americans themselves remain outside the interest group network and have little direct voice of their own.

These writers are members of the Writers Guild of America in Hollywood, California. If you were to classify this interest group, what kind would it be? (© Charley Gallay/Getty Images)

Environmental Groups

Environmental interest groups are not new. We have already mentioned the National Audubon Society, which was founded in 1905 to protect the snowy egret from the commercial demand for hat decorations. The patron of the Sierra Club, John Muir, worked for the creation of national parks more than a century ago. But the blossoming of national environmental groups with mass memberships did not occur until the 1970s. Since the first Earth Day, organized in 1970, many interest groups have sprung up to protect the environment in general or unique ecological niches. The groups range from the National Wildlife Federation, with a membership of more than 4 million and an emphasis on education, to the more elite Environmental Defense Fund, with a membership of 500,000 and a focus on influencing federal policy. The Nature Conservancy uses members' contributions to buy up threatened natural areas and either give them to state or local governments or manage them itself. Other groups include the more radical Greenpeace Society and Earth First.

In early 2007, twenty labor unions joined with the Theodore Roosevelt Conservation Partnership, a Republican-leaning group of conservationists, to form the Union Sportsmen's

5. R. Allen Hays, *Who Speaks for the Poor? National Interest Groups and Social Policy* (New York: Routledge, 2001).

This member of the environmentalist group Greenpeace collects samples of oil at the mouth of the Mississippi River after the massive leakage from a BP deep-water well in the Gulf of Mexico in 2010. What motivates individuals to join public-interest organizations? (AP Photo/Charlie Riedel)

Alliance. This unlikely combination of union and conservation interests was a response to the limitations placed in recent years on prime hunting and fishing areas on federal lands in the West. Many hunters and fishers belong to the labor unions, and union leaders also looked at the alliance with the conservation group as a way to expand union membership. The conservation group, in turn, thought that it would benefit from the funds and lobbying power of the unions. According to environmental expert Thomas Dunlap of Texas A&M University, the new alliance "may have a major effect in reshaping the environmental movement for this decade."[6]

Public-Interest Groups

Public interest is a difficult term to define because, as we noted in Chapter 6, there are many publics in our nation of more than 300 million. It is almost impossible for one particular public policy to benefit everybody, which makes it practically impossible to define the public interest. Nonetheless, over the past few decades, a variety of lobbying organizations have been formed "in the public interest."

Public Interest
The best interests of the overall community; the national good, rather than the narrow interests of a particular group.

Nader Organizations. The best-known and perhaps the most effective public-interest groups are those founded under the leadership of consumer activist Ralph Nader. Nader's rise to the top began in 1965 with the publication of his book *Unsafe at Any Speed,* a lambasting critique of the purported attempt by General Motors (GM) to keep from the public detrimental information about its rear-engine Corvair. Partly as a result of Nader's book, Congress began to consider an automobile safety bill. GM made a clumsy attempt to discredit Nader. Nader sued, the media exploited the story, and when GM settled out of court for $425,000, Nader became a recognized champion of consumer interests. Since then, Nader has turned over much of his income to the more than sixty public-interest groups that he has formed or sponsored. Nader ran for president in 2000 on the Green Party ticket and in 2004 and 2008 as an independent.

Partly in response to the Nader organizations, a variety of conservative public-interest law firms have sprung up that are often pitted against the consumer groups in court. Some of these are the Mountain States Legal Defense Foundation, the Pacific Legal Foundation, the National Right-to-Work Legal Defense Foundation, the Washington Legal Foundation, the Institute for Justice, and the Mid-Atlantic Legal Foundation.

Other Public-Interest Groups. One of the largest public-interest groups is Common Cause, founded in 1970. Its goal is to reorder national priorities toward "the public" and to make governmental institutions more responsive to the needs of the public. Anyone willing to pay dues of $40 a year can become a member ($15 for students). Members are polled regularly to obtain information about local and national issues. Some of the activities of Common Cause have been (1) helping to ensure the passage of the Twenty-sixth Amendment (giving eighteen-year-olds the right to vote), (2) achieving greater voter registration in all states, (3) supporting the complete withdrawal of all U.S. forces from South Vietnam in the 1970s, and (4) promoting legislation that would limit campaign spending.

Other public-interest groups include the League of Women Voters, founded in 1920. Although officially nonpartisan, it has lobbied for the Equal Rights Amendment and for government reform. The Consumer Federation of America is an alliance of about three hundred nonprofit organizations interested in consumer protection. The American Civil Liberties Union dates back to World War I (1914–1918), when, under a different name, it defended draft resisters. It generally enters into legal disputes related to Bill of Rights issues.

6. As cited in Blaine Harden, "Unions, Conservationists Join Hands," *The Washington Post,* January 16, 2007.

Other Interest Groups

A number of interest groups focus on just one issue. Single-interest groups, being narrowly focused, may be able to call attention to their causes because they have simple, straightforward goals and because their members tend to care intensely about the issues. Thus, such groups can easily motivate their members to contact legislators or to organize demonstrations in support of their policy goals.

The acting head of the federal Consumer Product Safety Commission wants to educate all-terrain vehicle (ATV) riders about how to use ATVs safely. Which interest groups would be in favor of such action? (AP Photo/Stephen J. Boitano)

The abortion debate has created various groups opposed to abortion (such as the National Right to Life Committee) and groups in favor of abortion rights (such as NARAL Pro-Choice America). Other single-issue groups are the National Rifle Association of America, the Right to Work Committee (an antiunion group), and the American Israel Public Affairs Committee (a pro-Israel group).

Still other groups represent Americans who share a common characteristic, such as age or ethnicity. Such interest groups may lobby for legislation that enhances the rights of their members or may just represent a viewpoint.

AARP, as mentioned earlier, is one of the most powerful interest groups in Washington, D.C., and, according to some, the strongest lobbying group in the United States. It is certainly the nation's largest interest group, with a membership of about 40 million. AARP has accomplished much for its members over the years. It played a significant role in the creation of Medicare and Medicaid, as well as in obtaining annual cost-of-living increases in Social Security payments. (Medicare pays for medical expenses incurred by those who are at least 65 years of age; Medicaid provides health-care support for the poor.)

In 2003, AARP supported the Republican bill to add prescription drug coverage to Medicare. (The plan also made other changes to the system.) Some observers believe that AARP's support tipped the balance and allowed Congress to pass the measure on a closely divided vote. In 2009 and 2010, AARP strongly supported the Democratic health-care reform bills and argued against those who feared that the new legislation might harm the Medicare program.

Foreign Governments

Homegrown interests are not the only players in the game. Washington, D.C., is also the center for lobbying by foreign governments as well as private foreign interests. The governments of the largest U.S. trading partners, such as Canada, the European Union (EU) countries, Japan, and South Korea, maintain substantial research and lobbying staffs. Even smaller nations, such as those in the Caribbean, engage lobbyists when vital legislation affecting their trade interests is considered. Frequently, these foreign interests hire former representatives or former senators to promote their positions on Capitol Hill. Should foreign interests be allowed to lobby Congress? We address this question in the *Beyond Our Borders* feature on the next page.

What Makes an Interest Group Powerful?

At any time, thousands of interest groups are attempting to influence state legislatures, governors, Congress, and members of the executive branch of the U.S. government. What characteristics make some of those groups more powerful than others and more likely to have influence over government policy? Generally, interest groups attain a reputation for being powerful through their membership size, financial resources, leadership, and cohesiveness.

Size and Resources

No legislator can deny the power of an interest group that includes thousands of his or her own constituents among its members. Labor unions and organizations such as AARP and the American Automobile Association are able to claim voters in every congressional district. Having a large membership—about 10 million in the case of the AFL-CIO—carries a great deal of weight with government officials. AARP now has about 40 million members and a budget of more than a billion dollars for its operations. In addition, AARP claims to represent all older Americans, who constitute close to 20 percent of the population, whether they join the organization or not.

Having a large number of members, even if the individual membership dues are relatively small, provides an organization with a strong financial base. Those funds pay for lobbyists, television advertisements, e-mailings to members, a Web site, pages on Facebook and MySpace, and many other resources that help an interest group make its point to politicians. The business organization with the largest membership is probably the U.S. Chamber of Commerce, which represents more than 3 million businesses. The Chamber uses its members' dues to pay for staff and lobbyists, as well as a sophisticated communications network so that it can contact members in a timely way. All of the members can receive e-mail and check the Chamber's Web site to get updates on the latest legislative proposals.

Other organizations may have fewer members but nonetheless can muster significant financial resources. The pharmaceutical lobby, which represents many of the major drug manufacturers, is one of the most powerful interest groups in Washington due to its financial resources. This interest group has more than 1,250 registered lobbyists and spent close to $200 million in the last presidential election cycle for lobbying and campaign expenditures.

BEYOND OUR BORDERS

FOREIGN LOBBYISTS AND THE AMERICAN CONGRESS

Thousands of lobbyists ply the halls of Congress on a daily basis. Many people don't know, however, that many of these lobbyists work for foreign governments and companies, seeking to advance their agendas. The use of American lobbyists ensures greater access and increases the possibility of legislative success.

Foreign governments seeking to present a good image of their countries often hire consulting firms in Washington, D.C. That's exactly what Saudi Arabia did after 9/11. That government hired Qorvis Communications to spread the message that Saudi Arabia backed the U.S.-led war on terrorism. Qorvis garnered at least $15 million in fees from Saudi Arabia.

Likewise, foreign companies that invest in the United States often hire American lobbying firms to safeguard their interests. When Borse Dubai (an Arab stock exchange) wanted to buy a 20 percent stake in NASDAQ (a U.S. stock exchange), it spent millions in lobbying to boost the image of Dubai and the United Arab Emirates.

Often, however, the U.S. government has pushed back against foreign investment, especially when foreign governments are involved. The Chinese government contacted U.S. lobbying firms as part of its attempt to purchase Unocal Oil Company in 2005. Members of Congress, however, claimed that Chinese government ownership of a U.S. oil company would be contrary to the national interest, and the deal failed. In 2006, Dubai Ports World purchased the right to operate six U.S. ports from a British company. Dubai Ports World is owned by the government of the United Arab Emirates. The firm was pressured into selling its interests after widespread negative publicity. Many people argued that Arab ownership of U.S. port operations represented a national security risk.

Leadership

Money is not the only resource that interest groups need. Strong leaders who can develop effective strategies are also important. For example, the American Israel Public Affairs Committee (AIPAC) has long benefited from strong leadership. AIPAC lobbies Congress and the executive branch on issues related to U.S.-Israeli relations, as well as general foreign policy in the Middle East. AIPAC has been successful in promoting the close relationship that the two nations have enjoyed, which includes foreign aid that the United States annually bestows on Israel, now down to about $2.8 billion a year, but more than $4 billion as recently as 2000. Despite its modest membership size, AIPAC has won bipartisan support for its agenda and is consistently ranked among the most influential interest groups in America.

Obama at an AIPAC meeting. (Alex Wong/Getty Images)

Other interest groups, including some with few financial resources, succeed in part because they are led by individuals with charisma and access to power. Sometimes, choosing a leader with a particular image can be an effective strategy for an organization. The National Rifle Association (NRA) had more than organizational skills in mind when it elected the late actor Charlton Heston as its president. The strategy of using an actor identified with powerful roles as the spokesperson for the organization worked to improve its image.

Cohesiveness

Regardless of an interest group's size or the amount of funds in its coffers, the motivation of an interest group's members is a key factor in determining how powerful it is. If the members of a group hold their beliefs strongly enough to send letters to their representatives, join a march on Washington, or work together to defeat a candidate, that group is considered powerful. As described earlier, the American labor movement's success in electing Democratic candidates made the labor movement a more powerful lobby.

Although groups that oppose abortion rights have had modest success in influencing policy, they are considered powerful because their members are vocal and highly motivated. Of course, the existence of countervailing pro-choice groups limits their influence. Other measures of cohesion include the ability of a group to get its members to contact Washington quickly or to give extra funds when needed. The U.S. Chamber of Commerce excels at both of these strategies. In comparison, AARP cannot claim that it can get many of its 40 million members to contact their congressional representatives, but it does seem to influence the opinions of older Americans and their views of political candidates.

Interest Group Strategies

Interest groups employ a wide range of techniques and strategies to promote their policy goals. Although few groups are successful at persuading Congress and the president to endorse their programs completely, many are able to block—or at least weaken—legislation injurious to their members. The key to success for interest groups is access to government officials. To gain such access, interest groups and their representatives try to cultivate long-term relationships with legislators and government officials. The best of these relationships are based on mutual respect and cooperation. The interest group provides the official with sources of information and assistance, and the official in turn gives the group opportunities to express its views.

The techniques used by interest groups can be divided into direct and indirect techniques. With **direct techniques,** the interest group and its lobbyists approach the officials personally to present their case. With **indirect techniques,** in contrast, the interest group uses the general public or individual constituents to influence the government on behalf of the interest group.

Direct Technique
An interest group activity that involves interaction with government officials to further the group's goals.

Indirect Technique
A strategy employed by interest groups that uses third parties to influence government officials.

Direct Techniques

Lobbying, publicizing ratings of legislative behavior, building coalitions, and providing campaign assistance are the four main direct techniques used by interest groups.

Lobbying Techniques. As might be guessed, the term *lobbying* comes from the activities of private citizens regularly congregating in the lobbies of legislative chambers before a session to petition legislators. In the latter part of the 1800s, railroad and industrial groups openly bribed state legislators to pass legislation beneficial to their interests, giving lobbying a well-deserved bad name. Most lobbyists today are professionals. They are either consultants to a company or interest group or members of one of the Washington, D.C., law firms that specialize in providing such services. Such firms employ hundreds of former members of Congress and former government officials—for example, former presidential candidates Bob Dole and Walter Mondale. Lobbyists are valued for their network of contacts in Washington. As Ed Rollins, a former White House aide, put it, "I've got many friends who are all through the agencies and equally important, I don't have many enemies. . . . I tell my clients I can get your case moved to the top of the pile."[7] Lobbyists of all types are becoming more numerous. The number of lobbyists in Washington, D.C., has more than doubled since 2000.

did you know?

That federal lobbying expenditures in the United States exceed the gross domestic product (GDP) of fifty-nine countries.

Lobbyists engage in an array of activities to influence legislation and government policy. These include the following:

- Engaging in private meetings with public officials to make known the interests of the lobbyists' clients. Although they are acting on behalf of their clients, lobbyists often furnish needed information to senators and representatives (and government agency appointees) that these officials could not easily obtain on their own. It is to the lobbyists' advantage to provide information that is useful to officials so that the policymakers will trust them in the future.
- Testifying before congressional committees for or against proposed legislation.
- Testifying before executive rulemaking agencies—such as the Federal Trade Commission or the Consumer Product Safety Commission—for or against proposed rules.
- Assisting legislators or bureaucrats in drafting legislation or prospective regulations. Often, lobbyists furnish advice on the specific details of legislation.
- Inviting legislators to social occasions, such as cocktail parties, boating expeditions, and other events, including conferences at exotic locations. Most lobbyists believe that meeting legislators in a social setting is effective.
- Providing political information to legislators and other government officials. Sometimes, the lobbyists have better information than the party leadership about how other legislators are going to vote. When this is so, the political information they furnish may be a key to legislative success.
- Suggesting nominations for federal appointments to the executive branch.

---

7. As quoted in H. R. Mahood, *Interest Groups in American National Politics: An Overview* (New York: Prentice Hall, 2000), p. 51.

The Ratings Game. Many interest groups attempt to influence the overall behavior of legislators through their rating systems. Each year, the interest group selects legislation that it believes is most important to the organization's goals and then monitors how legislators vote on it. Each legislator is given a score based on the percentage of times that he or she voted in favor of the group's position. The usual rating scheme ranges from 0 to 100 percent. In the scheme of the liberal Americans for Democratic Action, for example, a rating of 100 means that a member of Congress voted with the group on every issue and is, by that measure, very liberal.

Ratings are a shorthand way of describing members' voting records for interested citizens. Voting records can also be used to embarrass members. For example, an environmental group identifies the twelve representatives who the group believes have the worst voting records on environmental issues and labels them "the Dirty Dozen," and a watchdog group describes those representatives who took home the most "pork" for their districts or states as the biggest "pigs."

Building Alliances. Another direct technique used by interest groups is to form a coalition with other groups concerned about the same legislation. Often, these groups will set up a paper organization with an innocuous name to represent their joint concerns. In the early 1990s, for example, environmental, labor, and consumer groups formed an alliance called the Citizens Trade Campaign to oppose the passage of the North American Free Trade Agreement.

Members of such a coalition share expenses and multiply the influence of their individual groups by combining their efforts. Other advantages of forming a coalition are that it blurs the specific interests of the individual groups involved and makes it appear that larger public interests are at stake. These alliances also are efficient devices for keeping like-minded groups from duplicating one another's lobbying efforts.

Another example of an alliance was the K Street Project, launched by the Republicans during the Bush administration. The project, named for the street in Washington, D.C., where the largest lobbying firms have their headquarters, was designed to freeze Democrats out of the lobbying community. Republicans sought to pressure lobbying firms to hire Republicans in top positions, offering loyal lobbyists greater access to lawmakers in return. An indication of the success of the project was the increase in the donations given to Republican lawmakers by lobbyists, which rose from $1.2 million in 1994 to nearly $12 million in 2006. But the K Street Project also had a troubling aspect, as revelations of legislative favors being granted to special interests in return for campaign donations have made clear. This trend, and the many examples of corruption attendant on it, will be discussed further in Chapter 9.

The K Street Project essentially fell apart when the Democrats took control of Congress after the 2006 elections. With the likelihood that the Democrats would do even better in 2008, K Street lobbyists tilted to the Democrats in 2007 and 2008. Congress also passed new lobbying rules in 2007, described in detail later in this chapter. Among other things, the new rules criminalized efforts to influence private hiring at lobbying firms "solely on the basis of partisan political affiliation." This provision seeks to ensure that the K Street Project cannot be resurrected in the future by either party.

"Please understand. I don't sell access to the government. I merely sell access to the guys who do sell access to the government." (© The New York Collection, 1986. Ed Fisher, from cartoonbank.com. All Rights Reserved.)

Assistance with Campaigns. Interest groups have additional strategies to use in their attempts to influence government policies.

Groups recognize that the greatest concern of legislators is to be reelected, so they focus on the legislators' campaign needs. Associations with large memberships, such as labor unions, are able to provide workers for political campaigns, including precinct workers to get out the vote, volunteers to put up posters and pass out literature, and people to staff telephone banks for campaign headquarters.

Candidates vie for the groups' endorsements in a campaign. Gaining those endorsements may be automatic, or it may require that the candidates participate in debates or interviews with the interest groups. An interest group usually publicizes its choices in its membership publications, and the candidate can use the endorsement in her or his campaign literature. Traditionally, labor unions have endorsed Democratic Party candidates. Republican candidates, however, often try to persuade union locals at least to refrain from any endorsement. Making no endorsement can then be perceived as disapproval of the Democratic Party candidate.

Recent Developments. Despite attempts at campaign-finance reform, the 2008 elections boasted record campaign spending. The usual array of interest groups gathered contributions to their political action committees and distributed them to the candidates. Most labor contributions went to Democratic candidates, of course. For the first time in living memory, however, businesses, including the finance, health-care, and pharmaceutical industries, contributed larger sums to the Democrats than to their rivals. At the same time, new campaign groups—the so-called 527 organizations, tax-exempt associations focused on influencing political elections—raised hundreds of millions of dollars in unregulated contributions and used them for campaign activities and advertising. Some national interest groups, such as the Laborers' Union, the National Association of Realtors, and the Sierra Club, created their own 527 organizations to spend funds for advertising and other political activities.

In 2010, the United States Supreme Court shook up the campaign-finance system when it issued its opinion in *Citizens United v. FEC.*[8] The Court ruled that corporations (and implicitly, unions) may spend freely to support or oppose political candidates, so long as they do not contribute directly to candidate campaigns. The new freedom to make "independent expenditures" eases decades-old limits on corporate participation in federal elections. The Court held that the independent expenditures were a form of constitutionally protected free speech. The Court's decision was criticized by President Obama and many others. Some crit-

8. 558 U.S. ___ (2010).

ELECTIONS 2010

THE IMPACT OF INTEREST GROUPS

In some ways, the biggest interest group story in 2010 was not the impact of interest groups on the elections, but the impact of the elections on interest groups. Key industries began switching their donations from the Democrats to the Republicans in December 2009. Instead of giving three-fifths of their contributions to the Democrats, major industries began to give about that much to the Republicans. Such groups included the health-care and financial industries, both of which had a major stake in pending legislation. The timing of the change indicates that the donations could not have caused the growing disenchantment with the Democrats, because it took place right at the time when Democratic unpopularity was becoming obvious. Rather, business interests recognized that donations to Republicans would win the good graces of future congressional leaders.

One sector that swung against the Democrats somewhat earlier was energy. In January 2009, energy interests split their contributions evenly between the parties. By September 2009, three-quarters of energy funds went to the Republicans. The switch probably occurred because the House passed cap-and-trade legislation in June 2009. The bill, in effect a tax on carbon dioxide emissions, would have cost the energy industry dearly if it had not died in the Senate.

ics argued that the Court was granting to corporations rights that should only be given to flesh-and-blood humans. You will learn much more about campaign finance in Chapter 9.

Indirect Techniques

Interest groups can also try to influence government policy by working through others, who may be constituents or the general public. Indirect techniques mask an interest group's own activities and make the effort appear to be spontaneous. Furthermore, legislators and government officials are often more impressed by contacts from constituents than from an interest group's lobbyist.

Generating Public Pressure. In some instances, interest groups try to produce a "groundswell" of public pressure to influence the government. Such efforts may include advertisements in national magazines and newspapers, mass mailings, television publicity, and demonstrations. The Internet and satellite links make communication efforts even more effective. Interest groups may commission polls to find out what the public's sentiments are and then publicize the results. The intent of this activity is to convince policymakers that public opinion supports the group's position.

Some corporations and interest groups also engage in a practice that might be called **climate control.** With this strategy, public relations efforts are aimed at improving the public image of the industry or group and are not necessarily related to any specific political issue. Contributions by corporations and groups in support of public television programs, sponsorship of special events, and commercials extolling the virtues of corporate research are some ways of achieving climate control. For example, to improve its image in the wake of litigation against tobacco companies, Philip Morris began advertising its assistance to community agencies, including halfway houses for teen offenders and shelters for battered women. By building a reservoir of favorable public opinion, groups believe that their legislative goals will be less likely to encounter opposition from the public.

Climate Control
The use of public relations techniques to create favorable public opinion toward an interest group, industry, or corporation.

Using Constituents as Lobbyists. Interest groups also use constituents of elected officials to lobby for the groups' goals. In the "shotgun" approach, the interest group tries to mobilize large numbers of constituents to write, phone, or send e-mails to their legislators or the president. Often, the group provides postcards or form letters for constituents to fill out and mail. These efforts are effective on Capitol Hill only when there are a great many responses, however, because legislators know that the voters did not initiate the communications on their own. Artificially manufactured grassroots activity has been aptly labeled *Astroturf lobbying.*

did you know?
That lobbyists have their own lobbying organization, the American League of Lobbyists.

A more powerful variation of this technique uses only important constituents. With this approach, known as the "rifle" technique or the "Utah plant manager theory," the interest group might, for example, ask the manager of a local plant in Utah to contact the senator from Utah. Because the constituent is seen as responsible for many jobs and other resources, the legislator is more likely to listen carefully to the constituent's concerns about legislation than to a paid lobbyist.

Unconventional Forms of Pressure. Sometimes, interest groups may employ forms of pressure that are outside the ordinary political process. These can include marches, rallies, or demonstrations. Such assemblies, as long as they are peaceful, are protected by the First Amendment. In Chapter 5, we described the civil disobedience techniques of the African American civil rights movement in the 1950s and 1960s. The 1963 March on Washington in support of civil rights was one of the most effective demonstrations ever organized. The women's suffrage movement of the early 1900s also employed marches and demonstrations to great effect.

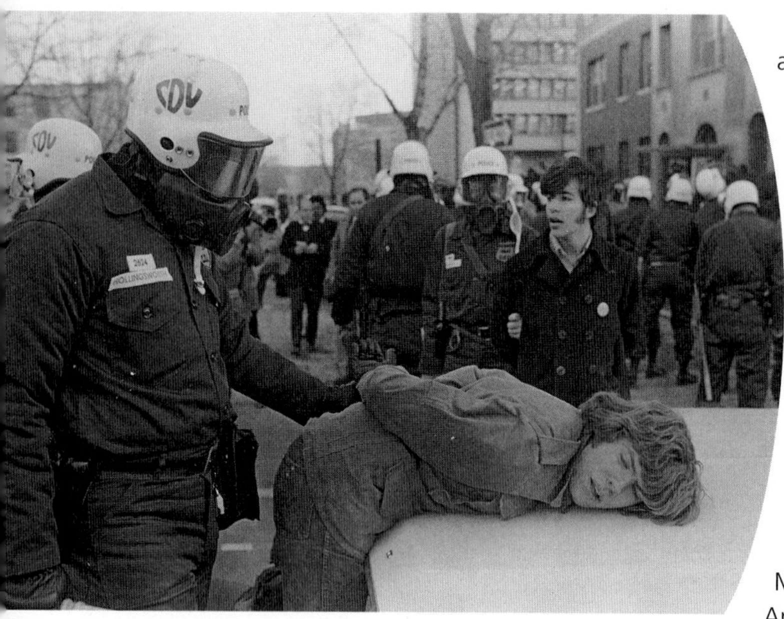

Some demonstrations are violent, and the police must be present. These young people were arrested for violent actions at an antiwar rally during the Vietnam War era (1964–1975). Why does such violence occur? (© Wally McNamee/ Corbis)

Demonstrations, however, are not always peaceable. Violent demonstrations have a long history in America, dating back to the antitax Boston Tea Party described in Chapter 2. The Vietnam War (1964–1975) provoked a large number of demonstrations, some of which were violent. Violent demonstrations can be counterproductive—instead of putting pressure on the authorities, they may simply alienate the public. For example, historians continue to debate whether the demonstrations against the Vietnam War were effective or counterproductive.

Another unconventional form of pressure is the **boycott**—a refusal to buy a particular product or deal with a particular business. To be effective, boycotts must command widespread support. One example was the African American boycott of buses in Montgomery, Alabama, in 1955, described in Chapter 5. Another was the boycott of California grapes that were picked by nonunion workers, as part of a campaign to organize Mexican American farmworkers. The first grape boycott lasted from 1965 to 1970; a series of later boycotts was less effective.

Boycott
A form of pressure or protest—an organized refusal to purchase a particular product or deal with a particular business.

Regulating Lobbyists

Congress made its first attempt to control lobbyists and lobbying activities through Title III of the Legislative Reorganization Act of 1946, otherwise known as the Federal Regulation of Lobbying Act. The law actually provided for public disclosure more than for regulation, and it neglected to specify which agency would enforce its provisions. The 1946 legislation defined a *lobbyist* as any person or organization that received funds to be used principally to influence legislation before Congress. Such persons and individuals were supposed to "register" their clients and the purposes of their efforts and to report quarterly on their activities.

The legislation was tested in a 1954 Supreme Court case, *United States v. Harriss*,[9] and was found to be constitutional. The Court agreed that the lobbying law did not violate due process, freedom of speech or of the press, or the freedom to petition. The Court narrowly construed the act, however, holding that it applied only to lobbyists who were influencing federal legislation *directly*.

The Results of the 1946 Act

The immediate result of the act was that a minimal number of individuals registered as lobbyists. National interest groups, such as the National Rifle Association and the American Petroleum Institute, could employ hundreds of staff members who were, of course, working on legislation but only register one or two lobbyists who were engaged *principally* in influencing Congress. There were no reporting requirements for lobbying the executive branch, federal agencies, the courts, or congressional staff. Approximately seven thousand individuals and organizations registered annually as lobbyists, although most experts estimated that ten times that number were actually employed in Washington to exert influence on the government.

9. 347 U.S. 612 (1954).

The Reforms of 1995

The reform-minded Congress of 1995–1996 overhauled the lobbying legislation, fundamentally changing the ground rules for those who seek to influence the federal government. The Lobbying Disclosure Act (LDA), passed in 1995, included the following provisions:

did you know?

That Washington's lobbying industry employs more than four times as many people today as it employed in the mid-1960s.

- A *lobbyist* is defined as anyone who spends at least 20 percent of his or her time lobbying members of Congress, their staffs, or executive-branch officials.
- Lobbyists must register with the clerk of the House and the secretary of the Senate within forty-five days of being hired or of making their first contacts. The registration requirement applies to organizations that spend more than $20,000 or to individuals who are paid more than $5,000 semiannually for lobbying work. These figures have since been raised to $24,500 and $6,000, respectively.
- Semiannual reports must disclose the general nature of the lobbying effort, the name of the client, specific issues and bill numbers, the estimated cost of the campaign, and a list of the branches of government contacted. The names of the individuals contacted need not be reported.
- Representatives of U.S.-owned subsidiaries of foreign-owned firms and lawyers who represent foreign entities also are required to register.
- The requirements exempt "grassroots" lobbying efforts and those of tax-exempt organizations, such as religious groups.

Also in 1995, both the House and the Senate adopted new rules on gifts and travel expenses provided by lobbyists: the House adopted a flat ban on gifts, and the Senate limited gifts to $50 in value and to no more than $100 in gifts from a single source in a year. There are exceptions for gifts from family members and for home-state products and souvenirs, such as T-shirts and coffee mugs. Both chambers banned all-expenses-paid trips, golf outings, and other such junkets. An exception applies for "widely attended" events, however, or if the member is a primary speaker at an event. These gift rules stopped the broad practice of taking members of Congress to lunch or dinner at high-priced restaurants, but the various exemptions and exceptions have allowed much gift giving to continue.

Lobbying Scandals and the Reforms of 2007

The regulation of lobbying activity resurfaced as an issue in 2005 when a number of scandals came to light. At the center of many of the publicized incidents was a highly influential and corrupt lobbyist, Jack Abramoff. Using his ties with numerous Republican, and a handful of Democratic, lawmakers, Abramoff brokered many deals for the special interest clients that he represented in return for campaign donations, gifts, and various perks. In January 2006, Abramoff pleaded guilty to three criminal felony counts alleging that he had defrauded American Indian tribes and engaged in the corruption of public officials. A number of politicians attempted to distance themselves from the embattled lobbyist by giving Abramoff's campaign donations to charity.

The corruption and scandals that occurred while the Republicans controlled Congress certainly had some effect on the 2006 elections. When the Democrats took control of Congress in January 2007, one of their first undertakings was ethics and lobbying reform. In the first one hundred hours of the session, the House tightened its ethics rules on gifts and on travel funded by lobbyists. The Senate followed shortly thereafter.

Lobbyist Jack Abramoff (left) was involved in one of the biggest lobbying scandals in recent times. He was sentenced to more than five years in prison. Is it possible to avoid such scandals completely? (Carlo Allegri/ Getty Images)

In September 2007, President George W. Bush signed the Honest Leadership and Open Government Act. Under the new law, lobbyists must report quarterly, and the registration threshold becomes $10,000 in spending per quarter. Organizations must report coalition activities if they contribute more than $5,000 to a coalition. The House and Senate must now post lobbying information in a searchable file on the Internet. In a significant alteration to legislative practices, "earmarked" expenditures, commonly called "pork," must now be identified and made public. This last change may not have its intended effect of reducing earmarks, however. It turns out that many legislators are actually proud of their pork and happy to tell the folks back home all about it. Many observers doubt whether the new rules will really change the congressional culture in which favors flow in one direction and legislation flows in the other.

Obama versus the Lobbyists?

During his presidential campaign, Barack Obama first claimed that there would be no former lobbyists in his administration. He later amended that statement to say that lobbyists would not "dominate my White House" and that former lobbyists could not work in areas where they had recently lobbied. Upon election, Obama made a considerable show of denying lobbyists access to administration officials. Many Washington insiders considered Obama's positions absurd and predicted that he would not be able to adhere to them.

As it happened, not long after taking office Obama was issuing dozens of waivers that allowed former lobbyists to serve in official posts. By 2010, more than forty ex-lobbyists had top jobs in the Obama administration, including three cabinet secretaries, the director of the Central Intelligence Agency, and numerous senior White House officials. In time, the administration found itself working with lobbyists from many industries. The Democrats could not have passed their health-care reform legislation if Obama had been unwilling to work closely with lobbyists representing physicians, hospitals, and the pharmaceutical industry.

Obama had no success in reducing the number of lobbyists in Washington, if that was ever his goal. Instead, the number increased sharply. We look at some of the reasons for the increase in this chapter's *Politics of Boom and Bust* feature on the facing page.

Interest Groups and Representative Democracy

The role played by interest groups in shaping national policy has caused many to question whether we really have a democracy at all. Most interest groups have a middle-class or upper-class bias. Members of interest groups can afford to pay the membership fees, are generally fairly well educated, and normally participate in the political process to a greater extent than the "average" American.

Furthermore, leaders of interest groups tend to constitute an "elite within an elite" in the sense that they usually are from a higher social class than other group members. The most powerful interest groups—those with the most resources and political influence—are primarily business, trade, and professional groups. In contrast, public-interest groups and civil rights groups make up only a small percentage of the interest groups lobbying Congress.

Interest Groups: Elitist or Pluralist?

Remember from Chapter 1 that the elite theory of politics presumes that most Americans are uninterested in politics and are willing to let a small, elite group of citizens make decisions for them. Pluralist theory, in contrast, views politics as a struggle among various interest groups to gain benefits for their members. The pluralist approach views compromise among various competing interests as the essence of political decision making. In reality, neither theory fully describes American politics. If interest groups led by elite, upper-class individuals are the dominant voices in Congress, then what we see is a conflict among elite groups—which would lend as much support to the elitist theory as to the pluralist approach.

Interest Group Influence

The results of lobbying efforts—congressional bills—do not always favor the interests of the most powerful groups, however. In part, this is because not all interest groups have an equal influence on government. Each group has a different combination of resources to use in the policymaking process. While some groups are composed of members who

THE POLITICS OF BOOM AND BUST

MORE LOBBYISTS IN SPITE OF THE RECESSION

During the winter of 2008 to 2009, the Great Recession hit major corporations very hard. Profits plummeted and some firms incurred losses. Some went bankrupt or were bought by stronger competitors. You might think that the recession would cause businesses to "count their pennies." In some ways they did—millions of people lost their jobs. Yet lobbying turned out to be an expense that was not reduced during tough times. Spending on lobbying was up considerably in 2009.

LOBBYING PROSPERS IN TOUGH TIMES

How much did the top twenty trade associations and companies increase expenditures on lobbyists in 2009? According to the Center for Responsive Politics, their spending increased by more than 20 percent compared to 2008. These same companies had laid off thousands of workers.

The U.S. Chamber of Commerce increased its lobbying expenditures by 60 percent over 2008. The only top company that reduced lobbying expenditures dramatically was General Motors (GM), which dropped out of the top twenty. Why? Because in 2009, the government took a 61 percent stake in the firm. Spending large sums to lobby the very government that owns you would draw unwanted attention from Congress. Still, GM's lobbying expenses did not go down to zero.

WHY DID SPENDING RISE?

Why, during a serious recession, did private companies spend so much on lobbying—a $3.5 billion in 2009? The answer lies in the increasing size and power of the federal government. The more the government does, the more lobbying we will see. Every interest affected by the increased government activity will swing into action. When Congress debated Obama's economic stimulus bill in February 2009, a headline in the *Washington Post* read "Lobbying Frenzy for Federal Funds." No surprise there.

Obama and the Democrats in Congress refashioned health-care funding, made major changes to the regulation of finance, and attempted to revamp the energy sector. These dramatic changes had a direct impact on a major share of the economy. Naturally, the affected interests hired an army of lobbyists to ensure that the new government efforts would help their clients—or at least not hurt them too badly.

Dave Levinthal of the Center for Responsive Politics puts it this way: "Companies have made the decision that they are going to spend more money today in order to protect their bottom line tomorrow, even if they are in the midst of layoffs, even if their profits are dwindling. When Congress is debating sweeping legislation, lobbyists are going to come out in force, regardless of economic conditions on the ground."

FOR CRITICAL ANALYSIS

Should companies that were "bailed out" by the federal government (that is, by the taxpayers) be allowed to lobby? Why or why not?

have high social status and significant economic resources, such as the National Association of Manufacturers, other groups derive influence from their large memberships. AARP, for example, has more members than any other interest group. Its large membership allows it to wield significant power over legislators. Still other groups, such as environmentalists, have causes that can claim strong public support even from people who have no direct stake in the issue. Groups such as the National Rifle Association are well organized and have highly motivated members. This enables them to channel a stream of letters or e-mails toward Congress with a few days' effort.

did you know?

That, on average, there are now sixty lobbyists for each member of Congress.

Even the most powerful interest groups do not always succeed in their demands. Whereas the U.S. Chamber of Commerce may be accepted as having a justified interest in the question of business taxes, many legislators might feel that the group should not engage in the debate over the future of Social Security. In other words, groups are seen as having a legitimate concern in the issues closest to their interests but not necessarily in broader issues. This may explain why some of the most successful groups are those that focus on very specific issues—such as tobacco farming, funding of abortions, and handgun control—and do not get involved in larger conflicts.

Complicating the question of interest group influence is the fact that many groups' lobbyists are former colleagues, friends, or family members of current members of Congress.

James and Sarah Brady are leading activists against gun violence. James Brady was President Ronald Reagan's first press secretary. In 1981, Reagan was shot and injured in an assassination attempt, but he recovered completely. Brady was shot in the same attempt and suffered permanent disabilities. (AP Photo/ Kenneth Lambert)

WHY SHOULD YOU CARE ABOUT... INTEREST GROUPS?

Why should you, as an individual, care about interest groups? True, some interest groups focus on issues that concern only a limited number of people. Others, however, are involved in causes in which almost everyone has a stake. Gun control is one of the issues that concerns a large number of people. The question of whether the possession of handguns should be regulated is at the heart of a long-running heated battle among organized interest groups. The fight is fueled by the one million gun incidents occurring in the United States each year—murders, suicides, assaults, accidents, and robberies in which guns are involved.

INTEREST GROUPS AND YOUR LIFE

The passionate feelings that are brought to bear on both sides of the gun control issue are evidence of its importance. The problem of crime is central to the gun control issue. Public opinion poll respondents cited crime as one of the nation's most important problems throughout the 1990s, and it continues to be a major concern today.

Does the easy availability of handguns promote crime? Are guns part of the problem of crime—or part of the solution? Either way, the question is important to you personally. Even if you are fortunate enough not to be victimized by crime, you will probably find yourself limiting your activities from time to time out of a fear of crime.

HOW YOU CAN MAKE A DIFFERENCE

Almost every year, Congress and the various state legislatures debate measures that would alter gun laws for the nation or for the individual states. As a result, there are plenty of opportunities to get involved.

Issues in the debate include child-safety features on guns and the regulation of gun dealers who sell firearms at gun shows. Proponents of gun control seek safety locks and more restrictions on gun purchases. Proponents of firearms claim that possessing firearms is a constitutional right and meets a vital defense need for individuals. They contend that the problem lies not in the sale and ownership of weapons but in their use by criminals.

The Coalition to Stop Gun Violence takes the position that handguns "serve no valid purpose, except to kill people." In contrast, the National Rifle Association (NRA) of America supports the rights of gun owners. The NRA, founded in 1871, is currently one of the most powerful single-issue groups in the United States. The NRA believes that gun laws will not reduce the number of crimes. It is illogical to assume, according to the NRA, that persons who refuse to obey laws prohibiting rape, murder, and other crimes will obey a gun law.

Many proponents of gun control insist that controlling the purchase of weapons would reduce the availability of guns to children. In response, some states have passed laws that hold adults liable for not locking away their firearms. In addition, a number of cities have sued gun manufacturers for not controlling the flow of their products to dealers who sell guns to criminals and gang members.

To find out more about the NRA's position, contact that organization at the following URL:

The National Rifle Association
home.nra.org

To learn about the positions of gun control advocates, contact:

The Coalition to Stop Gun Violence
www.csgv.org

Brady Campaign to Prevent Gun Violence
www.bradycampaign.org

questions for discussion and analysis

1. Review the *Beyond Our Borders* feature on page 232. Should foreign corporations be allowed to lobby the U.S. Congress and executive-branch officials? Why or why not? Should foreign governments be barred from lobbying? Explain.
2. Some interest groups are much more influential than others. Some interest groups famous for their clout are the National Rifle Association, AARP, business groups such as the National Federation of Independent Business, the American Israel Public Affairs Committee, and the American Association for Justice (formerly the Association of Trial Lawyers of America). What factors might make each of these groups powerful?
3. After 9/11, Congress passed new laws to increase airport security. The legislation was the subject of intense lobbying by airlines that wanted the government to pick up the expense of hiring new staff, labor groups that wanted the new federal employees to have civil service protections, and other interest groups as well. Is it appropriate for interest groups to lobby for their positions in times of national emergency? Why or why not?
4. "If guns are outlawed, only outlaws will have guns." This is a key slogan used by opponents of gun control. How much truth do you think there is to this slogan? Explain your reasoning.
5. About half of the paid lobbyists in Washington are former government staff members or former members of Congress. Why would interest groups employ such people? Why might some reformers want to limit the ability of interest groups to employ them? On what basis might an interest group argue that such limits are unconstitutional?

key terms

boycott 238
climate control 237
direct technique 234
free rider problem 223
indirect technique 234
interest group 221
labor movement 226
latent interests 222
lobbyist 225
material incentive 223
public interest 230
purposive incentive 224
service sector 227
social movement 222
solidary incentive 223

chapter summary

1. An interest group is an organization whose members share common objectives and actively attempt to influence government policy. Interest groups proliferate in the United States because they can influence government at many points in the political structure and because they offer solidary, material, and purposive incentives to their members. Interest groups are often created out of social movements.
2. Major types of interest groups include business, agricultural, labor, public employee, professional, and environmental groups. Other important groups may be considered public-interest groups. In addition, foreign governments and corporations lobby our government.
3. Interest groups use direct and indirect techniques to influence government. Direct techniques include testifying before committees and rulemaking agencies, providing information to legislators, rating legislators' voting records, aiding political campaigns, and building alliances. Indirect techniques to influence government include campaigns to rally public sentiment, letter-writing campaigns, efforts to influence the climate of opinion, and the use of constituents to lobby for the group's interest. Unconventional methods of applying pressure include demonstrations and boycotts.
4. The 1946 Legislative Reorganization Act was the first attempt to control lobbyists and their activities through

registration requirements. The United States Supreme Court narrowly construed the act as applying only to lobbyists who directly seek to influence federal legislation.

5. In 1995, Congress approved new legislation requiring anyone who spends 20 percent of his or her time influencing legislation to register as a lobbyist. Also, any organization spending more than $24,500 semiannually and any individual who is paid more than $6,000 semiannually for his or her work must register. Semiannual reports must include the names of clients, the bills in which they are interested, and the branches of government contacted. Grassroots lobbying and the lobbying efforts of tax-exempt organizations are exempt from the rules.

6. In 2007, in response to lobbying scandals, Congress tightened rules on giving gifts to legislators and increased reporting requirements for lobbyists to four times a year. Under the 2007 reform legislation, lobbyists now have to report contributions to coalition efforts. Congress has created a searchable online database of lobbying information.

selected print & media resources

SUGGESTED READINGS

Battista, Andrew. ***The Revival of Labor Liberalism.*** **Champaign, Ill.: University of Illinois Press, 2008. While labor unions have lost members in recent decades, it is still true that few interest groups are as large as organized labor. Until the late 1960s, the labor movement and political liberalism were close allies. Battista, a political science professor, analyzes the political decline of labor and liberalism, especially after the breakup of the labor-liberal coalition. He also looks at recent attempts to put the coalition back together.**

Feldman, Richard. ***Ricochet: Confessions of a Gun Lobbyist.*** **Hoboken, N.J.: Wiley, 2007. Feldman, a former NRA lobbyist and an engaging writer, tells the story of the NRA's lobbying efforts and its internal politics. Feldman strongly favors gun owners' rights, but his description of the NRA's internal conflicts is wry and cynical.**

Fleshler, Dan. ***Transforming America's Israel Lobby: The Limits of Its Power and the Potential for Change.*** **Dulles, Va.: Potomac Books, 2009. Fleshler contends that America's Israel lobby, like many other lobbies, is more resistant to compromise than the people it represents. Fleshler proposes strategies to encourage moderation and promote the peace process.**

Kaiser, Robert G. ***So Damn Much Money: The Triumph of Lobbying and the Corrosion of American Government.*** **New York: Vintage, 2010. A *Washington Post* journalist, Kaiser shows how lobbyists satisfy politicians' ever-growing need for campaign funds. He argues that behavior once considered corrupt has become commonplace.**

MEDIA RESOURCES

Bowling for Columbine—**A documentary by Michael Moore won an Academy Award in 2003. Moore seeks to understand why the United States leads the industrialized world in firearms deaths. While the film is hilarious, it takes a strong position in favor of gun control and is critical of the National Rifle Association.**

Norma Rae—**A 1979 Hollywood movie about an attempt by a northern union organizer to unionize workers in the southern textile industry; stars Sally Field, who won an Academy Award for her performance.**

Organizing America: The History of Trade Unions—**A 1994 documentary that incorporates interviews, personal accounts, and archival footage to tell the story of the American labor movement. The film is a Cambridge Educational Production.**

Under the Influence—**This 2007 episode from the CBS newsmagazine series *60 Minutes* focuses on the pharmaceutical lobby, which represents the major prescription drug manufacturers. Spending $100 million a year or more, the lobby has had a major impact on such legislation as President George W. Bush's Medicare prescription drug bill.**

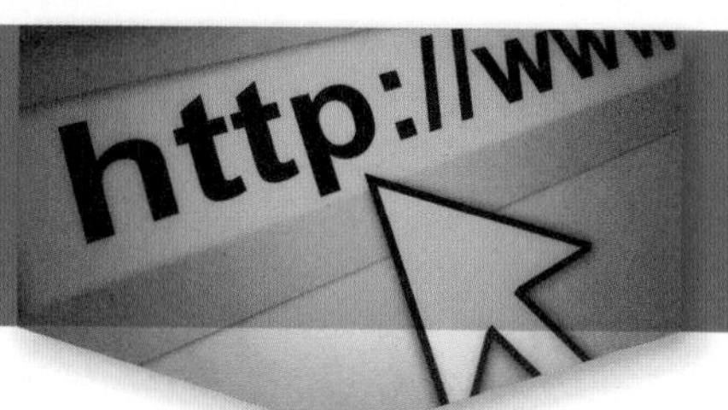

e-mocracy

INTEREST GROUPS AND THE INTERNET

The Internet may have a strong equalizing effect in the world of lobbying and government influence. The first organizations to use electronic means to reach their constituents and drum up support for action were the large economic coalitions, including the Chamber of Commerce and the National Association of Manufacturers. Groups such as these, as well as groups representing a single product such as tobacco, quickly realized that they could set up Web sites and mailing lists to provide information more rapidly to their members. Members could check the Web every day to see how legislation was developing in Congress or anywhere in the world. National associations could send e-mail to all of their members with one keystroke, mobilizing them to contact their representatives in Congress.

LOGGING ON

Today, almost every interest group or association has its own Web site. To find one, use your favorite search engine (Google or another search engine), and search for the association by name. For a sense of the breadth of the kinds of interest groups that have Web sites, take a look at one or two of those listed here.

Those interested in the gun control issue may want to visit the National Rifle Association's site at
home.nra.org

You can learn more about the labor movement by visiting the AFL-CIO's site at
www.aflcio.org

AARP (formerly the American Association of Retired Persons) has a site at
www.aarp.org

Information on environmental issues is available at a number of sites. The Environmental Defense Fund's site is
www.edf.org

You can also go to the National Resources Defense Council's site for information on environmental issues. Its URL is
www.nrdc.org

chapter 8

Political Parties

chapter contents

Representative John Boehner of Ohio became Speaker of the House after the 2010 midterm elections when Republicans retook the majority. (AP Photo/The Repository, Stan Myers)

WHAT IF... ...parties were supported solely by public funding?

These U.S. senators hold a news conference concerning campaign-finance reform. Senator Russ Feingold (D.,Wis.) answers reporters' questions. (AP Photo/Harry Hamburg)

BACKGROUND

Today's major political parties are supported by hundreds of millions of dollars offered by unions, corporations, other groups, and individuals. For years, members of both political parties have been linked to lobbying and campaign-contribution scandals, leading some critics to call for dramatic reforms. One of those reforms could be the public financing of political parties. Such public financing would, of course, come from taxpayers.

WHAT IF PARTIES WERE SUPPORTED SOLELY BY PUBLIC FUNDING?

If parties were supported solely by public funding, one question would immediately arise: What level of funding would be appropriate? Both major parties now spend millions of dollars each year to educate the public, register voters, recruit candidates, and support election campaigns. If that amount were significantly reduced, the effectiveness of the political parties would also be reduced.

In recent years, the United States has seen a rapid growth in nonparty political organizations that avoid regulation by not coordinating their activities with a party or campaign. If the political parties were limited to public funding, such nonparty groups would become vastly more important.

In 2010, the United States Supreme Court ruled that the national and state governments could not prevent corporations from running political ads that were independent of the candidate campaigns and, presumably, the parties. Over time, the resulting independent expenditures, aimed at supporting party tickets and electing candidates, may become very large. That, at any rate, is what the opponents of the Court's decision fear. If public funding were to counteract the effects of this decision, it would have to be fairly generous. That would be hard to achieve, given popular hostility to high levels of campaign spending.

WHAT HAS HAPPENED ALREADY

Several states now provide direct public financing to candidates. Other states provide minimal public financing to candidates or political parties, usually by collecting contributions to political parties from taxpayers through their state income tax returns. The federal government currently provides a limited amount of public funding for presidential candidates.

All such public financing of candidates' campaigns carries with it restrictions on acceptable sources of other funds. If both the major parties and candidates for election were publicly financed, the role of lobbies and lobbyists would be changed. No longer would they be holding fund-raising social events for candidates and parties. Instead, they would have to rely on their ability to inform or persuade legislators.

MORE POLITICAL PARTIES MIGHT BE POSSIBLE

Who is to say that public funding of political parties would be limited to only the two major parties? Public funds could be available for numerous political parties. The only requirement might be a minimum number of party members. The result could be dozens of small political parties. After all, if public funds are available, someone will figure out a way to obtain them. Even if minor parties became more important, however, the major political parties would still dominate. In our winner-take-all electoral system, few independent party candidates can win public office.

FOR CRITICAL ANALYSIS

1. If political parties were publicly funded, what would be the appropriate level of funding?
2. Currently, both major political parties have paid employees who function as "upper management." Would the type of person seeking such a job change if the parties were supported solely by public funds? Why or why not?

The state of the political parties is a matter of constant concern for the media. Even when an election is relatively far off, commentators obsessively assess the relative fortunes of the Republican and Democratic parties. In the years preceding the 2008 presidential elections, the most common question was: Has the unpopularity of Republican president George W. Bush inflicted a lasting injury to the Republican Party? Since 2009, the question has been reversed: How much damage has been done to the Democrats by the continuing high levels of unemployment and by their ambitious legislative agenda?

As elections draw closer, polls concentrate on determining which political party individual voters "belong" to or support. Prior to an election, a typical poll usually asks the following question: "Do you consider yourself to be a Republican, a Democrat, or an independent?" For many years, Americans divided fairly evenly among the three choices, with about a third describing themselves as **independents.** Of course, independents are not represented as such in Congress—for congressional purposes, they align themselves with either the Democratic Party or the Republican Party. In fact, three-quarters or more of all independents lean either toward the Republicans or the Democrats. This situation could change if public funding allowed for the creation of more parties, as discussed in the chapter-opening *What If . . .* feature.

Independent
A voter or candidate who does not identify with a political party.

Political Party
A group of political activists who organize to win elections, operate the government, and determine public policy.

Faction
A group or bloc in a legislature or political party that is trying to obtain power or benefits.

After the elections are over, the media publish the election results. Among other things, Americans learn which party controls the presidency and how many Democrats and Republicans will be sitting in the House of Representatives and the Senate when the new Congress convenes.

Notice that in the second paragraph, when discussing party membership, we put the word *belong* in quotation marks. We did this because hardly anyone actually "belongs" to a political party in the sense of being a card-carrying member. To become a member of a political party, you do not have to pay dues, pass an examination, or swear an oath of allegiance. Therefore, at this point we can ask an obvious question: If it takes nothing to be a member of a political party, what, then, is a political party?

What Is a Political Party?

A **political party** might be formally defined as a group of political activists who organize to win elections, operate the government, and determine public policy. This definition explains the difference between an interest group and a political party. Interest groups do not want to operate the government, and they do not put forth political candidates—even though they support candidates who will promote their interests if elected or reelected.

Political parties differ from **factions,** which are smaller groups that are trying to obtain power or benefits.[1] Factions generally preceded the formation of political parties in American history, and the term is still used to refer to groups within parties that fol-low a particular leader or share a regional identification or an ideological viewpoint. For example, until fairly recently the Democratic Party was seen as containing a southern faction that was much more conservative than the rest of the party. Factions are subgroups within parties that may try to capture a nomination or get a position adopted by the party. A key difference between factions and parties is that factions do not have a permanent organization, whereas political parties do.

Atlanta mayoral candidate Lisa Borders on the left visits an elementary school. She and her opponents spent more than a year on the campaign trail. Why would she be a member of one of the two major political parties? (AP Photo John Spink/ *Atlanta Journal Constitution*)

1. See James Madison's comments on factions in *Federalist Paper* No. 10 in Appendix C at the end of this book.

Political parties in the United States engage in a wide variety of activities, many of which are discussed in this chapter. Through these activities, parties perform a number of functions for the political system. These functions include the following:

1. *Recruiting candidates for public office.* Because it is the goal of parties to gain control of government, they must work to recruit candidates for all elective offices. Often, this means recruiting candidates to run against powerful incumbents. If parties did not search out and encourage political hopefuls, far more offices would be uncontested, and voters would have limited choices.
2. *Organizing and running elections.* Although elections are a government activity, political parties actually organize the voter-registration drives, recruit volunteers to work at the polls, provide much of the campaign activity to stimulate interest in the election, and work to increase voter participation.
3. *Presenting alternative policies to the electorate.* In contrast to factions, which are often centered on individual politicians or regions, parties are focused on a set of political positions. The Democrats or Republicans in Congress who vote together do so because they represent constituencies that have similar expectations and demands.
4. *Accepting responsibility for operating the government.* When a party elects the president or governor and members of the legislature, it accepts the responsibility for running the government. This includes staffing the executive branch with loyal party supporters and developing linkages among the elected officials to gain support for policies and their implementation.
5. *Acting as the organized opposition to the party in power.* The "out" party, or the one that does not control the government, is expected to articulate its own policies and oppose the winning party when appropriate. By organizing the opposition to the "in" party, the opposition party forces debate on the policy alternatives.

The major functions of American political parties are carried out by a small, relatively loose-knit nucleus of party activists. This arrangement is quite different from the more highly structured, mass-membership party organization typical of many European parties. American parties concentrate on winning elections rather than on signing up large numbers of deeply committed, dues-paying members who believe passionately in the party's program.

A History of Political Parties in the United States

Although it is difficult to imagine a political system in the United States with four, five, six, or seven major political parties, other democracies have three-party, four-party, or even ten-party systems. In some European nations, parties are clearly tied to ideological positions. Parties that represent Marxist, socialist, liberal, conservative, and ultraconservative positions appear on the political continuum. Some nations have political parties representing regions of the nation that have separate cultural identities, such as the French-speaking and Flemish-speaking regions of Belgium. Some parties are rooted in religious differences. Parties also exist that represent specific economic interests, such as agricultural, maritime, or industrial interests. Still other parties, such as monarchist parties, speak for alternative political systems.

Two-Party System
A political system in which only two parties have a reasonable chance of winning.

The United States has a **two-party system,** and that system has been around since before 1800. The function and character of the political parties, as well as the emergence of the two-party system itself, have much to do with the unique historical forces operating from this country's beginning as an independent nation. Indeed, James Madison (1751–1836) linked the emergence of political parties to the form of government created by the Constitution.

Generally, we can divide the evolution of the nation's political parties into seven periods:

1. The creation of parties, from 1789 to 1816.
2. The era of one-party rule, or personal politics, from 1816 to 1828.
3. The period from Andrew Jackson's presidency to just before the Civil War, from 1828 to 1856.
4. The Civil War and post–Civil War period, from 1856 to 1896.
5. The Republican ascendancy and the progressive period, from 1896 to 1932.
6. The New Deal period, from 1932 to about 1968.
7. The modern period, from approximately 1968 to the present.

did you know?

That the political party with the most seats in the House of Representatives chooses the Speaker of the House, makes any new rules it wants, obtains a majority of the seats on each important committee, chooses committee chairs, and hires most of the congressional staff.

The Formative Years: Federalists and Anti-Federalists

The first partisan political division in the United States occurred before the adoption of the Constitution. As you will recall from Chapter 2, the Federalists were those who pushed for adoption of the Constitution, whereas the Anti-Federalists were against ratification.

In September 1796, George Washington, who had served as president for two terms, decided not to run again. In his farewell address, he made a somber assessment of the nation's future. Washington felt that the country might be destroyed by the "baneful [harmful] effects of the spirit of party." He viewed parties as a threat to both national unity and the concept of popular government. Early in his career, Thomas Jefferson did not like political parties either. In 1789, he stated, "If I could not go to heaven but with a party, I would not go there at all."[2]

Thomas Jefferson was particularly adamant about his dislike of political parties. Nonetheless, he helped create a new party that we call the Jeffersonian Republicans. Why did he find it necessary to engage in party politics? (AP Photo)

Nevertheless, in the years after the ratification of the Constitution, Americans came to realize that something more permanent than a faction would be necessary to identify candidates for office and represent political differences among the people. The result was two political parties.

One party was the Federalists, which included John Adams, the second president (1797–1801). The Federalists represented commercial interests such as merchants and large planters. They supported a strong national government.

Thomas Jefferson led the other party, which came to be called the Republicans, or Jeffersonian Republicans. These Republicans should not be confused with the later Republican Party of Abraham Lincoln.[3] Jefferson's Republicans represented artisans and farmers. They strongly supported states' rights. In 1800, when Jefferson defeated Adams in the presidential contest, one of the world's first peaceful transfers of power from one party to another was achieved.

The Era of Good Feelings

From 1800 to 1820, a majority of U.S. voters regularly elected Republicans to the presidency and to Congress. By 1816, the Federalist Party had nearly collapsed, and two-party competition did not really exist at the national level. Although during elections the Republicans opposed the Federalists' call for a stronger, more active central government, they undertook such active government policies as acquiring the Louisiana Territory and Florida and establishing a national bank. Because there was no real political opposition to the Republicans and thus little political debate, the administration of James Monroe (1817–1825) came to be known as the **era of good feelings.** Since political competition

Era of Good Feelings
The years from 1817 to 1825, when James Monroe was president and there was, in effect, no political opposition.

2. Letter to Francis Hopkinson written from Paris while Jefferson was minister to France. In John P. Foley, ed., *The Jeffersonian Cyclopedia* (New York: Russell & Russell, 1967), p. 677.
3. To avoid confusion, some scholars refer to Jefferson's party as the Democratic-Republicans, but this name was never used during the time that the party existed.

now took place among individual Republican aspirants, this period can also be called the *era of personal politics.*

National Two-Party Rule: Democrats and Whigs

Organized two-party politics returned after 1824. Following the election of John Quincy Adams as president, the Republican Party split in two. The supporters of Adams called themselves National Republicans. The supporters of Andrew Jackson, who defeated Adams in 1828, formed the **Democratic Party.** Later, the National Republicans took the name **Whig Party,** which had been a traditional name for British liberals. The Whigs stood, among other things, for federal spending on "internal improvements," such as roads. The Democrats opposed this policy. The Democrats, who were the stronger of the two parties, favored personal liberty and opportunity for the "common man." It was understood implicitly that the "common man" was a white man—hostility toward African Americans was an important force holding the disparate Democratic groups together.[4]

Andrew Jackson
earned the name "Old Hickory" for his exploits during the War of 1812. In 1828, Jackson was elected president as the candidate of the new Democratic Party. (Corbis/Bettmann)

The Democrats' success was linked to their superior efforts to involve common citizens in the political process. Mass participation in politics and elections was a new phenomenon in the 1820s, as the political parties began to appeal to popular enthusiasm and themes. The parties adopted the techniques of mass campaigns, including rallies and parades. Lavishing food and drink on voters at polling places was also a common practice. Perhaps of greatest importance, however, was the push to cultivate party identity and loyalty. In large part, the spirit that motivated the new mass politics was democratic pride in participation. By making citizens feel that they were part of the political process, the parties hoped to win lasting party loyalty at the ballot box.

The Civil War Crisis

In the 1850s, hostility between the North and South over the issue of slavery divided both parties. The Whigs were the first to split in two. The Whigs had been the party of an active federal government, but southerners had come to believe that "a government strong enough to build roads is a government strong enough to free your slaves." The southern Whigs therefore ceased to exist as an organized party. In 1854, the northern Whigs united with antislavery Democrats and members of the radical antislavery Free Soil Party to found the modern **Republican Party.**

Democratic Party
One of the two major American political parties evolving out of the Republican Party of Thomas Jefferson.

Whig Party
A major party in the United States during the first half of the nineteenth century, formally established in 1836. The Whig Party was anti-Jackson and represented a variety of regional interests.

Republican Party
One of the two major American political parties. It emerged in the 1850s as an antislavery party and consisted of former northern Whigs and antislavery Democrats.

The Post–Civil War Period

After the Civil War, the Democratic Party was able to heal its divisions. Southern resentment of the Republicans' role in defeating the South and fears that the federal government would intervene on behalf of African Americans ensured that the Democrats would dominate the white South for the next century.

"Rum, Romanism, and Rebellion." Northern Democrats feared a strong government for other reasons. The Republicans thought that the government should promote business and economic growth, but many Republicans also wanted to use the power of government to impose evangelical Protestant moral values on society. Democrats opposed what they saw as culturally coercive measures. Many Republicans wanted to limit or even prohibit the sale of alcohol. They favored the establishment of public schools—with a Protestant curriculum. As a result, Catholics were strongly Democratic. In 1884, Protestant minister Samuel Burchard described the Democrats as the party of "rum, Romanism, and rebellion." This remark was

4. Edward Pessen, *Jacksonian America: Society, Personality, and Politics* (Homewood, Ill.: Dorsey Press, 1969). See especially pages 246–247. The small number of free blacks who could vote were overwhelmingly Whig.

offensive to Catholics, and Republican presidential candidate James Blaine later claimed that it cost him the White House.

The Triumph of the Republicans. In this period, the parties were very evenly matched in strength. The abolition of the three-fifths rule, described in Chapter 2, meant that African Americans would be counted fully when House seats and electoral votes were allocated to the South. The Republicans therefore had to carry almost every northern state to win, and this was not always possible. In the 1890s, however, the Republicans gained a decisive edge. In that decade, the Populist movement emerged in the West and South to champion the interests of small farmers, who were often heavily in debt. Populists supported inflation, which benefited debtors by reducing the real value of outstanding debts. In 1896, when William Jennings Bryan became the Democratic candidate for president, the Democrats embraced populism.

As it turned out, the few western farmers who were drawn to the Democrats by this step were greatly outnumbered by urban working-class voters who believed that inflation would reduce the purchasing power of their paychecks and who therefore became Republicans. William McKinley, the Republican candidate, was elected with a solid majority of the votes. Figure 8–1 below shows the states taken by Bryan and McKinley. The pattern of regional support shown in Figure 8–1 persisted for many years. From 1896 until 1932, the Republicans were successful at presenting themselves as the party that knew how to manage the economy.

President Abraham Lincoln ran on the Republican ticket for president in 1860. What political groups banded together to form the modern Republican Party? (Ohio Historical Society/www.ohiohistorycentral.org)

The Progressive Interlude

In the early 1900s, a spirit of political reform arose in both major parties. Called *progressivism,* this spirit was compounded of a fear of the growing power of large corporations and a belief that honest, impartial government could regulate the economy effectively. In 1912, the Republican Party temporarily split as former Republican president Theodore Roosevelt campaigned for the presidency on a third-party Progressive, or Bull Moose, ticket. The Republican split permitted the election of Woodrow Wilson, the Democratic candidate, along with a Democratic Congress.

FIGURE 8–1 The 1896 Presidential Elections

In 1896, the agrarian, Populist appeal of Democrat William Jennings Bryan (blue states) won western states for the Democrats at the cost of losing more populous eastern states to Republican William McKinley (red states). This pattern held in subsequent presidential elections.

President Woodrow Wilson (1913–1921) considered himself a progressive. (AP Photo)

Like Roosevelt, Wilson considered himself a progressive, although he and Roosevelt did not agree on how progressivism ought to be implemented. Wilson's progressivism marked the beginning of a radical change in Democratic policies. Dating back to its very foundation, the Democratic Party had been the party of limited government. Under Wilson, the Democrats became for the first time at least as receptive as the Republicans to government action in the economy. (Wilson's progressivism did not extend to race relations—for African Americans, the Wilson administration was something of a disaster.)

The New Deal Era

The Republican ascendancy resumed after Wilson left office. It ended with the election of 1932, in the depths of the Great Depression. Republican Herbert Hoover was president when the Depression began in 1929. Although Hoover took some measures to fight the Depression, they fell far short of what the public demanded. Significantly, Hoover opposed federal relief for the unemployed and the destitute. In 1932, Democrat Franklin D. Roosevelt was elected president by an overwhelming margin.

The Great Depression shattered the working-class belief in Republican economic competence. Under Roosevelt, the Democrats began to make major interventions in the economy in an attempt to combat the Depression and to relieve the suffering of the unemployed. Roosevelt's New Deal relief programs were open to all citizens, both black and white. As a result, African Americans began to support the Democratic Party in large numbers—a development that would have stunned any American politician of the 1800s.

Roosevelt's political coalition was broad enough to establish the Democrats as the new majority party, in place of the Republicans. In the 1950s, Republican Dwight D. Eisenhower, the leading U.S. general during World War II, won two terms as president. Otherwise, with minor interruptions, the Democratic ascendancy lasted until about 1968.

did you know?

That the Democrats and Republicans each had exactly one woman delegate at their conventions in 1900.

An Era of Divided Government

The New Deal coalition managed the unlikely feat of including both African Americans and whites who were hostile to African American advancement. This balancing act came to an end in the 1960s, a decade that was marked by the civil rights movement, by several years of "race riots" in major cities, and by increasingly heated protests against the Vietnam War (1964–1975). For many economically liberal, socially conservative voters, especially in the South, social issues had become more important than economic ones, and these individuals left the Democrats. These voters outnumbered the new voters who joined the Democrats—newly enfranchised African Americans and former liberal Republicans in New England and the upper Midwest.

Roosevelt's New Deal included federal spending on the Works Progress Administration during the Great Depression. (AP Photo/ Works Progress Administration)

The Parties in Balance. The result, after 1968, was a nation almost evenly divided in politics. In presidential elections, the Republicans had more success than the Democrats. Until 1994, Congress remained Democratic, but official party labels can be misleading. Some of the Democrats were southern conservatives who normally voted with the Republicans on issues. As these conservative Democrats retired, they were largely replaced by Republicans. In 1994, Republicans were able to take control of both the House and Senate for the first time in many years.

Red State, Blue State. In 2000, Democratic presidential candidate Al Gore won the popular vote, but lost the Electoral College by a narrow margin to Republican George W. Bush. The extreme closeness of the vote in the Electoral College led the press to repeatedly publish the map of the results state by state. Commentators discussed at length the supposed differences between the Republican "red states" and the Democratic "blue states."

"Am I a white man in a red state voting for a black president, or a blue man in a white state voting for a green president?" (© The New Yorker Collection, 2008. Drew Dernavich, from cartoonbank.com. All rights reserved.)

In the presidential elections of 2004, Bush won the popular vote by a margin of more than 3 million votes over Democrat John F. Kerry. Yet only three states changed hands. Bush picked up Iowa and New Mexico, which had voted Democratic in 2000, and lost New Hampshire. Clearly, the parties continued to be closely matched.

An interesting characteristic of the 2000 and 2004 red state–blue state divisions is that they were almost exact reversals of the presidential elections of 1896 (see Figure 8–1 on page 255). Except for the state of Washington, every state that supported Democrat William Jennings Bryan in 1896 supported Republican George W. Bush in 2000 and 2004. This reversal parallels the transformation of the Democrats from an anti–civil rights to a pro–civil rights party and from a party that supported limited government to a party that favors positive government action.

Tilting toward the Democrats. By 2006, the Republicans were in trouble. As the war in Iraq dragged on, ever-larger numbers of voters came to believe that U.S. intervention had been a mistake. In the 2006 midterm elections, the Democrats took control of the U.S. House and Senate. By 2007 and 2008, half or more of those polled claimed either to be Democrats or independents leaning Democratic, compared with about 40 percent on the Republican side. Bush's approval ratings were among the lowest ever recorded for a president.

The Elections of 2008—and After

It was clear from the beginning that 2008 was not going to be a good year for the Republicans. Still, many experts believed that the party had a chance to hold on to the presidency. John McCain, the Republican candidate, had a history of opposing his party on important issues, such as campaign-finance reform and immigration, and he had a proven track record in attracting independent voters. After September 15, however, the financial crisis dominated the headlines, and McCain's support faded. In the end, Obama received almost 53 percent of the popular vote (see Figure 8–2 on page 258). The Democrats also picked up eight seats in the U.S. Senate and twenty-one seats in the House, giving them commanding majorities in both chambers. In April 2009, when Pennsylvania Senator Arlen Specter switched from the Republicans to the Democrats, the Democratic Party was on the brink of controlling sixty Senate seats, enough to pass legislation in the face of united Republican opposition.[5]

The Republican Revival. By 2010, the Republicans seemed to have regained the support they lost during the previous five years. A Gallup poll reported that party identification, counting independents leaning toward a party, was now effectively tied at about 45 percent

---

5. The sixty votes included two independents who caucused with the Democrats, Joe Lieberman of Connecticut and Bernie Sanders of Vermont. The Democrats did not actually obtain their sixty votes until July 2009, when a contested Senate race in Minnesota was finally decided in favor of Democrat Al Franken.

support for each party. Such parity was last seen in 2005. Another Gallup survey suggested that the Republicans did not really gain support—the Democrats lost it. From 2000 to 2005, both parties had positive images among a majority of poll respondents. In 2005, however, the share of respondents with a positive image of the Republicans dropped into the 40 percent range and remained there through 2010. The Democrats' image polled above 50 percent until 2010, when it also fell to about 40 percent. The Republican recovery was confirmed in January 2010 when Scott Brown won a special U.S. Senate election in Massachusetts. This was a Republican victory in a normally Democratic state. Brown's victory cost the Senate Democrats their crucial sixty-vote margin.

Democratic Troubles. What happened to the Democrats? Two theories have been advanced, and both may be accurate. One explanation is that many independents now blamed the Democrats for persistent unemployment. True, through 2009 the net number of job losses steadily fell, but that simply meant that matters were getting worse more slowly. Not until 2010 did the economy actually begin to create more jobs than had been lost. It is hard to overestimate the impact of this type of economic disaster. Economist Douglas Hibbs, for example, has developed a model that explains most of the vote in U.S. presidential elections since 1952 with a single variable—national income growth during the preceding year.[6]

Many observers, however, focused on a second explanation. They argued that independents turned away from the Democrats in the belief that the party was expanding the scope of the federal government to an unacceptable degree. (This argument was introduced in Chapter 1 on page 17.) The economic stimulus package of February 2009, initially valued at $787 billion, may have been necessary. Had they been in power, the Republicans might have passed a stimulus program of their own (albeit probably less extensive). Any Republican measure, however, would have consisted almost entirely of tax cuts—as did the Republican counterproposal in February 2009. In contrast, the Democratic stimulus package contained major new federal spending initiatives.

---

6. In war years, Hibbs's model also depends on a second variable: military fatalities. See Douglas A. Hibbs, Jr., "Implications of the 'Bread and Peace' Model for the 2008 US Presidential Election," *Public Choice*, Vol. 137 (October 2008), pp.1–10.

FIGURE 8–2 The 2008 Presidential Elections

In the 2008 presidential elections, Democrat Barack Obama received a majority of the Electoral College votes, outdoing Republican John McCain by a large margin. Although Obama won nine more states than Democrat John Kerry had won in the 2004 presidential elections, the regional political preferences remained similar to those of previous elections.

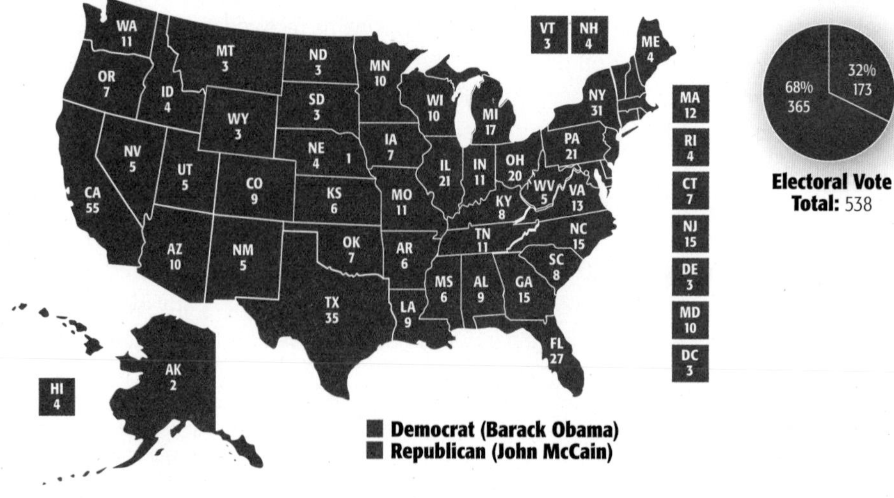

The Democratic health-care reform package, however, was crucial in fostering the perception of the party as committed to "big government." By passing this legislation, the Democrats attained a goal dating back half a century. Yet the victory meant that health care dominated public debate for almost nine months. In the public mind, health care had little or no relation to the economic crisis. Democrats could be accused of neglecting the nation's most important problems for almost a year in order to develop the most important new government program since the 1960s. By this analysis, the Democrats obtained a long-sought objective by burning through all the political capital they had accumulated during the previous five years.

The Two Major U.S. Parties Today

It is sometimes claimed that the major American political parties are like Tweedledee and Tweedledum, the twins in Lewis Carroll's *Through the Looking Glass.* Labels such as "Repubocrats" are especially popular among supporters of radical third parties, such as the Green Party and the Libertarian Party. Third-party advocates, of course, have an interest in claiming that there is no difference between the two major parties—their chances of gaining support are much greater if the major parties are seen as indistinguishable. Such allegations cannot disguise the fact that the major parties do have substantial differences, both in their policies and in their constituents.

The Parties' Core Constituents

You learned in Chapter 6 how demographic factors affect support for the two parties. Democrats receive disproportionate support not only from the least well-educated voters but also from individuals with advanced degrees. Businesspersons are much more likely to

ELECTIONS 2010

PARTISAN TRENDS IN THE 2010 ELECTIONS

In 2006, the Democrats opened up a margin of popularity over the Republicans. The thumping rejection of Democratic candidates in November 2010 certainly indicated that that margin was now dead. Republican John Boehner of Ohio, who was in line to become the Speaker of the House, proclaimed that the new Republican majority in the House would be "the voice of the American people." Boehner, however, may have been claiming too much. Polling data suggested that neither party had the trust or support of a majority of the country's citizens. Self-identified independents outnumbered the supporters of either party. Negative perceptions of both parties were about equally high. Clearly, the voters had given the Democrats a "shellacking," as President Obama put it. High unemployment and an extremely ambitious legislative program were both reasons for the voters to punish the Democrats. There were few signs, however, that the Democrats would stay in the doghouse forever.

Indeed, despite their current state of disarray, Democrats could point to certain positive signs of potential long-term growth. While the Tea Party movement provided the Republicans with much energy, one obvious characteristic of the movement was that its members were predominantly middle aged. Young voters remained predominantly Democratic, although that fact did not help in 2010 because young voters tended not to turn out in midterms. Latino citizens, the fastest growing part of the electorate, did turn out in reasonable numbers and proved to be more Democratic than ever. Support from tomorrow's voters gave the Democrats some hope that the future might be better for them than the highly depressing present.

For their part, the Republicans faced real challenges in solidifying their new-found strength. Americans might expect that the party in control of the House of Representatives would come up with concrete measures to improve the lives of ordinary citizens. Yet many observers expected that partisan gridlock would tie up Congress instead. It was by no means clear who would receive the blame if members of Congress did little but criticize each other.

vote Republican than labor union members. The Jewish electorate is heavily Democratic; white evangelical Christians who are regular churchgoers tend to be Republicans. Hispanics are strongly Democratic; African Americans are overwhelmingly so. City dwellers tend to be Democrats; rural people tend to be Republicans. Such tendencies represent the influences of economic interests and cultural values, which are often in conflict with each other.

A coalition of the labor movement and various racial and ethnic minorities has been the core of Democratic Party support since the presidency of Franklin D. Roosevelt. The social programs and increased government intervention in the economy that made up Roosevelt's New Deal were intended to ease the pressure of economic hard times on these groups. This goal remains important for many Democrats today. In general, Democratic identifiers are more likely to approve of social-welfare spending, to support government regulation of business, and to endorse measures to improve the situation of minorities. Republicans are more supportive of the private marketplace and believe more strongly in an ethic of self-reliance and limited government.

When President Bill Clinton announced in his 1996 State of the Union message that "the era of big government is over," what do you think he meant? Was he right? (AP Photo/ Denis Paquin)

Economic Convergence?

In his 1996 State of the Union address, Democratic president Bill Clinton announced that "the era of big government is over." One might conclude from this that both parties now favor limited government. Some political observers, however, argue that despite the tax cuts that Republicans have implemented, both parties in practice now favor "big government." Harvard University professor Jeffrey Frankel points out that budget deficits rose during the administrations of Republicans Ronald Reagan (1981–1989) and George W. Bush but fell under Bill Clinton. Federal employment grew under Reagan and George W. Bush but fell under Clinton. Reagan and Bush both introduced "protectionist" measures to restrict imports, such as Bush's tariffs on imported steel and timber. Clinton, despite the protectionist beliefs of many Democrats in Congress, was in practice more supportive of free trade.

During the presidency of George W. Bush, spending skyrocketed, in part due to the Iraq War. Bush signed into law more domestic government spending increases than any previous president since World War II (even correcting for inflation). By the time he left office in January 2009, the federal budget deficit had hit a record.

With the arrival of the Obama administration, however, the parties appeared to revert to their traditional positions on the size of government. Obama launched major new initiatives, including the February 2009 economic stimulus program, interventions into the automobile industry, a major health-care program, and reform of the financial industry. Depending on the initiative, Republicans responded either with monolithic or near-monolithic opposition. The question remained, however, whether the Republicans would maintain their antigovernment fervor if they should again gain control of the House, Senate, and presidency. (Republicans last enjoyed such control from January 2003 to January 2007.)

Cultural Politics

In the years that preceded the Great Recession, cultural values may have been unusually important in defining the beliefs of the two major parties. For example, in 1987, Democrats were almost as likely to favor stricter abortion laws (40 percent) as Republicans were (48 percent). Today, Republicans are twice as likely to favor stricter abortion laws (50 percent to 25 percent).

Cultural Politics and Socioeconomic Status. Some years ago, Thomas Frank reported seeing the following bumper sticker at a gun show in Kansas City: "A working person voting for the Democrats is like a chicken voting for Colonel Sanders." (Colonel Sanders is the iconic founder of KFC, the chain of fried chicken restaurants.) In light of the economic traditions of the two parties, this seems to be an odd statement. In fact, the sticker is an exact reversal of an earlier one directed against the Republicans.

You can make sense of such a sentiment by remembering what you learned in Chapter 6—although economic conservatism is associated with higher incomes, social conservatism is relatively more common among lower-income groups. The individual who displayed the bumper sticker, therefore, was in effect claiming that cultural concerns—in this example, presumably the right to own handguns—were far more important than economic ones. Frank argues that despite Republican control of both the White House and Congress during much of the George W. Bush administration, cultural conservatives continued to view themselves as embattled "ordinary Americans" under threat from a liberal, cosmopolitan elite.[7] Of course, the election of Barack Obama and a strongly Democratic Congress in 2008 was certain to magnify such fears. One result was the Tea Party movement that began in 2009.

This supporter of the health-care reform bill displays his view of corporate lobbying against the legislation in 2010. (Jewel Samad/AFP/Getty Images)

The Regional Factor in Cultural Politics. Conventionally, some parts of the country are viewed as culturally liberal, and others as culturally conservative. On a regional basis, cultural liberalism (as opposed to economic liberalism) may be associated with economic dynamism. The San Francisco Bay Area can serve as an example. The greater Bay Area contains Silicon Valley, the heart of the microcomputer industry; it has the highest per capita personal income of any metropolitan area in America. It also is one of the most liberal regions of the country. San Francisco liberalism is largely cultural—one sign of this liberalism is that the city has a claim to be the "capital" of gay America.

To further illustrate this point, we can compare the political preferences of relatively wealthy states with those of relatively poor ones. Of the fifteen states with the highest per capita personal incomes in 2008, fourteen voted for Democrat Barack Obama in the presidential elections of that year. Of the fifteen with the lowest per capita incomes in 2008, thirteen voted for Republican John McCain.

Given these data, it seems hard to believe that upper-income voters really are more Republican than lower-income ones. Still, within any given state or region, upscale voters are more likely to be Republican regardless of whether the area as a whole leans Democratic or Republican. States that vote Democratic are often northern states that contain large cities. At least part of this **reverse-income effect** may simply be that urban areas are more prosperous, culturally liberal, and Democratic than the countryside, and that the North is more prosperous, culturally liberal, and Democratic than the South.

Reverse-Income Effect
A tendency for wealthier states or regions to favor the Democrats and for less wealthy states or regions to favor the Republicans. The effect appears paradoxical because it reverses traditional patterns of support.

Cultural Divisions within the Democratic Party. The extremely close and hard-fought Democratic presidential primary contest between Senator Barack Obama and Senator Hillary Clinton in 2008 exposed a series of cultural divisions within the Democratic Party that political scientists have been aware of for some time. Of course, African Americans supported Obama strongly, and women tended to favor Clinton. Beyond these obvious patterns, Clinton appeared to do well among older people,

did you know?

That it took 103 ballots for John W. Davis to be nominated at the Democratic National Convention in 1924.

7. Thomas Frank, *What's the Matter with Kansas? How Conservatives Won the Heart of America* (New York: Holt, 2005).

white working-class voters, and Latinos, while Obama received more support from the young and from better-educated, upscale Democrats.

This division appears to be similar to the cultural divisions in the general population that we have just discussed. Yet the differences between the two candidates on policy issues were actually very small. Likewise, there was no evidence that Obama fans and the Clinton backers held significantly different positions on the issues—the two groups may have been somewhat different kinds of people, but they appeared to have similar politics.

To a degree, Obama's narrow victory reflects changes in the Democrats' core constituencies. Traditionally, the candidate with a stronger working-class appeal could expect to win over the largest number of Democrats. As we have noted, however, in recent years well-educated, professional individuals have shifted to the Democrats even as voters without college degrees have grown more Republican. By 2008, Obama's upscale supporters made up a larger share of the Democratic Party than in years past. Still, Obama could not have won without strong support from African Americans of all classes. Indeed, Obama's black support grew as the campaign progressed. Apparently, many African Americans saw the harsh criticisms he received during the campaign as attacks on the black community as a whole.

Tea Party protesters marked "tax day" April 15 with exhortations against "gangster government" and appeals to Republicans seeking their grassroots clout in November elections, a prospect both tempting and troubling to those in the loose movement. Why are Tea Party supporters against higher taxes? (AP Photo/Steve Bloom *The Olympian*)

Cultural Divisions among the Republicans. One wing of the Republican Party, often called the Religious Right, is energized by conservative religious beliefs. These conservatives are often evangelical Protestants but may also be Catholics, Mormons, or adherents of other faiths. For these voters, moral issues such as abortion and gay marriage are key. The other wing of the Republican Party is more oriented toward economic issues and business concerns. These voters often are small-business owners or have some other connection to commercial enterprise. Such voters oppose high taxes and are concerned about government regulations that interfere with the conduct of business.

Of course, many Republicans are pro-business and also support the Religious Right. Some economically oriented Republicans, however, are strongly libertarian and dislike government regulation of social issues as well as economic ones. Likewise, some on the Religious Right are not particularly committed to the free market ethos of the party's business wing and are willing to support a variety of government interventions in the economy.

did you know?

That in his first inaugural address, Thomas Jefferson proclaimed that "We are all Republicans, we are all Federalists."

Successful Republican presidential candidates, such as George W. Bush, tried to appeal to both wings of the party. Senator John McCain of Arizona, the Republican candidate for president in 2008, initially found it hard to appeal to the Religious Right until he chose Sarah Palin as his running mate. McCain's maverick positions on a number of issues in the past had led many to doubt his conservatism (which was actually quite strong). In the end, however, McCain was able to unite his party behind him.

The Republicans under Obama. In 2009 and 2010, divisions between business-oriented Republicans and the Religious Right grew less important. Both factions were united in their opposition to the Obama administration. A new fault line appeared to be opening up in the party, however—between moderate conservatives and more radical ones. The more radical wing was often highly critical of the existing Republican Party leadership, accusing it of being little better than the Democrats. The Tea Party movement, though it was officially nonpartisan and contained some Democrats and Libertarian Party members, was closely associated with the right wing of the Republican Party. It is notable that Tea Party activists tended to avoid issues dear to the Religious Right, such as abortion and same-sex marriage. The Tea Party movement appeared, rather, to represent a mobilization of the Republican Party's antigovernment wing. Together with celebrities such as talk-show host Rush Limbaugh and former Republican vice-presidential candidate Sarah Palin, plus groups such as the Club for Growth, Tea Party activists sought to purge the Republicans of so-called RINOs (Republicans in name only).

Between the newly resurgent political right and the apparent legislative overreach of the Democrats, it may be worth asking whether the two major parties are becoming too radical. We address that issue in this chapter's *Which Side Are You On?* feature on the following page.

The Three Faces of a Party

Although American parties are known by a single name and, in the public mind, have a common historical identity, each party really has three major components. The first component is the **party-in-the-electorate.** This phrase refers to all those individuals who claim an attachment to the political party. They need not participate in election campaigns. Rather, the party-in-the-electorate is the large number of Americans who feel some loyalty to the party or who use partisanship as a cue to decide who will earn their vote. Party membership is not really a rational choice; rather, it is an emotional tie somewhat analogous to identifying with a region or a baseball team. Although individuals may hold a deep loyalty to or identification with a political party, there is no need for members of the party-in-the-electorate to speak out publicly, to contribute to campaigns, or to vote all Republican or all Democratic. Nevertheless, the party leaders pay close attention to their members in the electorate.

Party-in-the-Electorate
Those members of the general public who identify with a political party or who express a preference for one party over another.

Party Organization
The formal structure and leadership of a political party, including election committees; local, state, and national executives; and paid professional staff.

Party-in-Government
All of the elected and appointed officials who identify with a political party.

The second component, the **party organization,** provides the structural framework for the political party by recruiting volunteers to become party leaders; identifying potential candidates; and organizing caucuses, conventions, and election campaigns for its candidates, as will be discussed in more detail shortly. It is the party organization and its active workers that keep the party functioning between elections, as well as ensure that the party puts forth electable candidates and clear positions in the elections. If the party-in-the-electorate declines in numbers and loyalty, the party organization must try to find a strategy to rebuild the grassroots following.

The **party-in-government** is the third component of American political parties. The party-in-government consists of those elected and appointed officials who identify with a political party. Generally, elected officials do not also hold official party positions within the formal organization, although they often have the informal power to appoint party executives.

The delegates to the Democratic National Convention in 2008 in Denver, Colorado, express their support for Barack Obama. Do delegates at such conventions reflect average voters in their respective parties? Why or why not? (AP Photo/Jae C. Hong)

Party Organization

Each of the American political parties is often seen as having a pyramid-shaped organization, with the national chairperson and committee at the top and the local precinct chairperson on the bottom. This structure, however, does not accurately reflect the relative power of the individual components of the party organization. If it did, the national chairperson of the Democratic Party

WHICH SIDE ARE YOU ON? ARE THE PARTIES BECOMING TOO RADICAL?

In 2009 and 2010, political rhetoric seemed to reach new heights of hysteria. Many Americans on the political right believed that President Obama was foreign-born and ineligible to be president—even though Obama produced his Hawaii birth certificate and the birth was announced in Honolulu newspapers. In one poll, a majority of Republicans affirmed that Obama was a Muslim. A quarter of the Republicans surveyed even agreed that "he may be the Anti-Christ." Among Republican leaders, former vice-presidential candidate Sarah Palin falsely accused the Democrats of sponsoring "death panels" that would refuse medical care to the elderly, and Texas governor Rick Perry predicted that his state might secede from the Union.

Meanwhile, the Democrats in Congress pushed through their health-care reform program, a massive change in how we fund one-sixth of the nation's economy. No national consensus existed in support of the program, but the Democrats proceeded regardless.

Irresponsible rhetoric, adventurous legislation—were these manifestations of a new radical spirit? Some observers contended that they were.

THE PARTIES HAVE NEVER BEEN SO RADICAL

Those who believe that our politics exhibits unprecedented levels of radicalism point to the extreme language used on the Web, on the airwaves, and in Congress. In addition, both parties seem willing to undertake ideologically motivated steps that can only hurt them. If passing health-care legislation that will damage you politically is not radical, what is?

On their side, Republicans sought to purge their party of candidates showing the least sign of moderation, even when purity meant losing elections. In 2009, for example, national figures such as Sarah Palin, Minnesota governor Tim Pawlenty, and former Tennessee senator Fred Thompson intervened to force Republican congressional candidate Dede Scozzafava out of a race in upstate New York on the ground that she was insufficiently conservative. They supported Conservative Party candidate Doug Hoffman instead. Hoffman then lost to Democrat Bill Owens. Parts of the district had not previously voted for a Democrat since the Civil War era.

RADICALISM EXISTS, ALL RIGHT, BUT IT IS NOT NEW

Those who disagree that the parties are more radical admit that the recession and Democratic dominance after the 2008 elections energized the political right. But anyone who thinks that the beliefs of the far right are unprecedentedly "out there" needs to learn more history. Well into the twentieth century, conservative Democrats made the most vicious statements about African Americans on the floor of the House and Senate. Radical conservatives would never countenance such language today. In 1958, Robert Welch, leader of the right-wing John Birch Society, claimed in all seriousness that Republican president Dwight D. Eisenhower was a "dedicated, conscious agent of the Communist conspiracy." That beats anything we've heard recently from a prominent figure.

As for the Democrats, passage of health-care legislation doesn't mean that the party has become more radical. It only means that with large majorities in the House and Senate, the party found itself in a position to pass measures it had supported for decades. What would happen if the Republicans had the power to win certain long-sought objectives supported by all wings of the party? Say that *Roe v. Wade* were repealed, thus allowing antiabortion legislation at the state and even the national level. Would rank-and-file members let the Republican Party back out on its right-to-life commitments? No. Would the party suffer at the next elections? Yes.

Many who do not believe the parties have become more radical will agree, however, that they have become more polarized—that is, more hostile to each other—than ever before. But that is a different issue, which we will turn to later in this chapter.

FOR CRITICAL ANALYSIS

Have the two major parties become too radical in recent years? Are Republicans justified in their anger at the Democrats? Are Democrats justified in pushing for long-time party objectives, regardless of current opinion poll results?

or the Republican Party, along with the national committee, could simply dictate how the organization was to be run, just as if it were the ExxonMobil Corporation or Ford Motor Company. In reality, the political parties have a confederal structure, in which each unit has significant autonomy and is linked only loosely to the other units.

During the last presidential campaign, these pro-McCain Puerto Ricans expressed their feelings near the city of San Juan. Why do individuals take time to attend such rallies? (AP Photo/ Andres Leighton)

The National Party Organization

Each party has a national organization, the most clearly institutional part of which is the **national convention,** held every four years. The convention is used to officially nominate the presidential and vice-presidential candidates. In addition, the **party platform** is developed at the national convention. The platform sets forth the party's position on the issues and makes promises to initiate certain policies if the party wins the presidency.

After the convention, the platform frequently is neglected or ignored whenever party candidates disagree with it. Because candidates are trying to win votes from a wide spectrum of voters, it can be counterproductive to emphasize the fairly narrow and sometimes controversial goals set forth in the platform. Political scientist Gerald M. Pomper discovered decades ago, however, that once elected, the parties do try to carry out platform promises and that roughly three-fourths of the promises eventually become law.[8] Of course, some general goals, such as economic prosperity, are included in the platforms of both parties.

Convention Delegates. The party convention provides the most striking illustration of the difference between the ordinary members of a party, or party identifiers, and party activists. As a series of studies by the *New York Times* shows, delegates to the national party conventions are different from ordinary party identifiers. Delegates to the Democratic National Convention, as shown in Table 8–1 on the next page, take stands on many issues that are far more liberal than the positions of ordinary Democratic voters. Typically, delegates to the Republican National Convention are far more conservative than ordinary Republicans. Why does this happen? In part, it is because a person, to become a delegate, must gather votes in a primary election from party members who care enough to vote in a primary or be appointed by party leaders. Also, the primaries generally pit presidential candidates against each other on intraparty issues. Competition within each party tends to pull candidates away from the center, and delegates even more so. Often, the most important activity for the convention is making peace among the delegates who support different candidates and persuading them to accept a party platform that will appeal to the general electorate.

National Convention
The meeting held every four years by each major party to select presidential and vice-presidential candidates, write a platform, choose a national committee, and conduct party business.

Party Platform
A document drawn up at each national convention, outlining the policies, positions, and principles of the party.

National Committee
A standing committee of a national political party established to direct and coordinate party activities between national party conventions.

The National Committee. At the national convention, each of the parties formally chooses a national standing committee, elected by the individual state parties. This **national committee** directs and coordinates party activities during the following four years. The Democrats include at least two members (a man and a woman) from each state, from the District of Columbia, and from the several territories. Governors, members of Congress, mayors, and other officials may be included as at-large members of the national committee. The Republicans, in addition, include state chairpersons from every state carried by the Republican Party in the preceding presidential, gubernatorial, or congressional elections. The selections of national committee members are ratified by the delegations to the national convention.

---

8. Gerald M. Pomper and Susan S. Lederman, *Elections in America: Control and Influence in Democratic Politics,* 2d ed. (New York: Longman, 1980).

TABLE 8–1 Convention Delegates and Voters: How Did They Compare on the Issues in 2008?

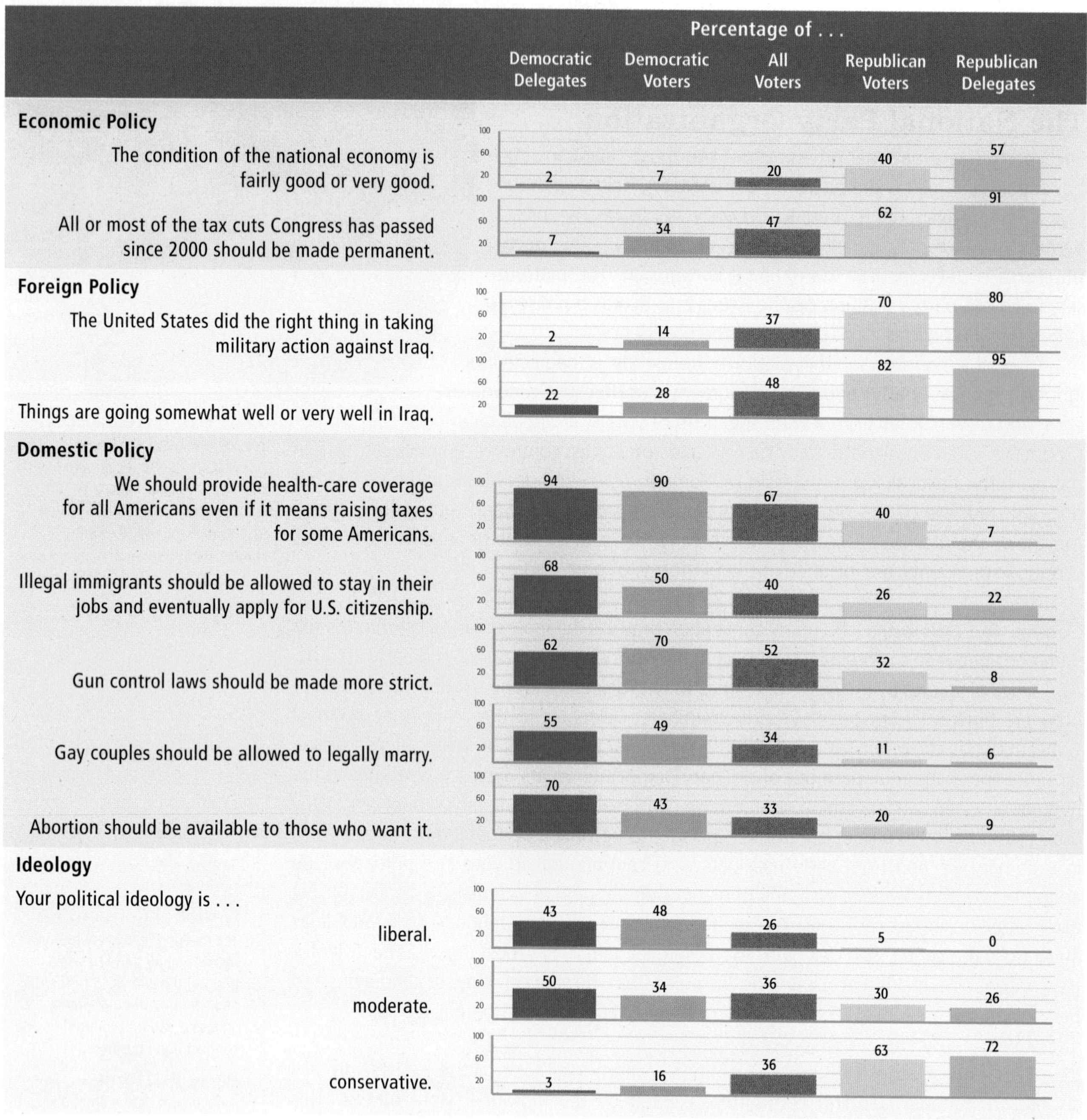

	Percentage of . . .				
	Democratic Delegates	Democratic Voters	All Voters	Republican Voters	Republican Delegates
Economic Policy					
The condition of the national economy is fairly good or very good.	2	7	20	40	57
All or most of the tax cuts Congress has passed since 2000 should be made permanent.	7	34	47	62	91
Foreign Policy					
The United States did the right thing in taking military action against Iraq.	2	14	37	70	80
Things are going somewhat well or very well in Iraq.	22	28	48	82	95
Domestic Policy					
We should provide health-care coverage for all Americans even if it means raising taxes for some Americans.	94	90	67	40	7
Illegal immigrants should be allowed to stay in their jobs and eventually apply for U.S. citizenship.	68	50	40	26	22
Gun control laws should be made more strict.	62	70	52	32	8
Gay couples should be allowed to legally marry.	55	49	34	11	6
Abortion should be available to those who want it.	70	43	33	20	9
Ideology					
Your political ideology is . . . liberal.	43	48	26	5	0
moderate.	50	34	36	30	26
conservative.	3	16	36	63	72

Source: Excerpted and adapted from *The New York Times*/CBS News polls, July 16–August 17, 2008 and July 23–August 26, 2008.

One of the jobs of the national committee is to ratify the presidential nominee's choice of a national chairperson, who in principle acts as the spokesperson for the party. The national chairperson and the national committee plan the next campaign and the next convention, obtain financial contributions, and publicize the national party.

Picking a National Chairperson. In general, the party's presidential candidate chooses the national chairperson. (If that candidate loses, however, the chairperson is often changed.) The national chairperson performs such jobs as establishing a national party headquarters, raising campaign funds and distributing them to state parties and to candidates, and appearing in the media as a party spokesperson. The national chairperson, along with the national committee, attempts to maintain some sort of liaison among the different levels of the party organization. The fact, though, is that the real strength and power of the party are at the state level.

Former Governor
Tim Kaine (D., Va.), chairman of the Democratic National Committee, left, and Michael Steele, chairman of the Republican National Committee, right, appear on NBC's *Meet the Press* in Washington, D.C. How much control over each party do these leaders have? (William B. Plowman/NBC NewsWire via AP Images)

The State Party Organization

There are fifty states in the Union, plus the District of Columbia and the territories, and an equal number of party organizations for each major party. Therefore, there are more than a hundred state parties (and even more, if we include local parties and minor parties). Because every state party is unique, it is impossible to describe what an "average" state political party is like. Nonetheless, state parties have several organizational features in common.

Each state party has a chairperson, a committee, and a number of local organizations. In theory, the role of the **state central committee**—the principal organized structure of each political party within each state—is similar in the various states. The committee, usually composed of members who represent congressional districts, state legislative districts, or counties, has responsibility for carrying out the policy decisions of the party's state convention. In some states, the state committee can issue directives to the state chairperson.

Also, like the national committee, the state central committee has control over the use of party campaign funds during political campaigns. Usually, the state central committee has little, if any, influence on party candidates once they are elected. In fact, state parties are fundamentally loose alliances of local interests and coalitions of often bitterly opposed factions.

State Central Committee
The principal organized structure of each political party within each state. This committee is responsible for carrying out policy decisions of the party's state convention.

Patronage
Rewarding faithful party workers and followers with government employment or contracts.

Local Party Machinery: The Grassroots

The lowest layer of party machinery is the local organization, supported by district leaders, precinct or ward captains, and party workers. Much of the work is coordinated by county committees and their chairpersons.

Patronage and City Machines. In the 1800s, the institution of **patronage**—rewarding the party faithful with government jobs or contracts—held the local organization together. For immigrants and the poor, the political machine often furnished important services and protections. The big-city machine was the archetypal example. Tammany Hall, or the Tammany Society, which dominated New York City government well into the twentieth century, was perhaps the most notorious example of this political form.

The last big-city local political machine to exercise substantial power was run by Chicago mayor Richard J. Daley, who was also an important figure in national Democratic politics. Daley, as mayor, ran the Chicago Democratic machine from 1955 until his death in 1976. Richard M. Daley, son of the former mayor, who served as Chicago mayor from 1989 until 2011, did not have the kind of political machine that his father had.

did you know?
That it takes about 700,000 signatures to qualify to be on the ballot as a presidential candidate in all fifty states.

City machines are now dead, mostly because their function of providing social services (and reaping the reward of votes) has been taken over by state and national agencies. This trend began in the 1930s, when the social legislation of the New Deal established Social Security and unemployment insurance. Today, local party organizations have little, if anything, to do with deciding who is eligible to receive social benefits.

Geraldine Ferraro, on the left, was the Democratic vice-presidential nominee in 1984. Alongside her is actress Kerry Washington. They launched WE Vote '08 in late 2007. The goal of this organization was to register more than one million female voters prior to the 2008 elections. Why did this organization target potential female voters? (AP Photo/Stuart Ramson)

Local Party Organizations Today. Local political organizations— whether located in cities, in townships, or at the county level—still can contribute a great deal to local election campaigns. These organizations are able to provide the foot soldiers of politics—individuals who pass out literature and get out the vote on election day, which can be crucial in local elections. In many regions, local Democratic and Republican organizations still exercise some patronage, such as awarding courthouse jobs, contracts for street repair, and other lucrative construction contracts. The constitutionality of awarding—or not awarding—contracts on the basis of political affiliation has been subject to challenge, however. The United States Supreme Court has ruled that firing or failing to hire individuals because of their political affiliation is an infringement of the employees' First Amendment rights to free expression.[9] Local party organizations are also the most important vehicles for recruiting young adults into political work, because political involvement at the local level offers activists many opportunities to gain experience.

The Party-in-Government

After the election is over and the winners are announced, the focus of party activity shifts from getting out the vote to organizing and controlling the government. As you will learn in Chapter 10, party membership plays an important role in the day-to-day operations of Congress, with partisanship determining everything from office space to committee assignments and power on Capitol Hill. For the president, the political party furnishes the pool of qualified applicants for political appointments to run the government. (Although it is uncommon to do so, presidents can and occasionally do appoint executive personnel, such as cabinet members, from the opposition party—one current example is Defense Secretary Robert Gates, a Republican.) As we note in Chapter 11, there are not as many of these appointed positions as presidents might like, and presidential power is limited by the permanent bureaucracy. Judicial appointments also offer a great opportunity to the winning party. For the most part, presidents are likely to appoint federal judges from their own party.

Divided Government. All of these party appointments suggest that the winning political party, whether at the national, state, or local level, has a great deal of control in the American system. The degree of control that a winning party can actually exercise, however, depends on several factors. At the national level, an important factor is whether the party controls both the executive and legislative branches of government. If it does, the party leadership in Congress may be reluctant to exercise congressional checks on presidential powers. If Congress is cooperating in implementing legislation approved by the president, the president, in turn, will not feel it necessary to exercise the veto power. Certainly, this situation existed while the Republicans controlled both the legislative and executive branches of government from January 2003 to January 2007, and when the Democrats controlled the government in the years following Obama's inauguration in January 2009.

Divided Government
A situation in which one major political party controls the presidency and the other controls one or more chambers of Congress, or in which one party controls a state governorship and the other controls part or all of the state legislature.

The winning party has less control over the government when the government is divided. A **divided government** is one in which the executive and legislative branches are controlled by different parties. After the 2006 elections, this was the situation facing the Democrats in Congress. The Democrats were unable to pass legislation that did not

9. *Rutan v. Republican Party of Illinois,* 497 U.S. 62 (1990).

President Barack Obama is surrounded by his cabinet, including Secretary of State Hillary Clinton, third from left, during a meeting in the Cabinet Room of the White House in Washington. (AP Photo/Susan Walsh)

meet with President Bush's approval because they did not have sufficient votes (a two-thirds majority) to override a presidential veto. Although Bush exercised only one veto from 2001 through 2006, after the Democrats took control of Congress in January 2007 he vetoed eleven bills.

The Limits of Party Unity. There are other ways in which the power of the parties is limited. Consider how major laws are passed in Congress. Traditionally, legislation was rarely passed by a vote strictly along party lines. Although most Democrats might oppose a bill, for example, some Democrats would vote for it. Their votes, combined with the votes of Republicans, were often enough to pass the bill. Similarly, support from some Republicans enabled bills sponsored by the Democrats to pass.

One reason that the political parties traditionally found it so hard to rally all of their members in Congress to vote along party lines was that candidates who won most elections largely did so on their own, without significant help from a political party. A candidate generally gained a nomination through her or his own hard work and personal political organization. In many other countries, most candidates are selected by the party organization, not by primary elections. This means, though, that in the United States the parties have very little control over the candidates who run under the party labels. In fact, a candidate could run as a Republican, for example, and advocate beliefs repugnant to the national party, such as racism. No one in the Republican Party organization could stop this person from being nominated or even elected.

Party Polarization. In recent years, it has become increasingly difficult for legislators in either party to obtain support for important legislation from members of the other party. More and more, voting takes place strictly along party lines. Discipline within the party caucuses has never been greater. The Republicans, who took the lead in the development of party unity, presented a united front throughout much of the 1990s. By 2009, the Democrats had largely caught up, although even then the party's congressional delegation contained a number of dissidents, notably the conservative Blue Dog caucus in the U.S. House. One reason for

This photo was taken when both John McCain and Barack Obama were active in the U.S. Senate. At that time, McCain unequivocally supported the war effort in Iraq whereas Obama did not. When they both became presidential candidates, national security and experience in foreign affairs became key points in their campaigns. Have American voters always been concerned about national security issues? (AP Photo/Dennis Cook, File)

"I think it was an election year."
(© The New Yorker Collection, 2000. Danny Shanahan, from cartoonbank.com. All Rights Reserved.)

party-line voting is that political overlap between the two parties has essentially vanished. Political scientists have calculated that in 2009, the most conservative Blue Dog Democrat in the House was still more liberal than the most liberal Republican—if a term such as *liberal Republican* still makes any sense.

For much of the twentieth century, however, liberal Republicans were a real presence in the nation's politics, and so were extremely conservative Democrats. Millions of Americans formed their party attachments not through ideology, but on the basis of tradition and sentiment. Old-stock New England Yankees were Republicans because New England Yankees had always been Republicans. White southerners were, by and large, Democrats because that party affiliation was part of what it meant to be a southerner. Ideologically, however, most of the southerners were well to the right of the average Yankee. Likewise, Yankee Republicans were, on average, more liberal than most southern Democrats. Today, liberal Yankees are usually Democrats, and conservative southerners are Republicans.

Blocking Tactics. One effect of the new polarization is that interpersonal relationships between members of the parties have deteriorated. True, some senators and representatives are able to maintain friendships across party lines, but such friendships have become less common. A second effect is the growing tactic of blocking bills to make the other party appear ineffective, without any attempt to reach a compromise. Republicans pioneered this tactic in the 1990s under House Speaker Newt Gingrich in an attempt to embarrass Democratic president Bill Clinton, and they tried it again in 2009 and 2010, with varying degrees of success. Democrats contended that the tactic demonstrated Republican irresponsibility. It is also possible to propose—rather than oppose—legislation for political ends, however. For example, in 2010 the Democrats introduced an immigration reform package, in the apparent hopes that it would mobilize their support among Latino voters, even though it had little chance of passing or even coming to a vote.

Why Has the Two-Party System Endured?

There are several reasons why two major parties have dominated the political landscape in the United States for almost two centuries. These reasons have to do with (1) the historical foundations of the system, (2) political socialization and practical considerations, (3) the winner-take-all electoral system, and (4) state and federal laws favoring the two-party system.

The Historical Foundations of the Two-Party System

As we have seen, at many times in American history there has been one preeminent issue or dispute that divided the nation politically. In the beginning, Americans were at odds over ratifying the Constitution. After the Constitution went into effect, the power of the federal government became the major national issue. Thereafter, the dispute over slavery divided the nation by section, North versus South. At times—for example, in the North after the Civil War—cultural differences have been important, with advocates of government-sponsored morality (such as banning alcoholic beverages) pitted against advocates of personal liberty.

During much of the twentieth century, economic differences were preeminent. In the New Deal period, the Democrats became known as the party of the working class, while the Republicans became known as the party of the middle and upper classes and commercial interests. When politics is based on an argument between two opposing points of view, advocates of each viewpoint can mobilize most effectively by forming a single, unified party, resulting in a two-party system. When such a system has been in existence for almost two centuries, it becomes difficult to imagine an alternative.

Political Socialization and Practical Considerations

Given that the majority of Americans identify with one of the two major political parties, it is not surprising that most children learn at a fairly young age to think of themselves as either Democrats or Republicans. This generates a built-in mechanism to perpetuate a two-party system. Also, most politically oriented people who aspire to work for change consider that the only realistic way to capture political power in this country is to be either a Republican or a Democrat.

The Winner-Take-All Electoral System

At almost every level of government in the United States, the outcome of elections is based on the **plurality,** winner-take-all principle. In a plurality system, the winner is the person who obtains the most votes, even if that person does not receive a majority (more than 50 percent) of the votes. Whoever gets the most votes gets everything. Most legislators in the United States are elected from single-member districts in which only one person represents the constituency, and the candidate who finishes second in such an election receives nothing for the effort.

Plurality
A number of votes cast for a candidate that is greater than the number of votes for any other candidate but not necessarily a majority.

Electoral College
A group of persons, called electors, who are selected by the voters in each state. This group officially elects the president and the vice president of the United States.

Presidential Voting. The winner-take-all system also operates in the election of the U.S. president. Recall that the voters in each state do not vote for a president directly but vote for **electoral college** delegates who are committed to the various presidential candidates. These delegates are called *electors.*

In all but two states (Maine and Nebraska), if a presidential candidate wins a plurality in the state, then *all* of the state's electoral votes go to that candidate. For example, let us say that the electors pledged to a particular presidential candidate receive a plurality of 40 percent of the votes in a state. That presidential candidate will receive all of the state's votes in the Electoral College. Minor parties have a difficult time competing under such a system. Because voters know that minor parties cannot win any electoral votes, they often will not vote for minor-party candidates, even if the candidates are in tune with them ideologically.

Popular Election of the Governors and the President. In most European countries, the chief executive (usually called the prime minister) is elected by the legislature, or parliament. If the parliament contains three or more parties, as is usually the situation, two or more of the parties can join together in a coalition to choose the prime minister and the other leaders of the government. In the United States, however, the people elect the president and the governors of all fifty states. There is no opportunity for two or more parties to negotiate a coalition. Here, too, the winner-take-all principle discriminates powerfully against any third party.

Proportional Representation. Many other nations use a system of proportional representation with multimember districts. If, during the national election, party X obtains 12 percent of the vote, party Y gets 43 percent of the vote, and party Z gets the remaining 45 percent of the vote, then party X gets 12 percent of the seats in the legislature, party Y gets 43 percent of the seats, and party Z gets 45 percent of the seats. Because even a minor party may still obtain at least a few seats in the legislature, the smaller parties have a greater incentive to organize under such electoral systems than they do in the United States.

Congressional pages carry the Electoral College votes to the House chamber where the election of Barack Obama as the forty-fourth president of the United States was certified on January 8, 2009. What effect does the Electoral College have on the political system? (Bill Clark/*Roll Call*/Getty Images)

The relative effects of proportional representation versus our system of single-member districts are so strong that many scholars have made them one of the few "laws" of political science. "Duverger's Law," named after French political scientist Maurice Duverger, states that electoral systems based on single-member districts tend to produce two parties, while systems of proportional representation produce multiple parties.[10] Still, many countries with single-member districts have more than two political parties—Britain and Canada are examples.

did you know?

That the Reform Party, established in 1996, used a vote-by-mail process for the first step of its nominating convention and also accepted votes cast by e-mail.

State and Federal Laws Favoring the Two Parties

Many state and federal election laws offer a clear advantage to the two major parties. In some states, the established major parties need to gather fewer signatures to place their candidates on the ballot than minor parties or independent candidates do. The criterion for determining how many signatures will be required is often based on the total party vote in the last general election, thus penalizing a new political party that did not compete in that election.

At the national level, minor parties face different obstacles. All of the rules and procedures of both houses of Congress divide committee seats, staff members, and other privileges on the basis of party membership. A legislator who is elected on a minor-party ticket, such as the Conservative Party of New York, must choose to be counted with one of the major parties to obtain a committee assignment. The Federal Election Commission (FEC) rules for campaign financing also place restrictions on minor-party candidates. Such candidates are not eligible for federal matching funds in either the primary or the general election. In the 1980 elections, John Anderson, running for president as an independent, sued the FEC for campaign funds. The commission finally agreed to repay part of his campaign costs after the election in proportion to the votes he received. Giving funds to a candidate when the campaign is over is, of course, much less helpful than providing funds while the campaign is still under way.

The Role of Minor Parties in U.S. Politics

Third Party
A political party other than the two major political parties (Republican and Democratic).

For the reasons just discussed, minor parties have a difficult, if not impossible, time competing within the American two-party political system. Nonetheless, minor parties have played an important role in our political life. Parties other than the Republicans or Democrats are usually called **third parties.** (Technically, of course, there could be fourth, fifth, or sixth parties as well, but we use the term *third party* because it has endured.) Third parties can come into existence in a number of ways. They may be founded from scratch by individuals or groups who are committed to a particular interest, issue, or ideology. They can split off from one of the major parties when a group becomes dissatisfied with the major party's policies. Finally, they can be organized around a particular charismatic leader and serve as that person's vehicle for contesting elections.

Third parties have acted as barometers of changes in the political mood, forcing the major parties to recognize new issues or trends in the thinking of Americans. Political scientists believe that third parties have acted as safety valves for dissident groups, preventing major confrontations and political unrest. In some instances, third parties have functioned as way stations for voters en route from one of the major parties to the other. On the following page, Table 8–2 lists significant third-party presidential campaigns in American history, and Table 8–3 provides a brief description of third-party beliefs.

10. As cited in Todd Landman, *Issues and Methods in Comparative Politics* (New York: Routledge, 2003), p. 14.

TABLE 8–2 The Most Successful Third-Party Presidential Campaigns since 1864

The following list includes all third-party candidates winning more than 5 percent of the popular vote or any electoral votes since 1864. (We ignore isolated "unfaithful electors" in the Electoral College who failed to vote for the candidate to which they were pledged.)

Year	Major Third Party	Third-Party Presidential Candidate	Percent of the Popular Vote	Electoral Votes	Winning Presidential Candidate and Party
1892	Populist	James Weaver	8.5	22	Grover Cleveland (D)
1912	Progressive	Theodore Roosevelt	27.4	88	Woodrow Wilson (D)
	Socialist	Eugene Debs	6.0	—	
1924	Progressive	Robert LaFollette	16.6	13	Calvin Coolidge (R)
1948	States' Rights	Strom Thurmond	2.4	39	Harry Truman (D)
1960	Independent Democrat	Harry Byrd	0.4	15*	John Kennedy (D)
1968	American Independent	George Wallace	13.5	46	Richard Nixon (R)
1980	National Union	John Anderson	6.6	—	Ronald Reagan (R)
1992	Independent	Ross Perot	18.9	—	Bill Clinton (D)
1996	Reform	Ross Perot	8.4	—	Bill Clinton (D)

*Byrd received fifteen electoral votes from unpledged electors in Alabama and Mississippi.

Source: *Dave Leip's Atlas of U.S. Presidential Elections* at **www.uselectionatlas.org**.

Ideological Third Parties

The longest-lived third parties have been those with strong ideological foundations that are typically at odds with the majority mind-set. The Socialist Party is an example. The party was founded in 1901 and lasted until 1972, when it was finally dissolved. (A smaller party later took up the name.) The Socialists were never very popular in the United States. Indeed, the term *socialist* has recently gained currency as a conservative insult directed at President Obama. In Europe, however, socialist parties became very important, and *socialist* is merely a description. We take a look at the "real" socialists in this chapter's *Beyond Our Borders* feature on the following page.

TABLE 8–3 Policies of Selected American Third Parties since 1864

Populist: This pro-farmer party of the 1890s advocated progressive reforms. It also advocated replacing gold with silver as the basis of the currency in hopes of creating a mild inflation in prices. (It was believed by many that inflation would help debtors and stimulate the economy.)

Socialist: This party advocated a "cooperative commonwealth" based on government ownership of industry. It was pro-labor, often antiwar, and in later years, anti-Communist. It was dissolved in 1972 and replaced by nonparty advocacy groups (Democratic Socialists of America and Social Democrats USA).

Communist: This left-wing breakaway from the Socialists was the U.S. branch of the worldwide Communist movement. The party was pro-labor and advocated full equality for African Americans. It was also closely aligned with the Communist-led Soviet Union, which provoked great hostility among most Americans.

Progressive: This name was given to several successive splinter parties built around individual political leaders. Theodore Roosevelt, who ran in 1912, advocated federal regulation of industry to protect consumers, workers, and small businesses. Robert LaFollette, who ran in 1924, held similar views.

American Independent: Built around George Wallace, this party opposed any further promotion of civil rights and advocated a militant foreign policy. Wallace's supporters were mostly former Democrats who were soon to be Republicans.

Libertarian: This party opposes most government activity.

Reform: The Reform Party was initially built around businessman Ross Perot but later was taken over by others. Under Perot, the party was a middle-of-the-road group opposed to federal budget deficits. Under Patrick Buchanan, it came to represent right-wing nationalism and opposition to free trade.

Green: The Greens are a left-of-center pro-environmental party. They are also generally hostile to globalization.

Ideology has at least two functions. First, the members of the minor party regard themselves as outsiders and look to one another for support; ideology provides great psychological cohesiveness. Second, because the rewards of ideological commitment are partly psychological, these minor parties do not think in terms of immediate electoral success. A poor showing at the polls does not dissuade either the leadership or the grassroots participants from continuing their quest for change in American government (and, ultimately, American society).

Currently active ideological parties include the Libertarian Party and the Green Party. As you learned in Chapter 1, the Libertarian Party supports a *laissez-faire* ("let it be") capitalist economic program, together with a hands-off policy on regulating matters of moral conduct. The Green Party began as a grassroots environmentalist organization with affiliated political parties across North America and Western Europe. It was established in the United States as a national party in 1996 and nominated Ralph Nader to run for president in 2000. Nader campaigned against what he called "corporate greed," advocated universal health insurance, and promoted environmental concerns.[11] He ran again for president as an independent in 2004 and 2008.

Splinter Party
A new party formed by a dissident faction within a major political party. Often, splinter parties have emerged when a particular personality was at odds with the major party.

Splinter Parties

Some of the most successful minor parties have been those that split from major parties. The impetus for these **splinter parties,** or factions, has usually been a situation in which a particular personality was at odds with the major party. The most successful of these

11. Ralph Nader offers his own entertaining account of his run for the presidency in 2000 in *Crashing the Party: How to Tell the Truth and Still Run for President* (New York: St. Martin's Press, 2002).

BEYOND OUR BORDERS

THE REAL SOCIALISTS

Not many American politicians accept the Socialist label, although Vermont senator Bernie Sanders answers to it. In most Western European nations, however, the main left-of-center party comes out of the Socialist tradition. Examples include the British Labour Party, the Socialist Party of France, and the Social Democratic Party of Germany. A hundred years ago, these parties were much more radical than they are today. Most called for the abolition of capitalism. Instead, the state, democratically elected by the people, would own the factories and shops, the banks and railroads. (Some Socialists advocated ownership by employee cooperatives instead.) Karl Marx was a patron saint of the movement. Many of these parties—most notably the British Labour Party—were tightly linked to labor unions.

From 1918 to 1920, some of the radical fervor left the Socialist parties as revolutionaries withdrew to form the new Communist movement. In Russia, the Communists actually succeeded in replacing capitalism with government ownership, but their methods were so brutal as to taint everything they did. In time, experiments revealed that government ownership of businesses was not helpful in democratic countries, either. In the years following World War II, one by one the Socialist parties formally gave up the goal of replacing capitalism. What was left was a commitment to a strong welfare state and to the labor movement.

Despite their growing moderation, substantial differences remain between Western European Socialists and American liberals. Socialists continue to champion a much larger and more active government than liberals ever would. European tax burdens prove the point.

FOR CRITICAL ANALYSIS

Socialist parties were far more effective at winning elections after World War II than before the war. What might have been the reason?

splinter parties was the Bull Moose Progressive Party, formed in 1912 to support Theodore Roosevelt for president. The Republican national convention of that year denied Roosevelt the nomination, despite the fact that he had won most of the primaries. He therefore left the Republicans and ran against Republican "regular" William Howard Taft in the general election. Although Roosevelt did not win the election, he did split the Republican vote, enabling Democrat Woodrow Wilson to become president.

Third parties have also been formed to back individual candidates who were not rebelling against a particular party. H. Ross Perot, for example, who challenged Republican George H. W. Bush and Democrat Bill Clinton in 1992, had not previously been active in a major party. Perot's supporters probably would have split their votes between Bush and Clinton had Perot not been in the race. In theory, Perot ran in 1992 as a nonparty independent; in practice, he had to create a campaign organization. By 1996, Perot's organization was formalized as the Reform Party.

Eugene V. Debs, a union leader, became a Socialist around 1895. He unsuccessfully ran for president of the United States as a Socialist several times. Why have Socialists had such a hard time gaining public support in this country? (AP Photo)

The Impact of Minor Parties

Third parties have rarely been able to affect American politics by actually winning elections. (One exception is that third-party and independent candidates have occasionally won races for state governorships—for example, Jesse Ventura was elected governor of Minnesota on the Reform Party ticket in 1998.) Instead, the impact of third parties has taken two forms. First, third parties can influence one of the major parties to take up one or more issues. Second, third parties can determine the outcome of a particular election by pulling votes from one of the major-party candidates in what is called the "spoiler effect."

Influencing the Major Parties. One of the most clear-cut examples of a major party adopting the issues of a minor party took place in 1896, when the Democratic Party took over the Populist demand for "free silver"—that is, a policy of coining enough new money to create an inflation. As you learned on page 255, however, absorbing the Populists cost the Democrats votes overall.

Affecting the Outcome of an Election. The presidential elections of 2000 were one instance in which a minor party may have altered the outcome. Green candidate Ralph Nader received almost 100,000 votes in Florida, a majority of which would probably have gone to Democrat Al Gore if Nader had not been in the race.

The real question, however, is not whether the Nader vote had an effect—clearly, it did—but whether the effect was important. The problem is that in elections as close as the presidential elections of 2000, *any* factor with an impact on the outcome can be said to have determined the results of the elections. Discussing his landslide loss to Democrat Lyndon Johnson in 1964, Republican Barry Goldwater wrote, "When you've lost an election by that much, it isn't the case of whether you made the wrong speech or wore the wrong necktie. It was just the wrong time."[12] With the opposite situation, a humorist might speculate that Gore would have won the election had he worn a better tie! Nevertheless, given that Nader garnered almost 3 million votes, many believe that the Nader campaign was an important reason for Gore's loss.

Mechanisms of Political Change

In the future, could one of the two parties decisively overtake the other and become the "natural party of government"? The Republicans held this status from 1896 until 1932, and the Democrats enjoyed it for many years after the election of Franklin D. Roosevelt in 1932.

12. Barry Goldwater, *With No Apologies* (New York: William Morrow, 1979).

Realignment
A process in which a substantial group of voters switches party allegiance, producing a long-term change in the political landscape.

Dealignment
A decline in party loyalties that reduces long-term party commitment.

Party Identification
Linking oneself to a particular political party.

Realignment

One mechanism by which a party might gain dominance is called **realignment.** In this process, major constituencies shift their allegiance from one party to another, creating a long-term alteration in the political environment. Realignment has often been associated with particular elections, called *realigning elections.* The election of 1896, which established a Republican ascendancy, was clearly a realigning election. So was the election of 1932, which made the Democrats the leading party.

Realignments in American Politics. A number of myths exist about the concept of realignment. One is that in realignment, a newly dominant party must replace the previously dominant party. Actually, realignment could easily strengthen an already dominant party. Alternatively, realignment could result in a tie. This has happened—twice. One example was the realignment of the 1850s, which resulted in Abraham Lincoln's election as president in 1860. After the Civil War, the Republicans and the Democrats were almost evenly matched nationally.

The most recent realignment—which also resulted in two closely matched parties—was a gradual process that took place over many years. In 1968, Republican presidential candidate Richard Nixon adopted a "southern strategy" aimed at drawing dissatisfied southern Democrats into the Republican Party.[13] At the presidential level, the strategy was an immediate success, although years would pass before the Republicans could gain dominance in the South's delegation to Congress or in state legislatures. Another milestone in the progress of the Republican realignment was Ronald Reagan's sweeping victory in the presidential elections of 1980.

Is Realignment Still Possible? The sheer size of our nation, combined with the inexorable pressure toward a two-party system, has resulted in parties made up of voters with conflicting interests or values. The pre–Civil War party system involved two parties—Whigs and Democrats—with support in both the North and the South. This system could survive only by burying, as deeply as possible, the issue of slavery. We should not be surprised that the structure eventually collapsed. The Republican ascendancy of 1896–1932 united capitalists and industrial workers under the Republican banner, despite serious economic conflicts between the two. The New Deal Democratic coalition after 1932 brought African Americans and ardent segregationists into the same party.

For realignment to occur, a substantial body of citizens must come to believe that their party can no longer represent their interests or values. The problem must be fundamental and not attributable to the behavior of an individual politician. Despite the divisions within the parties discussed earlier, it is not easy to identify groups of Republicans or Democrats today who might reach such a conclusion.

Dealignment

Among political scientists, one common argument has been that realignment is no longer likely because voters are not as committed to the two major parties as they were in the 1800s and early 1900s. In this view, called **dealignment** theory, large numbers of independent voters may result in political volatility, but the absence of strong partisan attachments means that it is no longer easy to "lock in" political preferences for decades.

Independent Voters. Figure 8–3 on the facing page shows trends in **party identification,** as measured by standard polling techniques from 1944 to the present. The chart displays a

13. The classic work on Nixon's southern strategy is Kirkpatrick Sales, *The Emerging Republican Majority* (New Rochelle, N.Y.: Arlington House, 1969).

FIGURE 8–3 Party Identification from 1944 to the Present

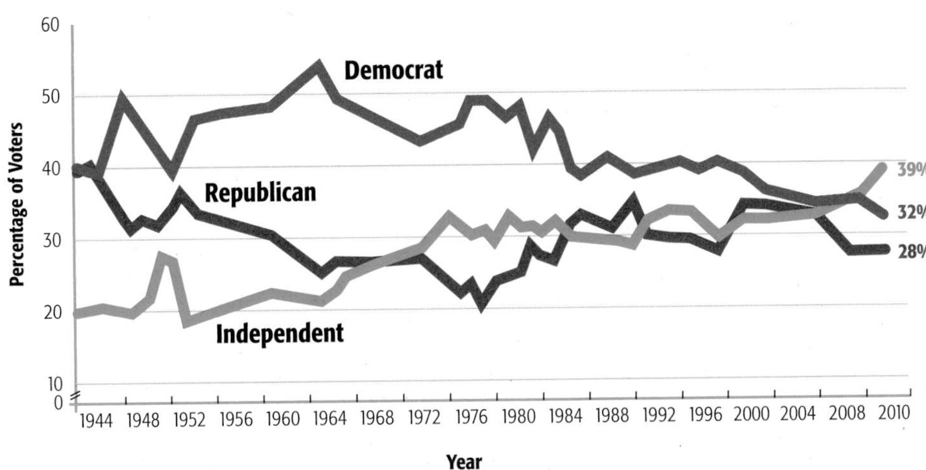

Sources: *Gallup Report,* August 1995; *New York Times*/CBS poll, June 1996; *Gallup Report,* February 1998; The Pew Research Center for the People and the Press, November 2003; Gallup polls, 2004 through 2010.

rise in the number of independent voters throughout the period combined with a fall in support for the Democrats from the mid-1960s on. The decline in Democratic identification may be due to the consolidation of Republican support in the South since 1968, a process that by now is substantially complete. In any event, the traditional Democratic advantage in party identification has largely vanished.

Not only has the number of independents grown over the last half century, but voters are also less willing to vote a straight ticket—that is, to vote for all the candidates of one party. In the early twentieth century, **straight-ticket voting** was nearly universal. By midcentury, 12 percent of voters engaged in **split-ticket voting**—voting for candidates of two or more parties for different offices, such as voting for a Republican presidential candidate and a Democratic congressional candidate. By the 1970s and 1980s, 25 to 30 percent of all ballots cast in presidential election years were split-ticket. A major reason was that many voters, especially in the South, were pairing a Republican for president with a conservative Democrat for Congress. In recent years, conservative Democrats have become scarce, and the incidence of split-ticket voting has ranged only from 17 to 19 percent.

Straight-Ticket Voting
Voting exclusively for the candidates of one party.

Split-Ticket Voting
Voting for candidates of two or more parties for different offices, such as voting for a Republican presidential candidate and a Democratic congressional candidate.

Swing Voters
Voters who frequently swing their support from one party to another.

Not-So-Independent Voters. A problem with dealignment theory is that many of the "independent" voters are not all that independent. For some time, about one-third of the voters who classified themselves as independents typically voted Democratic, and another one-third typically voted Republican. The remaining third consisted of true independents and became known as **swing voters**—they could swing back and forth between the parties.

By 2008, the Democratic-leaning share of the independent vote had risen as high as 50 percent, with the Republicans at 40 percent, and only about 10 percent remaining as true independents. By the spring of 2010, however, the parties were roughly even again, with about 40 percent of independents leaning to the Democrats, 40 percent leaning to the Republicans, and 20 percent as true independents.

The relatively modest number of true independents—currently less than a tenth of the total electorate—raises a strategic question for the parties. Is it more important to sway the independents, or can a party obtain better results by improving voter turnout among its natural supporters? We look at that issue in this chapter's *Politics of Boom and Bust* feature on the following page.

Tipping
A phenomenon that occurs when a group that is becoming more numerous over time grows large enough to change the political balance in a district, state, or country.

Tipping

Political transformation can also result from changes in the composition of the electorate. Even when groups of voters never change their party preferences, if one group becomes more numerous over time, it can become dominant for that reason alone. We call this kind of demographically based change **tipping.**

THE POLITICS OF BOOM AND BUST

THE IMPORTANCE OF INDEPENDENT VOTERS

True independents make up a relatively small share of the voters. In April 2010, a Gallup poll placed only 9 percent of its respondents in that category. A political strategy aimed at winning independents can therefore involve a tremendous effort to change the votes of a handful of people.

As it happens, the change in voter turnout from one election to the next exceeds the size of the true independent vote. Turnout in the presidential election year of 2008 was 62.3 percent. In 2006, an off-year with only senators and representatives on the national ballot, turnout was only 40.3 percent. That's a difference of 22 percent. This raises the questions: Do politicians need to care about independents? Might they be better off if they concentrated on turning out members of their "base," their most loyal supporters?

Karl Rove, President George W. Bush's chief political adviser, believed the answer was "yes." In the years leading up to the 2004 presidential elections, he recommended that Bush make no attempt to win over moderates, but to concentrate instead on motivating Republicans to come out and vote. In 2004, this was a successful strategy.

THE RETURN OF THE INDEPENDENTS

Beginning in 2006, however, such a strategy was no longer as effective. Politically, the years from 2000 to 2005 had been relatively quiet ones. Many things occurred in the world at large, beginning with the terrorist attacks of September 11, 2001, but few of these events seemed to push independents toward one party or the other. By 2006, however, many independents were angry with the Republicans over the war in Iraq. After the onset of the Great Recession and the financial crisis of September 2008, the independent vote was in play to an extent that had not been seen in years. In a time of economic crisis, in other words, the independent vote can decide elections.

Of course, political mobilization continues to be important. Obama's victory was guaranteed by high turnout among young, Latino, and African American voters—Democrats outvoted Republicans by about four to three in 2008. Obama's large win was confirmed, however, when he carried the independent vote by 52 to 44 percent. Independents were even more important in January 2010, when Republican Scott Brown won a special election to fill the late Democrat Ted Kennedy's old Senate seat. Brown carried independents by a stunning 64 to 34 percent. True, turnout matters, but no one will be able to ignore the independent vote as long as elections are dominated by the politics of boom and bust.

WHY THEY SWING

In theory, independent voters could possess a coherent set of independent ideas distinct from conservatism or liberalism. Many independents would accept such a description. Leading analysts disagree, however. Democrat George Lakoff, a cognitive scientist, contends that independents are capable of responding to either liberal or conservative arguments. Lakoff believes that independents carry both liberal and conservative value systems around in their heads, and either value system may be triggered, depending on context and language. For example, certain words, such as *taxes,* typically trigger the conservative value system. Republican analyst Frank Luntz makes similar arguments. As long as independents can be swayed by both progressive and conservative value systems, they will swing between the parties.

FOR CRITICAL ANALYSIS

How might a candidate increase the probability that her or his message appeals to independent voters?

Tipping in Massachusetts and California. Consider Massachusetts, where for generations Irish Catholics confronted Protestant Yankees in the political arena. Most of the Yankees were Republicans; most of the Irish were Democrats. The Yankees were numerically dominant from the founding of the state until 1928. In that year, for the first time, Democratic Irish voters came to outnumber the Republican Yankees. Massachusetts, which previously had been one of the most solidly Republican states, became one of the most reliably Democratic states in the nation.

California may have experienced a tipping effect during the 1990s. From 1952 through 1988, California normally supported Republican presidential candidates. Since 1992, however, no Republican presidential candidate has managed to carry California. The improved performance of the Democrats in California is almost certainly a function of demography. In 1999, California became the third state, after Hawaii and New Mexico, in which non-Hispanic whites do not make up a majority of the population.

Tipping in the Twenty-First Century? It is possible that states other than California may tip to a different party in future years. John B. Judis and Ruy Teixeira have argued that the Democrats are poised to become the new majority party due to a growth in the number of liberal professionals and Hispanic immigrants.[14] This thesis attracted much ridicule prior to 2006, as the Republicans continued to triumph in midterm and presidential elections. By 2008, however, the thesis had become more credible. In that year, a growing Hispanic vote clearly pushed several southwestern states, such as Nevada and Colorado, into the Democratic column, while larger numbers of upscale urban voters in the suburbs of Washington, D.C., helped Obama carry the traditionally Republican state of Virginia.

---

14. John B. Judis and Ruy Teixeira, *The Emerging Democratic Majority* (New York: Scribner, 2004).

Republican Scott Brown won a special election in January 2010 to represent Massachusetts in the U.S. Senate. His seat was once held by the late Edward (Ted) Kennedy, a Democratic legend. Brown's victory deprived the Democrats of their 60-vote majority in the Senate. (AP Photo/Cliff Owen)

WHY SHOULD YOU CARE ABOUT... POLITICAL PARTIES?

Why should you, as an individual, care about political parties? The most exciting political party event, staged every four years, is the national convention. State conventions also take place on a regular basis. These may seem like remote activities. Surprising as it might seem, though, there are opportunities for the individual voter to become involved in nominating delegates to a state or national convention or to become a delegate.

YOU CAN BE A CONVENTION DELEGATE

How would you like to exercise a small amount of real political power yourself—power that goes beyond simply voting in an election? You might be able to become a delegate to a county, district, or even state party convention. Many of these conventions nominate candidates for various offices. For example, in Michigan, the state party conventions nominate the candidates for the Board of Regents of the state's three top public universities. The regents set university policies, so these are nominations in which students have an obvious interest. In Michigan, if you are elected as a party precinct delegate, you can attend your party's state convention.

In much of the country, there are more openings for district-level delegates than there are people willing to serve. In such circumstances, almost anyone can become a delegate by collecting a handful of signatures on a nominating petition or by mounting a small-scale write-in campaign. You are then eligible to take part in one of the most educational political experiences available to an ordinary citizen. You will get a firsthand look at how political persuasion takes place, how resolutions are written and passed, and how candidates seek out support among their fellow party members. In some states, party caucuses bring debate even closer to the grassroots level.

A North Carolina delegate holds up a sign after Democratic presidential nominee Barack Obama (D., Ill.) gave his speech during the 2008 Democratic National Convention in Denver. (AP Photo/Matt Sayles)

HOW YOU CAN MAKE A DIFFERENCE

When the parties choose delegates for the national convention, the process begins at the local level—either the congressional district or the state legislative district. Delegates may be elected in party primary elections or chosen in neighborhood or precinct caucuses. Persons who want to run for delegate positions must first file petitions with the local board of elections. If you are interested in committing yourself to a particular presidential candidate and running for the delegate position, check with the local county committee or with the party's national committee about the rules you must follow.

It is even easier to get involved in the grassroots politics of presidential caucuses. In some states, delegates are first nominated at the local precinct caucus. According to the rules of the Iowa caucuses, anyone can participate in a caucus if he or she is eighteen years old, a precinct resident, and registered as a party member. These caucuses select delegates to the county conventions who are pledged to specific presidential candidates. This is the first step toward the national convention.

At the county caucus and the convention levels, both parties try to find younger members to fill some of the seats. Contact the state or county political party to find out when the caucuses or primaries will be held. Then gather local supporters, and prepare to join in an occasion during which political debate is at its best.

For further information about these opportunities, contact the state party office or your local state legislator. You can also contact the national committee for information on how to become a delegate.

Republican National Committee
www.gop.org

Democratic National Committee
www.democrats.org

questions for discussion and analysis

1. In America, party candidates for national office are typically chosen through primary elections. In some other countries, a party's central committee picks the party's candidates. How might primary elections limit the ability of political parties to present a united front on the issues?
2. Do you support (or lean toward) one of the major political parties today? If so, would you have supported the same party in the late 1800s—or would you have supported a different party? Explain your reasoning.
3. During 2009 and 2010, what political developments had an impact on the support that voters gave to the Republican and Democratic parties? To what extent were the Republicans able to take advantage of the unpopularity of the Democrats?
4. Suppose that the United States Supreme Court were to reverse itself on *Roe v. Wade,* with the result that abortions became illegal in many states. What impact do you think such a ruling might have on Republicans with strongly libertarian beliefs? How likely is it that some of these Republicans might leave the party?

key terms

dealignment 276
Democratic Party 254
divided government 268
Electoral College 271
era of good feelings 253
faction 251
independent 251
national committee 265
national convention 265
party identification 276
party-in-government 263
party-in-the-electorate 263
party organization 263
party platform 265
patronage 267
plurality 271
political party 251
realignment 276
Republican Party 254
reverse-income effect 261
splinter party 274
split-ticket voting 277
state central committee 267
straight-ticket voting 277
swing voters 277
third party 272
tipping 278
two-party system 252
Whig Party 254

chapter summary

1. A political party is a group of political activists who organize to win elections, operate the government, and determine public policy. Political parties recruit candidates for public office, organize and run elections, present alternative policies to the voters, assume responsibility for operating the government, and act as the opposition to the party in power.
2. The evolution of our nation's political parties can be divided into seven periods: (a) the creation and formation of political parties from 1789 to 1816; (b) the era of one-party rule, or personal politics, from 1816 to 1828; (c) the period from Andrew Jackson's presidency to the eve of the Civil War, from 1828 to 1856; (d) the Civil War and post–Civil War period, from 1856 to 1896; (e) the Republican ascendancy and progressive period, from 1896 to 1932; (f) the New Deal period, from 1932 to about 1968; and (g) the modern period, from approximately 1968 to the present. Throughout most of the modern period, the parties have been closely matched in strength.
3. Many of the differences between the two parties date from the time of Franklin D. Roosevelt's New Deal. The Democrats have advocated government action to help labor and minorities, and the Republicans have championed self-reliance and limited government. The constituents of the two parties continue to differ. A close look at policies actually enacted, however, suggests that despite rhetoric to the contrary, in recent years both parties have supported a large and active government. Today, cultural differences are at least as important as economic issues in determining party allegiance.
4. A political party consists of three components: the party-in-the-electorate, the party organization, and the party-in-government. Each party component maintains

linkages to the others to keep the party strong. Each level of the party—local, state, and national—has considerable autonomy. The national party organization is responsible for holding the national convention in presidential election years, writing the party platform, choosing the national committee, and conducting party business.

5. The party-in-government comprises all of the elected and appointed officeholders of a party. Increased ideological coherence in both major parties has resulted in growing political polarization.

6. Two major parties have dominated the political landscape in the United States for almost two centuries. The reasons for this include (a) the historical foundations of the system, (b) political socialization and practical considerations, (c) the winner-take-all electoral system, and (d) state and federal laws favoring the two-party system. For these reasons, minor parties have found it extremely difficult to win elections.

7. Minor, or third, parties have emerged from time to time, sometimes as dissatisfied splinter groups from within major parties, and have acted as barometers of changes in the political mood. Splinter parties have emerged when a particular personality was at odds with the major party, as when Theodore Roosevelt's differences with the Republican Party resulted in the formation of the Bull Moose Progressive Party. Other minor parties, such as the Socialist Party, have formed around specific issues or ideologies. Third parties can affect the political process (even if they do not win) if major parties adopt their issues or if they determine which major party wins an election.

8. One mechanism of political change is realignment, in which major blocs of voters switch allegiance from one party to another. Realignments were manifested in the elections of 1896 and 1932. Some scholars speak of dealignment—that is, the loss of strong party attachments. In fact, during the past fifty years, the share of the voters who describe themselves as independents has grown, and the share of self-identified Democrats has shrunk. Many independents actually vote as if they were Democrats or Republicans, however. Demographic change can also "tip" a district or state from one party to another.

selected print & media resources

SUGGESTED READINGS

Amato, Theresa. *Grand Illusion: The Fantasy of Voter Choice in a Two-Party Tyranny.* New York: The New Press, 2009. As Ralph Nader's campaign manager during his 2000 and 2004 presidential runs, Amato was in an excellent position to see how the political system makes it almost impossible for third-party candidates to succeed. She also examines the experiences of other challengers, including John Anderson, Ross Perot, and Pat Buchanan.

Callahan, David. *Fortunes of Change: The Rise of the Liberal Rich and the Remaking of America.* Hoboken, N.J.: Wiley, 2010. Callahan analyzes the surprising growth in support for the Democrats among the very richest Americans. He describes what these people want out of politics and how their rise affects ordinary Democrats and Republicans.

Conroy, Scott, and Shushannah Walshe. *Sarah from Alaska: The Sudden Rise and Brutal Education of a New Conservative Superstar.* New York: PublicAffairs, 2010. Like most political autobiographies, Sarah Palin's *Going Rogue* conceals as much as it reveals. In *Sarah from Alaska,* two reporters from Palin's home state attempt to present a more accurate, but not unsympathetic, picture of the political right's most charismatic new figure.

Dochuk, Darren. *From Bible Belt to Sunbelt: Plain-Folk Religion, Grassroots Politics, and the Rise of Evangelical Conservatism.* New York: W. W. Norton & Co., 2010. Dochuk uses new research to describe the impact of evangelicals on the conservative movement from the Barry Goldwater years to the time of Ronald Reagan. The book won the Allan Nevins prize awarded by the Society of American Historians.

Heilemann, John, and Mark Halperin. *Game Change: Obama and the Clintons, McCain and Palin, and the Race of a Lifetime.* New York: HarperCollins, 2010. *Game Change* is widely regarded as *the* insider's account of the 2008 presidential elections. Smoothly written, it is filled with tidbits of information that made headlines when the book was released.

MEDIA RESOURCES

The American President—A 1995 film starring Michael Douglas as a president who must balance partisanship and friendship (Republicans in Congress promise to approve the president's crime bill only if he modifies an environmental plan sponsored by his liberal girlfriend).

Last Man Standing: Politics, Texas Style—This 2004 documentary covers the 2002 race for governor of Texas and a battle for a state representative seat between a Democratic greenhorn and a hardened Republican veteran. Interviews feature Republican strategist Karl Rove and the late liberal columnist Molly Ivans.

Mr. Conservative: Goldwater on Goldwater—As the 1964 Republican presidential candidate, Arizona senator Barry Goldwater lost by a landslide. His conservative philosophy, however, transformed the Republican Party and triumphed in 1980 with the victory of Republican candidate Ronald Reagan. This 2006 production includes interviews with columnist George Will, United States Supreme Court Justice Sandra Day O'Connor, and others.

So Goes the Nation—As one observer correctly put it during the 2004 presidential elections, "As goes Ohio, so goes the nation." This 2006 film provides a close-up of the Republican and Democratic presidential campaigns in that state. Viewers come away with a better understanding of the two major parties.

A Third Choice—A film that examines America's experience with third parties and independent candidates throughout the nation's political history.

e-mocracy

POLITICAL PARTIES AND THE INTERNET

Today's political parties use the Internet to attract voters, organize campaigns, obtain campaign contributions, and the like. Voters, in turn, can go online to learn more about specific parties and their programs. Those who use the Internet for information on the parties, though, need to exercise some caution. Even the official party sites are filled with misinformation or outright lies about the policies and leaders of the other party. Besides the parties' official sites, there are satirical sites mimicking the parties, sites distributing misleading information about the parties, and sites that are raising money for their own causes rather than for political parties.

LOGGING ON

The political parties all have Web sites. The Democratic Party is online at
www.democrats.org

The Republican National Committee is at
www.gop.org

The Libertarian Party has a Web site located at
www.lp.org

The Green Party of the United States can be found at
www.gp.org

The Pew Research Center for the People and the Press offers survey data online on how the parties fared during the most recent elections, voter typology, and numerous other issues. To access this site, go to
people-press.org

chapter 9

Campaigns, Elections, and the Media

chapter contents

Well-known entertainers often participate in political campaigns, especially those for president. In this photo, Bruce Springsteen performs on the campus of Ohio State University in Columbus. Springsteen was in town to encourage Obama supporters to register to vote. (AP Photo/Terry Gilliam)

WHAT IF... ...there were no newspapers?

Local newspapers, such as the Minneapolis/St. Paul *Star Tribune*, have lost readership regularly for several years. Could all local newspapers disappear? (AP Photo/Jim Mone)

BACKGROUND

At the end of the Revolutionary War, Americans could buy any of a total of forty-three newspapers. By 1910, newspapers throughout the country looked much as they do today. Currently, however, many newspapers face extinction. Great newspapers in Chicago, Minneapolis, Philadelphia, and other cities have filed for bankruptcy protection. Some, such as the *Baltimore Examiner* and the *Cincinnati Post*, have folded completely. Some people have speculated that, ultimately, newspapers will disappear altogether. What would such a world look like?

WHAT IF THERE WERE NO NEWSPAPERS?

The trend is already here. Since 1994, the share of Americans saying they read a daily newspaper has dropped from almost 60 percent to around 30 percent. If this trend continues, newspapers could for the most part vanish. Gone, too, would be their reporters and management.

By 2008, for the first time, more people obtained their national and international news from the Internet than from newspapers. Obviously, without newspapers, everyone would obtain their news from the Internet, broadcast and cable television, and to a lesser extent, news magazines. Without newspapers, these other sources of news would increase in size, scope, and availability.

THE DEATH OF THE STANDARD NEWS PACKAGE

When you open a metropolitan newspaper today, it has a "newspaper look." When you visit that newspaper's Web site, it often has the same look, one that dates back a hundred years. You'll find a mixture of local, national, business, sports, and international news, plus weather forecasts. What you see online is not much different from what is in print, albeit easier perhaps to access.

If newspapers disappeared, the conventional news package also would disappear. People would find their news using online portals such as Yahoo! and Google News. Their news format consists of headlines, a sentence, and a link. Such operations are cheap to run. Google News has no editors as such—everything is automated. Of course, if newspapers disappeared, Google News would not be able to access newspaper stories. Such stories would have to be found elsewhere online.

NEWS BLOGS AND CABLE NEWS CHANNELS WOULD GAIN VIEWERS

Without newspapers, news blogs would grow. Currently, the Huffington Post (nicknamed HuffPo) has four reporters and a total staff of sixty. It has an unpaid army of about three thousand bloggers. Without newspapers, such news blogs would proliferate.

As of 2010, Fox News was the most popular cable news channel, but we also have MSNBC, CNN, and others. Without newspapers, more people would obtain some of their news from these cable sources. New cable news channels might pop up to serve niche audiences.

LOCAL NEWS WITHOUT NEWSPAPERS

Newspaper owners claim that it is not possible to obtain local news without the services of a local newspaper. Yet start-up companies are now creating "hyperlocal" news sites. These sites let people zoom in on what is happening in their neighborhoods. Check out **www.patch.com**, **outside.in**, and **www.everyblock.com**. These sites collect links to articles and blogs and often obtain data from municipal governments and other local sources.

FOR CRITICAL ANALYSIS

1. Would the quality of news gathering diminish if newspapers no longer existed?
2. Many news blogs are definitely biased, and often proud of it. Should this attitude worry us? Why or why not?

Free elections are the cornerstone of the American political system. Voters choose one candidate over another to hold political office by casting ballots in local, state, and federal elections. In 2008, the voters chose Barack Obama and Joe Biden to be president and vice president of the United States for the following four years. In 2010, voters elected all of the members of the House of Representatives and one-third of the members of the Senate. The campaigns were bitter, long, and expensive.

Voters and candidates frequently criticize the American electoral process. It is said to favor wealthier candidates, to further the aims of special interest groups, and to be dominated by older voters and those with better education and higher incomes. The most recent reforms of the campaign-finance laws were tested for the first time in 2004. Although the reforms had some effect on campaign strategy, fund-raising outside the system and extensive use of television advertising dominated the election season. Since then, campaign fund-raising has grown by leaps and bounds while the United States Supreme Court has progressively reduced the scope of the reforms.

The media play a major role in the political process and in election campaigns. Even though newspapers have become less important, new forms of media have taken their place, as we explained in the opening *What If . . .* feature. The role of the media is discussed in greater depth later in this chapter.

Who Wants to Be a Candidate?

There are thousands of elective offices in the United States. The major political parties strive to provide a slate of candidates for every election. Recruiting candidates is easier for some offices than for others. Political parties may have difficulty finding candidates for the board of the local water control district, for example, but they generally have a sufficient number of candidates for county commissioner or sheriff. The "higher" the office and the more prestige attached to it, the more candidates are likely to want to run. In many areas of the country, however, one political party may be considerably stronger than the other. In those situations, the minority party may have more difficulty finding nominees for elections in which victory is unlikely.

Presidential Primary
A statewide primary election of delegates to a political party's national convention, held to determine a party's presidential nominee.

The presidential campaign provides the most colorful and exciting look at candidates and how they prepare to compete for office—in this instance, the highest office in the land. The men and women who wanted to be candidates in the 2008 presidential campaign faced a long and obstacle-filled path. First, they needed to raise sufficient funds to tour the nation, particularly the states with early **presidential primaries,** to see if they had enough local supporters. They needed funds to create an organization and win primary votes. Finally, when they were nominated as their parties' candidates, they required funds to finance a successful campaign for president. Always, at every turn, there was the question of whether they had enough funds to effectively compete against their opponents.

Former Minnesota Governor Tim Pawlenty on the left is shown with former Massachusetts Governor Mitt Romney. Why do individuals seek public office? (AP Photo/Craig Lassig, File)

Why They Run

People who choose to run for office can be divided into two groups—the "self-starters" and those who are recruited. The volunteers, or self-starters, get involved in political activities to further their careers, to carry out specific political programs, or in response to certain issues or events.

Former Alaska Governor Sarah Palin on the right showing her support for South Carolina gubernatorial candidate Nikki Haley at the Statehouse in Columbia in 2010, Haley won. Why do some politicians support the candidacy of other politicians? (AP Photo/Mary Ann Chastain, File)

Self-interest and personal goals—status, career objectives, prestige, and income—are central in motivating some candidates to enter political life. A lawyer or an insurance agent may run for office only once or twice and then return to private life with enhanced status. Other politicians may aspire to long-term political office. For example, an office such as county sheriff is in itself a career goal. Finally, ambition is a major motivator for those seeking higher office.

The Nomination Process

Individuals become official candidates through the process of nomination. Generally, nominating processes for all offices are controlled by state laws and usually favor the two major political parties. For most minor offices, individuals become candidates by submitting petitions to the local election board. In most states, a candidate from one of the two major parties faces far fewer requirements to get on the ballot than a candidate who is an independent or who represents a minor or new party.

The American system of nominations and primary elections is one of the most complex in the world. In a majority of European nations, the political party's choice of candidates is final, and no primary elections are ever held.

Who Is Eligible?

There are few constitutional restrictions on who can become a candidate in the United States. As set out in the Constitution, the formal requirements for national office are as follows:

1. *President.* Must be a natural-born citizen, have attained the age of thirty-five years, and be a resident of the country for fourteen years by the time of inauguration.
2. *Vice president.* Must be a natural-born citizen, have attained the age of thirty-five years, and not be a resident of the same state as the candidate for president.[1]
3. *Senator.* Must be a citizen for at least nine years, have attained the age of thirty by the time of taking office, and be a resident of the state from which elected.
4. *Representative.* Must be a citizen for at least seven years, have attained the age of twenty-five by the time of taking office, and be a resident of the state from which elected.

New York Senator Hillary Clinton is shown in her first joint public appearance with then Illinois Senator Barack Obama after Obama won the 2008 Democratic presidential primary race. What was historic about this photo? (AP Photo/Elise Amendola)

The qualifications for state legislators are set by the state constitutions and likewise include age, place of residence, and citizenship. (Usually, the requirements for the upper chamber of a legislature are somewhat more stringent than those for the lower chamber.) The legal qualifications for running for governor or other state office are similar.

Who Runs?

In spite of these minimal legal qualifications for office at both the national and state levels, a quick look at the slate of candidates in any election—or at the current members of the U.S. House of Representatives—will reveal that not all segments of the population take advantage of these opportunities. Holders of political office in the United States are predominantly white and male. Until the twentieth century, presidential candidates were exclusively of northern European origin

1. Technically, a presidential and vice-presidential candidate on the same ticket can be from the same state, but if they are, one of the two must forfeit the electoral votes of his or her home state.

and of Protestant heritage.[2] Laws that effectively denied voting rights made it impossible to elect African American public officials in many areas in which African Americans constituted a significant portion of the population. As a result of the passage of major civil rights legislation in the 1960s, however, the number of African American public officials has increased throughout the United States, and in a groundbreaking vote, the nation elected an African American president in 2008.

2008 Republican presidential hopefuls included former Massachusetts Governor Mitt Romney on the left, Arizona Senator John McCain in the middle, and former Arkansas Governor Mike Huckabee. Who ultimately prevailed? (AP Photo/ Mary Ann Chastain)

Women as Candidates. Until recently, women generally were considered to be appropriate candidates only for lower-level offices, such as state legislator or school board member. The last twenty years have seen a tremendous increase in the number of women who run for office, not only at the state level but for the U.S. Congress as well. Figure 9–1 on the next page shows the increase in female candidates. In 2010, 154 women ran for the House or Senate on major party tickets, and 89 were elected. Today, a majority of Americans say they would vote for a qualified woman for president of the United States.[3] Indeed, Hillary Clinton came close to winning the Democratic presidential nomination in 2008, a year in which the eventual Democratic nominee was favored to win the general election.

Lawyers as Candidates. Candidates are likely to be professionals, particularly lawyers. Political campaigning and officeholding are simply easier for some occupational groups than for others, and political involvement can make a valuable contribution to certain careers. Lawyers, for example, have more flexible schedules than do many other professionals, can take time off for campaigning, and can leave their jobs to hold public office full-time. Furthermore, holding political office is good publicity for their professional practice. Perhaps most important, many jobs that lawyers aspire to—federal or state judgeships, state's attorney offices, or work in a federal agency—can be attained by political appointment.

did you know?

That five women received votes for vice president at the Democratic convention in 1924, the first held after women received the right to vote in 1920.

The Twenty-First-Century Campaign

After the candidates have been nominated, typically through a **primary election,** the most exhausting and expensive part of the election process begins—the **general election** campaign, which actually fills the offices at stake. The contemporary political campaign is becoming more complex and more sophisticated. Even with the most appealing of candidates, today's campaigns require a strong organization; expertise in political polling and marketing; professional assistance in fund-raising, accounting, and financial management; and technological capabilities in every aspect of the campaign.

Primary Election
An election in which political parties choose their candidates for the general election.

General Election
An election, normally held on the first Tuesday in November, that determines who will fill various elected positions.

2. A number of early presidents were Unitarian. The Unitarian Church is not Protestant, but it is historically rooted in the Protestant tradition.
3. According to a Gallup poll conducted prior to the 2008 elections, this majority varied according to party affiliation and ideology, ranging from 76 percent (for conservative Republicans) to 98 percent (for liberal Democrats).

FIGURE 9–1 Women Running for Congress (and Winning)

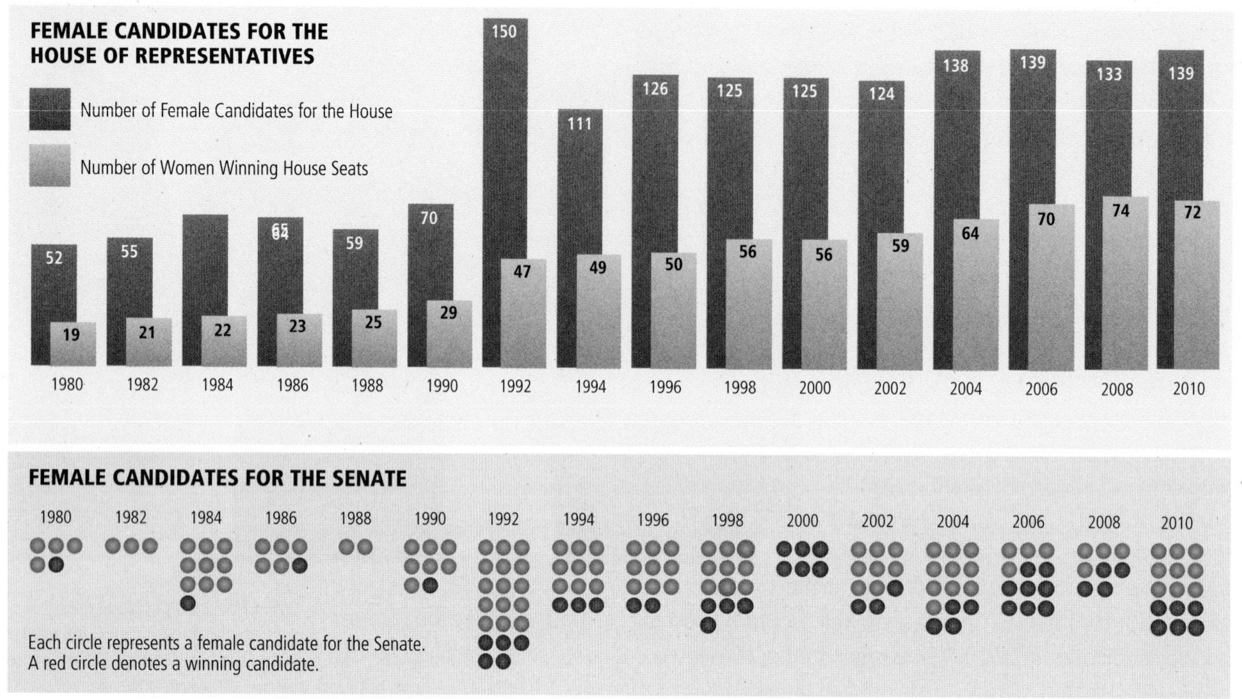

did you know?

That since 1945, the stock market (the Dow Jones Industrial Average) has gone up an average of 6.6 percent in years when a Republican was president—and 9.4 percent when the president was a Democrat.

The Changing Campaign

The goal is the same for all campaigns—to convince voters to choose a candidate or a slate of candidates for office. Part of the reason for the increased intensity of campaigns in the last decade is that they are now centered on the candidate, not on the party. The candidate-centered campaign emerged in response to changes in the electoral system, the increased importance of television in campaigns, technological innovations such as computers, and the increased cost of campaigning.

To run a successful and persuasive campaign, the candidate's organization must be able to raise funds for the effort, obtain coverage from the media, produce and pay for political commercials and advertising, schedule the candidate's time effectively, convey the candidate's position on the issues to the voters, conduct research on the opposing candidate, and get the voters to go to the polls. When party identification was stronger among voters and before the advent of television campaigning, a strong party organization at the local, state, or national level could furnish most of the services and expertise that the candidate needed. Parties used their precinct organizations to distribute literature, register voters, and get out the vote on election day. Less effort was spent on advertising each candidate's positions and character, because the party label presumably communicated that information to many voters.

One of the reasons that campaigns no longer depend on parties is that fewer people identify with them (see Chapter 8), as is evident from the increased number of political independents. In 1954, fewer than 20 percent of adults identified themselves as independents, whereas today that number exceeds 35 percent.

The Professional Campaign

Whether the candidate is running for the state legislature, for the governor's office, for the U.S. Congress, or for the presidency, every campaign has some fundamental tasks to accomplish. Today, in national elections, the lion's share of these tasks is handled by paid professionals rather than volunteers or amateur politicians.

The most sought-after and possibly the most criticized campaign expert is the **political consultant,** who, for a large fee, devises a campaign strategy, thinks up a campaign theme, oversees the advertising, and possibly chooses the campaign colors and the candidate's official portrait. Political consultants began to displace volunteer campaign managers in the 1960s, about the same time that television became a force in campaigns. The paid consultant monitors the campaign's progress, plans media appearances, and coaches the candidate for debates. The consultants and the firms they represent are not politically neutral. Most will work only for candidates from one party.

Political Consultant
A paid professional hired to devise a campaign strategy and manage a campaign.

Public appearances are a traditional part of any campaign, and they take up a considerable amount of the candidate's time. Candidates may appear before organized groups and in public forums to appeal for support, or they may organize their own campaign rallies. In the United States, such rallies typically are attended by loyal party supporters. In some countries, however, matters are handled differently, as you will learn in this chapter's *Beyond Our Borders* feature below.

The Strategy of Winning

In the United States, unlike some European countries, there are no rewards for a candidate who comes in second. The winner takes all. A winner-take-all system is also known as a *plurality voting system.* In most situations, the winning candidate does not need to have a majority of the votes. If there are three candidates, the one who gets the most votes wins—that is, "takes it all"—and the other two candidates get nothing. Given this system, the campaign organization must plan a strategy that maximizes the candidate's chances of winning. Candidates seek to capture all the votes of their party's supporters, to convince a majority of the independent voters to vote for them, and to gain a few votes from supporters of the other party. To accomplish these goals, candidates must consider their visibility, their message, and their campaign strategy.

BEYOND OUR BORDERS

RENT-A-CROWD IN UKRAINE

When politicians in the United States give a speech, they obviously want big crowds. So, too, do politicians in Ukraine, an independent country that until 1991 was part of the Russian-dominated Soviet Union. In Ukraine, when politicians wish to have a large crowd appear at a political rally, they sometimes turn to a company called Easy Work. This company pays young people—mostly college students—to cheer for politicians.

According to the head of the company, who is also a college student, "We'll do business with any political party. Ideology doesn't matter to us. We rally only for money." Easy Work pays about $4 an hour, more than four times the national minimum wage.

If you are a young Ukrainian, all you have to do is log on to **easywork.com.ua** using your fifteen-digit secret code. You can then view a list of rallies and click on the ones you wish to join. As a hired activist, you are supposed to show up on time, applaud, and not leave until the rally is over. Participants must not drink alcohol or fight, and should avoid talking to reporters.

Although the rent-a-crowd business in Ukraine is not illegal, politicians deny ever using it—the major parties claim that they have never paid people to rally for them and never will.

FOR CRITICAL ANALYSIS

How do politicians in the United States obtain crowds for their rallies?

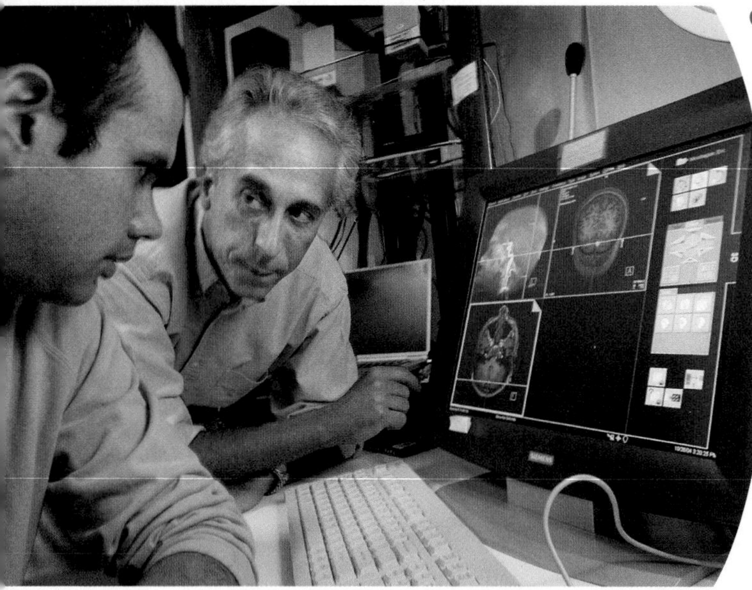

Instead of using focus groups and opinion polls, some political consultants have turned to magnetic resonance imaging (MRI) scans of volunteers' brains. What do these consultants hope to understand using MRI scanning? (AP Photo/ Reed Saxon)

Candidate Visibility and Appeal. One of the most important concerns is how well known the candidate is. If she or he is a highly visible incumbent, there may be little need for campaigning except to remind the voters of the officeholder's good deeds. If, however, the candidate is an unknown challenger or a largely unfamiliar character attacking a well-known public figure, the campaign requires a strategy to get the candidate before the public.

In the case of the independent candidate or the candidate representing a minor party, the problem of name recognition is serious. Such candidates must present an overwhelming case for the voter to reject the major-party candidates. Both Democratic and Republican candidates will label third-party candidates as "not serious" and therefore not worth the voter's time.

The Use of Opinion Polls. Opinion polls are a major source of information for both the media and the candidates. Poll taking is widespread during the primaries. Presidential hopefuls have private polls taken to make sure that there is at least some chance they could be nominated and, if nominated, elected. During the presidential campaign itself, polling is even more frequent. Polls are taken not only by the regular pollsters—Roper, Harris, Gallup, and others—but also privately by each candidate's campaign organization. These private polls are for the exclusive and secret use of the candidate and his or her campaign organization. As the election approaches, many candidates use **tracking polls,** which are polls taken almost every day, to find out how well they are competing for votes. Tracking polls enable consultants to fine-tune the advertising and the candidate's speeches in the last days of the campaign.

Focus Groups. Another tactic is to use a **focus group** to gain insights into public perceptions of the candidate. Professional consultants organize a discussion of the candidate or of certain political issues among ten to fifteen ordinary citizens. The citizens are selected from specific target groups in the population—for example, working women, blue-collar men, senior citizens, or young voters. Recent campaigns have tried to reach groups such as "soccer moms," "Wal-Mart shoppers," or "NASCAR dads."[4] The group discusses personality traits of the candidate, political advertising, and other candidate-related issues. Focus groups can reveal more emotional responses to candidates or the deeper anxieties of voters—feelings that consultants believe often are not tapped by more impersonal telephone surveys. The campaign then can shape its messages to respond to those feelings and perceptions.

did you know?

That a candidate can buy lists of all the voters in a precinct, county, or state for a few cents per name from a commercial firm.

Tracking Poll
A poll taken on a nearly daily basis as election day approaches.

Focus Group
A small group of individuals who are led in discussion by a professional consultant in order to gather opinions on and responses to candidates and issues.

Financing the Campaign

In a book published in 1932 entitled *Money in Elections,* Louise Overacker said the following about campaign financing:

> *The financing of elections in a democracy is a problem which is arousing increasing concern. Many are beginning to wonder if present-day methods of raising and spending*

4. NASCAR stands for the National Association of Stock Car Auto Racing.

campaign funds do not clog the wheels of our elaborately constructed mechanism of popular control, and if democracies do not inevitably become [governments ruled by small groups].[5]

Former comic actor Al Franken fought bitterly to prevail in a disputed race to represent Minnesota in the U.S. Senate in 2008. Ultimately he did. Why do candidates sometimes spend so many resources in disputing election results? (Win McNamee/Getty Images)

Although writing more than seventy-five years ago, Overacker touched on a sensitive issue in American political campaigns—the connection between money and elections. Total spending reached unprecedented heights during the 2007–2008 election cycle—$4.14 billion. Spending by the presidential candidates alone reached $2.4 billion.

In the mid-term elections of 2010, the average House incumbent raised about $1.7 million throughout the election cycle, and the average House challenger received close to $700,000. In the Senate, the average incumbent raked in more than $13 million, and the average challenger spent almost $5 million. Some races, of course, were much more expensive than the average. In several Senate races, spending passed the $50 million mark. House candidates spend less to retain or obtain their seat because they must run for election every two years, as opposed to every six years for senators. (The seats are also less valuable because the House has many more members than the Senate.)

Except for the presidential campaigns, all of these funds had to be provided by the candidates and their families, borrowed, or raised by contributions from individuals or *political action committees,* described later in this chapter. For the presidential campaigns, some of the funds may come from the federal government.

Regulating Campaign Financing

The way campaigns are financed has changed dramatically in the last two and a half decades. Today, candidates and political parties must operate within the constraints imposed by complicated laws regulating campaign financing.

A variety of federal **corrupt practices acts** have been designed to regulate campaign financing. The first, passed in 1925, contained many loopholes and proved to be ineffective. The **Hatch Act** (Political Activities Act) of 1939 is best known for restricting the political activities of civil servants. The act also, however, made it unlawful for a political group to spend more than $3 million in any campaign and limited individual contributions to a political group to $5,000. Of course, such restrictions were easily circumvented by creating additional political groups.

Corrupt Practices Acts
A series of acts passed by Congress in an attempt to limit and regulate the size and sources of contributions and expenditures in political campaigns.

Hatch Act
An act passed in 1939 that restricted the political activities of government employees. It also prohibited a political group from spending more than $3 million in any campaign and limited individual contributions to a campaign committee to $5,000.

The Federal Election Campaign Act

The Federal Election Campaign Act (FECA) of 1971, which became effective in 1972, essentially replaced all past laws. The act placed no limit on overall spending but restricted the amount that could be spent on mass media advertising, including television. It limited the amount that candidates could contribute to their own campaigns (a limit later ruled unconstitutional) and required disclosure of all contributions and expenditures over $100. In principle, the FECA limited the role of labor unions and corporations in political campaigns. It also provided for a voluntary $1 (now $3) checkoff on federal income tax returns for general campaign funds to be used by major-party presidential candidates.

did you know?
That Abraham Lincoln sold pieces of fence rail that he had split as political souvenirs to finance his campaign.

Further Reforms in 1974. For many, the 1971 act did not go far enough. Amendments to the FECA passed in 1974 did the following:

5. Louise Overacker, *Money in Elections* (New York: Macmillan, 1932), p. vii.

- *Created the Federal Election Commission (FEC).* This commission consists of six nonpartisan administrators whose duties are to enforce compliance with the requirements of the act. The FEC, however, is conspicuously ineffective, and typically does not determine that a candidate has violated the rules until the elections are over.
- *Provided public financing for presidential primaries and general elections.* Any candidate running for president who is able to obtain sufficient contributions in at least twenty states can obtain a subsidy from the U.S. Treasury to help pay for primary campaigns. The government also subsidizes the national conventions of the two major parties. Candidates who accept federal funding for the general elections are limited to spending what the government provides and cannot raise funds privately. The system began to break down after 2000, when many candidates rejected public funding in the belief that they could raise larger sums privately. George W. Bush opted out of primary financing in 2000, as did John Kerry in 2004. In the 2008 primaries, most of the major candidates refused public financing, and Barack Obama became the first candidate since the program was founded to opt out of federal funding for the general elections as well. As a result, he was able to raise unprecedented sums.
- *Limited presidential campaign spending.* Any candidate accepting federal support must agree to limit campaign expenditures to the amount prescribed by federal law.
- *Limited contributions.* Under the 1974 amendments, citizens could contribute up to $1,000 to each candidate in each federal election or primary; the total limit on all contributions from an individual to all candidates was $25,000 per year. Groups could contribute up to a maximum of $5,000 to a candidate in any election. (As you will read shortly, some of these limits were changed by the 2002 campaign-reform legislation.)
- *Required disclosure.* Each candidate must file periodic reports with the Federal Election Commission, listing who contributed, how much was spent, and for what the funds were spent.

Buckley v. Valeo. The original FECA of 1971 had limited the amount that each individual could spend on his or her own behalf. The Supreme Court overturned the provision in 1976, in *Buckley v. Valeo,*[6] stating that it was unconstitutional to restrict in any way the amount congressional candidates could spend on their own behalf: "The candidate, no less than any other person, has a First Amendment right to engage in the discussion of public issues and vigorously and tirelessly to advocate his own election." In 2006, the Court reaffirmed *Buckley v. Valeo* and extended its reach to candidates for state offices. It did so by holding unconstitutional a 1997 Vermont law that limited the amount that candidates for Vermont state offices could spend on their own campaigns.[7]

PACs and Political Campaigns

In the last two decades, interest groups and individual companies have found new, very direct ways to support elected officials through campaign donations. Elected officials, in turn, have become dependent on these donations to run increasingly expensive campaigns. Interest groups and corporations funnel money to political candidates through several devices, including **political action committees (PACs).**

Political Action Committee (PAC)
A committee set up by and representing a corporation, labor union, or special interest group. PACs raise and give campaign donations.

Laws Governing PACs. The 1974 and 1976 amendments to the Federal Election Campaign Act of 1971 allow corporations, labor unions, and other interest groups to set up PACs to raise funds for candidates. For a federal PAC to be legitimate, the funds must be raised from at least fifty volunteer donors and must be given to at least five candidates

6. 424 U.S. 1 (1976).
7. *Randall v. Sorrell,* 548 U.S. 230 (2006).

in the federal election. PACs can contribute up to $5,000 to each candidate in each election. Each corporation or each union is limited to one PAC. Campaign-financing regulations limit the amount that a PAC can give to any one candidate, but there is no limit on the amount that a PAC can spend on issue advocacy, either on behalf of a candidate or party or in opposition to one.

PACs and Campaign Financing. The number of PACs grew significantly after 1976, as did the amounts that they spent on elections. There were about 1,000 PACs in 1976. Today, there are more than 4,500. Since the 1990s, however, the number of PACs has leveled off because interest groups and activists have found alternate mechanisms for funneling resources into campaigns. Total spending by PACs exceeded $900 million in the 2003–2004 election cycle, when about 44 percent of all campaign funds raised by House candidates came from PACs. In subsequent years, the share of election financing provided by PACs fell, even as the dollar amount of PAC contributions continued to climb.

Interest groups funnel PAC funds to the candidates they think can do the most good for them. Frequently, they contribute to candidates who face little or no opposition. The great bulk of campaign contributions goes to incumbent candidates rather than to challengers. Table 9–1 on the following page shows the amounts contributed by the top twenty PACs during the 2009–2010 election cycle.

As Table 9–1 also shows, many PACs give most of their contributions to candidates of one party. Other PACs, particularly corporate PACs, tend to give funds to Democrats in Congress as well as to Republicans. Interest groups see PAC contributions as a way to ensure *access* to powerful legislators, even though the groups may disagree with the legislators some of the time.

Campaign Financing beyond the Limits

Within a few years after the establishment of the tight limits on contributions, new ways to finance campaigns were developed that skirted the reforms and made it possible for huge sums to be raised, especially by the major political parties.

Contributions to Political Parties. Candidates, PACs, and political parties found ways to generate **soft money**—that is, campaign contributions to political parties that escaped the limits of federal election law. Although the FECA limited contributions that would be spent on elections, there were no limits on contributions to political parties for activities such as voter education and voter-registration drives. This loophole enabled the parties to raise millions of dollars from corporations and individuals. Soft money contributions to the national parties were outlawed after Election Day 2002.

Soft Money
Campaign contributions unregulated by federal or state law, usually given to parties and party committees to help fund general party activities.

(PRICKLY CITY © 2007 Scott Stantis. Distributed by United Media. Reprinted with permission. All rights reserved.)

TABLE 9–1 The Top Twenty Political Action Committees Contributing to Federal Candidates, 2009–2010 Election Cycle*

Political Action Committee Name	Total Amount	Dem. %	Rep. %
Honeywell International	$3,183,100	55	45
AT&T, Inc.	2,776,875	48	51
Int'l Brotherhood of Electrical Workers	2,690,373	98	2
National Assn. of Realtors	2,685,054	58	41
National Beer Wholesalers Assn.	2,556,500	56	44
American Assn. for Justice	2,415,000	97	3
American Bankers Assn.	2,281,930	37	63
Operating Engineers Union	2,149,258	90	10
Carpenters & Joiners Union	2,004,875	86	14
American Crystal Sugar	1,962,500	68	32
Amer. Federation of State, County, & Mun. Employees	1,962,000	99	0
Teamsters Union	1,954,760	98	2
International Assn. of Fire Fighters	1,947,000	83	16
Machinists & Aerospace Workers Union	1,943,000	98	2
American Federation of Teachers	1,881,750	100	0
Credit Union National Assn.	1,879,196	57	42
Laborers Union	1,847,000	96	4
Boeing Co.	1,841,000	58	41
Lockheed Martin	1,759,250	58	42
Plumbers/Pipefitters Union	1,743,450	96	3

*Include subsidiaries and affiliated PACs, if any.

Source: Center for Responsive Politics, OpenSecrets.org.

Independent Expenditures
Nonregulated contributions from PACs, organizations, and individuals. The funds may be spent on advertising or other campaign activities so long as those expenditures are not coordinated with those of a candidate.

Issue Advocacy
Advertising paid for by interest groups that support or oppose a candidate or a candidate's position on an issue without mentioning voting or elections.

Independent Expenditures. Soon after soft money was banned, business corporations, labor unions, and other interest groups discovered that it was legal to make **independent expenditures** in an election campaign so long as the expenditures were not coordinated with those of the candidate or political party. Hundreds of committees and organizations blossomed to take advantage of this campaign tactic. Business and other types of groups were especially active in making independent expenditures on *issues*.

Issue Advocacy. Indeed, **issue advocacy**—spending unregulated funds on advertising that promotes positions on issues rather than candidates—has become a common tactic in recent years. Interest groups routinely wage their own issue campaigns. For example, the Christian Coalition, which is incorporated, annually raises millions of dollars to produce and distribute voter guidelines and other direct-mail literature to describe candidates' positions on various issues and to promote its agenda. Before the 2008 elections, AARP, which represents older Americans, aired a series of ads showcasing people who had been ruined by health-care costs. Ostensibly bipartisan, the campaign in fact benefited the Democrats.

Although promoting issue positions is very close to promoting candidates who support those positions, the courts repeatedly have held that interest groups have a First Amendment right to advocate their positions. The courts have also clarified that political parties may make independent expenditures on behalf of candidates—as long as the parties do so *independently* of the candidates. In other words, the parties must not coordinate such expenditures with the candidates' campaigns.

The Bipartisan Campaign Reform Act of 2002

Campaign reform had been in the air for so long that it was almost anticlimactic when President George W. Bush signed the Bipartisan Campaign Reform Act in March 2002. This act, also known as the McCain-Feingold Act after its chief sponsors in the Senate, amended the 1971 FECA. The act took effect on the day after the congressional elections were held on November 5, 2002.

Key Elements of the New Law. The 2002 law banned the large, unlimited contributions to national political parties that are known as soft money. It placed curbs on, but did not entirely eliminate, the use of campaign ads by outside special interest groups advocating the election or defeat of specific candidates. Such ads were allowed up to sixty days before a general election and up to thirty days before a primary election. (As you will read shortly, this rule was eased by the Supreme Court in 2007.)

In 1974, contributions by individuals to federal candidates were limited to $1,000 per individual. The McCain-Feingold Act increased this to $2,000. Also, the maximum amount that an individual can give to all federal candidates was raised from $25,000 per year to $95,000 over a two-year election cycle. The act did not ban soft money contributions to state and local parties, which can accept such contributions as long as they are limited to $10,000 per year per individual.

U.S. Senator Russell Feingold (D., Wis.) joined with Senator John McCain (R., Ariz.) to forge the 2002 Bipartisan Campaign Reform Act. In an upset, Feingold was defeated for reelection in 2010. What did that legislation do? (Mark Wilson/Getty Images)

Challenges to the 2002 Act. The constitutionality of the act was immediately challenged by groups that were negatively affected. In December 2003, the Supreme Court upheld almost all of the clauses of the act.[8] In 2007, however, the Court eased the restrictions on advocacy ads when it ruled that only those ads "susceptible of no reasonable interpretation other than as an appeal to vote for or against a specific candidate" could be restricted prior to an election.[9] In 2008, the Court found another provision of the act to be unconstitutional—one that penalized wealthy candidates by exempting their opponents from various campaign-finance rules.[10]

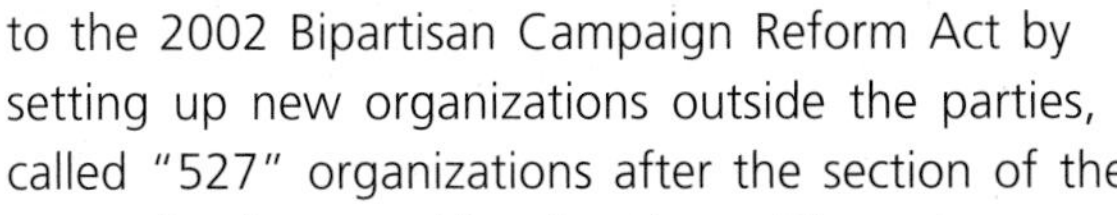

The Rise of the 527s. Interest groups that previously gave soft money to the parties responded to the 2002 Bipartisan Campaign Reform Act by setting up new organizations outside the parties, called "527" organizations after the section of the tax code that provides for them. These tax-exempt

8. *McConnell v. Federal Election Commission,* 540 U.S. 93 (2003).
9. *Federal Election Commission v. Wisconsin Right to Life, Inc.,* 551 U.S. 449 (2007).
10. *Davis v. Federal Election Commission,* 554 U.S. ___ (2008).

organizations first made a major impact in the 2003–2004 election cycle. The groups focused on encouraging voter registration and running issue ads aimed at energizing supporters. These groups continue to be active up to the present day, as you can see in Table 9–2 below.

New Types of Independent Committees. In the 2007–2008 election cycle, campaign-finance lawyers began recommending a new type of independent group—the 501(c)4 organization, which, like the 527 committee, is named after the relevant provision of the tax code. A 501(c)4 is ostensibly a "social-welfare" group and, unlike a 527, is not required to disclose the identity of its donors or report spending to the FEC.

Lawyers then began suggesting that 501(c)4 organizations claim a special exemption that would allow the organization to ask people to vote for or against specific candidates as long as a majority of the group's effort was devoted to issues. Only those funds spent directly to support candidates had to be reported to the FEC, and the 501(c)4 could continue to conceal its donors.

One result of the 501(c)4 was to make it all but impossible to determine exactly how much was really spent by independent groups on the 2007–2008 and 2009–2010 elections. Critics claimed that 501(c)4s were being used illegally. The FEC, however, has refused to issue any rule restricting the actions of 501(c)4 groups or requiring them to reveal their donors.

2010: *Citizens United v. Federal Election Commission*. In January 2010, the United States Supreme Court issued a new opinion on campaign finance that is expected to have a major influence on the conduct of future elections. The Court ruled that corporations, unions, and nonprofits may spend freely to support or oppose candidates for president and Congress, as long as the expenditures are made independently and are not coordinated with candidate campaign organizations. Corporations and unions also are allowed to spend whatever they wish on issue ads. Corporations and unions continue to be banned only from making direct contributions to candidates. The case, *Citizens United v. Federal Election Commission*, was soon called *Citizens* for short.[11] The Court's ruling, based on a five-to-four division, overturned campaign-finance laws dating back decades.

11. 558 U.S. ___ (2010).

TABLE 9–2 527 Committee Activity in 2009–2010 by Type of Group or Interest

Type of Group or Interest (top ten types)	Total Receipts	Total Expenditures
Republican/Conservative	$52,838,524	$47,616,886
Democratic/Liberal	19,413,806	21,735,282
Miscellaneous Unions	18,958,065	19,972,799
Miscellaneous Issues	14,428,289	13,232,474
Public Sector Unions	7,772,580	7,389,029
Women's Issues	7,724,469	8,815,483
Building Trade Unions	6,968,446	8,782,428
Candidate Committees	6,678,476	4,622,151
Industrial Unions	5,047,972	6,232,255
Human Rights	4,643,832	5,738,303

Source: Center for Responsive Politics, OpenSecrets.org.

Citizens provoked widespread criticism and was opposed by a majority of the public in opinion polls. President Obama condemned the decision in his State of the Union address, which was delivered shortly after the decision. The Court was in attendance at the address, and the members of the Court's majority were obviously discomfited by the president's remarks. Republican leaders and a variety of other prominent individuals defended *Citizens* as protecting freedom of speech. Democrats, plus many journalists and bloggers, accused the Court of granting corporations free speech rights that ought to be exercised only by flesh-and-blood humans. Many observers predicted a flood of campaign spending from the nation's wealthiest institutions and businesses.

did you know?

That in 1904, Florida became the first state to use primary elections to select delegates to the major-party national conventions, and although New Hampshire began using primary elections in 1916, it did not have a contested election until 1952.

Running for President: The Longest Campaign

The American presidential election is the culmination of two different campaigns: the presidential primary campaign and the general election campaign following the party's national convention. Traditionally, both the primary campaigns and the final campaigns take place during the first ten months of an election year. Increasingly, though, the states are holding their primaries earlier in the year, which has motivated the candidates to begin their campaigns earlier as well. Indeed, candidates in the 2008 presidential races began campaigning in early 2007, thus launching the longest presidential campaign to date in U.S. history.

Primary elections were first mandated in 1903 in Wisconsin. The purpose of the primary was to open the nomination process to ordinary party members and to weaken the influence of party bosses. Until 1968, however, there were fewer than twenty primary elections for the presidency. They were often **"beauty contests"** in which the candidates competed for popular votes, but the results had no impact on the selection of delegates to the national convention. National conventions were meetings of the party elite—legislators, mayors, county chairpersons, and loyal party workers—who were mostly appointed to their delegations. National conventions saw numerous trades and bargains

"Beauty Contest"
A presidential primary in which candidates compete for popular votes but the results do not control the selection of delegates to the national convention.

ELECTIONS 2010

CAMPAIGN SPENDING IN 2010

As expected, the 2010 elections were the most expensive mid-term elections in history. Spending totaled $3.23 billion by mid-October and was expected to approach $4 billion by the time the last dollar was counted. The record set in the previous mid-term election—2006—was about $3 billion. In part, spending was fueled by *Citizens United v. Federal Election Commission,* which opened the floodgates for outside spending by corporations, unions, and other interest groups. Many observers expected that the torrent of new cash would benefit Republicans, and this proved to be true. Democrats did not do badly, though. As of mid-October, their candidate committees had actually out-spent the Republicans. Spending by independent groups, however, pushed the Republicans into an overall lead. One notable development was huge expenditures by very rich—and very conservative—individuals, who provided much of the new independent spending. Several wealthy candidates also lavished fortunes on their own campaigns. Republican Meg Whitman dropped $140 million in her race for governor of California, an all-time record. Such self-financing had its limits. None of the five candidates who spent more than $6 million on their own campaigns, including Whitman, managed to win.

among competing candidates, and the leaders of large blocs of delegates could direct their delegates to support a favorite candidate.

Reforming the Primaries

In recent decades, the character of the primary process and the makeup of the national convention have changed dramatically. The public, rather than party elites, now generally controls the nomination process. After the disruptive riots outside the doors of the 1968 Democratic convention in Chicago, many party leaders pushed for serious reforms of the convention process. They saw the general dissatisfaction with the convention, and the riots in particular, as being caused by the inability of the average party member to influence the nomination system.

The Democratic National Committee appointed a special commission to study the problems of the primary system. Called the McGovern-Fraser Commission, during the next several years the group formulated new rules for delegate selection that had to be followed by state Democratic parties.

The reforms instituted by the Democratic Party, which were imitated in most states by the Republicans, revolutionized the nomination process for the presidency. The most important changes require that a majority of the convention delegates not be nominated by party elites; they must be elected by the voters in primary elections, in caucuses held by local parties (to be discussed shortly), or at state conventions. Delegates are normally pledged to a particular candidate, although the pledge is not always formally binding at the convention. The delegation from each state must also include a proportion of women, younger party members, and representatives of the minority groups within the party. At first, almost no special privileges were given to elected party officials, such as senators and governors. In 1984, however, many of these officials returned to the Democratic convention as **superdelegates** (party leaders, members of Congress, and others).

This voter submits his primary election ballot at the Codington Elementary School in Wilmington, North Carolina. Do you think fewer people vote in primary elections than in general elections? (Logan Mock-Bunting/Getty Images)

Superdelegate
A party leader or elected official who is given the right to vote at the party's national convention. Superdelegates are not elected at the state level.

Caucus
A meeting of party members designed to select candidates and propose policies.

Direct Primary
A primary election in which voters decide party nominations by voting directly for candidates.

Indirect Primary
A primary election in which voters choose convention delegates, and the delegates determine the party's candidate in the general election.

Primaries and Caucuses

A variety of types of primaries are used by the states. One notable difference is between proportional and winner-take-all primaries. Another important consideration is whether independent voters can take part in a primary, as we will explain shortly. Some states also use **caucuses** and conventions to choose candidates for various offices.

Direct and Indirect Primaries. A **direct primary** is one in which voters decide party nominations by voting directly for candidates. In an **indirect primary,** voters instead choose convention delegates, and the delegates determine the party's candidate in the general election. Delegates may be pledged to a particular candidate. Indirect primaries are used almost exclusively in presidential elections. Most candidates in state and local elections are chosen by direct primaries.

Proportional and Winner-Take-All Primaries. Most primaries are *winner-take-all. Proportional* primaries are used mostly to elect delegates to the national conventions of the two major parties—delegates who are pledged to one or another candidate for president. In 2008, all Democratic Party presidential primaries and caucuses allocated delegates on a proportional basis. This meant that if one candidate for president won 40 percent of the vote in a primary, that candidate would receive about 40 percent of the pledged delegates. If a candidate won 60 percent of the vote, he or she would obtain about 60 percent of the delegates. In contrast, the Republicans used the winner-take-all primary system in most, but not all, states. Under this system, the candidate who received the most votes won all of the states' delegates, no matter how narrow the margin of victory.

did you know?

That when David Leroy Gatchell changed his middle name to None of the Above and ran for the U.S. Senate representing Tennessee, a court ruled that he could not use his middle name on the ballot.

The use of different systems by the two major parties had a striking impact on the conduct and outcome of the 2008 presidential primaries. Because the Democratic contest between Barack Obama and Hillary Clinton was so close, the proportional distribution of delegates ensured that the winner was not established until June. Neither candidate actually accumulated enough delegates to win during the primary season—the nomination had to be settled by the unelected, unpledged superdelegates. Of course, a majority of the superdelegates eventually endorsed Obama, the candidate with the most pledged delegates. On the Republican side, the winner-take-all system let John McCain sew up his party's nomination by March 4.

Closed Primary. A closed primary is one of several types of primaries distinguished by how independent voters are handled. In a **closed primary,** only avowed or declared members of a party can vote in that party's primary. In other words, voters must declare their party affiliation, either when they register to vote or at the primary election. In a closed-primary system, voters cannot cross over into the other party's primary in order to nominate the weakest candidate of the opposing party or to affect the ideological direction of that party.

Closed Primary
A type of primary in which the voter is limited to choosing candidates of the party of which he or she is a member.

Open Primary
A primary in which any registered voter can vote (but must vote for candidates of only one party).

Open Primary. In an **open primary,** voters can vote in either party primary without declaring a party affiliation. Basically, the voter makes the choice in the privacy of the voting booth. The voter must, however, choose one party's list from which to select candidates. Open primaries place no restrictions on independent voters.

Blanket Primary. A *blanket primary* is one in which the voter can vote for candidates of more than one party. Until 2000, a few states, including Alaska, California, and Washington, had blanket primaries. In 2000, however, the United States Supreme Court effectively invalidated the use of the blanket primary. The Court ruled that the blanket primary violated political parties' First Amendment right of association. Because the nominees represent the party, party members—not the general electorate—should have the right to choose the party's nominee.[12]

In 2008, however, the Court upheld a revised version of the blanket primary that had been created by the state of Washington.[13] Under the new system, all candidates appear on a single ballot. Candidates may indicate their party, but are not required to do so. A party cannot prevent a candidate it does not support from appearing on the primary ballot—an insurgent Republican, for example, could appear on the primary ballot alongside the party-supported Republican. The two candidates receiving the most votes, regardless of party, then move on to the general election. In the general election, two Republicans might face each other in a conservative district. In other districts, both general election candidates could be Democrats. Louisiana has long used a similar system for filling some

12. *California Democratic Party v. Jones,* 530 U.S. 567 (2000).
13. *Washington State Grange v. Washington State Republican Party,* 552 U.S. 442 (2008).

offices. In June 2010, Californians voted in favor of a primary system based on the Washington plan.

These voters are manually filling out their primary election ballots in Oakland, California. What offices are at issue during such elections? (Justin Sullivan/Getty Images)

Run-Off Primary. Some states have a two-primary system. If no candidate receives a majority of the votes in the first primary, the top two candidates must compete in another primary, called a *run-off primary.*

Conventions. While primary elections are the most common way in which a party's candidates are selected, there are other procedures in use. The Virginia Republican Party, for example, chose its 2008 candidate for the U.S. Senate at its state convention, whereas the Democrats in that state used a primary. In Utah, the 2010 Republican state convention refused to endorse incumbent U.S. senator Bob Bennett, but instead nominated two Tea Party backed candidates. Voters in the Republican primary then decided between the two nominees.

Meetings below the statewide level may help nominate candidates for local, state, or national office. The most famous of such meetings are the caucuses that help nominate a party's candidate for president of the United States.

Caucuses. In 2008, twelve states relied entirely on the caucus system for choosing delegates to the Republican and Democratic national conventions—delegates committed to one presidential candidate or the other. Several other states used a combined system. Strictly speaking, the caucus system is actually a caucus/convention system. In North Dakota, for example, local citizens, who need not be registered as party members, gather in party meetings, called caucuses, at the precinct level. They choose delegates to district conventions. The district conventions elect delegates to the state convention, and the state convention actually chooses the delegates to the national convention. The national delegates, however, are pledged to reflect the presidential preferences that voters expressed at the caucus level.

Front-Loading the Primaries

When politicians and potential presidential candidates realized that winning as many primary elections as possible guaranteed them the party's nomination for president, their tactics changed dramatically. Candidates began to concentrate on building organizations in states that held early, important primary elections. By the 1970s, candidates recognized that winning early contests, such as the Iowa caucuses or the New Hampshire primary election (both now held in January), meant that the media instantly would label the winner as the **front-runner,** thus increasing the candidate's media exposure and escalating the pace of contributions to his or her campaign.

Front-Runner
The presidential candidate who appears to be ahead at a given time in the primary season.

Front-Loading
The practice of moving presidential primary elections to the early part of the campaign to maximize the impact of these primaries on the nomination.

The Rush to Be First. The state political parties began to see that early primaries had a much greater effect on the outcome of the presidential contest than later ones. Accordingly, in successive presidential elections, more and more states moved their primaries into the first months of the year, a process known as **front-loading** the primaries. One result was a series of "Super Tuesdays" when multiple states held simultaneous primaries. In 2008, twenty-four states held their primaries or caucuses on February 5, making it the largest Super Tuesday ever. The compressed primary schedule troubled many observers, who feared that a front-runner might wrap up the nomination before the voters were able to make a thorough assessment of the candidate. In the many months between the early primaries and the general election, the voters might come to regret their decision.

The National Parties Try to Regain Control of the Process. To keep primary dates from slipping into the preceding year, the national Republican and Democratic parties agreed that no state could hold a primary or caucus before February 5 without special permission. (This was the reason that so many states selected their delegates on that exact date.) The national parties let the traditional lead-off states, Iowa and New Hampshire, go first, and gave special permission to Nevada and South Carolina to hold their contests in January, giving the early primaries a national flavor.

State officials in Florida and Michigan refused to obey the rules and also scheduled primaries in January. The Republicans penalized the two states' delegations by cutting their representation at the national convention in half. After threatening even more severe penalties, the Democrats did likewise. (In the end, at the convention, the Democrats allowed Florida and Michigan to cast a full vote.)

The Consequences of Early Primaries. In 2008, so many states were in play on February 5 that it was impossible for the candidates to campaign strongly in all of them. Rather than winning more attention, many Super Tuesday states found that they were ignored. Because the Democratic race was not decided until the very end, the later Democratic primaries, such as those in Indiana, North Carolina, Ohio, Pennsylvania, and Texas, were hotly contested.

Front-loading, in short, had become counterproductive. As a result, it may be easier for the national parties to persuade states not to front-load the process so severely in 2012. Some have even suggested taking the power to set primary dates away from the states and replacing the current system with a series of nationally scheduled regional primaries.

Credentials Committee
A committee used by political parties at their national conventions to determine which delegates may participate. The committee inspects the claim of each prospective delegate to be seated as a legitimate representative of his or her state.

On to the National Convention

Presidential candidates have been nominated by the convention method in every election since 1832. Extra delegates are allowed from states that had voting majorities for the party in the preceding elections. Parties also accept delegates from the District of Columbia, the territories, and certain overseas groups.

Seating the Delegates. At the convention, each political party uses a **credentials committee** to determine which delegates may participate. Controversy may arise when rival groups claim to be the official party organization. For example, the Mississippi Democratic Party split in 1964 at the height of the civil rights movement, and two sets of delegates were selected. After much debate, the credentials committee seated the mixed-race, pro–civil rights delegation and excluded those who represented the traditional "white" party.

Convention Activities. Most delegates arrive at the convention committed to a presidential candidate. No convention since 1952 has required more than one ballot to choose a nominee. Conventions normally last four days. On each night, featured speakers seek to rally the

The late Democratic Senator Edward "Ted" Kennedy of Massachusetts is shown here addressing the most recent Democratic National Convention. Do such speakers attempt to change the opinions of those who are in attendance? (Paul J. Richards/AFP/Getty Images)

did you know?

That the 1976 Republican National Convention, where incumbent president Gerald Ford narrowly defeated former California Governor Ronald Reagan, was the last major party convention at which the party's nominee was not decided before the convention began.

party faithful and to draw in uncommitted voters who are watching on television. On day three, the vice-presidential nominee is featured. On day four the presidential candidate gives an acceptance speech. The national networks limit their coverage to the major speeches, but several cable networks and Internet sites provide gavel-to-gavel coverage. In 2008, more than 42 million people watched Democrat Barack Obama address an audience of 85,000 in Denver's Mile High Stadium. A week later, at least 37 million people tuned in to watch the Republican vice-presidential candidate, Alaska governor Sarah Palin. For most viewers (and for most Republican delegates), this was their first introduction to Palin, who was previously little known outside Alaska. The next night, John McCain's ratings matched or beat Obama's. At both conventions, the speakers were effective. Polls taken immediately after each convention showed substantial gains for each party.

The Electoral College

Elector
A member of the Electoral College, which selects the president and vice president. Each state's electors are chosen in each presidential election year according to state laws.

Some people who vote for the president and vice president think that they are voting directly for a candidate. In actuality, they are voting for **electors** who will cast their ballots in the Electoral College. Article II, Section 1, of the Constitution outlines in detail the method of choosing electors for president and vice president. The framers of the Constitution wanted to avoid the selection of president and vice president by the "excitable masses." Rather, they wished the choice to be made by a few supposedly dispassionate, reasonable men (but not women).

The Choice of Electors. Each state's electors are selected during each presidential election year. The selection is governed by state laws. After the national party convention, the electors normally are pledged to the candidates chosen. Each state's number of electors equals that state's number of senators (two) plus its number of representatives. The total number of electors today is 538, equal to 100 senators, 435 members of the House, and 3 electors for the District of Columbia. (The Twenty-third Amendment, ratified in 1961, added electors for the District of Columbia.)

South Carolina
Senator Lindsey Graham speaks at the 2008 Republican National Convention in St. Paul, Minnesota. What type of individuals are normally invited to speak at national party conventions? (AP Photo/ Ron Edmonds)

The Electors' Commitment. A plurality of voters in a state chooses a slate of electors (except in Maine and Nebraska, where electoral votes are partly based on congressional districts). Those electors are pledged to cast their ballots on the first Monday after the second Wednesday in December in the state capital for the presidential and vice-presidential candidates of their party. The Constitution does not, however, *require* the electors to cast their ballots for the candidates of their party, and on rare occasions so-called *faithless electors* have voted for a candidate to whom they were not pledged.

The ballots are counted and certified before a joint session of Congress early in January. The candidates who receive a majority of the electoral votes (270) are certified as president-elect and vice president elect. According to the Constitution, if no candidate receives a majority of the electoral votes, the election of the president is decided in the House from among the candidates with the three highest numbers of votes, with each state having one vote (decided by a plurality of each state delegation). The selection of the vice president is determined by the Senate in a choice between the two candidates with the most votes, each senator having one vote. The House was required to choose the president in 1801 (Thomas Jefferson) and again in 1825 (John Quincy Adams).[14]

It is possible for a candidate to become president without obtaining a majority of the popular vote. There have been many presidents in our history who did not win a majority of the popular vote, including Abraham Lincoln, Woodrow Wilson, Harry Truman, John F. Kennedy, Richard Nixon (in 1968), Bill Clinton, and George W. Bush (in 2000). Such an event becomes more likely when there are important third-party candidates.

did you know?

That forty-two states do not indicate on the ballot that the voter is casting a ballot for members of the Electoral College rather than for the president and vice president directly.

Perhaps more distressing is the possibility of a candidate's being elected when an opposing candidate receives a plurality of the popular vote. This has occurred on four occasions—in the elections of John Quincy Adams in 1824, Rutherford B. Hayes in 1876, Benjamin Harrison in 1888, and George W. Bush in 2000, all of whom won elections in which an opponent received more votes than they did.

How Are Elections Conducted?

The United States uses the **Australian ballot**—a secret ballot that is prepared, distributed, and counted by government officials at public expense. Since 1888, all states have used the Australian ballot. Before that, many states used the alternatives of oral voting and differently colored ballots prepared by the parties. Obviously, knowing which way a person was voting made it easy to apply pressure on the person to change his or her vote, and vote buying was common.

Office-Block and Party-Column Ballots

Two types of Australian ballots are used in the United States in general elections. The first, called an **office-block ballot,** or sometimes a **Massachusetts ballot,** groups all the candidates for a particular elective office under the title of that office. Parties dislike the office-block ballot because it places more emphasis on the office than on the party. It discourages straight-ticket voting and encourages split-ticket voting.

A **party-column ballot** is a form of general election ballot in which all of a party's candidates are arranged in one column under the party's label and symbol. It is also called the **Indiana ballot.** In some states, it allows voters to vote for all of a party's candidates for local, state, and national offices by simply marking a single "X" or by pulling a single lever. Most states use this type of ballot. Because it encourages straight-ticket voting, the two major parties favor this form. When a party has an exceptionally strong presidential or gubernatorial candidate to head the ticket, the use of the party-column ballot increases the **coattail effect** (the influence of a popular candidate on the success of other candidates on the same party ticket).

Australian Ballot
A secret ballot prepared, distributed, and tabulated by government officials at public expense. Since 1888, all states have used the Australian ballot rather than an open, public ballot.

Office-Block, or Massachusetts, Ballot
A form of general election ballot in which candidates for elective office are grouped together under the title of each office. It emphasizes voting for the office and the individual candidate, rather than for the party.

Party-Column, or Indiana, Ballot
A form of general election ballot in which all of a party's candidates for elective office are arranged in one column under the party's label and symbol. It emphasizes voting for the party, rather than for the office or individual.

Coattail Effect
The influence of a popular candidate on the success of other candidates on the same party ticket. The effect is increased by the party-column ballot, which encourages straight-ticket voting.

Voting by Mail

Although voting by mail has been accepted for absentee ballots for many decades (for example, for individuals who are doing business away from home or for members of the armed forces), recently several states have offered mail ballots to all of their voters. The rationale for using the mail ballot is to make voting easier for the voters. Oregon has gone one step further: since 1998, that state has employed postal ballots exclusively, and there are no polling places. (Voters who do not prepare their ballot in time for

did you know?

That when President Grover Cleveland lost the election of 1888, his wife told the White House staff to change nothing because the couple would be back in four years—and she was right.

14. For a detailed account of the process, see Michael J. Glennon, *When No Majority Rules: The Electoral College and Presidential Succession* (Washington, D.C.: Congressional Quarterly Press, 1993), p. 20.

did you know?

That in August 2000, six people offered to sell their votes for president on eBay, the online auction site (eBay quickly canceled the bidding).

the U.S. Postal Service to deliver it can drop off their ballots at drop boxes on Election Day.) In addition, most counties in Washington State now use mail ballots exclusively. Supporters of the system contend that it has enhanced voter participation, and Oregon's turnout in the 2010 elections was 56.9 percent, the nation's highest. Turnout was lower than in 2008, however.

Voting Fraud and Mistakes

Voting fraud is something regularly suspected but seldom proved. Voting in the 1800s, when secret ballots were rare and people had a cavalier attitude toward the open buying of votes, was probably much more conducive to fraud than modern elections are.

The Danger of Fraud. Some observers claim that the potential for voting fraud is high in many states, particularly through the use of phony voter registrations and absentee ballots. In California, for example, it is very difficult to remove a name from the polling list even if the person has not cast a ballot in the last two years. Thus, many persons are still on the rolls even though they no longer live in California. Enterprising political activists could use these names for absentee ballots. Other states have registration laws that are meant to encourage easy registration and voting. Such laws can be taken advantage of by those who seek to vote more than once.

After the 2000 elections, political scientist Larry Sabato emphasized the problem of voting fraud. "It's a silent scandal," said Sabato, "and the problem is getting worse with increases in absentee voting, which is the easiest way to commit fraud." Investigators in Milwaukee, Wisconsin, found that in the state's ultra-close 2004 presidential elections, more than two hundred felons voted illegally and more than one hundred people voted twice.[15]

Mistakes by Voting Officials. Some observers claim, however, that errors due to fraud are trivial in number and that a few mistakes are inevitable in a system involving millions of voters. These people argue that an excessive concern with voting fraud makes it harder for minorities and poor people to vote.

For example, in 2000, Katherine Harris, Florida's top election official, oversaw a purge of the voter rolls while simultaneously serving as co-chair of the Florida Bush campaign.

15. John Fund, "Voter-Fraud Showdown," *The Wall Street Journal*, January 9, 2008, p. A15.

The unsavory side of certain campaigns sometimes becomes public. Here the U.S. Attorney for the Eastern District of Kentucky talks to the media after the indictment of state senator Johnny Ray Turner for mail fraud and conspiracy. Turner allegedly sought to rig his 2000 campaign with bought votes and phantom contributors. What motivates candidates to violate the law when they are running for office? (AP Photo/Hobie Hiler)

According to the *New York Times,* when attempting to remove the names of convicted felons from the list of voters:

> *Ms. Harris's office overruled the advice of the private firm that compiled the felon list and called for removing not just names that were an exact match, but ones that were highly inexact. Thousands of Florida voters wound up being wrongly purged . . . . In Missouri, elected officials charged for years that large numbers of St. Louis residents were casting votes from vacant lots. A study conducted by* The *[St. Louis]* Post Dispatch *in 2001 found that in the vast majority of cases, the voters lived in homes that had been wrongly classified by the city.*[16]

In both the Florida and Missouri examples, a majority of the affected voters were African American.

Voter ID Requirements. In recent years, many states have adopted laws requiring enhanced proof of identity before voters can cast their ballots. Indiana imposed the nation's toughest voter identification (ID) law in 2005, which was challenged in a case that reached the United States Supreme Court. In 2008, the Court upheld the Indiana voter ID law.[17]

Reforming the Voting Process. In Florida in 2000, serious problems with the punch-card voting system may have determined the outcome of the presidential election. In response, Congress enacted the Help America Vote Act (HAVA) of 2002. The act provided funds to the states to help them implement a number of reforms. Among other things, the states were asked to replace outdated voting equipment with newer electronic voting systems. Critics of HAVA pointed out that by urging the adoption of electronic voting equipment, the act may have traded old problems for newer, more complicated ones.

These problems became particularly apparent during the 2006 midterm elections, when more than twenty-five states reported trouble at the polls on Election Day. Many of the problems involved failures in the new voting machines. In one Florida county, it was estimated that nearly 18,000 votes may have gone unrecorded by electronic voting machines, thus changing the outcome of a congressional election.

Sometimes ballots are disputed and must be recounted. This occurred after the votes were tallied for the U.S. senatorial candidates in Minnesota in 2008. Is there any way to reform the voting process to avoid such disputes? (AP Photo/Dawn Villella)

In 2008, therefore, many localities—including almost the entire state of California—retreated to using old-fashioned paper ballots. These ballots slowed the vote count, but they largely eliminated the problems with voting system errors that had plagued recent elections.

In 2010, voters reported isolated problems with voting systems, but the issue was not as serious as in earlier years. A growing problem that may require attention was voter intimidation and misinformation. Voters in some minority neighborhoods, for example, purportedly were told by "shadowy" groups that they would face legal trouble if they tried to vote.

Turning Out to Vote

In 2010, the number of Americans eligible to vote was about 218.05 million people. Of that number, about 90.5 million, or 41.5 percent of the eligible population, actually cast a ballot. When voter turnout is this low, it means, among other things, that the winner of

16. "How America Doesn't Vote," *The New York Times: The News of the Week in Review,* February 15, 2004, p. 10.
17. *Crawford v. Marion County Election Board,* 553 U.S. 181 (2008).

a close presidential election may be voted in by less than a third of those eligible to vote (see Table 9–3 below).

Voter Turnout
The percentage of citizens taking part in the election process; the number of eligible voters that actually "turn out" on election day to cast their ballots.

Figure 9–2 on the facing page shows **voter turnout** for presidential and congressional elections from 1908 to 2010. Each of the peaks in the figure represents voter turnout in a presidential election. Thus, we can also see that turnout for congressional elections is influenced greatly by whether there is a presidential election in the same year. Whereas voter turnout during the presidential elections of 2008 was 62.3 percent, it was only 40.3 percent in the midterm elections of 2006.

The same is true at the state level. When there is a race for governor, more voters participate both in the general election for governor and in the election for state representatives. Voter participation rates in gubernatorial elections are also greater in presidential

TABLE 9–3 Elected by a Majority?

Most presidents have won a majority of the votes cast in their election. We generally judge the extent of their victory by whether they have won more than 51 percent of the votes. Some presidential elections have been proclaimed *landslides,* meaning that the candidates won by an extraordinary majority of votes cast. As indicated below, however, no modern president has been elected by as many as 39 percent of the population eligible to vote. The best showing was by Johnson in 1964.

Year—Winner (party)	Percentage of Total Popular Vote	Percentage of Population Eligible to Vote
1936—Roosevelt (D)	60.8	34.6
1940—Roosevelt (D)	54.7	32.2
1944—Roosevelt (D)	53.4	29.9
1948—Truman (D)	49.6	25.9
1952—Eisenhower (R)	55.1	34.3
1956—Eisenhower (R)	57.4	34.6
1960—Kennedy (D)	49.7	31.7
1964—Johnson (D)	61.1	38.4
1968—Nixon (R)	43.4	27.6
1972—Nixon (R)	60.7	34.1
1976—Carter (D)	50.1	27.5
1980—Reagan (R)	50.7	27.5
1984—Reagan (R)	58.8	32.5
1988—Bush (R)	53.4	28.2
1992—Clinton (D)	43.3	25.2
1996—Clinton (D)	49.2	25.4
2000—Bush (R)	47.8	25.9
2004—Bush (R)	51.0	30.7
2008—Obama (D)	52.9	32.9
	0 10 20 30 40 50 60 70 80	0 10 20 30 40

Sources: Historical Data Archive, Inter-university Consortium for Political and Social Research; Michael P. McDonald and Samuel L. Popkin, "The Myth of the Vanishing Voter," *American Political Science Review,* Vol. 95, No. 4 (December 2001), p. 966; and the United States Elections Project.

FIGURE 9–2 Voter Turnout for Presidential and Congressional Elections, 1908–2010

The peaks represent voter turnout in presidential-election years; the troughs represent voter turnout in off-presidential-election years.

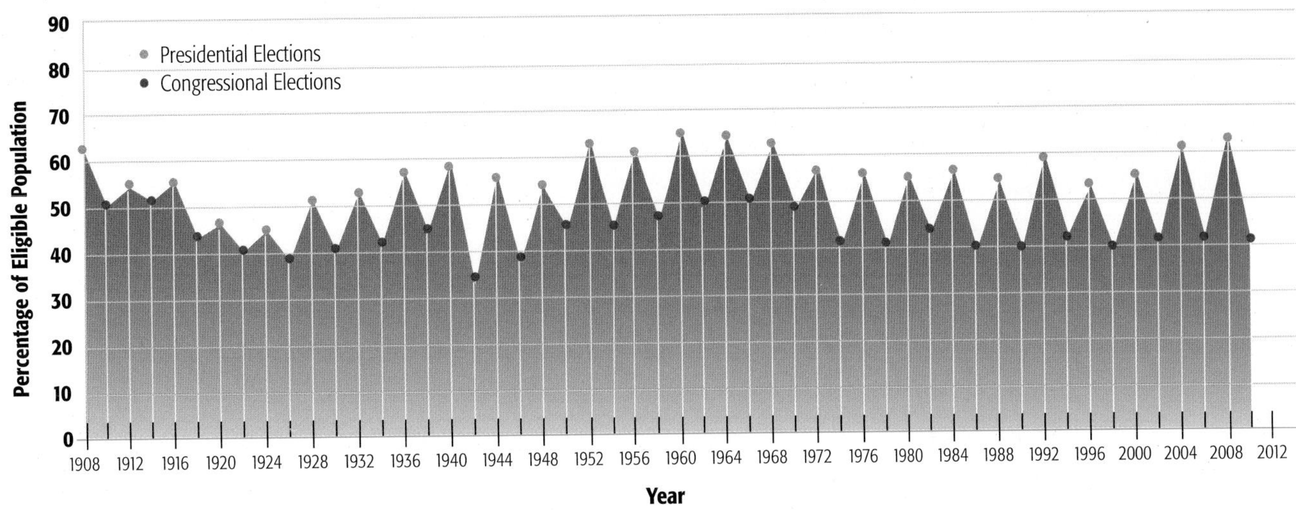

Note: Prior to 1948, the voting-age population is used as a proxy for the population eligible to vote.

Sources: Historical Data Archive, Inter-university Consortium for Political and Social Research; Michael P. McDonald and Samuel L. Popkin, "The Myth of the Vanishing Voter," *American Political Science Review*, Vol. 95, No. 4 (December 2001), p. 966; and the United States Elections Project.

election years. The average turnout in state elections is about 14 percentage points higher when a presidential election is held.

Now consider local elections. In races for mayor, city council, county auditor, and the like, it is fairly common for only 25 percent or less of the electorate to vote. Is something amiss here? It would seem that people should be more likely to vote in elections that directly affect them. At the local level, each person's vote counts more (because there are fewer voters). Furthermore, the issues—crime control, school bonds, sewer bonds, and the like—touch the immediate interests of the voters. In reality, however, potential voters are most interested in national elections when a presidential choice is involved. Otherwise, voter participation in our representative government is very low (and, as we have seen, it is not overwhelmingly great even in presidential elections).

The Effect of Low Voter Turnout

There are two schools of thought concerning low voter turnout. Some view low voter participation as a threat to representative democratic government. Too few individuals are deciding who wields political power in society. In addition, low voter participation presumably signals apathy about the political system in general. It also may signal that potential voters simply do not want to take the time to learn about the issues.

Others are less concerned about low voter participation. They contend that low voter participation simply indicates more satisfaction with the status quo. Also, they believe that representative democracy is a reality even if a very small percentage of eligible voters vote. If everyone who does not vote thinks that the outcome of the election will accord with his or her own desires, then representative democracy is working. The nonvoters are obtaining the type of government—with the type of people running it—that they want to have anyway.

did you know?

That computer software now exists that can identify likely voters and likely campaign donors by town, neighborhood, and street.

Is Voter Turnout Declining?

During the last decades of the twentieth century, the media regularly voiced concern that voter turnout was declining. Indeed, Figure 9–2 above shows relatively low voter turnout from 1972 through 2002—though turnout has gone back up in the last few elections.

Pundits have blamed the low turnout on negative campaigning and broad public cynicism about the political process. But is voter turnout actually as low as it seems?

did you know?

That noncitizens were allowed to vote in some states until the early 1920s.

One problem with widely used measurements of voter turnout is that they compare the number of people who actually vote with the **voting-age population,** not the population of *eligible voters*. These figures are not the same. The figure for the voting-age population includes felons and former felons who have lost the right to vote. Above all, it includes new immigrants who are not yet citizens. Finally, it does not include Americans living abroad, who can cast absentee ballots.

In 2010, the measured voting-age population included 3.1 million ineligible felons and former felons, and an estimated 19.6 million noncitizens. It did not include 5.0 million Americans abroad. The voting-age population in 2010 was 235.8 million people. The **vote-eligible population,** however, was only 218.05 million. Using the voting-age population to calculate national turnout would reduce the turnout percentage from 41.5 to 38.2 percent—a substantial error.

Voting-Age Population The number of people of voting age living in the country at a given time, regardless of whether they have the right to vote.

Vote-Eligible Population The number of people who, at a given time, enjoy the right to vote in national elections.

As you learned in Chapter 5, the United States has experienced high rates of immigration in recent decades. Political scientists Michael McDonald and Samuel Popkin concluded that the very low voter turnout reported in many sources after 1972 was a function of the increasing size of the ineligible population, chiefly due to immigration.[18]

Factors Influencing Who Votes

A clear association exists between voter participation and the following characteristics: age, educational attainment, minority status, income level, and the existence of two-party competition.

- *Age.* Look at Table 9–4 on the left, which shows the breakdown of voter participation by age group for the 2008 presidential elections. It would appear from these figures that age is a strong factor in determining voter turnout on Election Day. The reported turnout increases with older age groups. Older voters are more settled in their lives, are already registered, and have had more time to experience voting as an expected activity.
- *Educational attainment.* Education also influences voter turnout. In general, the more education you have, the more likely you are to vote. This pattern is clearly evident in the 2008 election results, as you can see in Table 9–5 on the facing page.

TABLE 9–4 Voting in the 2008 Presidential Elections by Age Group

Turnout is given as a percentage of the voting-age citizen population.

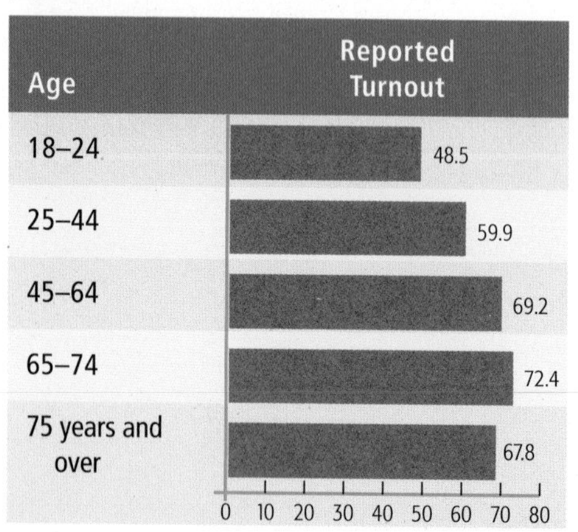

Source: U.S. Bureau of the Census, May 2010.

- *Minority status.* Race and ethnicity are important, too, in determining the level of voter turnout. According to census figures, non-Hispanic whites in 2008 voted at a 66.1 percent rate, whereas the non-Hispanic African American turnout rate was 64.7 percent. For Hispanics, the turnout rate was 49.9 percent, and for Asian Americans the rate was 47.6 percent. With an African American presidential candidate on the ballot in 2008, the African American vote took a considerable leap. Note that the Census Bureau did not correct its figures for felon status. If it had done so, the African American voting rate would have exceeded the rate for non-Hispanic whites.
- *Income level.* Differences in income also correlate with differences in voter turnout. Wealthier people tend to be overrepresented among voters who turn out on Election Day. In recent presidential elections,

18. Michael P. McDonald and Samuel L. Popkin, "The Myth of the Vanishing Voter," *American Political Science Review*, Vol. 95, No. 4 (December 2001), p. 963.

voter turnout for those with the highest annual family incomes has approached three times the turnout of those with the lowest annual family incomes.

- *Two-party competition.* Another factor in voter turnout is the extent to which elections are competitive within a state. More competitive states generally have higher turnout rates, and turnout increases considerably in states where there is an extremely competitive race in a particular year.

These statistics reinforce one another. For example, white voters are likely to be wealthier than African American voters, who are also less likely to have obtained a college education.

TABLE 9–5 Voting in the 2008 Presidential Elections by Education Level

Turnout is given as a percentage of the voting-age citizen population.

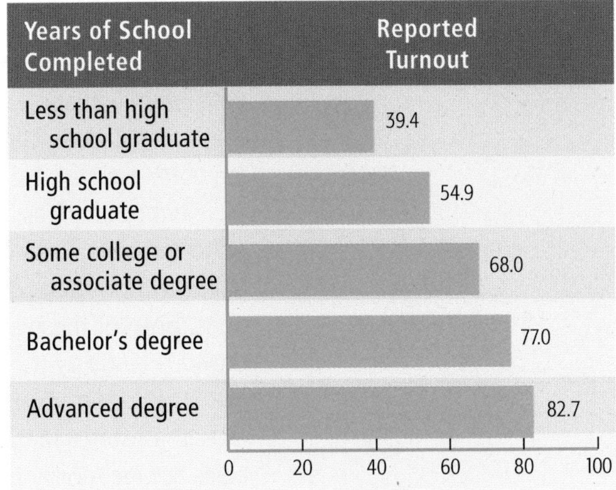

Years of School Completed	Reported Turnout
Less than high school graduate	39.4
High school graduate	54.9
Some college or associate degree	68.0
Bachelor's degree	77.0
Advanced degree	82.7

Source: U.S. Bureau of the Census, May 2010.

Why People Do Not Vote

For many years, political scientists believed that one reason voter turnout in the United States was so much lower than in other Western nations was that it was very difficult to register to vote. In most states, registration required a special trip to a public office far in advance of elections. During the last decade or so, however, laws have simplified the voter-registration process to a significant degree. Thus, many experts are now proposing other explanations for low U.S. voter turnout.

Uninformative Media Coverage and Negative Campaigning. Several scholars contend that one of the reasons why some people do not vote has to do with media coverage of campaigns. Many researchers have shown that the news media tend to provide much more news about "the horse race," or which candidates are ahead in the polls, than about the actual policy positions of the candidates. According to a 2006 study of voting behavior conducted by the Pew Research Center, lack of information about the candidates was cited by 68 percent of nonvoters as one of their reasons for not voting.[19]

Additionally, voters who are asked how a negative ad affects them typically respond that it makes them less likely to vote. Many commentators have concluded, therefore, that the epidemic of negative ads in recent years has depressed turnout. Studies of actual elections, however, suggest that voters subjected to barrages of negative ads vote in *greater* numbers. Political scientist Paul Martin of the University of Virginia contends that seeing negative ads makes people think that there are "more problems facing the country, which encourages people to vote." Stanford University professor Jon Krosnick notes that "turnout goes up when people don't just prefer their candidate, but strongly dislike the other guy."[20]

The Rational Ignorance Effect. Another explanation of low voter turnout suggests that citizens are making a logical choice in not voting. If citizens believe that their votes will not affect the outcome of an election, then they have little incentive to seek the information they need to cast intelligent votes. The lack of incentive to obtain costly (in terms of time, attention, and the like) information about politicians and political issues has been called the **rational ignorance effect.** That term may seem contradictory, but it is not. Rational ignorance is a condition in which people purposely and rationally decide not to obtain information—to remain ignorant.

Rational Ignorance Effect
An effect produced when people purposely and rationally decide not to become informed on an issue because they believe that their vote on the issue is not likely to be a deciding one; a lack of incentive to seek the necessary information to cast an intelligent vote.

Why, then, do even one-third to one-half of U.S. citizens bother to show up at the polls? One explanation is that most citizens receive personal satisfaction from the act of

19. Pew Research Center for the People and the Press, survey conducted September 21–October 4, 2006, and reported in "Who Votes, Who Doesn't, and Why," released October 28, 2006.
20. Sharon Begley, "Political Scientists Get More Scientific in Studying the Vote," *The Wall Street Journal,* August 18, 2006, p. A11.

voting. It makes them feel that they are fulfilling their duty as citizens and that they are doing something patriotic.[21] Even among voters who are registered and who plan to vote, however, if the cost of voting goes up (in terms of time and inconvenience), the number of voters who actually vote will fall. In particular, bad weather on Election Day means that, on average, a smaller percentage of registered voters will go to the polls.

Plans for Improving Voter Turnout. Mail-in voting, Internet voting, registering to vote when you apply for a driver's license, registering to vote on Election Day in all states—these are all ideas that have been either suggested or implemented in the hope of improving voter turnout. Nonetheless, voter turnout remains low.

Two other ideas have seemed promising. The first was to allow voters to visit the polls up to three weeks before Election Day. The second was to allow voters to vote by absentee ballot without having to give any particular reason for doing so. In the 2008 general elections, both of these plans were implemented by many states. The 2008 experience and a previous study by the Committee for the Study of the American Electorate suggest, however, that states with early voting or unrestricted absentee voting have no better turnout rates than states that require most people to show up at the polls. Apparently, these strategies appeal mostly to people who already intend to vote.

What is left? One possibility is to declare Election Day a national holiday. In this way, more eligible voters will find it easier to go to the polls.

Legal Restrictions on Voting

Legal restrictions on voter registration have existed since the founding of our nation. Most groups in the United States have been concerned with the suffrage issue at one time or another.

Historical Restrictions

In colonial times, only white males who owned property with a certain minimum value were eligible to vote, leaving more Americans ineligible to take part in elections than were eligible.

Property Requirements. Many government functions concern property rights and the distribution of income and wealth, and some of the founders of our nation believed it was appropriate that only people who had an interest in property should vote on these issues. The idea of extending the vote to all citizens was, according to Charles Pinckney, a South Carolina delegate to the Constitutional Convention, merely "theoretical nonsense."

The logic behind the restriction of voting rights to property owners was questioned by Thomas Paine in his pamphlet *Common Sense*:

> *Here is a man who today owns a jackass, and the jackass is worth $60. Today the man is a voter and goes to the polls and deposits his vote. Tomorrow the jackass dies. The next day the man comes to vote without his jackass and cannot vote at all. Now tell me, which was the voter, the man or the jackass?*[22]

The writers of the Constitution allowed the states to decide who should vote. Thus, women were allowed to vote in Wyoming in 1870 but not in the entire nation until the Nineteenth Amendment was ratified in 1920. By about 1850, most white adult males in

---

21. According to the Pew Research Center study cited in footnote 19, 88 percent of regular voters felt that they had a duty as citizens to always vote, whereas only 39 percent of nonvoters felt that they owed such a duty.
22. Thomas Paine, *Common Sense* (London: H. D. Symonds, 1792), p. 28.

nearly all the states could vote without any property qualification. North Carolina was the last state to eliminate its property test for voting—in 1856.

Further Extensions of the Franchise. Extension of the franchise to black males occurred with the passage of the Fifteenth Amendment in 1870. This enfranchisement was short lived, however, as the "redemption" of the South by white racists had rolled back those gains by the end of the century. As discussed in Chapter 5, it was not until the 1960s that African Americans, both male and female, were able to participate in the electoral process in all states. Women received full national voting rights with the Nineteenth Amendment in 1920. The most recent extension of the franchise occurred when the voting age was reduced to eighteen by the Twenty-sixth Amendment in 1971. One result of lowering the voting age was to depress voter turnout beginning in 1972, as you can see in Figure 9–2 on page 309. Young people are less likely to vote than older citizens.

These African American voters are shown in New York City in the mid-1940s. Until the 1965 Voting Rights Act, African Americans and other minorities faced numerous obstacles when trying to exercise their right to vote, especially in the South. If a significant part of the population is not allowed to vote, what effect is that likely to have on the types of legislation passed by Congress or by state legislatures? (Library of Congress/NAACP Collection)

Is the Franchise Still Too Restrictive? There continue to be certain classes of people who do not have the right to vote. These include noncitizens and, in most states, convicted felons who have been released from prison. They also include current prison inmates, election law violators, and people who are mentally incompetent. Also, no one under the age of eighteen can vote. A number of political activists have argued that some of these groups should be allowed to vote. Most other democracies do not prevent convicts from voting after they have completed their sentences. In the 1800s, many states let noncitizen immigrants vote.

One discussion concerns the voting rights of convicted felons who are no longer in prison or on parole. Those who oppose letting these people vote contend that voting should be a privilege, not a right, and we should not want the types of people who commit felonies participating in decision making. Others believe that it is wrong to further penalize those who have paid their debt to society. These people argue that barring felons from the polls injures minority groups, because minorities make up a disproportionately large share of former prison inmates.

Current Eligibility and Registration Requirements

Voting generally requires **registration,** and to register, a person must satisfy the following voter qualifications, or legal requirements: (1) citizenship, (2) age (eighteen or older), and (3) residency—the duration varies widely from state to state and with types of elections. Since 1972, states cannot impose residency requirements of more than thirty days.

Registration
The entry of a person's name onto the list of registered voters for elections. To register, a person must meet certain legal requirements of age, citizenship, and residency.

Each state has different qualifications for voting and registration. In 1993, Congress passed the "motor voter" bill, which requires that states provide voter-registration materials when people receive or renew driver's licenses, that all states allow voters to register by mail, and that voter-registration forms be made available at a wider variety of public places and agencies. In general, a person must register well in advance of an election, although voters in Idaho, Maine, Minnesota, Wisconsin, and Wyoming are allowed to register up to, or even on, Election Day. North Dakota has no voter registration at all.

Some argue that registration requirements are responsible for much of the nonparticipation in our political process. There also is a partisan dimension to the debate over registration and nonvoting. Republicans generally fear that an expanded electorate would help to elect more Democrats—because more Democrats than Republicans are the kinds of persons who have trouble registering.[23]

23. According to the 2006 Pew study of voting behavior cited earlier in footnote 19, of the approximately one-fifth of the U.S. voting-age population who are not registered to vote, 20 percent are Democrats and 14 percent are Republicans.

The question arises as to whether registration is really necessary. If it decreases participation in the political process, perhaps it should be dropped altogether. Still, as those in favor of registration requirements argue, such requirements may prevent fraudulent voting practices, such as multiple voting or voting by noncitizens.

Extension of the Voting Rights Act

In the summer of 2006, President George W. Bush signed legislation that extended the Voting Rights Act of 1965 for twenty-five more years. As we discussed in Chapter 5, the Voting Rights Act was enacted to assure that African Americans had equal access to the polls. Any new voting practices or procedures in jurisdictions with a history of discrimination in voting have to be approved by the U.S. Department of Justice or the federal district court in Washington, D.C., before being implemented.

did you know?

That the first "wire" story transmitted by telegraph was sent in 1846.

A provision of the Voting Rights Act permits jurisdictions to "bail out" of coverage if they can demonstrate a clean record on discrimination during the previous ten years. By 2009, however, seventeen Virginia counties were the only jurisdictions in the country to successfully bail out. In June 2009, the United States Supreme Court permitted a Texas utility district to file for a bailout, and strongly indicated that relief from the requirements of the act should be granted more freely. Indeed, several justices speculated on whether the act was still constitutional under modern circumstances, but the Court drew back from resolving that issue.[24]

The Media and Politics

The study of people and politics must take into account the role played by the media. Historically, the print media played the most important role in informing public debate. The print media developed, for the most part, our understanding of how news is to be reported. Today, however, more than 90 percent of Americans use television news as their primary source of information. In addition, the Internet has become a major source for news, political communications, and fund-raising. The Web is now the second most widely used source of information, displacing newspapers. As Internet use grows, the system of gathering and sharing news and information is changing from one in which the media have a primary role to one in which the individual citizen may play a greater part.

The mass media perform a number of different functions in any country. In the United States, we can list at least six. Almost all of them can have political implications, and some are essential to the democratic process. These functions are as follows: (1) entertainment, (2) reporting the news, (3) identifying public problems, (4) socializing new generations, (5) providing a political forum, and (6) making profits.

Many high-profile entertainers, such as actress America Ferrera, engage in charitable appearances to encourage voter registration. What might be the motivation for well-known entertainers to become part of this country's political process? (Gilbert Carrasquillo/FilmMagic/Getty Images)

Entertainment

By far the greatest number of radio and television hours are dedicated to entertaining the public. The battle for prime-time ratings indicates how important successful entertainment is to the survival of networks and individual stations.

Although there is no direct linkage between entertainment and politics, network dramas often introduce material that may be politically controversial and that may stimulate public discussion. Examples include the TV series *The West Wing* and *Commander in Chief,* which people believe promoted liberal political values. Made-for-TV movies have focused on a number of controversial topics, including AIDS, incest, and wife battering.

---

24. *Northwest Austin Municipal Utility District No. One v. Holder,* 557 U.S. ___ (2009).

Reporting the News

A primary function of the mass media in all their forms is the reporting of news. The media provide words and pictures about events, facts, personalities, and ideas. The protections of the First Amendment are intended to keep the flow of news as free as possible, because it is an essential part of the democratic process. If citizens cannot obtain unbiased information about the state of their communities and their leaders' actions, how can they make voting decisions? One of the most incisive comments about the importance of the media was made by James Madison, who said, "A people who mean to be their own governors must arm themselves with the power knowledge gives. A popular government without popular information or the means of acquiring it, is but a prologue to a farce or a tragedy or perhaps both."[25]

Identifying Public Problems

The power of the media is important not only in revealing what the government is doing but also in determining what the government ought to do—in other words, in setting the **public agenda.** The mass media identify public issues, such as convicted sex offenders living in residential neighborhoods on their release from prison. The media have influenced the passage of legislation, such as "Megan's Law," which requires police to notify neighbors about the release and/or resettlement of certain offenders. American journalists also work in a long tradition of uncovering public wrongdoing, corruption, and bribery and of bringing such wrongdoing to the public's attention. Closely related to this investigative function is that of presenting policy alternatives.

Public Agenda
Issues that are perceived by the political community as meriting public attention and governmental action.

Public policy is often complex and difficult to make entertaining, but programs devoted to public policy are often scheduled for prime-time television, especially on cable networks. Network shows with a "news magazine" format sometimes include segments on policy issues as well.

Socializing New Generations

As mentioned in Chapter 6, the media, and particularly television, strongly influence the beliefs and opinions of Americans. Because of this influence, the media play a significant role in the political socialization of the younger generation, as well as immigrants to this country. Through the transmission of historical information (sometimes fictionalized), the presentation of American culture, and the portrayal of the diverse regions and groups in the United States, the media teach young people and immigrants about what it means to be an American. TV talk shows, such as the *Oprah Winfrey Show,* sometimes focus on controversial issues (such as abortion or assisted suicide). Many children's shows are designed not only to entertain young viewers but also to instruct them in the moral values of American society.

As more young Americans turn to the Internet for entertainment, they are also finding an increasing amount of social and political information there. America's youth today are the Internet generation. Young people do not use the Internet just for chat and e-mail. They also participate in political forums, obtain information for writing assignments, and increasingly watch movies and news shows online.

Providing a Political Forum

As part of their news function, the media also provide a political forum for leaders and the public. Candidates for office use news reporting to sustain interest in their campaigns, while officeholders use the media to gain support for their policies or to present an

Young people (and others) often obtain their political information from political satire shows such as the one hosted by Jon Stewart on Comedy Central. How accurate are the impressions that viewers obtain from watching such shows? (Ethan Miller/Getty Images for Comedy Central)

25. James Madison, "Letter to W. T. Barry" (August 4, 1822), in Gaillard P. Hunt, ed., *The Writings of James Madison,* Vol. 103 (1910).

image of leadership. Presidential trips abroad are an outstanding way for the chief executive to get colorful, positive, and exciting news coverage that makes the president look "presidential." The media also offer ways for citizens to participate in public debate, through letters to the editor, blog posts, and other channels.

Making Profits

Most of the news media in the United States are private, for-profit corporate enterprises. One of their goals is to make profits for expansion and for dividends to the stockholders who own the companies. In general, profits are made as a result of charging for advertising. Advertising revenues usually are related directly to circulation or to listener/viewer ratings.

Several well-known media outlets, in contrast, are publicly owned—public television stations in many communities and National Public Radio. These operate without extensive commercials, are locally supported, and are often subsidized by the government and corporations.

did you know?

That the number of people watching the television networks during prime time has declined by almost 25 percent in the last ten years.

For the most part, however, the media depend on advertisers to obtain revenues to make profits. Consequently, reporters may feel pressure from media owners and from advertisers. Media owners may take their cues from what advertisers want. If an important advertiser does not like the political bent of a particular reporter, the reporter could be asked to alter his or her "style" of writing. According to the Pew Research Center's Project for Excellence in Journalism, 38 percent of local print and broadcast journalists know of instances in which their newsrooms were encouraged to do a story because it related to an owner, advertiser, or sponsor.[26]

Advertisers have been known to pull ads from newspapers and TV stations whenever they read or view negative publicity about their own companies or products. For example, CBS ran a *60 Minutes* show about Dillard's and other department stores that claimed store security guards used excessive force and racial profiling. In response, Dillard's pulled its ads from CBS. This example can be multiplied many times over.

Lately, newspapers have found it increasingly difficult to make a profit. Newspaper revenues have fallen because online services such as Craigslist have taken over a greater share of classified advertising. The recent economic crisis, which depressed all forms of advertising spending, pushed many large daily newspapers over the edge. Newspapers in Chicago, Denver, and Seattle went out of business. Even some of the most famous papers, such as the *New York Times* and the *Boston Globe,* were in serious financial trouble. Despite the recession, however, much of the new media has continued to grow and prosper. We provide examples in this chapter's *The Politics of Boom and Bust* feature on the facing page.

The Primacy of Television

Television is the most influential medium. It is also big business. National news TV personalities such as Katie Couric and Brian Williams may earn millions of dollars per year from their TV contracts alone. They are paid so much because they command large audiences, and large audiences command high prices for advertising on national news shows. Indeed, news *per se* has become a major factor in the profitability of TV stations.

The Increase in News-Type Programming

In 1963, the major networks—ABC, CBS, and NBC—devoted only eleven minutes daily to national news. A twenty-four-hour-a-day news cable channel—CNN—started operating in 1980. With the addition of CNN–Headline News, CNBC, MSNBC, Fox News, and other

26. Pew Research Center for the People and the Press and the Project for Excellence in Journalism, *The State of the News Media 2007: An Annual Report on American Journalism.*

news-format cable channels since the 1980s, the amount of news-type programming has continued to increase. By 2010, the amount of time the networks devoted to news-type programming each day amounted to about three hours. In recent years, all of the major networks have also added Internet sites to try to capture that market, but they face thousands of competitors on the Web.

THE POLITICS OF BOOM AND BUST

THE NEW MEDIA SUCCEED IN A RECESSION

The American economy was in terrible shape. The rate of inflation was higher than it had been since World War II. The housing market was faltering. The unemployment rate reached 9 percent, also a post–World War II record. The time was the mid-1970s, not today. During this grim recession, Microsoft and Apple were founded.

HIGH-TECH START-UPS DURING A BUST

Apple and Microsoft were then tiny start-up companies. Their founders, Steve Jobs and Bill Gates, respectively, begged and borrowed funds to get things going and paid their first workers in part with stock—now worth hundreds of millions of dollars. Today, we won't know which start-ups born during the latest recession will become tomorrow's Microsoft or Apple. Clearly, the recession reduced the amount of funding available from so-called angel investors and venture capital firms. What we do know is that in recent years, some of the most significant start-ups have been Internet media firms. Facebook and Twitter were founded in 2006 just before the recession began, but they have enjoyed their best years of growth during terrible economic conditions.

Consider Apple again. It started during a recession forty years ago. It introduced its most recent major innovation, the iPad, in April 2010 during the latest recession. In subsequent months, Apple's earnings and stock price hit all-time highs, propelled in part by sales of the iPhone, first released on the eve of the recession in 2007. For its part, the iPad sold 1 million units in its first two months on the market. Sales of the iPod continued to grow, too.

MAKING A PROFIT OFF THE NEW MEDIA

As you discovered in this chapter's opening *What If*. . . feature, more people, particularly younger people, are getting their news off the Web. How do people access the Web? In the old days, accessing the Internet required a desktop computer. Then laptops with WiFi came along, allowing access to the Web from multiple locations. Today, we can access the Internet through smartphones. These include the BlackBerry and the iPhone, which is gaining market share based on the many innovative applications available for it. Apple likewise hopes that the iPad will become a dominant player.

What do we read on the Web? Often, we go to the Web sites of traditional newspapers. These sites, however, have been unable to earn profits because they can't sell enough advertising. They also find it hard to charge for access. The Web is filled with vast quantities of free news, and sites that charge for access lose customers to sites that are free. Online newspapers are drowning in a sea of free content.

In contrast, Internet companies and high-tech firms that thrive financially have done so by dominating their markets, creating near-monopolies. Microsoft Windows is a famous example. Google is so pervasive that few users want to employ any other search engine. Apple dominates the market for music downloads, and the iTunes/iPod/iPhone combination is enormously profitable. Facebook now leads in social networking. There is only one Twitter.

As personal computers become Chinese-made commodities, sold for razor-thin profit margins, high-tech companies are frantic to find ways to become exclusive. "Control the channel" is the mantra. Apple demands the right to approve all iPhone applications—so that it can control the channel. That way, it believes, lies survival.

FOR CRITICAL ANALYSIS

Political news is more accessible than ever through new ways to access the Internet. Does this instant availability necessarily mean that people are more politically informed? Why or why not?

"Welcome to 'All About the Media,' where members of the media discuss the role of the media in media coverage of the media."

Television's Influence on the Political Process

Television's influence on the political process today is recognized by all who engage in that process. Television news is often criticized for being superficial, particularly compared with the detailed coverage available in newspapers and magazines. In fact, television news is constrained by its technical characteristics, the most important being the limitations of time—stories must be reported in only a few minutes.

The Impact of Video. The most interesting aspect of television is, of course, the fact that it relies on pictures rather than words to attract the viewer's attention. Therefore, the video that is chosen for a particular political story has exaggerated importance. Viewers do not know what other photos may have been taken or what other events may have been recorded—they see only those appearing on their screens. Television news can also be exploited for its drama by well-constructed stories. Some critics suggest that there is pressure to produce television news that has a "story line," like a novel or movie. The story should be short, with exciting pictures and a clear plot. In the extreme case, the news media are satisfied with a **sound bite,** a several-second comment selected or crafted for its immediate impact on the viewer.

did you know?

That the average length of a quote, or sound bite, for a candidate decreased from forty-nine seconds in 1968 to less than nine seconds today.

It has been suggested that these formatting characteristics—or necessities—of television increase its influence on political events. As you are aware, real life is usually not dramatic, nor do all events have a neat or an easily understood plot. Political campaigns are continuing events, lasting perhaps as long as two years. The significance of their daily turns and twists is only apparent later. The "drama" of Congress, with its 535 players and dozens of important committees and meetings, is also difficult for the media to present. Television requires, instead, dozens of daily three-minute stories.

Sound Bite
A brief, memorable comment that can easily be fit into news broadcasts.

Cable News Channels. A major change to television from its early days has been the growth in the number and popularity of cable channels. Cable has served to break the control that the three major broadcast networks formerly had on television news. The founding of the twenty-four-hour news channel Cable News Network (CNN) by entrepreneur Ted Turner in 1980 was the first major step in this direction. A second was the establishment of Fox News Channel by Australian American media magnate Rupert Murdoch in 1996. Fox has become well known for its conservative political positions, although the network itself disputes allegations that it is biased.

Some political scientists have argued that the development of twenty-four-hour news channels, operating internationally, has changed the way that political leaders address crises, such as international incidents, diplomatic initiatives, and natural disasters. Steven Livingston of George Washington University observes that this "CNN effect," by making the public immediately aware of such events, forces leaders to make decisions more rapidly. It can also complicate delicate diplomatic negotiations and compel nations to take positions on controversies they might prefer to avoid.

The Media and Political Campaigns

All forms of the media—television, newspapers, radio, magazines, the Internet and blogs and podcasts—have a significant political impact on American society. Media influence is most obvious during political campaigns. News coverage of a single event, such as the results of the Iowa caucuses or the New Hampshire primary, may determine whether a candidate is referred to in the media as the front-runner in a presidential campaign. It is not too much of an exaggeration to say that almost all national political figures, starting with the president, plan every public appearance and statement to attract media coverage.

Television Coverage

Because television is still the primary news source for the majority of Americans, candidates and their consultants spend much of their time devising strategies that use television to their benefit. Three types of TV coverage are generally employed in campaigns for the presidency and other offices: political advertising (including negative ads), management of news coverage, and campaign debates.

Political Advertising. Political advertising has become increasingly important for the profitability of television station owners. Hearst-Argyle Television, for example, obtains more than 10 percent of its revenues from political ads during an election year. In addition to typical print ads, online political advertising has been on the rise. Broadcast television still dominates media spending during campaigns, however, and the amounts spent continue to rise. During 2010, total spending on the media by candidates at all levels totaled close to $3 billion.

Negative Advertising. Perhaps one of the most effective political ads of all time was a thirty-second spot created by President Lyndon Johnson's media adviser in 1964. Johnson's opponent in the campaign was Barry Goldwater, a conservative Republican candidate known for his expansive views on the role of the U.S. military. In this ad, a little girl stood in a field of daisies. As she held a daisy, she pulled the petals off and quietly counted to herself. Suddenly, when she reached number ten, a deep bass voice cut in and began a countdown: "10, 9, 8, 7, 6 . . . ." When the voice intoned "zero," the mushroom cloud of an atomic bomb began to fill the screen. Then President Johnson's voice was heard: "These are the stakes. To make a world in which all of God's children can live, or to go into the dark. We must either love each other or we must die." At the end of the commercial, the message read, "Vote for President Johnson on November 3."

Negative campaign ads continue in full force. This one is aimed at former eBay chief executive officer Meg Whitman, who decided to run for governor of California in 2010. Do negative campaign ads work? Why or why not? (www.YouTube.com)

Since the daisy girl advertisement, negative advertising has come into its own. In recent elections, an ever-increasing percentage of political ads have been negative in nature. In 2008, one study found that two-thirds of the presidential campaign ads were negative, as opposed to one-third in previous presidential election cycles.

The public claims not to like negative advertising, but as one consultant put it, "Negative advertising works."[27] Negative ads can backfire, however, when there are three or more candidates in the race, a typical state of affairs in the early presidential primaries. If one candidate attacks another, the attacker as well as the candidate who is attacked may come to be viewed negatively by the public. A candidate who "goes negative" may thus unintentionally boost the chances of a third candidate who is not part of the exchange.

27. Interestingly, brain-imaging research bolsters this view. Studies conducted while subjects watched negative ads on TV indicated that viewers lost empathy for their own candidate once the candidate was attacked in an ad. See Seth Borenstein, "Scientists Track Effects of Negative Ads," *Seattle Post-Intelligencer,* November 3, 2006.

These are stills of a short television advertisement used by presidential candidate Lyndon Johnson in 1964. The "daisy girl" ad contrasted the innocence of childhood with the horror of an atomic bomb. How effective was this negative TV ad? (Doyle, Dane, Bernbach)

While many complain that negative ads undermine elections and even democracy, some scholars take a different approach. For example, John Geer, a political scientist at Vanderbilt University, argues that attack ads are actually beneficial to the democratic process. Geer claims that this is because negative ads tend to focus on important political issues, unlike positive ads, which are more likely to focus on the candidates' personal characteristics. Thus, negative ads enrich the democratic process by providing the voters with more information than can be gleaned from positive ads.[28]

Management of News Coverage. Using political advertising to get a message across to the public is a very expensive tactic. Coverage by the news media, however, is free. The campaign simply needs to ensure that coverage takes place. In recent years, campaign managers have shown increasing sophistication in creating newsworthy events for journalists to cover.

The campaign staff uses several methods to try to influence the quantity and type of coverage the campaign receives. First, the staff understands the technical aspects of media coverage—camera angles, necessary equipment, timing, and deadlines—and plans political events to accommodate the press. Second, the campaign organization is aware that political reporters and their sponsors—networks, newspapers, or blogs—are in competition for the best stories and can be manipulated through the granting of favors, such as a personal interview with the candidate. Third, the scheduler in the campaign has the important task of planning events that will be photogenic and interesting enough for the evening news.

Spin
An interpretation of campaign events or election results that is favorable to the candidate's campaign strategy.

Spin Doctor
A political campaign adviser who tries to convince journalists of the truth of a particular interpretation of events.

A related goal, although one that is more difficult to attain, is to convince reporters that a particular interpretation of an event is true. Today, the art of putting the appropriate **spin** on a story or event is highly developed. Press advisers, often referred to as **spin doctors,** try to convince the journalists that their interpretations of the political events are correct. For

28. John G. Geer, *In Defense of Negativity: Attack Ads in Presidential Campaigns* (Chicago: University of Chicago Press, 2006).

example, the Obama administration and the Republicans engaged in a major spinning duel over the stimulus package passed by Congress in February 2009. The administration called the bill essential to economic recovery; the Republicans described it as a dangerous increase in the size of government. Journalists have begun to report on the different spins placed on events and on how candidates and officeholders try to manipulate news coverage.

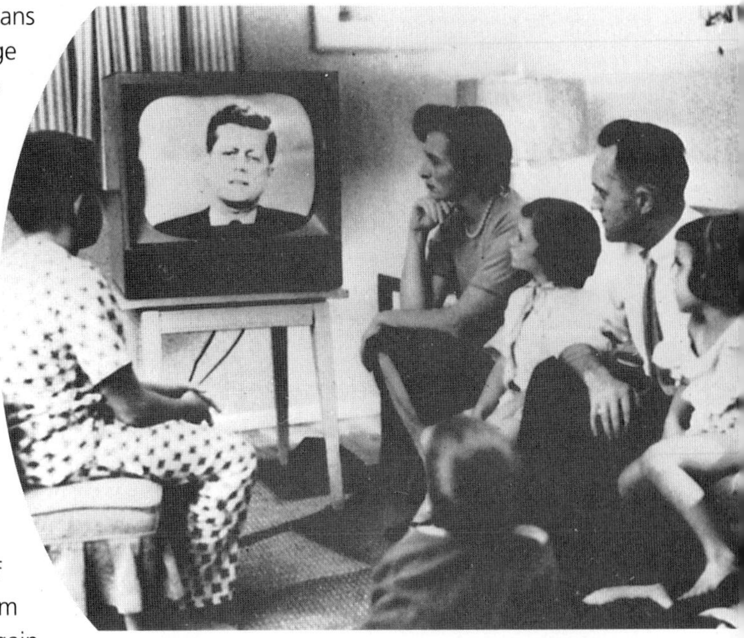

Going for the Knockout Punch—Televised Presidential Debates. In presidential elections, perhaps just as important as political advertisements and general news coverage is the performance of the candidate in televised presidential debates. After the first such debate in 1960, in which John Kennedy, the young senator from Massachusetts, took on the vice president of the United States, Richard Nixon, candidates became aware of the great potential of television for changing the momentum of a campaign. In general, challengers have much more to gain from debating than do incumbents. Challengers hope that the incumbent will make a mistake in the debate and undermine the "presidential" image. Incumbent presidents are loath to debate their challengers because it puts their opponents on an equal footing with them, but the debates have become so widely anticipated that it is difficult for an incumbent to refuse.

A family watches the 1960 Kennedy-Nixon debates on television. After the debate, TV viewers thought Kennedy had won, whereas radio listeners thought Nixon had won. Why have televised presidential debates become major media events? (Library of Congress)

Debates can affect the outcome of a race. In 2008, the three presidential debates may have given Democrat Barack Obama an added edge over Republican John McCain. Obama received a small positive bump in the polls after each debate, although the effect appeared to be temporary. More important, the debates gave Obama a chance to let the voters become more comfortable with him. His calm demeanor was viewed as a plus. McCain, in contrast, may have hurt himself in the third debate by being too aggressive. The vice-presidential debate was also important because Alaska Governor Sarah Palin, the Republican candidate, had not done well in earlier television interviews. Even some Republicans wondered whether she was knowledgeable enough to serve as president should McCain die or become incapacitated. Palin's confident performance in the debate reassured her supporters.

Although debates are justified publicly as an opportunity for the voters to find out how candidates differ on the issues, what the candidates want is to capitalize on the power of television to project an image. They view the debate as a strategic opportunity to improve their own images or to point out the failures of their opponents. Candidates also know that the morning-after interpretation of the debate by the news media may play a crucial role in what the public thinks.

The Internet, Blogging, and Podcasting

Without a doubt, the Internet has become an important vehicle for campaign advertising and news coverage, as well as for soliciting campaign contributions. The Internet became even more important during the 2007–2008 election cycle, when Democrat Barack Obama's fund-raising operation obliterated every political fund-raising and spending record in history. By mid-October, Obama had raised more than $650 million from about 3 million donors, in large part over the Internet. While about half of the funds came from people giving less than $200, larger donors were also generous. Obama was able to obtain this financing without extensive use of in-person fund-raising parties.

Monday, November 1, 2010 As of 5:22 PM EDT New York 49° | 35°

THE WALL STREET JOURNAL.

U.S. Edition Home | Today's Paper • Video • Blogs • Journal Community Log In

World • U.S. • New York • Business • Markets • Tech • Personal Finance • Life & Culture • Opinion • Careers • Real Estate • Small Business

QUICK LINKS: Campaign 2010 | Election Projection Map | Investing in Funds | The Foreclosure Crisis | World Series | Week Ahead | Heard on the Street

LATEST HEADLINES WSJ: Gut Check: Clothes That Make Men Look Slimmer

Vote Hints at Historic Political Volatility

The U.S. could be caught in a cycle of political volatility witnessed only four times in the past century, almost all during war or economic unease.

• Complete Coverage: Campaign 2010

• Get breaking email alerts

Google Sues Interior Department

Google is suing the Department of the Interior, alleging the federal agency wrote procurement requirements for a new email system to favor rival Microsoft over its own Google Apps.

Source of Bomb-Plot Tip-Off Is Named

The source of a tip that alerted security agencies around the world to the package-bomb plot late last week was Jabir al-Fayfi, a Saudi national and former Guantánamo Bay inmate.

Android Overtakes IPhone

A World Series That's Rich in Character

Death Toll in Iraq Church Siege Rises

Market Data Center

OVERVIEW | U.S. | EUROPE | ASIA | CURRENCY/RATES

DJIA*	11124.62	6.13 ↑	0.06%
Nasdaq*	2504.84	2.57 ↓	0.10%
S&P 500*	1184.38	1.12 ↑	0.09%
Global Dow*	2019.76	1.38 ↓	0.07%
FTSE 100*	5694.62	19.46 ↑	0.34%
Nikkei Average*	9154.72	47.73 ↓	0.52%

* at close Source: Dow Jones, Reuters 4:01 P.M. 11/1/10

MARKET NEWS Caution Limits Stocks

Quotes | MarketBeat | Market Data Center | Customize Your Markets Help

Highlights

Photos of the Day: Nov. 1

In Monday's pictures, Bulgarian students protest education cuts, separated Koreans say tearful goodbyes, a Pakistani boy celebrates a good fishing catch and more.

CAMPAIGN 2010 In The Polls Video Pictures Washington Wire Capital Journal Latest Coverage »

What's News —

SUBSCRIBER CONTENT LOG IN or SUBSCRIBE

Campaign 2010

Video

All major papers and magazines have their own Web sites, such as this one for the *Wall Street Journal*. How effective are these Web sites at informing the public about political matters? (© Dow Jones & Company, *Wall Street Journal*, 11/1/10. All rights reserved)

One highly effective characteristic of Obama's fund-raising machine was its decentralization, which was powerfully assisted by the nature of the Web. Obama was able to rely on thousands of individual fund-raising activists who solicited their friends and acquaintances, often for relatively small sums. No campaign had ever had so many volunteer fund-raisers or so many donors. Obama's site, MyBarackObama.com, was a major social networking hub.[29]

Today, the campaign staff of every candidate running for a significant political office includes an Internet campaign strategist—a professional hired to create and maintain the campaign Web site, blogs, and podcasts (blogs and podcasts will be discussed shortly). The work of this strategist includes designing a user-friendly and attractive Web site for the candidate, managing the candidate's e-mail communications, tracking campaign contributions made through the site, hiring bloggers to push the candidate's agenda on the Web, and monitoring Web sites for favorable or unfavorable comments or video clips about the candidate. Additionally, all major interest groups in the United States now use the Internet to promote their causes. Prior to elections, various groups engage in issue advocacy from their Web sites. At little or no cost, they can promote positions taken by favored candidates and solicit contributions.

Blogging. Within the last few years, politicians have also felt obligated to post regular blogs on their Web sites. The word *blog* comes from *Web log,* a regular updating of one's ideas at a specific Web site. Of course, many people besides politicians are also posting blogs. Not all of the millions of blogs posted daily are political in nature. Many are, though, and they can have a dramatic influence on events, giving rise to the term *blogosphere politics.*

Blogs are clearly threatening the mainstream media. They can be highly specialized, highly political, and highly entertaining. And they are cheap. The *Washington Post* requires thousands of employees, paper, and ink to generate its offline product and incurs delivery costs to get it to readers. A blogging organization such as RealClearPolitics can generate its political commentary with fewer than ten employees. Of course, all of the major newspapers and magazines have their own Web sites and blogs. The problem is how to gain revenue from these projects. Too often, sites operated by the traditional media cost more to maintain than they earn.

Podcasting. Once blogs—written words—became well established, it was only a matter of time before they ended up as spoken words. Enter **podcasting,** so called because the first Internet-communicated spoken blogs were downloaded onto Apple's iPods. Podcasts, though, can be heard on a computer or downloaded onto any portable listening device. Podcasting can also include videos. Hundreds of thousands of podcasts are now generated every day. Basically, anyone who has an idea can easily create a podcast and make it available for downloading. Like blogs, podcasting threatens traditional media sources. Publications that sponsor podcasts find it hard to make them profitable.

Podcasting
A method of distributing multimedia files, such as audio or video files, for downloading onto mobile devices or personal computers.

29. Joshua Green, "The Amazing Money Machine," *The Atlantic,* June 2008, p. 52.

Although politicians have been slower to adopt this form of communication, many now are using podcasts to keep in touch with their constituents, and there are currently thousands, if not tens of thousands, of political podcasts. Podcasting played a major part in campaigning during the 2007–2008 election cycle.

Are Candidates Losing Control of Their Campaigns? Blogs and Internet sites such as YouTube are threatening to make it difficult for candidates to manage the news coverage of their campaigns. Short video clips of candidates' bloopers can be propagated with lightning speed over the Internet. All it takes is an onlooker's camcorder or smart cell phone and an Internet connection. Candidates have discovered that apparent slurs and other offensive statements soon find their way onto YouTube or other Web sites. For example, at a private fund-raiser during the Democratic primaries, Barack Obama stated that small-town voters bitter over their economic circumstances "cling to guns or religion or antipathy to people who aren't like them" as a way to explain their frustrations. Four days later, a blogger reported the comment, and Obama's opponents immediately accused him of contempt for ordinary people.

Another problem for candidates is attempting to control their "Netroots" supporters. Online supporters of a candidate may engage in a type of campaigning that is at odds with the candidate's own agenda or ethics. The supporter may become the story, not the candidate. Obama certainly experienced this difficulty when ABC News obtained a "greatest hits" collection of controversial sermons from the Web site of Obama's church in Chicago. In one sermon, Jeremiah Wright, at that time Obama's personal pastor, cried out, "The government . . . wants us to sing 'God Bless America.' No, no, no, not God bless America. God damn America. . . ." Obama eventually broke with Wright, but the controversy dogged Obama throughout his campaign.

Republican John McCain began to have problems with his supporters toward the end of his presidential campaign. One of McCain's themes was that Obama was a dangerous

ELECTIONS 2010

THE MEDIA AND THE 2010 ELECTIONS

During the 2010 campaign, conservatives fiercely accused the mainstream media of liberal bias. Such charges were leveled by Tea Party supporters and by figures that included former Republican vice-presidential candidate Sarah Palin. Given the election results, however, it is difficult to conclude that the media did the Republicans much damage. For its part, Fox News, the leading conservative outlet, saw its impartiality questioned when its parent company, News Corporation, made two separate million-dollar contributions to Republican committees. Fox News also hired Palin as a commentator.

The use of negative advertising reached a new high. According to researchers at Wesleyan University, more than half of all ads were pure attack ads. If so-called "contrast spots" that compare the candidates are included, two out of three ads were negative. A striking development was the increase in Democratic ads that sought to discredit Republicans personally. In 2008, Republicans had been more likely to use such ads, but in 2010, Democrats took the lead. Presumably, in 2010, Democrats were less comfortable discussing policies than they had been in 2008—because in 2010 many were unpopular—and they went for personal attacks instead.

An additional factor driving up the level of political "dirt" was the striking increase in the number of ads by independent groups, as opposed to candidate committees. Because they were not tied to candidates, outside groups were under no pressure to avoid publicizing the most malicious accusations.

radical with unsavory associates. Some of McCain's supporters in the blogosphere and elsewhere took this line to the outer limits. Statements shouted by crowd members at Republican rallies became so heated that at one point they touched off a Secret Service investigation into possible threats against Obama's life. McCain, after much criticism, finally made attempts to calm his audiences.

Government Regulation of the Media

The United States has one of the freest presses in the world. Nonetheless, regulation of the media, particularly of the electronic media, does exist. We discussed some aspects of this regulation in Chapter 4, when we examined First Amendment rights and the press.

The First Amendment does not mention electronic media, which did not exist when the Bill of Rights was written. For many reasons, the government has much greater control over the electronic media than it does over printed media. Through the Federal Communications Commission (FCC), which regulates communications by radio, television, wire, and cable, the number of radio stations has been controlled for many years, even though technologically we could have many more radio stations than now exist. Also, the FCC created the environment in which for many decades the three major TV networks (NBC, CBS, and ABC) dominated broadcasting.

Controlling Ownership of the Media

Many FCC rules have dealt with ownership of news media, such as how many stations a network can own. In 1996, Congress passed legislation that had far-reaching implications for the communications industry—the Telecommunications Act. The act ended the rule that kept telephone companies from entering the cable business and other communications markets. What this means is that a single corporation—whether Time Warner or Disney—can offer long-distance and local telephone services, cable television, satellite television, Internet services, and, of course, libraries of films and entertainment. The act opened the door to competition and led to more options for consumers, who now can choose among multiple competitors for all of these services delivered to the home. At the same time, it launched a race among competing companies to control media ownership.

Media conglomerates own larger and larger shares of television networks, newspapers, and radio outlets. Shown here is Rupert Murdoch, chairman and chief executive officer of News Corporation. News Corporation has media interests throughout the world. In 2007, Murdoch bought Dow Jones & Company, publisher of the *Wall Street Journal*, for around $5 billion. What problems arise when one company owns television, radio, and newspaper companies? (AP Photo/ Jason DeCrow)

Media Conglomerates. Many media outlets are now owned by corporate conglomerates. A single entity may own a television network; the studios that produce shows, news, and movies; and the means to deliver that content to the home via cable, satellite, or the Internet. The question to be faced in the future is how to ensure competition in the delivery of news so that citizens have access to multiple points of view from the media.

All of the prime-time television networks are owned by major American corporations, including such corporate conglomerates as Disney (owner of ABC). The Turner Broadcasting/ CNN network was also purchased by a major corporation, Time Warner. Later, Time Warner was acquired by America Online (AOL), a merger that combined the world's then-largest media company with the world's then-largest online company. Fox Television has always been a part of Rupert Murdoch's publishing and media empire. In addition to taking part in mergers and acquisitions, many of these companies have formed partnerships with computer software makers, such as Microsoft, for joint electronic publishing ventures.

Increased Media Concentration. One measure of a conglomerate's impact is "audience reach," or the percentage of the national viewing public that has access to the conglomerate's outlets. The FCC places an upper limit on audience reach, known as the "audience-reach cap." A few years ago, the FCC raised the national audience-reach cap from 35 percent to 45 percent and also allowed a corporation to own a newspaper and a television station in the same market. Congress rebelled against this new rule, however, and pushed the national audience-reach cap back below 40 percent. Nevertheless, a corporation can still own up to three TV stations in its largest market. The reality today is that there are only a few independent news operations left in the entire country.

did you know?

That a thirty-second television advertisement shown during the Super Bowl costs more than $2.6 million.

This media concentration has led to the decline of localism in the news. Obviously, costly locally produced news cannot be shown anywhere except in that local market. In contrast, the costs of producing a similar show for national broadcast can be amortized over millions and millions of viewers and paid for by higher revenues from national advertisers. Another concern, according to former media mogul Ted Turner, is that the rise of media conglomerates may lead to a decline in democratic debate.

The emergence of independent news Web sites, blogs, and podcasts provides an offset to this trend, however. Consequently, the increased concentration of traditional media news organizations may not matter as much as it did in the past. This presumes, of course, that media conglomerates do not use their control over the Internet infrastructure to silence alternative voices.

Government Control of Content

On the face of it, the First Amendment would seem to apply to all media. In fact, the United States Supreme Court has often been slow to extend free speech and free press guarantees to new media. For example, in 1915, the Court held that "as a matter of common sense," free speech protections did not apply to cinema. Only in 1952 did the Court find that motion pictures were covered by the First Amendment.[30] In contrast, the Court extended full protection to the Internet by striking down almost immediately provisions of the 1996 Telecommunications Act.[31] Cable TV also received broad protection in 2000.[32]

While the Court has held that the First Amendment is relevant to radio and television, it has never extended full protection to these media. The Court has used a number of arguments to justify this stand—initially, the scarcity of broadcast frequencies. The Court later held that the government could restrict "indecent" programming based on the "pervasive" presence of broadcasting in the home.[33] On this basis, the FCC has the authority to fine broadcasters for indecency or profanity.

Bias in the Media

For decades, the contention that the mainstream media have a liberal **bias** has been repeated time and again. Bernard Goldberg, formerly a CBS broadcaster and now a commentator for Fox News, is among the most prominent of these critics. Goldberg argues that liberal bias, which "comes naturally to most reporters," has given viewers reason to distrust the big news networks.[34] Some progressives, however, believe that conservatives find liberal bias even in reporting that is scrupulously accurate. In the words of humorist Stephen Colbert: "Reality has a well-known liberal bias."

Bias
An inclination or preference that interferes with impartial judgment.

Other observers claim that, on the whole, the media actually have a conservative bias, especially in their coverage of economic issues. In an analysis of visual images on television

30. *Joseph Burstyn, Inc. v. Wilson,* 343 U.S. 495 (1952).
31. *Reno v. American Civil Liberties Union,* 521 U.S. 844 (1997).
32. *United States v. Playboy Entertainment Group,* 529 U.S. 803 (2000).
33. *FCC v. Pacifica Foundation,* 438 U.S. 726 (1978). In this case, the Court banned seven swear words (famously used by the late comedian George Carlin) during hours when children could hear them.
34. Goldberg's most recent book provides criticisms, widespread among conservatives, of the media's coverage of the Obama campaign. See Bernard Goldberg, *A Slobbering Love Affair: The True (and Pathetic) Story of the Torrid Romance between Barack Obama and the Mainstream Media* (Washington: Regnery Publishing, 2009).

news, political scientist Maria Elizabeth Grabe has concluded that "image bites" (as opposed to sound bites) more often favor the Republicans.[35] Certainly, the almost complete dominance of talk radio by conservatives has given the political right an outlet that the political left cannot counter. The rise of the blogosphere and other online outlets has complicated the picture of media bias considerably. Neither the left nor the right clearly dominates in this arena.

Other Theories of Media Bias

Some writers have concluded that the mainstream media are really biased toward stories that involve conflict and drama—the better to attract viewers. Still others contend the media are biased against "losers," and when a candidate falls behind in a race, his or her press quickly becomes negative. Coverage of the 2008 presidential campaigns suggests that the "loser" theory may have merit. The Center for Media and Public Affairs at George Mason University found that in July and August of 2008, the media were actually more critical of Barack Obama than of the Republican candidate, John McCain. In these months, McCain gained support, slowly but continuously, until the race was a dead heat. Thereafter, the media were far more critical of McCain, whose poll numbers dropped steadily until the general elections in November. Did the press cost McCain the election? Not even Goldberg believes that. It is possible that the economic crisis turned both the press *and* the voters against the Republicans.

did you know?

That the average age of CNN viewers is forty-four and that most people who watch the evening network news programs are over age fifty.

A Scientific Test for Bias?

Communications professor Tim Groeling has devised a test for media bias that may provide accurate results regardless of whether political events favor the Democrats or the Republicans. He has examined how ABC, CBS, NBC, and Fox News reported public opinion polls that assessed the job performance of Democratic president Bill Clinton and Republican president George W. Bush. Confirming what many suspect, Groeling found that ABC, CBS, and NBC gave Clinton more favorable coverage than Bush—and that Fox gave Bush more favorable coverage than Clinton.[36]

---

35. Maria Elizabeth Grabe and Erik Page Bucy, *Image Bite Politics: News and the Visual Framing of Elections* (New York: Oxford University Press, 2009).
36. Tim Groeling, "Who's the Fairest of Them All? An Empirical Test for Partisan Bias on ABC, CBS, NBC, and Fox News," *Presidential Studies Quarterly*, December 2008, p. 631.

WHY SHOULD YOU CARE ABOUT... THE MEDIA?

Why should you, as an individual, care about the media? Even if you do not plan to engage in political activism, you have a stake in ensuring that your beliefs are truly your own and that they represent your values and interests. To guarantee this result, you need to obtain accurate information from the media and avoid being swayed by subliminal appeals, loaded terms, or outright bias. If you do not take care, you could find yourself voting for a candidate who is opposed to what you believe in or voting against measures that are in your interest.

THE MEDIA AND YOUR LIFE

Television, print media, and the Internet provide a wide range of choices for Americans who want to stay informed. Still, critics of the media argue that a substantial amount of what you read and see is colored either by the subjectivity of editors and bloggers or by the demands of profit making. Even when journalists themselves are relatively successful in an attempt to remain objective, they will of necessity give airtime to politicians and interest group representatives who are far from impartial. The ratio of opinion to fact is even greater on the Web than in the traditional media.

It is worth your while to become a critical consumer of the news. You need the ability to determine what motivates the players in the political game and to what extent they are "shading" the news or even propagating outright lies. You also need to determine which news sources are reliable.

BP CEO Tony Hayward's reflection is seen in the lens of a TV camera as he talks to reporters while visiting a Coast Guard command center in Venice, Louisiana in May 2010. (AP Photo/Gerald Herbert)

HOW YOU CAN MAKE A DIFFERENCE

To become a critical news consumer, you must develop a critical eye and ear. For example, ask yourself what stories are given prominence at the top of a newspaper Web site. For a contrast to most daily papers, visit the sites of publications with explicit points of view, such as the *National Review* (**www.nationalreview.com**) or the *New Republic* (**www.tnr.com/politics**). Take note of how they handle stories.

Sources such as blogs often have strong political preferences, and you should try to determine what these are. Does a blog merely give opinions, or does it back up its arguments with data? It is possible to select anecdotes to support almost any argument—does a particular anecdote represent typical circumstances, or is it a rare occurrence highlighted to make a point?

Watching the evening news can be far more rewarding if you look at how much the news depends on video effects. You will note that stories on the evening news tend to be no more than three minutes long, that stories with excellent videotape get more attention, and that considerable time is taken up with "happy talk" or human interest stories.

Another way to critically evaluate news coverage is to compare how the news is covered by different outlets. For example, you might compare the coverage of events on Fox News with the presentation on MSNBC, or compare the radio commentary of Rush Limbaugh with that of National Public Radio's *All Things Considered*. When does a show cross the line between news and opinion?

A variety of organizations try to monitor news sources for accuracy and bias. Consider visiting the following sites:

- The American Journalism Review covers a wide variety of journalistic issues, including the migration from print media to online sources. See it at **www.ajr.org**
- The Committee of Concerned Journalists is a professional organization concerned with journalistic ethics. Its site is at **www.concernedjournalists.org**
- Fairness and Accuracy in Reporting is a media watchdog with a strong liberal viewpoint. Visit it at **www.fair.org**
- Accuracy in Media takes a combative conservative position on media issues. View it at **www.aim.org**

questions for discussion and analysis

1. Some have argued that limits on campaign contributions violate First Amendment guarantees of freedom of speech. How strong is this argument? Can contributions be seen as a form of protected expression? Under what circumstances can contributions be seen instead as a method of bribing elected officials?

2. Many observers believe that holding so many presidential primary elections at such an early point in an election year is a serious problem. How might the problem be resolved? Also, is it fair and appropriate that New Hampshire always holds the first presidential primary and Iowa always conducts the first caucuses? Why or why not?

3. Some people are more likely to vote than others. Older persons vote more frequently than younger people. Wealthy voters make it to the polls more often than poor voters. What might cause older and wealthier individuals to exhibit greater turnout?

4. Conservatives have long accused traditional media outlets of having a liberal bias. Are they correct? If so, to what degree? Regardless of whether this particular accusation is correct, what other kinds of bias might affect the reporting of prominent journalists? To the extent that the press exhibits political bias, what factors might cause this bias?

key terms

Australian ballot 305
"beauty contest" 299
bias 325
caucus 300
closed primary 301
coattail effect 305
corrupt practices acts 293
credentials committee 303
direct primary 300
elector 304
focus group 292
front-loading 302
front-runner 302
general election 289
Hatch Act 293
independent expenditures 296
indirect primary 300
issue advocacy 296
office-block, or Massachusetts, ballot 305
open primary 301
party-column, or Indiana, ballot 305
podcasting 322
political action committee (PAC) 294
political consultant 291
presidential primary 287
primary election 289
public agenda 315
rational ignorance effect 311
registration 313
soft money 295
sound bite 318
spin 320
spin doctor 320
superdelegate 300
tracking poll 292
vote-eligible population 310
voter turnout 308
voting-age population 310

chapter summary

1. The legal qualifications for holding political office are minimal at both the state and local levels, but holders of political office still are predominantly white and male and are likely to be from the professional class.

2. American political campaigns are lengthy and extremely expensive. In the last decade, they have become more candidate centered rather than party centered in response to technological innovations and decreasing party identification. Candidates have begun to rely on paid professional consultants to perform the various tasks necessary to wage a political campaign. The crucial task of professional political consultants is image building. The campaign organization devises a campaign strategy to maximize the candidate's chances of winning. Candidates use public opinion polls and focus groups to gauge their popularity and to test the mood of the country.

3. Interest groups are major sources of campaign funds. The contributions are often made through political action committees, or PACs. Other methods of contributing include issue advocacy advertising and setting up independent 527 organizations to register voters and run ads. The amount of money spent in financing campaigns is increasing steadily. A variety of corrupt practices acts have been passed to regulate campaign finance. The Bipartisan Campaign Reform Act of 2002 limited advertising by interest groups. The United States Supreme Court has chipped away at the limits imposed by the 2002 act, however. In 2010, the Court ruled that the government could not limit corporate political expenditures that were not coordinated with campaigns.

4. After the Democratic convention of 1968, the McGovern-Fraser Commission formulated new rules for primaries, which were adopted by all Democrats and by Republicans in most states. These reforms opened up the nomination process for the presidency to all voters.

5. A presidential primary is a statewide election to help a political party determine its presidential nominee at the national convention. Some states use the caucus method of choosing convention delegates. The primary campaign recently has been shortened to the first few months of the election year.

6. The voter technically does not vote directly for president but instead chooses between slates of presidential electors. In most states, the slate that wins the most popular votes throughout the state gets to cast all the electoral votes for the state. The candidate receiving a majority (270) of the electoral votes wins.

7. The United States uses the Australian ballot, a secret ballot that is prepared, distributed, and counted by government officials. The office-block ballot groups candidates according to office. The party-column ballot groups candidates according to their party labels and symbols.

8. Voter participation in the United States is often considered to be low, especially in elections that do not feature a presidential contest. Turnout is lower when measured as a percentage of the voting-age population than it is when measured as a percentage of the population actually eligible to vote. There is an association between voter turnout and a person's age, education, and income level.

9. In colonial times, only white males with a certain minimum amount of property were eligible to vote. The suffrage issue has concerned, at one time or another, most groups in the United States. Today, to be eligible to vote, a person must satisfy registration, citizenship, age, and residency requirements. Each state has different qualifications.

10. The media are enormously important in American politics today. They perform a number of functions, including (a) entertainment, (b) news reporting, (c) identifying public problems, (d) socializing new generations, (e) providing a political forum, and (f) making profits.

11. The political influence of the media is most obvious during political campaigns. Today's campaigns use political advertising and expert management of news coverage. For presidential candidates, how they appear in presidential debates is of major importance. Internet blogs, podcasts, and Web sites such as YouTube are transforming today's political campaigns and making it difficult for candidates to control their campaigns.

12. The electronic media are subject to government regulation. Many Federal Communications Commission rules have dealt with ownership of TV and radio stations. Legislation has removed many rules about coownership of several forms of media.

13. Frequently, the mainstream media have been accused of liberal bias, although some observers contend that these accusations result from true stories that offend conservatives. Other possible media biases include a bias against political "losers."

selected print & media resources

SUGGESTED READINGS

Boehlert, Eric. *Bloggers on the Bus: How the Internet Changed Politics and the Press.* New York: Free Press, 2010. Boehlert, a liberal blogger, describes how the American political left used the Web to rally its forces and reinvigorate itself in the years leading up to the 2008 elections.

Fuller, Jack. *What Is Happening to News: The Information Explosion and the Crisis in Journalism.* Chicago: University of Chicago Press, 2010. Fuller, formerly

the editor and publisher of the *Chicago Tribune,* seeks to explain the decline of conventional media and the growth of opinion-soaked television and Internet sources. Fuller believes the new media succeed by making an emotional connection with their audiences. To succeed, journalists must make similar connections while still preserving a commitment to objectivity.

Martinez, Michael D. *Does Turnout Matter?* Boulder, Colo.: Westview Press, 2009. Scholars have expended much effort in examining why voter turnout is lower in the United States than in many other countries, but the question of whether low turnout actually matters has received less attention. Martinez is a professor of political science at the University of Florida.

Nordlinger, Gary, and Dennis W. Johnson. *Campaigning in the Twenty-First Century: A Whole New Ballgame.* New York: Routledge, 2011. In this work, two political consultants examine how political campaigns have changed during the last decade. Topics include micro-targeting, online fund-raising, and the new media. Nordlinger and Johnson contend that campaigns have become much harder to manage, and the danger of chaos is ever present.

MEDIA RESOURCES

All the President's Men—A film, produced by Warner Brothers in 1976, starring Dustin Hoffman and Robert Redford as the two *Washington Post* reporters, Carl Bernstein and Bob Woodward, who broke the story on the Watergate scandal. The film is an excellent portrayal of the *Washington Post* newsroom and the decisions that editors make in such situations.

Bulworth—A 1998 satirical film starring Warren Beatty and Halle Berry. Jay Bulworth, a senator who is fed up with politics and life in general, hires a hit man to carry out his own assassination. He then throws political caution to the wind in campaign appearances by telling the truth and behaving the way he really wants to behave.

The Candidate—A 1972 film, starring the young Robert Redford, that effectively investigates and satirizes the decisions that a candidate for the U.S. Senate must make. A political classic.

Citizen Kane—A 1941 film, based on the life of William Randolph Hearst and directed by Orson Welles, that has been acclaimed as one of the best movies ever made. Welles himself stars as the newspaper tycoon. The film also stars Joseph Cotten and Alan Ladd.

Good Night, and Good Luck—A 2006 film about Edward R. Murrow, directed by George Clooney. Murrow's opposition to the tactics used by Senator Joe McCarthy's witch-hunters in 1953–1954 provides a powerful example of integrity to reporters today.

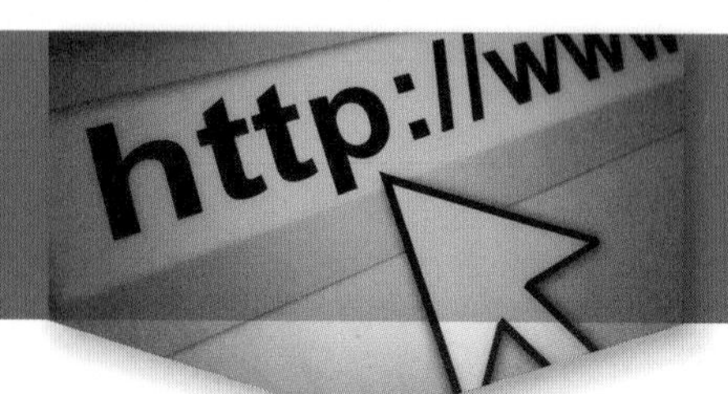

e-mocracy

CAMPAIGNS, ELECTIONS, AND THE MEDIA

Today's voters have a significant advantage over those in past decades. It is now possible to obtain extensive information about candidates and issues simply by going online. Some sites present point-counterpoint articles about the candidates or issues in an upcoming election. Other sites support some candidates and positions and oppose others. The candidates themselves all have Web sites that you can visit if you want to learn more about them and their positions. You can also obtain information online about election results by going to sites such as those listed in the *Logging On* section.

The Internet also offers a great opportunity to those who want to access the news. All of the major news organizations, including radio and television stations and newspapers, are online. Most local newspapers include at least some of their news coverage and features on their Web sites, and all national newspapers are online. Even foreign newspapers can now be accessed online within a few seconds. Also available are purely Web-based news publications, including e-zines (online news magazines) such as *Slate, Salon,* and *Hotwired.* Because it is relatively simple for anyone or any organization to put up a home page or Web site, a wide variety of sites have appeared that critique the news media or give alternative interpretations of the news and the way it is presented.

LOGGING ON

For detailed information about current campaign-financing laws and for the latest filings of finance reports, see the site maintained by the Federal Election Commission at
www.fec.gov

To find excellent reports on where campaign money comes from and how it is spent, be sure to view the site maintained

by the Center for Responsive Politics at
www.opensecrets.org

Another Web site for investigating voting records and campaign-financing information is that of Project Vote Smart. Go to
www.votesmart.org

To view *Slate,* the e-zine of politics and culture published by Microsoft, go to
www.slate.com

Blogs have become a major feature of the Internet. A large number of blogs deal with political topics. For a listing of several hundred political blogs, go to the Blog Search Engine at
www.blogsearchengine.com/category/political-blogs

To gain an international perspective on the news, you can check foreign news Web sites in English. The following sites all have broad worldwide coverage:

- The British Broadcasting Corporation: **www.bbc.co.uk**
- China Network Television (surprisingly informative given that it is owned by a Communist-controlled government): **english.cntv.cn**
- The Japan Broadcasting Corporation: **www.nhk.or.jp/daily/english**
- Al Jazeera (the Arab world's number-one television news network): **english.aljazeera.net**
- New Delhi Television (India): **www.ndtv.com**
- *Der Spiegel* (Germany): **www.spiegel.de/international**

chapter
10

The Congress

chapter contents

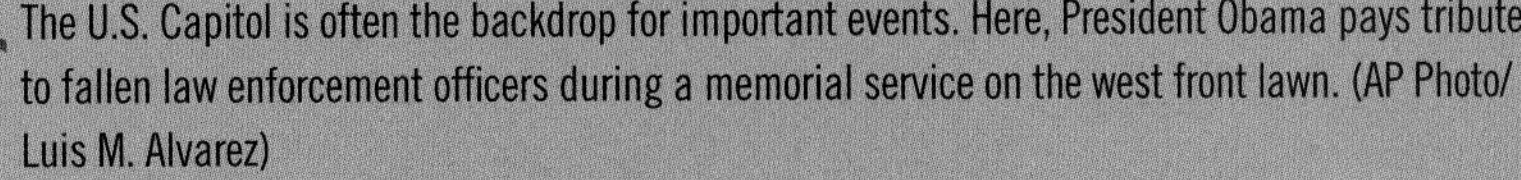

The U.S. Capitol is often the backdrop for important events. Here, President Obama pays tribute to fallen law enforcement officers during a memorial service on the west front lawn. (AP Photo/ Luis M. Alvarez)

WHAT IF... ...pork were banned?

The local U.S. representative in the House was able to obtain a $145,000 earmark to help pay for the renovation of the Opera House in McPherson, Kansas. Who actually paid these funds? (AP Photo/John Hanna)

BACKGROUND

Through *pork-barrel legislation,* members of Congress "bring home the bacon." Members directly help their constituents by inserting into legislation projects that create more jobs and generate more profits locally. The official name for pork is *earmarked spending*. In recent years, from 11,000 to 15,000 earmarks yearly, worth from $15 billion to $69 billion, have passed through Congress. Most earmarks are never discussed on the floor. The practice of earmarking is not new, but it has increased significantly over the last few decades. In 2006, Congress approved more than 13,000 earmarks worth about $67 billion.

Earmarking is a bipartisan activity. When the Democrats took control of Congress in 2007, they promised to "get tough" on earmarking. The volume of pork did decline somewhat, to $18.3 billion in 2008, $20 billion in 2009, and $16.5 billion in 2010. Still, this means that thousands of earmarks were inserted into legislation.

WHAT IF PORK WERE BANNED?

Without pork, earmarks could not simply be slipped into bills sent to the president as amendments. Because Congress does not have an unlimited amount of time for debate, eliminating pork might reduce federal spending. Realize, though, that the federal budget is about $3.8 trillion, so eliminating pork would not change much.

Banning pork would mean that most spending projects coming before Congress would have to pass through the normal budget process. Ordinarily, the various executive agencies of government receive proposals for spending on various projects. They rank all the requests in order of "need" and choose the ones with the most merit. The number of projects is limited by the president's Office of Management and Budget (OMB). The OMB submits the resulting budget to Congress. Before the budget reaches Congress, however, the White House routinely adds its own laundry list of politically desirable projects that were never reviewed by the bureaucracy. The president may actually be the biggest single "porkmeister" in government.

If all pork were really banned, "legitimate pork" would be eliminated, too. After all, members of Congress may at times have a better understanding than does the bureaucracy of local spending needs for hospitals, infrastructure repairs, and the like. If pork were banned, however, we would not see federal payments for a prison museum near Fort Leavenworth, Kansas, or the National Mule and Packers Museum in Bishop, California.

THE IMPACT ON CAMPAIGNS AND CAMPAIGN CONTRIBUTIONS

Currently, many lobbyist groups are rewarded for their campaign contributions through pork-barrel legislation. Earmarks are a way to show a legislator's appreciation for campaign contributions made by a specific group. For example, a defense contractor might contribute to the reelection of the local representative. If that representative is reelected, she or he can earmark funds for a weapons system that the contractor manufactures, even though the system was never requested by the Defense Department. In the absence of pork, candidates for election or reelection would probably receive fewer campaign contributions from lobbying groups representing local interests, and the number of registered lobbying groups would probably fall.

FOR CRITICAL ANALYSIS

1. In 2006, the Democrats campaigned on an "anti-pork" theme. Nonetheless, pork-barrel legislation continues. Why?
2. If Congress passed less legislation, would Americans be better off or worse off? Explain your answer.

Most Americans view Congress in a less-than-flattering light. In recent years, Congress has appeared to be deeply split, highly partisan in its conduct, and not very responsive to public needs. Polls show that at times the public has had notably unfavorable opinions about Congress as a whole. Yet individual members of Congress often receive much higher approval ratings from the voters in their districts. This is one of the paradoxes of the relationship between the people and Congress. Members of the public hold the institution in relatively low regard compared with the satisfaction they express with their individual representatives.

Part of the explanation for these seemingly contradictory appraisals is that members of Congress spend considerable time and effort serving their **constituents.** If the federal bureaucracy makes a mistake, the senator's or representative's office tries to resolve the issue. What most Americans see of Congress, therefore, is the work of their own representatives in their home states. One result is that members of Congress have exceptionally high reelection rates.

Constituent
One of the persons represented by a legislator or other elected or appointed official.

Bicameralism
The division of a legislature into two separate assemblies.

Congress, however, was created to work not just for local constituents but also for the nation as a whole. The national interest is sometimes hard to detect in Congress's everyday activities, though, as you learned in the chapter-opening *What If . . .* feature. Understanding the nature of the institution and the process of lawmaking is an important part of understanding how the laws and policies that shape our lives are made. In this chapter, we describe the functions of Congress, including constituent service, representation, lawmaking, and oversight of the government. We review how the members of Congress are elected and how Congress organizes itself when it meets. We also examine how bills pass through the legislative process and become laws.

The Nature and Functions of Congress

The founders of the American republic believed that the bulk of the power that would be exercised by a national government should be in the hands of the legislature. The leading role envisioned for Congress in the new government is apparent from its primacy in the Constitution. Article I deals with the structure, the powers, and the operation of Congress.

Bicameralism

The **bicameralism** of Congress—its division into two legislative houses—was in part the result of the Connecticut Compromise, which tried to balance the large-state population advantage, reflected in the House, and the small-state demand for equality in policymaking, which was satisfied in the Senate. Beyond that, the two chambers of Congress also reflected the social class biases of the founders. They wished to balance the interests and the numerical superiority of the common citizens with the property interests of the less numerous landowners, bankers, and merchants. They achieved this goal by providing that members of the House of Representatives should be elected directly by "the People," whereas members of the Senate were to be chosen by the elected representatives sitting in state legislatures, who were more likely to be members of the elite. (The latter provision was changed in 1913 by the passage of the Seventeenth Amendment, which provides that senators are also to be elected directly by the people.)

The logic of the bicameral Congress was reinforced by differences in length of tenure. Members of the House are required to face the electorate every two years, whereas senators can serve for a much more secure term of six years—even longer than the four-year term provided for the president. Furthermore, the senators' terms are staggered so that only one-third of the senators face the electorate every two years, along with all of the House members.

The bicameral Congress was designed to perform certain functions for the political system. These functions include lawmaking, representation, service to constituents, oversight, public education, and conflict resolution. Of these, the two most important and the ones that are most often in conflict are lawmaking and representation.

Lawmaking
The process of establishing the legal rules that govern society.

Logrolling
An arrangement in which two or more members of Congress agree in advance to support each other's bills.

Earmarks
Special provisions in legislation to set aside funds for projects that have not passed an impartial evaluation by agencies of the executive branch. Also known as *pork*.

Representation
The function of members of Congress as elected officials representing the views of their constituents.

Trustee
A legislator who acts according to her or his conscience and the broad interests of the entire society.

Instructed Delegate
A legislator who is an agent of the voters who elected him or her and who votes according to the views of constituents regardless of personal beliefs.

The Lawmaking Function

The principal and most obvious function of any legislature is **lawmaking.** Congress is the highest elected body in the country charged with making binding rules for all Americans. Lawmaking requires decisions about the size of the federal budget, about health-care reform and gun control, and about the long-term prospects for war or peace. This does not mean, however, that Congress initiates most of the ideas for legislation that it eventually considers. A majority of the bills that Congress acts on originate in the executive branch, and many other bills are traceable to interest groups and political party organizations. Through the processes of compromise and **logrolling** (offering to support a fellow member's bill in exchange for that member's promise to support your bill in the future), as well as debate and discussion, backers of legislation attempt to fashion a winning majority coalition. Logrolling often involves agreements to support another member's legislative **earmarks,** also known as *pork*. Earmarks, which were discussed in the opening *What If . . .* feature, are special provisions in legislation to set aside funds for projects that have not passed an impartial evaluation by agencies of the executive branch. (Normal spending projects pass through such evaluations.)

The Representation Function

Representation includes both representing the desires and demands of the constituents in the member's home district or state and representing larger national interests, such as the nation's security or the environment. Because the interests of constituents in a specific district may be in conflict with the demands of national policy, the representation function is often a source of conflict for individual lawmakers—and sometimes for Congress as a whole. For example, although it may be in the interest of the nation to reduce defense spending by closing military bases, such closures are not in the interest of the states and districts that will lose jobs and local spending. Every legislator faces votes that set local representational issues against lawmaking realities.

How should the legislators fulfill the representation function? There are several views on how this task should be accomplished.

The Trustee View of Representation. The first approach to the question of how representation should be achieved is that legislators should act as **trustees** of the broad interests of the entire society. They should vote against the narrow interests of their constituents if their conscience and their perception of national needs so dictate. For example, a number of Republican legislators have supported laws regulating the tobacco industry in spite of the views of some of their tobacco-growing constituents.

did you know?

That fewer than three in ten people can name the House member from their district, and fewer than half can name even one of the two senators from their state.

The Instructed-Delegate View of Representation. Directly opposed to the trustee view of representation is the notion that the members of Congress should behave as **instructed delegates.** That is, they should mirror the views of the majority of the constituents who elected them to power. On the surface, this approach is plausible and rewarding. For it to work, however, we must assume that constituents actually have well-formed views on the issues that are decided in Congress and, further, that they have clear-cut preferences about these issues. Neither condition is likely to be satisfied very often.

Generally, most legislators hold neither a pure trustee view nor a pure instructed-delegate view. Typically, they combine both perspectives in a pragmatic mix that is often called the "politico" style.

Service to Constituents

Individual members of Congress are expected by their constituents to act as brokers between private citizens and the imposing, often faceless federal government. This function of providing service to constituents usually takes the form of **casework.** The legislator and her or his staff spend a considerable portion of their time in casework activities, such as tracking down a missing Social Security check, explaining the meaning of particular bills to people who may be affected by them, promoting a local business interest, or interceding with a regulatory agency on behalf of constituents who disagree with proposed agency regulations.

Maine's two U.S. senators, Olympia Snowe, left, and Susan Collins, both Republicans, attend a rally in Kittery, Maine. What functions do members of Congress serve? (AP Photo/Pat Wellenbach)

Legislators and many analysts of congressional behavior regard this **ombudsperson** role as an activity that strongly benefits the members of Congress. A government characterized by a large, confusing bureaucracy and complex public programs offers innumerable opportunities for legislators to come to the assistance of (usually) grateful constituents. Morris P. Fiorina once suggested, somewhat mischievously, that senators and representatives prefer to maintain bureaucratic confusion to maximize their opportunities for performing good deeds on behalf of their constituents:

> *Some poor, aggrieved constituent becomes enmeshed in the tentacles of an evil bureaucracy and calls upon Congressman St. George to do battle with the dragon. . . . In dealing with the bureaucracy, the congressman is not merely one vote of 435. Rather, he is a nonpartisan power, someone whose phone call snaps an office to attention. He is not kept on hold. The constituent who receives aid believes that his congressman and his congressman alone got results.*[1]

The Oversight Function

Oversight of the bureaucracy is essential if the decisions made by Congress are to have any force. **Oversight** is the process by which Congress follows up on the laws it has enacted to ensure that they are being enforced and administered in the way Congress intended. This is done by holding committee hearings and investigations, changing the size of an agency's budget, and cross-examining high-level presidential nominees to head major agencies. Sometimes Congress establishes a special commission to investigate a problem. For example, after Hurricane Katrina devastated New Orleans and parts of surrounding states in 2005, Congress created a commission to determine how and why the federal government, particularly the Federal Emergency Management Agency (FEMA), had mishandled government aid both during and after that natural disaster. Sometimes a commission may take several years to complete its work. One example is the so-called 9/11 Commission, which investigated why the United States was unprepared for the terrorist attacks in 2001.

Senators and representatives traditionally have seen their oversight function as a critically important part of their legislative activities. In part, oversight is related to the concept of constituency service, particularly when Congress investigates alleged arbitrariness or wrongdoing by bureaucratic agencies.

Casework
Personal work for constituents by members of Congress.

Ombudsperson
A person who hears and investigates complaints by private individuals against public officials or agencies. (From the Swedish word *ombudsman,* meaning "representative.")

Oversight
The process by which Congress follows up on laws it has enacted to ensure that they are being enforced and administered in the way Congress intended.

---

1. Morris P. Fiorina, *Congress: Keystone of the Washington Establishment,* 2d ed. (New Haven, Conn.: Yale University Press, 1989), pp. 44, 47.

When the Republicans controlled both the executive and legislative branches of government from 2001 to 2007, many claimed that Congress failed to fulfill its oversight function. Serious allegations of wrongdoing by government officials, including some members of Congress, often went uninvestigated. After taking control of Congress in 2007, the Democrats let the nation know that they were taking their oversight function seriously. Within weeks, they had launched a series of investigations into alleged wrongdoing by various government officials. Some observers question whether the Democrats were able to maintain their enthusiasm for oversight after Democrat Barack Obama became president.

The Public-Education Function

Educating the public is a function that is performed whenever Congress holds public hearings, exercises oversight over the bureaucracy, or engages in committee and floor debate on such major issues and topics as immigration, global warming, aging, illegal drugs, and the concerns of small businesses. In so doing, Congress presents a range of viewpoints on pressing national questions. Congress also decides what issues will come up for discussion and decision. This **agenda setting** is a major facet of its public-education function.

Agenda Setting
Determining which public-policy questions will be debated or considered.

Enumerated Power
A power specifically granted to the national government by the Constitution. The first seventeen clauses of Article I, Section 8, specify most of the enumerated powers of Congress.

The Conflict-Resolution Function

Congress is commonly seen as an institution for resolving conflicts within American society. Organized interest groups and spokespersons for different racial, religious, economic, and ideological interests look on Congress as an access point for airing their grievances and seeking help. This puts Congress in the position of trying to resolve the differences among competing points of view by passing laws to accommodate as many interested parties as possible. To the extent that Congress meets pluralist expectations in accommodating competing interests, it tends to build support for the entire political process.

The Powers of Congress

The Constitution is both highly specific and extremely vague about the powers that Congress may exercise. The first seventeen clauses of Article I, Section 8, specify most of the **enumerated powers** of Congress—that is, powers expressly given to that body.

One of the expressed powers of Congress is the power to impose and collect taxes. Every year on April 15 (if it falls on a weekday), U.S. residents line up in front of post office buildings across America to file their tax returns before the midnight deadline. These New Yorkers have waited until the last minute and are standing in line inside the James A. Farley Post Office building. (Mario Tama/Getty Images)

Enumerated Powers

The enumerated, or expressed, powers of Congress include the right to impose a variety of taxes, including tariffs on imports; borrow funds; regulate interstate commerce and international trade; establish procedures for naturalizing citizens; make laws regulating bankruptcies; coin (and print) money and regulate its value; establish standards of weights and measures; punish counterfeiters; establish post offices and postal routes; regulate copyrights and patents; establish the federal court system; punish illegal acts on the high seas; declare war; raise and regulate an army and a navy; call up and regulate the state militias to enforce laws, to suppress insurrections, and to repel invasions; and govern the District of Columbia.

The most important of the domestic powers of Congress, listed in Article I, Section 8, are the rights to collect taxes, to spend, and to regulate commerce. The most important foreign policy power is the power to declare war. Other sections of the Constitution allow Congress to establish rules for its own members, to regulate the Electoral College, and to override a presidential veto. Congress may also regulate the extent of the Supreme Court's authority to review cases decided by the lower courts, regulate relations among states, and propose amendments to the Constitution.

Powers of the Senate. Some functions are restricted to one chamber. The Senate must advise on, and consent to, the ratification of treaties and must accept or reject presidential nominations of ambassadors, Supreme Court justices, and "all other Officers of the United States." But the Senate may delegate to the president or lesser officials the power to make lower-level appointments.

These specific powers granted to the Senate mean that the Senate is a more powerful chamber than the House. Interestingly, the United States is unique among the world's economically advanced nations in that its "upper house"—the Senate—is more powerful than the "lower house." Consider that in every nation with a parliamentary system, the lower house in effect chooses the nation's chief executive officer, the prime minister. We describe a few of the world's upper houses in the *Beyond Our Borders* feature below.

Constitutional Amendments. Amendments to the Constitution provide for other congressional powers. Congress must certify the election of a president and a vice president or itself choose those officers if no candidate has a majority of the electoral vote (Twelfth Amendment). It may levy an income tax (Sixteenth Amendment) and determine who will be acting president in case of the death or incapacity of the president or vice

BEYOND OUR BORDERS

THE EXCEPTIONAL POWER OF THE U.S. SENATE

Political scientists refer to the U.S. Senate as the "upper house" of Congress. Each senator represents an entire state and is one out of only a hundred, so he or she commands more prestige and press than a representative. The Senate is also more powerful than the "lower house"—the House of Representatives. The Senate must approve treaties. It advises and consents to presidential appointments. The House does not have such powers. In most of the world, however, the "lower house" is far more powerful than the upper one. (Latin America is the one region of the world where the U.S. model dominates.) Consider some examples:

- Canada has a Senate, but it mainly revises legislation passed by the lower house, the House of Commons. Only on rare occasions does it reject such bills altogether. Its seats are entirely filled by appointment; members are often former cabinet members and provincial leaders.
- In Britain, the House of Lords is almost powerless. Until 1958, all seats were inherited, thereby giving that body no democratic legitimacy. Finally, in 1999, all but ninety-two of the hereditary peers were expelled, and today, most members are appointed "life peers." The new Conservative-Liberal government in Britain has proposed making the Lords elective. The Lords are limited to making minor improvements to bills passed by the House of Commons.
- The senate in France, which is elected by local government officials, has an excellent wine cellar, but that is about it. When Charles de Gaulle became French president in 1959, he wondered aloud about the senate: "What is that little thing?"

FOR CRITICAL ANALYSIS

Why is the Senate so powerful in the United States?

president (Twentieth Amendment and Twenty-fifth Amendment). In addition, Congress explicitly is given the power to enforce, by appropriate legislation, the provisions of several other amendments.

The Necessary and Proper Clause

Beyond these numerous specific powers, Congress enjoys the right under Clause 18 of Article I, Section 8 (the "elastic," or "necessary and proper," clause), "to make all Laws which shall be necessary and proper for carrying into Execution the foregoing Powers [of Article I], and all other Powers vested by this Constitution in the Government of the United States, or in any Department or Officer thereof." As discussed in Chapter 3, this vague statement of congressional responsibilities has provided, over time, the basis for a greatly expanded national government. It also has constituted, at least in theory, a check on the expansion of presidential powers.

House–Senate Differences

Congress is composed of two markedly different—but co-equal—chambers. Although the Senate and the House of Representatives exist within the same legislative institution, each has developed certain distinctive features that clearly distinguish one from the other. A summary of these differences is given in Table 10–1 below.

Size and Rules

The central difference between the House and the Senate is simply that the House is much larger than the Senate. The House has 435 representatives, plus delegates from the District of Columbia, Puerto Rico, Guam, American Samoa, and the Virgin Islands, compared with just 100 senators. This size difference means that a greater number of formal rules are needed to govern activity in the House, whereas correspondingly looser procedures can be followed in the less crowded Senate.

TABLE 10–1 Differences between the House and the Senate

House*	Senate*
Members chosen from local districts	Members chosen from an entire state
Two-year term	Six-year term
Originally elected by voters	Originally (until 1913) elected by state legislatures
May impeach (indict) federal officials	May convict federal officials of impeachable offenses
Larger (435 voting members)	Smaller (100 members)
More formal rules	Fewer rules and restrictions
Debate limited	Debate extended
Less prestige and less individual notice	More prestige and more media attention
Originates bills for raising revenues	Has power to advise the president on, and to consent to, presidential appointments and treaties
Local or narrow leadership	National leadership
More partisan	Less party loyalty

*Some of these differences, such as the term of office, are provided for in the Constitution. Others, such as debate rules, are not.

The effect of the difference in size is most obvious in the rules governing debate on the floors of the two chambers. The Senate usually permits extended debate on all issues that arise before it. In contrast, the House operates with an elaborate system in which its **Rules Committee** normally proposes time limitations on debate for any bill, and a majority of the entire body accepts or modifies those suggested time limits. As a consequence of its stricter time limits on debate, the House, despite its greater size, often is able to act on legislation more quickly than the Senate.

Rules Committee
A standing committee of the House of Representatives that provides special rules under which specific bills can be debated, amended, and considered by the House.

Filibuster
The use of the Senate's tradition of unlimited debate as a delaying tactic to block a bill.

Debate and Filibustering

The Senate tradition of the **filibuster,** or the use of unlimited debate as a blocking tactic, dates back to 1790.[2] In that year, a proposal to move the U.S. capital from New York to Philadelphia was stalled by such time-wasting maneuvers. This unlimited-debate tradition—which also existed in the House until 1811—is not absolute, however.

Cloture. Under Senate Rule 22, debate may be ended by invoking *cloture.* Cloture shuts off discussion on a bill. Amended in 1975 and 1979, Rule 22 states that debate may be closed off on a bill if sixteen senators sign a petition requesting it and if, after two days have elapsed, three-fifths of the entire membership (sixty votes, assuming no vacancies) vote for cloture. After cloture is invoked, each senator may speak on a bill for a maximum of one hour before a vote is taken. In 1979, the Senate refined Rule 22 to ensure that a final vote must take place within one hundred hours of debate after cloture has been imposed. It further limited the use of multiple amendments to stall postcloture final action on a bill.

did you know?

That felons are not barred from serving in Congress, though a chamber can expel a convicted member by a two-thirds vote.

Increased Use of the Filibuster. Traditionally, filibusters were rare, and the tactic was employed only on issues of principle. Filibustering senators spoke for many hours, sometimes reading names from a telephone book. By the twenty-first century, however, filibusters could be invoked without such speeches, and senators were threatening to filibuster almost every significant piece of legislation to come before the body. The threats were sufficient to create a new, ad hoc rule that important legislation needed the support of sixty senators, not fifty. As a result of the increased use of the filibuster, some senators have called for its abolition. We discuss that issue in this chapter's *Which Side Are You On?* feature on the following page.

The Filibuster during 2009. A major issue in the 2008 elections was whether the Democrats could elect enough senators to reach the magic number of sixty without any Republican votes. In fact, the Senate convened in 2009 with fifty-eight Democratic members, which was set to rise to fifty-nine when the Minnesota Senate race was finally resolved.

Initially, it seemed that no legislation could pass the Senate without at least a few Republican votes, and indeed, the $787 billion stimulus bill was passed in February only after it was altered to win the votes of three Republican senators. In April, the Democrats came up with an antifilibuster tactic. Budget bills sent from the House of Representatives to the Senate can be handled under special *reconciliation* rules that do not permit filibusters. The Democrats therefore proposed to adopt major health-care legislation as part of a budget bill. Republicans protested, even though they had used the reconciliation tactic themselves in recent years. A problem with the reconciliation tactic is that under the rules, it can be used *only* to handle budgetary matters. Much of what needed to go into the health-care package could not properly be described as budgetary.

---

2. *Filibuster* comes from a Spanish word for pirate, which in turn came from the Dutch term *vrijbuiter,* or freebooter. The word was first used in 1851 to accuse senators of pirating or hijacking debate.

WHICH SIDE ARE YOU ON?

IS IT TIME TO GET RID OF THE FILIBUSTER?

It is not in the Constitution, but it is an important institution. It is the filibuster and it follows from Senate Rule 22, which allows for unlimited debate. Throughout American history, senators could tie up the Senate's business by talking indefinitely. In 1975, Rule 22 was revised. Since that year, a vote by sixty senators is required to stop floor debate instead of the previous sixty-seven. A second significant change in Senate practice developed, however—today, senators don't actually have to *talk* to hold a filibuster. All they have to do to maintain a filibuster is to announce that a filibuster exists. The practical effect has been to create a new rule that all important legislation requires sixty votes in the Senate. Some want the filibuster abolished. Others do not agree.

On August 29, 1957, Senator Strom Thurmond (D., S.C.) finished the longest one-man filibuster in the history of the Senate. It lasted for twenty-four hours and nineteen minutes. Thurmond was attempting to prevent the passage of a civil rights bill that nonetheless was later signed into law by the president. (AP Photo)

THE FILIBUSTER IS NOT EVEN CONSTITUTIONAL

Critics of the filibuster argue that it has no constitutional basis and implicitly violates many actual provisions of the Constitution. After all, the Constitution requires a *supermajority*—more than a simple majority—only for special situations such as ratifying treaties, proposing constitutional amendments, overriding presidential vetoes, and convicting impeached officials.

Consider this statement by Alexander Hamilton in *Federalist Paper* No. 75: "All provisions which require more than a majority of any [legislative] body to its resolutions have a direct tendency to embarrass the operations of the government and an indirect one to subject the sense of the majority to that of the minority." Hamilton was writing about a proposal to require that more than half of a chamber's members be present to convene a session, but his argument certainly applies to whether a body should need more than a majority of its members to take a vote.

THE FILIBUSTER AS DAMAGE CONTROL

True, filibusters today are not as colorful as they were before 1975, when senators were forced to read out of a telephone book or even wear diapers to keep a filibuster going. Yet the current filibuster system continues to provide an important protection for minority rights. Why shouldn't Congress be forced to obtain broad support for important legislation? It would be dangerous to allow major taxation and spending measures to be decided by a bare majority vote. Public opinion polling has shown that the filibuster is quite popular among the public at large. Clearly, Americans see the importance of slowing down legislation created by only a single party in Congress. The filibuster still serves a useful purpose, so let's keep it.

On April 28, Pennsylvania senator Arlen Specter left the Republican Party to join the Democrats. That switch, plus the seating of Minnesota's Al Franken, a Democrat, gave the Democrats their sixty votes. For a time, it seemed likely that the majority party would not need to use the reconciliation tactic.

Health-Care Legislation Dodges the Filibuster. By the end of 2009, both the House and the Senate had passed major health-care legislation, but the two bills were not identical. In the normal course of legislation, the two chambers would have negotiated a compromise. Bills with identical language would then have to be passed by both chambers before they could be sent to the president. In January 2010, however, Republican Scott Brown won a special senatorial election in Massachusetts, depriving the Democrats of their prized sixtieth vote. Republicans celebrated, believing that the Democratic health-care legislation was defeated.

The Republicans celebrated too quickly. A health-care bill could pass both chambers in identical language if the House simply adopted the Senate version of the legislation without alteration. In March 2010, the House did exactly that. It then adopted a package of amendments using the reconciliation process and sent it to the Senate, which passed the amendments four days later by a margin of fifty-six to forty-three. In accordance with the rules, the amendments package was purely budgetary. This meant that the House was forced to accept Senate language on nonbudgetary issues, such as abortion.

Prestige

As a consequence of the greater size of the House, representatives generally cannot achieve as much individual recognition and public prestige as can members of the Senate. Senators are better able to gain media exposure and to establish careers as spokespersons for large national constituencies. To obtain recognition for his or her activities, a member of the House generally must do one of two things. He or she might survive in office long enough to join the ranks of the leadership on committees or within the party. Alternatively, the representative could become an expert on some specialized aspect of legislative policy—such as tax laws, the environment, or education.

Judy Chu became the first Chinese American woman to be elected to Congress when she won a special election to the House for California's Thirty-Second District in July 2009. Do women and minorities have proportionate representation in Congress? Why or why not? (AP Photo/ Damian Dovarganes)

Congresspersons and the Citizenry: A Comparison

Members of the U.S. Senate and the U.S. House of Representatives are not typical American citizens. Members of Congress are older than most Americans, partly because of constitutional age requirements and partly because a good deal of political experience normally is an advantage in running for national office. Members of Congress are also disproportionately white, male, and trained in high-status occupations. Lawyers are by far the largest occupational group among congresspersons, although the proportion of lawyers in the House is lower now than it was in the past. Compared with the average American citizen, members of Congress are well paid. In 2010, annual congressional salaries were $174,000. Increasingly, members of Congress are also much wealthier than the average citizen. Whereas only about 3 percent of Americans have assets exceeding $1 million, more than one-third of the members of Congress are millionaires. Table 10–2 below summarizes selected characteristics of the members of Congress.

Compared with the composition of Congress over the past two hundred years, however, the House and Senate today are significantly more diverse in gender and ethnicity than ever before. There are seventy-four women in the House of Representatives (about 17 percent) and seventeen women in the Senate (17 percent). Minority group members fill over 15 percent of the seats in the House. The 112th Congress has significant numbers of members born in 1946 or later, the so-called Baby Boomers. A majority of House members and a large minority of the Senate belong to this postwar generation. This shift in the character of Congress may prompt consideration of the issues that will affect the Boomers, such as Social Security and Medicare.

Congressional Elections

did you know?

That one result of President Obama's election is that thirty-two African Americans ran for Congress as Republicans in 2010, the largest number to run as Republicans since the years following the Civil War.

The process of electing members of Congress is decentralized. Congressional elections are conducted by the individual state governments. The states, however, must conform to the rules established by the U.S. Constitution and by national statutes. The Constitution states that representatives are to be elected every second year by popular ballot, and the number of seats awarded to each state is to be determined every ten years by the results of the census. Each state has at least one representative, with most congressional districts having about 700,000 residents. Senators are elected by popular vote (since the passage of the Seventeenth Amendment) every six years; approximately one-third of the seats are chosen every two years. Each state has two senators. Under Article I, Section 4, of the Constitution, state legislatures are given control over "the Times, Places and Manner of holding Elections

TABLE 10–2 Characteristics of the 112th Congress, 2011–2013

Characteristic	U.S. Population	House	Senate
Age (median)	36.8	55.8	62.6
Percentage minority	34.9	17.7	4
Religion			
Percentage church or synagogue members	66.4	87.6	94
Percentage Roman Catholic	23.9	29.2	19
Percentage Protestant	51.3	53.3	57
Percentage Jewish	1.7	6.2	12
Percentage female	50.7	16.6	17
Percentage with advanced degrees			
Persons age 25 or above only	10.1	66.2	78
Occupation			
Percentage lawyers of those employed	0.8	38.6	57
Percentage blue-collar workers of those employed	23.0	1.6	3
Family income			
Percentage of families earning over $50,000 annually	44.9	100.0	100
Personal wealth*			
Percentage with assets over $1 million	4.7	44.0	58

*111th Congress.

Sources: CIA Factbook, 2010; Census Bureau; Association of Religion Data Archives and, authors' updates.

for Senators and Representatives"; however, "the Congress may at any time by Law make or alter such Regulations."

Only states can elect members of Congress. Therefore, territories such as Puerto Rico and Guam are not represented, though they do elect nonvoting delegates who sit in the House. The District of Columbia is also represented only by a nonvoting delegate.

Candidates for Congressional Elections

Candidates for congressional seats may be self-selected. In districts where one party is very strong, however, there may be a shortage of candidates willing to represent the weaker party. In such circumstances, leaders of the weaker party must often actively recruit candidates. Candidates may resemble the voters of the district in ethnicity or religion, but they are also likely to be very successful individuals who have been active in politics before. House candidates are especially likely to have local ties to their districts. Candidates usually choose to run because they believe they would enjoy the job and its accompanying status. They also may be thinking of a House seat as a stepping-stone to future political office as a senator, governor, or president.

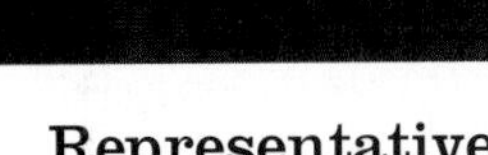

Representative Stephanie Herseth Sandlin (D., S. Dak.) was a leader of the Blue Dog Caucus of conservative Democrats. Almost half of the Blue Dogs lost their seats in 2010, including Sandlin. (AP Photo/Doug Dreyer)

Congressional Campaigns and Elections. Congressional campaigns have changed considerably in the past two decades. Like all other campaigns, they are much more expensive, with the average cost of a winning Senate campaign now $6.5 million and a winning House campaign averaging more than $1.1 million. Campaign funds include direct contributions by individuals and contributions by political action committees (PACs). As you read in Chapter 9, all of these contributions are regulated by laws, including the Federal Election Campaign Act of 1971, as amended, and most recently the Bipartisan Campaign Reform Act of 2002. Once in office, legislators spend time almost every day raising funds for their next campaign.

Most candidates for Congress must win the nomination through a direct primary, in which **party identifiers** vote for the candidate who will be on the party ticket in the general election. To win the primary, candidates may take more liberal or more conservative positions to get the votes of party identifiers. In the general election, they may moderate their views to attract the votes of independents and voters from the other party.

Party Identifier
A person who identifies with a political party.

Presidential Effects. Congressional candidates are always hopeful that a strong presidential candidate on the ticket will have "coattails" that will sweep in senators and representatives of the same party. In fact, coattail effects have been quite limited and in some recent presidential elections have not materialized at all. One way to measure the coattail effect is to look at the subsequent midterm elections, held in the even-numbered years following the presidential contests. In these years, voter turnout falls sharply. The party controlling the White House normally loses seats in Congress in the midterm elections, in part because the coattail effect ceases to apply. Members of Congress who are from contested districts or who are in their first term are more likely not to be reelected. Table 10–3 on the following page shows the pattern for midterm elections since 1946. As you can see, the "midterm effect" did not apply to Democrat Bill Clinton's second term (1998) or to Republican George W. Bush's first term (2002). In President Bush's second term, however, his job approval ratings were uncommonly low, often falling below 40 percent. In 2005 and 2006, the Gallup poll consistently found that voters would favor congressional candidates who opposed the president's policies. Not surprisingly, the midterm effect reappeared in the 2006 elections. As the table shows, in 2010 the midterm effect reasserted itself with a vengeance.

U.S. Senator Joe Lieberman, of Connecticut became an independent in 2006 but still caucuses with the Democrats. He supported Republican John McCain for president, which angered Democratic leaders. (Chris Kleponis/Getty Images)

TABLE 10–3 Midterm Gains and Losses by the Party of the President, 1946–2010

Seats Gained or Lost by the Party of the President in the House of Representatives		
Year	President's Party	Outcome
1946	D.	−55
1950	D.	−29
1954	R.	−18
1958	R.	−47
1962	D.	−4
1966	D.	−47
1970	R.	−12
1974	R.	−48
1978	D.	−15
1982	R.	−26
1986	R.	−5
1990	R.	−8
1994	D.	−52
1998	D.	+5
2002	R.	+5
2006	R.	−30
2010	D.	−64

The Power of Incumbency

The power of incumbency in the outcome of congressional elections cannot be overemphasized. Table 10–4 on the facing page shows that a sizable majority of representatives and a slightly smaller proportion of senators who decide to run for reelection are successful. This conclusion holds for both presidential-year and midterm elections. A number of scholars contend that the pursuit of reelection is the strongest motivation behind the activities of members of Congress. They pursue reelection in several ways. An incumbent can use the mass media, make personal appearances with constituents, and send newsletters—all to produce a favorable image and to make the incumbent's name a household word. Increasingly, members of Congress are using e-mail, blogs, and podcasts to communicate with constituents.

Members of Congress generally try to present themselves as informed, experienced, and responsive to people's needs. Legislators also can point to things that they have done to benefit their constituents—fulfilling the congressional casework function or bringing federal funds for highways or mass transit to the district, for example. Finally, incumbents can demonstrate the positions that they have taken on key issues by referring to their voting records in Congress.

Apportionment of the House

Two of the most complicated aspects of congressional elections are apportionment issues—**reapportionment** (the allocation of seats in the House to each state after each census) and **redistricting** (the redrawing of the boundaries of the districts within each state). In a landmark six-to-two vote in 1962, the United States Supreme Court made the districting of state legislative districts a **justiciable** (that is, a reviewable) **question.**[3] The Court did so by invoking the Fourteenth Amendment principle that no state can deny to any person "the equal protection of the laws." In 1964, the Court held that *both* chambers of a state legislature must be designed so that all districts are equal in population.[4] Later that year, the Court applied this "one person, one vote" principle to U.S. congressional districts on the basis of Article I, Section 2, of the Constitution, which requires that members of the House be chosen "by the People of the several States."[5]

Severe malapportionment of congressional districts before 1964 resulted in some districts containing two or three times the populations of other districts in the same state, thereby diluting the effect of a vote cast in the more populous districts. This system generally benefited the conservative populations of rural areas and small towns and harmed the interests of the more heavily populated and liberal cities. In fact, suburban areas have benefited the most from the Court's rulings, as suburbs account for an increasingly larger proportion of the nation's population, while cities include a correspondingly smaller segment of the population.

Reapportionment
The allocation of seats in the House of Representatives to each state after each census.

Redistricting
The redrawing of the boundaries of the congressional districts within each state.

Justiciable Question
A question that may be raised and reviewed in court.

Gerrymandering
The drawing of legislative district boundary lines for the purpose of obtaining partisan or factional advantage. A district is said to be gerrymandered when its shape is manipulated by the dominant party to maximize electoral strength at the expense of the minority party.

Gerrymandering

Although the general issue of apportionment has been dealt with fairly successfully by the one person, one vote principle, the **gerrymandering** issue has not yet been resolved. This term refers to the legislative-boundary-drawing tactics that were used under Elbridge Gerry, the governor of Massachusetts, in the 1812 elections (see Figure 10–1 on page 348). A district is said to have been gerrymandered when its shape is altered substantially

3. *Baker v. Carr,* 369 U.S. 186 (1962). The term *justiciable* is pronounced juhs-*tish*-a-buhl.
4. *Reynolds v. Sims,* 377 U.S. 533 (1964).
5. *Wesberry v. Sanders,* 376 U.S. 1 (1964).

TABLE 10–4 The Power of Incumbency

	Election Year													
	1984	1986	1988	1990	1992	1994	1996	1998	2000	2002	2004	2006	2008	2010
House														
Number of incumbent candidates	411	394	409	406	368	387	384	402	403	393	404	405	404	397
Reelected	392	385	402	390	325	349	361	395	394	383	397	382	381	338
Percentage of total	95.4	97.7	98.3	96.0	88.3	90.2	94.0	98.3	97.8	97.5	98.3	94.3	94.3	85.1
Defeated	19	9	7	16	43	38	23	7	9	10	7	23	23	59
In primary	3	3	1	1	19	4	2	1	3	3	1	2	5	4
In general election	16	6	6	15	24	34	21	6	6	7	6	21	18	55
Senate														
Number of incumbent candidates	29	28	27	32	28	26	21	29	29	28	26	29	30	24
Reelected	26	21	23	31	23	24	19	26	23	24	25	23	26	20
Percentage of total	89.6	75.0	85.2	96.9	82.1	92.3	90.5	89.7	79.3	85.7	96.2	79.3	86.7	83.3
Defeated	3	7	4	1	5	2	2	3	6	4	1	6	4	4
In primary	0	0	0	0	1	0	1	0	0	1	0	1*	0	3*
In general election	3	7	4	1	4	2	1	3	6	3	1	6	3	2

*In 2006, Joe Lieberman of Connecticut lost the Democratic primary but won the general election as an independent. He then caucused with the Democrats. In 2010, Alaska's Lisa Murkowski lost the Republican primary but won the general election as a write-in candidate. She continued to caucus with the Republicans.

Sources: Norman Ornstein, Thomas E. Mann, and Michael J. Malbin, *Vital Statistics on Congress, 2001–2002* (Washington, D.C.: The AEI Press, 2002); and authors' updates.

ELECTIONS 2010

PARTY CONTROL OF CONGRESS AFTER THE 2010 ELECTIONS

The elections left the congressional Republican Party in a much stronger position than before. Strong party unity meant that the Republicans would have had solid control of the House if their margin had been as little as five seats. (The Democrats could not have enjoyed effective control with a margin that small.) In fact, the Republican margin was fifty-one. In the Senate, the need to accumulate sixty votes to do anything meaningful meant that the fifty-three Democrats in that chamber were essentially stymied—although the Senate Republicans were in no position to move legislation, either.

Clearly, the only way legislation could pass the 112th Congress was through bipartisan consensus. In polls, voters strongly endorsed such cooperation. It is doubtful, however, whether the voters will get what they want. Many observers believed that partisan gridlock would ensure that very little would be accomplished. One factor likely to enhance gridlock was that in 2011 both parties were further from the center than they had been in 2010. In the House, almost half of the members of the moderate-to-conservative Democratic Blue Dog caucus lost their seats. More than one-third of all defeated Democrats were Blue Dogs. The remaining Democrats were therefore more liberal. On the Republican side, the many new Tea Party candidates were sworn to oppose any compromise with the Democrats. Some commentators thought it was a good thing that Congress would probably do little. Others, however, found this to be dangerous when the economy was so troubled.

FIGURE 10–1 The Original Gerrymander

The practice of "gerrymandering"—the excessive manipulation of the shape of a legislative district to benefit a certain incumbent or party—is probably as old as the republic, but the name originated in 1812. In that year, the Massachusetts legislature carved out of Essex County a district that historian John Fiske said had a "dragonlike contour." When the painter Gilbert Stuart saw the misshapen district, he penciled in a head, wings, and claws and exclaimed, "That will do for a salamander!" Editor Benjamin Russell replied, "Better say a Gerrymander" (after Elbridge Gerry, then governor of Massachusetts).

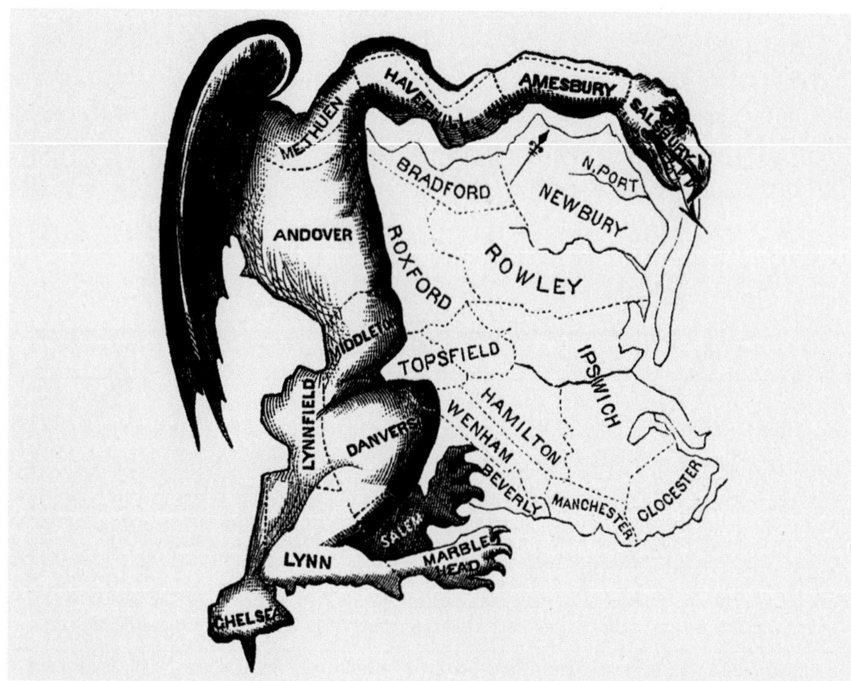

Source: *Congressional Quarterly's Guide to Congress,* 3d ed. (Washington, D.C.: Congressional Quarterly Press, 1982), p. 695.

by the dominant party to maximize its electoral strength at the expense of the minority party.

In 1986, the Supreme Court heard a case that challenged gerrymandered congressional districts in Indiana. The Court ruled for the first time that redistricting for the political benefit of one group could be challenged on constitutional grounds. In this specific case, *Davis v. Bandemer,*[6] however, the Court did not agree that the districts were drawn unfairly, because it could not be proved that a group of voters would consistently be deprived of influence at the polls as a result of the new districts.

Redistricting after the 2000 Census

In the meantime, political gerrymandering continues. For example, New York Democratic representative Maurice Hinchey's district resembles a soup ladle. Why? That shape guarantees that he will always be able to pick up enough votes in Ithaca and Binghamton to win reelection. Right next to that district is Republican representative Sherwood Boehlert's district, which has been said to resemble a "napping Bugs Bunny."

Congressional and state legislative redistricting decisions are often made by a small group of political leaders within a state legislature. Typically, their goal is to shape voting districts in such a way as to maximize their party's chances of winning state legislative seats, as well as seats in Congress. Two of the techniques they use are called "packing" and "cracking." With the use of powerful computers and software, they *pack* voters supporting the opposing party into as few districts as possible or *crack* the opposing party's supporters into different districts. Consider that in Michigan, the Republicans who dominated redistricting efforts succeeded in packing six Democratic incumbents into only three congressional seats.

Clearly, partisan redistricting aids incumbents. The party that dominates a state's legislature will be making redistricting decisions. Through gerrymandering tactics such as packing and cracking, districts can be redrawn in such a way as to ensure that party's continued strength in the state legislature or Congress. In most election years, only a small percentage of the 435 seats in the House of Representatives are open for any real competition.

In 2004, the United States Supreme Court reviewed an obviously political redistricting scheme in Pennsylvania. The Court concluded, however, that the federal judiciary would not address purely political gerrymandering claims.[7] Two years later, the Supreme Court

6. 478 U.S. 109 (1986).
7. *Vieth v. Jubelirer,* 541 U.S. 267 (2004).

reached a similar conclusion with respect to most of the new congressional districts created by the Republicans in the Texas legislature in 2003. Again, except for one district in Texas, the Court refused to intervene in what was clearly a political gerrymandering plan.[8]

"Minority–Majority" Districts

In the early 1990s, the federal government encouraged a type of gerrymandering that made possible the election of a minority representative from a "minority–majority" area. Under the mandate of the Voting Rights Act of 1965, the Justice Department issued directives to states after the 1990 census instructing them to create congressional districts that would maximize the voting power of minority groups—that is, create districts in which minority group voters were the majority. The result was a number of creatively drawn congressional districts—see, for example, the depiction of Illinois's Fourth Congressional District in Figure 10–2 below, which is commonly described as "a pair of earmuffs."

Constitutional Challenges. Many of these "minority–majority" districts were challenged in court by citizens who claimed that creating districts based on race or ethnicity alone violates the equal protection clause of the Constitution. In 1995, the Supreme Court agreed with this argument when it declared that Georgia's new Eleventh District was unconstitutional. The district stretched from Atlanta to the Atlantic, splitting eight counties and five municipalities along the way. The Court referred to the district as a "monstrosity" linking "widely spaced urban centers that have absolutely nothing to do with each other." The Court went on to say that when a state assigns voters on the basis

8. *League of United Latin American Citizens v. Perry,* 548 U.S. 399 (2006).

FIGURE 10–2 The Fourth Congressional District of Illinois

This district, which is mostly within Chicago's city limits, was drawn to connect two Hispanic neighborhoods separated by an African American majority district.

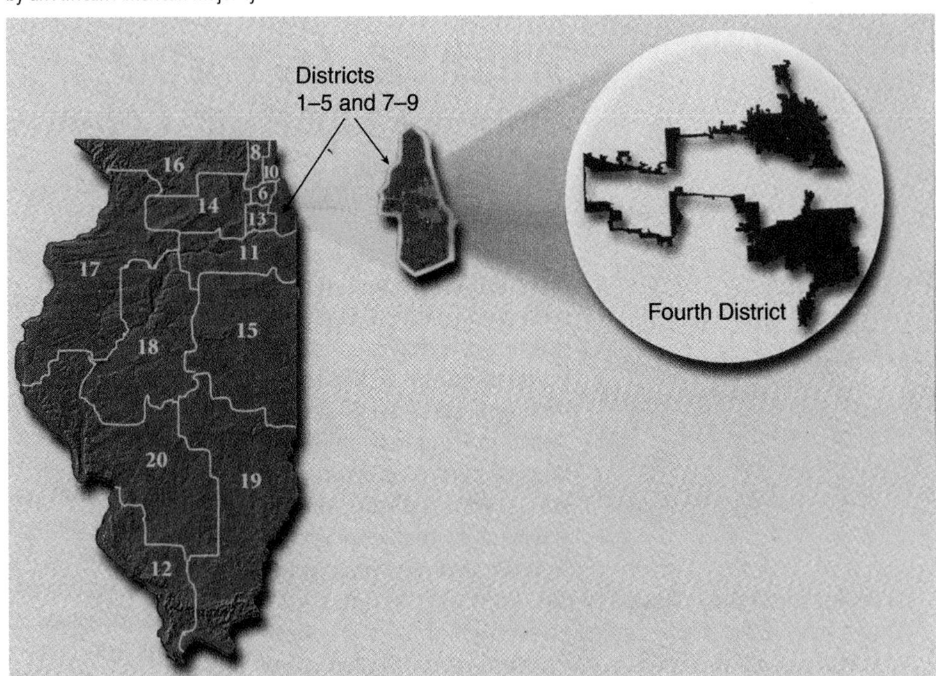

of race, "it engages in the offensive and demeaning assumption that voters of a particular race, because of their race, think alike, share the same political interests, and will prefer the same candidates at the polls." The Court also chastised the Justice Department for concluding that race-based districting was mandated under the Voting Rights Act of 1965: "When the Justice Department's interpretation of the Act compels race-based districting, it by definition raises a serious constitutional question."[9] In subsequent rulings, the Court affirmed its position that when race is the dominant factor in the drawing of congressional district lines, the districts are unconstitutional.

Changing Directions. In the early 2000s, the Supreme Court seemed to take a new direction on racial redistricting challenges. In a 2000 case, the Court limited the federal government's authority to invalidate changes in state and local elections on the basis that the changes were discriminatory. The case involved a proposed school redistricting plan in Louisiana. The Court held that federal approval for the plan could not be withheld simply because the plan was discriminatory. Rather, the test was whether the plan left racial and ethnic minorities worse off than they were before.[10]

In 2001, the Supreme Court reviewed, for a second time, a case involving North Carolina's Twelfth District. The district was 165 miles long, following Interstate 85 for the most part. According to a local joke, the district was so narrow that a car traveling down the interstate highway with both doors open would kill most of the voters in the district. In 1996, the Supreme Court had held that the district was unconstitutional because race had been the dominant factor in drawing the district's boundaries. Shortly thereafter, the boundaries were redrawn, but the district was again challenged as a racial gerrymander. A federal district court agreed and invalidated the new boundaries as unconstitutional. In 2001, however, the Supreme Court held that there was insufficient evidence for the lower court's conclusion that race had been the dominant factor when the boundaries were redrawn.[11] The Twelfth District's boundaries remained as drawn.

Franking
A policy that enables members of Congress to send material through the mail by substituting their facsimile signature (frank) for postage.

Perks and Privileges

did you know?

That before the Republicans reorganized House services in 1995, all members had buckets of ice delivered to their offices each day, at an annual cost of $500,000.

Legislators have many benefits that are not available to most workers. For example, members of Congress are granted generous **franking** privileges that permit them to mail newsletters, surveys, and other correspondence to their constituents without paying for postage.[12] The annual cost of congressional mail has risen from $11 million in 1971 to more than $70 million today. Typically, the costs for these mailings rise substantially during election years.

Permanent Professional Staffs

More than 30,000 people are employed in the Capitol Hill bureaucracy. About half of them are personal and committee staff members. The personal staff includes office clerks and assistants; professionals who deal with media relations, draft legislation, and satisfy constituency requests for service; and staffers who maintain local offices in the member's home district or state.

The average Senate office on Capitol Hill employs about thirty staff members, and twice that number work on the personal staffs of senators from the most populous states.

9. *Miller v. Johnson,* 515 U.S. 900 (1995).
10. *Reno v. Bossier Parish School Board,* 528 U.S. 320 (2000).
11. *Easley v. Cromartie,* 532 U.S. 234 (2001).
12. The word *franking* derives from the Latin *francus,* which means "free."

House office staffs typically are about half as large as those of the Senate. The number of staff members has increased dramatically since 1960. The bulk of those increases has been in assistants to individual members, leading some scholars to question whether staff members are really advising on legislation or are primarily aiding constituents and gaining votes in the next election.

Congress also benefits from the expertise of the professional staffs of agencies that were created to produce information for members of the House and Senate. For example, the Congressional Research Service, the Government Accountability Office, and the Congressional Budget Office all provide reports, audits, and policy recommendations for review by members of Congress.

did you know?

That the most recently constructed dormitory for Senate pages cost about $8 million, or $264,200 per bed, compared with the median cost of a university dormitory of $22,600 per bed.

Privileges and Immunities under the Law

Members of Congress also benefit from a number of special constitutional protections. Under Article I, Section 6, of the Constitution, they "shall in all Cases, except Treason, Felony and Breach of the Peace, be privileged from Arrest during their Attendance at the Session of their respective Houses, and in going to and returning from the same; and for any Speech or Debate in either House, they shall not be questioned in any other Place." The arrest immunity clause is not really an important provision today. The "speech or debate" clause, however, means that a member may make any allegations or other statements he or she wishes in connection with official duties and normally not be sued for libel or slander or otherwise be subject to legal action.

Congressional Caucuses: Another Source of Support

The typical member of Congress is part of a variety of caucuses. The most important caucuses are those established by the parties in each chamber. These Democratic and Republican meetings provide information to the members and devise legislative strategy for the party. Other caucuses have been founded, such as the Democratic Study Group and the Congressional Black Caucus, to support subgroups of members. In 1995, concerned with the growth of caucuses supported by public funds, the Republican majority in the House passed a rule that prohibited using free space for caucuses or using public funds to finance them.

There are numerous caucuses in Congress, including the Congressional Black Caucus. The current head of the caucus is Barbara Lee (D., Calif.), who is shown here with several other members. What is the purpose of such caucuses? (AP Photo/ Alex Brandon)

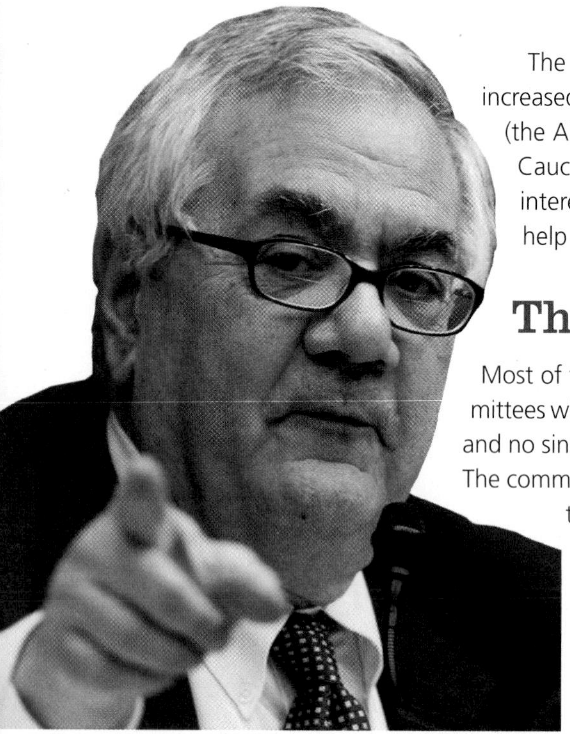

House Financial Services Committee Chairman Barney Frank (D., Mass.) presides over a committee hearing on Capitol Hill. Why do members of Congress want to become heads of committees? (AP Photo/Manuel Balce Ceneta)

The number of caucuses has not declined, however. Instead, the number has increased. There are now more than two hundred caucuses, including small ones (the Albanian Issues Caucus, the Potato Caucus) and large ones (the Sportsmen's Caucus). These organizations, which are now funded by businesses and special interests, provide staff assistance and information for members of Congress and help them build support among specific groups of voters.

The Committee Structure

Most of the actual work of legislating is performed by the committees and subcommittees within Congress. Thousands of bills are introduced in every session of Congress, and no single member can possibly be adequately informed on all the issues that arise. The committee system is a way to provide for specialization, or a division of the legislative labor. Members of a committee can concentrate on just one area or topic—such as taxation or energy—and develop sufficient expertise to draft appropriate legislation when needed. The flow of legislation through both the House and the Senate is determined largely by the speed with which the members of these committees act on bills and resolutions.

The Power of Committees

Sometimes called "little legislatures," committees usually have the final say on pieces of legislation.[13] Committee actions may be overturned on the floor by the House or Senate, but this rarely happens. Legislators normally defer to the expertise of the chairperson and other members of the committee who speak on the floor in defense of a committee decision. Chairpersons of committees exercise control over the scheduling of hearings and formal action on a bill. They also decide which subcommittee will act on legislation falling within their committees' jurisdiction.

Committees only very rarely are deprived of control over a bill—although this kind of action is provided for in the rules of each chamber. In the House, if a bill has been considered by a standing committee for thirty days, the signatures of a majority (218) of the House membership on a **discharge petition** can pry a bill out of an uncooperative committee's hands. From 1909 to 2010, however, although more than nine hundred such petitions were initiated, only slightly more than two dozen resulted in successful discharge efforts. Of those, twenty resulted in bills that passed the House.[14]

Discharge Petition
A procedure by which a bill in the House of Representatives can be forced (discharged) out of a committee that has refused to report it for consideration by the House. The petition must be signed by an absolute majority (218) of representatives and is used only on rare occasions.

Standing Committee
A permanent committee in the House or Senate that considers bills within a certain subject area.

Types of Congressional Committees

Over the past two centuries, Congress has created several different types of committees, each of which serves particular needs of the institution.

Standing Committees. By far the most important committees in Congress are the **standing committees**—permanent bodies that are established by the rules of each chamber of Congress and that continue from session to session. A list of the standing committees of the 112th Congress is presented in Table 10–5 on the facing page. In addition, most of the standing committees have created subcommittees to carry out their work. For example, the 112th Congress has 73 subcommittees in the Senate and 104 in the House. Each standing committee is given a specific area of legislative policy jurisdiction, and almost all legislative measures are considered by the appropriate standing committees.

13. The term *little legislatures* is from Woodrow Wilson, *Congressional Government* (New York: Meridian Books, 1956 [first published in 1885]).
14. Congressional Quarterly, Inc., *Guide to Congress,* 5th ed. (Washington, D.C.: CQ Press, 2000); and authors' update.

TABLE 10–5 Standing Committees of the 112th Congress, 2011–2013

House Committees	Senate Committees
Agriculture	Agriculture, Nutrition, and Forestry
Appropriations	Appropriations
Armed Services	Armed Services
Budget	Banking, Housing, and Urban Affairs
Education and Labor	Budget
Energy and Commerce	Commerce, Science, and Transportation
Financial Services	Energy and Natural Resources
Foreign Affairs	Environment and Public Works
Homeland Security	Finance
House Administration	Foreign Relations
Judiciary	Health, Education, Labor, and Pensions
Natural Resources	Homeland Security and Governmental Affairs
Oversight and Government Reform	Judiciary
Rules	Rules and Administration
Science and Technology	Small Business and Entrepreneurship
Small Business	Veterans' Affairs
Standards of Official Conduct	
Transportation and Infrastructure	
Veterans' Affairs	
Ways and Means	

Because of the importance of their work and the traditional influence of their members in Congress, certain committees are considered to be more prestigious than others. Seats on standing committees that handle spending issues are especially sought after because members can use these positions to benefit their constituents. Committees that control spending include the Appropriations Committee in either chamber and the Ways and Means Committee in the House. Members also normally seek seats on committees that handle matters of special interest to their constituents. A member of the House from an agricultural district, for example, will have an interest in joining the House Agriculture Committee.

Select Committees. In principle, a **select committee** is created for a limited time and for a specific legislative purpose. For example, a select committee may be formed to investigate a public problem, such as child nutrition or aging. In practice, a select committee, such as the Select Committee on Intelligence in each chamber, may continue indefinitely. Select committees rarely create original legislation.

Joint Committees. A **joint committee** is formed by the concurrent action of both chambers of Congress and consists of members from each chamber. Joint committees, which may be permanent or temporary, have dealt with the economy, taxation, and the Library of Congress.

Conference Committees. Special joint committees—**conference committees**—are formed for the purpose of achieving agreement between the House and the Senate on

Select Committee
A temporary legislative committee established for a limited time period and for a special purpose.

Joint Committee
A legislative committee composed of members from both chambers of Congress.

Conference Committee
A special joint committee appointed to reconcile differences when bills pass the two chambers of Congress in different forms.

Treasury Secretary Timothy Geithner, left, accompanied by Federal Reserve Chairman Ben Bernanke, center, and William Dudley, president and chief executive officer of the Federal Reserve Bank of New York, appear before a congressional committee. They are being questioned about the state of the economy. What do the members of such committees do with the testimony that they hear? (AP Photo/Evan Vucci)

the exact wording of legislative acts when the two chambers pass legislative proposals in different forms. No bill can be sent to the White House to be signed into law unless it first passes both chambers in identical form. Sometimes called the "third house" of Congress, conference committees are in a position to make significant alterations to legislation and frequently become the focal point of policy debates.

The House Rules Committee. Due to its special "gatekeeping" power over the terms on which legislation will reach the floor of the House of Representatives, the House Rules Committee holds a uniquely powerful position. A special committee rule sets the time limit on debate and determines whether and how a bill may be amended. This practice dates back to 1883. The Rules Committee has the unusual power to meet while the House is meeting as a whole, to have its resolutions considered immediately on the floor, and to initiate legislation on its own.

The Selection of Committee Members

In both chambers, members are appointed to standing committees by the Steering Committee of their party. The majority-party member with the longest term of continuous service on a standing committee is given preference when the committee selects its chairperson. This is not a law but an informal, traditional process, and it applies to other significant posts in Congress as well. The **seniority system,** although it deliberately treats members unequally, provides a predictable means of assigning positions of power within Congress. The most senior member of the minority party is called the *ranking committee member* for that party.

The general pattern until the 1970s was that members of the House or Senate who represented **safe seats** would be reelected continually and eventually would accumulate enough years of continuous committee service to enable them to become the chairpersons of their committees. In the 1970s, a number of reforms in the chairperson selection process somewhat modified the seniority system. The reforms introduced the use of a secret ballot in electing House committee chairpersons and allowed for the possibility of choosing a chairperson on a basis other than seniority. The Democrats immediately replaced three senior chairpersons who were out of step with the rest of their party. In 1995, under Speaker Newt Gingrich, the Republicans chose relatively junior House members as chairpersons of several key committees, valuing ideology over seniority and thus ensuring conservative control of the committees. The Republicans also passed a rule limiting the term of a chairperson to six years.

Seniority System
A custom followed in both chambers of Congress specifying that the member of the majority party with the longest term of continuous service will be given preference when a committee chairperson (or a holder of some other significant post) is selected.

Safe Seat
A district that returns a legislator with 55 percent of the vote or more.

The Formal Leadership

The limited amount of centralized power that exists in Congress is exercised through party-based mechanisms. Congress is organized by party. When the Democratic Party, for example, wins a majority of seats in either the House or the Senate, Democrats control the official positions of power in that chamber, and every important committee has a Democratic chairperson and a majority of Democratic members. The same process holds when Republicans are in the majority.

When the Republicans took control of the House of Representatives after the 2010 midterm elections, they were expected to elevate former minority leader John Boehner (R., Ohio, left) to the position of Speaker of the House. Eric Cantor (R., Va., center) was the leading candidate for majority leader. Nancy Pelosi (D., Calif., right), the former Speaker of the House, became a candidate for House minority leader. The leadership elections were scheduled for the week of November 15, 2010. What benefits could a state receive when one of its representatives obtains such a leadership post? (Photos left and right, courtesy of the U.S. Congress, center photo AP Photo/Cliff Owen)

We next consider the formal leadership positions in the House and Senate separately, but you will note some broad similarities in the way leaders are selected and in the ways they exercise power in the two chambers.

Leadership in the House

The House leadership is made up of the Speaker, the majority and minority leaders, and the party whips.

The Speaker. The foremost power holder in the House of Representatives is the **Speaker of the House.** The Speaker's position is technically a nonpartisan one, but in fact, for the better part of two centuries, the Speaker has been the official leader of the majority party in the House. When a new Congress convenes in January of odd-numbered years, each party nominates a candidate for Speaker. All Republican members of the House are expected to vote for their party's nominee, and all Democrats are expected to support their candidate. The vote to organize the House is the one vote in which representatives must vote with their party. In a sense, this vote defines a member's partisan status.

Speaker of the House
The presiding officer in the House of Representatives. The Speaker is always a member of the majority party and is the most powerful and influential member of the House.

The influence of modern-day Speakers is based primarily on their personal prestige, persuasive ability, and knowledge of the legislative process—plus the acquiescence or active support of other representatives. The major formal powers of the Speaker include the following:

- Presiding over meetings of the House.
- Appointing members of joint committees and conference committees.
- Scheduling legislation for floor action.
- Deciding points of order and interpreting the rules with the advice of the House parliamentarian.
- Referring bills and resolutions to the appropriate standing committees of the House.

A Speaker may take part in floor debate and vote, as can any other member of Congress, but recent Speakers usually have voted only to break a tie. Since 1975, the Speaker, when a Democrat, has also had the power to appoint the members of the Democratic Steering Committee, which determines new committee assignments for House party members.

In general, the powers of the Speaker are related to his or her control over information and communications channels in the House. This is a significant power in a large, decentralized institution in which information is a very important resource. With this control, the

Speaker attempts to ensure the smooth operation of the chamber and to integrate presidential and congressional policies.

Majority Leader of the House
A legislative position held by an important party member in the House of Representatives. The majority leader is selected by the majority party in caucus or conference to foster cohesion among party members and to act as spokesperson for the majority party in the House.

Minority Leader of the House
The party leader elected by the minority party in the House.

Whip
A member of Congress who aids the majority or minority leader of the House or the Senate.

President Pro Tempore
The temporary presiding officer of the Senate in the absence of the vice president.

Senate Majority Leader
The chief spokesperson of the majority party in the Senate, who directs the legislative program and party strategy.

Senate Minority Leader
The party officer in the Senate who commands the minority party's opposition to the policies of the majority party and directs the legislative program and strategy of his or her party.

The Majority Leader. The **majority leader of the House** is elected by a caucus of the majority party to foster cohesion among party members and to act as a spokesperson for the party. The majority leader influences the scheduling of debate and acts as the chief supporter of the Speaker. The majority leader cooperates with the Speaker and other party leaders, both inside and outside Congress, to formulate the party's legislative program and to guide that program through the legislative process in the House. The parties often recruit future Speakers from those who hold the position of majority leader.

The Minority Leader. The **minority leader of the House** is the candidate nominated for Speaker by a caucus of the minority party. Like the majority leader, the leader of the minority party has as her or his primary responsibility the maintaining of cohesion within the party's ranks. The minority leader works for solidarity among the party's members and speaks on behalf of the president if the minority party controls the White House. In relations with the majority party, the minority leader consults with both the Speaker and the majority leader on recognizing members who wish to speak on the floor, on House rules and procedures, and on the scheduling of legislation. Minority leaders have no actual power in these areas, however.

Whips. The leadership of each party includes assistants to the majority and minority leaders, known as **whips.**[15] The whips are members of Congress who assist the party leaders by passing information down from the leadership to party members and by ensuring that members show up for floor debate and cast their votes on important issues. Whips conduct polls among party members about the members' views on legislation, inform the leaders about whose vote is doubtful and whose is certain, and may exert pressure on members to support the leaders' positions. Serving as a whip is the first step toward positions of higher leadership.

Leadership in the Senate

The Senate is less than one-fourth the size of the House. This fact alone probably explains why a formal, complex, and centralized leadership structure is not as necessary in the Senate as it is in the House.

The two highest-ranking formal leadership positions in the Senate are essentially ceremonial in nature. Under the Constitution, the vice president of the United States is the president (that is, the presiding officer) of the Senate and may vote to break a tie. The vice president, however, is only rarely present for a meeting of the Senate. The Senate elects instead a **president pro tempore** ("pro tem") to preside over the Senate in the vice president's absence. Ordinarily, the president pro tem is the member of the majority party with the longest continuous term of service in the Senate. The president pro tem is mostly a ceremonial position. Junior senators take turns actually presiding over the sessions of the Senate.

The real leadership power in the Senate rests in the hands of the **Senate majority leader,** the **Senate minority leader,** and their respective whips. The Senate majority and minority leaders have the right to be recognized first in debate on the floor and generally exercise the same powers available to the House majority and minority leaders. They control the scheduling of debate on the floor in conjunction with the majority party's Policy Committee, influence the allocation of committee assignments for new members or for

15. *Whip* comes from "whipper-in," a fox-hunting term for someone who keeps the hunting dogs from straying.

When the Democrats took control of the U.S. Senate in the 2006 elections, Democratic senator Harry Reid, left, was elected the majority leader. Republican senator Mitch McConnell of Kentucky, right, became the minority leader. These two senators were expected to retain their leadership positions in the 112th Congress following the elections of 2010. (Photos Courtesy of Senator McConnell and Senator Reid)

senators attempting to transfer to a new committee, influence the selection of other party officials, and participate in selecting members of conference committees. The leaders are expected to mobilize support for partisan legislative or presidential initiatives. The leaders act as liaisons with the White House when the president is of their party, try to obtain the cooperation of committee chairpersons, and seek to facilitate the smooth functioning of the Senate through the senators' unanimous consent. The majority and minority leaders are elected by their respective party caucuses.

Senate party whips, like their House counterparts, maintain communication within the party on platform positions and try to ensure that party colleagues are present for floor debate and important votes. The Senate whip system is far less elaborate than its counterpart in the House, because there are fewer members to track and senators have a greater tradition of independence.

A list of the formal party leaders of the 112th Congress is presented in Table 10–6 on the next page.

did you know?

That the Constitution does not require that the Speaker of the House of Representatives be an elected member of the House.

How Members of Congress Decide

Each member of Congress casts hundreds of votes in each session. Each member compiles a record of votes during the years that he or she spends in the national legislature. There are usually a number of different reasons why any particular vote is cast. Research shows that the best predictor of a member's vote is party affiliation. Obviously, party members do have common opinions on some, if not all, issues facing the nation. In addition, the party leadership in each house works hard to build cohesion and agreement among the members through the activities of the party caucuses and conferences. In recent years, the increase in partisanship in both the House and the Senate has meant that most Republicans vote in opposition to most Democrats and vice versa.

The Conservative Coalition

The political parties have not always been so unified. In the 1950s and 1960s, the Democrats in Congress were often split between northern liberals and southern conservatives. This division gave rise to the **conservative coalition,** a voting bloc made up of southern Democrats and conservative (which is to say, most) Republicans. This coalition was able to win many votes

Conservative Coalition
An alliance of Republicans and southern Democrats that historically formed in the House or the Senate to oppose liberal legislation and support conservative legislation.

TABLE 10–6 Party Leaders in the 112th Congress, 2011–2013

Position	Incumbent	Party/State	Leader since
HOUSE			
Speaker	John Boehner	R., Ohio	Jan. 2011
Majority leader	Eric Cohen	R., Va.	Jan. 2011
Majority whip	Kevin McCarthy	R., Calif.	Jan. 2011
Chair of the Republican	to be determined		Jan. 2011
Conference			Jan. 2011
Minority leader	Nancy Pelosi	D., Calif.	Jan. 2011
Minority whip	to be determined		
Chair of the Democratic	John Larson	D., Conn.	Jan. 2011
Conference			
SENATE			
President pro tempore	Daniel Inouye	D., Hawaii	June 2010
Majority leader	Harry Reid	D., Nev.	Jan. 2007
Majority whip	Dick Durbin	D., Ill.	Jan. 2007
Chair of the Democratic			
Conference	Harry Reid	D., Nev.	Jan. 2007
Minority leader	Mitch McConnell	R., Ky.	Jan. 2007
Minority whip	Jon Kyl	R., Ariz.	Dec. 2007
Chair of the Republican			
Conference	Lamar Alexander	R., Tenn.	Dec. 2007

The named individuals are the leading contenders for the various positions in the 2010 leadership elections.

did you know?

That in 2004, on the urging of the Alaska congressional delegation, the House approved a $200 million bridge between a town of 7,845 people and an island with 50 residents—the famous "Bridge to Nowhere," which proved to be such a scandal that it had to be canceled.

over the years. Today, however, most southern conservatives are Republicans, so the coalition has disappeared.

"Crossing Over"

On some votes, individual representatives and senators will vote against their party, "crossing over to the other side," because the interests of their states or districts differ from the interests that prevail within the rest of their party. Additionally, members may vote a certain way because of the influence of regional or national interests, such as local opinion on the desirability of coal mining. Other voting decisions are based on the members' religious or ideological beliefs. Votes on such issues as abortion and gay rights may be motivated by a member's religious views.

There are, however, far too many voting decisions for every member to be fully informed on each issue. Research suggests that many voting decisions are based on cues provide by trusted colleagues or the party leadership. A member who sits on the committee that wrote a law may become a reliable source of information about that law. Alternatively, for cues on voting, a member may turn to a colleague who represents a district in the same state or one who represents a similar district. Cues may also come from fellow committee members, from leaders, and from the administration.

How a Bill Becomes Law

Each year, Congress and the president propose and approve many laws. Some are budget and appropriations laws that require extensive bargaining but must be passed for the government to continue to function. Other laws are relatively free of controversy and are passed with little dissension. Still other proposed legislation is extremely controversial and reaches to the roots of differences between Republicans and Democrats and between the executive and legislative branches.

As detailed in Figure 10–3 on page 360, each law begins as a bill, which must be introduced in either the House or the Senate. Often, similar bills are introduced in both chambers. A "money bill," however, must start in the House. In each chamber, the bill follows similar steps. It is referred to a committee and its subcommittees for study, discussion, hearings, and rewriting ("markup"). When the bill is reported out to the full chamber, it must be scheduled for debate (by the Rules Committee in the House and by the leadership in the Senate). After the bill has been passed in each chamber, if it contains different provisions, a conference committee is formed to write a compromise bill, which must be approved by both chambers before it is sent to the president to sign or veto.

Another form of congressional action, the *joint resolution,* differs little from a bill in how it is proposed or debated. Once it is approved by both chambers and signed by the president, it has the force of law.[16] A joint resolution to amend the Constitution, however, after it is approved by two-thirds of both chambers, is sent not to the president but to the states for ratification.

As a U.S. representative from Illinois, Rahm Emanuel had hopes someday of becoming Speaker of the House. Instead, he became President Obama's chief of staff. In late 2010, he resigned that position so that he could run for mayor of Chicago. Speaker, chief of staff, mayor of Chicago—which of these positions do you think has the most real power? Why? (Brendan Smialowski/Getty Images for *Meet The Press*)

How Much Will the Government Spend?

The Constitution is very clear about where the power of the purse lies in the national government: all taxing or spending bills must originate in the House of Representatives. Today, much of the business of Congress is concerned with approving government expenditures through the budget process and with raising the revenues to pay for government programs.

From 1922, when Congress required the president to prepare and present to the legislature an **executive budget,** until 1974, the congressional budget process was so disjointed that it was difficult to visualize the total picture of government finances. The president presented the executive budget to Congress in January. It was broken down into thirteen or more appropriations bills. Some time later, after all of the bills had been debated, amended, and passed, it was more or less possible to estimate total government spending for the next year.

Frustrated by the president's ability to impound, or withhold, funds and dissatisfied with the entire budget process, Congress passed the Budget and Impoundment Control Act of 1974 to regain some control over the nation's spending. The act required the president to spend the funds that Congress had appropriated, ending the president's ability to kill programs by withholding funds. The other major result of the act was to force Congress to examine total national taxing and spending at least twice in each budget cycle.

The budget cycle of the federal government is described in the rest of this section. (See Figure 10–4 on page 361 for a graphic illustration of the budget cycle.)

Executive Budget
The budget prepared and submitted by the president to Congress.

Fiscal Year (FY)
A twelve-month period that is used for bookkeeping, or accounting, purposes. Usually, the fiscal year does not coincide with the calendar year. For example, the federal government's fiscal year runs from October 1 through September 30.

Preparing the Budget

The federal government operates on a **fiscal year (FY)** cycle. The fiscal year runs from October through September, so that fiscal year 2012, or FY12, runs from October 1, 2011, through September 30, 2012. Eighteen months before a fiscal year starts, the executive branch begins preparing the budget. The Office of Management and Budget (OMB) receives advice from the Council of Economic Advisers and the Treasury Department. The OMB outlines the budget and then sends it to the various departments and agencies. Bargaining follows, in which—to use only two of many examples—the Department of Health and Human Services argues for more welfare spending, and the armed forces argue for more defense spending.

Even though the OMB has fewer than 550 employees, it is one of the most powerful agencies in Washington. It assembles the budget documents and monitors federal agencies

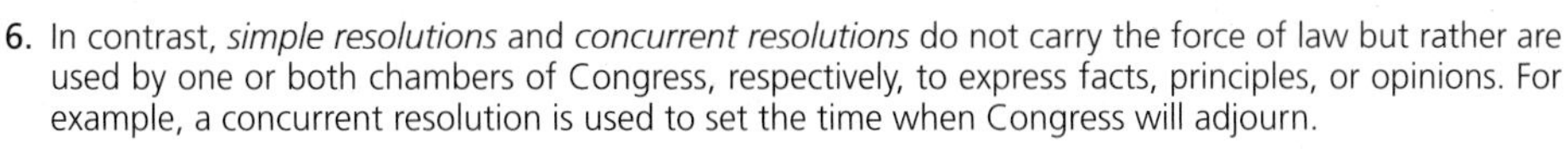

16. In contrast, *simple resolutions* and *concurrent resolutions* do not carry the force of law but rather are used by one or both chambers of Congress, respectively, to express facts, principles, or opinions. For example, a concurrent resolution is used to set the time when Congress will adjourn.

FIGURE 10–3 How a Bill Becomes Law

This illustration shows the most typical way in which proposed legislation is enacted into law. Most legislation begins as similar bills introduced into the House and the Senate. The process is illustrated here with two hypothetical bills, House bill No. 100 (HR 100) and Senate bill No. 200 (S 200). The path of HR 100 is shown on the left, and that of S 200, on the right.

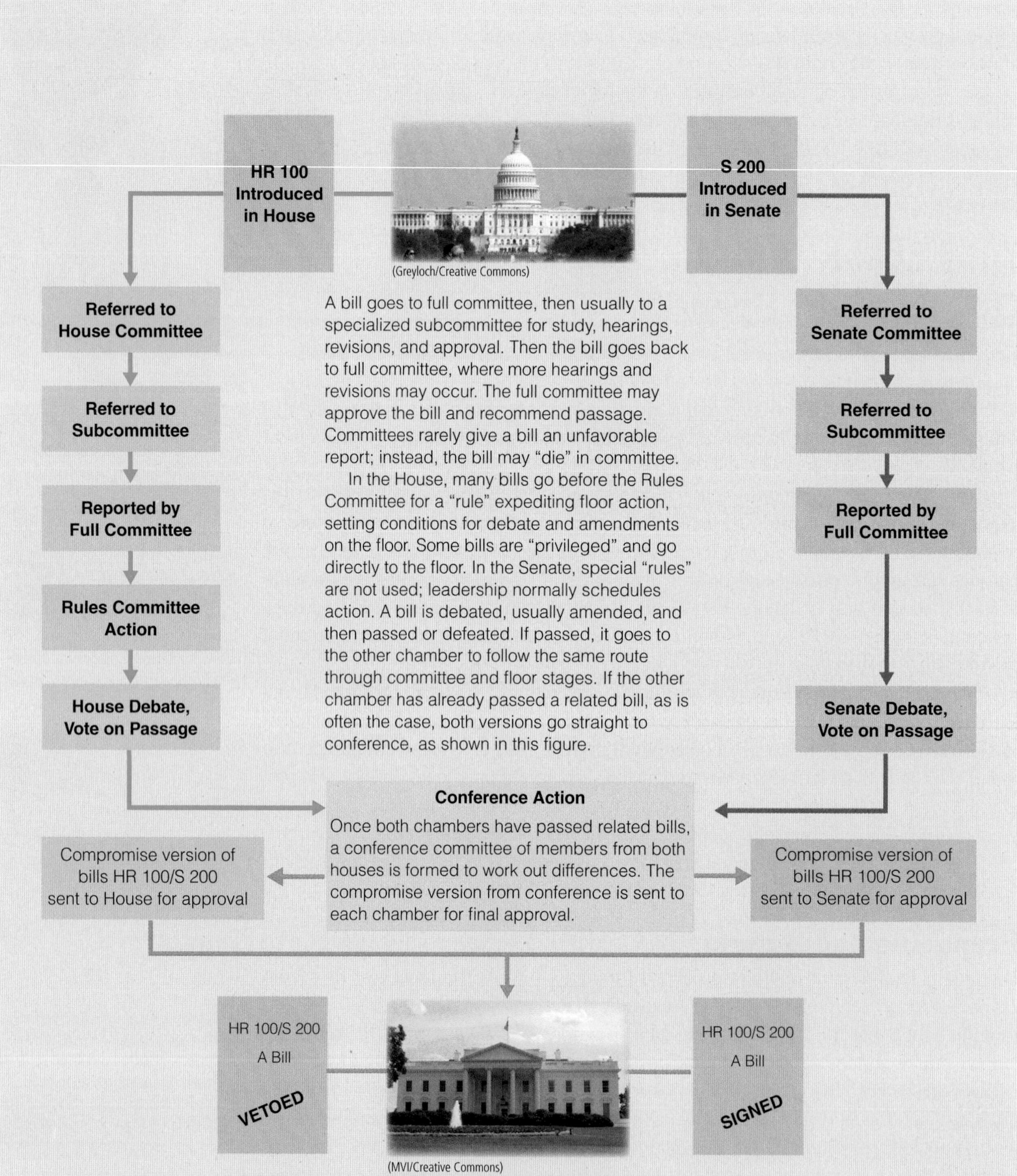

throughout each year. Every year, it begins the budget process with a **spring review,** in which it requires all of the agencies to review their programs, activities, and goals. At the beginning of each summer, the OMB sends out a letter instructing agencies to submit their requests for funding for the next fiscal year. By the end of the summer, each agency must submit a formal request to the OMB.

In actuality, the "budget season" begins with the **fall review.** At this time, the OMB looks at budget requests and, in almost all cases, routinely cuts them back. Although the OMB works within guidelines established by the president, specific decisions often are left to the OMB director and the director's associates. By the beginning of November, the director's review begins. The director meets with cabinet secretaries and budget officers. Time becomes crucial. The budget must be completed by January so that it can be included in the *Economic Report of the President*.

"The only solution I can see is to hold a series of long and costly hearings in order to put off finding a solution."
(© The New Yorker Collection, 2000. Jack Ziegler, from cartoonbank.com. All Rights Reserved.)

The Election-Year Budget

The schedule just described cannot apply to a year in which the voters elect a new president or to a year in which a new president is inaugurated. In 2008, George W. Bush did not engage in a fall review of the FY 2010 budget, because he would no longer be in office when the budget went into effect in October 2009. Barack Obama could hardly have undertaken the fall review either, given that he was still campaigning for the presidency.

Following the election of a new president, the budget process is compressed into the first months of the new administration. Indeed, Barack Obama released a budget document for FY 2010 on February 26, 2009, barely a month after he was inaugurated. Obama's budget predicted substantial deficits even after the end of the recession. Is that a problem? We discuss that issue in this chapter's feature *The Politics of Boom and Bust: Endless Federal Budget Deficits?* on the following page.

Spring Review
The annual process in which the Office of Management and Budget (OMB) requires federal agencies to review their programs, activities, and goals and submit their requests for funding for the next fiscal year.

Fall Review
The annual process in which the OMB, after receiving formal federal agency requests for funding for the next fiscal year, reviews the requests, makes changes, and submits its recommendations to the president.

FIGURE 10–4 The Budget Cycle

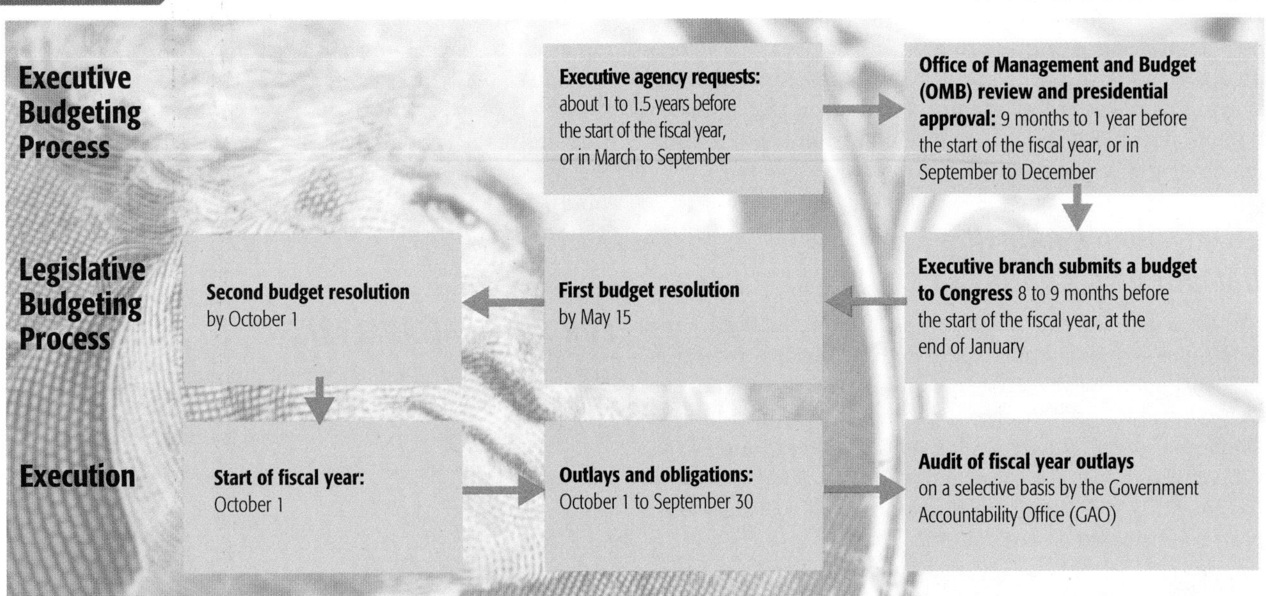

(© Tad Denson/MyShotz.com/Shutterstock)

THE POLITICS OF BOOM AND BUST

ENDLESS FEDERAL BUDGET DEFICITS?

Unless you've been vacationing on Mars, you know that the federal government has recently created the largest budget deficits in U.S. history. A deficit occurs each time the government spends more than it receives. To cover the deficit, the federal government borrows at home and abroad.

FIGHTING RECESSIONS (BUSTS) WITH DEFICIT SPENDING

Many economists and government officials believe that we can help the economy out of a recession if the federal government runs a deficit—by increasing spending or lowering taxes (or both). In a recession, not enough people are borrowing and spending, so the government should be the one to borrow and spend, jump-starting the economy. When the recession is over, the government should reverse course—reduce government spending or increase taxes (or both). Under this theory, we can smooth the busts and booms in the national economy with "countercyclical" budgets.

Congress and the president, however, have never been eager to increase taxes or reduce spending during a boom. In modern times, Bill Clinton (1993–2001) has been the only president willing to raise taxes and constrain spending in a boom by enough to balance the budget. In his last four budgets, Clinton (with the help of Congress) actually ran a surplus—the government spent less than what it received in revenues. In contrast, George W. Bush (backed by a Republican Congress during his first six years) created deficits with every budget he proposed. To be sure, there was a recession during 2001 after the "dot-com bubble" burst, but the Bush administration kept running deficits right through the subsequent good years.

ENTER OBAMA AND THE DEMOCRATIC CONGRESS

By the time Barack Obama was elected in 2008, the American economy was experiencing its worst recession in over sixty years. The response of Obama and the Democratic Congress was swift and monumental. At Obama's request, Congress passed the largest single stimulus package in the history of the United States. Initially valued at $787 billion over two years, the cost has since been re-estimated as $814 billion.

Federal budget documents reveal that, due in part to Obama's policies, the federal budget deficit was $1.4 trillion in 2009. That was 10 percent of the entire economy—the gross domestic product, or GDP. The estimated deficit for 2010 was $1.56 trillion—more than 10 percent of GDP. Ominously, the Congressional Budget Office (CBO) predicts that under current policies, the deficit will stay at about 5 percent of GDP all the way through 2019. That means large budget deficits even after the Great Recession.

CAN WE RUN FEDERAL BUDGET DEFICITS FOREVER?

If we run the deficits that the CBO predicts, the total debt of the federal government as a percentage of GDP will double by 2019. Can we do this? True, after the collapse of the financial markets in September 2008, the federal government had no trouble borrowing very large sums. Panicked investors saw the U.S. government as the world's safest borrower. But even Obama's first budget chief, Peter Orszag, admitted that indefinitely running deficits that amount to 5 percent of GDP is "ultimately not sustainable." Investors—such as the government of China, which already owns perhaps $1 trillion of the federal government's debt—might be reluctant to lend more to Uncle Sam. Higher taxes would be inevitable.

Of course, according to theory, the government is supposed to collect higher taxes in future good years. Opinions about taxes differ. For liberal economist Paul Krugman, "It's really a political question: are we willing, ultimately, to pay the modest costs of a better society?" The conservative editorial page of the *Wall Street Journal* fumes: "Republicans will spend the next two or three generations doing little more than collecting higher taxes from the middle class to finance the Obama revolution."

FOR CRITICAL ANALYSIS

One U.S. senator has said that increases in the federal deficit are the equivalent of mortgaging our grandchildren's future without their agreement. Is this a fair criticism? Why or why not?

Congress Faces the Budget

In January, nine months before the fiscal year starts, the president takes the OMB's proposed budget, approves it, and submits it to Congress. Then the congressional budgeting process takes over. The budgeting process involves two steps. First, Congress must authorize funds to be spent. The **authorization** is a formal declaration by the appropriate congressional committee that a certain amount of funding may be available to an agency. Congressional committees and subcommittees look at the proposals from the executive branch and the Congressional Budget Office in making the decision to authorize funds.

After the funds have been authorized, they must be appropriated by Congress. The appropriations committees of both the House and the Senate forward spending bills to their respective bodies. The **appropriation** of funds occurs when the final bill is passed. The budget process involves large sums. Representatives and senators who chair key committees find it relatively easy to slip additional spending proposals into a variety of bills. These proposals may have nothing to do with the ostensible purpose of the bill. Such earmarked appropriations are known as "pork," as discussed in the chapter-opening *What If . . .* feature.

Authorization
A formal declaration by a legislative committee that a certain amount of funding may be available to an agency. Some authorizations terminate in a year; others are renewable automatically without further congressional action.

Appropriation
The passage, by Congress, of a spending bill specifying the amount of authorized funds that actually will be allocated for an agency's use.

First Budget Resolution
A resolution passed by Congress in May that sets overall revenue and spending goals for the following fiscal year.

Second Budget Resolution
A resolution passed by Congress in September that sets "binding" limits on taxes and spending for the following fiscal year.

Continuing Resolution
A temporary funding law that Congress passes when an appropriations bill has not been decided by the beginning of the new fiscal year on October 1.

Budget Resolutions

The **first budget resolution** by Congress is due in May. It sets overall revenue goals and spending targets. Spending and tax laws that are drawn up over the summer are supposed to be guided by the first budget resolution. By September, Congress is scheduled to pass its **second budget resolution,** one that will set binding limits on taxes and spending for the fiscal year beginning October 1.

In actuality, Congress has finished the budget on time in only three years since 1977. The budget is usually broken up into a series of appropriations bills. If Congress has not passed one of these bills by October 1, it normally passes a **continuing resolution** that allows the affected agencies to keep on doing whatever they were doing the previous year with the same amount of funding. By the 1980s, continuing resolutions had ballooned into massive measures. Budget delays reached a climax in 1995 and 1996, when, in a spending dispute with Democratic president Bill Clinton, the Republican Congress refused to pass any continuing resolutions. As a result, some nonessential functions of the federal government were shut down for twenty-seven days. Since 1997, Congress has generally managed to limit continuing resolutions to their original purpose.

At some point during the beginning of each calendar year, the president submits a budget to Congress. Except for a few years under President Bill Clinton, all such budgets have shown expenditures exceeding revenues. Consequently, most U.S. government budgets have shown deficits. Why would a president submit a budget knowing that expenditures exceed revenues? (AP Photo/Pablo Martinez Monsivais)

WHY SHOULD YOU CARE ABOUT... CONGRESS?

Why should you, as an individual, care about Congress? Do you even know the names of your senators and your representative in Congress? A surprising number of Americans do not. Even if you know the names and parties of your elected delegates, there is still much more you could learn about them that would be useful.

CONGRESS AND YOUR LIFE

The legislation that Congress passes can directly affect your life. Consider, for example, the Medicare prescription drug benefit passed in November 2003. Some might think that such a benefit, which helps only persons over the age of sixty-five, would be of no interest to college students. Actually, legislation such as this could affect you long before you reach retirement age. Funding this benefit may mean that you will have to pay higher taxes when you join the workforce. Also, some students may be affected even sooner than that. Most students are part of a family, and family finances are often important in determining whether a family will help pay for the student's tuition. There are families in which the cost of medicine for the oldest members is a substantial burden.

You can make a difference in our democracy simply by going to the polls on Election Day and voting for the candidates you would like to represent you in Congress. It goes without saying, though, that to cast an informed vote, you need to know how your congressional representatives stand on the issues and, if they are incumbents, how they have voted on bills that are important to you.

(www.votesmart.org and www.opensecrets.org)

HOW YOU CAN MAKE A DIFFERENCE

To contact a member of Congress, start by going to the Web sites of the U.S. House of Representatives (at **www.house.gov**) and the U.S. Senate (at **www.senate.gov**).

Although you can communicate easily with your representatives by e-mail, using e-mail has some drawbacks. Representatives and senators are now receiving large volumes of e-mail from constituents, and they rarely read it themselves. They have staff members who read and respond to e-mail instead. Many interest groups argue that U.S. mail, or even express mail or a phone call, is more likely to capture the attention of the representative than e-mail. You can contact your representatives using one of the following addresses or phone numbers:

United States House of Representatives
Washington, DC 20515
202-224-3121

United States Senate
Washington, DC 20510
202-224-3121

Interest groups also track the voting records of members of Congress and rate the members on the issues. Project Vote Smart tracks the performance of more than 13,000 political leaders, including their campaign finances, issue positions, and voting records. You can view the Web site of Project Vote Smart at:

www.votesmart.org

Finally, if you want to know how your representatives funded their campaigns, contact the Center for Responsive Politics (CRP), a research group that tracks money in politics, campaign fund-raising, and similar issues. You can see the CRP site at:

www.opensecrets.org

questions for discussion and analysis

1. Review the *Which Side Are You On?* feature on page 342. Is the filibuster a legitimate legislative provision? Why or why not? Even if filibusters are legitimate, are they currently overused? Give your reasons. If filibusters were to be limited in frequency, how might this be done?
2. Some observers have proposed that nonpartisan panels draw congressional district boundaries in an attempt to curb gerrymandering. Who do you think would make good members of such panels? What types of people might be both knowledgeable and fair?
3. The District of Columbia is not represented in the Senate and has a single, nonvoting delegate to the House. Should D.C. be represented in Congress by voting legislators? Why or why not? If it should be represented, how? Would it make sense to admit it as a state? To give it back to Maryland? Explain your reasoning.
4. Identify some advantages to the nation that might follow when one party controls the House, the Senate, and the presidency. Identify some of the disadvantages that might follow from such a state of affairs.
5. When the Senate was first created, Americans were often more loyal to their individual states than they are today. Confederate general Robert E. Lee, for example, believed that his native land was Virginia, not the United States. Given the strong sense of national identity that exists in the country today, is it fair that the Senate gives equal representation to all states regardless of how many people live in each? Why or why not? If not, what (if anything) could be done to address the issue?

key terms

chapter summary

1. The authors of the Constitution believed that the bulk of national power should be in the legislature. The Connecticut Compromise established a balanced legislature, with the membership in the House of Representatives based on population and the membership in the Senate based on the equality of states.
2. The functions of Congress include (a) lawmaking, (b) representation, (c) service to constituents, (d) oversight, (e) public education, and (f) conflict resolution.
3. The Constitution specifies most of the enumerated, or expressed, powers of Congress, including the right to

impose taxes, to borrow funds, to regulate commerce, and to declare war. Congress also enjoys the right to "make all Laws which shall be necessary and proper for carrying into Execution the foregoing Powers, and all other Powers vested by this Constitution in the Government of the United States, or in any Department or Officer thereof." This is called the elastic, or necessary and proper, clause.

4. There are 435 members in the House of Representatives and 100 members in the Senate. Owing to its larger size, the House has a greater number of formal rules. The Senate tradition of unlimited debate dates back to 1790 and has been used over the years to frustrate the passage of bills.

5. Members of Congress are not typical American citizens. They are older and wealthier than most Americans, disproportionately white and male, and more likely to be lawyers.

6. Most candidates for Congress win nomination through a direct primary. Most incumbent representatives and senators who run for reelection are successful. Apportionment is the allocation of legislative seats to constituencies. The Supreme Court's "one person, one vote" rule means that the populations of legislative districts must be effectively equal.

7. Members of Congress are well paid and enjoy benefits such as free postage. Members have personal and committee staff and enjoy a number of legal privileges and immunities.

8. Most of the work of legislating is performed by committees and subcommittees within Congress. Legislation introduced into the House or Senate is assigned to standing committees for review. Joint committees are formed by the action of both chambers and consist of members from each. Conference committees are joint committees set up to achieve agreement between the House and the Senate on the exact wording of legislative acts that were passed by the chambers in different forms. The seniority rule, which is usually followed, specifies that the longest-serving member of the majority party will be the chairperson of a committee.

9. The foremost power holder in the House of Representatives is the Speaker of the House. Other leaders are the House majority leader, the House minority leader, and the majority and minority whips. Formally, the vice president is the presiding officer of the Senate. Actual leadership in the Senate rests with the majority leader, the minority leader, and their whips.

10. A bill becomes law by progressing through both chambers of Congress and their appropriate standing and joint committees to the president.

11. The budget process for a fiscal year begins with the preparation of an executive budget by the president. This is reviewed by the Office of Management and Budget and then sent to Congress, which is supposed to pass a final budget by the end of September. Since 1978, Congress generally has not followed its own time rules.

selected print & media resources

SUGGESTED READINGS

Just, Ward S. ***The Congressman Who Loved Flaubert.*** **New York: Carrol and Graf Publishers, 1990. This fictional account of a career politician was first published in 1973 and is still a favorite with students of political science. Ward Just is renowned for his political fiction, and particularly for his examination of character and motivation.**

Koger, Gregory. ***Filibustering: A Political History of Obstruction in the House and Senate.*** **Chicago: University of Chicago Press, 2010. Many people don't know it, but the rules under which the House and Senate consider legislation have changed considerably over the years. Koger traces the lively history of congressional obstruction.**

Koszczuk, Jackie, and Martha Angle, eds. ***CQ's Politics in America 2010: The 111th Congress.*** **Washington, D.C.: CQ Press, 2009. This "ultimate insider's guide to politics," as it is sometimes described, offers biographical data, voting behavior, ratings by interest groups, campaign-finance sources, and a wealth of information on each of the 535 members of the 111th Congress.**

Oleszek, Walter J. ***Congressional Procedures and the Policy Process.*** **Washington, D.C.: CQ Press, 2010. This regularly updated book offers a wealth of information for anyone seeking to understand the congressional procedures involved in initiating, debating, and enacting new laws.**

Peters, Jr., Ronald M., and Cindy Simon Rosenthal. ***Speaker Nancy Pelosi and the New American Politics.*** **New York: Oxford University Press, 2010. Peters and Rosenthal have authored the first full-length portrait of Nancy Pelosi. They describe her rise and how she has wielded power as one of America's most effective legislators.**

MEDIA RESOURCES

Charlie Wilson's War—One of the best movies of 2007, starring Tom Hanks and Julia Roberts. This hilarious film is based on the true story of how Wilson, a hard-living, hard-drinking representative from Texas, almost single-handedly wins a billion dollars in funding for the Afghans who are fighting a Russian invasion. When equipped with heat-seeking missiles, the Afghans win. Philip Seymour Hoffman steals the show portraying a rogue CIA operative.

The Congress—In one of his earliest efforts (1988), filmmaker Ken Burns profiles the history of Congress. Narration is by David McCullough, and those interviewed include David Broder, Alistair Cooke, and Cokie Roberts. PBS Home Video rereleased this film on DVD in 2003.

Congress: A Day in the Life of a Representative—From political meetings to social functions to campaigning, this 1995 program examines what politicians really do. Featured representatives are Tim Roemer (a Democrat from Indiana) and Sue Myrick (a Republican from North Carolina).

Mr. Smith Goes to Washington—A 1939 film in which Jimmy Stewart plays the naïve congressman who is quickly educated in Washington. A true American political classic.

Porked: Earmarks for Profit—A 2008 release from Fox News Channel that investigates congressional earmarks. Fox reporters contend that pork wastes tax dollars. Beyond that, the network also claims that some members of Congress have funded projects that benefited the members' own bank accounts.

The Seduction of Joe Tynan—A 1979 film in which Alan Alda plays a young senator who must face serious decisions about his political role and his private life.

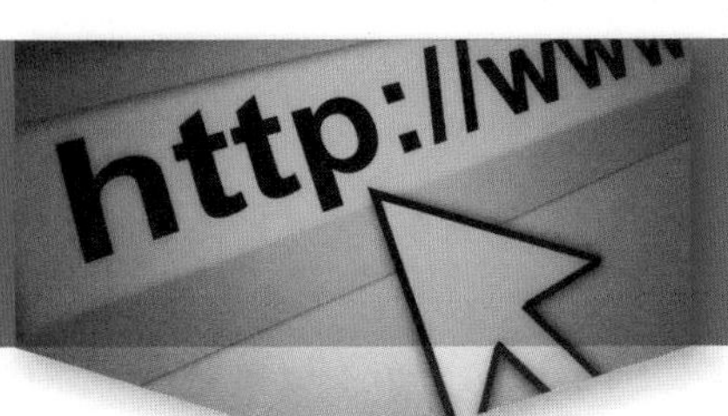

e-mocracy

CONGRESS AND THE WEB

Almost all senators and representatives have Web sites that you can find simply by keying in their names in a search engine. You can easily learn the names of your congressional representatives by going to the Web site of the House or Senate (see the following *Logging On* section for the URLs for these sites). Once you know the names of your representatives, you can go to their Web sites to learn more about them and their positions on specific issues.

Note that some members of Congress also provide important services to their constituents via their Web sites. Some sites, for example, allow constituents to apply for internships in Washington, D.C., apply for appointments to military academies, order flags, order tours of the Capitol, and register complaints electronically. Other sites may provide forms from certain government agencies, such as the Social Security Administration, that constituents can use to request assistance from those agencies or to register complaints.

LOGGING ON

To find out about the schedule of activities taking place in Congress, use the following Web sites:
www.senate.gov
www.house.gov

The Congressional Budget Office is online at
www.cbo.gov

The URL for the U.S. Government Printing Office is
www.gpoaccess.gov

For the real inside facts on what's going on in Washington, D.C., you can look at the following resources:

RollCall, the newspaper of the Capitol:
www.rollcall.com

Politico, a major Web site of political news:
www.politico.com

The Hill, which investigates various activities of Congress:
www.thehill.com

chapter 11

The President

chapter contents

<< President Obama leaves the White House for one of his many trips. Here he is going to give a college commencement speech. (AP Photo/Manuel Balce Ceneta)

WHAT IF... ...we could recall the president?

There are always Americans who don't like whoever is the current president. Negative signs were paraded at rallies against President Bush, too. (Sipa via AP Images)

BACKGROUND

The U.S. Constitution provides a way to remove the president or other high officials from office. For this to happen, the House of Representatives must impeach (indict) the official, and the Senate must then vote a conviction by a two-thirds majority. It is a sign of our current political polarization that in recent decades, many political hotheads have dreamed of deposing the president in this way. In 1998, Republicans in the House actually did impeach Democratic President Bill Clinton, but the Senate refused to convict. During the last years of Republican George W. Bush's administration, dozens of angry members of the political left published tracts demanding his ouster. Calls for President Obama's impeachment began almost as soon as he was inaugurated, and signs demanding impeachment have been commonplace at Tea Party rallies.

Calls to impeach Bush or Obama were never taken seriously by Congress, even when the Democrats had a majority of both chambers during Bush's last two years in office. Democrats remembered that the attempt to remove Clinton was unpopular and cost the Republicans votes. The constitutional standard for removal from office is high: An official must be found guilty of "Treason, Bribery, or other high Crimes and Misdemeanors."

The constitutions of many states, however, provide for the recall of elected officials by the voters. No finding of blame or criminal guilt is necessary. If the voters of a state or locality gather a sufficient number of signatures on a petition to remove an elected official, a special election is held in which citizens vote on whether to remove that official from office.

WHAT IF WE COULD RECALL THE PRESIDENT?

Recall of the president would require a constitutional amendment, of course. Let's assume that sometime in the future, such an amendment passes. The whole nation would then be involved in a decision to remove the president. Exactly such an event happened at the state level in California in 2003, when Governor Gray Davis was recalled barely a year after his reelection. Gray's opponents charged that he was incompetent and had misled the voters—nothing more.

RECALL: USEFUL OR DANGEROUS?

Supporters of recall might argue that the process could be a useful tool to keep government officials accountable. If officials knew that they could be removed from office if enough citizens were dissatisfied with their conduct, they might pay closer attention to public needs. Others might warn that such a process is dangerous. Imagine the kind of campaigning that would take place in the run-up to a recall election. Those who initiated the recall would attempt to bring out every unpleasant allegation about the president. Smears, lies, and character assassination would be commonplace. In addition, presidents might follow public opinion polls too slavishly if their ability to serve out their four-year term rested solely on public opinion. This could be a problem because many voters demand contradictory or impossible things. For example, some voters oppose tax increases and meaningful spending cuts, but are against budget deficits as well. Mathematically, that's an impossible combination.

FOR CRITICAL ANALYSIS

1. Given the responsibilities of the president, do you think it would be a good idea for the country to be able to recall the chief executive for unpopularity or partisan reasons?
2. Could the possibility of such recall make partisanship worse than it already is?

The writers of the Constitution created the presidency of the United States without any models to follow. Nowhere else in the world was there a democratically selected chief executive. What the founders did not want was a king. In fact, given their previous experience with royal governors in the colonies, many of the delegates to the Constitutional Convention wanted to create a very weak executive who could not veto legislation. Other delegates, especially those who had witnessed the need for a strong leader in the Revolutionary Army, believed a strong executive would be necessary for the new republic. The delegates, after much debate, created a chief executive who had enough powers granted in the Constitution to balance those of Congress.

The power exercised by each president who has held the office has been scrutinized and judged by historians, political scientists, the media, and the public. It would seem that Americans are fascinated by presidential power and by the persons who hold the office. Perhaps inevitably, the powers of the president lead many citizens to dream of his or her removal, as you learned in the chapter-opening *What If . . .* feature. In this chapter, after looking at who can become president and at the process involved, we examine closely the nature and extent of the constitutional powers held by the president.

did you know?

That President William McKinley's salary of $50,000 in 1900 would be worth $1,320,000 in today's dollars.

Who Can Become President?

The president receives a salary of $400,000, plus $169,000 for expenses and a vast array of free services, beginning with residence in the White House. The requirements for becoming president, as outlined in Article II, Section 1, of the Constitution, are not overwhelmingly stringent:

> *No person except a natural born Citizen, or a Citizen of the United States, at the time of the Adoption of this Constitution, shall be eligible to the Office of President; neither shall any Person be eligible to that Office who shall not have attained to the Age of thirty-five Years, and been fourteen Years a Resident within the United States.*

The only question that arises about these qualifications relates to the term *natural born Citizen.* Does that mean only citizens born in the United States and its territories? What about a child born to a U.S. citizen (or to a couple who are U.S. citizens) visiting or living in another country? Although the Supreme Court has never directly addressed the question, it is reasonable to expect that someone would be eligible if her or his parents were Americans. The first presidents, after all, were not even American citizens at birth, and others were born in areas that did not become part of the United States until later.

These questions were debated when George Romney, who was born in Chihuahua, Mexico, made a serious bid for the Republican presidential nomination in the 1960s.[1] The issue also came up when Arizona senator John McCain announced that he was a candidate for president. McCain was born in the Panama Canal Zone. Questions about McCain's eligibility were soon put to rest, however. Not only were McCain's parents both U.S. citizens (his father was an officer in the navy), but at the time McCain was born, the Canal Zone was a U.S. possession.

When Arnold Schwarzenegger became governor of California, many of his supporters suggested that he might be a potential presidential candidate. But Schwarzenegger, who was born in Austria, is a naturalized U.S. citizen and therefore is ineligible to become president under the Constitution. Although from time to time, movements have sought to amend the Constitution to allow *naturalized* citizens to become president, there has been little support for such an amendment.

---

1. George Romney was governor of Michigan from 1963 to 1969. Romney was not nominated for the presidency, and the issue remains unresolved.

The youngest president ever elected was John F. Kennedy (1961–1963). (AP Photo)

The oldest president ever elected was Ronald Reagan (1981–1989). (AP Photo)

did you know?

That the only president in U.S. history to be elected with every possible electoral vote was George Washington.

The American dream is symbolized by the statement that "anybody can become president of this country." It is true that in modern times, presidents have included a haberdasher (Harry Truman—for a short period of time), a peanut farmer (Jimmy Carter), and an actor (Ronald Reagan). But if you examine the list of presidents in Appendix F at the end of this book, you will see that the most common previous occupational field of presidents in this country has been the law. Out of forty-four presidents, twenty-seven have been lawyers, and many have been wealthy.

Although the Constitution states that the minimum-age requirement for the presidency is thirty-five years, most presidents have been much older than that when they assumed office. John F. Kennedy, at the age of forty-three, was the youngest elected president, and the oldest was Ronald Reagan, at age sixty-nine. The average age at inauguration has been fifty-four. There has clearly been a demographic bias in the selection of presidents. All have been male, white, and from the Protestant tradition, except for John F. Kennedy, a Roman Catholic, and Barack Obama, an African American. Presidents have been men of great stature, such as George Washington, and men in whom leadership qualities were not so pronounced, such as Warren Harding (1921–1923). A presidential candidate usually has experience as a vice president, senator, or state governor. Former governors have been especially successful at winning the presidency.

The Process of Becoming President

Major and minor political parties nominate candidates for president and vice president at national conventions every four years. As discussed in Chapter 9, the nation's voters do not elect a president and vice president directly but rather cast ballots for presidential electors, who then vote for president and vice president in the Electoral College.

Because victory goes to the candidate with a majority in the Electoral College, it is conceivable that someone could be elected to the office of the presidency without having a plurality of the popular vote cast. Indeed, on four occasions, candidates won elections even though their major opponents received more popular votes. One of those elections occurred in 2000, when George W. Bush won the Electoral College vote and became president even though his opponent, Al Gore, won the popular vote. In elections in which more than two candidates were running for office, many presidential candidates have won with less than 50 percent of the total popular votes cast for all candidates—including Abraham Lincoln, Woodrow Wilson, Harry Truman, John F. Kennedy, Richard Nixon, and, in 1992, Bill Clinton. Independent candidate Ross Perot garnered a surprising 19 percent of the vote in 1992. Remember from Chapter 9 that no president has won a majority of votes from the entire voting-age population.

did you know?

That twenty-one presidents have served only one term in office.

Thus far, on two occasions the Electoral College has failed to give any candidate a majority. At this point, the election is thrown into the House of Representatives. The president is then chosen from among the three candidates having the most Electoral College votes, as noted in Chapter 9. In 1800, Thomas Jefferson and Aaron Burr tied in the Electoral College. This happened because the Constitution had not been explicit in indicating which of the two electoral votes was for president and which was for vice president. In 1804, the **Twelfth Amendment** clarified the matter by requiring that the president and vice president be chosen separately. In 1824, the House again had to make a choice, this time among William H. Crawford, Andrew Jackson, and John Quincy Adams. It chose Adams, even though Jackson had more electoral and popular votes.

Twelfth Amendment
An amendment to the Constitution, adopted in 1804, that requires the separate election of the president and vice president by the Electoral College.

Head of State
The role of the president as ceremonial head of the government.

The Many Roles of the President

The Constitution speaks briefly about the duties and obligations of the president. Based on this brief list of powers and on the precedents of history, the presidency has grown into a very complicated job that requires balancing at least five constitutional roles. These are (1) head of state, (2) chief executive, (3) commander in chief of the armed forces, (4) chief diplomat, and (5) chief legislator of the United States. Here we examine each of these significant presidential functions, or roles. It is worth noting that one person plays all these roles simultaneously and that the needs of these roles may at times come into conflict.

Head of State

Every nation has at least one person who is the ceremonial head of state. In most democratic nations, the role of **head of state** is given to someone other than the chief executive, who leads the executive branch of government. In Britain, for example, the head of state is the queen. In much of Europe, the head of state is a relatively powerless president, and the prime minister is the chief executive. (In a further departure from American practice, prime ministers may lead coalitions of two or more political parties, as we explain in this chapter's *Beyond Our Borders* feature on the following page.) But in the United States, the president is both chief executive and head of state. According to William Howard Taft, as head of state the president symbolizes the "dignity and majesty" of the American people.

As head of state, the president engages in a number of activities that are largely symbolic or ceremonial, such as the following:

- Decorating war heroes.
- Throwing out the first ball to open the baseball season.
- Dedicating parks and post offices.
- Receiving visiting heads of state at the White House.
- Going on official state visits to other countries.
- Making personal telephone calls to astronauts.
- Representing the nation at times of national mourning, such as after the terrorist attacks of September 11, 2001, following the loss of the space shuttle *Columbia* in 2003, and subsequent to the destruction from Hurricane Katrina in 2005.

Some students of the American political system believe that having the president serve as both the chief executive and the head of state drastically limits the time available to do "real" work. Not all presidents have agreed with this conclusion, however—particularly

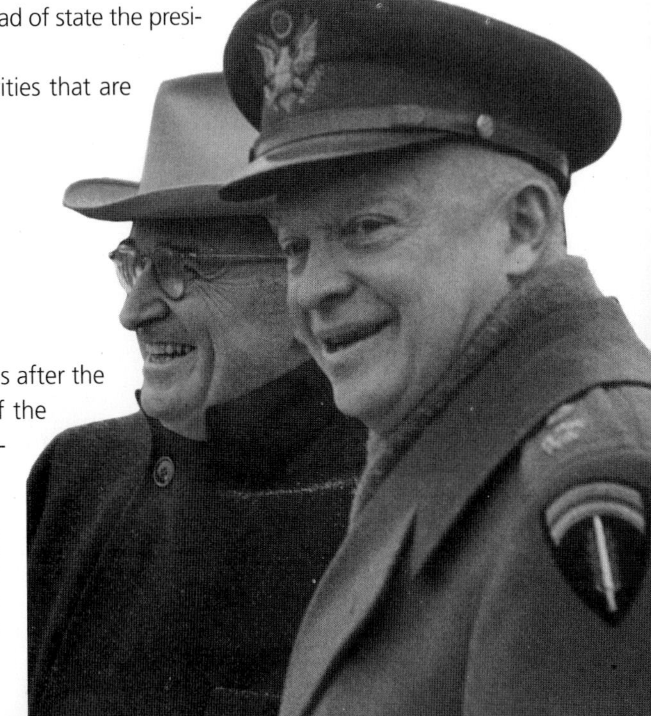

American president
Harry Truman (1945–1953), stands with General Dwight Eisenhower in 1951. A year later, Eisenhower successfully ran for president. Why might a general make a good president? (George Skadding/Time Life Pictures/Getty Images)

those presidents who have skillfully blended these two roles with their role as politician. Being head of state gives the president tremendous public exposure, which can be an important asset in a campaign for reelection. When that exposure is positive, it helps the president deal with Congress over proposed legislation and increases the chances of being reelected—or getting the candidates of the president's party elected.

Chief Executive

According to the Constitution, "The executive Power shall be vested in a President of the United States of America . . . . [H]e may require the Opinion, in writing, of the principal Officer in each of the executive Departments, upon any Subject relating to the Duties of

BEYOND OUR BORDERS

WHEN THE CHIEF EXECUTIVE ANSWERS TO A COALITION

In the United States, our chief executive—the president—works with a Congress that is made up of Democrats and Republicans. In each chamber, one of these two parties is in the majority at any given time. In countries with parliamentary systems, in contrast, the legislature may contain three, four, or even a dozen different parties. These are also systems in which the lower house of parliament chooses the prime minister and the rest of the cabinet. When no one party has a majority, therefore, a coalition of two or more parties may form to name the leaders of the executive.

For the first time in over half a century, Britain has a coalition government headed jointly by Prime Minister David Cameron (on the right) and Deputy Prime Minister Nick Clegg. Why don't we have coalition governments? (Christopher Furlong/AFP/Getty Images)

THE GERMAN EXAMPLE

The two largest parties in Germany are the Christian Democrats and the Social Democrats. Smaller parties include the Greens, the Left, and most importantly, the Free Democrats. For much of recent German history, the nation has been led by a coalition made up of the Free Democrats and either the Christian Democrats or the Social Democrats. The third-largest party, in other words, has often been the kingmaker. Coalition formation is a very formal process. A coalition agreement can be 150 pages long, and its negotiation may take six weeks or more. For example, after the last German elections, the Free Democratic Party became the junior party to Angela Merkel's Christian Democrats. The Free Democrats agreed to the coalition as long as Merkel agreed to tax cuts and a variety of other policy changes.

AND NOW THE BRITISH HAVE A COALITION AS WELL

After the 2010 British elections, no party had a majority in the House of Commons. The result was the first coalition government in 65 years. The Conservatives (or Tories) formed a partnership with the third-largest party, the Liberal Democrats, who are well to the left of the Tories. This broad coalition was widely applauded, but many in Britain doubt that it will last.

FOR CRITICAL ANALYSIS

Why don't we see coalitions in the U.S. Congress?

their respective Offices . . . and he shall nominate, and by and with the Advice and Consent of the Senate, shall appoint . . . Officers of the United States. . . . [H]e shall take Care that the Laws be faithfully executed." As **chief executive,** the president is constitutionally bound to enforce the acts of Congress, the judgments of federal courts, and treaties signed by the United States. The duty to "faithfully execute" the laws has been a source of constitutional power for presidents.

did you know?

That Thomas Jefferson was the first president to be inaugurated in Washington, D.C., where he walked to the Capitol from a boardinghouse, took the oath, made a brief speech in the Senate chamber, and then walked back home.

Signing Statements. Is the president allowed to refuse to enforce certain parts of legislation if he or she believes that they are unconstitutional? This question came to the forefront in recent years because of President George W. Bush's extensive use of signing statements. A **signing statement** is a written declaration that a president may make when signing a bill into law regarding the law's enforcement. A signing statement may point to sections of the law that the president thinks may be unconstitutional.

Presidents have been using such statements for decades, but President Bush used 161 statements to invalidate more than 1,000 provisions of federal law. No president before Bush used signing statements to make such sweeping claims on behalf of presidential power. Earlier presidents often employed statements to serve notice that parts of bills might be unconstitutional, but they were just as likely to issue statements that were purely rhetorical. Statements might praise Congress and the measure it just passed—or denounce the opposition party. During his campaign, Barack Obama criticized Bush's use of signing statements. As president, Obama's statements have been more in line with tradition. Five of the ten statements he issued through August 2010 were entirely rhetorical.

The Powers of Appointment and Removal. To assist in the various tasks of the chief executive, the president has a federal bureaucracy (see Chapter 12), which consists of 2 million federal civilian employees, not counting the U.S. Postal Service (700,000 employees). You might think that the president, as head of the largest bureaucracy in the United States, wields enormous power. The president, however, only nominally runs the executive bureaucracy. Most government positions are filled by **civil service** employees, who generally gain government employment through a merit system rather than presidential appointment.[2] Therefore, even though the president has important **appointment power,** it is limited to cabinet and subcabinet jobs, federal judgeships, agency heads, and several thousand lesser jobs—about 8,000 positions in total. This means that most of the 2.7 million federal employees owe no political allegiance to the president. They are more likely to owe loyalty to congressional committees or to interest groups representing the sector of the society that they serve. Table 11–1 on the following page shows what percentage of the total employment in each executive department is available for political appointment by the president.

The president's power to remove from office those officials who are not doing a good job or who do not agree with the president is not explicitly granted by the Constitution and has been limited. In 1926, however, a Supreme Court decision prevented Congress from interfering with the president's ability to fire those executive-branch officials whom the president had appointed with Senate approval.[3] There are ten agencies whose directors the president can remove at any time. These agencies include the Commission on Civil Rights, the Environmental Protection Agency, the General Services Administration, and the Small Business Administration. In addition, the president can remove all heads of cabinet departments, all individuals in the Executive Office of the President, and all of the political appointees listed in Table 11–1 on the following page.

Chief Executive
The role of the president as head of the executive branch of the government.

Signing Statement
A written declaration that a president may make when signing a bill into law. Such statements may point out sections of the law that the president deems unconstitutional.

Civil Service
A collective term for the body of employees working for the government. Generally, civil service is understood to apply to all those who gain government employment through a merit system.

Appointment Power
The authority vested in the president to fill a government office or position. Positions filled by presidential appointment include those in the executive branch and the federal judiciary, commissioned officers in the armed forces, and members of the independent regulatory commissions.

2. See Chapter 12 for a discussion of the Civil Service Reform Act.
3. *Meyers v. United States,* 272 U.S. 52 (1926).

TABLE 11–1 Total Civilian Employment in Cabinet Departments Available for Political Appointment by the President

Executive Department	Total Number of Employees	Political Appointments Available	Percentage
Agriculture	111,987	372	0.33
Commerce	52,063	336	0.65
Defense	754,963	695	0.09
Education	4,343	293	6.75
Energy	16,650	536	3.22
Health and Human Services	18,129	475	0.58
Homeland Security	186,797	287	0.15
Housing and Urban Development	9,742	146	1.50
Interior	81,796	296	0.36
Justice	115,299	474	0.41
Labor	16,483	226	1.37
State	11,974	555	4.64
Transportation	57,819	268	0.46
Treasury	116,375	202	0.17
Veterans Affairs	304,559	376	0.12

Sources: *Policy and Supporting Positions* (Washington, D.C.: Government Printing Office, 2008). This text, known as "The Plum Book" (see Chapter 12, page 419), is published after each presidential election. Also, U.S. Office of Personnel Management. Figures are for June 2010.

Harry Truman spoke candidly of the difficulties a president faces in trying to control the executive bureaucracy. On leaving office, he referred to the problems that Dwight Eisenhower, as a former general of the army, was going to have: "He'll sit here and he'll say do this! do that! and nothing will happen. Poor Ike—it won't be a bit like the Army. He'll find it very frustrating."[4]

Reprieve
A formal postponement of the execution of a sentence imposed by a court of law.

Pardon
A release from the punishment for, or legal consequences of, a crime; a pardon can be granted by the president before or after a conviction.

The Power to Grant Reprieves and Pardons. Section 2 of Article II of the Constitution gives the president the power to grant **reprieves** and **pardons** for offenses against the United States except in cases of impeachment. All pardons are administered by the Office of the Pardon Attorney in the Department of Justice. In principle, a pardon is granted to remedy a mistake made in a conviction.

The United States Supreme Court upheld the president's power to grant reprieves and pardons in a 1925 case concerning a pardon granted by the president to an individual convicted of contempt of court. A federal district court and circuit court had contended that only judges had the authority to convict individuals for contempt of court when court orders were violated and that the courts should be free from interference by the executive branch. The Supreme Court simply stated that the president could grant reprieves or pardons for all offenses "either before trial, during trial, or after trial, by individuals, or by classes, conditionally or absolutely, and this without modification or regulation by Congress."[5]

President Andrew Johnson set the record for the largest number of persons ever pardoned in 1868 when he issued a blanket amnesty to all former Confederate soldiers. In

4. Quoted in Richard E. Neustadt, *Presidential Power: The Politics of Leadership* (New York: Wiley, 1960), p. 9. Note that Truman may not have considered the amount of politics involved in decision making in the upper ranks of the army.
5. *Ex parte Grossman*, 267 U.S. 87 (1925).

1974, in a controversial decision, President Gerald Ford pardoned former president Richard Nixon for his role in the Watergate affair before any charges were brought in court. In 1977, President Jimmy Carter issued a blanket pardon to Vietnam War–era draft resisters, a group that probably included more than 100,000 persons. Just before George W. Bush's inauguration in 2001, President Bill Clinton announced pardons for almost two hundred persons. Some of those pardons were controversial. In early 2007, controversy arose over whether President Bush should pardon a member of his own administration. Lewis ("Scooter") Libby, Vice President Dick Cheney's former chief of staff, was convicted in March 2007 of several crimes, including perjury and obstruction of justice, in connection with a leak to the press revealing the identity of a CIA agent. Eventually, Bush commuted Libby's sentence so that he would not have to serve time in prison.

These military men are in charge of how the Army, Navy, Air Force, and Marines operate. The overall decision maker is Admiral Mike Mullen (on the left), who is chairman of the Joint Chiefs of Staff. While the leaders of the various branches of our armed forces confer with each other from time to time, they are also fiercely proud of their own branches and prefer to remain independent. Ultimately, who controls the admirals and generals of the various branches of our armed services? (Paul J. Richards/AFP/Getty Images)

Commander in Chief

The president, according to the Constitution, "shall be Commander in Chief of the Army and Navy of the United States, and of the Militia of the several States, when called into the actual Service of the United States." In other words, the armed forces are under civilian, rather than military, control.

Wartime Powers. Certainly, those who wrote the Constitution had George Washington in mind when they made the president the **commander in chief.** Although we do not expect our president to lead the troops into battle, presidents as commanders in chief have wielded dramatic power. Harry Truman made the awesome decision to drop atomic bombs on Hiroshima and Nagasaki in 1945 to force Japan to surrender and thus bring World War II to an end. Lyndon Johnson ordered bombing missions against North Vietnam in the 1960s, and he personally selected some of the targets. Richard Nixon decided to invade Cambodia in 1970. Ronald Reagan sent troops to Lebanon and Grenada in 1983 and ordered U.S. fighter planes to attack Libya in 1986. George H. W. Bush sent troops to Panama in 1989 and to the Middle East in 1990. Bill Clinton sent troops to Haiti in 1994 and to Bosnia in 1995, ordered missile attacks on alleged terrorist bases in 1998, and sent American planes to bomb Serbia in 1999. George W. Bush ordered the invasion of Afghanistan in 2001 and Iraq in 2003, and most recently, Barack Obama ordered additional troops into Afghanistan.

> **Commander in Chief**
> The role of the president as supreme commander of the military forces of the United States and of the state National Guard units when they are called into federal service.

The president is the ultimate decision maker in military matters. Everywhere the president goes, so too goes the "football"—a briefcase filled with all of the codes necessary to order a nuclear attack. Only the president has the power to order the use of nuclear force.

Presidents have probably exercised more authority in their capacity as commander in chief than in any other role. Constitutionally, Congress has the sole power to declare war, but the president can send the armed forces into a country in situations that are certainly the equivalent of war. Harry Truman dispatched troops to Korea in 1950. Kennedy, Johnson, and Nixon waged an undeclared war in Vietnam, where more than 58,000 Americans were killed and 300,000 were wounded. In neither of these situations had Congress declared war.

Power over the National Guard. One of the president's powers as commander in chief is the right to assume authority over National Guard units—that is, state militias.

Throughout American history, presidents have "nationalized" the Guard to handle domestic problems such as natural disasters or severe social disturbances, including strikes or urban riots. President George W. Bush sent 6,000 members of the National Guard to the Mexican border in 2006–2008 to assist the Border Patrol, and in 2010 President Obama sent 1,200 Guard troops to the border for the same purpose. The president also has the ability to send National Guard units abroad to supplement the regular armed forces. Bush sent Guard forces abroad on a massive scale. In 2005, National Guard troops comprised a larger percentage of frontline fighting forces than in any war in U.S. history—about 43 percent in Iraq and 55 percent in Afghanistan. Since then, the number of National Guard troops sent abroad has declined.

War Powers Resolution
A law passed in 1973 spelling out the conditions under which the president can commit troops without congressional approval.

Advice and Consent
Terms in the Constitution describing the U.S. Senate's power to review and approve treaties and presidential appointments.

Chief Diplomat
The role of the president in recognizing foreign governments, making treaties, and effecting executive agreements.

Diplomatic Recognition
The formal acknowledgment of a foreign government as legitimate.

The War Powers Resolution. In an attempt to gain more control over such military activities, in 1973 Congress passed the **War Powers Resolution**—over President Nixon's veto—requiring that the president consult with Congress when sending American forces into action. Once they are sent, the president must report to Congress within forty-eight hours. Unless Congress approves the use of troops within sixty days or extends the sixty-day time limit, the forces must be withdrawn. The War Powers Resolution was tested in the fall of 1983, when President Reagan requested that troops be left in Lebanon. The resulting compromise was a congressional resolution allowing troops to remain there for eighteen months. Shortly after the resolution was passed, however, more than 240 sailors and Marines were killed in a suicide bombing of a U.S. military housing compound in Beirut. That event provoked a furious congressional debate over the role American troops were playing in the Middle East, and Reagan withdrew all troops shortly thereafter.

Whether Congress had the constitutional power to set conditions on the continuation of the Iraq War was at issue in 2007 and 2008. President Bush threatened to veto any emergency war-funding legislation that conditioned the funds on a time line for the withdrawal or redeployment of the troops in Iraq.

In spite of the War Powers Resolution, the powers of the president as commander in chief are more extensive today than they were in the past. The so-called war on terror, which began after the terrorist attacks of September 11, 2001, led to an especially notable increase in presidential powers. Many people believe that the Bush administration claimed powers that were excessive or even unconstitutional. We discuss this controversy in the feature *Politics and . . . Terrorism: George W. Obama* on the facing page.

Chief Diplomat

The Constitution gives the president the power to recognize foreign governments, to make treaties with the **advice and consent** of the Senate, and to make special agreements with other heads of state that do not require congressional approval. In addition, the president nominates ambassadors. As **chief diplomat,** the president dominates American foreign policy, a role that has been supported many times by the Supreme Court.

Diplomatic Recognition. An important power of the president as chief diplomat is that of **diplomatic recognition,** or the power to recognize—or refuse to recognize—foreign governments. In the role of ceremonial head of state, the president has always received foreign diplomats. In modern times, the simple act of receiving a foreign diplomat has been equivalent to accrediting the diplomat and officially recognizing his or her government. Such recognition of the legitimacy of another country's government is a prerequisite to diplomatic relations or treaties between that country and the United States.

Deciding when to recognize a foreign power is not always simple. The United States, for example, did not recognize the Soviet Union until 1933—sixteen years after the Russian

POLITICS AND... terrorism

GEORGE W. OBAMA

Not long after President Obama took office, former Vice President Dick Cheney harshly criticized Obama's antiterrorism policies. Cheney claimed that Obama was endangering the country by overturning vigorous measures implemented during the Bush administration. These measures included holding prisoners indefinitely in a facility located at the Guantánamo Bay Naval Base in Cuba without charging them with crimes or granting them prisoner of war status. The measures also included harsh interrogation techniques that, in the opinion of many critics, amounted to torture.

WHEN DID ANTITERRORISM POLICY REALLY CHANGE?

Columnist David Brooks of the *New York Times,* however, makes an interesting observation: The real shift in America's antiterrorism policy did not occur after Obama's inauguration. Rather, it took place several years earlier, during the Bush administration. Already by 2006, dubious interrogation techniques such as waterboarding had been banned. The administration was frantically—and unsuccessfully—seeking ways to close the prison at Guantánamo. As a result, if you compare the policies of the Obama administration with those in place during Bush's last years in office, you see mainly continuity, not change.

Three people had reasons to pretend that the policy change occurred after Obama was sworn in, not before. Vice President Cheney, who was more responsible than any other Bush adviser for the initial harsh policies, wanted to defend them. It was in Cheney's interest to suggest that Bush had supported the policies right up to the end and to conceal the fact that by the end of the Bush administration, Cheney had lost much of his influence. President Obama believed that he could strengthen his political position by drawing a strong contrast between his policies and those of Bush, who was by then unpopular. For his part, President Bush was famous for his refusal ever to admit a mistake or a change in course. He was not about to alter his habits now.

Brooks believes that the chief difference between the two administrations was in the packaging of antiterrorism policy. Whereas the Bush administration was indifferent to process and how policy was presented to the public, the Obama administration has been far more concerned about public opinion, at home and abroad.

PLAYING HARDBALL IN AFGHANISTAN AND PAKISTAN

By moderating his rhetoric, Obama has been able to initiate new antiterrorism policies that have gone beyond those of the Bush administration—such as a major campaign to assassinate Taliban and al Qaeda leaders in Pakistan using unmanned drone aircraft.

The Bush administration was infamous for abducting individuals from across the world and detaining them at Guantánamo, a supposed "black hole" where no law applied. The Supreme Court, however, later ruled that the Constitution grants *habeas corpus* rights even to foreign nationals at Guantánamo, because the Guantánamo base is American soil. Guantánamo prisoners, in other words, have a right to challenge their detention in court. Bush got around this ruling by shipping detainees to the Bagram Air Force Base in Afghanistan.

Obama claimed that he would close Guantánamo—but as of 2011, the prison was still in business. Even more strikingly, Obama administration lawyers argued that detainees at Bagram had no legal rights to challenge their imprisonment. It was Bush all over again. In May 2010, the D.C. Circuit Court of Appeals ruled that the Bush/Obama position was legal—even detainees abducted outside Afghanistan, but shipped there, have no *habeas corpus* rights.

FOR CRITICAL ANALYSIS

Why do you think the Obama administration has kept in place so many of the Bush antiterrorism policies?

Revolution of 1917. It was only after all attempts to reverse the effects of that revolution—including military invasion of Russia and diplomatic isolation—had proved futile that Franklin Roosevelt extended recognition to the Soviet government. In December 1978, long after the Communist victory in China in 1949, Jimmy Carter granted official recognition to the People's Republic of China.[6]

A diplomatic recognition issue that faced the Clinton administration involved recognizing a former enemy—the Socialist Republic of Vietnam. Many Americans, particularly those who believed that Vietnam had not been forthcoming in the efforts to find the remains of missing American soldiers or to find out about former prisoners of war, opposed any formal relationship with that nation. After the U.S. government had negotiated with the Vietnamese government for many years over the missing-in-action issue and engaged in limited diplomatic contacts for several years, President Clinton announced on July 11, 1995, that the United States would recognize the government of Vietnam.

Proposal and Ratification of Treaties. The president has the sole power to negotiate treaties with other nations. These treaties must be presented to the Senate, where they may be modified and must be approved by a two-thirds vote. After ratification, the president can approve the senatorial version of the treaty. Approval poses a problem when the Senate has tacked on substantive amendments or reservations to a treaty, particularly when such changes may require reopening negotiations with the other signatory governments. Sometimes a president may decide to withdraw a treaty if the senatorial changes are too extensive—as Woodrow Wilson in 1919 did with the Versailles Treaty that concluded World War I. Wilson believed that the senatorial reservations would weaken the treaty so much that it would be ineffective. His refusal to accept the senatorial version of the treaty led to the eventual refusal of the United States to join the League of Nations.

President Jimmy Carter (1977–1981) was successful in lobbying for the treaties that provided for the return of the Panama Canal to Panama by the year 2000 and neutralizing the canal. President Bill Clinton won a major political and legislative victory in 1993 by persuading Congress to ratify the North American Free Trade Agreement (NAFTA). In so doing, he had to overcome opposition from Democrats and most of organized labor. In 2000, President Clinton won another major legislative victory when Congress voted to normalize trade relations with China permanently.

President George H. W. Bush (1989–1993) is shown here meeting with the foreign minister of Saudi Arabia. Why would a president spend time in such a meeting? (AP Photo/Barry Thumma)

Recent Treaty Efforts. Before September 11, 2001, President George W. Bush indicated his intention to steer the United States in a unilateral direction on foreign policy. He rejected the Kyoto Agreement on global warming and proposed ending the 1972 Anti-Ballistic Missile (ABM) Treaty, which was part of the first Strategic Arms Limitation Treaty (SALT I). After the terrorist attacks of September 11, 2001, however, President Bush sought cooperation from U.S. allies in the war on terrorism. Bush's return to multilateralism was exemplified in the signing of a nuclear weapons reduction treaty with Russia in 2002. Nonetheless, his attempts to gain international support for a war against Iraq to overthrow that country's government were not as successful as he had hoped.

---

6. The Nixon administration first encouraged new relations with the People's Republic of China by allowing a cultural exchange of table tennis teams.

In April 2010, President Obama and Russian president Dmitry Medvedev signed the New START Treaty, a follow-up to earlier arms control treaties. The ten-year pact will cut the number of nuclear warheads allowed to each party by 30 percent, to 1,550 warheads. The number of permitted missile launchers will be cut in half. The treaty includes a verification process. As of late 2010, the U.S. Senate had not yet voted on the treaty.

William Henry Harrison (1841) was the first president to die in office. He served only one month. (Library of Congress)

Executive Agreements. Presidential power in foreign affairs is enhanced greatly by the use of **executive agreements** made between the president and other heads of state. Such agreements do not require Senate approval, although the House and Senate may refuse to appropriate the funds necessary to implement them. Whereas treaties are binding on all succeeding administrations, executive agreements require each new president's consent to remain in effect.

Among the advantages of executive agreements are speed and secrecy. The former is essential during a crisis. The latter is important when the administration fears that open senatorial debate may be detrimental to the best interests of the United States or to the interests of the president.[7] There have been far more executive agreements (about 9,000) than treaties (about 1,300). Many executive agreements contain secret provisions calling for American military assistance or other support. For example, Franklin Roosevelt (1933–1945) used executive agreements to bypass congressional isolationists when he traded American destroyers for British Caribbean naval bases.

did you know?

That President William Henry Harrison gave the longest inaugural address (8,445 words) of any American president, lasting two hours (the weather was chilly and stormy, and Harrison caught a cold, developed pneumonia and pleurisy, and died a month later).

Chief Legislator

Constitutionally, presidents must recommend to Congress legislation that they judge necessary and expedient. Not all presidents have wielded their powers as **chief legislator** in the same manner. Some presidents have been almost completely unsuccessful in getting their legislative programs implemented by Congress. Presidents Franklin Roosevelt and Lyndon Johnson, however, saw much of their proposed legislation put into effect.

Creating the Congressional Agenda. In modern times, the president has played a dominant role in creating the congressional agenda. In the president's annual **State of the Union message,** which is required by the Constitution (Article II, Section 3) and is usually given in late January shortly after Congress reconvenes, the president presents a legislative program. The message gives a broad, comprehensive view of what the president wishes the legislature to accomplish during its session. It is as much a message to the American people and to the world as it is to Congress. Its impact on public opinion can determine the way in which Congress responds to the president's agenda.

Beginning with the presidency of Thomas Jefferson and for a century thereafter, the president's State of the Union message was a written document delivered to Congress and read aloud by a clerk. In 1913, Woodrow Wilson reinstated George Washington's practice of delivering the message himself in an address to Congress. Today, this address is one of the great formal ceremonies of American governance.

Many customs have grown up around the address. For example, one cabinet member, the "designated survivor," stays away to ensure that the country will always have a president even if someone manages to blow up the Capitol building. The president is not permitted to enter the House floor without the explicit permission of Congress, and granting that permission is part of the ceremony. Everyone gives the president an initial standing ovation out of

Executive Agreement
An international agreement made by the president, without senatorial ratification, with the head of a foreign state.

Chief Legislator
The role of the president in influencing the making of laws.

State of the Union Message
An annual message to Congress in which the president proposes a legislative program. The message is addressed not only to Congress but also to the American people and to the world.

7. The Case Act of 1972 requires that all executive agreements be transmitted to Congress within sixty days after the agreement takes effect. Secret agreements are transmitted to the foreign relations committees as classified information.

President George W. Bush gives a State of the Union address while Vice President Dick Cheney and Speaker of the House Nancy Pelosi listen. Where is that address given? (AP Photo/Charles Dharapak)

respect for the office, but this applause does not necessarily represent support for the individual who holds the office. During the speech, senators and House members either applaud or remain silent to indicate their opinion of the policies that the president announces.

Getting Legislation Passed. The president can propose legislation. Congress, however, is not required to pass—or even introduce—any of the administration's bills. How, then, does the president get those proposals made into law? One way is by exercising the power of persuasion. The president writes to, telephones, and meets with various congressional leaders; makes public announcements to influence public opinion; and, as head of the party, exercises legislative leadership through the congresspersons of that party.

A president whose party holds a majority in both chambers of Congress may have an easier time getting legislation passed than does a president who faces a hostile Congress. Note, though, that even with a Republican-dominated Congress (from 2001 to 2007), President George W. Bush failed to obtain Social Security reform legislation or to make headway with his proposed Federal Marriage Amendment to the Constitution. President Obama has been much more successful, as we explain in this chapter's feature *The Politics of Boom and Bust: The Audacity of Barack Obama* on the facing page.

Saying No to Legislation. The president has the power to say no to legislation through use of the veto,[8] by which the White House returns a bill unsigned to Congress with a **veto message** attached. Because the Constitution requires that every bill passed by the House and the Senate be sent to the president before it becomes law, the president must act on each bill:

1. If the bill is signed, it becomes law.
2. If the bill is not sent back to Congress after ten congressional working days, it becomes law without the president's signature.
3. The president can reject the bill and send it back to Congress with a veto message setting forth objections. Congress then can change the bill, hoping to secure presidential approval, and repass it. Or Congress can simply reject the president's objections by overriding the veto with a two-thirds roll-call vote of the members present in both the House and the Senate.
4. If the president refuses to sign the bill and Congress adjourns within ten working days after the bill has been submitted to the president, the bill is killed for that session of Congress. This is called a **pocket veto.** If Congress wishes the bill to be reconsidered, the bill must be reintroduced during the following session.

Veto Message
The president's formal explanation of a veto when legislation is returned to Congress.

Pocket Veto
A special veto exercised by the chief executive after a legislative body has adjourned. Bills not signed by the chief executive die after a specified period of time. If Congress wishes to reconsider such a bill, it must be reintroduced in the following session of Congress.

Presidents employed the veto power infrequently until after the Civil War, but it has been used with increasing vigor since then (see Table 11–2 on page 384). The total number of

8. *Veto* in Latin means "I forbid."

THE POLITICS OF BOOM AND BUST

THE AUDACITY OF BARACK OBAMA

In early 2008, the *National Journal,* a conservative magazine, claimed that Barack Obama was the most liberal member of the U.S. Senate. Skeptics recalled that the *Journal* named John Kerry the most liberal senator in 2004, when Kerry was the Democratic presidential candidate. More reliable sources identified Obama as a typical Senate Democrat. Obama championed standard liberal causes similar to those of the other Democratic candidates, such as Hillary Clinton.

Obama also called for a new tone in Washington, which many people interpreted as an appeal for bipartisanship. As president-elect, Obama appointed a series of moderate figures to his cabinet, and some Republicans began to believe they had nothing to fear. They soon learned otherwise. Obama had the will and the votes to implement an extensive agenda, something no Democrat had been able to do since Lyndon Johnson's Great Society of the 1960s. Obama was not the most liberal Democrat. Rather, he was the most audacious.

(Mandel Ngan/AFP/Getty Images)

HIT THE GROUND RUNNING

In his first one hundred days, Obama undertook a dazzling series of initiatives. Every day brought a new announcement. Obama directed the military to prepare a plan to leave Iraq even as he ordered 17,000 new troops into Afghanistan—and then 30,000 more in November 2009. He banned interrogation techniques widely considered to be torture and announced plans to close the Guantánamo Bay prison that housed terrorist suspects. At Obama's urging, Congress passed a long-stalled plan to fund children's health care.

COMBATING THE RECESSION

None of these steps addressed the major problem Obama faced on taking office—the economy. The economic scene on Inauguration Day in 2009 was not pretty, and Obama's reactions were characteristically bold. His first step was the February 2009 stimulus bill designed to jump-start the economy, passed without any Republican support in the House. Never in history had the Congress appropriated more new funding more quickly. Then on April 30, Congress approved Obama's $3.6 trillion budget for 2010, also without any Republican support.

Even while Bush was still president, a collapsing automobile industry had fallen into the federal lap. Thereafter, the responsibility was Obama's. A bankrupt Chrysler was forced to become a part of Fiat, the Italian automobile maker, and General Motors became a majority-owned subsidiary of the U.S. government. These steps represented unprecedented levels of federal involvement in private industry.

As a further step, in March 2010, after nine months of national debate, Obama steered a massive overhaul of the U.S. health-care financing system through Congress. Journalists agreed that the measures could not have succeeded without the unswerving support of Obama and House Speaker Nancy Pelosi. Republicans were aghast.

THE AUDACITY OF HOPE

Was Obama's call for a new spirit in Washington a hoax? Not quite. Charles Kesler of the Claremont Institute adopted the unusual strategy of reading Obama's own writings—especially his policy work, *The Audacity of Hope*—assuming that Obama meant what he said. Kesler was therefore able to predict Obama's behavior in office even before the 2008 elections. If there is a "villain" in *The Audacity of Hope,* it is former Democratic president Bill Clinton. According to Obama, Clinton wasted his enormous political talents and failed to advance a progressive agenda. Obama meant to do better. Obama indeed envisioned a new spirit in Washington based on resolving the conflict between conservatives and liberals. But for Obama, the fight ends *when the liberals win.* Indeed, Obama may be the most determined president of our times.

FOR CRITICAL ANALYSIS

What are the benefits of having the federal government more involved in banking, automobile manufacturing, health care, and other areas of the economy? What are the downsides?

vetoes from George Washington through the end of George W. Bush's second term in office was 2,562, with about two-thirds of those vetoes being exercised by Grover Cleveland, Franklin Roosevelt, Harry Truman, and Dwight Eisenhower.

George W. Bush was the first president since Martin Van Buren (1837–1841) to serve a full term in office without exercising the veto power. Bush, who had the benefit of a

TABLE 11–2 Presidential Vetoes, 1789 to Present

Years	President	Regular Vetoes	Vetoes Overrridden	Pocket Vetoes	Total Vetoes
1789–1797	Washington	2	0	0	2
1797–1801	J. Adams	0	0	0	0
1801–1809	Jefferson	0	0	0	0
1809–1817	Madison	5	0	2	7
1817–1825	Monroe	1	0	0	1
1825–1829	J. Q. Adams	0	0	0	0
1829–1837	Jackson	5	0	7	12
1837–1841	Van Buren	0	0	1	1
1841–1841	Harrison	0	0	0	0
1841–1845	Tyler	6	1	4	10
1845–1849	Polk	2	0	1	3
1849–1850	Taylor	0	0	0	0
1850–1853	Fillmore	0	0	0	0
1853–1857	Pierce	9	5	0	9
1857–1861	Buchanan	4	0	3	7
1861–1865	Lincoln	2	0	5	7
1865–1869	A. Johnson	21	15	8	29
1869–1877	Grant	45	4	48	93
1877–1881	Hayes	12	1	1	13
1881–1881	Garfield	0	0	0	0
1881–1885	Arthur	4	1	8	12
1885–1889	Cleveland	304	2	110	414
1889–1893	Harrison	19	1	25	44
1893–1897	Cleveland	42	5	128	170
1897–1901	McKinley	6	0	36	42
1901–1909	T. Roosevelt	42	1	40	82
1909–1913	Taft	30	1	9	39
1913–1921	Wilson	33	6	11	44
1921–1923	Harding	5	0	1	6
1923–1929	Coolidge	20	4	30	50
1929–1933	Hoover	21	3	16	37
1933–1945	F. Roosevelt	372	9	263	635
1945–1953	Truman	180	12	70	250
1953–1961	Eisenhower	73	2	108	181
1961–1963	Kennedy	12	0	9	21
1963–1969	L. Johnson	16	0	14	30
1969–1974	Nixon	26*	7	17	43
1974–1977	Ford	48	12	18	66
1977–1981	Carter	13	2	18	31
1981–1989	Reagan	39	9	39	78
1989–1993	G. H. W. Bush	29	1	15	44
1993–2001	Clinton	36†	2	1	37
2001–2009	G. W. Bush	11	4	1	12
2009–	Obama	0	0	2	2
TOTAL		1,489	110	1,069	2,564

*Two pocket vetoes by President Nixon, overruled in the courts, are counted here as regular vetoes.
†President Clinton's line-item vetoes are not included.
Sources: Office of the Clerk; plus authors' updates through 2011.

Republican Congress, did not veto any legislation during his first term. Only in the summer of 2006 did Bush finally issue a veto, saying "no" to stem-cell research legislation passed by Congress. Within months of the Democrats taking control of Congress in January 2007, however, the president issued several vetoes. President Obama, who also has enjoyed a Congress dominated by his own party, has made little use of the veto.

The Line-Item Veto. Ronald Reagan lobbied strenuously for Congress to give another tool to the president—the **line-item veto,** which would allow the president to veto *specific* spending provisions of legislation that was passed by Congress. In 1996, Congress passed the Line Item Veto Act, which provided for the line-item veto. Signed by President Clinton, the law granted the president the power to rescind any item in an appropriations bill unless Congress passed a resolution of disapproval. Of course, the congressional resolution could be, in turn, vetoed by the president. The law did not take effect until after the 1996 elections.

The act was soon challenged in court as an unconstitutional delegation of legislative powers to the executive branch. In 1998, by a six-to-three vote, the United States Supreme Court agreed and overturned the act. The Court stated that "there is no provision in the Constitution that authorizes the president to enact, to amend or to repeal statutes."[9]

Line-Item Veto
The power of an executive to veto individual lines or items within a piece of legislation without vetoing the entire bill.

Constitutional Power
A power vested in the president by Article II of the Constitution.

Statutory Power
A power created for the president through laws enacted by Congress.

Expressed Power
A power of the president that is expressly written into the Constitution or into statutory law.

Inherent Power
A power of the president derived from the statements in the Constitution that "the executive Power shall be vested in a President" and that the president should "take Care that the Laws be faithfully executed"; defined through practice rather than through law.

Congress's Power to Override Presidential Vetoes. A veto is a clear-cut indication of the president's dissatisfaction with congressional legislation. Congress, however, can override a presidential veto, although it rarely exercises this power. Consider that two-thirds of the members of each chamber who are present must vote to override the president's veto in a roll-call vote. This means that if only one-third plus one of the members voting in one of the chambers of Congress do not agree to override the veto, the veto holds. It was not until the administration of John Tyler (1841–1845) that Congress overrode a presidential veto. In American history, only about 7 percent of all vetoes have been overridden.

Other Presidential Powers

The powers of the president just discussed are called **constitutional powers,** because their basis lies in the Constitution. In addition, Congress has established by law, or statute, numerous other presidential powers—such as the ability to declare national emergencies. These are called **statutory powers.** Both constitutional and statutory powers have been labeled the **expressed powers** of the president, because they are expressly written into the Constitution or into law.

Presidents also have what have come to be known as **inherent powers.** These depend on the statements in the Constitution that "the executive Power shall be vested in a President" and that the president should "take Care that the Laws be faithfully executed." The most common example of inherent powers is those emergency powers invoked by the president during wartime. Franklin Roosevelt, for example, used his inherent powers to move the Japanese and Japanese Americans living in the United States into internment camps for the duration of World War II. As noted earlier, President George W. Bush often justified expanding the powers of his presidency by saying that such powers were necessary to fight the war on terrorism.

The President as Party Chief and Superpolitician

Presidents are by no means above political partisanship, and one of their many roles is that of chief of party. Although the Constitution says nothing about the function of the president within a political party (the mere concept of political parties was abhorrent to most

9. *Clinton v. City of New York,* 524 U.S. 417 (1998).

of the authors of the Constitution), today presidents are the actual leaders of their parties.

The President as Chief of Party

Patronage
The practice of rewarding faithful party workers and followers with government employment and contracts.

As party leader, the president chooses the national committee chairperson and can try to discipline party members who fail to support presidential policies. One way of exerting political power within the party is through **patronage**—appointing political supporters to government or public jobs. This power was more extensive in the past, before the establishment of the civil service in 1883 (see Chapter 12), but the president retains important patronage power. As we noted earlier, the president can appoint several thousand individuals to jobs in the cabinet, the White House, and the federal regulatory agencies.

Perhaps the most important partisan role that the president played in the late 1900s and early 2000s was that of fund-raiser. The president is able to raise large amounts of money for the party through appearances at dinners, speaking engagements, and other social occasions. President Clinton may have raised more than half a billion dollars for the Democratic Party during his two terms. President George W. Bush was even more successful than Clinton—until his popularity ratings dropped during his last years in office. Barack Obama's spectacular success in raising funds for his presidential campaign suggests that he will carry on this fund-raising tradition.

did you know?
That the 2008 presidential elections were only the second in the last twenty-eight years without a Bush on the ballot.

Presidents have a number of other ways of exerting influence as party chief. The president may make it known that a particular congressperson's choice for federal judge will not be appointed unless that member of Congress is more supportive of the president's legislative program.[10] The president may agree to campaign for a particular program or for a particular candidate. Presidents also reward loyal members of Congress with support for the funding of local projects, tax breaks for regional industries, and other forms of "pork."

The President's Power to Persuade

According to political scientist Richard E. Neustadt, without the power to persuade, no president can lead very well. After all, even though the president is in the news nearly every day, the Constitution gives Congress most of the authority in the U.S. political system. Therefore, the president must convince Congress to do what the president wants. As Neustadt argues, "presidential power is the power to persuade."[11] Neustadt argues that one can find a high correlation between effective presidents and those who are best at persuasion. Presidents have to persuade the public, too.

Some scholars, however, have argued that a president's powers extend far beyond the power to persuade. For example, political analysts Kenneth Mayer and William Howell both emphasize that presidents do not need to rely on persuasive powers and normal legislative processes to implement presidential policies. Rather, presidents can take direct action by using other presidential tools, an important one being the *executive order* (executive orders will be discussed shortly).[12]

Constituencies and Public Approval

All politicians worry about their constituencies, and presidents are no exception. Presidents are also concerned with public approval ratings.

---

10. "Senatorial courtesy" (see Chapter 13) often puts the judicial appointment in the hands of the Senate, however.
11. Richard E. Neustadt, *Presidential Power and the Modern Presidents: The Politics of Leadership from Roosevelt to Reagan,* rev. ed. (New York: Free Press, 1991).
12. See Kenneth R. Mayer, *With the Stroke of a Pen: Executive Orders and Presidential Power* (Princeton, N.J.: Princeton University Press, 2002); and William G. Howell, *Power without Persuasion: The Politics of Direct Presidential Action* (Princeton, N.J.: Princeton University Press, 2003).

Presidential Constituencies. Presidents have many constituencies. In principle, they are beholden to the entire electorate—the public of the United States—even those who did not vote. They are certainly beholden to their party, because its members helped to put them in office. The president's constituencies also include members of the opposing party whose cooperation the president needs. Finally, the president must take into consideration a constituency that has come to be called the **Washington community** (also known as those "inside the beltway"). This community consists of individuals who—whether in or out of political office—are intimately familiar with the workings of government, thrive on gossip, and measure on a daily basis the political power of the president.

Washington Community
Individuals regularly involved with politics in Washington, D.C.

Public Approval. All of these constituencies are impressed by presidents who maintain a high level of public approval, partly because doing so is very difficult to accomplish. Presidential popularity, as measured by national polls, gives the president an extra political resource to use in persuading legislators or bureaucrats to pass legislation.

As you can see from Figure 11–1 on the following page, President George W. Bush enjoyed spectacularly high approval ratings immediately after the terrorist attacks of 9/11. This popularity allowed him to win national security legislation such as the USA Patriot Act. It also allowed him to undertake a robust foreign policy that included the overthrow of the Afghan government and the occupation of Iraq. Bush's popularity declined steadily after 9/11, however, with a brief reprieve at the time of his reelection in late 2004. The year 2006, when public dissatisfaction with the war in Iraq reached a critical level, may have been a turning point. By 2008, Bush was so unpopular that other members of the administration, such as Treasury secretary Henry Paulson, took the public lead in begging Congress for help in combating the financial crisis that struck in September of that year.

The Popularaity of President Obama. Obama's initial popularity figures were also very high, but part of his support came from Republicans (who gave 40 percent approval) and was bound to dissipate. Obama retained the overwhelming favor of Democrats into 2010, but by that time his support among Republicans was in the teens. From August 2009 on, Obama's support among independents also eroded, presumably due to continued high levels of unemployment and concern about his ambitious progressive agenda. Obama therefore entered 2010 with favorability ratings at 50 percent or just under.

During 2010, Obama's approval rating continued to slide, but slowly. By the end of June, equal numbers of those surveyed approved and disapproved of Obama's performance—45 percent versus 45 percent, with the rest undecided. By October, the percentage of respondents who approved of his performance was still about 45 percent, but those disapproving had pulled into a narrow lead.

President John F. Kennedy (1961–1963) reached out to all Americans during a speech on November 2, 1962. He told television and radio listeners that he had reached an agreement with Soviet leaders to remove missile bases from Cuba. Why do some presidents "go public"? (AP Photo)

"Going Public." Since the early 1900s, presidents have spoken more to the public and less to Congress. In the 1800s, only 7 percent of presidential speeches were addressed to the public; since 1900, 50 percent have been addressed to the public. One scholar, Samuel Kernell, has proposed that the style of presidential leadership has changed since World War II, owing partly to the influence of television, with a resulting change in the balance of national politics.[13] Presidents frequently go over the heads of Congress and the political elites, taking their cases directly to the people.

13. Samuel Kernell, *Going Public: New Strategies of Presidential Leadership,* 4th ed. (Washington, D.C.: CQ Press, 2006).

FIGURE 11–1 Public Popularity of Modern Presidents

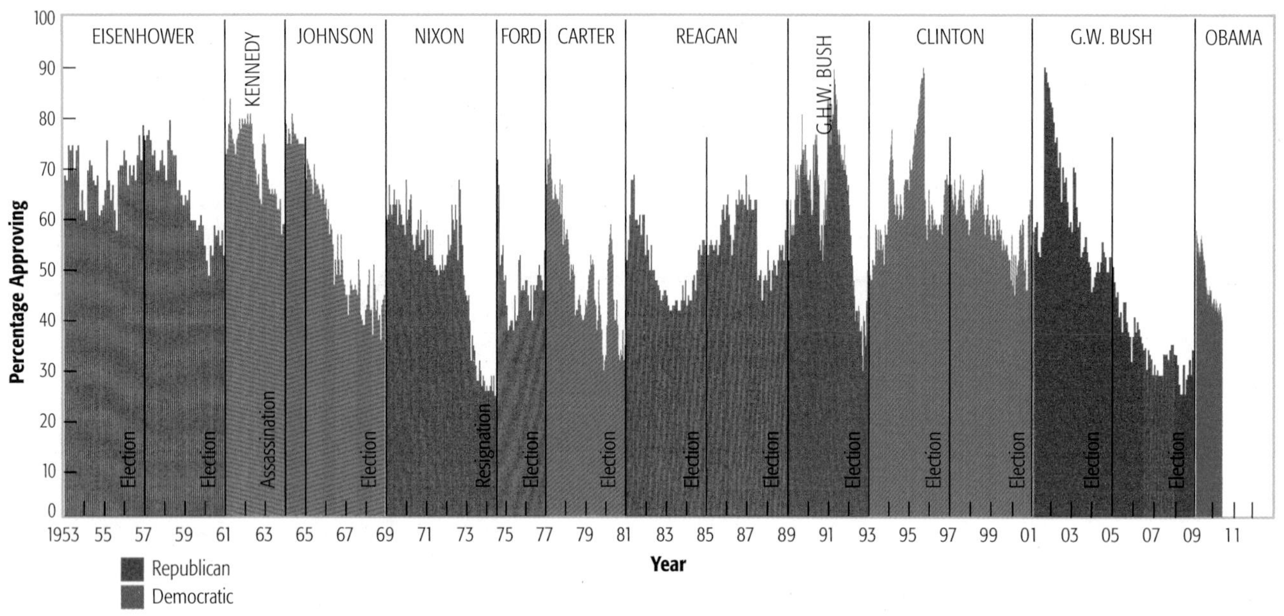

Sources: Adapted from The Roper Center for Public Opinion Research; Gallup and *USA Today*/CNN polls, March 1992 through June 2010.

This strategy, which Kernell dubbed "going public," gives the president additional power through the ability to persuade and manipulate public opinion. By identifying their own positions so clearly, presidents make compromises with Congress much more difficult and weaken the legislators' positions. Given the increasing importance of the media as the major source of political information for citizens and elites, presidents will continue to use public opinion as part of their arsenal of weapons to gain support from Congress and to achieve their policy goals. More than any previous president, Barack Obama has used new media such as YouTube, Facebook, and Twitter to enhance his relationship with the public. We take a quick look at one of these media in the feature *Politics and . . . Social Networking: When the President Tweets* on the facing page.

did you know?

That the shortest inaugural address was George Washington's second one, at 135 words.

Special Uses of Presidential Power

Presidents have at their disposal a variety of special powers and privileges not available in the other branches of the U.S. government. These include (1) emergency powers, (2) executive orders, and (3) executive privilege.

Emergency Powers

If you read the Constitution, you will find no mention of the additional powers that the executive office may exercise during national emergencies. Indeed, the Supreme Court has stated that an "emergency does not create power."[14] But it is clear that presidents have made strong use of their inherent powers during times of emergency, particularly in the realm of foreign affairs. The **emergency powers** of the president were first enunciated in the Supreme Court's decision in *United States v. Curtiss-Wright Export Corp.*[15] In that case, President Franklin Roosevelt, without authorization by Congress, ordered an

Emergency Power
An inherent power exercised by the president during a period of national crisis.

14. *Home Building and Loan Association v. Blaisdell,* 290 U.S. 398 (1934).
15. 299 U.S. 304 (1936).

POLITICS AND... social networking

WHEN THE PRESIDENT TWEETS

During his 2008 run for the U.S. presidency, Barack Obama became famous for the skillful way in which his campaign used the new social media to organize support. The campaign employed YouTube to distribute video to followers. Facebook brought followers together, often uniting supporters in a particular town or county. Obama's own Web site was a major social center. Of course, the campaign raised funds through the Internet to a degree never before seen.

The Obama campaign also made use of another tool—Twitter. It was not widely noticed at the time, but Twitter was important to the campaign. In March 2008, Barack Obama had more followers on Twitter than anyone else on planet Earth. Other politicians were not even close. Indeed, at the time, most of the other top ten twitterers were relative unknowns—the only other well-known member of the top ten was CNN. The Barack Obama Twitter feed went online in February 2007, making it one of the earliest such operations. Obama's tweets, as is common with politicians and news sources, largely consisted of pointers to various Web pages.

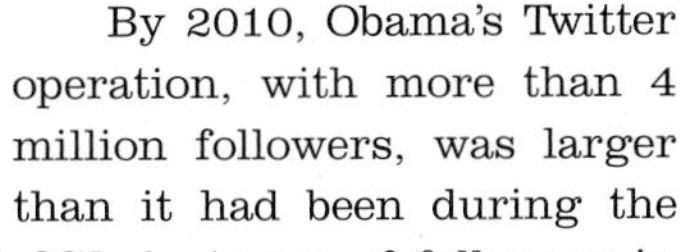

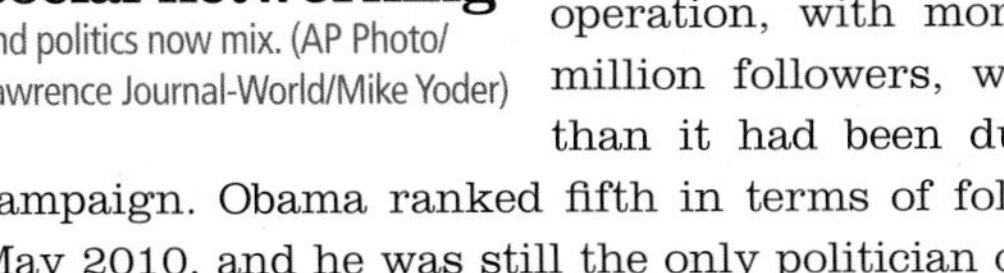

Social networking and politics now mix. (AP Photo/Lawrence Journal-World/Mike Yoder)

By 2010, Obama's Twitter operation, with more than 4 million followers, was larger than it had been during the campaign. Obama ranked fifth in terms of followers in May 2010, and he was still the only politician on the top ten. Now, however, he was outranked by such cultural icons as Britney Spears and Lady Gaga, most of whom did not begin tweeting until mid-2008 or 2009.

OBAMA'S LITTLE TWITTER SECRET

Obama's Twitter operation had one secret that was not widely publicized: It wasn't Obama himself who was doing the tweeting. Staff members did it all for him. The cat was let out of the bag in early 2010, when the president's campaign Web site advertised for a new social networks manager. Mia Cambronero, who previously held the position, said, "[I] will be stepping down from my infamous role as Barack Obama's twitterer. . . . We're looking for someone who is available to start immediately." Obama admitted in November 2009 that he had never used Twitter—"My thumbs are too clumsy to type in things on the phone," he said. In January 2010, however, during a visit to the American Red Cross headquarters in Washington, Obama finally entered his first real tweet, backing Red Cross assistance for earthquake victims in Haiti.

Further evidence that Obama's Twitter operation might not be as sophisticated as some thought surfaced in March 2010, when an unemployed French computer hacker was arrested for breaking into and taking over Obama's Twitter account. The hacker was no genius—he simply guessed Obama's password, which was based on the name of the presidential dog, Bo. In Congress, the Democrats also appeared not to be on the leading edge. By 2010, 42 percent of Republican House members were twittering, as opposed to only 15 percent of the Democrats.

GADGETS ARE "PUTTING NEW PRESSURES ON OUR DEMOCRACY"

Obama has long been known for his devotion to his BlackBerry cell phone. It therefore came as something of a surprise when he attacked the new electronic devices at Hampton University in Virginia in May 2010. Obama said: "With iPods and iPads and Xboxes and PlayStations—none of which I know how to work—information becomes a distraction, a diversion, a form of entertainment, rather than a tool of empowerment, rather than the means of emancipation." Back in 2008, however, Obama showed off his iPod playlist to reporters.

FOR CRITICAL ANALYSIS

How can more information be bad for democracy?

embargo on the shipment of weapons to two warring South American countries. The Court recognized that the president may exercise inherent powers in foreign affairs and that the national government has primacy in these affairs.

Examples of emergency powers are abundant, coinciding with crises in domestic and foreign affairs. Abraham Lincoln suspended civil liberties at the beginning of the Civil War (1861–1865) and called the state militias into national service. These actions and his subsequent governance of conquered areas—and even of areas of northern states—were justified by claims that they were essential to preserve the Union. Franklin Roosevelt declared an "unlimited national emergency" following the fall of France in World War II (1939–1945) and mobilized the federal budget and the economy for war.

President Harry Truman authorized the federal seizure of steel plants and their operation by the national government in 1952 during the Korean War. Truman claimed that he was using his inherent emergency power as chief executive and commander in chief to safeguard the nation's security, as an ongoing strike by steelworkers threatened the supply of weapons to the armed forces. The Supreme Court did not agree, holding that the president had no authority under the Constitution to seize private property or to legislate such action.[16] According to legal scholars, this was the first time a limit was placed on the exercise of the president's emergency powers.

Executive Orders

As we discussed in Chapter 2, Congress allows the president (as well as administrative agencies) to issue *executive orders* that have the force of law. These executive orders can do the following: (1) enforce legislative statutes, (2) enforce the Constitution or treaties with foreign nations, and (3) establish or modify rules and practices of executive administrative agencies.

An executive order, then, represents the president's legislative power. The only apparent requirement is that under the Administrative Procedure Act of 1946, all executive orders must be published in the ***Federal Register,*** a daily publication of the U.S. government. Executive orders have been used to establish procedures to appoint noncareer administrators, to restructure the White House bureaucracy, to ration consumer goods and to administer wage and price controls under emergency conditions, to classify government information as secret, to regulate the export of restricted items, to establish the Peace Corps, and to establish military tribunals for suspected terrorists.

Federal Register
A publication of the U.S. government that prints executive orders, rules, and regulations.

Executive Privilege
The right of executive officials to withhold information from or to refuse to appear before a legislative committee.

President Bush made use of such orders in executing the war on terrorism, and more generally in expanding presidential powers. President Obama's executive orders have covered matters such as the pay and practices of members of the executive branch, raising the fuel efficiency standards of cars and trucks, permitting federal grants to international organizations that support abortion, and lifting restrictions on the federal funding of embryonic stem-cell research. In 2010, Obama sought congressional repeal of the "Don't Ask, Don't Tell" policy that prohibited gay men and lesbians from openly serving in the armed forces. This step would allow the president to revoke the policy through executive order. It appeared likely that Obama would issue such an order in December 2010, after the armed forces finished a review of the implications of repeal.

Executive Privilege

Another inherent executive power that has been claimed by presidents concerns the ability of the president and the president's executive officials to withhold information from or refuse to appear before Congress or the courts. This is called **executive privilege,** and it relies on the constitutional separation of powers for its basis.

16. *Youngstown Sheet and Tube Co. v. Sawyer,* 343 U.S. 579 (1952).

Presidents have frequently invoked executive privilege to avoid having to disclose information to Congress on actions of the executive branch. Executive privilege rests on the assumption that a certain degree of secrecy is essential to the proper functioning of the executive branch. Critics of executive privilege believe that it can be used to shield from public scrutiny actions of the executive branch that should be open to Congress and to the American citizenry.

Limiting Executive Privilege. Limits to executive privilege went untested until the Watergate affair in the early 1970s. Five men had broken into the headquarters of the Democratic National Committee and were caught searching for documents that would damage the candidacy of the Democratic nominee, George McGovern. Later investigation showed that the break-in was planned by members of Richard Nixon's campaign committee and that Nixon and his closest advisers had devised a strategy for impeding the investigation of the crime. After it became known that all of the conversations held in the Oval Office had been tape-recorded on a secret system, Nixon was ordered to turn over the tapes to the special prosecutor.

Nixon refused to do so, claiming executive privilege. He argued that "no president could function if the private papers of his office, prepared by his personal staff, were open to public scrutiny." In 1974, in one of the Supreme Court's most famous cases, *United States v. Nixon,*[17] the justices unanimously ruled that Nixon had to hand over the tapes. The Court held that executive privilege could not be used to prevent evidence from being heard in criminal proceedings.

President Richard Nixon (1969–1974) says goodbye outside the White House after his resignation on August 9, 1974, as he prepares to board a helicopter for a flight to nearby Andrews Air Force Base. Nixon addressed members of his staff in the East Room prior to his departure. Was Nixon impeached? (AP Photo)

Executive Privilege and the Bush Administration. President George W. Bush also claimed executive privilege to prevent the disclosure to Congress of confidential communications or materials. For example, the Bush administration resisted attempts by the congressional Government Accountability Office to obtain information about meetings and documents related to Vice President Dick Cheney's actions as chair of the administration's energy policy task force. President Bush also asserted executive privilege on several occasions to prevent White House and Justice Department staffers from testifying before Congress about the firing of several U.S. attorneys, allegedly for political reasons. While he was a candidate, Barack Obama criticized Bush's use of executive privilege as excessive. Upon becoming president, however, Obama invoked the privilege on several occasions.

Abuses of Executive Power and Impeachment

Presidents normally leave office either because their first term has expired and they have not sought (or won) reelection or because, having served two full terms, they are not allowed to be elected for a third term (owing to the Twenty-second Amendment, passed in 1951). Eight presidents have died in office. But as you learned in the chapter-opening *What If . . .* feature, there is still another way for a president to leave office—by **impeachment** and conviction. Articles I and II of the Constitution authorize the House and Senate to remove the president, the vice president, or other civil officers of the United

Impeachment
An action by the House of Representatives to accuse the president, vice president, or other civil officers of the United States of committing "Treason, Bribery, or other high Crimes and Misdemeanors."

17. 318 U.S. 683 (1974).

On December 19, 1998, the House of Representatives voted to impeach President Bill Clinton (1993–2001), shown here with his vice president, Al Gore, and First Lady Hillary Clinton. Why was Clinton not forced to leave office because of this impeachment? (AP Photo/Doug Mills)

States for committing "Treason, Bribery, or other high Crimes and Misdemeanors." According to the Constitution, the impeachment process begins in the House, which impeaches (accuses) the federal officer involved. If the House votes to impeach the officer, it draws up articles of impeachment and submits them to the Senate, which conducts the actual trial.

In the history of the United States, no president has ever actually been impeached and also convicted—and thus removed from office—by means of this process. President Andrew Johnson (1865–1869), who succeeded to the office after the assassination of Abraham Lincoln, was impeached by the House but acquitted by the Senate. More than a century later, the House Judiciary Committee approved articles of impeachment against President Richard Nixon for his involvement in the cover-up of the Watergate break-in of 1972. Informed by members of his own party that he had no hope of surviving the trial in the Senate, Nixon resigned on August 9, 1974, before the full House voted on the articles. Nixon is the only president to have resigned from office.

The second president to be impeached by the House but not convicted by the Senate was President Bill Clinton. In September 1998, Independent Counsel Kenneth Starr sent to Congress the findings of his investigation of the president on the charges of perjury and obstruction of justice. The House approved two charges against Clinton: lying to the grand jury about his affair with Monica Lewinsky and obstruction of justice. The articles of impeachment were then sent to the Senate, which acquitted Clinton. As noted in the *What If . . .* feature, the attempt to remove Clinton was unpopular, although the allegations against him damaged his popularity as well. Part of the problem for Clinton's Republican opponents was that the charges against Clinton essentially boiled down to lying about sex. As one pundit put it, "Everyone lies about sex." Of course, not everyone lies about sex when under oath.

Eric Holder is attorney general in the Obama administration. How does he fit into the organization of the executive branch? (AP Photo/Charles Dharapak)

The Executive Organization

Gone are the days when presidents answered their own mail, as George Washington did. It was not until 1857 that Congress authorized a private secretary for the president, to be paid by the federal government. Woodrow Wilson typed most of his correspondence, even though he did have several secretaries. At the beginning of Franklin Roosevelt's long tenure in the White House, the entire staff consisted of thirty-seven employees. With the New Deal and World War II, however, the presidential staff became a sizable organization.

Today, the executive organization includes a White House Office staff of about 600, including some workers who are part-time employees and others who are borrowed from their departments by the White House. Not all of these employees have equal access to the president, nor are all of them likely to be equally concerned about the administration's political success. The more than 360 employees who work in the White House Office itself are closest to the president. They often include many individuals who worked on the president's campaign. These assistants are most concerned with preserving the president's reputation. Also included in the president's staff are a number of advisory personnel, such as the president's assistant for national security affairs. Although the individuals who hold staff positions in these offices are appointed by the president, they are often more concerned with their own responsibilities than with the president's overall success. The group of appointees perhaps least helpful to the president is the cabinet, each member of which is the principal officer of a government department.

The Cabinet

Although the Constitution does not include the word *cabinet,* it does state that the president "may require the Opinion, in writing, of the principal Officer in each of the executive Departments." Since the time of George Washington, these officers have formed an advisory group, or **cabinet,** to which the president turns for counsel.

Cabinet
An advisory group selected by the president to aid in making decisions. The cabinet includes the heads of fifteen executive departments and others named by the president.

Kitchen Cabinet
The informal advisers to the president.

Members of the Cabinet. Originally, the cabinet consisted of only four officials—the secretaries of state, treasury, and war, and the attorney general. Today, the cabinet numbers fourteen department secretaries and the attorney general. (See Table 11–1 on page 376 for the names of the cabinet departments and Chapter 12 for a detailed discussion of these units.)

The cabinet may include others as well. The president at his or her discretion can, for example, ascribe cabinet rank to the vice president, the head of the Office of Management and Budget, the national security adviser, the ambassador to the United Nations, or additional officials. Under President Barack Obama, the additional members of the cabinet are the following:

- The vice president.
- The chair of the Council of Economic Advisers.
- The administrator of the Environmental Protection Agency.
- The director of the Office of Management and Budget.
- The U.S. trade representative.
- The U.S. ambassador to the United Nations.
- The White House chief of staff.

Often, a president will use a **kitchen cabinet** to replace the formal cabinet as a major source of advice. The term *kitchen cabinet* originated during the presidency of Andrew Jackson, who relied on the counsel of close friends who allegedly met with him in the kitchen of the White House. A kitchen cabinet is a very informal group of advisers. Usually, they are friends with whom the president worked before being elected.

Presidential Use of Cabinets. Because neither the Constitution nor statutory law requires the president to consult with the cabinet, its use is purely discretionary. Some presidents have relied on the counsel of their cabinets more than others. Dwight Eisenhower was used to the team approach to solving problems from his experience as supreme allied commander during World War II, and therefore he frequently turned to his cabinet for advice on a wide range of issues. More often, presidents have solicited the opinions of their cabinets and then have done what they wanted to do anyway. Lincoln supposedly said—after a cabinet meeting in which a vote was seven nays against his one aye—"Seven nays and one aye, the ayes have it." In general, few presidents have relied heavily on the advice of their cabinet members.

It is not surprising that presidents tend to disregard their cabinet members' advice. Often, the departmental heads are more responsive to the wishes of their own

Steven Chu heads the Department of Energy. What might some of his duties be? (AP Photo/ Will Kinkaid *The Bismarck Tribune*)

Secretary of Defense
Robert Gates is in charge of our armed services. Why do civilians always head up the Defense Department? (AP Photo/ Alex Brandon)

staffs or to their own political ambitions than they are to the president. They may be more concerned with obtaining resources for their departments than with achieving the goals of the president. So there is often a conflict of interest between presidents and their cabinet members.

The Executive Office of the President

When President Franklin Roosevelt appointed a special committee on administrative management, he knew that the committee would conclude that the president needed help. Indeed, the committee proposed a major reorganization of the executive branch. Congress did not approve the entire reorganization, but it did create the **Executive Office of the President (EOP)** to provide staff assistance for the chief executive and to help coordinate the executive bureaucracy. Since that time, a number of agencies have been created within the EOP to supply the president with advice and staff help. Presidents reorganize the EOP and the White House Office constantly, and any table of organization is therefore temporary. As of late 2010, however, the EOP agencies under Barack Obama were the following:

- Council of Economic Advisers.
- Council on Environmental Quality.
- National Security Council and Homeland Security Council.
- Office of Administration.
- Office of Management and Budget.
- Office of National Drug Control Policy.
- Office of Science and Technology Policy.
- Office of the U.S. Trade Representative.
- Office of the Vice President.
- White House Office.

Several of the offices within the EOP are especially important, including the White House Office, the Office of Management and Budget, and the National Security Council. The activities of the Executive Office of the President are featured on the president's own Web site—**www.whitehouse.gov**. The site is a helpful source of information and also serves to promote the president and the president's initiatives.

The White House Office. The **White House Office** includes most of the key personal and political advisers to the president. Among the jobs held by these aides are those of legal counsel to the president, secretary, press secretary, and appointments secretary. Often, the individuals who hold these positions are recruited from the president's campaign staff. Their duties—mainly protecting the president's political interests—are similar to campaign functions. Under President Barack Obama, the White House Office is made up of the following units:

- National Security Adviser.
- Office of Cabinet Affairs.
- Office of the Chief of Staff.
- Office of Communications.
- Office of Energy and Climate Change Policy.
- Office of the First Lady.
- Office of Health Reform.
- Office of Legislative Affairs.
- Office of Management and Administration.
- Office of Political Affairs.
- Office of Presidential Personnel.
- Office of the Press Secretary.
- Office of Public Engagement and Intergovernmental Affairs.
- Office of Scheduling and Advance.
- Office of the Staff Secretary.
- Office of the White House Counsel.
- Office of White House Policy.
- Oval Office Operations.
- White House Military Office.

Executive Office of the President (EOP)
An organization established by President Franklin D. Roosevelt to assist the president in carrying out major duties.

White House Office
The personal office of the president, which tends to presidential political needs and manages the media.

Chief of Staff
The person who is named to direct the White House Office and advise the president.

In all recent administrations, one member of the White House Office has been named **chief of staff.** This person, who is responsible for coordinating the office, is also one of the president's chief advisers. As of October 2010, Pete Rouse was Obama's chief of staff.

In addition to civilian advisers, the president is supported by a large number of military personnel, who are organized under the White House Military Office. These members of the military provide communications, transportation, medical care, and food services to the president and the White House staff.

Employees of the White House Office have been both envied and criticized. The White House Office, according to most former staffers, grants its employees access and power. They are able to use the resources of the White House to contact almost anyone in the world by telephone, cable, fax, or electronic mail, as well as to use the influence of the White House to persuade legislators and citizens. Because of this influence, staffers are often criticized for overstepping the bounds of the office. It is the appointments secretary who is able to grant or deny senators, representatives, and cabinet secretaries access to the president. It is the press secretary who grants to the press and television journalists access to any information about the president.

"If I become President, I'm not giving any of my schoolfriends jobs." (©The New Yorker Collection, 1993. Victoria Roberts, from cartoonbank.com. All Rights Reserved.)

White House staff members are closest to the president and may have considerable influence over the administration's decisions. Often, when presidents are under fire for their decisions, the staff is accused of keeping the chief executive too isolated from criticism or help. Presidents insist that they will not allow the staff to become too powerful, but, given the difficulty of the office, each president eventually turns to staff members for loyal assistance and protection.

The Office of Management and Budget. The **Office of Management and Budget (OMB)** was originally the Bureau of the Budget, which was created in 1921 within the Department of the Treasury. Recognizing the importance of this agency, Franklin Roosevelt moved it into the White House Office in 1939. Richard Nixon reorganized the Bureau of the Budget in 1970 and changed its name to reflect its new managerial function. It is headed by a director, who makes up the annual federal budget that the president presents to Congress each January for approval. In principle, the director of the OMB has broad fiscal powers in planning and estimating various parts of the federal budget, because all agencies must submit their proposed budget to the OMB for approval. In reality, it is not so clear that the OMB truly can affect the greater scope of the federal budget. Rather, the OMB may be more important as a clearinghouse for legislative proposals initiated in the executive agencies. In July 2010, Jacob Lew became President Obama's OMB director.

Office of Management and Budget (OMB)
A division of the Executive Office of the President. The OMB assists the president in preparing the annual budget, clearing and coordinating departmental agency budgets, and supervising the administration of the federal budget.

National Security Council (NSC)
An agency in the Executive Office of the President that advises the president on national security.

The National Security Council. The **National Security Council (NSC)** is a link between the president's key foreign and military advisers and the president. Its members consist of the president, the vice president, and the secretaries of state and defense, plus other informal members. The NSC is managed by the president's special assistant for national security affairs, also known as the national security adviser. As of October 2010, Obama's national security adviser is Thomas Donilon.

The Vice Presidency

The Constitution does not give much power to the vice president. The only formal duty is to preside over the Senate—which is rarely necessary. This obligation is fulfilled when the Senate organizes and adopts its rules and when the vice president is needed to decide a tie vote. In all other cases, the president pro tem manages parliamentary procedures in the Senate. The vice president is expected to participate only informally in senatorial deliberations, if at all.

did you know?

That the 2008 presidential elections were the first since 1952 without an incumbent president or vice president running.

The Vice President's Job

Vice presidents have traditionally been chosen by presidential nominees to balance the ticket, attracting groups of voters or appeasing party factions. If a presidential nominee is from the North, it is not a bad idea to have a vice-presidential nominee who is from the South. If the presidential nominee is from a rural state, perhaps someone with an urban background would be most suitable as a running mate. Presidential nominees who are strongly conservative or strongly liberal would do well to have vice-presidential nominees who are more in the middle of the political road.

Strengthening the Ticket. In recent presidential elections, however, vice presidents have often been selected for other reasons. In 2000, both vice-presidential selections were intended to shore up the respective presidential candidates' perceived weaknesses. Republican George W. Bush, who was subject to criticism for his lack of government experience and his "lightweight" personality, chose Dick Cheney, a former member of Congress who had also served as secretary of defense. Democrat Al Gore chose Senator Joe Lieberman of Connecticut, whose reputation for moral integrity (as an Orthodox Jew) could help counteract the effects of Bill Clinton's sex scandals. In 2004, Democratic presidential candidate John Kerry made a more traditional choice in Senator John Edwards of North Carolina. Edwards provided regional balance and also a degree of socioeconomic balance because, unlike Kerry, he had been born into relatively humble circumstances.

In 2008, after a long, drawn out, and bitter primary season among Democratic candidates, Barack Obama had to decide whether to include Senator Hillary Clinton on his ticket. Many of her supporters argued for this "dream team." In the end, though, Obama chose a longtime senator, Joe Biden, who had extensive foreign affairs experience. For the Republican presidential ticket, John McCain shocked his party and the nation when he chose the governor of Alaska, Sarah Palin. Many criticized his choice of a relatively unknown politician who had previously been mayor of an Alaskan town with only 7,000 people and had been governor of Alaska for fewer than two years.

Vice President Joe Biden frequently appears on television talk shows and at conferences. What are the official duties of the vice president? (Chris Kleponis /AFP/Getty Images)

Supporting the President. Traditionally, the job of the vice president has not been very demanding. In recent years, however, presidents have granted their running mates increased responsibilities and power. President Jimmy Carter was the first modern president to rely on his vice president—Walter Mondale—as a major adviser. Under President Bush, Dick Cheney became the most powerful vice president in history. Cheney was able to place his supporters throughout the bureaucracy and exert influence on a wide range of issues. He could exercise this degree of power, however, only because he had the support of the president. In contrast, Vice President Biden's relationship to President Obama has been more conventional.

Vice presidents sometimes have become elected presidents in their own right. John Adams and Thomas Jefferson were the first to do so. Richard Nixon was elected president in 1968 after he had served as Dwight D. Eisenhower's vice president during 1953–1961. In 1988, George H. W. Bush was elected to the presidency after eight years as Ronald Reagan's vice president.

Presidential Succession

Eight vice presidents have become president because of the death of the president. John Tyler, the first to do so, took over William Henry Harrison's position after only one month. No one knew whether Tyler should simply be a caretaker until a new president could be elected

Only eight presidents have died in office, after which their vice presidents became president. When John F. Kennedy was assassinated in November 1963, then Vice President Lyndon B. Johnson was sworn in as president by a federal judge. Standing alongside Johnson (1963–1969) was Kennedy's widow, Jacqueline Kennedy. Who becomes president if both the president and the vice president are killed? (AP Photo/White House/Cecil Stoughton)

three and a half years later or whether he actually should be president. Tyler assumed that he was supposed to be the chief executive, and he acted as such—although he was commonly referred to as "His Accidency." Since then, vice presidents taking over the position of the presidency because of the incumbent's death have assumed the presidential powers.

But what should a vice president do if a president becomes incapable of carrying out necessary duties while in office? When James Garfield was shot in 1881, he remained alive for two and a half months. What was Vice President Chester Arthur's role?

This question was not addressed in the original Constitution. Article II, Section 1, says only that "in Case of the Removal of the President from Office, or of his Death, Resignation, or Inability to discharge the Powers and Duties of the said Office, the same shall devolve on [the same powers shall be exercised by] the Vice President." There have been many instances of presidential disability. When Dwight Eisenhower became ill a second time in 1958, he entered into a pact with Richard Nixon specifying that the vice president could determine whether the president was incapable of carrying out his duties if the president could not communicate. John F. Kennedy and Lyndon Johnson entered into similar agreements with their vice presidents. Finally, in 1967, the **Twenty-fifth Amendment** was passed, establishing procedures in the event of presidential incapacity.

Twenty-fifth Amendment
A 1967 amendment to the Constitution that establishes procedures for filling presidential and vice-presidential vacancies and makes provisions for presidential incapacity.

The Twenty-fifth Amendment

According to the Twenty-fifth Amendment, when a president believes that he or she is incapable of performing the duties of office, the president must inform Congress in writing. Then the vice president serves as acting president until the president can resume normal duties. When the president is unable to communicate, a majority of the cabinet, including the vice president, can declare that fact to Congress. Then the vice president serves as acting president until the president resumes normal duties. If a dispute arises over the return of the president's ability, a two-thirds vote of Congress is required to allow the vice president to remain acting president. Otherwise, the president shall resume normal duties.

When the Vice Presidency Becomes Vacant

The Twenty-fifth Amendment also addresses the issue of how the president should fill a vacant vice presidency. Section 2 of the amendment simply states, "Whenever there is a vacancy in the office of the Vice President, the President shall nominate a Vice President

did you know?

That President Richard Nixon served 56 days without a vice president, and that President Gerald Ford served 132 days without a vice president.

who shall take office upon confirmation by a majority vote of both Houses of Congress." This is exactly what occurred when Richard Nixon's first vice president, Spiro Agnew, resigned in 1973 because of his alleged receipt of construction contract kickbacks during his tenure as governor of Maryland. Nixon turned to Gerald Ford as his choice for vice president. After extensive hearings, both chambers of Congress confirmed the appointment. Then, when Nixon resigned on August 9, 1974, Ford automatically became president and nominated as his vice president Nelson Rockefeller. Congress confirmed Ford's choice. For the first time in the history of the country, neither the president nor the vice president had been elected to their positions.

The question of who shall be president if both the president and the vice president die is answered by the Succession Act of 1947. If the president and vice president die, resign, or are disabled, the Speaker of the House will become president, after resigning from Congress. Next in line is the president pro tem of the Senate, followed by the cabinet officers in the order of the creation of their departments (see Table 11–3 below).

TABLE 11–3 Line of Succession to the Presidency of the United States

1. Vice president	10. Secretary of commerce
2. Speaker of the House of Representatives	11. Secretary of labor
3. Senate president pro tempore	12. Secretary of health and human services
4. Secretary of state	13. Secretary of housing and urban development
5. Secretary of the treasury	14. Secretary of transportation
6. Secretary of defense	15. Secretary of energy
7. Attorney general (head of the Justice Department)	16. Secretary of education
8. Secretary of the interior	17. Secretary of veterans affairs
9. Secretary of agriculture	18. Secretary of homeland security

Senator Daniel K. Inouye (D., Hawaii), is president pro tempore of the U.S. Senate. (AP Photo/ Rick Bowmer)

WHY SHOULD YOU CARE ABOUT... THE PRESIDENCY?

When it comes to caring about the presidency, most people do not need much encouragement. The president is our most important official. The president serves as the public face of the government, and, indeed, of the nation as a whole. Many people, however, believe the president is such a remote figure that nothing they can do will affect what he or she does. That is not always true. On many issues, your voice—combined, of course, with the voices of many others—can have an impact. Writing to the president is a traditional way for citizens to express their opinions. Every day, the White House receives several thousand letters and other communications.

THE PRESIDENT AND YOUR LIFE

The president can influence many issues that directly affect your life. For example, in 2010, many voices began to raise the question of whether anything could be done soon about reforming the nation's immigration policies. If any change to immigration policies were to succeed, it would need strong support from the president. Immigration might be a topic on which you have strong opinions. If you have opinions on a subject such as this, you may well want to "cast your vote" by adding your letter to the many others that the president receives on this issue.

(PhotoDisc by Getty Images)

Lobbying the president on an issue such as immigration may have an impact, but there may also be issues on which the president refuses to consider popular opinion. President George W. Bush refused to be swayed by the public over the war in Iraq, even after the voters turned Congress over to the Democrats, and President Obama did not consult the opinion polls when pushing through health-care reform. The determination of these presidents should remind you of the importance of learning about presidential candidates and their positions on important issues, and then making sure to vote. Once a candidate is elected, it is possible that neither public opinion nor Congress will be able to alter presidential policies to any significant degree.

HOW YOU CAN MAKE A DIFFERENCE

The most traditional form of communication with the White House is, of course, by letter. Letters to the president should be addressed to

The President of the United States
The White House
1600 Pennsylvania Avenue N.W.
Washington, DC 20500

Letters may be sent to the First Lady at the same address. Will you get an answer? Almost certainly. The White House mail room is staffed by volunteers and paid employees who sort the mail for the president and tally the public's concerns. You may receive a standard response to your comments or a more personal, detailed response.

It is possible to call the White House on the telephone and leave a message for the president or First Lady. To call the switchboard, call 202-456-1414. In most circumstances, a better choice is the round-the-clock comment line, which you can reach at 202-456-1111. When you call that number, an operator will take down your comments and forward them to the president's office.

The home page for the White House is

www.whitehouse.gov

It is designed to be entertaining and to convey information about the president. You can also send your comments and ideas to the White House using e-mail. Send comments to the president at

comments@whitehouse.gov

Address e-mail to the vice president at

vice_president@whitehouse.gov

questions for discussion and analysis

1. Review the discussion of executive privilege beginning on page 390. The history of executive privilege dates back to 1796, when President George Washington refused a request by the House for certain documents. Given the changes that have taken place since that time, should executive privilege be eliminated—or is it even more necessary today than it was at that time? What would be the costs to the nation if executive privilege were eliminated?

2. What characteristics do you think voters look for when choosing a president? Might these characteristics change as a result of changes in the political environment and the specific problems facing the nation? If you believe voters almost always look for the same characteristics when selecting a president, why is this? If voters seek somewhat different people as president depending on circumstances, which circumstances favor which kinds of leaders?

3. In recent years, many presidents have been lawyers by profession, though George W. Bush was a businessman, Ronald Reagan was an actor, and Jimmy Carter was a naval officer and peanut farmer. What advantages might these three presidents have gained from their career backgrounds? In particular, what benefits might Ronald Reagan have derived from his experience as an actor?

4. Refer to Figure 11–1 on page 388. Note that with a single exception, every eight years since 1961 the presidency has been taken over by the other party. The only exception is Reagan's first term—had Carter been reelected instead, the pattern would have been perfect: eight of Democrats Kennedy and Johnson, eight of Republicans Nixon and Ford, eight of Democrat Carter, eight of Republicans Reagan and G. H. W. Bush, eight of Democrat Clinton, eight of Republican G. W. Bush, and finally a Democrat again, Barack Obama. Why might the voters prefer to pick a president from the other party every few years?

key terms

advice and consent 378
appointment power 375
cabinet 393
chief diplomat 378
chief executive 375
chief legislator 381
chief of staff 394
civil service 375
commander in chief 377
constitutional power 385
diplomatic recognition 378
emergency power 388
executive agreement 381
Executive Office of the President (EOP) 394
executive privilege 390
expressed power 385
***Federal Register* 390**
head of state 373
impeachment 391
inherent power 385
kitchen cabinet 393
line-item veto 385
National Security Council (NSC) 395
Office of Management and Budget (OMB) 395
pardon 376
patronage 386
pocket veto 382
reprieve 376
signing statement 375
State of the Union message 381
statutory power 385
Twelfth Amendment 373
Twenty-fifth Amendment 397
veto message 382
War Powers Resolution 378
Washington community 387
White House Office 394

chapter summary

1. The office of the presidency in the United States, combining as it does the functions of chief of state and chief executive, was unique upon its creation. The framers of the Constitution were divided over whether the president should be a weak or a strong executive.

2. The requirements for the office of the presidency are outlined in Article II, Section 1, of the Constitution. The president's roles include both formal and informal duties. The roles of the president include head of state, chief executive, commander in chief, chief diplomat, chief legislator, and party chief.

3. As head of state, the president is ceremonial leader of the government. As chief executive, the president is bound to enforce the acts of Congress, the judgments of the federal courts, and treaties. The chief executive has the power of appointment and the power to grant reprieves and pardons.

4. As commander in chief, the president is the ultimate decision maker in military matters. As chief diplomat, the president recognizes foreign governments, negotiates treaties, signs agreements, and nominates and receives ambassadors.

5. The role of chief legislator includes recommending legislation to Congress, lobbying for the legislation, approving laws, and exercising the veto power. In addition to constitutional and inherent powers, the president has statutory powers written into law by Congress. Presidents are also leaders of their political parties. Presidents use their power to persuade and their access to the media to fulfill this function.

6. Presidents have a variety of special powers not available in the other branches of the government. These include emergency powers and the power to issue executive orders and invoke executive privilege.

7. Abuses of executive power are dealt with by Articles I and II of the Constitution, which authorize the House and Senate to impeach and remove the president, vice president, or other officers of the federal government for committing "Treason, Bribery, or other high Crimes and Misdemeanors."

8. The president receives assistance from the cabinet and from the Executive Office of the President (including the White House Office).

9. The vice president is the constitutional officer assigned to preside over the Senate and to assume the presidency in the event of the death, resignation, removal, or disability of the president. The Twenty-fifth Amendment, passed in 1967, established procedures to be followed in case of presidential incapacity and when filling a vacant vice presidency.

selected print & media resources

SUGGESTED READINGS

Bush, George W. ***Decision Points.*** New York: Crown, 2010. Bush's memoirs, which focus on various crises that he faced, are essential reading material for understanding the modern presidency.

Obama, Barack. ***The Audacity of Hope: Thoughts on Reclaiming the American Dream.*** New York: Crown, 2006. In contrast to Obama's first book, *Dreams from My Father,* this work is not autobiographical. Rather, it presents Obama's political philosophy and program. As discussed in this chapter, *The Audacity of Hope* provides much insight into Obama's presidency.

Remnick, David. ***The Bridge: The Life and Rise of Barack Obama.*** New York: Knopf, 2010. This work of biographical journalism is more complete and inevitably more objective than Obama's own autobiography.

Sugrue, Thomas J. ***Not Even Past: Barack Obama and the Burden of Race.*** Princeton, N.J.: Princeton University Press, 2010. Sugrue, a civil rights historian, examines Obama as an intellectual, politician, and policymaker, with an emphasis on his thinking about class and race.

Wilentz, Sean. ***The Age of Reagan: A History, 1974–2008.*** New York: Harper, 2008. Wilentz, a prize-winning Princeton historian, believes that the American Right has defined and shaped the nation's political history since the 1970s. While Wilentz himself is no conservative, he makes the argument that Ronald Reagan was one of our great presidents.

MEDIA RESOURCES

The American President—A 1995 romantic comedy with plenty of ideas about both romance and government. Michael Douglas is the widower president who falls for a lobbyist, played by Annette Bening. Douglas's comedic performance has been called his best.

CNN—Election 2000—A politically balanced look at the extraordinarily close presidential elections of 2000, which pitted Republican George W. Bush against Democrat Al Gore. The race was eventually settled by the United States Supreme Court. CNN's Bill Hemmer narrates this 2001 production.

Fahrenheit 9/11—Michael Moore's scathing 2004 critique of the Bush administration. The film has been called "one long political attack ad." It is also the highest-grossing documentary ever made. While the film may be biased, it is—like all of Moore's productions—entertaining.

My Life—President Bill Clinton's autobiography, essential source material on a fascinating national leader. Many people consider the print version of this work to be excessively padded, so it is best experienced through the Random House audiobook—the CD and cassette versions of *My Life* are nicely abridged. Clinton's own narration adds considerable flavor to the production.

Nixon—An excellent 1995 film exposing the events of Richard Nixon's troubled presidency. Anthony Hopkins plays the embattled but brilliant chief executive.

W.—**A fictionalized account of the life of George W. Bush. This 2008 film by director Oliver Stone features Josh Brolin as Bush. Given Stone's well-known left-wing politics, the depiction is surprisingly sympathetic.**

e-mocracy

THE PRESIDENCY AND THE INTERNET

Today, the Internet has become such a normal part of most Americans' lives that it is almost hard to imagine what life was like without it. Certainly, accessing the latest press releases from the White House was much more difficult twenty years ago than it is today. It was not until the Clinton administration (1993–2001) that access to the White House via the Internet became possible. President Bill Clinton supported making many White House documents available on the White House Web site.

Correspondence with the president and the First Lady quickly moved from ordinary handwritten letters to e-mail. During the Clinton presidency, most agencies of the government, as well as congressional offices, also began to provide access and information on the Internet. Today, you can access the White House Web site (see the following ***Logging On*** section) to find White House press releases, presidential State of the Union messages and other speeches, historical data on the presidency, and much more.

LOGGING ON

This site offers extensive information on the White House and the presidency:
www.whitehouse.gov

Inaugural addresses of American presidents from George Washington to Barack Obama can be found at
www.bartleby.com/124

You can find an excellent collection of data and maps describing all U.S. presidential elections at Dave Leip's Atlas of U.S. Presidential Elections. Go to
uselectionatlas.org

chapter 12

The Bureaucracy

chapter contents

< This oil recovery vessel was deployed to help clean up the BP oil spill in the Gulf of Mexico during the spring and summer of 2010. Many critics of the federal bureaucracy blamed the agency in charge of deep-water drilling for not diligently overseeing BP's wells. (Joe Raedle/Getty Images)

WHAT IF... ...parts of the federal government were privatized?

The National Hurricane Center is located in Miami, Florida. If it were privatized, who would pay for its services? (Mark Elias/Bloomberg via Getty Images)

BACKGROUND

Many federal government agencies, such as the Central Intelligence Agency, provide services that are highly sensitive. Others, such as the U.S. Postal Service, provide for-fee services that in effect compete with private-sector businesses. Agencies such as the U.S. Weather Service provide their services to the U.S. public at no charge. The Weather Service, nonetheless, is in competition with private weather prediction organizations. The Tennessee Valley Authority (TVA) generates electric power for a seven-state region at relatively low rates. It is in direct competition with private companies that generate electricity.

WHAT IF PARTS OF THE FEDERAL GOVERNMENT WERE PRIVATIZED?

In recent decades, governments throughout the world have sold government-owned agencies and companies to private investors. Certainly, we cannot imagine auctioning off the Central Intelligence Agency to the highest private bidder. Nonetheless, many federal government agencies could be privatized. There are many methods by which privatization could take place. One option would be to issue and sell shares directly to anybody who wants to buy them. Eventually, a group would control a large enough percentage of shares to elect a board of directors so that the group could control the newly privatized agency.

Another option would be to offer to sell government agencies to existing corporations that already might be engaged in similar lines of business. The U.S. Postal Service, for example, could be offered for sale to existing delivery companies such as FedEx and UPS. The TVA could be sold in parts to private electric utility companies. The Federal Aviation Administration could be offered for sale in small chunks. For example, each airport control system could be offered for sale to investors in that particular city.

NOT EVERYONE WOULD BENEFIT FROM PRIVATIZATION

Any federal government agency that became privatized would be subject to the rigors of the marketplace. If the TVA were privatized, it would be forced to take account of the true costs of all of its operations. Ultimately, it might have to raise the price of electricity to its customers.

Consider other examples. The U.S. Postal Service probably would be run more like FedEx and UPS. If it were, U.S. postal workers, who now have a very strong union, would find private postal management much less willing to accept union demands for higher wages. Mail delivery to rural Americans might become more expensive—a private postal service might have to charge the true cost of delivering mail to out-of-the-way residents and businesses. If rural mail delivery service to remote areas became extremely expensive, some people might move closer to town.

If the National Mediation Board were privatized, it would have to bill unions and businesses for the full cost of its mediation services in labor-management disputes. As a result, some labor-management disputes might take longer to resolve because the parties would be reluctant to pay for mediation services.

FOR CRITICAL ANALYSIS

1. Which additional agencies and government operations are likely candidates for privatization? Why?
2. Which government agencies and operations clearly are not candidates for privatization? Why?

Faceless bureaucrats—this image provokes a negative reaction from many, if not most, Americans. Polls consistently report that the majority of Americans support "less government." The same polls, however, report that the majority of Americans support almost every specific program that the government undertakes. The conflict between the desire for small government and the desire for benefits that only a large government can provide has been a constant feature of American politics. For example, the goal of preserving endangered species has widespread support. At the same time, many people believe that restrictions imposed under the Endangered Species Act violate the rights of landowners. Helping the elderly pay their medical bills is a popular objective, but hardly anyone enjoys paying the Medicare tax that supports this effort.

In this chapter, we describe the size, organization, and staffing of the federal bureaucracy. We review modern attempts at bureaucratic reform and the process by which Congress exerts ultimate control over the bureaucracy. We also discuss the bureaucracy's role in making rules and setting policy.

The Nature of Bureaucracy

A **bureaucracy** is the name given to an organization that is structured hierarchically to carry out specific functions. Generally, most bureaucracies are characterized by an organization chart. The units of the organization are divided according to the specialization and expertise of the employees.

Bureaucracy
An organization that is structured hierarchically to carry out specific functions.

Weberian Model
A model of bureaucracy developed by the German sociologist Max Weber, who viewed bureaucracies as rational, hierarchical organizations in which decisions are based on logical reasoning.

Public and Private Bureaucracies

We should not think of bureaucracy as unique to government. Any large corporation or university can be considered a bureaucratic organization. The fact is that the handling of complex problems requires a division of labor. Individuals must concentrate their skills on specific, well-defined aspects of a problem and depend on others to solve the rest of it.

Public, or government, bureaucracies differ from private organizations in some important ways, however. A private corporation has a single set of leaders—its board of directors. Public bureaucracies do not have a single set of leaders. Although the president is the chief administrator of the federal system, all agencies are subject to Congress for their funding, staffing, and, indeed, their continued existence. Public bureaucracies supposedly serve all citizens, while private ones serve private interests.

One other important difference between private corporations and government bureaucracies is that government bureaucracies are not organized to make a profit. Rather, they are supposed to perform their functions as efficiently as possible to conserve the taxpayers' dollars. Perhaps it is this ideal that makes citizens hostile toward government bureaucracy when they experience inefficiency and red tape.

Every modern president, at one time or another, has proclaimed that his administration was going to "fix government." All modern presidents also have put forth plans to end government waste and inefficiency (see Table 12–1 on the following page). Their success has been, in a word, underwhelming. Presidents generally have been powerless to significantly affect the structure and operation of the federal bureaucracy.

Models of Bureaucracy

Several theories have been offered to help us better understand the ways in which bureaucracies function. Each of these theories focuses on specific features of bureaucracies.

Weberian Model. The classic model, or **Weberian model,** of the modern bureaucracy was proposed by the German sociologist Max Weber.[1] He argued that the increasingly

German sociologist
Max Weber (1864–1920) created the classic model of the modern bureaucracy. Does the power in the classic bureaucracy flow upward, downward, or horizontally? (Hulton Archive/Getty Images)

1. Max Weber, *Theory of Social and Economic Organization,* ed. Talcott Parsons (New York: Oxford University Press, 1974).

complex nature of modern life, coupled with the steadily growing demands placed on governments by their citizens, made the formation of bureaucracies inevitable. According to Weber, most bureaucracies—whether in the public or private sector—are organized hierarchically and governed by formal procedures. The power in a bureaucracy flows from the top downward. Decision-making processes in bureaucracies are shaped by detailed technical rules that promote similar decisions in similar situations. Bureaucrats are specialists who attempt to resolve problems through logical reasoning and data analysis instead of "gut feelings" and guesswork. Individual advancement in bureaucracies is supposed to be based on merit rather than on political connections. Indeed, the modern bureaucracy, according to Weber, should be an apolitical organization.

Acquisitive Model. Other theorists do not view bureaucracies in terms as benign as Weber's. Some believe that bureaucracies are acquisitive in nature. Proponents of the **acquisitive model** argue that top-level bureaucrats will always try to expand, or at least to avoid any reductions in, the size of their budgets. Although government bureaucracies are not-for-profit enterprises, bureaucrats want to maximize the size of their budgets and staffs which are the most visible trappings of power in the public sector. These efforts are also prompted by the desire of bureaucrats to "sell" their products—such as national defense, public housing, or agricultural subsidies—to both Congress and the public.

Acquisitive Model
A model of bureaucracy that views top-level bureaucrats as seeking to expand the size of their budgets and staffs to gain greater power.

Monopolistic Model
A model of bureaucracy that compares bureaucracies to monopolistic business firms. Lack of competition in either circumstance leads to inefficient and costly operations.

Monopolistic Model. Because government bureaucracies seldom have competitors, some theorists have suggested that these bureaucratic organizations may be explained best by a **monopolistic model.** The analysis is similar to that used by economists to examine the behavior of monopolistic firms. Monopolistic bureaucracies—like monopolistic firms—essentially have no competitors and act accordingly. Because monopolistic bureaucracies usually are not penalized for chronic inefficiency, they have little reason to adopt cost-saving measures or to make more productive use of their resources. Some economists have argued that such problems can be cured only by privatizing certain bureaucratic functions, as we discussed in this chapter's opening *What If . . .* feature.

Bureaucracies Compared

The federal bureaucracy in the United States enjoys a greater degree of autonomy than do federal or national bureaucracies in many other nations. Much of the insularity that is commonly supposed to characterize the bureaucracy in this country may stem from the sheer size of the government organizations needed to implement an annual budget of almost $4 trillion. Because lines of authority often are not well defined, some bureaucracies may be able to operate with a significant degree of autonomy.

TABLE 12–1 Selected Presidential Plans to End Government Inefficiency

President	Plan
Lyndon Johnson (1963–1969)	Programming, planning, and budgeting systems
Richard Nixon (1969–1974)	Management by Objectives
Jimmy Carter (1977–1981)	Zero-Based Budgeting
Ronald Reagan (1981–1989)	President's Private Sector Survey on Cost Control (the Grace Commission)
George H. W. Bush (1989–1993)	Right-Sizing Government
Bill Clinton (1993–2001)	Reinventing Government
George W. Bush (2001–2009)	Performance-Based Budgeting
Barack Obama (2009–present)	Appointment of a chief performance officer

The federal nature of the American government also means that national bureaucracies regularly provide financial assistance to their state counterparts. Both the Department of Education and the Department of Housing and Urban Development, for example, distribute funds to their counterparts at the state level. In contrast, most bureaucracies in European countries have a top-down command structure so that national programs may be implemented directly at the lower level. This is due not only to the smaller size of most European countries but also to the fact that public ownership of such businesses as telephone companies, airlines, railroads, and utilities is far more common in Europe than in the United States.

This U.S. Postal Service clerk sorts mail at the main post office in St. Louis, Missouri. Why are postal services provided by the federal government? (Bill Greenblatt/UPI/Landov)

Even though the U.S. government owns relatively few enterprises, this does not mean that its bureaucracies are comparatively powerless. Indeed, there are many **administrative agencies** in the federal bureaucracy—such as the Environmental Protection Agency, the Nuclear Regulatory Commission, and the Securities and Exchange Commission—that regulate private companies.

The Size of the Bureaucracy

Administrative Agency
A federal, state, or local government unit established to perform a specific function. Administrative agencies are created and authorized by legislative bodies to administer and enforce specific laws.

In 1789, the new government's bureaucracy was minuscule. There were three departments—State (with nine employees), War (with two employees), and Treasury (with thirty-nine employees)—and the Office of the Attorney General (which later became the Department of Justice). The bureaucracy was still small in 1798. At that time, the secretary of state had seven clerks and spent a total of $500 (about $9,000 in 2011 dollars) on stationery and printing. In that same year, the Appropriations Act allocated $1.4 million (or $25.7 million in 2011 dollars) to the War Department.[2]

Times have changed, as we can see in Figure 12–1 at the top of the following page, which shows the various federal agencies and the number of civilian employees in each. Excluding military service members but including employees of the legislative and judicial branches, the federal bureaucracy consists of approximately 2.8 million employees. That number has remained relatively stable for the past several decades. It is somewhat deceiving, however, because many other individuals work directly or indirectly for the federal government as subcontractors or consultants and in other capacities, as you will read later in this chapter. In fact, according to some studies, the federal workforce greatly exceeds the number of official federal workers.

The figures for federal government employment are only part of the story. Figure 12–2 at the bottom left of the following page shows the growth in government employment at the federal, state, and local levels. Since 1982, this growth has been mainly at the state and local levels. If all government employees are included, about 16 percent of all civilian employment is accounted for by government. Costs are commensurately high. Spending by all levels of government was equivalent to 11 percent of the nation's gross domestic product in 1929. For fiscal year 2011, it exceeds 45 percent.

---

2. Leonard D. White, *The Federalists: A Study in Administrative History, 1789–1801* (New York: Free Press, 1948).

FIGURE 12–1 Federal Agencies and Their Respective Numbers of Civilian Employees

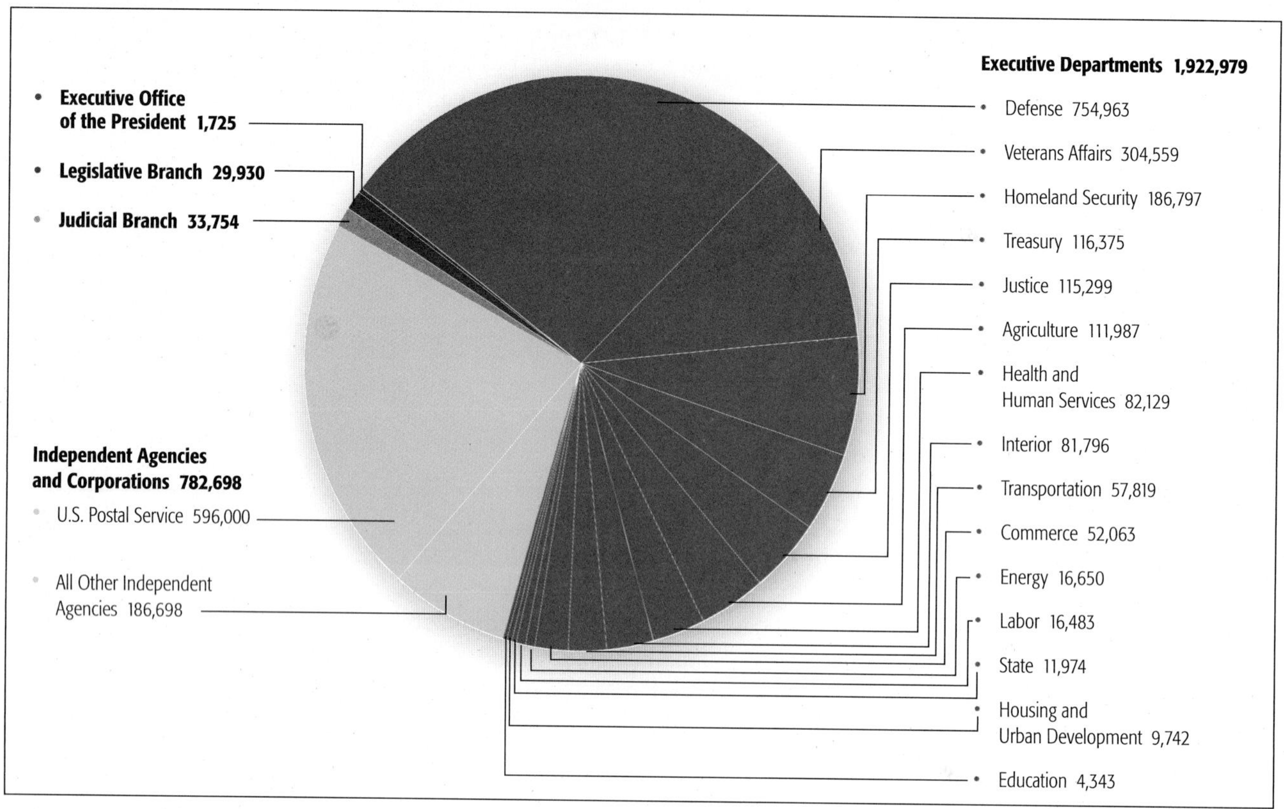

Sources: U.S. Office of Personnel Management, June 2010, and the U.S. Postal Service.

FIGURE 12–2 Government Employment at the Federal, State, and Local Levels

There are more local government employees than federal and state employees combined.

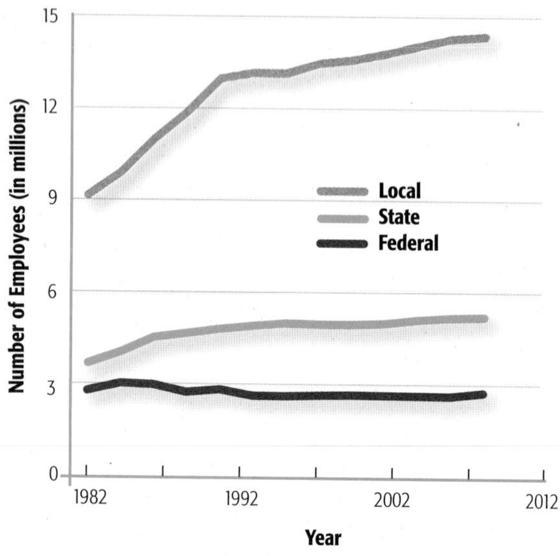

Sources: U.S. Census Bureau and U.S. Office of Personnel Management.

One factor driving up the amount of government spending has been legislation to combat the Great Recession that began in December 2007. Is the nation getting its money's worth from such policies? We address that question in this chapter's *Politics of Boom and Bust* feature on the facing page.

The Organization of the Federal Bureaucracy

Within the federal bureaucracy are a number of different types of government agencies and organizations. Figure 12–3 on page 412 outlines the several bodies within the executive branch, as well as the separate organizations that provide services to Congress, to the courts, and directly to the president. In Chapter 11, we discussed those agencies that are considered to be part of the Executive Office of the President.

The executive branch, which employs most of the government's staff, has four major types of structures. They are (1) cabinet departments, (2) independent executive agencies, (3) independent regulatory agencies, and (4) government corporations. Each has a distinctive relationship to the president, and some have unusual internal structures, overall goals, and grants of power.

THE POLITICS OF BOOM AND BUST

DID THE STIMULUS LEGISLATION CONTAIN TOO MUCH PORK?

In February 2009, President Obama signed an economic stimulus package initially valued at $787 billion. (It was estimated at $814 billion as of August 2010.) Of that sum, $284 billion consisted of tax breaks. A large share of the actual spending was distributed to state and local governments in response to grant requests. The stimulus bill soon became a centerpiece in the Republican campaign against the Obama administration, a campaign based largely on the accusation that the Democrats were spending dangerously excessive sums.

PORK, ANYONE?

Due to the way the bill was written, members of Congress had little scope for inserting pork—that is, specific requests for their constituents. With such a large part of the bill spent in response to state and local requests, however, much of the spending did resemble traditional pork. The Republicans also denounced specific items that were spelled out in the bill, such as:

- $8 billion for high-speed rail, possibly including a line between Disneyland and Las Vegas.
- $2 billion for the domestic lithium ion battery industry.
- $200 million for Filipino veterans, most of whom live abroad, for service in World War II.
- $600 million for new fuel-efficient cars for government employees.

As the spending was doled out, Republicans found other projects to criticize, including:

- $3.4 million for tunnels under a road in Florida to allow turtles to cross safely.
- $500,000 for Boston University research on whether meditation affects body temperature.

Republicans claimed that in the end, the stimulus package was little more than a collection of items from longtime Democratic wish lists.

THE STIMULUS DEFENDED

What, defenders responded, is wrong with wish lists? If you come into a small inheritance and decide to spend it all, will you spend it on things you long wanted but couldn't afford—or on things you'd never thought of before? Of course, you'll consult your wish list.

A more sweeping defense of the stimulus depends on an explanation of why the spending is helpful. The famous British economist John Maynard Keynes sought to determine how governments could combat the Great Depression of the 1930s. Keynes pointed out that in the Depression everyone was simultaneously trying to reduce both spending and borrowing. (Indeed, the same circumstances existed after September 2008.) Keynes argued that at such times, the government should step in to borrow—running up the deficit—and spend on projects that would rehire the unemployed and put idle resources back to work. Ideally, the government should spend the borrowed sums on useful projects, but the economy would be stimulated *even if the projects were pointless.* Keynes gave as an example hiring one huge team of workers to dig holes in the ground and a second huge team to fill them up.

This line of thought may sound absurd. Yet according to the traditional narrative (lately disputed by some economists), it was World War II that ended the Great Depression. From the Keynesian point of view, President Roosevelt's rather modest New Deal budget deficits just weren't large enough. Rather, the tremendous deficits incurred to finance World War II did the trick. From a purely economic standpoint, of course, the war was worse than pointless. It was a vast exercise in destruction. Tens of millions died. Much of Japan and continental Europe burned to the ground. Would that we could have dug holes instead.

BUT WAS KEYNES EVEN RIGHT?

Certain other economists believe that deficit-based spending and temporary tax reductions (such as one-time tax rebates) cannot actually stimulate the economy, even in the middle of a serious recession with much unemployment and idle resources. These economists believe that Keynes was wrong, and government spending can only move resources from one part of the economy to another. Such theories have significant support in university economics departments but are a minority view among politicians and their advisers.

FOR CRITICAL ANALYSIS

Large-scale initiatives, including government programs, often have consequences that their advocates did not anticipate. What unanticipated consequences could follow from the government's attempts to fight the recession? (*Hint:* What could be the long-range consequences of increased deficits?)

Cabinet Department
One of the fifteen major departments of the executive branch.

Line Organization
In the federal government, an administrative unit that is directly accountable to the president.

Cabinet Departments

The fifteen **cabinet departments** are the major service organizations of the federal government. They can also be described in management terms as **line organizations.** This means that they are directly accountable to the president and are responsible for performing government functions, such as printing money and training troops. These departments were created by Congress when the need for each department arose. The first department to be created was State, and the most recent one was Homeland Security, established in 2003. A president might ask that a new department be created or an old one abolished, but the president has no power to do so without legislative approval from Congress.

FIGURE 12–3 Organizational Chart of the Federal Government

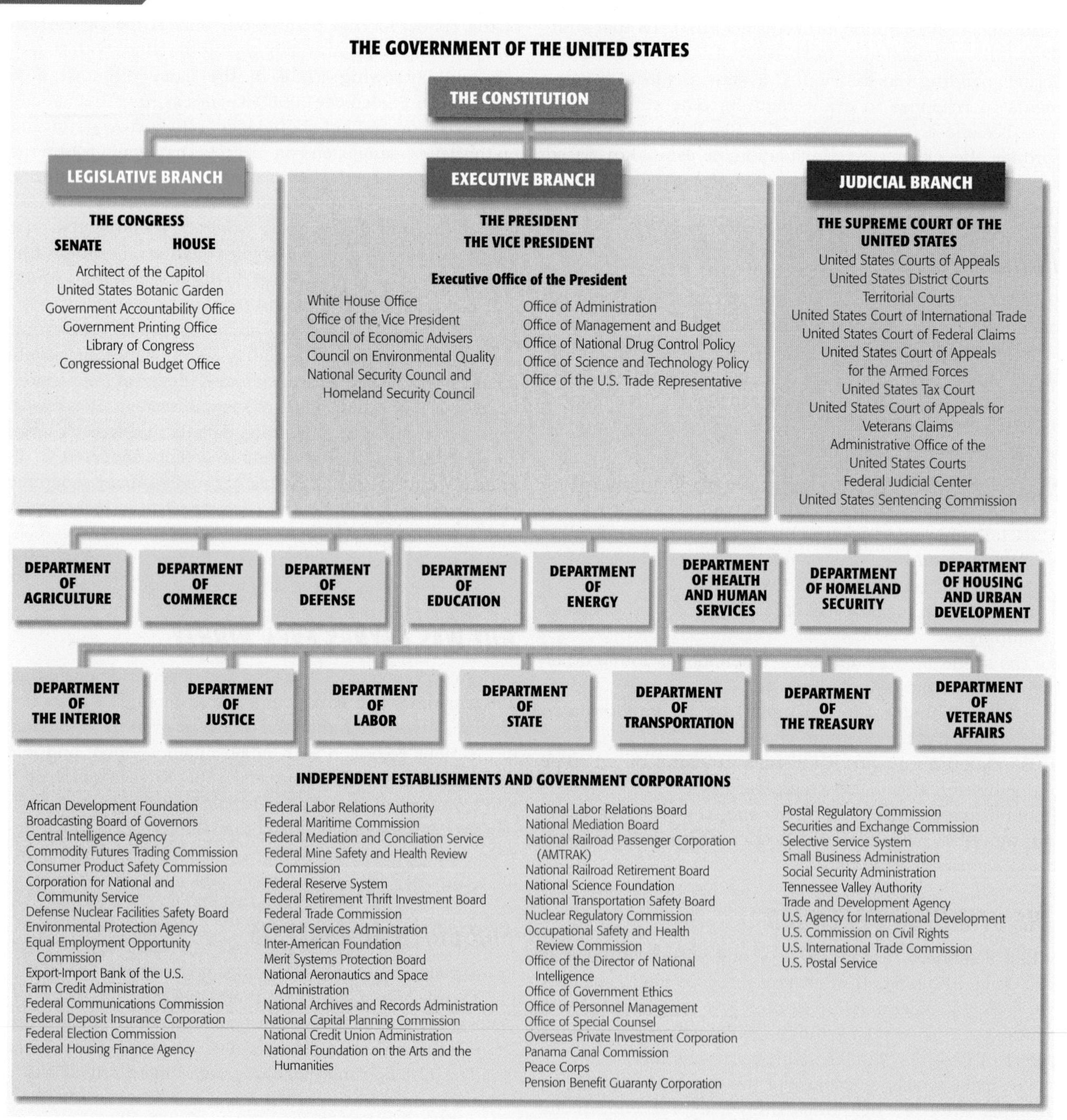

Source: *United States Government Manual*, 2009–2010 (Washington, D.C.: U.S. Government Printing Office, 2009).

Each department is headed by a secretary (except for the Justice Department, which is headed by the attorney general). Each department also has several levels of undersecretaries, assistant secretaries, and other personnel.

Presidents theoretically have considerable control over the cabinet departments, because presidents are able to appoint or fire all of the top officials. Even cabinet departments do not always respond to the president's wishes, though. One reason why presidents are frequently unhappy with their departments is that the entire bureaucratic structure below the top political levels is staffed by permanent employees, many of whom are committed to established programs or procedures and who resist change. Table 12–2 on the following page shows that each cabinet department employs thousands of individuals, only a handful of whom are under the control of the president. The table also describes some of the functions of each of the departments.

did you know?

That the federal, state, and local governments together spend about $1 billion every 78 minutes, every day of the year.

Independent Executive Agencies

Independent executive agencies are bureaucratic organizations that are not located within a department but report directly to the president, who appoints their chief officials. When a new federal agency is created—the Environmental Protection Agency, for example—Congress decides where it will be located in the bureaucracy. In recent decades, presidents often have asked that a new organization be kept separate or independent rather than added to an existing department, particularly if a department may be hostile to the agency's creation. Table 12–3 on page 415 describes the functions of several selected independent executive agencies.

Independent Executive Agency A federal agency that is not part of a cabinet department but reports directly to the president.

Independent Regulatory Agency An agency outside the major executive departments that is charged with making and implementing rules and regulations.

Independent Regulatory Agencies

The **independent regulatory agencies** are typically responsible for a specific type of public policy. Their function is to make and implement rules and regulations in a particular sphere of action to protect the public interest. The earliest such agency was the Interstate Commerce Commission (ICC), which was established in 1887 when Americans began to seek some form of government control over the rapidly growing business and industrial sector. This new form of organization, the independent regulatory agency, was supposed to make technical, nonpolitical decisions about rates, profits, and rules that would be for the benefit of all and that did not require congressional legislation. In the years that followed the creation of the ICC, other agencies were formed to regulate such areas as communication (the Federal Communications Commission) and nuclear power (the Nuclear Regulatory Commission). (The ICC was abolished in 1995.)

When the Federal National Mortgage Association (Fannie Mae) started to fail, the federal government took over. Who ultimately paid for its losses? (Mannie Garcia/Bloomberg via Getty Images)

TABLE 12–2 Executive Departments

Department and Year Established	Principal Functions	Selected Subagencies
State (1789) (11,974 employees)	Negotiates treaties; develops foreign policy; protects citizens abroad.	Passport Services Office; Bureau of Diplomatic Security; Foreign Service; Bureau of Human Rights and Humanitarian Affairs; Bureau of Consular Affairs.
Treasury (1789) (116,375 employees)	Pays all federal bills; borrows funds; collects federal taxes; mints coins and prints paper currency; supervises national banks.	Internal Revenue Service; U.S. Mint.
Interior (1849) (81,796 employees)	Supervises federally owned lands and parks; supervises Native American affairs.	U.S. Fish and Wildlife Service; National Park Service; Bureau of Indian Affairs; Bureau of Land Management.
Justice (1870)* (115,299 employees)	Furnishes legal advice to the president; enforces federal criminal laws; supervises federal prisons.	Federal Bureau of Investigation; Drug Enforcement Administration; Bureau of Prisons.
Agriculture (1889) (111,987 employees)	Provides assistance to farmers and ranchers; conducts agricultural research; works to protect forests.	Soil Conservation Service; Agricultural Research Service; Food Safety and Inspection Service; Federal Crop Insurance Corporation; Commodity Credit Corporation; Forest Service.
Commerce (1913)† (52,063 employees)	Grants patents and trademarks; conducts a national census; monitors the weather; protects the interests of businesses.	Bureau of the Census; Bureau of Economic Analysis; Patent and Trademark Office; National Oceanic and Atmospheric Administration.
Labor (1913)† (16,483 employees)	Administers federal labor laws; promotes the interests of workers.	Occupational Safety and Health Administration; Bureau of Labor Statistics; Employment Standards Administration; Employment and Training Administration.
Defense (1947)‡ (754,963 employees)	Manages the armed forces (army, navy, air force, and marines); operates military bases; is responsible for civil defense.	National Security Agency; Joint Chiefs of Staff; Departments of the Air Force, Navy, Army; Defense Advanced Research Projects Agency; Defense Intelligence Agency; the service academies.
Housing and Urban Development (1965) (9,742 employees)	Deals with the nation's housing needs; develops and rehabilitates urban communities; oversees resale of mortgages.	Government National Mortgage Association; Office of Community Planning and Development; Office of Fair Housing and Equal Opportunity.
Transportation (1967) (57,819 employees)	Finances improvements in mass transit; develops and administers programs for highways, railroads, and aviation.	Federal Aviation Administration; Federal Highway Administration; National Highway Traffic Safety Administration; Federal Transit Administration.
Energy (1977) (16,650 employees)	Promotes the conservation of energy and resources; analyzes energy data; conducts research and development.	Federal Energy Regulatory Commission; National Nuclear Security Administration.
Health and Human Services (1979)§ (82,129 employees)	Promotes public health; enforces pure food and drug laws; conducts and sponsors health-related research.	Food and Drug Administration; Public Health Service; Centers for Disease Control and Prevention; National Institutes of Health; Centers for Medicare and Medicaid Services.
Education (1979)§ (4,343 employees)	Coordinates federal programs and policies for education; administers aid to education; promotes educational research.	Office of Special Education and Rehabilitation Service; Office of Elementary and Secondary Education; Office of Postsecondary Education; Office of Vocational and Adult Education; Office of Federal Student Aid.
Veterans Affairs (1988) (304,559 employees)	Promotes the welfare of veterans of the U.S. armed forces.	Veterans Health Administration; Veterans Benefits Administration; National Cemetery Systems.
Homeland Security (2003) (186,797 employees)	Attempts to prevent terrorist attacks within the United States, control America's borders, and minimize the damage from natural disasters.	U.S. Customs and Border Protection; U.S. Coast Guard; Secret Service; Federal Emergency Management Agency; U.S. Citizenship and Immigration Services; U.S. Immigration Customs Enforcement.

*Formed from the Office of the Attorney General (created in 1789).
†Formed from the Department of Commerce and Labor (created in 1903).
‡Formed from the Department of War (created in 1789) and the Department of the Navy (created in 1798).
§Formed from the Department of Health, Education, and Welfare (created in 1953).

The Purpose and Nature of Regulatory Agencies. In practice, the regulatory agencies are administered independently of all three branches of government. They were set up because Congress felt it was unable to handle the complexities and technicalities required to carry out specific laws in the public interest. Regulatory agencies and commissions in fact combine some functions of all three branches of government—legislative, executive, and judicial. They are legislative in that they make rules that have the force of law. They are executive in that they provide for the enforcement of those rules. They are judicial in that they decide disputes involving the rules they have made.

did you know?

That the Commerce Department's U.S. Travel and Tourism Administration gave $440,000 in disaster relief loans to western ski resort operators because there hadn't been enough snow.

Heads of regulatory agencies and members of agency boards or commissions are appointed by the president with the consent of the Senate, although they do not report to the president. When an agency is headed by a board, not an individual, the members of the board cannot, by law, all be from the same political party. Members may be removed by the president only for causes specified in the law creating the agency. Presidents can influence regulatory agency behavior by appointing people of their own parties or individuals who share their political views when vacancies occur, in particular when the chair is vacant. For example, President George W. Bush placed people on the Federal Communications Commission (FCC) who shared his belief in the need to curb obscene language in the media. Not surprisingly, the FCC soon thereafter started to "crack down" on obscenities on the air. Table 12–4 on the following page describes the functions of selected independent regulatory agencies.

Agency Capture. Over the last several decades, some observers have concluded that regulatory agencies, although nominally independent, may in fact not always be so. They

TABLE 12–3 Selected Independent Executive Agencies

Name	Date Formed	Principal Functions
The Smithsonian Institution (4,930 employees)	1846	Runs the government's museums and the National Zoo.
Central Intelligence Agency (CIA) (number of employees not released)	1947	Gathers and analyzes political and military information about foreign countries; conducts covert operations outside the United States.
General Services Administration (GSA) (12,026 employees)	1949	Purchases and manages property of the federal government; acts as the business arm of the federal government in overseeing federal government spending projects; discovers overcharges in government programs.
National Science Foundation (NSF) (1,427 employees)	1950	Promotes scientific research; provides grants to all levels of schools for instructional programs in the sciences.
Small Business Administration (SBA) (3,872 employees)	1953	Protects the interests of small businesses; provides low-cost loans and management information to small businesses.
National Aeronautics and Space Administration (NASA) (18,354 employees)	1958	Is responsible for the U.S. space program, including the building, testing, and operating of space vehicles.
Environmental Protection Agency (EPA) (18,104 employees)	1970	Undertakes programs aimed at reducing air and water pollution; works with state and local agencies to help fight environmental hazards.
Social Security Administration (SSA)* (63,088 employees)	1995	Manages the government's Social Security programs, including Retirement and Survivors Insurance, Disability Insurance, Supplemental Security Income, and international programs.

*Separated from the Department of Health and Human Services (created in 1979).

Capture
The act by which an industry being regulated by a government agency gains direct or indirect control over agency personnel and decision makers.

contend that many agencies have been **captured** by the very industries and firms that they were supposed to regulate. For example, an agency may consult with leaders of an industry to be regulated and then be influenced by those leaders' suggestions when creating new rules. The results have been less competition rather than more competition, higher prices rather than lower prices, and less choice rather than more choice for consumers.

Deregulation and Reregulation. During the presidency of Jimmy Carter (1977–1981), significant deregulation (the removal of regulatory restraints—the opposite of regulation) was initiated. For example, Carter appointed a chairperson of the Civil Aeronautics Board (CAB) who gradually eliminated regulation of airline fares and routes. Deregulation continued under President Ronald Reagan (1981–1989), who eliminated the CAB in January 1985.

During the administration of George H. W. Bush (1989–1993), calls for reregulation of many businesses increased. Indeed, during that administration, the Americans with Disabilities Act of 1990, the Civil Rights Act of 1991, and the Clean Air Act Amendments of 1991, all of which increased or changed the regulation of many businesses, were passed. Additionally, the Cable Reregulation Act of 1992 was passed.

Under President Bill Clinton (1993–2001), the Interstate Commerce Commission was eliminated, and the banking and telecommunications industries, along with many other sectors of the economy, were deregulated. At the same time, there was extensive regulation to protect the environment, a trend somewhat reversed by the George W. Bush administration.

Regulation Today. After the financial crisis of September 2008, many people saw inadequate regulation of the financial industry as a major cause of the nation's economic difficulties. During President Obama's administration, therefore, reregulation of that industry became a major issue. After intense debate, Congress passed a comprehensive financial industry regulation plan in 2010.

TABLE 12–4 Selected Independent Regulatory Agencies

Name	Date Formed	Principal Functions
Federal Reserve System Board of Governors (Fed) (1,873 employees)	1913	Determines policy on interest rates, credit availability, and the money supply.
Federal Trade Commission (FTC) (1,131 employees)	1914	Prevents businesses from engaging in unfair trade practices; stops the formation of monopolies in the business sector; protects consumer rights.
Securities and Exchange Commission (SEC) (3,699 employees)	1934	Regulates the nation's stock exchanges, in which shares of stocks are bought and sold; requires full disclosure of the financial profiles of companies that wish to sell stocks and bonds to the public.
Federal Communications Commission (FCC) (1,850 employees)	1934	Regulates all communications by telegraph, cable, telephone, radio, and television.
National Labor Relations Board (NLRB) (1,614 employees)	1935	Protects employees' rights to join unions and bargain collectively with employers; attempts to prevent unfair labor practices by both employers and unions.
Equal Employment Opportunity Commission (EEOC) (2,178 employees)	1964	Works to eliminate discrimination based on religion, gender, race, color, national origin, age, or disability; examines claims of discrimination.
Nuclear Regulatory Commission (NRC) (4,094 employees)	1974	Ensures that electricity-generating nuclear reactors in the United States are built and operated safely; regularly inspects the operations of such reactors.

Americans have had conflicting views about the amount of regulation that is appropriate for various industries ever since the government began to undertake serious regulatory activities. Many people find regulation to be contrary to the spirit of free enterprise and the American tradition of individualism. Yet in cases such as BP's Deepwater Horizon oil spill disaster in the Gulf of Mexico in April 2010, citizens of all political stripes were outraged to learn that the relevant regulatory agency, the Minerals Management Service, had failed to do its job. Even so, real limits exist as to the ability of the federal government to protect the public, as you will learn in the feature *Politics and . . . National Security: Bureaucrats Can't Protect Us from Every Threat* on the following page.

did you know?

That the Pentagon and the Central Intelligence Agency once spent more than $11 million on psychics who were supposed to provide special insights regarding various foreign threats.

Government Corporations

Another form of bureaucratic organization in the United States is the **government corporation.** Although the concept is borrowed from the world of business, there are important differences between public and private corporations.

Government Corporation
An agency of government that administers a quasi-business enterprise. These corporations are used when activities are primarily commercial.

A private corporation has shareholders (stockholders) who elect a board of directors, who in turn choose the corporate officers, such as president and vice president. When a private corporation makes a profit, it must pay taxes (unless it avoids them through various legal loopholes). It then distributes the after-tax profits to shareholders as dividends, or plows the profits back into the corporation to make new investments, or both.

A government corporation has a board of directors and managers, but it does not have any stockholders. We cannot buy shares of stock in a government corporation, and if the entity makes a profit, it does not distribute the profit as dividends. Also, if it makes a profit, it does not have to pay taxes. The profits remain in the corporation. Table 12–5 below describes the functions of selected government corporations.

Bankruptcy. The federal government can also take control of a private corporation in a number of circumstances. One is bankruptcy. When a company files for bankruptcy, it asks a federal judge for relief from its creditors. The judge, operating under bankruptcy laws established by Congress (as specified in the Constitution), is ultimately responsible for the

TABLE 12–5 Selected Government Corporations

Name	Date Formed	Principal Functions
Tennessee Valley Authority (TVA) (11,498 employees)	1933	Operates a Tennessee River control system and generates power for a seven-state region and for the U.S. aeronautics and space programs; promotes the economic development of the Tennessee Valley region; controls floods and promotes the navigability of the Tennessee River.
Federal Deposit Insurance Corporation (FDIC) (5,276 employees)	1933	Insures individuals' bank deposits up to $250,000; oversees the business activities of banks.
Export-Import Bank of the United States (Ex-Im Bank) (374 employees)	1933	Promotes the sale of American-made goods abroad; grants loans to foreign purchasers of American products.
National Railroad Passenger Corporation (AMTRAK) (19,000 employees)	1970	Provides a national and intercity rail passenger service; controls 22,000 miles of track and serves 500 communities.
U.S. Postal Service (USPS)* (596,000 employees)	1970	Delivers mail throughout the United States and its territories; is the largest government corporation.

*Formed from the Post Office Department (an executive department) in 1970.

fate of the enterprise. When a bank fails, the government has a special interest in protecting customers who have deposited funds with the bank. For that reason, the failing institution is taken over by the Federal Deposit Insurance Corporation (FDIC), which ensures continuity of service to bank customers.

Government Ownership of Private Enterprises. The federal government can also obtain partial or complete ownership of a private corporation by purchasing its stock. Before 2008, such takeovers were rare, although they occasionally happened. When

POLITICS AND... national security

BUREAUCRATS CAN'T PROTECT US FROM EVERY THREAT

Since the terrorist attacks of September 11, 2001, billions have been spent to create a bureaucracy designed to protect Americans. Thousands of pages of regulations concerning airline travel as well as cargo movement into the United States have been written and applied. We are told by many, including those in government, that terrorism is the greatest threat facing the American people.

TERRORISM IS ONE THREAT AMONG OTHERS

While not downplaying the seriousness of the terrorist threat, we should put it into perspective. Compared to the few thousands who have died during and since 9/11, each year almost 40,000 Americans perish on our highways. Each year, between 30,000 and 50,000 of us die from seasonal flu. Each year, thousands die in household accidents. Terrorism is real, but so, too, are the other threats to our lives.

THE BUREAUCRATIC RESPONSE TO TERRORISM

Why must we take off our shoes to fly? Why the three-ounce bottles of shampoo and conditioner? Do such measures really help keep us safe? Possibly not. If once upon a time a terrorist smuggled explosives onto a plane in his shoes, the next terrorist will probably try something else. But for the Transportation Security Agency and its staff members, the worst thing that could possibly happen is a repetition of a successful attack. After such a repetition, no excuses, however reasonable, for having failed to prevent the attack would be accepted. So shoes will be checked forever after.

Some people, however, believe that current airport security measures send the wrong message. In *Time,* Amanda Ripley wrote: "By definition, terrorism succeeds by making us feel powerless. It is more often a psychological threat than an existential one. The authorities compound the damage when they overreact—by subjecting grandmothers to pat-downs and making it intolerable to travel."[a]

ORDINARY AMERICANS ARE KEY TO OUR SECURITY

The only successful antiterrorist action on September 11, 2001, was undertaken not by the government, but by the passengers of United Airlines Flight 93. (The passengers learned that their captors were on a suicide mission through surreptitious cell phone calls.) Since 2001, regular people without training or weapons have been primarily responsible for thwarting attacks aboard at least five commercial airplanes. The latest was on Christmas Day 2009 when passengers and flight attendants subdued the "underwear bomber" on board a plane flying into Detroit. The "thanks" that the passengers and crew received in Detroit was to be held in the baggage area for more than five hours without food—or the right to use their cell phones.

Realistically, it is ordinary people who are best positioned to see and respond to terrorist activities, according to Stephen Flynn, president of the Center for National Policy. Flynn does believe that better technology helps, but it is not enough. Flynn's solution? The government should "support regular people in being able to withstand, rapidly recover, and adapt to foreseeable risk."

FOR CRITICAL ANALYSIS

Our presidents have repeatedly assured us that the federal government is doing everything in its power to keep us safe. What limits the government's ability to do this?

a. Amanda Ripley, "The Lesson: Passengers Are Not Helpless," *Time,* January 11, 2010, p. 31.

Continental Illinois, then the nation's seventh-largest bank, failed in 1984, the FDIC wound up in control of the institution for ten years before it could find a buyer. When the federal government assumes ongoing control of a business, the action is called **nationalization.** Significantly, the FDIC nationalized Continental Illinois by purchasing *preferred stock* newly issued by the bank. **Preferred stock** is a special type of investment that typically pays interest but does not let the holders vote for the corporation's board of directors. By purchasing the stock, the FDIC pumped $4.5 billion of new capital—provided by the taxpayers—into the bank, ensuring its solvency.

Nationalization
The takeover of a business enterprise by the national government. Recently, the word has been used to describe temporary takeovers that are similar to bankruptcy proceedings.

Preferred Stock
A special share of ownership in a corporation that typically confers no right to vote for the company's board of directors, but does pay interest.

The Continental Illinois rescue provided a blueprint for the massive bank bailout initiated by Henry Paulson, President George W. Bush's Treasury secretary, in October 2008. Through 2010, the Treasury, using the Troubled Asset Relief Program (TARP), bought $466.5 billion in preferred stock and similar instruments from 829 businesses, including banks, automobile companies, and other firms. The largest businesses received tens of billions of dollars in new capital. By mid-2010, $185 billion had been repaid (mostly by banks), plus $24 billion in interest.

Some critics thought that the steps taken by Paulson and Obama's Treasury secretary Timothy Geithner were inadequate and that the government should have nationalized the troubled institutions instead. The government would then have settled the bad debts, wiped out the stockholders, and eventually sold the purified institutions back to private investors. At least where banks were concerned, such radical steps proved unnecessary. The nation's major banks were able to stabilize themselves by making large profits on loans in 2009 and 2010.

Government-Sponsored Enterprises. An additional type of corporation is the government-sponsored enterprise, a business created by the federal government itself, which then sells part or all of the corporation's stock to private investors. Up until 2008, the leading examples of this kind of company were the Federal Home Loan Mortgage Corporation, known as Freddie Mac, and the Federal National Mortgage Association, commonly known as Fannie Mae. Both of these firms buy mortgages from banks and bundle them into securities that can be sold to investors. When the housing market collapsed during the Great Recession, so—eventually—did Freddie Mac and Fannie Mae.

Investors had always assumed that the federal government backed up the obligations of the two enterprises, even though the government had never issued an explicit guarantee. On September 7, 2008, the implicit guarantee became real when Treasury secretary Paulson placed the two mortgage giants under a federal "conservatorship." Over time, $145 billion in fresh capital—also provided by the taxpayers—was pumped into them, in part through purchases of preferred and common stock. So far, the companies have paid $10 billion in interest on the government's investments. They have returned none of the $145 billion, however, and the Congressional Budget Office has estimated that the ultimate cost to the taxpayers may reach $350 billion, or higher.

Staffing the Bureaucracy

There are two categories of bureaucrats: political appointees and civil servants. As noted earlier, the president is able to make political appointments to most of the top jobs in the federal bureaucracy. The president can also appoint ambassadors to foreign posts. All of the jobs that are considered "political plums" and that usually go to the politically well connected are listed in *Policy and Supporting Positions,* a book published by the Government Printing Office after each presidential election. Informally (and appropriately), this has been called "The Plum Book." The rest of the national government's employees belong to the civil service and obtain their jobs through a much more formal process.

Political Appointees

To fill the positions listed in "The Plum Book,"[3] the president and the president's advisers solicit suggestions from politicians, businesspersons, and other prominent individuals. Appointments to these positions offer the president a way to pay off outstanding political debts. Presidents often use ambassadorships to reward individuals for their campaign contributions. But the president must also take into consideration such things as the candidate's work experience, intelligence, political affiliations, and personal characteristics. Presidents have differed in the importance they attach to appointing women and minorities to plum positions.

Difficulties in Making Appointments. We should note that just because the president has the power to appoint a government official does not mean that such an appointment will pass muster. Before making any nominations, the administration requires potential appointees to undergo a detailed screening process and answer questions such as the following: What are your accomplishments? Did you ever *not* pay taxes for your nannies or housekeepers? What kinds of investments have you made? What have your past partisan affiliations been?

Such a process takes months, and after completing it, the appointees must be confirmed by the Senate. Even with such a screening process, the Obama administration made some serious errors. For example, the president's appointment of Tom Daschle, formerly the Senate Democratic leader, to be secretary of health and human services, collapsed when it was discovered that he had failed to pay taxes on a car and driver assigned to him while he served as a lobbyist. In fact, an unusual number of Obama appointees had tax problems. Treasury secretary Timothy Geithner was confirmed despite his tax issues, however. Former New Mexico governor Bill Richardson had to withdraw his nomination to the post of secretary of commerce because he was the subject of a grand jury investigation into influence peddling. (Richardson was later cleared.) At least one nominee withdrew because of straightforward policy differences, however—Judd Gregg, a Republican senator from New Hampshire and candidate for the Commerce position, decided that his philosophy was simply not compatible with that of a Democratic administration.

The Food and Drug Administration can force pharmacists to remove diet drugs from their shelves if those drugs have dangerous side effects. What type of agency is the FDA? (Allan Tannenbaum//Time Life Pictures/Getty Images)

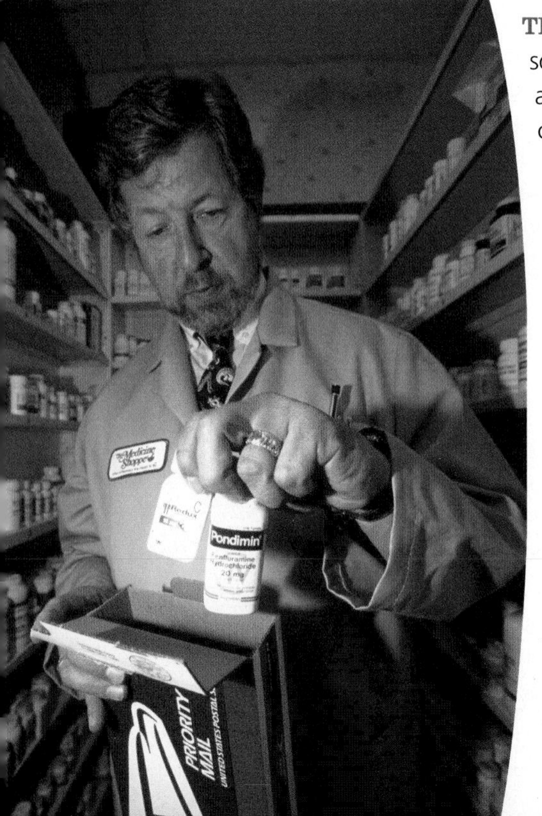

The Aristocracy of the Federal Government. Political appointees are in some sense the aristocracy of the federal government. But their powers, although appearing formidable on paper, are often exaggerated. Like the president, a political appointee will occupy her or his position for a comparatively brief time. Political appointees often leave office before the president's term actually ends. In fact, the average term of service for political appointees is less than two years. As a result, most appointees have little background for their positions and may be mere figureheads. Often, they only respond to the paperwork that flows up from below. Additionally, the professional civil servants who make up the permanent civil service may not feel compelled to carry out their current boss's directives quickly, because they know that he or she will not be around for very long.

The Difficulty in Firing Civil Servants. This inertia is compounded by the fact that it is very difficult to discharge civil servants. In recent years, fewer than one-tenth of 1 percent of federal employees have been fired for incompetence. Because discharged employees may appeal their dismissals, many months or even years can pass before the issue is resolved conclusively. This occupational

3. See Table 11–1 on page 376 for a list of the number of positions available for presidential appointments in the most recent edition of "The Plum Book."

rigidity helps to ensure that most political appointees, no matter how competent or driven, will not be able to exert much meaningful influence over their subordinates, let alone implement dramatic changes in the bureaucracy itself.

President James A. Garfield was assassinated in 1881 by a disappointed office seeker, Charles J. Guiteau. The long-term effect of this event was to replace the spoils system with a permanent career civil service. This process began with the passage of the Pendleton Act in 1883, which established the Civil Service Commission. (Library of Congress)

History of the Federal Civil Service

When the federal government was formed in 1789, it had no career public servants but rather consisted of amateurs who were almost all Federalists. When Thomas Jefferson took over as president, few federal administrative jobs were held by members of his party, so he fired more than one hundred officials and replaced them with his own supporters. Then, for the next twenty-five years, a growing body of federal administrators gained experience and expertise, becoming in the process professional public servants. These administrators stayed in office regardless of who was elected president. The bureaucracy had become a self-maintaining, long-term element within government.

To the Victor Belong the Spoils. When Andrew Jackson took over the White House in 1828, he could not believe how many appointed officials (appointed before he became president, that is) were overtly hostile toward him and his Democratic Party. Because the bureaucracy was reluctant to carry out his programs, Jackson did the obvious: he fired federal officials—more than had been fired by all of his predecessors combined. The **spoils system**—an application of the principle that to the victor belong the spoils—became the standard method of filling federal positions. Whenever a new president was elected from a party different from the party of the previous president, there would be an almost complete turnover in the staffing of the federal government.

Spoils System
The awarding of government jobs to political supporters and friends.

Merit System
The selection, retention, and promotion of government employees on the basis of competitive examinations.

Pendleton Act (Civil Service Reform Act)
An act that established the principle of employment on the basis of merit and created the Civil Service Commission to administer the personnel service.

Civil Service Commission
The initial central personnel agency of the national government; created in 1883.

The Civil Service Reform Act of 1883. Jackson's spoils system survived for a number of years, but it became increasingly corrupt. Also, as the size of the bureaucracy increased by 300 percent between 1851 and 1881, the cry for civil service reform became louder. Reformers began to look to the example of several European countries—in particular, Germany, which had established a professional civil service that operated under a **merit system** in which job appointments were based on competitive examinations.

In 1883, the **Pendleton Act**—or **Civil Service Reform Act**—was passed, placing the first limits on the spoils system. The act established the principle of employment on the basis of open, competitive examinations and created the **Civil Service Commission** to administer the personnel service. Only 10 percent of federal employees were covered by the merit system initially. Later laws, amendments, and executive orders, however, increased the coverage to more than 90 percent of federal employees. The effects of these reforms were felt at all levels of government.

The Supreme Court strengthened the civil service system in *Elrod v. Burns*[4] in 1976 and *Branti v. Finkel*[5] in 1980. In those two cases, the Court used the First Amendment to forbid government officials from discharging or threatening to discharge public employees solely for not being supporters of the political party in power unless party affiliation is an appropriate requirement for the position. Additional

did you know?

That according to a 2010 report, federal employees earn an average of $108,476 in total compensation (including benefits) for jobs equivalent to those in the private sector, while the comparable private-sector employees average $69,928.

4. 427 U.S. 347 (1976).
5. 445 U.S. 507 (1980).

enhancements to the civil service system were added in *Rutan v. Republican Party of Illinois*[6] in 1990. The Court's ruling effectively prevented the use of partisan political considerations as the basis for hiring, promoting, or transferring most public employees. An exception was permitted, however, for senior policymaking positions, which usually go to officials who will support the programs of the elected leaders.

The Civil Service Reform Act of 1978. In 1978, the Civil Service Reform Act abolished the Civil Service Commission and created two new federal agencies to perform its duties. To administer the civil service laws, rules, and regulations, the act created the Office of Personnel Management (OPM). The OPM is empowered to recruit, interview, and test potential government workers and determine who should be hired. The OPM makes recommendations to the individual agencies as to which persons meet the standards (typically, the top three applicants for a position), and the agencies then decide whom to hire. To oversee promotions, employees' rights, and other employment matters, the act created the Merit Systems Protection Board (MSPB). The MSPB evaluates charges of wrongdoing, hears employee appeals from agency decisions, and can order corrective action against agencies and employees.

Federal Employees and Political Campaigns. In 1933, when President Franklin D. Roosevelt set up his New Deal, an army of civil servants was hired to staff the many new agencies that were created. Because the individuals who worked in these agencies owed their jobs to the Democratic Party, it seemed natural for them to campaign for Democratic candidates. The Democrats who controlled Congress in the mid-1930s did not object. But in 1938, a coalition of conservative Democrats and Republicans took control of Congress and forced through the Hatch Act—or Political Activities Act—of 1939. The act prohibited federal employees from actively participating in the political management of campaigns. It also forbade the use of federal authority to influence nominations and elections and outlawed the use of bureaucratic rank to pressure federal employees to make political contributions.

The Hatch Act created a controversy that lasted for decades. Many contended that the act deprived federal employees of their First Amendment freedoms of speech and association. In 1972, a federal district court declared the act unconstitutional. The United States Supreme Court, however, reaffirmed the challenged portion of the act in 1973, stating that the government's interest in preserving a nonpartisan civil service was so great that the prohibitions should remain.[7] Twenty years later, Congress addressed the criticisms of the Hatch Act by passing the Federal Employees Political Activities Act of 1993. This act, which amended the Hatch Act, lessened the harshness of the 1939 act in several ways. Among other things, the 1993 act allowed federal employees to run for office in nonpartisan elections, participate in voter-registration drives, make campaign contributions to political organizations, and campaign for candidates in partisan elections.

Modern Attempts at Bureaucratic Reform

As long as the federal bureaucracy exists, there will continue to be attempts to make it more open, efficient, and responsive to the needs of U.S. citizens. The most important actual and proposed reforms in the last several decades include sunshine and sunset laws, privatization, incentives for efficiency, and more protection for so-called whistleblowers.

---

6. 497 U.S. 62 (1990).
7. *United States Civil Service Commission v. National Association of Letter Carriers,* 413 U.S. 548 (1973).

Sunshine Laws before and after 9/11

In 1976, Congress enacted the **Government in the Sunshine Act.** It required for the first time that all multiheaded federal agencies—agencies headed by a committee instead of an individual—hold their meetings regularly in public session. The bill defined meetings as almost any gathering, formal or informal, of agency members, including a conference telephone call. The only exceptions to this rule of openness are discussions of matters such as court proceedings or personnel problems, and these exceptions are specifically listed in the bill. Sunshine laws now exist at all levels of government.

"Who do I see to get big government off my back?" (©The New Yorker Collection, 2006. Mick Stevens, from cartoonbank.com. All Rights Reserved.)

Government in the Sunshine Act
A law that requires all committee-directed federal agencies to conduct their business regularly in public session.

Information Disclosure. Sunshine laws are consistent with the policy of information disclosure that for decades has been supported by the government for both the public and private sectors. For example, beginning in the 1960s, a number of consumer protection laws have required that certain information be disclosed to consumers when purchasing homes, borrowing funds, and the like. In 1966, the federal government passed the Freedom of Information Act (FOIA), which required federal government agencies, with certain exceptions, to disclose to individuals, on their request, any information about them contained in government files. (You will learn more about this act in the *Why Should You Care . . .* feature at the end of this chapter.)

FOIA requests are not just helpful to individuals. Indeed, the major beneficiaries of the act have been news organizations, which have used it to uncover government waste, scandals, and incompetence. For example, reporters learned that much of the $5 billion allocated to help small businesses recover from the effects of the 9/11 terrorist attacks went to companies that did not need such relief, including a South Dakota country radio station, a dog boutique in Utah, an Oregon winery, and a variety of Dunkin' Donuts and Subway franchises. After studying Veterans Administration records, the *Sacramento Bee* claimed in 2007 that the government was woefully unprepared to care for the flood of veterans returning from Iraq and Afghanistan with post-traumatic stress disorder. A Utah newspaper discovered through FOIA requests that a former air force acquisitions officer pressured a Utah airbase into approving contract changes that improperly benefited the Boeing Corporation. The former acquisitions officer went to prison.

Curbs on Information Disclosure. Since the terrorist attacks of September 11, 2001, the trend toward government in the sunshine and information disclosure has been reversed at both the federal and state levels. Within weeks after September 11, 2001, numerous federal agencies removed hundreds, if not thousands, of documents from Internet sites, public libraries, and the reading rooms found in various federal government departments. Information contained in some of the documents included diagrams of power plants and pipelines, structural details on dams, and safety plans for chemical plants. The military also immediately began restricting information about its current and planned activities, as did the Federal Bureau of Investigation. These agencies were concerned that terrorists could make use of this information to plan attacks. The federal government has also gone back into the archives to remove an increasing quantity of not only sensitive material but also sometimes seemingly unimportant information.

These members of North Dakota's Air and Army National Guard helped with flood prevention efforts in North Dakota. Under what circumstances might National Guard units undertake military activities within the United States? (AP Photo/ *The Forum*, Dave Walls)

In making official documents inaccessible to the public, the federal government was ahead of state and local governments, but they quickly followed suit. State and local governments control and supervise police forces, dams, electricity sources, and water supplies. Consequently, it is not surprising that many state and local governments followed in the footsteps of the federal government in curbing access to certain public records and information.

Such actions constitute a broad attempt by state and local governments to keep terrorists from learning about local emergency preparedness plans. It is possible, however, that as soon as the public starts to believe that the threat has lessened, some groups will take state and local governments to court in an effort to increase public access to state and local records by reimposing the sunshine laws that were in effect before 9/11.

Sunset Laws

Potentially, the size and scope of the federal bureaucracy can be controlled through **sunset legislation,** which places government programs on a definite schedule for congressional consideration. Unless Congress specifically reauthorizes a particular federally operated program at the end of a designated period, the program will be terminated automatically; that is, its sun will set.

The idea of sunset legislation was initially suggested by Franklin D. Roosevelt when he created the host of New Deal agencies in the 1930s. His assistant, William O. Douglas, recommended that each agency's charter should include a provision allowing for its termination in ten years. Only an act of Congress could revitalize it. The proposal was never adopted. It was not until 1976 that a state legislature—Colorado's—adopted sunset legislation for state regulatory commissions, giving them a life of six years before their suns set. Today, most states have some type of sunset law.

Privatization

Another approach to bureaucratic reform is **privatization,** which occurs when government services are replaced by services from the private sector. For example, the government has contracted with private firms to operate prisons. Supporters of privatization argue that some services could be provided more efficiently by the private sector. Another scheme is to furnish vouchers to "clients" in lieu of services. For example, instead of supplying housing, the government could offer vouchers that recipients could use to "pay" for housing in privately owned buildings.

The privatization, or contracting-out, strategy has been most successful on the local level. Municipalities, for example, can form contracts with private companies for such activities as trash collection. This approach is not a cure-all, however, because many functions, particularly on the national level, cannot be contracted out in any meaningful way. For example, the federal government could not contract out most of the Defense Department's functions to private firms (although the U.S. military has contracted out many services in Iraq and elsewhere).

Sunset Legislation Laws requiring that existing programs be reviewed regularly for their effectiveness and be terminated unless specifically extended as a result of these reviews.

Privatization The replacement of government services with services provided by private firms.

The increase in the amount of government work being contracted out to the private sector has led to significant controversy in recent years. Some have criticized the lack of competitive bidding for many contracts that the government has awarded to contractors. Another concern is the perceived lack of government oversight of the work done by private contractors. In order to exercise more oversight, in 2007 the government decided to have a study done to evaluate the performance of private contractors. Some reporters noted the irony of the government's decision to have a private contractor undertake this study. For a further discussion of contracting out government work to the private sector, see the *Which Side Are You On?* feature on the following page.

did you know?

That federal officials spent $333,000 building a deluxe, earthquake-proof outhouse for hikers in Pennsylvania's remote Delaware Water Gap recreation area.

Incentives for Efficiency and Productivity

An increasing number of state governments are beginning to experiment with a variety of schemes to run their operations more efficiently and capably. They focus on maximizing the efficiency and productivity of government workers by providing incentives for improved performance. For example, many governors, mayors, and city administrators are considering ways in which government can be made more entrepreneurial. Some of the most promising measures have included such tactics as permitting agencies that do not spend their entire budgets to keep some of the difference and rewarding employees with performance-based bonuses.

Government Performance and Results Act. At the federal level, the Government Performance and Results Act of 1997 was designed to improve efficiency in the federal workforce. The act required that all government agencies (except the Central Intelligence Agency) describe their goals and establish methods for determining whether those goals are met. Goals may be broadly crafted (for example, reducing the time it takes to test a new drug before allowing it to be marketed) or narrowly crafted (for example, reducing the number of times a telephone rings before it is answered).

Bureaucracy Has Changed Little. Efforts to improve bureaucratic efficiency are supported by the assertion that although society and industry have changed enormously in the past century, the form of government used in Washington, D.C., and in most states has remained the same. Some observers believe that the nation's diverse economic base cannot be administered competently by traditional bureaucratic organizations. Consequently, government must become more responsive to cope with the increasing demands placed on it. Political scientists Joel Aberbach and Bert Rockman take issue with this contention. They argue that the bureaucracy has changed significantly over time in response to changes desired by various presidential administrations. In their opinion, many of the problems attributed to the bureaucracy are, in fact, a result of the political decision-making process. Therefore, attempts to "reinvent" government by reforming the bureaucracy are misguided.[8]

"Look, all I'm asking is that we let market forces bring a greater degree of efficiency into our marriage."

Other analysts have suggested that the problem lies not so much with traditional bureaucratic organizations as with the people who run them. According to policy specialist Taegan Goddard and journalist Christopher Riback, what needs to be "reinvented" is not the machinery of government but public officials. After each election, new appointees to

8. Joel D. Aberbach and Bert A. Rockman, *In the Web of Politics: Three Decades of the U.S. Federal Executive* (Washington, D.C.: The Brookings Institution Press, 2000).

WHICH SIDE ARE YOU ON?

IS TOO MUCH GOVERNMENT WORK BEING CONTRACTED OUT?

When a job has to be undertaken by the government, those in charge have a choice: they can hire more government workers, or they can contract out the job to a private firm. During the George W. Bush administration, the practice of contracting out to private firms exploded. So, too, did the number of scandals associated with these private contractors. After armed guards belonging to the Blackwater security company killed seventeen Iraqi civilians in what the Iraqi government called indiscriminate gunfire, there were widespread calls for an end to the Blackwater contract. Nothing of the sort happened, however. Indeed, in May 2008, Blackwater's contract was renewed for at least another year. (Blackwater has since renamed itself as Xe Services.) "We cannot operate without private security firms in Iraq," said Patrick F. Kennedy, Bush's undersecretary of state for management. "If the contractors were removed, we would have to leave Iraq." In other words, contracting out has become so pervasive that the U.S. military cannot fight a war without it.

CONTRACTING OUT IS THE WAY TO MAKE GOVERNMENT MORE EFFICIENT

Today, federal contracting out exceeds $450 billion per year. Is this too much? Proponents of even more contracting out claim that government can never be efficient, but the private sector can. They point out that it is almost impossible to fire government employees, no matter how incompetent they are. Also, there is no "bottom line" for any operation undertaken by the government. Consequently, when the government does a job, it will do it at a higher cost, and with lower quality, than would a private contractor that did the same job.

The lack of a profit motive for government bureaucrats means that they will spend more time "feathering their own nests" than their counterparts in the private sector. More layers of management will therefore be evident in government bureaucracy than in the private sector doing the same job. Of course, there will be some waste among private contractors, but there is even more when the government undertakes a task. A few scandals among the thousands of private contractors the government is using do not mean that we have contracted out too much government work.

Contractors working for Blackwater USA take part in a firefight as Iraqi demonstrators loyal to Muqtada Al Sadr attempt to advance on a facility being defended by U.S. and Spanish soldiers in the city of Najaf. (AP Photo/Gervasio Sanchez/File)

TOO MUCH OF A GOOD THING MEANS WE HAVE GONE TOO FAR IN CONTRACTING OUT

Private contractors have become a virtual fourth branch of government. They now collect income taxes, build ships and satellites, and take down the minutes of policy meetings. More people currently work under private contracts for the U.S. government than work directly for the government as government employees. Fewer than half of the private contracts that have been issued by the federal government were the result of competitive bidding. The most successful private contractors do not necessarily do the best job. Rather, they have mastered the ability to market themselves to the federal government. In fewer than ten years, the top twenty private service contractors spent more than $300 million on lobbying and donated more than $25 million to political campaigns.

In 2007, when there was a scandal over the poor treatment of outpatients at Walter Reed Army Medical Center in Washington, D.C., the public learned that the maintenance job at that hospital had been contracted out. The head of Walter Reed, Major General George W. Weightman, testified before Congress that contracting out had "absolutely" contributed to the unsanitary conditions at the hospital. He was relieved of his duties soon thereafter.

bureaucratic positions may find themselves managing complex, multimillion-dollar enterprises, yet they often are untrained for their jobs. According to these authors, if we want to reform the bureaucracy, we should focus on preparing newcomers for the task of "doing" government.[9]

did you know?

That a report by the Government Accountability Office (GAO) revealed that the Department of Agriculture sent $1.1 billion in farm payments to more than 170,000 dead people over a seven-year period.

Saving Costs through E-Government. Many contend that the communications revolution brought about by the Internet has not only improved the efficiency with which government agencies deliver services to the public but also helped to reduce the cost of government. Agencies can now communicate with members of the public, as well as other agencies, via e-mail. Additionally, every federal agency now has a Web site to which citizens can go to find information about agency services instead of calling or appearing in person at a regional agency office. Since 2003, federal agencies have also been required by the Government Paperwork Elimination Act of 1998 to use electronic commerce whenever it is practical to do so and will save on costs.

Still, government agencies are often not very advanced in how they use the Internet. Some relatively poor countries, such as India, may actually outperform the rich world in their use of e-government, as we show in the *Beyond Our Borders* feature on the following page.

Helping Out the Whistleblowers

The term **whistleblower** as applied to the federal bureaucracy has a special meaning: it is someone who blows the whistle on a gross governmental inefficiency or illegal action. Whistleblowers may be clerical workers, managers, or even specialists, such as scientists.

Whistleblower
Someone who brings to public attention gross governmental inefficiency or an illegal action.

Laws Protecting Whistleblowers. The 1978 Civil Service Reform Act prohibits reprisals against whistleblowers by their superiors, and it set up the Merit Systems Protection Board as part of this protection. Many federal agencies also have toll-free hotlines that employees can use anonymously to report bureaucratic waste and inappropriate behavior. About 35 percent of all calls result in agency action or follow-up. Further protection for whistleblowers was provided in 1989, when Congress passed the Whistle-Blower Protection Act. That act established an independent agency, the Office of Special Counsel (OSC), to investigate complaints brought by government employees who have been demoted, fired, or otherwise sanctioned for reporting government fraud or waste.

Some state and federal laws encourage employees to blow the whistle on their employers' wrongful actions by providing monetary incentives to the whistleblowers. At the federal level, the False Claims Act of 1986 allows a whistleblower who has disclosed information about a fraud against the U.S. government to receive a monetary award. If the government chooses to prosecute the case and wins, the whistleblower receives between 15 and 25 percent of the proceeds. If the government declines to intervene, the whistleblower can bring suit on behalf of the government and, if the suit is successful, will receive between 25 and 30 percent of the proceeds.

The Problem Continues. Despite these endeavors to help whistleblowers, there is little evidence that potential whistleblowers truly have received more protection. More than 40 percent of the employees who turned to the OSC for assistance in a recent three-year period stated that they were no longer employees of the government agencies on which they blew the whistle.

---

9. Taegan D. Goddard and Christopher Riback, *You Won—Now What? How Americans Can Make Democracy Work from City Hall to the White House* (New York: Scribner, 1998).

During George W. Bush's administration, it was widely believed that the OSC was essentially useless in protecting whistleblowers. Allegedly, the agency closed hundreds of cases without bothering to investigate them. In May 2008, agents of the Federal Bureau of Investigation raided the OSC offices and the home of U.S. Special Counsel Scott Bloch. The raid was sparked by accusations that Bloch had destroyed evidence showing that he had retaliated against whistleblowers within the OSC itself.

Additionally, in a significant 2006 decision, the U.S. Supreme Court placed restrictions on lawsuits brought by public workers. The case, *Garcetti v. Ceballos,*[10] involved an assistant district attorney, Richard Ceballos, who wrote a memo asking if a county sheriff's deputy had lied in a search warrant affidavit. Ceballos claimed that he was subsequently demoted and

10. 547 U.S. 410 (2006).

BEYOND OUR BORDERS

INDIA, THE LAND OF BUREAUCRATIC PAPERWORK, GOES ONLINE

India is known for having one of the world's slowest bureaucracies. Nonetheless, one southern Indian state, Andhra Pradesh, is quickly entering the world of e-government. Hyderabad, the capital of the state, is one of the most important centers of India's rapidly growing high-tech economy. The state government of Andhra Pradesh has developed *eSeva,* a network of public Internet offices where citizens can pay bills online. In the past, citizens had to pay their electricity bills in person, which might have taken an eight-hour wait in a government office. The same was true for water and phone bills, as well as for taxes.

An increasing number of Indians can pay electricity bills with their cell phones. (Diptendu Dutta/AFP/Getty Images)

INTERACTING WITH GOVERNMENT ONLINE

Now, all government-provided services in Andhra Pradesh, such as electricity and water, can be paid for online. Citizens who have credit cards and computers can go to **esevaonline.com** to pay their bills. Those who do not can visit one of the *eSeva* centers. Today, the number of online transactions exceeds 150,000 per day, and the volume is growing by 25 percent a year. Over 60 percent of all payments for public services are electronic.

EXPANDING THE SYSTEM

Currently, there are about 140 *eSeva* centers. The government of Andhra Pradesh has plans to extend this number to 4,600, one for every six villages. By the time you read this, residents will be able to use *eSeva* centers and **esevaonline.com** to apply for driver's licenses.

THE MOVE TO MOBILE PHONES

Eventually, all of the services available on *eSeva* will be available through residents' cell phones. The mobile phone, rather than the computer, will become the main platform for payment. This is important because far more Indians have easy access to cell phones than to computers.

India's bankers have already taken major steps to give cell phone users access to banking services. For example, passengers arriving at the airport in Hyderabad are greeted by advertisements for bank accounts that allow payments to be authorized by a thumbprint—useful in a society in which many people are still illiterate. Some banks already offer *eSeva* services through a system called *m-banking,* for "mobile banking." Customers are able to pay for public services by using their cell phones to send a text message and a security code.

FOR CRITICAL ANALYSIS

Why might e-government be more important in rural areas of a country than in major cities?

denied a promotion for trying to expose the lie. The outcome of the case turned on an interpretation of an employee's right to freedom of speech—whether it included the right to criticize an employment-related action. In a close (five-to-four) and controversial decision, the Supreme Court held that when public employees make statements relating to their official duties, they are not speaking as citizens for First Amendment purposes. The Court deemed that when he wrote his memo, Ceballos was speaking as an employee, not a citizen, and was thus subject to his employer's disciplinary actions. The ruling will affect millions of governmental employees.

In 2007, the U.S. House of Representatives passed a new whistleblower protection act that would overturn the ruling in *Garcetti v. Ceballos.* The measure failed to clear the Senate, however. Protecting whistleblowers was an Obama campaign promise, but his administration has not yet acted on this issue.

did you know?

That each year, federal administrative agencies produce rules that fill an average of 7,500 pages in the *Code of Federal Regulations* and that the regulations now contained in this code cover 144,000 pages.

Bureaucrats as Politicians and Policymakers

Because Congress is unable to oversee the day-to-day administration of its programs, it must delegate certain powers to administrative agencies. Congress delegates the power to implement legislation to agencies through what is called **enabling legislation.** For example, the Federal Trade Commission was created by the Federal Trade Commission Act of 1914, the Equal Employment Opportunity Commission was created by the Civil Rights Act of 1964, and the Occupational Safety and Health Administration was created by the Occupational Safety and Health Act of 1970. The enabling legislation generally specifies the name, purpose, composition, functions, and powers of the agency.

Enabling Legislation
A statute enacted by Congress that authorizes the creation of an administrative agency and specifies the name, purpose, composition, functions, and powers of the agency being created.

In theory, the agencies should put into effect laws passed by Congress. Laws are often drafted in such vague and general terms, however, that they provide relatively little guidance to agency administrators as to how the laws should be implemented. This means that the agencies themselves must decide how best to carry out the wishes of Congress.

The discretion given to administrative agencies is not accidental. Congress has long realized that it lacks the technical expertise and the resources to monitor the implementation of its laws. Hence, the administrative agency is created to fill the gaps. This gap-filling role requires the agency to formulate administrative rules (regulations) to put flesh on the bones of the law. But it also forces the agency itself to become an unelected policymaker.

The Rulemaking Environment

Rulemaking does not occur in a vacuum. Suppose that Congress passes a new air-pollution law. The Environmental Protection Agency (EPA) might decide to implement the new law through a technical regulation on factory emissions. This proposed regulation would be published in the *Federal Register,* a daily government publication, so that interested parties would have an opportunity to comment on it. Individuals and companies that opposed parts or all of the rule might then try to convince the EPA to revise or redraft the regulation. Some parties might try to persuade the agency to withdraw the proposed regulation altogether. In any event, the EPA would consider these comments in drafting the final version of the regulation following the expiration of the comment period.

Waiting Periods and Court Challenges. Once the final regulation has been published in the *Federal Register,* there is a sixty-day waiting period before the rule can be enforced. During that period, businesses, individuals, and state and local governments can ask Congress to overturn the regulation. After that sixty-day period has lapsed, the regulation can still be challenged in court by a party having a direct interest in the rule, such as a company that expects to incur significant costs in complying with it. The company could argue that the rule misinterprets the applicable law or goes beyond the agency's statutory purview. An allegation by the company that the EPA made a mistake in judgment probably would not be enough to convince the court to throw out the rule. The company instead would have to demonstrate that the rule itself was "arbitrary and capricious." To meet this standard, the company would have to show that the rule reflected a serious flaw in the EPA's judgment.

Controversies. How agencies implement, administer, and enforce legislation has resulted in controversy. Decisions made by agencies charged with administering the Endangered Species Act have led to protests from farmers, ranchers, and others whose economic interests have been harmed. For example, the government decided to cut off the flow of irrigation water from Klamath Lake in Oregon in the summer of 2001. That action, which affected irrigation water for more than one thousand farmers in southern Oregon and northern California, was undertaken to save endangered suckerfish and salmon. It was believed that the lake's water level was so low that further use of the water for irrigation would harm these fish. The results of this decision were devastating for many farmers.

All vehicles that use internal combustion engines discharge carbon dioxide, which many researchers believe contributes to the threat of global warming. Who should regulate carbon dioxide emissions? (Daniel Acker/Bloomberg via Getty Images)

At times, a controversy may arise when an agency *refuses* to issue regulations to implement a particular law. When the EPA refused to issue regulations designed to curb the emission of carbon dioxide and other greenhouse gases, state and local governments, as well as a number of environmental groups, sued the agency. Thoses bringing the suit claimed that the EPA was not fulfilling its obligation to implement the provisions of the Clean Air Act. Ultimately, the Supreme Court held that the EPA had the authority to—and should—regulate such gases.[11]

Negotiated Rulemaking

Since the end of World War II (1939–1945), companies, environmentalists, and other special interest groups have challenged government regulations in court. In the 1980s, however, the sheer wastefulness of attempting to regulate through litigation became more and more apparent. Today, a growing number of federal agencies encourage businesses and public-interest groups to become directly involved in drafting regulations. Agencies hope that such participation may help to prevent later courtroom battles over the meaning, applicability, and legal effect of the regulations.

Congress formally approved such a process, which is called *negotiated rulemaking,* in the Negotiated Rulemaking Act of 1990. The act authorizes agencies to allow those who will be affected by a new rule to participate in the rule-drafting process. If an agency chooses to engage in negotiated rulemaking, it must publish in the *Federal Register* the subject and scope of the rule to be developed, the parties affected significantly by the rule, and other information. Representatives of the affected groups and other interested parties then may apply to be members of the negotiating committee. The agency is represented on the committee, but a neutral third party (not the agency) presides over the proceedings. Once the committee members have reached agreement on the terms of the proposed rule, a notice is published in the *Federal Register,* followed by a period for comments by any person or organization interested in the proposed rule. Negotiated rulemaking often is conducted under the condition that the participants promise not to challenge in court the outcome of any agreement to which they were a party.

11. *Massachusetts v. EPA,* 549 U.S. 497 (2007).

Bureaucrats as Policymakers

Theories of public administration once assumed that bureaucrats do not make policy decisions but only implement the laws and policies promulgated by the president and legislative bodies. Many people continue to make this assumption. A more realistic view, which is now held by most bureaucrats and elected officials, is that the agencies and departments of government play important roles in policymaking. As we have seen, many government rules, regulations, and programs are in fact initiated by bureaucrats, based on their expertise and scientific studies. How a law passed by Congress eventually is translated into concrete action—from the forms to be filled out to decisions about who gets the benefits—usually is determined within each agency or department. Even the evaluation of whether a policy has achieved its purpose usually is based on studies that are commissioned and interpreted by the agency administering the program.

The bureaucracy's policymaking role has often been depicted as an "iron triangle." Recently, many political scientists have come to see the concept of an "issue network" as a more accurate description of the policymaking process.

Iron Triangles. In the past, scholars often described the bureaucracy's role in the policymaking process by using the concept of an **iron triangle**—a three-way alliance among legislators in Congress, bureaucrats, and interest groups. Consider as an example the development of agricultural policy. Congress, as one component of the triangle, includes two major committees concerned with agricultural policy, the House Committee on Agriculture and the Senate Committee on Agriculture, Nutrition, and Forestry. The Department of Agriculture, the second component of the triangle, has about 100,000 employees, plus thousands of contractors and consultants. Agricultural interest groups, the third component of the iron triangle in agricultural policymaking, include many large and powerful associations, such as the American Farm Bureau Federation, the National Cattleman's Association, and the Corn Growers Association. These three components of the iron triangle work together, formally or informally, to create policy.

Iron Triangle
The three-way alliance among legislators, bureaucrats, and interest groups to make or preserve policies that benefit their respective interests.

For example, the various agricultural interest groups lobby Congress to develop policies that benefit their groups' interests. Members of Congress cannot afford to ignore the wishes of interest groups because those groups are potential sources of voter support and campaign contributions. The legislators in Congress also work closely with the Department of Agriculture, which, in implementing a policy, can develop rules that benefit—or at least do not hurt—certain industries or groups. The Department of Agriculture, in turn, supports policies that enhance the department's budget and powers. In this way, according to theory, agricultural policy is created that benefits all three components of the iron triangle.

These farmers raise beef cattle on an Iowa farm. To which part of the iron triangle in agriculture do they belong? (Gary Fandel/ Bloomberg via Getty Images)

Issue Networks. To be sure, the preceding discussion presents a much simplified picture of how the iron triangle works. With the growth in the complexity of government, policymaking also has become more complicated. The bureaucracy is larger, Congress has more committees and subcommittees, and interest groups are more powerful than ever. Although iron triangles still exist, often they are inadequate as descriptions of how policy is actually made. Frequently, different interest groups concerned about a certain area of policy have conflicting demands, making agency decisions difficult. Divided government in some years has meant that departments are sometimes pressured by the president to take one approach and by Congress to take another.

Issue Network
A group of individuals or organizations—which may consist of legislators and legislative staff members, interest group leaders, bureaucrats, the media, scholars, and other experts—that supports a particular policy position on a given issue.

Many scholars now use the term *issue network* to describe the policymaking process. An **issue network** consists of individuals or organizations that support a particular policy position on the environment, taxation, consumer safety, or some other issue. Typically, an issue network includes legislators and/or their staff members, interest groups, bureaucrats, scholars and other experts, and representatives from the media. Members of a particular issue network work together to influence the president, members of Congress, administrative agencies, and the courts to affect public policy on a specific issue. Each policy issue may involve conflicting positions taken by two or more issue networks.[12]

Congressional Control of the Bureaucracy

Many political pundits doubt whether Congress can meaningfully control the federal bureaucracy. Nevertheless, Congress does have some means of exerting control.

Ways Congress Does Control the Bureaucracy

These commentators forget that Congress specifies in an agency's "enabling legislation" the powers of the agency and the parameters within which it can operate. Additionally, Congress has the power of the purse and theoretically could refuse to authorize or appropriate funds for a particular agency (see the discussion of the budgeting process in Chapter 10). Whether Congress would actually take such a drastic measure would depend on the circumstances. Nevertheless, it is clear that Congress does have the legal authority to decide whether to fund or not to fund administrative agencies. Congress can also exercise oversight over agencies through investigations and hearings.

As discussed earlier in this text, Congress also has investigatory powers. Congressional committees conduct investigations and hold hearings to oversee an agency's actions, reviewing them to ensure compliance with congressional intentions. The agency's officers and employees can be ordered to testify before a committee about the details of various actions. Through these oversight activities, especially in the questions and comments of members of the House or Senate during the hearings, Congress indicates its positions on specific programs and issues.

Congress can ask the Government Accountability Office (GAO) to investigate particular agency actions as well. The Congressional Budget Office (CBO) also conducts oversight studies. The results of a GAO or CBO study may encourage Congress to hold further hearings or make changes in the law. Even if a law is not changed explicitly by Congress, however, the views expressed in any investigations and hearings are taken seriously by agency officials, who often act on those views.

In 1996, Congress passed the Congressional Review Act. The act created special procedures that can be employed to express congressional disapproval of particular agency actions. These procedures have rarely been used, however. Since the act's passage, the executive branch has issued more than 15,000 regulations. Yet only eight resolutions of disapproval have been introduced, and none of them were passed by either chamber.

12. For a landmark work on how the interests and priorities of government agencies, departments, and individuals influence the policymaking process, see Morton H. Halperin and Priscilla A. Clapp, with Arnold Kanter, *Bureaucratic Politics and Foreign Policy,* 2d ed. (Washington, D.C.: The Brookings Institution Press, 2006). Although the authors focus on foreign policymaking, their insightful analysis has much to say about the policymaking process in general.

Reasons Why Congress Cannot Easily Oversee the Bureaucracy

Despite the powers just described, one theory of congressional control over the bureaucracy suggests that Congress cannot possibly oversee all of the many federal government agencies that exist. Consider two possible approaches to congressional control—(1) the "police patrol" and (2) the "fire alarm" approach. Certain congressional activities, such as annual budget hearings, fall under the police patrol approach. This regular review occasionally catches *some* deficiencies in a bureaucracy's job performance, but it usually fails to detect most problems.

In contrast, the fire alarm approach is more likely to discover gross inadequacies in a bureaucracy's job performance. In this approach, Congress and its committees react to scandal, citizen disappointment, and massive negative publicity by launching a full-scale investigation into whatever agency is suspected of wrongdoing. Clearly, this is what happened when Congress investigated the inadequacies of the Central Intelligence Agency after the 9/11 terrorist attacks. Congress was also responding to an alarm when it investigated the failures of the Federal Emergency Management Agency after Hurricane Katrina. Under both the George W. Bush and the Obama administrations, however, Congress has often been reluctant to launch investigations when the president belongs to the same party that controls Congress. Fire alarm investigations will not catch all problems, but they will remind other bureaucracies that they may need to clean up their procedures before a problem arises in their own agencies.[13]

13. Matthew D. McCubbins and Thomas Schwartz, "Congressional Oversight Overlooked: Police Patrols versus Fire Alarms," *American Journal of Political Science*, February 28, 1984, pp. 165–179.

BP CEO Tony Hayward answers questions during a U.S. House hearing in June 2010 on the BP *Deepwater Horizon* explosion and oil spill. What responsibility does the government have when such disasters take place? (Rod Lamkey Jr/AFP/Getty Images)

WHY SHOULD YOU CARE ABOUT... THE BUREAUCRACY?

Why should you, as an individual, care about the bureaucracy? You might consider that the federal government collects billions of pieces of information on tens of millions of Americans each year. These data are stored in files and sometimes are exchanged among agencies. You are probably the subject of several federal records (for example, in the Social Security Administration; the Internal Revenue Service; and, if you are a male, the Selective Service).

THE BUREAUCRACY AND YOUR LIFE

Verifying the information that the government has on you can be important. On several occasions, the records of two people with similar names have become confused. Sometimes innocent persons have had the criminal records of other persons erroneously inserted in their files. Such disasters are not always caused by bureaucratic error. One of the most common crimes in today's world is "identity theft," in which one person makes use of another person's personal identifiers (such as a Social Security number) to commit fraud. In some instances, identity thieves have been arrested and even jailed under someone else's name.

These students are accessing their personal records to see if they are accurate. (AP Photo/ L.G. Patterson)

HOW YOU CAN MAKE A DIFFERENCE

The 1966 Freedom of Information Act (FOIA) requires that the federal government release, at your request, any identifiable information it has about you or about any other subject. Ten categories of material are exempted, however (classified material, confidential material on trade secrets, internal personnel rules, personal medical files, and the like). To request material, write directly to the Freedom of Information Act officer at the agency in question (say, the Department of Education). You must have a relatively specific idea about the document or information you want to obtain.

A second law, the Privacy Act of 1974, gives you access specifically to information the government may have collected about you. This law allows you to review records on file with federal agencies and to check those records for possible inaccuracies.

If you want to look at any records or find out if an agency has a record on you, write to the agency head or Privacy Act officer, and address your letter to the specific agency. State that "under the provisions of the Privacy Act of 1974, 5 U.S.C. 522a, I hereby request a copy of (or access to) _____." Then describe the record that you wish to investigate.

The General Services Administration (GSA) has published a citizen's guide, *Your Right to Federal Records,* that explains both the FOIA and the Privacy Act, and how to go about using them. You can locate this manual at the following Web site:

www.pueblo.gsa.gov/cic_text/fed_prog/foia/foia.htm

questions for discussion and analysis

1. Review the *Which Side Are You On?* feature on page 426. Do you think that too much government work is contracted out? Why or why not? What potential difficulties could contracting out present? What are the benefits? Is the private sector always more efficient in offering services than the government? Why or why not?
2. Consider the paradox described at the beginning of this chapter: the public believes strongly in "small government" but endorses almost all the activities that government actually performs. Why do you think Americans hold such contradictory beliefs?
3. If Congress tried to make civil servants easier to fire, what political forces might stand in the way?
4. The government's response to the BP Deepwater Horizon oil spill disaster in the Gulf of Mexico has been widely criticized. Why might the government have failed in this crisis? What could it have done instead?
5. The U.S. attorney general, head of the Justice Department, is appointed by the president and is frequently the president's close political ally. Should the attorney general and other U.S. attorneys be appointed on a partisan basis? Why or why not?

key terms

acquisitive model 408
administrative agency 409
bureaucracy 407
cabinet department 412
capture 416
Civil Service Commission 421
enabling legislation 429
government corporation 417
Government in the Sunshine Act 423
independent executive agency 413
independent regulatory agency 413
iron triangle 431
issue network 432
line organization 412
merit system 421
monopolistic model 408
nationalization 419
Pendleton Act (Civil Service Reform Act) 421
preferred stock 419
privatization 424
spoils system 421
sunset legislation 424
Weberian model 407
whistleblower 427

chapter summary

1. Bureaucracies are hierarchical organizations characterized by a division of labor and extensive procedural rules. Bureaucracy is the primary form of organization of most major corporations and universities, as well as governments.
2. Several theories have been offered to explain bureaucracies. The Weberian model posits that bureaucracies are rational, hierarchical organizations in which decisions are based on logical reasoning. The acquisitive model views top-level bureaucrats as pressing for ever-larger budgets and staffs to augment their own sense of power and security. The monopolistic model focuses on the environment in which most government bureaucracies operate, stating that bureaucracies are inefficient and excessively costly to operate because they have no competitors.
3. Since the founding of the United States, the federal bureaucracy has grown from 50 to about 2.8 million employees (including the U.S. Postal Service, but excluding the military). Federal, state, and local employees together make up about 16 percent of the nation's civilian labor force. The federal bureaucracy consists of fifteen cabinet departments, as well as a large number of independent executive agencies, independent regulatory agencies, and government corporations. These entities enjoy varying degrees of autonomy, visibility, and political support.
4. A federal bureaucracy of career civil servants was formed during Thomas Jefferson's presidency. Andrew Jackson implemented a spoils system through which he appointed his own political supporters. A civil service based on professionalism and merit was the goal of the Civil Service

Reform Act of 1883. Concerns that the civil service be freed from the pressures of politics prompted the passage of the Hatch Act in 1939. Significant changes in the administration of the civil service were made by the Civil Service Reform Act of 1978.

5. There have been many attempts to make the federal bureaucracy more open, efficient, and responsive to the needs of U.S. citizens. The most important reforms have included sunshine and sunset laws, privatization, strategies to provide incentives for increased efficiency and productivity, and protection for whistleblowers.

6. Congress delegates much of its authority to federal agencies when it creates new laws. The bureaucrats who run these agencies may become important policymakers because Congress has neither the time nor the technical expertise to oversee the administration of its laws. In the agency rulemaking process, a proposed regulation is published. A comment period follows, during which interested parties may offer suggestions for changes. Because companies and other organizations have challenged many regulations in court, federal agencies now are authorized to allow parties that will be affected by new regulations to participate in the rule-drafting process.

7. Congress exerts ultimate control over all federal agencies because it controls the federal government's purse strings. It also establishes the general guidelines by which regulatory agencies must abide. The appropriations process may provide a way to send messages of approval or disapproval to particular agencies, as do congressional hearings and investigations of agency actions.

selected print & media resources

SUGGESTED READINGS

Aab, Stacy Parker. ***Government Girl: Young and Female in the White House.*** New York: Ecco, 2010. In this delightfully written coming-of-age tale, Aab begins as an intern and graduates to becoming a staffer in the Clinton White House. The reader learns what it is like to work in a pressure-cooker environment populated by type A personalities.

Eggers, William D., and John O'Leary. ***If We Can Put a Man on the Moon: Getting Big Things Done in Government.*** Cambridge, Mass.: Harvard University Business School Press, 2009. This often-witty book looks at many examples of government initiatives that have failed—and some that have succeeded. Eggers and O'Leary identify traps that can undermine well-intended projects and offer management concepts from the business world that could produce better results.

Light, Paul C. ***A Government Ill Executed: The Decline of the Federal Service and How to Reverse It.*** Cambridge, Mass.: Harvard University Press, 2009. Light contends that young, talented workers are steering clear of jobs in the federal government. He believes that it is possible both to reduce the number of federal staff members and to improve their morale and effectiveness.

McGowan, Richard A. ***Privatize This? Assessing the Opportunities and Costs of Privatization.*** Santa Barbara, Calif.: Praeger, 2010. What happens when privatization is no longer a theory but is put to the test? McGowan examines nine case studies of privatization to learn where it works—and where it doesn't.

Steinzor, Rena, and Sidney Shapiro. ***The People's Agents and the Battle to Protect the American Public: Special Interests, Government, and Threats to Health, Safety, and the Environment.*** Chicago: University of Chicago Press, 2010. The authors contend that ceaseless attacks on the federal bureaucracy have led to a regulatory environment in which the government can no longer effectively protect the people.

MEDIA RESOURCES

The Bureaucracy of Government: John Lukacs—A 1988 Bill Moyers special. Historian John Lukacs discusses the common political lament over the giant but invisible mechanism called bureaucracy.

King Corn—A 2007 documentary that demonstrates the impact of corn growing on modern America. Ian Cheney and Curt Ellis learn that corn is in almost everything they eat. They move to Iowa for a year to grow corn and find out what happens to it. Inevitably, they come face-to-face with America's farm policy and its subsidies.

Yes, Minister—A new member of the British cabinet bumps up against the machinations of a top civil servant in a comedy of manners. This popular 1980 BBC comedy is now available on DVD.

When the Levees Broke: A Requiem in Four Acts—A strong treatment of Hurricane Katrina's impact on New Orleans by renowned African American director Spike Lee. We learn about the appalling performance of authorities at every level and the suffering that could have been avoided. Lee's anger at what he sees adds spice to this 2006 production.

e-mocracy

THE BUREAUCRACY AND THE INTERNET

All federal government agencies (and nearly all state agencies) have Web pages. Citizens can access these Web sites to find information and forms that, in the past, could normally be obtained only by going to a regional or local branch of the agency. For example, if you or a member of your family wants to learn about Social Security benefits available on retirement, you can simply access the Social Security Administration's Web site to find that information. A number of federal government agencies have also been active in discovering and prosecuting fraud perpetrated on citizens through the Internet.

LOGGING ON

Numerous links to federal agencies and information on the federal government can be found at the U.S. government's official Web site. Go to
www.usa.gov

You may want to examine two publications available from the federal government to learn more about the federal bureaucracy. The first is the *Federal Register,* which is the official publication for executive-branch documents. You can find it at
www.gpoaccess.gov/fr

The second is the *United States Government Manual,* which describes the origins, purposes, and administrators of every federal department and agency. It is available at
www.gpoaccess.gov/gmanual

"The Plum Book," which lists the bureaucratic positions that can be filled by presidential appointment, is online at
www.gpoaccess.gov/plumbook

To find telephone numbers for government agencies and personnel, you can go to
www.usa.gov/Agencies.shtml

chapter 13

The Courts

chapter contents

The building in which the United States Supreme Court meets remains a symbol of our system of justice. (Win McNamee/Getty Images)

WHAT IF... ...arguments before the Supreme Court were televised?

Many state appellate courts allow cameras in the courtroom. The United States Supreme Court has never done so, and many of its justices resist such a proposed action. Why would some justices oppose cameras in the courtroom? (AP Photo/Phil Coale)

BACKGROUND

Since 1955, the United States Supreme Court has allowed audio recordings of oral arguments before the Court. Also, during every session of the Supreme Court, a court reporter transcribes every word that is spoken, even with indications when there is laughter. You can find a written transcript of each oral argument at **www.supremecourt.gov**. At the end of every term, you can obtain all of the audio recordings online at **www.oyez.org**. Today, many states have gone one step further—they allow appellate court sessions to be televised. The federal appellate courts and the Supreme Court have resisted televising their proceedings, however.

WHAT IF ARGUMENTS BEFORE THE SUPREME COURT WERE TELEVISED?

Presumably, coverage of Supreme Court proceedings would be undertaken in the same way that sessions in the Senate and the House of Representatives are televised by C-SPAN. The C-SPAN coverage includes no commentaries about the proceedings in the chambers of Congress. The television coverage is straightforward, word for word, and often quite boring.

In the Supreme Court, similar television coverage would consist of one or two cameras and their operators discreetly positioned in the courtroom where the nine justices hear oral arguments and question the attorneys. Another third C-SPAN channel might have to be created to televise Supreme Court proceedings. As an alternative, we could envision Internet video streaming as a low-cost alternative. Internet video streaming would be available anywhere in the world, thereby allowing the rest of the world to better understand the American judicial system.

The Supreme Court could follow the states, which have already developed a wide variety of rules governing television coverage of court proceedings.[a] Most states' rules allow the presiding judge to limit or prohibit coverage. Most states also allow the parties to object to television coverage, and some require the parties' consent.

If Supreme Court proceedings were televised, we could expect a media "mini-industry" to follow, particularly on the Internet. There might be new Web sites with portions of Supreme Court proceedings shown in video along with commentary by legal and political experts.

GRANDSTANDING—A POSSIBILITY?

Certain sitting judges and others have argued against televising Supreme Court sessions because of the possibility of "grandstanding." In other words, they are worried that justices might ask questions and make comments during the proceedings in the hopes that such comments would become sound bites on the evening news. Justice Anthony M. Kennedy has said that televising proceedings would "change our collegial dynamic."

In contrast, Judge Diarmuid O'Scannlain of the U.S. Court of Appeals for the Ninth Circuit believes that the concerns about grandstanding and politicking in the courtroom are "overstated." He argues that televising appellate court proceedings depoliticizes them and improves the public's perception of the legal process.

FOR CRITICAL ANALYSIS

1. How wide an audience do you believe the television proceedings of the Supreme Court would have?
2. Do you think that televised proceedings of the Supreme Court would significantly increase public awareness of Supreme Court decisions? Why or why not?

---

a. See the information provided by the Radio Television Digital News Association at **www.rtdna.org/pages/media_items/cameras-in-the-court-a-state-by-state-guide55.php**.

As Alexis de Tocqueville, a French commentator on American society in the 1800s, noted, "scarcely any political question arises in the United States that is not resolved, sooner or later, into a judicial question."[1] Our judiciary forms part of our political process. The instant that judges interpret the law, they become actors in the political arena—policymakers working within a political institution.

The most important political force within our judiciary is the United States Supreme Court. The justices of the Supreme Court are not elected but rather are appointed by the president and confirmed by the Senate. The same is true for all other federal court judges. Because Supreme Court justices are so important in our governmental system, it has been suggested that arguments before the Court should be televised, as this chapter's opening *What If . . .* feature discussed.

How do courts make policy? Why do the federal courts play such an important role in American government? The answers to these questions lie, in part, in our colonial heritage. Most of American law is based on the English system, particularly the English *common law tradition*. In that tradition, the decisions made by judges constitute an important source of law. We open this chapter with an examination of this tradition and of the various sources of American law. We then look at the federal court system—its organization, how its judges are selected, how these judges affect policy, and how they are restrained by our system of checks and balances.

The Common Law Tradition

In 1066, the Normans conquered England, and William the Conqueror and his successors began the process of unifying the country under their rule. One of the ways in which they did this was to establish king's courts. Before the conquest, disputes had been settled according to local custom. The king's courts sought to establish a common, or uniform, set of rules for the whole country. As the number of courts and cases increased, portions of the most important decisions of each year were gathered together and recorded in *Year Books*. Judges settling disputes similar to ones that had been decided before used the *Year Books* as the basis for their decisions. If a case was unique, judges had to create new laws, but they based their decisions on the general principles suggested by earlier cases. The body of judge-made law that developed under this system is still used today and is known as the **common law.**

The practice of deciding new cases with reference to former decisions—that is, according to **precedent**—became a cornerstone of the English and American judicial systems and is embodied in the doctrine of ***stare decisis*** (pronounced *ster*-ay dih-*si*-*ses*), a Latin phrase that means "to stand on decided cases." The doctrine of *stare decisis* obligates judges to follow the precedents set previously by their own courts or by higher courts that have authority over them.

For example, a lower state court in California would be obligated to follow a precedent set by the California Supreme Court. That lower court, however, would not be obligated to follow a precedent set by the supreme court of another state, because each state court system is independent. Of course, when the United States Supreme Court decides an issue, all of the nation's other courts are obligated to abide by the Court's decision—because the Supreme Court is the highest court in the land.

Common Law
Judge-made law that originated in England from decisions shaped according to prevailing custom. Decisions were applied to similar situations and gradually became common to the nation.

Precedent
A court rule bearing on subsequent legal decisions in similar cases. Judges rely on precedents in deciding cases.

Stare Decisis
To stand on decided cases; the judicial policy of following precedents established by past decisions.

Sources of American Law

The body of American law includes the federal and state constitutions, statutes passed by legislative bodies, administrative law, and case law—the legal principles expressed in court decisions.

1. Alexis de Tocqueville, *Democracy in America* (New York: Harper & Row, 1966), p. 248

Constitutions

The constitutions of the federal government and the states set forth the general organization, powers, and limits of government. The U.S. Constitution is the supreme law of the land. A law in violation of the Constitution, no matter what its source, may be declared unconstitutional and thereafter cannot be enforced. Similarly, the state constitutions are supreme within their respective borders (unless they conflict with the U.S. Constitution or federal laws and treaties made in accordance with it). The Constitution thus defines the political playing field on which state and federal powers are reconciled. The idea that the Constitution should be supreme in certain matters stemmed from widespread dissatisfaction with the weak federal government that had existed previously under the Articles of Confederation adopted in 1781.

Statutes and Administrative Regulations

Although the English common law provides the basis for both our civil and criminal legal systems, statutes (laws enacted by legislatures) have become increasingly important in defining the rights and obligations of individuals. Federal statutes may relate to any subject that is a concern of the federal government and may apply to areas ranging from hazardous waste to federal taxation. State statutes include criminal codes, commercial laws, and laws covering a variety of other matters. Cities, counties, and other local political bodies also pass statutes, which are called *ordinances.* These ordinances may deal with such issues as zoning proposals and public safety. Rules and regulations issued by administrative agencies are another source of law. Today, much of the work of the courts consists of interpreting these laws and regulations and applying them to the specific circumstances of the cases that come before the courts.

Case Law
Judicial interpretations of common law principles and doctrines, as well as interpretations of constitutional law, statutory law, and administrative law.

Case Law

Because we have a common law tradition, in which the doctrine of *stare decisis* (see the discussion of this doctrine on the previous page) plays an important role, the decisions rendered by the courts also form an important body of law, collectively referred to as **case law.** Case law includes judicial interpretations of common law principles and doctrines, as well as interpretations of the types of law just mentioned—constitutional provisions, statutes, and administrative agency regulations. As you learned in previous chapters, it is up to the courts—and ultimately, if necessary, the Supreme Court—to decide what a constitutional provision or a statutory phrase means. In doing so, the courts, in effect, establish law. (We will discuss this policymaking function of the courts in more detail later in the chapter.)

Courts in many of the nations formerly governed or settled by Britain—Australia, Canada, Ireland, the United States, and others—exhibit some broad similarities. All make use of the common law, as well as statutes and administrative regulations. All share the basic judicial requirements that you will learn about shortly. In some lands formerly ruled by Britain, such as India, Nigeria, and Pakistan, the common law is supplemented by local traditional law, including Islamic family law. Islamic family law can have some interesting twists, as we explain in this chapter's *Beyond Our Borders* feature on the facing page. Nations that do not share the common law tradition typically rely on a statutory code alone, in what is called the civil law system. Judges under the civil law system are not bound by precedent in the way that judges are under the common law system.

Individuals sometimes band together to sue the federal government for what they believe is a violation of their constitutional rights. The woman on the right is one such individual. She joined together with other immigrants who had waited years to obtain U.S. citizenship. Their attorneys from the American Civil Liberties Union argued in court that the lengthy delays for their security checks were not constitutional. Who has the ultimate say on what is or is not constitutional? (AP Photo/ George Nikitin)

The Federal Court System

The United States has a dual court system. There are state courts and federal courts. Each of the fifty states, as well as the District of Columbia, has its own independent system of courts. This means that there are fifty-two court systems in total. Here we focus on the federal courts.

Basic Judicial Requirements

Before a case can be brought before a court in any court system, state or federal, certain requirements must be met. Two important requirements are *jurisdiction* and *standing to sue*.

BEYOND OUR BORDERS

TECHNOLOGY AND ISLAMIC DIVORCE

In 2003, a Malaysian court ruled that divorce via cell phone is legal. Why will such a method never be accepted in this country? (Jimin Lai/AFP/Getty Images)

Talaq. In Malaysia, this one word translates as "I divorce you." Under current Islamic law—called *sharia*—in Malaysia, if a man states the word *talaq* three times, he is divorced. Since the advent of text messaging, men in some areas of Malaysia can divorce their wives by stating "I divorce you" in their own language three times in a text message.

MULTIPLE WIVES AND DIVORCE IN MALAYSIA

Muslim men in Malaysia legally can take up to four wives. Any Muslim man in that country has the right to divorce. We don't know how many men have sent their wives text messages since the practice started in 2003, but we do know that the text-messaging divorce technique is growing as cell phone use also grows.

Muslim men in Malaysia divorce their wives at a rate five times higher than that of non-Muslims in their country. (Of course, this number is somewhat inflated because not many non-Muslim men have more than one wife.)

ABUSES OF ISLAMIC LAW

As it turns out, the ruling of a *sharia* court in one Malaysian state is not applicable in another. Consequently, a man may divorce one or more of his wives in one state and be required by that *sharia* court to provide child support. He can thereafter move to another Malaysian state and avoid paying child support. There are other differences in the application of *sharia* among the states in Malaysia. For example, two states give Muslim fathers the right to marry off a daughter without her consent.

FOR CRITICAL ANALYSIS

One government adviser on religious affairs in Malaysia stated that "mobile phone text messaging is just another form of writing." Do you believe that text messaging "I divorce you" should have the same legal effect as stating those words verbally to one's spouse? Why or why not?

Jurisdiction
The authority of a court to decide certain cases. Not all courts have the authority to decide all cases. Where a case arises and what its subject matter is are two jurisdictional issues.

Federal Question
A question that has to do with the U.S. Constitution, acts of Congress, or treaties. A federal question provides a basis for federal jurisdiction.

Diversity of Citizenship
The condition that exists when the parties to a lawsuit are citizens of different states or when the parties are citizens of a U.S. state and citizens or the government of a foreign country. Diversity of citizenship can provide a basis for federal jurisdiction.

Justiciable Controversy
A controversy that is real and substantial, as opposed to hypothetical or academic.

Jurisdiction. A state court can exercise **jurisdiction** (the authority of the court to hear and decide a case) over the residents of a particular geographic area, such as a county or district. A state's highest court, or supreme court, has jurisdictional authority over all residents within the state.

Because the Constitution established a federal government with limited powers, federal jurisdiction is also limited. Article III, Section 1, of the U.S. Constitution limits the jurisdiction of the federal courts to cases that involve either a federal question or diversity of citizenship. A **federal question** arises when a case is based, at least in part, on the U.S. Constitution, a treaty, or a federal law. A person who claims that her or his rights under the Constitution, such as the right to free speech, have been violated could bring a case in a federal court. **Diversity of citizenship** exists when the parties to a lawsuit are from different states or (more rarely) when the suit involves a U.S. citizen and a government or citizen of a foreign country. The amount in controversy must be at least $75,000 before a federal court can take jurisdiction in a diversity case, however.

Standing to Sue. Another basic judicial requirement is standing to sue, or a sufficient "stake" in a matter to justify bringing suit. The party bringing a lawsuit must have suffered a harm, or have been threatened by a harm, as a result of the action that led to the dispute in question. Standing to sue also requires that the controversy at issue be a justiciable controversy. A **justiciable controversy** is a controversy that is real and substantial, as opposed to hypothetical or academic. In other words, a court will not give advisory opinions on hypothetical questions.

Types of Federal Courts

As you can see in Figure 13–1 below, the federal court system is basically a three-tiered model consisting of (1) U.S. district courts and various specialized courts of limited jurisdiction (not all of the latter are shown in the figure), (2) intermediate U.S. courts of appeals, and (3) the United States Supreme Court.

FIGURE 13–1 The Federal Court System

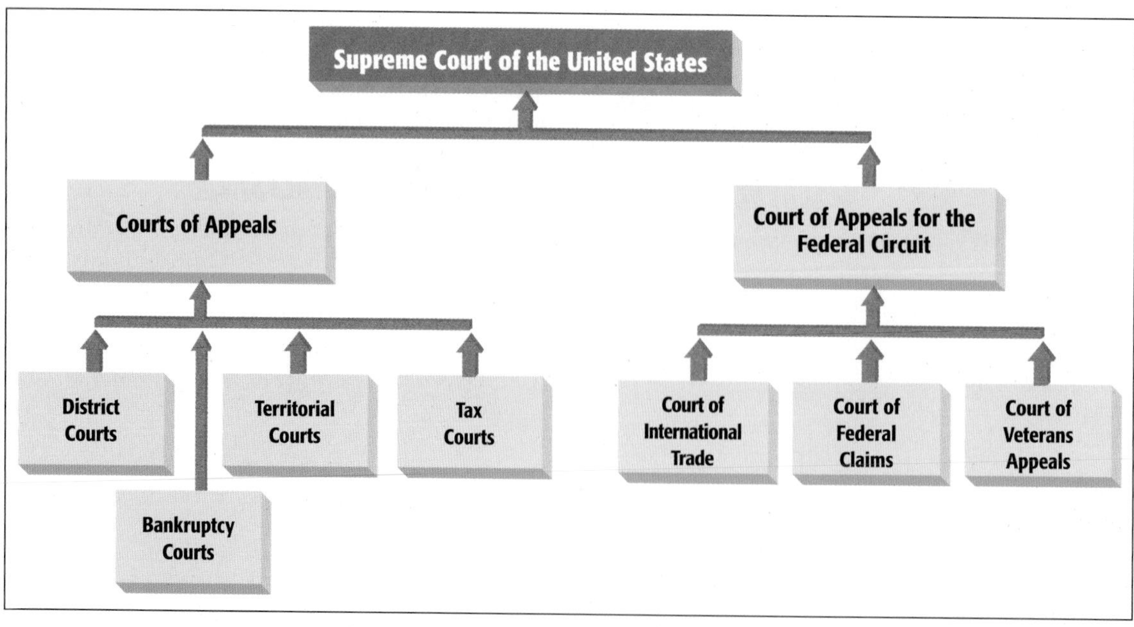

U.S. District Courts. The U.S. district courts are trial courts. A **trial court** is what the name implies—a court in which trials are held and testimony is taken. The U.S. district courts are courts of **general jurisdiction,** meaning that they can hear cases involving a broad array of issues. Federal cases involving most matters typically are heard in district courts. The other courts on the lower tier of the model shown in Figure 13–1 are courts of **limited jurisdiction,** meaning that they can try cases involving only certain types of claims, such as tax claims or bankruptcy petitions.

There is at least one federal district court in every state. The number of judicial districts can vary over time owing to population changes and corresponding caseloads. Currently, there are ninety-four federal judicial districts. A party who is dissatisfied with the decision of a district court can appeal the case to the appropriate U.S. court of appeals, or federal **appellate court.** Figure 13–2 below shows the jurisdictional boundaries of the district courts (which are state boundaries, unless otherwise indicated by dotted lines within a state) and of the U.S. courts of appeals.

Many federal administrative agencies and most executive departments also employ administrative law judges (ALJs) who resolve disputes arising under the rules governing their agencies. For example, the Social Security Administration might hold a hearing to determine whether a specific class of individuals is entitled to collect a particular benefit. If all internal agency appeals processes have been exhausted, a party may have a right to file an appeal in a federal district court.

Trial Court
The court in which most cases begin.

General Jurisdiction
Exists when a court's authority to hear cases is not significantly restricted. A court of general jurisdiction normally can hear a broad range of cases.

Limited Jurisdiction
Exists when a court's authority to hear cases is restricted to certain types of claims, such as tax claims or bankruptcy petitions.

Appellate Court
A court having jurisdiction to review cases and issues that were originally tried in lower courts.

U.S. Courts of Appeals. There are thirteen U.S. courts of appeals—also referred to as U.S. circuit courts of appeals. Twelve of these courts, including the U.S. Court of Appeals for the District of Columbia, hear appeals from the federal district courts located within

FIGURE 13–2 Geographic Boundaries of Federal District Courts and U.S. Courts of Appeals

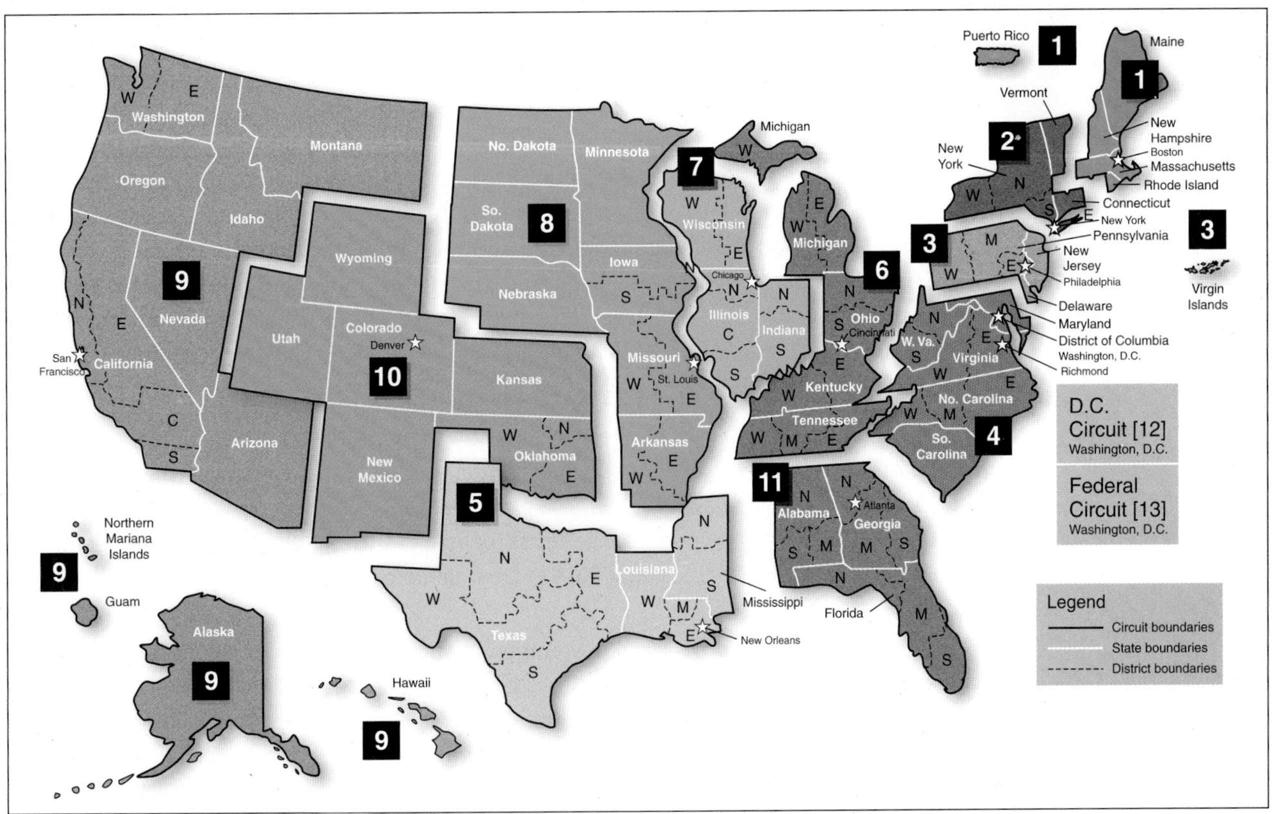

Source: Administrative Office of the United States Courts.

their respective judicial circuits (geographic areas over which they exercise jurisdiction). The Court of Appeals for the Thirteenth Circuit, called the Federal Circuit, has national appellate jurisdiction over certain types of cases, such as cases involving patent law and those in which the U.S. government is a defendant.

Note that when an appellate court reviews a case decided in a district court, the appellate court does not conduct another trial. Rather, a panel of three or more judges reviews the record of the case on appeal, which includes a transcript of the trial proceedings, and determines whether the trial court committed an error. Usually, appellate courts do not look at questions of *fact* (such as whether a party did, in fact, commit a certain action, such as burning a flag) but at questions of *law* (such as whether the act of burning a flag is a form of speech protected by the First Amendment to the Constitution). An appellate court will challenge a trial court's finding of fact only when the finding is clearly contrary to the evidence presented at trial or when there is no evidence to support the finding.

A party can petition the United States Supreme Court to review an appellate court's decision. The likelihood that the Supreme Court will grant the petition is slim, however, because the Court reviews very few of the cases decided by the appellate courts. This means that decisions made by appellate judges usually are final.

The United States Supreme Court. The highest level of the three-tiered model of the federal court system is the United States Supreme Court. When the Supreme Court came into existence in 1789, it had six justices. In the following years, more justices were added. Since 1869 there have been nine justices on the Court.

According to the language of Article III of the U.S. Constitution, there is only one national Supreme Court. All other courts in the federal system are considered "inferior." Congress is empowered to create other inferior courts as it deems necessary. The inferior courts that Congress has created include the district courts, the federal courts of appeals, and the federal courts of limited jurisdiction.

did you know?

That the Supreme Court was not provided with a building of its own until 1935, in the 146th year of its existence.

Although the Supreme Court can exercise original jurisdiction (that is, act as a trial court) in certain cases, such as those affecting foreign diplomats and those in which a state is a party, most of its work is as an appellate court. The Court hears appeals not only from the federal appellate courts but also from the highest state courts. Note, though, that the United States Supreme Court can review a state supreme court decision only if a federal question is involved. Because of its importance in the federal court system, we look more closely at the Supreme Court later in this chapter.

Federal Courts and the War on Terrorism

As noted, the federal court system includes a variety of trial courts of limited jurisdiction, dealing with matters such as tax claims or international trade. The government's attempts to combat terrorism have drawn attention to certain specialized courts that meet in secret. We look next at these courts, as well as at the role of the federal courts with respect to the detainees held at the U.S. Naval Base in Guantánamo Bay, Cuba.

The FISA Court. The federal government created the first secret court in 1978. In that year, Congress passed the Foreign Intelligence Surveillance Act (FISA), which established a court to hear requests for warrants for the surveillance of suspected spies. Officials can request warrants without having to reveal to the suspect or to the public the information used to justify the warrant. The FISA court has approved almost all of the thousands of requests for warrants that the U.S. attorney general's office and other officials have submitted. The seven judges on the FISA court meet in secret, with no published opinions or orders. There is also no public access to the court's proceedings or records. Hence, when the court authorizes surveillance, suspects normally do not even know that they are under scrutiny. During the Clinton administration (1993–2001), the court was given the additional authority to approve physical as well as electronic searches, which means that officials may search a suspect's property without obtaining a warrant in open court and without notifying the subject.

In the aftermath of the terrorist attacks on September 11, 2001, George W. Bush's administration expanded the powers of the FISA court. Previously, the FISA allowed secret domestic surveillance only if the "purpose" was to combat foreign intelligence gathering. Amendments to the FISA subsequent to the 9/11 terrorist attacks changed this wording to "a significant purpose"—meaning that warrants may now be requested to obtain evidence that can be used in criminal trials.

Chief Justice John Roberts, Jr., speaks at the University of Montana in Missoula. Do you think there are some subjects that he would avoid in any of his public speeches? (AP Photo/ Todd Goodrich)

Alien "Removal Courts." The FISA court is not the only court in which suspects' rights have been reduced. In the wake of the Oklahoma City bombing in 1995, Congress passed the Anti-Terrorism and Effective Death Penalty Act of 1996. The act included a provision creating an alien "removal court" to hear evidence against suspected "alien terrorists." The judges in this court rule on whether there is probable cause for deportation. If so, a public deportation proceeding is held in a U.S. district court. The prosecution does not need to follow procedures that normally apply in criminal cases. In addition, the defendant cannot see the evidence that the prosecution used to secure the hearing.

The Federal Courts and Enemy Combatants. Subsequent to the 9/11 terrorist attacks, the U.S. military took custody of hundreds of suspected terrorists and held them at the U.S. Naval Base in Guantánamo Bay, Cuba. The detainees were classified as *enemy combatants,* and, according to the Bush administration, they could be held indefinitely and without the normal legal protections available to U.S. citizens. Additionally, the Bush administration claimed that the detainees, because they had been designated enemy combatants and not prisoners of war, were not protected under international laws governing the treatment of prisoners of war. Since that time, the treatment of the prisoners at Guantánamo has been a source of ongoing controversy. The United States Supreme Court held, first in 2004 and then in 2006, that the Bush administration's treatment of these detainees violated the U.S. Constitution.[2]

In response to the Court's 2006 decision, Congress passed the Military Commissions Act of 2006. The act eliminated federal court jurisdiction over challenges by noncitizens held as enemy combatants based on *habeas corpus,* the right of a detained person to challenge the legality of his or her detention before a judge. Prisoners' challenges to their detention would be reviewed by military commissions, with a limited right of appeal to the federal courts. A federal appellate court held that the act was constitutional, and the case was then appealed to the United States Supreme Court. In June 2008, the Court ruled that the act's provisions restricting the federal courts' jurisdictional authority over detainees' *habeas corpus* challenges were illegal.[3] The decision gives Guantánamo detainees the

2. *Hamdi v. Rumsfeld,* 542 U.S. 507 (2004); *Hamdan v. Rumsfeld,* 548 U.S. 557 (2006).
3. *Boumediene v. Bush,* 553 U.S. 723 (2008).

"We've got a class-action suit if ever I saw one."
(© The New Yorker Collection, 1993. Mischa Richter, from www.cartoonbank.com. All Rights Reserved.)

right to challenge their detention in federal civil courts. The close (five-to-four) decision dealt a decisive blow to the Bush administration's detention policies.

In 2009, the Obama administration abolished the category of *enemy combatant* and promised to close the Guantánamo prison. President Barack Obama did not, however, seek to try all of the detainees in U.S. civil courts. Under the Military Commissions Act of 2009, some of the prisoners were to be tried in a revised system of military commissions. Further, in May 2009, Obama claimed the right to detain certain accused terrorists held at Guantánamo indefinitely without trial, possibly in a prison on the U.S. mainland. In May 2010, a federal appeals court ruled that the administration had the right to detain prisoners indefinitely at Bagram Air Force Base in Afghanistan because the prison is located on foreign soil and within a war zone.[4]

Parties to Lawsuits

In most lawsuits, the parties are the plaintiff (the person or organization that initiates the lawsuit) and the defendant (the person or organization against whom the lawsuit is brought). There may be a number of plaintiffs and defendants in a single lawsuit. In the last several decades, many lawsuits have been brought by interest groups (see Chapter 7). Interest groups play an important role in our judicial system, because they **litigate**—bring to trial—or assist in litigating most cases of racial or gender-based discrimination, almost all civil liberties cases, and more than one-third of the cases involving business matters. Interest groups also file ***amicus curiae*** (pronounced ah-*mee*-kous *kur*-ee-eye) **briefs,** or "friend of the court" briefs, in more than 50 percent of these kinds of cases.

Litigate
To engage in a legal proceeding or seek relief in a court of law; to carry on a lawsuit.

***Amicus Curiae* Brief**
A brief (a document containing a legal argument supporting a desired outcome in a particular case) filed by a third party, or *amicus curiae* (Latin for "friend of the court"), who is not directly involved in the litigation but who has an interest in the outcome of the case.

Class-Action Suit
A lawsuit filed by an individual seeking damages for "all persons similarly situated."

Sometimes interest groups or other plaintiffs will bring a **class-action suit,** in which whatever the court decides will affect all members of a class similarly situated (such as users of a particular product manufactured by the defendant in the lawsuit). The strategy of class-action lawsuits was pioneered by such groups as the National Association for the Advancement of Colored People (NAACP), the Legal Defense Fund, and the Sierra Club, whose leaders believed that the courts would offer a more sympathetic forum for their views than would Congress.

Procedural Rules

Both the federal and the state courts have established procedural rules that shape the litigation process. These rules are designed to protect the rights and interests of the parties and to ensure that the litigation proceeds in a fair and orderly manner. The rules also serve to identify the issues that must be decided by the court—thus saving court time and costs. Court decisions may also apply to trial procedures. For example, the Supreme Court has held that the parties' attorneys cannot discriminate against prospective jurors on the basis of race or gender. Some lower courts have also held that people cannot be excluded from juries because of their sexual orientation or religion.

The parties must comply with procedural rules and with any orders given by the judge during the course of the litigation. When a party does not follow a court's order, the court

4. *Maqaleh v. Gates,* ___ F.3d ___ (D.C.Cir. 2010).

can cite him or her for contempt. A party who commits *civil* contempt (failing to comply with a court's order for the benefit of another party to the proceeding) can be taken into custody, fined, or both, until that party complies with the court's order. A party who commits *criminal* contempt (obstructing the administration of justice or bringing the court into disrespect) also can be taken into custody and fined but cannot avoid punishment by complying with a previous order.

Throughout this text, you have read about how technology is affecting all areas of government. The judiciary is no exception. Today's courts post opinions and other information online. Increasingly, lawyers are expected to file court documents electronically. There is little doubt that in the future we will see more court business conducted through use of the Internet.

The Supreme Court at Work

The Supreme Court begins its regular annual term on the first Monday in October and usually adjourns in late June or early July of the next year. Special sessions may be held after the regular term ends, but only a few cases are decided in this way. More commonly, cases are carried over until the next regular session.

Of the total number of cases that are decided each year in U.S. courts, those reviewed by the Supreme Court represent less than one in four thousand. Included in these, however, are decisions that profoundly affect our lives. In recent years, the United States Supreme Court has decided issues involving freedom of speech, the right to bear arms, campaign finance, capital punishment, the rights of criminal suspects, affirmative action programs, religious freedom, abortion, property rights, sexual harassment, pornography, states' rights, and many other matters with significant consequences for the nation.

Because the Supreme Court exercises a great deal of discretion over the types of cases it hears, it can influence the nation's policies by issuing decisions in some types of cases and refusing to hear appeals in others, thereby allowing lower court decisions to stand. Indeed, the fact that George W. Bush assumed the presidency in 2001 instead of Al Gore, his Democratic opponent, was largely due to a Supreme Court decision to review a Florida court's ruling. The Supreme Court reversed the Florida court's order to manually recount the votes in selected Florida counties—a decision that effectively handed the presidency to Bush.[5]

United States
Supreme Court justice Clarence Thomas stands in his chambers with three of his clerks. What type of work do clerks do when they assist a Supreme Court justice? (David Hume Kennerly/ Getty Images)

Which Cases Reach the Supreme Court?

Many people are surprised to learn that in a typical case, there is no absolute right of appeal to the United States Supreme Court. The Court's appellate jurisdiction is almost entirely discretionary—the Court can choose which cases it will decide. The justices never

5. *Bush v. Gore,* 531 U.S. 98 (2000).

explain their reasons for hearing certain cases and not others, so it is difficult to predict which case or type of case the Court might select.

Factors That Bear on the Decision. A number of factors bear on the decision to accept a case. If a legal question has been decided differently by various lower courts, it may need resolution by the highest court. A ruling may be necessary if a lower court's decision conflicts with an existing Supreme Court ruling. In general, the Court considers whether the issue could have significance beyond the parties to the dispute.

Another factor is whether the solicitor general is asking the Court to take a case. The solicitor general, a high-ranking presidential appointee within the Justice Department, represents the national government before the Supreme Court and promotes presidential policies in the federal courts. He or she decides what cases the government should ask the Supreme Court to review and what position the government should take in cases before the Court.

did you know?

That before they take their seats at the bench, each justice shakes hands with the others? This practice began with Chief Justice Melville W. Fuller in the late 1800s as a way to remind justices that, although they may have differences of opinion, they share a common purpose.

Granting Petitions for Review. If the Court decides to grant a petition for review, it will issue a **writ of *certiorari*** (pronounced sur-shee-uh-*rah*-ree). The writ orders a lower court to send the Supreme Court a record of the case for review. Of the more than eight thousand petitions for review that the Court receives each term, only a small percentage are granted. A denial is not a decision on the merits of a case, nor does it indicate agreement with the lower court's opinion. (The judgment of the lower court remains in force, however.) Therefore, denial of the writ has no value as a precedent. The Court will not issue a writ unless at least four justices approve of it. This is called the **rule of four.**[6]

Court Procedures

Once the Supreme Court grants *certiorari* in a particular case, the justices do extensive research on the legal issues and facts involved in the case. (Of course, some preliminary research is necessary before deciding to grant the petition for review.) Each justice is entitled to four law clerks, who undertake much of the research and preliminary drafting necessary for the justice to form an opinion.

The Court normally does not hear any evidence, as is true with all appeals courts. The Court's consideration of a case is based on the abstracts, the record, and the briefs. The attorneys are permitted to present **oral arguments.** Unlike the practice in most courts, lawyers addressing the Supreme Court can be (and often are) questioned by the justices at any time during oral argument. All statements and the justices' questions during oral arguments are recorded.

The justices meet to discuss and vote on cases in conferences held throughout the term. In these conferences, in addition to deciding cases already before the Court, the justices determine which new petitions for *certiorari* to grant. These conferences take place in the oak-paneled chamber and are strictly private—no stenographers, audio recorders, or video cameras are allowed. Two pages used to be in attendance to wait on the justices while they were in conference, but fear of information leaks caused the Court to stop this practice.[7]

Writ of *Certiorari*
An order issued by a higher court to a lower court to send up the record of a case for review.

Rule of Four
A United States Supreme Court procedure by which four justices must vote to grant a petition for review if a case is to come before the full court.

Oral Arguments
The arguments presented in person by attorneys to an appellate court. Each attorney presents reasons to the court why the court should rule in her or his client's favor.

6. The "rule of four" is modified when seven or fewer justices participate, which occurs from time to time. When that happens, as few as three justices can grant *certiorari*.
7. It turned out that one supposed information leak came from lawyers making educated guesses.

Decisions and Opinions

When the Court has reached a decision, its opinion is written. The **opinion** contains the Court's ruling on the issue or issues presented, the reasons for its decision, the rules of law that apply, and other information. In many cases, the decision of the lower court is **affirmed,** resulting in the enforcement of that court's judgment or decree. If the Supreme Court believes that the lower courts made the wrong decision, however, the decision will be **reversed.** Sometimes the case will be **remanded** (sent back to the court that originally heard the case) for a new trial or other proceeding. For example, a lower court might have held that a party was not entitled to bring a lawsuit under a particular law. If the Supreme Court holds to the contrary, it will remand (send back) the case to the trial court with instructions that the trial go forward.

The Court's written opinion sometimes is unsigned; this is called an opinion *per curiam* ("by the court"). Typically, the Court's opinion is signed by all the justices who agree with it. When in the majority, the chief justice decides who writes the opinion and often writes it personally. When the chief justice is in the minority, the senior justice on the majority side assigns the opinion.

Types of Opinions. When all justices unanimously agree on an opinion, the opinion is written for the entire Court (all the justices) and can be deemed a **unanimous opinion.** When there is not a unanimous opinion, a **majority opinion** is written, outlining the views of the majority of the justices involved in the case. Often, one or more justices who feel strongly about making or emphasizing a particular point that is not made or emphasized in the unanimous or majority written opinion will write a **concurring opinion.** That means the justice writing the concurring opinion agrees (concurs) with the conclusion given in the majority written opinion, but for different reasons. Finally, in other than unanimous opinions, one or more justices who do not agree with the majority usually will write a **dissenting opinion.** The dissenting opinion is important because it often forms the basis of the arguments used years later if the Court reverses the previous decision and establishes a new precedent.

The Publication of Supreme Court Opinions. Shortly after the opinion is written, the Supreme Court announces its decision from the bench. At that time, the opinion is made available to the public at the office of the clerk of the Court. The clerk also releases the opinion for online publication. Ultimately, the opinion is published in the *United States Reports,* which is the official printed record of the Court's decisions.

The Court's Dwindling Caseload. Some have complained that the Court reviews too few cases each term, thus giving the lower courts less guidance on important issues. Indeed, the number of signed opinions issued by the Court has dwindled notably since the 1980s. For example, in its 1982–1983 term, the Court issued signed opinions in 151 cases. By the early 2000s, this number dropped to between 70 and 80 per term. In the term ending in June 2010, the number was 92.

Some scholars suggest that one of the reasons the Court hears fewer cases today than in the past is the growing conservatism of the judges sitting on lower courts. More than half of these judges have now been appointed by Republican presidents. As a result, the government loses fewer cases in the lower courts, which lessens the need for the government to appeal the rulings through the solicitor general's office. Some support for this conclusion is given by the fact that the number of petitions filed by that office declined by more than 50 percent during the administration of George W. Bush.

Opinion
The statement by a judge or a court of the decision reached in a case. The opinion sets forth the applicable law and details the reasoning on which the ruling was based.

Affirm
To declare that a court ruling is valid and must stand.

Reverse
To annul, or make void, a court ruling on account of some error or irregularity.

Remand
To send a case back to the court that originally heard it.

Unanimous Opinion
A court opinion or determination on which all judges agree.

Majority Opinion
A court opinion reflecting the views of the majority of the judges.

Concurring Opinion
A separate opinion prepared by a judge who supports the decision of the majority of the court but who wants to make or clarify a particular point or to voice disapproval of the grounds on which the decision was made.

Dissenting Opinion
A separate opinion in which a judge dissents from (disagrees with) the conclusion reached by the majority on the court and expounds his or her own views about the case.

The Selection of Federal Judges

All federal judges are appointed. The Constitution, in Article II, Section 2, states that the president appoints the justices of the Supreme Court with the advice and consent of the Senate. Congress has provided the same procedure for staffing other federal courts. This means that the Senate and the president jointly decide who shall fill every vacant judicial position, no matter what the level.

There are more than 850 federal judgeships in the United States. Once appointed to such a judgeship, a person holds that job for life. Judges serve until they resign, retire voluntarily, or die. Federal judges who engage in blatantly illegal conduct may be removed through impeachment, although such action is rare.

In contrast to federal judges, many state judges—including the judges who sit on state supreme courts—are chosen by the voters in elections. Inevitably, judicial candidates must raise campaign funds. What arguments favor the election of judges? What problems can such a system create? We examine such questions in this chapter's *Which Side Are You On?* feature on the facing page.

Judicial Appointments

Candidates for federal judgeships are suggested to the president by the Department of Justice, senators, other judges, the candidates themselves, and lawyers' associations and other interest groups. In selecting a candidate to nominate for a judgeship, the president considers not only the person's competence but also other factors, including the person's political philosophy (as will be discussed shortly), ethnicity, and gender.

The nomination process—no matter how the nominees are obtained—always works the same way. The president makes the actual nomination, transmitting the name to the Senate. The Senate then either confirms or rejects the nomination. To reach a conclusion, the Senate Judiciary Committee (operating through subcommittees) invites testimony, both written and oral, at its various hearings.

Federal District Court Judgeship Nominations. Although the president officially nominates federal judges, in the past the nomination of federal district court judges actually originated with a senator or senators of the president's party from the state in which there was a vacancy. In effect, judicial appointments were a form of political patronage. President Jimmy Carter (1977–1981) ended this tradition by establishing independent commissions to oversee the initial nomination process. President Ronald Reagan (1981–1989) abolished Carter's nominating commissions and established complete presidential control of nominations.

Senatorial Courtesy
In federal district court judgeship nominations, a tradition allowing a senator to veto a judicial appointment in his or her state.

A practice used in the Senate, called **senatorial courtesy,** is a constraint on the president's freedom to appoint federal district judges. Senatorial courtesy allows a senator of the president's political party to veto a judicial appointment in her or his state. During much of American history, senators from the "opposition" party (the party to which the president did not belong) also enjoyed the right of senatorial courtesy, although their veto power varied over time.

In 2000, Orrin Hatch, Republican chair of the Senate Judiciary Committee, announced that the opposition party (at that point, the Democrats) would no longer be allowed to invoke senatorial courtesy. The implementation of the new policy was delayed when Republican senator James Jeffords of Vermont left the Republican Party. Jeffords's departure turned control of the Senate over to the Democrats. After the 2002 elections, however, when the Republicans regained control of the Senate, they put the new policy into effect.

When the Democrats took over the Senate following the elections of 2006, Senator Patrick J. Leahy (D., Vt.), chairman of the Judiciary Committee, let it be known that the old bipartisan system of senatorial courtesy would return. Of course, the Republicans, who were now in the minority, were unlikely to object to a nomination submitted by Republican president George W. Bush, and the old practices did not become truly effective until Democratic president Barack Obama took office.

WHICH SIDE ARE YOU ON?

SHOULD STATE JUDGES BE ELECTED?

The nation's founders sought to insulate the courts from popular passions, and as a result, all of the judges and justices in the federal court system are appointed by the president and confirmed by the Senate. Federal judges and justices are appointed for life. In thirty-nine states, in contrast, some or all state judges must face election and reelection.

In many jurisdictions, judges must run for election and reelection. Here you see election campaign signs for judges (and commissioners). What are the arguments for and against state judicial elections? (AP Photo/Rogelio Solis)

The question of whether state judges should be elected or whether they should be appointed has proved to be very divisive. Many in the legal community agreed with a former Oregon Supreme Court justice, Hans A. Linde, when he pointed out that "to the rest of the world, American adherence to judicial elections is as incomprehensible as our rejection of the metric system." Public opinion polls, however, regularly show strong public support for electing judges.

THE PEOPLE'S WILL SHOULD PREVAIL

Those who advocate the election of state judges see the issue as a simple matter of democracy. Judges cannot be insulated from politics. Governors who appoint judges are highly political creatures and are likely to appoint members of their own party. If politics is going to play a role, the people ought to have their say directly. In addition, researchers at the University of Chicago School of Law found that elected judges wrote more opinions than appointed judges.

We let ordinary people participate in the legal process through the jury system, and they ought to be able to choose judges as well. That way, the people can be confident that judges will respond to popular concerns, such as the fear of crime. Without elections, judges living in safe, upscale neighborhoods may fail to appreciate what it is like to fear for your safety on an everyday basis.

ELECTING JUDGES LEADS TO CORRUPTION

Former United States Supreme Court justice Sandra Day O'Connor condemned the practice of electing judges: "No other nation in the world does that because they realize you are not going to get fair and impartial judges that way." Opponents of judicial elections observe that most voters do not have enough information to make sensible choices when they vote for judicial candidates. Therefore, campaign contributions wind up deciding judicial races. Governors fill hundreds of appointive positions. They can easily take the high road when appointing judges. The motives of campaign contributors, however, are *always* suspect.

Judicial candidates raise considerable funds from the lawyers who will appear before them if they win. Additional campaign funds are raised by special interest groups that want "their" candidate elected or reelected to the state court in question. People who want to elect judges think that the candidates they vote for will, for example, be "tough on crime." Often, they are. But those who oppose judicial elections contend that elected judges will also tilt toward the wealthy groups that put them in office, and away from the interests of ordinary people.

In a recent election to fill a Wisconsin state supreme court judgeship, the candidates spent more than $5.5 million in all, and more than 12,000 campaign commercials were aired on television. In the states in which there are state supreme court elections, more than 90 percent of the elections involve television campaign commercials.

Federal Courts of Appeals Appointments. Appointments to the federal courts of appeals are far less numerous than federal district court appointments, but they are more important. This is because federal appellate judges handle more important matters, at least from the point of view of the president, and therefore presidents take a keener interest in the nomination process for such judgeships. Also, the U.S. courts of appeals have become "stepping-stones" to the Supreme Court.

TABLE 13–1

Background of United States Supreme Court Justices to 2011

	Number of Justices (112 = Total)
Occupational Position before Appointment	
Federal judgeship	31
Private legal practice	25
State judgeship	21
Federal executive post	9
U.S. attorney general	7
U.S. senator	6
State governor	3
Deputy or assistant U.S. attorney general	2
U.S. solicitor general	3
U.S. representative	2
Other	3
Religious Background	
Protestant	83
Roman Catholic	14
Unitarian	7
Jewish	7
No religious affiliation	1
Age on Appointment	
Under 40	5
41–50	33
51–60	60
61–70	14
Political Party Affiliation	
Democrat	46
Republican	44
Federalist (to 1835)	13
Jeffersonian Republican (to 1828)	7
Whig (to 1861)	1
Independent	1
Educational Background	
College graduate	96
Not a college graduate	16
Gender	
Male	108
Female	4
Race	
Non-Hispanic White	109
African American	2
Hispanic	1

Sources: Congressional Quarterly, *Congressional Quarterly's Guide to the U.S. Supreme Court* (Washington, D.C.: Congressional Quarterly Press, 1996); and authors' updates.

Supreme Court Appointments. As we have described, the president nominates Supreme Court justices. As you can see in Table 13–1 alongside, which summarizes the background of all Supreme Court justices to 2011, the most common occupational background of the justices at the time of their appointment has been private legal practice or state or federal judgeship. Those nine justices who were in federal executive posts at the time of their appointment held the high offices of secretary of state, comptroller of the treasury, secretary of the navy, postmaster general, secretary of the interior, chairman of the Securities and Exchange Commission, and secretary of labor. In the "Other" category under "Occupational Position before Appointment" in Table 13–1 are two justices who were professors of law (including William H. Taft, a former president) and one justice who was a North Carolina state employee with responsibility for organizing and revising the state's statutes.

The Special Role of the Chief Justice. Ideology is always important in judicial appointments, as described next. When a chief justice is selected for the Supreme Court, however other considerations must also be taken into account. The chief justice is not only the head of a group of nine justices who interpret the law. He or she is also in essence the chief executive officer of a large bureaucracy that includes more than one thousand judges with lifetime tenure, hundreds of magistrates and bankruptcy judges with limited tenure, and a staff of about thirty thousand.

The chief justice is also the chair of the Judicial Conference of the United States, a policymaking body that sets priorities for the federal judiciary. That position means that the chief justice indirectly oversees the $6 billion budget of this group.

Finally, the chief justice appoints the director of the Administrative Office of the United States Courts. The chief justice and this director select judges who sit on judicial committees that examine international judicial relations, technology, and a variety of other topics.

Partisanship and Judicial Appointments

In most circumstances, the president appoints judges or justices who belong to the president's own political party. Presidents see their federal judiciary appointments as the one sure way to institutionalize their political views long after they have left office. By 1993, for example, Presidents Ronald Reagan and George H. W. Bush together had appointed nearly three-quarters of all federal court judges. This preponderance of Republican-appointed federal judges strengthened the legal moorings of the conservative social agenda on a variety of issues, ranging from abortion to civil rights. President Bill Clinton had the opportunity to appoint 371 federal district and appeals court judges, thereby shifting the ideological makeup of the federal judiciary. George W. Bush then appointed 322 federal district and appeals court judges, again creating a majority of Republican-appointed judges in the federal courts.

During the first two years of his second term, President Bush also had the opportunity to fill two Supreme Court vacancies—those left by the death of Chief Justice William Rehnquist and by the retirement of Justice Sandra Day O'Connor. Bush appointed two conservatives to these positions—John G. Roberts, Jr., who became chief justice, and Samuel Alito, Jr., who replaced O'Connor. The appointment of Alito, in particular, strengthened the rightward movement of the Court that had begun years before with the appointment of Rehnquist as chief justice. This was because Alito was a reliable member of the Court's conservative wing, whereas O'Connor had been a "swing voter."

President Obama had two opportunities to fill Supreme Court vacancies in the first two years of his term. The vacancies resulted from the retirement of Justices David Souter and John Paul Stevens. Both had been members of the Court's so-called liberal wing, so Obama's appointments did not change the ideological balance of the Court. Obama chose two women: Sonia Sotomayor, who had been an appeals court judge and was the Court's first Hispanic member, and Elena Kagan, who had been Obama's solicitor general.

Different courts have different procedures. In many state and local courts, the judge can ask the defense attorney to come to the "bench." The United States Supreme Court, in contrast, never asks attorneys to do so. Why not? (AP Photo/Zara Tzanev, Pool)

The Senate's Role

Ideology also plays a large role in the Senate's confirmation hearings, and presidential nominees to the Supreme Court have not always been confirmed. In fact, almost 20 percent of presidential nominations to the Supreme Court have either been rejected or not acted on by the Senate. There have been many acrimonious battles over Supreme Court appointments when the Senate and the president have not seen eye to eye about political matters.

Confirming Supreme Court Appointments. The U.S. Senate had a long record of refusing to confirm the president's judicial nominations from the beginning of Andrew Jackson's presidency in 1829 to the end of Ulysses Grant's presidency in 1877. From 1894 until 1968, however, only three nominees were not confirmed. Then, from 1968 through 1987, four presidential nominees to the highest court were rejected. One of the most controversial Supreme Court nominations was that of Clarence Thomas, who underwent an extremely volatile confirmation hearing in 1991, replete with charges against him of sexual harassment. He was ultimately confirmed by the Senate, however.

President Bill Clinton had little trouble gaining approval for both of his nominees to the Supreme Court: Ruth Bader Ginsburg and Stephen G. Breyer. President George W. Bush's nominees faced hostile grilling in their confirmation hearings, and various interest groups mounted intense media ad blitzes against them. Indeed, Bush had to forgo the nomination of Harriet Miers when he realized that he could not win the confirmation battle.

did you know?

That Jimmy Carter is the only president to serve a full term without nominating a Supreme Court justice.

Lower Court Appointments. Presidents have often found that appointments to district and appeals courts create even more trouble than Supreme Court appointments. For an extended period during the presidency of Bill Clinton, the Republican majority in Congress adopted a strategy of trying to block almost every action taken by the administration—and that included judicial appointments.

Attempts to block appointments have not been limited to times when the president faced a Congress dominated by the other party, however. The modern understanding that sixty votes are required before the Senate will consider a major measure has given the minority party a substantial degree of power. As a result, after the election of George W.

Bush in 2000, the Democratic minority in the Senate was able to hold up many of Bush's more controversial judicial appointments. Frustrated by this tactic, Republican senators threatened to use what some called the "nuclear option," under which Senate rules would be revised to disallow filibusters against judicial nominees. In the end, though, a bipartisan group engineered a temporary compromise to preserve the filibuster.

With the backing of sixty Democratic senators, President Obama initially had little trouble in getting his nominees approved. After Republican Scott Brown won the Massachusetts special senatorial election in January 2010, however, Republicans were able to slow, if not stop, the appointments process.

Policymaking and the Courts

The partisan battles over judicial appointments reflect a significant reality in today's American government: the importance of the judiciary in national politics. Because appointments to the federal bench are for life, the ideology of judicial appointees can affect national policy for years to come. Although the primary function of judges in our system of government is to interpret and apply the laws, inevitably judges make policy when carrying out this task. One of the major policymaking tools of the federal courts is their power of judicial review.

Judicial Review

Remember from Chapter 2 that the power of the courts to determine whether a law or action by the other branches of government is constitutional is known as the power of *judicial review.* This power enables the judicial branch to act as a check on the other two branches of government, in line with the system of checks and balances established by the U.S. Constitution.

The power of judicial review is not mentioned in the Constitution, however. Rather, it was established by the United States Supreme Court's decision in *Marbury v. Madison.*[8] In that case, in which the Court declared that a law passed by Congress violated the Constitution, the Court claimed such a power for the judiciary:

> *It is emphatically the province and duty of the Judicial Department to say what the law is. Those who apply the rule to a particular case must of necessity expound and interpret that rule. If two laws conflict with each other, the courts must decide on the operation of each.*

If a federal court declares that a federal or state law or policy is unconstitutional, the court's decision affects the application of the law or policy only within that court's jurisdiction. For this reason, the higher the level of the court, the greater the impact of the decision on society. Because of the Supreme Court's national jurisdiction, its decisions have the greatest impact. For example, when the Supreme Court held that an Arkansas state constitutional amendment limiting the terms of congresspersons was unconstitutional, laws establishing term limits in twenty-three other states were also invalidated.[9]

Some claim that the power of judicial review gives unelected judges and justices on federal court benches too much influence over national policy. Others argue that the powers exercised by the federal courts, particularly the power of judicial review, are necessary to protect our constitutional rights and liberties. Built into our federal form of government is a system of checks and balances. If the federal courts did not have the power of judicial review, there would be no governmental body to check Congress's lawmaking authority or the unconstitutional use of power by the executive branch.

---

8. 5 U.S. 137 (1803).
9. *U.S. Term Limits v. Thornton,* 514 U.S. 779 (1995).

Judicial Activism and Judicial Restraint

Judicial scholars like to characterize different judges and justices as being either "activist" or "restraintist."

Judicial Activism. The doctrine of **judicial activism** rests on the conviction that the federal judiciary should take an active role by using its powers to check the activities of Congress, state legislatures, and administrative agencies when those governmental bodies exceed their authority. One of the Supreme Court's most activist eras was the period from 1953 to 1969, when the Court was headed by Chief Justice Earl Warren. The Warren Court propelled the civil rights movement forward by holding, among other things, that laws permitting racial segregation violated the equal protection clause.

Judicial Restraint. In contrast, the doctrine of **judicial restraint** rests on the assumption that the courts should defer to the decisions made by the legislative and executive branches, because members of Congress and the president are elected by the people whereas members of the federal judiciary are not. Because administrative agency personnel normally have more expertise than the courts do in the areas regulated by the agencies, the courts likewise should defer to agency rules and decisions. In other words, under the doctrine of judicial restraint, the courts should not thwart the implementation of legislative acts and agency rules unless they are clearly unconstitutional.

Earl Warren served as chief justice of the United States Supreme Court for thirteen years starting in 1953. Was he known for judicial activism or for judicial restraint? (AP Photo)

Liberal and Conservative Activism. Judicial activism sometimes is linked with liberalism, and judicial restraint with conservatism. In fact, though, a conservative judge can be activist, just as a liberal judge can be restraintist. In the 1950s and 1960s, the Supreme Court was activist and liberal. Some observers believe that the Rehnquist Court, with its conservative majority, became increasingly activist during the early 2000s. The most conservative members on today's Roberts Court, (John Roberts, Antonin Scalia, Clarence Thomas, and Samuel Alito) however, are regarded by some scholars as restraintist justices because of their deference to laws and regulations reflecting the policy of the Bush administration.

With Democrat Barack Obama as president, some suggest that the Court's conservative wing may become more active in its approach to judicial interpretation. The *Citizens United v. Federal Election Commission* decision, in which the Court struck down longstanding campaign finance laws, lends credence to this view. (You learned about this ruling on page 298 in Chapter 9.) Recently, a coalition of state attorneys general has challenged the constitutionality of the Democrats' sweeping health-care reform measures—we discuss this issue in the *Politics of Boom and Bust* feature on the following page. If even a minority of the Court were to advocate overturning important parts of the health-care legislation, it would indeed represent a radical turn toward conservative judicial activism.

Judicial Activism
A doctrine holding that the federal judiciary should take an active role by using its powers to check the activities of governmental bodies when those bodies exceed their authority.

Judicial Restraint
A doctrine holding that the courts should defer to the decisions made by the elected representatives of the people in the legislative and executive branches.

Strict Construction
A judicial philosophy that looks to the "letter of the law" when interpreting the Constitution or a particular statute.

Broad Construction
A judicial philosophy that looks to the context and purpose of a law when making an interpretation.

Strict versus Broad Construction

Other terms that are often used to describe a justice's philosophy are *strict construction* and *broad construction.* Justices who believe in **strict construction** look to the "letter of the law" when they attempt to interpret the Constitution or a particular statute. Those who favor **broad construction** try to determine the context and purpose of the law.

As with the doctrines of judicial restraint and judicial activism, strict construction is often associated with conservative political views, whereas broad construction is often linked with liberalism. These traditional political associations sometimes appear to be reversed, however. Consider the Eleventh Amendment to the Constitution, which rules out lawsuits in federal courts "against one of the United States by Citizens of another State, or by Citizens or Subjects of any Foreign State." Nothing is said about citizens suing

THE POLITICS OF BOOM AND BUST

THE CONSTITUTIONALITY OF OBAMACARE

The 2010 health-care reform legislation advocated by President Obama and drafted by the Democrats in Congress will massively transform the health-care system, but the changes will be phased in over many years. The nation will not approach universal health-care insurance coverage until 2014. At that time, an *individual mandate* will go into effect that requires almost all persons either to have health insurance or to pay a penalty when filing their income tax returns.

After the passage of the legislation, twenty state governors or attorneys general, all but one of them Republicans, joined in a lawsuit against the federal government. These leaders argued that it is unconstitutional to require individuals to purchase health insurance. In March 2010, Virginia's legislature passed a law banning mandatory health insurance. The law states that Virginians cannot be required to buy health insurance nor can they be penalized for not having it. Idaho passed a similar law a week later. Thirty-five other states considered similar bills.

ARGUMENTS OVER THE CONSTITUTIONAL CHALLENGE

At the heart of the argument against the constitutionality of the individual mandate is the claim that the federal government cannot regulate *in*activity. Opponents of the individual mandate say that there will be no limits on government actions if this tax is deemed constitutional by the Supreme Court. After all, they claim, the government could go on to tax those who are overweight, those who don't exercise, those who smoke, or those who buy foreign cars. If the individual mandate were allowed to stand, Congress would have the power to regulate Americans "merely because they exist."

Many constitutional experts consider such arguments to be absurd. It is not the health-care legislation that grants Congress the right to regulate Americans "because they exist." Congress, these experts point out, has had that power since 1789. Right now, the government effectively imposes higher rates of income tax on those who do not marry, do not have children, or do not buy a house. If you believe that the government cannot penalize you for inactivity, try not filing your federal income tax return. You will discover that the government takes such inactivity very seriously. If you cannot pay what you owe, you may be able to work out a deal with the Internal Revenue Service. If you fail to file altogether, you could go to prison.

HOW CONGRESS SOUGHT TO AVOID CONSTITUTIONAL ISSUES

The Democratic members of Congress who drafted the health-care reform bills were aware that there might be constitutional challenges. They considered themselves on solid ground, however, with the argument that failing to buy insurance "substantially affects interstate commerce." This, of course, is the Supreme Court's standard for federal authority under the Constitution's commerce clause. Still, opponents argue that the federal government has never used the commerce clause to require that citizens buy a good or service. Liberal bloggers, however, have come up with a counterexample: The Militia Act of 1792 required all able-bodied adult white males not only to enroll in the militia, but to equip themselves with a musket and ammunition.

FOR CRITICAL ANALYSIS

Review the section of Chapter 3 entitled *Federalism and Today's Supreme Court,* beginning on page 103. What limits has the Supreme Court placed on the use of the commerce clause by Congress?

their own states, and strict construction would therefore find such suits to be constitutional. Conservative justices, however, have construed this amendment broadly to deny citizens the constitutional right to sue their own states in most circumstances. John T. Noonan, Jr., a federal appellate court judge who was appointed by a Republican president, has described these rulings as "adventurous."[10]

Broad construction is often associated with the concept of a "living constitution." Supreme Court justice Antonin Scalia, in contrast, has said that "the Constitution is not a living organism, it is a legal document. It says something and doesn't say other things." Scalia believes that jurists should stick to the plain text of the Constitution "as it was originally written and intended."

The Rightward Shift of the Rehnquist Court

William H. Rehnquist became the sixteenth chief justice of the Supreme Court in 1986, after fifteen years as an associate justice. He was known as a strong anchor of the Court's conservative wing until his death in 2005. With Rehnquist's appointment as chief justice, the Court began to take a rightward shift. The Court's rightward movement continued as other conservative appointments to the bench were made during the Reagan and George H. W. Bush administrations.

Interestingly, to counter the increasingly conservative movement of the Court, some previously conservative justices showed a tendency to "migrate" to a more liberal view of the law. Sandra Day O'Connor, the first female justice and a conservative, gradually shifted to the left on a number of issues, including abortion. Justice Anthony Kennedy also migrated to the left on occasion. Generally, O'Connor and Kennedy provided the "swing votes" on the Rehnquist Court.

did you know?

That a proclamation by President George Washington and a congressional resolution established the first national Thanksgiving Day on November 26, 1789? The reason for the holiday was to give thanks for the new Constitution.

Although the Court moved to the right during the Rehnquist era, its decisions were not always in line with conservative ideology. The Court was closely divided in many cases, making it difficult to predict how the Court might rule on any particular issue. Consider the Court's rulings with respect to states' rights. In 1995, the Court held, for the first time in sixty years, that Congress had overreached its powers under the commerce clause when it attempted to regulate the possession of guns in school zones. According to the Court, the possession of guns in school zones had nothing to do with the commerce clause.[11] Yet in a 2005 case, the Court ruled that Congress's power to regulate commerce allowed it to ban marijuana use even when a state's law permitted such use and the growing and use of the drug were strictly local in nature.[12] What these two rulings had in common was that they supported policies generally considered to be conservative—the right to possess firearms on the one hand, and a strong stand against marijuana use on the other.

The Roberts Court

During its first term, which ended on June 30, 2006, the Roberts Court (see Figure 13–3 on the following page) accepted few controversial cases for review. Some of the cases it did accept, however, revealed a rightward drift. In *Hudson v. Michigan*,[13] Roberts wrote the majority opinion in a five-to-four decision holding that it was not necessary to suppress evidence if the police did not knock and announce their presence before forcibly entering a home. This decision effectively removed the protections of the "knock and announce"

---

10. John T. Noonan, Jr., *Narrowing the Nation's Power: The Supreme Court Sides with the States* (Berkeley: University of California Press, 2002).
11. *United States v. Lopez*, 514 U.S. 549 (1995).
12. *Gonzales v. Raich*, 545 U.S. 1 (2005).
13. 547 U.S. 586 (2006).

rule for criminal suspects, and was generally considered to represent a conservative position on the rights of the accused. In several other close (five-to-four) decisions, however, Justice Kennedy sided with the Court's liberal wing in providing the deciding vote.

The Roberts Court's Second Term. In the second term of the Roberts Court (2006–2007), the addition of Justice Alito made it easier for Justices Roberts, Scalia, and Thomas to move the Court further to the right ideologically. Still, in an important decision challenging the George W. Bush administration's contention that the Environmental Protection Agency (EPA) did not have the authority under the Clean Air Act to regulate emissions of greenhouse gases, the majority on the Court held that the EPA *did* have this authority and should exercise it. Roberts, Scalia, Thomas, and Alito dissented from the majority's opinion.[14] Again, Justice Kennedy provided the swing vote, tipping the majority to the liberal-

14. *Massachusetts v. E.P.A.*, 549 U.S. 497 (2007).

FIGURE 13–3 The Roberts Court

The members of the United States Supreme Court as of 2011.

(Kagen–AP Photo/Alex Brandon, Sotomayor–AP/Charles Dharapak, remaining photos–The U.S. Supreme Court)

to-moderate side. In another 2007 case, however, the Court upheld a 2003 federal law banning partial-birth abortion, again by a close (five-to-four) vote. This time, Justice Kennedy sided with the conservatives on the Court, giving them a majority.[15]

The rightward drift of the Roberts Court resulted in some harsh criticisms, not all of which came from liberals. For example, Richard Posner, a well-known and relatively conservative federal appeals court judge in Chicago, has noted that what Roberts said during his confirmation hearings is often at odds with Roberts's actions as chief justice.[16] The case that drew the most negative public response may have been *Ledbetter v. Goodyear Tire & Rubber Co.*[17] The Court held, in a five-to-four decision, that employers are protected from lawsuits over racial or gender pay discrimination if the claims are based on decisions made by the employer more than 180 days before the claims are filed. Many observers argued that this verdict would make pay-discrimination suits almost impossible to win. The *Ledbetter* case was only the most conspicuous of a series of cases in which the Court sided with business interests. The U.S. Chamber of Commerce was successful in thirteen of the fifteen cases in which it filed *amicus curiae* (friend-of-the-court) briefs, an all-time high.

"I think it's high time we had an enigma on the Supreme Court."
(© The New Yorker Collection, 1990. Donald Reilly, from www.cartoonbank.com. All Rights Reserved.)

The Court Backpedals Slightly. The justices continued to chart a conservative course in the Roberts Court's third term, from 2007 to 2008. They drew back, however, from the strong pro-employer stance they had taken previously. In two cases, the Court held that workers who complain about racial or age-based bias may sue for damages if they face retaliation from their employers.[18] The Court also decided three other discrimination cases in favor of the employees. Still, it was not a bad term for business interests—several rulings restricted the extent to which corporations are exposed to lawsuits. Notably, the Court cut a $2.5 billion punitive damages award against ExxonMobil resulting from the *Exxon Valdez* supertanker oil spill in Alaska to about $500 million.[19]

Probably the most significant of the Court's right-of-center rulings came in *District of Columbia v. Heller,* when it overturned the District of Columbia's ban on handguns.[20] For the first time, the Court established the right of individuals to own guns for private use, not only as members of a militia. The five-to-four majority left considerable room for the states to regulate gun ownership, however. The Court also upheld Kentucky's method of execution by lethal injection,[21] Indiana's law requiring photo identification at the polls,[22] and a recent federal law that criminalizes offers to sell child pornography even if the pornography does not actually exist.[23]

The Court's next term, 2008 to 2009, was less dramatic. Many of the major decisions merely fine-tuned the law. These included rulings to clarify when evidence must be thrown

---

15. *Gonzales v. Carhart,* 550 U.S. 124 (2007).
16. Richard A. Posner, *How Judges Think* (Cambridge, Mass.: Harvard University Press, 2010).
17. 550 U.S. 618 (2007).
18. *CBOCS West, Inc. v. Humphries,* 128 S.Ct. 1951 (2008); and *Gomez-Perez v. Potter,* 128 S.Ct. 1931 (2008).
19. *Exxon Shipping Co. v. Baker,* 128 S.Ct. 2605 (2008).
20. 128 S.Ct. 2783 (2008).
21. *Baze and Bowling v. Rees,* 553 U.S. 35 (2008).
22. *Crawford v. Marion County Election Board,* 553 U.S. 181 (2008).
23. *United States v. Williams,* 553 U.S. 285 (2008).

President Barack Obama announces Judge Sonia Sotomayor as his nominee for the United States Supreme Court to replace retiring Justice David Souter. Vice President Joe Biden looks on at left. Sotomayor was confirmed. Why was this confirmation historic? (Larry Downing/Reuters/Landov)

out because it was improperly collected,[24] to extend protection to employees in sexual-harassment investigations,[25] and to establish clearer guidelines in cases of reverse discrimination.[26] In civil liberties cases, the Court ruled that the First Amendment does not require municipalities to accept donated monuments,[27] and that an unreasonable strip search of a middle school girl violated the Fourth Amendment.[28] The Court also held that state supreme court judges who receive large campaign contributions must recuse themselves from cases involving the contributors.[29]

With some exceptions, in the two terms from 2007 to 2009 the Court's opinions were often narrowly enough drawn to prevent the five-to-four splits that had characterized the Court in its earlier terms. When the Court was narrowly divided, Justice Kennedy continued to provide the swing vote.

The Court's 2009–2010 Term. In its most recent term, the Supreme Court issued few blockbuster opinions, but at least two of them were of prime constitutional importance. The Court's most striking move to the political right took place in January 2010. In *Citizens United v. Federal Election Commission,* the Court struck down long-standing campaign finance laws and extended First Amendment free speech rights to corporations and labor unions.[30] We have discussed *Citizens* on several occasions in this text—the fullest account is in Chapter 9 on page 298.

The second major ruling was *McDonald v. Chicago,* issued in June 2010. The Court held that, like the federal government, all state and local governments are bound to recognize the right to bear arms as an individual right, and not as a right that is limited to state militias.[31] This decision overturned a precedent dating back to 1939 and added the Second Amendment to the list of constitutional provisions incorporated into the Fourteenth Amendment, and therefore binding on the states. The issue of how to interpret the Second Amendment was discussed in the *Which Side Are You On?* feature in Chapter 2 on page 53, and incorporation theory was described in Chapter 4 on page 114.

In other significant decisions, the Court ruled in May 2010 that juveniles who commit crimes in which no one is killed may not be sentenced to life in prison without the possibility of parole.[32] Also in June 2010, the Court determined that state universities may deny funding to student groups that refuse to admit certain classes of students, in this case gay men and lesbians.[33]

---

24. *Herring v. United States,* 129 S.Ct. 695 (2009).
25. *Crawford v. Nashville,* 129 S.Ct. 846 (2009).
26. *Ricci v. DeStefano,* 129 S.Ct. 2658 (2009).
27. *Pleasant Grove City v. Summum,* 129 S.Ct. 1125 (2009).
28. *Safford Unified School District v. Redding,* 129 S.Ct. 2633 (2009).
29. *Caperton v. A. T. Massey Coal Co.,* 129 S.Ct. 2252 (2009).
30. 558 U.S. 50 (2010).
31. ___ S.Ct. ___ (2010).
32. *Graham v. Florida,* 560 U.S. ___ (2010).
33. *Christian Legal Society v. Martinez,* ___ S.Ct. ___ (2010).

What Checks Our Courts?

Our judicial system is one of the most independent in the world. But the courts do not have absolute independence, for they are part of the political process. Political checks limit the extent to which courts can exercise judicial review and engage in an activist policy. These checks are exercised by the executive branch, the legislature, the public, and, finally, the judiciary itself.

Executive Checks

President Andrew Jackson was once supposed to have said, after Chief Justice John Marshall made an unpopular decision, "John Marshall has made his decision; now let him enforce it."[34] This purported remark goes to the heart of **judicial implementation**—the enforcement of judicial decisions in such a way that those decisions are translated into policy. The Supreme Court simply does not have any enforcement powers, and whether a decision will be implemented depends on the cooperation of the other two branches of government. Rarely, though, will a president refuse to enforce a Supreme Court decision, as President Jackson did. To take such an action could mean a significant loss of public support and could even lead to impeachment hearings in the House.

Judicial Implementation
The way in which court decisions are translated into action.

More commonly, presidents exercise influence over the judiciary by appointing new judges and justices as federal judicial seats become vacant. Additionally, as mentioned earlier, the U.S. solicitor general plays a significant role in the federal court system, and the person holding that office is a presidential appointee.

Executives at the state level may also refuse to implement court decisions with which they disagree. A notable example of such a refusal occurred in Arkansas after the United States Supreme Court ordered schools to desegregate "with all deliberate speed" in 1955.[35] Arkansas governor Orval Faubus refused to cooperate with the decision and used the state's National Guard to block the integration of Central High School in Little Rock. Ultimately, President Dwight Eisenhower had to federalize the Arkansas National Guard and send federal troops to Little Rock to quell the violence that had erupted.

Legislative Checks

Courts may make rulings, but often the legislatures at local, state, and federal levels are required to appropriate funds to carry out the courts' rulings. A court, for example, may decide that prison conditions must be improved, but it is up to the legislature to authorize the funds necessary to carry out the ruling. When such funds are not appropriated, the court that made the ruling, in effect, has been checked.

Constitutional Amendments. Courts' rulings can be overturned by constitutional amendments at both the federal and state levels. Many of the amendments to the U.S. Constitution (such as the Fourteenth, Fifteenth, and Twenty-sixth Amendments) check the state courts' ability to allow discrimination, for example. Proposed constitutional amendments to reverse courts' decisions on school prayer, abortion, and same-sex marriage have failed.

Rewriting Laws. Finally, Congress or a state legislature can rewrite (amend) old laws or enact new ones to overturn a court's rulings if the legislature concludes that the court is interpreting laws or legislative intentions erroneously. For example, Congress passed the Civil Rights Act of 1991 in part to overturn a series of conservative rulings in employment-discrimination cases. In 2009, Congress passed (and President Obama signed) the Lilly

34. The decision referred to was *Cherokee Nation v. Georgia,* 30 U.S. 1 (1831).
35. *Brown v. Board of Education,* 349 U.S. 294 (1955)—the second *Brown* decision.

did you know?

That Justice Byron ("Whizzer") White (1962–1993) is the only Supreme Court justice to be in the College Football Hall of Fame.

Ledbetter Fair Pay Act, which resets the statute of limitations for filing an equal-pay lawsuit each time an employer issues a discriminatory paycheck. The law was a direct answer to *Ledbetter v. Goodyear,* in which the United States Supreme Court held that the statute of limitations begins at the date the pay was agreed on, not at the date of the most recent paycheck.[36] The new legislation made it much easier for employees to win pay-discrimination lawsuits.

According to political scientist Walter Murphy, "A permanent feature of our constitutional landscape is the ongoing tug and pull between elected government and the courts."[37] Certainly, over the last few decades the Supreme Court has been in conflict with the other two branches of government. Congress at various times has passed laws that, among other things, made it illegal to burn the American flag and attempted to curb pornography on the Internet. In each instance, the Supreme Court ruled that those laws were unconstitutional.

The states can also negate or alter the effects of Supreme Court rulings, when such decisions allow it. A good case in point is *Kelo v. City of New London.*[38] In that case, the Supreme Court allowed a city to take private property for redevelopment by private businesses. Since that case was decided, a majority of states have passed legislation limiting or prohibiting such takings.

When Elena Kagan was confirmed as a justice of the United States Supreme Court, she became only the fourth woman to hold this position. Why has it taken so long for women to win appointment as Supreme Court justices? (AP Photo/ Alex Brandon)

Public Opinion

Public opinion plays a significant role in shaping government policy, and certainly the judiciary is not excepted from this rule. For one thing, persons affected by a Supreme Court decision that is noticeably at odds with their views may simply ignore it. Officially sponsored prayers were banned in public schools in 1962, yet it was widely known that the ban was (and still is) ignored in many southern and rural districts. What can the courts do in this situation? Unless someone complains about the prayers and initiates a lawsuit, the courts can do nothing.

The public can also pressure state and local government officials to refuse to enforce a certain decision. As already mentioned, judicial implementation requires the cooperation of government officials at all levels, and public opinion in various regions of the country will influence whether such cooperation is forthcoming.

Additionally, the courts themselves necessarily are influenced by public opinion to some extent. After all, judges are not "islands" in our society; their attitudes are influenced by social trends, just as the attitudes and beliefs of all persons are. Courts generally tend to avoid issuing decisions that they know will be noticeably at odds with public opinion.[39] In part, this is because the judiciary, as a branch of the government, prefers to avoid creating divisiveness among members of the public. Also, a court—particularly the Supreme Court—may lose stature if it decides a case in a way that markedly diverges from public opinion. For example, in 2005 the Supreme Court ruled that the execution of persons who were under the age of eighteen when they committed the offense violates the Eighth Amendment's ban on cruel and unusual punishment.[40] In its ruling, the Court indicated that the standards of what constitutes cruel and unusual punishment are influenced by public opinion and that there is evidence that today our society views juvenile offenders as less culpable than the average criminal.

36. 550 U.S. 618 (2007).
37. As quoted in Neal Devins, "The Last Word Debate: How Social and Political Forces Shape Constitutional Values," *American Bar Association Journal,* October 1997, p. 48.
38. 545 U.S. 469 (2005).
39. One striking counterexample is the *Kelo v. City of New London* decision mentioned earlier.
40. *Roper v. Simmons,* 543 U.S. 551 (2005).

Judicial Traditions and Doctrines

Supreme Court justices (and other federal judges) typically exercise self-restraint in fashioning their decisions. In part, this restraint stems from their knowledge that the other two branches of government and the public can exercise checks on the judiciary, as previously discussed. To a large extent, however, this restraint is mandated by various judicially established traditions and doctrines. For example, in exercising its discretion to hear appeals, the Supreme Court will not hear a meritless appeal just so it can rule on the issue. Also, when reviewing a case, the Supreme Court typically narrows its focus to just one issue or one aspect of an issue involved in the case. The Court rarely makes broad, sweeping decisions on issues. Furthermore, the doctrine of *stare decisis* acts as a restraint because it obligates the courts, including the Supreme Court, to follow established precedents when deciding cases. Only rarely will courts overrule a precedent.

Hypothetical and Political Questions. Other judicial doctrines and practices also act as restraints. As already mentioned, the courts will hear only what are called justiciable disputes—disputes that arise out of actual cases. In other words, a court will not hear a case that involves a merely hypothetical issue. Additionally, if a political question is involved, the Supreme Court often will exercise judicial restraint and refuse to rule on the matter. A **political question** is one that the Supreme Court declares should be decided by the elected branches of government—the executive branch, the legislative branch, or those two branches acting together. For example, the Supreme Court has refused to rule on the controversy regarding the rights of gay men and lesbians in the military, preferring instead to defer to the executive branch's decisions on the matter. Generally, though, fewer questions are deemed political questions by the Supreme Court today than in the past.

Political Question
An issue that a court believes should be decided by the executive or legislative branch—or these two branches acting together.

The Impact of the Lower Courts. Higher courts can reverse the decisions of lower courts. Lower courts can act as a check on higher courts, too. Lower courts can ignore—and have ignored—Supreme Court decisions. Usually, this is done indirectly. A lower court might conclude, for example, that the precedent set by the Supreme Court does not apply to the exact circumstances in the case before the court. Alternatively, the lower court may decide that the Supreme Court's decision was ambiguous with respect to the issue before the lower court. The fact that the Supreme Court rarely makes broad and clear-cut statements on any issue makes it easier for the lower courts to interpret the Supreme Court's decisions in different ways.

The United States Supreme Court has decided that the right to bear arms is a constitutional question, not a political one. Some people argue that the question of whether guns should be banned in various locations ought to be settled by legislative bodies. Why would these people make that argument? (Kevin Dietsch/UPI/Landov)

WHY SHOULD YOU CARE ABOUT... THE COURTS?

Why should you, as an individual, care about the courts? The U.S. legal system may seem too complex to be influenced by one individual, but its power nonetheless depends on the support of individuals. The public has many ways of resisting, modifying, or overturning statutes and rulings of the courts.

A first-year student at Virginia Military Institute (VMI) waits to hear a welcoming statement from the school's superintendent in August 1997. That year was the first one in which women were allowed to attend VMI. (AP Photo/ *Richmond Times-Dispatch*, Bob Brown)

THE COURTS AND YOUR LIFE

You may find it worth your while to attend one or more court sessions to see how the law works in practice. Legislative bodies may make laws and ordinances, but legislation is given its practical form by court rulings. Therefore, if you care about the effects of a particular law, you may have to pay attention to how the courts are interpreting it. For example, do you believe that sentences handed down for certain crimes are too lenient—or too strict? Legislative bodies can attempt to establish sentences for various offenses, but the courts inevitably retain considerable flexibility in determining what happens in any particular case.

HOW YOU CAN MAKE A DIFFERENCE

Public opinion can have an effect on judicial policies. Whichever cause may interest you, there is probably an organization that pursues lawsuits to benefit that cause and that could use your support. A prime example is the modern women's movement, which undertook a long series of lawsuits to change the way women are treated in American life. The courts only rule on cases that are brought before them, and the women's movement changed American law by filing—and winning—case after case.

In 1965, a federal circuit court opened a wide range of jobs for women by overturning laws that kept women out of work that was "too hard" for them. In 1971, the United States Supreme Court ruled that states could not prefer men when assigning the administrators of estates. (This case was brought by Ruth Bader Ginsburg, who was later to sit on the Court herself.) In 1974, the Court ruled that employers could not use the "going market rate" to justify lower wages for women. In 1975, it ruled that women could not be excluded from juries. In 1978, an Oregon court became the first of many to find that a man could be prosecuted for raping his wife. In 1996, the Virginia Military Institute was forced to admit women as cadets. Today, groups such as the National Organization for Women continue to support lawsuits to advance women's rights.

If you want information about the Supreme Court, contact the following by telephone or letter:

Clerk of the Court
The Supreme Court of the United States
1 First St. N.E.
Washington, DC 20543
(202) 479-3011

You can access online information about the Supreme Court at the following site:
www.oyez.org

questions for discussion and analysis

1. Review the *Which Side Are You On?* feature on page 453. Why do you think that attorneys, as a group, contribute more to judicial campaigns than do members of other professions?
2. What are the benefits of having lifetime appointments to the United States Supreme Court? What problems might such appointments cause? What would be the likely result if Supreme Court justices faced term limits?
3. Under both presidents Bill Clinton and George W. Bush, members of the opposition party in the Senate often blocked the president's nominations to district and circuit courts. Under what circumstances are such blocking actions a legitimate exercise of the Senate's power? Under what circumstances can they rightly be described as inappropriate political maneuvers?
4. On page 459, we described how the Rehnquist Court ruled in favor of states' rights in a gun-control case and against states' rights on a matter concerning marijuana. Why do you think the justices might have come to different conclusions in these two cases?
5. Should Congress ever limit the jurisdiction of the federal courts for political reasons? Should Congress block the Court's ability to rule on cases raised by the prisoners at Guantánamo Bay? Why or why not?

key terms

affirm 451
***amicus curiae* brief 448**
appellate court 445
broad construction 457
case law 442
class-action suit 448
common law 441
concurring opinion 451
dissenting opinion 451
diversity of citizenship 444
federal question 444
general jurisdiction 445
judicial activism 457
judicial implementation 463
judicial restraint 457
jurisdiction 444
justiciable controversy 444
limited jurisdiction 445
litigate 448
majority opinion 451
opinion 451
oral arguments 450
political question 465
precedent 441
remand 451
reverse 451
rule of four 450
senatorial courtesy 452
***stare decisis* 441**
strict construction 457
trial court 445
unanimous opinion 451
writ of *certiorari* 450

chapter summary

1. American law is rooted in the common law tradition, which is part of our heritage from England. The common law doctrine of *stare decisis* (which means "to stand on decided cases") obligates judges to follow precedents established previously by their own courts or by higher courts that have authority over them. Precedents established by the United States Supreme Court, the highest court in the land, are binding on all lower courts. Fundamental sources of American law include the U.S. Constitution and state constitutions, statutes enacted by legislative bodies, regulations issued by administrative agencies, and case law.
2. Article III, Section 1, of the U.S. Constitution limits the jurisdiction of the federal courts to cases involving (a) a federal question, which is a question based, at least in part, on the U.S. Constitution, a treaty, or a federal law; or (b) diversity of citizenship—which arises when parties to a lawsuit are from different states or when the lawsuit involves a foreign citizen or foreign government. The federal court system is a three-tiered model consisting of (a) U.S. district (trial) courts and various lower courts of limited jurisdiction; (b) U.S. courts of appeals; and (c) the United States Supreme Court. Cases may be appealed from the district courts to the appellate courts. In most cases, the decisions of the federal appellate courts are final because the Supreme Court hears relatively few cases.
3. The Supreme Court's decision to review a case is influenced by many factors, including the significance of the issues involved and whether the solicitor general is asking the Court to take the case. After a case is accepted, the justices (with the help of their law clerks) undertake research on the issues involved in the case, hear oral

arguments from the parties, meet in conference to discuss and vote on the issues, and announce the opinion, which is then released for publication.

4. Federal judges are nominated by the president and confirmed by the Senate. Once appointed, they hold office for life, barring gross misconduct. The nomination and confirmation process, particularly for Supreme Court justices, is often extremely politicized. Democrats and Republicans alike realize that justices may occupy seats on the Court for decades and naturally want to have persons appointed who share their basic views. Nearly 20 percent of all Supreme Court appointments have been either rejected or not acted on by the Senate.

5. In interpreting and applying the law, judges inevitably become policymakers. The most important policymaking tool of the federal courts is the power of judicial review. This power was not mentioned specifically in the Constitution, but the Supreme Court claimed the power for the federal courts in its 1803 decision in *Marbury v. Madison*.

6. Judges who take an active role in checking the activities of the other branches of government sometimes are characterized as "activist" judges, and judges who defer to the other branches' decisions sometimes are regarded as "restraintist" judges. The Warren Court of the 1950s and 1960s was activist in a liberal direction, whereas the Rehnquist and Roberts Courts became increasingly activist in a conservative direction.

7. When William Rehnquist was appointed chief justice in 1986, the Supreme Court began a rightward shift and over time issued a number of conservative opinions. To date, the Roberts Court appears to be continuing the rightward movement of the Court. The Court, however, is fairly evenly divided between strongly conservative justices and liberal-to-moderate justices, with Justice Kennedy often providing swing votes in key cases before the Court.

8. Checks on the powers of the federal courts include executive checks, legislative checks, public opinion, and judicial traditions and doctrines.

selected print & media resources

SUGGESTED READINGS

Bach, Amy. ***Ordinary Injustice: How America Holds Court.*** **New York: Holt Paperbacks, 2010. In an investigation that moves from small-town Georgia to upstate New York, from Chicago to Mississippi, lawyer Amy Bach uncovers the chronic injustice meted out daily to ordinary Americans by a legal system so underfunded and understaffed that it is a menace to the people it is designed to serve.**

Barnhart, Bill, and Gene Schlickman. ***John Paul Stevens: An Independent Life.*** **DeKalb, Ill.: Northern Illinois University Press, 2010. This account details the personal and professional life of a recently retired Supreme Court justice. It shows how a sense of independence turned Stevens, a moderate Republican, into a member of the Court's liberal wing.**

Biskupic, Joan. ***American Original: The Life and Constitution of Supreme Court Justice Antonin Scalia.*** **New York: Farrar, Straus and Giroux, 2009. Biskupic, a longtime legal reporter currently at *USA Today,* earlier gave us the life of Justice Sandra Day O'Connor, the Court's first woman. Biskupic's latest biography, of Antonin Scalia, depicts the highly colorful anchor of the Court's conservative wing.**

Friedman, Barry. ***The Will of the People: How Public Opinion Has Influenced the Supreme Court and Shaped the Meaning of the Constitution.*** **New York: Farrar, Straus and Giroux, 2010. It has long been said that the Supreme Court follows the election returns. This history of the Court, by a New York University law professor, seeks to demonstrate that proposition in detail.**

Posner, Richard A. ***How Judges Think.*** **Cambridge, Mass.: Harvard University Press (paperback), 2010. Posner, a U.S. appeals court judge, is an astonishingly prolific writer on political, economic, and legal issues. In this volume, he returns to what he knows best, judicial philosophy. Posner contends that judges inevitably rely on their own experiences and prejudices, and that regardless of what Supreme Court justices may say, their rulings are highly political. Posner believes that the best guarantee of impartial justice is to fully understand the true consequences of each decision.**

MEDIA RESOURCES

Amistad—**A 1997 movie, starring Anthony Hopkins, about a slave ship mutiny in 1839. Much of the story revolves around the prosecution, ending at the Supreme Court, of the slave who led the revolt.**

Gideon's Trumpet—**A 1980 film, starring Henry Fonda as the small-time criminal James Earl Gideon, which makes clear the path a case takes to the Supreme Court and the importance of cases decided there.**

Justice Sandra Day O'Connor—In a 1994 program, Bill Moyers conducts Justice O'Connor's first television interview. Topics include women's rights, O'Connor's role as the Supreme Court's first female justice, and her difficulties breaking into the male-dominated legal profession. O'Connor defends her positions on affirmative action and abortion.

The Magnificent Yankee—A 1950 movie, starring Louis Calhern and Ann Harding, that traces the life and philosophy of Oliver Wendell Holmes, Jr., one of the Supreme Court's most brilliant justices.

Marbury v. Madison—A 1987 video on the famous 1803 case that established the principle of judicial review.

The Supreme Court—A four-part PBS series that won a 2008 Parents' Choice Gold Award. The series follows the history of the Supreme Court from the first chief justice, John Marshall, to the earliest days of the Roberts Court. Some of the many topics are the Court's dismal performance in the Civil War era, its conflicts with President Franklin D. Roosevelt, its role in banning the segregation of African Americans, and the abortion controversy.

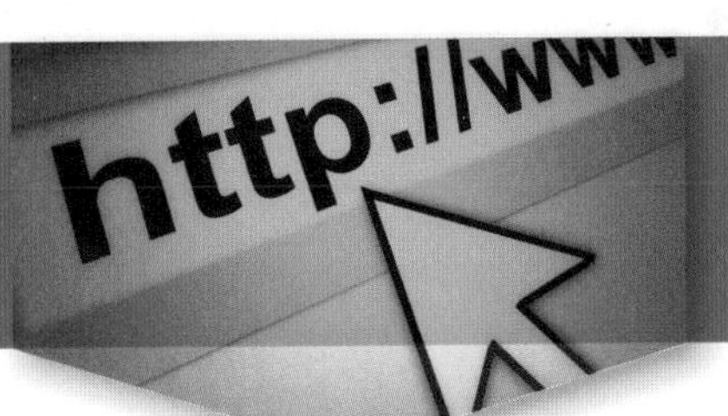

e-mocracy

COURTS ON THE WEB

Most courts in the United States have sites on the Web. These sites vary in what they include. Some courts simply display contact information for court personnel. Others include recent judicial decisions along with court rules and forms. Many federal courts permit attorneys to file documents electronically. The information available on these sites continues to grow as courts try to avoid being left behind in the information age. One day, courts may decide to implement *virtual courtrooms,* in which judicial proceedings take place totally via the Internet. The Internet may ultimately provide at least a partial solution to the twin problems of overloaded dockets and the high time and financial costs of litigation.

LOGGING ON

The home page of the federal courts is a good starting point for learning about the federal court system in general. At this site, you can even follow the path of a case as it moves through the federal court system. Go to
www.uscourts.gov

To access the Supreme Court's official Web site, on which Supreme Court decisions are made available within hours of their release, go to
www.supremecourt.gov

Several Web sites offer searchable databases of Supreme Court decisions. You can access Supreme Court cases since 1970 at FindLaw's site:
www.findlaw.com

The following Web site also offers an easily searchable index to Supreme Court opinions, including some important historic decisions:
www.law.cornell.edu/supct

You can find information on the justices of the Supreme Court, as well as their decisions, at
www.oyez.org

chapter 14

Domestic and Economic Policy

chapter contents

<< During the Great Recession, numerous families lost their homes to foreclosure because they no longer were paying off their mortgages. Many demonstrations protested these foreclosures. (Nader Khouri/MCT via Getty Images)

WHAT IF... ...every adult were guaranteed a job?

During the Great Depression in the 1930s, the federal government's Works Progress Administration (WPA) paid Americans to build new roads. (AP Photo)

BACKGROUND

Some psychologists say that unemployment is one of the most traumatizing events in a person's life. Certainly, unemployment imposes costs on the entire economy, not just on the unemployed themselves. Since the Great Depression of the 1930s, fighting unemployment has been a major goal of the federal government. Yet during the recent Great Recession, the unemployment rate reached 10 percent and remained close to that peak for months thereafter.

The government cannot force private businesses to hire employees. Therefore, the only way to guarantee a job to every adult would be for the government to become the employer of last resort. If such a program were implemented, what would it look like, and how would it work?

WHAT IF EVERY ADULT WERE GUARANTEED A JOB?

To get a sense of what a guaranteed jobs program would be like, consider the last time the federal government implemented a major jobs program. At the start of the Great Depression in the 1930s, the unemployment rate reached 25 percent. In response, the administration of President Franklin Roosevelt (1933–1945) adopted several emergency employment measures. Members of the Civilian Conservation Corps received a dollar a day (about $16.50 in 2011 dollars) plus room and board for disaster relief, reforestation, and flood control. Beginning in 1935, the Works Progress Administration (WPA) employed 8.5 million people. If a guaranteed jobs program were created today, presumably millions of Americans would be hired to pick up litter, look in on the elderly, care for the children of working mothers, and perform dozens of other hard-to-fill jobs.

Roosevelt's programs did not eliminate unemployment altogether. The programs also were expensive, and any modern-day guaranteed jobs program would be even more costly. Eventually, taxes would have to go up to pay for the program.

THE MINIMUM-WAGE PROBLEM

On average, WPA workers received approximately the minimum wage. (When the minimum wage was first created in 1938, it was twenty-five cents an hour.) Because unemployment was so widespread, paying WPA workers that much did not entice them away from private-sector jobs. Today, however, major sectors of the economy, including the retail and restaurant industries, depend on minimum-wage workers. If the government offered minimum-wage jobs to everyone, these industries might not be able to hire enough workers, unless we were in the middle of a serious recession. One solution would be to set the pay for government jobs of last resort at less than the minimum wage.

Even if the guaranteed jobs program offered a "sub-minimum wage," minimum-wage jobs would probably become harder to fill. Many minimum-wage jobs involve hard work, and employees often worry that they might be fired. Participants in a federal government jobs program would not have to be as concerned about losing their jobs and would probably not work that hard. Some employees might prefer such an environment.

THE IMMIGRATION PROBLEM

For many people in Asia, Africa, and Latin America, migrating to the United States is economically attractive. Of course, the government would not let illegal immigrants participate in a federal jobs program and might bar legal immigrants as well. But immigrants could perform minimum-wage jobs in the private sector that citizens did not want to take. If fewer citizens took minimum-wage jobs, the number of immigrants might increase. Therefore, a guaranteed jobs program could make the problem of illegal immigration worse.

FOR CRITICAL ANALYSIS

1. How would the problems created by a federal guaranteed jobs program compare with the benefits of such a program?
2. If some participants in a federal guaranteed jobs program did not perform satisfactory work, what should the government do?

Typically, whenever a policy decision is made, some groups will be better off and some groups will be hurt. All policymaking generally involves such a dilemma.

Part of the public-policy debate in our nation involves domestic problems. **Domestic policy** can be defined as all of the laws, government planning, and government actions that concern internal issues of national importance. Consequently, the span of such policies is enormous. Domestic policies range from relatively simple issues, such as what the speed limit should be on interstate highways, to more complex ones, such as how best to protect our environment or what we should do about unemployment, as discussed in this chapter's opening *What If . . .* feature. Many of our domestic policies are formulated and implemented by the federal government, but a number of others are the result of the combined efforts of federal, state, and local governments.

Domestic Policy
All of the laws, government planning, and government actions that concern internal issues of national importance, such as poverty, crime, and the environment.

We can define several types of domestic policy. *Regulatory policy* seeks to define what is and is not legal. Setting speed limits is obviously regulatory policy. *Redistributive policy* transfers income from certain individuals or groups to others, often based on the belief that these transfers enhance fairness. Social Security is an example. *Promotional policy* seeks to foster or discourage various economic or social activities, typically through subsidies and tax breaks. A tax credit for buying a fuel-efficient car would qualify as promotional.

In this chapter, we look at domestic policy issues involving health care, immigration, crime, and energy and the environment. We also examine national economic policies undertaken by the federal government. Before we start our analysis, though, we must look at how public policies are made.

The Policymaking Process

How does any issue get resolved? First, of course, the issue must be identified as a problem. Often, policymakers have only to open their local newspapers—or letters from their constituents—to discover that a problem is brewing. On rare occasions, a crisis, such as that brought about by the terrorist attacks of September 11, 2001, creates the need to formulate policy. Like most Americans, however, policymakers receive much of their information from the national media. Finally, various lobbying groups provide information to members of Congress.

As an example of policymaking, consider the Emergency Economic Stabilization Act of 2008, commonly known as the bank bailout bill. Enacted in response to the global financial crisis of 2008, the act granted the U.S. Treasury secretary under President George W. Bush, Henry Paulson, the power to spend up to $700 billion to support financial institutions. Although the bill was initially meant to fund the federal government's purchase of distressed mortgage-backed securities ("toxic assets") from banks, the language of the bill actually gave Paulson the ability to spend the funds on almost anything that could be considered support for the financial system.

No matter how simple or how complex the problem, those who make policy follow a number of steps. We can divide the process of policymaking into at least five steps: (1) agenda building, (2) policy formulation, (3) policy adoption, (4) policy implementation, and (5) policy evaluation.

Agenda Building

First of all, the issue must get on the agenda. In other words, Congress must become aware that a problem requires congressional action. Agenda building may occur as the result of a crisis, technological change, or mass media campaigns, as well as through the efforts of strong political personalities and effective lobbying groups.

At the beginning of the Great Recession, Treasury secretary Henry Paulson asked Congress to legislate a bank bailout. Could he have undertaken a bailout without congressional action? Why or why not? (AP Photo/Charles Dharapak)

Paulson proposed the bank bailout bill to Congress, with President Bush's backing, in response to a set of potentially catastrophic circumstances. On September 15, 2008, Lehman Brothers, a giant investment bank, failed. Lehman held more than $600 billion in assets and debts, making its bankruptcy the largest in U.S. history.

Earlier in the year, the federal government had intervened when a series of major financial institutions failed. These included Bear Stearns, an investment bank, and AIG, a giant insurance firm. By September, however, members of the Bush administration were increasingly reluctant to bail out such institutions. They feared that they were creating a dangerous degree of **moral hazard,** in which individuals and institutions take excessive risks, confident that they will be rescued if something goes wrong. The government therefore allowed Lehman to fail, wiping out not only the bank's owners (the stockholders) but also almost everyone who had lent or entrusted funds to the bank.[1] We discuss other examples of moral hazard in this chapter's *Politics of Boom and Bust* feature on the facing page.

Moral Hazard
The danger that protecting an individual or institution from the consequences of failure will encourage excessively risky behavior.

The government misjudged the situation. By September, banks were no longer taking excessive risks. The danger instead was that they would avoid taking any risks at all. After Lehman's collapse, banks became fearful that other banks might go under and fail to pay their debts. Banks therefore stopped making loans to each other. (See Figure 14–1 below.) The money market, which provides short-term corporate finance, froze up as well. Lending threatened to stop altogether. The resulting prospect was ominous: access to credit is essential for a vast share of the nation's firms, and a lending freeze could shut down much of the economy. Panicked financiers pleaded for the government to "do something."

Policy Formulation

During the next step in the policymaking process, various policy proposals are discussed among government officials and the public. Such discussions may take place in the printed media, on television, and in the halls of Congress. Congress holds hearings, the president voices the administration's views, and the topic may even become a campaign issue.

1. Investment banks such as Lehman Brothers do not have depositors as such, and funds at these banks are not covered by the Federal Deposit Insurance Corporation.

FIGURE 14–1 The Banking Crisis: September 15, 2008, and After

This chart depicts the differences between interbank interest rates and the interest rates on federal government debt. It shows that at the height of the financial crisis following September 15, 2008, banks were charging each other interest rates for three-month loans that were more than 4.5 percentage points above the rate that the U.S. government had to pay for its three-month borrowing. At these rates, few interbank loans actually took place.

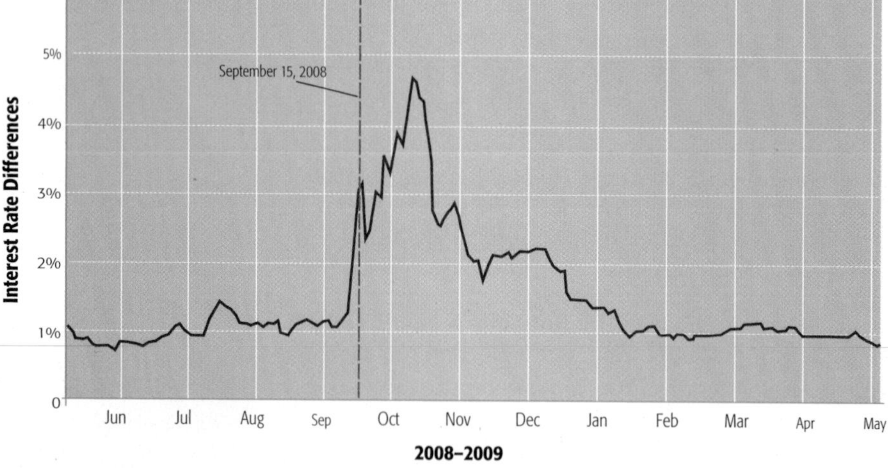

Source: The Federal Reserve System.

In the example of the bank bailout, Paulson and other officials concluded that the underlying cause of the crisis was bank losses due to the collapse in the value of the "toxic assets." The Treasury Department proposed to restore confidence by buying up these assets. To obtain congressional funding, Treasury drafted a three-page bill that granted Paulson the right to spend $700 billion on mortgage-related assets. The $700 billion figure was pulled out of a hat—the only consideration was that the sum be large enough to

THE POLITICS OF BOOM AND BUST

BAILOUTS AND THE DANGER OF MORAL HAZARD

During a "bust," those who are hurt seek help, often in the form of a government bailout. Banks were bailed out in the latest recession, as were automobile manufacturers, a giant insurance company (AIG), mortgage lenders, home borrowers, and others. All government actions have consequences, though, and bailouts are no different. Consumers, borrowers, investors, savers, and managers all react to changes in incentives. A serious problem that can result if incentives are badly designed is moral hazard, in which those who are protected against danger respond by taking greater risks. The term *moral hazard* comes from the insurance industry, which has recognized the problem for centuries.

THE BOOM IN MORTGAGE LENDING

Members of Congress decided long ago that home ownership should be promoted. In the 1990s, Congress and several lending regulatory agencies devised programs to increase homeownership among low-income Americans. Such programs increased the chance that borrowers would not be able to pay back their mortgages, resulting in default. Still, for many years these mortgages experienced few problems.

In time, however, lending to "subprime" borrowers began to get completely out of hand. A major reason was the securitization of mortgages, in which the mortgages of many different borrowers were piled together in large pools of debt. Shares in each pool were sold to investors. The semipublic institutions Freddie Mac and Fannie Mae were established years ago to create such bundles, but in the twenty-first century many private firms entered this market.

The housing boom started in earnest in 2002. Mortgage originators increasingly approved mortgage loan applications from individuals who had unstable incomes, low incomes, or no incomes at all. Why? Because the originators knew that they could sell the risky mortgages to someone else. All the risk that the mortgages would fail would be passed on to the next group down the line. No one was responsible for verifying that the loans were sound, that the borrowers responsible for making payments understood the papers that they had signed, or even that the paperwork existed and was in good order. Later investigations revealed that for a great number of securities, it was not. At institutions such as Washington Mutual Bank—which collapsed in September 2008—loan officers who attempted to verify the bona fides of mortgage applicants were fired. The lending environment, in short, was rife with moral hazard.

WHEN THE MUSIC STOPPED

When the housing bubble popped, persons who put no money down on a mortgage could walk away from the deal without loss (except to their credit rating). Likewise, mortgage originators had no investments to lose. Fannie Mae and Freddie Mac, however, were ruined. Banks and investment companies with large volumes of mortgage-backed securities on their books were in big trouble. The result was the bailout bill of October 2008, described in the text.

Bankers, especially investment bankers, were affected by moral hazard in other ways. Often, they would receive huge bonuses if a risky investment succeeded, but would lose little if it failed. If the bet failed, at most the banker might have to seek employment elsewhere—while collecting a large severance package.

FOR CRITICAL ANALYSIS

Is moral hazard a problem in health care? Would consumers reduce their use of medical services without harming their health if they had to help pay for medical care, or would the savings likely be limited to minor matters, rather than truly expensive procedures? Explain your answer.

During difficult economic times, trading on the floor of the New York Stock Exchange can become frenzied. What happened in the stock market after the first bank bailout bill failed to pass the House? (AP Photo/Richard Drew)

impress the financial markets. On September 20, 2008, five days after Lehman collapsed, Treasury sent the bill to the House.

Members of Congress were shocked by the onset of the crisis, but they were flabbergasted by Paulson's bill. Never in the history of the republic had Congress ever granted such uncontrolled spending power to an executive department, nor had it ever allocated hundreds of billions of dollars based on what was effectively a three-page memo. Still, the House set to work, adding desirable oversight mechanisms and a large dose of pork. The resulting 110-page bill was put to a vote on September 29. Members of both parties proceeded to vote it down. The next day, the Dow Jones Industrial Average, an index of stock market prices, sustained its biggest point drop in history.

Policy Adoption

The third step in the policymaking process involves choosing a specific policy from among the proposals that have been discussed.

After the House refused to pass the bank bailout bill, the Senate sought to rescue it. Senate leaders decided to amend an existing bill already passed by the House—this step circumvented the clause in the Constitution requiring that revenue bills originate in the House. By the time the Senate was done with the bill, it was 451 pages long and bursting with earmarks designed to win necessary votes. The Senate passed the measure on October 1, 2008, the House accepted it on October 3, and President Bush signed it into law within hours.

Policy Implementation

The fourth step in the policymaking process involves the implementation of the policy alternative chosen by Congress. Government action must be implemented by bureaucrats, the courts, police, and individual citizens.

The bank bailout, now known as the Troubled Assets Relief Program (TARP), actually expanded one grant of authority beyond what Treasury had included in the initial draft—it did not require that TARP funds be spent on mortgage-related assets. In the first weeks of October, Paulson and other officials began to realize that buying up toxic assets would not resolve the financial crisis. If Treasury paid market prices for the assets, banks would gain nothing of value. If Treasury overpaid, banks would gain financial stability, but taxpayers would be granting a huge subsidy to the banking industry that would never be returned.

On October 14, therefore, President Bush and Secretary Paulson announced that instead of buying toxic assets, TARP would buy preferred stock in banks, thereby adding to their capital. From the taxpayers' point of view, this step had two virtues: The preferred stock would pay interest, and the banks could eventually buy back the preferred stock, returning TARP funds to the government.

Policy Evaluation

After a policy has been implemented, it is evaluated. Groups inside and outside the government conduct studies to determine what actually happens after a policy has been in place for a given period of time. Based on this feedback and the perceived success or failure of the policy, a new round of policymaking initiatives may be undertaken to improve on the effort.

In the example of TARP, Congress developed a series of bodies to review Treasury's actions. These included a Financial Stability Oversight Board in the executive branch and a

Congressional Oversight Panel. Congress also created a special inspector general for the program. Given its size and importance, TARP was also a focus of intense interest by the media. Surprisingly, relatively few people objected to the complete transformation in the use of TARP funds from purchasing toxic assets to buying preferred stock. Many Americans were greatly interested, however, in whether the government's investments would promote lending and in how much bankers would be paid.

Furthermore, a great many citizens soon came to view the entire TARP program as a giant giveaway to large banks and to Wall Street, an example of the government serving the demands of special interests rather than meeting the needs of ordinary Americans. Still, as you learned in Chapter 12, most banks quickly repaid their TARP investments to the government, which earned a profit on the sums. Funds used to prop up Freddie Mac and Fannie Mae (the government-sponsored mortgage corporations), were apparently lost forever.

Health Care

Spending for health care is now estimated to account for 17.6 percent of the total U.S. economy. In 1965, about 6 percent of our income was spent on health care (as shown in Figure 14–2 below), but that percentage has been increasing ever since. Per capita spending on health care is greater in the United States than almost anywhere else in the world. Measured by the percentage of the **gross domestic product (GDP)** devoted to health care, America spends almost twice as much as Britain or Japan—see Figure 14–3 on the following page. (GDP is the dollar value of all final goods and services produced in a one-year period.)

Gross Domestic Product (GDP)
The dollar value of all final goods and services produced in a one-year period.

Medicare
A federal health-insurance program that covers U.S. residents over the age of sixty-five. The costs are met by a tax on wages and salaries.

Medicaid
A joint state-federal program that provides medical care to the poor (including indigent elderly persons in nursing homes). The program is funded out of general government revenues.

The Government's Role in Financing Health Care through 2009

As of January 2010, government spending on health care constituted about 50 percent of total health-care spending. Private insurance accounted for more than 30 percent of payments for health care. The remainder—less than 20 percent—was paid directly by individuals or by charity. The government programs Medicare and Medicaid have been the main sources of hospital and other medical benefits for about 100 million Americans—one-third of the nation's population. Many of these people are elderly.

Medicare is specifically designed to support the elderly, regardless of income. **Medicaid,** a joint state-federal program, is in principle a program to subsidize health care for the poor. In practice, it often provides long-term health care to persons living in nursing homes. (To become eligible for Medicaid, these individuals must first exhaust their financial assets.) Medicare, Medicaid, and private insurance companies are called *third parties.* Caregivers and patients are the two primary parties. When third parties pay for medical care, the quantity demanded of such services increases. Health-care recipients have no incentive to restrain their use of health care. One result is some degree of wasted resources.

FIGURE 14–2 Percentage of Total National Income Spent on Health Care in the United States

The portion of total national income spent on health care has risen steadily since 1965.

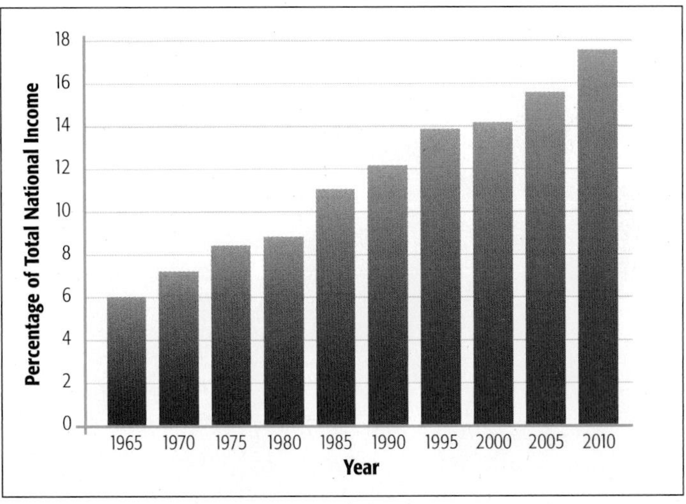

Sources: U.S. Department of Commerce; U.S. Department of Health and Human Services; Deloitte and Touche LLP; VHA, Inc.; and Centers for Medicare and Medicaid Services.

FIGURE 14–3 Cost of Health Care in Economically Advanced Nations

Cost is given as a percentage of total gross domestic product (GDP). The figures, for 2007, are the latest available.

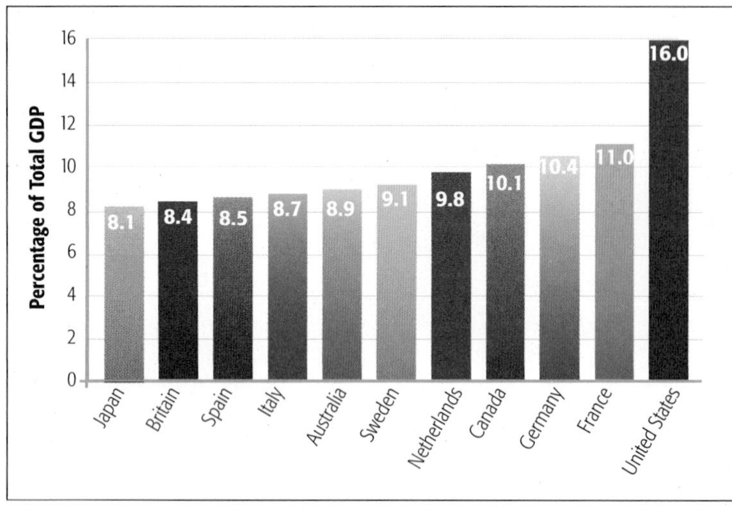

Source: Excerpted and adapted from the Organization for Economic Cooperation and Development, *OECD Health Data*, 2008.

Medicare. The Medicare program, which was created in 1965 under President Lyndon Johnson (1963–1969), pays hospital and physicians' bills for U.S. residents over the age of sixty-five. Since 2006, Medicare has also paid for at least part of the prescription drug expenses of the elderly. In return for paying a tax on their earnings (currently set at 2.9 percent of wages and salaries) while in the workforce, retirees are assured that the majority of their hospital and physicians' bills will be paid for with public funds.

Medicare is now the second-largest domestic spending program, after Social Security. Government expenditures on Medicare have routinely exceeded forecasts. The government has responded in part by imposing arbitrary reimbursement caps on specific procedures. To avoid going over Medicare's reimbursement caps, however, hospitals have sometimes discharged patients too soon or in an unstable condition. The government has also cut rates of reimbursement to individual physicians and physician groups, such as health maintenance organizations (HMOs). As a result, physicians and HMOs have become reluctant to accept Medicare patients. Several of the nation's largest HMOs have withdrawn from certain Medicare programs. A growing number of physicians now refuse to treat Medicare patients.

Medicaid. Within a few short years, the joint federal-state taxpayer-funded Medicaid program for the "working poor" has generated one of the biggest expansions of government entitlements ever. In 1997, federal Medicaid spending was around $150 billion. Ten years later, it easily exceeded $300 billion. At the end of the last decade, 34 million people were enrolled in the program. Today, there are about 60 million. When you add Medicaid coverage to Medicare and the military and federal employee health plans, the government has clearly become the nation's primary health insurer.

In recent years, the federal government has paid about 55 percent of Medicaid's total cost—the states pay the rest. Wealthy states must pick up a greater share of the tab than poor ones. Medicaid costs have imposed major strains on the budgets of many states. President Barack Obama's 2009 stimulus package included an extra $87 billion in federal spending for Medicaid, which substantially increased the federal share of the total. The stimulus allowed the states to control their Medicaid budgets. It also funded an expansion in the number of individuals covered—because of the recession, newly unemployed people joined the eligible population.

As you will learn later in this section, the new health-care reform legislation adopted in 2010 will expand considerably the share of

This child is receiving several inoculations at the same time. Are there situations in which her parents won't have to pay for such medical services? If so, what are they? (AP Photo/ J. Scott Applewhite)

the population that is eligible for Medicaid. Much—but not all—of the extra expense due to the new enrollees will be picked up by the federal government (i.e., the taxpayers).

Universal Health Insurance

On March 23, 2010, President Obama signed into law the Patient Protection and Affordable Care Act, a massive overhaul of the nation's health-care funding system crafted by the Senate and passed without alteration by the House of Representatives. On March 30, Obama signed the Health Care and Education Reconciliation Act of 2010, a series of adjustments to the Senate package prepared by the House and agreed to by the Senate. Together, these two measures constituted the most important political development in the United States between the 2008 and 2010 elections, and the largest expansion in the welfare state since the presidency of Lyndon B. Johnson (1963–1969).

During the run-up to the passage of health-care reform, many Americans attended rallies in favor of changing our system. Why were there so many differences of opinion? (AP Photo/Stephen Chernin)

The signing of these bills marked the climax of an approximately nine-month debate in the nation and in Congress over the future of our health-care system. When the new system is fully in place, which will take several years, the nation will approach the long-time progressive goal of universal health-care insurance coverage. The system will approach, rather than meet, this goal because it will be possible for an individual citizen to opt out—at a price. Also, unauthorized immigrants will not be covered.

Health-Care Reform: Building an Agenda

As you learn about how Congress came to pass these measures, keep in mind the five policymaking steps described earlier in this chapter: agenda building, policy formulation, policy adoption, policy implementation, and policy evaluation. In the example of health-care reform, the first three steps are complete. The fourth—implementation—will take place over several years. Policy evaluation remains a matter for the future. First, consider how the Democrats came to place the reforms on the national agenda.

The Problem of the Uninsured. In 2008, as the Great Recession was taking hold, more than 45 million Americans—almost 16 percent of the population—did not have health insurance. The uninsured population has been relatively young, in part due to Medicare, which covers almost everyone over the age of sixty-five. Also, younger workers are more likely to be employed in entry-level jobs without health-insurance benefits. The traditional system of health care in the United States was based on the assumption that employers would provide health insurance to working-age persons. Many small businesses, however, simply have not been able to afford to offer their workers health insurance. Average insurance benefits in 2009 cost more than $20,000 per year for each covered employee, according to the U.S. Chamber of Commerce.

A further problem that the uninsured have faced is that when seeking medical care, they usually have had to pay much higher fees than would be paid on their behalf if they had insurance coverage. Large third-party insurers, private or public, normally strike hard bargains with hospitals and physicians over how much they will pay for procedures and services. Individuals do not have that kind of bargaining power. As a result, hospitals have attempted to recover from individuals the revenues lost from underpaying third-party insurers. One result is that individual health-insurance policies (those not obtained through an employer) have been extremely costly, and for persons with preexisting health conditions, coverage has frequently been impossible to obtain at any price.

The Problem of High Costs. High medical costs are not only a problem for individuals with inadequate or nonexistent insurance coverage. Rather, high costs are a problem for the system as a whole. From 1975 to 2005, per capita spending on health care in the United States grew at an average rate of 4.2 percent per year. A main driver of the growth in health-care spending was new medical technologies and services. The increased number of elderly persons had a smaller effect on costs. Such rates of growth cannot continue indefinitely—at these rates, health-care spending would exceed the size of GDP by the year 2083. Using more realistic assumptions, the Congressional Budget Office (CBO) has calculated that if nothing were done, health-care spending would reach 31 percent of GDP by 2035.

Those over the age of sixty-five run up health-care bills that are far larger than those incurred by the rest of the population. As a federal problem, therefore, health-care spending growth has been and will remain chiefly a Medicare issue, even after the passage of the new health-care measures. In 2009, the government's Medicare trustees reported that the Medicare trust fund was projected to run out of funds in 2017. Such prospects explain why in 2009 health-care cost containment was almost as important an issue as universal coverage.

The International Experience. The concept of universal health insurance is not new. The first such program was implemented in 1883 and 1884 in Germany, under the leadership of Chancellor (prime minister) Otto von Bismarck. A conservative, Bismarck sought to use social legislation to steal the thunder of the socialists, who were popular in Germany. Throughout the twentieth century, other economically advanced nations adopted such systems. By the twenty-first century, the United States was the only advanced industrial country with a large pool of citizens who lacked health insurance. Australia, Canada, Japan, and the nations of Western Europe all provided systems of universal coverage. American progressives considered it shameful that the United States could not do what these other nations had done—another argument for placing reform on the agenda.

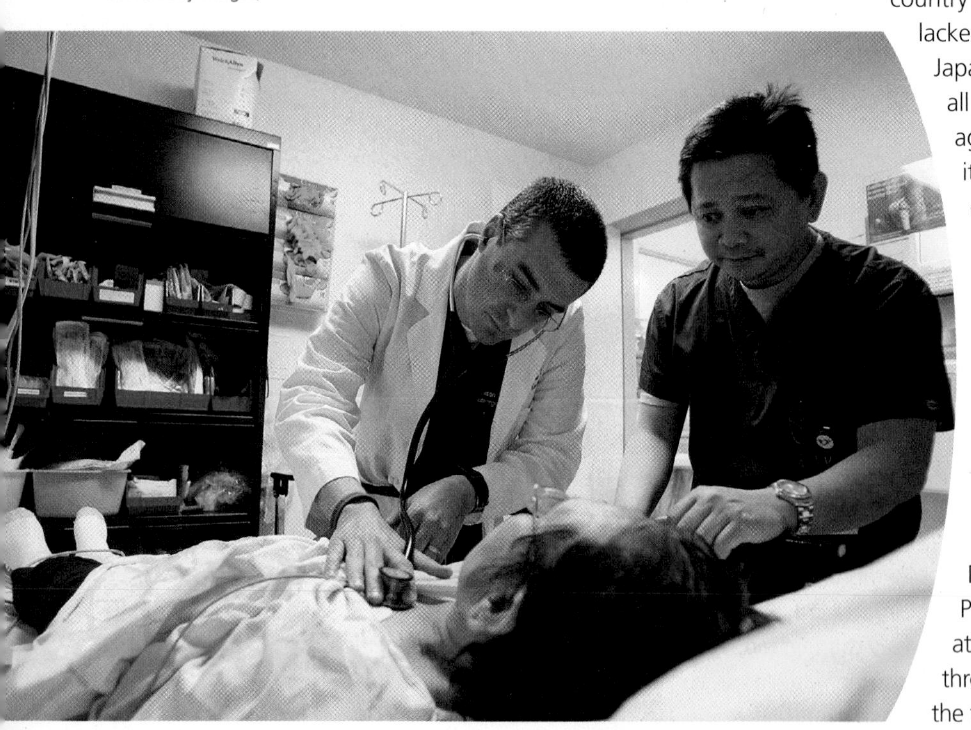

This physician and his assistant are treating a patient in the emergency room of Mission Community Hospital in Los Angeles, California. Will the use of emergency rooms increase or decrease as a result of health-care reform? Why? (David McNew/Getty Images)

Heath-Care Reform: Adopting a Policy

Since the time of President Harry Truman (1945–1953), some liberals have sought to establish a national health-insurance system in this country. During his first two years in office, President Bill Clinton (1993–2001) attempted to steer such a proposal through Congress, but his plan failed. In the first decade of the twenty-first century, however, **universal health insurance** began to reappear as a political issue. Unlike previous proposals, the new universal health-insurance plans did not provide for a federal monopoly on basic health insurance. Instead, universal coverage would result from a mandate that all citizens must obtain health insurance from some source—an employer, Medicare or Medicaid, or a new plan sponsored by the federal government or a state government. Low-income families would receive a subsidy to help them pay their insurance premiums. Insurers could not reject applicants. A program of this nature was adopted by the state of Massachusetts in 2006 in response to a proposal by Republican governor Mitt Romney. When, in 2008, the Democrats won the presidency and large majorities in both chambers of Congress, universal health insurance was again on the national agenda. But what kind of plan would the Democrats propose? Several major issues had to be addressed before a policy could be adopted.

Universal Health Insurance
Any of several possible programs to provide health insurance to everyone in the country. The central government does not necessarily provide the insurance itself, but may subsidize the purchase of insurance from private insurance companies.

Personal Mandate
In health-care reform, the requirement that all citizens obtain health-care insurance coverage from some source, public or private, also called *individual mandate*.

Public Option
In health-care reform, a government-run health-care insurance program that would compete with private-sector health-insurance companies.

Congress Takes Control. As president, Barack Obama largely delegated the drafting of a health-care plan to Congress, a tactic he employed with other measures such as the 2009 stimulus package and energy legislation. Obama's willingness to let Congress take the lead was a notable change—recent presidents such as George W. Bush and Bill Clinton had sought to push presidential proposals through the legislative process without significant alteration. Obama's tactics eliminated much of the tug-of-war between Congress and the president that was commonplace in past decades, but the political cost of letting Congress take the lead turned out to be larger than expected. Congress took a very long time to pass the necessary legislation, and much of the political maneuvering required for passage proved highly unpopular with the public.

The Issue of Mandated Coverage. One issue that needed to be resolved became known as the *personal mandate.* During the 2008 Democratic presidential primary campaigns, Obama's health-care plan differed from those of the other Democrats in that it did not require adults to obtain coverage, although coverage was required for children. Obama's plan, in other words, had no mandated coverage. Congressional Democrats, however, quickly adopted the **personal mandate**, also known as the *individual mandate,* in all of their draft proposals. Without the mandate, there was no way that the numbers would add up—universal coverage was impossible unless everyone chipped in, healthy and sick alike. Unfortunately for the Democrats, the personal mandate allowed the Republicans to accuse the Democrats of "forcing" people to do something, never a popular position in America.

did you know?

That in the three years ending in 2009, the U.S. government mailed out $180 million in benefit checks to 20,000 Americans—who were dead.

A Government-Backed Insurance Program? The most intense battle in Congress took place over the idea of a government-supported insurance program, or **public option,** that would compete with private insurance firms. President Obama and a majority of the Democrats supported a public option, arguing that competition from such a plan would hold down the cost of private insurance. The insurance industry, the Republicans, and some conservative Democrats were in vehement opposition. Their fear was that private companies could not compete with a program backed by the vast resources of the federal government. Although the House adopted the public option as part of its legislation, the Senate left it out.

New Taxes. It became clear that funding the legislation would require additional taxes. The House bill called for funding new coverage with heavier taxes on the rich. The Senate proposed a more complicated funding arrangement that included taxes on drug and insurance companies. In the end, the House and Senate settled on a compromise. The reconciliation act, the House's final adjustments to the Senate bill, contained smaller tax increases on the rich than the House had originally planned, plus a number of taxes on health-care corporations. The result was a package that, would reduce the federal budget deficit in forthcoming years, rather than increase it.

Public Reaction. Initially, popular support for health-care reform, as reported by public opinion polls, was relatively high, but support eroded quickly as Congress took up the actual legislation. Demonstrations against the Democratic proposals began in the late summer of 2009—many were organized by the new Tea Party movement. The process of moving the reform through congressional channels gave the public a very close look at how legislatures operate, and many citizens clearly were not happy with what they saw. Polls of Massachusetts voters in the days leading up to the January 2010 special Senate election won by Republican Scott Brown suggested that voters were more put off by the manner in which the legislation was handled than they were by its actual contents. Indeed, many voters admitted that they had little knowledge of what was in the reform legislation.

Passage. The House passed its bill in November 2009, and the Senate passed its version in December. As you learned in Chapter 10, passing the reform legislation became more complicated when Scott Brown deprived the Senate Democrats of their sixtieth vote, necessary to end filibusters. If the House and Senate versions of the bill were reconciled in a conference committee—the normal procedure—Senate Democrats would not be able to pass the resulting compromise, and the entire reform effort would collapse.

President Obama and House Speaker Nancy Pelosi, however, patiently assembled enough Democratic support in the House to pass the Senate bill unaltered, thus eliminating the need for a conference committee. On March 21, 2010, the House approved the Senate bill by a vote of 219–212. The House then immediately passed the reconciliation act, which was not subject to Senate filibuster. The Senate accepted it three days later. "Obamacare," as it was nicknamed, was the law of the land. Outraged Republicans accused the Democrats of "ramming" the legislation through Congress. Neither the Senate's bill nor the House's reconciliation measure received the vote of even a single Republican.

Health-Care Reform: Implementing the Policy

The health-care reform legislation is scheduled to become effective over an extended period of time. Most of the major provisions do not go into effect until 2014. The last scheduled provision is not imposed until 2018. The long delay was established in part to allow systems such as state insurance pools to be set up more effectively, but there was also a desire to keep costs down during the initial ten-year period. The lengthy implementation, however, presents political problems for the Democrats, who face two national elections before most of the program is in effect. Voters in those elections will have received few of the promised benefits of the program. Some provisions took effect quickly, however, and are in place now. These do the following:

- Bar insurance companies from dropping people when they get sick.
- Let young adults stay on their parents' health plans until age twenty-six.
- Set up insurer-of-last-resort programs for those denied coverage due to preexisting conditions.
- Take the first steps toward closing the "doughnut hole" coverage gap in the Medicare drug program.
- Grant a tax break to small businesses that insure their employees.
- Impose a 10 percent tax on indoor tanning services.

Immigration

In recent years, immigration rates for the United States have been among the highest they have been since their peak in the early twentieth century. Every year, more than 1 million people immigrate to this country legally, a figure that does not include the large number of unauthorized immigrants. People who were born on foreign soil now constitute about 13 percent of the U.S. population—more than twice the percentage of thirty years ago.

Since 1977, four out of five immigrants have come from Latin America or Asia. Hispanics have overtaken African Americans as the nation's largest minority group. As you learned in Chapter 5, if current immigration rates continue, by 2050, minority groups collectively will constitute the "majority" of Americans. If Hispanics, African Americans, and perhaps Asians were to form coalitions, they could increase their political power dramatically and would have the numerical strength to make significant changes. The "old guard" white majority would no longer dominate American politics.

Some regard the high rate of immigration as a plus for America because it offsets the low birthrate and aging population, which we also discussed in Chapter 5. Immigrants expand the workforce and help to support, through their taxes, government programs that benefit older Americans, such as Medicare and Social Security. If it were not for immigration, contend these observers, the United States would be facing even more serious problems with funding these programs than it already does. In contrast, nations that do not have high immigration rates, such as Japan, are experiencing serious fiscal challenges due to their aging populations.

A significant number of U.S. citizens, however, believe that immigration—both legal and illegal—negatively affects America. They argue, among other things, that the large number of immigrants seeking work results in lower wages for Americans, especially those with few skills. They also worry about the cost of providing immigrants with services such as schools and medical care.

Immigration remains a "hot button" issue, particularly in the states along the Mexican border. Why do so many foreigners wish to live in the United States, even if it means entering illegally? (AP Photo/Ralph Freso)

The Issue of Unauthorized Immigration

Illegal immigration—or unauthorized immigration, to use the terminology of the Department of Homeland Security—has become a major national issue. Latin Americans, especially those migrating from Mexico, constitute the majority of individuals entering the United States without permission. In addition, many unauthorized immigrants enter the country legally, often as tourists or students, and then fail to return home when their visa status expires. Naturally, the unauthorized population is hard to count, but recent estimates have put the number of such persons at about 12 million.

In the southwestern states bordering Mexico, Hispanic populations have surged dramatically, in part because of unauthorized immigration. The immigrants typically come to the United States to work, and in recent years their labor has been in high demand. The housing boom, which came to an abrupt end in the fall of 2007, was partially fueled by the steady stream of unauthorized immigrants seeking jobs. Until the Immigration Reform and Control Act of 1986, there was no law against hiring foreign citizens who lacked proper papers. Until recently, laws penalizing employers were infrequently enforced. In 2007, however, Arizona adopted a state law that imposed severe sanctions on businesses that employ unauthorized workers. As a result, many Arizona businesses have begun to report labor shortages.

Characteristics of the Undocumented Population. Studies of unauthorized immigrants have revealed that a large share of them eventually return to their home countries, where they frequently set up small businesses or retire. Many send remittances back to relatives in their homeland. In 2008, Mexico received $20.2 billion in such remittances. Vicente Fox, who was then president of Mexico, stated that remittances "are our biggest source of foreign income, bigger than oil, tourism, or foreign investment." In these ways, unauthorized immigrants are acting as immigrants to the United States always have. Throughout American history, immigrants frequently returned home or sent funds to relatives in the "old country."

Unauthorized immigrants very often live in mixed households, in which one or more members of a family have lawful resident status, but others do not. A woman from Guatemala with permanent resident status, for example, might be married to a Guatemalan man who is in the country illegally. A common circumstance is for the parents in a family to be unauthorized, whereas the children, who were born in the United States, possess American citizenship. Mixed families mean that deporting the unauthorized immigrant will either break up a family or force one or more American citizens into exile.

Concerns about Unauthorized Immigration. The number-one popular complaint about unauthorized immigrants is that they are breaking the law and "not playing by the rules." U.S. voters often have other concerns as well, some of which involve crime. "Coyotes," or smugglers who help such persons cross the border, may exploit or abuse their clients. Some people crossing the border have found themselves abandoned by "coyotes" in desert areas without sufficient water and have died of thirst or exposure. Illegal immigration may also contribute to the drug trade along the U.S.-Mexican border. In 2005, federal agents discovered an extensive underground tunnel that was used as a pipeline for a lucrative drug-trafficking scheme.

Attempts at Immigration Reform

In polls by Gallup and other organizations, Americans express opinions about illegal immigration (the term used in the questions) that are highly contradictory. A majority of respondents express sympathy toward the immigrants and believe that a way should be found to normalize their status. Only about a fifth favor immediate, permanent deportation. In the very same polls, however, four-fifths agree that illegal immigration is out of control, three-fifths believe that illegal immigration should be a crime, and half believe it should be a crime to assist illegal immigrants. While a majority of Americans believe that the illegal immigration problem is serious, most do not consider it a priority issue for the government. Those who do consider it a priority, however, have very strong feelings on the topic—and in American politics, a minority with strong feelings can often outbid a largely indifferent majority.

The split in the public's attitudes has been reflected in differences among the nation's leaders over how to handle the issue of illegal immigration. Although most Republicans in Congress have favored a harder line toward illegal immigrants than most Democrats, partisan divisions were blurred by the adherence of President George W. Bush and a number of Republican senators to the pro-immigration side of the debate.

Immigration and the Obama Administration. During his campaign, Barack Obama supported reforms that would give illegal immigrants a path toward citizenship. He also called for a crackdown on the employers that hire them. Obama criticized the Bush-era policy of raids on workplaces to round up undocumented workers, but it soon became clear that the new administration's policies were almost as harsh. Immigration reform was put off to allow Congress to concentrate on health-care reform, and as a result the Obama policy was all stick and no carrot. The subsequent Hispanic dissatisfaction with the Democrats raised the question of whether Hispanics would turn out and vote for Democratic candidates in the 2010 elections.

The Arizona Immigration Controversy. In April 2010, Arizona's governor signed the nation's toughest-ever bill on illegal immigration. The law criminalized the failure to carry immigration documents, and it required police to stop and question anyone suspected of being in the country illegally. Opponents contended that the act would lead to harassment of Hispanics regardless of their citizenship status. Arizona had earlier passed the nation's toughest law penalizing employers who hired undocumented workers. Latinos around the country mobilized against the new Arizona law.

Immigration reform was again a major issue. Democrats hoped that this issue would help turn out the Latino vote in 2010. Republican senators such as John McCain who had supported reform in the Bush years had changed their positions due to intense pressure from the political right, however, and the Republican Party was now substantially unified in opposition to reform. In July 2010, the U.S. government sued to overturn the Arizona law, claiming that it interfered with federal authority. A U.S. district court judge blocked enforcement of much of the law until the courts could rule on its constitutionality.

Crime in the Twenty-First Century

Almost all polls taken in the United States in the past several decades have shown that crime remains one of the major concerns of the public. A related issue that has been on the domestic policy agenda for decades is the status of the nation's prisons.

did you know?

That a University of Southern California evaluation of a gang prevention program discovered that when the program lost funding, the gang broke up and the gang's crime rate among the gang's former members declined.

Crime in American History

In every period in the history of this nation, people have voiced apprehension about crime. During the Civil War, mob violence and riots erupted in several cities. After the Civil War, people in San Francisco were told that "no decent man is in safety to walk the streets after dark; while at all hours, both night and day, his property is jeopardized by incendiarism [arson] and burglary."[2] In 1886, *Leslie's Weekly* reported, "Each day we see ghastly records of crime . . . murder seems to have run riot and each citizen asks . . . 'who is safe?'"

In fact, studies by historians have shown that preindustrial agricultural communities had very high levels of interpersonal violence, and that crime rates in the United States and other Western countries fell steadily from the second quarter of the nineteenth century into the twentieth century. Some historians suggest that this century-long decline came about because industrialization, urbanization, and the growth of bureaucratic institutions such as factories and schools socialized the lower classes into patterns of conformity and rule observance. It is notable that newly settled communities in the American West, where such socialization was incomplete, had much higher rates of crime—the "Wild West" was not entirely a myth.

The United States then experienced a substantial crime wave in the 1920s and the first half of the 1930s. This was the period of Prohibition, when the production and sale of alcoholic beverages was illegal. Criminals such as the famous Al Capone organized gangs to provide illicit alcohol to the public. After the end of Prohibition, crime rates dropped until after World War II (1939–1945).

2. President's Commission on Law Enforcement and Administration of Justice, *Challenge of Crime in a Free Society* (Washington, D.C.: Government Printing Office, 1967), p. 19.

FIGURE 14–4 Homicide Rates

Homicide rates recently declined to levels last seen in the 1960s. (The 2001 rate does *not* include deaths attributed to the 9/11 terrorist attacks.)

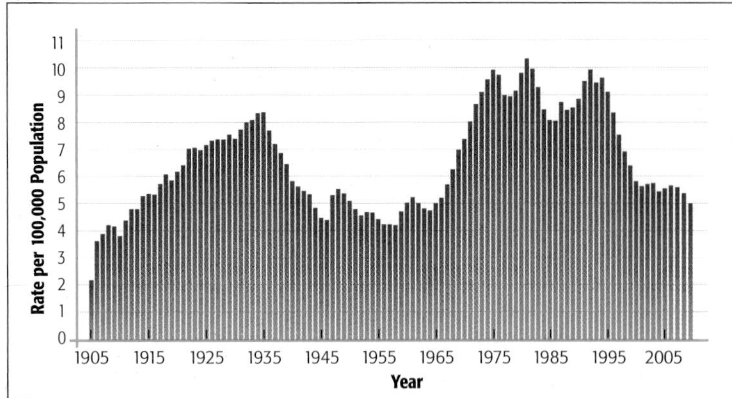

Sources: U.S. Department of Justice; and National Center for Health Statistics, *Vital Statistics.*

FIGURE 14–5 Violent Crime Rates

Violent crime rates began a steep decline in 1994. The crimes included in this chart are rape, robbery, aggravated and simple assault, and homicide.

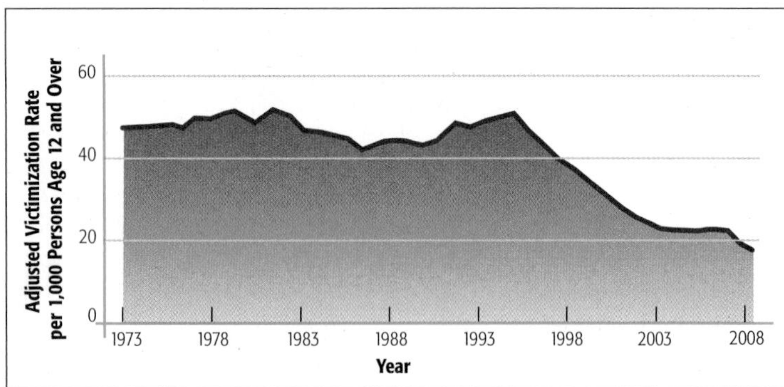

Sources: U.S. Department of Justice; rape, robbery, and assault data are from the *National Crime Victimization Survey;* the homicide data are from the Federal Bureau of Investigation's *Uniform Crime Reports.*

FIGURE 14–6 Theft Rates

Theft rates have declined significantly since the 1970s. *Theft* is defined as completed or attempted theft of property or cash without personal contact.

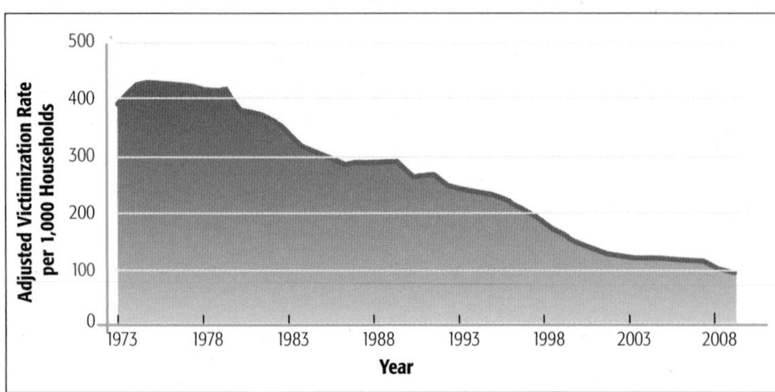

Source: U.S. Department of Justice, *National Crime Victimization Survey.*

Crime rates in Western countries began to rise in the 1950s. The United States, in particular, experienced an explosive growth in violent crime that began in the 1960s. The murder rate per 100,000 people in 1964 was 4.9, whereas in 1994 it was estimated at 9.3, an increase of almost 100 percent. Since 1995, however, violent crime rates have declined. Some argue that this decline was due to the growing economy the United States had generally enjoyed since about 1993. Others claim that the billions in additional funds the federal government has allotted to curbing crime in the last few years has led to less crime. Still others claim that an increase in the number of persons who are jailed or imprisoned is responsible for the reduction. Some have even argued that legalized abortion has reduced the population that is likely to commit crimes. In any event, the violent crime rate appears to be falling. You can see changes in the rates of homicides, violent crimes, and thefts in Figures 14–4, 14–5, and 14–6, respectively.

The Prison Population Bomb

Many Americans believe that the best solution to the nation's crime problem is to impose stiff prison sentences on offenders. Such sentences, in fact, have become national policy. By 2010, U.S. prisons and jails held 2.3 million people. About two-thirds of the incarcerated population were in state or federal prisons, with the remainder held in local jails. About 60 percent of the persons held in local jails were awaiting court action. The other 40 percent were serving sentences.

The number of incarcerated persons has grown rapidly in recent years. In 1990, for example, the total number of persons held in U.S. jails or prisons was still only 1.1 million. From 1995 to 2002, the incarcerated population grew at an average of 3.8 percent annually. The rate of growth has slowed since 2002, however.

The Incarceration Rate. Some groups of people are much more likely to find themselves behind bars than others. Men are more than ten times more likely to be incarcerated than women. Prisoners are also disproportionately African

American. To measure how frequently members of particular groups are imprisoned, the standard statistic is the **incarceration rate.** This rate is the number of people incarcerated for every 100,000 persons in a particular population group. To put it another way, an incarceration rate of 1,000 means that 1 percent of a particular group is in custody. Using this statistic, we can say that U.S. men have an incarceration rate of 1,403, compared with a rate of 135 for U.S. women. This figure, an all-time high, means that more than 1 male out of every 100 is in jail or prison in this country. Figure 14–7 above shows selected incarceration rates by gender, race, and age. Note the very high incarceration rate for African Americans between the ages of thirty and thirty-four—at any given time, more than 11 percent of this group is in jail or prison. How do American incarceration rates compare with those of other countries? We answer that question in this chapter's *Beyond Our Borders* feature on the following page.

FIGURE 14–7 Incarceration Rates per 100,000 Persons for Selected U.S. Population Groups

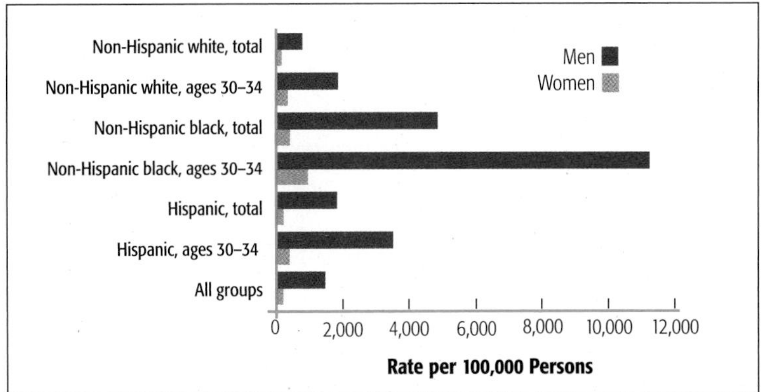

Source: "Prison Inmates at Midyear 2008," *Bureau of Justice Statistics Bulletin,* U.S. Department of Justice (2009).

Incarceration Rate
The number of persons held in jail or prison for every 100,000 persons in a particular population group.

Prison Construction and Conditions. To house a growing number of inmates, prison construction and management have become sizable industries in the United States. Ten years ago, prison overcrowding was a major issue. In 1994, for example, state prisons had a rated capacity of about 500,000 inmates but actually held 900,000 people. The prisons were therefore operating at 80 percent above capacity. Today, after a major prison construction program, many state prisons are operating within their capacity, but some state systems are still at 20 percent above capacity or more. The federal prison system is still 37 percent above capacity. Since 1980, Texas has built 120 new prisons, Florida has built 84, and California has built 83. In 1923, there were only 61 prisons in the entire United States.

did you know?
That the odds are one in twenty that an American born today will wind up in jail or prison at some point during his or her lifetime.

Effects of Incarceration. When imprisonment keeps truly violent felons behind bars longer, it prevents them from committing additional crimes. The average predatory street criminal commits fifteen or more crimes each year when not behind bars. But most prisoners are in for a relatively short time and are released on parole early, often because of prison overcrowding. Then many find themselves back in prison because they have violated parole, typically by using illegal drugs. Indeed, of the 1.5 million people who are arrested each year, the majority are arrested for drug offenses. Given that from 20 million to 40 million Americans violate one or more drug laws each year, the potential "supply" of prisoners seems almost limitless.

Energy and the Environment

A major part of President Obama's legislative agenda was directed at energy and environmental issues. Energy policy addresses two major problems: (1) America's reliance on foreign oil, much of which is produced by unfriendly regimes, and (2) potential global warming caused by increased emissions of carbon dioxide (CO_2) and other greenhouse gases.

Oil—A Strategic Issue

The United States now imports about three-fifths of the petroleum it consumes. Fortunately, about half of all U.S. imports come from two friendly neighbors, Canada and Mexico, and only about 16 percent from Middle Eastern countries, primarily Saudi Arabia. The world's largest oil exporters, however, include a number of nations that are not friends of the United States. Russia is the world's second-largest oil exporter, after Saudi Arabia. Other major exporters include Venezuela and Iran. Both are openly hostile to American interests, and Venezuela is a major source of U.S. imports.

The Government's Response. Although reducing America's dependence on foreign oil is widely considered to be desirable, in recent years the U.S. government has done little

BEYOND OUR BORDERS

HOW MANY PEOPLE DO OTHER COUNTRIES SEND TO PRISON?

The United States has more people in jail or prison than any other country in the world. That fact is not necessarily surprising, because the United States also has one of the world's largest total populations. More to the point, the United States has the highest reported incarceration *rate* of any country on earth. North Korea almost certainly has a higher incarceration rate than the United States, but that nation does not report its incarceration statistics. Figure 14–8 below compares U.S. incarceration rates, measured by the number of prisoners per 100,000 residents, with incarceration rates in other major countries.

FIGURE 14–8 Incarceration Rates around the World

Incarceration rates of major nations, measured by the number of prisoners per 100,000 residents.

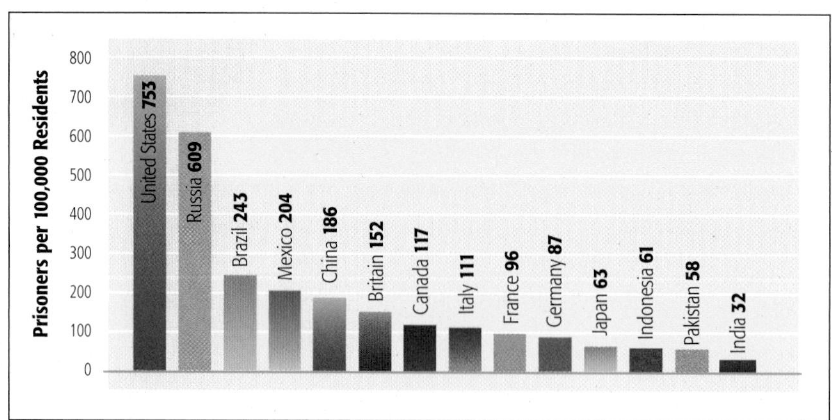

Source: International Centre for Prison Studies, King's College London.

to reach that goal. President Obama has been more active. In 2009, he issued higher fuel efficiency standards for vehicles. By 2016, the new requirement will be 39 miles per gallon for cars and 30 miles per gallon for light trucks. The standards, which took effect with 2011 models, will force major changes to vehicles and will inevitably add to their prices. At Obama's request, Congress has supported research into alternative fuels. Unlike many Democrats, Obama also favored building new energy plants that would use nuclear power—a carbon-free technology. Obama planned to open up additional territory for domestic oil drilling, although not nearly as much as the Republicans demanded. In 2010, Obama announced that major new offshore tracts in the Atlantic would be open to deep-sea drilling. A few weeks later, however, the BP Deepwater Horizon oil spill disaster in the Gulf of Mexico, discussed in a later section, resulted in a temporary moratorium on new offshore drilling.

Global Warming

In the 1990s, scientists working on climate change began to conclude that average world temperatures would rise significantly in the twenty-first century. Gases released by human activity, principally CO_2, are producing a "greenhouse effect," trapping the sun's heat and slowing its release into outer space.

The Global Warming Debate. Most scientists who perform research on the world's climate believe that global warming will be significant, but there is considerable disagreement as to how much warming will actually occur. It is generally accepted that world temperatures have already increased by about 0.74 degree Celsius during the last century. The United Nations' Intergovernmental Panel on Climate Change predicts increases ranging from 1.1 to 6.4 degrees Celsius by 2100. This range of estimates is rather wide and reflects the uncertainties involved in predicting the world's climate.

Global warming has become a major political football to be kicked back and forth by conservatives and liberals. Former vice president Al Gore's Oscar-winning and widely viewed documentary on global warming, released in 2006, further fueled the debate. (Gore received the Nobel Peace Prize in 2007 for his work.) Titled *An Inconvenient Truth,* the film stressed that actions to mitigate global warming must be taken now if we are to avert a planet-threatening crisis. Environmental groups and others have been pressing the federal government to do just that.

This family of polar bears finds itself on a shaky ice floe. Some experts on polar bears in the Arctic claim that if the warming trend in that part of the world continues, these majestic animals will have a hard time surviving into the second half of this century. (Johnny Johnson/Getty Images)

Their efforts are complicated by the fact that a major share of the American electorate does not believe that global warming is happening, or if it is happening, that it is caused by human activities. Disbelief in global warming is a partisan phenomenon. According to one poll, skepticism about global warming among Republicans rose by 11 percentage points from 2008 to 2009, and a majority of Republicans now believe that global warming does not exist. The opinions of Democrats have not changed—about four-fifths of them accept that global warming is a problem. If there were no global warming, of course, there would be no reason to limit emissions of CO_2 and other greenhouse gases.

The centerpiece of the Obama administration's legislative program on energy and the environment was a bill designed to limit greenhouse gas emissions. In June 2009, the House passed a 932-page bill replete with concessions to major energy consumers, including utility companies, heavy manufacturers, petroleum refiners, and others. In the Senate, this bill sank without a trace, to the considerable annoyance of House Democratic leaders. Senate attempts to agree on a different bill in 2010 were unsuccessful.

The BP *Deepwater Horizon* Oil Spill

On April 20, 2010, a torrent of methane gas began to spew out of the drill column of the *Deepwater Horizon,* an offshore oil-drilling platform in the Gulf of Mexico about forty-one miles from the Louisiana coast. The methane ignited and exploded. Eleven workers on the rig died, and the rest were evacuated. The *Deepwater Horizon* burned furiously for thirty-six hours and then sank. The platform was under lease to the BP oil company, formerly known as British Petroleum. BP had contracted with the Transocean company to perform the drilling, and at the time of the disaster, operations were being conducted by Halliburton Energy Services, which was placing cement around the drill site, five thousand feet below the surface. On April 22, a large oil slick began to spread at the former location of the rig. The largest oil spill in American history was under way.

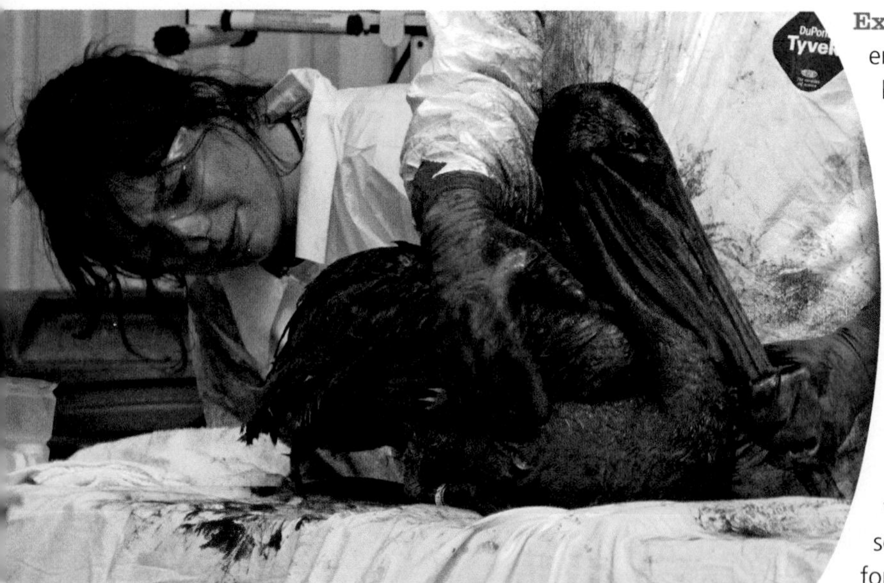

Workers clean a brown pelican at a rescue center at a facility set up by the International Bird Rescue Research Center in Buras, Louisiana, in the summer of 2010. Should the oil company BP be financially responsible for saving waterfowl along the Gulf coast? (AP Photo/Bill Haber)

Extent of the Spill. By April 30, the oil covered 3,850 square miles. On May 13, tar balls began washing up on the Louisiana shore. By June 4, oil was affecting 125 miles of Louisiana coast and was washing up on barrier islands in Mississippi, Alabama, and Florida. Sea birds and turtles became coated in oil and died. Not all of the oil made its way to the surface. In mid-May, scientists identified large oil plumes deep in the Gulf. The existence of these plumes explains why initial satellite imagery of the ocean surface put the spill rate at only five thousand barrels per day, whereas estimates based on underwater video of the gushing oil well put the rate at somewhere between twenty thousand and forty thousand barrels. The spill was 40 percent methane, in contrast to about 5 percent found in most oil deposits. The probable result of the methane was an enormous zone depleted of oxygen, where nothing could live.

Plugging the Leak. In the weeks following the explosion, BP made a series of attempts to plug the leak, all of which failed. First, the company used remote-controlled underwater vehicles in an attempt to close valves on the well head, without success. These valves were supposed to close automatically in a disaster, but had failed to do so. Attempts to place a dome over the leak failed due to interference from the methane. A smaller containment device, the "top hat," also failed. On May 26, BP began pumping mud into the well in a technique known as "top kill." When mud alone proved insufficient, BP added golf balls and rubber scrap to the mix, a process named "junk shot." The golf balls did not help.

Finally, the company attempted to cut away damaged tubing at the top of the well, creating a clean cut that might be more easily managed. The cut was made, but it was ragged, not clean. A cap fitted over the cut allowed oil and methane to be brought to the surface, where the methane was burned and the oil was collected by a series of ships. Unfortunately, as a result of the ragged cut, the amount of oil lost into the ocean was about as great as it had been before the procedure was performed.

In mid-July, BP was able to place a tighter-fitting cap on the well, which halted the leak. The ultimate solution was to drill relief wells and pump cement through them to form a permanent seal. Drilling takes time, however, and the BP well was not permanently sealed until September 19. By that time, 4.9 million barrels, or about 205 million gallons, of oil had spilled into the sea.[3]

Clean-up Efforts. A major part of the effort to control the spill was the use of dispersants to break up the oil. Dispersants are high-tech detergents—essentially soap. In addition to using dispersants on the ocean surface, BP began injecting large quantities of dispersants directly into the leak site at the bottom of the sea. By June, BP had pumped close to a million gallons of dispersants into the Gulf, a world record. Ecological experts were concerned that the dispersants themselves might cause serious environmental problems. Also, the dispersants BP used were neither the least toxic, nor the most effective, of the dispersants approved by the Environmental Protection Agency, and in fact were banned in Britain. They were, however, the only dispersants immediately available in enormous quantities.

Crews working to protect beaches, wetlands, and estuaries used skimmer ships, floating containment booms, anchored barriers, and sand-filled barricades along shorelines. By May 4, the effort involved 170 ships and about ten thousand workers and volunteers. By that time, almost one hundred miles of containment booms had been deployed along the coast. State and local officials proposed to build sand berms off the coast to catch the oil, but work on the berms was held up because the U.S. Army Corps of Engineers refused to approve the project. The holdup caused considerable anger in Louisiana, but the Army had reasons to balk—a variety of environmental experts believed that the sand would not work and might even make matters worse. In the end, however, the berm project was approved.

The Federal Government's Response. On April 28, the U.S. military announced that it was joining the clean-up effort. Military aircraft began applying dispersants to the ocean surface, and U.S. government ships participated in oil skimming. The federal government did not participate in the attempts to plug the leak, however, and was widely criticized for failing to do so. Some people began referring to the disaster as "Obama's Katrina," referring to the Bush administration's slow response to the flooding of New Orleans following Hurricane Katrina. The comparison was not entirely justified. Flood relief has always been the responsibility of local, state, and national governments. Prior to the *Deepwater Horizon* catastrophe, handling oil leaks and fires had always been the responsibility of the oil industry itself. The federal government lacked the personnel, equipment, and expertise that would have been necessary for it to participate in the plugging effort.

---

3. Although the spill was the largest in American history, it was only the second largest ever. During the First Gulf War in 1991, retreating Iraqi forces opened pipelines in Kuwait that spilled more than 7 million barrels into the Persian Gulf. The *Exxon Valdez* spill, the previous American record-holder, amounted to only 260,000 barrels.

During the oil spill crisis in 2010, President Obama flew to Louisiana to inspect the degradation of the beaches there. Why do Americans expect the president to solve every problem, or at least every problem that makes the headlines? (Redux/Stephen Crowley/*The New York Times*)

On April 30, Obama ordered the suspension of new offshore drilling leases, and on May 28 he placed a six-month moratorium on deepwater drilling projects. On June 1, Attorney General Eric Holder announced that he had opened a criminal investigation into the BP oil spill. Preliminary reports suggested that BP and the other companies involved might have cut corners at the *Deepwater Horizon* site in an attempt to reduce expenses and speed up operations, which were seriously behind schedule.

On June 15, Obama spoke from the Oval Office, saying, "We will fight this spill with everything we've got for as long as it takes. We will make BP pay for the damage their company has caused. And we will do whatever's necessary to help the Gulf Coast and its people recover from this tragedy." The next day, the administration announced that on its urging, BP had set aside a $20 billion response fund to pay for damage claims and response efforts. The company also suspended dividend payments to conserve cash. By August, BP had sold $10.6 billion in assets to raise additional funds.

The Failure of Regulation. At the time of the *Deepwater Horizon* spill, the federal agency in charge of monitoring the safety of offshore drilling was the Minerals Management Service (MMS), which was also responsible for issuing drilling permits and collecting royalty payments from the industry. In the wake of the *Deepwater Horizon* disaster, Americans learned that the MMS was a spectacular example of *regulatory capture,* as described in Chapter 12. MMS employees were completely under the industry's thumb—most expected to work for oil companies after leaving the agency.

In 2008, Department of the Interior investigators discovered that MMS employees had engaged in drug use and sexual activity with staff members of the energy firms that they were supposed to regulate. A May 2010 investigation revealed that MMS staff members in the Gulf allowed industry officials to fill in their own inspection reports. The Obama administration had replaced the head of MMS in 2009. After the spill, however, the rot had become so obvious that the agency was abolished altogether and replaced with three new ones, thus separating the functions of safety oversight, issuing leases, and collecting royalties.

Public Reaction. Opinion polls, as expected, showed considerable hostility to BP, which most people considered the responsible party. The public was not happy with the federal reaction either, with 60 percent rating the government's actions as "poor" and only 35 percent rating them as "good." Obama's handling of the affair was also viewed negatively. In one poll, 43 percent approved of his performance and 53 percent disapproved. Obama's overall job approval ratings remained level throughout the crisis, however, with about half of the public approving of his performance and about half disapproving.

The impact of the spill on the 2010 elections was not clear, but it could hardly be considered good news for the Democrats. As noted, the federal government was ill equipped to help stop the leak. Yet as the spill went on and on, week after week, it became clear that many people wanted President Obama to add a new role to the existing ones of head of state, chief executive, chief legislator, and the rest. For these citizens, Obama was now the nation's petroleum engineer in chief, whether he wanted the job or not.

The Politics of Economic Decision Making

Nowhere are the principles of public policymaking more obvious than in the economic decisions made by the federal government. The president and Congress (and to a growing extent, the judiciary) are constantly faced with questions of economic policy. Such issues become especially important when the nation enters a recession.

Protesters often attack any industrial activities that involve the creation of carbon dioxide. When we breathe, we create CO_2, so why are we so worried about it? (Theo Heimann/AFP/Getty Images)

Good Times, Bad Times

Like any economy that is fundamentally capitalist, the U.S. economy experiences ups and downs. Good times—booms—are followed by lean years. If a slowdown is severe enough, it is called a **recession.** Recessions are characterized by increased **unemployment,** the inability of those who are in the workforce to find a job. The government tries to moderate the effects of such downturns. In contrast, booms are historically associated with another economic problem that the government must address—rising prices, or **inflation.**

Recession
Two or more successive quarters in which the economy shrinks instead of grows.

Unemployment
The inability of those who are in the labor force to find a job; the number of those in the labor force actively looking for a job, but unable to find one.

Inflation
A sustained rise in the general price level of goods and services.

Measuring Unemployment. Estimates of the number of unemployed are prepared by the U.S. Department of Labor. The Bureau of the Census also generates estimates using survey research data. Critics of the published unemployment rate calculated by the federal government believe that it fails to reflect the true numbers of discouraged workers and "hidden unemployed." Although there is no exact definition or way to measure discouraged workers, the Department of Labor defines them as people who have dropped out of the labor force and are no longer looking for a job because they believe that the job market has little to offer them. To see an alternative depiction of job loss as it occurred in the most recent recession, see Figure 14–9 on the following page. Note that the number of job losses peaked in January 2009, at the very start of the Obama administration. Thereafter, the trend line was up, but that was cold comfort for job seekers. Throughout 2009, the employment picture merely got worse ever more slowly. Not until 2010 did the economy actually begin creating jobs again, and even then progress was slow and subject to reversals. If you look at how many jobs were lost in the previous two years, it is clear that the economic recovery had a long way to go.

Inflation. Rising prices, or inflation, can also be a serious economic and political problem. Inflation is a sustained upward movement in the average level of prices. Another way of defining inflation is as a decline in the purchasing power of money over time. The government measures inflation using the *consumer price index,* or CPI. The Bureau of Labor Statistics identifies a market basket of goods and services purchased by the typical consumer, and regularly checks the price of that basket. Over a period of many years, inflation can add up. For example, today's dollar is worth (very roughly) about a twentieth of what it was worth a century ago. In effect, today's dollar is a 1910 nickel.

The Business Cycle. Economists refer to the regular succession of economic expansions and contractions as the *business cycle.* An extremely severe recession is called a *depression,* as in the example of the Great Depression. By 1933, actual output was 35 percent below the nation's productive capacity. Unemployment reached 25 percent. Compared with this

FIGURE 14–9 Net Loss of U.S. Jobs during the Great Recession

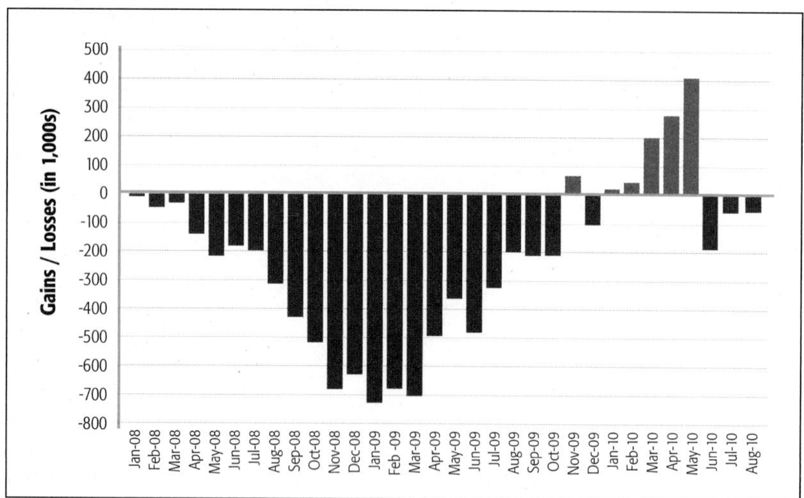

Source: Bureau of Labor Statistics.

catastrophe, recessions since 1945 have usually been mild. Nevertheless, the United States has experienced recessions with some regularity. Recession years since 1960 have included 1970, 1974, 1980, 1982, 1990, 2001, and 2008.

To try to control the ups and downs of the national economy, the government has several policy options. One is to change the level of taxes or government spending. Another possibility involves influencing interest rates and the money side of the economy. We will examine taxing and spending, or **fiscal policy,** first.

Fiscal Policy

Fiscal policy is the domain of Congress. A fiscal policy approach to stabilizing the economy is often associated with a twentieth-century British economist named John Maynard Keynes. Keynes (1883–1946) originated the school of thought called **Keynesian economics,** which supports the use of government spending and taxing to help stabilize the economy. (*Keynesian* is pronounced *kayn*-zee-un.) Keynes believed that there was a need for government intervention in the economy, in part because after falling into a recession or depression, a modern economy may become trapped in an ongoing state of less than full employment.

Fiscal Policy
The federal government's use of taxation and spending policies to affect overall business activity.

Keynesian Economics
A school of economic thought that tends to favor active federal government policymaking to stabilize economy-wide fluctuations, usually by implementing discretionary fiscal policy.

Budget Deficit
Government expenditures that exceed receipts.

Government Spending and Borrowing. Keynes developed his fiscal policy theories during the Great Depression. He believed that the forces of supply and demand operated too slowly on their own in such a serious recession. Unemployment meant people had less to spend, and because they could not buy things, more businesses failed, creating additional unemployment. It was a vicious cycle. Keynes's idea was simple: in such circumstances, the *government* should step in and undertake the spending that is needed to return the economy to a more normal state.[4]

Government spending can be financed in a number of ways, including increasing taxes and borrowing. For government spending to have the effect Keynes wanted, however, it was essential that the spending be financed by borrowing, and not by taxes. In other words, the government should run a **budget deficit**—it should spend more than it receives. If the government financed its spending during a recession by taxation, the government would be spending funds that would, for the most part, otherwise have been spent by taxpayers.

Criticisms of Keynes. Following World War II (1939–1945), Keynes's theories were integrated into the mainstream of economic thinking. There have always been economic schools of thought, however, that consider Keynesian economics to be fatally flawed. These schools argue either that fiscal policy has no effect or that it has negative side effects that outweigh any benefits. Some opponents of fiscal policy believe that the federal government should limit itself to monetary policy, which we will discuss shortly. Others even believe that it is best for the government to do nothing at all. For a further discussion of

4. Robert Skidelsky, *Keynes: The Return of the Master, 1920–1937: A Biography* (New York: Public Affairs, 2009).

Keynesian economics, see Chapter 12's *Politics of Boom and Bust* feature on page 411.

English economist John Maynard Keynes, (1883–1946). (Walter Stoneman/Samuel Bourne/ Getty Images)

Discretionary Fiscal Policy. Keynes originally developed his fiscal theories as a way of lifting an economy out of a major disaster such as the Great Depression. Beginning with the presidency of John F. Kennedy (1961–1963), however, policymakers have attempted to use Keynesian methods to "fine-tune" the economy. This is discretionary fiscal policy—*discretionary* meaning left to the judgment or discretion of a policymaker. For example, President George W. Bush advertised his tax cuts of 2001 and 2003 as a method of stimulating the economy to halt the economic slowdown of those years. Likewise, in February 2008, when the effects of the Great Recession were still modest, Bush obtained a $152 billion stimulus bill from Congress.

Attempts to fine-tune the economy face a timing problem. It takes a while to collect and assimilate economic data. Time may go by before an economic problem can be identified. After an economic problem is recognized, a solution must be formulated. There will be an action time lag between the recognition of a problem and the implementation of policy to solve it. Getting Congress to act can easily take a year or two. Finally, after fiscal policy is enacted, it takes time for the policy to act on the economy. Because fiscal policy time lags are long and variable, a policy designed to combat a recession may not produce results until the economy is already out of the recession.

Because of the timing problem, attempts by the government to employ fiscal policy in the past fifty years have typically taken the form of tax cuts or increases. Tax changes can take effect more quickly than government spending. In 2009, therefore, the Obama administration was employing a novel approach with its dramatic increase in government spending. Because the recession was worldwide and associated with a financial crisis, however, economists expected it to last for several years. That meant that there should be enough time for government spending to take effect.

Another problem with tax cuts is that taxpayers may use the income to pay down their debts, instead of spending it. According to Keynesian theory, this failure to spend reduces the stimulative effect of the tax cut—and in 2009, an unusually large number of people were trying to pay off their debts.

Deficit Spending and the Public Debt

The federal government typically borrows by selling U.S. Treasury bills, notes, and bonds, known collectively as *Treasury securities* and informally as **treasuries.** The sale of these federal obligations to corporations, private individuals, pension plans, foreign governments, foreign businesses, and foreign individuals adds to this nation's **public debt, or national debt.** In the past few years, foreign governments, especially those of China and Japan, have come to own about 50 percent of the net U.S. public debt. Thirty years ago, the share of the U.S. public debt held by foreigners was only 15 percent.

Treasuries
U.S. Treasury securities—bills, notes, and bonds. Debt issued by the federal government.

Public Debt, or National Debt
The total amount of debt carried by the federal government.

Deficit Spending. As noted, when the federal government spends more than it receives in revenues, it typically borrows by selling U.S. Treasury securities. Individuals, businesses, and foreigners buy these treasuries. Every time the federal government engages in deficit spending, it increases the size of its total debt.

Can deficit spending go on forever? Certainly, it can go on for quite a long time for the U.S. government. After all, as long as individuals, businesses, and foreigners (especially foreign governments) are willing to purchase Treasury securities, the government can continue to engage in deficit spending. If deficit spending goes on long enough,

Gross Public Debt
The net public debt plus interagency borrowings within the government.

Net Public Debt
The accumulation of all past federal government deficits; the total amount owed by the federal government to individuals, businesses, and foreigners.

however, the rest of the world—which owns about 50 percent of all Treasury securities—may lose faith in our government. Consequently, U.S. government borrowing might become more expensive. We, as taxpayers, are responsible for the interest that the federal government pays when it issues treasuries. A vicious cycle might occur—more deficit spending could lead to higher interest rate costs on the U.S. debt, leading in turn to even larger deficits.

So far, however, there has been little sign that such a problem is imminent. On the contrary, following the financial crisis that struck on September 15, 2008, panicked investors piled into treasuries in the belief that these were the safest instruments in existence. The interest that the U.S. government must pay on its borrowing is also very low. In 2009, the average interest rate on outstanding Treasury bills—the shortest-term Treasury obligations—was only 0.3 percent. In 2010, after a crisis in which it seemed possible that the government of Greece might default on its debts, investors again began to demand treasuries.

TABLE 14–1 Net Public Debt of the Federal Government

Year	Total (Billions of Current Dollars)
1940	$ 42.8
1945	235.2
1950	219.0
1960	236.8
1970	283.2
1980	811.9
1990	2,411.6
1992	2,999.7
1993	3,248.4
1994	3,433.1
1995	3,604.4
1996	3,734.1
1997	3,772.3
1998	3,721.1
1999	3,632.4
2000	3,405.3
2001	3,339.3
2002	3,553.2
2003	3,924.1
2004	4,307.3
2005	4,601.2
2006	4,843.1
2007	5,049.3
2008	5,808.7
2009	7,551.9
2010	9,022.8
2011	10,120.1*

*Estimate.

Source: 1945–1995, U.S. Office of Management and Budget; 2000–2011, U.S. Treasury.

The Public Debt in Perspective. Did you know that the federal government has accumulated trillions of dollars in debt? Does that scare you? It certainly would if you thought that we had to pay it back tomorrow. But we do not.

There are two types of public debt—gross and net. The **gross public debt** includes all federal government interagency borrowings, which really do not matter. This is similar to your taking an IOU ("I owe you") out of your left pocket and putting it into your right pocket. Today, federal interagency borrowings account for about $4.3 trillion of the gross public debt. What is important is the **net public debt**—the public debt that does not include interagency borrowing. Table 14–1 on the left shows the net public debt of the federal government since 1940. This table does not take into account two very important variables: inflation and increases in population. A better way to examine the relative importance of the public debt is to compare it with *gross domestic product (GDP),* as is done in Figure 14–10 on the facing page. (Remember from earlier in this chapter that gross domestic product is the dollar value of all final goods and services produced in a one-year period.) There you see that the public debt reached its peak during World War II and fell thereafter. From about 1960 until the onset of the Great Recession, the net public debt as a percentage of GDP ranged between 30 and 50 percent.

Are We Always in Debt? From 1960 until the last few years of the twentieth century, the federal government spent more than it received in all but two years. Some observers consider these ongoing budget deficits to be the negative result of Keynesian policies. Others argue that the deficits actually result from the abuse of Keynesianism. Politicians have been more than happy to run budget deficits in recessions, but they have often refused to implement the other side of Keynes's recommendations—to run a *budget surplus* during boom times.

In 1993, however, President Bill Clinton (1993–2001) obtained a tax increase as the nation emerged from a mild recession. For the first time, the federal government implemented the more painful side of Keynesianism. In any event, between the tax increase and the "dot-com boom," the United States had a budget surplus each year from 1998 to 2002. Some commentators predicted that we would be running federal government surpluses for years to come. All of those projections went by the wayside because of several events.

One event was the "dot-com bust" followed by the 2001–2002 recession, which lowered the rate of growth of not only the economy but also the federal government's tax receipts. In every recession that we have lived through, tax receipts have always fallen. The "bust" in 2008–2011 was no exception.

A major event took place on September 11, 2001. Basically, as a result of the terrorist attacks, the federal government spent much more than it had planned to spend on security against terrorism. Also, the government had to pay for the war in Iraq in 2003 and the occupation of that country thereafter. Finally, Congress authorized major increases in spending on discretionary programs.

Immediately upon taking office, President Obama obtained legislation from Congress that pushed the public debt to levels not seen since World War II. Such high levels of debt became a major political issue. For more details on Obama's approach to federal budget deficits, see Chapter 10's *Politics of Boom and Bust* feature on page 362.

FIGURE 14–10 Net Public Debt as a Percentage of Gross Domestic Product

During World War II, the net public debt as a percentage of GDP grew dramatically. It fell thereafter but rose again from 1980 to 1992, under Republicans Reagan and G.H.W. Bush. The percentage fell under President Clinton.

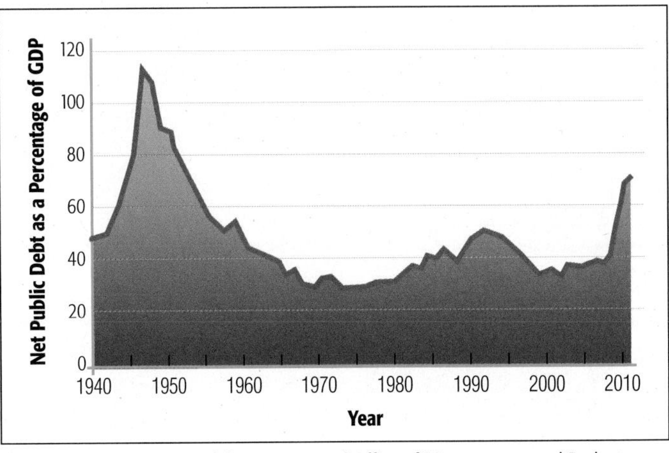

Sources: U.S. Department of the Treasury and Office of Management and Budget.

Monetary Policy

Controlling the rate of growth of the money supply is called *monetary policy.* This policy is the domain of the **Federal Reserve System,** also known simply as the **Fed.** The Fed is the most important regulatory agency in the U.S. monetary system.

The Fed performs a number of important functions. Perhaps the Fed's most important ability is that it is able to regulate the amount of money in circulation, which can be defined loosely as checking account balances and currency. The Fed also provides a system for transferring checks from one bank to another. In addition, it holds reserves deposited by most of the nation's banks, savings and loan associations, savings banks, and credit unions, and it plays a role in supervising the banking industry.

Organization of the Federal Reserve System. A board of governors manages the Fed. This board consists of seven full-time members appointed by the president with the approval of the Senate. The twelve Federal Reserve district banks have twenty-five branches. The most important unit within the Fed is the **Federal Open Market Committee.** This is the body that actually determines the future growth of the money supply and other important economy-wide financial variables. This committee is composed of the members of the Board of Governors, the president of the New York Federal Reserve Bank, and presidents of four other Federal Reserve banks, rotated periodically.

Federal Reserve System (the Fed)
The agency created by Congress in 1913 to serve as the nation's central banking organization.

Federal Open Market Committee
The most important body within the Federal Reserve System. The Federal Open Market Committee decides how monetary policy should be carried out.

Monetary Policy
The use of changes in the amount of money in circulation to alter credit markets, employment, and the rate of inflation.

The Board of Governors of the Federal Reserve System is independent. The president can attempt to influence the board, and Congress can threaten to merge the Fed into the Treasury Department, but as long as the Fed retains its independence, its chairperson and governors can do what they please. Hence, any talk about "the president's monetary policy" or "Congress's monetary policy" is inaccurate. To be sure, the Fed has, on occasion, yielded to presidential pressure, and for a while the Fed's chairperson had to observe a congressional resolution requiring him to report monetary targets over each six-month period. But now, more than ever before, the Fed remains one of the truly independent sources of economic power in the government.

Loose and Tight Monetary Policies. The Federal Reserve System seeks to stabilize nationwide economic activity by controlling the amount of money in circulation. Changing the amount of money in circulation is a major aspect of **monetary policy.** You may have read a news report in which a business executive complained that money is "too tight." You may have run across a story about an economist who has warned that money is "too loose." In these instances, the terms *tight* and *loose* refer to the monetary policy of the Fed.

The current chair of the Federal Reserve System is Ben Bernanke. What is his role in economic policymaking? (AP Photo/ Alex Brandon)

Credit, like any good or service, has a cost. The cost of borrowing—the interest rate—is similar to the cost of any other aspect of doing business. When the cost of borrowing falls, businesspersons can undertake more investment projects. When it rises, businesspersons will undertake fewer projects. Consumers also react to interest rates when deciding whether to borrow funds to buy houses, cars, or other "big-ticket" items.

If the Fed implements a **loose monetary policy** (often called an "expansionary" policy), the supply of credit increases and its cost falls. If the Fed implements a **tight monetary policy** (often called a "contractionary" policy), the supply of credit falls and its cost increases. A loose money policy is often implemented as an attempt to encourage economic growth. You may be wondering why any nation would want a tight money policy. The answer is to control inflation. If money becomes too plentiful too quickly, prices (and ultimately the price level) increase, and the purchasing power of the dollar decreases.

Loose Monetary Policy Monetary policy that makes credit inexpensive and abundant, possibly leading to inflation.

Tight Monetary Policy Monetary policy that makes credit expensive in an effort to slow inflation.

Time Lags for Monetary Policy. You learned earlier that policymakers who implement fiscal policy—the manipulation of budget deficits and the tax system—experience problems with time lags. The Fed faces similar problems when it implements monetary policy.

Sometimes accurate information about the economy is not available for months. Once the state of the economy is known, time may elapse before any policy can be put into effect. Still, the time lag in implementing monetary policy is usually much shorter than the lag involved in fiscal policy. The Federal Open Market Committee meets eight times a year and can put a policy into effect relatively quickly. Nevertheless, a change in the money supply may not have an effect for several months.

Monetary Policy during Recessions. A tight monetary policy is effective as a way of taming inflation. (Some would argue that it is the *only* way that inflation can be stopped.) If interest rates go high enough, people *will* stop borrowing. How effective, though, is a loose monetary policy at ending a recession? Under normal conditions, it is very effective. A loose monetary policy will spur an expansion in economic activity.

To combat the Great Recession, however, the Fed reduced its interest rate effectively to zero. It could not go any lower. Yet banks, seeking to rebuild their capital, did not lower their rates in response. Moreover, many businesses discovered that they could not obtain credit even to support obviously profitable investments. Also, even though consumers had credit, they were still reluctant to make major purchases. Monetary policy had run out of steam—using it was like "pushing on a string." The government has little power to force banks to lend, and it certainly has no power to make people borrow and spend. As a result, the Obama administration placed its bets on fiscal policy.

During 2008 and 2009, the Fed developed a new way to respond to the failure of banks to lend. Relying on its ability to create money, it began to make loans itself, without turning to Congress for appropriations. The Fed bought debt issued by corporations. It bought securities that were based on student loans and credit-card debt. By 2009, the Fed had loaned out close to $2 trillion in fresh credit.

Regulating Banks. In addition to managing the money supply, the Federal Reserve has a variety of responsibilities in the area of bank regulation. The Fed ensures that banks have a large enough quantity of reserve capital to back up the loans they are making. It also administers various regulations that protect consumers. In the past, not all banks fell under the regulatory oversight of the Fed. For example, the Fed did not supervise investment banks that do not take deposits from customers. This exemption came to an end in 2008 when the collapse of Bear Stearns, an investment bank, threatened to bring down large numbers of other institutions that had financial ties to the ailing firm. The Fed stepped in to extend Bear Stearns an emergency loan and to force it to sell out to JPMorgan Chase, a much stronger institution, for a nominal price. Subsequently, the president and Congress took action to provide $700 billion to "rescue" other financial firms facing collapse.

did you know?

That it costs the U.S. Mint 1.4 cents to make a penny and 7.8 cents to make a nickel.

The Politics of Taxes

Federal taxes are enacted by members of Congress. Today, the Internal Revenue Code, the federal tax code, encompasses tens of thousands of pages, thousands of sections, and thousands of subsections—our tax system is very complex.

Americans pay a variety of taxes. At the federal level, the income tax is levied on most sources of income. Social Security and Medicare taxes are assessed on wages and salaries. There is an income tax for corporations, which has an indirect effect on many individuals. The estate tax is collected from property left behind by those who have died. State and local governments also assess taxes on income, sales, and land. Altogether, the value of all taxes collected by the federal government and by state and local governments exceeds 25 percent of GDP. This is a substantial sum, but it is less than what many other countries collect, as you can see in Figure 14–11 below.

Federal Income Tax Rates

Individuals and businesses pay taxes based on tax rates. Not all of your income is taxed at the same rate. The first few dollars you make are not taxed at all. The highest rate is imposed on the "last" dollar you make. This highest rate is the *marginal* tax rate. Table 14–2 on the following page shows the 2010 marginal tax rates for individuals and married couples (tax forms filed in 2011). The higher the tax rate—the action on the part of the government—the greater the public's reaction to that tax rate. If the highest tax rate you pay on the income you make is 15 percent, then any method you can use to reduce your taxable income by one dollar saves you fifteen cents in tax liabilities that you owe to the federal government. Individuals paying a 15 percent rate have a relatively small incentive to avoid paying taxes, but consider the individuals who faced a marginal tax rate of 94 percent in the 1940s, during and after World War II. They had a tremendous incentive to find legal ways to reduce their taxable incomes.

FIGURE 14–11 Total Amount of Taxes Collected as a Percentage of Gross Domestic Product (GDP) in Major Industrialized Nations

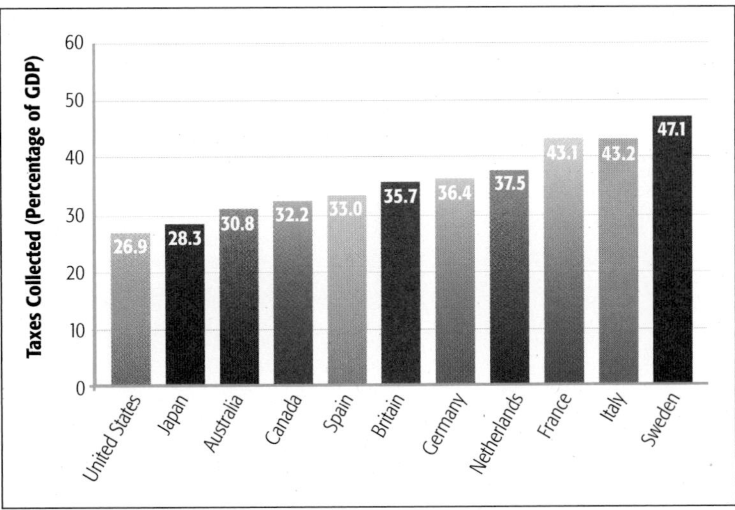

Source: Excerpted and adapted from the Organization for Economic Cooperation and Development.

For every dollar of income that was somehow deemed nontaxable, these taxpayers would reduce tax liabilities by ninety-four cents.

Loopholes and Lowered Taxes

Loophole
A legal method by which individuals and businesses are allowed to reduce the tax liabilities owed to the government.

Progressive Tax
A tax that rises in percentage terms as incomes rise.

Regressive Tax
A tax that falls in percentage terms as incomes rise.

Individuals and corporations facing high tax rates will adjust their earning and spending behavior to reduce their taxes. They will also make concerted attempts to get Congress to add **loopholes** to the tax law that allow them to reduce their taxable incomes. When Congress imposed very high tax rates on high incomes, it also provided for more loopholes than it does today. For example, special provisions enabled investors in oil and gas wells to reduce their taxable incomes.

In 2001, President George W. Bush fulfilled a campaign pledge by persuading Congress to enact new legislation lowering tax rates for a period of several years. In 2003, rates were lowered again, retroactive to January 2003. These rates are reflected in Table 14–2 below. As a result of other changes contained in the new tax laws, the U.S. tax code became even more complicated than it was before.

Progressive and Regressive Taxation. As Table 14–2 shows, the greater your income, the higher the marginal tax rate. Persons with large incomes pay a larger share of their income in income tax. A tax system in which rates go up with income is called a **progressive tax** system. The federal income tax is clearly progressive.

The income tax is not the only tax you must pay. For example, the federal Social Security tax is levied on wage and salary income at a flat rate of 6.2 percent. (Employers pay another 6.2 percent, making the total effective rate 12.4 percent.) In 2010, however, there was no Social Security tax on wages and salaries in excess of $106,800. (This threshold changes from year to year.) Persons with very high salaries therefore pay no Social Security tax on much of their wages. In addition, the tax is not levied on investment income (including capital gains, rents, royalties, interest, dividends, or profits from a business). The wealthy receive a much greater share of their income from these sources than do the poor. As a result, the wealthy pay a much smaller portion of their income in Social Security taxes than do the working poor. The Social Security tax is therefore a **regressive tax.** Note that three-quarters of all taxpayers owe more in payroll taxes, such as Social Security and Medicare taxes, than they do in income taxes.

Who Pays? The question of whether the tax system should be progressive—and if so, to what degree—is subject to vigorous political debate. Democrats in general and liberals in

TABLE 14–2 Marginal Tax Rates for Single Persons and Married Couples (2010)

Single Persons		Married Filing Jointly	
Marginal Tax Bracket	Marginal Tax Rate	Marginal Tax Bracket	Marginal Tax Rate
$ 0–$ 8,375	10%	$ 0–$ 16,750	10%
$ 8,376–$ 34,000	15%	$ 16,751–$ 68,000	15%
$ 34,001–$ 82,400	25%	$ 68,001–$137,300	25%
$ 82,401–$171,850	28%	$137,301–$209,250	28%
$171,851–$373,650	33%	$209,251–$373,650	33%
$373,651 and higher	35%	$373,651 and higher	35%

When Barack Obama campaigned for the presidency in 2008, he promised that there would be tax relief for the middle class. Why do most candidates favor some tax reductions and at the same time also favor increased government spending on many new programs? (Darren McCollester/ Getty Images)

particular favor a tax system that is significantly progressive. Republicans and conservatives are more likely to prefer a tax system that is proportional or even regressive. For example, President Bush's tax cuts made the federal system somewhat less progressive, largely because they significantly reduced taxes on nonsalary income.

Overall, what kind of tax system do we have? The various taxes Americans pay pull in different directions. The 1.45 percent Medicare tax, as applied to wages and salaries, is entirely flat—that is, neither progressive nor regressive. Because it is not levied on investment income, however, it is regressive overall. Sales taxes are regressive because the wealthy spend a relatively smaller portion of their income on items subject to the sales tax. Table 14–3 on the right lists the characteristics of major taxes. Add everything up, and the tax system as a whole is probably slightly progressive. Given all this, should the rich pay even more in taxes? We look at that question in the *Which Side Are You On?* feature on the following page.

The Recession's Impact on Taxes. As noted earlier, recessions lead to reduced tax collections. Furthermore, the government must spend more on measures such as helping the unemployed. As a result, federal budget deficits rise automatically in a recession—and in 2009 the Obama administration sharply increased spending as well. Meanwhile, the tax bite as a percentage of personal income actually fell. In 2010, taxes levied by all levels of government were only 24.8 percent of GDP. Given that spending by all levels of government was equivalent to almost 44 percent of GDP that year, it follows that less than three-fifths of total government expenditures were paid for by taxes. It is no surprise that the public debt rose rapidly, as shown in Figure 14–10 on page 497.

TABLE 14–3

Progressive versus Regressive Taxes

Progressive Taxes
Federal income tax
State income taxes
Federal corporate income tax
Estate tax
Regressive Taxes
Social Security tax
Medicare tax
State sales taxes
Local real estate taxes

WHICH SIDE ARE YOU ON?

SHOULD THE RICH PAY EVEN MORE IN TAXES?

The rich have gotten richer during the past few decades—of that we are certain. Go back to 1980—in that year, the top 1 percent of income earners made 9.3 percent of the nation's total income. Thirty years later, the top 1 percent of income earners made almost 19 percent of the nation's income.

IF THE RICH ARE RICHER, WHY SHOULDN'T THEY PAY MORE TAXES?

Not only have the rich increased their share of the nation's income, they have become wealthier. We are increasingly becoming a society divided by class. A small minority lives in opulence while the majority struggles. In the past ten years, the hourly wages of average workers, corrected for inflation, haven't risen at all. During the same decade, the number of millionaires and billionaires skyrocketed.

In this context, it seems perfectly appropriate to raise taxes on the rich. After all, they are now paying much lower marginal tax rates than during much of the postwar history of the United States. There have been periods when marginal federal income tax rates on the very rich exceeded 90 percent. Today, they are 35 percent. In addition, the tax on capital gains, which make up a much larger share of the income of the rich than of other people, is only 20 percent today for those with large incomes.

It seems appropriate that those who have benefited the most from America's economic system should pay more, particularly when many social needs are unmet and must be paid for by increased government expenditures. The rich will argue that they are the "engines of economic growth" and therefore should be encouraged to continue their hard work, but higher taxes are not going to keep the wealthy from striving.

DON'T KILL THE GEESE THAT LAY THE GOLDEN EGGS

It is true that the top 1 percent of income earners now receive 19 percent of the national income, whereas thirty years ago they made less than 10 percent. The part of the story that is less often told is that in those thirty years, even as marginal federal personal income tax rates fell, the share of total income taxes paid by the top 1 percent of income earners increased from 18.3 percent to 37 percent. The top 1 percent of income-earning U.S. residents paid more than one-third of all federal income taxes in the United States on the eve of the Great Recession.

The top 40 percent of all income earners pay 99.1 percent of federal income taxes. That means that the lower 60 percent of income earners pay less than 1 percent of the taxes. During the past few years, the richest 1.3 million tax filers paid more in federal income taxes than all of the 66 million U.S. tax filers below the median income in the United States—ten times more. The number of those who pay nothing to support the federal government through the income tax continues to rise every year.

Indeed, an increasingly large number of Americans actually receive more through the federal income tax than they pay. As part of the Earned Income Tax Program, 25 million families and individuals with incomes of less than about $40,000 receive payments that substantially reduce their Social Security and Medicare taxes.

It is true that the rich have benefited most from cuts in marginal federal income tax rates. After all, they are the individuals who pay the most federal income taxes. If we use taxes to "soak the rich," we will tax the most productive individuals in the country. High marginal tax rates discourage effort, and the higher the rate, the greater the discouragement. The cost of increasing the federal marginal income tax rate on the richest Americans will be a lower rate of economic growth. More income will be redistributed, but is that the ultimate goal of society?

(Newhouse News Service/Landov)

WHY SHOULD YOU CARE ABOUT... DOMESTIC POLICY?

Collectively, programs such as Medicare, Medicaid, Social Security, unemployment compensation, and several others are known as *entitlement programs.* They are called entitlements because if you meet certain qualifications—of age or income, for example—you are entitled to specified benefits. The federal government can estimate how much it will have to pay out in entitlements but cannot set an exact figure in advance. In this way, entitlement spending differs from other government spending. When Congress decides what it will give to the national park system, for example, it allocates an exact sum, and the park system cannot exceed that budget. Along with national defense, entitlements make up by far the greatest share of the federal budget. This fact led a Bush administration staff member to joke: "It helps to think of the government as an insurance company with an army."

ENTITLEMENT REFORM AND YOUR LIFE

What happens to entitlements will affect your life in two major ways. Entitlement spending will largely determine how much you pay in taxes throughout your working lifetime. Entitlement policy will also determine how much support you receive from the federal government when you grow old. Because entitlements make up such a large share of the federal budget, it is not possible to address the issue of budget deficits without considering entitlement spending. Further, as you learned in this chapter, under current policies, spending on Medicare and Social Security will rise in future years, placing ever-greater pressure on the federal budget. Sooner or later, entitlement reform will be impossible to avoid. However these programs are changed, you will feel the effects in your pocketbook throughout your life.

What kind of entitlements do seniors enjoy? (AP Photo/J Pat Carter)

HOW YOU CAN MAKE A DIFFERENCE

Should Medicare and Social Security benefits be high, with the understanding that taxes must therefore go up? Should these programs be cut back in the hope of avoiding deficits and tax increases? Do entitlements mean that the old are fleecing the young—or is that argument irrelevant because we will all grow old someday? Progressives and conservatives disagree strongly about these questions. You can develop your own opinions by learning more about entitlement reform. The following organizations take a conservative position on entitlements:

National Center for Policy Analysis
www.retirementreform.ncpa.org

The Heritage Foundation
www.heritage.org/Initiatives/Entitlements

The following organizations take a liberal stand on entitlements:

National Committee to Preserve Social Security and Medicare
www.ncpssm.org

AARP (formerly the American Association of Retired Persons)
www.aarp.org

questions for discussion and analysis

1. Just how serious an offense should illegal immigration be? Construct arguments in favor of considering it a felony and arguments for viewing it as a mere civil infraction.
2. Should the problem of illegal immigration be addressed by making legal immigration easier? Why or why not?
3. The federal income tax system collects a greater percentage of the income of wealthier persons than of poorer ones. The Social Security tax, in contrast, is a flat rate on all incomes—and it is not collected at all on income above a certain threshold. Are the higher income tax rates for wealthy people fair? Why or why not? Is the method of calculating the Social Security tax fair? Why or why not?
4. Review the *Which Side Are You On?* feature on page 502. How is it possible for the rich to pay more in taxes if their marginal tax rates go down?

key terms

budget deficit 494
domestic policy 473
Federal Open Market Committee 497
Federal Reserve System (the Fed) 497
fiscal policy 494
gross domestic product (GDP) 477
gross public debt 496
incarceration rate 487
inflation 493
Keynesian economics 494
loophole 500
loose monetary policy 498
Medicaid 477
Medicare 477
monetary policy 498
moral hazard 474
net public debt 496
personal mandate 481
progressive tax 500
public debt, or national debt 495
public option 481
recession 493
regressive tax 500
tight monetary policy 498
treasuries 495
unemployment 493
universal health insurance 481

chapter summary

1. Domestic policy consists of all of the laws, government planning, and government actions that concern internal issues of national importance. Policies are created in response to public problems or public demand for government action. The policymaking process is initiated when policymakers become aware—through the media or from their constituents—of a problem that needs to be addressed by the legislature and the president. The process of policymaking includes five steps: agenda building, policy formulation, policy adoption, policy implementation, and policy evaluation. All policy actions necessarily result in both costs and benefits for society.
2. Health-care spending accounts for about 17.6 percent of the U.S. economy and is growing. A major source of funding is Medicare, the federal program that pays the health-care expenses of U.S. residents over the age of sixty-five. The federal government has tried to restrain the growth in Medicare spending.
3. Almost 16 percent of the population does not have health insurance—a major political issue. Individual health-insurance policies (not obtained through an employer) are expensive and may be unobtainable at any price. In most wealthy countries, this problem is addressed by a national health-insurance system under which the government provides basic coverage to all citizens. In 2010, Congress passed a health-care reform package that in time will provide near-universal coverage in the United States. It would require residents not already covered to purchase coverage, which would be subsidized for low-income persons.
4. Today, more than 1 million immigrants from other nations enter the United States each year, and about 13 percent of the U.S. population consists of foreign-born persons. Illegal immigration, or unauthorized immigration (the Department of Homeland Security term), is a major political issue. Questions include how to improve

border control and whether the existing unauthorized population should be allowed to seek citizenship.

5. There is widespread concern in this country about violent crime. The overall rate of violent crime declined between 1995 and 2004, and has leveled off since. In response to crime concerns, the United States has incarcerated an unusually large number of persons.

6. Issues concerning energy and the environment are on the nation's agenda today. One problem is our reliance on petroleum imports, given that many petroleum exporters are hostile to American interests. Raising the average fuel efficiency of cars sold in the United States is one method of reducing imports. Global warming, caused by the emission of CO_2 and other greenhouse gases, is a second major problem, although some dispute how serious it is.

7. Fiscal policy is the use of taxes and spending to affect the overall economy. Time lags in implementing fiscal policy can create serious difficulties. The federal government has experienced ongoing budget deficits. A budget deficit is met by U.S. Treasury borrowing. This adds to the public debt of the U.S. government. Although the budget was temporarily in surplus from 1998 to 2002, deficits now seem likely for many years to come.

8. Monetary policy is controlled by the Federal Reserve System, or the Fed. Monetary policy involves changing the rate of growth of the money supply in an attempt to either stimulate or cool the economy. A loose monetary policy, in which more money is created, encourages economic growth. A tight monetary policy, in which less money is created, may be necessary to control inflation.

9. U.S. taxes exceed 25 percent of the gross domestic product, a percentage that is not particularly high by international standards. Individuals and corporations that pay taxes at the highest rates try to pressure Congress into creating exemptions and tax loopholes. Loopholes allow high-income earners to reduce their taxable incomes. The federal income tax is progressive; that is, tax rates increase as income increases. Some other taxes, such as the Social Security tax and state sales taxes, are regressive—they take a larger share of the income of poorer people. As a whole, the tax system is probably slightly progressive.

selected print & media resources

SUGGESTED READINGS

Broyles, Bill, and Mark Haynes. *Desert Duty: On the Line with the U.S. Border Patrol.* Austin, Tex.: University of Texas Press, 2010. The authors demonstrate that frontline border patrol work is a rugged and dangerous task. Officers frequently save the lives of illegal immigrants who will eventually be deported.

Krugman, Paul. *The Return of Depression Economics and the Crisis of 2008.* New York: W. W. Norton, 2009. Krugman is the leading liberal economist of our time. In this slim easy-to-read volume, he examines recent economic crises around the world, and concludes by arguing that Keynesian measures to address the Great Recession are essential.

Lewis, Michael. *The Big Short: Inside the Doomsday Machine.* New York: W. W. Norton, 2010. A brilliant writer, Lewis describes the handful of investors who knew that the housing market was about to collapse and who profited handsomely from that insight.

Miller, Roger LeRoy, *et al.* *The Economics of Public Issues,* 16th ed. Reading, Mass.: Addison-Wesley, 2009. Chapters 4, 8, 11, 13, 19, 20, 22, 24, and 27 are especially useful. The authors use short essays of three to seven pages to explain the purely economic aspects of numerous social problems, including health care, the environment, and poverty.

Lomborg, Bjørn. *Cool It: The Skeptical Environmentalist's Guide to Global Warming.* New York: Knopf, 2008. Lomborg, a critic of the environmental movement, believes that it would be more practical to take action against global warming later in the century, when the world is (presumably) richer and when renewable energy sources have become more competitive in price.

Roubini, Nouriel, and Stephen Mihm. *Crisis Economics: A Crash Course in the Future of Finance.* New York: Penguin Press, 2010. Roubini gained fame as one of the few economists who accurately predicted the Great Recession and its severity. This volume is his account of what went wrong and what we need to do next. Roubini is concerned that the buildup of government debt, which may have been necessary in the short run, will lead to future problems.

Staff of the *Washington Post*. *Landmark: The Inside Story of America's New Health Care Law and What It Means for Us All.* New York: PublicAffairs, 2010. This account, by top journalists, describes how the health-care reform bill survived several near-death experiences en route to passage. The book also explains the final legislation and its probable consequences.

Sterling, Terry Greene. *Illegal: Life and Death in Arizona's Immigration War Zone.* Augusta, Ga.: Lyons Press,

2010. Sterling gives us the lives of real people who seek to enter the country illegally—both saints and sinners.

MEDIA RESOURCES

Capitalism Hits the Fan: Richard Wolff on the Economic Meltdown—In this entertaining lecture given in 2009, an MIT economics professor attempts to show that the recent economic crisis was decades in the making.

De Nadie (Border Crossing)—An award-winning and heart-breaking documentary, this 2007 film follows a group of Central Americans as they attempt to pass through Mexico and enter the United States. Tin Dirdamal is the director.

An Inconvenient Truth—A 2006 Paramount Classics production of former vice president Al Gore's Oscar-winning documentary on global warming and actions that can be taken in response to this challenge.

i.o.u.s.a.—A 2009 film from the Peterson Foundation, *i.o.u.s.a.* depicts the dangers that can result from an uncontrolled rise in the national debt. It is based on the book *Empire of Debt* by William Bonner and Addison Wiggin.

Modern Marvels: Renewable Energy—This 2008 documentary from the A&E channel describes the rapidly evolving technologies that may help resolve our energy crisis.

Sicko—Michael Moore's 2007 effort, which takes on the U.S. health-care industry. Rather than focusing on the plight of the uninsured, Moore addresses the troubles of those who have been denied coverage by their insurance companies. In his most outrageous stunt ever, Moore assembles a group of 9/11 rescue workers who have been denied proper care and takes them to Cuba, where the government, perfectly aware of the propaganda implications, is more than happy to arrange for their treatment.

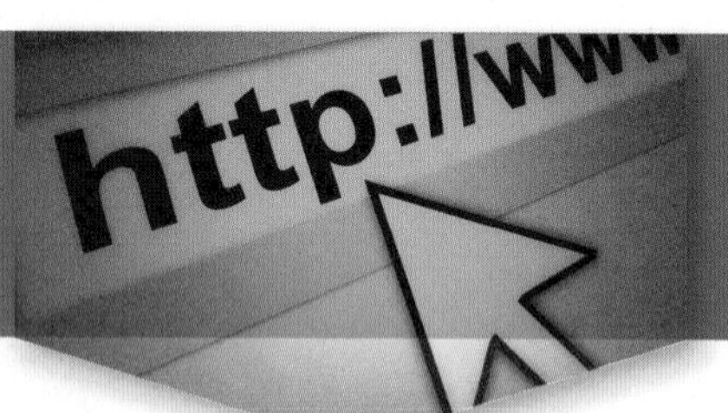

e-mocracy

PUBLIC POLICY

Today, the World Wide Web offers opportunities for you to easily access information about any domestic policy issue. The *Logging On* section that follows lists a variety of Web sites where you can learn more about domestic policy issues and how they affect you. Many other sites are available as well. For example, would you like to learn more about prisons and imprisonment rates in different countries? The Web site of the International Centre for Prison Studies (ICPS) can help. A URL for the ICPS is **www.kcl.ac.uk/depsta/rel/icps/worldbrief/world_brief.html**. Would you like to take a turn at proposing a federal budget and allocating spending among different programs, domestic or otherwise? You can find a budget simulation game at **www.kowaldesign.com/budget**. Of course, most news media outlets have their own Web sites, which are useful for keeping up to date on the latest domestic policy developments.

LOGGING ON

The National Governors Association offers information on the current status of Medicaid and other topics at
www.nga.org

The Federal Bureau of Investigation offers information about crime rates on its Web site at
www.fbi.gov/ucr/ucr.htm

For information on the BP oil spill and other energy topics, see the Department of Energy Web site at
www.energy.gov

You can keep up with actions taken by the Federal Reserve by checking the home page of the Federal Reserve Bank of San Francisco at
www.frbsf.org

For further information on Social Security, access the Social Security Administration's home page at
www.ssa.gov

For information on the 2012 budget of the U.S. government, go to
www.whitehouse.gov/omb/budget

chapter
15
ARMY STRONG.

Foreign Policy

chapter contents

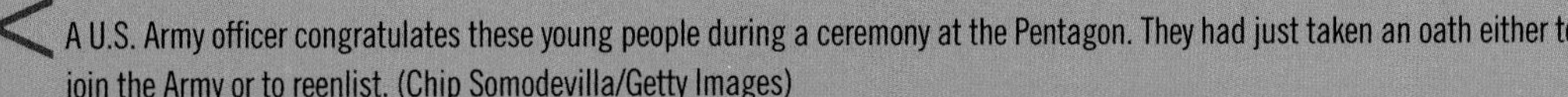

A U.S. Army officer congratulates these young people during a ceremony at the Pentagon. They had just taken an oath either to join the Army or to reenlist. (Chip Somodevilla/Getty Images)

WHAT IF... ...we brought back the draft?

What induces young people to voluntarily join the U.S. armed forces? (Chip Somodevilla/Getty Images)

BACKGROUND

Young people today have no direct memory of the draft—forced military conscription—because military service became voluntary in 1973. From 1948 to 1973, however, all American males were subject to the draft. Required military service provided large forces to confront the Soviet Union during the Cold War (a period you will read about in this chapter). The draft was used during the war in Vietnam (1964–1975), when it became a heated issue. In recent years, the idea of bringing back the draft has reappeared in public debate. In 2006, Representative Charles Rangel (D., N.Y.) called for the reinstatement of the draft. In 2006 and 2007, members of George W. Bush's administration also suggested that we bring back the draft. In recent years, however, because of the high unemployment caused by the Great Recession, the military has had no difficulty in filling its enlistment quotas. As a result, there has been less talk of a draft.

WHAT IF WE BROUGHT BACK THE DRAFT?

If we brought back the draft, the U.S. Selective Service would once again be a powerful bureaucratic organization. At the height of the Vietnam War, many young men over the age of eighteen focused much of their attention on avoiding the draft. The same might be true if we brought the draft back today.

Today, the pool of draft-eligible men (and women if they are included) is much larger than required by the U.S. military. Even though the military has recently been stretched thin, "boots on the ground" are becoming less important as the military continues to evolve toward technological warfare. At the peak of the Vietnam War, there were more than 500,000 U.S. troops in Southeast Asia. As of mid-2010, there were about 84,000 U.S. troops in Iraq and 78,000 in Afghanistan. Consequently, the Selective Service might have to create more deferments than were available during the Vietnam War. Another idea is to create a civilian service as an alternative to military service. Persons who opted for such a program might provide care for the elderly or assist with government services in the inner cities.

BENEFITS OF A DRAFT

At various times during the Iraq and Afghanistan wars, the Department of Defense was forced to extend tours of duty for units that were about to be brought home. A draft would prevent these kinds of troop shortages. In particular, a draft could eliminate the unfairness involved in stationing National Guard troops abroad for long periods of time.

If we brought the draft back, the U.S. military would include children of wealthy families, unlike the situation today. In principle, therefore, service to one's country would become more evenly distributed across social and economic classes, promoting fairness. Some argue that a draft would cause Congress and the president to think differently about military operations. If the children of senators and representatives were drafted and sent to dangerous regions, those leaders might be more cautious about military operations.

THE DRAFT AS A TAX ON THE YOUNG

Typically, draftees are paid nominal amounts—less than they could earn in the civilian sector. It is not necessary to pay draftees the relatively high salaries and benefits required to induce young Americans to volunteer for military service. As a result, with a draft, federal expenditures for the military would decline. The financial burden of staging military actions abroad would fall in part on the draftees themselves. They would effectively be paying a tax consisting of the difference between what they could earn outside the U.S. military and what they were paid by the military.

FOR CRITICAL ANALYSIS

1. Some argue that the volunteer nature of our U.S. military is responsible for the relatively small antiwar movement in this country today. Why might that be so?
2. What alternatives to military service might be possible?

On September 11, 2001, Americans were forced to change their view of national security and of our relations with the rest of the world—literally overnight. No longer could citizens of the United States believe that national security issues involved only threats overseas or that the American homeland could not be attacked. No longer could Americans believe that regional conflicts in other parts of the world had no direct impact on the United States.

Within a few days, it became known that the 9/11 attacks on the World Trade Center and on the Pentagon had been planned and carried out by a terrorist network named al Qaeda that was funded and directed by the radical Islamist leader Osama bin Laden. The network was closely linked to the Taliban government of Afghanistan, which had ruled that nation since 1996.

Americans were shocked by the complexity and the success of the attacks. They wondered how our airport security systems could have failed so drastically. How could the Pentagon, the heart of the nation's defense, have been successfully attacked? Shouldn't our intelligence community have known about and defended against this network? And, finally, how could our foreign policy have been so deaf to the anger voiced by Islamist groups throughout the world?

In this chapter, we examine the tools of foreign policy and national security policy in light of the many challenges facing the United States today. One of the major challenges for U.S. foreign policymakers is how best to respond to the threat of terrorism. One question raised by the resulting U.S. military commitments in Afghanistan and elsewhere is whether we need to bring back the draft, as we discussed in the chapter-opening *What If . . .* feature. The chapter concludes with a look at major themes in the history of American foreign policy.

Foreign Policy
A nation's external goals and the techniques and strategies used to achieve them.

Diplomacy
The process by which states carry on political relations with each other; settling conflicts among nations by peaceful means.

Economic Aid
Assistance to other nations in the form of grants, loans, or credits to buy the assisting nation's products.

Technical Assistance
The practice of sending experts in such areas as agriculture, engineering, or business to aid other nations.

Foreign Policy Process
The steps by which foreign policy goals are decided and acted on.

National Security Policy
Foreign and domestic policy designed to protect the nation's independence and political and economic integrity; policy that is concerned with the safety and defense of the nation.

Facing the World: Foreign and Defense Policy

The United States is only one nation in a world with almost two hundred independent countries, many located in regions where armed conflict is ongoing. What tools does our nation have to deal with the many challenges to its peace and prosperity? One tool is **foreign policy.** By this term, we mean both the goals the government wants to achieve in the world and the techniques and strategies to achieve them. For example, if one national goal is to achieve stability in the Middle East and to encourage the formation of pro-American governments there, U.S. foreign policy in that area may be carried out through **diplomacy, economic aid, technical assistance,** or military intervention. Sometimes foreign policies are restricted to statements of goals or ideas, such as helping to end world poverty, whereas at other times foreign policies are comprehensive efforts to achieve particular objectives, such as preventing Iran from obtaining nuclear weapons.

As you will read later in this chapter, in the United States, the **foreign policy process** usually originates with the president and those agencies that provide advice on foreign policy matters. Congressional action and national public debate often affect foreign policy formulation as well.

An American flag stands in the rubble of the World Trade Center towers two days after the September 11, 2001, terrorist attacks. In what ways did the events of 9/11 change U.S. foreign policy? (Beth A. Keiser/AFP/Getty Images)

National Security Policy

As one aspect of overall foreign policy, **national security policy** is designed primarily to protect the independence and the political integrity of the United States. It concerns itself with the defense of the United States against actual or potential future enemies.

U.S. national security policy is based on determinations made by the Department of Defense, the Department of State, and a number of other federal agencies, including the National Security Council (NSC). The NSC acts as an advisory body to the president, but it has increasingly become a rival to the State Department in influencing the foreign policy process.

Defense Policy
A subset of national security policies having to do with the U.S. armed forces.

Moral Idealism
A philosophy that sees nations as normally willing to cooperate and agree on moral standards for conduct.

Political Realism
A philosophy that sees each nation acting principally in its own interest.

Defense policy is a subset of national security policy. Generally, defense policy refers to the set of policies that direct the nature and activities of the U.S. armed forces. Defense policy also considers the types of armed forces units we need to have, such as Rapid Defense Forces or Marine Expeditionary Forces, and the types of weaponry that should be developed and maintained for the nation's security. Defense policies are proposed by the leaders of the nation's military forces and the secretary of defense, and these policies are greatly influenced by congressional decision makers.

Diplomacy

Diplomacy is another aspect of foreign policy. Diplomacy includes all of a nation's external relationships, from routine diplomatic communications to summit meetings among heads of state. More specifically, diplomacy refers to the settling of disputes and conflicts among nations by peaceful methods. Diplomacy is also the set of negotiating techniques by which a nation attempts to carry out its foreign policy. Of course, diplomacy can be successful only if the parties are willing to negotiate. The question of whether to negotiate with leaders such as Mahmoud Ahmadinejad, the president of Iran, became an issue in the 2008 U.S. presidential campaigns.

Morality versus Reality in Foreign Policy

Since the earliest years of the republic, Americans have felt that their nation had a special destiny. The American experiment in political and economic liberty, it was thought, would provide the best possible life for its citizens and be a model for other nations. As the United States assumed greater status as a power in world politics, Americans came to believe that the nation's actions on the world stage should be guided by American political and moral principles.

Moral Idealism

This view of America's mission has led to the adoption of many foreign policy initiatives that are rooted in **moral idealism.** This philosophy sees the world as fundamentally benign and assumes that most nations can be persuaded to take moral considerations into account when setting their policies.[1] In this perspective, nations should come together and agree to keep the peace, as President Woodrow Wilson (1913–1921) proposed for the League of Nations. Many of the foreign policy initiatives taken by the United States have been based on this idealistic view of the world. The Peace Corps, which was created by President John Kennedy in 1961, is one example of an effort to spread American goodwill and the technology.

Part of America's foreign policy involves humanitarian aid, as seen in this photo of members of the U.S. Navy helping a young Haitian after the devastating earthquake in early 2010. Who determines when U.S. armed forces will go to the assistance of a country after a natural disaster? (Win McNamee/ Getty Images)

Political Realism

In opposition to the moral perspective is **political realism,** often called *realpolitik* (a German word meaning "realistic politics"). Realists see the world as a dangerous place in which each nation strives for its own survival and interests regardless of moral considerations. The United States must also base its foreign

1. Eugene R. Wittkopf, Charles W. Kegley, and James M. Scott, *American Foreign Policy,* 7th ed. (Belmont, Calif.: Wadsworth Publishing, 2007).

policy decisions on cold calculations without regard for morality. Realists believe that the United States must be prepared militarily to defend itself, because other nations are, by definition, dangerous. A strong defense will show the world that the United States is willing to protect its interests. The practice of political realism in foreign policy allows the United States to sell weapons to military dictators who will support its policies, to support American business around the globe, and to repel terrorism through the use of force.

Al Qaeda leader
Osama bin Laden remains alive and at large, even though the United States has attempted to capture or kill him since 9/11. How does bin Laden differ from America's earlier enemies? (AP Photo)

American Foreign Policy—A Mixture of Both

It is important to note that the United States has never been guided by only one of these principles. Instead, both moral idealism and political realism affect foreign policymaking. President George W. Bush drew on the tradition of morality in foreign policy when he declared that the al Qaeda network of Osama bin Laden was "evil" and that fighting terrorism was fighting evil. The war against the Taliban government in Afghanistan, which had sheltered al Qaeda terrorists, was dubbed "Operation Enduring Freedom," a title that reflected the moral ideal of spreading democracy.

To actually wage war on the Taliban in Afghanistan, however, U.S. forces needed the right to use the airspace of India and Pakistan, neighbors of Afghanistan. The United States had previously criticized both of these South Asian nations because they had developed and tested nuclear weapons. In addition, the United States had taken the moral stand that it would not deliver certain fighter aircraft to Pakistan as long as that nation continued its weapons program. When it became absolutely necessary to work with India and Pakistan, the United States switched to a realist policy, promising aid and support to both regimes in return for their assistance in the war on terrorism.

The Iraq War that began in 2003 also revealed a mixture of idealism and realism. While the primary motive for invading Iraq was realistic (the interests of U.S. security), another goal of the war reflected idealism—the liberation of the Iraqi people from an oppressive regime and the establishment of a democratic model in the Middle East. The reference to the war effort as "Operation Iraqi Freedom" emphasized this idealistic goal.

Challenges in World Politics

The foreign policy of the United States, whether moralistic, realistic, or both, must be formulated to deal with world conditions. Early in its history, the United States was a weak, new nation facing older nations well equipped for war. In the twenty-first century, the United States faces different challenges. Now it must devise foreign and defense policies that will enhance its security in a world in which it is the global superpower and has no equal.

The Emergence of Terrorism

In years past, terrorism was a strategy typically employed by radicals who wanted to change the status of a particular nation or province. For example, over many years the Irish Republican Army undertook terrorist attacks in the British province of Northern Ireland with the aim of driving out the British and uniting the province with the Republic of Ireland. In Spain, the ETA organization continues to employ terrorism. Its goal is to create an independent Basque state in Spain's Basque region. In the twenty-first century, however, the United States has confronted a new form of terrorism that is not associated with such clear-cut aims.

September 11. In 2001, terrorism came home to the United States in ways that few Americans could have imagined. In a well-coordinated attack, nineteen terrorists hijacked four airplanes and crashed three of them into buildings—two into the World Trade Center towers in New York City and one into the Pentagon in Washington, D.C. The fourth airplane crashed in a field in Pennsylvania, after the passengers fought the hijackers.

Why did the al Qaeda network plan and launch attacks on the United States? One reason was that the leaders of the network, including Osama bin Laden, were angered by the presence of U.S. troops on the soil of Saudi Arabia, which they regard as sacred. They also saw the United States as the primary defender of Israel against the Palestinians and as the defender of the royal family that governs Saudi Arabia. The attacks were intended to so frighten and demoralize America that it would withdraw troops from the Middle East.

Al Qaeda's ultimate goals, however, were not limited to forcing the United States to withdraw from specific countries or even the entire Middle East. Al Qaeda envisioned worldwide revolutionary change, with all nations brought under the theocratic rule of an Islamist empire. Governments have successfully negotiated with terrorists who profess limited aims—today, radicals associated with the Irish Republican Army are part of a coalition government in Northern Ireland. There is no way to negotiate with an organization such as al Qaeda.

Acts of terrorism have occurred throughout the world in recent times. Here, rescue workers examine the destroyed remains of a suburban train in Madrid after terrorists planted bombs in early 2004. The attack killed 191 people. Hundreds more were injured. Why is it hard for countries that are targets of such terrorism to retaliate? (AP Photo/ Anja Niedringhaus, File)

Bombings in Madrid and London. Since September 11, 2001, al Qaeda has not undertaken another act of terrorism on American soil. Terrorists influenced by al Qaeda have committed serious crimes in other countries, however. On March 11, 2004, ten coordinated train bombings in Madrid killed 191 people and wounded more than 2,000 others. The subsequent investigation revealed that the attacks were carried out by Islamist extremists.

On July 7, 2005, terrorists carried out synchronized bombings of the London Underground (subway) and bus network. Four suicide bombers, British citizens of Middle Eastern descent, claimed the lives of fifty-two other people and wounded hundreds more in the attacks. It was later determined that the leader of this group had links to al Qaeda.

The War on Terrorism

After 9/11, President George W. Bush implemented stronger security measures to help ensure homeland security and protect U.S. facilities and personnel abroad. The president sought and received congressional support for heightened airport security, new laws allowing greater domestic surveillance of potential terrorists, and new funding for the military.

A New Kind of War. In September 2002, President Bush enunciated what has since become known as the "Bush Doctrine," or the doctrine of preemption:

> *We will . . . [defend] the United States, the American people, and our interests at home and abroad by identifying and destroying the threat before it reaches our borders. While the United States will constantly strive to enlist the support of the international community, we will not hesitate to act alone, if necessary, to exercise our right of self-defense by acting preemptively against such terrorists, to prevent them from doing harm against our people and our country.*[2]

The concept of "preemptive war" as a defense strategy was a new element in U.S. foreign policy. The concept is based on the assumption that in the war on terrorism, self-defense must be *anticipatory.* President Bush stated on March 17, 2003, just before launching the invasion of Iraq, "Responding to such enemies only after they have struck first is not self-defense, it is suicide."

Opposition to the Bush Doctrine. The Bush Doctrine had many critics. Some pointed out that preemptive wars against other nations have traditionally been waged by dictators and rogue states, not democratic nations. By employing such a strategy, the United States would seem to be contradicting its basic values. Others claimed that launching preemptive wars would make it difficult for the United States to pursue world peace in the future. By endorsing such a policy itself, the United States could hardly argue against the decisions of other nations to do likewise when they felt potentially threatened. While campaigning for the Democratic presidential nomination, Barack Obama rejected the Bush Doctrine with these words:

> *And part of the reason that we neglected Afghanistan, part of the reason that we didn't go after bin Laden as aggressively as we should have is we were distracted by a war of choice [in Iraq]. And that's the flaw of the Bush Doctrine. It wasn't that he went after those who attacked America. It was that he went after those who didn't.*

This London bus was destroyed by a bomb, as were several other buses and subway cars in that city. Four suicide bombers, all British citizens of Middle Eastern descent, ultimately killed fifty-two other people and wounded hundreds more. How might a city government prevent such terrorist actions? (AP Photo/Dylan Martinez, Pool)

Wars in Iraq

On August 2, 1990, the Persian Gulf became the setting for a major challenge to the international system set up after World War II (1939–1945). President Saddam Hussein of Iraq sent troops into the neighboring oil sheikdom of Kuwait, occupying that country. This was the most clear-cut case of aggression against an independent nation in half a century.

The First Gulf War. At the request of Saudi Arabia, American troops were dispatched to set up a defensive line at the Kuwaiti border. On January 17, 1991, U.S.-led coalition forces launched a massive air attack on Iraq. After several weeks, the ground offensive began. Iraqi troops retreated from Kuwait a few days later, and the First Gulf War ended.

As part of the cease-fire that ended the First Gulf War, Iraq agreed to allow United Nations (UN) weapons inspectors to search for, and oversee the destruction of, its missiles

2. George W. Bush, September 17, 2002. The full text of the document from which this statement is taken can be accessed at **georgewbush-whitehouse.archives.gov/nsc/nss/2002/nss3.html**.

These Taliban militants were photographed in the late summer of 2008 in an undisclosed location in Ghazni Province in Afghanistan. Many political analysts believe that the Taliban are regaining a foothold in Afghanistan and that additional troops will be needed to keep that country free of their radical influence. Is the United States capable of pursuing antiterrorist "wars" in several countries simultaneously? (AP Photo/Rahmatullah Naikzad)

and all weapons of mass destruction, including any chemical and nuclear weapons. Economic sanctions were to be imposed on Iraq until the weapons inspectors finished their work. In 1999, however, Iraq placed so many obstacles in the path of the UN inspectors that they withdrew from the country.

The Second Gulf War—The Iraq War. In 2002 and early 2003, President Bush called for "regime change" in Iraq and began assembling an international coalition that might support further military action in Iraq. Having tried and failed to convince the UN Security Council that the UN should take action to enforce its resolutions, Bush decided to take unilateral action against Iraq. In March 2003, U.S. and British forces invaded Iraq. Within three weeks, the coalition forces had toppled Hussein's decades-old dictatorship.

The process of establishing order and creating a new government in Iraq turned out to be extraordinarily difficult, however. In the course of the fighting, the Iraqi army, rather than surrendering, disbanded itself. Soldiers simply took off their uniforms and made their way home. As a result, the task of maintaining law and order fell on the shoulders of a remarkably small coalition expeditionary force. Coalition troops were unable to put an immediate halt to the wave of looting and disorder that spread across Iraq in the wake of the invasion.

Occupied Iraq. The people of Iraq are divided into three principal ethnic groups. The Kurdish-speaking people of the north were overjoyed by the invasion. The Arabs adhering to the Shiite branch of Islam live principally in the south and constitute a majority of the population. The Shiites were glad that Saddam Hussein, who had murdered many thousands of Shiites, was gone. They were deeply skeptical of U.S. intentions, however. The Arabs belonging to the Sunni branch of Islam live mainly to the west of Baghdad. Although the Sunnis constituted only a minority of the population, they had controlled the government under Hussein. Many of them considered the occupation to be a disaster.

The Insurgency. An American-led Coalition Provisional Authority (CPA) governed Iraq until the establishment of an Iraqi interim government in 2004. One of the first acts of the CPA was to formally disband the Iraqi army. In retrospect, this decision has been widely viewed as a disaster. It released hundreds of thousands of well-armed young men, largely Sunnis, who no longer had jobs but did possess a great resentment toward the American invaders. In short order, a guerrilla insurgency arose and launched attacks against the coalition forces. Occupation forces also came under attack by Shiite forces loyal to Muqtada al Sadr, a radical cleric who was the son of a famous Shiite martyr.

Coalition forces were soon suffering monthly casualties comparable to those experienced during the initial invasion. Iraq had begun to be a serious political problem for President Bush. By May 2004, a majority of Americans no longer believed that going to war had been the right thing to do.

The Threat of Civil War. In justifying its decision to invade Iraq, the Bush administration had claimed—incorrectly, as it turns out—that links existed between the Hussein regime and al Qaeda. Ironically, the occupation of Iraq soon led to the establishment of an al Qaeda operation in that country, which sponsored suicide bombings and other attacks against coalition troops and the forces of the newly established Iraqi government. Al Qaeda did not limit its hostility to the Americans but issued vitriolic denunciations of the Iraqi Shiites.

In February 2006, a bomb, believed to have been set by al Qaeda, destroyed much of the al Askari mosque, one of the holiest Shiite sites in Iraq. This attack marked a major turning point in the conflict. While Sunni and Shiite insurgents continued to launch attacks on coalition forces, the major bloodletting in the country now took place between Sunnis and Shiites.

Opposition to the War. By late 2006, polls indicated that about two-thirds of Americans wanted to see an end to the Iraq War—a sentiment clearly expressed in the 2006 elections, which were seen largely as a referendum on the Iraq War policy of President Bush and the Republican-led Congress. One immediate result of the elections was that Bush dismissed his secretary of defense, Donald Rumsfeld, who was closely associated with Iraq policy failures.

General David Petraeus presented his assessment of the situation in Iraq when he was called to testify before a congressional hearing in 2009. His testimony was criticized as being too optimistic. Nonetheless, in 2010 he was named head of our military forces in Afghanistan. Who ultimately decides the leadership of our military missions? (Alex Wong/Getty Images)

Signs of Progress. In January 2007, Bush announced a major increase, or "surge," in U.S. troop strength. Bush placed General David Petraeus, the U.S. Army's leading counterinsurgency expert, in charge of all forces in Iraq. Many observers thought that he was the first leader of the American war effort to truly understand the nature of the conflict. Nevertheless, skeptics doubted that either Petraeus or the new troop levels would have much effect on the outcome.

In April 2007, however, a new development transformed the situation in Iraq once again. Sunni tribal leaders rose up against al Qaeda and called in U.S. troops to help them. The new movement, called the Awakening, spread rapidly through most Sunni districts and Baghdad neighborhoods. Al Qaeda, it seems, had badly overplayed its hand by terrorizing the Sunni population. The Awakening did not solve Iraq's political problems, however. The Shiite-dominated central government resisted cooperation with it, fearing that the new movement might turn its U.S.-supplied weapons against the government.

Also in 2007, the radical cleric Muqtada al Sadr announced that his militia, the Mahdi Army, would begin observing a cease-fire. In March 2008, al Sadr suspended the cease-fire. On March 25, the Iraqi government launched an operation to drive the Mahdi Army out of the southern city of Basra. The government forces were forced to call on the Americans for support, but ultimately they prevailed.

Iraqi Endgame. The reconquest of Basra by the central government marked a final turning point in the war. During subsequent months, the government gained substantial control over its own territory. Still, American attitudes toward the war remained negative. The steep decline in terrorist and insurgent activities did push Iraq out of the headlines. Pundits had expected that the war would be a top issue in the 2008 presidential elections. As it turned out, the war was almost completely eclipsed as an issue by the economy.

Democratic candidate Barack Obama had opposed the Iraq War from the start, and he called for setting a deadline for the withdrawal of U.S. forces. In 2008, President Bush and Iraqi Prime Minister Nouri al-Maliki negotiated a deadline for the withdrawal of all U.S. forces, so the difference between Obama's position and that of Bush was now merely a matter of months. In 2009, President Obama announced that U.S. combat forces would leave Iraq by August 31, 2010, and the rest of the American troops would be out by the end of 2011. Combat forces left in mid-August 2010, ahead of schedule.

Afghanistan

The Iraq War was not the only military effort launched by the Bush administration as part of the war on terrorism. The first military effort was directed against al Qaeda camps in Afghanistan and the Taliban regime, which had ruled most of Afghanistan since 1996. In late 2001, after building a coalition of international allies and anti-Taliban rebels within Afghanistan, the United States began an air campaign against the Taliban regime. The anti-Taliban rebels, known as the Northern Alliance, were able to take Kabul, the capital, and oust the Taliban from power. The United States and other members of the international community then fostered the creation of an elected Afghan government.

The Return of the Taliban. The Taliban were defeated, but not destroyed. U.S. forces were never able to locate Osama bin Laden and other top al Qaeda leaders. The Taliban and al Qaeda both retreated to the rugged mountains between Afghanistan and Pakistan, where they were able to establish bases on the Pakistani side of the border. In 2003, the Taliban began to launch attacks against Afghan soldiers, foreign aid workers, and even American troops. Afghanistan's opium poppy crop served as a major source of Taliban revenue—Afghanistan was now supplying 95 percent of the world's opium, the raw material for morphine and heroin. Despite increases in coalition forces, the Taliban continued to gain strength. Through 2008 and 2009, the Taliban were able to take over a number of Pakistani districts, even as the United States began attacking suspected Taliban and al Qaeda targets in Pakistan using small unmanned aircraft. (For some interesting details about how these "drones" are controlled, see the feature *Politics and . . . Social Networking: Tipping Off the Troops* on the facing page.) In 2009, the government of Pakistan initiated military action in an attempt to retake Taliban-controlled districts.

Obama and Afghanistan. In his presidential campaign, Barack Obama called for increased American troop levels to deal with the emergency, and in February 2009 he dispatched 17,000 additional soldiers to Afghanistan. From September through November 2009, the administration conducted a policy review of the war. Lieutenant General Stanley McChrystal, who had been appointed by Obama as Afghanistan theater commander in May 2009, was requesting large numbers of additional troops. Several presidential advisers, including Vice President Joe Biden and U.S. Ambassador to Afghanistan Karl Eikenberry, thought that such a move would be a mistake.

McChrystal made his recommendations public, which led to accusations that he was attempting to force the president's hand and was therefore insubordinate. In December 2009, Obama announced that he would send an additional 30,000 troops to Afghanistan but would begin troop withdrawals in July 2011. In June 2010, *Rolling Stone* magazine published an interview in which McChrystal and his top aides made highly critical remarks about Biden, Eikenberry, and other administration officials. This act of insubordination made McChrystal a repeat offender. Obama dismissed him and replaced him with General David Petraeus, famous for leading the turnaround in Iraq.

Nuclear Weapons

In 1945, the United States was the only nation to possess nuclear weapons. Several nations quickly joined the "nuclear club," however, including the Soviet Union in 1949, Britain in 1952, France in 1960, and China in 1964. Few nations have made public their nuclear weapons programs since China's successful test of nuclear weapons in 1964. India and Pakistan, however, detonated nuclear devices within a few weeks of each other in 1998, and North Korea conducted an underground nuclear explosive test in October 2006. Several other nations are suspected of possessing nuclear weapons or the capability to produce them in a short time. Israel is known to possess more than one hundred nuclear warheads.

did you know?

That including the Civil War, more than 1 million American soldiers have been killed in the nation's wars.

With nuclear weapons, materials, and technology available worldwide, it is conceivable that terrorists could obtain a nuclear device and use it in a terrorist act. In fact, a U.S. federal indictment filed in 1998, after the attack on the American embassies in Kenya and Tanzania, charged Osama bin Laden and his associates with trying to buy components for a nuclear bomb "at various times" since 1992.

Nuclear Stockpiles. More than 22,000 nuclear warheads are known to be stocked worldwide, although the exact number is uncertain because some countries do not reveal

POLITICS AND... social networking

TIPPING OFF THE TROOPS

When the major military threat to the United States came from the Soviet Union, the U.S. Air Force focused on fixed targets such as military bases in that very large country. Times have changed now that the Cold War is over and we are fighting the Taliban in Afghanistan. The targets are terrorists and insurgents who plant roadside bombs or booby-trap helicopter-landing areas.

To combat this kind of irregular warfare, the United States currently uses a growing fleet of "drones"—unmanned, remote-controlled airplanes, called Predators and Reapers. Some of the drones drop bombs. Others send a steady flow of battlefield videos to our intelligence centers. No longer do our commanders in Afghanistan (and elsewhere) have to rely on information that is stale. In 2009, more drones were sent to Afghanistan than ever before.

USING SOCIAL NETWORKING SKILLS TO MANAGE A WAR

Eight thousand miles from Afghanistan, hundreds of military intelligence officers, most of them young, monitor video feeds from a variety of drones (as well as from high-flying U-2 spy planes). As these officers analyze the videos, they are in constant contact with troops on the ground. How? Usually through text messages. Young people who grew up on computers, interactive video games, Facebook, and now Twitter are adept at passing on important information to Marine or Army ground troops.

At any time during the day, hundreds of young texting whizzes each monitor four screens of video feeds. Each officer participates in designated chat rooms with commanders on the move throughout Afghanistan. Sometimes they just chat, but they also regularly relay information that indicates, for example, that a roadside bomb is ahead, or that enemy fire can soon be expected.

MORE MILITARY ANALYSTS ON THE WAY

As of 2010, the Air Force was using about four thousand analysts at bases in California and Florida and planned to recruit an additional two thousand. The Air Force was also sending liaisons to Afghanistan to learn more about our soldiers' priorities on the ground. Not only do the young analysts help save American lives, but they have reduced civilian casualties. They can report when their video feeds show that children or other innocents are in a proposed air strike target area. With this news, the troops in the field can abort the strike.

FOR CRITICAL ANALYSIS

Why does the military prefer intelligence analysts who are in their early twenties to undertake the job described above?

Cold War
The ideological, political, and economic confrontation between the United States and the Soviet Union following World War II.

the extent of their holdings. Although the United States and Russia have dismantled many of their nuclear weapons systems since the end of the **Cold War** (discussed later in this chapter), both still retain sizable nuclear arsenals. Also, since the dissolution of the Soviet Union in 1991, the security of its nuclear arsenal has declined. There have been reported thefts, smugglings, and illicit sales of nuclear material from the former Soviet Union in the past two decades.

Nuclear Proliferation: Iran. For years, the United States, the European Union, and the UN have tried to prevent Iran from becoming a nuclear power. In spite of these efforts, many observers believe that Iran is now in the process of developing nuclear weapons—although Iran maintains that it is interested in developing nuclear power only for peaceful purposes. Continued diplomatic attempts to at least slow down Iran's quest for a nuclear bomb have so far proved ineffectual. The group of nations attempting to talk with Iran includes Britain, China, France, Germany, Russia, and the United States. By 2009, the UN Security Council had already voted three rounds of sanctions against Iran in reaction to its nuclear program.

The international campaign against Iran's nuclear program was interrupted in June 2009, when the government of Iran announced that President Mahmoud Ahmadinejad had won a resounding victory in a presidential election. Considerable evidence existed that the election results had been manipulated. Street demonstrations appeared to threaten the government's survival, and under these circumstances, major pressure on the nuclear issue could have benefited the government by letting it claim the banner of nationalism. By late 2009, however, the protests had subsided. In October, the six nations that were attempting to negotiate offered Iran a proposal to enrich its uranium in Russia, thus placing international controls on the process. Iran initially agreed to the proposal, but then rejected it. In May 2010, Iran agreed with Turkey and Brazil that it would let some of its uranium be enriched in Turkey, but this did not satisfy the international community, and in June the UN imposed additional sanctions.

One problem with the attempt to develop meaningful international sanctions was resistance from Russia and China. By 2010, Russia appeared to have lost patience with Iran, but China was able to force a substantial reduction in the impact of the sanctions. China is Iran's number-one trading partner, and China relies heavily on oil imported from Iran.

This photo shows a successful North Korean missile launch. Why hasn't the United States been able to stop North Korea's nuclear armament program? (AP Photo/ KRT TV, File)

Nuclear Proliferation: North Korea. The George W. Bush administration participated in multilateral negotiations with North Korea, which tested a nuclear device in 2006. An agreement in February 2007 provided that North Korea would start disabling its nuclear facilities and allow UN inspectors into the country. In return, China, Japan, Russia, South Korea, and the United States—members of the six-party negotiations—would provide various kinds of aid to North Korea. North Korea was allowed to keep its nuclear arsenal, which American intelligence officials believe may include as many as six nuclear bombs or the fuel to make them. In July 2007, North Korea dismantled one of its nuclear reactors and admitted UN inspectors into the country. In October 2008, the United States removed North Korea from its list of states that sponsor terrorism.

In 2009, however, North Korea pulled back from its treaty obligations. In April, the country tested a long-range missile capable of delivering a nuclear warhead, in violation of a UN demand that it halt such tests. After the UN Security Council issued a statement condemning the test, North Korea ordered UN inspectors out of the country, broke off negotiations with the other members of the six-party talks, and conducted a second nuclear test. The United States and other parties have sought to persuade China to take the lead in bringing North Korea back to the negotiating table—China is the one nation that has significant economic leverage over North Korea. Tensions increased in March 2010 after a South Korean naval ship sank, with the loss of 104 lives. An investigation revealed that the ship had been sunk by a North Korean torpedo.

Is a nuclear-free world possible? We look at that question in the *Which Side Are You On?* feature below.

WHICH SIDE ARE YOU ON?

IS A NUCLEAR-FREE WORLD POSSIBLE?

The destructive capability of the atom bomb was obvious after the United States dropped one each on the Japanese cities of Hiroshima and Nagasaki in 1945. Since then, no more nuclear bombs have been used in war. Still, the spread of nuclear weapons, know-how, and material has accelerated. The biggest threat we face could be that the deadliest weapons ever invented might fall into the wrong hands.

During the Cold War against the Soviet Union and its Communist allies, a conflict between two ideologically opposed systems created the threat of nuclear war. After the Cold War ended, nuclear forces no longer seemed central to America's security strategy. Today, some people, notably including President Obama, would like to make the elimination of nuclear weapons a major goal of U.S. policy. Should we attempt to create a nuclear-free world?

OUR GOAL SHOULD BE NO MORE NUCLEAR WEAPONS ANYWHERE

The former head of the Soviet Union, Mikhail Gorbachev, wrote, "It is becoming clearer that nuclear weapons are no longer a means of achieving security; in fact, with every passing year, they make our security more precarious." Many past and present leaders argue that we must move toward a nuclear-free world. On our road to a nuclear-free world, we must provide the highest possible standards of security for any remaining nuclear weapons.

Men and women make mistakes. Consider that in 2007, six cruise missiles armed with nuclear warheads were erroneously loaded onto a U.S. Air Force plane and flown across the country. For more than a day, no one knew that these warheads were missing. Today, the United States and Russia still possess most of the world's nuclear weapons. We should undertake additional agreements to reduce the nuclear forces of these two countries. We also need to monitor secret attempts by countries to break agreements to eliminate nuclear weapons.

NUCLEAR DISARMAMENT IS NOT POSSIBLE

Even if the United States declared that it would eliminate nuclear weapons in the future, such a declaration would have no effect on countries attempting to "go nuclear" today. Some nations believe that nuclear weapons will improve their security. Certainly, nothing we say will stop attempts by terrorist groups to gain nuclear materials. Even if all nations that have "the bomb" agreed to get rid of it, many would probably keep a few weapons in secret, "just to be sure." No one can eliminate the knowledge that already exists about the making of nuclear weapons.

Given that nuclear weapons exist elsewhere, the United States must maintain its own weapons to deter potential opponents and to avoid intimidation by nuclear-armed nations. The United States has entered into negotiations with countries that have—or seek to have—nuclear weapons. We should continue such actions. But we should always remember that for the United States, nuclear weapons play an important deterrent role, and they must not be eliminated altogether.

The New Power: China

Since Richard Nixon's visit to China in 1972, American policy has been to engage the Chinese gradually in diplomatic and economic relationships in the hope of turning the nation in a more pro-Western direction. An important factor in U.S.-Chinese relations has been the large and growing trade ties between the two countries. In 1980, China was granted *most-favored-nation status* for tariffs and trade policy on a year-to-year basis. To prevent confusion, in 1998 the status was renamed **normal trade relations (NTR) status.** In 2000, over objections from organized labor and human rights groups, Congress approved a permanent grant of NTR status to China. In 2001, Congress endorsed China's application to join the World Trade Organization (WTO), thereby effectively guaranteeing China's admission to that body. For a country that is officially Communist, China already permits a striking degree of free enterprise, and the role of the private sector in China's economy is growing.

Normal Trade Relations (NTR) Status
A status granted through an international treaty by which each member nation must treat other members as well as it treats the country that receives its most favorable treatment. This status was formerly known as *most-favored-nation status.*

China exports substantially more goods and services to the United States than it imports, and as a result its central bank has built up a huge reserve of U.S. Treasury bonds and other American obligations. Ultimately, the books must balance, but instead of importing U.S. goods and services, the Chinese have imported U.S. bonds. The resulting economic imbalances are good for Chinese exporters, but bad for almost everyone else in both countries. The United States has repeatedly asked China to address these imbalances by allowing its currency to rise in value relative to the American dollar. Chinese authorities have been reluctant to do so, but they recently have allowed some movement.

Protesters gather in front of the Chinese embassy in Berlin, Germany. What are they protesting and why? (Sean Gallup/Getty Images)

China's Explosive Economic Growth. The growth of the Chinese economy during the last thirty-five years is one of the most important developments in world history. For the past several decades, the Chinese economy has grown at a rate of about 10 percent annually, a long-term growth rate previously unknown in human history. Never have so many escaped poverty so quickly.

China now produces more steel than America and Japan combined. It generates more than 40 percent of the world's output of cement. The new electrical generating capacity that China adds each year exceeds the entire installed capacity of Britain. (The new plants, which are usually coal fired, promote global warming and also generate some of the world's worst air pollution.) Skyscrapers fill the skyline of every major Chinese city.

In 2007, for the first time, China actually manufactured more passenger automobiles than the United States. China is building a limited-access highway system that, when complete, will be longer than the U.S. interstate highway system. Chinese demand for raw materials, notably petroleum, has led, in part, to dramatic increases in the price of oil and other commodities. Its people have begun to eat large quantities of meat, which adds to the strain on world food production. By 2050, if not before, the economy of China is expected to be larger than that of the United States. China, in short, will become the world's second superpower.

The Issue of Taiwan. Inevitably, economic power translates into military potential. Is this a problem? It could be if China had territorial ambitions. Currently, China does not appear to have an appetite for non-Chinese territory, and it does not seem likely to develop one. But China has always considered the island of Taiwan to be Chinese territory. In principle, Taiwan agrees. Taiwan calls itself the "Republic of China" and officially considers its government to be the legitimate ruler of the entire country. This diplomatic fiction has remained in effect since 1949, when the Chinese Communist Party won a civil war and drove the anti-Communist forces off the mainland.

China's position is that sooner or later, Taiwan must rejoin the rest of China. The position of the United States is that this reunification must not come about by force. Is peaceful reunification possible? China holds up Hong Kong as an example. Hong Kong came under Chinese sovereignty peacefully in 1997. The people of Taiwan, however, are far from considering Hong Kong to be an acceptable precedent.

Chinese Nationalism. A disturbing recent development—the growth in public expressions of Chinese nationalism—could have an impact on the Taiwan question. This increased expression has taken the form of heated rhetoric on the Web, cyber attacks against computers of other nations, and even violent demonstrations. The United States has been the target on several occasions. The Chinese government has sometimes appeared to support nationalist agitation because it benefits politically from the regime. When nationalism has seemed to be getting out of hand, however, the government has cracked down. Chinese nationalism has not only targeted foreign nations. Often, it has taken aim at ethnic minorities within China itself, such as the Tibetans or the Uighurs, a Muslim people who live in the far-western region of Xinjiang. Negative attitudes toward national minorities may create serious problems for China in the future.

The growth of Chinese economic power is not the only long-term development that is changing the shape of our world. We discuss the impact of population growth on world affairs in this chapter's *Beyond Our Borders* feature on the next page.

Israel and the Palestinians

As a longtime supporter of Israel, the United States has undertaken to persuade the Israelis to negotiate with the Palestinian Arabs who live in the territories occupied by the state of Israel. The conflict, which began in 1948, has been extremely hard to resolve. The internationally recognized solution is for Israel to yield the West Bank and the Gaza Strip to the Palestinians in return for effective security commitments and abandonment by the Palestinians of any right of return to Israel proper. The Palestinians, however, have been unwilling to stop terrorist attacks on Israel, and Israel has been unwilling to dismantle its settlements in the occupied territories. Further, the two parties have been unable to come to an agreement on how much of the West Bank should go to the Palestinians and on what compensation (if any) the Palestinians should receive for abandoning all claims to settlement in Israel proper.

In 1988, the United States began talking directly to the Palestine Liberation Organization (PLO), and in 1991, under pressure from the United States, the Israelis opened talks as well. In 1993, both parties agreed to set up Palestinian self-government in the West Bank and the Gaza Strip. The historic agreement was signed in Cairo on May 4, 1994. In the months that followed, Israeli troops withdrew from much of the occupied territory, and the new Palestinian Authority assumed police duties.

The Collapse of the Israeli-Palestinian Peace Process. Although negotiations between the Israelis and the Palestinians resulted in more agreements, the agreements were rejected by Palestinian radicals, who began a campaign of suicide bombings in Israeli cities. In 2002, the Israeli government responded by moving tanks and troops into Palestinian towns to kill or capture the terrorists. One result of the Israeli reoccupation was an almost complete collapse of the Palestinian Authority. Groups such as Hamas (the Islamic Resistance Movement), which did not accept the concept of peace with Israel even in principle, moved into the power vacuum.

In 2003, President Bush attempted to renew Israeli-Palestinian negotiations. In its weakened condition, however, the Palestinian Authority was unable to make any commitments. In February 2004, Israeli prime minister Ariel Sharon announced a plan under which Israel would withdraw from the Gaza Strip regardless of whether a deal could be reached with the Palestinians. Sharon's plan met with strong opposition, but ultimately the withdrawal took place.

In January 2006, the militant group Hamas won a majority of the seats in the Palestinian legislature. American and European politicians refused to talk to Hamas until it agreed to rescind its avowed desire to destroy Israel. In June 2007, the uneasy balance between the Hamas-dominated Palestinian legislature and the PLO president broke down. After open fighting between the two parties, Hamas wound up in complete control of the Gaza Strip, and the PLO retained exclusive power in the West Bank.

BEYOND OUR BORDERS

THE IMPACT OF POPULATION GROWTH ON AMERICA'S FUTURE ROLE IN THE WORLD

After World War II, the United States faced an adversary—the Union of Soviet Socialist Republics (U.S.S.R.)—which was alleged to have the second-largest economy in the world. Its military was definitely much larger than ours. Many believed that the Soviet army had defeated Hitler during World War II by the sheer force of numbers. By 1990, the Soviet population was 289 million, compared with America's 256 million. A year later, when the Soviet Union disintegrated, Russia was down to fewer than 149 million people. For a time, Russia's economy didn't even appear on lists of the world's ten largest. The United States was now the world's third most populous nation, with U.S. military spending approaching that of all other nations combined.

POPULATION CHANGES AND WORLD POWER RELATIONSHIPS

In forty years, both India and China will have around 1.5 billion residents each, compared with 400 million Americans. Populations in Arab and South Asian Muslim nations are growing. Pakistan's population, for example, will increase from 144 million to almost 300 million in the next forty years. China's population is stabilizing. Not so the population of Africa. The continent's population was only 224 million in 1950, reached 821 million in 2000, and by 2050 will be almost 2 billion. Africa's economy is growing, albeit slowly. We can predict, therefore, that over time, African nations should become more important in world affairs. Russia is another story, as is Japan. By 2050, these two nations won't even be among the top ten nations in the world with respect to population.

AND WHAT ABOUT THE UNITED STATES?

Currently, the United States is the only major power that is experiencing significant population growth. By 2050, the United States will have an estimated 4.37 percent of the world's population, down somewhat from 4.65 percent in 2000. In contrast, Russia's population is dwindling, sometimes at a shocking rate, because of poor diet, poor health care, and alcoholism. Many Western European countries are predicted to lose population as well. Russia may dwindle in significance, and Western Europe and Japan could lose clout. The United States should remain one of the world's superpowers for a long time to come, but it is likely to be joined by China and, later on, India as well.

FOR CRITICAL ANALYSIS

Does it really matter whether the United States remains a superpower? Why or why not?

Israel sought to pressure the Hamas regime in the Gaza Strip to relinquish power through an economic blockade. Hamas responded by firing a series of rockets into Israel. On January 3, 2009, in the final weeks of the Bush administration, Israeli ground forces entered the Gaza Strip. Israel declared a cease-fire on January 18, just days before Obama's inauguration.

President Obama meets with Israeli leader Benyamin Netanyahu at the White House to discuss the Israeli–Palestinian peace process. What are some of the reasons that this process has been unsuccessful? (Amos Moshe Milner/GPO via Getty Images)

Israel and the Obama Administration. In February 2009, Israelis elected a new, more conservative government under Prime Minister Benyamin Netanyahu. The tough positions advocated by the new government threatened to create fresh obstacles to the peace process. In particular, the new government accelerated the growth of Israeli settlements on the West Bank, even though the Obama administration opposed such settlements much more strongly than the Bush team ever had. In March 2010, the Israelis announced new construction projects during a visit by Vice President Joe Biden. The timing of the announcement was widely viewed as an act of rudeness directed at the U.S. government.

The Blockade of Gaza. The ongoing Israeli blockade of Gaza was thrust into prominence as an international issue in May 2010, when radical activists attempted to breach the blockade with six ships carrying humanitarian aid and construction materials. The flotilla was organized in Turkey, and a majority of the 663 activists on board were Turkish. Israeli commandos seized the ships while they were still well out to sea. Passengers on the largest ship resisted with improvised weapons. The commandos, who had reason to fear for their lives, employed live ammunition, resulting in the death of nine activists. The upshot was widespread condemnation of the commando raid and the blockade itself. The government of Turkey was particularly incensed. Israelis, who almost uniformly supported the raid, experienced a sense of international isolation. The blockade was officially justified as a way of keeping weapons out of the hands of Hamas, but the materials barred from Gaza were not limited to arms or even construction materials. Rather, they included such small luxuries as spices and pastries. In the weeks following the flotilla incident, Israel substantially reduced the list of prohibited imports.

These and other incidents continued to pose difficulties for peace-seekers. Despite the problems, the Obama administration persevered in its attempts to bring the Israelis and the Palestinians back to the negotiating table.

Humanitarian Efforts

U.S. foreign relations are not just a matter of waging wars or trying to prevent them. International economic coordination is another major field of action. Humanitarian assistance has also been a major component of America's foreign policy. Many voters are not aware, for example, that the Bush administration more than doubled the value of U.S. foreign aid provided to African nations, but many Africans are aware of this fact. As a result, Bush was relatively popular in much of Africa, in considerable contrast to his unpopularity in Western Europe and the Muslim world. (See the *Beyond Our Borders* feature in Chapter 6 on page 211.) Of course, as the son of a Kenyan father, Obama was even more popular in Africa.

Parts of the Israeli border with the Palestinian territories have separation barriers. Why did Israel decide to construct these barriers? (AP Photo/Emilio Morenatti)

did you know?

That the United States invaded and occupied part of Russia in 1919.

African Issues. Much of the assistance given to African nations was aimed at combating disease. Among the most important of these is AIDS (acquired immune deficiency syndrome), which remains extremely widespread in the southern part of the continent. One-fourth of the populations of Botswana and Zimbabwe are infected, for example. The economic and social impact of such high rates of infection has been tremendous. The Bush administration put together a special AIDS package amounting to $15 billion over five years. As a presidential candidate, Barack Obama spoke of a further doubling of U.S. foreign aid, but the nation's economic difficulties forced him to scale back his plans.

Another African humanitarian crisis took place in Darfur, part of the nation of Sudan. Following a 2003 rebellion in that area, government-backed militias drove up to 2.5 million residents out of their villages and into refugee camps. Hundreds of thousands died. The United States participated in international relief efforts organized under the UN, and in 2004 the U.S. Congress characterized the Sudanese government's actions as genocide. In 2009, the International Criminal Court (ICC) issued an arrest warrant for Sudan's president, charging him with war crimes. (The United States does not participate in the ICC.)

The Earthquake in Haiti. On January 12, 2010, a catastrophic earthquake struck the nation of Haiti. The epicenter of the quake was 16 miles west of Port-au-Prince, the capital. Fatality estimates ranged as high as 230,000. Haiti is the most impoverished nation in the Western Hemisphere. Even before the earthquake its infrastructure was heavily strained, but the quake blocked most roads with rubble and closed the Port-au-Prince seaport and airport. Roughly 250,000 structures were destroyed, including the Presidential Palace, the National Assembly, and the cathedral. The capital's three hospitals collapsed, as did the nation's prison, freeing four thousand inmates. Most of Port-au-Prince's population ended up camping out in the open. Sanitation facilities were nonexistent, and safe drinking water was desperately scarce. Most of the injured went many days without treatment.

The earthquake that hit Haiti during the winter of 2010 wreaked havoc throughout the island, causing the total destruction of houses, bridges, and roads. What role did the United States play in Haiti's reconstruction? (AP Photo/ Ryan Remiorz, CP)

First responders came from the next-door nation of the Dominican Republic, plus countries as varied as China, Iceland, Israel, and Qatar. Relief efforts were hampered at first by the destruction of the infrastructure. The United States, which eventually provided more assistance than any other nation, took control of the seaport and airport at the request of the Haitian government. The UN took charge of security within the city. The U.S. Navy deployed an aircraft carrier, two helicopter carriers, and a hospital ship. Canada provided the second-largest contingent of troops.

President Obama appointed former presidents Bill Clinton and George W. Bush to raise funds for Haiti's recovery. Fund-raising was facilitated by social networking sites. The American Red Cross pioneered a new donations system—it collected millions of dollars by letting people send $10 donations via text messages. Brazil marked its arrival as a world power by making the largest financial commitment of any single nation. Vice President Joe Biden stated that President Obama "does not view this as a humanitarian mission with a life cycle of a month. This will still be on our radar screen long after it's off the crawler at CNN. This is going to be a long slog."

Who Makes Foreign Policy?

Given the vast array of challenges in the world, developing a comprehensive U.S. foreign policy is a demanding task. Does this responsibility fall to the president, to Congress, or to both acting jointly? There is no easy answer to this question, because, as constitutional authority Edwin S. Corwin once observed, the U.S. Constitution created an "invitation to struggle" between the president and Congress for control over the foreign policy process. Let us look first at the powers given to the president by the Constitution.

Constitutional Powers of the President

The Constitution confers on the president broad powers that are either explicit or implied in key constitutional provisions. Article II vests the executive power of the government in the president. The presidential oath of office given in Article II, Section 1, requires that the president "solemnly swear" to "preserve, protect and defend the Constitution of the United States."

War Powers. In addition, and perhaps more important, Article II, Section 2, designates the president as "Commander in Chief of the Army and Navy of the United States." Starting with Abraham Lincoln, all presidents have interpreted this authority dynamically and broadly. Indeed, since George Washington's administration, the United States has been involved in at least 125 undeclared wars that were conducted under presidential authority. For example, in 1950 Harry Truman ordered U.S. armed forces in the Pacific to counter North Korea's invasion of South Korea. Bill Clinton sent troops to Haiti and Bosnia. In 2001, George W. Bush authorized an attack against the al Qaeda terrorist network and the Taliban government in Afghanistan, and in 2003 Bush sent military forces to Iraq to destroy Saddam Hussein's government.

did you know?

That it is estimated that the Central Intelligence Agency has more than 16,000 employees, with about 5,000 in the clandestine services.

Treaties and Executive Agreements. Article II, Section 2, of the Constitution also gives the president the power to make treaties, provided that two-thirds of the senators present concur. Presidents usually have been successful in getting treaties through the Senate. In addition to this formal treaty-making power, the president makes use of executive agreements (discussed in Chapter 11). Since World War II (1939–1945), executive agreements have accounted for almost 95 percent of the understandings reached between the United States and other nations.

Executive agreements have a long and important history. During World War II, Franklin Roosevelt reached several agreements with Britain, the Soviet Union, and other countries. In other important agreements, Presidents Eisenhower, Kennedy, and Johnson all promised support to the government of South Vietnam. In all, since 1946 more than eight thousand executive agreements with foreign countries have been made. There is no way to obtain an accurate count, because perhaps as many as several hundred of these agreements have been secret.

Other Constitutional Powers. An additional power conferred on the president in Article II, Section 2, is the right to appoint ambassadors, other public ministers, and consuls. In Section 3 of that article, the president is given the power to recognize foreign governments by receiving their ambassadors.

Other Sources of Foreign Policymaking

In addition to the president, there are at least four foreign policymaking sources within the executive branch. These are (1) the Department of State, (2) the National Security Council, (3) the intelligence community, and (4) the Department of Defense.

President Richard Nixon meets with Secretary of State Henry Kissinger, who received the Nobel Peace Prize for his role in ending the war in Vietnam. Does the Department of State have as much "clout" today as it did thirty-five years ago? Why or why not? (AP Photo)

The Department of State. In principle, the State Department is the executive agency that has primary authority over foreign affairs. It supervises U.S. relations with the nearly two hundred independent nations around the world and with the UN and other multinational groups, such as the Organization of American States. It staffs embassies and consulates throughout the world. It does all this with one of the smallest budgets of the cabinet departments.

Newly elected presidents usually tell the American public that the new secretary of state is the nation's chief foreign policy adviser. Nonetheless, the State Department's preeminence in foreign policy has declined since World War II. The State Department's image within the White House Executive Office and Congress (and even with foreign governments) is quite poor—it is seen as a slow, plodding, bureaucratic maze of inefficient, indecisive individuals. Reportedly, Premier Nikita Khrushchev of the Soviet Union urged President John F. Kennedy to formulate his own views rather than rely on State Department officials who, according to Khrushchev, "specialized in why something had not worked forty years ago."[3] In any event, since the days of Franklin D. Roosevelt, the State Department has often been bypassed or ignored when crucial decisions are made.

It is not surprising that the State Department has been overshadowed in foreign policy. It has no natural domestic constituency as does, for example, the Department of Defense, which can call on defense contractors for support. Instead, the State Department has what might be called **negative constituents**—U.S. citizens who openly oppose the government's policies.

Negative Constituents
Citizens who openly oppose the government's policies.

The National Security Council. The job of the National Security Council (NSC), created by the National Security Act of 1947, is to advise the president on the integration of "domestic, foreign, and military policies relating to the national security." Its larger purpose is to provide policy continuity from one administration to the next. As it has turned out, the NSC—consisting of the president, the vice president, the secretaries of state and defense, the director of emergency planning, and often the chairperson of the joint chiefs of staff and the director of the CIA—is used in just about any way the president wants to use it.

The role of national security adviser to the president seems to adjust to fit the player. Some advisers have come into conflict with heads of the State Department. Henry A. Kissinger, Richard Nixon's flamboyant and aggressive national security adviser, rapidly gained ascendancy over William Rogers, the secretary of state. More recently, Condoleezza Rice played an important role as national security adviser during George W. Bush's first term. Like Kissinger, Rice eventually became secretary of state. As of 2010, President

3. Theodore C. Sorensen, *Kennedy* (New York: Harper & Row, 1965), pp. 554–555.

Obama's national security adviser is Thomas Donilon, a long-time adviser and a former lobbyist for Fannie Mae.

The Intelligence Community. No discussion of foreign policy would be complete without some mention of the **intelligence community.** This consists of the forty or more government agencies or bureaus that are involved in intelligence activities. The CIA, created as part of the National Security Act of 1947, is the key official member of the intelligence community.

Intelligence Community
The government agencies that gather information about the capabilities and intentions of foreign governments or that engage in covert actions.

Covert Actions. Intelligence activities consist mostly of overt information gathering, but covert actions also are undertaken. Covert actions, as the name implies, are carried out in secret, and the American public rarely finds out about them. The CIA covertly aided in the overthrow of the Mossadegh regime in Iran in 1953 and the Arbenz government of Guatemala in 1954. The agency was instrumental in destabilizing the Allende government in Chile from 1970 to 1973.

During the mid-1970s, the "dark side" of the CIA was partly uncovered when the Senate undertook an investigation of its activities. One of the major findings of the Senate Select Committee on Intelligence was that the CIA had routinely spied on American citizens domestically, which was supposedly a prohibited activity. Consequently, the CIA came under the scrutiny of oversight committees within Congress.

did you know?
That in the name of national security, the United States spends at least $5.6 billion annually to keep information classified.

By 2001, the CIA had come under fire again for a number of lapses, including the discovery that one of its agents had been spying on behalf of a foreign power, the failure to detect the nuclear arsenals of India and Pakistan, and, above all, the failure to obtain advance knowledge about the 9/11 terrorist attacks.

President Bush is shown with his National Security Council (NSC) the day after the terrorist attacks on September 11, 2001. At that time, the NSC consisted of the director of the Central Intelligence Agency, the secretary of defense, the secretary of state, the vice president, the chairman of the joint chiefs of staff, and, of course, the national security adviser. How important is the NSC's role in determining U.S. foreign policy? (AP Photo/Doug Mills)

did you know?

That the Pentagon's stockpile of strategic materials includes 1.5 million pounds of quartz crystals used in pre–Great Depression radios and 150,000 tons of tannin used in tanning cavalry saddles.

The Intelligence Community and the War on Terrorism. With the rise of terrorism as a threat, the intelligence agencies have received more funding and enhanced surveillance powers, but these moves have also provoked fears of civil liberties violations. In 2004, the bipartisan 9/11 commission called for a new intelligence czar to oversee the entire intelligence community, with full control of all agency budgets. After initially balking at this recommendation, President George W. Bush eventually called for a partial implementation of the commission's report. Legislation enacted in 2004 established the Office of the Director of National Intelligence to oversee the intelligence community. As of mid-2010, President Obama's director of national intelligence was retired U.S. Air Force lieutenant general James R. Clapper, Jr.

A simmering controversy that came to a head in 2009 concerned the CIA's use of a technique called *waterboarding* while interrogating several prisoners in the years immediately following 9/11. Before 9/11, the government had defined waterboarding as a form of torture, but former vice president Dick Cheney, a public advocate of the practice, denied that it was. One concern was whether Bush administration officials would face legal action as a result of the practice. In May 2009, President Obama, even as he denounced waterboarding, assured CIA employees that no member of the agency would be penalized for following Justice Department rulings that had legitimized harsh interrogation methods. The Obama administration also declined to pursue cases against the Justice Department officials who made those rulings.

This aerial view of the five-sided Pentagon building shows where many of the defense personnel work in Arlington, Virginia. The Pentagon covers an area of twenty-nine acres. When was the Department of Defense created? (AP Photo)

The Department of Defense. The Department of Defense (DOD) was created in 1947 to bring all of the various activities of the American military establishment under the jurisdiction of a single department headed by a civilian secretary of defense. At the same time, the joint chiefs of staff, consisting of the commanders of the various military branches and a chairperson, was created to formulate a unified military strategy.

Although the Department of Defense is larger than any other federal department, it declined in size after the fall of the Soviet Union in 1991. In the subsequent ten years, the total number of civilian employees was reduced by nearly 400,000, to about 665,000. Military personnel were also reduced in number. The defense budget remained relatively flat for several years, but with the advent of the war on terrorism and the use of military forces in Afghanistan and Iraq, funding has again been increased.

Congress Balances the Presidency

A new interest in the balance of power between Congress and the president on foreign policy questions developed during the Vietnam War (1964–1975). Sensitive to public frustration over the long and costly war and angry at Richard Nixon for some of his other actions as president, Congress attempted to establish limits on the power of the president in setting foreign and defense policy.

The War Powers Resolution of 1973

In 1973, Congress passed the War Powers Resolution over President Nixon's veto. The act limited the president's use of troops in military action without congressional approval (see Chapter 11). Most presidents, however, have not interpreted the "consultation" provisions of the act as meaning that Congress should be consulted before military action is taken. Instead, Presidents Ford, Carter, Reagan, George H. W. Bush, and Clinton ordered troop movements and then informed congressional leaders.

The Power of the Purse

One of Congress's most significant constitutional powers is the so-called power of the purse. In other words, the president may order that a certain action be taken, but that decision cannot be executed unless it is funded by Congress. When the Democrats assumed control of Congress in January 2007, many expected that the new Congress would use its power of the purse to bring an end to the Iraq War, in view of the strong public opinion against the war. Congress's decision was to add conditions to a war-funding request that would require President George W. Bush to establish timelines for the redeployment of American troops in Iraq. Bush immediately threatened to veto any bill that imposed conditions on the funding.

In this circumstance, the power of Congress was limited by political considerations. Congress did not even consider the option of refusing to fund the war altogether. For one thing, there was little support in Congress for such an approach—the Democrats did not want to be accused of placing the troops in Iraq in danger. Additionally, the threat of a presidential veto significantly limited Congress's power. The Democrats simply did not have a large enough majority to override a veto.

The Major Foreign Policy Themes

Although some observers might suggest that U.S. foreign policy is inconsistent and changes with the current occupant of the White House, the long view of American diplomatic ventures reveals some major themes underlying foreign policy. In the early years of the nation, presidents and the people generally agreed that the United States should avoid foreign entanglements and concentrate instead on its own development. From the beginning of the twentieth century until the present, however, a major theme has been increasing global involvement. The theme of the post–World War II years was the containment of communism. The theme for at least the first part of the twenty-first century may be the containment of terrorism.

The Formative Years: Avoiding Entanglements

Foreign policy was largely nonexistent during the formative years of the United States. Remember that the new nation was operating under the Articles of Confederation. The national government had no right to levy or collect taxes, no control over commerce, no right to make commercial treaties, and no power to raise an army (the Revolutionary army was disbanded in 1783). The government's lack of international power was made clear when Barbary pirates seized American hostages in the Mediterranean. The United States was unable to rescue the hostages and ignominiously had to purchase them in a treaty with Morocco.

The founders of this nation had a basic mistrust of European governments. This was a logical position at a time when the United States was so weak militarily that it could not influence European developments directly. Moreover, being protected by oceans that took weeks to cross certainly allowed the nation to avoid entangling alliances. During the 1800s, therefore, the United States generally stayed out of European conflicts and politics.

James Monroe, the fifth president, is associated most commonly with what foreign policy doctrine? (AP Photo)

In this hemisphere, however, the United States pursued an active expansionist policy. The nation purchased Louisiana in 1803, annexed Texas in 1845, gained substantial territory from Mexico in 1848, purchased Alaska in 1867, and annexed Hawaii in 1898.

The Monroe Doctrine. President James Monroe, in his message to Congress on December 2, 1823, stated that the United States would not accept any new European intervention in the Western Hemisphere. In return, the United States would not meddle in European affairs. The **Monroe Doctrine** was the underpinning of the U.S. **isolationist foreign policy** toward Europe, which continued throughout the 1800s.

The Spanish-American War and World War I. The end of the isolationist policy started with the Spanish-American War in 1898. Winning the war gave the United States possession of Guam, Puerto Rico, and the Philippines (which gained independence in 1946). On the heels of that war came World War I (1914–1918). The United States declared war on Germany on April 6, 1917, because that country refused to give up its campaign of sinking all ships headed for Britain, including passenger ships from America. (Large passenger ships of that time commonly held over a thousand people, so the sinking of such a ship was a disaster comparable to the attack on the World Trade Center.)

In the 1920s, the United States went "back to normalcy," as President Warren G. Harding urged it to do. U.S. military forces were largely disbanded, defense spending dropped to about 1 percent of total annual national income, and the nation returned to a period of isolationism.

Monroe Doctrine
A policy statement by President James Monroe in 1823, which set out three principles: (1) European nations should not establish new colonies in the Western Hemisphere, (2) European nations should not intervene in the affairs of independent nations of the Western Hemisphere, and (3) the United States would not interfere in the affairs of European nations.

Isolationist Foreign Policy
A policy of abstaining from an active role in international affairs or alliances, which characterized U.S. foreign policy toward Europe during most of the 1800s.

Soviet Bloc
The Soviet Union and the Eastern European countries that installed Communist regimes after World War II and were dominated by the Soviet Union.

The Era of Internationalism

Isolationism was permanently shattered by the bombing of the U.S. naval base at Pearl Harbor, Hawaii, on December 7, 1941. The surprise attack by the Japanese caused the deaths of 2,403 American servicemen and wounded 1,143 others. Eighteen warships were sunk or seriously damaged, and 188 planes were destroyed at the airfields. President Franklin Roosevelt asked Congress to declare war on Japan immediately, and the United States entered World War II.

At the conclusion of the war, the United States was the only major participating country to emerge with its economy intact, and even strengthened. The United States was also the only country to have control over operational nuclear weapons. President Harry Truman had made the decision to use two atomic bombs, on August 6 and August 9, 1945, to end the war with Japan. (Historians still argue over the necessity of this action, which ultimately killed more than 100,000 Japanese and left an equal number permanently injured.) The United States truly had become the world's superpower.

The Cold War. The United States had become an uncomfortable ally of the Soviet Union after Adolf Hitler's invasion of that country. Soon after World War II ended, relations between the Soviet Union and the West deteriorated. The Soviet Union wanted a weakened Germany, and to achieve this, it insisted that Germany be divided in two, with East Germany becoming a buffer against the West. Little by little, the Soviet Union helped to install Communist governments in Eastern European countries, which began to be referred to collectively as the **Soviet bloc.** In response, the United States encouraged the rearming of Western Europe. The Cold War had begun.[4]

4. See John Lewis Gaddis, *The United Nations and the Origins of the Cold War* (New York: Columbia University Press, 1972).

Containment Policy. In 1947, a remarkable article was published in *Foreign Affairs.* The article was signed by "X." The actual author was George F. Kennan, chief of the policy-planning staff for the State Department. The doctrine of **containment** set forth in the article became—according to many—the bible of Western foreign policy. "X" argued that whenever and wherever the Soviet Union could successfully challenge the West, it would do so. He recommended that our policy toward the Soviet Union be "firm and vigilant containment of Russian expansive tendencies."[5]

Containment
A U.S. diplomatic policy adopted by the Truman administration to contain Communist power within its existing boundaries.

Truman Doctrine
The policy adopted by President Harry Truman in 1947 to halt Communist expansion in southeastern Europe.

The containment theory was expressed clearly in the **Truman Doctrine,** which was enunciated by President Harry Truman in 1947. Truman held that the United States must help countries in which a Communist takeover seemed likely. Later that year, he backed the Marshall Plan, an economic assistance plan for Europe that was intended to prevent the expansion of Communist influence there. In 1950, the United States entered into a military alliance with European nations commonly called the North Atlantic Treaty Organization, or NATO, to maintain a credible response to any Soviet military attack. Figure 15–1 on the following page shows the face-off between the U.S.-led NATO alliance and the Soviet-led Warsaw Pact—an agreement formed by Communist nations to counter the NATO alliance.

Superpower Relations

During the Cold War, there was never any direct military conflict between the United States and the Soviet Union. Only on occasion did the United States enter a conflict with any Communist country. Two such occasions were in Korea and in Vietnam.

After the end of World War II, northern Korea was occupied by the Soviet Union, and southern Korea was occupied by the United States. The result was two rival Korean governments. In 1950, North Korea invaded South Korea. Under UN authority, the United

5. X, "The Sources of Soviet Conduct," *Foreign Affairs,* July 1947, p. 575.

In a famous meeting in Yalta in February 1945, British prime minister Winston Churchill (left), U.S. president Franklin Roosevelt (center), and Soviet leader Joseph Stalin (right) decided on the fate of several nations in Europe, including Germany. What happened to Germany immediately after World War II? (Library of Congress)

FIGURE 15–1 Europe during the Cold War

This map shows the face-off between NATO (led by the United States) and the Soviet bloc (the Warsaw Pact). Note that West Germany did not join NATO until 1955, and Albania suspended participation in the Warsaw Pact in 1960. France was out of NATO from 1966 to 1996, and Spain did not join until 1982.

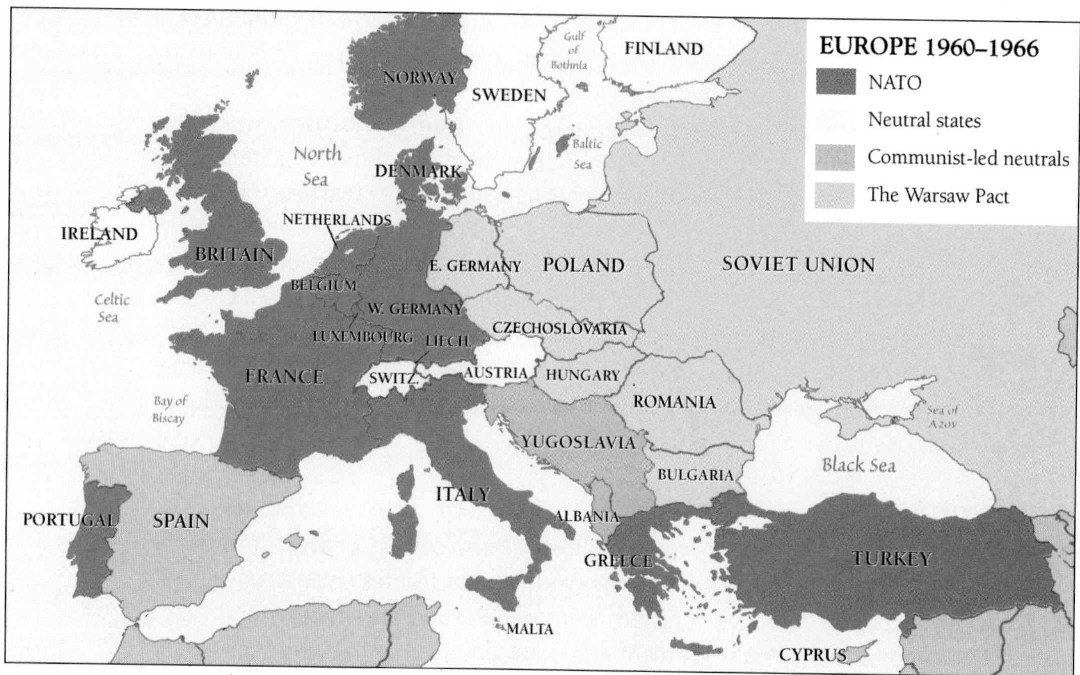

States entered the war, which prevented an almost certain South Korean defeat. When U.S. forces were on the brink of conquering North Korea, however, China joined the war on the side of the North, resulting in a stalemate. An armistice signed in 1953 led to the two Koreas that exist today. U.S. forces have remained in South Korea since that time.

The Vietnam War (1964–1975) also involved the United States in a civil war between a Communist North Vietnam and pro-Western South Vietnam. When the French army in Indochina was defeated by the Communist forces of Ho Chi Minh and the two Vietnams were created in 1954, the United States assumed the role of supporting the South Vietnamese government against North Vietnam. President John Kennedy sent 16,000 "advisers" to help South Vietnam, and after Kennedy's death in 1963, President Lyndon Johnson greatly increased the scope of that support. About 500,000 American troops were in Vietnam at the height of the U.S. involvement. More than 58,000 Americans were killed and 300,000 were wounded in the conflict. A peace agreement in 1973 allowed U.S. troops to leave the country, and in 1975 North Vietnam easily occupied Saigon (the South Vietnamese capital) and unified the nation.

Over the course of the Vietnam War, the debate over U.S. involvement became extremely heated and, as mentioned previously, spurred congressional efforts to limit the ability of the president to commit forces to armed combat. The military draft was also a major source of contention during the Vietnam War. Do recent events justify bringing back the draft? We examined this question in this chapter's opening *What If . . .* feature.

The Cuban Missile Crisis. Perhaps the closest the two superpowers came to a nuclear confrontation was the Cuban missile crisis in 1962. The Soviets installed missiles in Cuba, ninety miles off the U.S. coast, in response to Cuban fears of an American invasion and to try to balance an American nuclear advantage. President Kennedy and his advisers rejected the option of invading Cuba and set up a naval blockade around the island instead.

When Soviet vessels appeared near Cuban waters, the tension reached its height. After intense negotiations between Washington and Moscow, the Soviet ships turned around on October 25. On October 28 the Soviet Union announced the withdrawal of its missile operations from Cuba. In exchange, the United States agreed not to invade Cuba in the future and to remove some of its own missiles that were located near the Soviet border in Turkey.

A Period of Détente. The French word **détente** means a relaxation of tensions. By the end of the 1960s, it was clear that some efforts had to be made to reduce the threat of nuclear war between the United States and the Soviet Union. The Soviet Union gradually had begun to catch up in the building of strategic nuclear delivery vehicles in the form of bombers and missiles, thus balancing the nuclear scales between the two countries. Each nation had acquired the military capacity to destroy the other with nuclear weapons.

As the result of lengthy negotiations under Secretary of State Henry Kissinger and President Nixon, the United States and the Soviet Union signed the **Strategic Arms Limitation Treaty (SALT I)** in May 1972. That treaty "permanently" limited the development and deployment of antiballistic missiles (ABMs) and limited the number of offensive missiles each country could deploy.

The policy of détente was not limited to the U.S. relationship with the Soviet Union. Seeing an opportunity to capitalize on increasing friction between the Soviet Union and the People's Republic of China, Kissinger secretly began negotiations to establish a new relationship with China. President Nixon eventually visited that nation in 1972. The visit set the stage for the formal diplomatic recognition of that country, which occurred during the Carter administration (1977–1981).

Détente
A French word meaning a relaxation of tensions. The term characterized U.S.-Soviet relations as they developed under President Richard Nixon and Secretary of State Henry Kissinger.

Strategic Arms Limitation Treaty (SALT I)
A treaty between the United States and the Soviet Union to stabilize the nuclear arms competition between the two countries. SALT I talks began in 1969, and agreements were signed on May 26, 1972.

Nuclear Arms Agreements with the Soviet Union. President Ronald Reagan took a hard line against the Soviet Union during his first term, proposing the strategic defense initiative (SDI), or "Star Wars," in 1983. The SDI was designed to serve as a space-based defense against enemy missiles. Reagan and others in his administration argued that the program would deter nuclear war by shifting the emphasis of defense strategy from offensive to defensive weapons systems.

In November 1985, however, President Reagan and Mikhail Gorbachev, the Soviet leader, began to work on an arms reduction compact. In 1987, the negotiations resulted in the Intermediate-Range Nuclear Force (INF) Treaty, which required the superpowers to dismantle a total of four thousand intermediate-range missiles within the first three years of the agreement.

Beginning in 1989, President George H. W. Bush continued the negotiations with the Soviet Union to reduce the number of nuclear weapons and the number of armed troops in Europe. In July 1991, the United States and the Soviet Union signed the Strategic Arms Reduction Treaty (START). Implementation of the treaty was complicated when, on December 31, 1991, the Soviet Union ceased to exist as a nation and dissolved into its fifteen constituent republics. In 1992, however, the treaty was again signed by Russia, Belarus, Kazakhstan, and Ukraine, the four former Soviet republics in which nuclear facilities were located. Belarus, Kazakhstan, and Ukraine agreed to nuclear disarmament and transferred their weapons to Russia.

U.S. President
Ronald Reagan, right, and Soviet leader Mikhail Gorbachev exchange pens during a treaty signing ceremony in the White House East Room in December. Is the treaty still valid even though the Soviet Union no longer exists? (AP Photo/Bob Daugherty)

did you know?

That Russia has suffered more battle deaths in putting down the rebellion in Chechnya than the Soviet Union experienced in its decades-long attempt to subdue Afghanistan.

The Dissolution of the Soviet Union. After the fall of the Berlin Wall in 1989, it was clear that the Soviet Union had relinquished much of its political and military control over the states of Eastern Europe that formerly had been part of the Soviet bloc. No one expected the Soviet Union to dissolve into separate states as quickly as it did, however. Although Gorbachev tried to adjust the Soviet constitution and political system to allow greater autonomy for the republics within the union, demands for political, ethnic, and religious autonomy grew, and in December 1991 the Soviet Union was officially dissolved. Figure 15–2 below shows the situation in Europe today.

Russia after the Soviet Union. In 2000, Russian president Boris Yeltsin resigned because of poor health. He named Vladimir Putin, architect of the Russian military effort against an independence movement in the province of Chechnya, as acting president. A few months later, Putin won the presidency in a national election. He was reelected in 2004. Putin chipped away at Russia's democratic institutions, slowly turning the country into what was, in essence, an elected autocracy. When Putin's second term as president came to an end in 2008, he could not immediately run for reelection. He therefore engineered the election of one of his supporters, Dmitry Medvedev, as president. Medvedev promptly appointed Putin as prime minister. It was clear that Putin retained the real power in Russia.

In recent years, the United States has become concerned over Russia's aggressive attitude toward its neighbors. In 2007, Estonia was subjected to massive cyber attacks originating in Russia, apparently because Estonia had taken down a statue honoring fallen Soviet soldiers. In 2008, Russian troops entered Georgia to prevent that nation

FIGURE 15–2 Europe after the Fall of the Soviet Union

This map shows the growth in European unity as marked by participation in transnational organizations. The United States continues to lead NATO (and would be orange if it were on the map). Note the reunification of Germany and the creation of new states from the former Yugoslavia and the former Soviet Union.

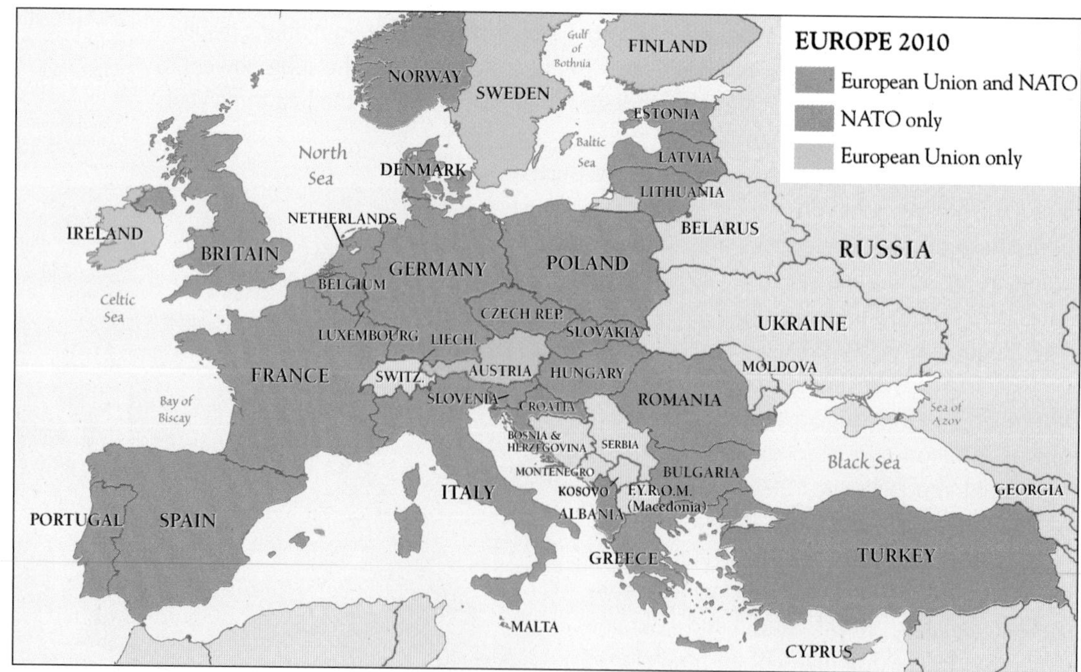

from retaking an autonomous region that was under Russian protection. The Georgian army was quickly defeated. On several occasions since 2005, Russia has cut off the transmission of natural gas to Ukraine as a result of disputes. The cutoffs have caused serious natural-gas shortages in several central European nations that rely on gas routed through Ukraine. Russia also reacted angrily to U.S. plans for antimissile defenses in Eastern Europe, aimed at protecting Europe from a possible future Iranian attack. Russia appeared to believe that the defenses were directed against it. By the end of 2008, relations between Russia and the Bush administration had grown chilly.

Still, the United States needed Russian assistance in matters such as curbing Iran's nuclear program. In 2009, Vice President Joe Biden spoke of "pressing the reset button" in Russian-American relations, a slogan that was taken up by other U.S. and Russian officials. The Obama administration developed a new, largely sea-based antimissile program aimed at Iran, which the Russians did not view as a threat. By 2010, Russian-American relations had thawed considerably, although there were occasional complications. In June 2010, for example, the United States arrested eleven people as deep-cover Russian agents. Apparently, the mission of these individuals dated back to Soviet times.

Nuclear Arms Agreements with Russia. After his election in 2000, President George W. Bush was initially unwilling to engage in nuclear weapons negotiations with Russia. In 2001, he announced that the United States was withdrawing from the 1972 ABM treaty (SALT I). Six months later, however, Bush and Putin signed an agreement greatly reducing the number of nuclear weapons on each side during the next few years. The 1992 START agreement expired in December 2009, but both Russia and the United States agreed to continue observing its terms until a new pact could be established. In April 2010, President Obama and Russian president Dmitry Medvedev signed New START, a follow-on treaty, at a meeting in Prague, Czech Republic. New START reduced the number of permitted warheads to 1,550 for each side, a drop of about 30 percent from previous agreements.

President Obama meets with the president of Russia, Dmitry Medvedev who is seated second from the left in this photo. Why would our president spend time with Russia's president? (Martin H. Simon-Pool/ Getty Images)

WHY SHOULD YOU CARE ABOUT... FOREIGN POLICY?

One foreign policy issue worth caring about is human rights. In many countries throughout the world, human rights are not protected. In some nations, people are imprisoned, tortured, or killed because they oppose the current regime. In other nations, certain ethnic or racial groups are oppressed by the majority population.

FOREIGN POLICY AND YOUR LIFE

The strongest reason for involving yourself with human rights issues in other countries is simple moral altruism—unselfish regard for the welfare of others. The defense of human rights is unlikely to put a single dollar in your pocket.

A broader consideration, however, is that human rights abuses are often associated with the kind of dictatorial regimes that are likely to provoke wars. To the extent that the people of the world can create a climate in which human rights abuses are unacceptable, they may also create an atmosphere in which national leaders believe that they must display peaceful conduct generally. This, in turn, might reduce the frequency of wars, some of which could involve the United States. Less war would mean preserving peace and human life, not to mention reducing the financial burden imposed by the military.

How do Amnesty International protesters hope to change our country's foreign policy? (Win McNamee/Getty Images)

HOW YOU CAN MAKE A DIFFERENCE

What can you do to work for the improvement of human rights in other nations? One way is to join an organization that attempts to keep watch over human rights violations. (Two such organizations are listed at the end of this feature.) By publicizing human rights violations, such organizations try to pressure nations into changing their practices. Sometimes, these organizations are able to apply enough pressure and cause enough embarrassment that victims may be freed from prison or allowed to emigrate.

Another way to work for human rights is to keep informed about the state of affairs in other nations and to write personally to governments that violate human rights or to their embassies, asking them to cease these violations.

If you want to receive general information about the position of the United States on human rights violations, you can contact the State Department:

U.S. Department of State
Bureau of Democracy, Human Rights, and Labor
2201 C St. N.W.
Washington, DC 20520
202-647-4000
www.state.gov/g/drl/hr

The following organizations are well known for their watchdog efforts in countries that violate human rights for political reasons:

Amnesty International U.S.A.
5 Penn Plaza
New York, NY 10001
212-807-8400
www.amnestyusa.org

American Friends Service Committee
1501 Cherry St.
Philadelphia, PA 19102
215-241-7000
www.afsc.org

questions for discussion and analysis

1. Review the *Which Side Are You On?* feature on page 521. Is a world free of nuclear weapons even possible? Why or why not? In what ways might the world be different if no nation had such weapons?
2. Why do you think that North Korea and Iran might want to possess nuclear weapons, even though they can never hope to match the nuclear arsenals of the original five nuclear powers?
3. Some people believe that if no U.S. military personnel were stationed abroad, terrorists would have less desire to harm Americans or the United States. Do you agree? Why or why not?
4. As of late 2010, no terrorist act remotely comparable to the attacks of 9/11 had taken place on U.S. soil. Why do you think that is so? How much credit can the government take? To what extent might terrorists experience practical difficulties in accomplishing anything like the damage inflicted on 9/11?

key terms

Cold War 520
containment 533
defense policy 512
détente 535
diplomacy 511
economic aid 511
foreign policy 511
foreign policy process 511
intelligence community 529
isolationist foreign policy 532
Monroe Doctrine 532
moral idealism 512
national security policy 511
negative constituents 528
normal trade relations (NTR) status 522
political realism 512
Soviet bloc 532
Strategic Arms Limitation Treaty (SALT I) 535
technical assistance 511
Truman Doctrine 533

chapter summary

1. Foreign policy includes the nation's external goals and the techniques used to achieve them. National security policy, which is one aspect of foreign policy, is designed to protect the independence and the political and economic integrity of the United States. Diplomacy involves the nation's external relationships and is an attempt to resolve conflict without resort to arms. U.S. foreign policy is sometimes based on moral idealism and sometimes on political realism.
2. Terrorism has become a major challenge facing the United States and other nations. The United States waged war on terrorism after the attacks of September 11, 2001. U.S. armed forces occupied Afghanistan in 2001 and Iraq in 2003.
3. Nuclear proliferation continues to be an issue. A current challenge for world leaders is how to contain the nuclear ambitions of Iran and North Korea.
4. The Middle East continues to be a hotbed of conflict despite efforts to continue the peace process between the Israelis and Palestinians. In 1991 and again in 2003, the United States sent combat troops to Iraq. The second war in Iraq, begun in 2003, succeeded in toppling that nation's decades-long dictatorship but led to a long, grinding conflict with insurgent forces. The current campaign in Afghanistan may prove to be equally difficult. Humanitarian assistance has also been a component of American foreign policy, as exemplified by relief efforts following a devastating earthquake in Haiti.
5. The formal power of the president to make foreign policy derives from the U.S. Constitution, which designates the president as commander in chief of the army and navy. Presidents have interpreted this authority broadly. They also have the power to make treaties and executive agreements. In principle, the State Department is the executive agency with primary authority over foreign affairs. The National Security Council also plays a major role. The intelligence community consists of government agencies engaged in activities varying from information gathering to covert operations. In response to presidential actions in the Vietnam War, Congress attempted to establish some limits on the power of the president to intervene abroad by passing the War Powers Resolution in 1973.

6. Three major themes have guided U.S. foreign policy. In the early years of the nation, isolationism was the primary strategy. With the start of the twentieth century, isolationism gave way to global involvement. From the end of World War II through the 1980s, the major goal was to contain communism and the influence of the Soviet Union.

7. During the 1800s, the United States stayed out of European conflicts and politics, so these years have been called the period of isolationism. The Monroe Doctrine of 1823 stated that the United States would not accept foreign intervention in the Western Hemisphere and would not meddle in European affairs. The United States pursued an active expansionist policy in the Americas and the Pacific area, however.

8. The end of the policy of isolationism toward Europe started with the Spanish-American War of 1898. U.S. involvement in European politics became more extensive when the United States entered World War I in 1917. World War II marked a lasting change in American foreign policy. The United States was the only major country to emerge from the war with its economy intact and the only country with operating nuclear weapons.

9. Soon after World War II, the Cold War began. A policy of containment, which assumed an expansionist Soviet Union, was enunciated in the Truman Doctrine. Following the frustrations of the Vietnam War and the apparent arms equality of the United States and the Soviet Union, the United States adopted a policy of détente, or loosening of tensions.

10. Although President Reagan took a tough stance toward the Soviet Union, he engaged in serious negotiations toward arms reduction, culminating in the Intermediate-Range Nuclear Force Treaty in 1987. After the fall of the Soviet Union, Russia emerged as a less threatening state and signed the Strategic Arms Reduction Treaty with the United States in 1992. Under President Vladimir Putin, Russia moved away from democracy and in part returned to its old autocratic traditions.

selected print & media resources

SUGGESTED READINGS

Asmus, Ronald. ***A Little War That Shook the World: Georgia, Russia, and the Future of the West.*** New York: Palgrave Macmillan, 2010. Asmus provides an in-depth description of the brief war between Russia and Georgia in 2008. He contends that Russia had prepared for the conflict for some time, and meant to use it to send a message to the West.

Fried, Charles, and Gregory Fried. ***Because It Is Wrong: Torture, Privacy and Presidential Power in the Age of Terror.*** New York: W. W. Norton, 2010. Charles Fried is a Harvard professor of law; his son, Gregory, is a philosophy professor. In this work, the two compare the behavior of Bush administration officials with the actions of earlier American leaders such as Lincoln, and examine the officials' justifications in relation to the thinking of major Western philosophers.

Gul, Imtiaz. ***The Most Dangerous Place: Pakistan's Lawless Frontier.*** New York: Viking Adult, 2010. Gul is a Pakistani reporter with decades of experience. In this volume, he gives a detailed account of Pakistan's tribal areas, lands on the Afghan border that provide refuge for the Taliban and al Qaeda.

Jones, Seth G. ***In the Graveyard of Empires: America's War in Afghanistan.*** New York: W. W. Norton, 2009. Jones's work is widely considered to be the best available study of America's involvement in Afghanistan. Vastly knowledgeable, Jones puts the conflict in historical context.

McGregor, Richard. ***The Party: The Secret World of China's Communist Rulers.*** New York: Harper, 2010. McGregor spent eight years in China as correspondent for the ***Financial Times*** of London. The Communist Party of China, which controls a fifth of the world's people, has succeeded because it is a self-aware and flexible social network. China is no longer ruled by an individual dictator, but by a committee of leaders, who in turn run an organism that permeates the entire society.

Ritter, Scott. ***Dangerous Ground: On the Trail of America's Failed Arms Control Policy.*** New York: Nation Books, 2009. Ritter, the chief weapons inspector for the United Nations Special Commission in Iraq from 1991 to 1998, believes that the George W. Bush administration misidentified the true dangers of nuclear proliferation. He presents a blueprint for addressing what he believes are the real dangers.

MEDIA RESOURCES

Black Hawk Down—A 2002 film that recounts the events in Mogadishu, Somalia, in October 1993, during which two U.S. Black Hawk helicopters were shot down. The film, which is based on reporter Mark Bowden's best-selling book by the same name, contains graphic scenes of terrifying urban warfare.

The 50 Years War—Israel and the Arabs—A two-volume PBS Home Video released in 2000. More balanced than some accounts, this film includes interviews with many leaders involved in the struggle, including the following: from Israel, Yitzhak Rabin, Shimon Peres, Benyamin Netanyahu, and Ariel Sharon; from the Arab world, Egypt's Anwar al-Sadat, Jordan's King Hussein, and Yasir Arafat; and from the United States, Presidents Jimmy Carter, George H. W. Bush, and Bill Clinton.

Senator Obama Goes to Africa—A documentary of Barack Obama's 2006 trip to Kenya, South Africa, and Chad. Despite the many questions Americans have had about Barack Obama, he has been more open about his unusual past than most politicians. One source of information is this film, which shows some of the advantages and disadvantages of Obama's international fame. In the end, he can do little about the suffering that he sees.

The Ugly American—One of the most intelligent political films of the 1960s, starring Marlon Brando as the U.S. ambassador to a Southeast Asian nation that is bursting with nationalism and beset by a Communist insurgency.

United 93—A 2006 documentary about the fourth airplane hijacked on 9/11. When they learned the fate of the other three planes through cell phones, the passengers decided to fight back, with the result that the flight crashed in a Pennsylvania field, far from its intended target. *United 93* takes place in real time and is almost unbearably moving. Several critics named it the best film of the year.

The World without US—A 2008 semidocumentary that poses the question: What would happen if the United States withdrew all of its military forces stationed abroad? The filmmakers, who are both thoughtful and politically conservative, believe the results of such a step would be disastrous. Historian Niall Ferguson is a star of this production.

e-mocracy

INTERNATIONAL ORGANIZATIONS

For years, international organizations have played a key role in world affairs, and these organizations are likely to become even more important in years to come. In the United States, the Obama administration has promised to place greater reliance on multilateral approaches when addressing problems abroad—in contrast to the Bush administration's "go it alone" approach.

International organizations do not only dispense aid, loans, and advice. Several of them field troops supplied by member nations. The "blue helmets" of the United Nations (UN) take part in seventeen missions, many in the Middle East or Africa. American forces in Afghanistan cooperate with those of other nations through the North Atlantic Treaty Organization (NATO). The UN, NATO, and other multinational organizations all have Web sites where you can learn about the history and status of current international conflicts.

LOGGING ON

In addition to materials on international crises, the United Nations Web site contains a treasure trove of international statistics. To access this site, go to
www.un.org/en/index.shtml

For news about NATO, visit
www.nato.int

The European Union, a confederation of twenty-seven nations, is one of the most important international bodies in existence. You can learn more about it at
www.europa.eu/index_en.htm

The Organisation for Economic Cooperation and Development (OECD) provides another major source of international statistics and economic analysis. You can access the OECD's Web site at
www.oecd.org

chapter
16

Texas History and Culture

chapter contents

The Alamo in San Antonio symbolizes the state's rich political history. (Larry Brownstein/Getty Images)

WHAT IF... ...Texas became five states?

BACKGROUND

Every day, every school child in every public school in Texas pledges from memory: "Honour the Texas flag; I pledge allegiance to thee, Texas, one and indivisible." This pledge is wrong, wrong, wrong! In fact, Texas is "divisible."

A provision of the Articles of Annexation, which admitted Texas into the Union, granted her the privilege of "creating . . . new states, of convenient size, not exceeding four in number, in addition to said State of Texas."* Thus, present-day Texans can politically carve Texas's geographic territory into a total of five states. This "privilege" was part of a political strategy to ensure an equal number of "slave" and "free" states in the existing Union. Although free-state representatives outnumbered slave-state members in the U.S. House, senators from slave states could block any federal legislation they deemed detrimental to their states' interests. It was assumed that the five states created from Texas would all be slave states, and their senators might be needed to maintain the tenuous balance between senators from free and slave states. As it turned out, the Senate remained balanced without dividing Texas for another 15 years, until slave states began withdrawing from the Union in 1860.

THE PLAN

However, the provision suggests fascinating possibilities for modern-day Texans. If the territory that is now the state of Texas consisted of five states instead of one, the geographic area would have 10 U.S. Senators instead of two and eight more votes in the electoral college. Modern Texans would thereby gain influence in the U.S. Senate, as well as in presidential politics.

It can also be argued that with five states, the political, ethnic, and historical diversity of Texas could be respected, and various cultural groups would be given better representation. Such a plan is shown in Figure 16–1 on the facing page. Lubbock would be West Texas's economic and political capital and include the oil-producing areas around Midland and Odessa. North Texas's capital would be the Dallas-Fort Worth Metroplex, with its western border along a line east of Abilene and Wichita Falls and including Waco to the south. East Texas would comprise the easternmost area of the state from Oklahoma to the Gulf of Mexico, including the eastern part of Houston and Texas City. Central Texas would include the western part of Houston, Victoria, northern San Antonio, and The Hill Country. South Texas would be bracketed by Brownsville and Corpus Christi on the east and El Paso on the west and include southern San Antonio.

* The Annexation of Texas, Joint Resolution of Congress, March 1, 1845, U.S. *Statutes at Large,* Vol. V, pp. 797–798. This document can be found online at www.pbs.org/weta/thewest/resources/archives/two/texannex.htm.

OPPOSITION TO THE PLAN

Modern Texans, however, seem uninterested in the prospect of carving four additional states from Texas. Republicans could oppose the plan in that South Texas, and possibly Central Texas and East Texas, could vote Democratic. Various interests would vie to be placed in one state or the other, and compromise boundaries would be difficult to achieve. Such a deal would require at least as much wily political talent as was needed to gerrymander Texas legislative and congressional districts. More importantly, the question of which state would have The Cowboys and The Alamo seems beyond resolution. So Texans will probably continue to be clustered in just one state, with only two U.S. senators and one governor.

FOR CRITICAL ANALYSIS

1. What arguments would you make against Texas becoming five states? Do Texans benefit from the combined economic and political power of being in a single state?
2. What are your arguments that favor five states? Should states be carved out to represent ethnic, cultural, and political groups?
3. Would you be more or less satisfied with your new state than you are with the present single-state arrangement? Why?

FIGURE 16–1 The Plan

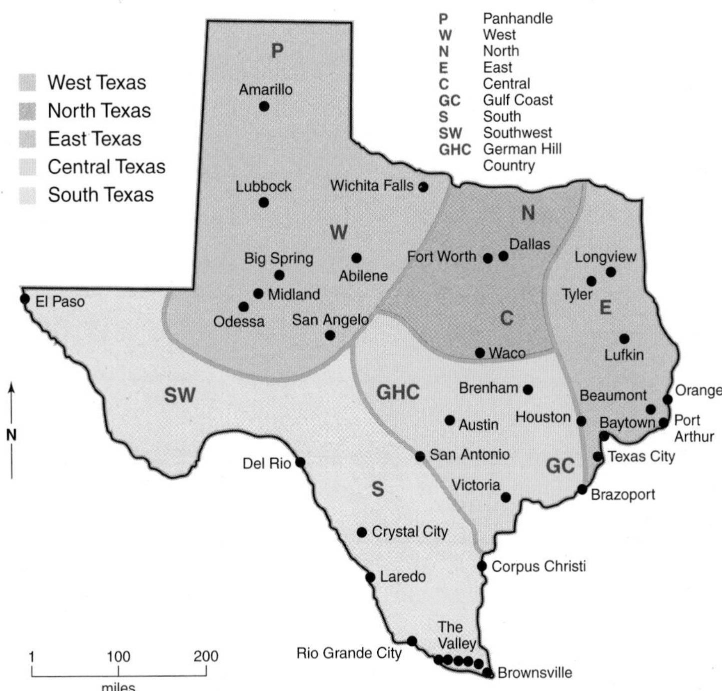

Almost 100 years before the *Mayflower* dropped anchor off Plymouth Rock, Núñez Cabeza de Vaca set foot on what was to become Texas. During the next three centuries, land-hungry settlers pushed the Cherokees and the Caddos from the eastern pine forests; the Karankawas from the sands of the coast; and the Comanches, Apaches, and Kiowas from the western plains. Texas culture and history were made under 37 Spanish governors, 15 Mexican governors, five presidents of the Republic of Texas, and 48 state governors.

The successful end of the Texas Revolution in 1836 saw the English/Scotch-Irish culture, as it had evolved in its migration through the Southern United States, become the dominant culture of the state. Anglo-Americans were the most numerous population group and controlled most of the political and economic systems in Texas. Anglo-American Protestant sects also became the dominant religious groups in Texas. As evidence of the dominance of this culture, all of the presidents of the Republic and the governors of the state have been Protestant and have had surnames linked to the British Isles.

Politics and Government: The Early Years

Politics in the Republic of Texas were simpler than politics in Texas today. There were no political parties, and conflict revolved around pro-Houston and anti-Houston policies. Sam Houston, the hero of the battle of San Jacinto (1836), advocated peaceful relations with the eastern Native Americans and U.S. statehood for Texas. The anti-Houston forces were led by Mirabeau B. Lamar, who believed that Native American and Anglo-American cultures could not coexist. He also envisioned Texas as a great nation extending from the Sabine River to the Pacific.[1]

did you know?

Sam Houston, David Crockett, and Jim Bowie were of Scotch-Irish descent and culture. Scotch-Irish immigrants from the Scot–English border, by way of Northern Ireland, led the Anglo-American movement west and had a major impact on the development of modern mid-American culture.

1. The information in this and subsequent sections depends heavily on Seymour V. Connor, *Texas: A History* (New York: Thomas Y. Crowell, 1971); Rupert N. Richardson, *Texas: The Lone Star State,* 3rd ed. (Englewood Cliffs, NJ: Prentice Hall, 1970); and T. R. Fehrenbach, *Lone Star: A History of Texas and the Texans* (New York: Collier Books, 1980).

Annexation
The incorporation of a territory into a larger political unit, such as a country, state, county, or city.

Joining the Union

Texas voters approved **annexation** to the United States in 1836, almost immediately after Texas achieved independence from Mexico. The slavery controversy in the United States, however, delayed final annexation until pro-annexation Democrat James K. Polk was elected president. On December 29, 1845, Texas officially became the 28th state in the Union.

Several articles of annexation were more or less peculiar to Texas. Most important was that Texas retained ownership of its public lands, because the U.S. Congress refused to

WHICH SIDE ARE YOU ON?

WHEN ART AND HISTORY CLASH

© Al Braden 2007

Texas has a long and rich history, one that is filled with heroes and villains. In an effort to commemorate these figures with art, the public's understanding of who is a villain and who is a hero can be brought into question. Such has been the case in El Paso. In 2007, the city of El Paso erected the world's largest equestrian statue. The work was created by the sculptor John Sherrill Houser, son of Ivan Houser, who worked on Mount Rushmore. John Sherrill Houser worked on the equestrian statue for a decade.

The sculpture is of Juan de Onate, who explored the region that is now the southwestern United States in the late 1500s and early 1600s. The 36-foot-tall statue honored the man who led an expedition that claimed the northern region of the Rio Grande for Spain. Onate would also help found Santa Fe, New Mexico. While Onate's stated mission in traveling to this region was to spread Catholicism, like other Spanish colonists he sought to mine minerals in the area. However, he is remembered by many as being particularly cruel to Native Americans, namely the Acoma Indians. After a skirmish with the Acoma that left Onate's nephew dead, Onate demanded that the left foot of every male Indian over the age of 25 be amputated.

This and other tyrannical actions against the Native American population were deemed so cruel that Onate was recalled back to Mexico City, where he was convicted of cruelty and other offenses. Eventually he would clear his name, but for many of the descendents of the Native American population in West Texas, his offenses have not been forgotten. In New Mexico, for instance, a smaller equestrian statue of Onate had its right foot removed in an act of vandalism. And in El Paso, the Native American population put pressure on the city council to name the statue simply as "the Equestrian." Onate's name does not appear on his statue.

Native Americans in the region are offended that the city would honor someone who had committed such atrocities. Protesters carried signs reading, "Onate butcher of 800 Acoma men, women and children," "A monument to a war criminal," and "Onate fue asesino" (Onate was an assassin). Native American populations protest that such a work is an insult to them because it honors the legacy of someone who did much harm to their people. Such insensitivity from the broader public is an affront to both the Native American and Mestizo populations. Supporters of the sculpture argue that Onate must be seen in a bigger picture. His exploration led people into areas previously unknown by Spanish colonists. In doing so, he brought new technology and ideas to the Southwest.

FOR CRITICAL ANALYSIS

What do you think? Should Onate be honored in this way? What about other such individuals? When artistic decisions are made, how much consideration should be given to descendents of long-dead victims of his actions? What roles do time and forgiveness play in a situation like this? How long is enough time for people to forgive and forget?

accept them in exchange for payment of the Republic's $10 million public debt. As we discuss in the *What If* . . . section, the annexation articles also granted Texas the privilege of "creating . . . new states, of convenient size, not exceeding four in number, in addition to said State of Texas."

This painting of Sam Houston shows him in the prime of life. Houston was commander in chief of the armies of Texas during the war for independence from Mexico and subsequently was elected the first president of the Republic of Texas. His lifelong friendship with the Native Americans and his opposition to secession set him apart from other Texans of his generation. He died in 1863 during the American Civil War. (Courtesy Huntsville Arts Commission)

Early Statehood and Secession: 1846–1864

The politics of early statehood immediately began to revolve around pro-Union and secessionist forces. Sam Houston, a strong Unionist alarmed at the support for **secession** in Texas, resigned his seat in the U.S. Senate and in 1857 ran for the office of governor of Texas. He was defeated, primarily because secession forces controlled the dominant Democratic Party. He was elected governor two years later, however.

After Abraham Lincoln was elected president of the United States in 1860, a Texas secessionist convention voted to secede from the Union. Branded as illegal by Sam Houston, the convention was nevertheless upheld as legitimate by the Texas legislature. Although Houston strongly opposed secession, he refused an offer from President Lincoln of 5,000 federal troops to force Texas to remain in the Union. Texas then seceded from the United States and was admitted into the Confederate States of America.

Texas politics during the Civil War primarily concerned the military. Besides supplying large numbers of troops to the conflict (primarily Confederate but also Union), Texas was responsible for the defense of the frontier and the Mexican border. Thus, the state—not the central Confederate government—filled the military vacuum created by the withdrawal of federal troops.

Post-Civil War Texas: 1865–1885

Following the collapse of the Confederacy, relative anarchy existed in Texas until it was occupied by federal troops on June 19, 1865. Only then were government functions and stability restored to the state.

Even before the end of the hostilities, a disagreement had arisen between radical and moderate Republicans in the U.S. Congress over Reconstruction policies for the defeated Southern states. Some of these states, including Texas, provided ammunition to Congressional radicals (called *Radical Republicans*) in this intraparty conflict by electing to office former Confederate officials and by passing **Black Codes.** Radical Republicans in Congress reacted by enacting legislation that strictly limited both voter registration and eligibility to hold public office for former Confederate soldiers and officials. This restriction even included former mayors and school board members.

Secession
The separation of a territory from a larger political unit. Specifically, the secession of Southern states from the Union in 1860 and 1861.

Black Codes
State laws passed after the Civil War that severely restricted the rights of freed slaves.

The Reconstruction of Texas under E. J. Davis. From 1865 through 1869, the Texas government was under the military rule of the U.S. Army. Following the adoption of the Constitution in 1869, E. J. Davis, a Texan and Radical Republican who had fought for the Union in the Civil War, was elected governor of Texas in an election in which the former slaves could vote—but the former leaders of the state could not. Texas was then readmitted to the Union and governed by civilian authority under Davis, who served a four-year term from 1870 through 1873. Under the 1869 Texas Constitution, political power was centralized in the office of the governor, and the state police and the militia were placed under the governor's direct control.

did you know?
That *Juneteenth,* or Emancipation Day, long celebrated by Texas African Americans, only became an official state holiday in 1979.

The Fall of Governor Davis. The perception of the Davis administration as a government imposed on a defeated people made it unpopular and prompted a strong anti-Republican reaction. In 1873, former Confederates were allowed to vote, and in 1874, Democrat Richard Coke was overwhelmingly elected governor in a vicious and hotly contested

Brigadier General E. J. Davis, U.S. Army. (Edmund J. Davis 1989.16; Courtesy State Preservation Board; Austin, TX; Photographer: Bill Kennedy 8/31/92 pre conservation/Texas State Preservation Board)

campaign. The Texas Supreme Court, handpicked by Davis, invalidated the election based on a technicality.

Davis locked himself in the Capitol, surrounded it with the state police, requested the support of federal troops from President Ulysses S. Grant, and refused to leave office. Only when serious violence seemed imminent between the state police and the numerically superior Coke forces did Davis withdraw.

The End of Republicanism. The new Texas officials immediately began to remove the last vestiges of Radical Republicanism. One of the first steps was to rewrite the state constitution. A constitutional convention of 90 members was elected (75 Democrats and 15 Republicans) that included many former officials of both the Union and Confederate governments. Forty members of the 1875 convention also belonged to the Grange, at that time a nonpartisan organization of farmers. Ratified in 1876, the new constitution cut expenditures, decentralized the state government, and strictly limited the flexibility of elected officials. Although often amended, it is still in use.

Politics and Government: 1886–1945

After 1886, increasing demands for change forced the Democratic Party to make political adjustments. Many reform measures were enacted and enforced in Texas in the 1880s, especially **antitrust legislation.** The election of James Stephen Hogg as attorney general in 1886 ensured the vigorous enforcement of the new laws against abuses by insurance companies, railroads, and other corporate interests.

Antitrust Legislation
Legislation directed against economic monopolies.

Governor Hogg

Hogg, who had strong support among small East Texas farmers, played an important reformist role in Texas politics and rapidly developed a reputation as a champion of the common people. Feeling that he needed more power to regulate the railroad interests that dominated many state governments, Hogg ran for governor. The 1890 Democratic state convention nominated him as its candidate for governor despite opposition from powerful political and corporate business enemies. A major issue in the campaign that followed was a proposed amendment giving the Texas legislature the power to establish a commission to regulate railroads. The voters gave both Hogg and the amendment a clear victory.

Norris Wright Cuney gained control of the Texas Republican party after 1883. (Prints and Photographs Collection, Norris Wright Cuney file, The Center for American History, The University of Texas at Austin; CN 01074)

The Railroad Commission. As governor, Hogg was able to persuade the legislature to establish a three-member Railroad Commission, despite intense opposition from special-interest legislators. His appointment of respected political figures to the commission, notably John H. Reagan as chairman, enabled it to become one of the most important railroad regulatory bodies in the United States.

The constitutionality of a railroad commission still had to be tested in the federal courts, but it was upheld after two years of litigation. The commission was later given the power to regulate the production and transportation of oil and natural gas and to regulate rubber-tired vehicles used in intrastate commerce.

Edward M. House. In 1894, an early Hogg supporter, Edward M. House, was able to take control of the Democratic Party from Hogg on a "promote unity" platform. House established himself as a behind-the-scenes political power in Texas for the next 40 years. House also wielded significant influence in national politics, first as a supporter and later as chief confidant of President Woodrow Wilson (served 1913–1921). Although he never sought elective office, House was one of the most astute politicians ever to operate in Texas.

Throughout the early 1900s, programs enacted by the legislature continued to identify Texas as one of the most progressive states in the nation. Texas pioneered the regulation of monopolies, railroads, child labor, and other employer abuses, as well as reform of prisons, taxes, and insurance companies. In 1905, state conventions were replaced with direct primaries to nominate major-party candidates.

James Stephen Hogg was a progressive newspaperman, a politician, and the first Texas-born governor of Texas. (Frontispiece, Speeches and State Papers of James Stephen Hogg, C. W. Raines, editor. The State Publishing Company, Austin, Texas, 1905. The University of Texas at Austin, Center for American History)

Farmer Jim: 1914–1918

James E. Ferguson entered the Texas political scene in 1914 and was a controversial and powerful force in Texas politics for the next 20 years. He had worked as a migrant laborer in California, Nevada, Colorado, and Texas. Although Ferguson had little formal education and only a few months' study of law, he was admitted to the Texas bar in 1897.

By 1914, when he announced his candidacy for governor, Ferguson owned varied business interests and was the president of the Temple State Bank. Ferguson was an anti-prohibitionist ("wet") at a time when **Prohibition** was a major political issue. Although his strongest opponent in the Democratic primary was a prohibitionist ("dry"), Ferguson tried to ignore the liquor issue. He was sensitive to the problems and interests of the business community, but Ferguson called himself "Farmer Jim" to emphasize his rural background and focused his campaign on the difficulties of the numerous **tenant farmers** in Texas.

Farmer Jim as Governor. The legislature was unusually receptive to Ferguson's programs, which were in the best tradition of the **Progressive Movement,** and enacted legislation designed to help alleviate the problems of tenant farmers, rural schools, and state courts. Governor Ferguson was re-elected in 1916, and although rumors of financial irregularities in the office had begun to gain credibility, his progressive legislative programs were again successful. This was especially true in the areas of public school and college education and the proposal to create a state highway commission. The latter agency was formed to take the construction and maintenance of state roads away from the counties, where there was great variation in quality and consistency.

did you know?

That Governor Hogg's daughter, Ima Hogg (Miss Ima), was a major benefactor and philanthropist to Texas institutions and charities. (Contrary to popular belief, Governor Hogg did not have a daughter named Ura Hogg.)

The Fall of Farmer Jim. Rumors of financial irregularities such as bribery and embezzlement continued during Ferguson's second term. Ultimately, he was impeached on 21 charges. In August 1917, following three weeks of hearings by the state senate, Ferguson was convicted on 10 of the charges, removed from office, and barred from holding public office in Texas.

Ferguson was found guilty of accepting funds from secret sources, tampering with state officials, depositing state funds in the Temple State Bank (which he partly owned), and using public funds for personal gain. His successor was Lieutenant Governor W. P. Hobby, Sr. The same legislature, in another session, ratified the Eighteenth Amendment to the U.S. Constitution, establishing national Prohibition. The prohibitionists had won.

Prohibition
Outlawing of the production, sale, and consumption of alcoholic beverages.

Tenant Farmer
A farmer who does not own the land that he or she farms but rents it from a landowner.

Progressive Movement
A political movement within both major parties in the early 20th century. Progressives believed that the power of the government should be used to restrain the growing power of large corporations.

World War I, the 1920s, and the Return of Farmer Jim: 1919–1928

As did the rest of the nation, Texas saw boom years during World War I. Its favorable climate and the Zimmerman Note (in which Germany allegedly urged Mexico to invade Texas) prompted the national government to station additional troops in the state. Texas became an important training area for the military, and many of the training camps later became permanent bases.

Progressive political programs, however, suffered during the war. Several of Governor Hobby's proposals—including women's suffrage, using the state's credit to help individuals purchase homes, and a new constitution—were defeated either by the legislature or by the voters.

In 1921, Pat M. Neff became governor of Texas. His proposals to reorganize the executive branch to eliminate duplication and waste and to rewrite the Texas Constitution both failed. Meanwhile, bootleggers—traffickers in illegal alcohol—often circumvented Prohibition. Governor Neff, an avid prohibitionist, used the Texas Rangers to find and destroy private stills used to produce illegal spirits. The Rangers were too few in number to be effective, though, and the legislature refused to give Neff the police powers necessary to enforce Prohibition effectively. Women's suffrage, crime, education, and the **Ku Klux Klan (KKK)** emerged as issues that demanded attention from the politicians and voters.

Ku Klux Klan (KKK)
A white supremacist organization. The first Klan was founded during the Reconstruction era following the Civil War.

Civil Rights. Civil rights remained an elusive concept during this period for racial minorities and women. Women were denied the right to vote by law specifically due to their gender. African Americans were effectively denied the right to vote by the poll tax law, the white primary, and unlawful terror tactics. Although these laws were not specifically directed at Tejanos (Hispanic Texans), they were enforced through social custom and coercion. The Ku Klux Klan, local law officers, and the Texas Rangers actively participated in violence and intimidation of Tejanos and African Texans to keep them "in their segregated place." Lynching was also used against both groups, often after torture.[2]

The Ku Klux Klan (first organized in the late 1860s to intimidate freed African-American slaves) was reborn in the 1920s with a somewhat modified mission. The new Klan saw itself as a patriotic, Christian, fraternal organization for native-born white Protestants. Its members perceived both a general moral decline in society, precipitated by "modern" young people, and a basic threat to the Protestant white Christian "race" and its values by African Americans, Jews, Catholics, Mexican Americans, German Americans, and other "foreigners."

In response to this racially charged atmosphere, several organizations committed to equality were founded or expanded during the 1920s. Founded in 1909, the National Association for the Advancement of Colored People (NAACP) chapters expanded, and the League of United Latin American Citizens (LULAC) was formed in Corpus Christi in 1929.

The women's suffrage movement also gained momentum in Texas during the early years of the 20th century, and by 1918, many suffrage organizations existed in the state. Groups opposing suffrage were also formed out of concern that the responsibilities of citizenship would be too hard on the "weaker sex." Nevertheless, Texas was one of the first states to ratify the Nineteenth Amendment to the U.S. Constitution, which gave women the right to vote. Other progressive measures during this period included free textbooks for public schools, the establishment of several colleges, and the beginning of the state park system.

did you know?

That "Ma" Ferguson was governor in name only, and that Farmer Jim exercised the real power of the office.

The Return of the Fergusons. The strongest anti-Klan candidate in the gubernatorial election of 1924 was Miriam A. "Ma" Ferguson, wife of the impeached (and convicted) Farmer Jim. Running successfully on a platform of "Two Governors for the Price of One," she became the first female governor of Texas. Ma's election indicated that Texas voters had forgiven Farmer Jim. Her success in getting legislation passed that prohibited wearing a mask in public led to the end of the Klan as an effective political force in Texas. Ma was criticized, however, for her lenient pardoning policy (occasionally a convicted felon was pardoned before reaching prison) and a high-

2. The Handbook of Texas Online.

way scandal. In the 1926 election, she was defeated by Attorney General Dan Moody, also a reformer and an anti-Klan candidate.

The Great Depression: 1929–1939

When the stock market crashed in 1929, Texas, along with the entire nation, was crushed under the blow. Almost overnight, prices dropped, farm products could not be sold, mortgages and taxes could not be paid, and many jobs ceased to exist. Numerous businesses and bank accounts were wiped out.

The Independent Oil Crisis. The discovery of the East Texas oil field near Kilgore in 1930 helped alleviate the situation until overproduction of oil forced the price to drop to as low as ten cents per barrel (about one dollar in today's currency). Unlike earlier discoveries, the East Texas field was developed and controlled largely by "independents"—oil producers not associated with the major oil companies. The "majors" owned the oil refineries, however, and because of the oil surplus, they often refused to purchase oil from independents for refining. Independents requested assistance from Governor Ross Sterling, but instead he ordered the East Texas field closed because of its threat to the entire oil industry. Outraged independents claimed that he had overreacted and refused to stop production.

Sterling declared martial law and sent in the National Guard. Eventually, the Railroad Commission (RRC) was given the power to control production of oil in Texas (first by executive order, later by law).

did you know?

That Governor Sterling was one of the founders of Humble Oil Company (later Exxon), and that the commander of the Texas National Guard was employed by Texaco Oil Company as an attorney.

"Ma" Ferguson Again. In 1932, Ma Ferguson, using economy in government as her campaign issue, was re-elected as governor. In an effort to promote efficiency, she hired a private consulting firm to recommend management changes in Texas government.

In 1933, the ratification of the Twenty-first Amendment to the U.S. Constitution ended nationwide Prohibition. Prohibition ended in Texas two years later with the adoption of local option elections, although selling liquor by the drink was still forbidden statewide. A board was established to administer the taxing and licensing of liquor dealers.

"Pass the Biscuits, Pappy": 1938–1945

W. Lee O'Daniel, certainly one of the most colorful and unusual characters in Texas politics, entered the Democratic gubernatorial primary in 1938. "Pappy" O'Daniel was a highly successful flour salesman and the host of a hillbilly music radio show that was liberally sprinkled with homespun poetry and moral advice.

In his gubernatorial campaign, O'Daniel used the slogan "Pass the biscuits, Pappy!" Touring Texas in a bus with the Light Crust Doughboys, O'Daniel ran on a platform of the Ten Commandments, the Golden Rule, and increased old-age pensions.

He had never run for public office, had never voted in Texas, had never paid a poll tax (saying that no politician was worth $1.75), and admitted that he knew nothing about politics. With no campaign manager and no campaign headquarters, and without a runoff, he defeated thirteen candidates in the Democratic primary—some of whom were well-known, prominent political figures.

did you know?

That Pappy O'Daniel was resurrected, buffoonized, and reincarnated as a Mississippi governor in the hit 2000 movie *O Brother, Where Art Thou?* by Joel and Ethan Coen.

"Pappy" as Governor. Governor O'Daniel was not successful as a legislative leader, but he was re-elected easily in 1940 against strong opposition in the Democratic primary.

"Pappy" O'Daniel is shown with the Hillbilly Boys—Pappy is on the right. For all his political and personal failings, O'Daniel was undeniably an important figure in the development of Western swing music. Because of his talent for publicity and his business acumen, his bands, the Light Crust Doughboys and the Hillbilly Boys, became nationally recognized performers. (Courtesy of the Texas State Library and Archives)

Again, he was notably unsuccessful in getting his proposals passed by the legislature. When the senior U.S. senator from Texas died, O'Daniel was urged to appoint himself to the post until a special election could be held. Instead, he appointed Andrew Jackson Houston, the last surviving son of Sam Houston. Houston, at age 87, became the oldest man ever to enter the U.S. Senate. There was some question as to whether he could survive the trip to Washington! He did, but he died 18 days later.

"Pappy" as Senator. Pappy then entered the special election for the Senate seat and won, defeating 29 other candidates. (His closest competitor was a young congressman from Central Texas, Lyndon B. Johnson.) Lieutenant Governor Coke R. Stevenson succeeded Pappy as governor. O'Daniel served with a notable lack of distinction in the Senate but was reelected to a full six-year term in 1942. His ineffectiveness in Washington was possibly related to his habit of making derogatory remarks about other politicians, such as "Washington is the only lunatic asylum in the world run by its own inmates."

Politics and Government Since World War II

Beauford Jester easily won the gubernatorial election of 1946 after an especially bitter primary victory over Homer P. Rainey, the former president of the University of Texas. A major campaign issue was university autonomy and academic freedom.

The 1948 senatorial campaign (for the seat of the retiring Pappy O'Daniel) is worth special note. Several qualified people announced their candidacies for the position. The runoff in the Democratic primary pitted former governor Coke R. Stevenson against 39-year-old U.S. Congressman Lyndon B. Johnson. The campaign was especially controversial, and the election was the closest in the state's history, with both candidates charging election fraud. At first, the election bureau gave the unofficial count as 494,330 votes for Stevenson and 493,968 for Johnson; then the revised returns for counties began to be reported, most of which favored Johnson. The final official election results were 494,191 for Johnson and 494,104 for Stevenson—a difference of 87 votes.

Civil Rights Revisited: Mexican Texans

Returning World War II veterans, fresh from fighting to make the world safe for democracy, found discrimination still existed in the homeland. Decorated veteran Major Hector Garcia settled in Corpus Christi and became convinced by conditions in the Mexican-American community in South Texas that still another battle was yet to be fought—and in his own backyard. Garcia, a medical doctor, found farm laborers enduring inhuman living conditions; deplorable medical conditions in slums; disabled veterans starving, sick, and ignored by the Veteran's Administration; and an entrenched, unapologetic Anglo-Texas elite maintaining public school segregation.

did you know?

That historian T. R. Fehrenbach, writing about Lyndon Johnson's 87-vote victory over Coke Stevenson for the U.S. Senate in 1948, said, "There was probably no injustice involved. Johnson men had not 'defrauded' Stevenson, but successfully 'out-frauded' him".

To begin his war, Dr. Garcia needed recruits for his "army." With other World War II veterans, Dr. Garcia organized The American GI Forum in a Corpus Christi elementary school classroom in March 1948. This organization spread throughout the United States and played a major role in giving Mexican Americans full citizenship and civil respect.[3]

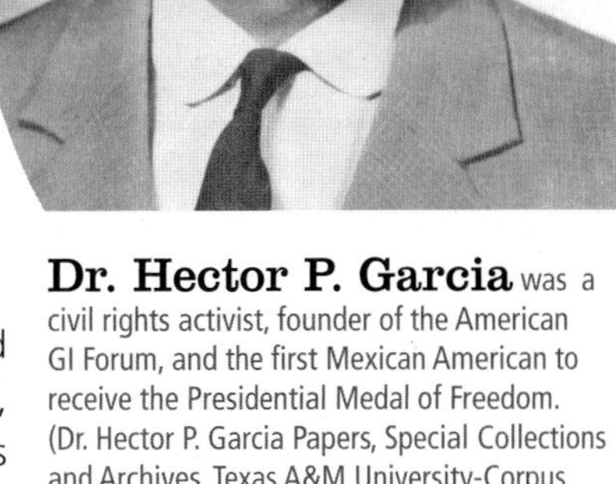

Dr. Hector P. Garcia was a civil rights activist, founder of the American GI Forum, and the first Mexican American to receive the Presidential Medal of Freedom. (Dr. Hector P. Garcia Papers, Special Collections and Archives, Texas A&M University-Corpus Christi Bell Library)

Herman Sweatt (far left) successfully integrated Texas public law schools after the U.S. Supreme Court began to chip away at the "separate but equal" doctrine in the landmark case *Sweatt v. Painter,* 339 U.S. 629 (1950). (Joseph Scherschel/Time & Life Pictures/Getty Images)

Civil Rights Revisited: African Texans

African Americans at last won the right to participate in the Texas Democratic primary when the U.S. Supreme Court ruled in *Smith v. Allwright*[4] that primaries were a part of the election process. Twenty years later, the first African Americans since Reconstruction were elected to the Texas legislature.

World War II Veteran Herman Sweatt applied for admission to the University of Texas Law School, which by Texas law was segregated. State laws requiring segregation were constitutional as long as the facilities were "equal." Because Texas had no African-American law school, the Texas legislature was forced to hurriedly establish a law school for Sweatt—conveniently in his hometown of Houston. The NAACP sued Texas, and the U.S. Supreme Court ruled that the new law school was not equal and ordered that Sweatt be admitted to the University of Texas. "Separate but equal" facilities were seldom equal, and the Court did not overturn the *Plessy v. Ferguson* case but ruled that the new law school was not equal to the University of Texas.[5]

The 1950s

Lieutenant Governor Allan Shivers became governor in 1949 following the death of Governor Jester. He was easily elected governor in 1950, setting the stage for the 1952 Texas political extravaganza in which a president, the governor, and a U.S. senator would be elected. Both state and national political issues captured the interest of the 1952 Texas voters. Harry Truman, a Democrat, had succeeded to the presidency in 1945 following the death of Franklin Roosevelt. Several scandals marred the Truman administration, and many conservative Texas Democrats were disillusioned with the New Deal and Fair Deal policies of the Roosevelt-Truman era.

The Tidelands Controversy. Another major issue was the **tidelands** question. Following the discovery of oil in the Gulf of Mexico, a jurisdictional conflict arose between the government of the United States and the governments of the coastal states.

Texas claimed three leagues (a Spanish unit of measure equal to about 10 miles) as its jurisdictional boundary; the U.S. government said that Texas had rights to only three miles. At stake were hundreds of millions of dollars in royalty revenue.

Tidelands
An area that extends three leagues (about 10 miles) off the Texas coast. The tidelands controversy developed when offshore oil was discovered and the federal government contended that Texas's jurisdiction extended only three miles out from the coast.

3. www.justiceformypeople.com/drhector2.html
4. 321 U.S. 649 (1944)
5. *Sweatt v. Painter,* 339 U.S. 629 (1950).

Governor Shivers was known for being all business. This photo shows him making a rare exception. To what extent might Shivers' hostility to the national Democratic Party have been the result of its refusal to give Texas the royalties from oil in the tidelands? (Texas State Library and Archives)

Governor Shivers and Attorney General Price Daniel, who were campaigning for the U.S. Senate, both attacked the national Democratic administration as being corrupt and soft on communism, eroding states' rights, and being outright thieves in attempting to steal the tidelands oil from the schoolchildren of Texas. State control would direct much of the oil income to the Permanent School Fund used for public education and would mean a lower school tax burden for Texans. The Democratic presidential nomination of Adlai Stevenson of Illinois, who disagreed with the Texas position on the tidelands, only intensified this opposition.

Loyalists and Shivercrats. The Republicans nominated Dwight Eisenhower, a World War II hero who was sympathetic to the Texas position on the tidelands issue. Eisenhower was born in Texas (but reared in Kansas), and his supporters used the campaign slogan "Texans for a Texan." The presidential campaign crystallized a split in the Texas Democratic Party that lasted for the next 40 years. The conservative "Texas Democrats" faction of the party, led by Shivers and Daniel, advocated "splitting the ticket"—voting for Eisenhower for president and for Texas Democrats for state offices. The liberal faction, or "Loyalist Democrats of Texas," led by Judge Ralph "Raff" Yarborough, campaigned for a straight Democratic ticket.

Texas voted for Eisenhower, and the tidelands dispute was eventually settled in favor of Texas. Shivers was re-elected governor, and Daniel succeeded in entering the U.S. Senate. Shivers, Daniel, and the Democratic candidates for several other statewide offices (including lieutenant governor and attorney general) were also nominated by the Republican Party. These candidates won in the general election as Democrats, however, because they received more votes as Democrats than as Republicans. For some time afterward, those who voted for conservative Democrats at the state level and for Republicans at the national level were known as **Shivercrats.**

Shivercrat
A follower of Governor Allan Shivers of Texas (1949–1957). Shivercrats split their votes between conservative Democrats for state office and Republicans for the U.S. presidency.

The 1960s

When Lyndon B. Johnson, majority leader of the U.S. Senate and one of the most powerful men in Washington, lost his bid for the Democratic presidential nomination to John F. Kennedy in 1960, he accepted the nomination for vice president. By the grace of the Texas legislature, Johnson was on the ballot of the general election as both a vice-presidential and senatorial nominee. When the Democratic ticket was successful, he was elected to both positions, and a special election was necessary to fill the Senate seat he chose to vacate. (The same law allowed Senator Lloyd Bentsen to run for both vice president and senator in 1988. He lost the vice-presidential election but was re-elected as senator.) In the special election, Republican John Tower was elected to fill Johnson's vacated seat in the Senate—the first Republican since Reconstruction to serve as a U.S. senator from Texas.

In 1962, John B. Connally, the Secretary of the Navy in the Kennedy administration, returned to Texas and was elected governor. Connally became a dominant force in Texas politics and was easily re-elected to second and third terms. He did not seek re-election for a fourth term and, in 1969, was succeeded by Lieutenant Governor Preston Smith.

did you know?

That Governor Allan Shivers, running as a Democrat, defeated himself running as a Republican in the 1952 election.

The 1960s is known for the victories of the national civil rights movement. Texan James Farmer was co-founder of the Congress of Racial Equality (CORE), and along with Dr. Martin Luther King, Jr., Whitney Young, and Roy Wilkins, was one of the "Big Four" African Americans who shaped the civil rights struggle in the 1950s and 1960s. Farmer followed the nonviolent principles of Mahatma Gandhi and initiated both sit-ins as a means of integrating public facilities and freedom rides as a means of registering African Americans to vote.

The first sit-in to protest segregation in Texas was organized with CORE support by students from Wiley and Bishop colleges in the rotunda of the Harrison County courthouse in Marshall, Texas. James Farmer was a graduate of Wiley College and was a member of its 1935 national champion debate team, which served as the inspiration for the popular movie *The Great Debaters,* starring Denzel Washington.[6]

The fight to organize into labor unions was the primary focus for much of the Mexican-American civil activism in the 1960s. In rural areas, large landowners controlled the political as well as the economic system and were largely united in opposition to labor unions. The United Farm Workers (UFW) led a strike against melon growers and packers in Starr County in the 1960s, demanding a minimum wage and resolution of other grievances. Starr County police officers, the local judiciary, and the Texas Rangers were accused of brutality as they arrested and prosecuted strikers for minor offenses.

Senator Ralph W. Yarborough was the leader of the Loyalist Democrats of Texas. (A. Y. Owen/Time & Life Pictures/Getty Images)

On July 4, 1966, members of the UFW, strikers, and other supporters began a march to Austin to demand the $1.25 minimum wage and other improvements for farm workers. Press coverage intensified as the marchers made their way north in the summer heat. Politicians, members of the AFL-CIO, and the Texas Council of Churches accompanied the protestors. Governor John Connally, who had refused to meet them in Austin, traveled to New Braunfels with then House Speaker Ben Barnes and Attorney General Waggoner Carr to intercept the march and inform strikers that their efforts would have no effect. Ignoring the governor, the marchers continued to Austin and held a 6,500-person protest rally at the State Capitol. The rally was broken up by Texas Rangers and law enforcement officers. Legal action was taken against the Rangers for their part in the strike and the protest. The eventual ruling of the Supreme Court held that the laws that the Rangers had been enforcing were in violation of the U.S. Constitution.[7] The Rangers were reorganized as a part of the Texas Department of Public Safety.

The 1970s

The Sharpstown scandal erupted in 1971. It began when attorneys for the U.S. Securities and Exchange Commission (SEC) filed a suit alleging stock fraud against a series of elected Texas officials. The SEC also filed suit against Frank Sharp, owner of the Sharpstown State Bank. Buried in the SEC's supporting material was the allegation that several prominent politicians, including Governor Preston Smith and house speaker Gus Mutscher, had accepted bribes to support legislation favorable to Sharp. Although Governor Smith was not found

6. See CORE-online.org for more information.
7. See Robert E. Hall, "Pickets, Politics and Power: The Farmworker Strike in Starr County," *Texas Bar Journal,* Vol. 70, No. 5; and *Allee v. Medrano,* 416 U.S. 802 (1974).

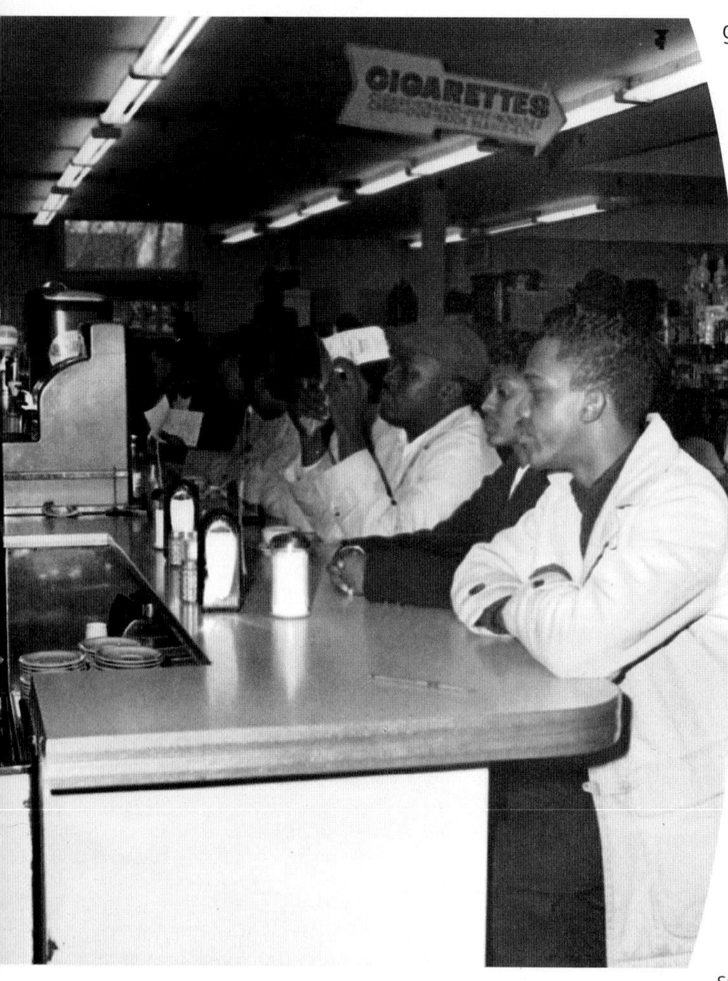

Texas Southern University students stage a sit-in at a Houston supermarket lunch counter, 1960. (AP Photo)

guilty of any wrongdoing, Mutscher, along with others, was convicted of conspiracy to accept a bribe.[8]

In the wake of the scandal, many "reform" advocates were elected in 1972. Dolph Briscoe, a wealthy Uvalde rancher and banker, won the governorship by a plurality of less than 100,000 votes over his Republican and **La Raza Unida** opponents—the first general election since the institution of the party primary in 1906 in which the Democratic gubernatorial candidate did not receive a majority of the votes. Briscoe was easily re-elected in 1974.

In 1979, William P. Clements became the first Republican governor of Texas since E. J. Davis vacated the office in 1874. The election of a Republican governor did not affect legislative-executive relations, however, because Clements received strong political support from conservative Democrats.

The 1980s

In 1982, a Democrat, Attorney General Mark White, displaced incumbent governor Bill Clements, despite Clements' unprecedented campaign spending. Teachers overwhelmingly supported White, who promised them salary increases and expressed support for education. Clements opposed the salary increases and was perceived as unsympathetic to education.

In 1986, voter unhappiness with education reform, a sour economy, and decreased state revenue was enough to return Republican Bill Clements to the governor's office in a sweeping victory over Democrat Mark White. In 1988, three Republicans were elected to the Texas Supreme Court and one to the Railroad Commission—the first Republicans elected to statewide office (other than governor or U.S. senator) since Reconstruction.

The 1990s

La Raza Unida
A party organized in the late 1960s as a means of getting Mexican Americans to unite politically and to identify ethnically as one people.

Down-ticket
Candidates for lower political offices are located further down the ballot.

With the 1990 election of Dan Morales (attorney general), Kay Bailey Hutchison (treasurer), and Rick Perry (agriculture commissioner), Texas elected the first Hispanic ever and the first Republicans since Reconstruction to **down-ticket** executive offices. (You will learn more about such offices in Chapter 25.) Austin voters elected the first openly gay legislator in 1991.

Texans also elected Ann Richards as their first female governor since Miriam "Ma" Ferguson. Through her appointive powers, she opened the doors of state government to unprecedented numbers of women, Hispanics, and African Americans. In 1992, Texas elected Kay Bailey Hutchison as its first female U.S. senator. She joined fellow Republican Phil Gramm, and they became the first two Republicans to hold U.S. Senate seats concurrently since 1874.

Two-Party Politics. When the smoke, mud, and sound bites of the 1994 general election settled, a new political age had dawned—Texas had truly become a two-party state. Republican candidates won victories from the top to the bottom of the ballot. For the first time since Reconstruction, with the election of Governor George W. Bush, Republicans held

8. For further discussion of the Sharpstown scandal, see Charles Deaton, *The Year They Threw the Rascals Out* (Austin: Shoal Creek Publishers, 1973); and Sam Kinch, Jr. and Ben Procter, *Texas under a Cloud: Story of the Texas Stock Fraud Scandal* (Austin and New York: Jenkins Publishing Co., 1972).

the governor's office and both U.S. Senate seats. Although both Democratic and Republican incumbents were re-elected to down-ticket administrative positions, Republicans held all of the Railroad Commission seats and a majority on the State Board of Education and the Texas Supreme Court.

In 1996, Republicans won a majority in the Texas Senate for the first time since Reconstruction. The 1997 legislature failed to enact campaign finance reform, nonpartisan election of judges, and Governor Bush's tax initiative to reduce public schools' reliance on local property taxes. The state's first comprehensive water management plan was enacted, however, along with voluntary surgical castration for child molesters, prohibition of tobacco possession by minors, and authorization for patients to sue health-maintenance organizations (HMOs) for malpractice. Voters also ratified an amendment to the Texas Constitution that allows them to use their *home equity* (the current market value of a home minus the outstanding mortgage debt) as collateral for a loan.

The Late Ann Richards was inaugurated governor in 1991. The first woman to be elected Texas governor on her own merits, Richards appointed more women, blacks, and Hispanics to office than any previous governor. Why are Texans (and other Americans) more willing to elect women to high office today than in years past? (Texas State Library and Archives)

Republican Dominance. The 1998 general election was a sweep year for Republicans, who won every statewide elective office. This overwhelming achievement also positioned Governor George W. Bush as the front-runner for the Republican nomination for president in 2000. In the Seventy-sixth Texas Legislature (1999), however, Democrats narrowly retained control of the state house of representatives, and Republican control of the state senate was diminished to a one-vote margin.

The 2000s

The Republicans Consolidate Their Power. The Republicans swept Texas statewide offices and both chambers of the legislature in the 2002 elections. A Republican governor, lieutenant governor, and speaker of the house ensured that Republican proposals would receive a sympathetic hearing in the 2003 legislative session. A nonpartisan policy, however, remained in effect in the legislature—the lieutenant governor and speaker appointed some Democrats to committee chair and vice-chair positions.

A projected $10 billion budget deficit created an uncomfortable environment for the Republicans. Politically and ideologically opposed to both new taxes and state-provided social services, the legislature and the governor chose to reduce funding for most state programs, but especially education, health care, children's health insurance, and social services for the needy.

Attempts to close some tax loopholes failed. For example, businesses and professions of all sizes continued to organize as "partnerships" to avoid the state corporate franchise tax. The legislature did place limits on pain-and-suffering jury awards for injuries caused by physician malpractice and hospital incompetence and made it more difficult to sue the makers of unsafe, defective products.

The Redistricting Controversy. Although the districts for electing U.S. representatives in Texas had been redrawn by a panel of one Democrat and two Republican federal judges following the 2000 census, Texas Congressman and U.S. House Majority Leader

Tom DeLay was unhappy that more Texas Republicans were not elected to Congress. Governor Rick Perry agreed to call a special session in order to redraw the already redrawn districts to favor Republican Congressional candidates. Minority-party Democrats argued that the districts had already been drawn to accommodate the decade's population shifts and that the Republicans were only trying to gerrymander Texas voters. (See Chapter 12 for a further discussion of the gerrymander.)

During Special Session One (June 30, 2003), most house Democrats (dubbed The Killer D's) left the state for Oklahoma to deny the state house of representatives the required two-thirds quorum necessary to conduct its business. Special Session Two (July 28, 2003) saw Republican Lieutenant Governor David Dewhurst change the senate rule that had required a two-thirds majority vote for bills to be heard on the senate floor. This denied the minority senate Democrats a procedural tool to block Congressional redistricting. In response, most senate Democrats left the state for New Mexico so that the Texas senate would not have the required quorum. For Special Session Three (September 15, 2003), senate Democrats were unable to muster enough members to block the quorum, and the new district lines were drawn. The redistricting generated numerous lawsuits challenging its legality, but the U.S. Supreme Court refused to overturn most of the actions of the Texas legislature, affirming that states could redistrict more than once each decade and rejected the argument that the redistricting was an illegal partisan gerrymander.

Congressman Tom DeLay was indicted for money laundering, which forced him to resign his seat in Congress and establish legal residence in Virginia. Nominated by his party for re-election, he attempted to get his name removed from the ballot but could not. The voters in his district elected a Democrat to Congress in 2006.

In 2007, the voters added 17 amendments to the Texas Constitution concerning a wide range of issues, such as extending property tax cuts to the elderly and disabled; abolishing the county inspector of hides and animals; requiring record votes on final passage of most bills; and issuing bonds for water development, highway improvement, cancer prevention, and student loans. The 2007 legislature saw almost continuous battles between the house and the speaker, the senate and the lieutenant governor, the senate and the house, and the legislature and the governor. Legislators did find time to restore some 127,000 poor children to the Children's Health Insurance Program (CHIP).

Texas Cultural Regions

D. W. Meinig found that the cultural diversity of Texas was more apparent than its homogeneity and that no unified culture has emerged from the various ethnic and cultural groups that settled Texas. He believed that the "typical Texan," like the "average American," does not exist but is an oversimplification used to broadly generalize the more distinctive social, economic, and political characteristics of all Texans.[9]

Both Meinig and Elazar see modern regional political culture as largely determined by migration patterns, because people take their culture with them as they move geographically. Meinig believed that Texas had evolved into the nine fairly distinct cultural regions shown in Figure 16–2. However, while political boundaries are distinct, cultural divisions are often blurred and transitional. For example, the East Texas region shares a political culture with much of the Upper South, while West Texas shares a similar culture with eastern New Mexico, and so forth.

The effect of the mass media, the mobility of modern Texans, and migration from the United States and immigration from Mexico also blur the cultural boundaries within Texas, between its bordering states, and with Mexico. Although limited by this reality, both

9. Information for this section is adapted from D. W. Meinig, *Imperial Texas: An Interpretive Essay in Cultural Geography* (Austin and London: University of Texas Press, 1969).

Meinig's and Elazar's explanations can serve as useful guides to help understand contemporary Texas culture, attitudes, and beliefs.

East Texas

East Texas is a social and cultural extension of the old South. It is basically rural and biracial. Despite the changes brought about by civil rights legislation, "black towns" still exist alongside "white towns," and there are many segregated social and economic institutions, such as churches, fraternal lodges, and chambers of commerce.

East Texas counties and towns are often dominated by old families, whose wealth is usually based on real estate, banking, construction, and retail merchandising. Cotton—once the "king" of agriculture in the region—has been replaced by beef cattle, poultry, and timber. Owing to a general lack of economic opportunity, young East Texans migrate to metropolitan areas, primarily Dallas-Fort Worth and Houston. The region is dominated spiritually by fundamentalist Protestantism, which permeates its political, social, and cultural activities.

FIGURE 16–2 **Texas Political Culture**

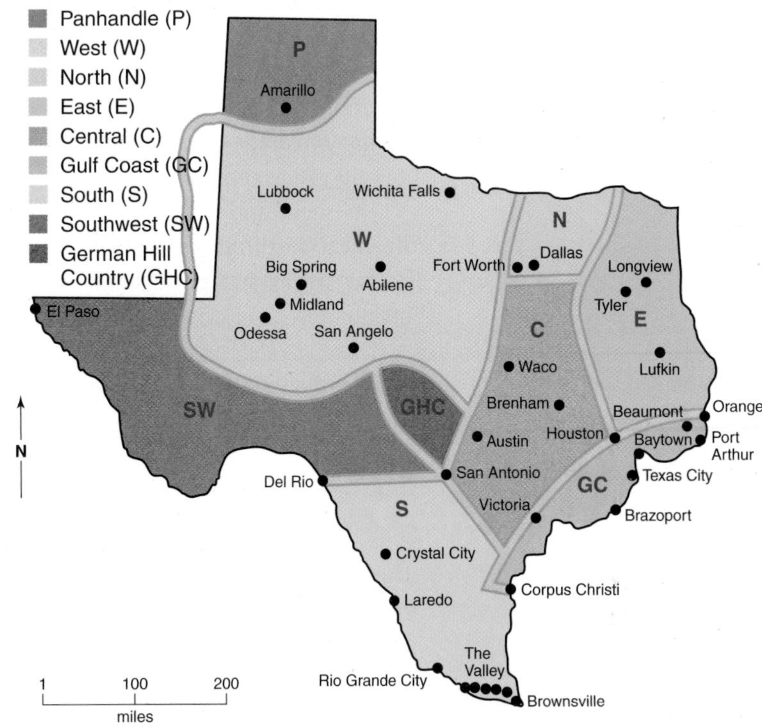

Source: Adapted from D. W. Meinig, *Imperial Texas: An Interpretive Essay in Cultural Geography* (Austin and London: University of Texas Press, 1969). Reproduced by permission of the publisher.

The Gulf Coast

Before 1900, Texas was an economic colony; it sold raw materials to the industrialized North and bought northern manufactured products. In 1901, however, an oil well named **Spindletop** was drilled near Beaumont, and the Texas economy began to change. Since Spindletop, the Gulf Coast has experienced almost continuous growth, especially during World War II, the Cold War defense buildup, and the various energy booms of the late 20th and early 21st centuries.

Spindletop
A major oil discovery in 1901 near Beaumont that began the industrialization of Texas.

In addition to being an industrial and petrochemical center, the Gulf Coast is one of the most important shipping centers in the nation. Spindletop was backed by out-of-state investors, largely from the Northeastern states, and its success stimulated increased out-of-state investment. Local wealth was also generated and largely reinvested in Texas to promote long-range development. Nevertheless, much of the economy is still supported by the sale of raw materials.

A Boom Based in Houston. Through boom and bust, the petrochemical industry, which is concentrated on the Gulf Coast, has experienced unprecedented growth, and a boomtown psychology developed. Rapid growth fed real estate development and speculation for the entire region. The Houston area especially flourished, and Harris County (Houston) grew to become the third most populous county in the United States.

did you know?

That Texas has the second largest population of any state in the country—an estimated 23,507,783 in 2006.

There continues to be extensive migration to Texas from the Frost Belt (Great Lake and mid-Atlantic states), which is still undergoing economic difficulty due to the metamorphosis of the U.S. economy from an industrial to a service base and the effects of the North American Free Trade Agreement (NAFTA). This migration includes large numbers of well-educated young executives and professionals, as well as skilled and unskilled laborers. The Gulf Coast economy also continues to attract heavy immigration from the Americas, Africa, and Asia.

The influx of job seekers from East Texas and other rural areas of the state tended to give the post-World War II Gulf Coast the flavor of rural Texas in an urban setting. The impact of this rural flavor has diminished and must now share its cultural influence with the many migrants and immigrants from outside the state. Houston's culture is now as international as those in Los Angeles or New York.

The social and economic elite is generally made up of second- and third-generation rich whose wealth comes from oil, insurance, construction, land development, or banking. The executives and professional support personnel of international corporations now headquartered in Houston contribute fresh blood to the elite pool.

There are still many large ranches and plantations in the Gulf Coast region. They are owned either by wealthy business executives who live in the large cities or by "old families." The collapse of the oil boom and drastic declines in the price of oil and other petroleum products in the 1980s and 1990s struck the Gulf Coast economy especially hard, because it relies heavily on the petrochemical industry. Conversely, rising prices in the 2000s have resulted in another oil-based boom for the region.

did you know?

That the Houston Astros baseball team changed the name of its stadium from Enron Field to Minute Maid Park after Enron's embarrassing collapse.

The implosion of the Houston-based Enron Corporation in the early 2000s affected financial markets and political attitudes nationwide, but it was especially damaging to Houston's economy, labor force, and national image. Enron was intertwined into the fabric of Houston's political, social, cultural, and financial existence to an extent rarely seen in corporate America. A dynamic corporate citizen, Enron made significant contributions to almost every aspect of Houston life. Its collapse left many Houstonians with dramatically decreased retirement incomes and investments. Despite the Enron collapse, the Gulf Coast continues to be a remarkably vibrant and energetic region. Houston, the worldwide oil and gas capital, boasts many corporate headquarters.

South Texas

The earliest area settled by Europeans, South Texas developed a **ranchero culture** based on livestock production that was similar to the feudal institutions in faraway Spain. **Creoles,** who descended from Spanish immigrants, were the economic, social, and political elite, while the first Texas cowboys, the **Mestizos,** and the Native Americans did the ranch work. Anglo-Americans first became culturally important in South Texas when they gained title to much of the real estate in the region following the Texas Revolution of 1836.

Modern South Texas still retains elements of the ranchero culture, including some of its feudal aspects. Large ranches, often owned by one family for several generations, are prevalent; however, wealthy and corporate ranchers from outside the area are becoming common.

Ranchero Culture
A quasi-feudal system—the owner or patron owed the workers protection and employment, while the workers owed the patron their loyalty and service. The rancher and workers all lived on the ranchero or ranch.

Creole
A descendant of European Spanish (or in some regions, French) immigrants to the Americas.

Mestizo
A person of both Spanish and Native American lineage.

The Valley (of the Rio Grande)
An area along the Texas side of the Rio Grande known for its production of citrus fruits.

Winter Garden
An area of South Texas known for its vegetable production.

South Texas Agriculture Today. Because of the semitropical South Texas climate, **The Valley (of the Rio Grande)** and the **Winter Garden** around Crystal City became major producers of vegetable and citrus products. They were developed by migrants from the northern United States in the 1920s and continue to be important agricultural assets.

The development of citrus and vegetable enterprises required intensive manual labor, which brought about increased immigration from Mexico. Modern South Texas Mexican Americans can usually trace their U.S. roots to the 1920s or later, because much of the

Hispanic population was driven south of the Rio Grande after the Texas Revolution. The La Raza Unida political movement of the 1960s began in Crystal City.[10]

The Mexican Connection. The border cities of South Texas are closely tied to the Mexican economy and tend to prosper along with Mexico. Although improving economically, the South Texas region remains one of the poorest in the United States.

South Texas also gains economically from ***maquiladoras,*** factories through which U.S. corporations pump needed revenue into Mexico's border regions by employing inexpensive Mexican labor for assembly and piecework. Unfortunately, lax environmental and safety standards result in high levels of air, ground, and water pollution in the general area. In fact, the Rio Grande is now one of America's most ecologically endangered rivers.

The **North American Free Trade Agreement (NAFTA),** which is still being implemented, has helped remove trade barriers among Canada, Mexico, and the United States, and is an economic benefit to South Texas because the region is a conduit for much of the U.S.'s commerce with Mexico.

Maquiladora
A factory in the Mexican border region that assembles goods imported duty-free into Mexico for export. In Spanish, it literally means "twin plant."

North American Free Trade Agreement (NAFTA)
A treaty among Canada, Mexico, and the United States that calls for the gradual removal of tariffs and other trade restrictions. NAFTA came into effect in 1994.

Bicultural
Encompassing two cultures.

Immigration and National Security. Economic poverty, political disorder, and suppression of civil liberties in Mexico, together with poverty, military conflicts, crime, and suppression of civil liberties in Central America, have driven hundreds of thousands of immigrants into the border states of the United States. This flow continues despite tightened security measures following September 11, 2001. South Texas remains a major staging ground for the migration of both legal and illegal immigrants into the interior of Texas and the rest of the United States.

South Texas is a "mingling pot" for Mexican-American and Anglo-American cultures. Roman Catholic Mexican Americans often retain strong links with Mexico through extended family and friends in Mexico and through Spanish-language newspapers. Many Mexican Americans continue to speak Spanish; in fact, Spanish is also the commercial and social language of choice for many of the region's Anglo-Americans.

Military expenditures by the U.S. government are also important to the economy of the region. A decision by the U.S. Navy to station a contingent of naval vessels in Ingleside has been an economic boost to the upper South Texas coast.

did you know?

That among the states in 2006, only Tennessee and Arkansas had a lower cost of living than Texas.

Southwest Texas

Southwest Texas exhibits many of the same **bicultural** characteristics as South Texas. Its large Mexican-American population often maintains strong ties with relatives and friends in Mexico. The Roman Catholic Church strongly influences social and cultural attitudes on both sides of the border.

Southwest Texas is a major commercial and social passageway between Mexico and the United States. El Paso, the "capital city" of Southwest Texas and the fifth largest city in Texas, is a military, manufacturing, and commercial center. El Paso's primary commercial partners are Mexico and New Mexico. The economy of the border cities of Southwest Texas, like that of South Texas, is closely linked to Mexico and has also benefited from the

---

10. *La Raza Unida* literally means "A United People." Officially named El Partido Nacional La Raza Unida, this party was organized in the late 1960s as a means of getting Mexican Americans to unite politically and to identify ethnically as one people. Its name is derived from *La Raza Cosmica (The Cosmic Race),* written by Mexican intellectual Jose Vasconcelos after the 1910 Mexican Revolution. Vasconcelos argued that the racially mixed Mestizos (whose racial heritage is both European and Native American) constituted a new race, and he urged them to unite regardless of national boundaries. For more information, see larazaunida.tripod.com.

economic opportunities brought about by NAFTA. The agricultural economy of much of the region depends on sheep, goat, and cattle production, although there is some irrigated row-crop agriculture. Most of the labor on ranches, as well as in manufacturing and commerce, is provided by Mexican Americans.

South and Southwest Texas together make up the area known as the Texas Border. A corresponding Mexico Border includes parts of the Mexican states of Chihuahua, Coahuila, Nuevo León, and Tamaulipas. It can be argued that the Texas Border and the Mexico Border are two parts of an economic, social, and cultural region with a substantial degree of communality that sets it off from the rest of the United States and Mexico. The region, which is expanding in size both to the north and to the south, has a **binational,** bicultural, and bilingual subculture in which **internationality** is commonplace, and the people, economies, and societies on both sides constantly interact.[11]

Binational
Belonging to two nations.

Internationality
Having family and/or business interests in two or more nations.

German Hill Country

The Hill Country was settled primarily by immigrants from Germany but also by immigrants who were Czech, Polish, and Norwegian. Although they mixed with Anglo-Americans, Central European culture and architecture was dominant well into the twentieth century. Skilled artisans were common in the towns; farms were usually moderate in size, self-sufficient, and family owned and operated. Most settlers were Lutheran or Roman Catholic, and these remain the most common religions for modern residents.

The German Hill Country is still a distinct cultural region. Although its inhabitants have become Americanized, they still cling to many of their Central European cultural traditions. Primarily a farming and ranching area, the Hill Country is socially and politically conservative and has long been a stronghold of the Texas Republican Party.

Migration into the region, primarily by Anglo-Americans and Mexican Americans, is increasing. The most significant encroachment into the Hill Country is residential growth from rapidly expanding urban areas, especially San Antonio and Austin. Resorts, country homes, and retirement villages for well-to-do urbanites from the Gulf Coast and the Dallas-Fort Worth area are also contributing to the cultural transformation of the German Hill Country.

did you know?

That Comfort, Texas, was settled by German "Freethinkers" seeking freedom *from* religion. They were both abolitionists and opponents of secession, and many were massacred by pro-Confederate raiders during the U.S. Civil War.

West Texas

The defeat of the Comanches in the 1870s opened West Texas to Anglo-American settlement. Migrating primarily from the southern United States, these settlers passed their social and political attitudes and Southern Protestant fundamentalism on to their descendants.

There are relatively few African Americans in modern West Texas, but Mexican Americans have begun to migrate into the region in significant numbers, primarily to the cities and the intensively farmed areas. West Texas is socially and politically conservative, and its religion is Bible Belt fundamentalism. West Texas voters traditionally supported conservative Democrats, but today favor the Republican Party. This is true of many conservative Texans throughout the state.

The southern portion of the area emphasizes sheep, goat, and cattle production. In fact, San Angelo advertises itself as the "Sheep and Wool Capital of the World." Southern West Texas, which is below the Cap Rock Escarpment, is the major oil-producing area of Texas. The cities of Snyder, Midland, and Odessa owe their existence almost entirely to oil and related industries.

---

11. John Sharp, Texas Comptroller of Public Accounts, "Bordering the Future: Challenge and Opportunity in the Texas Border Region," July 1998, p. 3; Jorge Bustamante, "A Conceptual and Operative Vision of the Population Problems on the Border," in *Demographic Dynamics on the U.S.-Mexico Border,* eds. John R. Weeks and Roberto Ham Chande (El Paso: Texas Western Press, 1992), cited in Sharp, "Bordering the Future."

Northern West Texas is part of the Great Plains and High Plains and is primarily agricultural, with cotton, grain, and feedlot cattle production predominating. In this part of semiarid West Texas, the outstanding agricultural production is due to extensive irrigation from the **Ogallala Aquifer.** The large amount of water used for irrigation is resulting in a gradual depletion of the Ogallala. This not only means higher costs to farmers but also serves as a warning signal for the economic future of the region.

The Panhandle

Railroads advancing from Kansas City through the Panhandle brought Midwestern farmers into this region. Wheat production was developed largely by these migrants from Kansas. Because the commercial and cultural focus of the region was, and still is, Kansas City rather than the developed areas of Texas, the Panhandle is basically Midwestern in both character and institutions. The social and political conservatism of the area is more Midwestern Republican than Southern Democrat, and its Protestant churches are Midwestern in philosophy and practice.

Economically, the Panhandle is similar to northern West Texas, with extensive irrigation of cotton and grains from the Ogallala Aquifer. Feedlots for livestock and livestock production are major economic enterprises. Effective conservation of the Ogallala Aquifer is critical to the economic future of both northern West Texas and the Panhandle.

did you know?

That the median age of Texans is 32.7 years and that only one state (Utah) has a younger population.

Ogallala Aquifer
A major underground reservoir and a source of water for irrigation and human consumption in northern West Texas and the Texas Panhandle, as well as other states.

La Réunion
A failed French socialist colony of the 1800s located within the city limits of modern Dallas. Its skilled and educated inhabitants benefited early Dallas.

Metroplex
The greater Dallas-Fort Worth metropolitan area.

North Texas

Located between East and West Texas, North Texas exhibits many characteristics of both regions. Early North Texas benefited from the failure of the French socialist colony of **La Réunion,** which included many highly trained professionals in medicine, education, music, and science. (La Réunion was located on the south bank of the Trinity River, across from modern downtown Dallas.) The colonists and their descendants helped give North Texas a cultural and commercial distinctiveness. North Texas today is dominated by the Dallas-Fort Worth **Metroplex.** Dallas is a banking and commercial center of national importance, and Fort Worth is the financial and commercial center of West Texas.

When railroads came into Texas from the North in the 1880s, Dallas became a rail center, and people and capital from the North stimulated its growth. Fort Worth became a regional capital that looked primarily to West Texas. The Swift and Armour meatpacking companies, which moved their plants to Fort Worth in 1901, became the first national firms to establish facilities close to Texas's natural resources. More businesses followed, and North Texas began its evolution from an economic colony to an industrially developed area.

North Texas experienced extraordinary population growth after World War II, with extensive migration from the rural areas of East, West, and Central Texas. The descendants of these migrants are now second- and third-generation urbanites and tend to display this in their attitudes and behavior. Recently, migration from other states, especially from the North, has been significant. Many international corporations have established headquarters in North Texas. Their executive and support staffs contribute to the region's diversity and cosmopolitan environment.

Although North Texas is more economically diverse than most other Texas regions, it relies heavily on the defense and aerospace industries. It also produces electronic equipment, computer products, plastics, and food products.

Central Texas

Central Texas is often called the "core area" of Texas. It is roughly triangular in shape, with its three corners being Houston, Dallas-Fort Worth, and San Antonio. The centerpiece of the region is Austin, one of the fastest-growing metropolitan areas in the nation. Already a center of government and education, the Austin metropolitan area has become the

Silicon Valley of high-tech industries in Texas. Although the worldwide downturn in the high-tech sector after 2000 dealt a serious blow to the area's economy, high-tech industries still make a major economic contribution.

Austin's rapid growth is a result of significant migration from the Northeastern United States and the West Coast, as well as from other regions in Texas. The influx of well-educated persons from outside Texas has added to the already substantial pool of accomplished Austinites, making the state's capital the intellectual and economic center of Central Texas. The cultural and economic traits of all the other Texas regions mingle here, with no single trait being dominant. Central Texas is a microcosm of Texas culture.

Cultural Diversity

Texas is one of the fastest-growing states in the nation. No longer predominantly rural and agrarian, Texas is becoming more culturally diverse than ever, as immigrants continue to find it a desirable place to call home. The 2000 census showed a significant trend toward greater ethnic diversity. Over the 10-year period from 1990 to 2000, the Anglo majority declined from 60.7 to 53.1 percent, while Hispanics increased from 25.5 to 32.0 percent, and the rapidly growing Other classification (primarily Asians, Pacific Islanders, Middle Easterners, and Native Americans) grew from 2.1 to 3.3 percent. The African American percentage of the total population also fell marginally, from 11.7 to 11.6 percent.

The Texas State Population Estimates and Projections Program is designed to aid government and corporate planners by developing estimates of Texas's future population growth. This group of researchers has proposed three possible population scenarios. One scenario assumes that net migration into Texas will be zero. We find this assumption to be unrealistic and therefore do not include that scenario here. Another scenario, in contrast, assumes that the relatively high immigration levels of the 1980s will continue. We have chosen, however, to use a third, middle-of-the-road scenario, which is what researchers recommend. This midrange scenario assumes a moderate degree of immigration. All scenarios show Anglo Texans losing their numerical majority by 2010.

The pie charts in Figure 16–3 illustrate the midrange scenario. The scenario predicts a Texas population of slightly more than 35 million by 2040, with a Hispanic plurality by 2025 and a Hispanic majority by 2035. A high-immigration scenario, in contrast, projects

FIGURE 16–3 Texas Population, Midrange Scenario

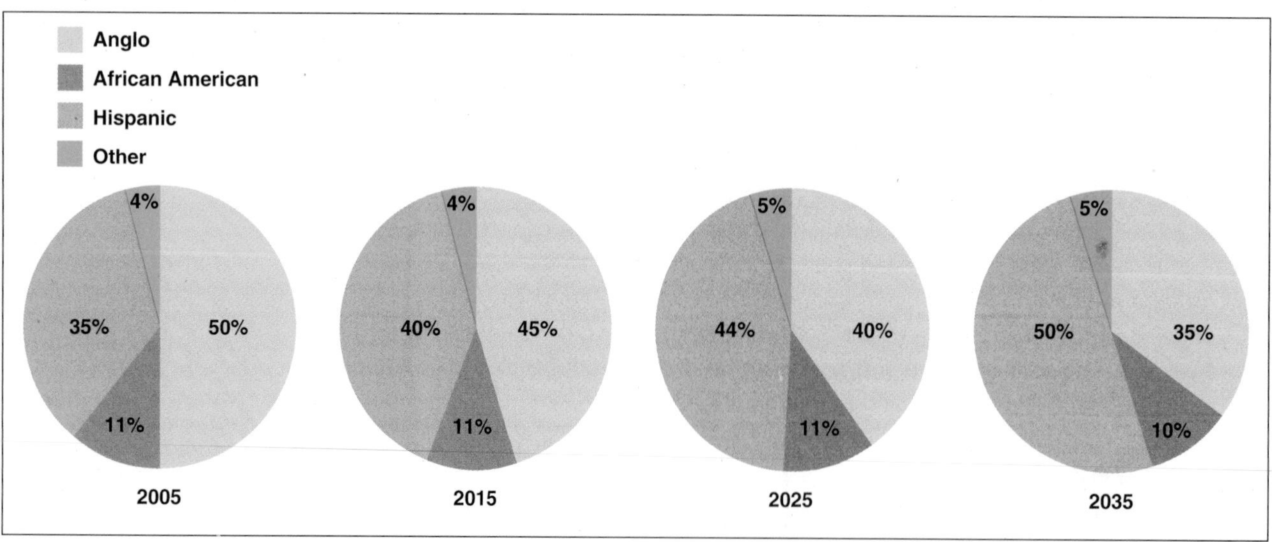

Source: Data from Population Estimates and Projections Program, "Projections of Texas and Counties in Texas by Age, Sex, and Race/Ethnicity for 1990–2040" (San Antonio: Texas State Data Center, Office of the State Demographer, 2004). Methodology and data are online at http://txsdc.utsa.edu/tpepp/2006projections/. Click on "Population Projections for the State of Texas."

FIGURE 16–4 Net Family Income in Texas

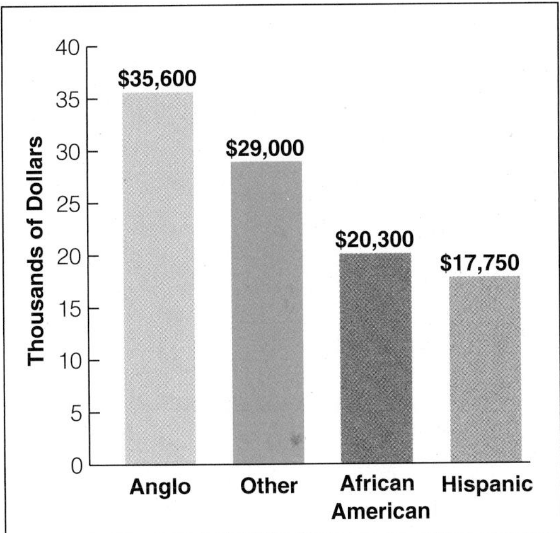

Source: The Henry J. Kaiser Family Foundation, "State Health Facts Online," www.statehealthfacts.kff.org.

FIGURE 16–5 Percentage of Persons in Poverty in Texas

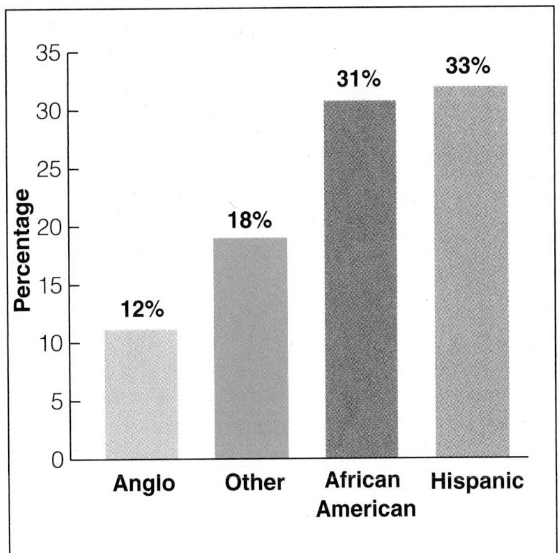

Source: The Henry J. Kaiser Family Foundation, "State Health Facts Online," www.statehealthfacts.kff.org.

a Texas population of more than 50 million by 2040. Hispanics achieve plurality status by 2015 and majority status by 2030. Furthermore, the Other classification surpasses African Americans and becomes the third largest group by 2040.

Clearly, Texans are becoming more diverse and now have the opportunity to continue to build on their already rich cultural pluralism. Increasing diversity could also have a significant impact on the political culture of Texas, because the interests of more groups would have to be seriously considered as public policy is formulated and implemented.

A downside of Texas diversity is an unequal distribution of wealth and access to medical care. As shown in Figures 16–4, 16–5, and 16–6, Hispanic Americans, African Americans, and Others are more likely to live in poverty, have significantly lower family income, and have lower levels of health insurance than the more favored Anglo-Americans.

Voter participation in Texas is historically low, even by U.S. standards. Social scientists argue that this is a result of political conditioning as well as social and economic reality. And Latino participation is low even by Texas standards, but the 2008 primary opened a floodgate of participation among all elements of Texas culture. What happened? Was it the birth of Texas political activism, or was it simply that at last Texans were presented with exciting candidates? Even the historically low voter turnout of Hispanics was reversed during the 2008 primary and election. Is this sleeping political giant really awake, or was this level of political participation simply an anomaly? What would be the impact of substantial Mexican-American political participation in the Texas political system?

FIGURE 16–6 Health Insurance Status of Persons Under the Age of 65 in Texas

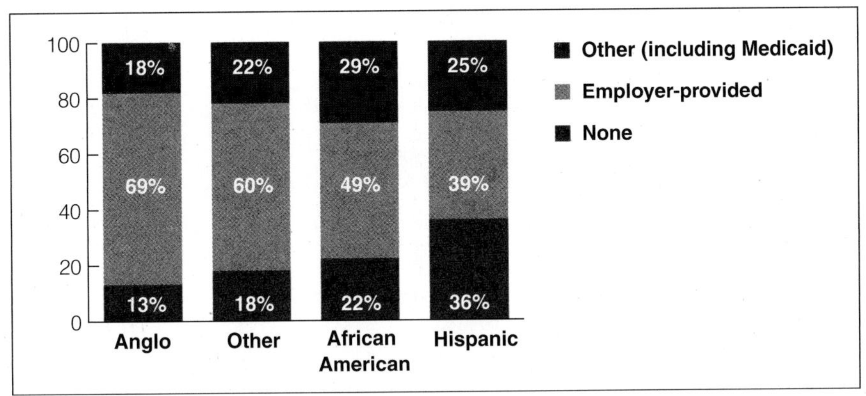

Source: The Henry J. Kaiser Family Foundation, "State Health Facts Online," www.statehealthfacts.kff.org.

WHY SHOULD YOU CARE ABOUT... TEXAS HISTORY AND CULTURE?

The United States is one of the most diverse nations in the world, and Texas is one of the most diverse states. It is made up of a rich variety of nationalities, ethnic groups, and religions that, when joined together, become the American mosaic. This does not mean that we are melted into one and have lost our individual distinctiveness. America is a mixing pot of all the races and nationalities of the world—different but united politically as one. Our individual uniqueness makes us different as a people; our unity in diversity makes us different as a nation.

TEXAS HISTORY AND YOUR LIFE

Our individual cultural and ethnic histories are, in a sense, who we are. Gaining knowledge of this history adds to your understanding of your own uniqueness. What you learn about your cultural and ethnic history will become a part of your understanding of yourself and can be a priceless gift to pass on to your children and to their children.

Learning to understand and appreciate the cultural and ethnic histories of others as well can only contribute to our understanding and appreciation of who we all are, both as individuals and as Americans. We can find both our national strength and the danger of internal conflicts among us in our individual differences. Collectively, our choice will determine which of these possibilities will predominate.

HOW CAN YOU MAKE A DIFFERENCE

Talk to your grandparents, parents, and uncles and aunts to learn what they know about your culture and family history. Record as much oral history as you can about their personal lives, experiences, and political recollections, as well as family myths and traditions. You may find this information priceless as you someday talk to your own children and grandchildren about their culture. Broaden your cultural and political experiences. Participate in activities and organizations of ethnic, religious, and ideological groups that are different from your own. This will help you better understand and appreciate the rich diversity of modern American life.

questions for discussion and analysis

1. How has Texas's history shaped its distinctive social, economic, and political characteristics?
2. Does your cultural region reflect the conclusions of Meinig and Elazar?
3. What social changes are most likely to dominate Texas's political future?

key terms

annexation 546
antitrust legislation 548
bicultural 561
binational 562
Black Codes 547
Creole 560
down-ticket 556
internationality 562
Ku Klux Klan (KKK) 550
La Raza Unida 556
La Réunion 563
maquiladora 561
Mestizo 560
Metroplex 563
North American Free Trade Agreement (NAFTA) 561
Ogallala Aquifer 563
Progressive Movement 549
Prohibition 549
ranchero culture 560
secession 547
Shivercrat 554
Spindletop 559
tenant farmer 549
tidelands 553
The Valley (of the Rio Grande) 560
Winter Garden 560

chapter summary

1. Originally part of Mexico, Texas was largely settled from the American South. Texas declared its independence from Mexico in 1836 and joined the United States in 1845. Early politics revolved around the slavery issue and the possibility of secession from the Union, which was strongly opposed by Sam Houston, one of the founders of the Texas Republic and the hero of the battle of San Jacinto (1836). After the election of Abraham Lincoln as U.S. president, Texas left the Union and joined the Confederacy. The collapse of the Confederacy meant anarchy until Union troops occupied Texas in June 1865.

2. After a period of military occupation, Radical Republican E. J. Davis (1870–1873) became governor in an election in which African Americans could vote, but many former Confederates could not. The Davis administration was enormously unpopular with the white majority in Texas, and after the former Confederates regained the franchise, Davis was swept from office. The Democratic Party was to control Texas politics for more than 100 years.

3. While conservatives normally dominated the Democratic Party, Texas experienced a degree of progressive reform with the election of several progressive governors between 1890 and 1939, including James Hogg (1891–1895) and both "Farmer Jim" and "Ma" Ferguson (1915–1917, 1925–1927, and 1933–1935). Another colorful governor was radio announcer W. "Pappy" Lee O'Daniel, a popular figure who nonetheless had little legislative success.

4. A key figure in the era following World War II (1939–1945) was governor Allan Shivers (1949–1957). A conservative Democrat, Shivers advocated voting for Republican presidents and conservative Democrats for all other offices. In 1960, Lyndon B. Johnson, U.S. senator from Texas and the Senate majority leader, became vice president under John F. Kennedy. In a special election in 1961, Republican John Tower filled Johnson's seat. Tower was the first Republican since Reconstruction to be elected to an important position in Texas, but he would not be the last. In 1963, following Kennedy's assassination, Johnson became U.S. president.

5. Civil rights have always been an issue, and the dominant Anglo-Americans thought the primary purpose for African Americans and Mexican Americans to be in Texas was to be sources of cheap labor. Modern Texans can take no pride in the historical treatment of either of these groups who were undereducated, exploited for their labor, and lived under a state-enforced caste system. The enduring consequences of discrimination are still with us, as illustrated by lower levels of health care, education, and income.

6. The election of Republican William Clements as governor in 1979 was a sign of the growing importance of the Republican Party. By 1994, Texas was clearly a two-party state. By 2002, the Republicans were in complete control of all levels of state government, including both chambers of the legislature. Texas seemed headed toward a one-party system again, but under a different party. In 2003, the Republicans consolidated their power by redistricting the U.S. House seats. As a result, in 2004 they gained control of the Texas delegation to the U.S. House.

7. Texas can be divided into a series of cultural regions with differing characteristics and traditions. We identify the following regions: (1) East Texas, (2) the Gulf Coast, (3) South Texas, (4) Southwest Texas, (5) the German Hill Country, (6) West Texas, (7) the Panhandle, (8) North Texas, and (9) Central Texas.

8. Projections of population growth and immigration predict a gradual shift in Texas's population away from an Anglo-American majority toward a Hispanic-American majority. Increased political clout can come with increased population, and Hispanic Americans could begin to challenge the political and economic dominance of Anglo-Americans. Regardless of the political outcome of population shifts, Texas is becoming more culturally diverse and now has an opportunity to build on its already rich cultural pluralism.

selected print & media resources

SUGGESTED READINGS

Brammer, Billy Lee. *The Gay Place.* Austin: University of Texas Press, 1995. This work is really three interlocking novels that use Texas politics as the setting and Texas politicians as the primary characters.

Campbell, Randolph B. *Gone to Texas: A History of the Lone Star State.* New York: Oxford University Press, 2003. A leading Texas historian, Campbell sets early Texas history firmly within the history of Mexico and also keeps African Americans, both slave and free, at the center of his story. Much of the book concerns the state's lively political history. Campbell exhibits considerable skepticism about claims that Texas is unique among the states.

Davidson, Chandler. *Race and Class in Texas Politics.* Princeton, NJ: Princeton University Press, 1992. The author examines the forces that shape Texas politics. The book is recommended by *The American Political Science Review.*

Farmer, James. *Lay Bare the Heart.* Fort Worth: Texas Christian University Press, 2005. James Farmer describes the battles, heroes, and knaves associated with the civil rights movement in the 1950s and 1960s.

Lind, Michael. *Made in Texas: George W. Bush and the Southern Takeover of American Politics.* New York: Basic Books, 2003. This book looks at how the political tradition of Texas is shaping U.S. and world politics.

Rogers, Mary Beth (with an introduction by Bill Moyers). *Cold Anger: A Story of Faith and Power Politics.* Denton: University of North Texas Press, 1990. Rogers writes the story of Ernesto Cortes, who employs religion and other tools to develop grassroots Mexican-American movements in South Texas.

Shabazz, Amilcar. *Advancing Democracy: African Americans and the Struggle for Access and Equity in Higher Education in Texas.* Chapel Hill: University of North Carolina Press, 2004. Shabazz chronicles the expansion of higher-education opportunities for African Americans.

Soltero, Carlos R. *Latinos and American Law: Landmark Supreme Court Cases.* Austin: University of Texas Press, 2006. This work documents major civil rights cases expanding the rights of Latinos.

MEDIA RESOURCES

The American Experience: Remember the Alamo—This PBS program is available in both Spanish and English versions. The documentary explores the life of prominent Mexican Texan José Antonio Navarro and the Tejanos (Mexican Texans) who fought alongside Anglo Texans for Texas independence.

Justice for My People: The Dr. Hector P. Garcia Story—This KEDT-TV public television production chronicles the rise of the Mexican-American civil rights movement from the 1920s to the 1980s, as lived by Dr. Hector Garcia.

Lone Star—Producer/director John Sayles explores the cultural and social interaction among Mexicans, Mexican Americans, African Americans, and Anglo-Americans along the Texas-Mexico border.

Mexican American Legislative Caucus: The Texas Struggle for Equality and Opportunity—A product of a team at Texas State University–San Marcos, this documentary was first aired by KLRN, a PBS station. Through interviews with several retired and present-day Tejano legislators, the story of the Caucus and its increasing influence on state affairs unfolds from its founding in the early 1970s to the present. It also traces the role of Tejanos from Texas independence through the period of political exclusion to the modern struggle for full citizenship.

Traffic—Director Steven Soderbergh examines the impact of the "war against drugs" on the people, institutions, and social structures along the Mexican border.

Two Towns of Jasper—Another PBS production from 2002, this program explores the separate reactions and viewpoints of the white and black communities of Jasper, Texas, following the murder of James Byrd, who was dragged to his death while chained to a pickup truck by three white men.

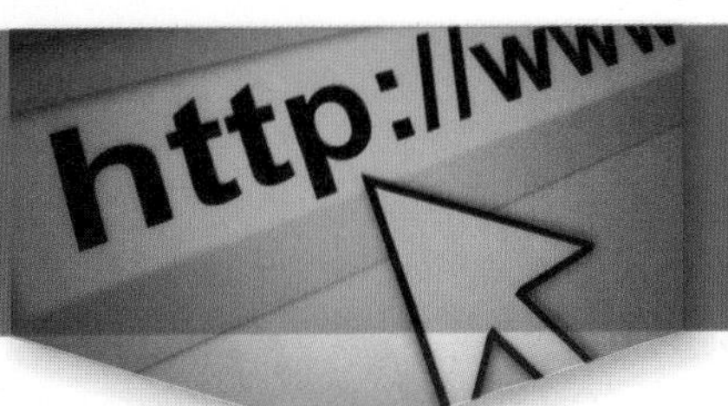

e-mocracy

CYBERPOLITICS IN TEXAS

Welcome to cyberpolitics in Texas. The rapid development of the World Wide Web on the Internet has created unprecedented opportunities for research, communication, and participation in Texas politics. Today, students can easily communicate with the authors of their textbooks, government leaders, and fellow students all across Texas.

To research the Texas cultural regions, we suggest you begin with the home page of the monthly magazine that presents Texas to Texans and to the rest of the country, *Texas Monthly.* Two recommended features are "Links across Texas," which includes a section on government and politics, and the "Texpertise" section, which answers a variety of questions about Texas. The site also lists more than 1,600 links, including a government and politics section and a "Texas Talks" section, which provides the opportunity to ask questions of famous Texans and of editors and writers at the magazine.

LOGGING ON

Texas Monthly can be found online at:
www.texasmonthly.com

Historical maps of interest can be found at the University of Texas Library Online. They include "State of Origin of the Old Stock Anglo-American Population;" "Black Slaves as a Percentage of Total Population, 1840 and 1860"; "German Element, 1850"; "Spanish and French Surnames, 1850"; and the "Vote on Secession, 1861." Go to:
www.lib.utexas.edu/maps/historical/history_texas.html

Look at the state of Texas home page for information on Texas history, early native populations, historical events and dates, historic sites, and population information, projections, and demographics at:
www.state.tx.us

The *New Handbook of Texas* is a great source for information on Texas history, culture, and geography. A joint project of the Texas State Historical Association and the University of Texas at Austin, it is an encyclopedia of all things Texan. It can be found online at:
www.tsha.utexas.edu/handbook/online

Factual information and statistics can be found in the *Texas Fact Book 2008,* written by Bob Bullock of the Texas State History Museum for the Legislative Budget Board. Go to:
www.lbb.state.tx.us/Fact_Book/Texas_Factbook_2008.pdf

Lone Star Junction is a nonprofit organization chartered by the state of Texas. It provides an online resource about Texas and its early history at:
www.lsjunction.com

ONLINE REVIEW

At **www.cengage.com/politicalscience/schmidt/agandpttexas14e**, you will find a Tutorial Quiz for this chapter, providing questions on the chapter contents, including the features. You'll gain access to other helpful study tools, including the book's glossary and flashcards, crossword puzzles, and Web links, as well as "Which Side Are You On?" and "Politics and . . ." features written by the authors of the book.

chapter 17

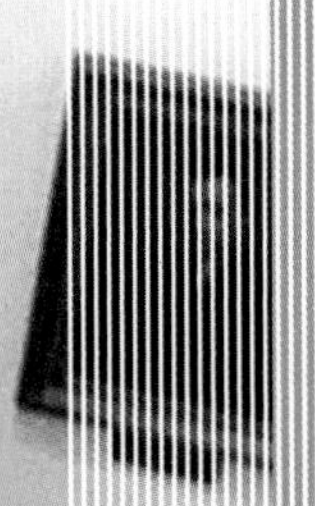

The Texas Constitution

chapter contents

<< The Texas seal on the floor of the capitol building. (AP Photo)

Constitutions establish major governing institutions, assign them power, and place both implicit and explicit limits on the power that has been assigned. And, because Americans respect constitutions, they promote *legitimacy,* a concept we discussed in Chapter 1 of this text. Texans' reactions to Reconstruction (1864–1877) led to the adoption of a constitution designed to curb government power. The legislature is hampered by numerous limitations on salary, sessions, and activities; power in the executive branch is fragmented; appeals courts are divided; and judges are elected rather than appointed. A rigid structure and ceilings on debt and tax restrictions limit local government, especially county government.

Therefore, it is difficult for the Texas state government to develop new programs without first amending the constitution. Amendments have been adopted for such seemingly minor purposes as abolishing the office of county surveyor in Jackson County and clearing some land titles in Fort Bend County. The division of executive power, which makes it difficult for the governor or any other official to become an effective leader, also obstructs problem solving. Although Texas has had some powerful governors, such as Allan Shivers, John Connally, and George W. Bush, they were effective despite the constitution, not because of it.

The Texas Constitution in History

Like all other state constitutions, the Texas Constitution reflects the interests and concerns of those who wrote and amended it. Some of its history parallels the histories of other state constitutions, but much of it is unique to Texas.

Foreclosure
The legal process by which a lender takes possession of a mortgaged property when the borrower defaults on the loan.

Community Property
Any property that a married couple has acquired during their marriage. In certain states, it is divided equally between them in the event of a divorce.

The First Texas Constitutions

The first constitution of Texas was written in 1836 after Texas had gained its independence from Mexico and become an independent republic. The constitutional convention established a *unitary,* as opposed to a *federal,* government (see Chapter 3). Several other provisions were direct reactions to policies experienced under the government of Mexico. The convention provided a constitution with strict separation of church and state, forbidding clergy of any faith from holding office. It reversed the antislavery policies of the old Mexican government by forbidding masters from freeing their slaves without consent of the Republic's congress. Remembering the abuses of Mexican president Santa Anna, Texans limited the terms of their presidents to three years and prohibited them from serving consecutive terms.

Aside from these provisions, the Texas Constitution was an almost word-for-word copy of the U.S. Constitution and those of several Southern states. It was clearly the product of the political culture from which the early Texans came—the Anglo-American traditions of Southern planters.

The Bob Bullock History Museum in downtown Austin tells the story of Texas with three floors of interactive exhibits and an IMAX theater, featuring Texas: *The Big Picture.* How has Texas history influenced the state's constitution? (Bob Daemmrich/ Image Works)

The Constitution of 1845. The constitution of 1845 was written in preparation for Texas's admission into the United States. Although similar to other Southern state constitutions, it also incorporated certain elements of Spanish political culture (some of which would later be adopted by other states). The constitution of 1845 exempted homesteads from **foreclosure,** protected a wife's property rights, and provided for **community property,** meaning that a husband and wife would equally own property acquired during their marriage. It also required a two-thirds vote in the Texas house to establish any corporation and made bank corporations

POLITICS AND... the Texas judicial system

DEFENDING THE INNOCENT

While two-thirds of Americans feel that the justice system is fair,[a] nearly half of the U.S. population believes the judicial system is unfair to the poor and to members of minority groups.[b] Whether deserved or not, the Texas judicial system is perceived as being particularly harsh toward indigent and minority defendants accused of crimes. For years, the judicial system has relied on faulty evidence to convict individuals of crimes. Because the judicial system relies on jailhouse snitches, eyewitness misidentification, inadequate scientific techniques, and overworked lawyers, many innocent people have been convicted of crimes they did not commit.[c]

In Texas, Jeff Blackburn, an Amarillo lawyer, and a team of university students, lawyers, and friends have reviewed the cases of hundreds of individuals convicted of crimes where faulty evidence or poor procedures may have been used. In one particular example from 1999, nearly half the African American population in the town of Tulia was arrested and charged with drug-related crimes on the testimony of one witness—Tom Coleman.[d] Jeff Blackburn defended many of these individuals, working with other lawyers to overturn their convictions. The tragedy of the Tulia cases eventually led to the enactment of legislation in 2001 that would outlaw the use of uncorroborated testimony from confidential informants. The story also gained Hollywood's attention, and plans for a movie are under way.

a. Heather Mason Kiefer, "Public on Justice System: Fair, But Still Too Soft," Gallup, February 3, 2004, www.gallup.com.
b. Linda Greenhouse, "47% in Poll View Legal System as Unfair to Poor and Minorities," *New York Times,* February 24, 1999, query.nytimes.com.
c. There have been 220 post-conviction DNA exonerations in United States history. Innocent Project Case Profiles, www.innocenceproject.org/know/.
d. Elizabeth Amon, "Jeff Blackburn: Tulia Defender," *National Law Journal,* January 13, 2003, www.truthinjustice.org/blackburn.htm.

Students from Texas Tech, Texas Wesleyan, South Texas College of Law, the University of Saint Thomas, and the University of Texas at Arlington have volunteered their time to investigate the cases of individuals convicted under questionable circumstances. These university students perform a significant amount of work for the newly formed Innocence Project of Texas, of which Jeff Blackburn is the Chief Counsel.

University professors are using their participation in the Innocence Project of Texas as a learning tool that provides university students real world experience that has a meaningful impact in the lives of others. Professor and attorney Nicole Casarez, who teaches a course on investigative journalism at the University of Saint Thomas, states, "I felt the Innocence Project was an excellent way to teach students about investigative reporting. It involves interviewing witnesses, searching public records, reviewing case files, public information requests, and reading court transcripts. These are all elements of investigative reporting."[e]

Jeff Blackburn, the Innocence Project of Texas, and their teams of lawyers and university students are working to protect the freedom of Texas's poor population, helping to ensure the fairness of the state's judicial system. The success of the Innocence Project of Texas depends in large part on the contributions of university students who contribute their time to review the evidence in court cases.

What do you think of the Innocence Project? Is the type of research it involves beyond your capabilities, or is this something you could do?

e. University of Saint Thomas, "Investigative Journalism: The UST Innocence Project," accessed August 6, 2008, at www.stthom.edu.

illegal altogether. The governor served a two-year term, and legislative sessions were biennial.

The Constitution of 1861. The constitution of 1861 was basically the same as that of 1845, except for changes required by the fact that Texas had become one of the Confederate states at war with the Union. It increased the debt ceiling and prohibited the emancipation of slaves.

Constitutions After the Civil War

Following the Civil War, the U.S. Army occupied Texas, as well as other Confederate states. Texans wrote the constitution of 1866, which they believed would permit the restoration of civilian government under President Andrew Johnson's mild Reconstruction program. The new constitution nullified secession, abolished slavery, and renounced Confederate war debts. Still, it did not fully satisfy the few requirements set down by President Johnson for the following reasons:

- It did not declare that secession was unconstitutional.
- It failed to ratify the Thirteenth Amendment (abolishing slavery).
- It did not adequately establish the civil status and rights of African Americans.

Freedmen's Bureau
The Bureau of Refugees, Freedmen and Abandoned Lands, a federal bureau established in 1865 to aid refugees of the Civil War (including former slaves) and to administer confiscated property. Among other tasks, it sought to provide education to the former slaves. It was disbanded in 1872.

Enabling Act
Legislation that confers on appropriate officials the power to implement or enforce the law.

Ironclad Oath
An oath of loyalty to the union required of former Confederates in order to participate in politics.

Texans, however, were correct in assuming that Johnson would accept it. Under its terms, a civilian government was elected and operated for several months despite some interference from the **Freedmen's Bureau** of the national government, which had responsibility for the former slaves.

Johnson's lenient policies were unacceptable to the Republican-controlled U.S. Congress, which took control of Reconstruction in 1867. Under the authority of the Reconstruction Act, the U.S. military purged the civilian-elected authorities and imposed military rule. Texas would be under military occupation until the Reconstruction era ended.

The Constitution of 1869. Under Congressional Reconstruction, top former Confederates and persons who refused to swear an oath of loyalty to the Union were temporarily barred from participation in politics. While those barred made up only about 10 percent of the population, they included almost the entire former leadership of Texas politics and society. The remaining voters, including newly enfranchised African Americans, elected 81 whites and nine blacks to the constitutional convention in 1868. The convention produced a document that centralized state power in the hands of the governor, lengthened the chief executive's term to four years, and allowed the governor to appoint all major state officers, including judges. It provided for annual legislative sessions; weakened local government, which was controlled by traditional elites; and centralized the public school system. The convention in 1868 reflected little of the fear of centralized government power that was later to become the hallmark of Texas government. The constitution it proposed was ratified in 1869.

In this 1868 drawing, a man representing the Freedman's Bureau stands between armed whites and African Americans. (Library of Congress Prints & Photographs Division, Washington, D.C.)

Reconstruction under the Constitution of 1869. The constitution of 1869 served as the instrument of government for an era that white Texans would regard as the most abusive in the state's history. An **enabling act** allowed Republican Governor E. J. Davis to fill about 8,500 jobs in state government that had been left vacant by enforcement of the **ironclad oath.** The legislature authorized a state police force that had the authority to operate anywhere in the state, overruling local law enforcement officials. The state police were hated by the white majority, because blacks made up a sizable portion of the force and because the force was used to put down violent opposition to Reconstruction. In four counties where law and order broke down, Governor Davis declared martial law and sent in the state police to regain state control. Davis also took control of voter registration, intimidated unsupportive newspapers, and arrested several political opponents.

The economic policies of the Davis administration were also unlike anything that had ever been seen in Texas. Both taxes and spending increased dramatically, in part to fund railroads and public schools. High taxes led to widespread tax evasion, and lavish government spending led to a large state debt. Subsidies to railroad companies, along with other legislation that financially benefited Republican-oriented interests, helped inspire the widespread view that the Davis administration was the most corrupt in Texas history. In 1874, Democrat Richard Coke was elected governor in a landslide. The Republican-dominated state supreme court, however, invalidated the election. Only when President Ulysses S. Grant refused to send federal troops to thwart the Democratic victory did Davis finally vacate his office.

The poster shows delegates to the Texas constitutional convention of 1875. The convention severely limited the powers of the state government. Why might Texans traditionally have been so resistant to strong government—an attitude that dates back to well before the Civil War? (Courtesy of Prints and Photographs Collection, The Center for American History, The University of Texas at Austin, CN 01063)

The Constitution of 1876

Most Texans were determined to strip power away from state government by writing a new constitution. The Texas Grange (whose members were called Grangers) organized in 1873. Campaigning on a platform of "retrenchment and reform," it managed to elect at least 40 of its members to the constitutional convention of 1875. Like most of the 90 delegates, they were Democrats who were determined to strike at the heart of big government.

Retrenchment. To reduce expenses, the convention did not publish a journal, reflecting the frugal tone of the final constitution. When the convention ended, some of the funds appropriated for its expenses remained unspent. The constitution created by the convention cut salaries for governing officials, placed strict limits on property taxes, and restricted state borrowing. The new regime was also miserly with the power it granted to government officials. Most of the governor's powers were stripped, the term of office was reduced from four to two years, and the salary was cut. In addition, the new constitution required that the attorney general and state judges be elected rather than appointed by the governor.

Restrictions on the Legislature. The legislature did not escape the convention's pruning. Regular legislative sessions were to be held only once every two years, and legislators were encouraged to limit the length of the sessions. Legislative procedure was detailed in the constitution of 1876, with severe restrictions placed on the kinds of policies the legislature might enact. In fact, several public policies were written directly into the Texas Constitution. Local government was strengthened, and counties were given many of the administrative and judicial functions of the state.

did you know?

That the Texas Supreme Court invalidated the 1874 election based on the placement of a semicolon in the state constitution.

Ratification. The convention had largely reacted to the abuse of state power by attempting to abolish it. Despite opposition from blacks, Republicans, most cities, and railroad interests, voters ratified the constitution in 1876, and it remains in effect today.

The Texas Constitution Today

There is no ideal constitution that would serve well in each of the diverse fifty states. Nor is it possible to write a state constitution that could permanently meet the dynamically changing needs and concerns of the state's citizens. Further, because government is much more than its constitution, honest and effective government must be commanded by the political environment—by leaders, citizens, parties, and interest groups. Constitutions alone cannot guarantee good government. Scoundrels will be corrupt and unconcerned citizens will be apathetic under even the best constitution.

This pragmatic view of the role of state constitutions, however, should not lead to the conclusion that these documents are only incidental to good government. A workable constitution is necessary for effective government even if it is not sufficient to guarantee it. Low salaries may discourage independent, high-caliber leaders from seeking office. Constitutional restrictions may make it virtually impossible for government to meet the changing needs of its citizens. Institutions may be set up so that they will operate inefficiently and irresponsibly.

The events preceding the adoption of the current Texas Constitution in 1876 did not provide the background for developing a constitution capable of serving well under the pressures and changes that would take place in the century to follow. The decade of the 1870s was an era of paranoia and reaction, and the constitution it produced was directed more toward solving the problems arising from Reconstruction than toward meeting the challenges of generations to follow. It was literally a reactionary document.

Separation of Powers

Like the Bill of Rights, Article 2 of the Texas Constitution limits government. To prevent the concentration of power in the hands of any single institution, the national government and all states have provided for a *separation of powers* among three branches: legislative, executive, and judicial branches (see Chapter 2).

Because any of these three branches can still potentially abuse whatever powers they have been given, the Texas Constitution also follows American tradition in subsequent constitutional articles—it sets up a system of *checks and balances.* So that each branch of government can check the others, functions normally assigned to one branch of government are given to another. For example, the veto power that deals with lawmaking (a legislative function) is given to the governor (an executive). Impeachment and conviction, which deal with determining guilt (a judicial function), are given to the legislature. The state senate (a chamber of the legislature) confirms appointments made by the governor in the executive branch.

Despite the separation of powers, the checks-and-balances system requires that each branch have the opportunity to influence the others. The three branches specialize in separate functions, but they share some powers as well.

did you know?

That although many of the framers of the constitution of 1876 opposed the idea of public education, they were persuaded to allow it only if segregated schools were established by local governments.

Legislative Branch

The legislative article (Article 3) is by far the longest in the Texas Constitution. It assigns legislative power to a bicameral (two-chamber) legislature consisting of the 31-member senate and the 150-member house of representatives. Each senator is elected for a four-year term from a single-member district. Representatives are elected to two-year terms, also from single-member districts.

The Texas constitutional provisions concerning bicameralism, number of members of the legislature, and length of terms are typical of state constitutions (see Table 17–1). Minimum qualifications for Texas senators, however, are somewhat more restrictive than average.

Salaries of Legislators. The Texas Constitution sets annual salaries at $7,200, unless the Texas Ethics Commission recommends an increase and voters approve it. The commission has made no such recommendation but has exercised its power to increase the *per diem* allowance (for daily expenses) to $139 while the legislature is in session. No other large state sets legislative salaries so low. Table 17–2 lists legislative salaries in the 50 states, along with the frequency of legislative sessions.

Regular Session
A legislative session scheduled by the constitution. Texas regular sessions are biennial (once every two years) rather than annual as in most states and in Congress.

Special Session
Any legislative session that is not specifically scheduled by the constitution or by statute. In some states, the legislature may call itself into special session, but in Texas only the governor may call the legislature into special session.

Limited Sessions. Texas is one of very few states that have a constitution restricting their legislatures to biennial **regular sessions.** Because sessions are also limited to 140 days, important legislation may receive inadequate consideration, and many bills are ignored altogether. The 2007 legislature introduced 10,990 bills, concurrent resolutions, and joint resolutions (78 per calendar day). Of these, it passed 5,899 (54 percent).

Unlike legislatures in most states, the Texas legislature may not call itself into **special sessions** or determine the issues to be decided in such sessions. Special sessions are convened by the governor to consider only the legislative matters he or she presents, and the length of a special session is limited to 30 days. Special sessions are more restricted than in any other state. The legislature has also adopted laws to permit it to call itself into special session for the sole purpose of impeachment.

TABLE 17–1 Requirements for Election to Various Legislatures

Constitutional and Statutory Provisions for Legislative Bodies	Texas Legislature	U.S. Congress	The 50 State Legislatures
Bicameral	Yes	Yes	Only Nebraska's legislature is unicameral.
Number of members			
Senate	31	2 per state	39.4 is average.
House	150	435 by statute	108.2 is average.
Term			
Senate	4 years; no limit on number of terms	6 years; no limit on number of terms	4 years in 38 states; 2 in the remainder. Fifteen states impose term limits.
House	2 years; no limit on number of terms	2 years; no limit on number of terms	2 years in all but 5 states, which have extended it to 4 years. Fifteen states impose term limits.
Qualifications			
Senate			
Age	26 years	30 years	Only 6 states set higher age requirements than Texas.
Residence in state	5 years	Citizen 9 years and current resident of state	Three years or less in 42 states; 2 states require more than 5 years.
Residence in district	1 year	—	Three states require more than 1 year.
House			
Age	21 years	25 years	Only 6 states set higher age requirements than Texas, while 17 states allow 18-year-olds to serve.
Residence in state	2 years	Citizen 7 years and current resident of state	Only 11 states require more than 2 years.
Residence in district	1 year	None	Only 2 states require more than 1 year.

Source: Council of State Governments, *Book of the States 2007.*

TABLE 17–2 State Legislative Sessions and Annual Salaries

State	Frequency of Regular Session	Salary*
Alabama	Annual**	$10(d)†
Alaska	Annual	24,012†
Arizona	Annual	24,000†
Arkansas	Biennial	14,765†
California	Annual	113,098†
Colorado	Annual	30,000†
Connecticut	Annual	28,000
Delaware	Annual	42,000
Florida	Annual	30,996†
Georgia	Annual	17,342†
Hawaii	Annual	35,900†
Idaho	Annual	16,116†
Illinois	Annual	57,619†
Indiana	Annual	11,600†
Iowa	Annual	25,000†
Kansas	Annual	84.80(d)†
Kentucky	Annual	180.54(d)†
Louisiana	Annual	16,800†
Maine	Annual	12,713†
Maryland	Annual	43,500†
Massachusetts	Annual	58,237†
Michigan	Annual	79,650†
Minnesota	Annual	31,141†
Mississippi	Annual	10,000†
Missouri	Annual	31,351†
Montana	Biennial	82.67(d)†
Nebraska‡	Annual	12,000†
Nevada	Biennial	137.90(d)†
New Hampshire	Annual	200(b)

(Continued)

House and Senate Journals
The official public records of the actions of the two chambers of the Texas legislature. The two journals are issued daily during sessions.

Setting Legislative Procedures. The Texas Constitution establishes more specific procedural requirements than most other state constitutions. Although the provision is often suspended, the Texas Constitution requires that a bill must be read on three separate days unless four-fifths of the legislature set aside the requirement. It stipulates when bills may be introduced and how they will be reported out of committee, signed, and entered into the **house and senate journals** once enacted. It even specifies how the enacting clause will read. (The enacting clause is formal language in any bill that gives the bill the force of law if it is approved.)

Mandating a Balanced Budget. Most states legally require a balanced budget, but the restrictions imposed by the Texas Constitution seem more effective than most. Article 3 (Section 49) prohibits the legislature from authorizing state debt except under rare con-

TABLE 17–2 State Legislative Sessions and Annual Salaries *(continued)*

State	Frequency of Regular Session	Salary*
New Jersey	Annual	49,000
New Mexico	Annual	0†
New York	Annual	79,500†
North Carolina	Biennial††	13,951†
North Dakota	Biennial	125(d)†
Ohio	Annual	58,934
Oklahoma	Annual	38,400†
Oregon	Biennial	18,408†
Pennsylvania	Annual	73,613†
Rhode Island	Annual	13,089
South Carolina	Annual	10,400†
South Dakota	Annual	12,000†
Tennessee	Annual	18,123†
Texas	Biennial	7,200†
Utah	Annual	130(d)†
Vermont	Annual	600.78(w)†
Virginia	Annual	18,000‡‡
Washington	Annual	36,311†
West Virginia	Annual	15,000†
Wisconsin	Annual	47,413†
Wyoming	Annual	150(d)†

*Salaries annual unless otherwise noted as (d)—per day, (b)—biennium, or (w)—per week.
†Plus *per diem* living expenses.
‡Unicameral (single-house) legislature.
**Includes legislative sessions that convene every year and those that meet in continuous sessions.
††Annual at option of legislature.
‡‡Senate; House is $17,640.

Source: Council of State Governments, *Book of the States 2007.*

ditions. The comptroller of public accounts is required to certify that funds are available for each appropriations measure adopted. Although specific constitutional amendments have authorized the sale of bonds for such purposes as veterans' real estate programs, student loans, cancer prevention, parks, highways, water projects, and prison construction, per capita state debt remains among the lowest in the nation.

Statute-Like Details. The Texas Constitution further confines the legislature by establishing detailed policies on subjects that normally would be handled by legislative statute.

By including such **statute-like details** in the Texas Constitution, its framers guaranteed that even relatively unimportant decisions that might easily be handled by the legislature could instead be changed only by constitutional amendment. Events may outstrip detailed constitutional provisions, leaving behind **deadwood**—provisions that are no longer functional. Only by amending the constitution can Texans remove such provisions. In

Statute-Like Details
Detailed state constitutional provisions characterized by the narrow scope usually found in statutory law.

Deadwood
In the context of state government, constitutional provisions made inoperative by changing circumstances or by conflicting federal constitutional or statutory law.

brief, basic distrust of the legislature—however much it may have been deserved in 1876—put a straitjacket on the state's ability to cope with the challenges of the 21st century.

Executive Branch

Article 4 establishes the executive branch, with the governor as its head. Since the passage of a constitutional amendment in 1974, the governor is elected to a four-year term. The governor's salary is no longer constitutionally limited; according to statute, it is $115,345. Table 17–3 compares the governor of Texas with other governors and the U.S. president.

did you know?

That Texas's constitution even explains how the state must purchase stationery.

A Plural Executive. Provisions for terms, qualifications, and salary may be somewhat less restrictive than in most states, but other constitutional provisions restrict the power of the office more severely. The governor of Texas remains among the weakest in the nation. Although the Texas Constitution provides that the governor is the chief executive, it actually establishes a **plural executive** by dividing executive powers among several independently elected officers—the governor, the lieutenant governor, the attorney general, the comptroller of public accounts, the commissioner of the general land office, and three railroad commissioners. There are also provisions for a state board of education to be either elected or appointed.

Plural Executive
An executive branch with power divided among several independent officers and a weak chief executive.

Few states elect as many officials as Texas. Eight states have abolished the office of lieutenant governor as an independent, publicly elected executive, and a few have made offices as important as the attorney general appointive rather than elective. Comptrollers, and land, educational, and agricultural officers, are rarely elected in states other than Texas.

did you know?

That, unlike the president of the United States and most governors, the Texas governor is not subject to term limits and, legally, could be re-elected every four years for life.

In the tradition of the constitutional plural executive, the legislature by statute has established an elected commissioner of agriculture and has exercised its option to have the state board of education elected independently of the governor. Most of the remaining agencies the legislature establishes to administer state programs are headed by appointed multimember boards with substantial independence from the governor. Generally, the governor appoints only supervisory boards for the agencies, with the approval of two-thirds of the state senate. Each board in turn appoints the agency's director. The governor does not appoint the agency administrator directly. Texas is one of eight states lacking a formal cabinet.

TABLE 17–3 Constitutional Provisions for Chief Executives' Qualification

Constitutional Provisions	Texas Governor	U.S. President	The 50 States' Governors
Age	30 years	35 years	33 states set the minimum age at 30.
Residence	5 years	14 years	Five years or less in 37 states.
Term	4 years with no limit on the number of terms	4 years (limited to 2 terms or 10 years)	48 states allow a 4-year term, but unlike Texas, 38 states impose term limits.

Source: Council of State Governments, *Book of the States 2007.*

FIGURE 17–1 The Texas Court System

Texas is the only state, other than Oklahoma, with two "supreme courts," or courts of final appeal.

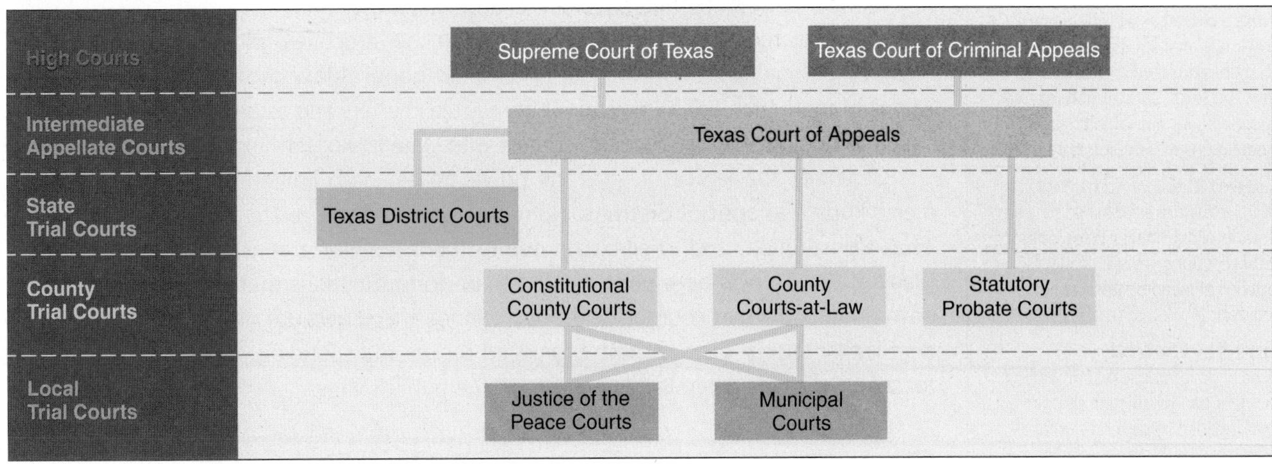

Source: University of North Texas libraries.

The Courts

Just as the Texas Constitution limits the power of the chief executive, it also fragments the court system, which is governed by Article 5. Texas is the only state other than Oklahoma that has two courts of final appeal. The highest court for civil matters is the nine-member Texas Supreme Court; the other, for criminal matters, is the nine-member Court of Criminal Appeals. Leaving some flexibility as to number and jurisdiction, the constitution also creates intermediate courts of appeals and district, county, and justice of the peace courts. (The structure of the Texas court system is displayed in Figure 17–1.) The same article describes the selection of grand and trial juries and such administrative officers as sheriff, county clerk, and county and district attorney.

Judicial Problems. The number and variety of courts confuse the average citizen, and coordination among courts is minimal, as is supervision of lower-level judges. Some have also claimed that the state courts lack qualified judges. The Texas Constitution specifies only general qualifications for county judges and justices of the peace, who need not be lawyers. There may have been good reason for nonlawyers to serve as judges in a simple, rural setting, but today such judges may be an anachronism.

Partisan Election
An election between candidates who are nominated by their parties and whose party affiliation is designated on the ballot. In Texas, all state and county officials (including judges) are selected in this manner. Only municipal and some special district elections are nonpartisan in Texas.

Partisan Election of Judges. The manner of selecting judges is another factor that affects their qualifications—Texas judges are chosen in **partisan elections** in which they run as Democrats or Republicans. Trial judges are elected to four-year terms and appeals court judges to six-year terms, but the governor has frequent opportunities to fill temporary vacancies when judges leave office before the end of their terms.

Local Government

The Texas Constitution decentralizes governmental power by assigning many functions to units of local government, especially counties. Much of the counties' rigid organizational structure is set down in Articles 9 and 16. As a result of these provisions, voters of the entire state were once required to approve constitutional amendments to allow individual counties to abolish unneeded offices such as treasurer, weigher, and surveyor. The

did you know?

That although no county has elected a county inspector of hides and animals in modern times, the office was not removed from the Texas Constitution until 2007.

Home Rule
The right of a local government to write a charter establishing any organizational structure or program that does not conflict with state law. The Texas Constitution reserves home rule for municipalities with populations of 5,000 or more.

General-Law Charter
A city structure established by statute. Most smaller Texas cities choose among several available options allowed by the state legislature.

Special District
A local government that provides services to a jurisdiction that are not provided by general-purpose governments. Examples are municipal utility districts, hospital authorities, and transit authorities.

Texas Constitution now authorizes county voters to abolish some offices, but there is no provision for county **home rule.** As in state government, the constitution divides and diffuses county powers through a plural executive system.

The legislature, which has the power to set up structures for city governments, has offered municipalities several standard alternative **general-law charters.** Cities with populations of more than 5,000 may adopt home-rule charters and establish any organizational structure or program that does not conflict with state law or the Texas Constitution.

Generally, the legislature has the power to establish limited-purpose local governments known as **special districts.** Numerous special districts, are also established by the Texas Constitution, and to eliminate one of them requires a constitutional amendment. Many of the districts have been created to perform functions that general-purpose local governments, such as counties and cities, cannot afford because of constitutional tax and debt limits. Special districts have multiplied taxing and spending authorities and, except for school districts, operate largely outside the public's view.

The Constitution and the People

The Texas Constitution defines the relationship between the state's government and its people, and in doing so it reflects basic American political culture. For example, its bill of rights contains provisions similar to those found in other state constitutions and the U.S. Constitution. Important areas in which the constitution affects the people of Texas include civil rights and liberties and voting rights.

Civil Rights and Liberties

As you learned in Chapter 4, the United States Supreme Court has interpreted the Fourteenth Amendment to extend many national constitutional guarantees to the states. The U.S. Constitution establishes only minimum standards for the states, however. The Texas Bill of Rights (Article 1) guarantees additional rights not specifically mentioned by the U.S. Constitution.

Texans' Rights Under the State Constitution. Notably, Texas has adopted an amendment to prohibit discrimination based on gender. Similar guarantees were proposed as an Equal Rights Amendment to the U.S. Constitution, but it was never ratified by the states (see Chapter 5). The Texas Constitution also guarantees victims' rights and forbids imprisonment for debt. A person who is mentally ill may not be committed for an extended period without a jury trial. The constitution also prohibits the suspension of the writ of *habeas corpus* under any circumstances. Article 16 protects homesteads and prohibits garnishment of wages except for court-ordered child support. There is general agreement that the Texas bill of rights and other provisions guarantee the average citizen a greater variety of protections than most other state constitutions.

Rights Established by the Courts and the Legislature. Texas courts have interpreted some state constitutional provisions in a way that broadens basic rights beyond the minimum standards set by the U.S. Constitution. While the United States Supreme Court has refused to interpret the Fourteenth Amendment as guaranteeing equal public school funding,[1] the Texas Supreme Court interpreted the efficiency clause of the Texas Constitution (Article 7, Section 1) to require greater equality in public school funding between rich and poor school districts.[2]

1. *San Antonio Independent School District v. Rodriguez,* 411 U.S. 1 (1973).
2. *Edgewood v. Kirby,* 777 S.W. 2d 391 (Texas 1989).

Using Texas constitutional and **statutory law** (law passed by the legislature), Texas courts have struck down polygraph (lie-detector) tests for public employees, required workers' compensation for farm workers, expanded free-speech rights of private employees, and affirmed free-speech rights at privately owned shopping malls.

Statutory Law
Law passed by legislatures and eventually compiled in law codes.

Suffrage

A major way in which state and local governments determine the character of our democracy is by setting suffrage requirements and administering elections. Article 6 of the Texas Constitution deals with suffrage requirements. It denies the right to vote to persons under age eighteen, to certain convicted felons, and to those found mentally incompetent by a court of law.

Although constitutional restrictions on the qualifications of voters are now as minimal in Texas as in any other state, Texas voters still lack certain opportunities to participate in state government. The *initiative* (a vote on statutory or constitutional changes brought about by petition), the referendum (a vote on laws submitted to the people by the legislature or by initiative), and the recall (a special election to remove an official before his or her term expires) are available in many other states and even in some Texas cities, but not for statewide issues in Texas. Texas limits voters to ratifying constitutional amendments, approving a state income tax, and increasing legislative salaries. Political parties in Texas sometimes place referenda on their primary ballots, but they are not legally binding.

Amending and Revising the Constitution

Given the level of detail in the Texas Constitution, the ability to amend that document is of great importance. It is much easier to amend the Texas Constitution than the U.S. Constitution.

Rules for Amending the Constitution

The Texas Constitution provides that constitutional amendments must be proposed by two-thirds of the total membership of each chamber of the legislature (at least 21 senators and 100 representatives). Ratification requires approval by a majority of those persons voting on the amendment in either a general or a special election. Because an extraordinary majority of legislators must agree merely to propose constitutional amendments, many are relatively uncontroversial. Historically, voters have approved more than 70 percent of proposed constitutional amendments. Since 1876, Texans have amended their constitution 456 times, more than twice as frequently as the average state. Only three states have amended their constitutions more than Texas: Alabama (794), California (514), and South Carolina (492). Table 17–4 compares the process of amending the Texas Constitution with the methods used to amend the constitutions of the federal government and the other states.

Difficulties in Revising the Constitution

Although the Texas Constitution has been frequently amended, successive attempts to revise it have met with failure. Ironically, in 1972, Texas voters had to amend the constitution in order to provide for its revision. Under the provisions of that amendment, the legislature established a constitutional revision commission of 37 members appointed by the governor, lieutenant governor, speaker of the house, attorney general, chief justice of the supreme court, and presiding judge of the Court of Criminal Appeals.

did you know?

That the Texas constitution even mentions public notaries—who are not elected—making them constitutional officers.

TABLE 17–4 Procedures for Amending Constitutions

Amending Procedures	Texas Constitution	U.S. Constitution	The 50 States' Constitutions
Proposal	Two-thirds of the entire membership of both chambers of the legislature	(1) Two-thirds of those voting in both chambers of Congress or (2) a national convention called by petition of two-thirds of the states	Twenty-one states require a two-thirds vote, but 9 permit a three-fifths vote, and 20 permit a simple majority vote; 18 permit proposal by initiative.
Ratification	A majority of those voting on the amendment	(1) Three-fourths of state legislatures or (2) three-fourths of state ratifying conventions	Forty-three other states have the same requirement as Texas; 4 require a majority of those voting in the entire election; New Hampshire and Florida require more than a simple majority; Delaware requires no ratification by voters; and some states allow alternative methods.

Source: Council of State Governments, *Book of the States 2007.*

The Proposed Constitution of 1975. The commission made several proposals for revising the constitution. Meeting in 1974, the legislature acted as a constitutional convention and agreed to many of these recommendations. Ultimately, though, the convention divided over the issue of a right-to-work provision (under which workers have the right not to join labor unions), and supporters could not muster the two-thirds vote needed to submit the final document to the electorate.

The New Constitution Goes to the People. The proposed revision remained alive, however, in another form. In the 1975 regular session, the legislature proposed eight constitutional amendments to the voters. Together, these amendments were substantially the same as the proposal defeated in the convention. If the amendments had been adopted, they would have shortened the constitution by 75 percent through reorganization and through elimination of statute-like detail and deadwood. The legislature would have been strengthened by annual sessions, and a salary commission would have set the legislators' salary. Although limited to two terms, the governor would have been designated as the chief planning officer and given removal powers and certain powers of fiscal control. The court system would have been unified and its administrative procedure simplified. Local governments would have operated under broader home-rule provisions, and counties would have been authorized to pass ordinances and abolish offices.

The People Turn It Down. Opponents' chief arguments against the amendments focused on fear that they would result in more power for the legislature, greater government costs, and the possibility of an income tax—all of which are serious issues for many Texans. Because the legislature had written the proposals, it was easy for Texas voters to see such things as annual sessions and changes in legislative salaries as a "grab for power" that would substantially increase government expenditures. Despite an emotional campaign, only 23 percent of registered voters cast ballots in the election, and they overwhelmingly rejected the proposed amendments.

The Texas Constitution Compared

The U.S. Constitution is widely regarded as a model and is revered by most scholars. State constitutions, including the Texas Constitution, have attracted more criticism. Here, we compare the various constitutions and examine the reasons that many state constitutions have been so frequently criticized.

The National Constitution

As of 2009, the U.S. Constitution has been in effect for 220 years but has been formally amended only 27 times. It has endured mammoth and fundamental changes in government and society largely because it does not lock government into a rigid framework. Because the U.S. Constitution deals only with the most basic elements of government and leaves much to Congress, the president, and the courts, few formal amendments have been necessary.

did you know?

That the Texas Constitution has more amendments (456) than 46 other states.

Although the U.S. Constitution provides for a representative government, the nation's government was hardly democratic in the earliest years. During the Jeffersonian and Jacksonian eras, it became more democratic as political parties developed, states lowered suffrage requirements, and voters were allowed to choose electors in the electoral college.

The 1800s saw the growth of the new nation from thirteen fledgling agricultural states on the Atlantic coast to a vast industrial nation stretching across a continent. In the modern era, America moved from the position of a third-rate international power to a dominant role in the world. Since the New Deal of the 1930s, government has increasingly provided a safety net for disadvantaged Americans. Much of the nature of the national government is determined by statute, executive order, and court interpretation, so these changes did not require changing the language of the U.S. Constitution.

Criticisms of the Texas Constitution

The Texas Constitution has been characterized as an example of poor writing. Only two state constitutions are as concise as the U.S. Constitution (fewer than 10,000 words). Nevertheless, at almost 90,000 words, the Texas Constitution is one of the least concise in the nation. One sentence rambles on for 765 words, and several approach 300 words in length. The document is ambiguous, overlapping, and poorly organized. For example, the provisions dealing with local government are scattered throughout Articles 3, 5, 8, 9, 11, and 16. This poor draftsmanship has led to a restrictive interpretation of the constitution's provisions and, on the part of Texas citizens, ignorance of its contents and confusion as to its intentions.

did you know?

That only Alabama's state constitution is longer than Texas's.

The continuing need to amend a detailed and restrictive state constitution means that citizens are frequently called to pass judgment on proposed amendments. Although some maintain that giving Texas voters the opportunity to express themselves on constitutional amendments reaffirms popular control of government, there is little voter interest in amendment elections. Faced with trivial, confusing, or technical amendments, often as few as 10 to 15 percent of the voting-age population vote on constitutional amendments, and turnout has occasionally dropped even lower.

WHY SHOULD YOU CARE ABOUT...

AMENDING THE TEXAS CONSTITUTION?

The Texas Constitution is often criticized because it is so frequently amended. On the one hand, as you know, frequent amendment of the constitution has drawbacks. On the other hand, it gives you an extraordinary opportunity to participate in the continual rewriting of the state's fundamental law.

Because so many detailed provisions of Texas law are spelled out in the state constitution, much legislative business is of necessity placed before the voters at large. This gives you and other Texas citizens a degree of control over legislation that may affect your life. Such control is not possible at the national level and is available in few other states to the same extent as in Texas.

HOW YOU CAN MAKE A DIFFERENCE

You can express your approval or disapproval of proposed constitutional amendments by voting in general and special elections, by writing letters to the local newspaper or other publications, or by participating in campaigns for or against an amendment. Although many amendments deal with technicalities and details, they will be explained in local newspapers, and summaries are available through the Texas Legislative Council, a research body set up by the legislature. Constitutional amendment analyses can be found in Texas Legislative Council publications and at the council's Web site at **www.tlc.state.tx.us**. The Legislative Reference Library (**www.lrl.state.tx.us**) is another good resource for reading about constitutional amendments. The League of Women Voters (**www.lwvtexas.org**) often provides good analyses as well. Be aware that special-interest groups often pay for television and newspaper ads on amendments, and their ads often reflect their biases.

questions for discussion and analysis

1. How do cultural and political forces help shape a state's constitution?
2. How do constitutional limitations on government prevent the abuse of individual liberties?
3. How do constitutional restrictions hinder the effective and efficient operation of government?

key terms

community property 572
deadwood 579
enabling act 574
foreclosure 572
Freedmen's Bureau 574
general-law charter 582
home rule 582
house and senate journals 578
partisan election 581
plural executive 580
regular session 577
special district 582
special session 577
statute-like details 579
statutory law 583

chapter summary

1. A constitution sets forth fundamental law that establishes basic governing principles and structures. Some constitutions, like that of Texas, also establish many details of routine government and require frequent amendment to reflect new realities. In such circumstances, it is difficult for the state government to develop effective programs without first amending the constitution. Numerous amendments dealing with minor issues are added, like patches, to the constitution.

2. Constitutions are always the result of a political process in which framers reflect their values, hopes, and fears. The current Texas Constitution was written in the period following Reconstruction after the U.S. Civil War. Most white Texans viewed the Reconstruction state government as extravagant, tyrannical, and abusive. In 1875, an elected state constitutional convention reacted to the Reconstruction regime by limiting state government in almost every imaginable way. Voters overwhelmingly approved the convention's work in 1876.

3. The Texas Constitution strictly limits the sessions and salaries of state legislators and includes many statute-like details that the legislature cannot change without a constitutional amendment. Special sessions are especially restricted, and procedures in both regular and special sessions are circumscribed.

4. The governor of Texas is limited in his or her role as chief executive, because Texas has a plural executive system that includes many independently elected executives over which the governor has no control. The governor lacks most of the powers of typical executives to hire, fire, direct, and budget. Although Texas has had some powerful governors, such as Allan Shivers and John Connally (discussed in Chapter 16), they were effective despite the constitution, not because of it.

5. The power of the courts to interpret the Texas Constitution is limited by its detail. Texas divides its final court of appeal into two bodies—the Court of Criminal Appeals and the Texas Supreme Court—and also establishes intermediate courts of appeals and district, county, and justice of the peace courts. Judges are chosen in partisan elections. Critics say that judges elected in this way may become too concerned with political matters.

6. County and special district governments are particularly limited by constitutional and statutory requirements. Only large cities have the considerable flexibility of home rule. All local governments face debt and tax restrictions.

7. The Texas Constitution includes a bill of rights that is more expansive than that in most constitutions. At the state level, the constitution does not provide for the initiative, referendum, or recall, though such mechanisms may be available at the municipal level.

8. Critics find the Texas Constitution confusing. It contains not only the fundamentals of government but also detailed provisions concerning matters that might better be left to the ongoing institutions of government. It is long, it contains much deadwood, and many say that it is poorly drafted and disorganized. Reformers argue that a constitution should include only organic law; that is, it should organize responsible institutions of government. If it goes beyond fundamentals, it becomes a rigid legislative code, difficult to change and baffling to voters.

9. Texas has one of the longest, most detailed, and most frequently amended state constitutions in the United States, but it does reflect Texans' general political culture and their skeptical view of government. It is clear why Texans wrote such a constitution and have held to its principles for so long.

selected print & media resources

SUGGESTED READINGS

Angell, Robert H. ***A Compilation and Analysis of the 1998 Texas Constitution and the Original 1876 Text.*** Lewiston, NY: Edwin Mellon Press, 1998. This work contains a version of the Texas Constitution with amendments placed in appropriate spots and obsolete text deleted, thus yielding a more coherent document. In his thoroughgoing analysis of the text, Angell argues against assertions that the original 1876 constitution was excessively limited.

Campbell, Randolph B. ***Grass-Roots Reconstruction in Texas, 1865–1880.*** Baton Rouge: Louisiana State University Press, 1998. Campbell, who later authored Gone to Texas: *A History of the Lone Star State,* uses statistics and case studies to determine the actual impact of Reconstruction at the county level. Campbell notes that the counties with the largest number of freed slaves experienced the greatest degree of political controversy and armed violence.

May, Janice C. ***The Texas State Constitution: A Reference Guide.*** Reference Guides to the State Constitutions of the United States, no. 26. Westport, CT: Greenwood Press, 1996. May, of the University of Texas, is an expert on the Texas Constitution. Her work analyzes Texas constitutional and political history from Spanish and Mexican rule to the present. An analytical commentary on the current constitution, with amendments, makes up the heart of the book.

Moneyhon, Carl H. ***Texas after the Civil War: The Struggle of Reconstruction.*** College Station: Texas A&M University Press, 2004. This new account of Reconstruction in Texas may become a standard. Moneyhon argues that the Civil War shook, but did not destroy, antebellum society. He pays due attention to the violence that accompanied the end of Reconstruction.

MEDIA RESOURCES

The American Experience: Reconstruction, The Second Civil War—This dramatic PBS mini-series recounts the aftermath of the Civil War and the social and political struggles that set the stage for the Texas Constitution.

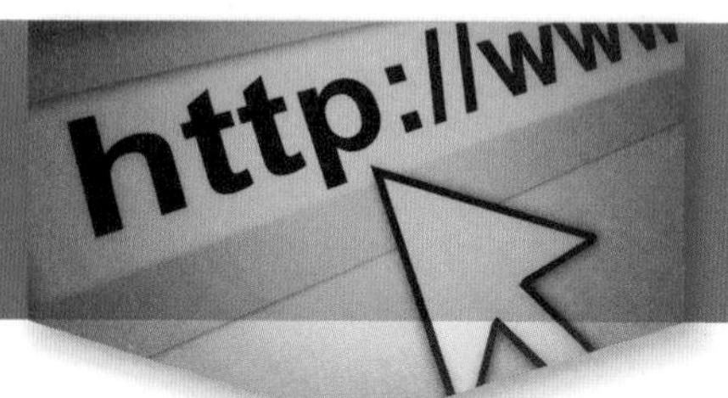

e-mocracy

CONSTITUTIONS ONLINE

You can easily research constitutions and constitutional documents using the Internet. A wide variety of sites provide annotated copies of the U.S. Constitution. Other sites provide collections of URLs that lead you to constitutions of nations around the world. Finally, several sites can direct you to the constitutions of the various American states. Cornell University and FindLaw sponsor two sites that provide access to state constitutions. The FindLaw site is of particular interest, because it is probably the most comprehensive source of free legal information on the Internet. The addresses of the Cornell and FindLaw sites are in the following *Logging On* section. For additional Web resources on constitutional topics, see the *Logging On* section in Chapter 2 of this text.

LOGGING ON

The U.S. Constitution sets the context for the powers of the state of Texas in relation to the national government and the other 49 state governments. Search for key cases such as *Marbury v. Madison, Fletcher v. Peck,* and *McCulloch v. Maryland* at:
www.findlaw.com

Search for the U.S. Constitution—Articles 4 and 6 and the Tenth and Eleventh Amendments. Click on annotations to read United States Supreme Court interpretations of these important constitutional provisions. The complete text of the Texas Constitution, with all 17 articles, is at:
www.constitution.legis.state.tx.us

Click on "3—Legislative Department." Then click on "Sec. 29" and notice that even the enacting clause for legislation is included in the constitution. Click on "16—General Provisions" and then "Sec. 6" and notice the detail. Read deadwood provisions in Article 9, Section 14. Contrast the legislative and executive articles (3 and 4) of the Texas Constitution with those of Illinois (Articles 4 and 5) at:
ilga.gov/commission/lrb/conmain.htm

Read constitutional amendments that have been proposed by the Texas legislature at:
www.lrl.state.tx.us

Read a history of Texas constitutional amendments since 1876 published at:
www.tlc.state.tx.us

Several sites on the Web provide collections of links to state constitutions. The Cornell University Law School maintains one such collection. Go to:
www.law.cornell.edu/states/listing.html

Another collection is part of the highly useful FindLaw site at:
www.findlaw.com/11stategov/indexconst.html

ONLINE REVIEW

At **www.cengage.com/politicalscience/schmidt/agandpttexas 14e**, you will find a Tutorial Quiz for this chapter, providing questions on the chapter contents, including the features. You'll gain access to other helpful study tools, including the book's glossary and flashcards, crossword puzzles, and Web links, as well as "Which Side Are You On?" and "Politics and . . ." features written by the authors of the book.

chapter
18

Texas Interest Groups

chapter contents

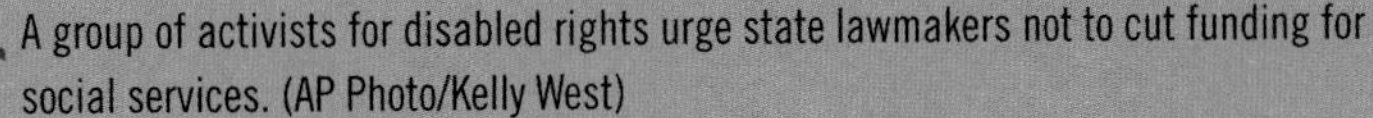

A group of activists for disabled rights urge state lawmakers not to cut funding for social services. (AP Photo/Kelly West)

WHAT IF... ...former Texas lawmakers were banned from lobbying?

BACKGROUND

In recent years, a peculiar practice has developed among many former members of state legislative bodies. Many ex-lawmakers are becoming lobbyists for the very interest groups they once regulated. Their familiarity with the policy-making process, their policy expertise, and their kinship with other lawmakers make them very attractive candidates for the lobbying profession.

Despite their fitness to serve as lobbyists, there are some dangers to permitting former lawmakers to serve as lobbyists. *Ex*-lawmakers, after all, were once *lawmakers*. That is to say, they were once in the position of creating legislation, regulating industry, and providing oversight of government agencies. Lawmakers planning their next career move might feel compelled to reward their future employers with favorable public policy.

Unlike the federal government and many other states, Texas does not ban former lawmakers from becoming lobbyists. Furthermore, Texas pays its citizen legislators a mere $7,200 per year. A legislator's poor pay does not compare to the salaries of successful lobbyists. In a recent study conducted by the Center for Public Integrity, 70 former members of the Texas Legislature were working as lobbyists—the largest number of any state. California and New York, which have full-time legislative bodies, reported only 35 and 19 ex-lawmakers-turned-lobbyists, respectively.*

WHAT'S WRONG WITH FORMER LAWMAKERS LOBBYING?

If ex-lawmakers were banned from lobbying, the legislator's freedom to choose a career path would be denied for the sake of assumed improved representation. As former lawmakers, these individuals have developed skills that can be parlayed into a lobbying career that could allow them to address the personal financial needs that they were unable to fully address as public servants.

Unfortunately, the risk of affording lawmakers the freedom to choose lobbying careers upon leaving office creates a more sinister outcome. Lawmakers are in a position to exploit their positions for the sake of future returns. Unscrupulous lawmakers can sponsor legislation that rewards those interest groups that will provide such lawmakers employment upon leaving the legislature.

Others are critical that the use of public service as a stepping stone to a more lucrative career as a lobbyist is simply unseemly. Public service should be its own reward. Most public servants do not enter public service because it is lucrative, but because they care about creating good public policy.

ONE- OR TWO-YEAR BAN?

A ban on lobbying would limit the career paths of many public servants. It would also ensure that ex-lawmakers do not seek personal gain from their positions upon leaving office.

A compromise that many state legislative bodies have reached, and one upon which the federal government relies, is a one- or two-year ban on lobbying. Ex-lawmakers must wait either one or two years before they can lobby their former colleagues. This still does not avoid the problems mentioned previously, but some believe that a one- or two-year ban reduces the number of ex-lawmakers who become lobbyists. Relying on the Center for Public Integrity's data for 2005, one can gauge the effectiveness of these programs. While states with no ban on lobbying produced an average of 29 ex-lawmakers who became lobbyists, states with a one-year ban averaged 22 lawmakers who became lobbyists, and the six states with a two-year ban averaged 28 lawmakers who became lobbyists.

Further contributing to the number of former lawmakers who become lobbyists is the number of states that have set term limits for lawmakers. Term limits help produce more ex-lawmakers in need of employment—employment that ex-lawmakers tend to find as lobbyists. A complete ban on postlegislative service would ensure that ex-lawmakers do not use their public service as a stepping stone to a more lucrative lobbying career. Such a ban, however, would deny the ex-lawmaker the liberty to choose a career after public service.

FOR CRITICAL ANALYSIS

1. What other factors might explain why ex-lawmakers become lobbyists?
2. Is the cost of denying a lawmaker the freedom to choose a lobbying career outweighed by the public's expectation for good public policy?

* Center for Public Integrity, "Ex-legislators Registered to Lobby 2005," accessed March 1, 2008, at www.publicintegrity.org/hiredguns/reg.aspx.

People in the United States endorse participation in the political process. As discussed in Chapter 7, when individuals join with others in an organizational structure designed to express their preferences to government, they act as an *interest group*. Usually, they hire *lobbyists* to represent them to public officials.

What Are Interest Groups?

Interest groups are also sometimes called *pressure groups*. The two terms basically mean the same thing. The term *pressure group* comes from the fact that interest groups try to apply pressure on decision makers as they seek favorable policy outputs. Pressure on the officeholder can come from the voting power of the group and the value of its endorsement, campaign contributions, and volunteer help in elections.

Constitutional Guarantees

The constitutions of the United States and of Texas guarantee to citizens the right to political participation through voting, speaking, writing, and petitioning government "for redress of grievances." To peaceably assemble *for political expression* is likewise clearly encouraged. The Texas constitution says it very well:

> *The citizens shall have the right . . . to . . . apply to those invested with the powers of government for redress of grievances or other purposes, by petition, address or remonstrance [formal protest]. (Article I, Section 27)*

The First Amendment to the U.S. Constitution makes our liberties even more clear:

> *Congress shall make no law . . . abridging the freedom of speech, or of the press; or the right of the people peaceably to assemble, and to petition the Government for a redress of grievances.*

In these constitutional expressions, free speech, a free press, and the right to join together in political parties and interest groups "to petition the government" are guaranteed. These guarantees and the right to vote are essential to democracy. Representative democracy, however, creates dangers. The liberty that comes with it requires citizens to inform themselves about political issues and involve themselves in the choices to be made. Both extreme zealousness and apathy can present dangers to democracy. Highly organized and active groups can threaten the well-being of the unorganized majority. The organized and zealous can be expected to triumph over the apathetic or unorganized. Hence, small factions of the population, rather than the majority, may control selected policy areas.

What Interest Groups Do

The primary goal of interest groups is to influence the branches of government to produce policies favorable to their members. States like Texas, which have a diverse and complex economic system, tend to produce a greater diversity of interest groups. The diversity of interest groups that exist in Texas makes it difficult for any one special interest group to dominate Texas politics. And, as a result, the public is protected from public policy that benefits one group. The agricultural, energy, legal, banking, medical, religious, racial, ethnic, and educational interest groups are just a few organized interests in Texas, and all compete with one another for favorable legislation. Because there are so many interest groups in Texas, no one group is the sole recipient of public goods.

Interest groups also provide policy makers with valuable information. This information is often provided in the form of testimony before committees. Because the information is provided under oath, special-interest groups are careful to provide truthful information. Failure to testify truthfully can lead to charges of perjury. The information provided by interest groups can be costly to gather both in terms of time and money. Because interest groups provide the information free of cost, taxpayers are spared the burden.

Critics focus on the harm that can result when powerful groups demand that public policy reflect their values. Private meetings with public officials present no opportunity for rebuttal of the views that are advanced. Critics worry about corruption and intimidation of public officials by what they call "special interests." The need for campaign contributions, they believe, makes elected officials especially vulnerable to pressure.

Conflict of Interest
A situation that arises when a legislator, bureaucrat, executive official, or judge can make an official decision that results in a personal economic advantage. The result is a potential or real conflict between the personal interests of the officeholder and the general interests of the public.

Subsidies
Grants or special tax exemptions provided by the government to individuals or businesses in the private sector.

A **conflict of interest** is a situation that arises when a legislator, bureaucrat, executive official, or judge can make an official decision that results in a personal economic advantage. The result is a potential or real conflict between the personal interests of the officeholder and the general interests of the public.

Types of Interest Groups

Interest groups can be classified in a multitude of ways. The most simple is to categorize them as economic, noneconomic, or mixed. Table 18–1 provides classification and examples of Texas interest groups.

Economic. Economic interests operating at the state level include business and the professions, education, local government, agriculture, and labor. Each interest seeks financial advantages for its members. Business and agriculture are always interested in keeping their taxes low, securing benefits called **subsidies,** avoiding regulation, and obtaining government contracts. Labor unions seek legislation to obtain workers' compensation and workplace safety benefits and to make it easier to organize (unionize) labor.

Noneconomic. Noneconomic groups seek the betterment of society as a whole or reform of the political, social, or economic system in ways that do not directly affect their

TABLE 18–1 Examples of Texas Interest Groups

Economic Type of Group	Examples	Noneconomic Type of Group	Examples	Mixed Type of Group	Examples
Agriculture	Texas Farm Bureau	**Patriotic**	American Legion	**Education**	Texas State Teachers Association Texas Association of School Administrators
Business	Texas Association of Business and Chambers of Commerce	**Public interest**	Texas Common Cause Texans for Public Justice	**Race and ethnicity**	League of United Latin American Citizens NAACP (African Americans)
Labor	American Federation of Labor–Congress of Industrial Organizations (AFL-CIO)	**Religious**	Texas Christian Life Commission	**Local government**	Texas Municipal League Texas County Judges and Commissioners Association
Occupations and professions	Texas Association of Realtors Texas Trial Lawyers Association	**Environment and recreation**	Texas Nature Conservatory Texas Committee on Natural Resources		

members' pockets. Environmental and political reformers maintain that society in general benefits from their programs. Clean air, clean water, and fair elections are said to promote the well-being of all. Patriotic, civic, and religious groups also fall within this classification.

Government. Levels and branches of government also lobby. They are not generally recognized as interest groups, but they are affected by what other political institutions and jurisdictions decide. Governors have staffs that promotes their political agenda in the legislature. Cities, school districts, and other local governments are seriously affected by legislative decisions on finances and local government authority. They are also affected by rules set by state executive-branch agencies. Therefore, they must protect and/or promote their interests by employing lobbyists or reassigning employees to be lobbyists as needed.

Mixed. Many groups do not fit neatly into economic or noneconomic classifications because they pursue social goals that have clear economic effects. For example, discrimination on the basis of age, disability, ethnicity, gender, or native language is a social problem that also has negative consequences on wages and promotion within the workplace. Groups pursuing equality in society and the workplace can thus be classified as mixed or hybrid organizations.

Similarly, education and local government groups want economic benefits such as greater state support and increased salaries and benefits for their employees. In addition, blocking **unfunded mandates** imposed by the state and obtaining more local control over their affairs are often objectives. Many of the goals of such groups can also be characterized as noneconomic. Improvements to the educational system, for example, can be seen as contributing to the betterment of persons other than the educators.

Unfunded Mandate
A requirement imposed on a lower level of government by a higher level of government. The requirement is not accompanied by the funds to pay for the resulting expenses.

Implementation
The carrying out of laws by executive officials and the bureaucrats who work for them.

Influencing Government

As you learned in Chapter 7, the techniques used by interest groups can be divided into direct and indirect techniques. With *direct techniques,* groups attempt to influence government officials by dealing with them personally. With *indirect techniques,* groups attempt to influence officials by influencing other parties, such as the electorate at large.

Direct Techniques of Exercising Influence

Using lobbyists to contact government officials is the most obvious direct technique. Lawsuits and demonstrations can also fall under this heading.

Lobbying the Legislative and Executive Branches. Lobbying is direct contact between an interest-group representative and a legislative- or executive-branch official or employee to influence a specific public-policy outcome.[1] Most people understand that the legislature creates, finances, and changes government programs. Therefore, it comes as no surprise that individuals and groups affected by these decisions attempt to participate in the lawmaking process by lobbying legislators. Awareness that privilege, prestige, and funds are at stake in the executive decision-making process that follows the lawmaking is not so common.

The executive branch, or the administration, is charged with the **implementation** of legislative policy. The legislature delegates a great

Governor Rick Perry signs House Bill 3011, authorizing creation of the Houston Ship Channel Security District in 2007. (Courtesy of the Office of the Governor, Austin, Texas)

1. Texas Government Code Section 305.003a.

POLITICS AND... interest groups

TUITION DEREGULATION AND PUBLIC UNIVERSITIES

In 2003, the state of Texas deregulated tuition rates, allowing university regents to raise tuition as they saw fit. Since this time, designated tuition has risen by 113 percent.[a] Students at the University of Texas at Dallas watched their tuition rise from $690 in 2003 to $2,022 in the fall of 2007—a 193 percent increase for 15 semester credit hours.[b] Such dramatic increases ignore the fact that Texas university students pay an average of $2,952 in mandatory fees and course fees.[c] In the end, middle-class students are feeling the pinch most directly. Not wealthy enough to afford the increase and not poor enough to qualify for grants, middle-class students are finding themselves having to make difficult choices. Many of these students find their way to community colleges, which have their own sources of revenue such as taxing property owners in their jurisdictions; others are organizing. In doing so, they are letting lawmakers know how they feel.

The legislature supported the idea of tuition deregulation because it meant that the state would not have to come up with more revenue to adequately fund public universities. Governor Rick Perry continues to support tuition deregulation, arguing that universities can be more efficient,[d] but lawmakers are feeling the pressure from their constituents. Senator Rodney Ellis reports receiving phone calls, e-mails, and letters asking for some kind of protection from tuition increases.[e]

University students have begun to organize to protect their interests. They are demanding that the legislature rein in state universities and the authority granted to university regents to raise tuition rates. At the University of Texas, the Tuition Accountability Coalition has brought students from disparate groups together to protest tuition increases. Across the state, the Texas Student Association has been revived after years of dormancy. Among the issues it hopes to bring to the forefront is tuition deregulation.

Editorial boards of many local newspapers have been reading angry letters from students and parents. In many opinion pieces, local papers are asking the state to repeal tuition deregulation. While many state lawmakers have followed the strategy of rebuking boards of regents, recent attempts to repeal the law have not been very successful. If university students are successful at organizing, they may very well force the legislature to repeal the law.

FOR CRITICAL ANALYSIS

Do you think that the law should be repealed? How much of the burden of funding public universities should fall on the state?

---

a. Texas Higher Education Coordinating Board, "Academic Charges (Tuition, Mandatory Fees, and Average College and Course Fees) Fall 2002–Fall 2007," July 10, 2008, www.thecb.state.tx.us/reports.
b. *Ibid.*
c. *Ibid.*
d. Christy Hoppe, "Higher Education—Perry Asks Regents to Shift Their Thinking—Proposals Include Giving Students, Not Schools, Public Money," *Dallas Morning News*, May 22, 2008, p. 3A.
e. Jeannie Kever, "Complaints Rising Right Along with Tuition, Fees: Legislators Feel the Heat, Wonder if Deregulation Needs New Look," *Houston Chronicle*, July 10, 2008, p. A1.

Discretion
An official's power to make decisions based on personal judgment rather than on the specific requirements of the law; the freedom to decide or make choices.

deal of **discretion** to executive agencies, both directly and indirectly. This freedom allows the administrative agencies to complete the policy-making process by issuing rules or regulations that specify how the law will be applied to actual situations. Interest groups seek to shape the regulations that will apply to them.

Filing Suit in Court. There are several reasons why organized interests use the courts to further their causes. It can be less expensive to file a suit than to successfully influence the legislature. Furthermore, public opinion is supposed to be irrelevant to judicial outcomes. An interest group that has lost the political struggle may be able to challenge the constitutionality of the law or the means of enforcement selected by the administering agency.

Courts often postpone implementation of the law or rule while the case is pending. The members of the group bringing the litigation can then continue to operate as before, in (presumably) a more profitable and unrestrained manner. The publicity that results from being sued may provide an incentive for the government to enter into negotiation with the lawsuit's filer to change the policy without the necessity of judicial action. Suits, then, can be utilized to delay, stop, or start action. The goal depends on the needs of the interest group.

Faculty, staff, and students from the University of Texas at Austin and UT Hearts of Texas volunteers form the "Heart of Texas" on the main mall of the campus in Austin. The UT Hearts of Texas promotes charitable giving and volunteerism and participates in the Texas State Employee Charitable Campaign. Organizations affiliated with UT and other large universities are important interest groups. (AP Photo/ UT Austin)

Advising and Serving on State Boards. State law in Texas generally requires that a majority of the members of appointed boards come from the profession, occupation, business, or activity the board is regulating. The mere existence of such a requirement is testimony to the power of special-interest groups to shape government decisions in Texas. The board members and commissioners appointed as a result of this requirement are part-time officials but full-time practitioners of the activity they have the power to regulate. They simultaneously exercise power as state officials and function as members of a special-interest group that may testify and present information to the agency.

We can call this blurring of the line between the state and the special interest **co-optation.** Critics of interest groups believe that the public interest is endangered when state officials can act as representatives of the group the agency regulates. As mentioned earlier, a conflict of interest exists when the decision maker is personally affected by the decision she or he makes.

Co-optation
The "capturing" of an agency by members of an interest group. In effect, governmental power comes to be exercised by a private interest.

Public Demonstrations. Marches and demonstrations are used periodically to obtain publicity for a cause. Press coverage is all but guaranteed. This sort of "theater" is especially suited to television news. In 2006, Governor Rick Perry fast-tracked approval to build several coal-fired power plants in Texas. To bring attention to these plans, several environmental groups protested in the streets of Austin in December 2006, asking passersby to sign their names to envelopes of coal that would be delivered to the governor just in time for Christmas. This stunt, although comical, garnered serious media attention.[2] The challenge for interest groups using this method of pressuring the state is to simultaneously enlist enough members to be impressive and still control the activity. Violating the law, blocking traffic, damaging property, and using obscenities are usually counterproductive. Such conduct may antagonize fellow citizens or public officials who have the power to change the conditions at which the protest is aimed.

Indirect Techniques of Influencing Government

Attempts to influence the voting public are the most obvious indirect technique used by interest groups. We can also characterize as indirect those interactions with government officials that are not specific attempts to address a particular piece of legislation or a particular administrative rule. Socializing at parties and other recreational events may allow lobbyists to create a positive impression on officials they may later seek to influence.

Electioneering. Although interest groups do not nominate candidates for office, one candidate may be more favorable to their cause than another. The organization may

2. See video of protest on YouTube, "Austin Sends Dirty Coal Back to Gov. Perry," December 19, 2006, www.youtube.com/watch?v=DEGlbXGKnDw, accessed March 15, 2008.

More than 40 organizations gathered outside the Texas capitol in February 2007 asking the Texas legislature to pass a resolution calling for a moratorium on coal-fired generating plants and supporting cleaner energy solutions. (AP Photo/Harry Cabluck)

endorse that candidate and recommend that its members vote for that person. The organization's newsletter or magazine will be used to carry this message.

A second means of helping candidates who are favorable to the group's interests is to create a political action committee (PAC). This structure, separated from the interest group legally, is solely intended to funnel funds to candidates for office.

Educating the Public. An interest group clearly benefits from providing the general public with messages that build a positive image of the interest the group supports. Everyone knows that reputation is important. Industry interest groups may employ the services of public relations people to enhance the industry's reputation for honesty, satisfactory products and services, concern for the well-being of customers, and good citizenship. Organizational magazines, annual reports to stockholders, and press releases to newspapers are some of the ways to build a reputation and educate the public about the wisdom of policy proposals supported by the organization. Occasionally, a group purchases advertisements on radio and television and in magazines and newspapers to shape and mobilize public opinion on behalf of the interest group or to neutralize opposition to what the interest group wants to do.

Socializing. Interest-group representatives know that friendships can be formed at social functions. Informal occasions allow people to interact in comfortable settings. A lobbyist may invite a public official to lunch or to a social gathering to establish a positive relationship. Formal occasions designed to honor a person can also build positive relationships. Invitations to speak before a group are another way to cultivate relationships with public officials.

The purpose of social invitations is to establish a positive impression that pays off in favorable votes or other friendly decisions by government officials. Interest groups view socializing with public officials as a good investment, whether or not there is an immediate need for the official's support.

Access
The ability to contact an official either in person or by telephone. Campaign contributions are often given in hopes of gaining access to elected officials.

Access to public officials is the prerequisite for influencing public decisions. Lobbyists seek to "get in the door" to discuss a matter of concern in time to shape the public-policy outcome. Indirect techniques of influencing government often pave the road for direct techniques. Groups that have established good relations with public officials are more likely to enjoy access, but even the most successful groups can expect to lose sometimes.

Which Interests Are Powerful?

Twenty years ago, businesses and the professions tended to be the most powerful interests in Texas. They still are, despite an explosion in the number of interest groups in recent years. Generally speaking, the newer interest groups, such as environmentalists, have not supplanted the old. In conservative, pro-business Texas, that is not surprising. The National

Institute on Money in State Politics identifies the major industries in Texas by the amount of money they contribute.[3] In 2008, those industries were:

Lawyers and lobbyists	$4,882,963
Oil and gas	$2,078,455
Real estate industry	$1,417,329
Home builders	$1,019,786
Liberal policy organizations	$891,451
Telecom services and equipment	$803,659
Health professionals	$716,126
Securities and investments	$616,737
Beer, wine and liquor	$588,860
Business associations	$538,325
Commercial banks	$481,765
Pharmaceuticals and health products	$464,732
Electric utilities	$462,468
Miscellaneous finance, insurance, and real estate	$374,399
General contractors	$344,408

These sectors of the economy have strong membership associations like the Texas Association of Realtors, Texas Medical Association, and the Texas State Teachers Association, which have the funds to maintain permanent headquarters in Austin and to employ clerical and research staff, as well as lobbyists, to make their presence felt. These resources, when competently managed, enable some interest groups to create a need for themselves within the halls of government. Research shows that the number-one element determining the political power of a group is how much public officials need the group. Officials may need the group's expertise to help the state solve problems. They may depend on the group for campaign contributions. Perhaps the state's economy depends on the economic sector the group represents. There are many explanations of public officials' need for a particular interest group.[4]

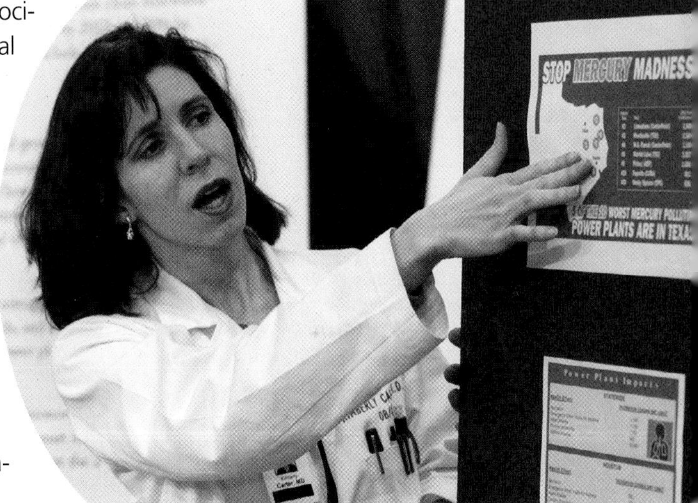

A physician representing Physicians for Social Responsibility refers to a map that locates mercury pollution sites in Texas during a news conference. She joined a group of environmentalists who laid out a legislative agenda to reduce pollution and protect public health. How might other interest groups argue against additional environmental legislation? (AP Photo/Harry Cabluck)

The Strength of the Business Lobby

Records of registered lobbyists kept by the Texas Ethics Commission show that two-thirds of the registered groups represent some form of business. Business is a comprehensive category. Therefore, we should not think of all business interests as being alike. There are both powerful and weak interests within this classification. Furthermore, independent and small businesses frequently seek policy outcomes opposed by larger enterprises. This diversity within the business sector ensures that no one business group dominates other groups.

The number of lobbyists by subject-matter category, shown in Table 18–2, reflects the importance of business interests. Unraveling the lobbyist registration reports to determine the number of lobbyists representing specific trade groups, business associations, or other interests is challenging. Many organizations listed may be supported by the

3. National Institute on Money in State Politics, "Top 15 Industries," *Legislative Committee Analysis Tool,* 2006, www.followthemoney.org/database/state_overview.phtml?s=TX&y=2006, accessed March 5, 2008.
4. Ronald Hrebenar and Clive Thomas, "Who's Got Clout? Interest Group Power in the States," *State Legislatures,* April 1999.

TABLE 18–2 Number of Lobbyists Reporting by Subject-Matter Category, 2007

Subject-Matter Category	Number of Lobbyists
Taxation	1,087
Business and commerce	1,035
State agencies, boards, and commissions	929
Health and health care	847
Corporations and associations	818
Utilities	804
Economic and industrial development	803
Insurance	794
Environment	785
State finance	785
Transportation	755
Tourism	718
Education	682
Occupational regulation	666
Water	654
City government	639
Consumer protection	605
Labor	604
County government	596
Civil remedies	558

Sources: Texas Ethics Commission, *2007 Lobbyists Subject Matter Categories, Sorted by Subject Matter Code Parts 1-4*, March 21, 2008. www.ethics.state.tx.us/tedd/sublob2007a.htm, accessed March 21, 2008.

same benefactors and represent the same industry, business, or activity. It is easier to identify the lobbyists representing a particular company, profession, union, or employee association. Among business interests, 57 percent are associated with an identifiable company. Many companies, however, are also represented through **umbrella organizations,** in which industries, wholesalers, producers, retailers, and others join together to promote their collective interests. In other words, a firm may employ lobbyists directly and also through these umbrella organizations. (Refer back to Table 18–1.)

The Effects of Poverty

Not all interests are well represented in the political system. Low levels of political participation in Texas are associated with the below-average educational attainment of many Texas citizens. Education and income are also related. Compared with the rest of the country, Texas has a relatively high proportion of poor people in its population. The poor and marginalized do not participate actively in politics. These factors bias the political system toward the upper-middle and upper classes. For the most part, people in these classes have the income to obtain education that pays off economically and socially.

Iron Triangles and Issue Networks

Political scientist Ernest Griffin observed nearly 70 years ago that the relationships and interactions among members of the legislature are generally weaker than the relationships between the legislators and the lobbyists, academics, and high-ranking bureaucrats who interact to address specific needs and solve specific problems.[5] When these participants are active, they become a subsystem of the legislative or administrative decision-making process.

Umbrella Organization
An organization created by interest groups to promote common goals. Several interest groups may choose this mechanism to coordinate their efforts to influence government when they share the same policy goals. The umbrella organization may be temporary or permanent.

Iron Triangles. In the literature of political science, a stable interaction pattern among legislative committee members, high-ranking bureaucrats, and representatives of special interests is called an *iron triangle,* which we first discussed in Chapter 14. The members of such a triangle can be very powerful when they operate out of public view; they may even control policy outcomes. This is especially likely if the policy issue is very narrow and affects only a small segment of society.

Issue Networks. The iron triangle arrangement does not describe the environment of all or even most decision making. Another kind of arrangement, called an *issue network,* was also discussed in Chapter 14. Participants in a network are interested in a general policy area, such as health, transportation, or rural economic development, but as the specific topics change, the participants may change. For example, some participants concerned about health care focus on cost and access to services, whereas others are concerned more with professionalism and the supply of health-care providers. Thus,

5. Ernest Stacey Griffin, *The Impasse of Democracy* (New York: Harrison-Hilton Books, 1939), p. 182.

people representing interests move into and out of the subsystem as the issue focus changes.[6]

Another key difference between issue networks and iron triangles is that typically, networks exist that are opposed to each other on policy issues. As a result, more players are drawn into issue networks than are likely to participate in an iron triangle. While issue networks have more participants than iron triangles, the numbers involved are still small. The general public is absent from most public policy-making and policy-implementing events.

Broad and Narrow Concerns. Iron triangles are most likely to control rather routine decisions. Economic concerns dominate their agenda. Often, what motivates the actors is subsidies in the form of grants or tax deductions that favor specific economic interests.

Issue networks are broader in their interests and, hence, have more participants. Their focus may be economic, social, or both. The participants may be members of professional and social organizations that are national in scope and that distribute information through newsletters and other publications. They may strive to bring legislative and bureaucratic actors together in agreement on an approach to a problem.

Factors that Affect Interest Group Power

The Texas political environment has its peculiarities, and it differs from the national political environment and the environments in many other states. The special characteristics of Texas politics affect organized interest groups in several ways. Here, we look at a variety of factors that determine the strength of interest groups in general relative to other players in the political game.

A Culture of Nonparticipation

One hundred and fifty years of one-party politics has probably given many Texans less incentive to participate in political affairs than citizens living in states with competitive parties. The absence of two competitive parties has also helped empower elites and strengthen special interests. Historically, conservative Texas political elites used their control of state government to enact laws that discouraged mass political participation. The poll tax, annual voter registration, and the white primary were examples. (We discussed historical barriers to voting in Chapter 5.) These barriers to participation promoted a culture of nonparticipation by the masses that has yet to be undone.

Party Competition

Studies by political scientists consistently show that where political parties are weak, interest groups are strong. States with a long history of two-party competition have weaker interest groups than states with weak party development.[7]

In Texas, one-party politics has left the parties weak. In the 1990s, the growth of the Republican Party raised the possibility that Texas would, for the first time, enjoy competition between two strong parties. The elections since 2002, however, suggest that Texas has simply been in transition from one dominant party (Democratic) to another (Republican). The two-party system in Texas may simply have been a passing fancy. Republican Party

6. Hugh Heclo, "Issue Networks and the Executive Establishment," in Anthony King, ed., *The New American Political System,* 2nd ed. (Washington, DC: American Enterprise Institute Press, 1990).
7. Ronald Hrebenar and Clive Thomas, "Who's Got Clout? Interest Group Power in the States," *State Legislatures,* April 1999.

Texas Lieutenant Governor David Dewhurst, left, applauds with Texas Railroad Commission Chairperson Victor Carrillo during the commission's oil and gas industry annual meeting. In other states, administrators appointed by the governor wield the powers that in Texas are exercised by the elected Railroad Commission. What kinds of issues might be raised during an election campaign for a seat on the commission? (AP Photo/Jack Plunkett)

control now extends to the two highest courts in the state, both houses of the legislature, and all elected officers in the executive branch. We can expect that a one-party Republican system will be as vulnerable to interest-group domination as a one-party Democratic system.

The Part-Time Legislature

Texas is the only large state with legislative sessions that are limited in length and frequency. In addition, legislative pay is very low, and member turnover is fairly high. The result is a legislative body that is easily influenced by special-interest groups. Professor Cal Jillson of Southern Methodist University has put it this way: "If you meet only occasionally, get paid little and have weak staffs, you are at the disposal of the lobby because you have to go to them to get information."[8]

There is no question that the quality of staff in the legislative and executive branches has significantly improved since the 1950s. Better sources of information and research are now available within the government. Therefore, public officials may depend somewhat less on special interests for information. Still, this change may be nullified by the dependence of elected officials on campaign funds. The Center for Public Integrity claims that the percentage of Texas legislators with financial ties to special interests is the highest in the United States.[9] The author of this report suggests that the low pay of Texas legislators makes them highly vulnerable to interest-group pressure. While that may be true, it is also clear that in the political culture of Texas, politicians accept large campaign contributions as "the way it is done," and the public is resigned to this system.

The Decentralization of Executive-Branch Power

Texas has a plural executive. Power is divided among numerous independently elected executives—the governor, the lieutenant governor, the attorney general, the comptroller, an agricultural commissioner, a land commissioner, and the multiple members of the Railroad Commission and the State Board of Education.

Fragmentation
In state government, a division of power among separately elected executive officials. A plural executive is a fragmented executive.

Government by Commission. The **fragmentation,** or division of power, within the executive branch is enhanced by the practice of establishing independent boards and commissions as structures for implementing the law. The governor appoints the membership of most unelected boards and commissions—usually one-third of the membership every two years—but has little power to remove those appointed. Reformists have argued that if each agency were headed by a single executive who was appointed and removable by the governor, agencies would be more responsive to the broader values represented by the governor rather than those of the specific clientele the agencies serve.

Fragmentation and Interest Group Power. The plural executive and fragmentation of authority mean that no strong central executive authority has the legal power to control the executive branch of government. This situation increases the vulnerability of each exec-

8. Clay Robison, "Weak State Government Paved Way for Lobbyists," *Houston Chronicle,* December 29, 2002, p. A1.
9. John Dunbar, "Low-Paid Texas Lawmakers Tops in Connections to Lobbyists: Is Their Pay a Factor?" *The Center for Public Integrity,* October 28, 2000.

utive agency to special-interest influence. The result may be policies established with less regard for the general public interest than for special interests. Increasing this likelihood is the requirement (previously discussed) that a majority of members on many boards and commissions be engaged in the profession, business, or activity that the board or commission regulates.

Governor Rick Perry talks with the media. Any governor of Texas has a high profile and can therefore use the media to communicate his or her agenda to the public effectively. How do the media create problems for a governor? (AP Photo/ Harry Cabluck)

Laws

Reformers have long advocated laws to regulate the relationship between public officials and private parties who seek special favors from government. Texas, as we see later in this chapter, does have laws that define lobbying and require reporting of information about the lobbyist, his or her employer, and the expenses associated with trying to influence government decisions. The Texas Ethics Commission makes this information generally available. The press has a special obligation to examine this information and report it to the public in a usable form. If the voters receive this information, they may be able to act on it.

The Media

The media are essential to the democratic system. Radio, television, Internet, and print journalists serve as watchdogs of government. Public officials and bureaucrats know that every decision they make, as well as their general conduct, is fair game for the news media. In a democracy, the public has a right to know what public officials are doing, and the public relies on the media to tell it.

The media not only relay the activities of government to the people but also transmit the people's moods and messages to the state leaders. In addition, members of the media communicate their own opinions to both the public and the government. The media are a link between the people and the government, but they are not necessarily a neutral one.

The Media and Open Government. The media's interests are allied with the interests of the people when the media demand that the government's business be conducted in public view. The media work to promote open meetings, open records, and recorded votes on policy decisions in the legislature and in administrative boards and commissions. Openness is the enemy of conflicts of interest and other questionable conduct, and the press delights in exposing such behavior to the public. Thus, the interaction of lobbyists and public officials is a matter of interest to the media.

did you know?

That in terms of per capita federal support for homeland security, only one state (California) received less than Texas in 2006.

Coverage of News from the Capital. The media, however, labor under self-imposed restraints on reporting. These restraints may be based on the fact that newspapers, news magazines, and radio and television stations are businesses concerned with making a profit. Austin, the state capital, is not the home of the largest newspapers or broadcasting channels in Texas. It is costly for media outlets not located in the capital to employ journalists stationed in Austin, and declining newspaper readership has led to the closing of several Austin news bureaus. In 2004, the last of the TV news bureaus, A. H. Belo Corporation (owner of the *Dallas Morning News* and WFFA), "destaffed" its Austin operation. KHOU Houston and KENS San Antonio had previously closed their operations, except for the presence of the local Austin news manager.

This has affected TV coverage of state government as well, because media chains generally own newspapers as well as radio and TV stations in their market areas. Increasingly, local station managers deemphasize coverage of the legislature, governor, and high courts, saying that members of the public are uninterested.

The Media versus the Government. The media thrive on scandals, corruption, inefficiencies, mistakes, and conspiracies in the public sector. Money in politics and cozy relationships between public officials and interest groups make good news stories. This seems true even though most of the Texas mass-distribution dailies appear to share the conservative politics that are dominant in Texas. It is true even though competition between newspapers and broadcast media is limited because major newspapers own radio stations and can own at least one key television station in their market area.

Evidence that Texas media, slimmed down as they are, remain important in informing the public and pointing out potential wrongdoing in Texas can be appreciated from the following headlines and programming:

"Craddick Denies Pushing Insurance Law to Help Daughter," *Austin American-Statesman,* December 4, 2002.

"Questioning the Ethics of Perry's Bahamas Trip" (editorial), Houston *Chronicle,* April 25, 2004.

"Special Session's Winners: Lobbyists," *Dallas Morning News,* May 9, 2004.

"Special Session," KLRU and selected PBS stations in Texas, 2006.

New Technologies

Perhaps the biggest change affecting existing power relationships in the state in recent years is the increasing use of the computer as a political tool. Databases allow groups to keep track of members and finances more easily than in the past. Also, interest groups that are starved for economic resources now have a medium—the Internet—that connects them to their members and to state decision makers. Contacting public officials has never been easier. The Internet cannot completely overcome the disadvantages of scarce funds and other resources, but it does make possible the raising of new and underrepresented voices.

Constituent Influence

Texas has a part-time legislature that is only in regular session for 140 days every odd-numbered year. Hence, members are home in their districts 590 days out of 730 in every two-year period. Furthermore, they are home almost every weekend during the four and a half months of the session. Members do not have to exert much effort to find out what their constituents want (presuming that the constituents *know* what they want).

In contrast, when the voters back home have no consensus on an issue, then interest groups, fellow legislators, the governor, and the legislator's party may struggle for the legislator's vote.

Campaign Contributions

Money in politics is a hot topic, in part because of a startling increase in the amount of funds raised and spent by candidates for elective office at all levels. A candidate for state representative in a metropolitan area of Texas may spend more than $200,000 to win an office that pays $7,200 per year.

Campaign contributions for legislative and statewide offices often come from large donors. These donors may represent banks, insurance companies, the petrochemical industry, physicians, trial lawyers, real estate agents, teachers, and others who use political action committees (PACs) to funnel money to candidates. These donors participate because the state legislature, the governor, the Railroad Commission, and other agencies and officers make decisions that affect their economic well-being. Donors contribute to gain access to public officials. A substantial contribution may create a sense of obligation on the part of an elected official to listen when the contributor calls. Ordinary citizens may find access more difficult.

According to Texans for Public Justice, statewide and legislative candidates raised $186 million in the 2006 election cycle, $42 million being raised by the gubernatorial candidates alone. An estimated $60 million was raised by the 309 major candidates vying for a seat in the Texas House, and an estimated $27 million raised by the 48 candidates vying for seats on the Texas Senate.[10] Sixty-two percent of the dollars raised by house candidates went to incumbents, and 51 percent of money raised by senate candidates went to incumbent senators.[11]

Texans for Public Justice report that 141 individual donors contributed more than $100,000 in 2006. These 141 donors contributed $51.8 million. The top 132 institutional donors that contributed more than $150,000 raised $64.9 million during the 2006 election cycle. Combined, these two groups of major donors account for 63 percent of the money donated to campaigns.[12] PACs and businesses contributed $63.8 million. Individuals contributed $91.7 million.[13] Even when candidates face little or no opposition, they raise large amounts of money. Their success in raising campaign contributions indicates the state's economic and political importance.

A member of Texans for Public Justice, a group that monitors money in Texas politics, shows a report entitled "Ain't Nobody's Business." The report concluded that few politicians and officials in Texas fully report lobbyists' payments. How might Texas do a better job of tracking lobbying activities? (AP Photo/Harry Cabluck)

"Late-Train" Contributions

One of the biennial rituals in Austin occurs after each election when special-interest groups hold fundraising events to honor selected legislators. State law forbids giving and accepting campaign contributions 30 days before the start of a legislative session and throughout the session, causing a rush of fundraising activity during the five weeks following election day. Note that the fundraising occurs after the election, not before. The reason, as one lobbyist has said, is to "pay the price of admission," or to obtain good access to legislators. Postelection contributions, or **"late-train" contributions,** are commonly given to the winning candidates in the executive branch as well. Losers are rarely the beneficiaries of such largesse. During the five-week period before the start of the 80th legislative session, $14 million was distributed among the (winning) candidates.[14]

Late-Train Contribution
A contribution given to a candidate in the period that begins after an election and ends 30 days before a regular legislative session.

The Effect of Contributions on the System

Do campaign contributions buy sponsorship of bills and special favors? The press—and much of the public—thinks that they do.[15] Lobbyists and legislators claim they do not. The increasing volume of campaign contributions noted earlier, and the 12 percent increase in the number of lobbyists from 1998 to 2007, are evidence that would tend to support the perceptions of the press and the public.[16] In 2007, there were 9.8 lobbyists

10. Texans for Public Justice, *Money in PoliTex: A Guide to Money in the 2006 Texas Elections,* September 2007, www.tpj.org/reports/politex2006, accessed March 13, 2008.
11. *Ibid.*
12. *Ibid.*
13. *Ibid.*
14. Texans for Public Justice, "Who Bankrolls Your Legislator?" News Release, September 27, 2007, www.tpj.org/reports/politex2006/pressrelease06.html, accessed March 14, 2008.
15. James Gibbons, "Officials Come and Go; the Lobby Rules," *Austin American-Statesman,* January 27, 2003.
16. The Texas Ethics Commission listed 1,561 registered lobbyists in 1999. In 2007, the number of registered lobbyists increased to 1,780. See Texas Ethics Commission, *Lobby Lists and Reports,* www.ethics.state.tx.us/dfs/loblists.htm, accessed March 14, 2008.

for every legislator.[17] Records of the 2005 legislative session show that lobbyists earned $304 million trying to influence decisions of the Texas legislature—up from $172 million in 1995.[18] These figures do not include expenditures to influence the members of the executive branch.

The Regulation of Lobbying

Lobbyists and organizations that spend more than a specified amount attempting to shape public decisions are required to register and file reports with the Texas Ethics Commission. Appropriate behavior of both lobbyists and public officials is spelled out in Chapter 305 of the Government Code of Texas.

Who Must Register and Report Lobbying Costs?

Not all lobbyists are required by state law to register and report their activities. Classes of lobbyists not required to register and report include state officials and state employees who lobby, even if lobbying is their principal function. Also exempt are individuals from the private sector who are not paid for their services and do not directly spend any money to influence legislative or administrative action.

Those who do have to register and report are private-sector lobbyists who pass the "compensation threshold" of $1,000 in salary per quarter-year or the "expenditure threshold" of $500 per quarter-year. These rules seem simple and straightforward, but an examination of the law reveals that not all compensation and expenditures are counted as lobbying. Exempted from reporting are the following:

- Compensation received to prepare for lobbying.
- Office expenses, including telephone, fax, copying, office supplies, postage, dues and subscriptions, transportation, and the costs of clerical help.
- Costs associated with events to which all members of the legislature are invited.[19]

These and other exemptions in the law mean that an incomplete picture of the investment in lobbying by interest groups is made available to the people.

What Must a Lobbyist Report?

The lobbyist registration form requires the lobbyist to reveal the following:

- For whom he or she lobbies—information about these clients and employers.
- The policy areas of concern.
- The compensation category into which the salary or reimbursement received falls.
- The name of, and information about, anyone who assists the principal lobbyist through direct contact with public officials.

Activity reports must be filed by the tenth day of each month for any lobbyist who foresees expending more than $1,000 per year. Those who spend less need only file annually.[20]

Reporting on Clients. A firm or entity often represents multiple clients before the state legislature and administrative agencies. The reporting law requires a lobbyist working for

17. The ratio of lobbyists to lawmakers is calculated by dividing the number of registered lobbyists in 2007 (1,780) by 181—the number of legislators in the Texas House and Senate.
18. Texans for Public Justice, *Austin's Oldest Profession: Texas's Top Lobby Clients and Those Who Support Them, 2005 Edition,* www.tpj.org/reports/austinsoldest06/facts.html.
19. Texas Ethics Commission, "Texas Ethics Commission Rules: Chapter 34. Regulation of Lobbyists," 2007, www.ethics.state.tx.us/legal/ch34.html, accessed March 16, 2008.
20. *Ibid.*

a lobbying firm to report who pays the firm to represent its interests to the government. Without such a requirement, those who wanted to influence legislative and executive officials anonymously could simply hire someone else to lobby on their behalf. For many years, in fact, this guarantee of anonymity existed in Texas.

did you know?

That during the 2006 election cycle, Republicans raised 66 percent of the money contributed to campaigns, Democrats 25 percent, and Independents 10 percent.[21]

Financial Reporting. As noted, the lobbyist's compensation and expenditures are reported in broad categories rather than in actual amounts. Some believe that this practice understates the influence of money on policy making. In 2003, Southwestern Bell Telephone reported having 12 paid and 14 unpaid lobbyists at the time of filing, and 65 "prospective" lobbyists with salaries set but not paid. The payroll for the session was between $3,935,000 and $7,600,000. Again in 2005, Southwestern Bell, renamed AT&T, led all others in lobby contracts and expenditures.[22]

Criticisms of the Reporting Standards. Critics have suggested that the actual compensation and expenditures of a lobbyist should be disclosed, rather than broad categories. This additional detail would require little effort, because the lobbyist must have the actual figures to know which category to mark on the form.

Reporting on which policy area a lobbyist seeks to influence can also be rather vague. The lobbyist, again, need only check a box on the form. Such a requirement may hide as much as it reveals. Requiring lobbyists to reveal more specifically what they are lobbying about would enable the public to see where corporations, trade associations, labor unions, and individuals were concentrating their efforts.

To provide a clear picture of lobbying activity, Texas could require lobbyists to list the numbers of the bills they have lobbied for and the rule-making hearings before executive agencies at which they have testified. This would require more time and expense in filling out the activity forms. Many believe that Texas does not require this additional information because special interests have successfully lobbied the legislature to keep the lobbying law relatively weak.

What We Know about Lobbying. Thanks to the research of Texans for Public Justice and the Texas Ethics Commission, several interesting facts about the lobbying industry in Texas are clear:

- Special interests entered into 7,455 lobby contracts with 1,525 lobbyists in 2005.[23]
- Sixteen identifiable industry groupings spent more than $1 million each to have their interests protected or advanced.[24]
- Most lobbyists are affiliated with law firms in Texas.

Table 18–3 shows details on the industries spending the most money to influence Texas state government and the number of lobby contracts entered into by each. We also have information about expenditures in a few categories that do require detailed reporting. Expenditures of more than $50 per day on members of the state legislature for food, drink, transportation, or lodging or in the form of a gift must be reported by name, date,

---

21. Texans for Public Justice, *Money in PoliTex: A Guide to Money in the 2006 Texas Elections,* September 2007, www.tpj.org/reports/politex2006, accessed March 13, 2008.
22. Texans for Public Justice, *Austin's Oldest Profession: Texas's Top Lobby Clients and Those Who Service Them: 2004 Edition,* Part II, "Lobby Clients," p. 1; Texans for Public Justice, *Austin's Oldest Profession: Texas's Top Lobby Clients and Those Who Support Them, 2005 Edition,* www.tpj.org/reports/austinsoldest06/facts.html.
23. *Ibid.*
24. *Ibid.*

TABLE 18–3 Number and Maximum Value of Lobby Contracts Issued by Industry Groupings

Industry Grouplng	Number of Contracts	Value of Contracts
Energy and natural resources	910	$20,790,311
Ideological and single issue	1,224	20,035,596
Health	911	17,970,371
Miscellaneous business	870	16,398,372
Finance	538	10,275,279
Communications	400	9,400,143
Lawyers and lobbyists	334	9,380,153
Real estate	336	8,770,123
Insurance	536	8,565,309
Electronics and computers	313	6,310,091
Transportation	348	5,039,182
Construction	242	4,630,134
Agriculture	179	3,230,072
Labor	137	2,690,042
Unknown	66	810,033
Other	91	1,440,033
Total	**7,455**	**$304,122,043**

Source: Texans for Public Justice, *Austin's Oldest Profession: Texas's Top Lobby Clients and Those Who Service Them, 2005 Edition,* available at www.tpj.org/reports/austinsoldest06/clients.html.

place, and purpose.[25] Expenditures for broadcast or print advertisements, mass mailings, and other communications designed to support or oppose legislation or administrative actions also must be identified.

What Is Not Reported as Lobbying. Campaign and late-train contributions to public officials are not lobbying expenses as defined by law, even though the state recognizes their potential to influence policy making. As noted earlier, such contributions cannot be made fewer than 30 days before a legislative session or during the session. This restriction is intended to prevent corruption or the appearance of corruption. Campaign contributions are thus reported to the Texas Ethics Commission separately from lobbying expenses.

Registration and the Legislature

Members of the Texas legislature are provided with a list of registered lobbyists and their clients by February 1 of each legislative (odd-numbered) year.[26] The public may obtain copies of registration and activity reports from the Texas Ethics Commission. Much of the information is available from the Ethics Commission on the Internet or on paper.

There is much evidence that lawmakers' regulation of lobbying remains, in the public's mind, unfinished business and controversial. The legislature tweaks the laws frequently in response to suspected or verifiable scandal. In 2001, for example, a new conflict-of-interest statute directed the Ethics Commission to write rules requiring lobbyists to provide

25. Texas Ethics Commission, *Lobbying in Texas,* Part IVB.
26. Texas Government Code, Section 305.011.

written notice to the commission and to their clients when they represent multiple clients who may have incompatible legislative goals. It is a common practice for a lobbyist in Texas to represent multiple clients. Because many firms represent many clients, the possibility of a conflict exists when different people in the firm represent clients with opposing legislative objectives. It can be argued that this change to the law benefits the interests that hire lobbyists more than it does the general public.

The Craft of Lobbying

Those who directly contact public officials to influence their behavior will find their work easier if they are extroverted and enjoy socializing. The lobbyist's first job is to become known and recognized by members of the legislature and by any executive officials relevant to the interest he or she represents.

Lobbying Before the Legislative Session Begins

Before a legislative session begins, a lobbyist must have successfully completed several tasks:

- Learn who is predisposed to support the lobbyist's cause, who is on the other side, and which members can be swayed.
- Memorize the faces of the members, their nonlegislative occupations, the counties they represent, and a little about their families.
- Establish rapport through personal contact with the members of the legislature.
- Get to know the staffs of legislators, because the members can be influenced through them.
- Know the legislative issues, including the arguments of opponents.

Honesty Is the Best Policy. To maintain relationships with legislators, the lobbyist must provide sound, accurate information about the legislation the lobbyist's group supports or opposes. This includes off-the-record admission of the pluses and minuses of the legislation. Honesty is, in fact, often the best policy for a lobbyist when dealing with a public official.

Wining and Dining Also Helps. A lobbyist can befriend a legislator in several ways that may eventually pay off in support. Lobbyists have information that may be valuable to a legislator, and they may be able to help draft an important piece of legislation for her or him. Providing an occasional free meal or acknowledging a helpful legislator at a banquet in his or her honor also has merit from the lobbyist's perspective. All of these actions are necessary to create and maintain goodwill, without which nothing is possible.

Approaching the Legislators. How does a lobbyist approach a member of the legislature or a member of the leadership? How do you get in the door, and what do you say when you get in? How important is the staff of a legislator to a lobbyist? Is it necessary to see all 181 members of the legislature, the lieutenant governor, and the governor?

Given that there are only 140 days in a session, lobbying must precede the convening of the legislature. The 18-month period between regular sessions leaves ample time to do the following:

- Work on relationships.
- Learn what proposals have a chance of receiving favorable responses.
- Draft legislation.
- Line up sponsors to introduce bills in the house and senate at the beginning of the next session.

Key Endorsements. Not all members of the legislature are equal. Establishing rapport with, and obtaining feedback from, the powerful presiding officers—the speaker of the house and the lieutenant governor, who presides over the senate—are especially useful. No endorsements are more important to an interest group than those of the presiding officers. If an endorsement for the group's legislative proposal is not forthcoming, the lobbyist must at least persuade the presiding officers to remain neutral in the legislative struggle.

Securing the endorsement of the chairs of committees through which the legislation must pass before it can go to the floor for a vote is an advantage second only to that of securing the support of the presiding officers. In addition, legislation sought by a local government must have the endorsement of the members representing the relevant legislative districts, or it is doomed to fail.

Lobbying Administrative Agencies

Administrators and interest-group representatives seek each other out to provide and obtain information. For example, the Texas Educational Diagnosticians Association (TEDA) and the state colleges of education may wish to know whether the examination for the certification of diagnosticians is scheduled for revision. They will therefore contact the State Board for Educator Certification to obtain an answer. The issue is important to the TEDA, because the content and difficulty of the exam affect the number of recruits to the profession. Colleges of education know that changes in the state exam mean changes in the curriculum. Inquiries about the exam also allow the interest groups to communicate their professional opinion about the current exam and suggest any changes.

Administrators seek to discover the impact of their programs and rules on the clientele they serve. They may well seek input from those they serve about present and planned programs. In so doing, they surrender some of their power to the clientele to maintain the political support that is in turn necessary to retain the support of the legislature and governor. An agency's clientele is especially interested in influencing the rules and guidelines that control how they do business, because these rules directly affect profits.

The Rule Making Process. Agencies issue formal rules that prescribe the standards of conduct to be followed by citizens who are subject to the law. Agencies also issue guidelines to govern the actions of their staffs in applying the law. The rule making process in Texas gives all interested parties an opportunity to influence an agency's decision. Notice of intent to make a rule must be published in the ***Texas Register.*** A time for written public comment on the proposed rule is established. At the close of the comment period, the agency analyzes the public's views. It then publishes a "final rule" having the force of law.

Texas Register
A publication that contains all official notices of the Texas state government and some notices of regional bodies. It is found in all university libraries and large municipal libraries in Texas.

While all citizens have the right to participate in the rule making process, it is obvious that only those who are aware of, and interested in, the proposed rule will participate. Ordinary citizens do not subscribe to the *Texas Register.* Corporations, labor unions, law firms, and interest groups do. Hence, they know when to mobilize their members to influence decision making.

The Co-optation of Agencies. There is a natural linkage from agency to clientele and clientele to agency. As you learned earlier in this chapter, most state agencies are headed by boards and commissions drawn from the industry, trade, profession, or activity the agency regulates. It is normal for individuals who engage in an economic activity to join the state board or commission regulating that activity and then return to the private sector and resume the regulated activity.

The purpose of this staffing system is to fill the need for expertise in board membership. The question is how the interests of the larger society can be protected when roles become so blurred. Can those regulating an economic activity be objective public servants when they have been, and will be, participants in that activity? Many observers argue that such arrangements endanger the public interest and benefit only special interests. The *Economist* has noted that, in Texas, "the state's business and political elites are hopelessly intertwined."[27]

> **did you know?**
>
> That for a brief period in 2006 and 2007, it was permissible for the policy makers who were given gifts in the form of checks to simply report the check as a gift without having to disclose the amount that the check was made out for.

Lobbying the Courts

Filing suit to affect government activities is not lobbying or pressure politics. Rather, it involves using a long-established set of legal procedures to challenge the substance of laws, administrative rules, or other government actions. Only persons licensed to practice law can handle cases in the state's major trial courts.

Grounds for Lawsuits. Anyone negatively affected by a law, an administrative rule, or a government action may seek relief from the courts. The challenge may be made on the ground that the agency failed to follow proper procedures in making the rule or that it misinterpreted the law in writing guidelines or rules. The allegation that the laws or rules are applied unfairly is another basis for suit.

Using the courts is typically a last resort. Nevertheless, major corporations, labor unions, interest groups, and local governments employ staff attorneys to protect their interests. Smaller and less wealthy organizations may keep attorneys on retainer or use attorneys on their boards of directors to represent their interests as needed.

The Impact of Judicial Elections. Between 1994 and 2006, CBS ran programs about "justice for sale" on *60 Minutes,* alleging that the Texas Supreme Court overwhelmingly identifies with specific interests. These reports have led to demands for campaign-finance regulations to reduce any possible conflicts of interest caused by justices accepting campaign contributions. Thus far, however, the legislature has resisted enactment of anything but voluntary compliance standards for judicial campaigns.[28]

Legislators and elected executives are expected to be highly partisan. Judges are expected to be as impartial as humanly possible. Currently, Texas is one of 15 states that elects its judges in partisan elections. Even though most voters do not know who the judicial candidates are, they prefer to elect their judges rather than allow an independent commission or some other body to nominate nonpartisan judges. Political parties and campaign consultants also have a vested interest in maintaining the status quo. Reformers, however, will continue to seek changes in the method of selecting judges, even when they do not advocate changes in the other branches of government.

Dan Lambe, executive director of Texas Watch, displays what he calls the ten most harmful Texas Supreme Court decisions for consumers. He says that the Texas Supreme Court routinely favors business over consumer and family rights in deciding cases. Does this type of campaign have any chance of influencing the Texas court? (AP Photo/Harry Cabluck)

27. "The Future Is Texas," *The Economist,* December 19, 2002.
28. Clay Robison, "Campaign 96: 'Justice for Sale' Charges Leveled Anew," *Houston Chronicle,* September 22, 1996, p. 1A.

WHY SHOULD YOU CARE ABOUT... TEXAS INTEREST GROUPS?

The Texas legislature decided in 2003 to allow each university to set tuition, rather than having it set by the legislature. This decision has led to rapidly rising tuition costs in Texas. Were you represented during the policy formulation and policy adoption stages of that policy-making event? Probably not. Many students may not know why tuition has risen.

The new tuition policy in Texas affects how many people can go to the state universities and which institutions they can afford to attend. We can see similar effects in other policy areas. State policies, in other words, affect the quality of life of every citizen. That is why groups organize to control the political agenda and policy outcomes. Those who do not participate do not have a say about what rules apply to them or how state programs may benefit or harm them.

HOW YOU CAN MAKE A DIFFERENCE

Time is precious. Working, studying, sleeping, and socializing consume the lion's share of any student's time. Citizens, however, still have the opportunity to become informed and use their knowledge to influence the decisions of their state and local governments. How? Become a joiner. Allow an organization that shares your values to monitor government activities and represent you at the state capitol and city hall.

Organizations can analyze the political environment and summarize the information that you need to know to understand the political situation. The organization you join can notify you whenever a phone call, e-mail, or letter from you could help affect the outcome of votes and rule making activities. Such participation will not take much of your time.

Almost every organized interest has a Web site that you can locate using popular search engines. Size and wealth are assets that help groups to become powerful, but good leadership and good issues are also important. One group that you might consider is Common Cause of Texas. Founded more than 30 years ago, it has never had a membership in excess of 6,000 or a budget in excess of $100,000, yet it is constantly called on for advice by the Texas Ethics Commission and the state legislature. Why? Because of the consistency of its opinions, the length of time it has spent in the political arena, the stability of its leadership, and its focus on "good government" issues. You can contact Common Cause at:

Common Cause of Texas
603 W. 13th, Suite 2-D
Austin, TX 78701
512-474-2374
e-mail: commoncause@ccsi.com

www.commoncause.org

Click on "State Organizations" and then on Texas on the U.S. map.

questions for discussion and analysis

1. What are the positive and negative effects of interest groups in Texas politics? How can the negative effects be controlled?
2. What techniques do interest groups use to influence state policies?
3. What factors determine the relative power of interest groups in Texas?

key terms

access 598
conflict of interest 594
co-optation 597
discretion 596
fragmentation 602
implementation 595
late-train contribution 605
subsidies 594
Texas Register 610
umbrella organization 600
unfunded mandate 595

chapter summary

1. Interest groups are organizations of people who agree on policy issues that affect their members. Interest groups do not nominate candidates for office but do care about the ideologies of those who stand for election. They therefore may form political action committees (PACs) to support candidates favorable to their causes.

2. The constitutions of the United States and Texas promote political expression. The right to organize to petition officials is explicit. This right recognizes that representatives of the people can represent their constituents only when they are informed of their wishes. Interest groups are therefore constitutionally protected.

3. Groups with sufficient resources employ staff to monitor the government. They proactively bring issues before decision makers and reactively move into the political process to stop or alter proposals that negatively affect their membership.

4. Business groups are among the strongest interests. Large corporations lobby decision makers both through umbrella organizations and directly. It is not uncommon for large interests to have more than 20 paid lobbyists working for them during a legislative session. Between sessions, groups conduct research, draft proposed legislation for the next session, and monitor and influence the executive branch, which writes the rules to carry out laws.

5. Interest groups have been powerful in Texas due to the historical absence of competitive two-party politics, restrictive election laws, low voter turnout, and the below-average educational attainment of many citizens.

6. As happens at the national level, "iron triangles" often form in Texas. These triangles unite interest groups that represent a particular industry or activity with the bureaucracy that regulates the activity and with the members of the legislative committee that oversees the bureaucracy. Iron triangles are especially potent in Texas, because regulatory boards and commissions are required to have members who actively participate in the regulated activity. This requirement almost guarantees conflicts of interest. Looser alliances called issue networks also form. These may consist of legislators, legislative staff members, interest-group leaders, bureaucrats, journalists, scholars, and others who support a particular policy position on a given issue.

7. The media, a few nonprofit and officially nonpartisan special interests, and the Texas Ethics Commission are the sources of most of the information we have about the relationship between interest groups and public officials in Texas. Most lobbyists are required to file reports with the Ethics Commission, which in turn publishes the names, addresses, employers, expenditures, and salaries (in broad categorical ranges) of lobbyists. The media and the nonpartisan interests "blow the whistle" about conflicts of interest and official behavior that is suspect.

selected print & media resources

SUGGESTED READINGS

Hrebenar, Ronald, and Clive Thomas. *Interest Group Politics in the Southern States.* Tuscaloosa: University of Alabama Press, 1992 (reprinted in 2002). This is one of four regional analyses of special-interest power in the United States by these authors. It gives a comprehensive look at power structures, types of interests, lobbying tactics, and state regulations. It contains very good, although somewhat dated, information.

———. "Who's Got Clout? Interest Group Power in the States." *State Legislatures,* April 1999. This article serves to update the authors' previous works. The title pinpoints the focus.

Prindle, David. *Petroleum Politics in Texas and the Texas Railroad Commission.* Austin: University of Texas Press, 1981. This work looks inside one of the most powerful regulatory agencies in the United States, the Texas Railroad Commission. Internal politics, conflicts of interest, external pressure groups and their agents, methods of operation, and consequences of the Commission's policy choices are all examined.

Texas Ethics Commission. *Lobbying in Texas.* Austin: Texas Ethics Commission, published annually. This document defines lobbying and summarizes the law governing lobbying. Information on who should register, how to fill out reports, and dates of submission are included. Available in paper and online.

Texans for Public Justice. *Austin's Oldest Profession: Texas's Top Lobby Clients and Those Who Service Them.* Austin: Texans for Public Justice, published annually. Through this publication, Texans for Public Justice compiles information from the Texas Ethics Commission and disseminates it widely throughout the state in press releases, in publications, and electronically. Registered lobbyists in Texas are identified, along with their employers. Lobbyists are grouped by interests, such as energy and natural resources, ideological and single issues, health, and miscellaneous business.

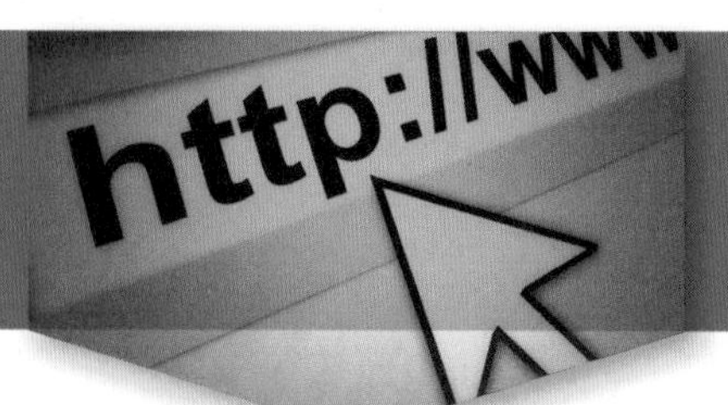

e-mocracy

TEXAS INTEREST GROUPS ON THE WEB

The Internet has given interest groups a very useful tool to mobilize and inform their members. An organization cannot really claim to be "in the game" if it does not have a Web site. Mailing lists are another tool for disseminating information and soliciting donations. At the national level, some of the larger interest groups have organized their home pages to tempt their more ardent supporters to use the home pages as gateways to the entire Internet. Texas interest groups and the Texas branches of national interest groups also strive to maintain a Web presence, as you can see from the examples in the *Logging On* section that follows.

LOGGING ON

You can view the Web sites of leading economic interest groups in Texas at the following addresses. The Texas Association of Business is at:
www.txbiz.org

The Texas Association of Mexican-American Chambers of Commerce (TAMACC) is at:
www.tamacc.org

For the American Federation of Labor–Congress of Industrial Organizations (AFL-CIO) in Texas, go to:
www.texasaflcio.org

For the Texas Trial Lawyers Association, go to:
www.ttla.com/tx

For the Texas Farm Bureau, go to:
www.txfb.org

Education-oriented groups are well represented on the Web. For the Texas State Teachers Association (TSTA), go to:
www.tsta.org

For interesting information available on the TSTA Web site, click on "Legislative" and then "Guide to Lobbying." For the Texas Association of School Boards (TASB), go to:
www.tasb.org

Hispanics in Texas are represented by a variety of groups. The Texas branch of the League of United Latin American Citizens (LULAC), for example, has a site at:
www.tx-lulac.org

You can find out who made major campaign contributions on a state-by-state or even ZIP-code-by-ZIP-code basis at the Web site of the Center for Responsive Politics at:
www.opensecrets.org

For Web sites of selected think tanks in Texas, go to the following addresses:
The Center for Public Policy Priorities is at:
www.cppp.org

Texas Citizens for a Sound Economy have a Web site at:
www.freedomworks.org/texas

The Texas Public Policy Foundation can be found at:
www.texaspolicy.com

ONLINE REVIEW

At **www.cengage.com/politicalscience/schmidt/agandpttexas14e**, you will find a Tutorial Quiz for this chapter, providing questions on the chapter contents, including the features. You'll gain access to other helpful study tools, including the book's glossary and flashcards, crossword puzzles, and Web links, as well as "Which Side Are You On?" and "Politics and . . ." features written by the authors of the book.

chapter

19

Political Parties In Texas

chapter contents

< Texas delegates at the Republican National Convention. (Mike Segar/Reuters/Corbis)

WHAT IF... Texas nominated its candidates by conventions?

BACKGROUND

In Texas and most other states, political parties use the direct primary election for selecting nominees to national, state, and some local offices. Voters in Texas go to the polls in the spring and vote in either the Democratic or Republican primary election to select their party's nominee. This method of selecting party nominees through elections is unique to the American political system. In most Western democracies, party leaders and delegates meeting in conventions or caucuses select party candidates; rank-and-file voters do not participate in the nomination process.

The direct primary emerged in the early twentieth century as part of the American Progressive reform movement. Reformers, disenchanted with the autocratic and corrupt influence of party leaders, pressed for more involvement of ordinary voters in the nomination process. In addition, in states where there was very little party competition, the primary election helped ensure meaningful popular participation. This was certainly the case in Texas, which, like the South in general, was dominated by the Democratic Party. Up until the early 1980s, the Democratic primary was the only competitive election in Texas.

These days, competitors for the party nominations in Texas and other states are self-selected; that is, the individuals decide to run and, consequently, are primarily responsible for their own campaign organization, strategy, and spending.

NOMINATION BY CONVENTION

Nominating by convention allows parties much more control over the nomination. Party leaders can ensure that candidates are those loyal to the party's platform; they can also select nominees they believe will be stronger candidates in the general election. For example, in Great Britain, the national party organization sends a list of approved party nominees to the local party organization. The local party organization then interviews the potential nominees and selects them based on several factors, including the candidate's loyalty to party goals and his or her potential for winning. The party is able to concentrate its resources behind its nominee and play a dominant role in organizing the campaign.

Although the prospect of this kind of party control seems unthinkable to Texans and most other Americans, there are consequences of the convention nomination process that appeal to some, particularly party activists. Texas parties would be able to exercise more control over those that bear their party label. For example, a Republican candidate in Texas who supports abortion rights would have little chance of being the GOP nominee (the GOP's official position is pro-life). Others argue that it is easier to assign credit or blame to the party in power if nominees are closely tied to the party and the party's program. That is, a convention system may result in greater accountability in government, particularly if both the executive and legislative branches are controlled by the same party. Some observers maintain that there would be less need for the massive amounts of funding that characterize competitive primary races.

Although every state in the United States allows for nomination by the direct primary, some states either permit or require conventions to nominate candidates for governor or U.S. Senator. For example, in New York, primaries are not mandatory and are held only if two or more candidates receive 25 percent of the convention delegates' votes. In Colorado, if a candidate receives more than 50 percent of the votes of the delegates, he or she may avoid a primary. Some states, such as Massachusetts and Minnesota, allow for preprimary endorsements by party conventions. While candidates endorsed by party conventions do not always win the primary, the party's endorsement gives the recipient visibility and some advantage over well-financed challengers.

As long as the Republican Party continues to dominate Texas politics at the state level, a formal role for state conventions in the nominating process is not likely. As this chapter points out, for many offices in Texas, the Republican primary may be the only competitive election. However, if the state moves toward two truly competitive parties, there may be incentives for the Democratic and Republican party leaders to exert more influence over the nomination process.

FOR CRITICAL ANALYSIS

1. Other than GOP dominance, what other factors would make it difficult for Texas to adopt a convention system of nominating candidates?
2. Describe the major issue positions of Democrats or Republicans in Texas. How would a convention system of nominating candidates make it easier for the state party to enact its positions into law?

The American founders created our complicated federal system and provided for the election of a president and Congress. But the U.S. Constitution makes no mention of political parties. Indeed, early American leaders held negative attitudes about parties. George Washington warned of the "baneful effects of the spirit of party" in his farewell address. James Madison, in *Federalist Paper* No. 10 (see Appendix B), criticized parties or "factions" as divisive, although he admitted they were inevitable. Madison and others thought that parties would encourage conflict and undermine consensus on public policy. Yet despite their condemnation of parties, these early American politicians engaged in partisan politics and initiated a competitive two-party system, as described in Chapter 8.

Development of the Texas Party System

Although the two-party system characterizes American politics, many states and localities—Texas, for one—have been dominated by just one party at various times in history. Texas was formerly a one-party Democratic state, but that is no longer the case. To understand political parties in Texas, it is necessary to examine the history of one-party dominance by the Democratic Party, the emergence of two-party competition in the state, and the emerging Republican Party domination of Texas, which can be expected to last years into the future.

did you know?

That in the 1890s, the journalist O. Henry wrote, "We have only two or three laws [in Texas], such as against murder before witnesses and being caught stealing horses and voting the Republican ticket".

The One-Party Tradition in Texas

Under the Republic of Texas, there was little party activity. Political divisions were usually oriented around support of, or opposition to, Sam Houston (a leading founder of the Republic). After Texas became a state, however, the Democratic Party dominated Texas politics until the 1990s. This legacy of dominance was firmly established by the Civil War and the era of Reconstruction, as described in Chapters 19 and 20. During this period, Northern troops occupied the South under the direction of a Republican U.S. Congress. From the time Republican and former Union soldier Edmund J. Davis's single term as governor ended in 1874 until Republican Bill Clements's surprising victory in the 1978 gubernatorial election, the Democrats exercised almost complete control over Texas politics.

The Populist Challenge. The Democratic Party was, at times, challenged by the emergence of more liberal third parties. The most serious of these challenges came in the late 1800s with the Populist revolt. The Populist Party grew out of the dissatisfaction of small farmers, who demanded government regulation of rates charged by banks and railroads, as well as an inflationary monetary policy.

These farmers—joined by sharecroppers, laborers, and African Americans—mounted a serious election bid in 1896 by taking 44 percent of the vote for governor. Eventually,

Official photograph of the 1928 Democratic National Convention, held in Houston. Holding the convention in Texas did little to help the Democratic nominee, Governor Al Smith of New York. Smith was the first Catholic ever nominated as a presidential candidate by a major party, and he lost many Southern states, including Texas. Why might many Protestants have been unwilling to accept a Catholic presidential candidate in those days? (Calvin Wheat Studio, Library of Congress Prints & Photographs Division, Washington, D.C. [LC-USZ62-128459])

however, the Democratic Party diffused the threat of the Populists by co-opting many of the issues of the new party. The Democrats also effectively disenfranchised African Americans and poor whites in 1902 with the establishment of a poll tax.

The Democratic Primary. Two events in the early 20th century solidified the position of the Democrats in Texas politics. The first was the institution of party primary reforms in 1906. For the first time, voters could choose the party's nominees by a vote in a **direct primary.** Thereafter, the Democratic primary became the substitute for the two-party contest—the general election. In the absence of Republican competition, the Democratic primary was the only game in town, and it provided a competitive arena for political differences within the state.

Direct Primary
An intraparty election in which the voters select the candidates who will run on a party's ticket in the subsequent general election. In Texas, nominees must win a majority of the votes, which often means that there are primary runoff elections between the top two candidates.

The Great Depression. The second event that helped the Democrats was the Great Depression. Although Republican presidential candidate Herbert Hoover carried Texas in 1928, the Republicans were blamed for failing to do enough to combat the Great Depression of the 1930s. The effect of this crisis, added to the effects of the Civil War and Reconstruction, ensured Democratic dominance in state government until the early 1990s.

Ideological Basis of Factionalism: Conservatives and Liberals

Although members of a political party may be similar in their views, *factions,* or divisions, within the party inevitably develop. These conflicts may involve a variety of different personalities and issues, but the most important basis for division is ideology.

To understand the ideological basis for factionalism in political parties in Texas, it is necessary to define the terms *conservative* and *liberal*—a difficult task, because the meanings change with time and may mean different things to different people. You learned about conservative and liberal ideologies in Chapter 1; we review these concepts here.

Conservatives. Modern conservatives typically combine support for the free market with support for traditional values. Conservatives believe that individuals should be left alone to compete in a free market unfettered by government control; they prefer that government regulation of the economy be kept to a minimum. Conservatives, though, often support government subsidies and promotion of business. They may favor construction of highways, tax incentives for investment, and other government aids to business. The theory is that these aids will encourage economic development and hence prosperity for the entire society. In contrast, conservatives are likely to oppose government programs that involve redistribution of wealth, such as welfare, health-care assistance, and unemployment compensation.

As the label suggests, conservatives may view change suspiciously. They may tend to favor the status quo—things as they are now and as they have been in the recent past. They emphasize traditional values associated with the family and close communities, and they often favor government action to preserve what they see as the proper moral values of society. Because conservatives hold a more skeptical view of human nature than do liberals, they are more likely to be tougher on perceived threats to personal safety and the public order. For example, conservatives are more likely to favor stiffer penalties for criminals, including capital punishment.

Liberals. Modern liberals believe that it is often necessary for government to regulate the economy. They point to concentrations of wealth and power that have threatened to control government, destroy economic competition, and weaken individual freedom.

Government power, they believe, should be used to protect the disadvantaged and to promote equality. Liberals generally support the social-welfare programs that conservatives oppose.

Liberals possess a more optimistic view of human nature than conservatives. They tend to believe that individuals are essentially rational and, therefore, that consciously planned change will ultimately bring improvements in the human condition. Liberals want government to protect the civil rights and liberties of individuals and are critical of interference with the exercise of constitutional rights of free speech, press, religion, assembly, association, and privacy. They are often suspicious of conservatives' attempts to "legislate morality" because of the potential for interference with individual rights.

Conservative and Liberal Factions in the Democratic Party

For many years, factions within the Texas Democratic Party resembled a two-party system, and the election to select the Democratic Party's nominees—the primary—was the most important election in Texas. Until the 1990s, conservative Democrats were much more successful than their liberal counterparts in these primaries, in part because Republican voters, facing no significant primary race of their own, regularly "crossed over" and supported conservative Democratic candidates. Voters in the general elections, faced with a choice between a conservative Democrat and a conservative Republican, usually went with the traditional party—the Democrats. These Republican crossover votes enabled conservative Democrats, with few exceptions, to control the party and state government for many years—until 1978, when Bill Clements was elected as the first Republican governor of Texas in 105 years.

Conservative Democrats. Conservative Democrats in Texas provided a good example of the semi-independent relationship of national, state, and local party organizations (as illustrated in Figure 19–1). Texas conservatives traditionally voted Democratic in state and local races but often refused to support the national Democratic candidates for president. The development of the conservative Democratic faction in Texas was an outgrowth of conservative dissatisfaction with many New Deal proposals of Franklin D. Roosevelt in the 1930s and Fair Deal proposals of Harry Truman in the late 1940s. Conservative Democrats in Texas continued their cool relationship with the national party when many of them supported Republican presidential candidates Dwight D. Eisenhower in 1952 and 1956, Richard Nixon in 1968 and 1972, and Ronald Reagan in 1980 and 1984.

Governor Allan Shivers (right) was nationally known for his break with the Democratic Party over the tidelands issue. Shivers endorsed Dwight Eisenhower's presidential candidacy in 1952 and was instrumental in delivering the electoral votes of Texas to the Republicans. A few months after taking office, Eisenhower signed a law that endorsed the state's claim to the tidelands. (Texas State Library and Archives)

The Success of the Conservative Democrats. In the past, the conservative wing of the Democratic Party enjoyed almost continuous success in Texas politics. This faction supplied almost every governor elected from the mid-1930s to the 1970s. These governors included Allan Shivers (served 1949–1957), John Connally (served 1963–1969), and Preston Smith (served 1969–1973), all of whom later switched to the Republican Party. It also included governors Dolph Briscoe (served 1973–1979) and Mark White (served 1983–1987). Until recently, conservative Democrats held almost all of the state's congressional seats; they also dominated both chambers of the Texas legislature.

Several factors accounted for this success, but the most important were the power and resources of the conservative constituency. Conservatives have traditionally made up the state's power elite and represent such interests as the oil, gas, and sulfur industries; other large corporations; bigger farms and ranches, or "agribusiness"; owners and publishers of most of the state's major daily newspapers; and veterans. In other words, the most affluent persons in the state have been able and willing to contribute their considerable resources to the campaigns of like-minded politicians. These segments of the population are also the most likely to turn out to vote in elections. This was a significant advantage to conservative Democrats competing in the party primaries, where turnout has generally been low.

The Impact of Governor Shivers. As described in Chapter 19, Governor Allan Shivers, elected in 1948, did more than any individual to establish the dominance of the conservative faction of the Democratic Party. The Shivers faction (labeled *Shivercrats* by liberals) announced its support for the 1952 Republican presidential nominee, Dwight D. Eisenhower, and urged Texas Democrats to vote Republican for president and Democratic for state offices. That same year, Shivers, along with all other Democratic state officeholders at the time (with the exception of state agriculture commissioner John White), received the nomination of both the Democratic and Republican parties. This dual nomination was a unique situation in Texas politics.

Liberal Democrats. Liberals in the Texas Democratic Party consist of those groups that have supported the national Democratic Party ticket and its presidents (Roosevelt, Truman, Kennedy, Johnson, Carter, Clinton, and Obama). These groups include the following:

- Organized labor, in particular the AFL-CIO.
- African American groups, such as the National Association for the Advancement of Colored People (NAACP).
- Mexican American groups, such as the American G.I. Forum, the League of United Latin American Citizens (LULAC), Mexican American Democrats (MAD), and the Mexican American Legal Defense and Educational Fund (MALDEF).
- Various professionals, teachers, and intellectuals.
- Small farmers and ranchers, sometimes belonging to the Texas Farmers Union.
- Environmental groups, such as the Sierra Club.
- Abortion-rights groups, such as the Texas Abortion Rights Action League.
- Trial lawyers—that is, lawyers who represent plaintiffs in civil suits and defendants in criminal cases.

Success for liberal Democratic politicians in Texas has been infrequent and has rarely persisted for more than a few years. The heyday of Texas liberalism came in a period from the 1890s through the 1930s with the election of several progressive governors. The latter included governors James Hogg (served 1891–1895), "Pa" and "Ma" Ferguson (served 1915–1917, 1925–1927, and 1933–1935), Dan Moody (served 1927–1931), and James V. Allred (served 1935–1939). Since the Great Depression of the 1930s, liberals have been able to capture a U.S. Senate seat only once, in 1957, with the election of Ralph Yarborough. In 1970, Yarborough was defeated for re-election by the moderate-to-conservative Democrat Lloyd Bentsen, who held the seat until he became President Bill Clinton's treasury secretary in 1992.

did you know?

That when Texas voted for Republican presidential candidate George H. W. Bush in 1992, it was the first time in history that Texas voted for a Republican presidential candidate who was unable to win nationally.

Today, liberal Texas Democrats enjoy more success in capturing their party's nomination, largely because conservatives are voting in the Republican primary. In recent years, liberal or moderate Democrats have been routinely nominated for all statewide offices. This presents an irony for liberal Democrats: although they have gained strength within the party from the defection of conservatives, this very defection has permitted the Republicans to dominate Texas politics.

The Rise of the Republican Party

Before the presidential election of 1988, only three modern-day Republicans had won statewide races in Texas: U.S. senator John Tower (served 1961–1985), Governor Bill Clements (served 1979–1983 and 1987–1991), and U.S. Senator Phil Gramm (served 1985–2003). Why had the Republican Party failed to compete in Texas in the past? As we have seen, the most important reason was the bitter memory that was left by the state's experience in the Civil War and during Reconstruction. The Republican administration of Governor E. J. Davis (served 1870–1874) was widely considered by the white majority to be the most corrupt and abusive in Texas history. Only in the last few years has the Republican Party been able to shake its image as "the party of Reconstruction."

The Republicans Become Competitive. The revival of the Republican Party was foreshadowed in the 1950s by the development of the so-called presidential Republicans (those who vote Republican for national office but Democratic for state and local office). Conservative Democrats objected to the liberal policies of the national Democratic Party and often voted for Republican presidential candidates.

The first major step in the rejuvenation of the Republican Party in Texas came in 1961, when John Tower, a Republican, was elected to the U.S. Senate. Tower won a special nonpartisan election held when Lyndon B. Johnson gave up his Senate seat to assume the vice presidency. Tower initially won with the help of many liberal Democrats and was reelected until he retired in 1984. The Republicans retained his seat with the election of former Congressman Phil Gramm over his liberal Democratic opponent Lloyd Doggett in 1984. In November 2002, John Cornyn, a Republican and the state's former attorney general, was elected to replace Gramm.

In November 1978, the Republicans achieved their most stunning breakthrough when Republican Bill Clements defeated Democrat John Hill in the race for governor. After losing the governor's seat to moderate-to-conservative Democrat Mark White in 1982, the Republicans regained their momentum in 1986, when Clements turned the tables on White and recaptured the governor's chair.

The Republicans Become Dominant. Developments in the 1990s and early 2000s transformed Texas into Republican country. With the election in 1992 of U.S. Senator Kay Bailey Hutchison, Republicans held both U.S. Senate seats for the first time since Reconstruction. In 1994, Republican George W. Bush (son of former president George H. W. Bush) defeated incumbent Democratic governor Ann Richards.

By far the most impressive gains for the Republicans came in the November 1998 elections, when incumbent governor George W. Bush led the Republicans to victory in every statewide election. For the first time in living memory, no Democrats occupied any statewide executive or judicial office. Republicans have continued to maintain their monopoly on statewide offices. In 2004, after a successful effort at congressional redistricting, the GOP captured a majority in Texas's congressional delegation.

The Republican Party is also extremely competitive in lower-level offices in the state, where Democrats have been most firmly entrenched. In 1974, the GOP held only 53 offices at the county level; they now hold more than 2,000 county offices. In 1996, the Republicans gained a majority of seats in the state senate, the first time in 126 years that Republicans had held a majority in either chamber of the legislature; and in 2002, they captured the state house of representatives.

Table 19–1 shows the dramatic increases by Republicans in the Texas legislature and the Texas delegation to the U.S. House of Representatives. The extent to which these gains signal a Republican-dominated party system in Texas is discussed later in this chapter.

TABLE 19–1 Changes in the Number of Republican and Democratic Officeholders in Texas

	1973		2011	
	Democrats	Republicans	Democrats	Republicans
Texas House of Representatives	132	17	49	101
Texas Senate	28	3	12	19
U.S. House of Representatives	20	4	9	23
U.S. Senate	1	1	0	2

Sources of Republican Strengths and Weaknesses. Republican voting strength in recent years has been concentrated in several clusters of counties (see Figure 19–1):

- The Houston area
- The Dallas-Fort Worth area
- The Midland-Odessa area
- The Northern Panhandle
- The East Texas oil field counties of Smith, Rusk, and Gregg
- The Hill Country-Edwards Plateau area

FIGURE 19–1 2006 Texas Agriculture Commissioner Election: Democrat Hank Gilbert versus Republican Todd Staples

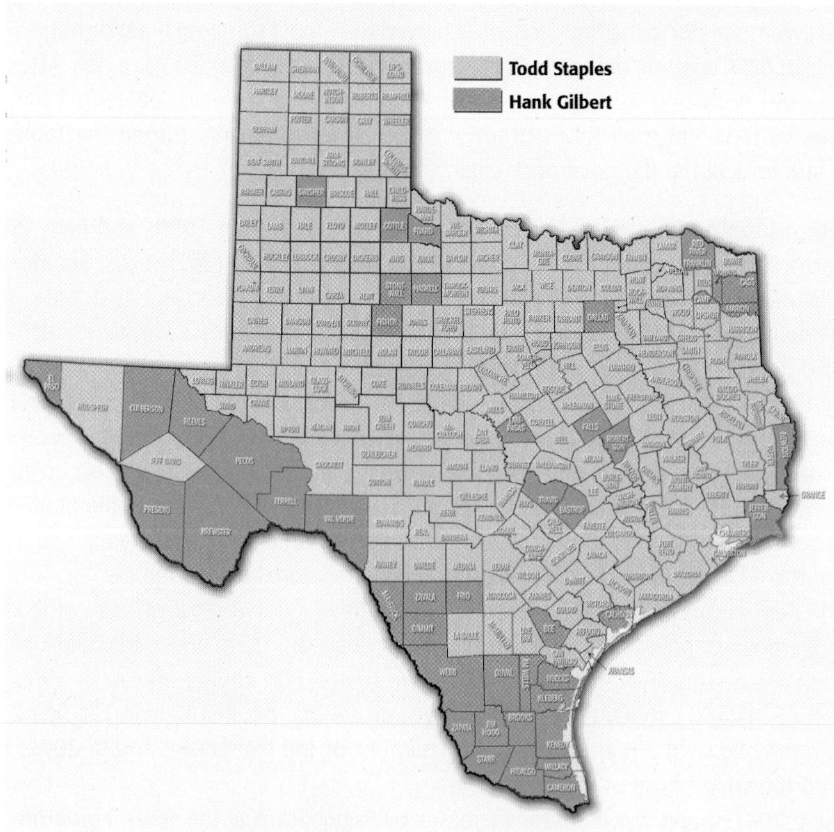

Source: Office of the Texas Secretary of State.

Results from the 2006 Agricultural Commissioner's race reveal that the Republican Party is weaker in the following areas:

- South and South Central Texas
- Pockets of Northwest Texas
- Far West Texas
- Far pockets of East Texas

The Republican Party seems to appeal primarily to the following groups:

- Middle- and upper-class individuals in urban and suburban communities
- Rural, high-income ranchers
- White Anglo-Saxon Protestants (WASPs)
- German Americans whose ancestors were strong supporters of the Union during the Civil War
- Active and retired military officers
- Traditional conservatives who find themselves in a new urban setting

The party has benefited from the economic growth and prosperity that occurred in Texas from the end of World War II to the early 1980s. During this period, newcomers from more Republican parts of the country were lured to the state by a sympathetic business climate or by the promise of jobs. These transplanted Texans joined more prosperous native Texans to provide a political climate more conducive to Republican Party politics.

Conservative and Moderate Factions Within the Republican Party

As the Republican Party becomes more prominent in Texas politics, it is beginning to experience some of the factional differences that characterized the Democratic Party in Texas for years. For example, a bloc of conservative Christians, sometimes loosely referred to as **evangelical** or fundamentalist Christians, has increasingly dominated the Texas Republican Party.[1] This group is concerned with such issues as family, religion, and community morals, and it has been effective in influencing the *party platform.*

Evangelical
Having to do with a broad spectrum of Protestant Christianity that emphasizes salvation and traditional values. Evangelical voters are likely to support culturally conservative politics.

The Success of the Conservative Christian Bloc. In 1992, conservative Christians in the Texas Republican Party easily gained control of the Republican state convention and strengthened the antiabortion and antihomosexuality planks in the party's platform. They also captured more than half the seats on the Republican State Executive Committee. Since 1994, the state party chair and a majority of the members of the state executive committee have been conservative Christians. This dominance of leadership positions has given the conservative Christians a degree of control of the party machinery that continues today.

Republican Moderates. The control of the state's Republican Party by the conservative, or right, wing is opposed by the more moderate, or centrist, wing. Many of these moderates fear that the radicalism of the right will interfere with the party's ability to win elections. Many moderates represent business interests, and they are more concerned with keeping taxes low and limiting the government's interference in business decision making than with moral issues.

---

1. Actually, a majority of American Protestants can be characterized as evangelical. Not all are politically conservative. Some are politically liberal, such as former Democratic presidents Jimmy Carter and Bill Clinton. Conservative Protestants are also sometimes referred to as *fundamentalists.* Fundamentalists are a subset of evangelicals who believe in several doctrines not held by all evangelicals. In particular, fundamentalists believe in *biblical inerrancy*—that is, that every word of the Bible is literally true. In politics, fundamentalists are notably more conservative than other evangelicals; liberal fundamentalists are rare. See George M. Marsden, *Understanding Fundamentalism and Evangelicalism* (Grand Rapids, MI: Eerdmans Publishing, 1991); and Karen Armstrong, *The Battle for God* (New York: Ballantine Books, 2001).

Republicans and Minorities

In general, the Republican Party has failed to generate much support among the state's minority voters. African American identification with the Republicans consistently hovers around 5 percent. Party strategists have made no great effort to attract African Americans, since they are unlikely to switch parties.

Although George W. Bush did well among Texas Hispanic voters in the 2004 presidential elections, Mexican Americans in Texas have traditionally identified with the Democratic

POLITICS AND... third parties

CRYSTAL CITY HIGH SCHOOL AND THE CREATION OF THE RAZA UNIDA PARTY

Political parties have generally been viewed with suspicion by the American people. In spite of that trepidation, they formed as soon as the country was founded. Except for a brief period known as the "era of good feelings," when the country experimented with one party, the U.S. has operated under a two-party system. Given that candidates are generally selected from single-member districts and must win a plurality of votes, it is difficult for more than two parties to compete effectively.

Every now and then, however, a third party develops, causing a restructuring among the larger parties. Texas had precisely such an experience in the 1970s, when the Raza Unida Party formed. The Raza Unida Party arose from the ethnic conflicts experienced by Mexican Americans in the town of Crystal City, Texas. While the town had served as an internment camp for German, Japanese, and Italian Americans during World War II, by the 1960s its spinach fields had attracted a growing Mexican American population. This group had long been denied political power. Poll taxes and intimidation were used to dissuade Hispanics from voting in the town.[a] In 1963, the Hispanic population organized, getting a substantial number to pay the poll tax and vote. The result was a turnover in control of city council from white to Hispanic control.

A few years later, Hispanic students at Crystal City High School, led by José Ángel Gutiérrez, protested the unequal treatment Hispanic students experienced at the school. After several walk-outs, protests, and even federal intervention, the Mexican American population was successful in electing Hispanics to the school board.[b] The movement also led to the creation of the Mexican American Youth Organization (MAYO), which led to the creation of the Raza Unida Party in 1970. The leaders of MAYO—Mario Compean, José Ángel Gutiérrez, Ignacio Pérez, and Willie Velásquez—would lead the Raza Unida Party into other states. They would field candidates for office, having their greatest electoral success at the local level.[c]

Twice the Raza Unida Party fielded Ramsey Muñiz as their gubernatorial candidate. In 1972, he ran a campaign with a focus on improving the lives of Mexican Americans. In 1974, he expanded the focus of the campaign to include improved transportation, education, and health care,[d] but attracted less support.

While the Raza Unida Party was unsuccessful in electing statewide office holders, it was successful in electing school board members and city and county officials. More importantly, the party mobilized thousands of previously disenfranchised voters. Young Hispanics became politically involved in ways not seen before. The Raza Unida Party's influence would wane, but its efforts demonstrate the influence young people can have on politics. Moreover, the party accomplished what many third parties can do—bring the issues of a previously ignored population to the forefront. The Raza Unida Party brought the concerns of Mexican Americans to the attention of the two major political parties. These concerns would become part of the Democratic Party's platform.

FOR CRITICAL ANALYSIS

What were some of the ramifications of creating a third party like the Raza Unida Party? Why is it that third parties have such a difficult time in winning elections? What would have to change for the U.S. to have a multiparty system?

a. John Staples Shockley, *Chicano Revolt in a Texas Town* (Notre Dame, Indiana: University of Notre Dame Press, 1974).

b. Ibid.

c. Ignatio M. Garcia, *United We Win: The Rise and Fall of La Raza Unida Party* (Tucson: University of Arizona Mexican American Studies Research Center, 1989).

d. Teresa Palomo Acosta, "Raza Unida Party," in The Handbook of Texas Online, www.tshaonline.org/handbook/online/articles/RR/war1.html, accessed May 21, 2008.

Party. However, in 2008, Barack Obama captured 63 percent of the Hispanic vote in Texas. Democrats typically capture elections in heavily Hispanic counties, such as those found in the southern and southwestern areas of the state. Nevertheless, observers note that a substantial number of Hispanic voters are *swing voters* (see Chapter 8) not bound by party identification. The Democratic Party cannot afford to take this portion of the electorate for granted, and the Republican Party cannot assume that Hispanic party identification will trend its way. Do the Republicans have a chance of winning enough of the Hispanic vote to maintain their dominance in the state?

An Example of a Third Party: The Libertarian Party

Chances are, if you have voted in a Texas election, you have seen many Libertarian candidates on the ballot. In recent years, the Libertarian Party has become an active, if not always influential, force in Texas politics. The Libertarian Party has a hands-off philosophy of government that combines the conservative emphasis on free markets with the liberal skepticism toward legislating morality. The party's general philosophy is one of individual liberty and personal responsibility. Applying their doctrine to the issues, Libertarians oppose Social Security, campaign-finance reform, and military intervention abroad. The Libertarian Party faces the same hurdles as other third parties: poor financing, a lack of media coverage, and in some states, getting access to the ballot. A key problem for the Libertarians is that some of their ideas may be taken over by one of the major parties, in particular the Republicans. They have managed, however, to elect more than three hundred Libertarians to public office at the local and state levels throughout the country.

A lawn sign supporting Bob Smither, the Libertarian Party's candidate for District 22 in the 2006 elections. This district was vacated by the scandal-plagued Tom DeLay. Smither received 6 percent of the vote, breaking the Texas Libertarian Party's record for a congressional candidate. (Nick Lampson won.) In total, the Libertarian Party of Texas had 168 candidates on the ballot, its highest count ever. (Photo courtesy of Advocates for Self-Government and Bob Smither's campaign)

How the Party Machinery Is Organized in Texas

To better understand how political parties are organized in Texas, we can divide the party machinery into two parts: the *temporary,* consisting of a series of short-lived conventions at various levels; and the *permanent,* consisting of people elected to continuing leadership positions in the party (see Figure 19–2).

Temporary Party Organization

Conventions are held at all levels of party organization in Texas. Conventions draw in a much larger number of party members than the ongoing permanent bodies can mobilize.

The Precinct Convention. The voting precinct is the starting point of party activity, for it is the scene of the precinct convention, a gathering of the faithful that is open to all who voted earlier in the day in that party's primary. It is also the key to getting involved in politics. (See the *You Can Make a Difference* feature at the end of this chapter.)

On a Tuesday early in March in even-numbered years, both the Democratic and the Republican parties hold conventions in almost all the voting precincts in the state. The ticket of admission is usually a voter-registration card stamped to indicate that the holder voted in the party's primary earlier in the day. The agenda of the precinct convention includes the following:

- Adoption of resolutions to be passed on to the county or state senatorial district convention.
- Selection of delegates to the county or senatorial district convention.

FIGURE 19–2 Texas Political Party Organization

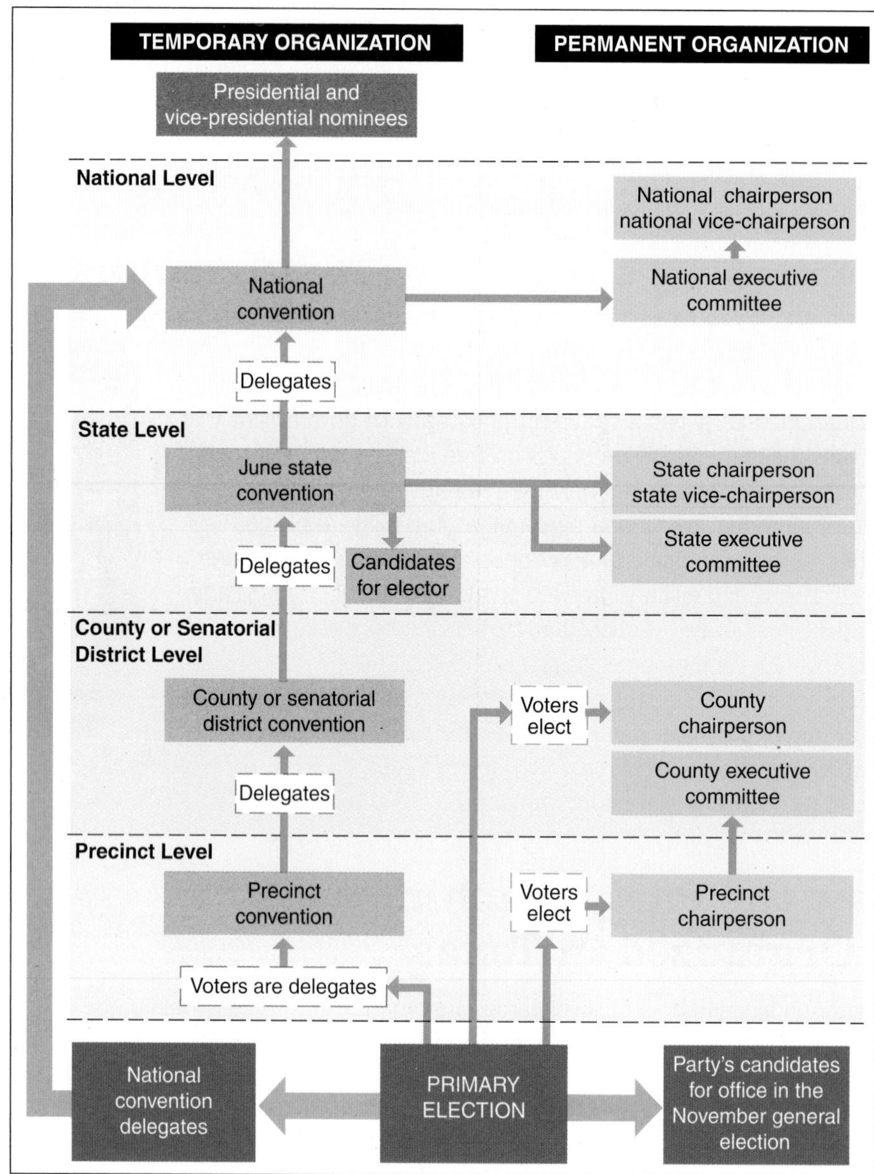

Although eligibility for participation in this grassroots level of democracy is open to all who vote in the first primary election, the attendance is low—usually only 2 or 3 percent of those who vote. This low attendance makes it possible for a small, determined minority of the electorate to assume control of the precinct convention and dominate its affairs.

Political Divisions at the Precinct Level. A precinct convention normally starts with signing in those present and certifying that they voted in the party's primary. In presidential election years, those signing in also indicate their preference for a presidential candidate, while in nonpresidential election years, delegates may organize themselves in different ways, such as by indicating support for a "conservative caucus," "moderate-progressive caucus," and so forth. The preferences are used to evaluate the strength of support for each candidate or caucus. Those factions with the largest numbers present are able to dominate the selection of delegates to the county convention.

If contending factions in a precinct are closely divided, one side or the other may walk out if it loses a key vote and claim a grave injustice was done. Such a group may conduct its own convention, called a **rump convention,** going through the same procedures; then both precinct groups will appeal to a credentials committee appointed by the county executive committee. The credentials committee will decide which set of rival delegates is to be officially seated at the county convention. Although fairness and justice sometimes determine the results, the decision on which group to seat usually depends on which faction is in the majority on the credentials committee.

Rump Convention
A meeting of members from a larger convention who secede and organize their own convention elsewhere.

County and Senatorial District Conventions. In the weeks following the primary and precinct conventions, county and state senatorial district conventions are held. In the most populous counties, the county convention has given way to state senatorial district conventions within those counties, yielding several state senatorial district conventions instead of one county convention. Delegates vote on adoption of resolutions to be considered at the state convention and select delegates and alternates to attend that convention.

As with the precinct convention, liberal or conservative factions or factions representing different presidential candidates will seek to dominate the selection of delegates. Walkouts followed by rump conventions may occur at the county or even the state level, as well as the precinct level. In Texas, bitter intraparty conflict has historically characterized the Democratic Party to a greater extent than the Republican Party, but that is changing as Republican primaries and conventions grow in importance.

State Convention. Both the Democratic and Republican parties in Texas hold state conventions in June of even-numbered years. The major functions of these biennial state conventions are as follows:

- Elect state party officers.
- Elect the 62 members of the state executive committee (one member for each senatorial district).
- Adopt a party platform.
- Certify the candidates nominated by the party in its March primary to the secretary of state.

In addition, in presidential election years, the state convention performs the following tasks:

- Elects the party's nominees from Texas to the national committee of the party.
- Selects the 34 candidates to the electoral college who, if chosen, will vote for the party's candidate for U.S. president.
- Elects some of the delegates to the party's national nominating convention, held in July or August. The number of delegates selected is determined by national party rules.

The role of state convention delegates in selecting delegates to the national convention has diminished in recent years. Most of the delegates for both parties are now selected on the basis of the party's presidential primary. A presidential primary allows voters in the party primary to vote directly on the party's presidential nominee.

In 2008, Texas held its presidential primary on March 4. Both Democrats and Republicans, voting in their separate primaries, indicated their selections for presidential candidates, as well as candidates for state and local offices. Texas Democrats were given the opportunity to express their preference for either Senator Hillary Clinton or Senator Barack Obama—twice. Dubbed the "Texas Two-Step" by the national press, Democrats voted once in the presidential primary election, and, if they chose, voted again in the precinct convention or caucus held in the evening after polls

did you know?

The number of votes cast in the 2008 presidential primaries was almost 4.3 million, breaking the previous record of 2.8 million set in 1988.

Senators Hillary Clinton and Barack Obama engaged in a fierce battle for Texas delegates in the spring 2008 primary for the Democratic presidential nomination. Although Clinton won the popular vote in the primary, Obama captured the lead in the state's caucuses. (Clinton photo: Carolyn Kaster/AP Photo. Obama photo: Michael Short/AP Photo)

had closed. Democrats were allocated 228 delegates to the Democratic national convention, 126 of which were chosen by the primaries, 67 by precinct conventions or caucuses, and 35 by unpledged superdelegates or party leaders. The assignment of delegates to candidates at the precinct convention distinguishes the Democratic from the Republican parties in Texas. The GOP also holds precinct conventions, but only to choose who gets to attend the higher level party conventions. Texas Republicans were allocated 140, all but three of which were determined by the primary vote. The rules for selecting delegates to the respective parties' national conventions are somewhat complex; each state party organization describes these rules in detail on their Web sites.

For the Democrats, the 67 "pledged" caucus-chosen delegates are assigned based on who shows up to the precinct conventions after the polls close in the evening. When Democrats established this system in 1988, the sentiment was that the caucuses would give party regulars an opportunity to exert some influence over both the nominating process and the party platform. The system was supposed to encourage turnout by rewarding those who had participated in the primary.

In the past, the precinct conventions had very few attendees, even in presidential election years. With the stakes so much higher in 2008, an estimated 1.1 million people turned out for the precinct convention-caucuses, four times what party officials were expecting. The unprecedented numbers caused a myriad of problems. Hundreds of people were squeezed into child-sized cafeterias or other small spaces. Some even caucused outside. Voters who arrived at 7:15 P.M. were kept waiting for hours while party officials tried to figure out obtuse procedures (including a curious rule that no one is in charge when the event begins). Some left because of the time it took to sign in, figure out the rules, and find a place to caucus. In some polling places, the police were called to address clashes between highly charged supporters of both candidates. The confusion drew the attention of the national media and complaints from the candidates, particularly the Clinton campaign, which threatened to file suit over irregularities. It took weeks to finalize the final results.

Those who defended the caucuses claimed that the process energized the party and attracted those who had never participated in the past. Still, the negative publicity had many party activists calling for changes in the system.

Permanent Party Organization

The permanent structure of the party consists of people selected to lead the party organization and provide continuity between election campaigns.

Precinct-Level Organization. At the bottom, or grassroots, level of the party structure is the precinct chair. Voters in the precinct's primary election choose the precinct chair for a two-year term. Often the position is uncontested, and in some precincts the chair is elected by write-in votes. The chair's role is to serve as party organizer in the precinct, regularly contacting known and potential party members. He or she may help organize party activities in the neighborhood, such as voter-registration drives. The precinct chair is responsible for arranging and presiding over the precinct convention and serving as a member of the county executive committee.

County-Level Organization. The county chair has a much more active and important role than the precinct chair. The voters choose the county chair for a two-year term in the party primary. The chair presides over the county executive committee, which is composed of all precinct chairs.

The county chair determines where the voting places will be for the primaries and appoints all primary **election judges.** (These choices must later be approved by the county commissioners court.) Accepting candidates for places on the primary ballot and printing paper ballots or renting voting machines are also the chair's responsibilities. Finally, the chair, along with the county executive committee, must certify the names of official nominees of the party to the secretary of state's office.

Election Judge
A public official who is responsible for enforcing election rules at a polling place on election day.

The county executive committee has three major functions:

1. Assemble the temporary roll of delegates to the county convention.
2. Canvass (that is, examine and certify) the returns from the primary for local offices.
3. Help the county chair prepare the primary ballot, accept filing fees, and determine the order of candidates' names on the ballot. The order of names is an important consideration if there is a great deal of "blind voting" in which ill-informed voters opt for the first name they come to on the ballot.

State-Level Organization. Delegates to the state convention choose the state chair—the titular head of the party—for a two-year term. The duties of the chair are to:

- Preside over meetings of the state executive committee;
- Call the state convention to order;
- Handle the requests of statewide candidates on the ballot; and
- Certify any runoff primary election winners to the state convention.

Each party's state executive committee has 64 members and is led by a chair and a vice chair (who must be of opposite genders). In addition, the Democratic and Republican state convention delegates choose one man and one woman from each of the 31 state senate districts. The main legal duties of the state executive committee are as follows:

- Determine the site of the next state convention—sometimes a crucial factor in determining whose loyal supporters can attend, since the party does not pay delegates' expenses.
- Canvass statewide primary returns and certify the nomination of party candidates.

The state executive committee also has some political duties, including issuing press releases and other publicity, encouraging organizational work in precincts and counties, raising money, and coordinating special projects. The state committee may work closely with the national party. These political chores are so numerous that the executive committees of both parties now employ full-time executive directors and staff assistants.

A New Era of Republican Dominance

In the elections of 2006, the Democrats fielded a full slate of candidates for state offices. Yet even with a national political climate that led to Democratic control of Congress, incumbent governor Rick Perry led the Republicans to victory in every statewide office. The results of the election demonstrate that although two-party competition now exists in Texas, in practice the Republican Party dominates Texas politics.

Republicans hold 76 of the 150 seats in the Texas House and 19 of the 31 seats in the Texas Senate. In 1978, the Republicans held just 92 elected offices across all of Texas. Following the November 2004 elections, the total was well over 2,100. Clearly, the old pattern of Texans' voting Republican at the top of the ticket and Democratic at the bottom of the ticket is no longer true.

Most observers now agree that Texas has experienced a political *realignment*—that is, a transition from one stable party system to another. After a hundred years of Democratic Party domination following the Civil War, the pendulum has swung to the Republican Party. (We discussed realignment in Chapter 8.)

Emergence of Republican Party Dominance

Realignment involves more than just casting a vote for a Republican Party candidate. It refers to a shift in *party identification.* Evidence that Texas is becoming a two-party or even a Republican-dominated state comes from public opinion polls that show more Texans are identifying with the Republican Party than in the past. Table 19–2 indicates that in 1952, an overwhelming percentage of those who identified with a political party in Texas were Democrats. In 2008, polls showed that the number of voters who identified with the Republican Party exceeded the number who identified with the Democratic Party.

The Slow Progress of Realignment in Texas. As we have already suggested, there are several reasons for the rise of Republican Party dominance in Texas. The first was the shift among existing voters as conservative middle- and upper-class white Democrats gradually switched their allegiance to the Republican Party during the decades following 1968. After years of voting Republican in presidential elections but identifying themselves as Democrats, these conservatives began thinking of themselves as Republicans. Many white voters defected to the Republican Party because they were alienated by the national Democratic Party's emphasis on civil rights in the 1960s and 1970s. The existence of popular and powerful Democratic leaders from Texas, such as President Lyndon B. Johnson (served 1963–1969), may have slowed the transition briefly but could not stop it.

TABLE 19–2 Democratic and Republican Party Identifiers

	Democrats (%)	Republicans (%)	Total (%)
1952	66	6	72
1972	57	14	71
1990	34	30	64
2008	35	37	72

Sources: Statewide polls in 1952 and 1972 conducted by Belden Associates of Dallas and archived at the Roper Center. Data for 1990 from the Texas poll, Texas A&M University Policy Resources Laboratory, Harte-Hanks Communications. Data for 2008 from University of Texas, Austin, Texas Politics Poll.

This shift in partisan identification was also spurred, in part, by the election of an extremely popular Republican president. Ronald Reagan, elected in 1980 and re-elected in 1984, combined clearly conservative positions with a charismatic personality that attracted conservative Democrats into the Republican camp. The impact of Reagan's leadership was reinforced by the election of George W. Bush to the presidency in 2000 and 2004. Bush had been a very popular governor, and his election to the presidency helped solidify the Republican realignment in Texas.

Interstate Immigration, Industrialization, and Urbanization. Party switching by native Texans has not been the only cause of realignment. Another factor involves newcomers to the state. A majority of recent migrants to Texas from other states have been Republicans or independents. These newcomers, who came to Texas in large numbers in the 1970s and 1980s, have helped break down traditional partisan patterns.

Finally, long-term economic trends have provided opportunities for political change. Texas has slowly become an industrialized and urbanized state, a pattern that accelerated after the 1940s. Industrialization, urbanization, and the rise of an affluent middle class have created a new environment for many Texans, and many Texans have been willing to adopt a new party as part and parcel of their new lives. In some parts of the country, urbanization and affluence have been associated with support for the Democratic Party, but in Texas these phenomena may have benefited the Republicans.

Can the Democrats Still Be Competitive?

Some observers still believe that Texas will continue as a competitive two-party state. Supporters of this view cite the unique influence of George W. Bush, a popular governor and later president. Now that he has left office, Bush will no longer influence party politics in Texas. They note that Democrats still have considerable resources in many local governments, especially in some central cities and South and Southwest Texas. For example, in 2006, Democrats swept every contested countywide race in Dallas County. Ironically, it was anger against George W. Bush's military policy in Iraq that helped the Democrats to victory.

Democratic strategists are also encouraged by the state's growing population of ethnic minorities, particularly Hispanics. These voters tend to support Democratic candidates. In spring 2008, many Hispanics and African Americans were energized by the race for the Democratic presidential nominee and turned out in record numbers. Ethnic minorities now make up a majority of the state's population. If their energy and commitment to politics continue, a significant Democratic resurgence will probably occur.

Dealignment

There is also some speculation that what is occurring in Texas is not realignment but *dealignment,* meaning that the voters are refusing to identify with either political party and are more inclined to call themselves independents. Evidence for dealignment comes from evaluating the percentage of voters engaging in *ticket splitting*—that is, voting for candidates of both parties in the general election rather than voting for all the candidates of one party or the other (a straight ticket). Increased numbers of ticket splitters suggest that dealignment is occurring. Recent surveys show that in both parties, straight-ticket and split-ticket voting occur in equal proportions—about 50 percent each. This pattern probably means that in Texas, both realignment and dealignment are occurring at the same time. In other words, voters are less willing to identify with either political party (dealignment) and also are more willing to change their professed party (realignment).

WHY SHOULD YOU CARE ABOUT... GRASSROOTS POLITICS?

Have you ever wondered how politicians get their start? Chances are they become involved with a political party at the grassroots level. In Texas, as in many other states, the most basic level of partisan participation is the party precinct. Precincts are this country's smallest political unit and are generally composed of about 2,000 to 3,000 voters. Political activity at the precinct level involves personal face-to-face activity, such as registering voters in your precinct, attending the precinct conventions, and getting voters to the polls on election day.

Political participation is one of the most important principles of democracy. The American federal system provides many access points for participation; some would say the most important point of access is the local level. Through your involvement, you influence the leadership and activities of your party and, ultimately, the issues that directly affect your life. In a practical sense, a strong and vital precinct organization is a key component in building the success of your county or district and state party organizations.

HOW YOU CAN MAKE A DIFFERENCE

Participating at the precinct level can include several activities, but one of the most important is participating in the precinct convention. In early March, during even-numbered years, both the Democratic and Republican parties in Texas hold their primary elections. Voters in the party primary may attend their party's precinct convention or caucus, which begins around 7:15 P.M. after the polls close at 7:00 P.M. Resolutions are passed, and delegates to the next level of party conventions (the county or senate district level) are selected. Because attendance is often sparse (2008 was an exception), an individual has a good chance of being heard and even being elected as a delegate. Delegates at the county or district level will pass more resolutions and will elect delegates to the state level. If you are persistent and lucky, you may be selected as a delegate to the state party convention. At this point, you will have become a significant player in politics.

For further information on Texas party conventions and events, leaders, rules, and issue positions, you can check the Web sites of both state political parties at:

Texas Democratic Party
www.txdemocrats.org

Texas Republican Party
www.texasgop.org

questions for discussion and analysis

1. What features describe American political parties?
2. What are the differences between liberal and conservative views?
3. Why was Texas politics dominated by the Democratic Party until the early 1990s?
4. Why have a majority of Texans come to identify with the Republican Party?

key terms

direct primary 620
election judges 631
evangelical 625
rump convention 629

chapter summary

1. Despite the hostility of the founders, political parties have become an important part of American political life. This is because parties perform critically important functions in a democracy. They nominate and elect their members to public office, educate and mobilize voters and provide them with cues on how to vote, and run the government at whatever level (local, state, or national) they are active.

2. In discussing political parties in the United States, we must look at three fundamental characteristics: (1) pragmatism, (2) decentralization, and (3) the effects of the two-party system. Pragmatism follows from the major goal of American parties, which is to build majority coalitions and win elections. This means that both Republican and Democratic Party candidates are often fuzzy on issues. The candidates try to accommodate many different interests and viewpoints and alienate as few voters as possible. Because there are few voters on the extremes, left or right, serious third parties have great difficulty developing and surviving, and they are often co-opted by one of the two major parties.

3. Parties are relatively decentralized, with much of the control of the nominating process (the primary) and party machinery in the hands of state and local voters and their leaders. In the recent past, however, both the Democratic and Republican national party organizations have increased their control over state and local parties because of their capacity to raise large amounts of money and provide various services. The McCain-Feingold Act of 2002 may end this trend by cutting off the flow of "soft money" to the major parties.

4. For much of its history, Texas was a one-party Democratic state. Until recently, one-party dominance meant that the election to select the Democratic Party's nominees—the Democratic primary—was the most important election in Texas. Moderate and conservative factions within the Democratic Party became the key political players.

5. After years of domination by the Democratic Party, Texas began to experience strong two-party competition. As a result, both parties strengthened their party machinery and made aggressive appeals to their traditional constituencies. By the late 1990s, the Republicans had become the dominant party in Texas. The transition from a party system in which the Democrats were overwhelmingly dominant to a new system in which the Republicans have a clear edge can be described as a political realignment. The realignment process was foreshadowed in the 1950s by the Shivercrats—Democrats who advocated voting for Republican presidential candidates and conservative Democrats at the state level. After the 1960s, the Republicans slowly but surely gained strength at the state level. In 1978, they gained the governorship. By 2002, they controlled both chambers of the state legislature, and in 2004 captured a majority in the state's congressional delegation. The Republicans will no doubt remain dominant in the foreseeable future.

6. Republicans have attracted voters in the expanding suburban areas of the state and have increased their appeal to white voters in rural areas. Democrats have attracted votes in inner cities and among ethnic minorities. The state's increasing ethnic diversity could thus augur well for the Democratic Party.

7. A second political mechanism that may be at work, in addition to realignment, is political dealignment. In this process, voters become detached from both political parties and begin to see themselves as independents.

selected print & media resources

SUGGESTED READINGS

Black, Earl, and Merle Black. ***The Rise of Southern Republicans.*** Cambridge, MA: Harvard University Press, 2002. This book discusses the slow but sure rise of Republican strength in the previously solid Democratic South over the past five decades.

Burnham, Walter Dean. ***Critical Elections and the Mainsprings of American Politics.*** New York: W. W. Norton, 1970. This classic work develops the concept of critical elections and electoral realignments. According to Burnham, critical elections establish new dominant parties. Burnham's theories have been criticized on the ground that political realignments are not always tied to specific elections.

Davidson, Chandler. ***Race and Class in Texas Politics.*** Princeton, NJ: Princeton University Press, 1992. This work on Texas politics explores the complicated relations between the politically disorganized Texas blue-collar class and the wealthy elite and illustrates the tactics used by the latter to largely control policy making in the state.

Keefe, William J., and Marc J. Hetherington. ***Parties, Politics, and Public Policy in America.*** Washington, DC: Congressional Quarterly Press, 2003. This fine, up-to-date textbook examines the two-party system in America. The authors discuss how parties have changed and what role partisanship plays among the elites and among ordinary voters.

Key, V. O. ***Southern Politics.*** New York: Knopf, 1949. This classic work describes the one-party Democratic system that existed in the South until recent years.

Richards, David. ***Once Upon a Time in Texas: A Liberal in the Lone Star State.*** Austin: University of Texas Press, 2002. This is a lively account of the experiences of Texas liberals from the 1950s to the 1990s. It includes a description of policy battles and profiles of prominent politicians and journalists.

MEDIA RESOURCES

Giant—A 1956 film that tells the story of rival ranchers in Texas in the middle years of the 20th century. It stars Elizabeth Taylor, Rock Hudson, James Dean, and Carroll Baker.

Last Man Standing: Politics Texas Style—A 2004 PBS video that documents the successful challenge to a Republican incumbent legislator by a 24-year-old Democratic "upstart." It features comments by such important figures as George W. Bush strategist Karl Rove, former Democratic Governor Ann Richards, and President Bill Clinton appointees Henry Cisneros and Paul Begala.

Lone Star—A 1996 film that offers a realistic portrait of the political machine in a South Texas border town. The story involves characters from the middle and younger generations of three ethnic communities who uncover and confront the surprising truth about their elders' past.

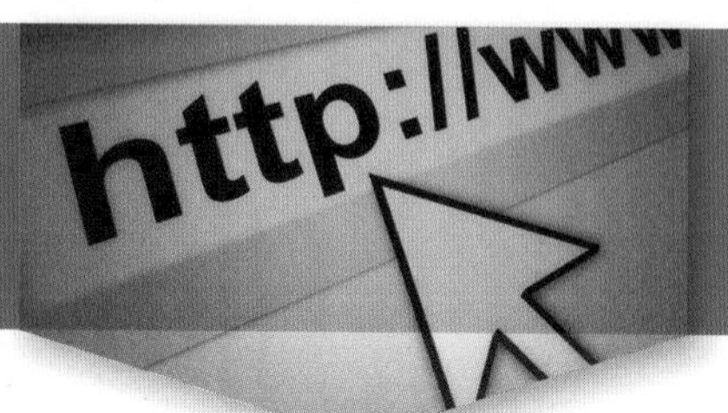

e-mocracy

TEXAS POLITICAL PARTIES AND THE INTERNET

The Internet offers a variety of information about Texas political parties. Citizens of the state can locate official party platforms, research party rules for participating in grassroots and state conventions, learn about the party history of Texas, and even view video clips of party officials. The Internet also makes it easy for political parties to mobilize supporters and seek donations.

For those who like a more informal or opinionated discussion of party views and activities, several unofficial Web logs, or blogs, offer individuals and columnists a chance to express their own views. These vary from the columns of media professionals to individual sites that may be fleeting. Be very careful when using information gleaned from a blog. Individuals who publish blogs are often highly opinionated, although most are straightforward about their ideological leanings.

By accessing the Web sites of the parties listed as follows in the *Logging On* section, you can see how the parties promote themselves. Voter registration is a major concern for both parties. Try accessing the home pages of the Texas Democratic and Republican parties. List at least three major differences in the official platforms of the two parties. Then go to the sites of the blogs mentioned, or find others by using the search engines described. Read through columns and comments from these blogs, and compare the information with that on the official sites. Can you identify points that may legitimately support either platform? Can you identify columns or statements that should be viewed skeptically?

LOGGING ON

The two major political parties have Web sites both nationally and in Texas. See the Republicans in Texas at:
www.texasgop.org

See the Republicans nationally at:
www.gop.com

See the Democrats in Texas at:
www.txdemocrats.org

See the Democrats nationally at:
www.democrats.org

The University of Texas offers an excellent Web site describing Texas politics in general. The site has a unit on Texas political parties that includes the history and functions of political parties in the state, as well as features such as graphs and video clips. To access this site, go to:
texaspolitics.laits.utexas.edu

Blog search engines allow you to find blogs of all types. One site that lists such engines is:
www.faganfinder.com/blogs

A popular blog search engine is:
www.blogsearchengine.com

Many newspapers have political blogs. For example, the *Austin American Stateman's* blog "Postcards from the Lege" by W. Gardner Selby regularly discusses Texas politics and events:
www.statesman.com/blogs/content/shared-gen/blogs/austin/politics/

ONLINE REVIEW

At **www.cengage.com/politicalscience/schmidt/agandpttexas14e**, you will find a Tutorial Quiz for this chapter, providing questions on the chapter contents, including the features. You'll gain access to other helpful study tools, including the book's glossary and flashcards, crossword puzzles, and Web links, as well as "Which Side Are You On?" and "Politics and . . ." features written by the authors of the book.

chapter
20

Voting and Elections In Texas

chapter contents

<< Chris Bell, Kinky Friedman, Governor Rick Perry, and Carole Keeton Strayhorn, the four candidates for Texas governor, debate in 2006. (Bob Daemmrich/The Image Works)

WHAT IF... ... voting were required by law?

BACKGROUND

The 2008 presidential elections were fairly close. Nationally, Barack Obama received a 6.4 percent larger share of the votes than John McCain (or about 8 million more votes). Only about 61.5 percent of those who were eligible to vote actually did so, however. In Texas, about 54.6 percent of the eligible population turned out to vote.

In the United States and most other countries, voting is voluntary, and people can decide whether or not to go to the polls. In some countries, however, voting is mandatory. In Australia, for example, all citizens are required to vote. Those who do not vote risk a fine and even imprisonment. The same is true in a handful of other countries, including Belgium. Turnout in these countries (not surprisingly) is high.

POSSIBLE CHANGES RESULTING FROM MANDATORY VOTING

Suppose voting had been required by law in the 2008 presidential elections. Would it have made a difference at the national level? In other words, would John McCain have emerged victorious? What about in Texas? John McCain took 55 percent of the Texas vote in 2008, but what would have happened if the 45.4 percent of the eligible population that did not vote had turned out?

Voters and nonvoters are different. Voters are on average better educated. They also tend to have better jobs and higher incomes. Not surprisingly, voters tend to be more Republican than nonvoters. It would seem to follow that if everyone voted, Democratic candidates would do better on election day. But is this true? Do Democrats stand to gain and Republicans to lose? We cannot be sure what would happen if everyone voted. Based on what we know about how people with certain characteristics vote, however, we can simulate how nonvoters would behave. Such an analysis suggests that most of the time, Democrats would gain more than Republicans, but by only a small margin.

There are two main reasons for this prediction. First, the differences in the preferences of voters and nonvoters are actually not very great.* Second, nonvoters are more likely to be influenced by short-term forces such as the state of the economy.** Therefore, their support might go disproportionately to the victor. Expanding the voting population might merely widen the winner's margin. Some evidence for this argument comes from the presidential election of 2004, where voter turnout was up significantly from 2000. Democrat John Kerry received about 8 million more votes nationally in 2004 than Democrat Al Gore did in 2000, but George W. Bush received about 11.5 million more votes than he did four years previously.

WHAT IF EVERYONE VOTED IN TEXAS?

Even if the partisan balance at the national level remained largely unchanged, it might conceal some measure of variance among individuals, states, and localities. This may be especially true in states such as Texas. It would take a very large change to overcome the current state-level Republican dominance. In state legislative races, however, the parties are often more closely balanced, and turnout is much lower. In local races, turnout tends to be lower still. In such races, expanding participation could have significant effects.

OTHER EFFECTS

Mandatory voting might have effects in addition to altering the balance between the parties. Some believe that it could cause a "dumbing down" of election campaigns as parties and candidates targeted the votes of people participating only to avoid paying a fine or going to jail. Alternatively, the new voters might seek to learn more about politics. Either result might change the political preferences of those who currently do not vote.

FOR CRITICAL ANALYSIS

1. Consider whether mandatory voting would work in the United States and specifically in Texas. Would the public support mandatory voting? How could we enforce it?
2. Would mandatory voting change the types of candidates who run for office and the positions they take? Might it ultimately change public policies?

---

* See the report by Benjamin Highton and Raymond Wolfinger at www.igs.berkeley.edu/publications/par/July1999/HightonWolfinger.html.

** Glenn Mitchell II and Christopher Wlezien, "The Impact of Legal Constraints on Voter Registration, Turnout, and the Composition of the American Electorate," *Political Behavior*, June 1995, pp. 179–202.

Voting in elections is the most basic and common form of political participation, but other forms of participation exist as well. Many people discuss political issues with friends and coworkers, write letters to local representatives or to newspaper editors, distribute campaign literature, make contributions to campaigns, or place bumper stickers on their cars. Some people are members of interest groups, such as neighborhood or trade associations, or serve on political party committees or as delegates to conventions. Voting is fundamental, yet not everyone votes, as we point out in this chapter's *What If . . .* feature on page 640.

Political Participation

Elections are a defining characteristic of representative democracies. We hold elected officials accountable through our votes. Votes are what matter to politicians, at least those interested in winning and holding office. If we vote—and thereby reward or punish elected officials for what they do while in office—politicians have an incentive to do what we want. If we do not vote, elected officials are largely free to do what they want. Clearly, voting is important in a representative democracy.

The Participation Paradox

Our individual votes rarely have any effect on the outcome, yet people still vote. Among political scientists, this is known as the **participation paradox.** The purpose for mentioning this paradox is not to say that you or other people should not vote. Rather, it is to point out that people vote for other reasons (and chiding people to vote because their votes "make a difference" probably is not very effective).

Participation Paradox
The fact that people vote even though their individual votes rarely influence the outcome of an election.

Who Votes?

Over the years, political scientists have learned much about why people go to the polls. It now is clear that a relatively small number of demographic and political variables are especially important.[1]

Education, Income, and Age. The most important demographic variables are education, income, and age. The more education a person has, the more likely the person is to vote. The same is true for income, regardless of how much education a person has. Age also matters. As people grow older, they are more likely to vote, at least until they become very old. Why do these factors matter? The answer is straightforward: People who are educated, have high incomes, and are older are more likely to care about, and pay attention to, politics. Thus, they are more likely to vote.

Interest in Politics and Partisan Identification. In addition to demographic factors, certain political factors influence the likelihood of voting, especially a person's expressed interest in politics and intensity of identification with a political party. The greater the interest in politics, the more likely a person is to vote. The effect is obvious but nevertheless quite important. A person who does not have much education or income still is very likely to vote if she or he has an intense interest in politics.

Identification with either of the political parties also makes a person more likely to vote. People who are strong partisan identifiers, on average, care much more about politics than those who do not identify with the parties. Parties also attempt to mobilize their identifiers—that is, the more you

did you know?

That in a recent election year, 21 percent of the voters wore a button or displayed a bumper sticker, 13 percent made political contributions, 7 percent attended a political meeting or rally, and 3 percent worked for a party or candidate.

1. Raymond E. Wolfinger and Steven Rosenstone, *Who Votes?* (New Haven, CT: Yale University Press, 1980). Also see Sydney Verba and Norman H. Nie, *Participation in America* (New York: Harper & Row, 1972).

identify with a party, the more likely it is that you will be contacted by the party and its candidates during election campaigns.

The Price of Voting

The legal qualifications for voting in Texas are surprisingly few and simple. Anyone who meets the following requirements is eligible to register and vote in Texas:

1. Be a citizen of the United States.
2. Be at least 18 years of age.
3. Be a resident of the state.

The only individuals prohibited from voting in Texas are those who have been declared "mentally incompetent" in formal court proceedings and those convicted of a felony whose civil rights have not been restored by a pardon or by the passage of two calendar years from the completion of the sentence.

Registration. Meeting these qualifications does not mean that a person can simply walk into the voting booth on election day. To vote, a person must be registered. As a result of the Voting Rights Acts of 1965 and 1970, several United States Supreme Court rulings, and recent Congressional action, the registration procedure is almost as simple as voting itself. A person may register in person or by mail at any time of the year up to 30 days before the election. Since the passage of federal "motor voter" legislation, a person can also register when renewing a driver's license; every person renewing a driver's license is asked whether he or she wants to register. Spouses, parents, or offspring also can register the applicant, provided they are qualified voters.

A future voter at the polls. Children of voters are much more likely to vote when they come of age. Is this true in your case? Are your parents voters or nonvoters? Do you think it influences what you do? (Tom Carter/Photoedit, Inc.)

The present Texas registration system is as open and modern as that of any other state that requires advance registration. (Note that a number of states, including Maine, Minnesota, and Wisconsin, permit election day registration, while North Dakota requires no registration at all. There, you simply walk in, show your identification, and vote.) The Texas system, established by law in 1975, provides for the mailing of a new two-year voter-registration certificate to every registered voter by January 1 in even-numbered years. The system is permanent; once a voter is on the rolls, he or she will not be removed unless the nonforwardable certificate is returned. Since 1977, Texas law requires the secretary of state to make postage-free registration applications available at any county clerk's office. They are also available at various other public offices.

The "Strike List." Names on returned certificates are stricken from the list of eligible voters and placed on a "strike list." The strike list is attached to the list of voters for each precinct. What if you move? For three months, registered voters who have moved and whose names are therefore on the strike list can vote in their old precincts—provided they have filled out a new voter-registration card for the new residence. They can vote, however, only for those offices that both residences have in common. Coroner's death reports, lists of felony convictions, and adjudications of mental incompetence are also used to purge the list of eligible voters.

Residency Requirements. Establishing residence for voting is no longer a matter of living at a place for a specified time. Residence is defined primarily in terms of intent (that is, people's homes are where they intend them to be). No delay in qualifying to vote is permitted under United States Supreme Court rulings, except for a short period of time during which the application is processed and the registrant's name is entered on the rolls. Under a federal court ruling, that delay in Texas is fixed at 30 days.[2]

Voting. Once a person is registered, voting is easy. This is especially true in Texas, which has passed laws to make voting easier. In 1975, for example, the legislature required that all ballots and election materials be printed in Spanish as well as English in counties with a Hispanic population of 5 percent or more. In 1991, the legislature established early voting, which allows people to vote at several different sites before election day.[3]

Central Texas Voters enter their polling place in Temple, Texas on Tuesday, Nov. 2, 2010. (AP Photo/The Temple Daily Telegram, Rusty Schramm)

Voter Turnout in the United States and Texas

Easier registration and voting was expected to result in increased *voter turnout*—that is, the proportion of Americans who vote. Many people believe that, instead, voter turnout has fallen during recent decades. Political scientists and pundits alike have made this claim. Some commentators have blamed the falling turnout on negative campaigning and broad public cynicism about the political process. The striking upturn in voter turnout during the 2004 presidential elections has tended to put this issue to rest, at least for now.

Is Voter Turnout Declining?

Is it true that voter turnout had been declining in the years before 2004? If you look at the percentage of the **voting-age population (VAP)** that actually cast a ballot, there seems to be some evidence of this decline. The national voter turnout as measured by the voting-age population is shown by the green bars in Figure 20–1.

> **Voting-Age Population (VAP)**
> The total number of persons in the United States or a state who are 18 years of age or older, regardless of citizenship, military status, felony conviction, or mental state.
>
> **Vote-Eligible Population (VEP)**
> The total number of persons actually eligible to cast a ballot, excluding noncitizens, felons, and other ineligible persons but including citizens who are temporarily abroad (and who may vote absentee).

One problem with using the VAP figure to gauge voter turnout is that it is not a very accurate measure of the number of *eligible voters.* The VAP figure includes felons who have lost the right to vote. Above all, it includes new immigrants who are not yet citizens. Finally, it does not include Americans living abroad, who can cast absentee ballots. As we stated in Chapter 9, the national voting-age population in 2008 was 231 million people. The number of eligible voters, however, was only 213 million. We call this second, more accurate figure the **vote-eligible population (VEP).** Using the VEP measure, voter turnout in 2008 was not 56.6 percent, as it is sometimes reported, but 61.5 percent.

As you read in Chapter 1, the United States has experienced high rates of immigration in recent decades. Political scientists Michael McDonald and Samuel Popkin argue that the apparent decline in voter turnout since 1972 is entirely a function of the increasing size of the ineligible population, chiefly due to immigration. Voter turnout as measured by McDonald and Popkin using VEP figures that they have calculated is shown by the upper (orange) bars in Figure 20–1. (Even if voter turnout has not declined in the United States, however, it is low by international standards, as we explain in this chapter's *Beyond Our Borders* feature.)

Midterm Elections. The national elections that take place halfway between presidential elections are called *midterm elections.* Voter turnout for midterm elections is substantially

---

2. *Beare v. Smith,* 321 F.Supp. 1100 (1971). In later cases—*Burns v. Fortson,* 410 U.S. 686 (1973) and *Martson v. Lewis,* 410 U.S. 679 (1973)—the United States Supreme Court upheld delays of up to 50 days in Georgia and Arizona.
3. Texas was one of the first states to institute early voting for all voters.

FIGURE 20–1 **U.S. Voter Turnout in Presidential Elections Since 1948**

This figure shows voter turnout in presidential elections based both on the vote-eligible population (VEP) and on the voting-age population (VAP). Note that a drop-off in voter turnout took place in 1972, in part because the minimum voting age was lowered to 18 and young people are less likely to vote. As measured by the more accurate VEP figure, turnout since then has gone up and down but has shown no consistent tendency to drop.

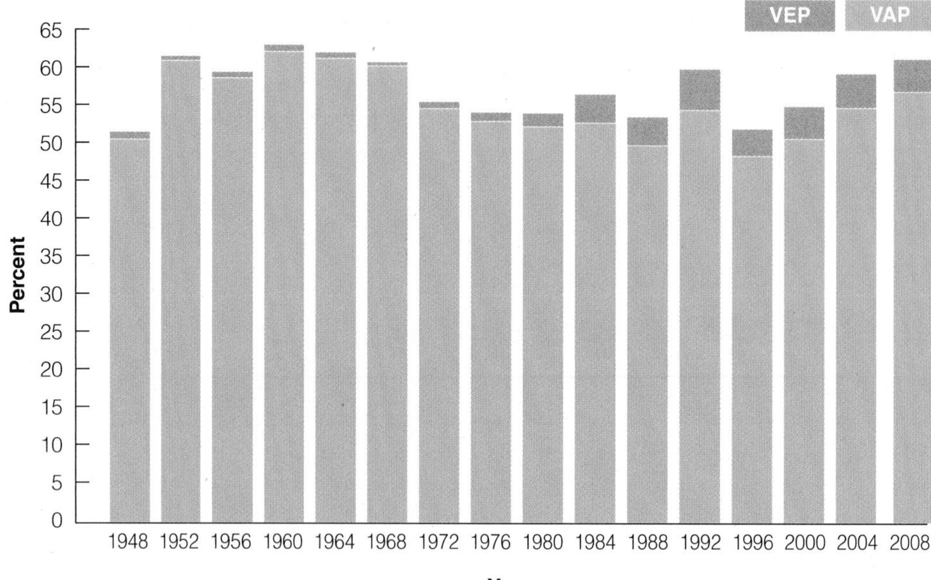

Sources: Data through 2000 are from Michael P. McDonald and Samuel Popkin, "The Myth of the Vanishing Voter," *American Political Science Review,* Vol. 95, No. 4, 2001, p. 963–974. The 2004 and 2008 figures are from the United States Elections Project and are available at elections.gmu.edu/voter_turnout.htm.

lower than for presidential elections, even though many states—including Texas—choose their governors in these elections. As measured by VEP, presidential election turnout has fluctuated around an average of 55 percent since 1972. Turnout for the midterm elections has been more constant, rarely moving very far from an average of 40 percent.[4]

Young Voters. As we have observed, young people are much less likely to vote than the average American. Since 1972, citizens in the 18- to 20-year-old age group have rarely posted turnout rates as high as 40 percent, even in a presidential year. In fact, there is some evidence that turnout rates among the youngest voters have fallen since 1972, reaching a low point of 30 percent in 2000. Young citizens increased their turnout markedly in 2004, however (as did all other groups). In 2004, turnout among the 18- to 24-year-old age group rose by almost 6 percentage points over 2000.[5]

In 2006, voter turnout actually dipped to 26 percent despite an open field of four gubernatorial candidates, including Republican Governor Rick Perry and Democrat challenger Chris Bell, and two independent candidates—Republican State Comptroller Carole Keeton Strayhorn and singer-writer Richard "Kinky" Friedman (pictured). Do you think that Friedman's campaign increased or decreased voter turnout? Why or why not? (Peter Silva/Reuters/Landov)

Voter Turnout in Texas

In past years, voter turnout in Texas (and in most of the South) has been consistently lower than the turnout nationwide. Figure 20–3 shows that turnout in Texas (as measured by VEP) has tracked national turnout but has regularly been six to seven percentage points lower than the national number. In 2004, only four states posted lower turnout rates than Texas.

Turnout for midterm elections in Texas shows a greater amount of variation. Since 1982, it has fluctuated between 30 and 40 percent. The turnout rate was

4. Michael P. McDonald and Samuel Popkin, "The Myth of the Vanishing Voter," *American Political Science Review,* Vol. 95, No. 4, 2001, p. 966.
5. *Ibid.* For 2004 figures, see reports issued by the Center for Information and Research on Civic Learning and Engagement (CIRCLE) at www.civicyouth.org.

BEYOND OUR BORDERS

AMERICAN VOTER TURNOUT COMPARED WITH TURNOUT IN OTHER COUNTRIES

Turnout in American general elections is significantly lower than voter turnout in other industrialized democracies of the world. A study found that among the 13 most comparable nations—those without compulsory voting—the turnout between 1972 and 1980 averaged 80 percent, substantially higher than the rate in the United States.* The more comprehensive numbers in Figure 20–2 show much the same pattern. They also show that U.S. turnout figures are well below those attained by many economically underdeveloped nations.

Some have argued that Americans are less likely to vote than Europeans because welfare spending is much lower (on a per capita basis) in the United States than in most European countries. Because low-income persons in the United States are less likely to depend on government spending than low-income persons in Europe, they have less of an incentive to follow politics and may find it easier to believe that election results are irrelevant to their lives. As we have seen, low-income persons are less likely to vote than high-income individuals.

* G. Bingham Powell, Jr., "American Voter Turnout in Comparative Perspective," *American Political Science Review,* Vol. 80, March 1986, pp. 17, 23.

FOR CRITICAL ANALYSIS

Political observers often wonder about whether who votes matters. We know that low-income citizens are less likely to vote in the U.S. than in other countries and less likely in Texas than in other states in the U.S.

1. What consequences does this have for policy?
2. Do politicians in the U.S. and especially Texas have much incentive to represent the interests of the poor?

FIGURE 20–2 Voter Turnout in Selected Countries Around the World

The turnout figures given here are based on the voting-age population (VAP) and not the vote-eligible population (VEP). The extent to which this makes a difference varies by country (we know that it depresses the U.S. figure). The turnout figures are not for any particular election but represent an average of national elections held since 1945. The U.S. figure is an average of presidential and midterm elections.

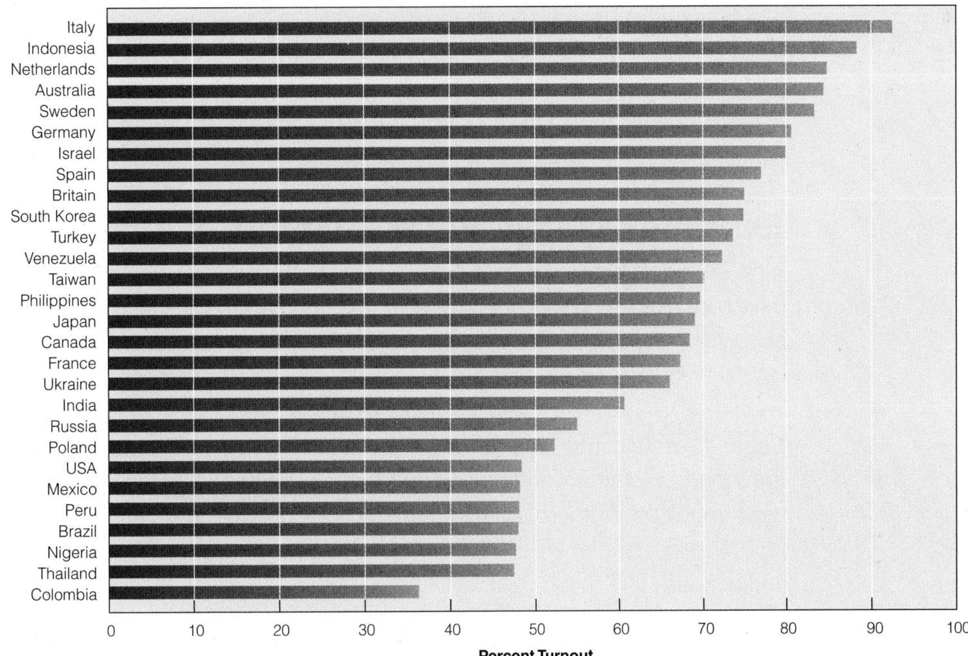

Source: International Institute for Democracy and Electoral Assistance, *Voter Turnout since 1945: A Global Report* (Stockholm, Sweden, 2002). The specific data shown above are available at www.idea.int/vt/index.cfm.

FIGURE 20–3 Texas Versus National Voter Turnout

The chart shows turnout in presidential election years since 1980. The figures do not appear to show any long-term trend upward or downward, though some elections have clearly been more interesting to the voters than others. The difference between the Texas voting-age population (VAP) and vote-eligible population (VEP) figures has grown, primarily because of a growing number of noncitizen residents.

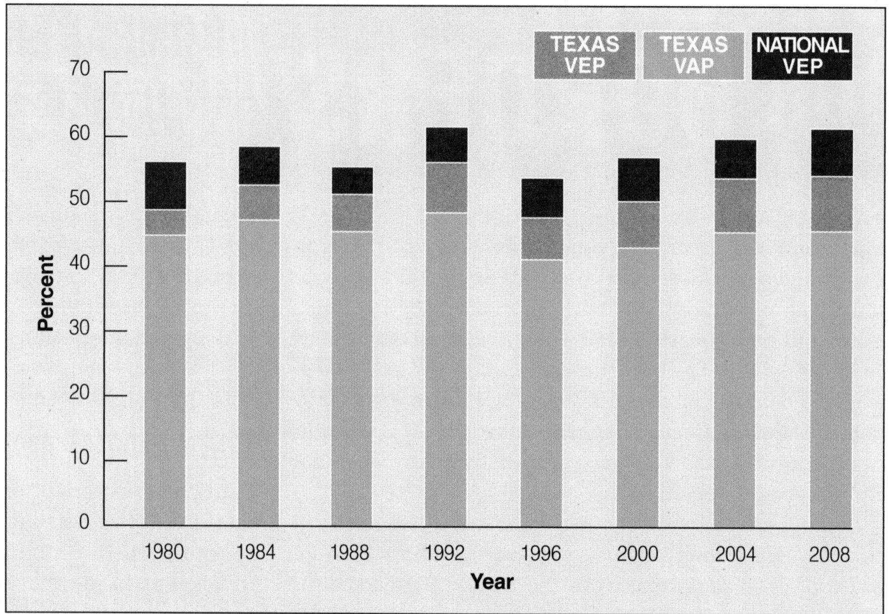

Sources: National VEP figures through 2000 are from Michael P. McDonald and Samuel Popkin, "The Myth of the Vanishing Voter," *American Political Science Review,* Vol. 95, No. 4, 2001, p. 963–974. Texas VEP and VAP figures are from Michael P. McDonald, "State Turnout Rates among Those Eligible to Vote," *State Politics and Policy Quarterly,* Vol. 2, No. 2, 2002. All 2004 figures are from the United States Elections Project and are available at elections.gmu.edu/voter_turnout.htm.

especially good in 1990 and 1994, at 36.2 percent and 38.9 percent, respectively. These relatively high figures may have resulted from fierce competition between Republicans and Democrats at the state level in those years.[6] In 2006, turnout surged to more than 40 percent, seemingly because of the open field of four candidates, which included not only Republican Governor Perry and Democrat challenger Chris Bell but two independent candidates as well—Republican state comptroller Carole Keeton Strayhorn (who ran as an independent) and singer-writer Kinky Friedman.

Reasons for Low Voter Turnout in Texas

Most Texans probably think that Texas is in the mainstream of American society. Why, then, is there such a difference between Texas and other urbanized and industrialized states in political behavior? Why is Texas closer to the states of the Deep South in voter turnout? The answer may lie in its laws, socioeconomic characteristics, political structure, and political culture.

Legal Constraints. Traditionally, scholars interested in the variation in turnout across the American states have focused on laws regulating registration and voting. Clearly, the most important of these laws were restrictions on who was allowed to vote, such as the poll tax, property ownership requirements, and the outright exclusion of African Americans and women.

Today, nearly all of these restrictions have been abolished by amendments to the U.S. Constitution, changes to state and national laws, rulings by the U.S. Department of Justice,

6. Michael P. McDonald, "State Turnout Rates among Those Eligible to Vote," *State Politics and Policy Quarterly,* Vol. 2, No. 2, 2002. The 2002 and 2004 figures are from the United States Elections Project and are available at elections.gmu.edu/voter_turnout.htm.

and judicial decisions. Even a cursory examination of the restrictions and the conditions under which they were removed makes us appreciate the extent to which Texas elections were at one time closed. Consider these changes in Texas voting policies:

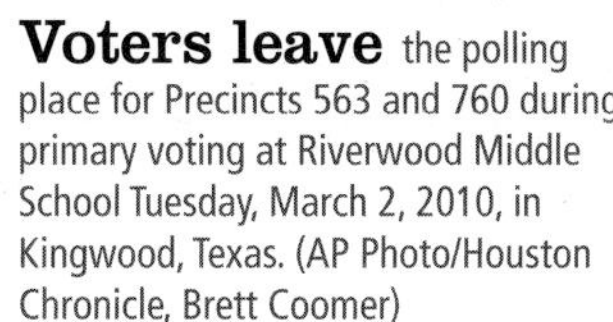

Voters leave the polling place for Precincts 563 and 760 during primary voting at Riverwood Middle School Tuesday, March 2, 2010, in Kingwood, Texas. (AP Photo/Houston Chronicle, Brett Coomer)

1. *Poll tax.* The payment of a poll tax was made a prerequisite for voting in 1902. The cost was $1.75 ($1.50 plus $0.25 optional for the county) and represented more than a typical day's wages at that time. Many poor Texans were therefore kept from voting. When the Twenty-fourth Amendment was ratified in 1964, it voided the poll tax in national elections. Texas was one of only two states to keep it for state elections, until it was held unconstitutional in 1966.[7]
2. *Women's suffrage.* Texas made an attempt to grant the ballot to women in 1917, but the effort failed by four votes in the Texas legislature. Women were allowed to vote in the primaries of 1918, but not until ratification of the Nineteenth Amendment in 1920 did women gain full suffrage in Texas.
3. *The white primary.* African Americans were barred from participating when the first Democratic Party primary was held in 1906. This measure was based on the theory that the Democratic Party was a private institution, as we explained in Chapter 5. When movement toward increased participation seemed likely, Texas took several steps to avoid a United States Supreme Court ruling allowing African Americans to vote. Not until 1944 were the legislature's efforts to deny African Americans access to the primaries finally overturned.[8]
4. *The military vote.* Until 1931, members of the National Guard were not permitted to vote. Members of the regular military began to enjoy the full rights of suffrage in Texas in 1965, when the United States Supreme Court voided the Texas constitutional exclusion.[9]
5. *Long residence requirement.* The Texas residency requirement of one year in the state and six months in the county was modified slightly by the legislature to allow new residents to vote in the presidential part of the ballot, but not until a United States Supreme Court ruling in 1972 were such requirements abolished altogether.[10]
6. *Property ownership.* Texas required property ownership for voting in bond elections until the United States Supreme Court ruled out property ownership as a requirement for revenue bond elections in 1969[11] and for tax elections in 1969 and in 1975.[12]
7. *Annual registration.* Even after the poll tax was voided, Texas continued to require voters to register every year until annual registration was prohibited by the federal courts in 1971.[13]
8. *Early registration.* Texas voters were required to meet registration requirements by January 31, earlier than the cutoff date for candidates' filings and more than nine months before the general election. This restriction was also voided in 1971.[14]

did you know?

That Texas has the nation's seventh largest percentage of people living in poverty—more than 15.6 percent in 2006.

---

7. *U.S. v. Texas,* 384 U.S. 155 (1966).
8. *Smith v. Allwright,* 321 U.S. 649 (1944).
9. *Carrington v. Rash,* 380 U.S. 89 (1965).
10. *Dunn v. Blumstein,* 405 U.S. 330 (1972).
11. *Kramer v. Union Free District,* No. 15, 395 U.S. 621 (1969).
12. *Cipriano v. City of Houma,* 395 U.S. 701 (1969); and Hill v. Stone, 421 U.S. 289 (1975).
13. *Beare v. Smith,* 321 F.Supp. 1100 (1971).
14. *Ibid.*

Courtesy Texas Secretary of State, http://www.votexas.org

9. *Jury duty.* Texas law provided that the names of prospective jurors must be drawn from the voting rolls. Some Texans did not want to serve on juries, and not registering to vote ensured against a jury summons. (Texas counties now use driver's licenses for jury lists.)

Texas used almost every technique available except the literacy test and the grandfather clause[15] to deny the vote to some citizens or to make voting time consuming, expensive, and psychologically difficult. This is not the case today. Most barriers to voting in Texas have been removed. In fact, as mentioned previously, the legislature has instituted provisions that make voting easier than in most states. Thus, the laws in Texas may help us understand why turnout was low in the past and, with the relaxing of restrictions, why turnout has increased somewhat since 1960. The current laws do not help us understand why turnout in Texas remains low today. For this, we need to look elsewhere.

Socioeconomic Factors. Texas, with its cattle barons and oil tycoons, is known as the land of the "big rich." What is not so well known is that Texas is also the land of the "big poor," and that more persons live in poverty in Texas than in any other state of the Union. While nationally the proportion of people living below the poverty level in 2006 was 12.3 percent, in Texas the proportion was 16.3 percent. More than 25 percent of African-American and Mexican-American Texans have incomes below the poverty level. More than 3 million individuals in Texas live in poverty, and more than 1 million of these are children. Understandably, formal educational achievement also is low. Of all Texans who are older than age 25, one out of four has not graduated from high school. Among African Americans, the ratio is slightly less than one out of three, and among Mexican Americans it is almost one out of two.[16]

Given that income and education are such important determinants of electoral participation, low voter turnout is exactly what we should expect in Texas. Because income and education levels are particularly low among African Americans and especially Mexican Americans, turnout is particularly low for these groups. Voting by Texas minorities is on the rise, however, and this has led to much greater representation of both groups in elected offices, as we will see. These trends should continue as income and education levels among minorities increase.

Political Structure. Another deterrent to voting in Texas is the length of the ballot and the number of different elections. Texas uses a long ballot that provides for the popular election of a large number of public officers. (Critics believe that some of these officers should be appointed rather than elected.) In an urban county, the ballot may call for the voter to choose among 150 and 200 candidates vying for 50 or more offices. The frequency of referendums on constitutional amendments also contributes to the length of the ballot in Texas. In addition, voters are asked to go to the polls for various municipal, school board, bond, and special district elections. Government simply is far more fragmented in Texas than in other states, and this makes particular elections less meaningful and perhaps more frustrating to voters.

Primary, General, and Special Elections in Texas

Winning an office typically is a two-stage process. First, the candidate must win the Democratic or Republican nomination in the primary election. Second, the candidate must win the general election against the nominee of the other party. It is possible for a candi-

15. Grandfather clauses were found unconstitutional by the United States Supreme Court in Guinn v. United States, 238 U.S. 347 (1915).
16. U.S. Census Bureau. The definition of poverty depends on the size and composition of the family. For a family of four, two of whom are children, the poverty-level threshold in 2007 was $21,027.

date to get on the general-election ballot without winning a primary election (as we explain shortly), but this is rare. As in most other states, elections in Texas are dominated by the Democratic and Republican parties.

Primary Elections

Three devices for selecting political party nominees have been used in U.S. history, each perceived as a cure for the ills of a previous system that was considered corrupt, inefficient, or inadequate. The first was the *caucus,* consisting of the elected party members serving in the legislature. The "insider" politics of the caucus room motivated the reformers of the Jacksonian era to institute the party convention system in 1828. In this system, ordinary party members select delegates to a party convention, and these delegates then nominate the party's candidates for office and write a party platform. The convention system was hailed as a surefire method of ending party nominations by the legislative bosses.

The Direct Primary. By 1890, however, the backroom politics of the convention halls again moved reformers to action, and the result was the direct primary, which most states adopted between 1890 and 1920. The first direct primary in Texas was held in 1906, under the Terrell Election Law (passed in 1903). This law enables party members to participate directly in their party's selection of candidates to represent them in the general election.

POLITICS AND... elections

WHO CAN RUN FOR OFFICE?

Members of the Texas Legislature must meet a few minimum constitutional requirements to hold office. House members must be at least 21 years old, and senators must be at least 26. House members must also have lived in the state for at least two years. Senators must have lived in the state for at least five. All members of the Texas Legislature must be U.S. citizens, qualified voters, and residents of the district they will represent for at least one year. Any individual who meets these requirements can run for office.

Overcoming the cost of an election to the Texas legislature can seem quite daunting to many. After all, an average Texas House race can cost as much $153,000. Senate races can be even more costly, averaging more than $452,000. While it is true that most lawmakers are older, many young, ambitious candidates have successfully won seats in the Texas legislature. Countless members of the Texas legislature got there while they were either still in college or recent college graduates. Many spent modest amounts of money to win seats that they have turned into powerful positions, making meaningful contributions to the state of Texas. Many have won these seats in races in which a few thousand votes were cast. Others have won with no real competition. Some races for elective offices can be costly, challenging, and highly competitive; many others are not. Many highly ambitious, smart young people have run successful campaigns.

Representative Jessica Farrar was a 27-year-old engineering student at the University of Houston when she first ran for office in 1994. She spent some $10,000 to purchase door knockers and yard signs. She then took to pounding the pavement and meeting as many constituents as she could. Fourteen years later, she serves on the powerful House Committee on State Affairs and the House Committee on Juvenile Justice and Family Issues. In 1997, Representative Dennis Bonnen was only 24 years old when he was elected to the Texas House. He is now in his sixth term.

FOR CRITICAL ANALYSIS

Do you think it is a good idea or a bad idea to elect young people to the Texas House or Senate? Why?

The White Primary. Traditionally regarded as private activities, primaries were at one time largely beyond the concern of legislatures and courts. Costs of party activities, including primaries, were paid through donations and through assessments of candidates who sought a party's nomination. Judges attempted to avoid suits among warring factions of the parties in the same way that they avoided those suits involving church squabbles over the division of church property. On the basis of the theory that primaries were private activities, the United States Supreme Court in 1935 upheld the decision of the Texas Democratic Party convention to continue barring African Americans from participating in the Democratic Party primary.[17]

Recognizing that political party activities were increasingly circumscribed by law, the Court reversed itself in 1944 and threw out the white primary system.[18] The Court argued that in a one-party state, which Texas was at the time, the party primary may be the only election in which any meaningful choice is possible. Because the Democratic Party seldom had any real opposition in the general election, winning the nomination was, for all practical purposes, winning the office. Therefore, African Americans could not constitutionally be prevented from participating in the primary.

Who Must Hold a Primary? Texas, like most other states, has for decades required that major political parties—those whose candidates for governor received a fixed minimum number of votes in the last general election—select their nominees through the primary. Other parties, however, were at one time allowed to nominate candidates by primary or convention, whichever they chose. In 1973, the Texas legislature amended the Texas election code to provide that any party receiving 20 percent or more of the gubernatorial vote must hold a primary, and that all other parties must use the convention system.[19]

Limits on New Parties. New parties must meet additional requirements if their nominees are to be on the general-election ballot. In addition to holding a convention, these parties must file with the secretary of state a list of supporters equal to 1 percent of the total vote for governor in the last general election. The list may consist of the names of those who participated in the party's convention, those who signed a nominating petition, or a combination of the two groups. Persons named as supporters must be registered voters who have not participated in the activities (primaries or conventions) of either of the two major parties. Each page (though not each name) on the nominating petition must be notarized. This requirement is, as intended, difficult to meet and therefore inhibits the creation of new political parties.

Getting on the Ballot through a Petition. So that no person is forced to bear an unreasonable expense when running for political office, the legislature (prodded by the federal courts) provided the petition as an alternative to the filing fee. For those seeking nomination to statewide office, the petition must bear the names of 5,000 voters. For district and lesser offices, the number of signatures must equal 2 percent of the votes cast for the party's candidate for governor in the last election, up to a maximum of 500 required signatures. A sample county primary ballot is reproduced in Figure 20–4.

Administering Primaries. In a county primary, the chair and the county executive committee of each party receive applications and filing fees and hold drawings to determine the order of names on the ballot for both party and government offices. They then

17. *Grovey v. Townsend,* 295 U.S. 45 (1935).
18. *Smith v. Allwright,* 321 U.S. 649 (1944).
19. La Raza Unida Party challenged this limitation. The U.S. Justice Department and federal courts sustained the challenge, but only as applied to La Raza Unida, which was permitted to conduct a primary in 1978. Otherwise, the law stands as written.

FIGURE 20–4 Sample Ballot for 2006 Republican Party Primary Election

Vote Both Sides *Vote en Ambos Lados de la Página*

March 7, 2006 Joint Primary Election
Elección Primaria Junta 7 de marzo de 2006
Travis County
Condado de Travis
March 07, 2006 - *07 Marzo 2006* **Precinct** *Precinto* ***REP SAMPLE***

Instruction Note:
Use a BLUE or BLACK pen to mark your ballot. To vote, completely fill in the square to the left of your candidate or proposition choice. To vote for a write-in candidate, completely fill in the square to the left of "Write-in" and enter the name of the certified write-in candidate on the line provided.

Nota de Instruccion:
Marque su boleta con una pluma negra o azul. Para votar, llene completamenta el espacio cuadrado a la izquierda del nombre del candidato o selección de proposición de su preferencia. Para votar por un candidato por voto escrito, llene completamente el espacio cuadrado a la izquierda de Voto Escrito y escriba el nombre del candidato certificado en la linea provista.

UNITED STATES SENATOR - REP
SENADOR DE LOS ESTADOS UNIDOS - REP
- Kay Bailey Hutchison

DISTRICT 10, UNITED STATES REPRESENTATIVE - REP
DISTRITO NÚM. 10, REPRESENTANTE DE LOS ESTADOS UNIDOS - REP
- Michael T. McCaul

DISTRICT 21, UNITED STATES REPRESENTATIVE - REP
DISTRITO NÚM. 21, REPRESENTANTE DE LOS ESTADOS UNIDOS - REP
- Lamar Smith

GOVERNOR - REP
GOBERNADOR - REP
- Rhett R. Smith
- Larry Kilgore
- Rick Perry
- Star Locke

LIEUTENANT GOVERNOR - REP
GOBERNADOR TENIENTE -REP
- David Dewhurst
- Tom Kelly

ATTORNEY GENERAL - REP
PROCURADOR GENERAL - REP
- Greg Abbott

COMPTROLLER OF PUBLIC ACCOUNTS - REP
CONTRALOR DE CUENTAS PÚBLICAS - REP
- Susan Combs

COMMISSIONER OF THE GENERAL LAND OFFICE - REP
COMISIONADO DE LA OFICINA GENERAL DE TIERRAS - REP
- Jerry Patterson

COMMISSIONER OF AGRICULTURE - REP
COMISIONADO DE AGRICULTURA - REP
- Todd Staples

RAILROAD COMMISSIONER - REP
COMISIONADO DE FERROCARRILES - REP
- Major Buck Werner
- Elizabeth Ames Jones

CHIEF JUSTICE, SUPREME COURT, UNEXPIRED TERM - REP
JUEZ PRESIDENTE, CORTE SUPREMA, DURACIÓN RESTANTE DEL CARGO - REP
- Wallace Jefferson

PLACE 2, JUSTICE, SUPREME COURT - REP
LUGAR NÚM. 2, JUEZ, CORTE SUPREMA - REP
- Steve Smith
- Don Willett

PLACE 4, JUSTICE, SUPREME COURT - REP
LUGAR NÚM. 4, JUEZ, CORTE SUPREMA - REP
- David M. Medina

PLACE 6, JUSTICE, SUPREME COURT - REP
LUGAR NÚM. 6, JUEZ, CORTE SUPREMA - REP
- Nathan Hecht

PLACE 8, JUSTICE, SUPREME COURT, UNEXPIRED TERM - REP
LUGAR NÚM. 8, JUEZ, CORTE SUPREMA, DURACIÓN RESTANTE DEL CARGO - REP
- Phil Johnson

PRESIDING JUDGE, COURT OF CRIMINAL APPEALS - REP
JUEZ PRESIDENTE, CORTE DE APELACIONES CRIMINALES - REP
- Sharon Keller
- Tom Price

PLACE 7, JUDGE, COURT OF CRIMINAL APPEALS - REP
LUGAR NÚM. 7, JUEZ, CORTE DE APELACIONES CRIMINALES - REP
- Barbara Parker Hervey

PLACE 8, JUDGE, COURT OF CRIMINAL APPEALS - REP
JUEZ, CORTE DE APELACIONES CRIMINALES, LUGAR NÚM. 8 - REP
- Robert W. Francis
- Charles Holcomb
- Terry Keel

DISTRICT 5, MEMBER, STATE BOARD OF EDUCATION - REP
DISTRITO NÚM. 5, MIEMBRO DE LA JUNTA ESTATAL DE EDUCACIÓN PÚBLICA - REP
- Ken Mercer
- Mark Loewe
- Dan Montgomery

DISTRICT 10, MEMBER, STATE BOARD OF EDUCATION - REP
DISTRITO NÚM. 10, MIEMBRO DE LA JUNTA ESTATAL DE EDUCACIÓN PÚBLICA - REP
- Tony Dale
- Cythnia Dunbar

STATE SENATOR, DISTRICT 25 - REP
SENADOR ESTATAL, DISTRITO NÚM. 25 - REP
- Jeff Wentworth

DISTRICT 47, STATE REPRESENTATIVE - REP
DISTRITO NÚM. 47, REPRESENTANTE ESTATAL - REP
- Dick Reynolds
- Bill Welch
- Rich Phillips
- Terry Dill
- Alex Castano

DISTRICT 48, STATE REPRESENTATIVE - REP
DISTRITO NÚM. 48, REPRESENTANTE ESTATAL - REP
- Ben Bentzin

Sample Ballot 21000433110 0 1000000021 Sample Ballot 18520300

Vote Both Sides *Vote en Ambos Lados de la Página*

certify the ballot, select an election judge for each voting precinct (usually the precinct chair), select the voting devices (paper ballots, voting machines, or punch cards), and arrange for polling places and for printing. After the primary, the county chair and the executive committee canvass (count) the votes and certify the results to their respective state executive committees.

In the state primaries, the state party chair and the state executive committee of each political party receive applications of candidates for state offices, conduct drawings to determine the order of names, certify the ballot to the county-level officials, and canvass the election returns after the primary.

The Dual Primary. In Texas, as in other Southern states that once had a Democratic one-party system (except Tennessee and Virginia), nominations are decided by a majority (50 percent plus one) of the popular vote. If no candidate receives a majority of votes cast for a particular office in the first primary, a second **runoff primary** is required, in which the two candidates receiving the highest number of votes are pitted against each other.

Runoff Primary
A second primary election that pits the two top vote-getters from the first primary against each other. Such an election is held in states such as Texas when the winner of the first primary did not receive a majority of the votes.

Primary elections in Texas usually are held on the second Tuesday in March of even-numbered years. The runoff primary is scheduled for the second Tuesday in April, roughly a month after the initial primary election. Although there are earlier presidential primaries, no other state schedules primaries to nominate candidates for state offices so far in advance of the general election in November.

Presidential Aspirations and Early Primaries. Until 1960, the primaries were held much later in the year, on the fourth Saturday in July and the fourth Saturday in August. The dates were moved up so that presidential aspirant Lyndon B. Johnson could "lock up" his renomination to the U.S. Senate before the Democratic National Convention began in Los Angeles.

The presidential ambitions of another Texan, vice president George H. W. Bush, contributed to the adoption of an even earlier primary. Believing an early primary victory in Texas would benefit their candidate, Bush's Republican supporters joined conservative Democrats in urging Texas to join most other Southern states holding a regional primary on Super Tuesday. In a special session in 1986, the Texas legislature rescheduled the primary to nominate all state officials on the second Tuesday in March in both presidential and midterm election years. In 1996, Super Tuesday included primary elections in Florida, Louisiana, Mississippi, Oklahoma, Oregon, Tennessee, and Texas. (In later years, several states made further changes to their primary schedules, and these changes broke up the Super Tuesday primary.) By 2008, most states already had their primaries before March, but Texas (and Ohio, which held its primary on the same day) may have had a bigger impact on the process than in previous years. Both Texas and Ohio went for Hillary Clinton, temporarily disrupting Barack Obama's path to the Democratic nomination. The states also sealed the nomination for Republican presidential candidate John McCain.

Turnout in Primaries. Turnout in Texas primaries is much lower than in general elections. Take 2002, for example: Although 4.5 million Texans voted in the general election, only 1.6 million participated in either the Democratic or the Republican primary—that is, approximately 12 percent of the vote-eligible population. Matters were even worse in 2006, when 1.2 million people, less than 10 percent of the eligible population, voted in either primary. Turnout in presidential election years is higher but still averages below 30 percent. Participation was up a little in 2008, especially for the Democrats, as 2.9 million citizens turned out to support either Obama or Clinton. Another 1.4 million voted in the much-less-competitive Republican primary in that year. The people who vote in primary elections are not representative of the overall population: they tend to be better educated, more affluent, and more extreme ideologically.

Open versus Closed Primaries. Party primaries are defined as either open or closed. These terms specify whether or not participation is limited to party members. Because the purpose of a primary is to choose the party's nominee, it would seem logical to exclude anyone who is not a party member. Not every state accepts this argument, however.

Alaska and Washington used to have a blanket primary, in which voters could "mix and match" among the various parties' candidates, but the United States Supreme Court declared it unconstitutional in 2004. Seven states have an *open primary,* in which voters decide at the polls in which primary they will participate. Texas and the remaining 40 states use what is called a *closed primary.*

The Closed Primary in Texas Although Texas is classified technically as a closed-primary state, it operates as an open-primary state in practice. As in other closed-primary states, the primary voter is morally—but not legally—bound to vote only in his or her own party's elections. This means that people can participate in either the Democratic or the Republican primary whether they are party members or not. Only two minor legal restrictions make Texas technically a closed-primary state:

1. A person is forbidden to vote in more than one primary on the day of the primary elections.
2. Once a person has voted in the first primary, he or she cannot switch parties and participate in the runoff election or convention of any other party.

Closed Primaries in Other States. In contrast, the closed primary used in many other states requires that when registering to vote, a person must specify a party preference. The party's name is then stamped on the registration card at the time it is issued. A voter may change his or her party registration between elections, up to a set time (often 30 days) before the primary or convention. Voters are limited to participating in the activities of the party for which they have registered. Furthermore, an individual who registers as an independent (no party preference) is excluded from the primaries and conventions of all parties. Note that how a person votes (or fails to vote) in any type of primary does not limit in any way that person's choice in the general election in November.

Crossover Voting. The opportunity always exists in Texas for members of one political party to invade the other party's primary. This is called **crossover voting.** It is often done to increase the chances that the nominee from the other party will be someone whose philosophy is similar to that of the invader's own party. For example, if Republicans can ensure the nomination of a strong conservative in the Democratic primary, either of the two major party's candidates may be quite acceptable in November.

In the past, the Republican Party "institutionalized" crossover voting to a degree by not holding a Republican primary in some counties. In those counties, Republicans had no place to go except to the Democratic primary. The decision to forgo the primary was not necessarily based on a lack of support for Republican candidates. Although that was true in some counties, it was certainly not true of all. Of the 22 counties that did not hold a Republican primary in 1980, President Ronald Reagan carried 10; in 1984 he carried 18 of 26. This is because a large number of Democrats voted for Reagan in the general election.

Crossover Voting
A circumstance in which members of one political party vote in the other party's primary to influence which nominee is selected by the other party.

Plurality
The number of votes cast for a candidate who receives more votes than any other candidate but not necessarily a majority. Most national, state, and local election laws provide for winning elections by a plurality vote.

General Elections

The purpose of party primaries is to choose each party's candidates from among the competing intraparty factions. General elections, in contrast, allow the voters to choose the people who will actually serve in national, state, and county offices from among the competing political party nominees and write-in candidates. General elections differ from primaries in at least two other important ways. First, general elections are administered completely by public (as opposed to party) officials of state and county governments. Second, unlike Texas primaries, in which a majority vote is required, the general election is decided by **plurality** vote, in which

did you know?

That while Texas does not limit the number of terms for either legislators or the governor, most neighboring states, including Arkansas, Colorado, Louisiana, and Oklahoma, limit both.

the winning candidate only need receive at least one more vote than any opponent.

Scheduling General Elections. General elections in Texas are held biennially on the same day as national elections—the first Tuesday after the first Monday in November of even-numbered years. In years divisible by four, Americans elect the president, the vice president, all U.S. representatives, and one-third of the U.S. senators. In Texas, the voters elect all 150 members of the state house in these elections and roughly half (15 or 16) of the 31 senators. Texas voters also elect the winners of a number of board and court positions at the state level, as well as about half of the county positions.

President Ronald Reagan and First Lady Nancy Reagan are joined on the podium by his vice-presidential running mate, George H. W. Bush, and his wife, Barbara, at the Republican National Convention in Dallas, Texas, in 1984. How much of a benefit do you think the Republicans gained from holding the convention for Reagan's nomination to his second term in Texas? How much might Reagan have benefited from having a Texan—George H. W. Bush—as his vice-presidential running mate? (Courtesy of Reagan Presidential Library)

Most major state executive positions (governor, lieutenant governor, attorney general, and others) are not filled until the midterm election, when all U.S. representatives and one-third of U.S. senators (but not the president) again face the voters. All state house representatives and half of the state senators are elected in these years. Some board members, judges, and county officers are chosen as well.

The Effects of Simultaneous State and National Elections. Holding simultaneous national and state elections has important political ramifications. During the administration of Andrew Jackson, parties first began to tie the state and the national governments together politically. A strong presidential candidate and an effective candidate for state office can benefit significantly by cooperating and campaigning under the party label. This usually works best if the candidates are in fundamental agreement on political philosophy and the issues.

In Texas, which is more politically conservative than the average American state, such fundamental agreement has often been lacking. This has been especially true for the Democrats. Popular Democrats in the state have often disassociated themselves from the more liberal presidential nominee of the party. As you learned in Chapter 19, Democratic governor Allan Shivers openly endorsed and worked for the election of the Republican candidate for president in 1952 and again in 1956. In 1980, four former governors (all Democrats) joined Republican Governor Bill Clements in endorsing Ronald Reagan for president. State leaders are often hesitant to be identified with a presidential nominee who may "drag them down," because the candidate is less popular with the Texas voters than they are.

The Effects of Separating State and National Elections. When the Texas Constitution was amended in 1972 to extend the terms of the governor and other major administrative officials from two years to four years, the elections for these offices were scheduled for the midterm election years. This change had two major effects. First, the separation of presidential and state campaigns insulates public officials from the ebb and flow of presidential politics and allows them to disassociate themselves from the national political parties. Elections for statewide office now largely reflect Texas issues and interests.

Second, the separation reduces voter turnout in statewide elections and makes the outcomes much more predictable. As was shown earlier, turnout is much lower in midterm elections than in presidential elections, when many people are lured to the polls by the importance and the visibility of the presidential campaign. Independent and marginal voters are more likely to turn out, and election results for congressional and state-level offices are less predictable. In midterm election years, however, the less informed and the less predictable voters are more likely to stay home, and the contest is largely confined to party regulars. Most incumbent state politicians prefer to cast their lot with this more limited and predictable midterm electorate.

Special Elections

As the name implies, special elections are held to meet special or emergency needs, such as to ratify a constitutional amendment or to fill a vacant office. Special elections are held to fill vacancies only in those legislative bodies having general (rather than limited) lawmaking power. Legislative bodies with general power are the U.S. Senate and House of Representatives, state legislatures, and city councils in home-rule cities. All other vacancies, including judgeships and county commissioner seats, are filled by appointment. The special election fills a vacancy only until the end of the regular term or until the next general election, whichever comes first.

Special elections are nonpartisan, and so the process of getting on the ballot is relatively easy and does not involve a primary.[20] All that is required is the filing of the application form in a timely and appropriate manner and the payment of the designated filing fee. Unlike the winner of a general election, the winner of a special election must receive a majority of the votes. Thus, a runoff special election may be necessary when no candidate wins an absolute majority the first time around.

Senator Hutchison. In 1993, after U.S. Senator Lloyd Bentsen was nominated to serve as secretary of the treasury by President Bill Clinton, a special election was necessary to fill the vacancy. Democratic Governor Ann Richards appointed Robert Krueger, a former member of Congress and ambassador-at-large, to fill in until the special election, in which he was the Democratic candidate. Republican Kay Bailey Hutchison ultimately won the special election, however, becoming the first woman elected to represent Texas in the U.S. Senate.

Senator Kay Bailey Hutchison calls the 2004 Republican National Convention to order at Madison Square Garden in New York. (Joe Cavaretta/AP Photo)

The Conduct and Administration of Elections

In 1967 the Texas legislature designated the secretary of state as the chief election officer of Texas. In this capacity, the secretary of state interprets legislation and issues guidelines. Under the Voting Rights Act, the U.S. Department of Justice must approve these decisions, so they appear to carry the weight of federal authority as well.

Since 1973, the secretary of state has had the responsibility for disbursing funds to the state and county party executive committees to pay for the primary elections. The secretary of state is the keeper of election records, both party and governmental. The secretary also receives certificates of nomination from parties that have conducted primaries and conventions and uses these certificates to prepare the ballot for statewide offices. The governor, the secretary of state, and a gubernatorial appointee are the members of a three-person board that canvasses election returns for state and district offices.

County-Level Administration

Except for the preparation of the statewide portion of the ballot, county-level officials actually conduct general elections. In 1977, the legislature created three options from which the counties may choose when administering general elections.

---

20. Here, *nonpartisan* means only that the party label does not appear on the ballot, and certification by the party is not necessary. Special elections are, in fact, often partisan because regular party supporters work for their candidates.

The Traditional System. The first option is to maintain the decentralized system that the counties have used for decades. Under this system, the major responsibility rests with the county clerk. By the time the clerk receives the state portion of the ballot from the secretary of state, she or he will have certified the candidates' names for the county-level and precinct-level portions of the ballot. The board of elections—consisting of the county judge, sheriff, and clerk and the chairs of the county executive committees of the two major parties—arranges for polling places and for the printing of ballots. The county tax assessor-collector processes all voter applications and updates the voting rolls. The county commissioners' court draws precinct voting lines, appoints election judges, selects voting devices, canvasses votes, and authorizes payment of all election expenses from the county treasury.

Alternative County Options. The two other options are designed to promote efficiency. One is for the county commissioners' court to transfer the voter-registration function from the office of the tax assessor-collector to that of the county clerk, thus removing the assessor-collector from the electoral process.

The third option, available for the first time in 1979, involves more extensive changes and may represent the direction that election administration will take in the future. It calls for all election-related duties of both the assessor-collector and the county clerk to be transferred to a county election administrator. This officer is appointed for a term of two years by the county elections commission, which, in counties that choose this option, replaces the board of elections. (The membership of the commission is the same as that of the board, except that the sheriff is not included.)

Ballot Construction

Like so many other features of an election system, ballot construction reflects both practical and political considerations. Two basic types of general-election ballots are available: the party-column ballot and the office-block ballot.

The Party-Column Ballot. In the *party-column ballot* (which we first described in Chapter 9), the names of all the candidates of each party are listed in parallel columns. This is the type of ballot that has traditionally been used in Texas. For an example, see Figure 20–5. This ballot itemizes the offices as prescribed by law in descending order of importance, and the candidates are listed in each row. Beside each name is a box (on paper ballots) or lever (on voting machines) that the voter must mark or pull if she or he wishes to vote a split ticket. At the top of each column is the party's name and a box or lever. To vote a straight ticket, the voter need only mark the box or pull the lever for the party of his or her choice.

The Office-Block Ballot. In the *office-block ballot* (which we also described in Chapter 9), the names of the candidates for each office are listed underneath the title of the office. (See Figure 20–6 for an example.) To vote a straight party ticket, a voter must pick his or her party's candidate for each office. Several states use the office-block ballot, which also is called the Massachusetts ballot because it originated there. Minor parties in Texas (which once included the Republican Party) and independent voters advocate the use of this ballot type because it makes straight-ticket voting for the major parties more difficult.

The Politics of Ballot Construction. Understandably, supporters of the major Texas political parties strongly support the use of the party-column ballot. It enables lesser-known candidates to ride on the coattails of the party label or of a popular candidate running for major office. There also may be an extra advantage in the use of this type of ballot for the party that is listed in the first column.

FIGURE 20–5 Party-Column Ballot Used in Texas for the 2004 General Election

No. 0000

GENERAL ELECTION *(ELECCION GENERAL)*
***(Condado de)* SAMPLE COUNTY, TEXAS**
NOVEMBER 2, 2004 *(2 de noviembre de 2004)*
SAMPLE BALLOT *(BOLETA DE MUESTRA)*

INSTRUCTION NOTE: Vote for the candidate of your choice in each race by placing an "X" in the square beside the candidate's name. You may cast a straight-party vote (that is, cast a vote for all the nominees of one party) by placing an "X" in the square beside the name of the party of your choice. If you cast a straight-party vote for all the nominees of one party and also cast a vote for an opponent of one of that party's nominees, your vote for the opponent will be counted as well as your vote for all the other nominees of the party for which the straight-party vote was cast.

(NOTA DE INSTRUCCION: Vote por el candidato de su preferencia para cada candidatura marcando una "X" en el espacio cuadrado a la izquierda del nombre del candidato. Usted podrá votar por todos los candidatos de un solo partido político ("straight ticket") marcando una "X" en el espacio cuadrado a la izquierda del nombre de ese partido politico. Si usted vota por uno de los partidos políticos y también vota por el contrincante de uno de los candidatos de dicho partido político, se contará su voto por el contrincante tanto como su voto por todos los demás candidatos del partido político de su preferencia.)

Candidates for: *(Candidatos para:)*	❑ REPUBLICAN PARTY *(Partido Republicano)*	❑ DEMOCRATIC PARTY *(Partido Democrático)*	❑ LIBERTARIAN PARTY *(Partido Libertariano)*	❑ INDEPENDENT *(Independiente)*	❑ WRITE-IN *(Voto Escrito)*
President and Vice President *(Presidente y Vice Presidente)*	❑ George W. Bush/ Dick Cheney	❑ John F. Kerry/ John Edwards	❑ Michael Badnarik/ Richard V. Campagna		❑
United States Representative, District _______ *(Representante de los Estados Unidos, Distrito Núm _______)*					❑
Railroad Commissioner *(Comisionado de Ferrocarriles)*	❑ Victor G. Carrillo	❑ Bob Scarborough	❑ Anthony Garcia		
Justice, Supreme Court, Place 3 *(Juez, Corte Suprema, Núm 3)*	❑ Harriet O'Neill				
Justice, Supreme Court, Place 5 *(Juez, Corte Suprema, Núm 5)*	❑ Paul Green				
Justice, Supreme Court, Place 9 *(Juez, Corte Suprema, Núm 9)*	❑ Scott Brister	❑ David Van Os			
Judge, Court of Criminal Appeals, Place 2 *(Juez, Corte de Apelaciones Criminales, Lugar Núm 2)*	❑ Lawrence "Larry" Meyers		❑ Quanah Parker		
Judge, Court of Criminal Appeals, Place 5 *(Juez, Corte de Apelaciones Criminales, Lugar Núm 5)*	❑ Cheryl Johnson		❑ Tom Oxford		
Judge, Court of Criminal Appeals, Place 6 *(Juez, Corte de Apelaciones Criminales, Lugar Núm 6)*	❑ Michael E. Keasler	❑ J.R. Molina			

In the past, candidates of the once-dominant Democratic Party were always listed first, and the practice was accepted without challenge. In 1963, however, the legislature enacted a requirement that the parties be slated from left to right on the ballot according to the proportion of votes that each party's candidate for governor received in the most recent gubernatorial election. Next come candidates of parties that were not on the ballot in the last election, and last come independents. After the election of Governor Bill Clements in 1979, the Republicans achieved the favored ballot position.

Beginning with the 2002 elections, many Texas counties moved away from a strict party-column ballot. Partly because of the adoption of electronic voting systems (discussed later), ballots in these counties combine features of the office-block and party-column designs. As with the office-block ballot, candidates are listed underneath each office. As with the party-column ballot, however, one can vote a straight party ticket with a single mark; that is, before turning to specific offices, voters are first given the option to vote a straight ticket.

Getting on the Ballot

For a candidate to get his or her name on the general-election ballot, the candidate must be either a party nominee or an independent. If a party received at least 5 percent of the vote for any statewide office in the previous general election, its full slate of candidates is placed on the ballot automatically. Thus, the Democratic and Republican parties have no problems, and certification by the appropriate party officials of the winner of a primary or convention is routine.

FIGURE 20–6 Office-Block Ballot Used in Massachusetts

OFFICIAL BALLOT

TO VOTE FOR A PERSON MARK A CROSS X IN THE SQUARE AT THE RIGHT OF THE NAME.

SENATOR IN CONGRESS — Vote for ONE
JOHN F. KERRY 43 Commonwealth Ave., Boston + Democratic Candidate for Re-election
JIM RAPPAPORT 701 Strawberry Hill Rd., Concord + Republican

GOVERNOR AND LIEUTENANT GOVERNOR — Vote for ONE
SILBER and CLAPPROOD
WELD and CELLUCCI
UMINA and DeBERRY

ATTORNEY GENERAL — Vote for ONE
L. SCOTT HARSHBARGER - 14 Sacramento St., Cambridge
WILLIAM C. SAWYER - 15 Spring Hill Rd., Acton

SECRETARY OF STATE — Vote for ONE
MICHAEL JOSEPH CONNOLLY - 42 Cerdan Ave., Boston Candidate for Re-election
PAUL McCARTHY - 12 Lakeview Dr., Lynnfield
BARBARA F. AHEARN - 86 So. Main St., Templeton

TREASURER — Vote for ONE
WILLIAM FRANCIS GALVIN - 46 Lake St., Boston
JOSEPH D. MALONE - 15 Cushman St., Watertown
C. DAVID NASH - 2 Scott Dr., Framingham

AUDITOR — Vote for ONE
A. JOSEPH DeNUCCI - 119 Warwick Rd., Newton Candidate for Re-election
DOUGLAS J. MURRAY - 40 Everett Ave., Somerville
STEVEN K. SHERMAN - 85 Tremont St., Marlborough

REPRESENTATIVE IN CONGRESS — SECOND DISTRICT — Vote for ONE
RICHARD E. NEAL - 36 Atwater Ter., Springfield Candidate for Re-election

COUNCILLOR — SEVENTH DISTRICT — Vote for ONE
JAMES D. O'BRIEN, JR. - 31 Old English Rd., Worcester Candidate for Re-election

SENATOR IN GENERAL COURT — WORCESTER, FRANKLIN, HAMPDEN, HAMPSHIRE DISTRICT — Vote for ONE
ROBERT D. WETMORE - Hubbardston Rd., Barre Candidate for Re-election
JOHN LaPOINTE - Dugway Rd., Petersham

REPRESENTATIVE IN GENERAL COURT — FIFTH WORCESTER DISTRICT — Vote for ONE
STEPHEN M. BREWER - Pleasant St., Barre Candidate for Re-election
GEORGE R. LEFEBVRE - 23 Chestnut St., North Brookfield

DISTRICT ATTORNEY — MIDDLE DISTRICT — Vote for ONE
JOHN J. CONTE - 29 Elnora Dr., Worcester Candidate for Re-election

REGISTER OF PROBATE — WORCESTER COUNTY — Vote for ONE
LEONARD P. FLYNN - 679 Main St., Shrewsbury Candidate for Re-election

COUNTY TREASURER — WORCESTER COUNTY — Vote for ONE
MICHAEL J. DONOGHUE - 54 Summerhill Ave., Worcester Candidate for Re-election

COUNTY COMMISSIONER — WORCESTER COUNTY — Vote for ONE
FRANCIS J. HOLLOWAY - 12 Greenleaf Farm Cir., Shrewsbury Candidate for Re-election

Making Life Hard for Third Parties and Independents. Minor parties have a more difficult time. For instance, neither the Libertarian Party nor the Green Party received the necessary votes in 2002, and both had to petition to get their candidates on the ballot in 2004. Independent candidates for president have the most difficult challenge, for they must present a petition with signatures equaling 1 percent of the total state vote for president in the last election. For John Anderson, an independent candidate who ran in 1980, that meant a minimum of 40,719 names on the petition. In 1992, Ross Perot's supporters presented 54,275 signatures to get his name on the ballot.

For all offices except president, the total vote for governor is the basis for determining the required number of signatures for both independents and third-party candidates. A candidate for statewide office needs signatures equaling 1 percent of the total gubernatorial vote in the entire state. For multicounty district offices, the requirement is 3 percent of the gubernatorial vote in the district. For all other district and local offices, it is 5 percent of the gubernatorial vote in the district (a maximum of 500 signatures at the local level). Further requirements add to the difficulty of gaining access to the ballot by petition. Signers must be registered voters and must not have participated in the selection of a nominee for that office in another party's primary. In addition, each page of the petition must be notarized.[21]

21. In 1976, the secretary of state interpreted the law as requiring that each signature be notarized. The next year, the legislature specified that a notary need only sign each page of the petition. Difficulties involving technical aspects of the law and adverse interpretations of the law represent only part of the harassment that minor parties and independents have traditionally encountered in their quest for a place on the ballot. See Ernest Crain, et al., *Understanding Texas Politics,* 12th ed. (Belmont, CA: Wadsworth Publishing Company, 2006).

As a general rule, candidates using the petition route seek twice the required number of signatures to ensure the petition's certifiability. For example, in 1980, the Libertarian Party submitted 55,000 signatures, and the Socialist Workers Party (SWP) turned in 30,000 to ensure that each had 23,698 persons who were legally qualified to sign. Only the Libertarians succeeded in placing their candidates' names on the ballot, however. The SWP fell below the minimum when almost half of the petitioners' signatures were found to be those of persons not qualified to sign.[22]

Write-in Candidates. Write-in candidates are seldom successful. Often, they are individuals who have entered a party primary and lost.

Write-in candidates may have an easier task in the future as a result of a law passed by the legislature. It requires a candidate to register with the secretary of state before the start of absentee voting in general elections and 45 days before a primary election. The names of write-in candidates must be posted at the election site, possibly in the election booth. A candidate not properly registered cannot win, regardless of the number of votes he or she receives. Write-ins in primary elections are permitted only for party offices.

Presidential candidate Ralph Nader on the campaign trail in 2008. Some argue that he is the reason Al Gore did not win the election in 2000. What difference do you think he made in 2008? (Alex Wong/Getty Images)

The Secret Ballot and the Integrity of Elections

Most people believe that the right to vote includes the rights to cast a ballot in secret, have the election conducted fairly, and have the ballots counted correctly. These rights have not always been available, however. The *Australian ballot* (see Chapter 9), adopted by Texas in 1892, includes names of the candidates of all political parties on a single ballot printed at public expense and available only at the voting place.[23] Given a reasonably private area in which to mark the ballot, the voter was offered a secret ballot for the first time.

Election Judges and Poll Watchers. Protection of the integrity of the electoral process in Texas is primarily addressed through political remedies. As a result, minor parties have reason to be concerned that irregularities in elections administered by members of the majority parties may not be observed and, if observed, may not be reported.

Traditional practice has been that, in general and special elections, the county board of elections appoints as election judges the precinct chairs of the political party that has a majority on the elections board. Since 1967, each election judge has been required to select at least one election clerk from each of the lists submitted by the county chairs of the two major political parties. Moreover, law now recognizes the status of "poll watchers," and both primary candidates and county chairs are authorized to appoint them. These oversight options mark a significant improvement over the days when the only possible (and usually ineffective) remedy was to go to court.

Rechecks and Recounts. If there is a question about the election results, candidates can ask for either a recheck or a recount of the ballots. A recheck applies primarily to voting machines. It checks for counting errors and costs $3 per precinct. The loser of an election also can ask for a recount (this is discussed in greater detail in the section on "Voting Problems"). The candidate who requests a recount must put up a deposit and is liable for the entire cost

22. The SWP was founded in 1938 by followers of the Russian Communist leader Leon Trotsky, who was Joseph Stalin's chief opponent in the struggle for control of the Soviet Union. (Trotsky lost.) In recent decades, the SWP has looked less to Trotsky for inspiration and more to former Cuban leader Fidel Castro.
23. Optional at first, the Australian ballot was made mandatory in 1903.

unless she or he wins or ties in the recount. Moreover, a recount (but not a recheck) must include all precincts. In a large county, the cost of a recount can be prohibitive.

Multilingualism

Ballots in most Texas counties are printed in English. In more than 100 counties, the ballot is printed in both English and Spanish. In some parts of the United States, other languages are required, including Chinese, Eskimo, Filipino, Japanese, and Korean. In Los Angeles County alone, ballots are printed in seven different languages.

Vietnamese Ballots in Houston. In 2002, the U.S. Department of Justice ordered several counties around the country, including Harris County (which contains Houston), to provide ballots and voting materials in Vietnamese as well as Spanish. Harris County was the only county in Texas required to provide Vietnamese ballots and the only county outside California to face this requirement. The requirement was due to the Voting Rights Act of 1965 and its 1992 amendments. According to Section 203 of the Act, a political subdivision (typically a county) must provide such help if significant numbers of voting-age citizens are members of a single-language minority who do not speak or understand English "well enough to participate in the electoral process."

When Are Multilingual Ballots Required? Specifically, the legal requirement is triggered when more than 5 percent of the voting-age citizens or 10,000 of these citizens meet the criteria. The 2000 census showed that more than 55,000 people living in Harris County identified themselves as Vietnamese. The Department of Justice determined that at least 10,000 of them were old enough to vote and not proficient in English. Thus, the requirement was triggered. Given the current record levels of immigration into the United States, the number of ballot languages is almost certain to increase. We show a sample multilingual ballot in Figure 20–7.

Voting Absentee and Voting Early

All states allow members of the U.S. armed forces to vote absentee, and Texas, along with forty other states, also permits absentee voting for reasons such as illness or anticipated absence from the county. Traditionally, absentee voting in Texas (and other states) was mostly a convenience for the middle class and served as a boost for conservative candidates.

Current Rules for Absentee Voting. In 1987, the legislature made changes that appear to have far-ranging effects:

- To vote absentee in person (rather than by mail), you need not swear that you intend to be out of the city or county on election day.
- Absentee ballots can be cast in substations in the urban counties.

Since 1989, the absentee-voting period has begun 22 days before the election and ended on the sixth day before the election. Moreover, substation voting places now remain open 12 hours a day Monday through Friday, with shorter hours on Saturdays and Sundays. As a result, absentee voting has increased tremendously. Whether cast by mail or in person, on paper ballots or by punch card or electronic machines, absentee votes are not counted until election day.

Early Voting. In 1991, the Texas legislature instituted early voting.[24] All Texas voters now are able to cast their ballots before election day. Unlike absentee voting, early voting is available to any registered voter. In addition to traditional election day voting sites, such

---

24. For a description of early voting and a preliminary assessment of its effects, see Robert M. Stein and Patricia A. Garcia-Monet, "Voting Early but Not Often," *Social Science Quarterly,* Vol. 78, December 1997, p. 657–671.

FIGURE 20–7 English-Vietnamese Language Ballot Used in Harris County for the 2006 General Election

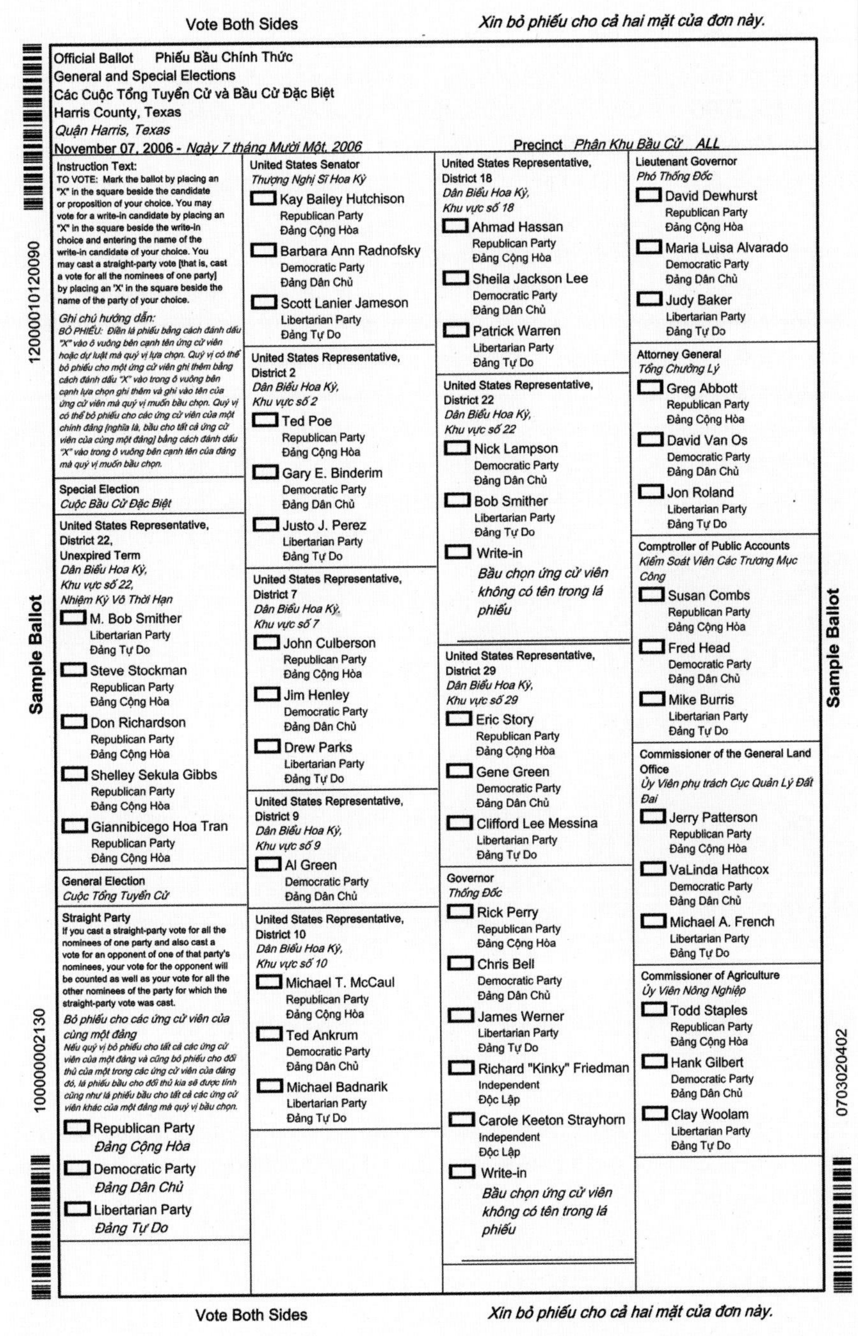

Vote Both Sides — *Xin bỏ phiếu cho cả hai mặt của đơn này.*

Official Ballot Phiếu Bầu Chính Thức
General and Special Elections
Các Cuộc Tổng Tuyển Cử và Bầu Cử Đặc Biệt
Harris County, Texas
Quận Harris, Texas
November 07, 2006 - *Ngày 7 tháng Mười Một, 2006*
Precinct *Phân Khu Bầu Cử* ALL

Instruction Text:
TO VOTE: Mark the ballot by placing an "X" in the square beside the candidate or proposition of your choice. You may vote for a write-in candidate by placing an "X" in the square beside the write-in choice and entering the name of the write-in candidate of your choice. You may cast a straight-party vote [that is, cast a vote for all the nominees of one party] by placing an 'X' in the square beside the name of the party of your choice.

Ghi chú hướng dẫn:
BỎ PHIẾU: Điền lá phiếu bằng cách đánh dấu "X" vào ô vuông bên cạnh tên ứng cử viên hoặc dự luật mà quý vị lựa chọn. Quý vị có thể bỏ phiếu cho một ứng cử viên ghi thêm bằng cách đánh dấu "X" vào trong ô vuông bên cạnh lựa chọn ghi thêm và ghi vào tên của ứng cử viên mà quý vị muốn bầu chọn. Quý vị có thể bỏ phiếu cho các ứng cử viên của một chính đảng [nghĩa là, bầu cho tất cả ứng cử viên của cùng một đảng] bằng cách đánh dấu "X" vào trong ô vuông bên cạnh tên của đảng mà quý vị muốn bầu chọn.

Special Election
Cuộc Bầu Cử Đặc Biệt

United States Representative, District 22, Unexpired Term
Dân Biểu Hoa Kỳ, Khu vực số 22, Nhiệm Kỳ Vô Thời Hạn
- M. Bob Smither — Libertarian Party, Đảng Tự Do
- Steve Stockman — Republican Party, Đảng Cộng Hòa
- Don Richardson — Republican Party, Đảng Cộng Hòa
- Shelley Sekula Gibbs — Republican Party, Đảng Cộng Hòa
- Giannibicego Hoa Tran — Republican Party, Đảng Cộng Hòa

General Election
Cuộc Tổng Tuyển Cử

Straight Party
If you cast a straight-party vote for all the nominees of one party and also cast a vote for an opponent of one of that party's nominees, your vote for the opponent will be counted as well as your vote for all the other nominees of the party for which the straight-party vote was cast.

Bỏ phiếu cho các ứng cử viên của cùng một đảng
Nếu quý vị bỏ phiếu cho tất cả các ứng cử viên của một đảng và cũng bỏ phiếu cho đối thủ của một trong các ứng cử viên của đảng đó, lá phiếu bầu cho đối thủ kia sẽ được tính cũng như lá phiếu bầu cho tất cả các ứng cử viên khác của một đảng mà quý vị bầu chọn.
- Republican Party — *Đảng Cộng Hòa*
- Democratic Party — *Đảng Dân Chủ*
- Libertarian Party — *Đảng Tự Do*

United States Senator
Thượng Nghị Sĩ Hoa Kỳ
- Kay Bailey Hutchison — Republican Party, Đảng Cộng Hòa
- Barbara Ann Radnofsky — Democratic Party, Đảng Dân Chủ
- Scott Lanier Jameson — Libertarian Party, Đảng Tự Do

United States Representative, District 2
Dân Biểu Hoa Kỳ, Khu vực số 2
- Ted Poe — Republican Party, Đảng Cộng Hòa
- Gary E. Binderim — Democratic Party, Đảng Dân Chủ
- Justo J. Perez — Libertarian Party, Đảng Tự Do

United States Representative, District 7
Dân Biểu Hoa Kỳ, Khu vực số 7
- John Culberson — Republican Party, Đảng Cộng Hòa
- Jim Henley — Democratic Party, Đảng Dân Chủ
- Drew Parks — Libertarian Party, Đảng Tự Do

United States Representative, District 9
Dân Biểu Hoa Kỳ, Khu vực số 9
- Al Green — Democratic Party, Đảng Dân Chủ

United States Representative, District 10
Dân Biểu Hoa Kỳ, Khu vực số 10
- Michael T. McCaul — Republican Party, Đảng Cộng Hòa
- Ted Ankrum — Democratic Party, Đảng Dân Chủ
- Michael Badnarik — Libertarian Party, Đảng Tự Do

United States Representative, District 18
Dân Biểu Hoa Kỳ, Khu vực số 18
- Ahmad Hassan — Republican Party, Đảng Cộng Hòa
- Sheila Jackson Lee — Democratic Party, Đảng Dân Chủ
- Patrick Warren — Libertarian Party, Đảng Tự Do

United States Representative, District 22
Dân Biểu Hoa Kỳ, Khu vực số 22
- Nick Lampson — Democratic Party, Đảng Dân Chủ
- Bob Smither — Libertarian Party, Đảng Tự Do
- Write-in — *Bầu chọn ứng cử viên không có tên trong lá phiếu*

United States Representative, District 29
Dân Biểu Hoa Kỳ, Khu vực số 29
- Eric Story — Republican Party, Đảng Cộng Hòa
- Gene Green — Democratic Party, Đảng Dân Chủ
- Clifford Lee Messina — Libertarian Party, Đảng Tự Do

Governor
Thống Đốc
- Rick Perry — Republican Party, Đảng Cộng Hòa
- Chris Bell — Democratic Party, Đảng Dân Chủ
- James Werner — Libertarian Party, Đảng Tự Do
- Richard "Kinky" Friedman — Independent, Độc Lập
- Carole Keeton Strayhorn — Independent, Độc Lập
- Write-in — *Bầu chọn ứng cử viên không có tên trong lá phiếu*

Lieutenant Governor
Phó Thống Đốc
- David Dewhurst — Republican Party, Đảng Cộng Hòa
- Maria Luisa Alvarado — Democratic Party, Đảng Dân Chủ
- Judy Baker — Libertarian Party, Đảng Tự Do

Attorney General
Tổng Chưởng Lý
- Greg Abbott — Republican Party, Đảng Cộng Hòa
- David Van Os — Democratic Party, Đảng Dân Chủ
- Jon Roland — Libertarian Party, Đảng Tự Do

Comptroller of Public Accounts
Kiểm Soát Viên Các Trương Mục Công
- Susan Combs — Republican Party, Đảng Cộng Hòa
- Fred Head — Democratic Party, Đảng Dân Chủ
- Mike Burris — Libertarian Party, Đảng Tự Do

Commissioner of the General Land Office
Ủy Viên phụ trách Cục Quản Lý Đất Đai
- Jerry Patterson — Republican Party, Đảng Cộng Hòa
- VaLinda Hathcox — Democratic Party, Đảng Dân Chủ
- Michael A. French — Libertarian Party, Đảng Tự Do

Commissioner of Agriculture
Ủy Viên Nông Nghiệp
- Todd Staples — Republican Party, Đảng Cộng Hòa
- Hank Gilbert — Democratic Party, Đảng Dân Chủ
- Clay Woolam — Libertarian Party, Đảng Tự Do

Sample Ballot

12000010120090

10000002130

07030020402

Vote Both Sides — *Xin bỏ phiếu cho cả hai mặt của đơn này.*

as schools and fire stations, there are many other places to vote early, including grocery and convenience stores.

This innovation clearly has made voting easier in Texas, and people are taking advantage of it. In 1992, for example, about 25 percent of all votes were cast before election day. In 1996, approximately 33 percent of votes were cast early. In 2000, the number was slightly less than 39 percent. In 2004, more than 50 percent of all votes were cast early. Although people are voting earlier, turnout has not increased greatly. Still,

did you know?

That in 2004, two-thirds of the votes in the state of Washington and approximately half of the votes in Colorado, Nevada, and New Mexico were cast early, before election day.

the tendency to vote early may have serious implications for when and how politicians campaign, as late campaign activities cannot influence those whose votes have already been cast.

Voting Problems

We take for granted that when we vote, the system will work correctly. As we learned in Florida in the 2000 presidential elections, this is not always ensured. Experts have known for a long time that voting involves a degree of error. By most accounts, the error rate averages 1 to 2 percent, although it can be higher, depending on the system used.

Recounts. Texas has specific laws about recounts. A candidate can request a recount if he or she loses by less than 10 percent. This is a fairly generous rule compared with other states. The candidate who requests the recount does have to pay for it, however, which means that most candidates do not request a recount unless the margin is much closer, say, 1 percentage point.

The Texas election code states that "only one method may be used in the recount [and] a manual recount shall be conducted in preference to an electronic recount." The procedures are fairly detailed. What may be most interesting is the set of rules for how chads should be interpreted. Canvassing authorities are allowed to determine whether "an indentation on the chad from the stylus or other object is present" and whether "the chad reflects by other means a clearly ascertainable intent of the voter to vote."[25] This leaves ample room for discretion on the part of canvassing authorities in the various Texas counties.

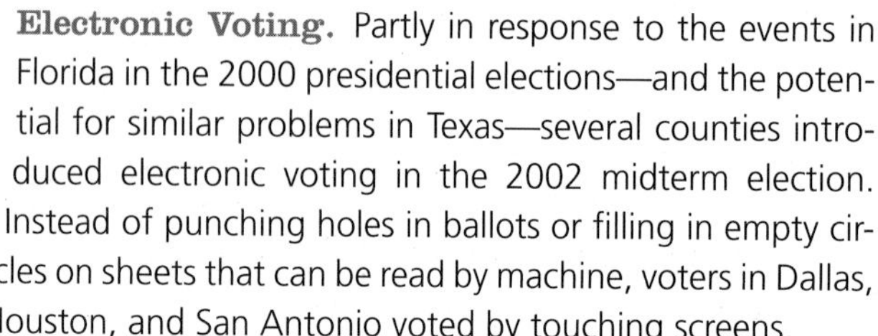

Under Texas election law, hand recounts include "hanging chads." Here, an election worker holds a ballot filled with undetached chads (squares of paper that are pushed out of punch-card ballots) that will have to be manually removed before the ballot can be counted. Why might some states refuse to count ballots unless they are perfectly formed? (AP Photo/ Ted S. Warren)

Electronic Voting. Partly in response to the events in Florida in the 2000 presidential elections—and the potential for similar problems in Texas—several counties introduced electronic voting in the 2002 midterm election. Instead of punching holes in ballots or filling in empty circles on sheets that can be read by machine, voters in Dallas, Houston, and San Antonio voted by touching screens.

The technology is similar to what is used for e-ticket check-in at many airports and promises an exact count of votes. Electronic voting is being used in various jurisdictions throughout the United States. As with any new technology, however, problems have occurred with the new systems in Texas and elsewhere.[26]

Election Campaigns in Texas

The aim of party activity is to nominate candidates in the party primary or convention and then get them elected in the general election. The pattern in Texas before 1978 was for Republicans and other minor parties to run only token, poorly financed candidates for most contested offices, so the real choices were made in the Democratic primary. Today, the battle has moved from the Democratic primary to the general election.

---

25. Texas Code 127.130. Also see Carlos Guerra, "Texas Is Far Friendlier to All Our Chad," *San Antonio Express-News*, November 25, 2000, p. B1.
26. Rachel Konrad, "Reports of Electronic Voting Trouble Top 1,000," *USA Today*, accessed November 4, 2004, at www.usatoday.com/tech/news/techpolicy/evoting/2004-11-04-1000-reports_x.htm.

Who Gets Elected

It is useful to think of the elective offices in Texas as a pyramid. At the bottom of the pyramid are the most local of offices, and at the top is the governor. Moving from bottom to top, the importance of the office increases, and the number of officeholders decreases. It thus becomes increasingly difficult for a politician to ascend higher up the pyramid, and only the best politicians rise to the top. This tells us much about candidates and elections in Texas and elsewhere.

Candidates for Statewide Office. In the most local elections, the pool of candidates is diverse. Contenders may vary in educational background, income, and profession. As we move up the pyramid, however, candidates become more homogeneous. For statewide office, the typical candidate is middle or upper class, is from an urban area, and has strong ties to business and professional interests in the state. Most officers who are elected statewide, including the governor, lieutenant governor, and attorney general, must be acceptable to the state's major financial and corporate interests and to its top law firms. These interests help a statewide candidate to raise the large volume of funds that is critical to a successful race.

A lineup of people voting electronically. This fairly recent voting technology promises to be more accurate than paper ballots. Some argue that this is not correct. What do you think? Does electronic voting solve the problems with paper ballots? How can you tell? (Bob Daemmrich/ Image Works)

Successful candidates for statewide office in Texas traditionally have been white Protestant males. Before 1984, when Raul Gonzalez was elected to the state supreme court, no Mexican American or African American had been elected to statewide office, although these two ethnic groups combined represent half of the state's population. The only female governor had been Miriam A. "Ma" Ferguson, who in the 1920s served as surrogate for her husband, Jim. In 1982, Ann Richards was elected state treasurer, becoming the second woman ever to be elected to statewide office in Texas.

Gains by Women and Minorities. Since then, women and minority group members have made substantial gains in statewide offices. In 1990, Democrat Ann Richards (1933–2006) became the first woman elected governor in her own right. That same year, Republican Kay Bailey Hutchison captured the state treasurer's office. In 1993, Hutchison won a special election to become the first woman from Texas elected to the U.S. Senate. Dan Morales became the first Mexican American to win a state executive office when he was elected attorney general in 1990.[27] More history was made in 1992 when Morris Overstreet of Amarillo won a seat on the Texas Court of Criminal Appeals and became the first African American elected to a statewide office.

Women and ethnic groups are starting to make inroads in other elected offices in Texas as well. In the seventy-ninth legislature (2005–2006), 32 women were elected to the 150-member house and four to the 31-member senate. Women have also held the post of mayor in five of the state's largest cities—Austin, Dallas, El Paso, Houston, and San Antonio. Mexican Americans hold 35 seats in the state legislature, and African Americans occupy 16 seats. Among the state's 32 U.S. congressional representatives are three women, six Mexican Americans, and three African Americans. Clearly, Texas politics has changed quite a bit.

---

27. Morales was convicted of mail and tax fraud in 2003 and was sentenced to four years in prison.

The General-Election Campaign

To a large extent, election outcomes are predictable. Despite all the media attention paid to conventions, debates, advertising, and other elements of political campaigns, certain factors powerfully structure the vote in national and state elections.[28] In state elections, two factors predominate: party identification and incumbency.

Governor Rick Perry waits to be introduced at a gun shop in Dallas. Perry emphasized his pro-gun credentials in his re-election campaign and received the endorsement of the National Rifle Association. (AP Photo/LM Otero)

Party Identification. First, if the voters in a state tend to identify more with one political party than the other, the candidates of the favored party have an advantage in general elections. When most Texans identified with the Democratic Party, Democratic candidates dominated elected offices throughout the state. As Texans have become more Republican in their identification, Republican candidates have done very well. As we pointed out in Chapter 22, Republicans now hold every statewide elective office.

Party identification varies considerably within Texas, however, and this has implications for state legislative elections. In some parts of the state, particularly in urban districts, a majority of the voters identify with the Democratic Party. Democratic candidates typically represent those areas in the state house and senate. Thus, party identification in the state and in the various districts has much to do with which candidates win general elections. How the boundaries of the various districts are drawn also has an important effect on the outcome.

Incumbency. Second, incumbent candidates—those who hold office and are up for re-election—are more likely to win in general elections. This is particularly true in state legislative elections, where the districts are fairly homogeneous and the campaigns are not very visible, but incumbency also is important in elections for statewide office. Incumbents have several advantages over challengers, the most important of which is that they have won before. To become an incumbent, a candidate has to beat an incumbent or win in an open-seat election, which usually includes strong candidates. By definition, therefore, incumbents are good candidates. In addition, incumbents have the advantages of office. They are in a position to do things for their constituents, and thus increase their support among voters.

While party identification and incumbency are important in Texas elections, they are not the whole story. What they really tell us is the degree to which candidates are advantaged or disadvantaged as they embark on their campaigns. Other factors also matter on election day, and we consider some of those factors next.[29]

Mobilizing Groups. Groups play an important role in elections for any office. A fundamental part of campaigns is getting out the vote among those groups that strongly support the candidate. To a large extent, candidates focus on groups aligned with the political par-

---

28. Most of the research has focused on presidential elections. See Christopher Wlezien, "On Forecasting the Presidential Vote," *PS: Political Science and Politics,* Vol. 34, March 2001, p. 25–31, available at www.apsanet.org/imgtest/CJ312-ElectionIntro%5B23-24%5D.pdf. There is some research on state gubernatorial and legislative elections. See, for example, Mark E. Tompkins, "The Electoral Fortunes of Gubernatorial Incumbents," *Journal of Politics,* Vol. 46, May 1984, p. 520–543; and Ronald E. Weber, Harvey J. Tucker, and Paul Brace, "Vanishing Marginals in State Legislative Elections," *Legislative Studies Quarterly,* Vol. 16, February 1991, pp. 29–47.
29. For a detailed analysis of election campaigns in Texas in a single election year, see Richard Murray, "The 1996 Elections in Texas," in Kent L. Tedin, Donald S. Lutz, and Edward P. Fuchs, eds., *Perspectives on American and Texas Politics,* 5th ed. (Dubuque, IA: Kendall/Hunt, 1998), p. 247–286.

ties.[30] At the state level, business interests and teachers are particularly important; Republican candidates tend to focus their efforts on the former and Democratic candidates on the latter.

Candidates also attempt to mobilize other groups, including African Americans and Mexican Americans. Traditionally, Democratic candidates emphasized these minority groups, although Governor George W. Bush broke somewhat with this tradition and focused substantial attention on the Hispanic community in Texas. Mobilizing groups does not necessarily involve taking strong public stands on their behalf. Mobilization of such groups may be conducted quietly, often through targeted mailings and phone calls.

Texas Democratic gubernatorial candidate Bill White greets supporters in Corpus Christi, Texas on the day before election day, 2010. (AP Photo/Corpus Christi Caller-Times, Todd Yates)

Choosing Issues. Issues play a role in any campaign. In campaigns for state office, the issues of taxes, education, and crime are relevant, and the abortion issue is important in many states. As with the mobilization of groups, the issues that candidates select tend to reflect their party affiliations, but issue stands are often not so clear-cut. Very few candidates, after all, are in favor of higher taxes and less spending on education and crime prevention.

Where candidates do differ is in their emphasis on particular issues and their policy proposals. Their choices depend heavily on carefully crafted opinion polls. Using polls, candidates attempt to identify the issues that the public considers important and then develop policy positions to address those issues. The process is ongoing, and candidates pay close attention to changes in public opinion and, perhaps most important, to the public's response to the candidates' own positions. Polling is thus fundamental in modern political campaigns in America.

The Campaign Trail. Deciding where and how to campaign is a critical part of campaign strategy. Candidates spend countless hours "taking the stump," or traveling around the state or district to speak before diverse groups. In a state as large as Texas, candidates for statewide office must pick and choose areas to maximize their exposure. This means that candidates spend most of their time in urban areas.

Today, no candidate is elected by stumping alone. The most direct route to the voters is through the media. There are some 17 media markets in Texas. These include approximately 200 television and cable stations and more than 500 radio stations. In addition, there are 79 daily and 403 weekly papers dispersed throughout the state's 254 counties.[31] Candidates hire public relations firms in their effort to take advantage of all these media outlets, and media consultants and advertising play a large role.

These days, a successful campaign often relies on **negative campaigning,** in which candidates attack opponents' issue positions or character. As one campaign consultant said, "Campaigns are about definition. Either you define yourself and your opponent or they do . . . Victory goes to the aggressor."[32] While many consider negative campaigning

Negative Campaigning
A strategy in political campaigns of attacking the opposing candidate's issue positions or—especially—his or her character.

30. For an analysis of how membership in various demographic groups influences voting behavior, see Robert S. Erikson, Thomas B. Lancaster, and David W. Romero, "Group Components of the Presidential Vote, 1952–1984," *Journal of Politics,* Vol. 50, May 1988, p. 337–346. For an analysis of how identification with various social groups influences voting behavior, see Christopher Wlezien and Arthur H. Miller, "Social Groups and Political Judgments," *Social Science Quarterly,* Vol. 78, December 1997, p. 625–640.
31. *Gale Directory of Publications and Broadcast Media,* Vol. 2, 129th ed. (Detroit, MI: Gale Research, 1997).
32. Quoted in Dave McNeely, "Campaign Strategists Preparing Spin Systems," *Austin American-Statesman,* October 21, 1993, p. A11.

an unfortunate part of American politics, such campaigning can provide voters with information about the candidates and their issue positions.

Timing. The timing of the campaign effort can be very important. Unlike presidential campaigns, campaigns for state offices, including the governorship, begin fairly late in the election cycle. It is common to hear little from gubernatorial candidates until after Labor Day and not much from candidates for the legislature until a month before the election.

Candidates often reserve a large proportion of their campaign advertising budget for a last-minute media blitz. Early voting may affect this strategy, however. In 2004, half of the votes in Texas were cast early, which means that any final campaign blitz came far too late to have any effect on those voters. Because of this trend, in the future candidates may be less likely to concentrate their efforts on the final days of the campaign.

Financing Political Campaigns

Political campaigns are expensive, which means that candidates need to raise substantial funds to be competitive. The amount a candidate raises can be the deciding factor in the campaign. How much a candidate needs depends on the level of the campaign and the competitiveness of the race. High-level campaigns for statewide office are usually multimillion-dollar affairs.

In recent years, the race for governor has become especially expensive. In 1990, Republican Clayton Williams spent a reported $20 million but lost to Democrat Ann Richards, who spent almost $12 million. George W. Bush spent almost $15 million to defeat Ann Richards in 1994. In 2002, Tony Sanchez spent almost $70 million, mostly his own funds, but lost to incumbent governor Rick Perry, who spent slightly less than $30 million.

Although lower-level races in Texas are usually not million-dollar affairs, they too can be expensive. This is certainly true if a contested office is an open seat (where the incumbent is not running for re-election) or if the district is a marginal one (where the incumbent won office with less than 55 percent of the vote). It is not unusual for a candidate in a competitive race for the state house to spend between $100,000 and $200,000.

Where Does the Funding Come From? Where do contributions of this size come from? Candidates often try to solicit small individual contributions through direct-mail campaigns. But to raise the millions required for a high-level state race, they must solicit "big money" from wealthy friends or from business and professional interests that have a stake in the outcome of the campaign. Banks, corporations, law firms, and professional associations—such as those representing physicians, real estate agents, or teachers—organize and register their political action committees (PACs) with the secretary of state's office. PACs serve as the vehicle through which interest groups collect donations and then contribute them to political candidates. (You learned about PACs at the national level in Chapter 10.) Another source of big money is loans. Candidates often borrow heavily from banks or wealthy friends or even from themselves.[33]

Where Do the Contributions Go? Today's political campaign involves a multitude of different expenses. Newspaper ads, billboards, radio messages, bumper stickers, yard signs, and phone banks are all staples in the traditional campaign. Candidates for statewide and urban races must rely on media advertising, particularly television, to get the exposure they need in the three- or four-month campaign period. These candidates are likely to hire consulting firms to manage their campaigns. Consultants contract with public opinion pollsters, arrange advertising, and set up direct-mail campaigns that can target certain areas of the state.

---

33. For a comprehensive treatment of campaign finance, see Frank J. Sorauf, *Inside Campaign Finance: Myths and Realities* (New Haven, CT: Yale University Press, 1992).

We can get some idea about spending in campaigns from what candidates pay for advertising and political consultants in Houston (and Harris County):[34]

- A 30-second TV spot costs about $1,500 for a daytime ad, $2,000 to $5,000 for an ad during the evening news, and $5,000 to $20,000 for an ad during a prime-time show, depending on the show's popularity rating. For some very popular programs, such as *CSI,* the cost can be even higher, as much as $25,000.
- Prime time for most radio broadcasting corresponds with "drive time" (5:00 A.M. to 10:00 A.M. and 3:00 P.M. to 8:00 P.M.), when the largest number of people are driving to or from work. Drive-time rates range from $250 to $2,000 per 60-second spot.

  Billboards can run anywhere from $600 to $15,000 per month, depending on the location. Understandably, billboards on busy freeways are the most expensive.

  Newspaper ads cost from $300 to $500 per column inch in the Sunday paper and $250 per column inch in the daily paper. In November 2004, a half-page ad in the *Houston Chronicle* run on the day before the election cost about $15,000. Advertising rates for political campaigns actually are higher than the rates charged to commercial customers because campaigns are not given the discounts that regular advertisers receive.

  Hiring a professional polling organization to conduct a poll in Harris County costs $15,000 to $30,000.
- Hiring a political consulting firm to manage a campaign in Harris County costs up to $50,000, plus a percentage of the media buys. (Technically, the latter cost is paid by the television and radio stations.) Most firms also get a bonus ranging from $5,000 to $25,000 if the candidate wins.

Clearly, finance is important in political campaigns. While the candidate who spends the most does not always win, a certain amount of spending is necessary for a candidate to be competitive. Speaking with his tongue halfway in his cheek, one prominent politician noted, in regard to high-level statewide races in Texas, that even if "you don't have to raise $10 million, you have to raise $8 million."[35]

Controlling Campaign Finance. Prompted by the increasing use of television in campaigns and the increasing amount of funds needed to buy television advertisements, the federal government and most state governments passed laws regulating campaign finance in the early 1970s. (We first discussed campaign finance in Chapter 10.) The Federal Elections Campaign Act of 1971, substantially amended in 1974, established regulations that apply only to federal elections (president, vice president, and members of Congress). It provided for public financing of presidential campaigns through tax dollars, limited the size of the contributions that individuals and PACs could make to campaigns, and required disclosure of campaign donations. In 1976, the United States Supreme Court declared that it was unconstitutional to set spending limits for campaigns that are not publicly funded. This means there are no spending limits for Congressional races.[36]

did you know?

That PACs active in Texas include AQUAPAC (the Water Quality Association), NUTPAC (the Nut Processors Association), SIX-PAC (the National Beer Wholesalers Association), WAFFLEPAC (Waffle House, Inc.), and WHATAPAC (Whataburger Corporation of Texas).

Growing Campaign Expenditures. Not surprisingly, expenditures in election campaigns continue to increase. The Federal Election Commission reported that $211.8 million was spent in the 1976 election of the president

34. Nancy Sims of Pierpont Communications, with offices in both Austin and Houston, graciously provided this information.
35. Interview with Jim Hightower, "The Senate Can Wait," in *The Texas Observer,* January 27, 1989, p. 6.
36. *Buckley v. Valeo,* 424 U.S. 1 (1976).

Texas Secretary of State Hope Andrade reaches into a hat for numbers that represent proposed constitutional amendments. Her drawing determines the order of the 11 proposed amendments that appeared on the 2009 election ballot. (AP Photo/Harry Cabluck)

and members of Congress, with $122.8 million spent in the presidential race alone. Of the $60.9 million spent in the elections of the 435 House members, more was spent on behalf of candidates in Texas ($4.5 million) than on those of any other state except California. Such expenditure levels appear modest by today's standards. In 1998, outlays for all congressional races (House and Senate combined) totaled $740 million.[37] In the same year, candidates for the 30 U.S. House seats allocated to Texas spent $27 million in their election efforts, an average of almost $1 million per seat. In 2002, spending totaled more than $40 million, more than $1.25 million each for the 32 seats Texas has after redistricting. In 2002, the average ballooned again to more than $1.75 million per seat. Costs of campaigns for state offices in Texas are at least proportionately high, and Texas has joined other states in enacting legislation designed to control the flow of funds.

Current Texas Campaign Law. The most important provisions of current Texas law on campaign finance are as follows:

1. Candidates may not raise or spend funds until an official campaign treasurer is appointed.
2. Candidates and PACs may not accept contributions in currency for more than an aggregate of $100.
3. Direct contributions from corporations and labor unions are prohibited.
4. Candidates and treasurers of campaign committees are required to file sworn statements listing all contributions and expenditures for a designated reporting period to the Texas secretary of state's office.
5. Both criminal and civil penalties are imposed on those who violate the law's provisions. Primary enforcement of campaign regulations is the responsibility of the Texas Ethics Commission.

Although these provisions may sound imposing, in fact raising and spending funds in Texas campaigns still is fairly wide open. For example, while corporations and labor unions may not give directly to a candidate, they may give through their PACs. Note that the amount a candidate may spend of his or her own funds is unlimited. Probably the most important effect of the campaign-finance law in Texas comes from the disclosure requirements. How much a candidate raises, who makes contributions, and how campaign funds are spent are matters of open record. This information may be newsworthy to reporters or other individuals motivated to inform the public.

Soft Money and Independent Expenditures. In 1979, amendments to the Federal Elections Campaign Act made it legal for political parties to raise and spend unlimited

37. Federal Election Commission data, reported in *Congressional Quarterly Almanac 1977* (Washington, DC: Congressional Quarterly, 1977), p. 35A; and *Congressional Quarterly Weekly Report,* March 5, 1989, p. 478. Since 1976, the federal government actually has expanded the role of contributions in elections.

amounts of *soft money.* Party funds could be used to help candidates in a variety of ways, especially through voter-registration and Get Out the Vote drives. The United States Supreme Court further opened up spending in 1985 by deciding that *independent expenditures* could not be limited.[38] As a result, individuals and organizations can spend as much as they want to promote a candidate so long as they are not working or communicating directly with the candidate's campaign organization. (Soft money and independent expenditures were discussed in Chapter 10.)

In 2002, the Campaign Reform Act deprived the parties of their soft money resources, but activists simply set up nonparty organizations to collect and disperse such funds. Understandably, it has been very difficult to effectively control spending in political campaigns in Texas or anywhere else in the United States.

---

38. Federal Election Commission data are available at www.fec.gov.

WHY SHOULD YOU CARE ABOUT... LOCAL ELECTIONS?

"Think globally, act locally" is a common slogan in American politics. The phrase reflects a simple and well-known logic. While it may be a good thing to care about the really big issues, such as global warming and the war in Iraq, it makes more sense to act locally, where the effects of our actions are much greater. The math is quite convincing: If I am one of 100 million, my contribution is likely to be a small share of the total. If I am one of 50, however, I can make a noticeable difference. Ironically, we are much more likely to vote in national-level elections, where we have an almost imperceptible effect, than in local-level elections, where we can make a big impact. To have really tangible effects, we should play a bigger role in local politics.

Elections for local office seem much less important than national elections, and there is truth in this perception. Whether we go to war in Iraq is a question decided by our national politicians. The largest taxes are collected nationally. Social Security is a federal program. The states are the next biggest players. Much of the funding for higher education and welfare comes from the states.

Counties and cities still have a big role to play, however, as do other local governing bodies. They are largely responsible for streets and garbage collection. These services may seem basic, but they are important, as you probably know all too well. Take roads, for instance. Poorly designed roads can create unnecessary gridlock. Badly managed traffic lights can have the same effect. Potholes have an obvious impact on our cars and our patience. Local governments also largely fund and oversee our schools. Do we tax a lot or a little for education? Do we fund classrooms or teachers or athletic facilities?

These are big decisions, obviously, and they are largely in the hands of local governments. In addition to basic services and schools, local governments are responsible for policing the streets where we live, work, and shop. Whether the police are well trained, well equipped, and properly managed clearly matters. Indeed, it can be a matter of life or death.

HOW YOU CAN MAKE A DIFFERENCE

The obvious thing to do is to get involved in local elections. First, find out more about local politics. Newspapers are a good source, and the Internet is, too, but do not forget about your family and your fellow students. They also can be sources of information. You might be surprised by how much of what happens locally is not only interesting but also important. You may find yourself getting involved in an election campaign or an interest group. There, you could really make a difference.

questions for discussion and analysis

1. Why is voter turnout in Texas lower than it is in most other states?
2. What is the majority election rule, and why do we use it in Texas primaries?
3. Why are some candidates more likely than others to win elections in Texas?

key terms

crossover voting 653
negative campaigning 665
participation paradox 641
plurality 653
runoff primary 652
vote-eligible population (VEP) 643
voting-age population (VAP) 643

chapter summary

1. Elections are the defining characteristic of representative democracy. We hold elected officials accountable through our votes.
2. A small number of demographic and political variables are important in predicting who will vote. The most important demographic variables are education, income, and age. Certain political factors also influence the likelihood of voting, especially a person's level of interest in politics and intensity of identification with a political party. Other factors are important as well, but with this small set of demographic and political variables, we can pretty well predict whether a person will vote in a particular election.
3. Voting in Texas (and most other states) is a two-stage process. Before you can vote, you must first register. Traditionally a barrier for women and minorities, the registration procedure today is as simple as voting—perhaps even simpler. Since the passage of federal "motor voter" legislation, a person can register when renewing a driver's license.
4. Traditionally, voter turnout was measured as a percentage of the voting-age population (VAP). That figure has become increasingly inaccurate, mainly because it includes a growing number of noncitizens, who cannot vote. We can use estimates of the vote-eligible population (VEP) instead. By that measure, national turnout in presidential elections has fluctuated around 55 percent in recent years. In midterm elections, turnout is around 40 percent. These numbers are significantly lower than what we find in other advanced democracies. Voter turnout in Texas is even below the U.S. national average.
5. Low voter turnout in Texas may be partly related to the state's socioeconomic characteristics. A comparatively large percentage of the population live below the poverty level. An even larger percentage have not graduated from high school, and these people are not very likely to vote. Income and education levels are low for African Americans and Mexican Americans, so turnout is particularly low for these groups. Political factors, such as political structure and political culture, may also play a role in low turnout.
6. In Texas, as in other Southern states that once were predominantly Democratic, a majority rule is used in primary elections. If no candidate receives a majority of the votes cast for a particular office in the first primary, a second, runoff primary is used to determine the winner. Outside the South, only a plurality of the votes is typically required.
7. Ballot design is an important factor in elections. Texas traditionally has used the party-column ballot, in which the names of all the candidates of each party are listed in parallel columns. The main alternative is the office-block ballot, in which the names of candidates are listed underneath each office. Beginning with the 2002 election, many Texas counties adopted electronic voting systems, which combine features of the office-block and party-column designs.
8. Texas is a diverse state, and the pool of candidates for local offices reflects this diversity. As we move up the pyramid of elected offices, however, the candidates become much more homogeneous. Successful candidates for statewide office traditionally have been white males. While this remains true today, women and minorities have made substantial gains, which are likely to continue as more women and minorities enter politics.
9. In a state as large as Texas, media advertising, political consultants, and polling are required for any candidate seeking to win statewide office or the most competitive state legislative and local elections. These services are expensive.
10. Without a certain amount of funding, it is impossible to be competitive in Texas elections. The high and rising cost of campaigns means that serious candidates must collect contributions from a variety of sources. Most candidates must rely on PACs and wealthy individuals. Although the Texas legislature has passed laws regulating campaign finance in state races, raising and spending funds is still fairly wide open.

selected print & media resources

SUGGESTED READINGS

Brischetto, Robert, David Richards, Chandler Davidson, and Bernard Grofman. "Texas." In Chandler Davidson and Bernard Grofman, eds., *Quiet Revolution in the South: The Impact of the Voting Rights Act, 1965–1990.* Princeton, NJ: Princeton University Press, 1994. This chapter chronicles how the Voting Rights Act influenced Texas elections and politics in the 25 years after its enactment.

Davidson, Chandler. *Race and Class in Texas Politics.* Princeton, NJ: Princeton University Press, 1992. This wide-ranging book by a Texas sociologist highlights the power of business interests in Texas politics.

Murray, Richard. "The 1996 Elections in Texas." In Kent L. Tedin, Donald S. Lutz, and Edward P. Fuchs, eds., *Perspectives on American and Texas Politics,* 5th ed. Dubuque, IA: Kendall/Hunt, 1998. In this article, a leading analyst of Texas elections and politics offers a view of Texas campaigns through the prism of the 1996 elections.

Murray, Richard, and Sam Attlesey. "Texas: Republicans Gallop Ahead." In Alexander Lamis, ed., *Southern Politics in the 1990s.* Baton Rouge: Louisiana State University Press, 1999. This very accessible chapter traces the rise of Republicans in Texas state politics during the 1990s.

Stein, Robert M. "Early Voting." *Public Opinion Quarterly,* Vol. 62, No. 1 (1998), pp. 57–69. This article by a well-known Texas political scientist analyzes the effects of early voting in Texas on both the level of turnout and the composition of the electorate.

Tolleson-Rinehart, Sue, and Jeanie Ricketts Stanley. *Claytie and the Lady: Ann Richards, Gender, and Politics in Texas.* Austin: University of Texas Press, 1994. The authors of this book examine the influence of gender in Texas politics, focusing especially on the 1990 gubernatorial election, in which Ann Richards defeated Clayton Williams after a truly fascinating campaign.

MEDIA RESOURCES

Hispanic Voters *on Cengage's Texas Political Theatre 2008*—This is a feature on the Houston mayoral election, during which a Hispanic conservative, with strong support from the party establishment, nearly defeated a black Democrat. The election, according to political observers, demonstrates that both parties have an opportunity to gain strength by promoting Hispanic candidates.

Populism *on Cengage's Texas Political Theatre 2008*—During an interview, Kinky Friedman, an unsuccessful candidate for governor in 2006, discusses unusual political stances, his friendship with former President Bush, and his attempt to challenge the two-party system.

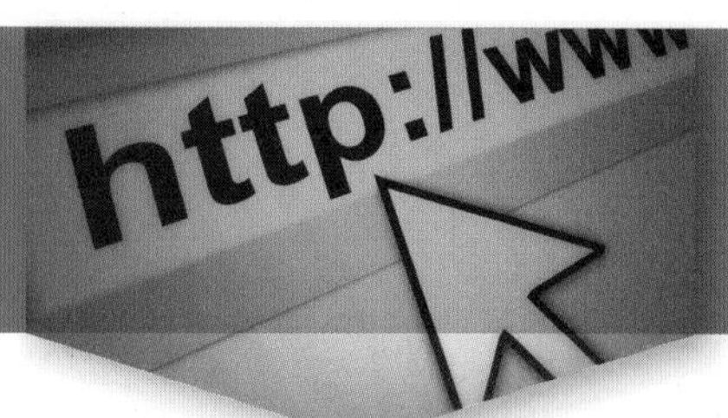

e-mocracy

ALL THOSE ELECTIONS

One of the distinguishing features of Texas politics is the number and variety of elections held in the state. Texas elects a very large number of officials to do different things at different levels of government. See for yourself: go to your county Web site and locate a sample ballot. To find your county's URL, go to **www.state.tx.us**. On this home page, under "Helpful Links," click on "Texas Counties."

Once you have located your county Web site, find a sample ballot. Ballots usually are stored on the county clerk's section of the site. You may be able to click on a link marked "Elections" or "County Clerk," although a site's structure is sometimes not so straightforward. In some instances, you may find that your county simply does not post a sample ballot. You might mention this in an e-mail to the county clerk. Perhaps the clerk's office will send you one.

If your county has no sample ballot, you can go to another county site, such as that of Bexar, Dallas, Denton, El Paso, Harris, Jefferson, or Travis, all of which include a full sample ballot before primary and general elections. Examine the ballot from top to bottom, keeping in mind that it may take a while. In some areas, people may be asked to vote for more than 100 different offices, from governor to railroad commissioner, from state representative to city council member, from state judges to county judges, justices of the peace, and constables. There are other offices as well, and often a constitutional amendment or two.

LOGGING ON

A very large number of Web sites relate to voting, elections, and campaigns. The political parties have Web sites, as do the political candidates, and there are many independent sites.

For specific information about voting and elections in Texas, go to the secretary of state's election page at:
www.sos.state.tx.us

The Federal Election Commission makes its wide array of campaign finance data available at:
www.fec.gov

The Pew Center on the States provides an up-to-date digest of election reform developments in Texas and other states at:
www.electionline.org

The Southwest Voter Registration Education Project, which is specifically interested in enrolling Hispanic Americans, is at:
www.svrep.org

ONLINE REVIEW

At **www.cengage.com/politicalscience/schmidt/agandpttexas 14e**, you will find a Tutorial Quiz for this chapter, providing questions on the chapter contents, including the features. You'll gain access to other helpful study tools, including the book's glossary and flashcards, crossword puzzles, and Web links, as well as "Which Side Are You On?" and "Politics and . . ." features written by the authors of the book.

chapter
21

The Texas Legislature

chapter contents

<< Voting in the Texas House of Representatives. (AP Photo/Harry Cabluck/File)

WHAT IF... the Texas legislature were a full-time legislature?

Lawmakers and family members crowded the chamber of the Texas House of Representatives as the 79th Texas Legislature began its regular session in January 2005. What is special about Texas legislative sessions? (AP Photo/Harry Cabluck)

The Texas legislature meets for 140 days on odd-numbered years, unless the governor calls a special session. Members of the Texas legislature are paid $7,200 per year plus a ***per diem*** (daily allowance) for days when the legislature is in session. Members of the Texas House average a staff of about three people, while senators average a staff of a little more than seven. The Texas legislature is considered a part-time legislative body.

Texas legislators often must depend on outside sources of income to earn a living, making them vulnerable to the temptations of special-interest groups. Some lawmakers will work in areas in which their clients are the very interest groups that also lobby these lawmakers when the legislature is in session.[a] Legislators who are not paid adequately are also more likely to leave their posts after a short period of service, leading to greater instability in the legislative body.[b] As lawmakers leave the legislature, they take with them policy and political expertise that is necessary to adequately represent the public.

WHAT IF TEXAS HAD A FULL-TIME LEGISLATURE?

If the Texas legislature were a full-time legislative body, one would expect to see improvements in the quality of representation that Texans receive. Legislators would certainly receive better salaries if the Texas legislature were a full-time legislative body. Better pay would attract more qualified individuals to run for public office, and better pay would help retain experienced legislators who would otherwise seek higher office.

BETTER LEGISLATION

Some have argued that a part-time legislature is better because it governs less, but in Texas, this is not always the case. In the 140 days of the 80th Legislative Session, more than 1,400 bills became law.[c] The 109th (U.S.) Congress, by contrast, produced 482 laws in twice as many days. With fewer resources and less time, the Texas legislature produces many more pieces of legislation than does the U.S. Congress. While the Texas legislature is certainly not governing less (as measured by legislative activity), some have speculated about the quality of so much legislation produced in such a short period of time.

As it stands, legislators rely on lobbyists to write bills that lawmakers then introduce. Because of time constraints, it is difficult for lawmakers to properly vet bills. As a result, legislators are often not familiar with the legislation on which they are asked to vote. A full-time legislative body would provide lawmakers with the necessary resources to better represent the public.

IS REFORM LIKELY?

Current lawmakers have been successful under this system and are unlikely to want to change the legislature to a system that would bring uncertainty into their lives. The public is also unlikely to want to go along with such a change because it assumes that Texas legislators are compensated more than adequately. Or, when it is familiar with the part-time nature of the Texas legislature, the public assumes that the Texas legislature governs best when it governs least. Such assumptions from the public, and concerns about the future from legislators, make it unlikely that the Texas legislature will be reformed anytime soon.

FOR CRITICAL ANALYSIS

1. What other reasons would lawmakers have for not wanting to reform the legislature from a part-time to a full-time legislative body?
2. In what ways does a part-time or full-time legislative body improve representation?

a. Center for Public Integrity, "Low-Paid Texas Lawmakers Tops in Connections to Lobbyists," accessed February 15, 2008, at projects.publicintegrity.org/hiredguns.

b. Peverill Squire, "Career Opportunities and Membership Stability in Legislatures," *Legislative Studies Quarterly,* Vol. 13, February, p. 65–82.

c. House Research Organization, "Focus Report: Major Issues of the 80th Legislature, *Regular Session,*" accessed February 25, 2008, at www.hro.house.state.tx.us/focus/major80.pdf.

The Texas legislature, like the U.S. Congress and all other state legislatures, except that of Nebraska, is a bicameral (two-chamber) legislature composed of a senate and a house of representatives. Although the two chambers have approximately equal power, the smaller, 31-member Texas Senate is more prestigious, and its individual members generally exercise greater power and influence than the 150 members of the Texas House. The Texas legislature has several unusual features. One such feature is the great power of the **presiding officers** in each body. A second is the no-party system of organizing the two chambers, which allows each presiding officer to recruit members of the other party to his or her team. Texas is also one of the few large states that relies on a **part-time legislature.**

Presiding Officers
In Texas, the chief officers of the state senate and house. They are the lieutenant governor, who presides over the senate, and the speaker of the house.

Part-time Legislature
A legislative body that meets for short periods of time. Its members are often provided limited resources, including small salaries.

The Limited Session

The Texas legislature meets on the second Tuesday in January in odd-numbered years for a 140-day session. It is the only legislature among those of the ten most populous states that meets biennially. Although forty-three states have instituted annual sessions to conduct state business, Texas has refused to do so. Many Texans believe that the legislature does more harm than good when it is in session and that a longer session would simply give legislators more time to make mischief.

In these short, infrequent sessions, the volume of legislation can overwhelm legislators. Most bills are passed or killed with little consideration. As a result, many important bills are never granted a legislative hearing. In 2007, for example, the Texas legislature debated several air toxics bills. In a state with some of the most serious air-quality problems in the country, not a single bill became law.

Special Sessions

The short biennial sessions and the increasingly complex problems of a modern society make thirty-day special sessions, which can be called only by the governor, more frequent. They are, however, usually unpopular with both the general public and the legislators. The public tends to see the added expense as wasteful, and legislators may be distressed by calls away from their homes, families, and primary occupations. Furthermore, any interest that was able to get the legislature to kill an item of legislation during the regular session will strongly oppose a special session to reconsider the item that was already killed.

Time Pressures

Because most of the legislative work is done during the regular session, time is valuable. Legislators, lacking adequate staff support, find it difficult to obtain even rudimentary knowledge of the content of much of the legislation that must be considered, whether in committee or on the *floor,* which will be discussed later in this chapter. The time constraints dictated by the limited session tend to isolate individual legislators and deepen their reliance on the information provided by lobbyists, administrators, and the legislative leadership. Thus, bills that lack interest-group, administrative agency, or legislative leadership support have no chance of passage or even serious consideration.

did you know?

That the Texas legislature passed a bill during the 80th Legislative Session that allows school districts to offer classes in Bible studies to students in high school.

Historically, much questionable legislation was passed in the last days of the session. In 1993, the house adopted new rules to address the end-of-session legislative crunch. During the last 17 days of the session, the house may consider only bills that originated in the senate or that received previous house approval. The new rules also give house members 24 hours to study major legislation before taking floor action. These reforms diminish the volume of last-minute legislation and give legislators time to become better acquainted with bills.

Qualifications, Terms, and Compensation of Members

Texas has citizen legislators who meet for only 140 days every other year and receive most of their income from outside sources. It is reasonable to expect the lawmakers to be more focused on their full-time careers and outside sources of income than on the Texas public's business. Texas lawmakers are not constrained in the amount of outside sources of income they can have. As a result, entrepreneurial lawmakers will often work as consultants for special-interest groups that have issues pending before the committees on which the lawmakers serve.

Formal Qualifications

Although an individual must meet legal, or formal, qualifications before he or she can serve in the Texas legislature, the criteria are broad enough to allow millions of Texas residents the opportunity to run. To be a state senator, a person must be a U.S. citizen, a registered voter, at least 26 years of age, and must have lived for five years in the state and one year in the district in which he or she seeks election. Qualifications for house membership are even more easily met. To be a representative, an individual must be a U.S. citizen, at least 21 years of age, and have lived in Texas for two years and in the district for one year.

Terms

Texas senators are elected for four-year staggered terms; representatives are elected for two-year terms. This means that the entire house and half the senate are elected every two years.

Redistricting, which is based on the census, takes place every 10 years and triggers a special senate procedure in the first election following redistricting. The last such election took place in 2002. Because of redistricting, the entire senate was up for election. At the start of the first session after the redistricting, senators drew lots to determine who would serve a four-year term and who would serve for two years. Unlucky senators faced re-election in 2004, while the lucky ones did not have to run for re-election until 2006. Thereafter, all senators will serve four-year terms until the election that follows the next census (in 2012). The relative competitiveness of a senator's district determines whether the result of the lottery is only an inconvenience or an incident of major significance.

did you know?

That in the 140 days of the 2007 regular session 1,481 bills were enacted into law? With 6,190 bills filed, nearly one-quarter of the bills became law.

Texas legislators experience a more rapid turnover than their counterparts in the U.S. Congress, where seniority brings political power. Frustrated by low salaries and the inability to achieve legislative goals that are not supported by powerful interests or the presiding officers, many house members leave office to pursue full-time careers or to seek higher political office. Senators and the members of the house power structure tend to serve longer. Redistricting also brings significant legislative turnover when district lines are redrawn and power bases shift. The median length of service for senators is about 12 years and for house members about seven.

Compensation

Texas Ethics Commission
A constitutionally authorized body that has the power to investigate ethics violations and to penalize violators of Texas ethics laws.

Legislators receive an annual salary of $7,200 plus $128 *per diem* (per day) for expenses during both regular and special sessions. They also have a travel allowance on a reimbursement basis when the legislature is in session. The **Texas Ethics Commission** is constitutionally empowered to propose salary increases, subject to voter approval, for legislators and the lieutenant governor. Lawmakers have not received a pay increase since

1975, when Texas voters approved a pay raise for lawmakers. An attempt to increase their salaries failed in 1991. As a result, lawmakers often rely on campaign contributions to offset the cost of public service. A 2004 study of Texas senators found that 40 percent of the senators' campaign dollars were spent on campaign activity, and the remaining 60 percent was spent on housing and office expenses.[1] While state law prohibits using campaign funds for personal use, the law does allow for the use of campaign contributions for paying rent and other household expenses in Travis County. Texas lawmakers are among the worst-paid legislators in the country, but the law allows them to rely on campaign contributions to offset their living expenses.

The Texas Ethics Commission. The eight-member Texas Ethics Commission enforces state ethics and campaign-finance law. The governor, lieutenant governor, and speaker appoint the commission from a list provided by the Democratic and Republican legislative caucuses. Legislators are excluded from serving on the commission.

Conflicts of Interest. There is little motivation for a Texas legislator to keep his or her position solely for the salary. Present legislative salaries are so low that legislators must receive their primary income from other sources. While Texans require that their legislators seek additional income to subsist, they rarely question the nature of this income. People tend to be responsible to those who pay them, and the public does not furnish most of the legislators' income.[2]

The potential for conflict between the public interest and the interests of a lawmaker's business or employer is obvious. Some legislators recognize the dilemma. For example, Bob Bullock faced it in 1991 when he left the comptroller's office, which paid $74,698 per year, and became the lieutenant governor for a salary of $7,200. Although many employers were eager to hire the lieutenant governor, the appearance of a conflict of interest concerned Bullock enough that he rejected several lucrative offers and accepted employment as a counselor and consultant with View Point Recovery Centers, a network of alcohol rehabilitation hospitals. His salary from View Point, his state employees' retirement income, and his salary as lieutenant governor gave Bullock approximately the same income he had received as comptroller. Many Texas officials have not shared Bullock's desire to avoid even the appearance of impropriety. (Bullock retired in 1998 and died in 1999. The Texas State History Museum is named in his honor.)

Legislative Districts

The members of the Texas House of Representatives, like the members of the Texas Senate, are elected from single-member districts—one member per house district and one senator per senate district. These districts are required by the U.S. Constitution to be approximately equal in population.[3] Following every 10-year census, each state must undertake a redistricting process to correct for changes in the populations of the districts. Today, the average population of an electoral district for the Texas House is approximately 159,000. State senators represent an average of about 771,000 people. Because the state senate has 31 members and the Texas delegation to the U.S. Congress includes 32 representatives, U.S. Congressional districts are about the same size as senate districts and contain an average of 747,000 people (see Figure 21–1 on the following page).

1. Fred Lewis, "Money in all the Wrong Places: How Texas Senators Spend Their Campaign Contributions," *Campaigns for People,* 2004.
2. See Chapter 25 for a further discussion of the interaction among administrators, lobbyists, and legislators.
3. *Reynolds v. Sims,* 377 U.S. 533 (1964).

FIGURE 21–1 U.S. Congressional Districts, 111th Congress, 2009–2011

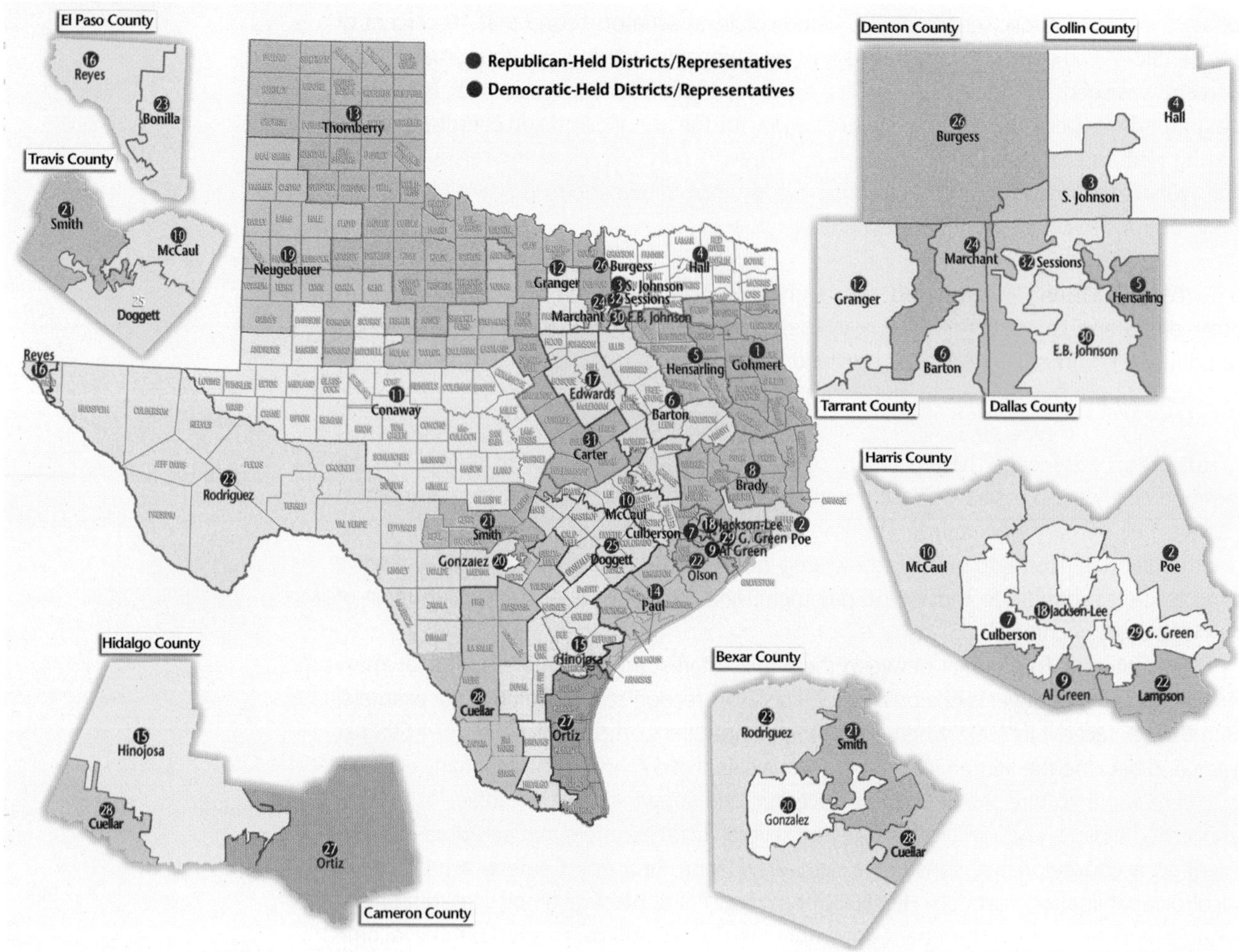

Source: Texas Legislative Council.

> **Ex Officio**
> Having a position by virtue of holding a particular office. For example, the lieutenant governor of Texas serves *ex officio* as the presiding officer of the Texas Senate.

In Texas, as in most other states, the state legislature redraws its own districts, as well as those of the state's delegation to the U.S. Congress. In the event the Texas legislature fails to redistrict, the state constitution provides for the function to be performed by the Legislative Redistricting Board. The board is ***ex officio,*** which means that members hold other offices. It is made up of the lieutenant governor, the speaker of the house, the attorney general, the comptroller, and the commissioner of the General Land Office.

Gerrymandering

The once-per-decade ritual of redistricting may take place with little notice by the casual observer of politics. For the political practitioner and the political activist, however, it may resemble a life-or-death struggle. The way districts are drawn at any level of government to a large extent determines the political, ideological, and ethnic makeup of the legislative body. When districts are subject to *gerrymandering,* political careers may be made or broken, public policy determined for at least a decade, and the power of ethnic or political minorities enhanced or diminished. (Gerrymandering was discussed in Chapter 12.) Three gerrymandering techniques are common: cracking, packing, and pairing.

Cracking and Packing. One technique is to diffuse a concentrated political or ethnic minority among several districts so that its votes within any one district are negligible *(cracking).* A second tactic is used if the minority's numbers are great enough when diffused to affect the outcome of elections in several districts. In this circumstance, the minority is concentrated within the smallest possible number of districts *(packing),* thereby ensuring that it will influence the fewest possible elections and that its influence within the legislature as a whole will be minimal. (See Figure 21–2.)

FIGURE 21–2 Cracking and Packing

The diagram at the top is balanced, having eight red "voters" and eight blue "voters" represented by the dots in each of the four "districts." Redrawing the electoral districts in the lower example results in a guaranteed three-to-one advantage in representation for the blue voters. Here, 14 red dots are "packed" into the green-tinted district and the remaining 18 are "cracked" across the three gray-tinted districts.

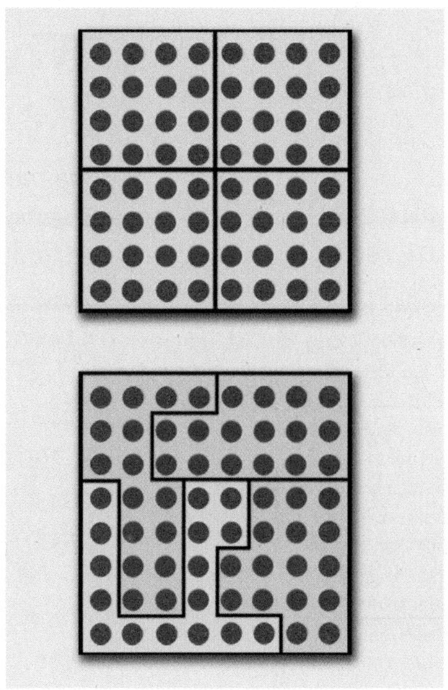

Pairing Incumbents. A third tactic is the **pairing** technique, which redistricts in such a way that two or more **incumbent** legislators must run in the same district, thereby ensuring that one will be defeated. Pairing can be used to punish legislators who have fallen from grace with the legislative leadership.

Redistricting after the 1990 and 2000 Censuses

Redistricting after the last two censuses substantially changed the makeup of both the Texas legislature and the Texas delegation to the U.S. House of Representatives.

Redistricting after 1990. Following the 1990 census, it took a special session of the Texas legislature, eleven lawsuits, and various other legal actions in both state and federal courts from 1990 through 1994 to settle the placement of district boundaries. Republican membership in the Texas Senate immediately increased from nine in 1991 to 13 in 1993. By 1996, Republicans controlled the Texas Senate, although Democrats continued to be the majority in the house.

State House and Senate Redistricting after 2000. Controversy flared again after the 2000 census. Because of the state's dramatic population growth, driven by the growth in the Hispanic population, Texas picked up two additional Congressional seats from the previous decade. In the 1990s, Texas was awarded 30 seats to the U.S. House of Representatives. After the 2000 census, 32 House seats were allocated to Texas. These two additional seats, in conjunction with shifts in the population, meant that districts would have to be redrawn so that they would be equal in size. Republican lawmakers refused to accept the legislative redistricting that followed the census and forced the redistricting effort into the Legislative Redistricting Board, where Republicans enjoyed a four-to-one majority. Subsequent to the board's redistricting, the 2002 election increased the senate Republican majority to 19 and gave Republicans a majority in the Texas House for the first time since Reconstruction.

Pairing
In political redistricting, placing two incumbent officeholders from the same party in the same district. (Only one of these officeholders can be re-elected.)

Incumbent
The current holder of an office.

Redistricting for the U.S. Congress after 2000. Following a series of lawsuits, the Texas districts that elect members of the U.S. House were redesigned in 2000 by a panel of one Democratic and two Republican U.S. district judges. Despite the political tendencies of the judges, the Democrats still maintained a 17-to-15 majority in the Texas Congressional delegation after the 2002 elections. Given the narrow majority that the Republicans possessed in the U.S. House, its former majority leader, Tom DeLay (a Texan), encouraged Republican-controlled legislatures in Texas, Colorado, and other states to redraw Congressional districts before the 2010 census to favor Republican candidates.

In Texas, Governor Rick Perry called a special session to revise the 2000 judicial plan. The first two special sessions were unsuccessful, because first the house and then the senate Democrats fled the state. The Congressional district boundaries were finally redrawn in a third special session in 2003.

As shown by the irregular district shapes in Figure 21–1, the Republican majority in the third legislative special session used classic gerrymandering techniques to redraw the boundaries for the Texas Congressional districts. Although the federal courts prohibit racial gerrymandering, they are reluctant to become involved in **partisan gerrymandering.**[4]

Partisan Gerrymandering
The drawing of district lines for the purpose of providing electoral advantage to members of one political party.

Following the 2006 elections, the Texas Congressional delegation still had a Republican majority. Anglo-American Democratic members of Congress and rural constituents appear to have been the principal losers.

Who Can Become a Member of the Legislature?

We have already described the legal requirements for holding legislative office in Texas. The most important requirements, though, are not the legal ones but the informal ones. Political, social, and economic criteria largely determine who is elected not only to the state legislature but also to offices at all levels of government—national, state, county, city, and special district.

Race and Gender

In 2004, Texas became a majority-minority state.[5] Texas is a state where no one racial or ethnic group accounts for the majority of the population. The change in the state's demographics has impacted the makeup of the Texas legislature.

Hispanics make up 36 percent of the Texas population but hold just over 21 percent of the seats in the Texas House and 19 percent in the Texas Senate. It is important to note that many Hispanics are not eligible to vote because they are not U.S. citizens. As Hispanic immigrants become U.S. citizens and vote, their levels of representation are expected to improve. African Americans, with just over 11 percent of the population, are represented by about 9 percent of the Texas House and 6 percent in the Texas Senate. Asian Americans, accounting for 3 percent of the population, are represented by two Asian Americans in the Texas House and none in the Texas Senate. During the 81st Legislative Session, two Asian Americans served in the Texas House: Republican Angie Chen Button and Democrat Hubert Vo. Martha Wong, who also served in the Texas House, was defeated in 2006.

Nicholas V. "Nick" Lampson, shown here campaigning in September 2006, was a Democratic member of Congress representing Texas's 9th District from 1997 to 2005. After the redistricting orchestrated by former Republican majority leader Tom DeLay, the Ninth District was renumbered the Second and radically redrawn to favor the Republican Ted Poe, who won the district from Lampson in the 2004 election. In 2006, following the scandal-tainted resignation of DeLay, Lampson delivered DeLay's seat in the Twenty-second district to the Democrats. Does this mean that Texas is truly becoming a two-party state? (Pat Sullivan/AP Photo)

The female population is perhaps the most underrepresented of the major groups. Although females account for slightly more than half of the state's population, only 21 percent of the members of the Texas house and 13 percent of Texas senators are female. As the number of female candidates increases, one can expect to see more women serving in the Texas legislature.

The Anglo population in the state is 49 percent of the total population, but accounts for 69 percent of the

4. The United States Supreme Court, by a six-to-three vote, refused to hear an appeal from Colorado Republicans following a Colorado Supreme Court ruling that nullified political gerrymandering similar to that in Texas. The gerrymandering was found by the state court to be in conflict with the Colorado Constitution.
5. Robert Bernstein, "Texas Becomes Nation's Newest 'Majority-Minority' State, Census Bureau Announces," *US Census Bureau News,* accessed February 24, 2008, at www.census.gov/Press-Release/www/releases/archives/population/005514.html.

members of the Texas House and 74 percent of the Texas Senate. Anglo males account for a larger percentage of the members of the Texas legislature than their numbers in the population would indicate.

did you know?

That the Institute for Women's Policy Research ranked Texas 49th among the 50 states in women's voter turnout.

Campaign Funding

Another qualification for winning legislative office is access to campaign funds. Many competent, motivated individuals who want to serve are excluded because they are unable to raise the funds necessary to finance an adequate campaign. Thus, the voters' pool of potential candidates may be limited to persons who can appeal to the economic interests that provide most campaign contributions. Securing office space, printing campaign literature, buying postage stamps, building a campaign organization, and purchasing advertisements are all among the necessary ingredients for a successful campaign—and all are expensive. In 2006, the National Institute on Money in State Politics found that of the 426 candidates who ran for the Texas House, an average of $153,706 was raised for their campaigns. Among the 46 candidates who ran for the Texas Senate, they raised an average of $452,966 for their campaigns.[6] Candidates raised more than $94 million for their campaigns in the national House and Senate races.[7] The key ingredient in Texas politics is money![8]

Business and the Law as Sources of Legislators. Few wage earners or small-business owners can afford to leave their jobs and businesses for four-and-a-half months every other year to take a temporary job that pays $600 per month. In contrast, persons who serve as executives in large businesses, practice law, or engage in certain other professions may more easily find the time required for service in the state legislature. Legislators from these groups may actually increase their incomes through political service if the prestige and contacts they develop as members of the legislature benefit their law firms or companies. Economic interests may retain the services of an attorney from a particular firm or steer business toward a specific company to ingratiate themselves with a legislator. Paying a public official in exchange for legislative influence is illegal, but paying for goods and services is not.[9]

Even when there is no overt intent to bribe a legislator, an individual who works closely with a particular industry or organization and is handsomely compensated for that work may find that superhuman effort is required to distinguish between the public interest and the client's interest. Because some legislators do not appear to strive very hard to separate the two, an interest can, in effect, "buy a legislator."

When Legislators Appear before Boards and in Court. Legislators who are lawyers may also be employed to represent clients in adversary proceedings before the various state administrative boards and commissions. The legislature is responsible for the appropriations to state boards and commissions, and the fact that the concerned agency may be generous in evaluating the legal arguments of a lawyer-legislator is not lost on the litigants. In this instance, both the lawyer and her or his client may benefit from the lawyer's legislative position.

A state judge may also grant a trial delay in civil or criminal litigation to a lawyer serving in the legislature. This right of delay lasts from 30 days before a legislative session begins until 30 days after it ends. Either the plaintiff or the defendant may benefit from

---

6. National Institute on Money in State Politics, "Election Summary," accessed January 19, 2008, at www.followthemoney.org.
7. *Ibid.*
8. See www.followthemoney.org for comprehensive information on Texas campaign contributions.
9. See John Dunbar, "Public Service, Personal Gain in Texas," Center for Public Integrity, available at www.publicintegrity.org/oi/iys.aspx?st=TX&sub=pub.

such a delay. Thus, when either party to a suit seeks a delay, and the legislature is in session, that party may find a lawyer-legislator desirable as a counsel.

Organization of the Texas Legislature

The Texas legislative system places an unusual degree of power in the hands of the presiding officers of each chamber. As in most legislative bodies, the house and senate committees do much of the actual work of the legislature. The presiding officers appoint the chairpersons of committees and most of the committee members. In the Texas legislature, committees are often seen as extensions of the presiding officers' power.

The Presiding Officers

The presiding officers in the Texas legislature are the lieutenant governor in the senate and the speaker of the House of Representatives. Although these are primarily legislative offices, their holders exercise significant influence throughout Texas government.

Lieutenant Governor. The presiding officer in the Texas Senate is the lieutenant governor, who serves as its president. Although not a senator, the lieutenant governor is in the unique situation of being a member of both the legislative branch and the executive branch. The lieutenant governor is elected in a statewide, partisan election, and can have a party affiliation that is different from that of the governor or other members of the Texas executive branch. In the event the office becomes vacant through death, disability, or resignation, the senate elects one of its members to serve as acting lieutenant governor until the next regular election. The senators have adopted rules that grant the lieutenant governor extensive legislative, organizational, procedural, administrative, and planning authority.

The election of the lieutenant governor, who serves a four-year term, attracts far less public attention than the power of the office merits; the lieutenant governor is one of the most influential officials in Texas government. Organized interests are well aware of the importance of the office and contribute sizable sums to influence the election.

Although lieutenant governors in many states exercise a hybrid executive-legislative function, their influence rarely approaches that of the lieutenant governor of Texas. The political power of the lieutenant governor of Texas is largely based on senate rules and could be weakened by a majority of the senate. Therefore, the lieutenant governor must maintain a working relationship with the majority of the senators. The Republican-dominated 79th Senate (2005), however, enacted rules that maintained the power of the Republican lieutenant governor.

Speaker of the House. The Texas House of Representatives, by a majority vote of its membership, chooses its presiding officer from among its members by a recorded vote. The actual campaign can be very competitive and may attract candidates from all parts of the ideological spectrum. Yet because the vote for speaker is not secret, the successful candidate may take punitive action against opponents and their supporters. As a result, incumbent speakers have rarely faced serious opposition. When Republicans gained a majority in the Texas House in 2002, however, they ousted the Democratic incumbent and elected the first Republican speaker since Reconstruction, Tom Craddick. Surprisingly, Craddick was himself ousted in 2009 by a coalition of disgruntled Democratic and Republican legislators and was replaced by Republican representative Joe Straus of San Antonio.

did you know?

That in Texas, a state legislator cannot legally receive a campaign contribution 30 days before the start of a regular legislative session or 20 days after its adjournment.

House members who support the winning candidate can become part of the speaker's team, even if they are members of the opposition party. As mentioned earlier, this Texas legislative idiosyncrasy is known as the no-party system. The speaker appoints team members to serve on prestigious committees and selects her or his most reliable supporters as committee chairs. Tom Craddick, the former Speaker of the Texas House of Representatives, has relied on Democrats to chair or vice chair committees. Of the 40 standing committees in the Texas House, 10 were headed by Democrats during the 80th Legislature. Another 15 vice chairs were Democrats. Lobbyists attempt to form alliances with powerful team members by making campaign contributions and supporting their legislative agendas.

Republican Joe Straus of San Antonio is sworn in as speaker of the Texas House of Representatives. Administering the oath is Wallace Jefferson, Chief Justice of the Texas Supreme Court. In a rare move Straus ousted incumbent speaker, and fellow Republican, Tom Craddick. (AP Photo/Eric Gay)

Legislative Committees

Because several thousand bills are introduced into the Texas legislature each session, a division of labor is necessary for an orderly operation. The committee system exists to carry out this distribution of tasks. Each committee has a chair and a vice chair. The chair controls the committee's agenda, its schedule of hearings, the witnesses to be called, and the voting schedule.

Types of Committees. There are several types of committees in the Texas House and Texas Senate: standing, conference, joint, and select committees. The latter of these are also referred to as special committees and can have features of joint committees. Committees are classified based on function, membership, and longevity. The function of some committees is to draft legislation (standing and conference committees), while others are charged with a specific purpose, such as studying a problem or making recommendations (select and joint committees). The membership of some committees may only include members of one chamber (standing and select committees), while others may consist of members from both chambers (conference and joint committees). Some special committees may even include members of the public. Some tend to be temporary or ad hoc committees (conference and select committees), while others are more permanent (standing and joint committees). Table 21–1 summarizes the characteristics of each type of committee.

Standing Committees. There are two types of standing committees—substantive and procedural committees. All of the standing committees are listed in Table 21–2. Substantive and procedural committees are marked accordingly. Most committees are standing substantive committees. Each committee of this type is given authority over a subject of political interest, such as education, taxes, appropriations, or agriculture. Each committee also may have subcommittees with authority over specific topics within the general subject area of the committee. Substantive committees have been called "little legislatures," because they normally conduct the real legislative business of conflict, compromise, and accommodation.

TABLE 21–1 Types of Committees in Texas Legislature

	Standing	Conference	Joint	Select
Function	Lawmaking authority	Lawmaking authority	Advisory	Advisory
Longevity	Permanent	Temporary	Permanent	Temporary
Membership	From one chamber only	From both the house and senate	From both the house and senate	May include members of one chamber, both chambers, or members of the legislature and non-legislators
Examples	House: Agriculture and Livestock Committee Senate: Criminal Justice Committee		Legislative Budget Board	House Select Committee Electric Generation Capacity and Environmental Effects

Mark Up
In legislation, to amend, change, or rewrite bills while they are in committee.

Calendars Committee
The committee in the Texas House of Representatives that assigns bills to the calendars for floor action. (The less important Local and Consent Calendars Committee also performs this function.)

Pigeonhole
The action by which a legislative committee tables a bill and then ignores it.

Each bill brought before the Texas legislature is assigned to a substantive standing committee in each chamber, where witnesses—both for and against the proposal—may be heard, debates are held, and bills are **marked up** (changed) or killed. Successful bills are seldom reported out of a committee in their original form. Because standing committees do the basic legislative work, the general membership relies heavily on them for guidance on how to vote on a bill being considered on the floor. In fact, attempting to amend some bills, or even questioning the work of the committee, violates the norms of the Texas Senate.

The most important standing procedural committee is the **Calendars Committee** in the Texas House of Representatives. It controls the flow of legislation from the substantive committees to the floor of the house. No bill can reach the floor of the house without authorization from the Calendars Committee (or the much less important Local and Consent Calendars Committee).

Pigeonholing Bills. An important function of committees in the Texas legislature is to serve as a burial ground for bills. A legislator may introduce a bill as a favor to some group or constituent who feels very strongly about the matter, even though the legislator knows full well that the bill will be killed, or **pigeonholed,** in committee (and that the committee will take the blame). Other bills may be assigned to hostile committees with the expectation that they will be totally rewritten, if not pigeonholed.

Expertise. Where a seniority system is used, committee members and committee chairs are usually returned to the same committee posts each session, and legislators can thus become reasonably well informed, if not expert, on a given subject. This expertise is important, because members must hear interest-group lobbyists and administrative officials and evaluate their arguments on the merits of proposed legislation.

Compared with the U.S. Congress and most other state legislatures, the Texas legislature operates under a very limited seniority system. Therefore, the expertise of committee members may come from their occupational backgrounds rather than from legislative experience. As a result, many Texas legislators are *preference outliers.* These are legislators who self-select into one particular committee. Texas legislators, as we have seen, are seldom politicians to the exclusion of other occupations, and their interest in their primary occupations may create conflicts with the public interest.

TABLE 21–2 List of Substantive and Procedural Standing Committees in the Texas House and Senate Committees

House Committees	Senate Committees
Agriculture & Livestock	Administration (Procedural)
Appropriations	Business & Commerce
Border & International Affairs	Subcommittee on Emerging
Business & Industry	Technologies & Economic Development
Calendars (Procedural)	Criminal Justice
Civil Practices	Education
Corrections	Subcommittee on Higher Education
County Affairs	Finance
Criminal Jurisprudence	Government Organization
Culture, Recreation, & Tourism	Health & Human Services
Defense Affairs & State-Federal Relations	Intergovernmental Relations
Economic Development	Subcommittee on Flooding
Elections	& Evacuations
Energy Resources	International Relations and Trade
Environmental Regulation	Jurisprudence
Financial Institutions	Natural Resources
General Investigating & Ethics (Procedural)	Subcommittee on Agriculture, Rural
Government Reform	Affairs & Coastal Resources
Higher Education	Nominations (Procedural)
House Administration (Procedural)	State Affairs
Human Services	Transportation & Homeland Security
Insurance	Veteran Affairs & Military Installations
Judiciary	Subcommittee on Base Realignment and
Juvenile Justice & Family Issues	Closure
Land & Resource Management	
Law Enforcement	
Licensing & Administrative Procedures	
Local & Consent Calendars (Procedural)	
Local Government Ways & Means	
Natural Resources	
Pensions & Investments	
Public Education	
Public Health	
Redistricting (Procedural)	
Regulated Industries	
Rules & Resolutions (Procedural)	
State Affairs	
Transportation	
Urban Affairs	
Ways & Means	

Bureaucratic Oversight. In the United States, legislatures function as watchdogs over the executive branch; that is, the legislature oversees the administrative bureaucracy as it executes the law and implements public programs. The vehicle for oversight is usually the legislative committee. Legislators wish to determine whether the bureaucrats are administering the laws in the way the legislature intended. They also must determine if new or revised legislation is needed. Accordingly, committees hold hearings and ask bureaucrats under their jurisdiction about the laws and programs that they are implementing.

Control of Committees

Committees are central to the legislative process. Those who have the authority to name a committee's members are able to influence the policy decisions of the legislative body. In Texas, this authority belongs to the lieutenant governor and the speaker. Control of committees also provides a degree of control over scheduling, though the presiding officers have additional tools to control scheduling.

Committee Membership in the House. In the house, the speaker appoints the total membership as well as the chairs and vice chairs of the procedural committees. The speaker also appoints all members of the powerful Appropriations Committee, whose members serve as *ex officio* chairs of the subcommittees for budget and oversight of the substantive committees. Thus, the speaker's appointees to the Appropriations Committee also control the budget requests of the other committees. The Appropriations Committee strongly influences funding for all divisions of state government.

did you know?

That the house legislative calendars are Emergency, Major State, Constitutional Amendments, General State, Local Consent and Resolutions, and Congratulatory and Memorial Resolutions.

The House Calendars Committee controls the flow of legislation from the committees to the house floor. The speaker uses his or her influence with this procedural committee to determine if and when bills are heard on the house floor.

For all substantive committees other than Appropriations, a limited seniority system in the house determines up to one-half of the membership; the speaker appoints the other half. The speaker also appoints the committee's chair and vice chair, which ensures that the committee leadership, as well as a numerical majority of each substantive committee, will be speaker appointees. The standing committee chairs appoint the membership and the chairs and vice chairs of the subcommittees.

Committee Membership in the Senate. The lieutenant governor officially appoints the total membership, as well as the chairs and vice chairs, of all senate committees and permanent subcommittees. In practice, an informal seniority system allows the most senior senators to choose the committee on which they wish to serve until one-third of the committee's positions are filled. This ensures that senior senators will serve on the more powerful committees. The chairs of the standing committees, at their discretion, may appoint subcommittees from the committee membership.

Results of Control by the Presiding Officers. The appointive power of the presiding officers means that the action of a committee on specific legislation is usually predictable. The presiding officers can also use the power of appointment to reward friends and supporters as well as to punish opponents. Interest groups often attempt to influence the presiding officer's decision to their advantage. Interest groups need to have sympathetic members on a committee that reviews legislation important to their interests.

The relative power of the committee and the legislator's position on it (as committee or subcommittee chair) can largely determine that person's influence with administrators, lobbyists, and other legislators. Members actively seek appointments to committees that consider taxes, spending, or legislation for powerful economic interests or control the house calendar.

Selection of Committee Chairs. The presiding officers, by virtue of their power to appoint the chairs of all committees, have a tool that works like a magnet to attract legislators to their teams. If legislators want to get along in the legislature, they go along (with the presiding officers). This power also increases the bargaining position of the presiding officers relative to interest groups. The lobbyist who can help get a sympathetic legislator appointed as chair of an important committee has earned the salary paid by the interest group that employs her or him. At the same time, the lobbyist owes the presiding officer a real favor for appointing the "right" committee chair.

The appointive power of the presiding officers, although significant, does not provide absolute power over the legislature. The presiding officers may also appoint to important positions legislators who have political power in their own right, such as legislators with close ties to powerful special-interest groups. The presiding officers may then have the support of some of the most powerful members of the legislature in a reciprocally beneficial relationship. The presiding officers can usually count on the loyalty of the chairs, who in turn can usually depend on support from the presiding officers.

The No-Party System. The Texas legislature has historically been organized on the basis of ideology, rather than political party, with a coalition of Republicans and conservative-to-moderate Democrats usually in control. Under this no-party system, party affiliation has less significance than ideology and interest-group ties.

Historically, the conservative Democratic speakers appointed mostly Democrats—but some Republicans—to committee chair positions. Today, the no-party system has been modified and continued under conservative Republican leadership, with the ratio of Republican to Democrat chairs reversed. The chairs of the most powerful committees are usually, but not always, appointed from the presiding officers' party.

It is important to understand that although the Texas legislature is organizationally a no-party system, party differences are important on matters of policy. Political party caucuses do not fill the positions of power as they do in the U.S. Congress, and members of the minority party may join the presiding officers' team, serve on important committees, and become committee chairs. Differences on public-policy issues are sometimes intense, however, and are becoming increasingly partisan.

Committee Action

Committee members can deliver to the leadership such things as substantial changes in bills, support for legislation favored by the leadership team, and opposition to legislation the leadership wants to defeat. A politically knowledgeable leadership that astutely uses its power over committee members can thus consolidate support for its policies.

Committee Jurisdiction. The presiding officers in the Texas legislature are responsible for assigning bills to particular committees. Because committee jurisdiction in the Texas legislature is often poorly defined, the officers have considerable discretion when making these assignments. The speaker may even reconsider a bill's assignment and change its committees during the legislative session.

The presiding officers do not hesitate to assign a bill they oppose to a committee they know will act unfavorably on the bill—and likewise, assign a bill they support to a committee that will report on it positively. Because the presiding officers can stack the committees to their liking, this is a simple process.

Killing Bills. There are several reasons why a presiding officer may oppose a specific bill (other than that the bill is simply bad public policy):

1. The backers and financial supporters of the presiding officer may view the bill as a threat to their economic or political well-being.
2. The presiding officer and his or her team may feel that supporters of the bill have been uncooperative in the past and should be punished.
3. The supporters of the bill may be outbargained by the bill's opponents.
4. The presiding officer and his or her supporters may believe that the bill, if it became law, would take funds away from programs that they favor.

When a legislator who does not serve on the committee opposes a bill, the legislator may bargain with the members of the committee to pigeonhole it. There are several reasons for this. The most obvious is that the legislator—or an interest that she or he represents—is ideologically opposed to the substance of the bill. In addition, a legislator may want to kill a bill on which his or her political supporters are evenly divided, for no matter how the legislator voted, he or she would lose political support and face political or economic repercussions from angered interest groups or constituents.

Tagging
In the Texas Senate, a rule that allows a senator to halt a standing committee's consideration of a bill for 48 hours.

Calendar
In the Texas legislature, the schedule that serves as a conduit for legislation between the committees and the primary legislative body.

Tagging in the Senate. The Texas Senate also practices **tagging.** Once each session, any senator may require the chair of a senate committee to give that senator 48 hours' advance notice as to when the committee will hold hearings on a bill. This means that, in effect, the senator can delay the hearings for 48 hours. The tagging procedure is not debatable; any committee action on the bill within the 48-hour period is void. If the bill's sponsors can get the senator to remove the tag, however, the bill can be immediately cleared for committee hearings. The effect of tagging would be minimal if it were not for the limited legislative session. Under the existing system, tagging late in the session enables a single senator to kill or force the modification of a bill.

The Discharge Petition. All legislative bodies have some procedure whereby bills can be extracted from reluctant committees, but it is usually difficult to accomplish. Even though they may support a bill that is buried in a committee, legislators are reluctant to vote to discharge it. They see the discharge petition as a threat to the privileges of the entire committee system—privileges that they too enjoy.

The Relative Weakness of Committees in Texas. The importance of legislative committees within the political system varies from state to state. In Texas, the power of legislative committees is proportionately less, and the power of the bureaucracy and special interests is proportionately more, than in some other political jurisdictions. The reasons include the following:

1. Because legislative sessions are infrequent and short, committees seldom meet and cannot provide ongoing oversight.
2. Members often move from one committee to another, hampering the development of expertise and long-term working relationships.
3. Texas legislators serve for relatively short periods compared with top administrators and lobbyists.

The Calendar and the Floor

The instrument for controlling the flow of legislation from the committees to the floor is the **calendar.** Control of the calendar of bills is important in any legislative body. In Texas, it is of paramount importance because of the short biennial sessions.

With the calendar schedules, as with other important aspects of the legislative process, power in the Texas legislature is centralized in the offices of the presiding officers. Unlike many of their other organizational and procedural powers, however, the ability of the speaker and the lieutenant governor to control scheduling is based as much on their influence with other legislators as on the formal powers of the offices.

Because timing a bill for consideration on the floor is critical to its eventual passage or defeat, control of the schedule is a powerful weapon that can be used to aid or to hinder legislation, to reward allies, or to punish enemies. For example, any of the following situations may occur:

1. Supporters may want floor consideration of a bill delayed until they can muster the necessary votes to get it passed. (Opponents, in contrast, may favor quick action because they have the necessary votes to defeat the bill but believe those votes could erode if the supporters are given time to consolidate their forces.)
2. Conversely, supporters may want early consideration of a bill because the opposition appears to be gaining strength. (Opponents would want delay under these circumstances.)
3. If a bill has been placed far down on the calendar, opponents can kill it through the filibuster, tagging, or parliamentary maneuvers even if they are in the minority.

House Calendars

The speaker of the house exercises no formal control over the house calendars. The Calendars Committee (and the much less important Local and Consent Calendars Committee) performs this function. This apparent decentralization of power, however, is more illusion than reality. The members and the chairs of the two committees are appointed by the speaker, are allies of the speaker, and can usually be persuaded to be amenable to the speaker's wishes.

There are several calendars for different kinds of bills. Unimportant or trivial bills are placed on special schedules and are usually disposed of promptly with little debate by the body of the house. The process is not so automatic for major or controversial legislation, however. In fact, the speaker and the committee chair often use the Calendars Committee as a black hole into which bills simply disappear. The process was once even more opaque than it is today. In a much-applauded action, the 1993 house, under the leadership of Speaker Pete Laney, adopted rules making the process more open to the general house membership.

Democratic Representative Terri Hodge of Dallas sits at a desk in the Texas House after learning that several members had bills hung up in the Local and Consent Calendars Committee. Why might the leadership use this committee to pigeonhole a bill of purely local interest? (AP Photo/Harry Cabluck)

The Senate Calendar

Unlike the house, the senate has only one calendar. Officially, the senate has a rule that requires bills to be placed on the calendar and then considered on the senate floor in the same chronological order in which they were reported from the committees. In practice, bills are taken off the calendar for senate consideration only by a suspension of this rule. The **suspension of the rule** requires a two-thirds majority vote of the entire membership of the senate.

The Blocking Bill. The procedure for consideration goes something like this: The first bill placed on the senate calendar each session is called a **blocking bill.** It is usually a bill dealing with a proposed horticultural change somewhere around the state capitol. It will never be taken off the calendar. It does, however, block all other bills' access to the floor except by the two-thirds vote to suspend the rule.

A Two-Thirds Majority for Action. This senate practice affects the senate's entire legislative process. The irony is that while only a simple majority is necessary for final passage in the senate, a two-thirds majority is necessary to get the bill to the floor for consideration. It can be said that this process protects the minority from the majority. It is also a means whereby the senate can kill a bill without having a floor vote for or against—the bill simply fails to reach the floor and so dies on the calendar. Although lobbyists are keenly interested in which bills die for lack of two-thirds support in a consideration vote, the general public and some members of the press are often unaware that an important vote has even occurred.

The two-thirds rule is a tool that can be used to enhance the powers of the presiding officer. By using this requirement, the lieutenant governor can keep a bill from reaching the floor of the senate by simply persuading eleven members to vote against it. The bill then lacks the necessary two-thirds majority and cannot advance to the floor of the senate. Any coalition of eleven senators can achieve the same result—occasionally against the wishes of the lieutenant governor.

Suspension of the Rule
Setting aside of the rules of a legislative body so that another set of rules can be used.

Blocking Bill
In Texas, a bill placed early on the senate calendar that will never actually be considered. A rule—which can be suspended by a two-thirds vote—requires that the senate address bills in chronological order. The blocking bill ensures that a measure must win the vote of two-thirds of the senate even to be considered.

The Quorum Requirement

At least two-thirds of the members of each chamber must be present to conduct business. Absence of 11 or more senators brings any senate action to a halt, as does the absence of 51 or more house members. The quorum rule is written into the state constitution, and lack of a quorum is an absolute bar to legislative action. This fact has led to a series of incidents in which members have absented themselves to halt business. Texas has an unusually high figure for a legislative quorum. Half the membership is a more common rule, and the U.S. Constitution establishes that quorum for the U.S. House and Senate.

The Floor

Floor
The place where a legislative body debates, amends, votes on, enacts, and defeats proposed legislation; the entire house or senate acting as a whole.

Floor Leaders
Legislators who are responsible for getting party members to vote for or against particular legislation.

The Texas Constitution requires that bills must be "read on three consecutive days in each house." The purpose of this action on the **floor** is to ensure that laws are not passed without adequate opportunity for debate. Bills are read once on being introduced before the presiding officer assigns them to a committee. In practice, the entire bill is seldom read at this time. Instead, a caption, or brief summary, is read to acquaint the members of the legislature with the subject of the bill. The bill is read the second time before floor debate in each chamber, and if an entire bill is to be read, it is usually on this second reading. The third reading usually occurs at least one day after floor passage.

Bills containing a statement that they are "cases of imperative public necessity" may be read for the third time on the same day as floor passage, as long as four-fifths of the membership agree. All bills now routinely contain this provision and usually receive the third reading immediately following floor passage. A simple majority is required for passage on the third reading, while a two-thirds majority is necessary for the addition of an amendment.

The House Floor. As bills reach the floor of the house, a loudspeaker system allows the members and visitors to follow the debate. **Floor leaders** usually stand at the front of the chamber, answer questions, and speak in favor of or against the bill. Microphones located elsewhere in the house chamber serve opponents of the bill and other concerned lawmakers as they argue against the bill, speak for the bill, or simply ask questions.

The consideration of bills on the floor of the house would seem to be a study in confusion and inattention. Throughout the process, members of the house may be laughing, talking, reading papers, or sleeping at their desks. Because many members often know very little about a bill under consideration, however, this is an excellent opportunity for both proponents and opponents of the legislation to seek support for their positions. Eloquent speeches seldom change votes. In fact, many members vote for or against legislation based on who is supporting it or who is against it and only then ask what the bill was all about. This practice is especially true of specialized bills that have generated little statewide interest. Voting time usually brings both supporters and opponents of the bill up and down the aisles pleading with either one finger (vote yes) or two fingers (vote no).

Electronic Voting in the House. House members insert cards into a voting panel on their desks that allows them to push buttons to record a vote of yes, no, or present but not voting. The tallies are displayed on a large electronic scoreboard with green, red, and white bulbs next to each legislator's name. (Green means yes, red means no, and white means present but not voting.)

Although the use of the electronic voting machine in the Texas House is a major innovation, it has made the practice of "ghost voting" more visible. The house rules prohibit ghost voting, whereby legislators cast votes for absent colleagues. The practice, however, persists. Nanci Wilson, an Austin reporter for CBS Channel 42, caught many lawmakers casting votes for absent colleagues.[10] The practice has real implications. Suspecting that

10. Nanci Wilson, "One Lawmaker, Many Votes?" *CBS 42 Investigates,* May 14, 2007. The video can be seen on YouTube under "Texas Politicians' multiple voting breaks legislature rules."

the defeat of a 1993 bill to increase the penalties for having drugs or weapons near schools was a result of ghost voting, the bill's supporters requested a roll-call vote. Ten members, eight of whom had voted against the bill, had been present only in spirit. The bill was then passed 65 to 58 by the roll-call vote.

Points of Order in the House. Throughout the voting, the speaker recognizes members from the floor, rules on **points of order,** and so forth. If a point of order is sustained late in the session, there may not be time to correct the error, and in that case the bill dies.

Although raising a point of order is not uncommon, it seldom has the impact that it did during the 1997 legislature. Representative Debra Danburg, a Democrat from Houston, raised a point of order that killed a bill requiring parental notification before a minor could have an abortion. In reaction, Arlene Wohlgemuth, a Republican representative from Burleson and a proponent of the antiabortion bill, raised points of order that killed some 80 pending bills, many of which were supported by Governor George W. Bush and other Republican legislators.[11]

Points of Order
A formal question to the chairperson about the legitimacy of a parliamentary process. A successful point of order can result in the postponement or defeat of legislation.

Committee of the Whole
An entire legislative body (such as the Texas Senate) acting as a committee. The committee's purpose is to allow the body to relax its rules and thereby expedite legislation.

Cloture
An action by which legislative debate is ended so that a floor vote must be taken.

The Senate Floor. The senate scene may be similar to that in the house in one sense—usually, few members are paying attention to the debate. Senate debates on even important bills are usually much shorter than debates in the house, primarily due to the all-important rule that requires a two-thirds vote before a bill can be brought to the floor out of its calendar sequence. Bringing a bill to the floor requires the cooperation of the lieutenant governor (who can recognize senators from the floor) and at least 21 senators. Such support suggests that compromises have been made and deals have been brokered well before the legislation ever reaches the floor.

The senate may also form itself into a **committee of the whole,** at which time the lieutenant governor appoints a senator to preside. Only a simple majority rather than the usual two-thirds is necessary to consider legislation, and the lieutenant governor may debate and vote on all questions. Otherwise, the senate rules are observed. No journal is kept of the proceedings.

Filibustering in the Senate. The *filibuster,* which was discussed in Chapter 12, is a threat to bills in the Texas Senate, just as it is in the U.S. Senate. The difference in the Texas Senate is that a member may not give the floor to other senators who also want to filibuster. In Texas, the lieutenant governor controls the floor, so in effect only one senator may filibuster for as long as he or she can physically last. Then the vote is taken. **Cloture** to force a vote is not an option in the Texas Senate.

The purpose of a filibuster is either to attract public attention to a bill that is sure to pass without the filibuster or to delay legislation in the closing days of the session. In fact, the mere threat of a filibuster may be enough to compel a bill's supporters to change the content of the bill to reach a compromise with the disgruntled senator. If a filibuster does occur, it means that no compromise was possible—usually because the senators who favor the bill, by virtue of their numbers, refuse to be intimidated by the threat of a filibuster.

Senator Bill Meier set the world record for a filibuster in the 1977 legislative session by talking for 43 hours. This feat broke the old record of 42 hours and 33 minutes set in 1972 by Senator Mike McKool. There have been several other notable filibusters in the Texas Senate. In 1993, Senator Gonzalo Barrientos filibustered for 17 hours and 50 minutes in an attempt to kill legislation that overturned an Austin ordinance designed to

11. "In Session: Notes on the Legislature," *Austin American-Statesman,* May 30, 1997, p. B7.

protect the Barton Springs watershed from development. During the filibuster, Barrientos was required to stand and was restricted to a three-square-foot area. The bill eventually passed 22 to 7.[12]

Finally, the Senate Votes. Following the debate, the senators usually vote by hand signals directed toward a recording clerk—one finger for a yes vote and two fingers for a no. During the voting process, senators plead for their colleagues' votes using the same hand signals directed toward the senators. Only a simple majority is necessary for passage.

12. Diana R. Fuentes, *San Antonio Express-News,* May 1, 1993, p. 17A.

POLITICS AND... the Texas legislature

UNIVERSITY STUDENTS

Members of the Texas legislature are given a monthly stipend to run their offices that is generally not enough to be an effective representative. As a result, state lawmakers depend heavily on interns for assistance to run their offices while the legislature is in and out of session. Many interns are involved in reviewing bills before the legislature. Interns are asked to provide lawmakers feedback on bills, meet with lobbyists, address constituency concerns, and work with the staff of other legislators. These very important functions are often assigned to university students with little or no experience with legislative work.

Some lobbyists complain that interns are given too many responsibilities, and are underprepared for the important work assigned to them. Others believe that the use of interns creates an unstable environment where office staff members come and go with such frequency that it is difficult to develop institutional memory, or the know-how and experiences learned over many years. With the exception of lawmakers, who have longer tenures, few lawmakers retain their interns or their staff for a very long period of time, diminishing the experience of legislative office staff.

Nevertheless, the internship experience has a profound impact on the lives of university students who take part in such programs. Christopher Smith, an associate with Thompson and Knight L.L.P., an international law firm with four Texas offices, writes that his internship experience provided him "an unparalleled opportunity to understand the legislative process by being part of the legislative process. The insight I gained and the relationships I developed as a TLIP intern are assets that will serve me well in my legal career."[a] Similarly, Chris Lopez, an associate attorney with Weil, Gotshal and Manges L.L.P., another of Texas's largest firms, writes, "The Texas Legislative Internship Program provided me with the best opportunity to enhance my understanding of the Texas Legislature and contributed to my success as an attorney."[b] Young people who serve as interns develop a sense of self confidence in their ability to make a difference in public policy and in the lives of others.

Many find their way back into public service after having served as interns in Austin. Before Texas State Representative Ana Hernandez served in Austin as a lawmaker, she served as an intern. Similarly, Shelley Davis, who now serves as an assistant to the Reverend Jesse Jackson, credits his internship experience for preparing him for public office as a Georgetown City Council Member.[c]

Every year, thousands of university students who are interested in politics get involved in politics in a truly fundamental way—by serving as interns in the offices of state lawmakers. Such involvement has a direct impact in the enactment of public policy and in the casework assigned to interns. But, most importantly, such service has a meaningful and positive impact in the lives of those young people who serve as interns. What do you think about the role of interns in the Texas legislature? Is this something you think you could do?

a. Texas Legislative Internship Program, accessed August 3, 2008, at www.rodneyellis.com/tlip/.
b. *Ibid.*
c. *Ibid.*

Conference Committees

A unique byproduct of bicameralism is the need to resolve differences in similar bills passed by the two chambers. A temporary (or ad hoc) committee known as a *conference committee* is appointed for each bill to resolve these differences. To determine the acceptability of proposed compromises, the membership of this committee remains in contact with interested legislators, lobbyists, administrators, and the presiding officers.

Conference Committee Membership. In Texas, conference committees are composed of five members from each chamber (known as conferees), appointed by each chamber's presiding officer. At least two of the senate conferees must be from the standing committee that heard the bill, and the chair of the senate conferees is either the author or sponsor of the bill for which the conference committee is called. The compromise proposal must win the support of a majority of the committee members from each chamber to be reported out of the conference committee. Because the members of the committee may alter or even kill a bill, the attitudes of the legislators appointed to the committee are of crucial concern to the various interests involved. Bargaining before the selection of the committee is common, and bargaining continues among the committee members during deliberations. Both the presiding officers and the conference committee members are well placed to affect the outcome.

Conference Committee Reports. After a bill has been reported from the conference committee, it cannot be amended by either chamber but must be accepted or rejected as written or sent back to the conference committee for further compromise. In practice, because of the volume of legislation that must be considered and the limited time available, the Texas legislature tends to accept conference committee reports on most legislation.

How a Bill Becomes a Law

Bills may be introduced in either chamber or, to speed the process, in both chambers at the same time. Consider as an example a bill that is introduced in the senate before it is sent to the house. The numbers in Figure 21–3 on the next page correspond to the numbers in the following discussion.

1. **Introduction in the Senate.** A senator must introduce a bill in the senate. It is not difficult to find a legislator who is willing to perform this somewhat clerical function. More difficult is finding a sponsor who will use her or his political skills and bargaining prowess to help get the bill through the intricacies of the legislative process. On introduction, the bill is assigned a number—for example, Senate Bill 13 (SB 13).
2. **Assignment to a Senate Committee.** The lieutenant governor assigns bills to committees in the senate and can, for many bills, choose between two or more committees. It is very important to proponents of the bill that the chosen committee not oppose the spirit of the bill. If possible, proponents of the bill and their allies will gain the lieutenant governor's support and receive a friendly committee assignment. This may be granted in exchange for their support of or opposition to some other bill of particular interest to the lieutenant governor.
3. **Senate Committee Action.** In the relevant subcommittee, supporters and opponents of the bill are allowed to testify. Witnesses are often lobbyists or concerned bureaucrats affected by the bill. The subcommittee then marks up (makes changes to) the bill and sends it to the whole committee. The committee may hear additional testimony and further mark up the bill. Some senate committees do not have subcommittees. In that circumstance, the entire committee initially hears testimony and marks up the bill. The committee may then report on the bill favorably or unfavorably or may refuse to report on it at all.

FIGURE 21–3 How a Bill Becomes a Law in Texas

The procedure shown in this figure follows a bill that is first introduced in the Texas Senate and eventually reaches the governor's desk. If a bill is first introduced in the Texas House of Representatives, the procedure is much the same, but the diagram would be a mirror image of what you see here, and the bill would be introduced as HB 13.

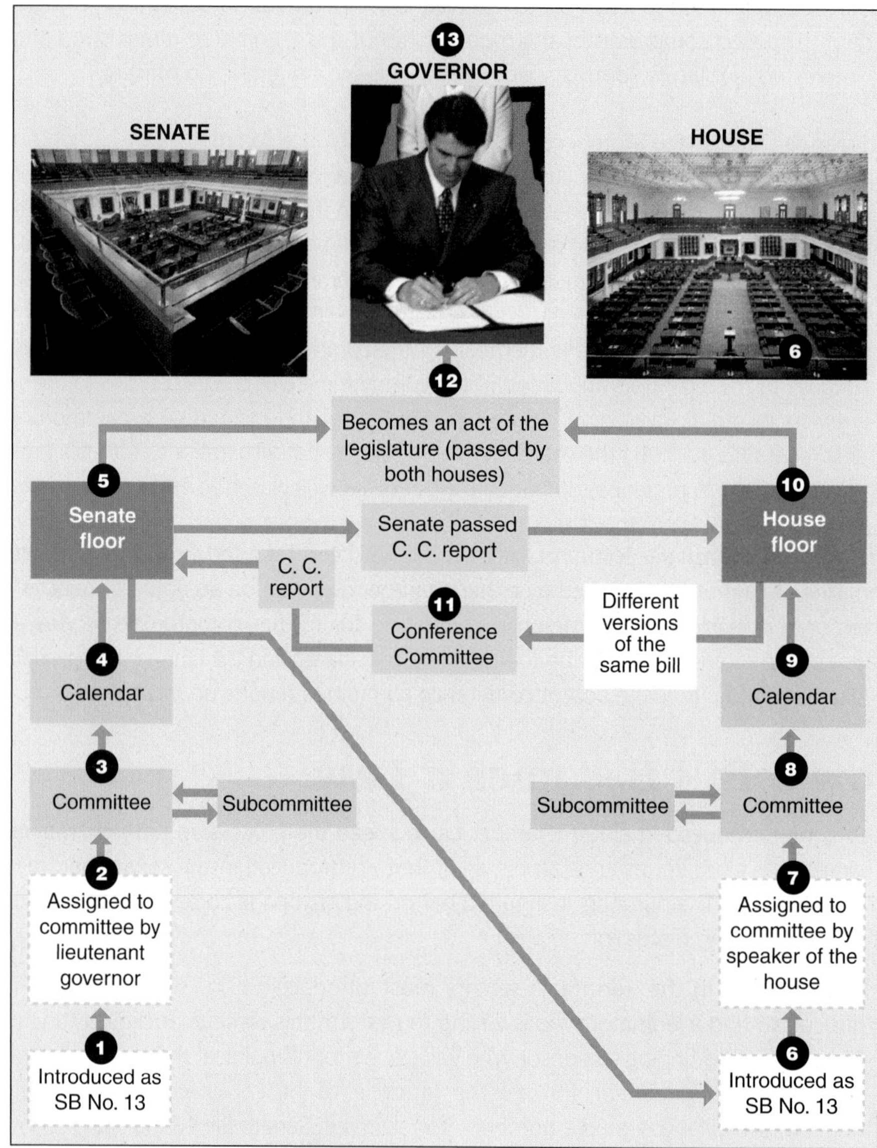

All photos courtesy of the Governor's Office, Austin, TX.

4. **The Senate Calendar.** The senate has only one calendar of bills, and it is rarely followed. In the usual procedure, as described earlier, a senator makes a motion to suspend the regular calendar order and consider a proposed bill out of its sequence. For this parliamentary maneuver to succeed, prior arrangements must be made for the lieutenant governor to recognize the senator who will make the motion. If two-thirds of the senators agree to the motion, the bill, with the blessings of the lieutenant governor, is ready for action on the senate floor.
5. **The Senate Floor.** The president of the senate (the lieutenant governor) has the power to recognize senators who wish to speak and to interpret rules and points of order. Rarely does the senate overrule these interpretations. Unlimited debate is the rule in the Texas Senate. This does not mean that the Texas Senate is a deliberative

body, for it is not; such luxury is not possible in the short legislative session. Unlimited debate could, however, lead to a filibuster—an attempt to either "talk the bill to death" or force a compromise. If a bill is successful in reaching the senate floor, it has already cleared its major obstacle (the two-thirds majority necessary for senate consideration) and will usually pass in some form. A simple majority is necessary for a bill to pass. The lieutenant governor may vote only to break ties.

6. **Introduction to the House.** Following senate passage, the bill is sent to the house. A procedure similar to that in the senate is followed there.
7. **Assignment to a House Committee.** The speaker of the house assigns each bill to a committee. The speaker, like the lieutenant governor, has some freedom of choice in selecting a committee, because the jurisdiction of house committees is vague.
8. **House Committee Action.** Committee action in the house is similar to that in the senate. Each bill is assigned to a committee and then to a subcommittee, which may hold public hearings. The subcommittee as well as the committee may amend, totally rewrite, pigeonhole, or report favorably or unfavorably on a bill.
9. **House Calendars.** A bill that is reported favorably by a standing committee, or receives a favorable minority report by the required number of committee members, is placed on one of the eight house calendars by one of the two calendars committees. This establishes the approximate order in which the whole house will consider the legislation. If a calendars committee fails to assign the bill to a calendar, it can be forced to do so by the action of a simple majority of the house. If a bill has the blessings of the speaker, however, it is sure to be promptly placed on the appropriate calendar.
10. **The House Floor.** The speaker of the house has the power to recognize representatives on the house floor and also to interpret the rules and points of order. Although the speaker may be overruled, he or she seldom is. The size of the house necessitates that debate be more limited than in the senate—usually each member is allowed 10 minutes. A bill may be amended, **tabled** (which usually kills the measure), defeated, or sent back to committee. The "yes" votes of only a simple majority of members present and voting are necessary for a bill to pass.

Table
In a legislature or similar body, to cease action on a particular measure. A motion to table is not debatable.

11. **Conference Committee.** If the house makes a change in the senate-passed version of a bill, a conference committee is necessary to reconcile the differences between the two versions of the bill. The lieutenant governor appoints five senators and the speaker appoints five representatives to sit on the committee. The compromise bill must be approved by a majority of both the senators and the representatives before it can be reported out of the conference committee.
12. **Final Passage.** A bill reported out of a conference committee is sent first to the chamber where it originated and then to the other chamber for final approval. Neither one may amend the reported bill but must accept it, reject it, or send it back to the conference committee. If both the senate and the house pass the conference committee version of the bill, it becomes an act of the legislature and is sent to the governor.
13. **The Governor.** The governor has several options for dealing with an act of the legislature. First, she or he may sign it into law. Second, he or she may choose not to sign it, in which circumstance it becomes law in 10 days if the legislature is in session or in 20 days if the legislature is not in session. Third, the governor may choose to veto the act, but the veto can be overridden by a two-thirds vote in each chamber. (The Texas legislature almost never overrides a governor's vetoes, in large part because the legislature typically is no longer in session when the veto is issued.) The governor cannot veto a portion of an act unless it is a clause that actually appropriates funds. This is

the power known as line-item veto power. The governor may strike out an item of appropriation, but he or she does not have a reduction veto (to reduce spending for an item).

If the governor signs an act of the legislature, it becomes a law in ninety days—or sooner if it is an appropriations act or an act that the legislature has designated as emergency legislation. If the act requires the expenditure of funds, the comptroller of public accounts must certify that adequate revenue is available for its implementation. If revenue is lacking, the act goes back to the legislature, where either adequate funds are provided or a four-fifths majority in each chamber approves the act. If neither option is successful, the act cannot be implemented.

Institutional Tools of Leadership

The Texas legislature has established a series of bodies that are active even when the legislature is not in session. To a limited degree, the work of these bodies may counteract the negative effects of the very short legislative sessions.[13]

Legislative Budget Board

Legislative Budget Board
The primary budgeting entity for Texas state government.

Legislative Council
In Texas, a body that provides research support, information, and bill-drafting assistance to legislators.

Most states, the U.S. government, and most countries have only one budget. Texas has two. Each agency in the state government presents its budget requests both to the governor's office and to the **Legislative Budget Board.** The board then provides to the governor and the legislature a draft of the appropriations bill. The Legislative Budget Board has also been given broad authority over strategic planning for the state, bill analyses, and policy and impact analyses affecting education, criminal justice, and other policy areas.

The Legislative Budget Board operates continuously, even when the legislature is not in session. It is made up of the lieutenant governor and the speaker (who serve as joint chairs), as well as four members from each chamber who are appointed by their presiding officers. These 10 members include the chairs of the senate Finance Committee and the house Ways and Means and Appropriations Committees. The board appoints an administrative director.

Clearly, the control of the board is in the hands of the two presiding officers, who are in a position to strongly influence state government from the budgeting stage through the final appropriations stage. The board staff assists the appropriating committees and their chairs, and it also has the watchdog function of overseeing to some extent the expenditures of the executive agencies and departments. Thus, in this critical area of finance, the concentration of power in the hands of the presiding officers is even greater than in other legislative areas.

Legislative Council

Another instrument of influence is the 14-member **Legislative Council,** which includes six senators, the chair of the house Administration Committee, five other representatives, and the lieutenant governor and the speaker of the house, who serve as joint chairs. The lieutenant governor appoints the senate members, and the speaker appoints the house members. A director and staff who serve at the pleasure of the council perform the administrative work.

---

13. Sources for this material are *Guide to Texas State Agencies,* 9th ed. (Austin: Lyndon B. Johnson School of Public Affairs, University of Texas at Austin, 1996); the Legislative Budget Board Web site at www.lbb.state.tx.us; the Texas Legislative Council Web site at www.tlc.state.tx.us; the State Auditor's Office Web site at www.sao.state.tx.us; and the Sunset Advisory Commission Web site at www.sunset.state.tx.us.

The Legislative Council functions as a source of information and support to the legislature, state agencies, and other governmental institutions. It provides research support to legislators and helps draft legislative proposals.

Legislative Audit Committee

The primary function of the **Legislative Audit Committee** is to audit (formally check) the expenditures of the state agencies and departments. The committee is composed of the presiding officers and the chairs of the taxing committees, the house Appropriations Committee, and the senate State Affairs Committee. The state auditor, who serves at the pleasure of the committee, heads the State Auditor's Office. Here, too, management of the fiscal affairs of the Texas government is firmly under the influence of the presiding officers.

Legislative Audit Committee
In Texas, a committee that performs audits of state agencies and departments for the legislature.

Sunset Advisory Commission
In Texas, a body that periodically evaluates most government agencies and departments. The commission may recommend the restructuring, abolition, or alteration of the jurisdiction of an agency.

Sunset Advisory Commission

The Texas Sunset Act requires that most state agencies undergo reevaluation, usually on a 12-year cycle, to determine the need for their continuance. Agencies are automatically terminated if they are not renewed—that is, the "sun sets" on those agencies not specifically renewed by the legislature. Reauthorization may result in altered scope and authority for the agency.

The 12-member **Sunset Advisory Commission** enforces the Act. The lieutenant governor appoints four senators and one public member, and the speaker appoints four representatives and one public member. The presiding officers also serve on the commission. Public members are appointed for two-year terms and legislators for four-year staggered terms, with two positions from each chamber filled every two years. The commission appoints the agency's chief executive officer.

In the Sunset Advisory Commission's more than 30-year history, the commission has abolished more than 52 state agencies, saving taxpayers hundreds of millions of dollars. In recent years, however, abolishing state agencies has proven politically unpopular. As a result, the Sunset Advisory Commission has worked to improve state agencies, rather than attempt to abolish them.

WHY SHOULD YOU CARE ABOUT... THE TEXAS LEGISLATURE?

A democratic republic such as ours is a unique form of government. Under most other forms of government, citizen participation is neither important nor encouraged, but a democratic republic does not function well without the participation of its citizens. All of us have interests and issues that concern us directly, and it is important for us to become informed and to support the legislators and interest groups that are our allies.

CITIZEN PARTICIPATION

What is your opinion of your legislators' positions on the issues? Do your elected representatives work in your best interest? In our political system, it is our business to find out where our legislators stand on the issues. If you raise your voice—and if those who share your views raise their voices as well—you may be able to sway your legislator on an issue of concern to you.

Learn who finances the campaigns of your elected representatives. Go to "Follow the Money: The Institute on Money in State Politics" at **www.followthemoney.org**. Under "State-at-a-Glance," scroll to Texas, and use the date of the last election. In the "Election Summary" section, click on "House" or "Senate," and then click on your representative or senator. You will find a list of his or her top contributors, along with contributions by industry, by economic interest, and by geographic location. This information can help you understand who has access to your representative and, to a large extent, where she or he stands on various issues.

HOW YOU CAN MAKE A DIFFERENCE

You can follow legislation. The best time to learn how the legislature works is when the legislature is in session. By going to **www.capitol.state.tx.us**, you can find a bill that affects you personally. Click on "Legislation," then scroll to and click on "Bills by Subject." Now click on the legislative session desired and then on your subject of interest. There will be a list of bills from which to choose.

1. Adopt a bill as your project, and follow the bill through the legislative process. Did your bill pass, or was it killed? If it was killed, where did it die?
2. Try to determine what interest groups favored or opposed your bill. Why did they take these positions? Most interest groups have Web pages, and you can go to a group's Web page to learn about the group and its view on the issues before the legislature.
3. What action did the governor take on the bill? If your bill became law, which agency is responsible for its administration?

questions for discussion and analysis

1. How does the political and legal environment affect the way Texas's legislature operates?
2. What are the main power structures in the Texas legislature?
3. What are the major steps by which laws are passed?

key terms

blocking bill 691
calendar 690
Calendars Committee 686
cloture 693
committee of the whole 693
ex officio 680
floor 692
floor leaders 692
incumbent 681
Legislative Audit Committee 699
Legislative Budget Board 698
Legislative Council 698
mark up 686
pairing 681
partisan gerrymandering 682
part-time legislature 677
pigeonhole 686
point of order 693
presiding officers 677
Sunset Advisory Commission 699
suspension of the rule 691
table 697
tagging 690
Texas Ethics Commission 678

chapter summary

1. The Texas legislature meets on odd-numbered years for 140 days. Texas alone, among the large states, has such a restricted period of time in which to conduct legislative business. The Texas legislator tends to be a white, male, Protestant businessperson or lawyer with enough personal wealth or interest-group support to adequately finance a campaign.

2. There are 31 senators and 150 representatives. The Texas two-chamber legislature is presided over by the lieutenant governor in the senate and the speaker in the house of representatives. Actual power in the legislative process rests with these presiding officers. Through appointive, jurisdictional, and other procedural powers, they are able to strongly influence state policy.

3. Historically, Texas government has been dominated by a coalition of conservative Democrats and Republicans. This coalition dominated the legislature through ideology rather than using party membership as the basis for control. Under Republican control of the legislature, the no-party system of legislative organization remains superficially intact, and Democrats continue to be appointed to chair committees under Republican leadership. The viability of the no-party system may be nearing its end as state politics becomes more partisan.

4. Legislative action is based on the committee system. The presiding officers appoint the committee chairs and many of the committee members. The officers assign bills to committees and have discretion over which committee to use. If a committee does not report on a bill (but instead pigeonholes or tables it), the measure is most likely dead for the session.

5. To reach the floor of the house, a bill must also be placed on a calendar by one of the two calendar committees. These committees are firmly under the control of the speaker. A bill that does not receive a calendar assignment is probably out of the running.

6. The senate calendar is an artificial device. The first item on the calendar is a "blocking bill," which is never brought to the floor. Actually bringing a bill to the floor requires a vote by two-thirds of the senators to "suspend the rule" and vote on the bill out of its calendar order. Given that two-thirds of the senate must vote in the affirmative even to bring a measure to the floor, most bills that reach the floor are approved.

7. To become an act of the legislature, a bill must pass both chambers with identical language. To iron out any differences, bills are sent to a conference committee, a special joint committee with members from both chambers. The presiding officers appoint these committees. Once a conference committee report is accepted by both chambers, the bill is sent to the governor.

8. The governor can sign or refuse to sign a bill (in which circumstance it eventually becomes law without the governor's signature). The governor can also veto a bill. If the bill contains an appropriations clause, the governor can strike it out with an item veto. In theory, the legislature could override a veto, but by the time the veto is issued, the legislature is usually no longer in session.

9. The institutional powers of the presiding officers include control over legislative boards and commissions that manage the budgeting function of state government (the Legislative Budget Board), the auditing function (the Legislative Audit Committee), and policy research (the Legislative Council).

selected print & media resources

SUGGESTED READINGS

Bickerstaff, Steve. ***Lines in the Sand: Congress Redistricting in Texas and the Downfall of Tom Delay.*** Austin: University of Texas Press, 2007. This book provides a detailed account of the redistricting controversy in 2003, often through the personal stories of members of both parties and of minority activist groups. It examines the political aftermath and criminal prosecution of Delay.

Crawford, Ann Fears, and Frances "Sissy" Farenthold. ***Frankie: Mrs. R. D. Randolph and Texas Liberal Politics.*** Austin, TX: Eakin Press, 1999. This book describes the life and political impact of Mrs. Randolph. the founder of the *Texas Observer,* a patron of liberal Democratic candidates, and an unelected leader of liberal Democrats in their conflicts with Shivercrats and Republicans.

Hanna, Betty Elliott. ***Ladies of the House: How to Survive as the Wife of a Texas Legislator.*** Austin, TX: Eakin Press, 1993. This book describes Texas politics from the spousal viewpoint.

Jones, Nancy Baker. ***Capitol Women: Texas Female Legislators, 1923–1999.*** Austin: University of Texas Press, 2000. The lives, memories, and political strategies of 87 female Texas legislators.

Kinch, Sam, and Anne Marie Kilday. ***Too Much Money Is Not Enough: Political Power and Big Money in Texas Politics.*** Austin, TX: Campaigns for People, 2001. This book includes interviews with Texas legislators and commentary about Texas's campaign-finance system and the resulting concentration of political power in the hands of wealthy contributors.

Spaw, Patsy McDonald, ed. ***Texas Senate, Volume 1: Republic to Civil War, 1836–1861;*** and ***Texas Senate, Volume 2: Civil War to the Eve of Reform, 1861–1889.*** College Station: Texas A&M University Press, 1991 and 1999. Written by the Senate Engrossing and Enrolling Department, this two-volume set is a narrative account of issues, personalities, and events that shaped the economy, politics, and personality of the state.

MEDIA RESOURCES

Last Man Standing: Politics—Texas Style—In a documentary shown on the PBS program *POV* in 2004, Paul Stekler highlights two 2002 election campaigns. One pits the Democratic "dream team" of Tony Sanchez, Ron Kirk, and John Sharp against Rick Perry and the Republican political operatives of President George W. Bush and Karl Rove for, as Stekler says, "the future of Texas politics." The second campaign pits an Anglo-American Republican against an Anglo-American Democrat in a race for the Texas House of Representatives. The documentary is available in DVD format through Netflix.com.

NOW with Bill Moyers— In the May 16, 2003, episode, Moyers interviews columnist Molly Ivins about the redistricting conflict in the Texas legislature.

Tussle in Texas—In a 2003 interview available on PBS's *Online NewsHour,* Tom Bearden reports on Texas congressional redistricting designed to increase the number of Republicans in the U.S. Congress.

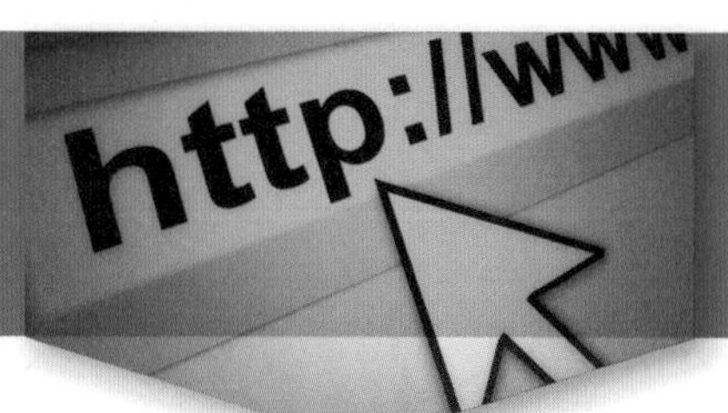

e-mocracy

FIND YOUR LEGISLATORS

Texas Legislature Online—the Web site of the Texas legislature—serves as the front door to a wide variety of information. Be sure to check out the links to the presiding officers' sites, "Speaker of the House" and "Lieutenant Governor." Another interesting feature of the site is "Who Represents Me?" Click on this link, and it will take you to a form that lets you find your state representative, state senator, U.S. representative, and State Board of Education member. Additional links then let you visit the home pages of these individuals. Use the "Who Represents Me?" feature to identify your legislators, and send them e-mail about an issue that concerns you.

LOGGING ON

The Texas Legislature Online site is at:
www.capitol.state.tx.us

The lieutenant governor has a site at:
www.senate.state.tx.us/75r/LtGov/Ltgov.htm

The Web site of the speaker of the house is at:
www.house.state.tx.us/speaker/welcome.htm

The Legislative Budget Board, which helps the legislature to prepare the budget, has a site at:
www.lbb.state.tx.us

The Texas State Library is a source for legislative, administrative, and judicial research, as well as general information about many political, economic, and social aspects of Texas. The library's Web site is at:
www.tsl.state.tx.us

The Legislative Reference Library is another good source of information about the Texas legislature. Go to:
www.lrl.state.tx.us

For information on the Texas Legislative Council, go to:
www.tlc.state.tx.us

The State Auditor's Office is at:
www.sao.state.tx.us

The Sunset Advisory Commission is at:
www.sunset.state.tx.us

You can find the Web site for any state newspaper at the following site:
www.refdesk.com/tx.html

ONLINE REVIEW

At **www.cengage.com/politicalscience/schmidt/agandpttexas14e**, you will find a Tutorial Quiz for this chapter, providing questions on the chapter contents, including the features. You'll gain access to other helpful study tools, including the book's glossary and flashcards, crossword puzzles, and Web links, as well as "Which Side Are You On?" and "Politics and . . ." features written by the authors of the book.

chapter

22

The Texas Executive Branch

chapter contents

<< The Governor's mansion. (AP Photo/Harry Cabluck)

WHAT IF...

... Texas used private contractors to administer state government?

The 21st century is seeing a movement away from the concept of government employees administering the laws and policies of American government. Private contractors are prevalent at all levels of the U.S. government. For example, they are a prime force in the logistics, administration, and fighting of the Iraq and Afghanistan wars.

Private contractors also play a prominent role in Texas government. Operation of prisons and jails, highway construction and repair, management of the Children's Health Insurance Program (CHIP), various education services, and the proposed ownership and operation of the Trans Texas Corridor are just a few of the functions private contractors perform for state government.

WHAT IF TEXAS DISBANDED THE STATE'S ADMINISTRATION?

State services could be run more cheaply by private contractors than by the state. Contractors could hire employees for the going wage rate and not necessarily be bound by the more restrictive framework of government employee pay grades. Work could be outsourced to subcontractors in developing countries, providing even greater savings. Using private contractors also eliminates the need for costly health and retirement benefits.

USING FEES INSTEAD OF TAXES

State services could be funded primarily by fees, which would be charged by the contractor to defray expenses and to make a profit. Fee-for-service is already an integral part of Texas government, and it need only be expanded to ensure a profit and to cover the expense of providing the service.

What to do if some citizens cannot afford essential services? For example, some families may have a problem paying the full cost for educating their children. The state could remedy this by giving contracts to lending institutions that would in turn lend money to these families so they could fund their children's education. Something similar to the existing college student loan program could be expanded to finance other public services as well.

SELLING GOVERNMENT ASSETS

Existing physical assets could also be sold to corporations. This would be a financial boon to Texas, because these proceeds could be used to reduce taxes or placed in an emergency fund in the event of a future economic or environmental catastrophe. The state could also save millions of tax dollars that are currently used to maintain offices, schools, highways, dams, bridges, and so forth by shifting the burden of upkeep and operation to private contractors.

DEVELOPING A CONTRACT SPOILS SYSTEM

Contracting the state administration would provide politicians with a way to reward political supporters. People are often reluctant to invest their time or resources in political campaigns unless they see personal and immediate gain. President Andrew Jackson solved this problem by hiring supporters to government positions, and he popularized the slogan "to the victors belong the spoils!" Modern political campaigns rely even more heavily on financial contributions. Politicians could reward their campaign contributors with contracts to provide public services. To paraphrase Andrew Jackson, to the victor go the contract spoils.

OPPOSITION TO PRIVATIZATION

Opponents of privatization would argue that one of the basic functions of a political system is to provide services to its citizens. Furthermore, corporations cannot be trusted, because there is no regulatory oversight in place to ensure equitable enforcement of state law and policies. Also, some citizens could not afford state services if they were not largely funded by taxpayers, and services like education are so important that they should be made available to everyone regardless of ability to pay. Private business already makes services available to those who can afford them.

FOR CRITICAL ANALYSIS

1. What is your opinion of the present private-contractor system?
2. Do you think private contractors should replace government employees?
3. Would this proposal be a logical expansion of the existing private-contractor system?
4. What are the problems with privatization?

The legislative function is to create law, and the executive function is to carry it out. For example, the legislative function is to determine who will pay how much in taxes, but the executive function is to actually collect those taxes. The legislative function is to determine how much will be appropriated for each agency and to set financial priorities, but the executive function is to actually spend the appropriations—write the checks and make the contracts. The legislative function is to define crime and prescribe punishment, but the executive function is to arrest, prosecute, and punish criminals. The legislative function is to determine which services will be provided, but the executive function is to actually provide those services—to hire personnel and manage their day-to-day conduct. The executive function is basically to do what the government does. Although more executive functions are now being outsourced (as we discuss in the *What If . . .* section), almost all of a citizen's contacts with the government are with the executive branch.

The administrators' function is to see that the law is enforced, but also imbedded within this function are elements of functions of the other branches of government. Administrators make law when they write rules and regulations that are designed to clarify and specify the more general wording of the actual statute. In other words, the bureaucracy interprets the meaning of the law (a **quasi-judicial function**) and then writes the rules and regulations (a **quasi-legislative function**) that are used to implement the enforcement.

Quasi-judicial Functions
Actions by a branch other than the courts that involve interpreting the law.

Quasi-legislative Functions
Legislative actions by entities other than the legislature; for example, executive branch agencies adopting rules and regulations that are binding on citizens.

Structure and Politics of the Governor's Office

More than 200 state agencies (the bureaucracy) administer Texas public policy. The state constitution designates the governor as the chief executive (chief bureaucrat) but then proceeds to systematically deny him or her the power to control state agencies. The executive branch of the Texas government is divided into many elective and appointive offices, primarily because Texans traditionally have feared concentration of power anywhere in government, particularly in the executive branch. The effect of this fear is compounded by legislators' reluctance to pass laws that would increase the powers of the chief executive relative to their own powers. As a result, the Texas executive branch has evolved into a mixture of elective offices, boards, and commissions, most separate from, and largely independent of, the governor. Texas, in other words, has a *plural executive* system.

Despite these constitutional and statutory restrictions, the governor can influence state policy by persuading and bargaining with others. The governor's legislative powers, media access, party influence, and appointive powers enable an astute, politically savvy officeholder to exert meaningful influence on both legislative and administrative decisions.

Who Can Become Governor?

As is usual with elective offices, the legal requirements for becoming governor are minimal: a candidate must be (1) 30 years of age, (2) an American citizen, and (3) a citizen of Texas for five years before election. While the formal qualifications for governor are easily met, the informal criteria are more restrictive.

White Protestant. Since the Texas Revolution, governors have all been white Protestants, usually Methodists or Baptists. They have also been Anglo, with family names originating in the British Isles.

Male. The governor is historically male. The only female governor of Texas before Ann Richards (served 1991–1995) was Miriam A. Ferguson, who

did you know?

That when Ann Richards was elected state treasurer in 1982, she was the first woman to win a statewide election to any post in Texas since "Ma" Ferguson was elected governor in 1932.

Texas Governor
Rick Perry delivers his State of the State address at the state capitol in Austin. As the most prominent leader in the state, the governor has the opportunity to supplement his or her rather limited formal powers by appealing to the people. How might the governor turn popular support to his or her advantage when seeking new legislation? (Photo courtesy of the Governor's Office)

served for two nonconsecutive terms (1925–1927 and 1933–1935). Ferguson ran on the slogan "Two Governors for the Price of One" and did not really represent a deviation from male domination of Texas politics, because it was clear that her husband, former governor James E. Ferguson, actually exercised the power of the office.[1] Only Ann Richards was a female governor in her own right.

Middle-Aged Businessperson or Attorney. The governor will probably be successful in business or law—more than half of the governors who have served in the last 100 years have been lawyers. The governor will most likely be between 40 and 60 years old; have a record of elective public service in state government or some other source of name recognition; and be a participant in service, social, and occupational organizations.

Today, a Republican. Democrats historically dominated Texas politics. Between 1952 and 1988, the Republicans became competitive in top-of-the-ticket elections—president, U.S. senator, and governor—but the state was basically Democratic for most other offices. Texas became an authentic two-party state with the 1990 election of two Republicans to the down-ticket offices of state treasurer and commissioner of agriculture.

Fourteen years later, Texas had completed its evolution into a strongly Republican state. Republicans first swept statewide offices in 1998, electing the governor, lieutenant governor, and all elected down-ticket administrators, including members of the Texas Railroad Commission. The down-ticket Republican victories have additional political significance. Statewide elective offices can provide political experience and name recognition. They also can serve as a springboard to higher office, as Kay Bailey Hutchison demonstrated by moving from state treasurer to the U.S. Senate. In 1998, Rick Perry rose from commissioner of agriculture to lieutenant governor, and in 2002 he was elected governor. That same year, Texas Attorney General John Cornyn was elected to the U.S. Senate. Like most states from the Old South, Texas's electorate now strongly favors Republican candidates for public office.

Support by Interest Groups. Most successful candidates for governor have substantial interest-group support. For example, the expenses of the 2003 inauguration of Governor Perry and Lieutenant Governor David Dewhurst were mostly paid by large corporations, including AT&T, Philip Morris, SBC Communications, Sprint, insurance companies, and the state's primary Medicaid contractor. Consumer lobbyists and liberals voiced concern about the likely impact on the pending agenda for insurance, health care, and other legislation facing the 2003 legislature. The festivities cost about $1.5 million, of which $500,000 was raised by ticket sales to the event.[2]

Well-Funded Campaigns. A hefty bankroll is necessary even for serious consideration. Challengers usually must spend more than incumbents to buy name recognition. Spending

1. Rupert N. Richardson, *Texas: The Lone Star State,* 2nd ed. (Englewood Cliffs, NJ: Prentice Hall, 1958), p. 317.
2. Associated Press, *Dallas Morning News,* January 2, 2003, available at www.dallasnews.com; and J. Taylor Rushing, "One Big Party," *Fort Worth Star-Telegram,* January 21, 2003, available at www.dfw.com.

does not buy all elections, however. In the 2002 Texas gubernatorial election, Democrat Tony Sanchez and Republican Rick Perry together spent $95 million to win a job that pays $115,345 per year. The incumbent, Perry, spent $29.9 million, and the challenger, Sanchez, spent a record $67.2 million, including $60 million of his own personal wealth. Sanchez spent $36 per vote and lost; Perry spent $9 per vote and won. Regardless of campaign spending, Texans seem to strongly favor Republican issues and values.

Tenure, Removal, and Succession

Texas governors serve a four-year term, as do governors in 47 other states. Unlike most states, however, Texas imposes no limit on the number of terms a governor may serve. The governor may be removed from office before the end of his or her term only by impeachment by the Texas House of Representatives and conviction by the Texas Senate. Impeachment is the legislative equivalent of **indictment** and requires only a simple majority of members present. Conviction requires a two-thirds majority.

Indictment
A formal accusation issued by a grand jury against a party charged with a crime when the jury determines that there is sufficient evidence to bring the accused to trial.

If the governor is removed or vacates the office, the lieutenant governor becomes governor for the remainder of the elected term. The Texas Senate then elects a senator as acting lieutenant governor, who also serves as president pro tem until the next general election.

Compensation

The governor's annual salary is set by the legislature. Now at $115,345, it stands in marked contrast to the low salaries paid to legislators. However, nine other Texas state officials earn more than the governor.

The governor receives free use of the governor's mansion, and there is an expense account to keep it maintained and staffed. The governor has a professional staff with offices in the capitol. This is important, because a modern chief executive depends heavily on staff personnel to carry out the duties of office.

Staff

The growing role of the executive in legislative affairs, the need to make appointments, and increased demands on government by the general public have placed greater claims on the time and resources of the executive branch. The Texas governor—like all executives in modern government—depends on others for advice, information, and assistance when making decisions and recommendations. A good staff is a key resource for a successful chief executive.

Assisting the Governor. Some administrative assistants head executive offices that compile and write budget recommendations and manage and coordinate activities within the governor's office. Staff personnel also exercise administrative control over the governor's schedule of ceremonial and official duties. The governor's staff, although primarily designed to assist in the everyday duties of the office, also attempts to persuade legislators, administrators, and the representatives of various local governments to follow the governor's leadership in solving common problems.

Evaluating Appointees. Among the most important concerns of the governor's staff are political appointments. Each year, the governor makes several hundred appointments to various boards, commissions, and executive agencies. He or she also fills newly created judicial offices and those vacated because of death or resignation. Staff evaluation of potential appointees is necessary, because the governor may not personally know many of the individuals under consideration.

Legislative Liaison. Legislative assistants act as liaisons between the office of the governor and the legislature. Their job is to stay in contact with key legislators, committee chairs, and the legislative leadership. These assistants are, in fact, the governor's lobbyists. They keep legislators informed and attempt to persuade them to support the governor's position on legislation. Often, the success of the governor's legislative program rests on the ability and political expertise of the staff.

The Governor's Powers of Persuasion

A governor's ability to influence the creation and execution of government policy depends in part on his or her bargaining skills, persuasiveness, and ability to broker effectively among competing interests—the tools of persuasion. Thus, the **informal powers** of office are as important as the **formal powers** (those granted by the constitution or by law). The ability to use informal powers is largely determined by the extent of the formal powers.

Informal Powers
Powers not directly granted by law. The governor's informal powers may follow from powers granted by law but may also come from the governor's persuasive abilities, which are affected by the governor's personality, popularity, and political support.

Formal Powers
Legal powers granted to the governor by constitution or statute. Powers of this type, when exercised by the U.S. president, are called expressed powers.

Chief of State
Nationally, the head of state—the president of the United States, for example. In Texas and other states, the governor—who serves as the symbol of the state and performs ceremonial duties—is the chief of state.

Compared with the governors of other states (especially other populous, industrialized states), the governor of Texas has very weak formal administrative powers. Yet some Texas governors have been able to exert significant influence on policy formulation and execution. Generally, this occurs when the governor's formal and informal powers are enhanced by a blending of other conditions, such as the following:

- A strong personality
- Political expertise
- Prestige
- A knack for public relations and political drama
- Good relations with the press
- Supporters with political and economic strength
- A favorable political climate

The Governor as Chief of State

The governor, as the first citizen of Texas, serves as a symbol of Texas as surely as the bluebonnet or the pecan tree. A significant part of the governor's job is related to the pomp and ceremony of the office. These ceremonial duties include throwing out the first baseball of the season; greeting Boy Scout troops at the state capitol; visiting disaster areas; and riding in parades for peanut festivals, county fairs, and cow chip-throwing contests.

The ceremonial role of **chief of state** is important because it can contribute indirectly to the governor's leadership effectiveness through increased popularity and prestige. The governor also broadens the image of first citizen to that of first family of Texas whenever possible. Voters identify with the governor's family, and the governor's spouse often is included in photo opportunities, particularly if the spouse is photogenic and articulate.

The Governor as Party Chief

The governor usually maintains the leadership of his or her party by controlling the membership of its executive committee (though there may be varying degrees of competition from other elected officials and from political activists). The chair and a majority of the executive committee of the party are formally elected at the party's state convention but are typically selected by the governor.

Control of the party is a useful channel of influence for a governor. It permits what many consider to be one of the most effective tools of gubernatorial persuasion—rewarding supporters with political patronage. Influential party members who support the governor's party choices and proposals and who contribute to his or her election may be permitted to influence the several hundred appointments the governor makes each year.

Taking Positions on National Issues. National politics also affords the governor an opportunity to build a clear public image within Texas. The governor can take positions on political issues that do not involve the Texas government and that the governor cannot control (such as foreign aid and national defense), but that nevertheless are of great concern to the voters. State government issues are often difficult for voters to understand (because of the complexities of the issues or inadequate reporting by the media). As a result, the electorate can more easily make political identifications through national issues.

Legislative Tools of Persuasion

Ironically, the governor's most important bargaining tools are often legislative. How these tools are used frequently determines the governor's effectiveness.

The Veto. One of the most powerful formal legislative tools of the governor is the veto. After a bill has passed both chambers of the legislature (as described in Chapter 24), it is sent to the governor. If the governor signs the bill, it becomes law. If the governor vetoes the bill, it is sent back to the legislature with a message stating the reasons for the governor's opposition. The legislature has the constitutional power to override a veto by a two-thirds vote, but in practice vetoes are usually final.

Because legislative sessions in Texas are short, the vast majority of important bills are passed and sent to the governor in the final days of the session. The governor need take no action on the legislation for 10 days when the legislature is in session (20 days when it is not in session), so he or she can often wait until the legislature has adjourned, and thereby ensure that a veto will not be overridden. In fact, it is so difficult to override a veto that this has happened only once since World War II (1939–1945). Thus, the veto gives the Texas governor a strong bargaining position with legislators.

No Pocket Veto. The Texas governor lacks the pocket veto that is available to many other chief executives, including the president of the United States. A pocket veto permits an executive to kill legislation passed at the end of a session by ignoring it. If the Texas governor neither signs nor vetoes a bill, it becomes law without her or his signature. By not signing a bill and allowing it to become law, the governor may register protest against the bill or some of its sections.

The Item Veto. The single most important bill that the legislature passes is the appropriations bill. If it should be vetoed in its entirety, funds for the operation of the government would be cut off, and a special session would be necessary. Thus, Texas, like most other states, allows the governor an *item veto,* which can be used to veto funds for specific items or projects without killing an entire bill.

The item veto is potentially a very effective legislative tool. Funding is necessary to administer laws, so by vetoing an item or a category of items, the governor can, in effect, kill either programs or classes of programs. Because the appropriations bill is normally passed at the end of the session, the governor usually employs the item veto after the legislature has adjourned. As a result, there is no opportunity for an override.

The Threat of a Veto. An informal legislative power of the governor that is not mentioned in the constitution or the law is the **threat to veto.** This power nevertheless is a very real and effective tool, which depends on the formal power of the veto. Both the veto and the item veto are negative tools that simply kill bills or programs; they do not help the governor shape legislation. Threatening a veto is effective in this regard, however, because the legislature knows how difficult it is to override a veto, and usually lawmakers will at least partially meet the governor's wishes in response to such a threat.

Threat to Veto
An informal power by which a state governor (or the U.S. president) threatens to veto legislation so as to affect the content of the legislation while it is still in the legislature.

Bargaining. The governor's bargaining with legislators, lobbyists, and administrators is often intense. These other political forces may attempt to convince the governor to support, oppose, or maintain neutrality toward certain legislation. If the governor or the governor's political and financial supporters have not made this legislation an explicit part of their legislative program, avenues are left open for political bartering. Whoever seeks the governor's support must be willing to give something of real political value in return. All sides of the negotiation want to gain as much as possible and give as little as they can. There is, of course, a vast difference in political resources among politicians, just as there is among interest groups.

POLITICS AND... conflicts of interest

Political participation can take many shapes. Some vote; others join interest groups and political parties. Campaign contributions are the one form of political participation that is greatly welcomed by both candidates and political parties alike. Monetary contributions to political campaigns are appreciated greatly by candidates because of the growing cost of political campaigns. Gone are the days when political campaigns were inexpensive affairs. Political campaigns can cost millions of dollars, and Texas political campaigns are no exception. Races for the governor's seat have become costly affairs.

In 2006, gubernatorial candidates in Texas raised $53,434,828.[a] This was a huge sum of money to be raised in a state where Republicans have defeated Democrats by nearly two to one. Nevertheless, this was hardly the costliest gubernatorial race. In 2002, the gubernatorial candidates raised $125,326,728.[b] In this race, the Texas billionaire Tony Sanchez spent $66 million dollars for an unsuccessful bid for the governorship.[c] Governor Rick Perry spent $20,674,811, and was successful in defeating the Democratic challenger from Laredo.[d]

While candidates like Tony Sanchez have their own wealth to contribute to a political campaign, most candidates do not. Most rely heavily on the campaign contributions made by individuals, institutions, party committees, and other groups.[e] Many contributors may have business pending before the Texas legislature or the executive branch. The perception of conflict of interest abounds in politics. The public has strong disdain for lawmakers who offer favorable policies in exchange for campaign contributions. Such was the case with Governor Rick Perry's executive order requiring that all girls be immunized from the human papillomavirus, which causes cervical cancer. When it was revealed that the governor received a campaign contribution from Gardasil, the vaccine's manufacturer, the legislature reversed the governor's executive order.

The perception of conflicts of interest such as in the papillomavirus case is difficult to avoid in an environment where gubernatorial candidates must raise huge amounts of money to run strong campaigns. While the perception that candidates are beholden to special interest groups is firmly in place in the minds of the American people, some point out that because so many special interest groups make contributions, candidates do not have to be beholden to any one contributor or any one interest group. Others argue, however, that economically powerful interest groups do influence public policy since the opponents of the proposed policy may be either the aggregate, unorganized community or interests with few economic resources.

How do you think that elected officials' policy positions impact the campaign contributions that they receive? How do you think incumbency affects this?

a. National Institute on Money in State Politics, "Total Dollars for all Gubernatorial Candidates in Texas 2006," accessed July 25, 2008, at www.followthemoney.org/database.
b. National Institute on Money in State Politics, "Total Dollars for all Gubernatorial Candidates in Texas 2002," accessed July 25, 2008, at www.followthemoney.org/database/.
c. *Ibid.*
d. *Ibid.*
e. Corporations and unions are banned from making direct contributions to political candidates.

Special Sessions. As mentioned in Chapter 24, the constitution gives the governor exclusive power to call the legislature into *special session* and to determine the legislative subjects to be considered by the session. The legislature may, however, consider nonlegislative subjects, such as confirmation of appointments, resolutions, impeachment, and constitutional amendments, even if the governor does not include them in the call. Special sessions are limited to 30 days' duration, but the governor may call them as often as he or she wants.

did you know?

That in 2003, Governor Perry refused to take a position on controversial budget cuts and simply proposed a budget of $0.

Message Power. As a constitutional requirement, the governor must deliver a State of the State message at the beginning of each legislative session. This message includes the outline for the governor's legislative program. Throughout the session, the governor may also submit messages calling for action on individual items of legislation. The receptiveness of the legislature to the various messages is influenced by the governor's popularity, the amount of favorable public opinion generated for the proposals, and the governor's political expertise.

The **message power** of the governor is a formal power that is enhanced by the visibility of the office. Through the judicious use of the mass media (an informal power), the governor can focus public attention on a bill when it might otherwise be buried in the legislative maze. He or she must not overuse the mass media, however, for too many attempts to urge legislative action can result in public apathy toward all gubernatorial appeals. An effective governor "goes to the people" only for legislation considered vital to the interest of the state or to her or his political and financial supporters.

Message Power
The ability of a governor (or a U.S. president) to focus the attention of the press, legislators, and citizens on legislative proposals that he or she considers important. The visibility of the office gives the chief executive instant public attention.

Blue-Ribbon Commission
A commission composed of public personalities or authorities on the subject that is being considered. In Texas, such a commission may have both fact-finding and recommending authority.

Fact-Finding Commissions. Governors sometimes appoint **blue-ribbon commissions** consisting of influential citizens, politicians, and members of concerned special-interest groups. Such commissions can serve either as trial balloons to measure public acceptance of a proposal or as a means to provide information and increase public and interest-group support for a proposal. Blue-ribbon commissions are also commonly used to delay the actual consideration of a political "hot potato" until it has cooled. Politicians know that the attention span of the public is short and that other personally important issues, such as the Dallas Cowboys, jobs, and families, draw people's attention away from politics.

The Governor as Chief Executive

The Texas Constitution charges the governor, as the chief executive, with broad responsibilities. Yet it systematically denies the governor the power to meet these responsibilities through direct executive action. In fact, four other important elective executive offices are established in the same section of the constitution and are legally independent of the governor.

Other provisions in the constitution further fragment executive power. For example, the constitution establishes the Railroad Commission and states that its members are to be elected. It provides that the State Board of Education can be either elected or appointed. (It is elected independently of the governor.) Moreover, the Texas legislature, by statute, has systematically continued to assume executive functions such as budgeting and auditing. The legislature has also created the Department of Agriculture and a multitude of boards and commissions that are independent of direct gubernatorial control to administer state laws. Elected officials in Texas are shown in Figure 22–1. Given the present fragmented executive branch in Texas, few executive bargaining tools are available to the governor, making that officer one of the weakest state chief executives in the nation.

FIGURE 22–1 Elected Administrative Officials in Texas

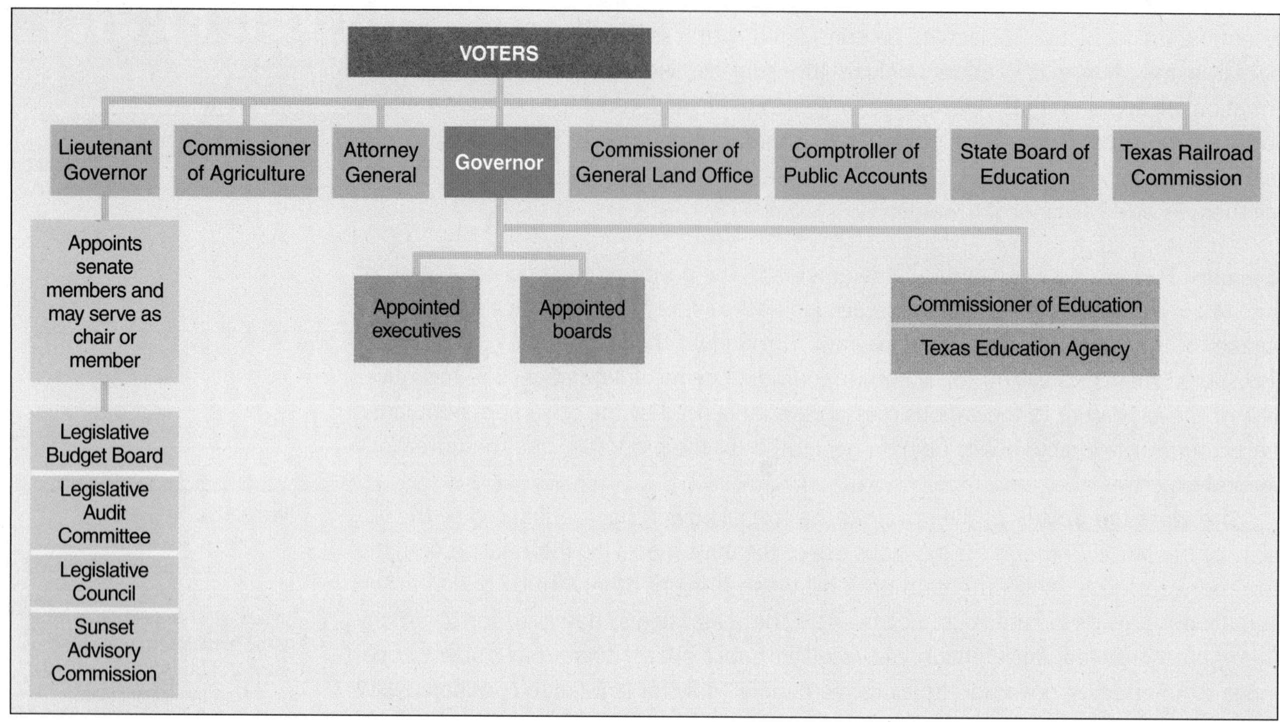

Appointive Powers

Boards and Commissions
In Texas, bodies consisting of three to 18 members that supervise most state agencies.

An effective governor will use the power of appointment to the maximum. Probably the most important appointments the governor makes are to certain independent **boards and commissions.** The members of these boards establish general administrative and regulatory policy for state agencies or institutions and choose the top administrators to carry out these policies.

The governor's ability to affect board policy through appointments is not immediate, however, because the boards are usually appointed for fixed, six-year staggered terms. Because only one-third of these positions become vacant every two years, the governor will have appointed a majority of the members of most boards only in the second half of his or her term.

The Influence of the Senate. The Texas Senate must confirm appointments, and individual senators have some influence over appointments from their districts as a result of the practice of *senatorial courtesy.* The senate will usually refuse to vote for confirmation if a senator announces that an appointee from his or her district is "personally obnoxious." The senators thereby show courtesy to the disgruntled senator by refusing to confirm his or her political enemy.

Judicial Appointments. The governor can exert a great deal of influence on the state's judiciary. It is common for judges to retire or resign before their terms end. The governor is empowered to fill these vacancies until the next general election. The result is that the governor is able to repay political supporters with judicial appointments, and the appointees enjoy the advantage of incumbency in the general election.

Removal Powers

Although the governor possesses broad powers of appointment, powers of removal are limited. She or he may remove members of the executive office and a few minor administrators. The governor may also remove—for cause and with the consent of two-thirds of the senate—his or her own appointees to boards and commissions. (The governor cannot remove those appointed by previous governors even through this difficult procedure.)

In general, the governor cannot issue directives or orders to state agencies, nor remove executive officials who do not abide by her or his wishes. If the governor believes that an official is administering the law so as to violate its spirit, there is no official way to force that official to administer the law differently. Only by focusing public attention on the agency and garnering public support can the governor force an administrator to change positions or resign.

Planning Powers

Mostly because of national government requirements concerning federal grants, the governor has gained some powers to engage in planning for state and local governments. With federal encouragement, the state government developed rudimentary coordination and cooperation activities to link the various government units and subunits in the state. The natural center for such statewide planning is the governor's office, which is in a position to determine whether grant requests are in accord with statewide plans. The result is some centralization of planning in the governor's office. The governor also serves as a member of (or appoints representatives to) many multistate organizations and conferences that work to coordinate relations between Texas and other states.

Texas created the Office of State-Federal Relations in Washington, D.C., to facilitate the governor's job of coordinating the activities of state agencies and local governments with the federal government. The governor appoints (and may remove) the director. The office provides information to state officials about federal initiatives and also advocates for the interests of the Texas government with Congress, the administration, and federal agencies. The governor may request federal aid when the state has suffered disaster, drought, or economic calamity. As chief of state, he or she often flies over or visits a disaster area to personally assess the damage—and also to show the unfortunate victims that the governor is concerned for their welfare.

Budget Powers

Many state executives find their power to propose a budget to the legislature important in dealing with state agencies. The Texas governor also is legally designated as the state's chief budget officer, and each biennium the various agencies and institutions submit their appropriation requests to the governor's staff and to the staff of the Legislative Budget Board (LBB). Working from these estimates, the governor and staff may prepare a budget based on both the state's estimated income and the estimated cost of program proposals. When completed, the budget is submitted to the legislature.

The independent Legislative Budget Board also submits a plan for state spending, however. Because the LBB includes the legislature's most powerful officers, the governor's budget may be largely ignored in favor of the LBB proposals.

Law Enforcement Powers

The governor has little law enforcement power. In the basic tradition of Texas government, law enforcement is decentralized. The governor does have the power to extradite fugitives from Texas law and to grant or refuse such requests from other states.

At the state level, the Texas Rangers and the Highway Patrol conduct law enforcement. Both agencies are under the administrative direction of a director of public safety, who is appointed by an independent board, the Public Safety Commission. At the local level, police functions are under the jurisdiction of county sheriffs and constables (who are elected) and city chiefs of police (who are appointed by city officials).

Criminal acts are prosecuted either by elected district or county attorneys or by appointed city attorneys. The judiciary, which tries and sentences criminals, is elective (except for municipal judges, who are appointed by city officials).

Military Powers

The governor is commander in chief of the state militia, which has two basic parts: the Texas National Guard and the Texas State Guard. The governor appoints (and can remove) an **adjutant general,** who exercises administrative control over both units.

Adjutant General
The principal staff officer of an army, who passes communications to the commanding general and distributes the general's orders to subordinates. In the example of the Texas National Guard and Texas State Guard, the "commanding general" is the governor. *Adjutant* comes from a Latin word meaning "helper."

Clemency
Relief from criminal punishment granted by an executive. In Texas, the power of the governor to grant clemency is strictly limited.

The governor may send units of the militia to keep the peace and protect public property (usually following a natural disaster). She or he may also employ the militia to "execute the laws of the state, suppress insurrection and repel invasions." The governor does not have the power to order evacuations in the event of terrorist attacks, hurricanes, or other natural disasters; only county judges have that power.

The Texas National Guard is made up of both army and air force components and is financed by the U.S. government. It must meet federal standards and may be called to active duty by the president. In the event the Guard is nationalized, command passes from the governor to the president.

The Texas State Guard was established during World War II and serves as a backup organization in the event the National Guard is called to active duty by the president. It cannot be called into active duty by the federal government, and its members receive no pay unless mobilized by the governor.

Clemency Powers

The 1876 constitution granted the governor virtually unlimited power to pardon, parole, and grant reprieves. Several governors were very generous with these powers, resulting in a 1936 constitutional amendment that established the Board of Pardons and Paroles. Many of the powers that had been held by the governor were transferred to the board, which grants, revokes, and determines the conditions for parole and makes **clemency** recommendations to the governor. The governor appoints the board's membership and can grant less clemency than recommended by the board, but not more. He or she can no longer exercise a check on the parole process by blocking early releases from prison. The governor can postpone executions for 30 days.

Governor Perry visits Texas troops in Baghdad. (Photo courtesy of the Governor's Office)

The Texas Bureaucracy

The most distinctive characteristic of the Texas administration is that no one is really in charge of the administrative apparatus. As in many other states, the administration of laws in Texas is fragmented into several elective and many appointive positions. No single official in the Texas government bears the ultimate responsibility for the actions of the Texas bureaucracy, and no single official can coordinate either planning or program implementation among the many agencies, commissions, and departments. The Texas bureaucracy can be visualized as more than 200 separate entities, each following its own path, often oblivious to the goals and ambitions of other agencies. Texas, in other words, has a *plural executive* system.

Elected Executives

The constitutional and statutory requirement that several administrators (in addition to the governor) be elected was a deliberate effort to decentralize administrative power and prevent any one official from gaining control of the government. Under the Texas plural executive system, the governor shares executive power with several other independently elected executives and boards.

These elected officials are directly responsible to the people rather than to the governor. The fact that few Texans can name the individuals who hold these offices, much less judge their competence or honesty, tends to weigh against the theory that the popular election of multiple administrators enhances democracy.

Lieutenant Governor David Dewhurst is shown here during a campaign stop in 2006. He won the election with almost 60 percent of the vote. Does the lieutenant governor in Texas necessarily work with the governor to form a "team"? Why or why not? (Photo courtesy of the Lieutenant Governor's Office)

Lieutenant Governor. Although the lieutenant governor technically is part of the executive branch, the source of his or her power comes from the legislative branch. The lieutenant governor, as president of the senate, is the *ex officio* co-chair of the Legislative Budget Board, the Legislative Council, and the Legislative Audit Board and, if he or she desires, exercises considerable personal influence in the Sunset Advisory Commission and the Legislative Criminal Justice Board. (You learned about most of these bodies in Chapter 24.) These legislative boards and commissions are not part of the bureaucracy, but they conduct continuing studies of administrative policies and make recommendations to the legislature. The lieutenant governor is also the acting governor when the governor is outside the state, and would succeed the governor upon a vacancy in the office.

Attorney General. The attorney general is elected for a four-year term and holds one of the four most powerful offices in Texas government. The attorney general is the lawyer for all officials, boards, and agencies in state government. The legal functions of the office range from antitrust actions and consumer protection to activities concerning insurance, banking, and securities. A broad spectrum of the state's business—oil and gas, law enforcement, environmental protection, highways, transportation, and charitable trusts, to name only a few—is included under the overall jurisdiction of the attorney general.

> **Attorney General's Opinion**
> An interpretation of the state's constitution or laws by the state attorney general. Officials may request such opinions, and although the opinions are not legally binding, they are usually followed.

The attorney general performs two major functions: (1) to give advisory opinions to state officers and (2) to represent the state in major civil actions. Because Texas courts, like other American courts, will not issue advisory opinions or rule on hypothetical cases, the attorney general's opinions perform this function. As the state's lawyer, the attorney general advises his or her clients on the meaning of the constitution, state law, and administrative regulations. Although these **attorney general's opinions** are no more than legal advice, they are in effect a quasi-judicial opinion that fills the gap between legislative statute or administrative regulation and judicial interpretation. Although the opinion lacks official enforcement authority, the fact that the attorney general will not defend ignored opinions in court usually ensures compliance by legislators and administrators.

The attorney general also represents the state and the state government in civil litigation, including conflicts with the national government. The attorney general has defended Texas positions on such past issues as the poll tax and segregation and on current issues such as:

- Abortion
- Obscenity laws
- Challenges to state legislative districts
- Affirmative-action programs

Texas Attorney General Greg Abbott, with a playground behind him, discusses with the media his crackdown on child sex predators. (Photo courtesy of the Attorney General's Office)

Susan Combs is the Texas state comptroller. As manager of the state's financial activities, she holds a powerful position. (Harry Cablluck/AP Photo)

The attorney general also initiates suits in cooperation with the governments of other states on antitrust violations or consumer protection. For example, the Texas attorney general, along with the attorneys general from most other states, sued the tobacco industry to recover the state's Medicaid expenses for tobacco-related injuries. The attorney general's power to prosecute crimes is relatively narrow, however, because the primary responsibility for criminal prosecution in Texas lies with the locally elected district and county attorneys.

Comptroller of Public Accounts. The comptroller, who has become one of the state's most powerful officials, is elected for a four-year term to manage most financial activities of state government. She or he is the state's chief tax collector, accountant, and treasurer. The constitution requires that the comptroller certify the estimated two-year state revenue, and the state legislature may not constitutionally appropriate more than the comptroller certifies.

The comptroller also certifies the financial condition of the state at the close of each fiscal year. The governor and legislature are anxious to learn if they must reduce spending or increase taxes. (Unlike the federal government, Texas cannot simply balance the books by borrowing.) In recent years, the economy has forced them to do both. In better times, the legislature has had the luxury of increasing spending.

Commissioner of the General Land Office. The commissioner of the General Land Office is elected for a four-year term. Principal duties of the commissioner are managing public lands and leasing mineral rights beneath them and overseeing riverbeds, tidelands, bays, and inlets.

The land commissioner also serves *ex officio* on several boards and chairs the important Veterans' Land Board and the School Land Board, whose programs are administered by the General Land Office. The Veterans' Land Board lends sums to veterans for land purchases and home purchases and improvements. The School Land Board oversees approximately 20 million acres of public land and mineral rights properties, a large portion of which are dedicated to the **Permanent School Fund** (for public schools) and the Permanent University Fund, which benefits the University of Texas and Texas A&M University.

Permanent School Fund
In Texas, a fund that provides support to the public school system. Leases, rents, and royalties from designated public school lands are deposited into the fund.

Commissioner of Agriculture. The commissioner of agriculture is elected for a four-year term to oversee the Texas Department of Agriculture. The department has more than 500 employees and is responsible for the administration of all laws relating to agriculture, as well as research, educational, and regulatory activities. The duties of the department range from checking the accuracy of scales in meat markets and gas pumps at service stations to determining labeling procedures for pesticides and promoting Texas agricultural products in national and world markets. The commissioner also administers the Texas Agricultural Finance Authority, which provides grants and low-interest loans to businesses that produce, process, market, and export Texas agricultural products. The possibility of conflict between the interests of producers and the interests of consumers is ever present in the department's activities.

Appointed Executives

The governor of Texas does have the power to appoint a limited number of officials. In general, these officials are less powerful than the ones who are directly elected by the public.

Secretary of State. The governor appoints the secretary of state with confirmation by the state senate. The secretary of state is keeper of the seal of the state. She or he serves as the chief election officer for Texas, administers Texas election laws, maintains voter-registration records, and receives election results. The office of the secretary of state provides a repository for official, business, and commercial records required to be filed with the office. The secretary publishes government rules and regulations and commissions notaries public. By executive order, Governor Rick Perry has also directed the secretary of state to serve as his liaison for Texas border and Mexican affairs and to represent him and the state at international and diplomatic occasions.

Adjutant General. The adjutant general is appointed by the governor with the consent of the senate for a two-year term. The adjutant general serves as the state's top-ranking military officer and exercises administrative jurisdiction over the Texas National Guard and Texas State Guard. These are among the few state agencies under the direct administrative control of the governor.

Commissioner of Health and Human Services. The office of commissioner of health and human services was created in the first special session in 1991 and is filled by the governor with the consent of the senate for a two-year term. The commissioner heads an umbrella agency that oversees and manages 11 health and welfare agencies.

Insurance Commissioner. The commissioner of insurance is appointed directly by the governor for a two-year term, subject to senate confirmation. The commissioner oversees the Department of Insurance, which monitors and regulates the Texas insurance industry. The department provides consumer information; monitors corporate solvency; prosecutes violators of insurance law; licenses agents and investigates complaints against them; develops statistics for rate determination; and regulates specific lines of insurance such as property, liability, and life insurance.

Boards and Commissions

Texas government includes at least 200 boards and commissions. These administrative bodies may be elective, appointive, *ex officio,* or some combination of the three. Members may be salaried or may serve only for reimbursement of expenses. Boards differ considerably in their political power. Generally speaking, the most important boards are those that affect the largest number of people and have the largest budgets. Other important boards charter or regulate the state's business, industrial, and financial powers. Their rules and regulations, which often have the force of law, are called **administrative law.**

Administrative Law
Rules and regulations written by administrators to implement laws. The effectiveness of a law is often determined by how the corresponding administrative law is written.

Elective Boards—The Railroad Commission. One of the most important state regulatory boards in the United States has been the Texas Railroad Commission, a constitutionally authorized elective board whose three members serve for overlapping six-year terms. The governor fills any midterm vacancies on the board, and these appointees serve until the first election, at which time they may win election to the board in their own right.

The board is politically partisan, and its members must first win their party's nomination before running in the general election. The chair position is rotated so that each member becomes the chair during the last two years of his or her term. This forces any candidate who is challenging an incumbent commissioner to run against the chair of the commission.

The commission regulates gas utilities, oil and gas pipelines, oil and gas drilling and pumping activities, and intrastate railroad transportation. It is also responsible for regulation of waste disposal by the oil and gas industry and the protection of both surface and subsurface water supplies from oil- or gas-related residue. Formerly, the Railroad Commission

This screen capture from the Texas Railroad Commission web site shows its three Republican commissioners. From left are Elizabeth A. Jones (chair), Michael L. Williams, and David Porter. To what extent may declining production of oil and natural gas reduce the importance of the commission in the future? (Photos courtesy of the Texas Railroad Commission and the Governor's Office)

(RRC) regulated **intrastate** truck freight in Texas, but the national government preempted the commission's powers in this area because the RRC's rules of regulation interfered with **interstate** commerce.

Elective Boards—The State Board of Education. The elected State Board of Education (SBOE) sets policy for the Texas Education Agency (TEA), which oversees and regulates the Texas public school system below the college level and administers national and state education law and SBOE rules and regulations. The TEA writes regulations for and compels local compliance with legislative and judicial mandates and reforms, dispenses state funds, serves as a conduit for some funds from the national government to the local schools, and approves the textbooks to be purchased at state expense for use by local districts.

Members of the SBOE are elected on a partisan basis from 15 single-member districts and serve four-year staggered terms. The governor appoints the chair for a two-year term from the SBOE membership. The SBOE establishes policy, implements policy established by law, and, as mentioned, oversees the TEA. The board also recommends three nominees for commissioner of education (the TEA's chief executive officer), who is appointed by the governor with the senate's consent to a four-year term.

Intrastate
Within the state.

Interstate
Between two or more states.

***Ex Officio* Boards.** A number of boards have memberships that are completely or partially *ex officio*—that is, some or all of their members belong automatically because of other offices they hold. There are two basic reasons for creating such boards. One is that when travel to Austin was expensive and time consuming, it seemed logical to establish a board consisting of persons already in Austin. Another reason is that *ex officio* members may have relevant subject-matter expertise.

The Texas Bond Review Board is an example of an *ex officio* board. It has four *ex officio* members—the governor, the lieutenant governor, the speaker of the house, and the comptroller of public accounts—and has 12 full-time employees. It reviews and approves all bonds and other long-term debt issued by state agencies and universities. It also engages in various other functions pertaining to state and local long-term debt.

A number of agencies' boards have some *ex officio* members. The Agriculture Resources Protection Authority (15 members, nine *ex officio*), the Texas Cosmetology Commission (seven members, one *ex officio*), and the Texas Turnpike Authority (12 members, three *ex officio*) are examples of such boards.

Appointive Boards. Appointive boards vary extensively in importance, administrative power, and salary. The members of these boards, who are usually not salaried, set the policies for their agencies and appoint their own chief administrators. The governor, with the consent of the senate, usually appoints board members, but there are many mixed boards whose members are appointed by the governor or by some other official or whose membership is partially *ex officio*. Due to the usual practice of appointing members to staggered terms, six years may lapse before a governor can appoint a complete board.

Board appointees are often representatives of groups that have an economic interest in the rules and policies of the board. Appointments may be either a reward for political support or an attempt to balance competing interest groups whose economic well-being is affected by board rules and policies.

The governor can remove board members before the expiration of their terms only if he or she appointed those board members, and then only with the concurrence of two-thirds of the senate. The governor may encourage board members to resign, however, by publicly criticizing the members or policies of a board.

The Bureaucracy and Public Policy Neutrality

Texans have not only decentralized public functions, but they have also attempted to depoliticize the bureaucracy by establishing the independent board and commission system. This is an attempt to insulate the bureaucracy from the politics of the legislature and the governor.

Attempts to depoliticize the bureaucracy, however, have simply replaced one kind of politics with another. Most political observers today agree that the Texas bureaucracy is deeply engaged in politics, that politics strongly affects public policy, and that policy formulation cannot be separated from policy administration. Public administration is "in politics" because it operates in a political environment and must seek political support from somewhere if it is to accomplish goals, gain appropriations, or even survive. The result of strong political support for an agency is increased size, jurisdiction, influence, and prestige. The less successful agency may suffer reduced appropriations, static employment, narrowed administrative jurisdiction, and possibly extinction. Where, then, does a unit of the bureaucracy look for the political support so necessary for its well-being? It may look to clientele interest groups, the legislature, the chief executive, and the public. Political power also comes from factors within the bureaucracy, such as expertise, control of information, and discretion in the interpretation and administration of laws.

Public Support

Good public relations benefits any agency, both in appropriations and jurisdictional battles with other agencies. Favorable propaganda, myth, and literature create broad-based public support for such agencies as the Texas Department of Criminal Justice, the Texas Rangers, and to some extent, the Texas Highway Patrol.

Clientele Groups. The most natural allies for an agency are its **clientele** (or constituent) interest groups—the private groups that benefit directly from agency programs. At the national level, examples of close-knit alliances of interest groups and agencies are defense contractors and the Department of Defense, agribusiness and the Department of Agriculture, and the airlines and the Federal Aviation Administration. In Texas, close bedfellows include the Texas Good Roads and Transportation Association and the Texas Department of Transportation; the oil, gas, and transportation industries and the Texas Railroad Commission; the banking industry and the Department of Banking; and the Texas Medical Association and the Department of Health.

Clientele
Persons represented by a government agency or a politician.

The Agency-Clientele Alliance. Agitation by interest groups often leads to the establishment of a state agency, and the agency's power and importance may be directly related to the power and influence of its clientele groups and the intensity of their support. The agency and its clientele groups are therefore usually allied from the very beginning, and this alliance continues to grow and mature as mutual convenience, power, and prosperity increase. Economic and political ties are cemented by mutual self-interest. Agencies and clients share information, have common attitudes and goals, exchange employees, and lobby together with the legislature for both agency appropriations and government policies that favor the interest groups.

Reciprocity. Mutual accommodation has become so accepted that clientele groups often speak of "our agency" and devote considerable time and funds to lobbying for it. The agency reciprocates by protecting its clients within the administration. Of course, both the bureaucracy and the various clientele groups are made up of many entities, and there is often competition for appropriations, so both agencies and special interests seek allies in the legislative branch.

The Legislature, the Lieutenant Governor, and the Speaker

Bureaucratic power is enhanced by the support of powerful legislators, often including the chairperson of the committee that exercises legislative oversight over the agency. The agency depends on legislative allies for laws that expand its powers, increase the scope of its duties, protect it from unfriendly interests, and appropriate the funds for its operation. Therefore, administrators seek the favor of influential lawmakers.

Although the committee chairs are important in the Texas legislature, the short session and the power of the presiding officers limit their influence. For this reason, an agency seeks the support of the lieutenant governor and the speaker of the house, as well as members of the finance and appropriations committees, the Legislative Budget Board, and the Legislative Council.

Campaigns for the Leadership. The importance of legislative support explains the intense lobbying activity that surrounds the appointment of legislators to powerful committees and the campaign activity that precedes election to positions of legislative leadership. If an interest group and its agency are unable to get allies appointed or elected to positions of influence in the legislature, they are forced to try to win support after the influential legislators are chosen—a more difficult endeavor.

The Revolving Door. Relationships among interest groups, agencies, and lawmakers can be enhanced by the exchange of personnel. The practice by which corporations employ former administrators and legislators as executives, lobbyists, or consultants is known as the **revolving door.** A government employee may resign and accept lucrative employment with an individual, a corporation, or some other organization that has profited financially by that employee's actions. In this environment, legislators, administrators, and regulators often become promoters of the regulated industry. The revolving door negatively affects public perception of public servants and prompts cynicism toward government.

Revolving Door
The interchange of employees among the legislature, government agencies, and related private special-interest groups.

The Governor

Although the governor has few direct administrative powers, agencies still need support from the governor. The governor's cooperation is especially important because of his or her power to appoint policy-making boards and commissions. Moreover, the governor's support gives the agency greater bargaining power with legislators and interest groups. The Texas governor can influence and shape agency programs and success through veto power as well as through appointments.

Agency employees develop shared attitudes, an esprit de corps, and a sense of communality with the employees of the agency's clientele interest groups. Because an agency's interests are usually similar to those of its clientele, both want the governor to appoint board members who will advance their mutual political goals.

The Iron Texas Star

The iron triangle model (first discussed in Chapter 14) is commonly used to provide a conceptual understanding of the alliance among legislative committees, administrative agencies, and economic special-interest groups (clientele groups). The iron triangle, however, is better as a description of the common interests that develop at the federal level than as a description of what happens in Texas. The Texas system can better be described using the **iron Texas star** model. The iron star has five points, not three. Figure 22–2 shows a model of the national iron triangle, while Figure 22–3 displays the iron Texas star.

Iron Texas Star
The Texas version of the iron triangle. A policy-making coalition that includes interest groups; the lieutenant governor and the speaker of the house; standing committees of the legislature; the governor; and administrators, boards, and commissions.

The Five Points of the Star. The coalitions that make policy in Texas can be thought of as consisting of the following five players:

1 and **2.** *Presiding officers and the legislative institutions and committees that they control.* Due to the hands-on authority exercised by the lieutenant governor and the speaker of the house of representatives, each of the presiding officers and the legislative institutions and committees that they control warrant a point on the Texas star. Although individual legislators often have independent political support, the power of the lieutenant governor and the speaker to select most of the membership and all of the chairs of the standing committees, the conference committees, and the legislative boards and commissions gives each presiding officer undeniable influence within both the legislature and the bureaucracy.

3. *Elected and appointed boards and elected administrators.* These individuals are also important players in the Texas political process. Usually appointed or elected with the support of economic special interests, these administrators and board members often possess political support independent of the legislature and the governor. Their influence within the bureaucracy itself is amplified due to the virtual absence of a civil service system for Texas government employees, making them especially vulnerable to political influence.

4. *The governor.* Strong legislative, appointive, and other powers ensure the inclusion of the governor as the fourth point on the Texas star.

5. *Economic interest groups.* These groups provide campaign funds for elected officials, political and financial support for friendly legislators and administrators, and employment and investment opportunities for former, present, and future state officials.

FIGURE 22–2 The National Iron Triangle

Interest Groups
Legislative Committees
Administrative Agencies

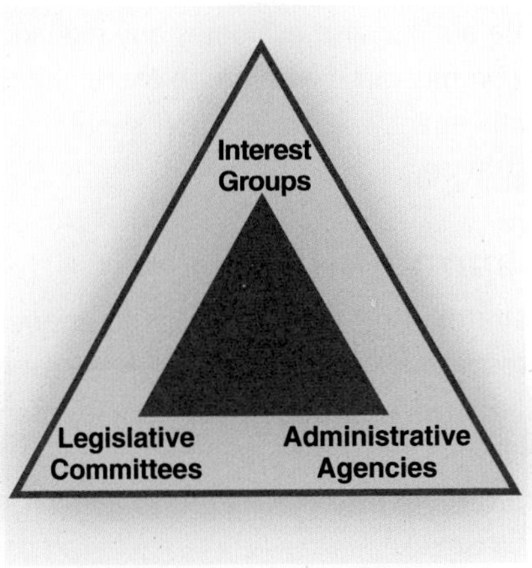

FIGURE 22–3 The Iron Texas Star Model

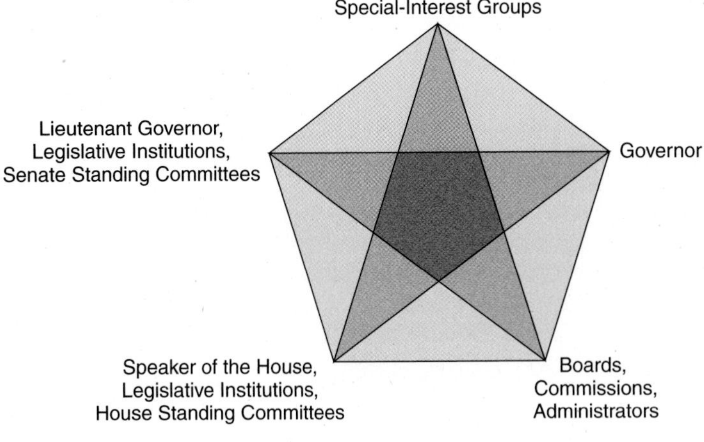

Economic special interests provide both the plans and the mortar that builds and holds together the five-cornered coalition that we call the Texas government.

Acquiring "Friends." The basic goal for special interests is to accumulate "friends" in the policy-making and regulatory areas of government. It is equally critical for political operatives to acquire friends among economically powerful individuals and special-interest groups. The members of the coalition also support the friends of their friends at the other points of the iron star, and thereby develop a system of mutual support from which all can benefit.

Legislators, administrators, the presiding officers, and the governor rely to varying degrees on the support of their interest-group friends for campaign contributions, supplemental income, political advancement, financial advice and opportunity, and after-office employment and income. As time passes and members of the coalition become more interdependent, each looks to the others for support. Legislators bargain for the interest of the coalition in the legislature. Administrators issue favorable regulations and support their friends' viewpoints in administrative decisions. The presiding officers may shepherd the proposals of their friends through the legislative process and also place the friends of economic special interests on powerful legislative committees and legislative boards and commissions. Finally, the governor appoints friends and friends of friends to various boards and commissions that make policy affecting these same friends. Other government officials may also broker with political operatives for decisions favorable to their friends in the iron star coalition.

Again, the Revolving Door. Appointees to boards and administrative positions are usually chosen from the industry concerned, and the policy decisions they make tend to benefit the most influential operatives in the industry. In turn, when government employees leave government service, many find jobs in the industry where their expertise lies. This interchange of employees between the public and private sectors is the revolving door we mentioned earlier in this chapter, and it undermines the independence of government employees. Literally hundreds of former administrators and legislators work for special interests as lobbyists, consultants, and executives.

The Sunset Advisory Commission. As an important oversight step, the Texas legislature established the Sunset Advisory Commission in 1977 to make recommendations on whether to alter, terminate, or continue most state boards, commissions, and agencies. Currently, about 150 state administrative entities and their operations are reviewed periodically, usually in 12-year cycles. At the end of its cycle, an agency ceases to exist unless the legislature takes specific action to renew it. If an agency is renewed, the Sunset Commission evaluates its compliance with legislative directives. In addition, agency functions may be expanded, diminished, or reassigned to other agencies by legislative action. The state auditor also evaluates any management changes recommended by the commission. Some argue that periodic legislative evaluation together with agency self-evaluation should result in better, more efficient administration.

did you know?

That at the beginning of this decade, Southwestern Bell's parent corporation (SBC) had seven former state legislators on its payroll as lobbyists? SBC was one of several clients that paid more than $1 million to former attorney general Dan Morales, who had supported a Southwestern Bell suit to gain early entry into the long-distance market.

Bureaucratic Responsibility

To whom is a Texas administrator really responsible? The answer may well be to the economic interest groups that benefit from the programs that the officer administers. Politics works on the basic principles of mutual accommodation among allies, conflict among opponents, coalition building, and compromise. Agency officials are often obligated to administer the laws and make policy decisions in ways that support the goals and aspirations of their political allies among private economic interests.

Open Meetings and Open Records. How, then, can the Texas administration be made more accountable to the public? There is no single answer. More openness in government offers one possibility. A basic concept of democratic government is that policy made in the name of the public should be made in full view of the public. Texas has made great strides in this area.

Open-meetings laws require that meetings of government bodies at all levels be open to the general public, except when personnel, land acquisition, and litigation are discussed. The laws further prohibit holding unannounced sessions and splitting up to avoid a quorum, and they require that public notice be posted for both open and closed sessions. These laws are continuously being tested by policy makers, however, who feel more comfortable operating in secret.

Open-Meetings Law
A law that requires meetings of government decision-making bodies to be open to public scrutiny (with some exceptions).

Open-Records Law
A law requiring that records of all government proceedings and decisions are made available to the public.

Openness is further encouraged by the state's **open-records law,** which requires that records of all government proceedings and decisions be available to the public. The only cost in obtaining such records is the expense involved in assembling and reproducing them, which is low when using the Internet.

Whistle-blowers and Ombudspersons. Another source of openness is whistle-blowers—government employees who expose bureaucratic excesses, blunders, corruption, or favoritism. These employees could be commended and protected from retribution, but too often they are instead exiled to the minor agencies or fired for their effort. To its credit, the Texas whistle-blowers' law prohibits governments from acting against employees who report law violations. Enforcement is difficult and time consuming, however. Whistle-blowers must often hire attorneys at great expense and lose years of their careers.

Still another option is for government to provide an ombudsperson, an official who hears and investigates complaints by private individuals against public officials or agencies. The appointment of ombudspersons at every level of government would give individuals increased access to the bureaucracy and a single impartial office with which to lodge complaints against administrative decisions.

WHY SHOULD YOU CARE ABOUT... STATE AGENCIES?

The state's executive branch follows many antiquated traditions, but state agencies are beginning to join the information age and provide a wealth of information and conveniences to residents. Some agency Web sites are not user friendly, but many provide information that can serve as an excellent original source for academic research. Quite a few of these sites also offer online services that can make life easier for Texans.

BECOME A SMART CONSUMER

Democracy depends on an informed electorate. In addition, Texas state agencies provide vital services, and students may benefit directly from many of those services. Some of the best information about crime is available online at the Texas Department of Public Safety site, for example. The most comprehensive analyses of tax and spending issues are available through the Texas Office of the Comptroller of Public Accounts and the Legislative Budget Board.

HOW YOU CAN MAKE A DIFFERENCE

You can browse through the Legislative Budget Board's latest *Fiscal Size-Up, 2006–2007* at **www.lbb.state.tx.us** to see what services the state offers. From which of these services can you benefit? Guaranteed student loans and grants are one possibility.

You can contact the Consumer Protection Division of the Office of the Attorney General to learn about your rights and how to exercise them. Also available are copies of the Deceptive Practices Act and consumer brochures. The office provides instructions on how to file a complaint, along with a copy of a consumer complaint form. You can contact the office at:

Consumer Protection Division Office
of the Attorney General
P.O. Box 12548
Austin, TX 78711-2548
www.oag.state.tx.us/consumer/index.shtml

Complaints against health-care professionals can be lodged with the Health Professions Council at 800-821-3205.

Privately owned electric utility rates will no longer be set by the Texas Public Utility Commission. In the new competitive environment, shop for lower utility bills at **www.powertochoose.org**.

questions for discussion and analysis

1. What is the basic function of the executive branch of government? Does the Texas administration accomplish this function?
2. How does the structural organization of the Texas administration compare with that of the United States government?
3. Which organizational structure best meets the principles of accountability, openness, and administrative efficiency?
4. What is your concept of how government works, based on a comparison of the Iron Texas Star model with the more common descriptions of government processes?

key terms

adjutant general 716
administrative law 719
attorney general's opinion 717
blue-ribbon commission 713
boards and commissions 714
chief of state 710
clemency 716
clientele 721
formal powers 710
indictment 709
informal powers 710
interstate 720
intrastate 720
iron Texas star 723
message power 713
open-meetings law 725
open-records law 725
Permanent School Fund 718
quasi-judicial functions 707
quasi-legislative functions 707
revolving door 722
threat to veto 711

chapter summary

1. The government of Texas was conceived in the post-Reconstruction era, following an unfortunate and unhappy experience with a centralized, unpopular, minority government. Texas government has been systematically weakened and decentralized by both constitution and statute, reflecting voters' basic distrust of government in general and the executive branch in particular.
2. Distrust of the chief executive's power led the constitution's authors to establish a weak governorship as part of a plural executive system in which executive power is shared among many independently elected officers, as well as appointed boards and commissions.
3. As the executive branch evolved, the legislature established as many as 200 state agencies headed by appointed boards and commissions. These boards and commissions make general rules and appoint chief administrative directors. Although a governor has extensive powers to appoint members of boards and commissions, this appointive power does not give the governor effective control of state agencies. The governor usually does not appoint the actual administrators of state agencies.
4. The governor lacks meaningful removal, budgetary, or directive powers (to issue executive orders to state agencies). The result is an executive branch that is fragmented, uncoordinated, and insufficiently supervised. The governor is not a true chief executive.
5. To be effective, the governor, as the state's most highly visible officer, must develop the personal power to persuade. In addition to appealing to the public, the governor has strong legislative powers to veto bills (or, with the item veto, parts of bills) and to call special sessions. The patronage power to appoint board and commission members can be used to reward political allies and punish enemies.
6. In the absence of effective gubernatorial power, interest groups and legislative leaders usually fill the power vacuum. Bureaucrats and agency heads have greater latitude to follow their own agendas.
7. Important elected officials other than the governor include the following: (1) the lieutenant governor, who has a powerful role as the presiding officer in the senate; (2) the attorney general, who serves as the lawyer

for the state and can issue opinions on the legality of various measures and practices in response to official requests; (3) the comptroller of public accounts, who handles tax collection and state accounting tasks; (4) the commissioner of the General Land Office, who manages state-owned land and mineral rights; and (5) the commissioner of agriculture, who both serves the agricultural industry and oversees consumer protection laws.

8. Important officials who are appointed by the governor include (1) the secretary of state, who oversees elections and records; (2) the adjutant general, who is in charge of the Texas National Guard and Texas State Guard; (3) the commissioner of health and human services; and (4) the insurance commissioner. Major elective boards and commissions include the Railroad Commission, which regulates the oil and gas industries as well as intrastate rail services, and the State Board of Education, which oversees the Texas Education Agency.

9. Texas has adopted some administrative reforms. Although the state continues to use a patronage system of hiring with no systematic requirements to hire the most qualified, Texas has passed sunset legislation, open-meetings and open-records laws, and laws to protect whistleblowers. As with all modern governments around the world, the goal of holding bureaucrats accountable remains elusive.

selected print & media resources

SUGGESTED READINGS

Gantt, Fred, Jr. ***The Chief Executive in Texas.*** **Austin: University of Texas Press, 1964. This is the classic study of the governor's office in Texas.**

Gantt, Fred, Jr. ***The Impact of the Texas Constitution on the Executive.*** **Houston: Institute for Urban Studies, University of Houston, 1973. This book presents an analysis of the state constitution as it affects the executive branch and provides some insights by comparing the Texas governor with governors of other states. Some provisions in the Texas Constitution have been changed since the book was written.**

Gray, Virginia, and Russell L. Hanson. ***Politics of the American States: A Comparative Analysis.*** **Washington, DC: Congressional Quarterly, 2003. This publication offers an interesting comparison of politics in the various states.**

Prindle, David F. ***Petroleum Politics and the Texas Railroad Commission.*** **Austin: University of Texas Press, 1981. This book offers perhaps the best description available of relations between a Texas agency and its clientele group.**

MEDIA RESOURCES

The Best Little Whorehouse in Texas—**A lighthearted play and later a movie starring Dolly Parton and Burt Reynolds. It shows the governor's frustration with Texas values and the tradition of local control. Although based partly on fact, neither the play nor the movie reveals that the Texas attorney general finally closed the house with a public-nuisance civil suit.**

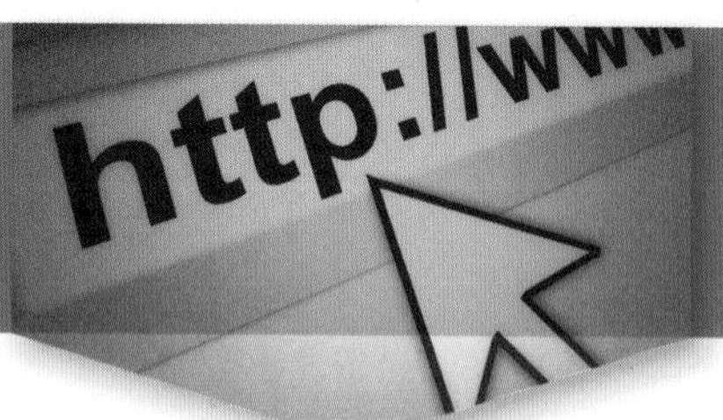

e-mocracy

CONTACTING THE GOVERNOR

You can send e-mail to the governor of Texas about an issue of concern to you. First, go to the governor's Web site, listed below. Click on "Major Initiatives." Select one of the priority issues for the governor in the upcoming term. Do some research on the issue by using a search engine or by visiting a few of the sites listed in other chapters of this textbook.

Once you have completed your research, go back to the governor's Web site to send a message. At the bottom of the home page is a button labeled "Contact." Click on that button, and scroll to the bottom of the next page. Click on "Electronic Mail," and an e-mail form will appear that will allow you to send your message to the governor's office.

LOGGING ON

The governor's Web site is located at:
www.governor.state.tx.us

From the governor's home page, you can investigate the governor's legislative initiatives. To check out the governor's appointive power, go to:
www.governor.state.tx.us/divisions/appointments

The governor's mansion, which is open to the public, is displayed at:
www.governor.state.tx.us/about/governors_mansion

For the governor's commander-in-chief powers, visit the site of the Texas adjutant general at:
www.agd.state.tx.us

Each of the statewide elected executives has a Web site. Notice how these officials try to outdo one another on their Web sites. The attorney general is at:
www.oag.state.tx.us

The comptroller of public accounts is at:
www.cpa.state.tx.us

The commissioner of the General Land Office is at:
www.glo.state.tx.us

The commissioner of agriculture is at:
www.agr.state.tx.us

The lieutenant governor is at:
www.senate.state.tx.us/75r/LtGov/Ltgov.htm

The key appointed executives also have Web sites. The site of the adjutant general is given above. The secretary of state is at:
www.sos.state.tx.us

The key elected boards have sites as well. The Texas Railroad Commission is at:
www.rrc.state.tx.us

The Texas Education Agency is at:
www.tea.state.tx.us

The Texas State Board of Education is at:
www.tea.state.tx.us/sboe

For a list of all state agencies, go to:
info.texas.gov
Scroll to "Government" and click on "State Agencies" to research the Texas bureaucracy. Select one agency, and go to its site to find out all you can. Does the agency have an e-mail address that you can use to contact it for more information?

ONLINE REVIEW

At **www.cengage.com/politicalscience/schmidt/agandpttexas14e**, you will find a Tutorial Quiz for this chapter, providing questions on the chapter contents, including the features. You'll gain access to other helpful study tools, including the book's glossary and flashcards, crossword puzzles, and Web links, as well as "Which Side Are You On?" and "Politics and . . ." features written by the authors of the book.

chapter
23

The Texas Judiciary, Law, and Due Process

chapter contents

Civil Law and Criminal Law

Issues in Civil Law

Issues and Elements in Criminal Law

Due Process of Law

Texas Court Organization

Selection of Judges

< Wallace B. Jefferson, chief justice of the Supreme Court of Texas. (AP Photo/Harry Cabluck)

American society has increasingly turned to the judiciary to find answers to personal, economic, social, and political problems. Courts are often asked to determine our rights. Important legal questions touch almost every aspect of our lives. For example, what level of privacy should we expect in our cars, offices, and homes? What level of safety and reliability should consumers expect from the merchandise they buy? Should manufacturers be responsible for work hazards and pollution at their factories? How about accountability for incompetence and neglect in hospitals? Should workers feel safe from discrimination at their workplaces? Should a convicted person go to jail, and if so, for how long? What about the death penalty, should it be abolished? These are among the thousands of questions asked and answered daily by courts in the United States.

In this chapter, our focus will be the Texas judicial system and general attributes of American legal procedure and *due process.* What will quickly become clear is the sheer size and complexity of the Texas court system. We describe political influences on the courts and examine how those influences create controversy about how we choose Texas judges.

Civil Law and Criminal Law

did you know?

That in 2007, Texas had the nation's ninth-highest crime rate—4,599.6 crimes per each 100,000 in population.

America is often considered the most litigious (anxious to go to court to settle differences) society in the world. We have approximately one-quarter of the world's lawyers.[1] There are more than 1 million attorneys in the United States today.[2] In 1951, one out of every 700 people was a lawyer; today, that figure is now about one out of 342.[3] Cases in American courts have included, for example, a legal action by parents blaming McDonald's food for obesity in teens, a $54 million lawsuit by a judge against dry cleaners for losing his suit pants, a case in which a wife sued her husband for not shoveling the snow in front of their home, and a lawsuit in which a woman asked for $12 million because she was "pawed" and "humiliated" when a fur-costumed actor interacted with her during a Broadway performance of the musical *Cats.*[4] You should understand, though, that even if people file outrageous-sounding suits, it does not follow that they will win in court. There are few restrictions on what kinds of suits Americans can bring, even if they have little or no chance of success.

Litigation In Texas

Texas clearly fits into this general pattern of using the courts often. The Chamber of Commerce ranks Texas as having the 10th worst litigation environment in America.[5] In 2000, it had one attorney for every 309 people.[6] Texas also has more than 2,600 courts and approximately 3,200 justices or judges.[7] These courts dealt with more than 13 million cases in 2007—on average, more than one case for every two residents of the state.[8] In addition,

---

1. G. Alan Tarr, *Judicial Process and Judicial Policymaking,* 3rd ed. (Belmont, CA: Wadsworth Publishing, 2003), p. 107.
2. American Bar Association, "Lawyer Demographic," accessed February 2, 2008, at www.abanet.org.
3. U.S. Department of State, "Outline of the United States Legal System: Lawyers, Litigants, and Interest Groups in the Judicial Process," accessed April 2, 2006, at usinfo.state.gov/products/pubs/legalotln/lawyers.htm.
4. "Civil Wars," *Newsweek,* December 15, 2003, p. 45; "Scenes from a Maul: Suit Targets 'Cats,'" *Dallas Morning News,* January 23, 2003, p. 4A, and February 8, 1997, p. C6.
5. "Lawsuit Climate 2008: Where Does Your State Rank?," accessed October 1, 2008, at www.instituteforlegalreform.com/states/lawsuitclimate2008/.
6. American Bar Association, "National Lawyer Population by State," accessed February 2, 2008, from www.abanet.org; figures from the Census of 2000, quickfacts.census.gov.
7. *Annual Statistical Report for the Texas Judiciary, 2007,* p. 13; Texas Judiciary Online, "Texas Courts Online," accessed January 25, 2008, at www.courts.state.tx.us. We also wish to acknowledge Mia Romano and Jered Little for their efforts in this project.
8. *Annual Statistical Report for the Texas Judiciary, 2007.*

in recent years, Texas courts have heard important or controversial cases involving topics such as flag-burning, the death penalty, school desegregation, school finance, sexual orientation, and the freedom-of-association rights of the Ku Klux Klan, as well as a case involving two large oil companies, in which one was found liable for more than $10 billion.

Civil Law Versus Criminal Law

In the American legal system, court actions are generally classified as cases under either the civil law or the criminal law. Civil law concerns private rights and remedies and usually involves private parties or organizations (for example, *Smith v. Jones*), although the government may be involved. A personal-injury suit, a divorce case, a child-custody dispute, a breach of contract case, a challenge to utility rates, and a dispute over water rights are all examples of civil suits.

Criminal law involves violations of laws established by the government. If convicted, the lawbreaker may be punished by a fine or imprisonment, or both. The action is taken by the state against the accused (for example, *State of Texas v. Smith*). Typical examples of grounds for prosecution are arson, rape, murder, armed robbery, speeding, jaywalking, and embezzlement. With exceptions, the characteristics laid out in Figure 23–1 generally distinguish civil and criminal cases.

One of the most important distinctions between civil and criminal cases involves the issue of **burden of proof.** In civil cases, the standard used is a "preponderance of the evidence." This means that whichever party has more evidence or proof on its side should win the case. In a criminal case, however, the burden of proof falls heavily on the government, or prosecution. The prosecution must prove that the defendant is guilty "beyond a reasonable doubt." The evidence must overwhelmingly (without serious question or doubt) point to the defendant's guilt, or the defendant should be found not guilty.

In practice, judges determine our legal rights. Indeed, a large part of our system of laws is judge-made and dates back before the Texas Revolution—or even the American Revolution. This system is the "common law," and it can be traced back to medieval England, when judges began codifying standard answers to legal questions. When a state legislature or the U.S. Congress passes a law, the new statute takes precedence over the common law. Judges must also interpret the meaning of every new statute whenever there is a question that bears on a case. (AP Photo/Irwin Thompson)

Burden of Proof
In a court case, a party's duty to convince a judge or jury that the party's version of the facts is true. The standard of proof is higher in a criminal case than in a civil one.

FIGURE 23–1 Civil Law Versus Criminal Law

Civil Law	Criminal Law
1 Deals primarily with individual or property rights. Civil law involves a concept of responsibility but not guilt.	1 Deals with public concepts of proper behavior and morality as defined in law. The case is initiated by a government prosecutor on behalf of the public.
2 The plaintiff, or petitioner, is often a private party, as is the defendant, or respondent.	2 Specific charges of wrongdoing are spelled out in a grand jury indictment or a writ of information.
3 A dispute is usually set out in a petition.	3 On arraignment, the defendant enters a plea of guilty or not guilty.
4 A somewhat more relaxed procedure is used to weigh the evidence than in criminal law; the side with the preponderance of the evidence wins the suit.	4 Strict rules of procedure are used to evaluate evidence. The standard of proof is guilt beyond a reasonable doubt.
5 The final court remedy is relief from or compensation for the violation of legal rights.	5 Determination of guilt results in punishment.

Issues In Civil Law

Some argue that society has become too litigious. These people claim that frivolous lawsuits overcrowd court **dockets,** and excessive damages awards unnecessarily drive up insurance premiums and other business costs. When then-Texas Governor George W. Bush urged **tort reform** to limit awards for injury, he was supported by groups representing conservatives and defendants in civil actions, by the Texas Civil Justice League, by insurance companies, and by a wide range of business and medical interest groups.

As a result, the Texas legislature passed bills to restrict lawsuits by prison inmates, reduce frivolous lawsuits, limit liability in civil cases involving multiple defendants and government employees, enforce residency requirements for plaintiffs, and cap **punitive damages awards.** Texans narrowly approved a constitutional amendment to allow the legislature to limit all medical malpractice and other damages, such as those for pain and suffering, except actual economic damages. Are allegedly frivolous lawsuits sometimes more serious than one might gather from media reports?

Dockets
The schedule of court activity.

Tort Reform
In civil law, a tort is a wrong or injury (other than a breach of contract). Tort reform is an effort to limit liability in tort cases.

Punitive Damages Awards
A financial payment that may be awarded to a plaintiff in a civil case to punish the defendant and deter similar conduct in the future.

Felony
A crime—such as arson, murder, rape, or robbery—that carries the most severe sanctions, usually ranging from one year in prison to death.

Misdemeanor
A lesser crime than a felony, punishable by a fine or imprisonment for up to one year.

Issues and Elements In Criminal Law

Crime is a national issue, but despite the popularity of "law and order" as a campaign slogan in national elections, only 5 percent of crimes are prosecuted under federal law. The activities of the criminal justice system are primarily state, not federal, functions.

Congress has made the following crimes, among many others, federal offenses:

1. Those committed on the high seas.
2. Those committed on federal property, territories, and reservations.
3. Those that involve the crossing of state or national boundaries.
4. Those that interfere with interstate commerce.
5. Those committed against the national government or its employees while they are engaged in official duties.

Otherwise, most crimes are violations of state rather than federal law.

The Crime

As commonly used, the word *crime* refers to an act that violates whatever an authorized body (usually a state legislature) defines as the law. Many people obey the law simply because it is the law; others may obey out of fear of punishment. Attitudes and values usually determine whether a person will respect or disobey a law. If a law reflects the values of most of society, as the law against murder does, then it is usually obeyed. If, however, a large part of society does not accept the values protected by law, as happened with the national prohibition of alcoholic beverages in the 1920s, then violations become widespread.

Felonies are serious crimes. *Murder* is the illegal, willful killing of another human being. *Robbery* is attempting to take something from a person by force or threat of force. It is inaccurate to say that "a house was robbed"—only people can be robbed. Buildings are *burglarized*—unlawfully entered for the purpose of committing a felony or theft.

Theft (larceny) is simply taking property from the rightful possession of another. Grand larceny—taking something valued at more than $1,500—is a felony. In Texas, regardless of value, livestock rustling is a felony.

In Texas, it is a crime for a commercial fisher to possess a flounder less than 12 inches in length. Minors may not possess alcohol. Most traffic violations are crimes, and the resulting fine is a form of punishment. Such minor crimes are called **misdemeanors,** punishable by a sentence in a county jail, a fine, or both. We list the various types of felonies and misdemeanors in Texas in Table 23–1.

TABLE 23–1 Crime and Punishment under the Texas Penal Code

Offense	Terms*	Maximum Fine
Capital Murder Including murder of a police officer, firefighter, prison guard, or child under age six; murder for hire; murder committed during certain other felonies; and mass murder.	Life sentence or execution	
First Degree Felony Including aggravated sexual assault, theft of more than $200,000, robbery, noncapital murder, and sale of more than four grams of "hard" drugs such as heroin	5 to 99 years	$10,000
Second Degree Felony Including theft of more than $100,000 and burglary of a habitation	2 to 20 years	$10,000
Third Degree Felony Including theft of more than $20,000, drive-by shootings (that do not result in murder), and involuntary manslaughter	2 to 10 years	$10,000
State Jail Felony Including theft of more than $1,500, burglary of a building other than a habitation, sale of less than one gram of narcotics, auto theft, and forgery	180 days to 2 years probation**	$10,000
Class A Misdemeanor Including theft of more than $500, driving while intoxicated, resisting arrest, and stalking	1 year maximum	$4,000
Class B Misdemeanor Including theft of more than $50, possession of small amounts of marijuana, and reckless conduct (such as pointing a gun at someone)	180 days maximum	$2,000
Class C Misdemeanor Including theft of less than $50, smoking on a public elevator, and disorderly conduct (such as indecent exposure)	None	$500

*Punishments may be reduced for murder committed in "sudden passion" or may be enhanced to the next level if gang activity (involving three or more persons) or the use of deadly weapons is involved, if the person who committed the crime has had previous convictions, or if the murder is a hate crime (motivated by bias based on ethnicity, religion, or sexual orientation).

**Although probation must be granted, a judge may order a 60-day jail sentence as a condition for probation. If the conviction is for narcotics, the term may be one year. Repeat offenders are not given automatic probation.

Due Process of Law

The courts enforce the most general concepts of justice and the broadest norms of society against specific individuals. The courts must blend two conflicting goals of society:

1. To protect society according to the state's legal concepts of right and wrong.
2. To protect the rights of the individual charged with wrongdoing.

As a result of these conflicting goals, elaborate traditions of court process and procedure have developed over the centuries, dating back to when the American states were still colonies of Britain. Many of these traditional procedures derive from the English experience, whereas others were developed more recently in the American states. Some court procedures have been written into state and national constitutions and statutes; others are included in written and unwritten traditional codes of court process. Such procedures are designed to promote justice and protect the individual from the government, and together they constitute what is called **due process.**

Due Process
Established rules and principles for the administration of justice designed to safeguard the rights of the individual. The right to due process of law is provided by the U.S. Constitution and state constitutions.

Pretrial Court Activities

Following arrest, the suspect is jailed while reports are completed and the district attorney's office decides whether to file charges and what bail to recommend. As soon as is practical, the accused is presented before a justice of the peace or other magistrate for arraignment, at which time the court performs the following actions:

1. It explains the charges against the accused.
2. It reminds the suspect of the rights to remain silent, to be represented by counsel, and to request a written acknowledgment that the Miranda warning (see Chapter 4) was given and understood.
3. It sets bail.
4. It informs the accused of the right to an **examining trial**.

Examining Trial
A relatively uncommon procedure that may be requested by felony defendants in Texas. In an examining trial, a justice of the peace reviews the facts and decides whether a defendant should have to face trial in criminal court.

The Right to Know the Nature of the Accusation. The suspect is usually told the charges (1) on arrest, (2) in the arraignment, and (3) again in subsequent proceedings. Being told the nature of the charges against you is one of the most fundamental aspects of due process. Because the states have governments of "laws and not men," no one should be held in custody on a whim, but only for legal cause. Although a person need not necessarily be guilty of a crime to be held, there must be "probable cause" for the confinement. If it is determined that a person is being held unlawfully, counsel may secure release by a writ of *habeas corpus* (a court order requiring that the prisoner be presented in person and legal cause shown for imprisonment discussed in Chapter 4).

did you know?

That in 1999, the federal Fifth Circuit Court of Appeals reversed the death penalty conviction of Calvin Burdine because his attorney had slept during much of the trial.

The Right to Legal Counsel. The right to counsel is vital to the accused. Aside from clearly understanding the constitutional rights of an accused person, an attorney will be familiar with the baffling intricacies of the law. So important is the assistance of counsel that many suspects will contact an attorney before they appear in front of a magistrate. Yet this right to counsel has never been absolute.

Guaranteed in both the U.S. and Texas constitutions, the right to counsel was traditionally interpreted to mean that a person had a right to counsel if he or she could afford it. In 1932, the United States Supreme Court ruled that the Sixth Amendment requires state courts to appoint counsel for the poor, but only in capital cases.[9] Later, the Court extended the indigent's right to counsel to other felony cases and serious misdemeanor cases in which imprisonment might be involved, but the right does not extend to petty offenses such as traffic violations.[10]

The Right to Bail. Bail is the security required for the release of a suspect awaiting trial. When the suspect appears at trial, the bail is refunded. Some persons released on bail fail to appear in court, and their security is forfeited. Others commit still more crimes while on bail. The legal system presumes, however, that an individual is innocent unless convicted, and bail supports this assumption by permitting the accused to resume his or her professional and social life while preparing a defense.

The Texas Constitution guarantees the right to bail immediately after arrest, except when proof is "evident" in capital cases or when the defendant is being charged with a third felony after two prior felony convictions. The state constitution allows bail to be denied if the defendant is charged with committing a felony while released on bail or under indictment for another felony.

The Right to an Examining Trial. Although few defendants request one, in Texas the accused has the right to an examining trial in felony cases, as mentioned earlier. In an examining trial, a justice of the peace reviews the facts and decides whether the case should be recommended for criminal proceedings. If the facts warrant, the charges may be dismissed or bail adjusted.

---

9. *Powell v. Alabama,* 287 U.S. 45 (1932).
10. *Gideon v. Wainwright,* 372 U.S. 335 (1963); and *Argersinger v. Hamlin,* 407 U.S. 25 (1972).

Formal Charges

Although an *indictment,* or formal charge, sometimes precedes arrest, a felony case is usually bound over to a **grand jury** for indictment following arraignment. A grand jury should not be confused with a petit, or trial, jury. Grand juries do not determine a person's guilt or innocence, as trial juries do. Often, the accused does not even appear before the grand jury. The grand jury primarily weighs the evidence in the hands of the prosecutor to determine whether the case will be taken to trial. If the grand jury determines that the evidence could be sufficient to convict, it issues an indictment, which constitutes a formal charge that enables the case to go to trial.

A determination that the evidence is sufficient to convict is necessary, because if the prosecutor does not have enough evidence to convict, there is no point in bringing the case to trial. Trying a case on flimsy evidence not only costs the taxpayers financially, but it also costs the accused in terms of needless expense, lost time, and damaged reputation. The right to a grand jury indictment is guaranteed in both the Texas and the federal courts to protect innocent citizens against harassment on unjustified charges.

Grand Jury
A jury that sits in pretrial proceedings to determine if sufficient evidence exists to try an individual and, therefore, approve an indictment.

Change of Venue
A change in the site of a trial.

Plea Bargaining
Negotiations that take place between the prosecution and the defense in a criminal case in which the defendant normally is offered a lighter sentence or other benefits in return for a guilty plea.

Pretrial Hearings

After the indictment, the defendant has the right to another hearing, sometimes called the second arraignment. A district judge (rather than a justice of the peace) presides as the formal indictment is read and the defendant enters a plea. If the plea is guilty, a later hearing is scheduled to set punishment. Most often, the defendant pleads not guilty at this point, and the case is placed on the docket (schedule of court activity) for subsequent trial. A variety of motions may be presented, including a motion for delay or for the suppression of certain evidence.

The Insanity Defense. Another subject of pretrial hearings concerns possible insanity. A person cannot be held morally and criminally responsible for a crime if, at the time of the offense, mental disorder made it impossible for him or her to recognize that it was wrong. There is considerable controversy regarding the effects of mental disorder, so professional testimony may be necessary to establish legal insanity, and psychiatric opinion is frequently divided. The courts rarely find a defendant not guilty by reason of insanity.

Change of Venue. A change in the site of a trial (a **change of venue**) may be necessary when the news media have so publicized a case that an unbiased jury cannot be selected or when inflamed public opinion may prevent a fair trial. A real tension exists between the rights of the free press and the rights of the accused.

Plea Bargaining

Ideally, the trial is the final step in society's elaborate guarantees of due process. Yet for most of those who are accused of a crime, the final day in court never comes. In fact, the system is designed to discourage and even punish those who choose to exercise the right to a trial. Most cases end in a secret bargaining session with the prosecutor (**plea bargaining**).

Faced with overcrowded dockets and limited staffs, prosecuting attorneys usually meet with the accused and offer a deal in exchange for a plea of guilty, which eliminates the necessity of a trial. The usual deal is to offer to drop some of the charges, to recommend probation or a lighter sentence, or to charge the accused with a lesser

Andrea Yates drowned her five children in a bathtub after discontinuing antipsychotic drugs for 13 days. A second trial resulted in a verdict of not guilty by reason of insanity—an exceedingly rare outcome in Texas. Like most insane convicts, Yates will spend most, if not all, of her life in a mental institution operated by the Texas prison system. (Steve Ueckert/ AP Photo/Pool)

Deferred Adjudication
A procedure that allows a judge to postpone final sentencing in a criminal case; charges are dismissed if the defendant completes a satisfactory probationary period.

Adversary System
A legal system in which parties to a legal action are opponents and are responsible for bringing the facts and law related to their case before the court.

crime. The prosecutor may agree to delay prosecution (**deferred adjudication**) and later drop charges if the defendant agrees to meet certain probation-like conditions. Such agreements cut costs and court time, and may be useful to law enforcement when defendants are given a lighter sentence in exchange for acting as witnesses and testifying against fellow criminals.

The Trial

Unless the defense waives the right to a trial by jury, the first major step in the trial is the selection of a jury. The right to a jury trial is often regarded as one of the most valuable rights available in the U.S. criminal justice system. In fact, every state provides for trial by jury in all but the most minor cases, and Texas goes even further, providing for the right to trial by jury in every criminal case.[11]

Nevertheless, the right to trial by jury in a criminal case is one of the most frequently waived rights, especially in cases in which the defendant is an object of community prejudice (a member of an unpopular political group or ethnic minority) or in which the alleged crime is particularly outrageous. If the right to a jury trial is waived, the presiding judge determines the verdict. Regardless of whether a person chooses to exercise the right to trial by jury, that right remains a valuable alternative to decisions by possibly arbitrary judges.

Selecting the Jurors. During an initial questioning, prospective jurors may be asked about possible biases, their prior knowledge of the case, or any opinions they may have formed about the case. Either the prosecution or the defense may challenge a prospective juror for reason of prejudice, and the presiding judge will evaluate that challenge.

In addition to asking the judge to dismiss a prospective juror on the ground that he or she is prejudiced, both the prosecution and the defense may dismiss several jurors by *peremptory challenges* (challenges without cause). Experienced attorneys and prosecutors use peremptory challenges to eliminate jurors who may be hostile to their side of the case. The defense and the prosecution may consider the occupations, social status, and attitudes of possible jurors. In principle, race and gender are not legitimate grounds for peremptory challenges, but bias is hard to prove. Some lawyers have been known to employ psychologists to assist in the selection process, and lucrative consulting businesses have developed to assist attorneys in jury selection.

The Adversary System. The United States has an **adversary system,** in which two parties to the case (the prosecution and the defense in criminal cases) arm themselves with whatever evidence they can muster and battle in court, under the rules of law, to final judgment. An adversary system cannot operate fairly unless both the defense and the prosecution have an equal opportunity to influence the decision of the court. Hence, procedural guarantees are designed to ensure that both sides have equal access to (1) knowledge of the law and (2) the evidence. So that equal knowledge of the law is guaranteed, the legal knowledge of the prosecution is balanced by the right of the defendant to have legal counsel. Because the government (in the person of the prosecutor) has the power to seize evidence and to force witnesses to testify under oath, the defense must be given that same power (called *compulsory process*).

Presenting Evidence. In the adversary system, each side can challenge the material evidence and cross-examine the witnesses presented by the opposition. Only evidence

---

11. The United States Supreme Court held, in the case of *Duncan v. Louisiana,* 391 U.S. 145, 149 (1968), that trial by jury is an essential part of due process when state criminal proceedings involve more than petty offenses.

that is presented can be evaluated in court. The fact that both parties to a case have opposite biases means that each has an interest in concealing evidence that could benefit the opposition.

In jury trials, once the evidence has been presented, the presiding judge reads the charge to the jury; this charge constitutes the judge's instructions and the law that applies in the case. He or she will instruct the jurors to ignore such things as hearsay testimony and other illegal evidence to which they may have been exposed during the course of the trial. (Still, it is difficult for jurors to erase from their minds the impact of illegal testimony.) The judge is supposedly neutral and cannot comment on the weight of the evidence that has been presented.

Concluding the Trial. Following the judge's charge to the jury, the prosecution and defense are allowed to summarize the case. During their summary remarks, the prosecutor will argue that the evidence points toward guilt, and the defense will conclude that the evidence is insufficient to prove guilt beyond a reasonable doubt.

The jury then retires to decide between verdicts of guilty and not guilty. Texas law requires that all the jurors agree on the verdict in criminal cases. If the jury cannot agree, it is said to be a hung jury, and the judge will declare a **mistrial,** but the defendant may be tried again.

Sentencing. Regardless of whether the judge or the jury determines guilt, the judge usually prescribes a sentence, unless the defendant demands that the jury do so. After considering the character of the defendant, any past criminal record, and the circumstances surrounding the crime, the judge may assess a penalty between the minimum and maximum provided by law.

A first offender may be given **probation,** which allows her or him to serve the sentence in free society according to specific terms and restrictions and under the supervision of a probation officer. Similarly, deferred adjudication allows judges to postpone final sentencing in criminal cases; and after a satisfactory probationary period, the charges are dismissed. Judges have a great deal of latitude in assessing penalties, so the fate of a defendant will depend in large part on the attitudes of the presiding judge. Different judges sometimes assess vastly different penalties for similar crimes committed under similar circumstances.

did you know?

That Texas imprisons a larger percentage of its population than China, Russia, Cuba, or Iran.

Posttrial Proceedings

To protect the accused from double jeopardy, a person who is **acquitted** (found not guilty) cannot be tried again for the same offense. Protection from double jeopardy is much more limited than many citizens realize. In the event of a mistrial or an error in procedure, the trial may end in neither a conviction nor an acquittal. The defendant may then be tried for the same offense on the theory that he or she was never put in jeopardy by the first trial.

Multiple Charges. A person found not guilty of one crime may be tried for a related offense. For example, a person accused of driving 75 miles per hour through a school zone, going the wrong way on a one-way street, striking down a child in the crosswalk, and then leaving the scene of the accident may have committed several crimes. Being acquitted for speeding does not free the defendant of possible charges for each of the other offenses—they were separate crimes.

Likewise, such acts as bank robbery and kidnapping may violate both federal and state law, and the accused may be tried by both jurisdictions. Finally, even if a person is found not guilty of a crime, a victim of that crime can sue the defendant under civil law.

Mistrial
A trial judged to be invalid because of fundamental error. When a mistrial is declared, the trial may start again, beginning with the selection of a new jury.

Probation
A sentencing alternative to imprisonment in which the court releases convicted defendants under supervision as long as certain conditions are observed.

Acquitted
Found not guilty.

Because the standards of proof under civil law are lower than under criminal law, an acquitted individual may still be forced to pay monetary damages to the alleged victim or the alleged victim's heirs.

Appeals. A defendant may appeal a guilty verdict. Although the state cannot appeal a not-guilty verdict, because doing so would constitute double jeopardy, prosecutors may appeal the reversal of a guilty verdict by a higher court. Appellate procedure is designed to review the law as applied by lower courts. In most cases, the appellate court will not

POLITICS AND... judicial elections

In a four-year period, Texans are asked to elect more than a hundred public officials. Many of these are down-ballot candidates, candidates appearing toward the bottom of a ballot, who hold important positions but are not well-known by the electorate. Unlike federal judges, many of these are judicial candidates who are nominated by the president and approved by the Senate.

CREATIVE SENTENCING AND NAME RECOGNITION

Most Texas judges are elected to their positions. They know that very few voters know who they are, and yet they are beholden to the voters for their positions. One strategy that some incumbent judicial candidates are now employing is the use of creative sentencing. *Creative sentencing* is a punishment handed down by a judge that deviates from normal punishments. For example, a judge might sentence a man who slapped his wife to "yoga classes," as was the sentence handed down in January 2004 by Judge Larry Standley with the Harris County Criminal Court.[a]

Other judges have gone beyond what would be considered appropriate by most. In June 2004, Judge Michael Peters, another Harris County Criminal Court judge, sentenced a woman who starved her horses to "thirty days in jail and to have a diet restricted to bread and water for the first three days."[b] Judge Peters also sentenced a man found guilty of dumping chromium to drink water containing the substance.[c] Neither of these orders was carried out. The State Commission on Judicial Conduct admonished the judge for his use of creative sentences, stating, "Judge Peters failed to comply with the law and failed to act at all times in a manner that promotes public confidence in the integrity of the judiciary by issuing orders that he knew or should have known were unenforceable and in violation of state law."[d]

Congressman Ted Poe was successful at parlaying his judgeship into a Congressional seat by using creative sentences. Judge Poe used his power on the bench to punish law breakers with unusual sentences that got his name in the newspaper time and time again. In so doing, his constituents became sufficiently familiar with his name that when he ran for Congress in 2004, he had the name recognition to win a seat in Congress.

Judges often justify their use of creative sentencing by calling it a strategy to deal with overcrowding in jails and prisons. However, the press coverage judges receive for such rulings is a likely motivation for creative sentencing—and the more outrageous the ruling, the more press coverage.

FOR CRITICAL ANALYSIS

What do you think of judges using their power as a way of getting media attention? What do you think the benefits are to creative sentencing, if any? Does the electoral process ensure that judges with questionable ethics are kept off the bench?

a. Donna Leinwand, "Judges Write Creative Sentences," USA Today, February 24, 2004, accessed August 3, 2008, at www.usatoday.com.

b. State Commission on Judicial Conduct, "Public Admonition: Honorable Michael Peters Criminal County Court at Law Number 2 Houston, Harris County, Texas," *CJC* No. 04-1044-CC, May 4, 2006, accessed August 7, 2008, at www.scjc.state.tx.us.

c. *Ibid.*

d. *Ibid.*

assess the evidence. Its major concern is procedure. If serious procedural errors are found, the appellate court may return the case to a lower court for retrial. Such a retrial does not constitute double jeopardy.

Having exhausted the rights of appeal in the Texas courts, a very few defendants appeal their cases to the federal courts, which have jurisdiction in federal law. A ground for appeal to federal courts is the assertion that the state courts have violated the U.S. Constitution or other federal laws.

did you know?

That only Louisiana had a higher incarceration rate (number of prison inmates per 100,000 population) than Texas in 2007.

Texas Court Organization

Figure 23–2 outlines the organizational structure of the Texas court system. This figure shows the various types and levels of courts in the system. It should be noted that some courts within this rather large and complicated system have overlapping jurisdiction.

Municipal Courts

Although *municipal courts* are authorized by state statute, they are set up by incorporated cities and towns. Their status and organization are normally recognized in the city charter or municipal ordinances.

Legally, the municipal courts have exclusive jurisdiction to try violations of city ordinances. They also handle minor violations of state law—class C misdemeanors, for which the punishment is a fine of $500 or less and does not include a jail sentence. (Justice of the peace courts have overlapping jurisdiction to handle such minor violations.) Approximately 80 percent of the cases filed in municipal courts involve traffic violations.[12]

Courts of Record? The legislature has authorized city governments to determine whether their municipal courts are courts of record. Normally, they are not. When a municipal court is designated as a court of record, however, its records are the basis of appeal to the appropriate county court. (Only 0.2 percent of cases are appealed from municipal courts.)[13] Otherwise, records are not kept, and defendants may demand a completely new trial in overworked county courts, in which most such cases are simply dismissed. Where it is available, drivers frequently use this procedure to avoid traffic convictions and higher auto insurance rates.

Those favoring the court-of-record concept point to the large amount of revenue lost because new trials usually result in dismissal. Those opposing the concept argue that municipal courts are too often a means of raising revenue rather than achieving justice. Municipal courts collect more than $500 million per year, giving some support to the latter argument.

Judicial Qualifications and Selection. Judges of the municipal courts meet whatever qualifications are set by the city charter or ordinances. Some cities require specific legal training or experience. Other charters say very little about qualifications. In 2007, 50 percent of municipal court judges were licensed attorneys. Judges may serve one year or indefinitely. Most are appointed for two-year terms but serve at the pleasure of the governing bodies that have selected them. Furthermore, these judges' salaries are paid entirely by their respective cities and vary widely. Where statutes permit, some cities have established

12. *Annual Statistical Report for the Texas Judiciary, 2007,* p. 53; Texas Judiciary Online, accessed January 29, 2008, at www.courts.state.tx.us/pubs/AR2007/AR07.pdf.
13. *Ibid.,* p. 55.

FIGURE 23–2 Court Structure of Texas

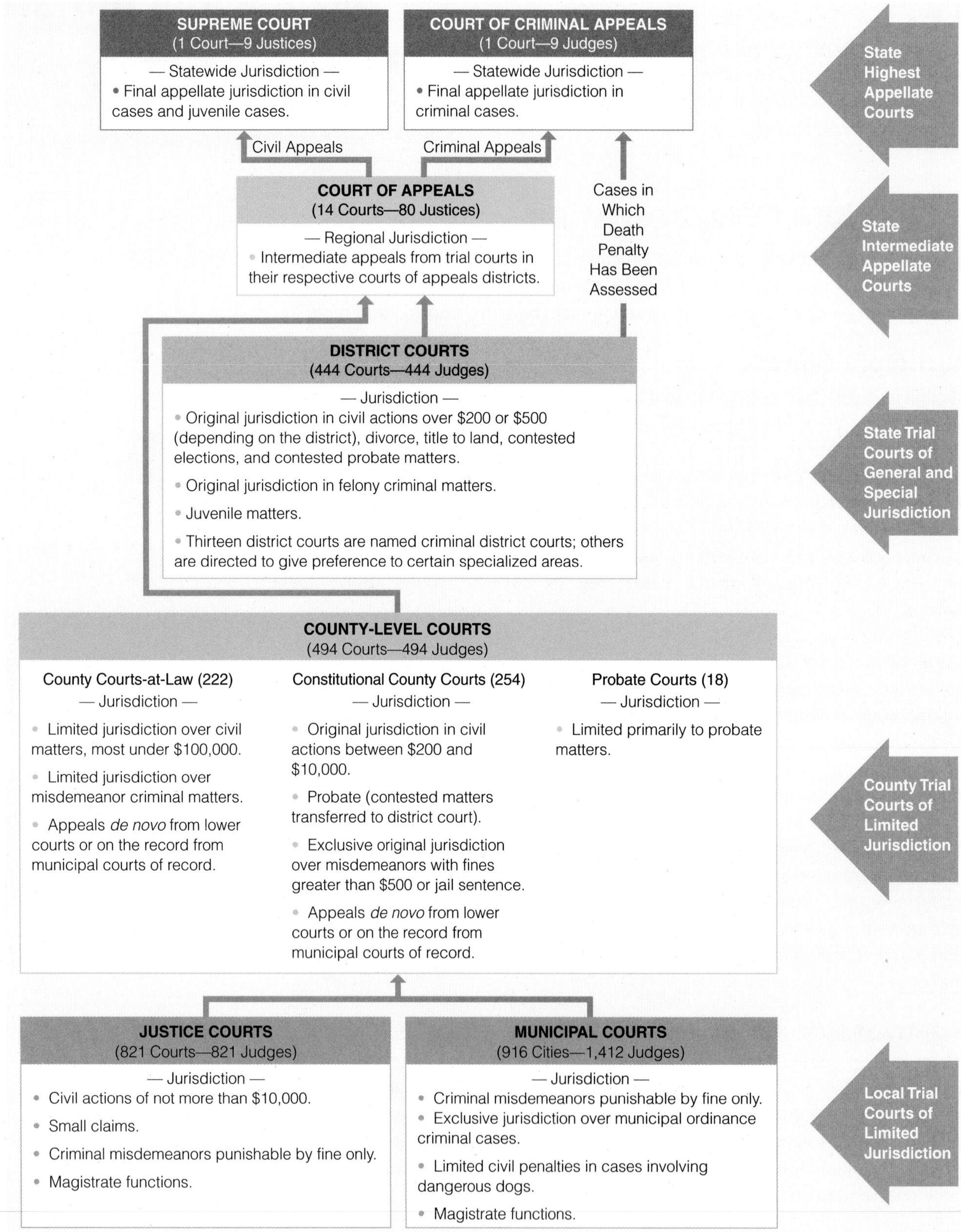

SUPREME COURT
(1 Court—9 Justices)

— Statewide Jurisdiction —

- Final appellate jurisdiction in civil cases and juvenile cases.

COURT OF CRIMINAL APPEALS
(1 Court—9 Judges)

— Statewide Jurisdiction —

- Final appellate jurisdiction in criminal cases.

Civil Appeals

Criminal Appeals

Cases in Which Death Penalty Has Been Assessed

COURT OF APPEALS
(14 Courts—80 Justices)

— Regional Jurisdiction —

- Intermediate appeals from trial courts in their respective courts of appeals districts.

DISTRICT COURTS
(444 Courts—444 Judges)

— Jurisdiction —

- Original jurisdiction in civil actions over $200 or $500 (depending on the district), divorce, title to land, contested elections, and contested probate matters.
- Original jurisdiction in felony criminal matters.
- Juvenile matters.
- Thirteen district courts are named criminal district courts; others are directed to give preference to certain specialized areas.

COUNTY-LEVEL COURTS
(494 Courts—494 Judges)

County Courts-at-Law (222)

— Jurisdiction —

- Limited jurisdiction over civil matters, most under $100,000.
- Limited jurisdiction over misdemeanor criminal matters.
- Appeals *de novo* from lower courts or on the record from municipal courts of record.

Constitutional County Courts (254)

— Jurisdiction —

- Original jurisdiction in civil actions between $200 and $10,000.
- Probate (contested matters transferred to district court).
- Exclusive original jurisdiction over misdemeanors with fines greater than $500 or jail sentence.
- Appeals *de novo* from lower courts or on the record from municipal courts of record.

Probate Courts (18)

— Jurisdiction —

- Limited primarily to probate matters.

JUSTICE COURTS
(821 Courts—821 Judges)

— Jurisdiction —

- Civil actions of not more than $10,000.
- Small claims.
- Criminal misdemeanors punishable by fine only.
- Magistrate functions.

MUNICIPAL COURTS
(916 Cities—1,412 Judges)

— Jurisdiction —

- Criminal misdemeanors punishable by fine only.
- Exclusive jurisdiction over municipal ordinance criminal cases.
- Limited civil penalties in cases involving dangerous dogs.
- Magistrate functions.

State Highest Appellate Courts

State Intermediate Appellate Courts

State Trial Courts of General and Special Jurisdiction

County Trial Courts of Limited Jurisdiction

Local Trial Courts of Limited Jurisdiction

more than one municipal court or more than one judge for each court. In view of the volume of cases pending before these courts, the need for several judges is obvious.

Justices of the Peace

The justice of the peace courts in Texas are authorized by the Texas Constitution, which requires that the county commissioners in each county establish at least one, and not more than eight, justice precincts (the areas from which justices of the peace are elected for four-year terms). County commissioners determine how many justices of the peace will be elected (based on the population) and where their courts will sit. Changes are made continuously, making it difficult to determine the number of justices of the peace at any given time. The Texas Judicial Council determined that there were 821 justices of the peace during 2007.[14]

The functions of the justice of the peace courts are varied. Justice of the peace courts have **original jurisdiction** in criminal misdemeanor cases only when the maximum punishment is a fine less than $500, and in civil matters where the amount in controversy does not exceed $200. They also have concurrent jurisdiction with the county courts in civil matters as long as the amount in controversy does not exceed $10,000. Justices of the peace may issue warrants for search and arrest, serve *ex officio* as notaries public, conduct preliminary hearings, perform marriages, serve as coroners in counties having no medical examiner, and hear cases involving small claims. Approximately 89 percent of cases filed in justice courts are criminal, and most involve traffic violations.[15]

Original Jurisdiction
The authority of a court to consider a case in the first instance; the power to try a case, as opposed to appellate jurisdiction, which involves the power to review cases decided by other courts.

Qualifications. All the functions just mentioned are performed by an official whose only qualification is to be a registered voter. No statutory or constitutional provisions require that a justice of the peace be a lawyer, and only about 7 percent of Texas's justices of the peace are lawyers.

When a justice of the peace is not a licensed attorney, he or she is required by statute to take a 40-hour course in the performance of the duties of the office, plus a 20-hour course each year thereafter, at an accredited state-supported institution of higher education. Some people have questioned the constitutionality of this provision, because it adds a qualification for the office not specified in the constitution.

did you know?
That 93 percent of Texas justices of the peace are not lawyers.

Compensation. For many years, counties in Texas varied widely as to whether they paid their justices of the peace a specific salary or paid them fees based on services performed. Some counties had a mixed system, wherein some justices were salaried while others were paid according to a fee system. Since January 1973, all justices of the peace have been paid a salary,[16] but the salary may vary a great deal from county to county and from justice to justice within the same county.

County Courts

Each of the 254 counties in Texas has a county court presided over by the county judge. (The county judge is sometimes referred to as the constitutional county judge, and his or her court may be called the constitutional county court.) The Texas Constitution requires that county judges be elected by voters for four-year terms and be "well informed in the law of the state," which can mean almost anything.

---

14. Texas Judiciary Online, "Texas Courts Online," accessed January 25, 2008, at www.courts.state.tx.us.
15. *Annual Statistical Report for the Texas Judiciary, 2007,* p. 50; Texas Judiciary Online, accessed January 29, 2008, at www.courts.state.tx.us/pubs/AR2007/AR07.pdf.
16. Article 16.61 of the Texas Constitution, as amended in November 1972.

These photos show four of the 254 county courthouses in Texas. Clockwise from the upper left are the courthouses that serve Tarrant County, Somervell County, Hood County, and Anderson County. In 1999, the Texas legislature and then-Governor George W. Bush established the Texas Historic Courthouse Preservation Program. The program provides partial matching grants to Texas counties for the restoration of their historic county courthouses. The legislature has approved $145 million for the program since it began. (Photos courtesy of Texas Historical Commission)

Their salaries are paid by the county and vary greatly. About 12 percent of county judges are licensed to practice law. County courts handle probate and other civil matters in which the amount in dispute is between $200 and $10,000. Their criminal jurisdiction is confined to serious misdemeanors for which punishment is a fine of more than $500, a jail sentence, or both.

County Courts-at-Law. Because the constitutional county judge also has administrative responsibilities as presiding officer of the commissioners court (the governing body for Texas counties and not a judicial entity at all), the judge may have little time to handle judicial matters. The legislature has responded by establishing **county courts-at-law** in certain counties to act as auxiliary, or supplemental, courts. Their judges are elected for four-year terms. There are 222 of these statutory courts-at-law in 84 Texas counties.[17] For example, Dallas County has 15 and Harris County, 19. They have either civil or criminal jurisdiction or a combination of both, as determined by the legislative act that established them. Their civil jurisdiction includes cases involving claims of less than $100,000. Their criminal jurisdiction includes misdemeanors that are more serious than those tried by the justice of the peace and municipal courts, or misdemeanors that include a jail sentence or a fine in excess of $500.

The qualifications of the judges of the statutory county courts-at-law vary according to the statute that established the particular court. In addition to residence in the county, a court-at-law judge usually must have four years' experience as a practicing attorney or judge.

More than two-thirds of cases filed in county-level courts are criminal. Cases involving theft and driving while intoxicated or under the influence of drugs are the most common. Civil cases include probate matters and suits to collect debt.

County Courts-at-Law
In Texas, county courts in addition to the constitutional county court. They are established by the legislature in all but the smallest Texas counties and may have criminal or civil jurisdiction. They form a level of courts superior to justice of the peace and municipal courts but inferior to district courts.

District Courts

The district courts are often described as the chief trial courts of the state, and as a group these courts are called the general trial courts. The names of the courts and their jurisdictions vary. There are constitutional district courts, civil district courts, criminal district courts, and so on, through more than 40 other jurisdictions.

Texas has 444 district courts, all of which are single-judge courts.[18] Each judge must be at least 25 years of age, a resident of the district for two years, and a citizen of the United States and a judge or a licensed practicing attorney for four years. Judges are elected for four-year terms by voters in their districts. The state of Texas pays $125,000 of the salary of each district judge. Each county may supplement the state salary up to a maximum of $140,000.

17. Texas Judiciary Online, "Court Structure of Texas," Accessed October 1, 2008, at www.courts.state.tx.us.
18. *Ibid.*

Jurisdiction of the District Courts. District courts have jurisdiction in felony cases, which make up about one-third of their caseloads. Civil cases in which the claim exceeds $200 may also be tried in district courts, and such cases constitute the greatest share of their workload (approximately 69 percent). Juvenile cases are usually tried in district courts. While most district courts exercise both criminal and civil jurisdiction, there is a tendency for courts in metropolitan areas to specialize in criminal, civil, or family law matters.

Appellate Jurisdiction The authority vested in an appellate court to review and revise the judicial actions of inferior courts.

Plea Bargaining. The caseload for district courts is heavy, and plea bargaining is often used to dispose of criminal cases at this level. Plea bargaining saves the state a great amount of time and expense. It is estimated that about 90 percent of criminal cases in district courts are disposed of in this way.[19] If plea bargaining were not used in many urban areas, court delays would be increased by months, if not years. While efficient, plea bargaining raises serious issues concerning equity and justice; it often encourages innocent people to plead guilty and allows guilty people to escape with less punishment than the law provides.

Civil Settlements. Similarly, many civil lawsuits are resolved through negotiated settlements between the parties. At times, settlements may be appropriate and just. In many urban areas, however, there is such a backlog of civil cases before the courts that it can take years for a matter to be heard and settled. Therefore, litigants often choose to settle their cases out of court for reasons other than justice.

A man hugs his daughters in 2003 after his release at the Swisher County courthouse in Tulia, Texas. He was one of 46 Tulia residents—15 percent of the town's African American population—who were arrested in 1999 during a drug "sting." That operation was conducted by a lone police officer, Tom Coleman. No drugs, money, or weapons were seized in any of the cases. Still, all defendants were convicted and sentenced to prison terms running from 20 to 434 years. Coleman's uncorroborated testimony was later discredited; Governor Rick Perry pardoned the wrongly convicted; and Swisher County paid $5 million in damages to 45 of the defendants. In 2005, Coleman was convicted of perjury and sentenced to 10 years' probation and a $7,500 fine. This case is discussed in the *Politics and . . .* feature in Chapter 17. (AP Photo /LM Otero)

Courts of Appeals

Fourteen courts of appeals hear immediate appeals in both civil and criminal cases from district- and county-level courts in their areas. These courts are said to have **appellate jurisdiction.** Only a small percentage of trial court cases are appealed. For example, during 2007, the courts of appeals disposed of 11,286 cases.[20] In these cases, the appeals courts reversed, at least in part, the decision of the trial court 7.8 percent of the time.[21]

The state pays each chief appeals justice $140,000 and each associate justice $137,500. Counties may pay a supplement to appeals judges, but the total salary cannot exceed $147,500 for the chief appeals justice and $145,000 for an associate justice. Appeals judges are elected from their districts for six-year terms. They must be at least 35 years of age, with at least 10 years' experience as a lawyer or judge.

Court of Criminal Appeals

An 1891 constitutional amendment established the present system of dual courts of last resort. The Texas Supreme Court is the highest state appellate court in civil matters, and the Court of Criminal Appeals is the highest state appellate court in criminal matters. Only Oklahoma has a similar system.

19. *Texas Crime, Texas Justice* (Austin: Comptroller's Office, 1994), p. 51.
20. *Annual Statistical Report for the Texas Judiciary, 2007,* p. 27; Texas Judiciary Online, accessed January 29, 2008, at www.courts.state.tx.us/pubs/AR2007/AR07.pdf.
21. *Ibid.,* p. 27.

Although most criminal cases decided by the 14 courts of appeals go no further, some are heard by the Court of Criminal Appeals, which consists of a presiding judge and eight other judges. In 2007, Criminal Appeals Court judges wrote 575 opinions, of which 444 (77 percent) were "determinative opinions" that disposed of cases, and the remainder were dissents, concurrences, or opinions on rehearings.[22]

Criminal Appeals Court judges are elected statewide in partisan elections for six-year overlapping terms. They must be at least 35 years old and be lawyers or judges with 10 years' experience. The presiding judge of the Court of Criminal Appeals receives a salary of $152,500; the other judges receive $150,000.

Reversing Criminal Verdicts. Historically, the Texas Court of Criminal Appeals has generated a large measure of public controversy due to its alleged coddling of criminals. Between 1900 and 1927, the court reversed 42 percent of all the cases it reviewed. As early as 1910, the court was cited by the American Institute of Criminal Law as being "one of the foremost worshippers, among the American appellate courts, of the technicality." In the 1940s, largely in response to both professional and public criticism, the reversal rate began to drop, and by 1966 it was only 3 percent.[23] Today's Court of Criminal Appeals reverses a very small percentage of the cases that it takes on appeal.

The nature of its work makes the Court of Criminal Appeals a highly visible court, even if its individual members are not so visible. When the court reverses convictions based on inadmissible arguments by prosecutors or the introduction of unacceptable or tainted evidence, protests are sure to follow from prosecutors, newspaper editorial writers, and civic club luncheon speakers. Remarks concerning legal technicalities are frequent when a conviction is overturned, even though the real reason for the reversal might be the overkill of a zealous prosecutor or other inappropriate behavior by the state. Ordinarily, a reversal means only that the case will be retried.

The Court of Criminal Appeals and the Texas Bill of Rights. The Court of Criminal Appeals has been involved in another controversy. Previously criticized for its nitpicking opinions, the court has recently been accused of unfounded interpretations of the Texas Bill of Rights. For example, in a 1991 decision, *William Randolph Heitman v. State,* the court ruled that the Texas Constitution provides criminal defendants more protection against illegal searches and seizures than the U.S. Constitution does.[24] Critics argue that the court should guarantee the accused no broader rights than those protected by the U.S. Constitution. Those supporting the court's decisions point out that the bill of rights in the Texas Constitution is not identical to the Bill of Rights in the U.S. Constitution and therefore lends itself to different interpretations.

did you know?

That Michael Richard was executed because Texas Court of Criminal Appeals Judge Sharon Keller refused to take his appeal after 5 P.M.

The Death Penalty. The Court of Criminal Appeals has exclusive jurisdiction over automatic appeals in death penalty cases. In 2007, the court received 19 death penalty appeals.[25] Since the United States Supreme Court restored the use of capital punishment in 1976, Texas has executed far more individuals than any other state. By 2007, the state had executed more than 400 convicted murderers (more than three times as many as the state with the second-highest total). For several years, the rate of executions averaged approximately 25 to 30 per year (including a

22. *Ibid.,* p. 25.
23. Paul Burka, "Trial by Technicality," *Texas Monthly,* April 1982, p. 131.
24. 815 S.W. 2d 681 (1991).
25. *Annual Statistical Report for the Texas Judiciary, 2007,* p. 24; Texas Judiciary Online, accessed January 29, 2008, at www.courts.state.tx.us/pubs/AR2007/AR07.pdf.

record of 40 in 2000).[26] This rate has recently been dropping, however (26 individuals were executed in 2007).[27] Death penalty cases have led to headline stories, including controversies over the use of lethal injections, executing a woman (Karla Faye Tucker), a 66-year-old man, persons who were juveniles when they committed the crimes for which they were sentenced to death, individuals who were mentally retarded or mentally ill, those who had received poor legal counsel (including a sleeping attorney), and persons who might actually have been innocent of the crimes.[28]

The State Supreme Court

The Texas Supreme Court is the final court of appeals in civil and juvenile cases. The court has original jurisdiction over issuing writs and conducting proceedings for involuntary retirement or removal of judges. In its other cases, the court has appellate jurisdiction. The court also has the power to make rules for the administration of justice—rules of civil practice and procedure for courts having civil jurisdiction. In addition, it makes rules governing licensing of members of the state bar.

The Texas Supreme Court consists of one chief justice and eight associate justices. All are elected statewide after being nominated in party primaries. Three of the nine justices are elected every two years for six-year terms. The Texas Constitution specifies that a justice must be at least 35 years of age and a citizen of the United States and of Texas and must have been a lawyer or judge of a court of record for at least 10 years. The salary of the chief justice is $152,500, and the salary of associate justices is $150,000.

The Supreme Court's Workload. During 2007, the court acted on 3,676 matters.[29] The justices wrote 170 opinions, of which 131 (77.1 percent) were deciding opinions that disposed of cases.[30] The court also reversed (at least in part) approximately 73 percent of the 111 cases that came to it from the 14 courts of appeals on petitions for review (formerly "applications for writs of error").[31]

The Role of the Texas Supreme Court. The Texas Supreme Court spends much of its time deciding which petitions for review will be granted, because not all appeals are heard. Generally, it only takes the cases it views as presenting the most significant legal issues. It should also be noted that the Texas Supreme Court plays a policy-making role in the state. As discussed in Chapter 21, for example, in 1989 the court unanimously decided the *Edgewood v. Kirby* case.[32] In this decision, the court ordered major changes in how public schools were financed in Texas. It found unacceptable the huge disparities between rich and poor school districts in the state.

---

26. "Retarded Man's Impending Execution Prompts Scrutiny of Death-Penalty Laws," *Dallas Morning News,* February 15, 2000; "Who Really Deserves to Die?", *Fort Worth Star-Telegram,* January 14, 2001.
27. Texas Department of Criminal Justice, "Executed Defenders," accessed February 4, 2008, at www.tdcj.state.tx.us/stat/executedoffenders.htm.
28. "High Court looks at Lethal Injections," *Dallas Morning News,* September 26, 2007; "Karla Faye Tucker Executed," *Dallas Morning News,* February 4, 1998; "Questions of Competence Arise in Death Row Appeal," *Dallas Morning News,* September 11, 2000; "Man Denied New Trial Despite Sleeping Lawyer," *Fort Worth Star-Telegram,* October 28, 2000; "Death-Penalty Trials Rife with Errors, Study Finds," *Dallas Morning News,* June 12, 2000; "Man Executed for 1988 Revenge Killing," *Fort Worth Star-Telegram,* November 21, 2002; "Death Penalty Debate Reopens," *Fort Worth Star-Telegram,* November 8, 2002; "At Last Name Is Cleared," *Dallas Morning News,* October 6, 2004; "Supreme Court, 5–4, Forbids Execution in Juvenile Crime," *The New York Times,* March 2, 2005, p. A1.
29. *Annual Statistical Report for the Texas Judiciary, 2007,* p. 21; Texas Judiciary Online, accessed January 29, 2008, at www.courts.state.tx.us/pubs/AR2007/AR07.pdf.
30. *Ibid.,* p. 22.
31. *Ibid.,* p. 22.
32. 777 S.W. 2d 391 (Tex. 1989).

(© Ben Sargent. Reprinted by permission of Universal Press Syndicate)

Selection of Judges

Officially, Texas elects its judges (except municipal court judges) in partisan elections. This statement oversimplifies the process, however, and can be somewhat misleading. Former Chief Justice Robert W. Calvert referred many times to the system as an "appointive-elective" one. Approximately 45 percent of the trial judges (those who serve in district courts, criminal district courts, county courts-at-law, and probate courts) first assume office through appointment to fill vacancies created when judges leave office before their terms expire.[33] Likewise, about 40 percent of the judges of the appellate courts first assume office through appointment. These appointments between elections are made by the governor with the advice and consent of the senate. In the elections for judicial offices, approximately 80 percent of all Texas judges are re-elected unopposed. Even when there is no incumbent running for re-election, serious competition for judicial posts is uncommon.

An Uninformed Electorate

Because Texas elects judges, a natural question arises: How knowledgeable are voters in these judicial elections? In other words, do voters know who the candidates are and what their records in office look like? Research on the United States Supreme Court has repeatedly shown that the vast majority of the public knows little about its rulings and actions.[34] If most Americans know very little about the United States Supreme Court, the court that receives the most media attention in this country, how much can we expect voters to know about state and local courts?

A voter in Texas could be asked to vote for candidates running for the Texas Supreme Court, the Court of Criminal Appeals, a court of appeals, a district court, and a county court, as well as justice of the peace. Not surprisingly, polls and research indicate that most voters enter the voting booth with scant knowledge of the candidates running for various judicial posts.[35] For example, a poll taken in Texas after a presidential general election found that only 14.5 percent of voters could recall the name of one of the candidates for either the Texas Supreme Court or the Court of Criminal Appeals.

33. "Profile of Appellate and Trial Judges," *Texas Judicial System Annual Report, 2002* (Austin: Office of Court Administration), p. 54.
34. For example, see John Kessel, "Public Perceptions of the Supreme Court," *Midwest Journal of Political Science,* Vol. 10, 1966, pp. 167–191; Kenneth Dolbeare, "The Public Views the Supreme Court," in Herbert Jacob, ed., *Law, Politics, and the Federal Courts* (Boston: Little, Brown, 1967); Gregory Casey, "Popular Perceptions of Supreme Court Rulings," *American Politics Quarterly,* Vol. 4, 1976, pp. 3–45; *Gallup Report,* Vol. 264, 1987, pp. 29–30; Thomas Marshall, *Public Opinion and the Supreme Court* (New York: Longman, 1989); and Lee Epstein et al., *The Supreme Court Compendium* (Washington, DC: CQ Press, 2003).
35. For example, see Philip Dubois, *From Ballot to Bench: Judicial Elections and the Quest for Accountability* (Austin: University of Texas Press, 1980); and Anthony Champagne and Gregory Thielemann, "Awareness of Trial Court Judges," *Judicature,* Vol. 74, 1991, pp. 271–276.

In addition to systematic research, anecdotal evidence also indicates that most voters in Texas are unaware of candidates' qualifications or experience. Thus, name recognition of any sort can lead people to cast their votes for a candidate. Consequently, candidates with names the same as or similar to those of movie stars, historical figures, or public personages are often candidates for judicial positions.

Party Identification

Because voters know so little about individual candidates, they may use party identification as a cue to determine how to vote. In other words, if a voter has no knowledge of the views or backgrounds of the candidates on the ballot, he or she may make a choice based on the candidates' political party affiliation. In Texas, this appears to be a common way for voters to make selections in judicial elections.

The Rise of the Republicans. Historically, Texas was part of the "Solid South," and as in other Southern states, the Democratic Party monopolized politics. This monopoly was reflected in the judicial posts throughout the state. When Texas became a competitive two-party state in the 1980s, many Republicans were elected to judicial positions. One researcher noted, "In one decade the Republican party moved from a position of being locked out of power in the court house to controlling 36 of 37 district seats" in the city of Dallas.[36] This dramatic change included both the Texas Supreme Court and the Court of Criminal Appeals. Both high courts are entirely Republican; not a single Democrat serves as a justice on either court. Republican successes led many incumbent Democratic judges to switch to the Republican Party in hopes of continuing their judicial careers.[37] In the 2006 and 2008 elections, however, the Democratic party began to show some renewed signs of life in Harris and Dallas Counties and a few other areas.

The Effects of Partisan Voting. It has been argued that because judges, especially at the appellate level, make significant policy decisions, it is reasonable for voters to select judges on the basis of political party affiliation.[38] Party affiliation may provide accurate information concerning the general ideology and, thus, the decision-making patterns of judges. Even if this is true, voting based solely on a candidate's political party can lead to controversial results. Some critics point to the 1994 election of Steve Mansfield to the Texas Court of Criminal Appeals as evidence of what can happen when voters do not educate themselves about a candidate's qualifications or background. During the campaign, it was revealed that Mansfield had very limited legal experience and that he had lied in his campaign literature about his experience and his personal and political background. He won nonetheless, apparently because many voters supported every Republican on the ballot (that is, they voted a *straight ticket*).

Judicial Campaign Spending

Because voters often look for simple voting cues (such as name familiarity or party identification), candidates often want to spend as much money as possible to make their names or candidacy well known. In recent years, spending in judicial races has risen dramatically. Candidates need to win two elections: their party's nomination and the general election. This can be an expensive endeavor. In the 1988 races for six open seats on the Texas Supreme Court, the candidates spent more than $10 million.[39] In the 1996 races for the

---

36. Champagne and Thielemann, "Awareness of Trial Court Judges."
37. Office of the Secretary of State, *Race Summary Report for the 2006 General Election,* accessed at elections.sos.state.tx.us/elchist.exe.
38. Dubois, *Judicial Elections.*
39. Anthony Champagne, "Campaign Contributions in Texas Supreme Court Races," *Crime, Law, and Social Change,* Vol. 17, 1992, pp. 91–106; Kyle Cheek and Anthony Champagne, "Money in Texas Supreme Court Elections: 1980–1998," *Judicature,* Vol. 84, 2000, pp. 20–25.

same seats, three of four incumbent Republican candidates raised about $1 million each (the fourth incumbent received about $700,000, although he was running unopposed).[40]

None of the three Democrats in the race raised even $100,000. For example, Chief Justice Tom Phillips received more than $1.1 million, while his challenger raised a little more than $15,000.[41] Not surprisingly, all four Republicans were re-elected. In the three races in 1998 in which the Republicans most outspent their rivals, the funding ratio was 15 to one (nearly $2.9 million collected compared with $190,000 for the Democrats).[42] In 2002, the results were similar. The Republicans won or held onto all five seats that were up for election and outspent Democrats approximately three to one (even with Chief Justice Phillips accepting no new campaign contributions).[43]

Plaintiffs' lawyers and their related interest group, the Texas Trial Lawyers Association, have made a concerted effort in the past few decades to make the judiciary more open to consumer suits. Such suits are often filed against businesses, physicians, and their insurance companies. The plaintiffs' lawyers have poured millions of dollars into the political funds of candidates they believed would be more favorable to their perspective. Defense and business attorneys have responded with millions of dollars of their own contributions. Plaintiff and defense lawyers alike then often appear before the very judges to whom they have given these large sums.

Minority Representation

A final major criticism of the current partisan elective system involves questions about diversity and minority representation. In 1988, African American and Hispanic groups challenged in federal court the way judges were elected in urban areas of Texas, citing the Voting Rights Act of 1965, as amended. They argued that the at-large (countywide) election of district and county court judges in Bexar, Dallas, Ector, Harris, Jefferson, Lubbock, Midland, Tarrant, and Travis counties made the election of minority candidates difficult because it diluted minority voting strength. Attorney General Dan Morales pointed out that African Americans and Hispanics made up 40 percent of Texas's population but held only 5 percent of state district judgeships. In August 1993, the full federal Court of Appeals for the Fifth Circuit upheld the current system. In January 1994, the United States Supreme Court rejected an appeal of the decision without comment.

did you know?

That only 2.8 percent of Texas district judges are African Americans.

In recent decades, however, minority judicial candidates have won several high-profile victories. For example, in 1984, Raul A. Gonzalez became the first Hispanic to serve on the Texas Supreme Court. In 1990, Morris Overstreet became the first African American to serve on the Texas Court of Criminal Appeals. In 2001, Governor Rick Perry filled two vacancies on the Texas Supreme Court with minorities—and one of these individuals, Wallace Jefferson, was appointed chief justice in 2004.[44] Nevertheless, these changes have been modest, and ethnic minorities are still underrepresented among trial court judges. In 2007, only 13.8 percent of 398 district court judges were Hispanic, and only 2.8 percent were African American.[45]

---

40. "Republican Judges Lead Money Race," *Dallas Morning News,* October 27, 1996, p. A45.
41. *Ibid.*
42. "Justice Spector Hopes to Win Tough Race against Well-Financed Republican O'Neill," *Dallas Morning News,* October 18, 1998, p. A47.
43. "Report: Justice Candidates Raise about $3 Million," *Fort Worth Star-Telegram,* August 28, 2002.
44. "First Black Named to Texas High Court," *Fort Worth Star-Telegram,* March 15, 2001.
45. *Annual Statistical Report for the Texas Judiciary, 2007,* p. 13; Texas Judiciary Online, accessed January 29, 2008, at www.courts.state.tx.us/pubs/AR2007/AR07.pdf.

WHY SHOULD YOU CARE ABOUT... LAW ENFORCEMENT?

Many students may become involved in the criminal justice process as victims, witnesses, or perpetrators. (Legally, traffic offenses are crimes.) As a victim or witness of crime, you must decide whether to report it. Many criminals get away with their crimes because many citizens (especially in minority communities) fear dealing with law enforcement. Others fear that crime reports will increase their insurance rates. Some fail to report crimes because the perpetrator is a friend or relative. Still others fear the perpetrator's vengeance. Some (especially rape victims) are embarrassed by the fact they have become victims. Failure to report crime, however, creates an environment that supports it. The individual must personally evaluate the costs and benefits of filing a report.

Sooner or later, many of us will be arrested—if only through a traffic stop. Do not take such an arrest lightly. In some instances, your life, liberty, property, and reputation may be at stake. Even a traffic ticket can affect your insurability, and accumulating several tickets may now result in a large annual state fee to keep your driver's license.

HOW TO DEAL INTELLIGENTLY WITH LAW ENFORCEMENT OFFICERS

Let's consider how you might deal with traffic violations. The best advice is to avoid them. Law-enforcement officers do not often ticket drivers traveling less than 10 miles per hour above the posted speed limit except in school zones—there, 20 miles per hour means exactly that, and absolutely no more! Regardless of posted speed limits, Texas law provides that you must travel at safe and reasonable speeds, and this provision is usually taken to mean that about one-sixth of the traffic will pass you.

Since 1998, it has been illegal to possess open alcoholic beverages in a car in Texas. Therefore, keep any opened alcoholic beverage containers in the trunk of the car or, if the vehicle has no trunk, behind the last seat.

If you are arrested for a traffic violation or any other crime, be respectful and obey the officer or officers. Sometimes a polite, reasoned explanation can prevent the ordeal of a traffic ticket. Do not confess guilt or argue your innocence—these matters will be settled in court later. If you believe a police order is unlawful, you should politely state that you believe the order is unlawful. For example, it is not legal for an officer to demand that you open any locked compartment without probable cause.

If you ultimately are given a ticket, take advantage of the opportunity to take a safe-driving course to absolve your responsibility. Other alternatives include hiring a lawyer to have the ticket dismissed or obtaining a plea bargain with the prosecutor or judge to plead guilty to the crime of "failure to appear" in exchange for having the ticket dismissed. Deferred adjudications are also a real possibility. Good drivers may get help finding lower insurance rates through the Texas Department of Insurance.

questions for discussion and analysis

1. What are the differences between the kinds of cases tried in Texas's criminal courts and those tried in its civil courts?
2. How does due process in Texas's courts balance the rights of individuals and the mores of the community as a whole?
3. What are the advantages and disadvantages of Texas's judicial selection process?

key terms

acquitted 739
adversary system 738
appellate jurisdiction 745
burden of proof 733
change of venue 737
county courts-at-law 744
deferred adjudication 738
docket 734
due process 735
examining trial 736
felony 734
grand jury 737
misdemeanor 734
mistrial 739
original jurisdiction 743
plea bargaining 737
probation 739
punitive damages award 734
tort reform 734

chapter summary

1. Within the American legal system, cases are classified as either civil or criminal. Civil cases primarily involve the rights of private parties or organizations (e.g., *Smith v. Jones*). Resolution is based on the concept of responsibility rather than guilt. Tort actions are common in civil law—a tort is a wrong suffered by a party. Disputes are usually set out in a petition, and the side with the preponderance of the evidence wins the suit. The Texas legislature, in an effort to lighten overcrowded court dockets and limit allegedly unnecessary suits, has undertaken tort reform. It has, for example, passed bills that restrict lawsuits by prison inmates, reduce frivolous lawsuits, and cap punitive damages awards.
2. Criminal cases deal with public concepts of proper behavior and morality as defined by law. Punishment for a conviction ranges from a fine to imprisonment to a combination of both. Initiated by a government prosecutor on behalf of the public, a criminal case is brought by the state against the accused (e.g., *State of Texas v. Smith*). Specific charges of wrongdoing are spelled out in a grand jury indictment or a writ of information. In addition, in criminal cases the prosecutor must prove that the defendant is guilty beyond a reasonable doubt, a much higher standard than in civil cases.
3. The court procedures that constitute due process aim to promote justice and protect individuals from the government. These procedures are generally either written into state and national constitutions and statutes or included in written and unwritten traditional codes of court process. Court procedures have been greatly influenced by tradition. Unfortunately, the goal of due process is often an ideal rather than a reality. It is largely through due process, though, that the courts aim to blend two conflicting goals of society: (1) to protect society according to the state's legal concepts of right and wrong and (2) to protect the rights of the individual charged with wrongdoing.
4. The Texas court system is a large and complicated structure. There are many municipal courts, fewer county-level courts, still fewer district courts and courts of appeals, and only one Texas Supreme Court and one Court of Criminal Appeals. With jurisdictions frequently overlapping, the organization of courts in Texas is often confusing.
5. The system of judicial selection in Texas has been described as appointive-elective. The system has come under attack due to its political nature. For example, voters are often ignorant of the candidates and their records in office, qualifications, and experience. Many vote along party lines. Finally, individuals or organizations often appear before judges after contributing large amounts to their election campaigns, thereby fueling perceptions of apparent or real conflicts of interest.

selected print & media resources

SUGGESTED READINGS

Abraham, Henry. *The Judicial Process,* 7th ed. New York: Oxford University Press, 1998. This work is a comparative review of courts and court systems throughout the world.

Abramsky, Sasha. *Vengeance in the Age of Mass Imprisonment.* New York: Beacon Press, 2007. This provocative book argues against the conventional wisdom that a "get tough" approach to crime can reduce crime rates.

Abramson, Jeffrey. *We, the Jury.* New York: Basic Books, 1994. Abramson reviews various issues surrounding the jury system and its connection to democracy.

Baum, Lawrence. *American Courts: Process and Policy,* 5th ed. Boston: Houghton Mifflin, 2001. This volume is a broad review of lawyers, judges, and U.S. courts.

Dubois, Philip. *From Ballot to Bench: Judicial Elections and the Quest for Accountability.* Austin: University of Texas Press, 1980. Dubois discusses the concepts of competition and accountability in judicial elections.

Epstein, Lee, ed. *Contemplating Courts.* Washington, DC: CQ Press, 1995. This edited collection of essays in political science deals with the law, the courts, and the judicial process.

Marquart, James W., Sheldon Ekland-Olson, and Jonathan R. Sorensen. *The Rope, the Chair, and the Needle: Capital Punishment in Texas, 1923–1990.* Austin: University of Texas Press, 1994. James W. Marquart, now director of the Crime and Justice Studies Program at The University of Texas at Dallas, and his co-authors explore the history of the death penalty in Texas and discuss some of the most interesting issues surrounding it.

Segal, Jeffrey, and Harold Spaeth. *The Supreme Court and the Attitudinal Model.* New York: Cambridge University Press, 1993. This research attempts to show how the behavior and decision making of justices are affected by their personal policy preferences and attitudes.

Zimbardo, Philip. *The Lucifer Effect: Understanding How Good People Turn Evil.* New York: Random House, 2007. Using a classic Stanford psychology experiment, the author shows that prison roles are toxic to both prisoners and guards.

MEDIA RESOURCES

Dead Man Walking–A movie starring Susan Sarandon and Sean Penn that examines both sides of the death penalty issue.

The Executed–A PBS *Frontline* case study of an execution in Texas.

The Exonerated–A play by Jessica Blank and Erik Jenson that brings together characters whose lives were affected by wrongful death sentences, including some that occurred in Texas. It is based on real-life interviews.

Justice for Sale–A provocative film that critically examines the election of judges in three states, including Texas. It is available from the Center for Investigative Reporting and the WGBH Education Foundation.

Not Guilty by Reason of Insanity–An A&E production that questions why the mentally ill find their way into the criminal justice system and whether it is difficult to get out of it.

The Plea–A video produced by PBS *Frontline* that focuses on the judicial process and trial by jury.

To Kill a Mockingbird–A 1962 film, based on Harper Lee's Pulitzer Prize-winning novel, that combines a coming-of-age story with a racially charged rape trial in 1930s Alabama.

Twelve Angry Men–A classic 1957 movie starring Henry Fonda. Almost the entire film takes place in a jury room. In the film, we witness how 12 strangers come together to make a decision concerning the life of a young man, and we see the interplay of the law and personal biases during the jury's high-pressure decision making.

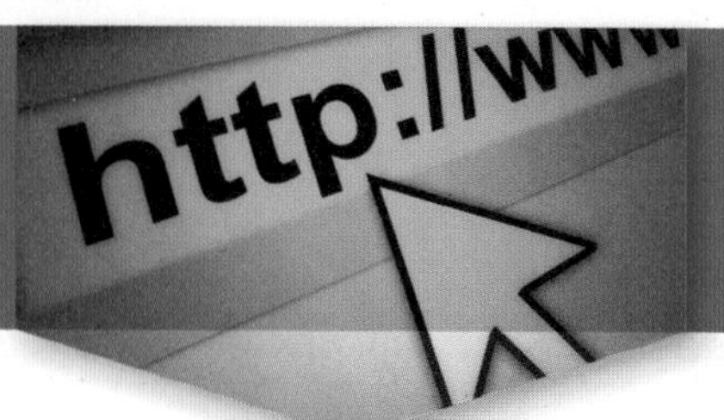

e-mocracy

GETTING TIPS ON DO-IT-YOURSELF AND LOW-COST LEGAL SERVICES

Many of the legal services that ordinary citizens require during their everyday lives can be fairly simple and cost very little. Citizens can handle some of these legal procedures themselves with the help of the Internet.

Commercial businesses sell legal forms online to declare bankruptcy, transfer real estate, file no-fault divorces, write wills, enter wills into probate, and grant power of attorney. The Texas Bar provides helpful online advice on landlord and tenant rights, how to file cases in small claims (JP) courts, family law, consumer issues, and other common legal issues. The Texas attorney general's Web site offers good advice about settling consumer complaints and provides access to parents seeking to collect child support payments. Other Web sites offer advice on low-cost legal solutions, and numerous community legal aid organizations and law school–sponsored legal aid clinics can also be searched online.

Citizens should always do as much research as possible about their legal problems before turning to an attorney. Although many legal issues require that a person retain an attorney, lawyers appreciate clients who are able to ask intelligent questions and actively assist in their cases. And, Texas laws (statutes) are surprisingly easy to navigate.

LOGGING ON

Get tips on low-cost and do-it-yourself civil legal strategies at:
http://texaslawhelp.org/

To learn about family law, tenants' rights, and how to sue in small claims court, go to the Texas Bar Web site:
www.texasbar.com/template.cfm?section=pamphlets

Find out about Texas speed traps and help identify them at the Speed Trap Exchange:
www.speedtrap.org

Texas laws (statutes) can be found at:
www.capitol.state.tx.us

You can access the courts of the state of Texas online at the Texas Judicial Server:
www.courts.state.tx.us

The Texas Supreme Court site, which features Webcasts of oral arguments, is at:
www.supreme.courts.state.tx.us

The Texas Civil Justice League works with corporate legal departments to support tort reform to limit civil court awards. Go to:
www.tcjl.com

On the other side of the issue are plaintiffs' attorneys, who argue cases for consumers, patients, and the insured. Their views are represented by the Texas Trial Lawyers Association at:
www.ttla.com

You can renew your driver's license, identify registered sex offenders in your neighborhood, and get the latest crime statistics from the Texas Department of Public Safety (DPS) at:
www.txdps.state.tx.us

You can compare Texas crime figures with the national index crime figures in the Uniform Crime Reports:
www.fbi.gov/ucr/ucr.htm

The state attorney general's office has a Criminal Victims Services Division. Go to:
www.oag.state.tx.us/victims

Visit the Bureau of Justice Statistics Web site for a rich source of national data about crime, victims, prosecution, prison, probation, and capital punishment:
www.ojp.usdoj.gov/bjs/

ONLINE REVIEW

At **www.cengage.com/politicalscience/schmidt/agandpttexas 14e**, you will find a Tutorial Quiz for this chapter, providing questions on the chapter contents, including the features. You'll gain access to other helpful study tools, including the book's glossary and flashcards, crossword puzzles, and Web links, as well as "Which Side Are You On?" and "Politics and . . ." features written by the authors of the book.

chapter 24

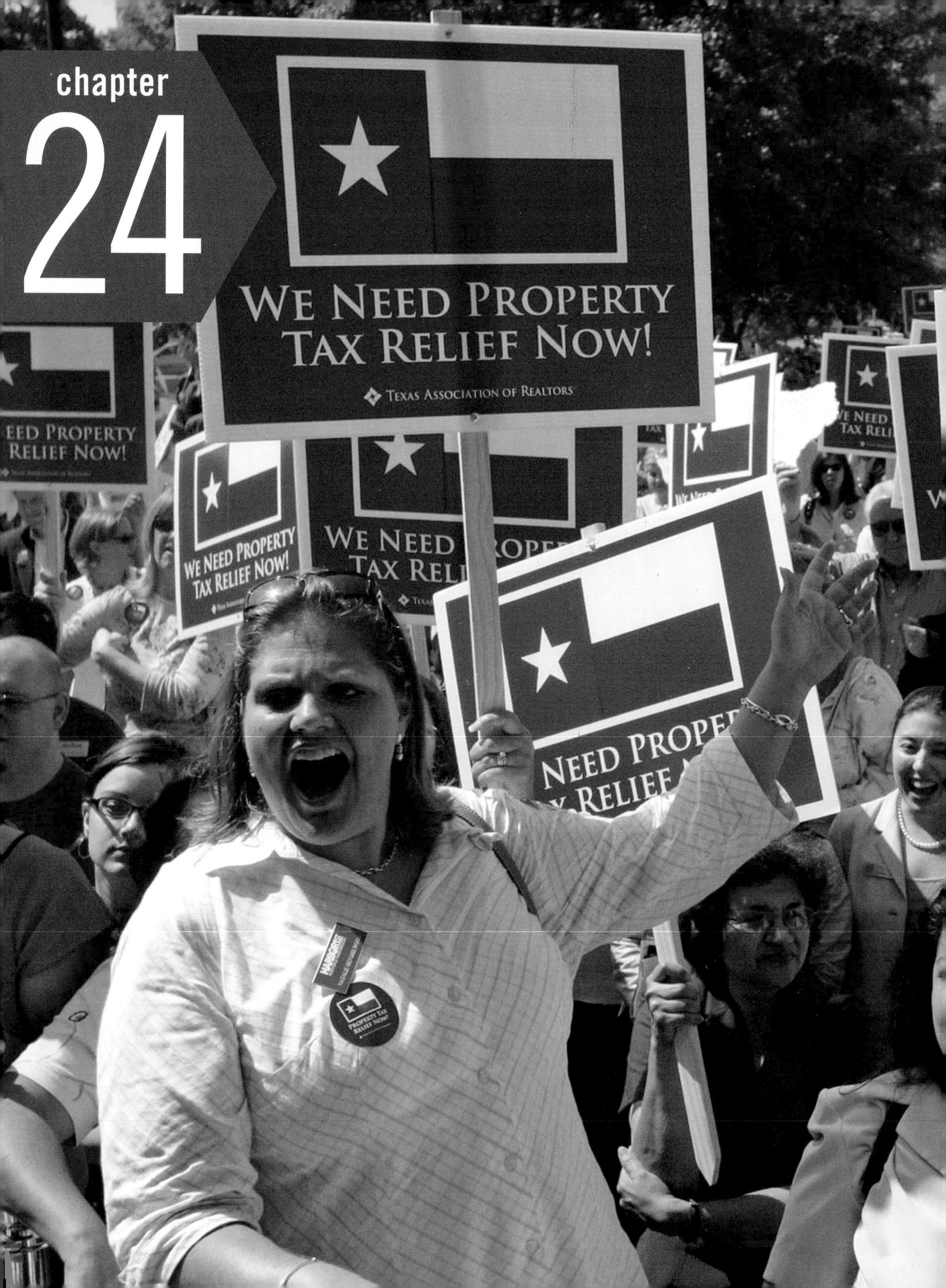

Texas Public Policy

chapter contents

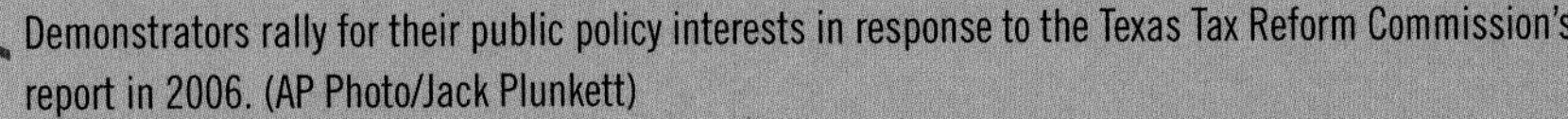

Demonstrators rally for their public policy interests in response to the Texas Tax Reform Commission's report in 2006. (AP Photo/Jack Plunkett)

WHAT IF... ...Texas required individuals to have health insurance?

The uninsured commonly clog hospital emergency rooms seeking extremely costly treatment for relatively minor afflictions that could be easily treated by primary care physicians and local clinics. (Gary Kazanjian/AP Photo)

About three out of four Texans are insured through Medicare, Medicaid, employer group plans, or individual policies. At any point in time, however, approximately 25 percent—a larger proportion than in any other state—have no insurance at all. Because the uninsured have little access to preventive care, their illnesses progress until they become a serious threat to public health and a costly burden to the medical care system.

Medical providers of all types are forced to raise paying patients' fees to cover losses resulting from unpaid medical services to the uninsured. Costs that are not reimbursed are passed on to Texans in the form of higher taxes and insurance premiums.

MANDATING HEALTH INSURANCE

Under former Governor Mitt Romney's lead, Massachusetts made health insurance mandatory for most of its residents, and Governor Arnold Schwarzenegger proposed a similar plan for California. If Texas followed those examples, it would penalize individuals for failing to have health insurance, much as it now fines drivers who lack liability insurance. The state would require employers of more than 10 workers to offer state-approved plans or contribute to a pool to cover the uninsured. Individuals and small businesses could buy health insurance through the state-administered pool, and insurance companies would compete to offer a choice of approved plans to pool customers. The state would subsidize health care on a sliding scale for those earning up to 300 percent of the poverty level.

BENEFITS AND COSTS

Mandatory health insurance would broaden access to health care to near-universal coverage. A more orderly health-care system could clear backlogs in emergency rooms, and expanded access to preventive care would reduce long-term costs. Bringing younger, healthier persons into the insurance system would lower rates for older, sicker consumers. Universal coverage would reduce financial risks to health-care providers and allow them to pass savings onto patients and their insurance companies. Pooling of insurance buyers would give patients market power to demand lower insurance premiums.

Mandating health insurance would not necessarily reduce premiums as some advocates argue. Whatever the efficiencies universal coverage may offer, they do not pay for themselves or offset the costs of government subsidies to low-income families. Government costs have risen in Massachusetts beyond the expectations of the plan's supporters.

Universal health insurance does not address many of the problems in our medical-care system. It does not eliminate costs associated with processing claims. Insurance companies are deft at imposing cost controls that inconvenience patients and limit medical choices. Physicians have no incentive to reduce unnecessary procedures when they are paid on a fee-for-service basis, and patients have little incentive to shop among competing medical providers when insurance is available to pick up most of the tab.

FOR CRITICAL ANALYSIS

1. How should Texas balance the costs against the benefits of a universal health insurance system? How much would such a system limit choices in a free society?
2. It has been asserted that the United States has the best health care in the world for those who can afford it. If the United States spends more for health care than any other country, why is it that the United States ranks 42nd, behind even Jordan, in life expectancy? Is this low ranking entirely a result of unequal access to health care, or do lifestyles explain poor health outcomes in the United States?

At the end of its 2007 session, the Texas legislature passed and sent to the governor the largest budget in the state's history—a total of almost $152.5 billion for fiscal years 2008 and 2009. Texas has the third largest state budget, exceeded only by those of California and New York.

In a sense, though, the size of the most recent Texas budget is not surprising. Each successive budget over the past several years has been larger than the preceding one, resulting in a long succession of record expenditures, as shown in Figure 24–1.

Inflation alone explains some of the rise in government spending, as you can see in the figure. Just as the cost of what individuals and families buy has increased, the cost of what government buys has increased as well. Nevertheless, inflation has also driven up the salaries and profits with which residents pay their taxes.

Population growth also has played a role in the growth in state spending. Texas's population has grown more rapidly than that of most other states. Each new person must be served, protected, and educated. Of course, the demands of a larger population for increased state services are offset by the fact that more people are also paying taxes to support them. Adjusted for population and inflation, state spending has grown at an average annual rate of 1.8 percent during the past 14 years.

Revenues

What are the sources of the funds that the state spends? In 2008–2009, the state comptroller's office estimated that about half of the state's revenues (51.1 percent) would come from various taxes. Federal funding, mostly grants-in-aid, accounted for 31.2 percent, interest and investment income for 3.9 percent, and other sources for the remaining 13.8 percent, as shown in Figure 24–2. In addition, the Texas legislature has some limited ability to borrow funds.

FIGURE 24–1 Trends in Texas State Expenditures, All Funds, by Biennial Budget Periods 1991–2008 (in millions of dollars)

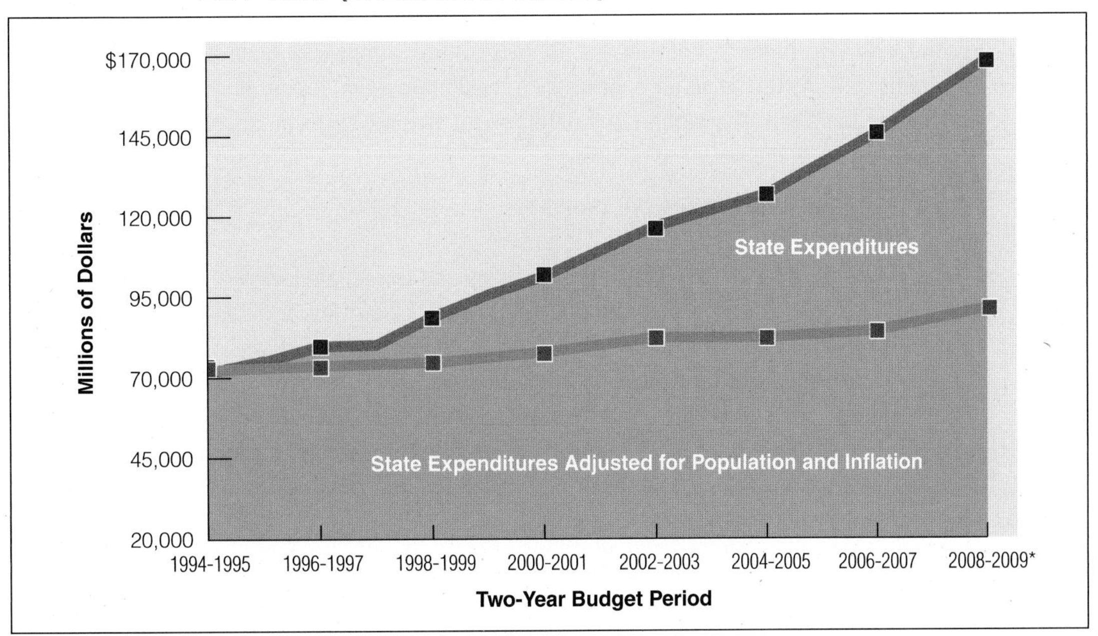

*Estimated.
*Source: *Legislative Budget Board, Fiscal Size-Up, 2008–2009* (Austin: Legislative Budget Board, 2008), p. 8.

FIGURE 24–2 Sources of Estimated State Revenues, 2008–2009 Budget Period

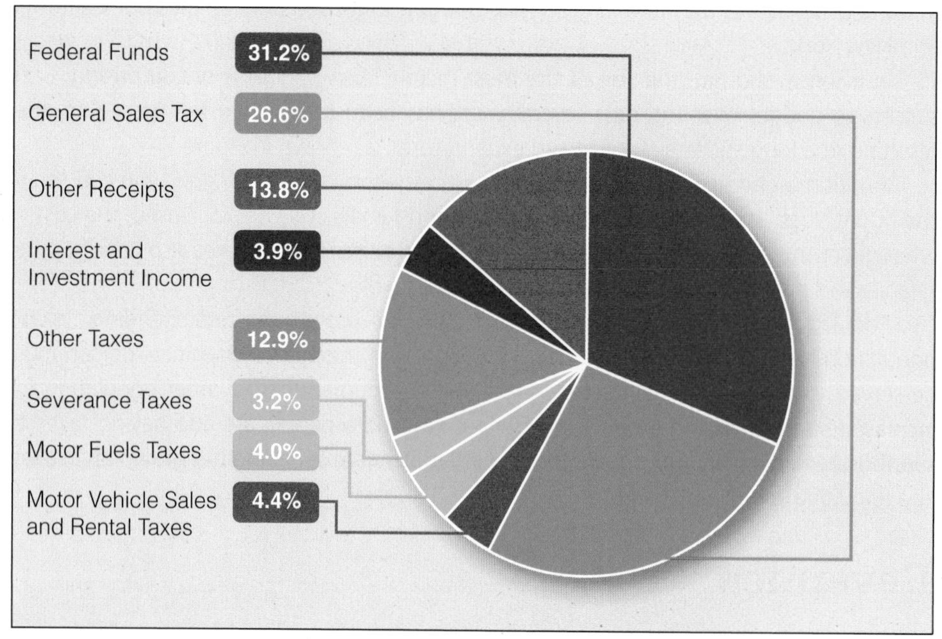

Source: Texas Comptroller of Public Accounts, *Biennial Revenue Estimate, 2008–2009*, Table A-18.

Taxation

Property taxes (which are *ad valorem taxes*) were once the major source of state revenue, but property values collapsed during the Great Depression of the 1930s, and with them went the property tax base. At the same time, demands for economic assistance and other public services skyrocketed. Forced to seek other revenue sources, states came to rely on various sales taxes. Texas adopted a tax on cigarettes in 1931, on beer in 1933, and on distilled spirits in 1935. Additional selective sales taxes were adopted in the 1940s and 1950s, but it became apparent that a more general and more broad-based tax would be necessary to meet revenue needs. In 1961, Texas adopted a general sales tax on most items sold. At the same time, Texas, like most states, first drastically reduced its property taxes, and then abandoned them for exclusive use by local governments. Texas has adopted several types of sales taxes:

General Sales Tax
A broad-based tax collected on the retail price of most items.

Selective Sales Tax, or Excise Tax
A tax levied on specific items only.

Hidden Tax
A tax that is reflected in higher prices of the goods and services sold.

Gross-Receipts Tax
A tax on the gross revenues of certain enterprises.

1. **General sales taxes** are broad-based taxes collected on the retail price of most items.
2. **Selective sales taxes,** also known as **excise taxes,** are levied on the sale, manufacture, or use of particular items, such as liquor, cigarettes, and gasoline. Because these taxes are usually included in the items' purchase price, they are often **hidden taxes.**
3. **Gross-receipts taxes** are taxes on the total gross revenue (sales) of certain enterprises, such as utilities and insurance companies. A new broad-based margins tax applies to the gross sales of most corporations and limited partnerships after taking a deduction for cost of goods or personnel. Small companies, sole proprietorships, and general partnerships are exempt.

As shown in Figure 24–2, most state tax revenue in 2008–2009 came from various sales tax collections. The general sales tax (6.25 percent on retail sales of most items) yielded 26.6 percent of the state's revenues; motor fuels taxes, 4.0 percent; and motor vehicle sales and rental taxes, 4.4 percent. Once a major source of state revenue, *severance taxes* (production taxes on oil and natural gas) now account for only 3.2 percent. Texas also collects special taxes on a range of items and activities, such as tobacco, alcohol, registration of motor vehicles, hotel and motel occupancy, insurance company operations, and bingo games.

Most states, like Texas, rely heavily on sales and gross-receipts taxes, but few are as dependent on them as Texas. Texas is one of seven states without a personal income tax, and it is one of only four states without a corporate income tax. In 15 states, income taxes account for the largest share of revenues.

State taxes remain low in Texas compared with those in other states. Whereas the average state collects 6.0 percent of its residents' incomes in taxes, Texas collects 4.5 percent. Even taking into account Texas's relatively high local taxes, the Tax Foundation calculated that Texas state and local governments collect only 9.3 percent of personal income. In 2007, residents of only seven states paid less in state and local taxes.

did you know?

That Texans have the third lowest state taxes (as a percentage of income) in the nation.

Other Revenues

Besides state taxes, Texas has several other sources of revenue. The federal government represents an important source of funds, and the state legislature can also borrow funds by issuing bonds, although borrowing is severely restricted. The remainder of the state's revenues comes from miscellaneous sources.

Federal Grants-in-Aid. Federal funds are provided for Texas state and local government programs. For the 2008–2009 period, Texas received about $51 billion in federal funds, which represents more than 30 percent of state revenues (see Figure 24–3). A large majority of the funds Texas spends for health and human services and more than 40 percent of its expenditures for transportation originate as federal grants. Although there has been movement toward consolidating federal grant-in-aid programs, they are so numerous that it is only possible to generalize in discussing them.

The evolution of federal grants to state and local governments has a long and controversial history. Although some grants from the national government to the states began as early as 1785, the adoption of the income tax in 1913 drastically altered the financial relationship between the national and state governments by making possible extensive aid to state and local governments.

FIGURE 24–3 Federal Funds as a Share of All Texas Funds, 2008–2009

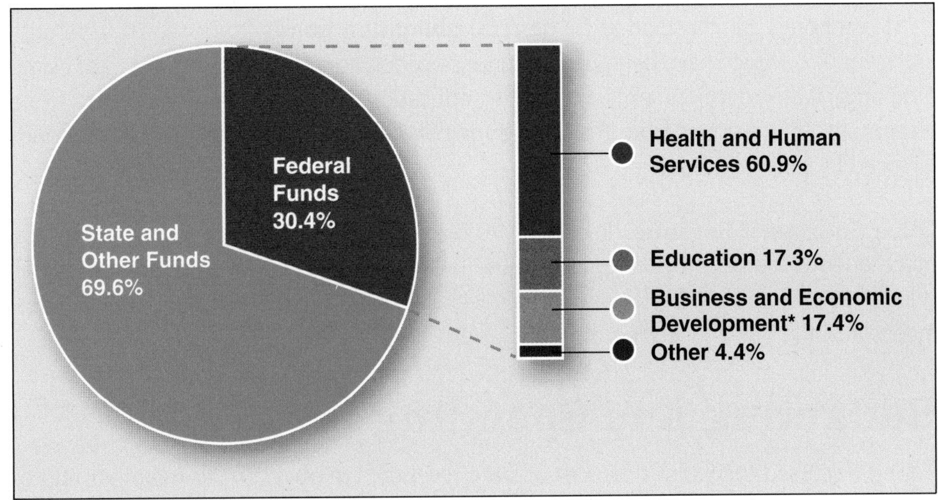

*Primarily highways.
Legislative Budget Board.

As discussed in Chapter 3, the Great Depression of the 1930s brought with it a series of financial problems more severe than any that state and local governments had previously experienced. Increased demands for state and local services when revenues were rapidly declining stimulated a long series of New Deal grant-in-aid programs, ranging from welfare to public health and unemployment insurance.

As discussed previously in Chapter 3, most of these early grant-in-aid programs were *categorical grants.* Under such aid programs, Congress appropriates funds for a specific purpose and sets up a formula for their distribution. Certain conditions are attached to these grant programs:

1. The receiving government agrees to match the federal funds with its own at a ratio fixed by law (between 10 and 90 percent of the cost of the program).
2. The receiving government administers the program. For example, federal funds are made available for Medicaid, but the state actually pays client benefits.
3. The receiving government must meet minimum standards of federal law. For example, states are forbidden to spend federal funds in any way that promotes racial segregation.

Sometimes additional conditions are attached to categorical grants, such as regional planning and accounting requirements.

Today, most federal aid is in the form of *block grants* (see Chapter 3) specifying general purposes, such as job training or community development, but allowing the state or local government to determine precisely how the funds should be spent. Conditions may also be established for receipt of block grants, but state and local governments have greater administrative flexibility than with categorical grants. In recent years, federal transportation, welfare, and many other grants have been reformed to allow for significant devolution of power to the states through block grants.

Borrowing. Forty state constitutions or statutes require the legislature to pass a balanced budget. The Texas Constitution is more effective at limiting state borrowing than the constitutions of most other states. At the beginning of each legislative session, the comptroller of public accounts reports to the legislature the total amount of revenues expected from current taxes and other sources, and the legislature can in turn appropriate no more than this amount unless it enacts new tax laws. There are a few exceptions to this general limit: (1) the legislature, by a nearly impossible four-fifths vote, may borrow in emergencies; and (2) the 1876 constitution may be amended to provide for the issuance of bonds for specific programs. Such restrictions have been very effective; only Nebraska and Tennessee have a lower per capita state debt than Texas.

State bonds are classified as (1) **general-obligation bonds** (to be repaid from general revenues), which have been used to finance prison construction, veterans' real estate programs, water development, and higher education, and (2) **revenue bonds,** to be repaid with the revenues from the service they finance, such as higher education bonds financed by tuition revenue.

General-Obligation Bond
A bond to be repaid from general taxes and other revenues; such bond issues usually must be approved by voters.

Revenue Bond
A bond to be repaid with revenues from the project financed, such as utilities or sports stadiums.

Other Sources of Revenue. In addition to taxing, grants-in-aid, and borrowing, several miscellaneous sources provide revenue to the Texas government. The state receives a small share of its income from the lottery; various licenses, fines, and fees; dividends from investments; and the sale and leasing of public lands.

Budgeting and Spending

Having discussed the various sources of state revenue, we now turn to the other end of the income stream—budgeting and spending. We begin by describing the budgetary process and then discuss spending policies.

The Budgetary Process

The budgetary process includes two basic steps. First, a budget plan must be formulated. Then, the legislature must appropriate the funds necessary to implement the plan.

Budget Planning. Every state has developed some sort of central budgeting agency. Typically, such agencies are set up within the executive branch and are provided with a staff to analyze and evaluate budget requests before submitting a comprehensive budget to the legislature for its consideration. In some states, budget preparation is the joint responsibility of both the legislative and the executive branches.

Texas has established a dual system of budget preparation in which the legislative and executive branches each have separate budget agencies: (1) the Legislative Budget Board (LBB), a legislative agency made up of the presiding officers of the Texas House and Senate plus four other members from each of the two houses, and (2) the governor's office.

These two budgeting agencies engage in some joint activities. A full year before the legislature meets, they jointly prepare forms on which the state's operating agencies submit their budgetary requests. After these requests are submitted, joint hearings are held, but the LBB's staff and the governor's staff independently prepare budget proposals. Not surprisingly, these two proposed budgets differ considerably, as each of the two branches, the legislative and the executive, has its own distinct perspectives, goals, and political considerations.

In preparing their budgetary requests, agencies have a strong tendency toward **incremental budgeting**—that is, they tend to base their current budget requests on past appropriations plus some additional amount. In the rush of the short 140-day session, the legislature cannot conscientiously evaluate billions of dollars in budget requests, so it reviews ongoing programs in light of past expenditures, whereas new spending programs are viewed more critically. This process inherently assumes that past appropriations reflect current needs. Reformers frequently advocate **zero-based budgeting,** which would instead evaluate existing programs as if they were new programs for which funding had to be justified.

Incremental Budgeting
A budgeting practice in which an agency bases its budget requests on past appropriations plus increases to cover inflation and increased demand for services; this process assumes that past appropriations justify current budgetary requests.

Zero-based Budgeting
A budgeting practice in which existing programs are evaluated as if they were new programs rather than on the basis of past levels of funding.

Appropriations Process
The process by which a legislative body legally authorizes a government to spend specific sums of money to provide various programs and services.

Dedicated Funds
Revenues dedicated for a specific purpose by the constitution or by statute.

Appropriations. The legislature legally authorizes the state to spend money to provide its various programs and services through the **appropriations process.** Appropriations bills follow the same steps as other legislation (described in Chapter 24), through standing committee consideration, floor action, conference committee compromise, final voting, and approval by the governor. During most of the legislative process, the recommendations of the LBB carry greater weight than those of the governor, because they usually reflect the wishes of the legislature's powerful presiding officers.

Perhaps the governor's most effective influence in the appropriations process results from the item veto. Like 42 other governors, the Texas chief executive can veto particular items of expenditure without vetoing the whole bill. Although all vetoes can be legally overridden by a two-thirds vote of the legislature, in practice, item vetoes on appropriations bills are final. The legislature finishes its work on the appropriations bill so late in the session that it has usually gone home by the time the governor takes up the bill; obviously, such after-session vetoes are immune to an override attempt.

Despite the importance of the appropriations process, the legislature's control over state expenditures is limited in several ways. **Dedicated funds** prevent the legislature from systematically reviewing the state's expenditures. For example, three-fourths of revenues from motor fuel taxes are dedicated to the State Highway Fund and one-fourth to the Available School Fund. Earnings from state lands are automatically directed to the Permanent University Fund and the Permanent School Fund. Contributions to the Teacher Retirement Fund may be used only for their specified purpose. The Texas Constitution and state statutes automatically channel 45 percent of state revenues to specified purposes with little or no legislative involvement. Federal grants, court orders, and other restrictions also limit the legislature as it adopts appropriations bills. Only one-sixth of the state's budget is discretionary funding (unaffected by federal, state, statutory, or court requirements).

Biennial legislative sessions make it difficult to spend state funds rationally. It is impossible to predict with precision, say, how many students will enroll in a college for the upcoming semester. Nevertheless, the legislature is expected to predict the state's financial needs two years in advance based on how many students will enroll in all public colleges in the state as well as elementary and secondary schools, how many applicants will be found eligible for unemployment and welfare benefits, how many potholes will develop along state highways, how many criminals will be sentenced to state prison, how many patients will be admitted to state hospitals, and so on. Inevitably, some agencies will be overfunded and others will have too little. Overfunded agencies always find ways to spend whatever money they have, whereas others literally run out of money during the two-year budget period.

did you know?

That if you counted one dollar every second, it would take you about 2,660 years to count the state's average annual expenditures.

The Politics of Spending

A wide variety of factors affects the level of state spending and complicates efforts toward rational budget planning. Nowhere is the dynamic nature of politics as evident as in public finance; nowhere is the conflict between competing economic interests more visible than in the budgetary process. Behind the large figures that represent the state's final budget are vigorous conflict, compromise, and coalition building. Most of society's programs are evaluated not only according to their merit but also in light of the competing demands of other programs and other economic interests. Government programs and problems, including highways, education, urban decay, poverty, crime, and the environment—in short, all the problems and challenges of a modern society—compete for a share of the public treasury.

Powerful political constituencies, interest groups, and their lobbyists join forces with state agencies to defend the programs that benefit them. This alliance between administrative agencies and interest groups brings great pressure to bear on the legislative process. Legislators trade votes (a process called logrolling) to gain funding to benefit their districts or their political supporters.

No single decision better typifies the political character of a state than its budget decision. The whole pattern of spending is, in a sense, a shorthand description of which problems the state has decided to face and which challenges it has chosen to meet. The budget shows how much of which services the state will offer and to whom. Figure 24–4 shows how Texans spent their state revenues in the 2008–2009 budget period. The most costly service in Texas remains education. Public and higher education accounted for 44.4 percent of the state budget. Health and human services (including Medicaid and public assistance), in second place, accounted for 31.6 percent. Transportation, primarily highways, accounted for 10.1 percent. These three services consumed more than four-fifths of the state's budget, with a wide variety of miscellaneous services using up the remainder.

Education

The educational system in Texas includes elementary and secondary schools (the public schools) and the college and university system (higher education).

Elementary and Secondary Schools

Public schools were accepted institutions in the North by the early 19th century, but they did not take root in the South (including Texas) until after the Civil War. Not until the constitution of 1876 provided that alternate sections of public land grants must be set aside

FIGURE 24–4 State Appropriations by Function, 2008–2009 Budget Period (in Billions of Dollars)

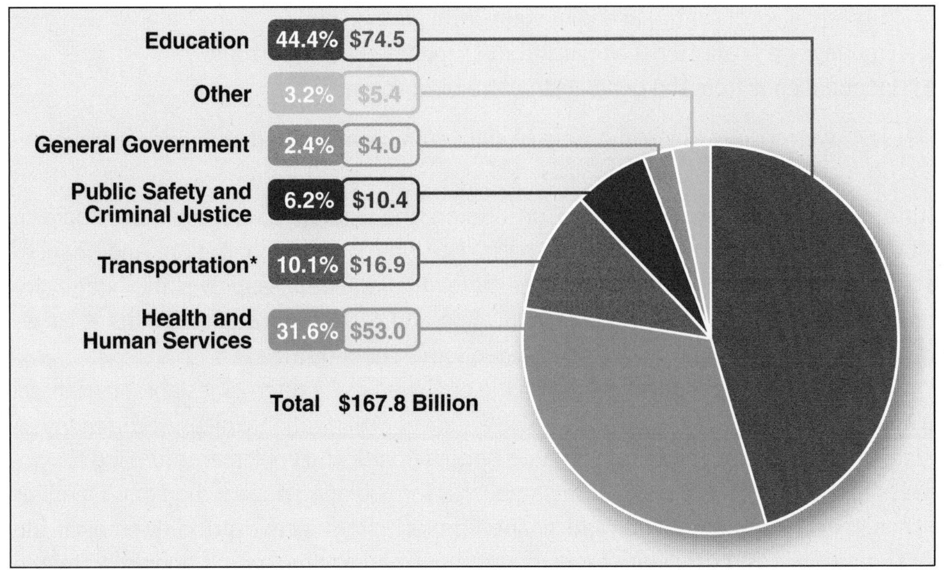

*Primarily highways.
Legislative Budget Board.

to finance schools did the state begin to commit itself to locally administered, optional public schools.

Meaningful state support for public education started with a compulsory attendance law, enacted in 1915, and a constitutional amendment that provided for free textbooks in 1918. In 1949, the Gilmer-Aikin law increased state funding and established the Texas Education Agency (TEA), which carries out the state's educational program.

Recent Trends. Sweeping changes in education resulted when House Bill 72 passed in 1984 to establish statewide **accountability** standards for student test performance and teacher competence. Former President George W. Bush later took the use of high-stakes testing nationwide with his No Child Left Behind program.

> **Accountability**
> Responsibility for a program's results—for example, using measurable standards to hold public schools responsible for their students' performance.

Although the standards used to measure public school performance are sometimes controversial, there has been a recent trend toward using them to bring market forces to the public school system. Some teachers and administrators receive merit pay, bonuses for improved student achievement. To introduce the element of competition, the state legislature authorized the State Board of Education to establish schools with special program charters, able to recruit students from across existing school district boundaries.

Entire school districts may also exempt themselves from most state regulations by adopting a home-rule school district charter. Texas was the first state to allow such districts; adoption of home-rule charters is difficult, requiring a majority vote in an election in which at least 25 percent of registered voters participate. Many state legislators now also favor *privatization* by providing vouchers to help students buy their education from private and religious organizations.

Today, public elementary and secondary education has grown from a fledgling, underfinanced local function into a major state–local partnership. The TEA administers approximately 30 percent of all state expenditures, helping local school districts educate the approximately 90 percent of Texas students who attend public elementary and secondary schools. Public policy decisions affect the knowledge, attitudes, and earning potential of these 4.6 million students and the approximately 300,000 individuals who teach them.

Public School Administration. As in other states, public school administration in Texas has three basic aspects:

1. Substantial local control in a joint state–local partnership.
2. Emphasis on professional administration supervised by laypersons.
3. Independence from the general structure of government.

Next, we consider the relationship of state administration and local administration.

State Administration. The Texas Constitution, the legislature, and the State Board of Education (SBOE) have established the basic decision-making organizations and financial arrangements for public education in the state. The legislature approves the budget for the state's share of the cost of public education and sets certain standards, but it leaves most routine decision making to the TEA and local school districts.

The State Board of Education, which we discussed in Chapter 25, establishes general rules and guidelines for the TEA. The SBOE approves organizational plans, recommends a budget to the governor and the Legislative Budget Board, and implements funding formulas established by the legislature. It sets standards for operating public schools and requires management, cost-accounting, and financial reports from local districts. Moreover, the SBOE recommends a candidate for commissioner of education, who is appointed by the governor with the consent of the senate.

The commissioner serves as the state's principal executive officer for education; she or he is assigned several assistant and associate commissioners and has a professional staff. They carry out the regulations and policies established by the legislature and the SBOE concerning public school programs. As professionals, the commissioner and staff have enough experience to make recommendations to the SBOE and to influence substantially its decisions.

did you know?

That Texas students taking the Scholastic Aptitude Test (SAT) in 2007 ranked 42nd among the 50 states.

Local Administration. Texas has 1,031 school districts (more than any other state), and these districts are the basic structure for local control. Voters in independent school districts elect seven or nine trustees (depending on the district's population) at large or from single-member electoral districts for either three- or four-year terms. These trustees set the district's tax rate and determine school policies within the guidelines established by the TEA. They approve the budget, contract for instructional supplies and construction, and hire and fire personnel. Their most important decision is the hiring of a professional superintendent, who is responsible for the executive or administrative functions of the school district.

Elected state and local school boards usually follow the recommendations of professional administrators (the commissioner and the superintendents). Most educational decisions are made independently of general government. Nevertheless, we should not conclude that this constitutes independence or that localization or professionalism keeps education free of politics. On the contrary, whenever important public decisions are made, political controversy and conflict arise.

The Politics of Public Education. One of the most important decisions concerning public education is what education should be. Should it promote traditional views of society, reinforce the dominant political culture, and teach "acceptable" attitudes? Alternatively, should it teach students to be independent thinkers, capable of evaluating ideas for themselves? Because the Texas state educational system determines the curriculum, selects textbooks, and hires and fires teachers, it must answer these fundamental questions.

Curriculum. The TEA determines most of the basic curriculum for Texas public schools. Some school districts supplement this basic curriculum with a variety of elective and specialized courses, but in the basic courses—history, civics, biology, and English—students are most likely to be exposed to issues that may fundamentally affect their attitudes. How should a student be exposed to the theory of evolution? What about a course in sex education? In the social sciences, should the political system be pictured in terms of its ideals or as it actually operates, with all of its mistakes and weaknesses? How should the roles of women and minorities be presented? Should students who do not speak standard English be gradually taught English through bilingual education, or should they immediately be immersed in the core curriculum taught in English?

The substance of education in Texas is important in other respects as well. Although a large proportion of public school students will never enroll in an institution of higher learning, much educational effort and testing have been directed toward college preparatory courses that provide graduates few, if any, usable job skills. Historically, vocational, agricultural, and home economics programs were viewed as "burial grounds" for pupils who had failed in the traditional academic programs. Today, almost half of public school students are enrolled in "career and technology" programs, and one in five are in "family and consumer sciences." Although program titles have changed, much remains to be done to meet the need for highly skilled technical workers who possess other practical life skills.

did you know?

That the percentage of adults with a high school diploma is lower in Texas than in any other state.

Textbooks. The SBOE selects a list of approved textbooks that the state will buy for public school courses. The selection process generates intense political battles between conservative organizations (such as the Texas Public Policy Foundation, Mel Gabler's Educational Research Analysts, and Texas Freedom Works) and liberal groups (such as the Texas Freedom Network). In general, the conservatives dominate the battle. Some publishers withdraw their text offerings, whereas others change the content of their texts to satisfy the SBOE, which controls the second largest textbook market in the nation. As a result, Texas's textbook decisions effectively determine the content of texts used in public schools in much of the nation.

Legally, the State Board of Education can determine only the accuracy of textbooks, but it has used this power to pressure publishers to submit texts that reflect the political and religious values of its members. One publisher eliminated references to "fossil fuels formed millions of years ago" from a science text because it conflicts with some interpretations of the timeline in the Bible. Another publisher eliminated sections that were perceived as too kind to Muslims because they asserted that Osama bin Laden's actions were inconsistent with commonly accepted Islamic teachings (even though this was the official policy view of the president and the U.S. government). An environmental science text was rejected because it favorably mentioned the Endangered Species Act and warned of the threat of global warming—one group argued that it was unpatriotic to refer to the fact that the U.S. represents 5 percent of the world's population, but produces 25 percent of greenhouse gases. Under recent pressure from religious conservatives, publishers submitted health textbooks that presented an abstinence-only approach to sex education, excluding essential information about how to prevent unwanted pregnancies and sexually transmitted diseases.

State Board of Education members are shown at their desks with samples of health textbooks before a meeting of the Board in 2004. Social conservatives and sex education advocates squared off at the final public hearing before the Board adopted new health textbooks for Texas school students. A Texas Department of Public Safety officer stands in the background as people look at some of the books. (AP Photo/Harry Cabluck)

A Texas government text was rejected because it included an article that asserted that religious conservatives influence the SBOE!

did you know?

That on average, Texas physicians earn $158,060; lawyers, $114,980; pharmacists, $96,290; and elementary school teachers, $42,660.

Faculties. A 15-member state board for educator certification establishes standards for qualification, conduct, and certification of public school teachers. Actual hiring of teachers is a local matter. Most districts do not follow a publicly announced policy of hiring or dismissing teachers because of their political viewpoints, but in many districts, teachers are carefully screened for their attitudes. Salary and working conditions are perpetual issues of dissatisfaction among teachers because they affect morale and recruitment. The student-to-teacher ratios in Texas schools remain similar to those in other states, but increasing public demands for accountability have added reporting and other paperwork to teachers' workloads beyond the standard expectations for lesson planning, grading, and communicating with parents.

Expected income is certainly a factor when people choose their careers, and education simply does not rank favorably among the professions. Furthermore, Texas teachers' average salary of $41,744 in 2005–2006 ranked 35th among the 50 states (15 percent below the national average), according to the National Education Association. The TEA reported that one-third of beginning teachers leave the profession by their fifth year.

Students. Public schools have changed considerably in recent years. The number of students attending Texas public schools has been increasing at a rate of about 2 percent per year, and that increase is expected to continue for the next decade. Students are also more ethnically diverse than in the past.

Scores on the Texas Assessment of Knowledge and Skills (TAKS) test measure student achievement but will soon be phased out for high school students to be replaced with 12 end-of-course exams in core classes. Student accountability programs limit *social promotion* (promotion to the next grade based on age rather than level of learning) and a "no pass, no play" rule forbids students from participating in extracurricular activities without obtaining a passing grade in academic subjects. Most high school students are required to take four years of math and science.

Perhaps as a result of these efforts, student performance on standardized tests has been improving somewhat. Sixty-seven percent of all students taking TAKS were able to meet standards in 2007 (80 percent of whites, 59 percent of Hispanics, and 52 percent of African Americans passed). Texas students taking the National Assessment of Educational Progress ("The Nation's Report Card") scored close to the national average in math and reading.

Public School Finance. In 2005–2006, expenditures for public school operations in Texas were $7,547 per student, ranking Texas 44th among the 50 states (17 percent below the national average). The actual distribution of these funds is so complex that it has been said that there are probably only four or five people in the state who fully understand Texas's system of school finance. Public school funding comes from three sources: federal, state, and local.

Federal grants have been declining in recent years. Most of the funds from federal grants are used for child nutrition and special needs, military, and low-income students. *State funding* comes from a variety of sources. The Permanent School Fund invests receipts of rentals, sales, and mineral royalties from Texas's public lands. Only the interest and dividends from this permanent endowment may be spent. Earnings from the Permanent School Fund and one-fourth of the motor fuels tax make up the Available School Fund. Part of this fund is used for textbooks; the remainder is distributed to local school districts based on students in average daily attendance. Basing distribution of state funds on attendance focuses a school district's attention on truancy.

did you know?

That Texas per-student expenditures were less than in 43 other states.

The Foundation School Program (FSP) accounts for the largest portion of state and local funding by far. State funds are from general revenues, a new broad-based business gross-receipts tax, and higher tobacco taxes and are distributed to districts according to a complex formula based on district and student characteristics. The FSP is structured as a state–local partnership to bring some financial equality to local districts, despite vast differences in local tax resources.

Local funding comes primarily from ad valorem property taxes. The market value of property is determined by the county appraisal authority for all local governments within the county, and local district boards then set the property tax rate stated as an amount per $100 of property value. Local school district trustees may set the property tax rate for maintenance and operations up to $1 per $100 valuation.

These property taxes are used to pay about 40 percent of the FSP basic operating expenses, with the state paying for the remainder. The state supplements local funds to ensure that each district has a basic allotment per student ($3,218 in 2009) and guarantees that each additional cent in local tax above the minimum must yield at least $36.45 per student.

In addition, to provide greater equality in local funding, the richer districts must reduce their taxable property per student to a ceiling of $374,200 by sharing directly with poorer districts or by sending money to the state for redistribution to other districts. Most wealthy districts simply send money to the state.

Some local tax revenues are not subject to these "recapture" requirements. Districts may tax up to an additional 50 cents per $100 for construction, other capital improvements, and debt service; they may also tax a small amount for educational enrichment.

Higher Education

Like public schools, higher education is a major state service, accounting for 12 percent of state expenditures during the 2008–2009 budget period. Texas public institutions of higher education include 35 general academic institutions and universities, nine health-related institutions, and seven technical and state colleges. Fifty public community colleges operate on more than 70 campuses.

Figure 24–5 shows that public institutions enroll 90 percent of all students in Texas higher education. The majority of students enroll in public community colleges where average tuition and fees cost about one-third as much as at public universities.

FIGURE 24–5 Texas Higher Education Enrollments, Fall 2007

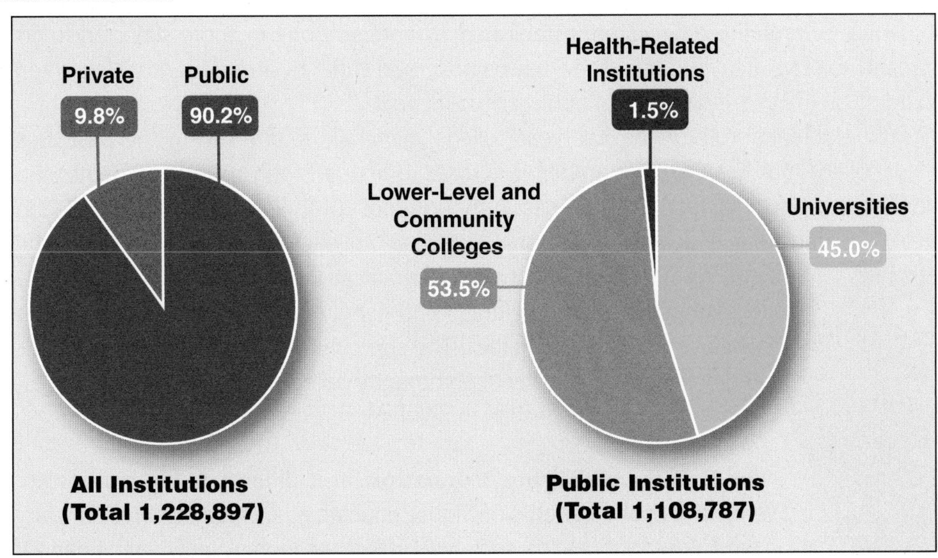

Source: Texas Higher Education Coordinating Board.

Administration of Colleges and Universities. The Texas Higher Education Coordinating Board was established to coordinate the complex system of higher education in the state. The governor, with the consent of the senate, appoints its 18 members, and they serve for six-year terms. The Coordinating Board appoints the commissioner of higher education to supervise its staff. Together, the board and staff outline the role of each public college and university and determine future needs for programs, curricula, and physical plants.

Because Texas's colleges and universities were not established systematically, the Coordinating Board has difficulty imposing a sensible plan for them to relate to one another. Politically powerful boards of regents compete to impose their views on higher education, as do other groups. Regents and trustees set basic policies for these institutions, within the limits of state law and the rules and guidelines established by the Coordinating Board.

Some boards of regents govern single-campus institutions. Others govern institutions located on several campuses:

- The University of Texas system includes the University of Texas at Austin (with the nation's third largest student population on a single campus) and other campuses located at Arlington, Brownsville, Dallas, El Paso, Permian Basin, San Antonio, and Tyler, as well as the University of Texas—Pan American and several medical and health units.
- The Texas A&M system has its main campus at College Station, with additional campuses at Corpus Christi, Commerce, Texarkana, Galveston, Kingsville, Prairie View A&M, Tarleton State, West Texas A&M, and Texas A&M International.
- The Texas State University system includes Sam Houston State, Texas State University at San Marcos, Sul Ross State, Sul Ross State—Rio Grande Valley, Lamar University, Lamar Institute of Technology, and Lamar State College in Orange and Port Arthur.
- The University of Houston has its main campus in Houston, as well as a downtown campus and campuses at Clear Lake and Victoria.
- The Texas Tech System includes the main campus at Lubbock, several other Western Texas campuses, health science centers, and Angelo State University.

The administrative structure of senior colleges and universities may include systemwide administrators (chancellors), campus presidents, deans, and other officers. The Coordinating Board also generally supervises community colleges, which are authorized and financed largely by the state. Unlike four-year institutions (which are usually designed to attract students from larger regions of the state and nation as well as international students), community colleges are established by voters in one or more school districts primarily to serve area residents. They may be governed either by an independently elected board or by the trustees of a local public school district.

The traditional role of the two-year college, generally referred to in the past as a junior college, has been to offer academic courses to first- and second-year students who would later transfer to four-year colleges. Although most of their students are enrolled in transferable academic courses, two-year colleges have responded to the demands resulting from economic diversification by adopting a community college approach—adding adult, continuing, and special education courses as well as technical specialties. The curriculum, low cost, and geographic and financial accessibility of community colleges have resulted in increasing enrollments, especially in academic programs.

did you know?

That the University of Texas at Austin ranks 44th and Texas A&M University—College Station 62nd in *U.S. News and World Report*'s 2008 ranking of top national universities.

The Politics of Higher Education. It is difficult to measure objectively many of the benefits of higher education, such as personal satisfaction and contributions to society and the economy. Individual financial benefits, however, are very clear. High school graduates have an average annual income of $31,071; those with an associate's degree earn $39,724; and college graduates have an average income of $65,395.[1]

Despite its benefits, legislative bodies and boards of regents and trustees have often been critical in their evaluations of higher education and its results. Calls for faculty and student accountability have been frequent. Yet there are no generally agreed-upon answers to the questions raised about higher education: What should its goals be? How should it measure success in achieving those goals? To whom should it be accountable? We examine some issues concerning higher education in the remainder of this section.

Faculty Issues. Salaries are a perpetual issue when Texas institutions of higher education recruit new faculty. Average full-time public college and university faculty salaries, for example, are still significantly below the national average.

Rationalizing their attempts as an effort to promote faculty accountability, college and university administrators have long sought to dilute job-protection guarantees for professors. State law requires governing boards to adopt procedures for periodic reevaluation of all tenured faculty. Faculties generally fear such policies as a threat to academic freedom and a tool for political repression by administrators.

Financial Issues. Financing higher education is a continuing issue. Like elementary and secondary schools, most colleges and universities in Texas must struggle with relatively small budgets. Meanwhile, increasing college enrollments and demands for specialized, high-cost programs are increasing at a time when prisons, health care, and other services are also placing more demands on state revenues. Revenues in turn are limited by the legislature's reluctance to increase taxes. Proposals to cope with financial pressures include closing institutions with smaller enrollments, reducing duplication, restricting student services, raising tuitions, and delaying construction plans or the implementation of new degree programs.

Student Retention. Related to these financial issues is the question of affordability. College and university boards have been raising tuitions, mandatory student fees, and housing costs. Table 24–1 shows that between 2003 and 2007, average tuition and fees at Texas public universities rose 62 percent, to $5,569. At community colleges, tuition and fees increased to $1,639.[2] Financial accessibility of higher education is thus a growing concern.

1. U.S. Census Bureau, Current Population Reports, 2007 *Annual Social and Economic Supplement,* Table PINC-04.
2. Texas Higher Education Coordinating Board data, cited in Susan Combs, *Texas in Focus: A Statewide View of Opportunities* (Austin: Office of the Comptroller of Public Accounts, January 2008).

TABLE 24–1 Texas Resident Tuition and Fees, 30 Credit Hours

Fiscal Year	Universities	Community Colleges
2003	3,441	1,120
2004	3,782	1,245
2005	4,332	1,453
2006	4,867	1,483
2007–2008*	5,569	1,693

*2007–2008 is for the academic year.
Source: Texas Higher Education Coordinating Board.

did you know?

That college graduates typically earn at least $1 million more than high school graduates during their working lifetimes.

High costs, lack of course availability, inadequate academic preparation, and personal factors all contribute to the problem of student retention. Among full-time degree-seeking students at public universities, 24 percent graduate within four years and 57 percent receive degrees within six years. Retaining students is also a significant issue at other institutions of higher learning, especially community colleges.

Inequalities. Inequality in the distribution of limited public resources is also an issue. General legislative appropriations have been more generous for the University of Texas (UT) at Austin and Texas A&M University than for other colleges and universities. Furthermore, the state constitution earmarked more than 2 million acres of public land for the Permanent University Fund (PUF). Two-thirds of the earnings from the PUF go to the campuses of the UT system, and one-third goes to Texas A&M University campuses. A long-awaited constitutional amendment now requires the legislature to establish a higher-education fund of $2 billion in permanent endowments for the benefit of state universities that do not participate in PUF funding. The legislature has been slow to provide this funding, however.

did you know?

That, in 2007, only Harvard, Yale, Stanford, and Princeton had total endowments larger than the University of Texas System, with its $15.6 billion.

Affirmative Action. Institutions of higher education have struggled with other inequities as well. One issue concerns efforts to recruit minority students to increase ethnic diversity and offer more services to underserved populations. Those efforts became especially difficult when the federal Fifth Circuit Court of Appeals ruled that race could not be considered in affirmative action admissions policies.[3] The Texas legislature responded by requiring that general college and university academic institutions automatically admit students from the top 10 percent of their high school graduating class regardless of test scores (as discussed in Chapter 24). This policy guaranteed that the top-ranking students in predominantly minority high schools would be able to attend a public university in Texas. Other states attempted to achieve diversity by considering low family income and other special nonracial obstacles that make it difficult for students to meet standard admission criteria.

The United States Supreme Court has begun to allow race to be considered in college admissions policies so long as specific point advantages are not assigned to minorities.[4] These decisions have sent most administrators scrambling to find acceptable affirmative action policies.

Health and Human Services

The second most costly category of state spending can be broadly classified as health and human services. This category encompasses public assistance, Medicaid for the poor, and a variety of other programs. In the 2008–2009 budget period, these programs cost $53 billion (32 percent of the state's total budget). About 60 percent of this funding originates as grants-in-aid from the federal government.

did you know?

That one in six Texans lives in poverty.

The Texas Health and Human Services Commission provides a variety of social services, including Temporary Assistance to Needy Families, Medicaid, and the Children's Health Insurance Program, as shown in Figure 24–6 on the following page. The commission also coordinates planning, rule making, and budgeting among its four subsidiary social-service agencies: the Department of Aging and Disability Services, the Department of Assistive and Rehabilitative

3. *Hopwood v. Texas,* 84 F.3d 720 (5th Cir. 1996).
4. *Grutter v. Bollinger,* 539 U.S. 306 (2003); and *Gratz v. Bollinger,* 539 U.S. 234 (2003).

FIGURE 24–6 Texas Health and Human Services Agencies

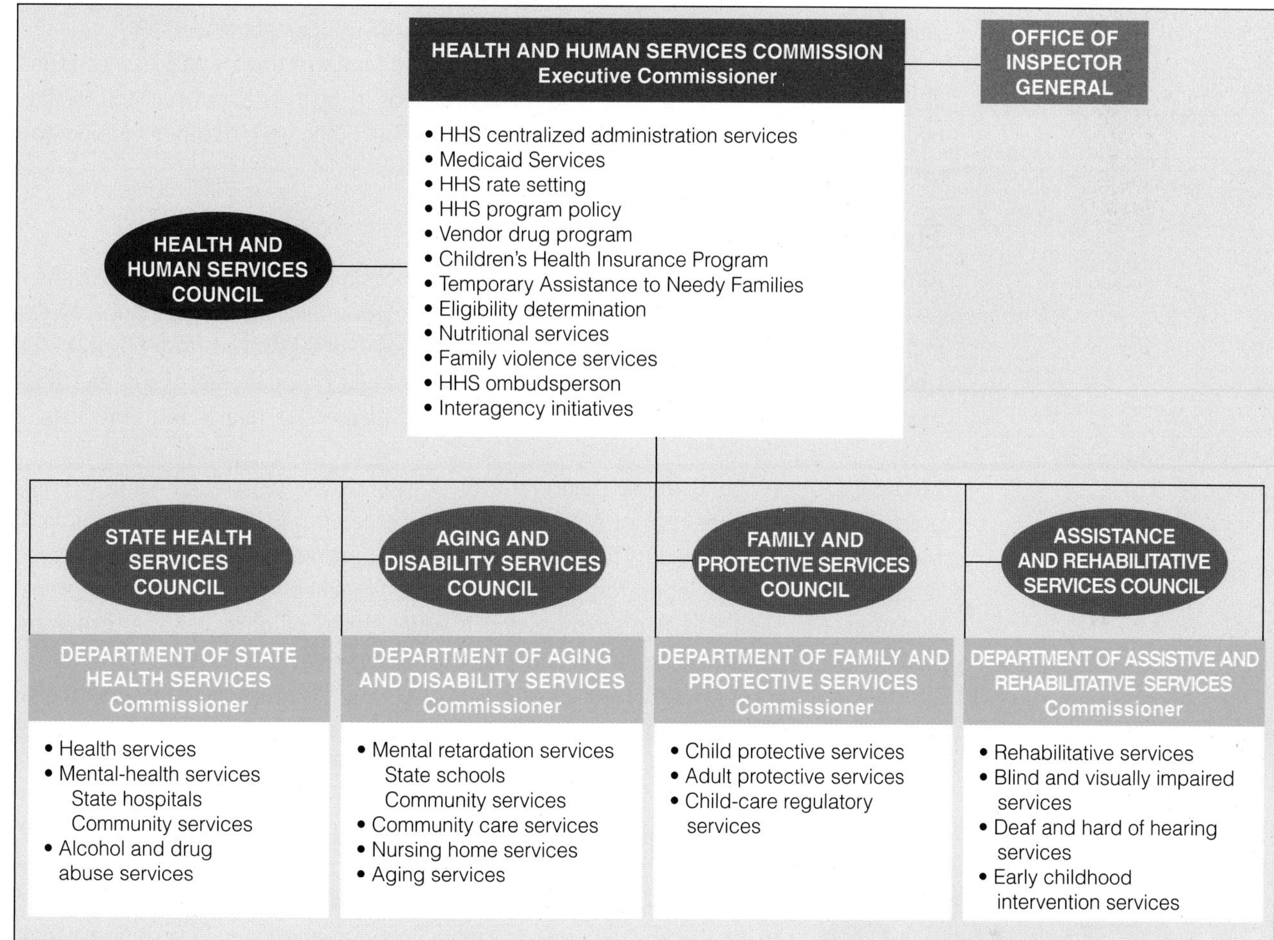

Source: Health and Human Services Commission.

Services, the Department of Family and Protective Services, and the Department of State Health Services. In general, social services can be categorized as income-support programs, health programs, or unemployment programs.

Income Support Programs

One important income-support program is Temporary Assistance to Needy Families (TANF), designed for children whose parents are incapable of providing for the children's basic needs. More than two-thirds of TANF recipients are children. Unless they are disabled or needed at home to care for very young children, adult TANF recipients are referred for employment counseling, assessment, and job placement.

The TANF-Basic program serves those who are deprived of support as a result of the absence or disability of one or both parents. TANF grants are also available for two-parent families in which the principal wage earner is unemployed and the family income does not exceed the criteria established for the basic program. Because TANF eligibility requires that family income must be at least 86 percent below the poverty level, the vast majority of the 3.7 million Texans living in poverty cannot receive benefits.

Federal and state regulations now place additional limits on TANF benefits. Adult eligibility is usually limited to two years at a time, with a maximum five-year lifetime benefit. These welfare reforms were intended to force able-bodied individuals out of dependency and into productive work. Some federal funds are distributed as block grants to the states to allow them flexibility in developing support services, child care, job training and placement, and rehabilitation programs to help welfare recipients find work. These reforms have reduced the number of TANF recipients in Texas by 75 percent since 1996.

In 2007, the maximum monthly TANF grant for a family of three was $243, considerably below the national average. The median benefit in Texas is about half the median benefit nationwide, and adjusting for inflation, TANF benefits have declined considerably over the years.

Health Programs

Although opponents of government's assuming responsibility for public health describe it as "socialized medicine," health care has concerned public authorities since Moses imposed strict hygienic codes on the Jews during their biblical exodus from Egypt. In the United States, the federal government began to provide hospital care to the merchant marine in 1798. Today, health care is the second most expensive service Texas provides.

Medicaid. Texas spends more than one-fifth of its state budget on the Medicaid program, but about 60 percent of Medicaid funding comes from the federal government. Medicaid reimburses providers for most health services, including eyeglasses, prescription drugs, physicians' fees, laboratory and X-ray services, family planning, ambulance transportation, Medicare Part B premiums, and a wide variety of other medical expenses. Generally, these providers are in managed care (HMO-type) systems.

Medicaid should not be confused with *Medicare,* which is available to all persons over age 65, is financed by federal payroll taxes, and is administered by the U.S. Department of Health and Human Services. In contrast, only certain categories of individuals are eligible for the state-administered Medicaid program: (1) any persons eligible for TANF or Supplemental Security Income (SSI), a federal program that may be available to aged, blind, or disabled individuals; (2) low-income persons residing in institutions who qualify for SSI except for certain income requirements; (3) children up to 19 years of age whose family financial status would qualify for TANF but who reside in families with two able-bodied parents; (4) pregnant women who would qualify for TANF but have no other children; (5) children ages six through 18 who reside in families with income below the federal poverty level; (6) children under age six whose families' income is at or below 133 percent of the federal poverty level; (7) pregnant women and infants under one year of age who reside in families with income below 185 percent of the federal poverty level; (8) medically needy individuals whose income is not more than one-third higher than that allowed for TANF participation; and (9) Medicare beneficiaries whose incomes are no more than 135 percent of the federal poverty level.[5] More than 90 percent of Medicaid patients are elderly persons, persons with disabilities, or children.

did you know?

That one in four Texans lacks health insurance, the highest uninsured rate in the nation.

Other Health Programs. For low-income children who are not eligible for Medicaid, the Children's Health Insurance Program (CHIP) helps parents with incomes of less than 200 percent of the poverty level obtain health insurance for their children. Despite these programs, one in five Texas children remains uninsured.[6]

The state Department of Health Services licenses hospitals and provides personal health programs for special populations. The Women, Infants, and Children (WIC) pro-

5. Texas Health and Human Services Commission, "Texas Medicaid Program," available at www.hhsc.state.tx.us/medicaid/index.html.
6. U.S. Census Bureau, "Table HIA-5: Health Insurance Coverage Status and Type of Coverage by State, Children Under 18, 1999 to 2006."

gram provides nutrition and health assistance for women who are pregnant, have just given birth, or are breastfeeding infants. In addition, the health department operates a lung and tuberculosis hospital in San Antonio and a general-services hospital in Harlingen. Because this department deals with communicable diseases, it is likely to be a center of attention in the event of an epidemic or a biological terrorist attack.

The Department of Health Services also operates general psychiatric hospitals and locally governed special or contract mental-health facilities and community centers. Most such problems, however, are treated privately or not at all. For individuals who are treated at public expense, Texas, like most states, provides treatment on a community, outpatient basis. Some 3 million Texans suffering from mental illness require mental-health services,

POLITICS AND... public policy

REGULATING CELL PHONE USE

Many Americans believe that using a cell phone while driving an automobile can be dangerous. Many of these same individuals admit to using their cell phones while doing so. In a survey conducted by the Insurance Research Council, 84 percent of cell phone users reported that using cell phones while driving could increase the likelihood of accidents, while another 61 percent reported using their cell phones while driving.[a] Some studies have also found delayed reaction time, "especially in the beginning stages of the telephone conversation."[b] Whether talking on cell phones or texting, these electronic devices are perceived to be a danger to drivers. Given this evidence, state lawmakers are trying to figure out how best to regulate cell phone use in automobiles.

NEGATIVE SIDE EFFECTS OF NEW TECHNOLOGY

Some states have already taken steps to either ban or limit hand-held cell phone use in automobiles. In 2008, California, Connecticut, New Jersey, New York, Utah, and Washington were the only states to ban the use of hand-held cell phones while driving. Texas and 16 other states have banned the use of cell phones while operating a school bus. Texas also bans intermediate license holders from using a cell phone for the first six months that they hold this license.[c] These limitations on cell phone use may very well be the beginning of a flood of laws regulating cell phone use.

Some state lawmakers are more concerned with drivers using their cell phones to text message. In May 2007, Washington became the first state to ban sending and receiving text messages while driving, and New Jersey soon followed. Texting while driving is proving to be as controversial as, if not more than, talking on a cell phone. Since 2007, 21 states have looked into regulating texting. In Texas, West University Place has banned using cell phones in school zones—the first municipality to do so. If this policy leads to improvements in driving habits, one can expect state lawmakers and other municipalities to do the same.

Public policy is inspired by a variety of factors. When new technology is introduced into society, lawmakers, like those in the Texas legislature, react to the impact of technology on society and respond to regulate the negative side effects of it. In doing so, lawmakers attempt to limit government intrusion without compromising public safety.

FOR CRITICAL ANALYSIS

Do you think that these attempts have been successful? What do you think about the regulation of cell phone use? What other factors contribute to the enactment of legislation?

a. Insurance Research Council (IRC), "Cell Phone Owners Prefer to Ignore the Risks," accessed at www.ircweb.org/.
b. Andrew Parkes and Victor Hooijmeijer, "The influence of the Use of Mobile Phones on Driver Situation Awareness," accessed August 20, 2008, at www-nrd.nhtsa.dot.gov/.
c. Insurance Institute for Highway Safety: Highway Loss Data Institute, "Cell Phone Laws," accessed August 25, 2008, at www.iihs.org/laws/CellPhoneLaws.aspx.

but only 5 percent of them receive services from the state. Another half-million Texans are developmentally disabled, but only 30,000 of them receive direct state services.

Unemployment Programs

As discussed previously in Chapter 17, with the Social Security Act of 1935, the U.S. Congress established a system of unemployment insurance that would become a partnership program between the states and the federal government. This Act imposed a tax on covered employers to establish a nationwide system of unemployment insurance administered by the federal government. The Act provided that most of this tax would be set aside in the states that adopted an acceptable state program. Thus, every state in the union was pressured into adopting a state system of unemployment insurance.

Today, benefits are financed from state taxes on employers, but some administrative costs are paid with federal funds. These programs are actually administered by the state. In Texas, unemployment insurance is administered by the Texas Workforce Commission (TWC), a three-member board appointed by the governor, with the consent of the senate, for six-year overlapping terms.

did you know?

That between 2001 and 2007, Texas health insurance costs rose 78 percent to $12,106 for the average family policy.

Under Texas's rather restrictive laws, a worker who loses his or her job may be able to collect a weekly benefit payment for a maximum of 26 weeks. The payments are based on past earnings regardless of need or family size. A worker receiving benefits must register for job placement with the TWC. In addition, a worker is ineligible to receive benefits (at least for a time) if he or she voluntarily quit, was fired for cause, or was unemployed because of a labor dispute. Because the rate at which employers are taxed is based on claims made by former employees, employers have an interest in contesting employee claims.

Handling unemployment insurance claims is a minor part of the TWC's activities; its major functions are to provide a workforce for employers, gather employment statistics, enforce child-labor laws, and provide various special job-training and rehabilitation services. Able-bodied welfare recipients are referred to the TWC for training and child-care services. Regional workforce development boards plan one-stop career development centers in 28 areas across the state.

Transportation

The third most costly service provided by the state of Texas is transportation. As we mentioned earlier, transportation (primarily highways) accounted for about 10.1 percent of expenditures in 2008–2009.

Highway Programs

In the early days of Texas history, road construction was primarily a county responsibility. Most Texas counties still maintain a property tax dedicated to the construction and maintenance of roads, and in rural areas, road building remains a major function of county government. The efforts are too small and too poorly financed, however, to provide the expensive, coordinated, statewide network of roads needed by highly mobile Texans in the modern world.

In contrast to county roads, state highways in Texas are better financed. In 1916, the national government encouraged state governments to assume the major responsibility for highway construction and maintenance. The 1916 Federal Aid Road Act made available federal funds to cover one-half of the construction costs for state highways. To become eligible for those funds, a state was required to establish an agency to develop a coordinated plan for the state highway system and to administer construction and main-

TABLE 24–2 The Texas Highway System

Type of Roadway	Total Miles	% of Traffic Accommodated
Interstate highways	9,953	26%
Farm-to-market roads	40,996	11
Federal and state highways	28,357	36

Note: Figures do not include more than 222,000 miles of city streets and county roads, which accommodate approximately one-third of traffic.
Source: Susan Combs, *Texas in Focus: A Statewide View of Opportunities* (Austin: Office of the Comptroller of Public Accounts, January 2008).

tenance programs. Texas responded by establishing the Texas Highway Department, now known as the Texas Department of Transportation (TxDOT). The department is supervised by a five-member commission appointed by the governor, with the consent of the senate, for six-year overlapping terms. The commission appoints an executive director, who oversees the department and supervises the work of regional district offices.

Newer federal aid programs and increased funding for existing ones have expanded the responsibilities of the transportation department. The earliest highway-building program was designed to provide only major highways along primary routes. Federal funding later became available for secondary roads, and Texas established the farm-to-market program to assume state maintenance of many county roads as the rural road network was paved, extended, and improved. Finally, beginning in 1956, Congress made funds available for 90 percent of the cost of constructing express, limited-access highways to connect major cities in the United States. Altogether, the state highway system today consists of 79,645 miles of highways (including 339 miles of park and recreation roads) and carries almost three-fourths of the state's motor vehicle traffic (see Table 24–2).

Funding for the highway program is a joint federal–state responsibility. In the 2008–2009 period, the federal government, mostly from the federal gasoline tax, provided more than 40 percent of the transportation department's revenues. The federal government pays for 90 percent of the construction cost of interstate highways and 80 percent of the cost of other primary and secondary highways. This large federal contribution has allowed the national government to demand such restrictions as meeting clean-air standards and setting a minimum drinking age of 18 as conditions for receiving federal aid.

State monies account for close to 60 percent of TxDOT funding. The state highway fund is supported through a sales tax on lubricants, motor vehicle registration fees, and three-fourths of the 20-cent-per-gallon motor fuels tax. The majority of TxDOT's expenditures are for construction, and most of the remainder is for highway maintenance. The department also handles federal funding for mass public transportation, issues motor vehicle titles, and regulates commercial motor carriers.

did you know?

That recently, Texas ranked last among the 50 states in per capita spending (28 percent below the national average).

The Politics of Transportation

The Good Roads and Transportation Association, a private organization supported by highway contractors and other groups, lobbied for the establishment of the state highway fund and for increases in motor fuel taxes and still attempts to guard the fund against those who would spend any part of it for other purposes. Despite the organization's efforts, per capita state highway funding in Texas is now among America's lowest.

Texans have, so far, been unreceptive to alternatives. Automobile transportation is as close to the hearts of Texans as it is to other Americans; no other mode of transportation seems as convenient because no other is as individualized. Buses, trains, and airplanes cannot take individuals exactly where they want to go exactly when they want to go there.

Only in New England, New York, Washington, D.C., and Chicago is mass transit a viable alternative to the personal vehicles that have become a way of life as well as a status symbol. The manufacture, maintenance, and fueling of automobiles have become dominant elements of the economy. Drive-through restaurants, drive-through banking facilities, and even drive-through churches have influenced people's habits. For the young, motor vehicles have influenced dating and mate selection. They have become a manner of personal expression as well; small efficient hybrids, large luxurious sedans, SUVs, pickup trucks, and finely tuned sports cars express different personal images and self-concepts.

So dependent are Texans on their automobiles that they ignore the cost of using their vehicles to themselves individually and to society. Texas's annual highway death toll is close to 4,000, and thousands more are injured every year. The motor vehicle is also the single most important contributor to atmospheric pollution, a factor in global warming (the greenhouse effect), and a significant source of refuse that finds its way into junkyards and landfills. As the least efficient mode of transportation now available, the individual motor vehicle is in direct conflict with the need to conserve energy and reduce our strategic dependence on foreign oil (a factor in terrorism and foreign wars).

Because of these problems, some people advocate increasing the investment of public funds in alternative means of transportation. With adequate financing, railroads could once again become rapid and comfortable. In many big cities, mass transportation provided by buses and trains could become an attractive alternative. Nevertheless, in some areas where significant investment has been made in mass transportation, the public has not responded with increased use. Given Texans' love affair with the automobile and their strong individualism, it seems doubtful that the state would seriously consider significant funding for any of these alternatives.

In spite of its many costs, the automobile is the preferred method of transportation in Texas, making it difficult to introduce more efficient alternatives. This photo shows highway IH-30 traffic with the Dallas skyline in the background. (AP Photo/Tony Gutierrez)

WHY SHOULD YOU CARE ABOUT... STATE SERVICES?

Texas students or their families pay local property taxes either directly, if they are homeowners, or indirectly as hidden taxes if they rent their dwellings. Texas has among the lowest state taxes in the nation partly because the state has pushed the cost of many services down to the local level. As a result, Texans pay relatively high local property tax rates.

BECOME AN INTELLIGENT TAXPAYER

You (or your family) may be among many local property taxpayers who have seen taxes grow much more rapidly than their incomes. In fact, your property may be taxed disproportionately higher than your neighbors.' You can have a direct impact on the property taxes you (or your family) pay.

Your local property taxes are based on the appraised value of your real estate. Local governments in your area use a central countywide appraisal district usually accessible online. It determines the value of your property.

You can protest the appraised value of your property with this appraisal authority. You may find your efforts rewarded—in some jurisdictions, fewer than 10 percent of owners protest their property appraisals, but as many as 75 percent of those who do succeed in lowering their taxes. Be prepared with photos, specific measurements of floor space and land area, and a list of any defects that might diminish the value of the property. How do you know what the appraised value of your property should be? You can research the appraised values of other comparable properties in your neighborhood; these values are a matter of public record and are available in the appraisal district of the county where you live.

HOW YOU CAN MAKE A DIFFERENCE . . . AND SAVE MONEY!

You may be eligible for a homestead exemption if you live in a home you own. Such an exemption allows you to pay less in property taxes than you would otherwise. A special exemption is also available for the elderly. It is the taxpayer's responsibility to apply for these exemptions. To locate your county appraisal authority and to find the appraised value of any property, go to **www.txcountydata.com**.

Much state and federal tuition assistance goes undistributed. Visit your school's financial aid office to determine if you qualify for tuition help. Find help at the Texas Higher Education Coordinating Board Web site at **www.collegefortexans.com** and the comptroller's Web site at **www.window.state.tx.us/scholars/aid/aidtx.html**.

A parent's failure to make child-support payments may force the other parent to apply for Temporary Assistance to Needy Families. If you have this problem, call the attorney general's child-support enforcement office at the number listed in your local telephone directory, or visit the attorney general's Web site at **www.oag.state.tx.us/cs/index.shtml**.

Find lower electric and telephone rates and stop unwanted telephone solicitations at the Public Utilities Website at **www.puc.state.tx.us**.

See if your family and friends are eligible for state social services by checking links at **www.hhsc.state.tx.us/about_hhsc/HHS_Agencies.html**. Or, dial 211 for human service needs. Compare health insurance plans at **www.texashealthoptions.com**.

Before you buy a new vehicle, contact the Texas Department of Transportation, which maintains "lemon law" records at **www.dot.state.tx.us**.

When you buy auto and homeowner's insurance, check with the Texas Department of Insurance, which publishes rates and numbers of customer complaints. Go to **www.tdi.state.tx.us/consumer/index.html**.

Apply for a job or unemployment compensation at the Texas Workforce Commission, **www.twc.state.tx.us**.

The most comprehensive Web site for state services is at **www.state.tx.us**.

questions for discussion and analysis

1. In the politics of taxation, how are different groups' views of the "public interest" affected by their social and economic positions?
2. How do Texas's public policy decisions result from political bargaining, compromise, and coalition building among competing interests?
3. Which political values do Texas public policy priorities reflect?

key terms

accountability 765
appropriations process 763
dedicated funds 763
general-obligation bond 762
general sales tax 760
gross-receipts tax 760
hidden tax 760
incremental budgeting 763
revenue bond 762
selective sales tax, or excise tax 760
zero-based budgeting 763

chapter summary

1. State tax rates are low in Texas compared with other states and are not rising as a percentage of personal income. Nevertheless, about half of state revenues are raised through taxes. A substantial portion (about one-third) comes from federal grants-in-aid, and miscellaneous sources account for the rest. State borrowing is limited.
2. Although political self-interest determines which kinds of taxes are used, taxing decisions may be rationalized as serving some regulatory purpose or reflecting benefits received or ability to pay.
3. Both narrow- and broad-based taxes are used in Texas. The largest single state tax is the general sales tax, which is regressive relative to income because it falls most heavily on middle- and lower-income people. Other state taxes, as well as the ad valorem tax employed by local governments, are also regressive in their effect. The federal income tax is somewhat progressive.
4. The Legislative Budget Board, the state legislature, and the governor become involved in state spending decisions. The process is political. Perhaps no other type of decision evokes more consistent and passionate political efforts from interest groups and administrative agencies.
5. Education, health and human services, and transportation are the major services that state government offers, together constituting more than four-fifths of the total cost of Texas's state government. These services have a significant effect on the way Texans live and even on the way they think. It is nearly impossible to evaluate them objectively because they affect varying groups so differently.
6. The educational system of Texas is generally decentralized and independent of the normal course of partisan politics. Its administrators and curricula are conservative, as is much of Texas politics. Compared with other states, per capita expenditures, per-student expenditures, and teacher salaries are below average.
7. Health-care services are both publicly and privately financed in Texas, as in the rest of the nation, and they are plagued by a similar problem: the rising costs of providing better services to more people. A smaller proportion of residents are insured to cover these costs in Texas than in any other state, however.
8. In many ways, the Texas system of public welfare reflects the same values that are present in the state educational system. It too is poorly financed, and the public-assistance programs that the state has adopted were established only with the financial support of the national government. Few of these programs are designed to eliminate the root causes of poverty.

9. The highway system has consistently lost funding despite the efforts of the Good Roads and Transportation Association, and per capita spending for highways is less than in most other states. Texans refuse to consider increased spending for highways or alternative means of transportation. Privatization of highways has been proposed as an alternative to the inadequate public highway system.

10. Individual and group positions on these and virtually all public policies differ according to who benefits and who pays the cost for which public services. The process of allocating costs and benefits is the very essence of politics.

selected print & media resources

SUGGESTED READINGS

Blau, Joel, and Mimi Abramovitz. ***The Dynamics of Social Welfare Policy.*** **New York: Oxford University Press, 2004. This work examines national social-welfare policy in the context of history, social change, and the economy.**

Combs, Susan. ***Exemptions and Tax Incidence*** **(Austin: Office of the Comptroller of Public Accounts, February 2007). This excellent analysis of major Texas taxes demonstrates who bears the burden of each tax and how business taxation ultimately falls on consumers.**

——. ***Texas in Focus: A Statewide View of Opportunities*** **(Austin: Office of the Comptroller of Public Accounts, January 2008). This wide-ranging report discusses state problems and programs ranging from education to health to the environment in an authoritative but provocative style.**

Heller, Donald E., ed. ***The States and Public Higher Education Policy: Affordability, Access, and Accountability.*** **Baltimore, MD: Johns Hopkins University Press, 2001. In this series of essays, various authors explore some of the most serious issues states face in making decisions about higher education.**

Legislative Budget Board. ***Fiscal Size-Up, 2008–2009.*** **Austin, TX: Legislative Budget Board, 2008. This state publication details state taxing and spending programs as well as recent developments in Texas public policy.**

Norton, Peter D. ***Fighting Traffic: The Dawn of the Motor Age in the American City.*** **Cambridge, MA: MIT Press, 2008. This insightful book describes the dramatic changes in society that were necessary to accommodate motor vehicle transportation.**

MEDIA RESOURCES

The Battle over School Choice—**This PBS *Frontline* video explores the heated debate over whether public school reform or privatization (including voucher plans) is a better choice.**

The Merrow Report: In Schools We Trust—**Americans rarely agree on what public education should do: Teach basics? Train workers? Inculcate democratic values and tolerance? This PBS video explores varying views on public education.**

NOW with Bill Moyers: Medicaid Mess—**This PBS feature deals with the tough choices concerning Medicaid and also discusses the cultural values that divide America.**

Promoting Prosperity for Texas: Role of State and Local Governments—**Produced by Texas's Center for Public Policy Priorities and available at the group's Web site, www.cppp.org, this short feature engages the state's challenges in funding public services.**

Tax Me If You Can—**Produced by PBS *Frontline,* this video offers an inside look at how big corporations and wealthy individuals use tax shelters to avoid paying income taxes.**

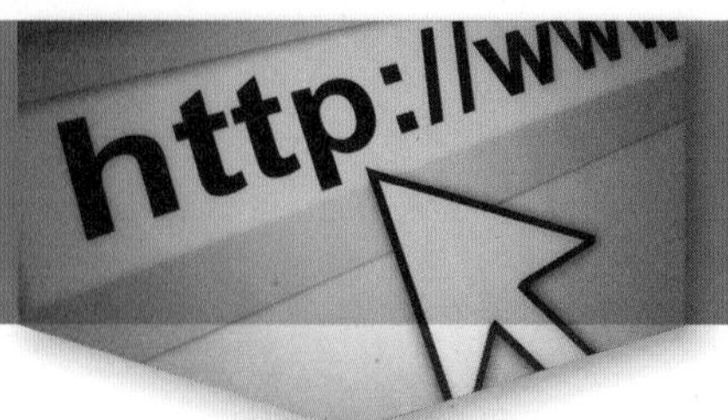

e-mocracy

TAP INTO TEXAS THINK TANKS AND EXPLORE PUBLIC POLICY

Taxing and spending policies generate much political controversy. The Internet makes it possible for various interest groups and individuals to publicize their positions on these issues. As you read in the Chapter 18 *Making a Difference* feature, many special-interest groups sponsor public-policy research institutes, sometimes referred to as think tanks, with Web sites that students can access for diverse views on state policy. At the same time, the Internet makes available more-reliable public resources that students can use to evaluate state policies and services.

LOGGING ON

The key government site for taxes and the budget is the Window on State Government of the Comptroller of Public Accounts at:
www.window.state.tx.us
Scroll down to "Find a Comptroller Publication" to find some of the most complete financial information about Texas that is available.

You can also research tax and budget issues and the latest state appropriations bills at the Legislative Budget Board Web site at:
www.lbb.state.tx.us

The Texas Education Agency is the key site for public education. Visit the TEA site at:
www.tea.state.tx.us

To examine the complex funding of Texas public schools, go to:
www.capitol.state.tx.us
Click on "Statutes" and then on "Education Code." Scroll to Chapters 41, 42, and 43.

Many special-interest groups provide persuasive arguments for their views of taxation. The Texas Taxpayers and Research Association represents the conservative and business perspective on taxation. Go to:
www.ttara.org
Click on "Documents" to examine the group's lobbying positions.

For other antitax, business-oriented tax arguments, go to the Tax Foundation site at:
www.taxfoundation.org
Click on "Research Areas" and select "State Policy and Data."

For the liberal and labor positions on taxes, browse the Citizens for Tax Justice site at:
www.ctj.org
Select "State Issues" and go to Texas.

See how Texas public schools compare to other states and note the standards used for comparison at the Chamber of Commerce Web site at:
www.uschamber.com/icw/reportcard/default

Tap into Texas-based "think tanks" with public policy Web sites that offer contrasting conclusions about a wide range of issues. Even though they are funded by special-interest groups, they can still provide interesting perspectives and useful information. Decide where you stand on welfare, education, transportation, and health-care reforms. Visit think tank Web sites and determine where your views fit into the conservative or liberal spectrum.

Conservative think tanks include:
The Institute for Policy Innovation at **www.ipi.org**
Lone Star Foundation at **www.lonestarfoundation.org**
Private Enterprise Research Center at **www.tamu.edu/perc**
Texas Conservative Coalition Research Institute at **www.txccri.org**
Texas Public Policy Foundation at **www.texaspolicy.com**

Liberal/progressive think tanks include:
The Center for Public Policy Priorities at **www.cppp.org**
Public Citizen—Texas State Office at **www.citizen.org/texas**
Texas Center for Policy Studies at **www.texascenter.org**
Texans for Public Justice at **www.tpj.org**

ONLINE REVIEW

At **www.cengage.com/politicalscience/schmidt/agandpttexas 14e**, you will find a Tutorial Quiz for this chapter, providing questions on the chapter contents, including the features. You'll gain access to other helpful study tools, including the book's glossary and flashcards, crossword puzzles, and Web links, as well as "Which Side Are You On?" and "Politics and . . ." features written by the authors of the book.

chapter
25

Local Government

chapter contents

Municipalities

Counties

Special Districts

Councils of Governments

<< Critically important decisions that affect the well-being of a community are made at City Hall. (David R. Frazier/The Image Works)

WHAT IF... ... Texas cities appointed students to city councils?

Concerned citizens meet in Austin, Texas, with police and city council members regarding crime, gangs, and drugs. (Bob Daemmrich/Image Works)

Politicians want to hear the perspectives of students. In Texas, the governor appoints a student regent to the board of regents of every public university for a one-year term. Student regents are not board members, but they still enjoy the "powers and duties" that come with board service, except they cannot vote on or second a motion, and their presence will not count toward the quorum needed for the board to meet or cast votes.[a]

Other states have student representation on higher education boards, and in some cases students have voting privileges. City councils throughout the nation appoint high school students to youth commissions in an effort to learn more about the challenges facing young people in their communities. While youth commissioners serve only in an advisory capacity, their perspectives are of great value to mayors and council members whose votes on safety, education, recreation, and health issues can have a direct bearing on a city's youth.

By appointing student regents and creating youth commissions, public officials demonstrate that they value student participation in the political decision-making process. Texas cities could make student input at city hall even more meaningful if they went one step further and added a student seat to their city councils.

Even as a nonvoting member, a student serving on a city council would routinely interact with the mayor, council members, and city staff about council agendas, ordinances, zoning proposals, tax hikes and abatements, and the budget process. City council service would give a student an in-depth look at the inner workings of city government and municipal politics. Mayors and councils would have the benefit of a student's perspective on a wider range of issues than those typically labeled youth issues.

a. Texas Education Code, Sections 51.355 and 51.356.

CIVIC ENGAGEMENT

A 2006 survey of local governments reveals that officials recognize a variety of ways the public can make their views known, including attending city council meetings and public hearings, serving on boards and commissions, and completing citizen surveys. But Evelina R. Moulder and Robert J. O'Neill Jr. point out that "There is an important distinction between providing input and participating in the solution."[b] They also note that the survey reveals differences in the amount of resources (such as staff assistance, funding and budget information) local governments provide to boards and commissions.[c] A student who holds a seat on the city council, even in a nonvoting capacity, would have access to the same resources as the elected members of the council, and that would make the student a more knowledgeable, engaged, and effective participant in the deliberation process.

According to the National Civic League, "Citizens who are educated about their community, their government, and their history will come to believe that their actions matter and that they can make a difference."[d] Appointing a student to the city council would strengthen the student voice in a community in a way that would benefit students, city hall, and society as a whole.

FOR CRITICAL ANALYSIS

1. What qualifications should a student have in order to be appointed to a city council?
2. If a city has a youth commission, should the city council select only from a list of candidates approved by the commission when appointing a student to the council?
3. If the youth commission and the student appointed to serve on the city council disagree on a proposed ordinance, which perspective should the city council weigh more heavily?

b. Evelina R. Moulder and Robert J. O'Neill Jr., "Citizen Engagement and Local Government Management," *The Municipal Yearbook 2007* (Washington, DC: the International City/County Management Association), p. 33.

c. Moulder and O'Neill Jr., p. 34.

d. "Life-Long Learning for Life-Long Civic Participation," *National Civic Review,* accessed April 4, 2008, at www.ncl.org/cs/articles/okubo7.html.

Should a city place red-light cameras at high-traffic intersections? Or annex a neighboring unincorporated area against the wishes of those who live there? How should counties provide for mentally ill prisoners? These are just a few issues that have been placed on the agendas of local governments throughout the nation, including Texas.

These examples are of a local nature, but a visit to the Web sites of the U.S. Conference of Mayors and the National Association of Counties (NACo) underscores the following point: issues of national importance are also highly relevant to local governments. In 2008, the U.S. Conference of Mayors emphasized several objectives, including anticrime measures, climate protection, public housing assistance, infrastructure improvements, and youth employment opportunities in "Strong Cities . . . Strong Families . . . for a Strong America: Mayors' 10-Point Plan." That same year, NACo legislative priorities focused on a variety of goals, including food safety, renewable and alternative energy, reauthorization and expansion of the State Children's Health Insurance Program, and improving health care for veterans. It selected the theme of "Protecting Our Children" for National County Week. Both organizations stressed homeland security concerns.

The use of red light cameras has grown throughout the nation. (Jim Mahoney/Dallas Morning News)

The sheer number of local governments in Texas can challenge even the most interested members of a community who want to contact local officials occasionally or routinely about pressing concerns, ranging from fixing potholes to the need for better street lighting and more police to the rise in the number of homeless families. (See Table 25–1 for a comparison of local governments in Texas and in the United States as a whole.) Anyone who lives in a metropolitan area is likely to be governed by several special districts (such as a hospital district, a metropolitan transit authority, and a municipal utility district), in addition to the two **general-purpose governments**—the municipal and county governments.

General-Purpose Government
A municipal or county government. In contrast to special districts, general-purpose governments provide a wide range of services.

In an effort to shed more light on the inner workings of local government, we examine in the following sections the various institutional features of cities, counties, and special districts. We also look at issues and trends facing local government. Finally, given the growing interest in finding regional solutions to local problems, we discuss the role of councils of governments (COGs) at the local level.

TABLE 25–1 Local Governments and Public School Systems, U.S. and Texas, 2007

Total	County*	Municipal	Town or Township	Special Districts	School Districts
United States					
89,476	3,033	19,492	16,519	37,381	13,051
Texas					
4,835	254	1,209	0	2,291	1,081

*Excludes areas corresponding to counties but having no organized governments.
Source: U.S. Census Bureau, *2007 Census of Governments.* Available at www.census.gov/govs/cog/GovOrgTab03ss.html.

Municipalities

Cities hire police and firefighters to protect the community. Cities enforce building and safety codes, pass antilitter ordinances, issue garage sale permits, maintain recycling programs, launch antigraffiti programs, impound stray animals for the safety of the community, and enforce curfews. Some cities have passed ordinances in the interest of public safety and the health of a community. In some cases, an ordinance can be subject to amendments, or several ordinances pertaining to one issue are proposed, as was the case with the smoking ban issue in Corpus Christi. (See Figure 25-1.)

All local governments in Texas are bound by federal and state laws as well as the U.S. and Texas constitutions. The relationship between state and local governments follows from the fact that states, including Texas, have a *unitary* form of government. (We discussed unitary governments, as opposed to federal systems, in Chapter 3.) Municipalities—like counties, special districts, and school districts—are creatures of the state and have only as much power as the Texas Constitution and Texas legislature grant them. Texas has seen a marked increase in the number of municipalities in the state since the 1950s (see Table 25–2).

General-Law City
A city operating under general state laws that apply to all local government units of a similar type. In Texas, cities with a population of 5,000 or less are (in most instances) general-law cities.

Home-Rule City
A city with the state-granted right to frame, adopt, and amend its own charter.

Charter
An organizing document for corporations or municipalities.

General-Law and Home-Rule Cities

Texas cities are classified as either general-law or home-rule cities. According to the Texas Municipal League, the vast majority of Texas cities—about 75 percent—are general-law cities, and more than 5,000 unincorporated communities have no municipal government.

A **general-law city** is an incorporated community with a population of 5,000 or less and is limited in the subject matter on which it may legislate. A city with a population of more than 5,000 may, by majority vote, become a **home-rule city.** This means it can adopt its own **charter** and structure its local government as it sees fit, as long as these

FIGURE 25–1 The Many Iterations of an Ordinance

An ordinance may undergo many changes between the time it is first voted on by a governing body and the time it is finally approved.

	Brent Chesney	Javier Colmenero	Melody Cooper	Henry Garrett	Bill Kelly	Rex Kinneson	Loyd Neal	Jesse Noyola	Mark Scott	
Amendment to add bingo halls to areas exempted from smoking ban	👍	👍	👎	👎	👎	👎	👍	👍	👍	5–4 PASS
Amendment to add private clubs to areas exempted from smoking ban	Abstain	👎	👎	👎	👎	👍	👎	👎	👍	2–6 FAIL
Ordinance banning smoking in all public places, including restaurants and bars	👎	👎	👍	👎	👍	👍	👍	👎	👎	4–5 FAIL
Ordinance banning smoking in all restaurants and bars	👎	👎	👍	👎	👍	👍	👍	👎	👎	4–5 FAIL
Ordinance allowing smoking in restaurant bars with sealed areas and separated ventilation	👍	👍	👎	👎	👎	👎	👎	👍	👍	4–5 FAIL
Ordinance banning smoking in Corpus Christi restaurants	👍	👍	👍	👍	👍	👍	👍	👍	👍	9–0 PASS

Leanne Libby, "Smoke Ban Passes," *The Corpus Christi Caller-Times,* January 12, 2005, p. A5.

TABLE 25–2 **Municipal Governments in Texas, 1952–2007**

1952	1962	1972	1982	1992	1997	2002	2007
738	866	981	1,121	1,171	1,177	1,196	1,209

Source: U.S. Census Bureau, *2002 Census of Governments,* Vol. 1, No. 1, available at www.census.gov/prod/2003pubs/gc021x1.pdf; U.S. Census Bureau, *2007 Census of Governments,* available at www.census.gov/govs/cog/GovOrgTab03ss.html.

provisions do not conflict with state and national laws and the U.S. and Texas constitutions. Municipal home rule was established in 1912 by a state constitutional amendment. The Texas Constitution allows a home-rule city whose population has dropped to 5,000 or less to retain its home-rule designation.

Direct Democracy at the Municipal Level. In addition to enabling a city to establish its own charter and laws (also called *ordinances*), home rule permits local voters to impose their will directly on the city government through the initiative, the referendum, and the recall. According to the Texas Municipal League, most home-rule cities have all three provisions.

With the initiative power, after a campaign obtains signatures from a designated percentage of registered voters, it can force a sometimes-reluctant city council to place a proposed ordinance on the ballot. If the proposal passes by a majority vote, it becomes law. Voters who wish to remove an existing ordinance can petition the council to hold a referendum election to determine whether the law should remain in effect. For example, smoking bans were put to a referendum vote in Lubbock and Baytown. In both cases, voters decided to retain the ban.

Finally, voters can, by petition, force the council to hold a recall election that would permit the people to remove the mayor or a member of the council. Texas Attorney General Greg Abbott ruled that recalled members of a city council must step down once the election results are certified—even if that leaves the council without a quorum.[1]

The Limits of Home Rule. While home-rule cities have wider latitude than general-law cities in their day-to-day operations, they still must contend with state limitations on their authority. For example, state law determines the specific dates on which municipal elections can be held. Voters are free to amend city charters, but the Texas Constitution permits cities to hold charter elections only every two years. In addition, an election establishing a metropolitan transit authority can be held only in cities that meet a population requirement determined by the Texas legislature.

Forms of Municipal Government

There are three common forms of municipal government: the council-manager system, the mayor-council system, and the commission system.

The Council-Manager System. In a **council-manager system** (see Figure 25–2), an elected city council makes laws and hires a professional manager who is responsible for both executing council policies and managing the day-to-day operations of city government. The manager serves at the pleasure of the council.

The powers of the city manager come from the city charter and from the delegation of authority by the council through direct assignment and passage of ordinances. For

Council-Manager System
A municipal system featuring an elected city council and a city manager who is hired by the council. The council makes policy decisions, and the manager is responsible for the day-to-day operations of the city government.

1. Texas Attorney General Opinion No. GA-0175 (2004).

FIGURE 25–2 Common Forms of Municipal Government

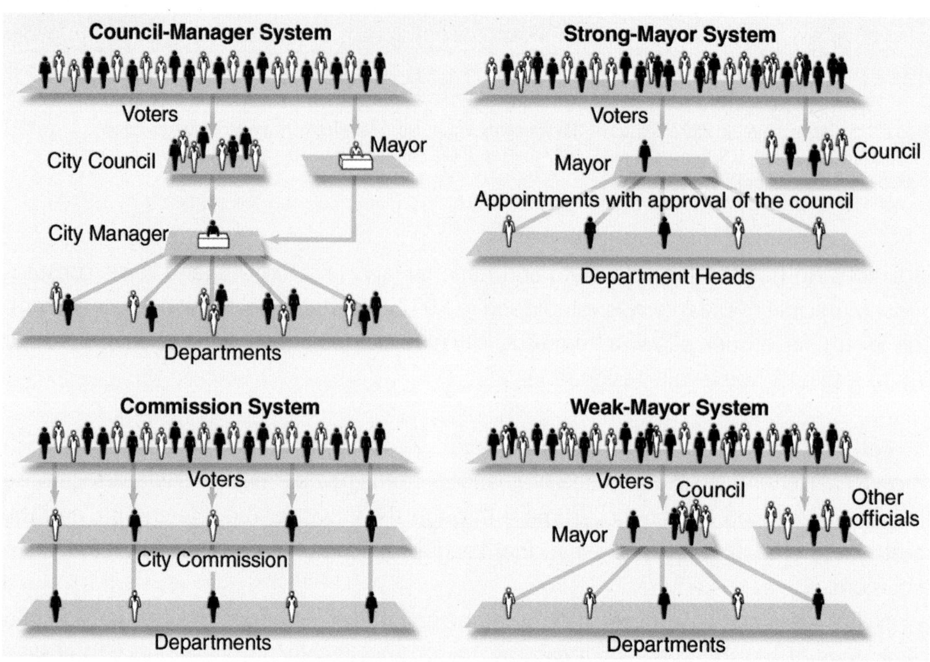

did you know?

During World War II, the U.S. government maintained internment camps in three Texas cities—Seagoville, Kenedy, and Crystal City.

example, the city manager is responsible for selecting key personnel and for submitting a proposed budget to the council for its approval. The city council will probably seek the manager's opinion on a wide variety of matters, including what tax rate the city should adopt, whether the city should call a bond election, and the feasibility of recommendations made by interest groups. But these issues are ultimately up to the council, and the city manager is expected to implement whatever decisions the council makes.

The Mayor's Role. In a council-manager form of government, a mayor may be either selected by the council from among its members or independently elected by the voters. The mayor presides over council meetings, has limited or no veto power, and has, for the most part, only the same legislative authority as other members of the council. The salaries of the mayor and council members are minimal compared with that of the full-time city manager. However, a 2008 survey of 20 Texas cities conducted by the City of Corpus Christi Legal Department revealed that some council-manager cities provide council members expense or travel allowances, cell phones, laptops, and BlackBerrys—all for official use—and health insurance. In 2008 a district judge ordered the City of Corpus Christi to discontinue allowing members of the city council health insurance benefits because the provision was not in the city charter.

The Powers of the Mayor. The mayor in a council-manager system does have important ceremonial powers, such as signing proclamations and issuing keys to the city to important dignitaries. While the office is institutionally weak, a high-profile mayor can wield considerable influence. Henry Cisneros, who served as Secretary of Housing and Urban Development under President Bill Clinton, first achieved national attention as mayor of San Antonio in the 1980s. Ron Kirk, former Texas secretary of state, made history in 1995 as the first African American elected to the position of Dallas mayor in the city's history. San Antonio and Dallas are the two largest Texas cities that use the council-manager system.

The council-manager government was initiated as part of a reform movement during the Progressive Era (1900–1917). Reformers were attempting to substitute "efficient and businesslike management" for the then-prevalent system of "boss rule," in which politics was the key consideration in city hall decisions. While the council-manager system is seen as a means of separating politics from the administration of city government, critics charge that its principal shortcoming is that the voters do not directly elect the chief executive officer of the city.

The Mayor-Council System—Strong Mayor. Mayor-council systems take two common forms—the strong-mayor and weak-mayor forms—each with many variations. In the **strong-mayor system** (see Figure 25–2), the mayor, who is chosen in a citywide election, is both the chief executive and the leader of the city council (a legislative position). The mayor makes appointments, prepares the budget, and is responsible for the management of city government. The mayor also sets the council agenda, proposes policy, and (in many cities) may veto council actions.

Strong-Mayor System
A form of municipal government in which substantial authority (such as authority over appointments and the budget) is lodged in the office of the mayor, who is elected in a citywide election.

Weak-Mayor System
A form of municipal government in which an elected mayor and city council, often along with other elected officers, share administrative responsibilities.

Commission System
A system that allows the members of a city council to serve as heads of city departments.

Although it was criticized by early 20th-century reformers, the strong-mayor form of government did not die out. It was often restructured, however, to include an elected city comptroller (or controller), thus preventing the mayor from having complete control of city finances. (Houston, for example, elects a city controller, who serves as the chief financial officer for the city.) Rules were also adopted to require that contracts be awarded to the lowest and best bidders. Other restrictions in place today that political bosses did not have to contend with include nonpartisan elections; ethics and campaign finance laws; Voting Rights Act coverage in many states, including Texas, that protects minority voting rights; and mayoral and city council term limits in cities throughout the nation.

Houston and Pasadena are the two largest Texas cities with a strong-mayor form of government. El Paso was the second largest city with such a system until 2004. That year, El Paso voters approved the establishment of the council-manager form of government, and a city manager was hired. In 2005, Dallas voters rejected two attempts to replace the city's council-manager system with a strong-mayor form of government.

The Mayor-Council System—Weak Mayor. The **weak-mayor system** (see Figure 25–2) lacks clear lines of authority because the mayor and council share administrative duties. Power, in effect, is decentralized. Under this system, voters may have difficulty determining who should be held accountable when problems and mismanagement occur. This type of government is not common in Texas, although it is used by many small cities.

The Commission System. The **commission system** (see Figure 25–2) is another variety of municipal government found across the United States. In this system, voters elect one set of officials, who act as both executives and legislators. The commissioners, sitting together, are the municipal legislature, but each administers a city department individually. A manager or administrative assistant may be employed, but the ultimate administrative authority still remains with the elected commissioners.

Commissioners may possess technical knowledge about city government because they supervise city departments. Because power in the city bureaucracy is fragmented among separately elected commissioners, however, coordination is difficult, and the checks-and-balances system is impaired.

Municipal Elections Systems

The election systems used by Texas municipalities have sparked a considerable amount of legal and political controversy. The debate has primarily focused on the choice between at-large and single-member district elections.

At-Large Election
A citywide (or, in some states, countywide) election.

Pure At-Large System
An at-large election system in which all voters elect all the members of the city council, and candidates do not run for specific seats.

At-Large Place System
An at-large election system in which all voters elect all the members of the city council, and each candidate runs for a specific seat on the council.

Single-Member District
A district in which the voters elect a single member of a legislative body, who runs for election only in that district.

At-large elections—citywide elections—usually take one of two forms. In the **pure at-large system,** all of the voters elect all of the members of the city council. The voters simply choose among all of the candidates to fill the available council seats, and the winning candidates are those who receive the most votes. With the **at-large place system,** each candidate runs for a specific seat on the council (place 1, place 2, and so forth) and is elected by either a plurality or a majority of votes cast citywide for that particular seat. Variations of either system may require that a candidate live in a particular district of the city, but the candidates are still elected by all of the voters in the city. In contrast, with **single-member districts,** each council member is elected from a particular district by the voters who live in that district.

At-Large Systems Versus District Systems. Supporters of at-large elections say that they promote the public interest because council members must take a citywide view of problems. They charge that council members elected from districts are focused on the needs of their districts rather than the interests of the community as a whole.

Critics of at-large elections maintain that the system allows a simple majority of voters to elect all council members (who typically come from the upper-income brackets and live in the higher-income areas of town). When a citywide majority elects all council members, the interests of racial, ethnic, and ideological minorities in the community are not represented at city hall. These critics charge that effective neighborhood representation serves the interest of the entire city and is more likely to occur when each district elects its own representative to the council.

Single-Member Districts and Minorities. Although major Texas cities have usually resisted single-member districts, successful legal action in the federal courts by civil rights organizations—such as the Mexican American Legal Defense and Educational Fund, the League of United Latin American Citizens, the American GI Forum, the National Association for the Advancement of Colored People, Texas Rural Legal Aid, and the Southwest Voter Registration Education Project—has forced them to abandon at-large elections. Several cities have instituted a mixed system in which a majority of the council members live in, and are elected from, single-member districts, while the mayor and some additional council members are elected at large. One study found that Mexican-American candidates in Texas cities were more likely to win the district positions than the at-large seats in mixed systems.[2] Another investigation drew similar conclusions about African-American candidates in the state but found that, for Mexican-American candidates, "the pattern was less clear primarily because they were sharply underrepresented in both components."[3]

According to the National Association of Latino Elected and Appointed Officials (NALEO) Educational Fund, in 2007 there were 2,127 locally elected Latino officials in the state. Further, Texas ranks number one among the states in the number of Latinos holding elective offices, and the vast majority (98 percent) are local officials. In 2001, according to the Joint Center for Political and Economic Studies, of the 5,452 African American county and municipal elected officials in the nation, 302 were elected in Texas.

Another Alternative: Cumulative Voting. While the single-member district system has been the primary means of increasing minority representation on city councils, some cities have adopted other methods of achieving this goal. One alternative system is

2. J. L. Polinard, Robert D. Wrinkle, Tomas Longoria, and Norman E. Binder, *Electoral Structure and Urban Policy: The Impact on Mexican-American Communities* (Armonk, NY: M. E. Sharpe, 1994), p. 55.
3. Robert Brischetto, David R. Richards, Chandler Davidson, and Bernard Grofman, "Texas," in *Quiet Revolution in the South: The Impact of the Voting Rights Act 1965–1990,* eds. Chandler Davidson and Bernard Grofman (Princeton, NJ: Princeton University Press, 1994), p. 252.

cumulative voting (CV). Under this plan, city council members are elected in at-large elections. The number of votes a voter can cast corresponds to the number of seats on the council.

The key characteristic of CV is that the voter can cast more than one vote for a particular candidate. If, for example, there are five seats on the city council, a voter can cast all five votes for one candidate or can cast, say, three votes for one candidate and the remaining two votes for another candidate. Theoretically, members of a voting minority in the city could cast all of their votes for a single candidate and increase the chances of that candidate's winning. Two political scientists have concluded, however, that "CV systems . . . guarantee no electoral outcomes. Minority voters must be mobilized and vote cohesively to take advantage of the opportunities CV provides."[4]

According to the organization FairVote, more than 50 local jurisdictions in Texas have adopted CV since the 1990s. Most are school districts. In about 20 percent of the communities where CV is found, both the school board and the city council have adopted the method. The Amarillo Independent School District resolved a lawsuit by adopting CV and is the largest jurisdiction in the nation to use this election system.

Cumulative Voting (CV)
An at-large election system in which voters can cast one or more votes for a single candidate. For example, a voter who can cast up to five votes in a city council election can cast all five votes for one candidate or spread the votes among several candidates.

Sales Tax
A tax collected on the retail price of purchased items.

Revenue Sources and Limitations

Sources and amounts of revenue vary greatly among Texas municipalities according to various factors, including the following:

- The size of the city's population
- The amount and type of taxes the city is allowed and willing to levy
- The total assessed value of taxable property within the city limits

The local political culture determines expectations about appropriate standards of services and tolerable levels of taxation (see Table 25–3). External forces—such as a downturn in the national economy, the closing of a military base, the downsizing of industries, federal and state mandates, and natural disasters—also influence the economic climate of a community. In Texas, state aid represents a considerably lower percentage of municipal revenue than is the norm in many other states. Thus, sales and property taxes are important sources of revenue for Texas cities.

did you know?

Grant money from the Governor's Criminal Justice Division was used to launch tattoo-removal programs in four Texas cities—Amarillo, Austin, El Paso, and San Antonio.

The Sales Tax. A 1 percent municipal **sales tax** was authorized by the legislature in 1968, and since then Texas cities have become heavily dependent on it. Although all taxes are affected by economic conditions, sales tax revenues vary more sharply during economic cycles of recession and recovery than do property tax revenues. In addition, the budgetary problems of state and national governments make their assistance to cities unreliable. Cities, therefore, need to build a reserve fund into their budgets to compensate for these somewhat inconsistent sources of revenues.

TABLE 25–3 Property Taxes Levied by Texas Local Governments in 2006 (in Billions of Dollars)

Counties	Cities	Special Districts	School Districts	Total
5.3	5.3	3.9	20.9	35.5

Totals may not add due to rounding.
Source: Texas Comptroller of Public Accounts, Property Tax Division.

4. Robert R. Brischetto and Richard L. Engstrom, "Cumulative Voting and Latino Representation: Exit Surveys in Fifteen Texas Communities," *Social Science Quarterly,* December 1997.

Property Tax
A tax on the assessed value of real estate.

Property Taxes. Municipalities, school districts, and counties depend heavily on **property taxes,** in which the tax rate is a percentage of the assessed value of real estate. In a community with a low *tax base,* or total assessed value, the local government has a limited capacity to raise taxes from this source. Thus, a poor city must have a high tax rate to provide adequate services. Furthermore, any loss in assessed property values causes a decline in the city's tax base.

Texas has established a countywide appraisal authority for property taxes, and all local governments must accept its property appraisals. However, Texas state law does not require full disclosure when it comes to the price of home sales, which poses challenges when attempting to appraise property with accuracy. According to a 2003 survey by the Texas comptroller's office, chief appraisers concluded that a mandatory disclosure law would increase property values by more than $18 billion. Attempts to pass a mandatory disclosure law in the Texas state legislature in 2007 were unsuccessful.

POLITICS AND... public policy

SCHOOL UNIFORMS

In recent years, school districts have begun to ask their students to wear school uniforms. School districts have moved in this direction for several reasons, some of which address financial burdens on poor families, while others address questions of equality in the classroom.

The requirement that all students wear school uniforms may decrease the pressure on parents to purchase, or students to wear, expensive name-brand clothing that can be a financial hardship on families. In the classroom, students look as identical to one another as clothing can possibly make them. Teachers have always been expected to treat all students the same, but the implementation of school uniform policies give teachers visual cues that promote equal treatment.

When the school uniform policies were being implemented in a large urban school district in Texas, a group of researchers gathered data on all of the middle schools in the district to find out whether the students improved academically and behaviorally. Academic and disciplinary measures were gathered for the two years before and after implementation of the school uniform policies.

While the implementation of school uniforms did not have a significant impact on the students' academic performance, the data indicated a dramatic increase in disciplinary problems. This led to speculation that the school uniforms policy contributed to the increase in disciplinary problems. They did, but in an unexpected way. Students did not rebel against the uniform policies; instead, students were getting into serious trouble for seemingly innocuous infractions of the rules. In-school suspensions were imposed for chewing gum, not wearing uniforms, talking in class, or failing to tuck their shirts in their pants.

The school uniform policy happened to coincide with zero-tolerance policies in the school district. As the name implies, zero-tolerance policies mean that students are disciplined for any and all rule infractions, which suddenly included violations that may have been pardoned in previous years. The uniforms assisted teachers in identifying violators because rule violators stood out.

The implementation of school uniform policies raises an interesting question about our country's two most fundamental values—liberty and equality. Texans believe that the government should protect our liberties while promoting equality. Local governments, like school districts, are expected to treat everyone equally. School districts are expected to teach every child within their jurisdiction. Schools and teachers are also expected to treat every child the same regardless of their economic background, gender, race, or ethnicity. In doing so, governments are forced to make difficult choices balancing the values of liberty and equality.

Evaluations of public policy like this one have been made possible thanks in large part to the access of data available on the Internet. What policy areas would you be interested in evaluating? How would you go about conducting such research?

The property tax rate in general-law cities depends on the size of the city. The maximum property tax rate of a general-law city, however, is $1.50 per $100 of assessed value. Home-rule municipalities can set property tax rates as high as $2.50 per $100 of assessed value.

did you know?

Eighteen states permit local income taxes but Texas does not.

Limits on Property Taxes. Some Texas cities have taken measures to limit increases in property taxes. For example, the Corpus Christi city charter contains a property tax cap of $0.68 per $100 valuation. (The tax hikes that are tied to voter-approved bonds are not applied toward the cap.) In 2003, Texas voters approved Proposition 13, which allows cities, towns, counties, and junior college districts to freeze property taxes for people who are disabled or elderly. Once the freeze is in place, the governing body cannot repeal it. Texas cities (as well as counties and hospital districts) may also call an election to lower property taxes by raising sales and use taxes.

Voters in non-school-district jurisdictions (cities, counties, and special districts) may petition for a **rollback election** to limit an increase in the property tax rate to no more than 8 percent, plus additional revenue to meet debt-service requirements. For school districts, an election to decide if a tax increase will stand is automatically held if the increase exceeds $0.06 per $100 of assessed valuation; no petition is necessary. According to the Texas comptroller's office, close to 400 local governments have held rollback elections since 1982.

Rollback Election
In Texas, an election that permits voters to lower a local property tax increase to 8 percent.

User Fee
A charge paid by an individual who receives a particular government service, such as water provision or garbage collection.

Public Debt
Sums owed by governments.

User Fees. When citizens are charged for services received, the charges are called **user fees.** These fees are increasingly popular for two reasons: (1) citizens' opposition to higher taxes and (2) the notion that people should pay for what they actually use. User fees may be collected for city-provided electricity, water, sewage, and garbage collection, as well as for swimming pools, golf courses, and ambulance services. The Texas Municipal League has found that user fees bring in 21 percent of municipal revenue. Permits, business licenses, and inspection fees round out the usual sources of city revenue.

Borrowing. Local governments use **public debt**—normally, bond issues that must be approved by the voters in a referendum—to fund infrastructure projects such as roads, buildings, and public facilities. The amount and use of the debt are determined by the same legal, political, economic, and cultural factors that determine the source and amount of tax revenues. The law in Texas explicitly limits the amount of long-term debt to a percentage of assessed valuation of property within the boundaries of the government. This restriction is intended to keep governments from falling into bankruptcy, as many did during the Great Depression of the 1930s.

Seventy-one percent of Ameriquest Field in Arlington was financed with a city sales tax, and 29 percent was funded by the owners of the Texas Rangers baseball team. In all, taxpayers funded $135 million of the project that was completed in 1994. Who benefits from taxpayer-financed stadiums? (Andy Sharp/AP Photo)

Trends and Issues

A series of trends and issues are important in understanding the current circumstances of Texas municipalities. These include population changes, economic development issues, federal and state mandates, annexation issues, and term limits for local officials.

Population Trends. Table 25–4 shows the populations of the 15 largest counties and cities in Texas based on 2007

TABLE 25–4 Population Estimates for the Largest Counties and Incorporated Cities in Texas, 2007 and 2000

Geographic Area	Population 2007	2000	% Increase
County			
Harris	3,935,855	3,400,578	15.7%
Dallas	2,366,511	2,218,899	6.6
Tarrant	1,717,435	1,446,219	18.7
Bexar	1,594,493	1,392,931	14.4
Travis	974,365	812,280	19.9
El Paso	734,669	679,622	8.0
Collin	730,690	491,675	48.6
Hidalgo	710,514	569,463	24.7
Denton	612,357	432,976	41.0
Fort Bend	509,822	354,452	43.8
Montgomery	412,638	293,768	40.4
Cameron	387,210	335,227	15.4
Williamson	373,363	249,967	49.3
Nueces	321,135	313,645	2.3
Brazoria	294,233	241,767	21.7
City			
Houston	2,208,180	1,953,631	13.02%
San Antonio	1,328,984	1,144,646	16.1
Dallas	1,240,499	1,188,580	4.3
Austin	743,074	656,562	13.17
Fort Worth	656,562	534,694	22.7
El Paso	606,913	563,662	7.67
Arlington	371,038	332,969	11.4
Corpus Christi	285,507	277,454	2.9
Plano	260,796	222,030	17.4
Garland	218,792	215,768	1.40
Laredo	217,506	176,576	23.17
Lubbock	217,326	199,564	8.9
Irving	199,505	191,615	4.1
Amarillo	186,106	173,627	7.18
Brownsville	172,806	139,722	23.67

Source: U.S. Census Bureau, Estimates of Population Change for Counties of Texas and County Rankings: July 1, 2006 to July 1, 2007 (CO-EST2007-03-48). Release Date: March 2008.

Census Bureau estimates. A community's size as well as its rate of growth can have a significant impact on the public-policy decisions made by local officials. Even a city with overall limited growth may see an internal shift in population, with one area of the city facing dramatic growth in a short span of time, while other areas contend with a loss of population and businesses.

Like other local governments, cities must be aware of demographic changes that produce new demands on city services. For example, a survey of more than 1,000 local governments revealed "challenges in meeting the needs of or planning for older adults," including "accessibility, availability, affordability" when it comes to housing.[5] Cities can also feel the impact of countywide trends on such variables as income. According to the Census Bureau's 2006 American Community Survey, of the 10 counties in the nation with the lowest median incomes, five are in Texas: Lubbock, Nueces, El Paso, Hidalgo, and Cameron.

Development Corporation Act
A state law that allows select Texas cities to raise the sales tax for economic development, subject to voter approval.

Mandate
A requirement or standard imposed on one level of government by a higher level of government.

Economic Development. The **Development Corporation Act** allows many Texas cities to adopt a sales tax for economic development projects, subject to voter approval. The adopting cities have either a 4A or 4B designation, and the classifications determine how the funds can be spent. According to the Texas attorney general's *Economic Development Handbook for Texas Cities 2006,* 4A status is open only to cities that meet certain population standards, while all cities are eligible for the 4B designation.

Sales tax revenue based on 4A status is used for projects related to industry and manufacturing and can be tied to a decrease in the property tax rate. The 4B designation is more expansive in scope, allowing cities to use revenue for a wide range of projects, including professional and amateur sports facilities, public park improvements, and affordable housing. Since 1989, more than 500 cities have approved a sales tax hike for economic development under one of the designations, and more than 90 have passed increases under both the 4A and 4B designations. The economic development sales tax is particularly popular with small jurisdictions. According to the Texas Economic Development Council, more than half of the cities that have adopted the tax have a population of less than 5,000.

Government Mandates. Texas cities—like most cities in the nation—have seen both a decline in federal and state government dollars and an increase in the number of mandates imposed by these governments. A **mandate** is a law passed by Congress or a state legislature requiring a lower-level government to meet an obligation. Some notable examples of federal mandates are the Americans with Disabilities Act, the National Voter Registration Act (Motor Voter Act), the Help America Vote Act, and the No Child Left Behind Act. Supporters of mandates argue that they permit the federal and state governments to meet important needs in a uniform fashion. Critics charge that mandates—particularly those that are unfunded—impose a heavy financial burden on those governments required to fulfill the obligations.

In the late 1990s, the Texas legislature passed House Bill 66, which established the Unfunded Mandates Interagency Work Group. The state auditor, the state comptroller, the director of the Legislative Budget Board, a senator (selected by the lieutenant governor), and a representative (selected by the speaker) make up the group. Its charge is to record unfunded mandates that are passed by the legislature so that lawmakers have a sense of the impact of these mandates on other governments. Several types of unfunded mandates are exempt from the list, however, including those that are passed in compliance with the Texas Constitution, federal law, or a court order, as well as those that are established as a result of a popular election.

did you know?

According to the Texas Department of State Health Services, more than 250 Texas cities restrict smoking in public places, such as restaurants, bars, and workplaces, but some of the cities have stricter enforcement and punishment than others.

Annexation. Big cities in Texas have not suffered as much as many other U.S. cities from "white flight," urban decay, the evacuation of industry, and declining tax bases. Texas cities have escaped some of the worst of these problems because of the state's liberal annexation laws.

5. Evelina R. Moulder, "The Maturing of America: How Local Governments Are Preparing for a Wave of Retirees," *The Municipal Year Book 2007* (Washington, DC: International City/County Management Association, 2007), p. 9.

Extraterritorial Jurisdiction (ETJ)
In Texas, a buffer area that extends beyond a city's limits. Cities can enforce some laws, such as zoning and building codes, in an ETJ.

Colonia
In Texas, an unincorporated urban district along the U.S.–Mexican border. Colonias are often impoverished and are chiefly inhabited by Mexican Americans.

Term Limit
A restriction on the number of times a person can be elected to a particular office.

The Municipal Annexation Act establishes a buffer area, known as **extraterritorial jurisdiction (ETJ),** that extends from one-half mile to five miles beyond the city's limits, depending on the city's population. The city may enforce zoning and building codes in the outlying area, and new cities may not be incorporated within the ETJ. The law also gives home-rule cities the power to annex an area equal to 10 percent of their existing area each year without the consent of the inhabitants of the area to be annexed. With this protection and with long-range planning, Texas cities can avoid being boxed in by suburban bedroom cities.

One strategy involves annexing "fingers" of land outward from the existing city limits and placing the area between the fingers into the ETJ. The unincorporated areas within the ETJ may then be annexed as they become sufficiently populated to warrant it. Central cities that plan ahead are therefore free to extend their boundaries and recapture both the tax base and the population that may have left the city. Increasingly, though, inhabitants of outlying areas are raising objections to the state's municipal annexation laws. These persons resent the fact that their jurisdictions can be annexed without their permission.

The Texas legislature passed a comprehensive annexation bill—the first in more than three decades—in 1999. The measure requires cities to give notice of annexation plans three years in advance, participate in arbitration with areas to be annexed, and deliver services within two and a half years. (Exceptions to the last requirement can be triggered under certain circumstances.) Outlying areas face limits on what they can do if they want to avoid annexation.

did you know?

That Texas has more than 2,000 colonias, which is more than any other state.

A special annexation issue involves **colonias.** A colonia is an unincorporated urban district along the U.S.–Mexican border. They are typically severely impoverished and must contend with a multitude of problems, including substandard housing, unsanitary drinking water, and lack of proper sewage disposal. The Texas attorney general's office has identified more than 1,800 colonias in 29 Texas counties, most of which lie along the U.S.–Mexico border.

These colonias are eligible for financial aid from the state. But what happens to the aid a colonia receives if it is annexed? In 1999, the Texas legislature passed a law that allows a colonia eligible for state aid to continue to receive it for five years after annexation.

Term Limits. While there are no **term limits** for members of Congress, 15 states limit the terms of their state legislatures, according to the National Conference of State Legislatures. In a 2003 survey of cities, responses revealed that only 9 percent have term limits for their chief elected official or the city council, but the measure is more likely to be adopted in larger cities.[6] Proponents of term limits believe that city hall is best governed by new blood and fresh ideas and that limiting the number of terms council members may serve is the best way to achieve that goal. Opponents, though, worry that cities stand to lose experienced, effective council members.

According to the Texas Municipal League, term-limit laws have been approved by the voters in more than 60 cities in the state, with the bulk of the adoptions occurring in the early 1990s. These laws are less than uniform. Corpus Christi, for example, allows a person who has held a seat for four two-year terms to run again for the seat after sitting out a term. In Austin, a council member is limited to two consecutive three-year terms, but that limit can be waived with a petition signed by 5 percent of the registered voters represented by the council member. In Dallas, city council members are subject to term limits, but the mayor is not.

6. Susan A. MacManus and Charles S. Bullock III, "The Form, Structure, and Composition of America's Municipalities in the New Millennium," *The Municipal Year Book 2003* (Washington, DC: International City/County Management Association, 2003), pp. 9, 15.

Counties

The responsibilities of county governments also have a direct impact on the public. For example, the March 2008 Democratic primary and precinct conventions (caucuses)—commonly referred to as the "Texas two-step"—saw a huge turnout as a result of the intense competition between Barack Obama and Hillary Clinton for the Democratic Party nomination. The county commissioners court decided the precinct voting locations in each county. The county clerk is responsible for early voting, issues marriage licenses, and records birth and death certificates. Property taxes are paid to the county Tax Office, which also issues license plates and stickers, and processes vehicle transfers. County Dispute Resolution Services help resolve conflicts between landlords and tenants through mediation.

did you know?

That according to the Texas Hospital Association, approximately 63 Texas counties do not have a hospital.

Like the counties in most other states, Texas counties are established and structured by the state constitution and the legislature. The county serves as a general-purpose government and as an administrative arm of the state, carrying out the state's laws and collecting certain state taxes. Although the county is an arm of the state, state supervision is minimal.

County government is far less flexible than municipal government in its organization and functions. Texas counties do not have home rule. At one time, a constitutional provision authorized county home rule. The provision was so poorly written and so difficult to implement that no county in the state was able to use it to reorganize, and it was subsequently repealed.

The Presidio county courthouse in Marfa, Texas. Courthouses are not only the home for the courts, but they are the nerve center of county government, where the county commissioners meet, taxes are collected, and important records are kept. (Dave G. Houser/Corbis)

Because counties cannot pass ordinances unless specifically authorized by the state, new state statutes or constitutional amendments are often necessary to allow a county to deal with contemporary problems. The needs of Harris County, for example, with an estimated population of 3,886,207 in 2006, are significantly different from those of Loving County, which had only an estimated 60 inhabitants in that year. Yet Texas law allows only modest variations in county governments to accommodate these differences. (Many state laws, however, are unique to specific counties because of their population or their location—a law pertaining to a coastal county, for example.)

Counties are also limited in their ability to tax their citizens. Counties can impose property taxes at a maximum rate of $0.80 per $100 of assessed valuation, but they have the power to collect additional taxes beyond this limit—if the voters approve—to cover long-term debt for infrastructure, such as courthouses, criminal justice buildings, farm-to-market roads, flood control, and county road and bridge maintenance.

Functions of Counties

County government is responsible for administering county, state, and national elections, but not those for municipalities, school districts, and other special districts. County government acts for the state in the following areas:

1. Securing rights-of-way for highways
2. Providing law enforcement
3. Registering births, deaths, and marriages
4. Housing state district courts
5. Registering motor vehicles
6. Recording land titles and deeds
7. Collecting some state taxes and fees

Optional Powers. County government also has optional powers specifically authorized by state law, and these powers are found in various state codes. For example, according to the Local Government Code, a county government may undertake the following activities:

1. Establish and maintain libraries
2. Operate and maintain parks
3. Establish recreational and cultural facilities (such as auditoriums and convention centers)
4. Appoint a county historical commission
5. Regulate sexually oriented businesses

According to the Health and Safety Code, a county government has the authority to maintain a county hospital.

Commissioners Court
In Texas, the policy-making body of a county. A commissioners court consists of a county judge (the presiding officer), who is elected in countywide elections, and four county commissioners elected from individual precincts.

County Judge
In Texas, an official elected countywide to preside over the commissioners court and to try certain minor cases.

County Commissioner
One of a group of officials elected to administer a county; in Texas, a member of the commissioners court who is elected from a district, or precinct.

Sheriff
The chief law enforcement officer of a county—in most states, an elected official. In Texas, the sheriff's budget must be approved by the commissioners court, which limits the sheriff's authority.

Intergovernmental Cooperation. A county government may also enter into an agreement with another local government to provide a service or program. For example, the Local Government Code permits county–city partnerships to purchase and maintain parks, museums, and historic sites. The Interlocal Cooperation Act, a part of the code, authorizes various local governments, including counties, cities, and special districts, to contract with each other for the provision of various administrative functions, such as tax assessment and collection and records management. The various governmental units may also jointly provide governmental functions and services, including police and fire protection, streets and roads, public health and welfare, and waste disposal.

Structure and Organization of Counties

County government consists of several independently elected officials (see Figure 28–3). The county governing body, the **commissioners court,** consists of the **county judge** and four **county commissioners.** The commissioners court is not a judicial body but a legislature of limited authority that approves the budget for all operations of the county, sets the tax rate, and passes ordinances.

Maintaining libraries is an optional power of counties. (Marjorie Kamys Cotera/Daemmrich Photography/ The Image Works)

The commissioners court does not have direct control over the many elected department heads of county government, but it wields considerable influence through its budgetary power. The county **sheriff,** for example, is responsible to county voters for enforcing the law and maintaining order and security in the county jail. The commissioners court, however, must provide the funds to build the jail and must approve its staff; authorize expenditures for each vehicle and its gas and repairs; and authorize deputies, clerks, and their salaries. The sheriff, therefore, is accountable not only to the voters but also to other elected county officials.

FIGURE 25–3 Texas County Officials Elected by Voters

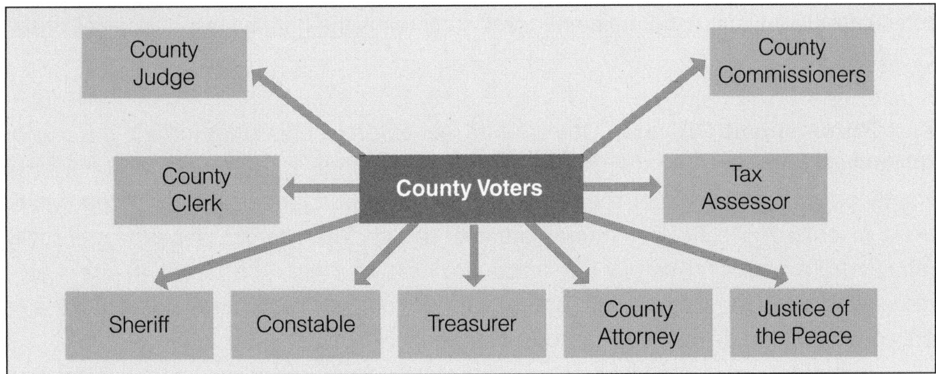

County Judges. The county judge is elected for a four-year term from the county at large to preside over the commissioners court. According to the Texas comptroller's office, the powers of the county judge are found in more than 50 provisions of the Local Government Code, as well as many other state codes. The Texas Association of Counties lists many powers held by Texas county judges, including the following:

1. Preparing the budget (a responsibility the county judge shares with the county clerk or auditor in counties with populations under 225,000)
2. Supervising election-related activities (calling elections, posting election notices, and receiving and canvassing election results)
3. Conducting hearings for beer and wine permits
4. Performing marriage ceremonies
5. Conducting hearings on state hospital admittance for people with mental illness and other mental disabilities
6. Serving as the head of civil defense and disaster relief for the county

Additionally, a county judge may have judicial authority, but the obligations in this area depend on the county.

The County Commissioners. Four county commissioners make up the remaining membership of the court and are elected for four-year terms. Commissioners are elected in single-member districts (or precincts, as they are called in Texas). In 1968, the United States Supreme Court ruled that commissioner districts must be drawn on the basis of the one-person, one-vote principle.[7] During the next two decades, county governments faced many legal challenges because of malapportioned precincts. For example, between 1974 and 1984, the Mexican American Legal Defense and Educational Fund and the Southwest Voter Registration Education Project filed voting-rights lawsuits in more than 80 counties.[8]

Commissioners are frequently called "road commissioners" because they are responsible for the county roads and bridges within their precincts (unless a county engineer has been hired

Lupe Valdez was re-elected sheriff of Dallas County in 2008. With a relatively large budget and staff of deputies to assist them in enforcing state law throughout the county, sheriffs, next to county judges, are usually the most powerful county officers. (AP Photo/LM Otero)

7. *Avery v. Midland County,* 390 U.S. 474 (1968).
8. David Montejano, *Anglos and Mexicans in the Making of Texas, 1836–1986* (Austin: University of Texas Press, 1987), p. 296.

to do that job). Each commissioner is given a certain amount of revenue and has almost total authority to determine how it will be spent on roads and bridges. Rural residents often consider building and maintenance of rural roads the primary responsibilities of the commissioners.

Law-Enforcement Officers. Officers with law-enforcement duties include the county sheriff and constables. The sheriff, next to the county judge, is usually the most powerful county officer, because he or she has a relatively large budget and a staff of deputies to assist in enforcing state law throughout the county. The sheriff's department usually refrains from patrolling within the corporate limits of cities, the better to use scarce resources and avoid jurisdictional disputes with city police. The department also operates the county jail and delivers and executes court papers (such as court orders).

Constables are elected from the same precincts as justices of the peace and serve as process officers of that court. They are also general law-enforcement officers. In metropolitan counties such as Harris and Montgomery, constables have many deputies and are the heads of important law-enforcement agencies.

In some counties, the office of constable has remained unfilled for years. Because the office is provided for in the Texas Constitution, however, the only way to abolish it has been by constitutional amendment. In 2002, voters approved an amendment that allows a commissioners court to abolish a constable office that has been vacant for more than seven years. An abolished office can be restored by the commissioners court or by voter approval.

Constable
A law-enforcement officer. In Texas, constables are elected at the county level and serve as process officers of justice of the peace courts.

Tax Assessor-Collector
In Texas, a county financial officer whose responsibilities include collecting county taxes or fees and registering voters.

County Treasurer
A county official who is responsible for receiving, depositing, and disbursing county funds.

County Auditor
In Texas, a county financial officer whose duties, depending on the population of the county, may include reviewing county financial records and (in large counties) serving as the chief budget officer.

County Clerk
The chief record keeper and elections officer of a county.

County Financial Officers. Officials with financial duties include the tax assessor-collector, the treasurer, and the auditor. The **tax assessor-collector** is probably the most important of these. The office has the following responsibilities:

1. Collecting various county taxes and fees
2. Collecting certain state taxes and fees, particularly motor vehicle registration fees (license plate fees) and the motor vehicle sales tax
3. Registering voters

The **county treasurer** is responsible for receiving, depositing, and disbursing funds. Some counties have done away with the treasurer's office. When a county wishes to do this, the commissioners court must petition the legislature for a constitutional amendment to allow its county's voters to eliminate the county treasurer's office. The most likely recipient of the treasurer's duties will be the auditor.

The **county auditor** reviews all county financial records and ensures that expenditures are made in accordance with law. Whereas other key county officials are elected, county auditors are appointed for two-year terms by district judges.

Clerical Officers. Officials with clerical duties include county and district clerks. The **county clerk** serves as the county's chief record keeper and election officer. In some ways, the office parallels that of the Texas secretary of state. The county clerk has the following duties:

1. Serving as clerk for the county commissioners court
2. Maintaining records for justices of the peace, for county courts, and for district courts in counties with populations of less than 8,000
3. Recording deeds, mortgages, wills, and contracts
4. Issuing marriage licenses and maintaining certain records of births and deaths
5. Serving on the county election board, certifying candidates running for county office, and carrying out other "housekeeping" functions in connection with elections, including preserving the results of state, county, and local elections

In counties with populations of more than 8,000, the **district clerk** assumes the county clerk's role as record keeper for the district courts. (The county clerk continues to maintain records for the constitutional county court and any county courts-at-law in existence; these courts were discussed in Chapter 26.)

Legal Officers. **County attorneys** and **district attorneys** perform a variety of functions. Some counties have only one of these officials—either a county or a district attorney. This official prosecutes all criminal cases, gives advisory opinions to county officials that define their authority, and represents the county in civil proceedings.

If a county has both a district attorney and a county attorney, the district attorney specializes in prosecuting cases in district court, while the county attorney handles lesser cases. District attorneys are neither subordinate to nor part of county government in Texas, but their office space and salaries are partly paid by the counties. County attorneys are wholly county officials.

Other Officials. In some counties, commissioners courts or voters have created other executive officers. There may be five or more members of a county board of school trustees, a county superintendent of schools, a county surveyor, a county weigher, and even a county inspector of hides and animals. Counties may also authorize such appointive officers as the county election administrator, county health officer, county medical examiner, county agricultural agent, and home demonstration agent.

District Clerk
In Texas, the record keeper for the district court in a county with a population that exceeds 8,000.

County Attorney
In Texas, a county legal officer who gives legal advice to the commissioners court, represents the county in court, and prosecutes crimes. If a county has both a county attorney and a district attorney, the latter prosecutes felony crimes.

District Attorney
An official who prosecutes felony cases.

Long Ballot
An election ballot listing many independently elected offices.

Short Ballot
An election ballot listing only a few independently elected offices.

Issues and Trends

The institutional features of Texas county government date to the 1800s. The demands of modern society are placing an increasingly heavy burden on this level of government. Next, we review some frequent criticisms of county government that follow from outdated structures and discuss the measures counties can take to deal with contemporary problems.

Constitutional Rigidity. The great mass of detailed and restrictive material in the Texas Constitution creates problems of rigidity and inflexibility, and additional controls are scattered throughout the civil statutes. The result is a collection of legal requirements that are applied equally to the four largest counties in the state—Harris, Dallas, Tarrant, and Bexar—and to the scores of counties that have populations of less than 20,000. This standardized approach gives little consideration to the special needs of individual counties. Two political scientists have observed that the nation's "state legislatures have exercised virtually unlimited authority in prescribing the limits of county discretion."[9] This general observation clearly applies to Texas. Under the current system, change has to come from the state legislature.

The Long Ballot. So many county officials are independently elected, and the operations of county government are so decentralized, that voters may find it difficult to monitor the many positions involved in county government. The current system of electing county officials is sometimes said to use a **long ballot,** because the ballot includes a long list of county offices to be filled. Reformers recommend a **short ballot** with fewer elected county officials. More officials would be appointed, and a county-manager system or an elected county executive would be established. Defenders of the long ballot counter that the direct election of public officials ensures that government will remain responsive to the needs and demands of the voters.

---

9. David R. Berman and Tanis J. Salant, "The Changing Role of Counties in the Intergovernment System," in *The American County: Frontiers of Knowledge,* ed. Donald C. Menzel (Tuscaloosa: University of Alabama Press, 1996), p. 24.

Unit Road System
In Texas, a system that concentrates the day-to-day responsibilities of roads in the hands of a professional engineer rather than individual county commissioners. The engineer is ultimately responsible to the commissioners court.

City-County Consolidation
The union of a county and cities within the county to form a single unit of government.

Unit Road System. One reform that counties are permitted to undertake is to establish a **unit road system.** This system takes the day-to-day responsibility for roads away from individual county commissioners and concentrates it in the hands of a professional engineer, who is responsible to the commissioners court. The voters may petition for an election to establish the unit road system, or commissioners may initiate the change themselves.

Supporters of this system maintain that it brings greater coordination and professionalism to the building of roads in rural areas. The current practice in most counties—dividing funds for roads and bridges among the four commissioners—is defended by those who believe these activities should remain the direct responsibility of elected officials.

The Civil Service System. Students of government often criticize the use of the spoils system to hire employees. Under this system, political loyalty rather than competence may be the main factor in the recruitment and retention of government workers. A county worker's job security may depend on political allegiance to a particular official and on that official's re-election. When a new official is elected, there may be a substantial turnover of county employees.

Opponents of these practices propose a civil service system that bases employment and promotion on specific qualifications and performance. Because civil service systems also prohibit termination of employment except for proven cause, such systems offer job security, which allegedly attracts qualified personnel. Supporters of this system maintain that it encourages professionalism, increases efficiency, and allows uniform application of equal opportunity requirements.

In contrast, supporters of the spoils system point out that elected officials are responsible for their employees' performance and therefore should have the authority to hire and fire at will. They also argue that an elected official would be foolish to release competent employees simply because they had gained their experience under a predecessor. Finally, they argue that the civil service system provides so much job security that complacency and indifference to the public interest may result.

Eligibility for Civil Service Systems. Texas counties with populations of 200,000 or more may establish a civil service system for county employees, while counties with populations of more than 500,000 may also establish a civil service system for the sheriff's office. According to the Texas Association of Counties, a civil service system exists in half of the 20 counties that meet the eligibility requirement. All seven counties that can establish this system in their sheriff's department have done so.

Consolidation. Students of county government reform point to **city-county consolidation** as a means of reducing both the number of local governments and the duplication of government services, as well as providing greater government efficiency. With consolidation, a county and cities within the county are merged into a single government. According to the National Association of Counties, there are 37 city-county governments in the United States.

There are several major challenges to the consolidation of governments. Consolidation requires action on the part of the state legislature, followed by local voter approval. Independently elected officials at the local level are likely to resist a move that would merge local responsibilities and reduce the number of political offices. Suzanne M. Leland and Kurt Thurmaier conclude that "The most critical elements that can affect the passage or defeat of the consolidation attempt involve the county sheriff, the status of the new chief executive, taxation, minority representation on the new city-county council, public

TABLE 25–5 Special Districts in Texas, 1952–2007

1952	1962	1972	1982	1992	2002	2007
491	733	1,215	1,681	2,266	2,245	2,291

Source: U.S. Census Bureau, *2002 Census of Governments,* Vol. 1, No. 1, available at www.census.gov/prod/2003pubs/gc021x1.pdf; U.S. Census Bureau, *2007 Census of Governments,* available at www.census.gov/govs/cog/GovOrgTab03ss.html.

employees' job security, and the status of minor municipalities."[10] Additionally, "public choice" theorists maintain that government fragmentation is preferable to a monopoly, that smaller governments are more responsive than larger ones, and that the current system forces governments to be competitive.[11] While many cities and counties enter into agreements to provide services, city-county consolidation bills have failed to win passage in the Texas legislature.

Special Districts

Special districts are local governments that provide single or closely related services that are not provided by general-purpose county or municipal governments. (Although the more than 1,000 independent school districts in Texas constitute a type of special-purpose government, other districts are the focus of this chapter. School districts were discussed in Chapter 27.) Special districts do not always receive attention comparable to cities and councils, but they are no less important when it comes to serving the needs of the public. In a suburban area outside the city limits, for example, a special district may be established to provide water and sewer facilities for a housing development. This government unit will have the authority to borrow to build the system and may assess taxes and user fees on property owners and residents.

The number of special districts has grown considerably since the 1950s, as shown in Table 25–5. In fact, special districts are the most numerous of all local governments in Texas (see Table 25–1). According to the Census Bureau, two-thirds of the special districts in Texas provide a single service. The rest are classified as multiple-function districts, and most of those provide sewerage and water supply. Examples of special districts in the state include the following:

- Airport authorities
- Drainage districts
- Hospital authorities
- Municipal utility districts (MUDs)
- Library districts
- Navigation districts
- Metropolitan transit authorities (MTAs—see Figure 25–4 on the following page)
- River authorities
- Rural fire-prevention districts
- Noxious weed-control districts

Some individuals who serve on the governing boards of special districts are elected, whereas city councils and county commissioners appoint others. In some cases, council members and commissioners serve on these boards themselves.

10. Suzanne M. Leland and Kurt Thurmaier, "Lessons from 35 Years of City-County Consolidation Attempts," in *The Municipal Year Book, 2006* (Washington, DC: International City/County Management Association, 2006), p. 8.
11. A thorough discussion of metropolitan fragmentation can be found in Virginia Gray and Peter Eisinger, *American States and Cities,* 2nd ed. (New York: Addison-Wesley Educational Publishers, 1997), Chapter 11.

FIGURE 25–4 Cities and Counties Served by Public Transportation Systems (Metropolitan Transit Authorities, or MTAs)

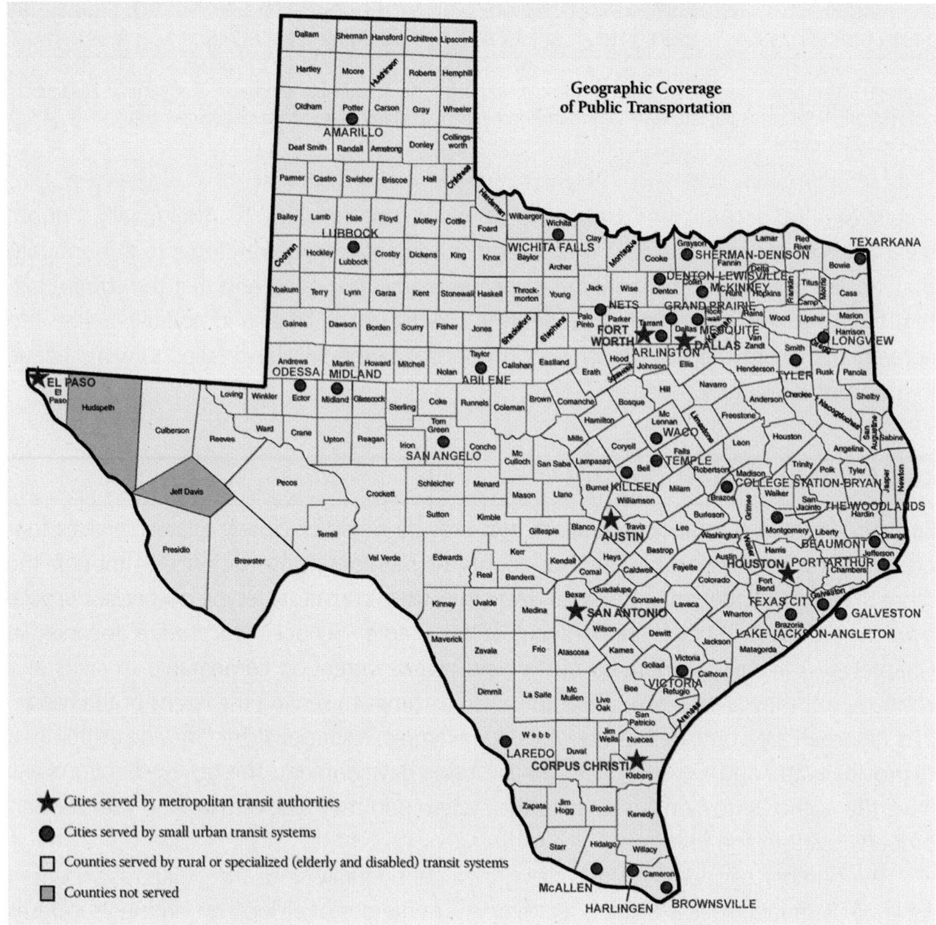

Source: Texas Department of Transportation.

> **Dependent Agency**
> A government entity that is closely linked to general-purpose governments. Dependent agencies do not have the independence of special districts.

Dependent Agencies

Special districts should not be confused with **dependent agencies.** The Bureau of the Census recognizes some government entities as dependent agencies rather than special districts because they are closely tied to general-purpose governments and do not have as much independence as special districts in budgeting and administration.

An example of a dependent agency is a crime-control and prevention district, which is subject to voter approval and remains in existence for only a designated number of years unless the voters approve an extension. A crime-control district (as it is sometimes called) also collects a voter-approved sales tax. This type of dependent agency has become increasingly popular since the 1990s, particularly in cities located in Tarrant County. Fort Worth became the first Texas city to approve such a district in 1995. In 2008, the Texas comptroller's office reported 46 crime-control districts with most collecting either a one-half cent or one-fourth cent sales tax. In some communities, an increase in the number of police officers is due to money generated by a voter-approved Crime Control and Prevention District.

Reasons For Using Special Districts

Having a service provided by a special district rather than a general-purpose government is appealing to many residents for a variety of reasons. A city or county may have limited revenue because of a downturn in the economy, the loss of a major industry, new unfunded mandates, or fewer federal dollars. The general-purpose government may have hit its sales tax ceiling (2 percent) as mandated by the state. Popular or political sentiment may be that city and county property taxes are already too high, and there may be a strong antitax organization in the community eager to make that point. Little or no support may exist for raising taxes or cutting other services to accommodate another service responsibility.

Furthermore, the service need in question may be unique to only a small area within a city or county. Why tax the entire jurisdiction? A district may be created for the benefit of underserved areas, as is the case with the 15 library districts in Texas, according to the Texas comptroller, that serve rural and suburban areas. Finally, the demand for a service may extend beyond a single jurisdiction, calling for a special district that is multicity or multicounty in scope. For a host of reasons, a special district as an alternative revenue source can become an attractive option.

did you know?

Four of the top 10 ports in the United States (in terms of cargo tonnage) are located in Texas cities—Houston, Beaumont, Corpus Christi, and Texas City.

Issues and Trends

Special districts can be dissolved. According to the Local Government Code, a municipality can annex a special district. The municipality then takes ownership of the district's property and assets and assumes responsibility for the district's debts, liabilities, and services. The national trend, though, has clearly been toward an increase in the number of special districts, and this trend is also evident in Texas. (See again Table 25–5.) Some people believe that the growing number of special districts may be a problem.

"Hidden" Governments. Special districts are sometimes called "hidden" governments. For one thing, the actions of district officials and employees are less visible than if a county or city provided the services. In addition, when elections are held at times or places other than those for general elections, voter turnout is quite low.

Cost. Because special districts are often small, they may purchase in limited quantities at higher prices than larger governments. Additionally, if special districts have little or no authority to tax, they are forced to borrow by issuing revenue bonds, which are paid from fees collected for the service provided, rather than from general-obligation bonds, which are paid from tax revenue.

Because revenue bonds are less secure than general-obligation bonds, residents are forced to pay higher interest rates just to service the bonded indebtedness. Special districts may also have a lower bond rating than larger, general-function governments, which further increases their cost of borrowing.

As stated earlier, local governments sometimes enter into interlocal governments to meet the needs of their respective jurisdictions. Many governments also recognize that problems and fiscal challenges often transcend city, county, and special-district jurisdictions, and that solutions of a regional nature must be sought.

A 2004 survey of city officials conducted by the National League of Cities revealed that "Three-fourths of city officials (75 percent) rate their municipality's relations with other cities in their region and metropolitan area as either excellent (28 percent) or good (47 percent),"[12] which is encouraging to those who seek intergovernmental cooperation. However, the survey also shows that the degree of cooperation among municipalities varies depending on the policy. For example, cities are more optimistic about working together on traffic congestion problems and business development issues than on concentrated poverty and the physical conditions of neighborhoods. Furthermore, looking at the three classifications of cities—central, suburban, and rural—the survey concludes that "Different

12. *The State of America's Cities 2004: The Annual Opinion Survey of Municipal Elected Officials* (Washington DC: National League of Cities, 2004), p. 10.

types of cities within a region perceive the benefits of interlocal and regional cooperation in different ways."[13]

Councils of Government

Councils of governments (COGs) represent an attempt by the state to encourage coordination of local government activities on a regional basis. The first COG in Texas was formed in 1966, and today there are 24 COGs encompassing all regions of Texas. Figure 25–5 shows the boundaries, populations, and Web site addresses of the 24 Texas COGs. According to the Texas Association of Regional Councils (TARC), more than 2,000 governments in Texas belong to COGs. Most of the members are municipal and county governments.

13. *Ibid.*

FIGURE 25–5 Councils of Governments in Texas

This map shows the comptroller's 13 regions and the 24 corresponding regional governments. Regional governing bodies are shown with Web site addresses and the U.S. Census 2000 population. Texas's total population in 2000 was 20,851,820.

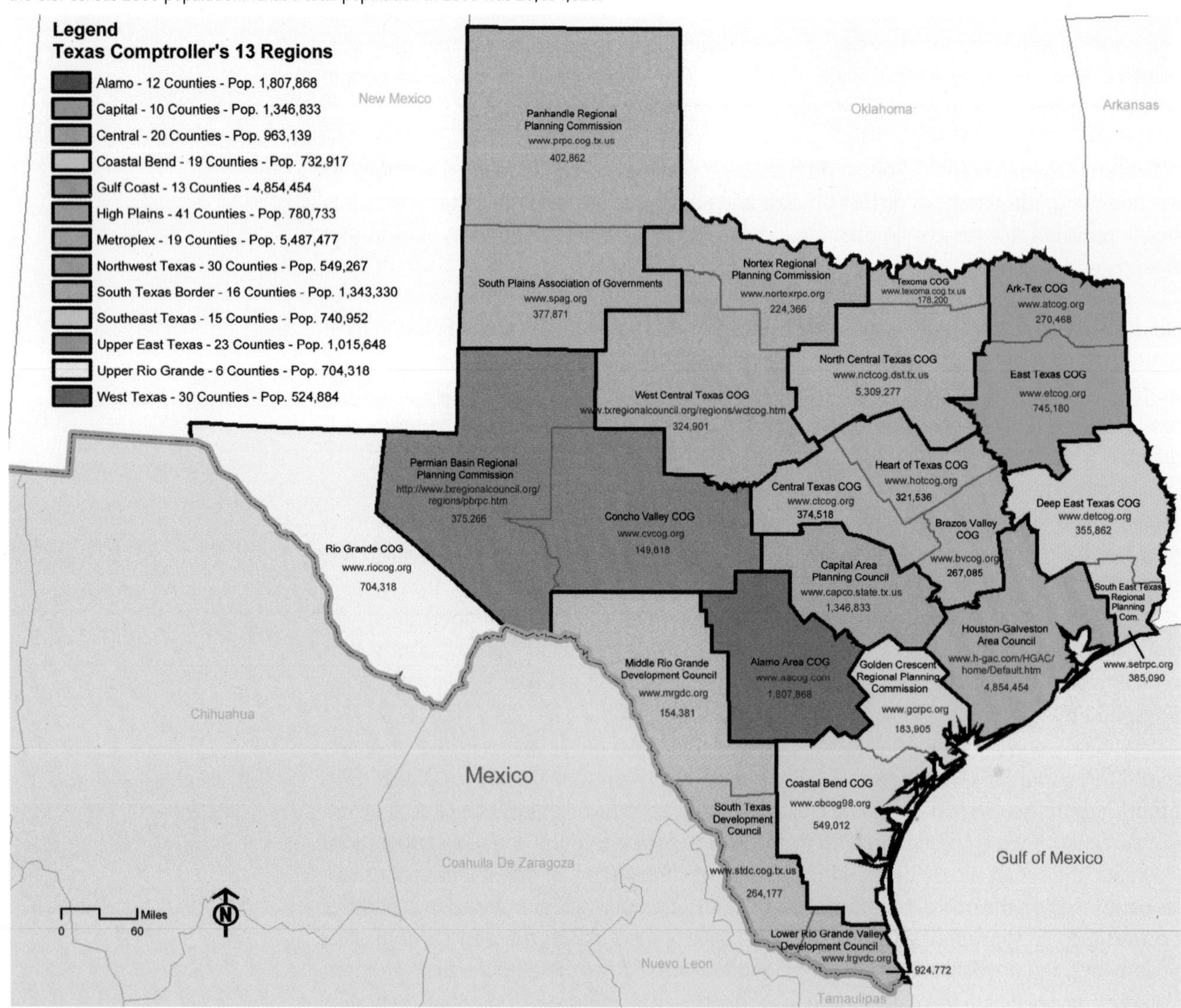

Note: Map data provided "as is" with no warranties of any kind. Colors have no specific representation other than cartographic display.
Sources: ESRI data, Texas comptroller, and U.S. Census Bureau's 2000 Population Statistics Disclaimer.

A COG is not another government and has no jurisdiction over the various local governments within its borders. Rather, it is a voluntary grouping of governments that have not relinquished any of their self-government rights. COGs provide several significant services to their members, including regional planning, technical services, and help in applying for grants. When requested by member governments, COGs provide research into problem areas and organize and operate training facilities, such as police academies.

One of the major issues on the agenda of Texas COGs is homeland security. The Texas Association of Regional Councils is working with the Texas Engineering Extension Service and the governor's Texas homeland security coordinator to facilitate the implementation of the state's Homeland Security Project. The TARC Web site (**www.txregionalcouncil.org**) lists homeland security training workshops that were held at COGs throughout the state, including workshops entitled "Operational Weapons of Mass Destruction Response for Law Enforcement Train-the-Trainer," "Counterterrorism Training," "Multihazard Program for Schools," and "Radiation Safety Training."

did you know?

That Plano was the first Texas city to establish a Youth Police Academy.

According to the TARC, the South East Texas Regional Planning Commission, Deep East Texas Council of Governments, and the Houston-Galveston Area Council have distributed $40 million of Hurricane Rita relief money to Southeast Texas. In 2008, the Bexar County Commissioners Court commissioned the Alamo Area Council of Governments to establish an inventory of all greenhouse gases in the county.

By bringing local officials together, COGs provide a base for the exchange of ideas and knowledge. Although COGs do not solve the problems facing local governments, they do encourage local officials to recognize the magnitude of these problems and cooperate in managing some of them.

WHY SHOULD YOU CARE ABOUT... LOCAL GOVERNMENT?

Like the laws handed down by the national and state governments, the policies made by cities, counties, and special districts have a major bearing on our lives. While we can correspond with elected officials and bureaucrats at every level of government in one fashion or another, the best chance of communicating with government officials in an immediate manner—and sometimes even face to face—is at the local level. In addition, we share a common bond with those who fill our local government offices: like us, they live in our community.

Local government issues often create strong differences of opinion in the community. Should a city council pass a smoking ban? Should it replace an at-large election system with single-member districts? Should it change from a city-manager to a strong-mayor form of government? Should a municipality and a county government share the expense of a jail, or should they maintain separate jail facilities? Should two neighboring counties join forces to establish and fund a park? Should a metropolitan transit authority change bus routes or suspend service on holidays?

Elected and appointed officials may disagree on what to do about these matters, but unless they decide to take no action at all, they will cast votes or adopt policies that affect everyone in the community. Local government officials should, and often do, seek the views of the public. The public also has many other opportunities to express informed opinions.

HOW YOU CAN MAKE A DIFFERENCE

You can take the following steps to influence local governments:

1. **Observe and learn about local government**. Organize a City Hall Day at your college or university. Hold panel discussions on key issues facing your community. Invite local elected officials (such as the mayor and members of the city council), appointed officials (such as the city manager, the city secretary, and the heads of various city departments), and city hall reporters to serve on the panels. Attend a city council meeting or a county commissioners court meeting. If your local cable system carries these meetings, watch them regularly. Attend a court trial, and watch the county attorney or district attorney in action. If a constable maintains a ride-along program, ask if you can participate.
2. **Get your message out.** At a meeting of the city council, a special-district board, or the county commissioners court, sign up to speak about an issue that matters to you during the public comments part of the meeting. Write a letter to the editor of a newspaper about a local issue that is important to you. Your letter could spark an exchange of ideas in your community. It might even lead local elected officials to take action.
3. **Participate.** Participate in a local campaign. Candidates often need volunteers to help organize rallies and Get Out the Vote drives, stuff envelopes, work phone banks, and pass out campaign literature.
4. **Advise local lawmakers and officials.** Apply for membership on a city advisory board or commission. Go to your city's official Web site and check out the many boards and commissions that offer you the chance to advise the city council and city officials on matters of critical importance to your community such as health, education, transportation, housing, and ethics.

questions for discussion and analysis

1. What are the key differences in the organization of Texas municipal and county governments?
2. What are the benefits of establishing special district governments? What are the drawbacks?
3. What factors can influence a city's budget?
4. What revenue sources can Texas cities use to meet their budget needs and obligations?

key terms

at-large election 792
at-large place system 792
charter 788
city-county consolidation 804
colonia 798
commissioners court 800
commission system 791
constable 802
council-manager system 789
county attorney 803
county auditor 802
county clerk 802
county commissioner 800
county judge 800
county treasurer 802
cumulative voting (CV) 793
dependent agency 806
Development Corporation Act 797
district attorney 803
district clerk 803
extraterritorial jurisdiction (ETJ) 798
general-law city 788
general-purpose government 787
home-rule city 788
long ballot 803
mandate 797
property tax 794
public debt 795
pure at-large system 792
rollback election 795
sales tax 793
sheriff 800
short ballot 803
single-member district 792
strong-mayor system 791
tax assessor-collector 802
term limit 798
unit road system 804
user fee 795
weak-mayor system 791

chapter summary

1. Municipalities, counties, and special districts provide many services that have a direct impact on our daily lives. It is important, then, to examine these governments in both their historical and contemporary contexts.
2. The municipal reform movement of the early 20th century had a major effect on Texas cities. Key features of the reform era—nonpartisan elections, the council-manager form of government, and at-large elections—are characteristic of many Texas cities. Some cities with Hispanic and African-American populations have (often by court order) replaced at-large elections with single-member districts, modified election systems, or cumulative voting to enhance the chances that minority candidates can be elected to the city council.
3. The initiative, the referendum, recall elections, rollback elections, term-limit laws, and economic development sales tax elections offer voters the opportunity to exert direct influence over municipal government.
4. Texas county government is largely a product of the 1800s, yet the county is increasingly being called on to resolve problems once considered almost exclusively urban.
5. Local governments rely on a variety of revenue sources—property and sales taxes, user fees, public debt, and state and federal dollars—to provide services to the people.
6. Government is largely fragmented at the local level. While there can be friction between governments (e.g., in the area of annexation), there can also be cooperation (such as interlocal agreements). Any significant changes in the structural relationship among cities, counties, and special districts, however, will probably be incremental rather than sweeping.

selected print & media resources

SUGGESTED READINGS

Bowler, Shaun, and Todd Andrew Donovan. ***Demanding Choices: Opinion, Voting, and Direct Democracy.*** Ann Arbor: University of Michigan Press, 1998. The authors give a comprehensive overview of the role the voter plays in referendums.

García, Sonia R., Valerie Martinez-Ebers, Irasema Coronado, Sharon A. Navarro, and Patricia A. Jaramillo. ***Políticas: Latina Public Officials in Texas.*** Austin: University of Texas Press, 2008. This study includes insightful interviews with some of the first Latinas to serve as mayors or on city councils in the state.

Grey, Lawrence. ***How to Win a Local Election: A Complete Step-by-Step Guide,*** 3rd ed. New York: M. Evans & Co., 2007. A former Ohio appellate judge offers sound advice on the many aspects of running for local office.

Kaufmann, Karen M. ***The Urban Voter: Group Conflict and Mayoral Voting Behavior in American Cities.*** Ann Arbor: The University of Michigan Press, 2004. The author explores the role of race when it comes to voting in big-city elections.

Pelissero, John, ed. ***Cities, Politics, and Policy: A Comparative Analysis.*** Washington, DC: CQ Press, 2003. This book is a collection of articles focusing on major urban issues, including intergovernmental relations, political participation, race and ethnicity, power, decision making, economic development, urban service delivery, finance, and suburban and metropolitan government.

Riordon, William L. ***Plunkitt of Tammany Hall: A Series of Very Plain Talks on Very Practical Politics.*** Boston, MA: Bedford/St. Martin's, 1994. This book offers the perspective of George Washington Plunkitt, a Tammany Hall ward boss, on why the political machine is preferable to political reform.

Rosales, Rodolfo. ***The Illusion of Inclusion: The Untold Political Story of San Antonio.*** Austin: University of Texas Press, 2000. The author provides a comprehensive examination of the role of Chicano and Chicana electoral politics in San Antonio municipal elections from the early 1950s to the early 1990s.

Shaw, Catherine. ***The Campaign Manager: Running and Winning Local Elections,*** 3rd ed. Boulder, CO: Westview Press, 2004. This book offers an in-depth examination of campaigning at the local level.

Strachan, J. Cherie. ***High-Tech Grass Roots: The Professionalism of Local Politics.*** New York: Rowman & Littlefield Publishers, 2003. This book demonstrates that candidates running for local office in small and medium-districts are using resources that in the past were more commonly associated with big-city elections.

Woodworth, James R., W. Robert Gump, and James R. Forrester. ***Camelot: A Role Playing Simulation of Political Decision Making,*** 5th ed. Belmont, CA: Thomson Wadsworth, 2006. The authors provide a variety of simulation exercises that reveal the inner workings of local political decision making.

MEDIA RESOURCES

City Hall—A 1996 film that depicts a New York mayor (Al Pacino) and the corruption that can surface in big-city politics.

Lone Star—A 1996 murder mystery that depicts the interaction among the residents of a small South Texas border community.

Street Fight—A 2005 documentary on the 2002 Newark, New Jersey, mayoral contest between Cory Booker, a 32-year-old Rhodes Scholar and Yale Law School graduate, and the veteran four-term incumbent, Sharpe James.

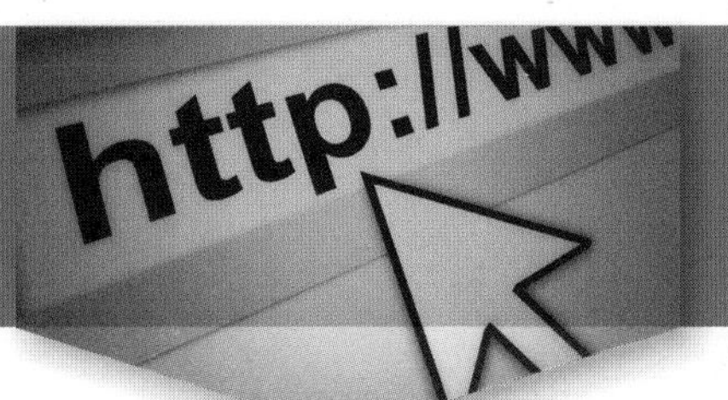

e-mocracy

DEALING WITH LOCAL GOVERNMENT ONLINE

Individuals conduct only a tiny fraction—less than 1 percent—of their fund-related transactions with federal, state, and local governments over the Internet each year. This percentage should increase sharply over the next decade as more governments make it possible for citizens to pay fines, register automobiles, and more via the Internet.

The range of information we can access on the Internet is also growing and is certainly not limited to government resources. Now, the number of places where we can access that information is growing as well. Children are becoming more exposed to cyberspace as public schools add computers to their classroom tools. Community centers, public libraries, and other local organizations and entities often have computers that can be used by patrons who otherwise would not have access to the Internet. As a result of these innovations, standing in long lines at the post office to file taxes or at the employment office to apply for a job might one day be a thing of the past.

LOGGING ON

A useful source of information about local government in Texas is the U.S. Census Bureau's "People QuickFacts," which provides an abundance of data on all Texas counties and cities. Go to:
http://quickfacts.census.gov/qfd/index.html

Click on Texas on the map, then click on the name of a county or a city, and click on "Go."

Most major cities in Texas have their own Web sites. You can use these sites to compare different types of city government. Cities that use the council-manager system include Austin, Dallas, and San Antonio:
www.ci.austin.tx.us
www.dallascityhall.com
www.ci.sat.tx.us

Houston and Pasadena use the mayor-council system:
www.houstontx.gov
www.ci.pasadena.tx.us

For links to other Texas cities and to Texas counties, go to:
www.state.tx.us

Click on "Texas Cities" or "Texas Counties."

Special districts can provide almost any kind of governmental service. A hospital district is one example. Information about hospital and other health-related districts can be found at the Texas comptroller's Web site:
www.window.state.tx.us/specialrpt/hcs/pg57.html

Another example is a metropolitan transit authority (MTA). The Texas Department of Transportation provides information about MTAs in the state at:
www.dot.state.tx.us/services/

Councils of governments are regional planning organizations that try to coordinate the activities of local governments in their regions. See the regions at:
www.txregionalcouncil.org

ONLINE REVIEW

At **www.cengage.com/politicalscience/schmidt/agandpttexas14e**, you will find a Tutorial Quiz for this chapter, providing questions on the chapter contents, including the features. You'll gain access to other helpful study tools, including the book's glossary and flashcards, crossword puzzles, and Web links, as well as "Which Side Are You On?" and "Politics and . . ." features written by the authors of the book.

APPENDIX A

THE DECLARATION OF INDEPENDENCE

In Congress, July 4, 1776

A Declaration by the Representatives of the United States of America, in General Congress assembled. When in the Course of human Events, it becomes necessary for one People to dissolve the Political Bands which have connected them with another, and to assume among the Powers of the Earth, the separate and equal Station to which the Laws of Nature and of Nature's God entitle them, a decent Respect to the Opinions of Mankind requires that they should declare the causes which impel them to the Separation.

We hold these Truths to be self-evident, that all Men are created equal, that they are endowed by their Creator with certain unalienable Rights, that among these are Life, Liberty, and the Pursuit of Happiness–That to secure these Rights, Governments are instituted among Men, deriving their just Powers from the Consent of the Governed, that whenever any Form of Government becomes destructive of these Ends, it is the Right of the People to alter or to abolish it, and to institute new Government, laying its Foundation on such Principles, and organizing its Powers in such Forms, as to them shall seem most likely to effect their Safety and Happiness. Prudence, indeed, will dictate that Governments long established should not be changed for light and transient Causes; and accordingly all Experience hath shewn, that Mankind are more disposed to suffer, while Evils are sufferable, than to right themselves by abolishing the Forms to which they are accustomed. But when a long Train of Abuses and Usurpations, pursuing invariably the same Object, evinces a Design to reduce them under absolute Despotism, it is their Right, it is their Duty, to throw off such Government, and to provide new Guards for their future Security. Such has been the patient Sufferance of these Colonies; and such is now the Neces-sity which constrains them to alter their former Systems of Government. The History of the present King of Great-Britain is a History of repeated Injuries and Usurpations, all having in direct Object the Establishment of an absolute Tyranny over these States. To prove this, let Facts be submitted to a candid World.

He has refused his Assent to Laws, the most wholesome and necessary for the public Good.

He has forbidden his Governors to pass Laws of immediate and pressing Importance, unless suspended in their Operation till his Assent should be obtained; and when so suspended, he has utterly neglected to attend to them.

He has refused to pass other Laws for the Accommodation of large Districts of People, unless those People would relinquish the Right of Representation in the Legislature, a Right inestimable to them, and formidable to Tyrants only.

He has called together Legislative Bodies at Places unusual, uncomfortable, and distant from the Depository of their Public Records, for the sole Purpose of fatiguing them into Compliance with his Measures.

He has dissolved Representative Houses repeatedly, for opposing with manly Firmness his Invasions on the Rights of the People.

He has refused for a long Time, after such Dissolutions, to cause others to be elected; whereby the Legislative Powers, incapable of Annihilation, have returned to the People at large for their exercise; the State remaining in the mean time exposed to all the Dangers of Invasion from without, and Convulsions within.

He has endeavoured to prevent the Population of these States; for that Purpose obstructing the Laws for Naturalization of Foreigners; refusing to pass others to encourage their Migrations hither, and raising the Conditions of new Appropriations of Lands.

He has obstructed the Administration of Justice, by refusing his Assent to Laws for establishing Judiciary Powers.

He has made Judges dependent on his Will alone, for the Tenure of their offices, and the Amount and payment of their Salaries.

He has erected a Multitude of new Offices, and sent hither Swarms of Officers to harass our People, and eat out their Substance.

He has kept among us, in Times of Peace, Standing Armies, without the consent of our Legislatures.

He has affected to render the Military independent of, and superior to the Civil Power.

He has combined with others to subject us to a Jurisdiction foreign to our Constitution, and unacknowledged by our Laws; giving his Assent to their Acts of pretended Legislation:

For quartering large Bodies of Armed Troops among us:

For protecting them, by a mock Trial, from Punishment for any Murders which they should commit on the Inhabitants of these States:

For cutting off our Trade with all Parts of the World:

For imposing Taxes on us without our Consent:

For depriving us, in many cases, of the Benefits of Trial by Jury:

For transporting us beyond Seas to be tried for pretended Offences:

For abolishing the free System of English Laws in a neighbouring Province, establishing therein an arbitrary Government, and enlarging its Boundaries, so as to render it at once an Example and fit Instrument for introducing the same absolute Rule into these Colonies:

For taking away our Charters, abolishing our most valuable Laws, and altering fundamentally the Forms of our Governments:

For suspending our own Legislatures, and declaring themselves invested with Power to legislate for us in all Cases whatsoever.

He has abdicated Government here, by declaring us out of his Protection and waging War against us.

He has plundered our Seas, ravaged our Coasts, burnt our towns, and destroyed the Lives of our People.

He is, at this Time, transporting large Armies of foreign Mercenaries to compleat the works of Death, Desolation, and Tyranny, already begun with circumstances of Cruelty and

Perfidy, scarcely paralleled in the most barbarous Ages, and totally unworthy the Head of a civilized Nation.

He has constrained our fellow Citizens taken Captive on the high Seas to bear Arms against their Country, to become the Executioners of their Friends and Brethren, or to fall themselves by their Hands.

He has excited domestic Insurrections amongst us, and has endeavoured to bring on the Inhabitants of our Frontiers, the merciless Indian Savages, whose known Rule of Warfare, is an undistinguished Destruction, of all Ages, Sexes and Conditions.

In every state of these Oppressions we have Petitioned for Redress in the most humble Terms: Our repeated Petitions have been answered only by repeated Injury. A Prince, whose Character is thus marked by every act which may define a Tyrant, is unfit to be the Ruler of a free People.

Nor have we been wanting in Attentions to our British Brethren. We have warned them from Time to Time of Attempts by their Legislature to extend an unwarrantable Jurisdiction over us. We have reminded them of the Circumstances of our Emigration and Settlement here. We have appealed to their native Justice and Magnanimity, and we have conjured them by the Ties of our common Kindred to disavow these Usurpations, which, would inevitably interrupt our Connections and Correspondence. They too have been deaf to the Voice of Justice and of Consanguinity. We must, therefore, acquiesce in the Necessity, which denounces our Separation, and hold them, as we hold the rest of Mankind, Enemies in War, in Peace, Friends.

We, therefore, the Representatives of the UNITED STATES OF AMERICA, in General Congress Assembled, appealing to the Supreme Judge of the World for the Rectitude of our Intentions, do, in the Name, and by the Authority of the good People of these Colonies, solemnly Publish and Declare, That these United Colonies are, and of Right ought to be, Free and Independent States; that they are absolved from all Allegiance to the British Crown, and that all political Connection between them and the State of Great-Britain, is and ought to be totally dissolved; and that as Free and Independent States, they have full Power to levy War, conclude Peace, contract Alliances, establish Commerce, and to do all other Acts and Things which Independent States may of right do. And for the support of this declaration, with a firm Reliance on the Protection of divine Providence, we mutually pledge to each other our lives, our Fortunes, and our sacred Honor.

APPENDIX B

FEDERALIST PAPERS NOS. 10, 51, AND 78

In 1787, after the newly drafted U.S. Constitution was submitted to the thirteen states for ratification, a major political debate ensued between the Federalists (who favored ratification) and the Anti-Federalists (who opposed ratification). Anti-Federalists in New York were particularly critical of the Constitution, and in response to their objections, Federalists Alexander Hamilton, James Madison, and John Jay wrote a series of eighty-five essays in defense of the Constitution. The essays were published in New York newspapers and reprinted in other newspapers throughout the country.

For students of American government, the essays, collectively known as the Federalist Papers, *are particularly important because they provide a glimpse of the founders' political philosophy and intentions in designing the Constitution—and, consequently, in shaping the American philosophy of government.*

We have included in this appendix three of these essays: Federalist Papers *Nos. 10, 51, and 78. Each essay has been annotated by the authors to indicate its importance in American political thought and to clarify the meaning of particular passages.*

Federalist Paper No. 10

Federalist Paper *No. 10, penned by James Madison, has often been singled out as a key document in American political thought. In this essay, Madison attacks the Anti-Federalists' fear that a republican form of government will inevitably give rise to "factions"—small political parties or groups united by a common interest—that will control the government. Factions will be harmful to the country because they will implement policies beneficial to their own interests but adverse to other people's rights and to the public good. In this essay, Madison attempts to lay to rest this fear by explaining how, in a large republic such as the United States, there will be so many different factions, held together by regional or local interests, that no single one of them will dominate national politics.*

Madison opens his essay with a paragraph discussing how important it is to devise a plan of government that can control the "instability, injustice, and confusion" brought about by factions.

Among the numerous advantages promised by a well-constructed Union, none deserves to be more accurately developed than its tendency to break and control the violence of faction. The friend of popular governments never finds himself so much alarmed for their character and fate as when he contemplates their propensity to this dangerous vice. He will not fail, therefore, to set a due value on any plan which, without violating the principles to which he is attached, provides a proper cure for it. The instability, injustice, and confusion introduced into the public councils have, in truth, been the mortal diseases under which popular governments have everywhere perished, as they continue to be the favorite and fruitful topics from which the adversaries to liberty derive their most specious declamations. The valuable improvements made by the American constitutions on the popular models, both ancient and modern, cannot certainly be too much admired; but it would be an unwarrantable partiality to contend that they have as effectually obviated the danger on this side, as was wished and expected. Complaints are everywhere heard from our most considerate and virtuous citizens, equally the friends of public and private faith and of public and personal liberty, that our governments are too unstable, that the public good is disregarded in the conflicts of rival parties, and that measures are too often decided, not according to the rules of justice and the rights of the minor party, but by the superior force of an interested and overbearing majority. However anxiously we may wish that these complaints had no foundation, the evidence of known facts will not permit us to deny that they are in some degree true. It will be found, indeed, on a candid review of our situation, that some of the distresses under which we labor have been erroneously charged on the operation of our governments; but it will be found, at the same time, that other causes will not alone account for many of our heaviest misfortunes; and, particularly, for that prevailing and increasing distrust of public engagements and alarm for private rights which are echoed from one end of the continent to the other. These must be chiefly, if not wholly, effects of the unsteadiness and injustice with which a factious spirit has tainted our public administration.

Madison now defines what he means by the term faction.

By a faction I understand a number of citizens, whether amounting to a majority or minority of the whole, who are united and actuated by some common impulse of passion, or of interest, adverse to the rights of other citizens, or the permanent and aggregate interests of the community.

Madison next contends that there are two methods by which the "mischiefs of faction" can be cured: by removing the causes of faction or by controlling their effects. In the following paragraphs, Madison explains how liberty itself nourishes factions. Therefore, to abolish factions would involve abolishing liberty—a cure "worse than the disease."

There are two methods of curing the mischiefs of faction: the one, by removing its causes; the other, by controlling its effects.

There are again two methods of removing the causes of faction: the one, by destroying the liberty which is essential to its existence; the other, by giving to every citizen the same opinions, the same passions, and the same interests.

It could never be more truly said than of the first remedy that it was worse than the disease. Liberty is to faction what air is to fire, an aliment without which it instantly expires. But it could not be a less folly to abolish liberty, which is essential to political life, because it nourishes faction than it would be to wish the annihilation of air, which is essential to animal life, because it imparts to fire its destructive agency.

The second expedient is as impracticable as the first would be unwise. As long as the reason of man continues fallible, and he is at liberty to exercise it, different opinions will be formed. As long as the connection subsists between his reason and his self-love, his opinions and his passions will have a reciprocal influence on each other; and the former will be objects to which the latter will attach themselves. The diversity in the faculties of men, from which the rights of property originate, is not less an insuperable obstacle to a uniformity of interests. The protection of these faculties is the first object of government. From the protection of different and unequal faculties of acquiring property, the possession of different degrees and kinds of property immediately results; and from the influence of these on the sentiments and views of the respective proprietors ensues a division of the society into different interests and parties.

The latent causes of faction are thus sown in the nature of man; and we see them everywhere brought into different degrees of activity, according to the different circumstances of civil society. A zeal for different opinions concerning religion, concerning government, and many other points, as well of speculation as of practice; an attachment to different leaders ambitiously contending for pre-eminence and power; or to persons of other descriptions whose fortunes have been interesting to the human passions, have, in turn, divided mankind into parties, inflamed them with mutual animosity, and rendered them much more disposed to vex and oppress each other than to co-operate for their common good. So strong is this propensity of mankind to fall into mutual animosities that where no substantial occasion presents itself the most frivolous and fanciful distinctions have been sufficient to kindle their unfriendly passions and excite their most violent conflicts. But the most common and durable source of factions has been the various and unequal distribution of property. Those who hold and those who are without property have ever formed distinct interests in society. Those who are creditors, and those who are debtors, fall under a like discrimination. A landed interest, a manufacturing interest, a mercantile interest, a moneyed interest, with many lesser interests, grow up of necessity in civilized nations, and divide them into different classes, actuated by different sentiments and views. The regulation of these various and interfering interests forms the principal task of modern legislation and involves the spirit of party and faction in the necessary and ordinary operations of government.

No man is allowed to be a judge in his own cause, because his interest would certainly bias his judgment, and, not improbably, corrupt his integrity. With equal, nay with greater reason, a body of men are unfit to be both judges and parties at the same time; yet what are many of the most important acts of legislation but so many judicial determinations, not indeed concerning the rights of single persons, but concerning the rights of large bodies of citizens? And what are the different classes of legislators but advocates and parties to the causes which they determine? Is a law proposed concerning private debts? It is a question to which the creditors are parties on one side and the debtors on the other. Justice ought to hold the balance between them. Yet the parties are, and must be, themselves the judges; and the most numerous party, or in other words, the most powerful faction must be expected to prevail. Shall domestic manufacturers be encouraged, and in what degree, by restrictions on foreign manufacturers? [These] are questions which would be differently decided by the landed and the manufacturing classes, and probably by neither with a sole regard to justice and the public good. The apportionment of taxes on the various descriptions of property is an act which seems to require the most exact impartiality; yet there is, perhaps, no legislative act in which greater opportunity and temptation are given to a predominant party to trample on the rules of justice. Every shilling with which they overburden the inferior number is a shilling saved to their own pockets.

It is in vain to say that enlightened statesmen will be able to adjust these clashing interests and render them all subservient to the public good. Enlightened statesmen will not always be at the helm. Nor, in many cases, can such an adjustment be made at all without taking into view indirect and remote considerations, which will rarely prevail over the immediate interest which one party may find in disregarding the rights of another or the good of the whole.

The inference to which we are brought is that the *causes* of faction cannot be removed and that relief is only to be sought in the means of controlling its *effects*.

Having concluded that "the causes of faction cannot be removed," Madison now looks in some detail at the other method by which factions can be cured—by controlling their effects. This is the heart of his essay. He begins by positing a significant question: How can you have self-government without risking the possibility that a ruling faction, particularly a majority faction, might tyrannize over the rights of others?

If a faction consists of less than a majority, relief is supplied by the republican principle, which enables the majority to defeat its sinister views by regular vote. It may clog the administration, it may convulse the society; but it will be unable to execute and mask its violence under the forms of the Constitution. When a majority is included in a faction, the form of popular government, on the other hand, enables it to sacrifice to its ruling passion or interest both the public good and the rights of other citizens. To secure the public good and private rights against the danger of such a faction, and at the same time to preserve the spirit and the form of popular government, is then the great object to which our inquiries are directed. Let me add that it is the great desideratum by which alone this form of government can be rescued from the opprobrium under which it has so long labored and be recommended to the esteem and adoption of mankind.

Madison now sets forth the idea that one way to control the effects of factions is to ensure that the majority is rendered incapable of acting in concert in order to "carry into effect schemes of oppression." He goes on to state that in a democracy, in which all citizens participate personally in government decision making, there is no way to prevent the majority from communicating with each other and, as a result, acting in concert.

By what means is this object attainable? Evidently by one of two only. Either the existence of the same passion or interest in a majority at the same time must be prevented, or the majority, having such coexistent passion or interest, must be rendered, by their number and local situation, unable to concert and carry into effect schemes of oppression. If the impulse and the opportunity be suffered to coincide, we well know that neither moral nor religious motives can be relied on as an adequate control. They are not found to be such on the injustice and violence of individuals, and lose their efficacy in proportion to the number combined together, that is, in proportion as their efficacy becomes needful.

From this view of the subject it may be concluded that a pure democracy, by which I mean a society consisting of a small number of citizens, who assemble and administer the government in person, can admit of no cure for the mischiefs of faction. A common passion or interest will, in almost every case, be felt by a majority of the whole; a communication and concert results from the form of government itself; and there is nothing to check the inducements to sacrifice the weaker party or an obnoxious individual. Hence it is that such democracies have ever been spectacles of turbulence and contention; have ever been found incompatible with personal security or the rights of property; and have in general been as short in their lives as they have been violent in their deaths. Theoretic politicians, who have patronized this species of government, have erroneously supposed that by reducing mankind to a perfect equality in their political rights, they would at the same time be perfectly equalized and assimilated in their possessions, their opinions, and their passions.

Madison now moves on to discuss the benefits of a republic with respect to controlling the effects of factions. He begins by defining a republic and then pointing out the "two great points of difference" between a republic and a democracy: a republic is governed by a small body of elected representatives, not by the people directly; and a republic can extend over a much larger territory and embrace more citizens than a democracy can.

A republic, by which I mean a government in which the scheme of representation takes place, opens a different prospect and promises the cure for which we are seeking. Let us examine the points in which it varies from pure democracy, and we shall comprehend both the nature of the cure and the efficacy which it must derive from the Union.

The two great points of difference between a democracy and a republic are: first, the delegation of the government, in the latter, to a small number of citizens elected by the rest; secondly, the greater number of citizens and greater sphere of country over which the latter may be extended.

In the following four paragraphs, Madison explains how in a republic, particularly a large republic, the delegation of authority to elected representatives will increase the likelihood that those who govern will be "fit" for their positions and that a proper balance will be achieved between local (factional) interests and national interests. Note how he stresses that the new federal Constitution, by dividing powers between state governments and the national government, provides a "happy combination in this respect."

The effect of the first difference is, on the one hand, to refine and enlarge the public views by passing them through the medium of a chosen body of citizens, whose wisdom may best discern the true interest of their country and whose patriotism and love of justice will be least likely to sacrifice it to temporary or partial considerations. Under such a regulation it may well happen that the public voice, pronounced by the representatives of the people, will be more consonant to the public good than if pronounced by the people themselves, convened for the purpose. On the other hand, the effect may be inverted. Men of factious tempers, of local prejudices, or of sinister designs, may, by intrigue, by corruption, or by other means, first obtain the suffrages, and then betray the interests of the people. The question resulting is, whether small or extensive republics are most favorable to the election of proper guardians of the public weal; and it is clearly decided in favor of the latter by two obvious considerations.

In the first place, it is to be remarked that however small the republic may be the representatives must be raised to a certain number in order to guard against the cabals of a few; and that however large it may be, they must be limited to a certain number in order to guard against the confusion of a multitude. Hence, the number of representatives in the two cases not being in proportion to that of the constituents, and being proportionally greater in the small republic, it follows that if the proportion of fit characters be not less in the large than in the small republic, the former will present a greater option, and consequently a greater probability of a fit choice.

In the next place, as each representative will be chosen by a greater number of citizens in the large than in the small republic, it will be more difficult for unworthy candidates to practice with success the vicious arts by which elections are too often carried; and the suffrages of the people being more free, will be more likely to center on men who possess the most attractive merit and the most diffusive and established characters.

It must be confessed that in this, as in most other cases, there is a mean, on both sides of which inconveniencies will be found to lie. By enlarging too much the number of electors, you render the representative too little acquainted with all their local circumstances and lesser interests; as by reducing it too much, you render him unduly attached to these, and too little fit to comprehend and pursue great and national objects. The federal Constitution forms a happy combination in this respect; the great and aggregate interests being referred to the national, the local and particular to the State legislatures.

Madison now looks more closely at the other difference between a republic and a democracy—namely, that a republic can encompass a larger territory and more citizens than a democracy can. In the remaining paragraphs of his essay, Madison concludes that in a large republic, it will be difficult for factions to act in concert. Although a factious group—religious, political, economic, or otherwise—may control a local or regional government, it will have little chance of gathering a national following. This is because in a large republic, there will be numerous factions whose work will offset the work of any one particular faction ("sect"). As Madison phrases it, these numerous factions will "secure the national councils against any danger from that source."

The other point of difference is the greater number of citizens and extent of territory which may be brought within the compass of republican than of democratic government; and it is this circumstance principally which renders factious combinations less to be dreaded in the former than in the latter. The smaller the society, the fewer probably will be the distinct parties and interests composing it; the fewer the distinct parties and interests, the more frequently will a majority be found of the same party; and the smaller the number of individuals composing a majority, and the smaller the compass within which they are placed, the more easily will they concert and execute their plans of oppression. Extend the sphere and you take in a greater variety of parties and interests; you make it less probable that a majority of the whole will have a common motive to invade the rights of other citizens; or if such a common motive exists, it will be more difficult for all who feel it to discover their own strength and to act in unison with each other. Besides other impediments, it may be remarked that, where there is a consciousness of unjust or dishonorable purposes, communication is always checked by distrust in proportion to the number whose concurrence is necessary.

Hence, it clearly appears that the same advantage which a republic has over a democracy in controlling the effects of faction is enjoyed by a large over a small republic—is enjoyed by the Union over the States composing it. Does this advantage consist in the substitution of representatives whose enlightened views and virtuous sentiments render them superior to local prejudices and to schemes of injustice? It will not be denied that the representation of the Union will be most likely to possess these requisite endowments. Does it consist in the greater security afforded by a greater variety of parties, against the event of any one party being able to outnumber and oppress the rest? In an equal degree does the increased variety of parties comprised within the Union increase this security. Does it, in fine, consist in the greater obstacles opposed to the concert and accomplishment of the secret wishes of an unjust and interested majority? Here again the extent of the Union gives it the most palpable advantage.

The influence of factious leaders may kindle a flame within their particular States but will be unable to spread a general conflagration through the other States. A religious sect may degenerate into a political faction in a part of the Confederacy; but the variety of sects dispersed over the entire face of it must secure the national councils against any danger from that source. A rage for paper money, for an abolition of debts, for an equal division of property, or for any other improper or wicked project, will be less apt to pervade the whole body of the Union than a particular member of it, in the same proportion as such a malady is more likely to taint a particular county or district than an entire State.

In the extent and proper structure of the Union, therefore, we behold a republican remedy for the diseases most incident to republican government. And according to the degree of pleasure and pride we feel in being republicans ought to be our zeal in cherishing the spirit and supporting the character of federalists.

Publius
(James Madison)

Federalist Paper No. 51

Federalist Paper *No. 51, also authored by James Madison, is another classic in American political theory. Although the Federalists wanted a strong national government, they had not abandoned the traditional American view, particularly notable during the revolutionary era, that those holding powerful government positions could not be trusted to put national interests and the common good above their own personal interests. In this essay, Madison explains why the separation of the national government's powers into three branches—executive, legislative, and judicial—and a federal structure of government offer the best protection against tyranny.*

To what expedient, then, shall we finally resort, for maintaining in practice the necessary partition of power among the several departments as laid down in the Constitution? The only answer that can be given is that as all these exterior provisions are found to be inadequate the defect must be supplied, by so contriving the interior structure of the government as that its several constituent parts may, by their mutual relations, be the means of keeping each other in their proper places. Without presuming to undertake a full development of this important idea I will hazard a few general observations which may perhaps place it in a clearer light, and enable us to form a more correct judgment of the principles and structure of the government planned by the convention.

In the next two paragraphs, Madison stresses that for the powers of the different branches (departments) of government to be truly separated, the personnel in one branch should not be dependent on another branch for their appointment or for the "emoluments" (compensation) attached to their offices.

In order to lay a due foundation for that separate and distinct exercise of the different powers of government, which to a certain extent is admitted on all hands to be essential to the preservation of liberty, it is evident that each department should have a will of its own; and consequently should be so constituted that the members of each should have as little agency as possible in the appointment of the members of the others. Were this principle rigorously adhered to, it would require that all the appointments for the supreme executive, legislative, and judiciary magistracies should be drawn from the same fountain of authority, the people, through channels having no communication whatever with one another. Perhaps such a plan of constructing the several departments would be less difficult in practice than it may in contemplation appear. Some difficulties, however, and some additional expense would attend the execution of it. Some deviations, therefore, from the principle must be admitted. In the constitution of the judiciary department in particular, it might be inexpedient to insist rigorously on the principle: first, because peculiar qualifications being essential in the members, the primary consideration ought to be to select that mode of choice which best secures these qualifications; second, because the permanent tenure by which the appointments are held in that department must soon destroy all sense of dependence on the authority conferring them.

It is equally evident that the members of each department should be as little dependent as possible on those of the others for the emoluments annexed to their offices. Were the executive magistrate, or the judges, not independent of the legislature in this particular, their independence in every other would be merely nominal.

In the following passages, which are among the most widely quoted of Madison's writings, he explains how the separation of the powers of government into three branches helps to counter the effects of personal ambition on government. The separation of powers allows personal motives to be linked to the constitutional rights of a branch of government. In effect, competing personal interests in each branch will help to keep the powers of the three government branches separate and, in so doing, will help to guard the public interest.

But the great security against a gradual concentration of the several powers in the same department consists in giving to those who administer each department the necessary constitutional means and personal motives to resist encroachments of the others. The provision for defense must in this, as in all other cases, be made commensurate to the danger of attack. Ambition must be made to counteract ambition. The interest of the man must be connected with the constitutional rights of the place. It may be a reflection on human nature that such devices should be necessary to control the abuses of government. But what is government itself but the greatest of all reflections on human nature? If men were angels, no government would be necessary. If angels were to govern men, neither external nor internal controls on government would be necessary. In framing a government which is to be administered by men over men, the great difficulty lies in this: you must first enable the government to control the governed; and in the next place oblige it to control itself. A dependence on the people is, no doubt, the primary control on the government; but experience has taught mankind the necessity of auxiliary precautions.

This policy of supplying, by opposite and rival interests, the defect of better motives, might be traced through the whole system of human affairs, private as well as public. We see it particularly displayed in all the subordinate distributions of power, where the constant aim is to divide and arrange the several offices in such a manner as that each may be a check on the other—that the private interest of every individual may be a sentinel over the public rights. These inventions of prudence cannot be less requisite in the distribution of the supreme powers of the State.

Madison now addresses the issue of equality between the branches of government. The legislature will necessarily predominate, but if the executive is given an "absolute negative" (absolute veto power) over legislative actions, this also could lead to an abuse of power. Madison concludes that the division of the legislature into two "branches" (parts, or chambers) will act as a check on the legislature's powers.

But it is not possible to give to each department an equal power of self-defense. In republican government, the legislative authority necessarily predominates. The remedy for this inconveniency is to divide the legislature into different branches; and to render them, by different modes of election and different principles of action, as little connected with each other as the nature of their common functions and their common dependence on the society will admit. It may even be necessary to guard against dangerous encroachments by still further precautions. As the weight of the legislative authority requires that it should be thus divided, the weakness of the executive may require, on the other hand, that it should be fortified. An absolute negative on the legislature appears, at first view, to be the natural defense with which the executive magistrate should be armed. But perhaps it would be neither altogether safe nor alone sufficient. On ordinary occasions it might not be exerted with the requisite firmness, and on extraordinary occasions it might be perfidiously abused. May not this defect of an absolute negative be supplied by some qualified connection between this weaker department and the weaker branch of the stronger department, by which the latter may be led to support the constitutional rights of the former, without being too much detached from the rights of its own department?

If the principles on which these observations are founded be just, as I persuade myself they are, and they be applied as a criterion to the several State constitutions, and to the federal Constitution, it will be found that if the latter does not perfectly correspond with them, the former are infinitely less able to bear such a test.

In the remainder of the essay, Madison discusses how a federal system of government, in which powers are divided between the states and the national government, offers "double security" against tyranny.

There are, moreover, two considerations particularly applicable to the federal system of America, which place that system in a very interesting point of view.

First. In a single republic, all the power surrendered by the people is submitted to the administration of a single government; and the usurpations are guarded against by a division of the government into distinct and separate departments. In the compound republic of America, the power surrendered by the people is first divided between two distinct governments, and then the portion allotted to each subdivided among distinct and separate departments. Hence a double security arises to the rights of the people. The different governments will control each other, at the same time that each will be controlled by itself.

Second. It is of great importance in a republic not only to guard the society against the oppression of its rulers, but to guard one part of the society against the injustice of the other part. Different interests necessarily exist in different classes of citizens. If a majority be united by a common interest, the rights of the minority will be insecure. There are but two methods of providing against this evil: the one by creating a will in the community independent of the majority—that is, of the society itself; the other, by comprehending in the society so many separate descriptions of citizens as will render an unjust combination of a majority of the whole very improbable, if not impracticable. The first method prevails in all governments possessing an hereditary or self-appointed authority. This, at best, is but a precarious security; because a power independent of the society may as well espouse the unjust views of the major as the rightful interests of the minor party, and may possibly be turned against both parties.

The second method will be exemplified in the federal republic of the United States. Whilst all authority in it will be derived from and dependent on the society, the society itself will be broken into so many parts, interests and classes of citizens, that the rights of individuals, or of the minority, will be in little danger from interested combinations of the majority.

In a free government the security for civil rights must be the same as that for religious rights. It consists in the one case in the multiplicity of interests, and in the other in the multiplicity of sects. The degree of security in both cases will depend on the number of interests and sects; and this may be presumed to depend on the extent of country and number of people comprehended under the same government. This view of the subject must particularly recommend a proper federal system to all the sincere and considerate friends of republican government, since it shows that in exact proportion as the territory of the Union may be formed into more circumscribed Confederacies, or States, oppressive combinations of a majority will be facilitated; the best security, under the republican forms, for the rights of every class of citizen, will be diminished; and consequently the stability and independence of some member of the government, the only other security, must be proportionally increased. Justice is the end of government. It is the end of civil society. It ever has been and ever will be pursued until it be obtained, or until liberty be lost in the pursuit. In a society under the forms of which the stronger faction can readily unite and oppress the weaker, anarchy may as truly be said to reign as in a state of nature, where the weaker individual is not secured against the violence of the stronger; and as, in the latter state, even the stronger individuals are prompted, by the uncertainty of their condition, to submit to a government which may protect the weak as well as themselves; so, in the former state, will the more powerful factions or parties be gradually induced, by a like motive, to wish for a government which will protect all parties, the weaker as well as the more powerful.

It can be little doubted that if the State of Rhode Island was separated from the Confederacy and left to itself, the insecurity of rights under the popular form of government within such narrow limits would be displayed by such reiterated oppressions of factious majorities that some power altogether independent of the people would soon be called for by the voice of the very factions whose misrule had proved the necessity of it. In the extended republic of the United States, and among the great variety of interests, parties, and sects which it embraces, a coalition of a majority of the whole society could seldom take place on any other principles than those of justice and the general good; whilst there being thus less danger to a minor from the will of a major party, there must be less pretext, also, to provide for the security of the former, by introducing into the government a will not dependent on the latter, or, in other words, a will independent of the society itself. It is no less certain than it is important, notwithstanding the contrary opinions which have been entertained, that the larger the society, provided it lie within a practicable sphere, the more duly capable it will be of self-government. And happily for the republican cause, the practicable sphere may be carried to a very great extent by a judicious modification and mixture of the *federal principle*.

Publius
(James Madison)

Federalist Paper No. 78

In this essay, Alexander Hamilton looks at the role of the judicial branch (the courts) in the new government fashioned by the Constitution's framers. The essay is historically significant because, among other things, it provides a basis for the courts' power of judicial review, which was not explicitly set forth in the Constitution (see Chapters 2 and 13).

After some brief introductory remarks, Hamilton explains why the founders decided that federal judges should be appointed and given lifetime tenure. Note how he describes the judiciary as the "weakest" and "least dangerous" branch of government. Because of this, claims Hamilton, "all possible care" is required to enable the judiciary to defend itself against attacks by the other two branches of government. Above all, the independence of the judicial branch should be secured, because if judicial powers were combined with legislative or executive powers, there would be no liberty.

We proceed now to an examination of the judiciary department of the proposed government.

In unfolding the defects of the existing Confederation, the utility and necessity of a federal judicature have been clearly pointed out. It is the less necessary to recapitulate the considerations there urged, as the propriety of the institution in the abstract is not disputed; the only questions which have been raised being relative to the manner of constituting it, and to its extent. To these points, therefore, our observations shall be confined.

The manner of constituting it seems to embrace these several objects: 1st. The mode of appointing the judges. 2d. The tenure by which they are to hold their places. 3d. The partition of the judiciary authority between different courts, and their relations to each other.

First. As to the mode of appointing the judges; this is the same with that of appointing the officers of the Union in general, and has been so fully discussed in the last two numbers, that nothing can be said here which would not be useless repetition.

Second. As to the tenure by which the judges are to hold their places; this chiefly concerns their duration in office; the provisions for their support; the precautions for their responsibility.

According to the plan of the convention, all judges who may be appointed by the United States are to hold their offices during good behavior; which is conformable to the most approved of the State constitutions and among the rest, to that of this State. Its propriety having been drawn into question by the adversaries of that plan, is no light symptom of the rage for objection, which disorders their imaginations and judgments. The standard of good behavior for the continuance in office of the judicial magistracy, is certainly one of the most valuable of the modern improvements in the practice of government. In a monarchy it is an excellent barrier to the despotism of the prince; in a republic it is a no less excellent barrier to the encroachments and oppressions of the representative body. And it is the best expedient which can be devised in any government, to secure a steady, upright, and impartial administration of the laws.

Whoever attentively considers the different departments of power must perceive, that, in a government in which they are separated from each other, the judiciary, from the nature of its functions, will always be the least dangerous to the political rights of the Constitution; because it will be least in a capacity to annoy or injure them. The Executive not only dispenses the honors, but holds the sword of the community. The legislature not only commands the purse, but prescribes the rules by which the duties and rights of every citizen are to be regulated. The judiciary, on the contrary, has no influence over either the sword or the purse; no direction either of the strength or of the wealth of the society; and can take no active resolution whatever. It may truly be said to have neither force nor will, but merely judgment; and must ultimately depend upon the aid of the executive arm even for the efficacy of its judgments.

This simple view of the matter suggests several important consequences. It proves incontestably, that the judiciary is beyond comparison the weakest of the three departments of power; that it can never attack with success either of the other two; and that all possible care is requisite to enable it to defend itself against their attacks. It equally proves, that though individual oppression may now and then proceed from the courts of justice, the general liberty of the people can never be endangered from that quarter; I mean so long as the judiciary remains truly distinct from both the legislature and the Executive. For I agree, that "there is no liberty, if the power of judging is not separated from the legislative and executive powers." And it proves, in the last place, that as liberty can have nothing to fear from the judiciary alone, but would have everything to fear from its union with either of the other departments; that as all the effects of such a union must ensue from a dependence of the former on the latter, notwithstanding a nominal and apparent separation; that as, from the natural feebleness of the judiciary, it is in continual jeopardy of being overpowered, awed, or influenced by its co-ordinate branches; and that as nothing can contribute so much to its firmness and independence as permanency in office, this quality may therefore be justly regarded as an indispensable ingredient in its constitution, and, in a great measure, as the citadel of the public justice and the public security.

Hamilton now stresses that the "complete independence of the courts" is essential in a limited government, because it is up to the courts to interpret the laws. Just as a federal court can decide which of two conflicting statutes should take priority, so can that court decide whether a statute conflicts with the Constitution. Essentially, Hamilton sets forth here the theory of judicial review—the power of the courts to decide whether actions of the other branches of government are (or are not) consistent with the Constitution. Hamilton points out that this "exercise of judicial discretion, in determining between two contradictory laws," does not mean that the judicial branch is superior to the legislative branch. Rather, it "supposes" that the power of the people (as declared in the Constitution) is superior to both the judiciary and the legislature.

The complete independence of the courts of justice is peculiarly essential in a limited Constitution. By a limited Constitution, I understand one which contains certain specified exceptions to the legislative authority; such, for instance, as that it shall pass no bills of attainder, no ex-post-facto laws, and the like. Limitations of this kind can be preserved in practice no other way than through the medium of courts of justice, whose duty it must be to declare all acts contrary to the manifest tenor of the Constitution void. Without this, all the reservations of particular rights or privileges would amount to nothing. Some perplexity respecting the rights of the courts to pronounce legislative acts void, because contrary to the Constitution, has arisen from an imagination that the doctrine would imply a superiority of the judiciary to the legislative power. It is urged that the authority which can declare the acts of another void, must necessarily be superior to the one whose acts may be declared void. As this doctrine is of great importance in all the American constitutions, a brief discussion of the ground on which it rests cannot be unacceptable.

There is no position which depends on clearer principles, than that every act of a delegated authority, contrary to the tenor of the commission under which it is exercised, is void. No legislative act, therefore, contrary to the Constitution, can be valid. To deny this, would be to affirm, that the deputy is greater than his principal; that the servant is above his master; that the representatives of the people are superior to the people themselves; that men acting by virtue of powers, may do not only what their powers do not authorize, but what they forbid.

If it be said that the legislative body are themselves the constitutional judges of their own powers, and that the construction they put upon them is conclusive upon the other departments, it may be answered, that this cannot be the natural presumption, where it is not to be collected from any particular provisions in the Constitution. It is not otherwise to be supposed, that the Constitution could intend to enable the representatives of the people to substitute their will to that of their constituents. It is far more rational to suppose, that the courts were designed to be an intermediate body between the people and the legislature, in order, among other things, to keep the latter within the limits assigned to their authority. The interpretation of the laws is the proper and peculiar province of the courts. A constitution is, in fact, and must be regarded by the judges, as a fundamental law. It therefore belongs to them to ascertain its meaning, as well as the meaning of any particular act proceeding from the legislative body. If there should happen to be an irreconcilable variance between the two, that which has the superior obligation and validity ought, of course, to be preferred; or, in other words, the Constitution ought to be preferred to the statute, the intention of the people to the intention of their agents.

Nor does this conclusion by any means suppose a superiority of the judicial to the legislative power. It only supposes that the power of the people is superior to both; and that where the will of the legislature, declared in its statutes, stands in opposition to that of the people, declared in the Constitution, the judges ought to be governed by the latter rather than the former. They ought to regulate their decisions by the fundamental laws, rather than by those which are not fundamental.

This exercise of judicial discretion, in determining between two contradictory laws, is exemplified in a familiar instance. It not uncommonly happens, that there are two statutes existing at one time, clashing in whole or in part with each other, and neither of them containing any repealing clause or expression. In such a case, it is the province of the courts to liquidate and fix their meaning and operation. So far as they can, by any fair construction, be reconciled to each other, reason and law conspire to dictate that this should be done; where this is impracticable, it becomes a matter of necessity to give effect to one, in exclusion of the other. The rule which has obtained in the courts for determining their relative validity is, that the last in order of time shall be preferred to the first. But this is a mere rule of construction, not derived from any positive law, but from the nature and reason of the thing. It is a rule not enjoined upon the courts by legislative provision, but adopted by themselves, as consonant to truth the propriety, for the direction of their conduct as interpreters of the law. They thought it reasonable, that between the interfering acts of an equal authority, that which was the last indication of its will should have the preference.

But in regard to the interfering acts of a superior and subordinate authority, of an original and derivative power, the nature and reason of the thing indicate the converse of that rule as proper to be followed. They teach us that the prior act of a superior ought to be preferred to the subsequent act of an inferior and subordinate authority; and that accordingly, whenever a particular statute contravenes the Constitution, it will be the duty of the judicial tribunals to adhere to the latter and disregard the former.

It can be of no weight to say that the courts, on the pretense of a repugnancy, may substitute their own pleasure to the constitutional intentions of the legislature. This might as well happen in the case of two contradictory statutes; or it might as well happen in every adjudication upon any single statute. The courts must declare the sense of the law; and if they should be disposed to exercise will instead of judgment, the consequence would equally be the substitution of their pleasure to that of the legislative body. The observation, if it prove anything, would prove that there ought to be no judges distinct from that body.

If, then, the courts of justice are to be considered as the bulwarks of a limited Constitution against legislative encroachments, this consideration will afford a strong argument for the permanent tenure of judicial offices, since nothing will contribute so much as this to that independent spirit in the judges which must be essential to the faithful performance of so arduous a duty.

The independence of the judges is equally requisite to guard the Constitution and the rights of individuals from the effects of those ill humors, which the arts of designing men, or the influence of particular conjunctures, sometimes disseminate among the people themselves, and which, though they speedily give place to better information, and more deliberate reflection, have a tendency, in the meantime, to occasion dangerous innovations in the government, and serious oppressions of the minor party in the community. Though I trust the friends of the proposed Constitution will never concur with its enemies, in questioning that fundamental principle of republican government, which admits the right of the people to alter or abolish the established Constitution, whenever they find it inconsistent with their happiness, yet it is not to be inferred from this principle, that the representatives of the people, whenever a momentary inclination happens to lay hold of a majority of their constituents, incompatible with the provisions of the existing Constitution, would, on that account, be justifiable in a violation of those provisions; or that the courts would be under a greater obligation to connive at infractions in this shape, than when they had proceeded wholly from the cabals of the representative body. Until the people have, by some solemn and authoritative act, annulled or changed the established form, it is binding upon themselves collectively, as well as individually; and no presumption, or even knowledge, of their sentiments, can warrant their representatives in a departure from it, prior to such an act. But it is easy to see, that it would require an uncommon portion of fortitude in the judges to do their duty as faithful guardians of the Constitution, where legislative invasions of it had been instigated by the major voice of the community.

But it is not with a view to infractions of the Constitution only, that the independence of the judges may be an essential safeguard against the effects of occasional ill humors in the society. These sometimes extend no farther than to the injury of the private rights of particular classes of citizens, by unjust and partial laws. Here also the firmness of the judicial magistracy is of vast importance in mitigating the severity and confining the operation of such laws. It not only serves to moderate the immediate mischiefs of those which may have been passed, but it operates as a check upon the legislative body in passing them; who, perceiving that obstacles to the success of iniquitous intention are to be expected from the scruples of the courts, are in a manner compelled, by the very motives of the injustice they meditate, to qualify their attempts. This is a circumstance calculated to have more influence upon the character of our governments, than but few may be aware of. The benefits of the integrity and moderation of the judiciary have already been felt in more States than one; and though they may have displeased those whose sinister expectations they may have disappointed, they must have commanded the esteem and applause of all the virtuous and disinterested. Considerate men, of every description, ought to prize whatever will tend to beget or fortify that temper in the courts; as no man can be sure that he may not be tomorrow the victim of a spirit of injustice, by which he may be a gainer today. And every man must now feel, that the inevitable tendency of such a spirit is to sap the foundations of public and private confidence, and to introduce in its stead universal distrust and distress.

That inflexible and uniform adherence to the rights of the Constitution, and of individuals, which we perceive to be indispensable in the courts of justice, can certainly not be expected from judges who hold their offices by a temporary commission. Periodical appointments, however regulated, or by whomsoever made, would, in some way or other, be fatal to their necessary independence. If the power of making them was committed either to the Executive or legislature, there would be danger of an improper complaisance to the branch which possessed it; if to both, there would be an unwillingness to hazard the displeasure of either; if to the people, or to persons chosen by them for the special purpose, there would be too great a disposition to consult popularity, to justify a reliance that nothing would be consulted but the Constitution and the laws.

Hamilton points to yet another reason why lifetime tenure for federal judges will benefit the public: effective judgments rest on a knowledge of judicial precedents and the law, and such knowledge can only be obtained through experience on the bench. A "temporary duration of office," according to Hamilton, would "discourage individuals [of 'fit character'] from quitting a lucrative practice to serve on the bench" and ultimately would "throw the administration of justice into the hands of the less able, and less well qualified."

There is yet a further and a weightier reason for the permanency of the judicial offices, which is deducible from the nature of the qualifications they require. It has been frequently remarked, with great propriety, that a voluminous code of laws is one of the inconveniences necessarily connected with the advantages of a free gov-ernment. To avoid an arbitrary discretion in the courts, it is indispensable that they should be bound down by strict rules and precedents, which serve to define and point out their duty in every particular case that comes before them; and it will readily be conceived from the variety of controversies which grow out of the folly and wickedness of mankind, that the records of those precedents must unavoidably swell to a very considerable bulk, and must demand long and laborious study to acquire a competent knowledge of them. Hence it is, that there can be but few men in the society who will have sufficient skill in the laws to qualify them for the stations of judges. And making the proper deductions for the ordinary depravity of human nature, the number must be still smaller of those who unite the requisite integrity with the requisite knowledge. These considerations apprise us, that the government can have no great option between fit character; and that a temporary duration in office, which would naturally discourage such characters from quitting a lucrative line of practice to accept a seat on the bench, would have a tendency to throw the administration of justice into hands less able, and less well qualified, to conduct it with utility and dignity. In the present circumstances of this country, and in those in which it is likely to be for a long time to come, the disadvantages on this score would be greater than they may at first sight appear; but it must be confessed, that they are far inferior to those which present themselves under other aspects of the subject.

Upon the whole, there can be no room to doubt that the convention acted wisely in copying from the models of those constitutions which have established good behavior as the tenure of their judicial offices, in point of duration; and that so far from being blamable on this account, their plan would have been inexcusably defective, if it had wanted this important feature of good government. The experience of Great Britain affords an illustrious comment on the excellence of the institution.

Publius
(Alexander Hamilton)

APPENDIX C

PRESIDENTS OF THE UNITED STATES

	Term of Service	Age at Inauguration	Political Party	College or University	Occupation or Profession
1. George Washington	1789–1797	57	None		Planter
2. John Adams	1797–1801	61	Federalist	Harvard	Lawyer
3. Thomas Jefferson	1801–1809	57	Jeffersonian Republican	William and Mary	Planter, Lawyer
4. James Madison	1809–1817	57	Jeffersonian Republican	Princeton	Lawyer
5. James Monroe	1817–1825	58	Jeffersonian Republican	William and Mary	Lawyer
6. John Quincy Adams	1825–1829	57	Jeffersonian Republican	Harvard	Lawyer
7. Andrew Jackson	1829–1837	61	Democrat		Lawyer
8. Martin Van Buren	1837–1841	54	Democrat		Lawyer
9. William H. Harrison	1841	68	Whig	Hampden-Sydney	Soldier
10. John Tyler	1841–1845	51	Whig	William and Mary	Lawyer
11. James K. Polk	1845–1849	49	Democrat	U. of N. Carolina	Lawyer
12. Zachary Taylor	1849–1850	64	Whig		Soldier
13. Millard Fillmore	1850–1853	50	Whig		Lawyer
14. Franklin Pierce	1853–1857	48	Democrat	Bowdoin	Lawyer
15. James Buchanan	1857–1861	65	Democrat	Dickinson	Lawyer
16. Abraham Lincoln	1861–1865	52	Republican		Lawyer
17. Andrew Johnson	1865–1869	56	National Union†		Tailor
18. Ulysses S. Grant	1869–1877	46	Republican	U.S. Mil. Academy	Soldier
19. Rutherford B. Hayes	1877–1881	54	Republican	Kenyon	Lawyer
20. James A. Garfield	1881	49	Republican	Williams	Lawyer
21. Chester A. Arthur	1881–1885	51	Republican	Union	Lawyer
22. Grover Cleveland	1885–1889	47	Democrat		Lawyer
23. Benjamin Harrison	1889–1893	55	Republican	Miami	Lawyer
24. Grover Cleveland	1893–1897	55	Democrat		Lawyer
25. William McKinley	1897–1901	54	Republican	Allegheny College	Lawyer
26. Theodore Roosevelt	1901–1909	42	Republican	Harvard	Author
27. William H. Taft	1909–1913	51	Republican	Yale	Lawyer
28. Woodrow Wilson	1913–1921	56	Democrat	Princeton	Educator
29. Warren G. Harding	1921–1923	55	Republican		Editor
30. Calvin Coolidge	1923–1929	51	Republican	Amherst	Lawyer
31. Herbert C. Hoover	1929–1933	54	Republican	Stanford	Engineer
32. Franklin D. Roosevelt	1933–1945	51	Democrat	Harvard	Lawyer
33. Harry S. Truman	1945–1953	60	Democrat		Businessman
34. Dwight D. Eisenhower	1953–1961	62	Republican	U.S. Mil. Academy	Soldier
35. John F. Kennedy	1961–1963	43	Democrat	Harvard	Author
36. Lyndon B. Johnson	1963–1969	55	Democrat	Southwest Texas State	Teacher
37. Richard M. Nixon	1969–1974	56	Republican	Whittier	Lawyer
38. Gerald R. Ford‡	1974–1977	61	Republican	Michigan	Lawyer
39. James E. Carter, Jr.	1977–1981	52	Democrat	U.S. Naval Academy	Businessman
40. Ronald W. Reagan	1981–1989	69	Republican	Eureka College	Actor
41. George H. W. Bush	1989–1993	64	Republican	Yale	Businessman
42. Bill Clinton	1993–2001	46	Democrat	Georgetown	Lawyer
43. George W. Bush	2001–2009	54	Republican	Yale	Businessman
44. Barack Obama	2009–	47	Democrat	Columbia	Lawyer

*Church preference; never joined any church.

†The National Union Party consisted of Republicans and War Democrats. Johnson was a Democrat.

**Inaugurated Dec. 6, 1973, to replace Agnew, who resigned Oct. 10, 1973.

Religion	Born	Died	Age at Death	Vice President	
1. Episcopalian	Feb. 22, 1732	Dec. 14, 1799	67	John Adams	(1789–1797)
2. Unitarian	Oct. 30, 1735	July 4, 1826	90	Thomas Jefferson	(1797–1801)
3. Unitarian*	Apr. 13, 1743	July 4, 1826	83	Aaron Burr George Clinton	(1801–1805) (1805–1809)
4. Episcopalian	Mar. 16, 1751	June 28, 1836	85	George Clinton Elbridge Gerry	(1809–1812) (1813–1814)
5. Episcopalian	Apr. 28, 1758	July 4, 1831	73	Daniel D. Tompkins	(1817–1825)
6. Unitarian	July 11, 1767	Feb. 23, 1848	80	John C. Calhoun	(1825–1829)
7. Presbyterian	Mar. 15, 1767	June 8, 1845	78	John C. Calhoun Martin Van Buren	(1829–1832) (1833–1837)
8. Dutch Reformed	Dec. 5, 1782	July 24, 1862	79	Richard M. Johnson	(1837–1841)
9. Episcopalian	Feb. 9, 1773	Apr. 4, 1841	68	John Tyler	(1841)
10. Episcopalian	Mar. 29, 1790	Jan. 18, 1862	71		
11. Methodist	Nov. 2, 1795	June 15, 1849	53	George M. Dallas	(1845–1849)
12. Episcopalian	Nov. 24, 1784	July 9, 1850	65	Millard Fillmore	(1849–1850)
13. Unitarian	Jan. 7, 1800	Mar. 8, 1874	74		
14. Episcopalian	Nov. 23, 1804	Oct. 8, 1869	64	William R. King	(1853)
15. Presbyterian	Apr. 23, 1791	June 1, 1868	77	John C. Breckinridge	(1857–1861)
16. Presbyterian*	Feb. 12, 1809	Apr. 15, 1865	56	Hannibal Hamlin Andrew Johnson	(1861–1865) (1865)
17. Methodist*	Dec. 29, 1808	July 31, 1875	66		
18. Methodist	Apr. 27, 1822	July 23, 1885	63	Schuyler Colfax Henry Wilson	(1869–1873) (1873–1875)
19. Methodist*	Oct. 4, 1822	Jan. 17, 1893	70	William A. Wheeler	(1877–1881)
20. Disciples of Christ	Nov. 19, 1831	Sept. 19, 1881	49	Chester A. Arthur	(1881)
21. Episcopalian	Oct. 5, 1829	Nov. 18, 1886	57		
22. Presbyterian	Mar. 18, 1837	June 24, 1908	71	Thomas A. Hendricks	(1885)
23. Presbyterian	Aug. 20, 1833	Mar. 13, 1901	67	Levi P. Morton	(1889–1893)
24. Presbyterian	Mar. 18, 1837	June 24, 1908	71	Adlai E. Stevenson	(1893–1897)
25. Methodist	Jan. 29, 1843	Sept. 14, 1901	58	Garret A. Hobart Theodore Roosevelt	(1897–1899) (1901)
26. Dutch Reformed	Oct. 27, 1858	Jan. 6, 1919	60	Charles W. Fairbanks	(1905–1909)
27. Unitarian	Sept. 15, 1857	Mar. 8, 1930	72	James S. Sherman	(1909–1912)
28. Presbyterian	Dec. 29, 1856	Feb. 3, 1924	67	Thomas R. Marshall	(1913–1921)
29. Baptist	Nov. 2, 1865	Aug. 2, 1923	57	Calvin Coolidge	(1921–1923)
30. Congregationalist	July 4, 1872	Jan. 5, 1933	60	Charles G. Dawes	(1925–1929)
31. Friend (Quaker)	Aug. 10, 1874	Oct. 20, 1964	90	Charles Curtis	(1929–1933)
32. Episcopalian	Jan. 30, 1882	Apr. 12, 1945	63	John N. Garner Henry A. Wallace Harry S. Truman	(1933–1941) (1941–1945) (1945)
33. Baptist	May 8, 1884	Dec. 26, 1972	88	Alben W. Barkley	(1949–1953)
34. Presbyterian	Oct. 14, 1890	Mar. 28, 1969	78	Richard M. Nixon	(1953–1961)
35. Roman Catholic	May 29, 1917	Nov. 22, 1963	46	Lyndon B. Johnson	(1961–1963)
36. Disciples of Christ	Aug. 27, 1908	Jan. 22, 1973	64	Hubert H. Humphrey	(1965–1969)
37. Friend (Quaker)	Jan. 9, 1913	Apr. 22, 1994	81	Spiro T. Agnew Gerald R. Ford**	(1969–1973) (1973–1974)
38. Episcopalian	July 14, 1913	Dec. 26, 2006	93	Nelson A. Rockefeller§	(1974–1977)
39. Baptist	Oct. 1, 1924			Walter F. Mondale	(1977–1981)
40. Disciples of Christ	Feb. 6, 1911	June 5, 2004	93	George H. W. Bush	(1981–1989)
41. Episcopalian	June 12, 1924			J. Danforth Quayle	(1989–1993)
42. Baptist	Aug. 19, 1946			Albert A. Gore	(1993–2001)
43. Methodist	July 6, 1946			Dick Cheney	(2001–2009)
44. United Church of Christ	Aug. 4, 1961			Joe Biden	(2009–)

‡Inaugurated Aug. 9, 1974, to replace Nixon, who resigned that same day.
§Inaugurated Dec. 19, 1974, to replace Ford, who became president Aug. 9, 1974.

APPENDIX D

PARTY CONTROL OF CONGRESS SINCE 1900

Congress	Years	President	Majority Party in House	Majority Party in Senate
57th	1901–1903	McKinley/T. Roosevelt	Republican	Republican
58th	1903–1905	T. Roosevelt	Republican	Republican
59th	1905–1907	T. Roosevelt	Republican	Republican
60th	1907–1909	T. Roosevelt	Republican	Republican
61st	1909–1911	Taft	Republican	Republican
62d	1911–1913	Taft	Democratic	Republican
63d	1913–1915	Wilson	Democratic	Democratic
64th	1915–1917	Wilson	Democratic	Democratic
65th	1917–1919	Wilson	Democratic	Democratic
66th	1919–1921	Wilson	Republican	Republican
67th	1921–1923	Harding	Republican	Republican
68th	1923–1925	Harding/Coolidge	Republican	Republican
69th	1925–1927	Coolidge	Republican	Republican
70th	1927–1929	Coolidge	Republican	Republican
71st	1929–1931	Hoover	Republican	Republican
72d	1931–1933	Hoover	Democratic	Republican
73d	1933–1935	F. Roosevelt	Democratic	Democratic
74th	1935–1937	F. Roosevelt	Democratic	Democratic
75th	1937–1939	F. Roosevelt	Democratic	Democratic
76th	1939–1941	F. Roosevelt	Democratic	Democratic
77th	1941–1943	F. Roosevelt	Democratic	Democratic
78th	1943–1945	F. Roosevelt	Democratic	Democratic
79th	1945–1947	F. Roosevelt/Truman	Democratic	Democratic
80th	1947–1949	Truman	Republican	Democratic
81st	1949–1951	Truman	Democratic	Democratic
82d	1951–1953	Truman	Democratic	Democratic
83d	1953–1955	Eisenhower	Republican	Republican
84th	1955–1957	Eisenhower	Democratic	Democratic
85th	1957–1959	Eisenhower	Democratic	Democratic
86th	1959–1961	Eisenhower	Democratic	Democratic
87th	1961–1963	Kennedy	Democratic	Democratic
88th	1963–1965	Kennedy/Johnson	Democratic	Democratic
89th	1965–1967	Johnson	Democratic	Democratic
90th	1967–1969	Johnson	Democratic	Democratic
91st	1969–1971	Nixon	Democratic	Democratic
92d	1971–1973	Nixon	Democratic	Democratic
93d	1973–1975	Nixon/Ford	Democratic	Democratic
94th	1975–1977	Ford	Democratic	Democratic
95th	1977–1979	Carter	Democratic	Democratic
96th	1979–1981	Carter	Democratic	Democratic
97th	1981–1983	Reagan	Democratic	Republican
98th	1983–1985	Reagan	Democratic	Republican
99th	1985–1987	Reagan	Democratic	Republican
100th	1987–1989	Reagan	Democratic	Democratic
101st	1989–1991	G. H. W. Bush	Democratic	Democratic
102d	1991–1993	G. H. W. Bush	Democratic	Democratic
103d	1993–1995	Clinton	Democratic	Democratic
104th	1995–1997	Clinton	Republican	Republican
105th	1997–1999	Clinton	Republican	Republican
106th	1999–2001	Clinton	Republican	Republican
107th	2001–2003	G. W. Bush	Republican	Democratic
108th	2003–2005	G. W. Bush	Republican	Republican
109th	2005–2007	G. W. Bush	Republican	Republican
110th	2007–2009	G. W. Bush	Democratic	Democratic
111th	2009–2011	Obama	Democratic	Democratic
112th	2011–2013	Obama	Republican	Democratic

GLOSSARY

A

Access The ability to contact an official either in person or by telephone. Campaign contributions are often given in hopes of gaining access to elected officials.

Accountability Responsibility for a program's results—for example, using measurable standards to hold public schools responsible for their students' performance.

Acquisitive Model A model of bureaucracy that views top-level bureaucrats as seeking to expand the size of their budgets and staffs to gain greater power.

Acquitted Found not guilty.

Actual Malice Either knowledge of a defamatory statement's falsity or a reckless disregard for the truth.

Adjutant General The principal staff officer of an army, who passes communications to the commanding general and distributes the general's orders to subordinates. In the example of the Texas National Guard and Texas State Guard, the "commanding general" is the governor. *Adjutant* comes from a Latin word meaning "helper."

Administrative Agency A federal, state, or local government unit established to perform a specific function. Administrative agencies are created and authorized by legislative bodies to administer and enforce specific laws.

Administrative Law Rules and regulations written by administrators to implement laws. The effectiveness of a law is often determined by how the corresponding administrative law is written.

Adversary System A legal system in which parties to a legal action are opponents and are responsible for bringing the facts and law related to their case before the court.

Advice and Consent Terms in the Constitution describing the U.S. Senate's power to review and approve treaties and presidential appointments.

Affirm To declare that a court ruling is valid and must stand.

Affirmative Action A policy in educational admissions or job hiring that gives special attention or compensatory treatment to traditionally disadvantaged groups in an effort to overcome present effects of past discrimination.

Agenda Setting Determining which public-policy questions will be debated or considered.

***Amicus Curiae* Brief** A brief (a document containing a legal argument supporting a desired outcome in a particular case) filed by a third party, or *amicus curiae* (Latin for "friend of the court"), who is not directly involved in the litigation but who has an interest in the outcome of the case.

Anarchy The condition of no government.

Annexation The incorporation of a territory into a larger political unit, such as a country, state, county, or city.

Anti-Federalist An individual who opposed the ratification of the new Constitution in 1787. The Anti-Federalists were opposed to a strong central government.

Antitrust Legislation Legislation directed against economic monopolies.

Appellate Court A court having jurisdiction to review cases and issues that were originally tried in lower courts.

Appellate Jurisdiction The authority vested in an appellate court to review and revise the judicial actions of inferior courts.

Appointment Power The authority vested in the president to fill a government office or position. Positions filled by presidential appointment include those in the executive branch and the federal judiciary, commissioned officers in the armed forces, and members of the independent regulatory commissions.

Appropriation The passage, by Congress, of a spending bill specifying the amount of authorized funds that actually will be allocated for an agency's use.

Appropriations Process The process by which a legislative body legally authorizes a government to spend specific sums of money to provide various programs and services.

Aristocracy Rule by the "best"; in reality, rule by an upper class.

Arraignment The first act in a criminal proceeding, in which the defendant is brought before a court to hear the charges against him or her and enter a plea of guilty or not guilty.

At-Large Election A citywide (or, in some states, countywide) election.

At-Large Place System An at-large election system in which all voters elect all the members of the city council, and each candidate runs for a specific seat on the council.

Attorney General's Opinion An interpretation of the state's constitution or laws by the state attorney general. Officials may request such opinions, and although the opinions are not legally binding, they are usually followed.

Australian Ballot A secret ballot prepared, distributed, and tabulated by government officials at public expense. Since 1888, all states have used the Australian ballot rather than an open, public ballot.

Authoritarianism A type of regime in which only the government itself is fully controlled by the ruler. Social and economic institutions exist that are not under the government's control.

Authority The right and power of a government or other entity to enforce its decisions and compel obedience.

Authorization A formal declaration by a legislative committee that a certain amount of funding may be available to an agency. Some authorizations terminate in a year; others are renewable automatically without further congressional action.

B

"Beauty Contest" A presidential primary in which candidates compete for popular votes but the results do not control the selection of delegates to the national convention.

Bias An inclination or preference that interferes with impartial judgment.

Bicameral Legislature A legislature made up of two parts, called chambers. The U.S. Congress, composed of the House of Representatives and the Senate, is a bicameral legislature.

Bicameralism The division of a legislature into two separate assemblies.

Bicultural Encompassing two cultures.

Binational Belonging to two nations.

Black Codes State laws passed after the Civil War that severely restricted the rights of freed slaves.

Bill of Rights The first ten amendments to the U.S. Constitution.

Block Grants Federal programs that provide funds to state and local governments for broad functional areas, such as criminal justice or mental-health programs.

Blocking Bill In Texas, a bill placed early on the senate calendar that will never actually be considered. A rule—which can be suspended by a two-thirds vote—requires that the senate address bills in chronological order. The blocking bill ensures that a measure must win the vote of two-thirds of the senate even to be considered.

Blue-Ribbon Commission A commission composed of public personalities or authorities on the subject that is being considered. In Texas, such a commission may have both fact-finding and recommending authority.

Boards and Commissions In Texas, bodies consisting of three to 18 members that supervise most state agencies.

Boycott A form of pressure or protest—an organized refusal to purchase a particular product or deal with a particular business.

Broad Construction A judicial philosophy that looks to the context and purpose of a law when making an interpretation.

Budget Deficit Government expenditures that exceed receipts.

Burden of Proof In a court case, a party's duty to convince a judge or jury that the party's version of the facts is true. The standard of proof is higher in a criminal case than in a civil one.

Bureaucracy A large organization that is structured hierarchically to carry out specific functions.

Busing In the context of civil rights, the transportation of public school students from areas where they live to schools in other areas to eliminate school segregation based on residential patterns.

C

Cabinet An advisory group selected by the president to aid in making decisions. The cabinet includes the heads of fifteen executive departments and others named by the president.

Cabinet Department One of the fifteen departments of the executive branch (Agriculture, Commerce, Defense, Education, Energy, Health and Human Services, Homeland Security, Housing and Urban Development, Interior, Justice, Labor, State, Transportation, Treasury, and Veterans Affairs).

Calendar In the Texas legislature, the schedule that serves as a conduit for legislation between the committees and the primary legislative body.

Calendars Committee The committee in the Texas House of Representatives that assigns bills to the calendars for floor action. (The less important Local and Consent Calendars Committee also performs this function.)

Capitalism An economic system characterized by the private ownership of wealth-creating assets, free markets, and freedom of contract.

Capture The act by which an industry being regulated by a government agency gains direct or indirect control over agency personnel and decision makers.

Case Law Judicial interpretations of common law principles and doctrines, as well as interpretations of constitutional law, statutory law, and administrative law.

Casework Personal work for constituents by members of Congress.

Categorical Grants Federal grants to states or local governments that are for specific programs or projects.

Caucus A meeting of party members designed to select candidates and propose policies.

Change of Venue A change in the site of a trial.

Charter An organizing document for corporations or municipalities.

Checks and Balances A major principle of the American system of government whereby each branch of the government can check the actions of the others.

Chief Diplomat The role of the president in recognizing foreign governments, making treaties, and effecting executive agreements.

Chief Executive The role of the president as head of the executive branch of the government.

Chief Legislator The role of the president in influencing the making of laws.

Chief of Staff The person who is named to direct the White House Office and advise the president.

Chief of State Nationally, the head of state—the president of the United States, for example. In Texas and other states, the governor—who serves as the symbol of the state and performs ceremonial duties—is the chief of state.

City-County Consolidation The union of a county and cities within the county to form a single unit of government.

Civil Disobedience A nonviolent, public refusal to obey allegedly unjust laws.

Civil Law The law regulating conduct between private persons over noncriminal matters, including contracts, domestic relations, and business interactions.

Civil Liberties Those personal freedoms, including freedom of religion and freedom of speech, that are protected for all individuals. The civil liberties set forth in the U.S. Constitution, as amended, restrain the government from taking certain actions against individuals.

Civil Rights Generally, all rights rooted in the Fourteenth Amendment's guarantee of equal protection under the law.

Civil Service A collective term for the body of employees working for the government. Generally, *civil service* is understood to apply to all those who gain government employment through a merit system.

Civil Service Commission The initial central personnel agency of the national government; created in 1883.

Class-Action Suit A lawsuit filed by an individual seeking damages for "all persons similarly situated."

Clear and Present Danger Test The test proposed by Justice Oliver Wendell Holmes for determining when government may restrict free speech. Restrictions are permissible, he argued, only when speech creates a *clear and present danger* to the public order.

Clemency Relief from criminal punishment granted by an executive. In Texas, the power of the governor to grant clemency is strictly limited.

Clientele Persons represented by a government agency or a politician.

Climate Control The use of public relations techniques to create favorable public opinion toward an interest group, industry, or corporation.

Closed Primary A type of primary in which the voter is limited to choosing candidates of the party of which he or she is a member.

Cloture An action by which legislative debate is ended so that a floor vote must be taken.

Coattail Effect The influence of a popular candidate on the electoral success of other candidates on the same party ticket. The effect is increased by the party-column ballot, which encourages straight-ticket voting.

Cold War The ideological, political, and economic confrontation between the United States and the Soviet Union following World War II.

Colonia In Texas, an unincorporated urban district along the U.S.–Mexican border. Colonias are often impoverished and are chiefly inhabited by Mexican Americans.

Commander in Chief The role of the president as supreme commander of the military forces of the United States and of the state National Guard units when they are called into federal service.

Commerce Clause The section of the U.S. Constitution in which Congress is given the power to regulate trade among the states and with foreign countries.

Commercial Speech Advertising statements, which increasingly have been given First Amendment protection.

Commissioners Court In Texas, the policy-making body of a county. A commissioners court consists of a county judge (the presiding officer), who is elected in countywide elections, and four county commissioners elected from individual precincts.

Commission System A system that allows the members of a city council to serve as heads of city departments.

Committee of the Whole An entire legislative body (such as the Texas Senate) acting as a committee. The committee's purpose is to allow the body to relax its rules and thereby expedite legislation.

Common Law Judge-made law that originated in England from decisions shaped according to prevailing customs. Decisions were applied to similar situations and thus gradually became common to the nation.

Community Property Any property that a married couple has acquired during their marriage. In certain states, it is divided equally between them in the event of a divorce.

Concurrent Powers Powers held jointly by the national and state governments.

Concurring Opinion A separate opinion prepared by a judge who supports the decision of the majority of the court but who wants to make or clarify a particular point or to voice disapproval of the grounds on which the decision was made.

Confederal System A system consisting of a league of independent states, each having essentially sovereign powers. The central government created by such a league has only limited powers over the states.

Confederation A political system in which states or regional governments retain ultimate authority except for those powers they expressly delegate to a central government; a voluntary association of independent states, in which the member states agree to limited restraints on their freedom of action.

Conference Committee A special joint committee appointed to reconcile differences when bills pass the two chambers of Congress in different forms.

Conflict of Interest A situation that arises when a legislator, bureaucrat, executive official, or judge can make an official decision that results in a personal economic advantage. The result is a potential or real conflict between the personal interests of the officeholder and the general interests of the public.

Consensus General agreement among the citizenry on an issue.

Consent of the People The idea that governments and laws derive their legitimacy from the consent of the governed.

Conservatism A set of beliefs that includes a limited role for the national government in helping individuals, support for traditional values and lifestyles, and a cautious response to change.

Conservative Coalition An alliance of Republicans and southern Democrats that historically formed in the House or the Senate to oppose liberal legislation and support conservative legislation.

Constable A law-enforcement officer. In Texas, constables are elected at the county level and serve as process officers of justice of the peace courts.

Constituent One of the persons represented by a legislator or other elected or appointed official.

Constitutional Power A power vested in the president by Article II of the Constitution.

Containment A U.S. diplomatic policy adopted by the Truman administration to contain Communist power within its existing boundaries.

Continuing Resolution A temporary funding law that Congress passes when an appropriations bill has not been decided by the beginning of the new fiscal year on October 1.

Cooperative Federalism A model of federalism in which the states and the national government cooperate in solving problems.

Co-optation The "capturing" of an agency by members of an interest group. In effect, governmental power comes to be exercised by a private interest.

Corrupt Practices Acts A series of acts passed by Congress in an attempt to limit and regulate the size and sources of contributions and expenditures in political campaigns.

Council-Manager System A municipal system featuring an elected city council and a city manager who is hired by the council. The council makes policy decisions, and the manager is responsible for the day-to-day operations of the city government.

County Attorney In Texas, a county legal officer who gives legal advice to the commissioners court, represents the county in court, and prosecutes crimes. If a county has both a county attorney and a district attorney, the latter prosecutes felony crimes.

County Auditor In Texas, a county financial officer whose duties, depending on the population of the county, may include reviewing county financial records and (in large counties) serving as the chief budget officer.

County Clerk The chief record keeper and elections officer of a county.

County Commissioner One of a group of officials elected to administer a county; in Texas, a member of the commissioners court who is elected from a district, or precinct.

County Courts-at-Law In Texas, county courts in addition to the constitutional county court. They are established by the legislature in all but the smallest Texas counties and may have criminal or civil jurisdiction. They form a level of courts superior to justice of the peace and municipal courts but inferior to district courts.

County Judge In Texas, an official elected countywide to preside over the commissioners court and to try certain minor cases.

County Treasurer A county official who is responsible for receiving, depositing, and disbursing county funds.

Credentials Committee A committee used by political parties at their national conventions to determine which delegates may participate. The committee inspects the claim of each prospective delegate to be seated as a legitimate representative of his or her state.

Creole A descendant of European Spanish (or in some regions, French) immigrants to the Americas.

Criminal Law The law that defines crimes and provides punishment for violations. In criminal cases, the government is the prosecutor.

Crossover Voting A circumstance in which members of one political party vote in the other party's primary to influence which nominee is selected by the other party.

Cumulative Voting (CV) An at-large election system in which voters can cast one or more votes for a single candidate. For example, a voter who can cast up to five votes in a city council election can cast all five votes for one candidate or spread the votes among several candidates.

D

Deadwood In the context of state government, constitutional provisions made inoperative by changing circumstances or by conflicting federal constitutional or statutory law.

Dedicated Funds Revenues dedicated for a specific purpose by the constitution or by statute.

***De Facto* Segregation** Racial segregation that occurs because of past social and economic conditions and residential racial patterns.

***De Jure* Segregation** Racial segregation that occurs because of laws or administrative decisions by public agencies.

Dealignment A decline in party loyalties that reduces long-term party commitment.

Defamation of Character Wrongfully hurting a person's good reputation. The law imposes a general duty on all persons to refrain from making false, defamatory statements about others.

Defense Policy A subset of national security policies having to do with the U.S. armed forces.

Deferred Adjudication A procedure that allows a judge to postpone final sentencing in a criminal case; charges are dismissed if the defendant completes a satisfactory probationary period.

Democracy A system of government in which political authority is vested in the people. The term is derived from the Greek words *demos* ("the people") and *kratos* ("authority").

Democratic Party One of the two major American political parties evolving out of the Republican Party of Thomas Jefferson.

Democratic Republic A republic in which representatives elected by the people make and enforce laws and policies.

Dependent Agency A government entity that is closely linked to general-purpose governments. Dependent agencies do not have the independence of special districts.

Détente A French word meaning a relaxation of tensions. The term characterized U.S.-Soviet relations as they developed under President Richard Nixon and Secretary of State Henry Kissinger.

Development Corporation Act A state law that allows select Texas cities to raise the sales tax for economic development, subject to voter approval.

Devolution The transfer of powers from a national or central government to a state or local government.

Diplomacy The process by which states carry on political relations with each other; settling conflicts among nations by peaceful means.

Diplomatic Recognition The formal acknowledgment of a foreign government as legitimate.

Direct Democracy A system of government in which political decisions are made by the people directly, rather than by their elected representatives; probably attained most easily in small political communities.

Direct Primary An intraparty election in which the voters select the candidates who will run on a party's ticket in the subsequent general election. In Texas, nominees must win a majority of the votes, which often means that there are primary runoff elections between the top two candidates.

Direct Technique An interest group activity that involves interaction with government officials to further the group's goals.

Discharge Petition A procedure by which a bill in the House of Representatives can be forced (discharged) out of a committee that has refused to report it for consideration by the House. The petition must be signed by an absolute majority (218) of representatives and is used only on rare occasions.

Discretion An official's power to make decisions based on personal judgment rather than on the specific requirements of the law; the freedom to decide or make choices.

Dissenting Opinion A separate opinion in which a judge dissents from (disagrees with) the conclusion reached by the majority on the court and expounds his or her own views about the case.

District Attorney An official who prosecutes felony cases.

District Clerk In Texas, the record keeper for the district court in a county with a population that exceeds 8,000.

Diversity of Citizenship The condition that exists when the parties to a lawsuit are citizens of different states or when the parties are citizens of a U.S. state and citizens or the government of a foreign country. Diversity of citizenship can provide a basis for federal jurisdiction.

Divided Government A situation in which one major political party controls the presidency and the other controls the chambers of Congress, or in which one party controls a state governorship and the other controls the state legislature.

Divided Opinion Public opinion that is polarized between two quite different positions.

Docket The schedule of court activity.

Domestic Policy All government laws, planning, and actions that concern internal issues of national importance, such as poverty, crime, and the environment.

Down-ticket Candidates for lower political offices are located further down the ballot.

Dual Federalism A model of federalism in which the states and the national government each remain supreme within their own spheres. The doctrine looks on nation and state as coequal sovereign powers. Neither the state government nor the national government should interfere in the other's sphere.

Due Process Established rules and principles for the administration of justice designed to safeguard the rights of the individual. The right to due process of law is provided by the U.S. Constitution and most state constitutions.

E

Earmarks Special provisions in legislation to set aside funds for projects that have not passed an impartial evaluation by agencies of the executive branch. Also known as "pork."

Economic Aid Assistance to other nations in the form of grants, loans, or credits to buy the assisting nation's products.

Elastic Clause, or Necessary and Proper Clause The clause in Article I, Section 8, that grants Congress the power to do whatever is necessary to execute its specifically delegated powers.

Election Judge A public official who is responsible for enforcing election rules at a polling place on election day.

Elector A member of the electoral college, which selects the president and vice president. Each state's electors are chosen in each presidential election year according to state laws.

Electoral College A group of persons, called electors, who are selected by the voters in each state. This group officially elects the president and the vice president of the United States.

Elite Theory A perspective holding that society is ruled by a small number of people who exercise power to further their self-interest.

Emergency Power An inherent power exercised by the president during a period of national crisis.

Enabling Act Legislation that confers on appropriate officials the power to implement or enforce the law.

Enabling Legislation A statute enacted by Congress that authorizes the creation of an administrative agency and specifies the name, purpose, composition, functions, and powers of the agency being created.

Enumerated Powers Powers specifically granted to the national government by the Constitution. The first seventeen clauses of Article I, Section 8, specify most of the enumerated powers of Congress.

Equality As a political value, the idea that all people are of equal worth.

Era of Good Feelings The years from 1817 to 1825, when James Monroe was president and there was, in effect, no political opposition.

Establishment Clause The part of the First Amendment prohibiting the establishment of a church officially supported by the national government. It is applied to questions of the legality of giving state and local government aid to religious organizations and schools, allowing or requiring school prayers, and teaching evolution versus intelligent design.

Evangelical Having to do with a broad spectrum of Protestant Christianity that emphasizes salvation and traditional values. Evangelical voters are likely to support culturally conservative politics.

Examining Trial A relatively uncommon procedure that may be requested by felony defendants in Texas. In an examining trial, a justice of the peace reviews the facts and decides whether a defendant should have to face trial in criminal court.

Exclusionary Rule A judicial policy prohibiting the admission at trial of illegally seized evidence.

Executive Agreement An international agreement between chiefs of state that does not require legislative approval.

Executive Budget The budget prepared and submitted by the president to Congress.

Executive Office of the President (EOP) An organization established by President Franklin D. Roosevelt to assist the president in carrying out major duties.

Executive Order A rule or regulation issued by the president that has the effect of law. Executive orders can implement and give administrative effect to provisions in the U.S. Constitution, treaties, or statutes.

Executive Privilege The right of executive officials to withhold information from or to refuse to appear before a legislative committee.

Ex Officio Having a position by virtue of holding a particular office. For example, the lieutenant governor of Texas serves ex officio as the presiding officer of the Texas Senate.

Exports Goods and services produced domestically for sale abroad.

Expressed Power A power of the president that is expressly written into the Constitution or into statutory law.

Extraterritorial Jurisdiction (ETJ) In Texas, a buffer area that extends beyond a city's limits. Cities can enforce some laws, such as zoning and building codes, in an ETJ.

F

Faction A group or bloc in a legislature or political party that is trying to obtain power or benefits.

Fairness Doctrine A Federal Communications Commission rule enforced between 1949 and 1987 that required radio and television to present controversial issues and discuss them in a manner that was (in the commission's view) honest, equitable, and balanced.

Fall Review The annual process in which the Office of Management and Budget, after receiving formal federal agency requests for funding for the next fiscal year, reviews the requests, makes changes, and submits its recommendations to the president.

Federal Mandate A requirement in federal legislation that forces states and municipalities to comply with certain rules.

Federal Open Market Committee The most important body within the Federal Reserve System. The Federal Open Market Committee decides how monetary policy should be carried out.

Federal Question A question that has to do with the U.S. Constitution, acts of Congress, or treaties. A federal question provides a basis for federal jurisdiction.

Federal Register A publication of the U.S. government that prints executive orders, rules, and regulations.

Federal Reserve System (the Fed) The agency created by Congress in 1913 to serve as the nation's central banking organization.

Federal System A system of government in which power is divided between a central government and regional, or subdivisional, governments. Each level must have some domain in which its policies are dominant and some genuine political or constitutional guarantee of its authority.

Federalist The name given to one who was in favor of the adoption of the U.S. Constitution and the creation of a federal union with a strong central government.

Felony A crime—such as arson, murder, rape, or robbery—that carries the most severe sanctions, usually ranging from one year in prison to death.

Feminism The movement that supports political, economic, and social equality for women.

Fertility Rate A statistic that measures the average number of children that women in a given group are expected to have over the course of a lifetime.

Filibuster The use of the Senate's tradition of unlimited debate as a delaying tactic to block a bill.

First Budget Resolution A resolution passed by Congress in May that sets overall revenue and spending goals for the following fiscal year.

Fiscal Policy The federal government's use of taxation and spending policies to affect overall business activity.

Fiscal Year (FY) A twelve-month period that is used for bookkeeping, or accounting, purposes. Usually, the fiscal year does not coincide with the calendar year. For example, the federal government's fiscal year runs from October 1 through September 30.

Floor The place where a legislative body debates, amends, votes on, enacts, and defeats proposed legislation; the entire house or senate acting as a whole.

Floor Leaders Legislators who are responsible for getting party members to vote for or against particular legislation.

Focus Group A small group of individuals who are led in discussion by a professional consultant in order to gather opinions on and responses to candidates and issues.

Foreclosure The legal process by which a lender takes possession of a mortgaged property when the borrower defaults on the loan.

Foreign Policy A nation's external goals and the techniques and strategies used to achieve them.

Foreign Policy Process The steps by which foreign policy goals are decided and acted on.

Formal Powers Legal powers granted to the governor by constitution or statute. Powers of this type, when exercised by the U.S. president, are called expressed powers.

Fragmentation In state government, a division of power among separately elected executive officials. A plural executive is a fragmented executive.

Franking A policy that enables members of Congress to send material through the mail by substituting their facsimile signature (frank) for postage.

Freedmen's Bureau The Bureau of Refugees, Freedmen and Abandoned Lands, a federal bureau established in 1865 to aid refugees of the Civil War (including former slaves) and to administer confiscated property. Among other tasks, it sought to provide education to the former slaves. It was disbanded in 1872.

Free Exercise Clause The provision of the First Amendment guaranteeing the free exercise of religion. The provision constrains the national government from prohibiting individuals from practicing the religion of their choice.

Free Rider Problem The difficulty interest groups face in recruiting members when the benefits they achieve can be gained without joining the group.

Front-Loading The practice of moving presidential primary elections to the early part of the campaign to maximize the impact of these primaries on the nomination.

Front-Runner The presidential candidate who appears to be ahead at a given time in the primary season.

G

Gag Order An order issued by a judge restricting the publication of news about a trial or a pretrial hearing to protect the accused's right to a fair trial.

Gender Discrimination Any practice, policy, or procedure that denies equality of treatment to an individual or to a group because of gender.

Gender Gap The difference between the percentage of women who vote for a particular candidate and the percentage of men who vote for the candidate.

General Election An election, normally held on the first Tuesday in November, that determines who will fill various elected positions.

General Jurisdiction Exists when a court's authority to hear cases is not significantly restricted. A court of general jurisdiction normally can hear a broad range of cases.

General-Law Charter A city structure established by statute. Most smaller Texas cities choose among several available options allowed by the state legislature.

General-Law City A city operating under general state laws that apply to all local government units of a similar type. In Texas, cities with a population of 5,000 or less are (in most instances) general-law cities.

General-Obligation Bond A bond to be repaid from general taxes and other revenues; such bond issues usually must be approved by voters.

General-Purpose Government A municipal or county government. In contrast to special districts, general-purpose governments provide a wide range of services.

General Sales Tax A broad-based tax collected on the retail price of most items.

Generational Effect A long-lasting effect of the events of a particular time on the political opinions of those who came of political age at that time.

Gerrymandering The drawing of legislative district boundary lines for the purpose of obtaining partisan or factional advantage. A district is said to be gerrymandered when its shape is manipulated by the dominant party to maximize electoral strength at the expense of the minority party.

Government The preeminent institution within society in which decisions are made that resolve conflicts or allocate benefits and privileges. It is unique because it has the ultimate authority for making decisions and establishing political values.

Government Corporation An agency of government that administers a quasi-business enterprise. These corporations are used when activities are primarily commercial.

Government in the Sunshine Act A law that requires all committee-directed federal agencies to conduct their business regularly in public session.

Grandfather Clause A device used by southern states to disenfranchise African Americans. It restricted voting to those whose grandfathers had voted before 1867.

Grand Jury A jury that sits in pretrial proceedings to determine if sufficient evidence exists to try an individual and, therefore, approve an indictment.

Great Compromise The compromise between the New Jersey and Virginia Plans that created one chamber of the Congress based on population and one chamber representing each state equally; also called the Connecticut Compromise.

Gross Domestic Product (GDP) The dollar value of all final goods and services produced in a one-year period.

Gross-Receipts Tax A tax on the gross revenues of certain enterprises.

Gross Public Debt The net public debt plus interagency borrowings within the government.

H

Hatch Act An act passed in 1939 that restricted the political activities of government employees. It also prohibited a political group from spending more than $3 million in any campaign and limited individual contributions to a campaign committee to $5,000.

Head of State The role of the president as ceremonial head of the government.

Hidden Tax A tax that is reflected in higher prices of the goods and services sold.

Hispanic Someone who can claim a heritage from a Spanish-speaking country (other than Spain). The term is used only in the United States or other countries that receive immigrants—Spanish-speaking persons living in Spanish-speaking countries do not normally apply the term to themselves.

Home Rule The right of a local government to write a charter establishing any organizational structure or program that does not conflict with state law. The Texas Constitution reserves home rule for municipalities with populations of 5,000 or more.

Home-Rule City A city with the state-granted right to frame, adopt, and amend its own charter.

House and Senate Journals The official public records of the actions of the two chambers of the Texas legislature. The two journals are issued daily during sessions.

I

Ideology A comprehensive set of beliefs about the nature of people and about the role of an institution or government.

Impeachment An action by the House of Representatives to accuse the president, vice president, or other civil officers of the United States of committing "Treason, Bribery, or other high Crimes and Misdemeanors."

Implementation The carrying out of laws by executive officials and the bureaucrats who work for them.

Incarceration Rate The number of persons held in jail or prison for every 100,000 persons in a particular population group.

Income Transfer A transfer of income from some individuals in the economy to other individuals. This is generally done by government action.

Incorporation Theory The view that most of the protections of the Bill of Rights apply to state governments through the Fourteenth Amendment's due process clause.

Incremental Budgeting A budgeting practice in which an agency bases its budget requests on past appropriations plus increases to cover inflation and increased demand for services; this process assumes that past appropriations justify current budgetary requests.

Incumbent The current holder of an office.

Independent A voter or candidate who does not identify with a political party.

Independent Executive Agency A federal agency that is not part of a cabinet department but reports directly to the president.

Independent Expenditures Nonregulated contributions from PACs, organizations, and individuals. The funds may be spent on advertising or other campaign activities so long as those expenditures are not coordinated with those of a candidate.

Independent Regulatory Agency An agency outside the major executive departments charged with making and implementing rules and regulations.

Indictment A formal accusation issued by a grand jury against a party charged with a crime when the jury determines that there is sufficient evidence to bring the accused to trial.

Indirect Primary A primary election in which voters choose convention delegates, and the delegates determine the party's candidate in the general election.

Indirect Technique A strategy employed by interest groups that uses third parties to influence government officials.

Inflation A sustained rise in the general price level of goods and services.

Informal Powers Powers not directly granted by law. The governor's informal powers may follow from powers granted by law but may also come from the governor's persuasive abilities, which are affected by the governor's personality, popularity, and political support.

Inherent Power A power of the president derived from the statements in the Constitution that "the executive Power shall be vested in a President" and that the president should "take Care that the Laws be faithfully executed"; defined through practice rather than through law.

Initiative A procedure by which voters can propose a law or a constitutional amendment.

In-Kind Subsidy A good or service—such as food stamps, housing, or medical care—provided by the government to low-income groups.

Institution An ongoing organization that performs certain functions for society.

Instructed Delegate A legislator who is an agent of the voters who elected him or her and who votes according to the views of constituents regardless of personal beliefs.

Intelligence Community The government agencies that gather information about the capabilities and intentions of foreign governments or that engage in covert actions.

Interest Group An organized group of individuals sharing common objectives who actively attempt to influence policymakers.

Internationality Having family and/or business interests in two or more nations.

Interstate Between two or more states.

Interstate Compact An agreement between two or more states. Agreements on minor matters are made without congressional consent, but any compact that tends to increase the power of the contracting states relative to other states or relative to the national government generally requires the consent of Congress.

Intrastate Within the state.

Iron Triangle The three-way alliance among legislators, bureaucrats, and interest groups to make or preserve policies that benefit their respective interests.

Isolationist Foreign Policy A policy of abstaining from an active role in international affairs or alliances, which characterized U.S. foreign policy toward Europe during most of the 1800s.

Issue Advocacy Advertising paid for by interest groups that support or oppose a candidate or a candidate's position on an issue without mentioning voting or elections.

Issue Network A group of individuals or organizations—which may consist of legislators and legislative staff members, interest group leaders, bureaucrats, the media, scholars, and other experts—that supports a particular policy position on a given issue.

Iron Texas Star The Texas version of the iron triangle. A policy-making coalition that includes interest groups; the lieutenant governor and the speaker of the house; standing committees of the legislature; the governor; and administrators, boards, and commissions.

J

Joint Committee A legislative committee composed of members from both chambers of Congress.

Judicial Activism A doctrine holding that the federal judiciary should take an active role by using its powers to check the activities of governmental bodies when those bodies exceed their authority.

Judicial Implementation The way in which court decisions are translated into action.

Judicial Restraint A doctrine holding that the courts should defer to the decisions made by the elected representatives of the people in the legislative and executive branches.

Judicial Review The power of the Supreme Court and other courts to declare unconstitutional federal or state laws and other acts of government.

Jurisdiction The authority of a court to decide certain cases. Not all courts have the authority to decide all cases. Where a case arises and what its subject matter is are two jurisdictional issues.

Justiciable Controversy A controversy that is real and substantial, as opposed to hypothetical or academic.

Justiciable Question A question that may be raised and reviewed in court.

K

Keynesian Economics A school of economic thought that tends to favor active federal government policymaking to stabilize economy-wide fluctuations, usually by implementing discretionary fiscal policy.

Kitchen Cabinet The informal advisers to the president.

Ku Klux Klan (KKK) A white supremacist organization. The first Klan was founded during the Reconstruction era following the Civil War.

L

Labor Movement Generally, the economic and political expression of working-class interests; politically, the organization of working-class interests.

La Raza Unida A party organized in the late 1960s as a means of getting Mexican Americans to unite politically and to identify ethnically as one people.

La Réunion A failed French socialist colony of the 1800s located within the city limits of modern Dallas. Its skilled and educated inhabitants benefited early Dallas.

Latent Interests Public-policy interests that are not recognized or addressed by a group at a particular time.

Late-Train Contribution A contribution given to a candidate in the period that begins after an election and ends 30 days before a regular legislative session.

Latino An alternative to the term Hispanic that is preferred by many.

Lawmaking The process of establishing the legal rules that govern society.

Legislative Audit Committee In Texas, a committee that performs audits of state agencies and departments for the legislature.

Legislative Budget Board The primary budgeting entity for Texas state government.

Legislative Council In Texas, a body that provides research support, information, and bill-drafting assistance to legislators.

Legislature A governmental body primarily responsible for the making of laws.

Legitimacy Popular acceptance of the right and power of a government or other entity to exercise authority.

Libel A written defamation of a person's character, reputation, business, or property rights.

Liberalism A set of beliefs that includes the advocacy of positive government action to improve the welfare of individuals, support for civil rights, and tolerance for political and social change.

Libertarianism A political ideology based on skepticism or opposition toward most government activities.

Liberty The greatest freedom of the individual that is consistent with the freedom of other individuals in the society.

Lifestyle Effect A phenomenon in which certain attitudes occur at certain chronological ages.

Limited Government A government with powers that are limited either through a written document or through widely shared beliefs.

Limited Jurisdiction Exists when a court's authority to hear cases is restricted to certain types of claims, such as tax claims or bankruptcy petitions.

Line Organization In the federal government, an administrative unit that is directly accountable to the president.

Line-Item Veto The power of an executive to veto individual lines or items within a piece of legislation without vetoing the entire bill.

Literacy Test A test administered as a precondition for voting, often used to prevent African Americans from exercising their right to vote.

Litigate To engage in a legal proceeding or seek relief in a court of law; to carry on a lawsuit.

Lobbyist An organization or individual who attempts to influence legislation and the administrative decisions of government.

Logrolling An arrangement in which two or more members of Congress agree in advance to support each other's bills.

Long Ballot An election ballot listing many independently elected offices.

Loophole A legal method by which individuals and businesses are allowed to reduce the tax liabilities owed to the government.

Loose Monetary Policy Monetary policy that makes credit inexpensive and abundant, possibly leading to inflation.

M

Madisonian Model A structure of government proposed by James Madison in which the powers of the government are separated into three branches: executive, legislative, and judicial.

Majoritarianism A political theory holding that in a democracy, the government ought to do what the majority of the people want.

Majority The age at which a person is entitled by law to the right to manage her or his own affairs and to the full enjoyment of civil rights. Or more than 50 percent.

Majority Leader of the House A legislative position held by an important party member in the House of Representatives. The majority leader is selected by the majority party in caucus or conference to foster cohesion among party members and to act as spokesperson for the majority party in the House.

Majority Opinion A court opinion reflecting the views of the majority of the judges.

Majority Rule A basic principle of democracy asserting that the greatest number of citizens in any political unit should select officials and determine policies.

Mandate A requirement or standard imposed on one level of government by a higher level of government.

Maquiladora A factory in the Mexican border region that assembles goods imported duty-free into Mexico for export. In Spanish, it literally means "twin plant."

Mark Up In legislation, to amend, change, or rewrite bills while they are in committee.

Material Incentive A reason or motive based on the desire to enjoy certain economic benefits or opportunities.

Media The channels of mass communication.

Medicaid A joint state-federal program that provides medical care to the poor (including indigent elderly persons in nursing homes). The program is funded out of general government revenues.

Medicare A federal health-insurance program that covers U.S. residents over the age of sixty-five. The costs are met by a tax on wages and salaries.

Merit System The selection, retention, and promotion of government employees on the basis of competitive examinations.

Message Power The ability of a governor (or a U.S. president) to focus the attention of the press, legislators, and citizens on legislative proposals that he or she considers important. The visibility of the office gives the chief executive instant public attention.

Mestizo A person of both Spanish and Native American lineage.

Metroplex The greater Dallas-Fort Worth metropolitan area.

Minority Leader of the House The party leader elected by the minority party in the House.

Misdemeanor A lesser crime than a felony, punishable by a fine or imprisonment for up to one year.

Mistrial A trial judged to be invalid because of fundamental error. When a mistrial is declared, the trial may start again, beginning with the selection of a new jury.

Monetary Policy The utilization of changes in the amount of money in circulation to alter credit markets, employment, and the rate of inflation.

Monopolistic Model A model of bureaucracy that compares bureaucracies to monopolistic business firms. Lack of competition in either circumstance leads to inefficient and costly operations.

Monroe Doctrine A policy statement made by President James Monroe in 1823, which set out three principles: (1) European nations should not establish new colonies in the Western Hemisphere, (2) European nations should not intervene in the affairs of independent nations of the Western Hemisphere, and (3) the United States would not interfere in the affairs of European nations.

Moral Hazard The danger that protecting an individual or institution from the consequences of failure will encourage excessively risky behavior.

Moral Idealism A philosophy that sees nations as normally willing to cooperate and agree on moral standards for conduct.

N

National Committee A standing committee of a national political party established to direct and coordinate party activities between national party conventions.

National Convention The meeting held every four years by each major party to select presidential and vice-presidential candidates, write a platform, choose a national committee, and conduct party business.

Nationalization The takeover of a business enterprise by the national government. Recently, the word has been used to describe temporary takeovers that are similar to bankruptcy proceedings.

National Security Council (NSC) An agency in the Executive Office of the President that advises the president on national security.

National Security Policy Foreign and domestic policy designed to protect the nation's independence and political and economic integrity; policy that is concerned with the safety and defense of the nation.

Natural Rights Rights held to be inherent in natural law, not dependent on governments. John Locke stated that natural law, being superior to human law, specifies certain rights of "life, liberty, and property." These rights, altered to become "life, liberty, and the pursuit of happiness," are asserted in the Declaration of Independence.

Necessaries Things necessary for existence. In contract law, necessaries include whatever is reasonably necessary for suitable subsistence as measured by age, state, condition in life, and the like.

Negative Campaigning A strategy in political campaigns of attacking the opposing candidate's issue positions or—especially—his or her character.

Negative Constituents Citizens who openly oppose the government's policies.

Net Public Debt The accumulation of all past federal government deficits; the total amount owed by the federal government to individuals, businesses, and foreigners.

Normal Trade Relations (NTR) Status A status granted through an international treaty by which each member nation must treat other members at least as well as it treats the country that receives its most favorable treatment. This status was formerly known as *most-favored-nation status.*

North American Free Trade Agreement (NAFTA) A treaty among Canada, Mexico, and the United States that calls for the gradual removal of tariffs and other trade restrictions. NAFTA came into effect in 1994.

O

Obscenity Sexually offensive material. Obscenity can be illegal if it is found to violate a four-part test established by the United States Supreme Court.

Office of Management and Budget (OMB) A division of the Executive Office of the President. The OMB assists the president in preparing the annual budget, clearing and coordinating departmental agency budgets, and supervising the administration of the federal budget.

Ogallala Aquifer A major underground reservoir and a source of water for irrigation and human consumption in northern West Texas and the Texas Panhandle, as well as other states.

Office-Block, or Massachusetts, Ballot A form of general election ballot in which candidates for elective office are grouped together under the title of each office. It emphasizes voting for the office and the individual candidate, rather than for the party.

Oligarchy Rule by a few.

Ombudsperson A person who hears and investigates complaints by private individuals against public officials or agencies.

Open-Meetings Law A law that requires meetings of government decision-making bodies to be open to public scrutiny (with some exceptions).

Open Primary A primary in which any registered voter can vote (but must vote for candidates of only one party).

Open-Records Law A law requiring that records of all government proceedings and decisions are made available to the public.

Opinion The statement by a judge or a court of the decision reached in a case. The opinion sets forth the applicable law and details the reasoning on which the ruling was based.

Opinion Leader One who is able to influence the opinions of others because of position, expertise, or personality.

Opinion Poll A method of systematically questioning a small, selected sample of respondents who are deemed representative of the total population.

Oral Arguments The verbal arguments presented in person by attorneys to an appellate court. Each attorney presents reasons to the court why the court should rule in her or his client's favor.

Order A state of peace and security. Maintaining order by protecting members of society from violence and criminal activity is the oldest purpose of government.

Original Jurisdiction The authority of a court to consider a case in the first instance; the power to try a case, as opposed to appellate jurisdiction, which involves the power to review cases decided by other courts.

Oversight The process by which Congress follows up on laws it has enacted to ensure that they are being enforced and administered in the way Congress intended.

P

Pairing In political redistricting, placing two incumbent officeholders from the same party in the same district. (Only one of these officeholders can be re-elected.)

Pardon A release from the punishment for, or legal consequences of, a crime; a pardon can be granted by the president before or after a conviction.

Participation Paradox The fact that people vote even though their individual votes rarely influence the outcome of an election.

Partisan Election An election between candidates who are nominated by their parties and whose party affiliation is designated on the ballot. In Texas, all state and county officials (including judges) are selected in this manner. Only municipal and some special district elections are nonpartisan in Texas.

Partisan Gerrymandering The drawing of district lines for the purpose of providing electoral advantage to members of one political party.

Part-time Legislature A legislative body that meets for short periods of time. Its members are often provided limited resources, including small salaries.

Party Identification Linking oneself to a particular political party.

Party Identifier A person who identifies with a political party.

Party Organization The formal structure and leadership of a political party, including election committees; local, state, and national executives; and paid professional staff.

Party Platform A document drawn up at each national convention, outlining the policies, positions, and principles of the party.

Party-Column, or Indiana, Ballot A form of general-election ballot in which all of a party's candidates for elective office are arranged in one column under the party's label and symbol. It emphasizes voting for the party, rather than for the office or individual.

Party-in-Government All of the elected and appointed officials who identify with a political party.

Party-in-the-Electorate Those members of the general public who identify with a political party or who express a preference for one party over another.

Patronage Rewarding faithful party workers and followers with government employment and contracts.

Peer Group A group consisting of members sharing common social characteristics. These groups play an important part in the socialization process, helping to shape attitudes and beliefs.

Pendleton Act (Civil Service Reform Act) An act that established the principle of employment on the basis of merit and created the Civil Service Commission to administer the personnel service.

Permanent School Fund In Texas, a fund that provides support to the public school system. Leases, rents, and royalties from designated public school lands are deposited into the fund.

Personal Mandate In health-care reform, the requirement that all citizens obtain health-care insurance coverage from some source, public or private.

Picket-Fence Federalism A model of federalism in which specific programs and policies (depicted as vertical pickets in a picket fence) involve all levels of government–national, state, and local (depicted by the horizontal boards in a picket fence).

Pigeonhole The action by which a legislative committee tables a bill and then ignores it.

Plea Bargaining Negotiations that take place between the prosecution and the defense in a criminal case in which the defendant normally is offered a lighter sentence or other benefits in return for a guilty plea.

Plural Executive An executive branch with power divided among several independent officers and a weak chief executive.

Pluralism A theory that views politics as a conflict among interest groups. Political decision making is characterized by compromise and accommodation.

Plurality A number of votes cast for a candidate that is greater than the number of votes for any other candidate but not necessarily a majority.

Pocket Veto A special veto exercised by the chief executive after a legislative body has adjourned. Bills not signed by the chief executive die after a specified period of time. If Congress wishes to reconsider such a bill, it must be reintroduced in the following session of Congress.

Podcasting A method of distributing multimedia files, such as audio or video files, for downloading onto mobile devices or personal computers.

Point of Order A formal question to the chairperson about the legitimacy of a parliamentary process. A successful point of order can result in the postponement or defeat of legislation.

Police Power The authority to legislate for the protection of the health, morals, safety, and welfare of the people. In the United States, most police power is reserved to the states.

Political Action Committee (PAC) A committee set up by and representing a corporation, labor union, or special interest group. PACs raise and give campaign donations.

Political Consultant A paid professional hired to devise a campaign strategy and manage a campaign.

Political Culture A patterned set of ideas, values, and ways of thinking about government and politics.

Political Party A group of political activists who organize to win elections, operate the government, and determine public policy.

Political Question An issue that a court believes should be decided by the executive or legislative branch.

Political Realism A philosophy that sees each nation acting principally in its own interest.

Political Socialization The process by which people acquire political beliefs and values.

Political Trust The degree to which individuals express trust in the government and political institutions, usually measured through a specific series of survey questions.

Politics The process of resolving conflicts and deciding "who gets what, when, and how." More specifically, politics is the struggle over power or influence within organizations or informal groups that can grant or withhold benefits or privileges.

Poll Tax A special tax that must be paid as a qualification for voting. In 1964, the Twenty-fourth Amendment to the Constitution outlawed the poll tax in national elections, and in 1966 the Supreme Court declared it unconstitutional in all elections.

Popular Sovereignty The concept that ultimate political authority is based on the will of the people.

Precedent A court rule bearing on subsequent legal decisions in similar cases. Judges rely on precedents in deciding cases.

Preferred Stock A special share of ownership in a corporation that typically confers no right to vote for the company's board of directors, but does pay interest.

President Pro Tempore The temporary presiding officer of the Senate in the absence of the vice president.

Presiding Officers In Texas, the chief officers of the state senate and house. They are the lieutenant governor, who presides over the senate, and the speaker of the house.

Presidential Primary A statewide primary election of delegates to a political party's national convention, held to determine a party's presidential nominee.

Primary Election An election in which political parties choose their candidates for the general election.

Prior Restraint Restraining an activity before it has actually occurred. When expression is involved, this means censorship.

Privatization The replacement of government services with services provided by private firms.

Probation A sentencing alternative to imprisonment in which the court releases convicted defendants under supervision as long as certain conditions are observed.

Progressive Movement A political movement within both major parties in the early 20th century. Progressives believed that the power of the government should be used to restrain the growing power of large corporations.

Progressive Tax A tax that rises in percentage terms as incomes rise.

Prohibition Outlawing of the production, sale, and consumption of alcoholic beverages.

Property Anything that is or may be subject to ownership. As conceived by the political philosopher John Locke, the right to property is a natural right superior to human law (laws made by government).

Property Tax A tax on the assessed value of real estate.

Public Agenda Issues that are perceived by the political community as meriting public attention and governmental action.

Public Debt, or National Debt The total amount of debt carried by the federal government.

Public Figure A public official, a public employee who exercises substantial governmental power, or any other person, such as a movie star, known to the public because of his or her position or activities.

Public Interest The best interests of the overall community; the national good, rather than the narrow interests of a particular group.

Public Opinion The aggregate of individual attitudes or beliefs shared by some portion of the adult population.

Punitive Damages Awards A financial payment that may be awarded to a plaintiff in a civil case to punish the defendant and deter similar conduct in the future.

Pure At-Large System An at-large election system in which all voters elect all the members of the city council, and candidates do not run for specific seats.

Public Option In health-care reform, a government-run health-care insurance program that would compete with private-sector health-insurance companies.

Purposive Incentive A reason for supporting or participating in the activities of a group that is based on agreement with the goals of the group. For example, someone with a strong interest in human rights might have a purposive incentive to join Amnesty International.

Q

Quasi-judicial Functions Actions by a branch other than the courts that involve interpreting the law.

Quasi-legislative Functions Legislative actions by entities other than the legislature; for example, executive branch agencies adopting rules and regulations that are binding on citizens.

R

Ranchero Culture A quasi-feudal system—the owner or patron owed the workers protection and employment, while the workers owed the patron their loyalty and service. The rancher and workers all lived on the ranchero or ranch.

Ratification Formal approval.

Rational Ignorance Effect An effect produced when people purposely and rationally decide not to become informed on an issue because they believe that their vote on the issue is not likely to be a deciding one; a lack of incentive to seek the necessary information to cast an intelligent vote.

Realignment A process in which a substantial group of voters switches party allegiance, producing a long-term change in the political landscape.

Reapportionment The allocation of seats in the House of Representatives to each state after each census.

Recall A procedure allowing the people to vote to dismiss an elected official from state office before his or her term has expired.

Recession Two or more successive quarters in which the economy shrinks instead of grows.

Redistricting The redrawing of the boundaries of the congressional districts within each state.

Referendum An electoral device whereby legislative or constitutional measures are referred by the legislature to the voters for approval or disapproval.

Registration The entry of a person's name onto the list of registered voters for elections. To register, a person must meet certain legal requirements of age, citizenship, and residency.

Regressive Tax A tax that falls in percentage terms as incomes rise.

Regular Session A legislative session scheduled by the constitution. Texas regular sessions are biennial (once every two years) rather than annual as in most states and in Congress.

Remand To send a case back to the court that originally heard it.

Representation The function of members of Congress as elected officials representing the views of their constituents.

Representative Assembly A legislature composed of individuals who represent the population.

Representative Democracy A form of government in which representatives elected by the people make and enforce laws and policies; may retain the monarchy in a ceremonial role.

Reprieve A formal postponement of the execution of a sentence imposed by a court of law.

Republic A form of government in which sovereign power rests with the people, rather than with a king or a monarch.

Republican Party One of the two major American political parties. It emerged in the 1850s as an antislavery party and consisted of former northern Whigs and antislavery Democrats.

Revenue Bond A bond to be repaid with revenues from the project financed, such as utilities or sports stadiums.

Reverse To annul, or make void, a court ruling on account of some error or irregularity.

Reverse Discrimination The situation in which an affirmative action program discriminates against those who do not have minority status.

Reverse-Income Effect A tendency for wealthier states or regions to favor the Democrats and for less wealthy states or regions to favor the Republicans. The effect appears paradoxical because it reverses traditional patterns of support.

Revolving Door The interchange of employees among the legislature, government agencies, and related private special-interest groups.

Rollback Election In Texas, an election that permits voters to lower a local property tax increase to 8 percent.

Rule of Four A United States Supreme Court procedure by which four justices must vote to grant a petition for review if a case is to come before the full court.

Rules Committee A standing committee of the House of Representatives that provides special rules under which specific bills can be debated, amended, and considered by the House.

Rump Convention A meeting of members from a larger convention who secede and organize their own convention elsewhere.

Runoff Primary A second primary election that pits the two top vote-getters from the first primary against each other. Such an election is held in states such as Texas when the winner of the first primary did not receive a majority of the votes.

S

Safe Seat A district that returns a legislator with 55 percent of the vote or more.

Sales Tax A tax collected on the retail price of purchased items.

Sampling Error The difference between a sample's results and the true result if the entire population had been interviewed.

Secession The separation of a territory from a larger political unit. Specifically, the secession of Southern states from the Union in 1860 and 1861.

Second Budget Resolution A resolution passed by Congress in September that sets "binding" limits on taxes and spending for the following fiscal year.

Select Committee A temporary legislative committee established for a limited time period and for a special purpose.

Selective Sales Tax, or Excise Tax A tax levied on specific items only.

Senate Majority Leader The chief spokesperson of the majority party in the Senate, who directs the legislative program and party strategy.

Senate Minority Leader The party officer in the Senate who commands the minority party's opposition to the policies of the majority party and directs the legislative program and strategy of his or her party.

Senatorial Courtesy In federal district court judgeship nominations, a tradition allowing a senator to veto a judicial appointment in his or her state.

Seniority System A custom followed in both chambers of Congress specifying that the member of the majority party with the longest term of continuous service will be given preference when a committee chairperson (or a holder of some other significant post) is selected.

Separate-but-Equal Doctrine The doctrine holding that separate-but-equal facilities do not violate the equal protection clause of the Fourteenth Amendment to the U.S. Constitution.

Separation of Powers The principle of dividing governmental powers among different branches of government.

Service Sector The sector of the economy that provides services—such as health care, banking, and education—in contrast to the sector that produces goods.

Sexual Harassment Unwanted physical or verbal conduct or abuse of a sexual nature that interferes with a recipient's job performance, creates a hostile work environment, or carries with it an implicit or explicit threat of adverse employment consequences.

Sheriff The chief law enforcement officer of a county—in most states, an elected official. In Texas, the sheriff's budget must be approved by the commissioners court, which limits the sheriff's authority.

Shivercrat A follower of Governor Allan Shivers of Texas (1949–1957). Shivercrats split their votes between conservative Democrats for state office and Republicans for the U.S. presidency.

Short Ballot An election ballot listing only a few independently elected offices.

Signing Statement A written declaration that a president may make when signing a bill into law. Usually, such statements point out sections of the law that the president deems unconstitutional.

Single-Member District System A system that allows only one candidate to be elected from each electoral district. This system discourages the formation of third parties.

Slander The public uttering of a false statement that harms the good reputation of another. The statement must be made to, or within the hearing of, persons other than the defamed party.

Social Contract A voluntary agreement among individuals to secure their rights and welfare by creating a government and abiding by its rules.

Social Movement A movement that represents the demands of a large segment of the public for political, economic, or social change.

Socialism A political ideology based on strong support for economic and social equality. Socialists traditionally envisioned a society in which major businesses were taken over by the government or by employee cooperatives.

Socioeconomic Status The value assigned to a person due to occupation or income. An upper-class person, for example, has high socioeconomic status.

Soft Money Campaign contributions unregulated by federal or state law, usually given to parties and party committees to help fund general party activities.

Solidary Incentive A reason or motive that follows from the desire to associate with others and to share with others a particular interest or hobby.

Sound Bite A brief, memorable comment that can easily be fit into news broadcasts.

Soviet Bloc The Soviet Union and the Eastern European countries that installed Communist regimes after World War II and were dominated by the Soviet Union.

Speaker of the House The presiding officer in the House of Representatives. The Speaker is always a member of the majority party and is the most powerful and influential member of the House.

Special District A local government that provides services to a jurisdiction that are not provided by general-purpose governments. Examples are municipal utility districts, hospital authorities, and transit authorities.

Special Session Any legislative session that is not specifically scheduled by the constitution or by statute. In some states, the legislature may call itself into special session, but in Texas only the governor may call the legislature into special session.

Spin An interpretation of campaign events or election results that is favorable to the candidate's campaign strategy.

Spindletop A major oil discovery in 1901 near Beaumont that began the industrialization of Texas.

Spin Doctor A political campaign adviser who tries to convince journalists of the truth of a particular interpretation of events.

Splinter Party A new party formed by a dissident faction within a major political party. Often, splinter parties have emerged when a particular personality was at odds with the major party.

Split-Ticket Voting Voting for candidates of two or more parties for different offices, such as voting for a Republican presidential candidate and a Democratic congressional candidate.

Spoils System The awarding of government jobs to political supporters and friends.

Spring Review The annual process in which the Office of Management and Budget requires federal agencies to review their programs, activities, and goals and submit their requests for funding for the next fiscal year.

Standing Committee A permanent committee in the House or Senate that considers bills within a certain subject area.

Stare Decisis To stand on decided cases; the judicial policy of following precedents established by past decisions.

State A group of people occupying a specific area and organized under one government; may be either a nation or a subunit of a nation.

State Central Committee The principal organized structure of each political party within each state. This committee is responsible for carrying out policy decisions of the party's state convention.

State of the Union Message An annual message to Congress in which the president proposes a legislative program. The message is addressed not only to Congress but also to the American people and to the world.

Statute-Like Details Detailed state constitutional provisions characterized by the narrow scope usually found in statutory law.

Statutory Law Law passed by legislatures and eventually compiled in law codes.

Statutory Power A power created for the president through laws enacted by Congress.

Straight-Ticket Voting Voting exclusively for the candidates of one party.

Strategic Arms Limitation Treaty (SALT I) A treaty between the United States and the Soviet Union to stabilize the nuclear arms competition between the two countries. SALT I talks began in 1969, and agreements were signed on May 26, 1972.

Strict Construction A judicial philosophy that looks to the "letter of the law" when interpreting the Constitution or a particular statute.

Strong-Mayor System A form of municipal government in which substantial authority (such as authority over appointments and the budget) is lodged in the office of the mayor, who is elected in a citywide election.

Subsidies Grants or special tax exemptions provided by the government to individuals or businesses in the private sector.

Suffrage The right to vote; the franchise.

Sunset Advisory Commission In Texas, a body that periodically evaluates most government agencies and departments. The commission may recommend the restructuring, abolition, or alteration of the jurisdiction of an agency.

Sunset Legislation Laws requiring that existing programs be reviewed regularly for their effectiveness and be terminated unless specifically extended as a result of these reviews.

Superdelegate A party leader or elected official who is given the right to vote at the party's national convention. Superdelegates are not elected at the state level.

Supremacy Clause The constitutional provision that makes the Constitution and federal laws superior to all conflicting state and local laws.

Supremacy Doctrine A doctrine that asserts the priority of national law over state laws. This principle is rooted in Article VI of the Constitution, which provides that the Constitution, the laws passed by the national government under its constitutional powers, and all treaties constitute the supreme law of the land.

Suspension of the Rule Setting aside of the rules of a legislative body so that another set of rules can be used.

Swing Voters Voters who frequently swing their support from one party to another.

Symbolic Speech Expression made through articles of clothing, gestures, movements, and other forms of nonverbal conduct. Symbolic speech is given substantial protection by the courts.

T

Table In a legislature or similar body, to cease action on a particular measure. A motion to table is not debatable.

Tagging In the Texas Senate, a rule that allows a senator to halt a standing committee's consideration of a bill for 48 hours.

Tax Assessor-Collector In Texas, a county financial officer whose responsibilities include collecting county taxes or fees and registering voters.

Technical Assistance The practice of sending experts in such areas as agriculture, engineering, or business to aid other nations.

Tenant Farmer A farmer who does not own the land that he or she farms but rents it from a landowner.

Term Limit A restriction on the number of times a person can be elected to a particular office.

Texas Ethics Commission A constitutionally authorized body that has the power to investigate ethics violations and to penalize violators of Texas ethics laws.

Texas Register A publication that contains all official notices of the Texas state government and some notices of regional bodies. It is found in all university libraries and large municipal libraries in Texas.

Theocracy Literally, rule by God or the gods; in practice, rule by religious leaders, typically self-appointed.

Third Party A political party other than the two major political parties (Republican and Democratic).

Threat to Veto An informal power by which a state governor (or the U.S. president) threatens to veto legislation so as to affect the content of the legislation while it is still in the legislature.

Tidelands An area that extends three leagues (about 10 miles) off the Texas coast. The tidelands controversy developed when offshore oil was discovered and the federal government contended that Texas's jurisdiction extended only three miles out from the coast.

Tight Monetary Policy Monetary policy that makes credit expensive in an effort to slow the economy.

Tipping A phenomenon that occurs when a group that is becoming more numerous over time grows large enough to change the political balance in a district, state, or country.

Tort Reform In civil law, a tort is a wrong or injury (other than a breach of contract). Tort reform is an effort to limit liability in tort cases.

Totalitarian Regime A form of government that controls all aspects of the political and social life of a nation.

Tracking Poll A poll taken on a nearly daily basis as election day approaches.

Treasuries U.S. Treasury securities—bills, notes, and bonds. Debt issued by the federal government.

Trial Court The court in which most cases begin.

Truman Doctrine The policy adopted by President Harry Truman in 1947 to halt Communist expansion in southeastern Europe.

Trustee A legislator who acts according to her or his conscience and the broad interests of the entire society.

Twelfth Amendment Adopted in 1804, an amendment to the Constitution that requires the separate election of the president and vice president by the electoral college.

Twenty-fifth Amendment A 1967 amendment to the Constitution that establishes procedures for filling presidential and vice-presidential vacancies and makes provisions for presidential incapacity.

Two-Party System A political system in which only two parties have a reasonable chance of winning.

U

Umbrella Organization An organization created by interest groups to promote common goals. Several interest groups may choose this mechanism to coordinate their efforts to influence government when they share the same policy goals. The umbrella organization may be temporary or permanent.

Unanimous Opinion A court opinion or determination on which all judges agree.

Unemployment The inability of those who are in the labor force to find a job; the number of those in the labor force actively looking for a job, but unable to find one.

Unfunded Mandate A requirement imposed on a lower level of government by a higher level of government. The requirement is not accompanied by the funds to pay for the resulting expenses.

Unicameral Legislature A legislature with only one legislative chamber, as opposed to a bicameral (two-chamber) legislature, such as the U.S. Congress. Today, Nebraska is the only state in the Union with a unicameral legislature.

Unit Road System In Texas, a system that concentrates the day-to-day responsibilities of roads in the hands of a professional engineer rather than individual county commissioners. The engineer is ultimately responsible to the commissioners court.

Unit Rule A rule by which all of a state's electoral votes are cast for the presidential candidate receiving a plurality of the popular vote in that state.

Unitary System A centralized governmental system in which ultimate governmental authority rests in the hands of the national, or central, government.

Universal Health Insurance Any of several possible programs to provide health insurance to everyone in the country. The central government does not necessarily provide the insurance itself, but may subsidize the purchase of insurance from private insurance companies.

Universal Suffrage The right of all adults to vote for their representatives.

User Fee A charge paid by an individual who receives a particular government service, such as water provision or garbage collection.

V

The Valley (of the Rio Grande) An area along the Texas side of the Rio Grande known for its production of citrus fruits.

Veto Message The president's formal explanation of a veto when legislation is returned to Congress.

Vote-Eligible Population (VEP) The total number of persons actually eligible to cast a ballot, excluding noncitizens, felons, and other ineligible persons but including citizens who are temporarily abroad (and who may vote absentee).

Voter Turnout The percentage of citizens taking part in the election process; the number of eligible voters that actually "turn out" on election day to cast their ballots.

Voting-Age Population (VAP) The total number of persons in the United States or a state who are 18 years of age or older, regardless of citizenship, military status, felony conviction, or mental state.

W

War Powers Resolution A law passed in 1973 spelling out the conditions under which the president can commit troops without congressional approval.

Washington Community Indiviuals regularly involved with politics in Washington, D.C.

Watergate Break-In The 1972 illegal entry into the Democratic National Committee offices by participants in President Richard Nixon's reelection campaign.

Weak-Mayor System A form of municipal government in which an elected mayor and city council, often along with other elected officers, share administrative responsibilities.

Weberian Model A model of bureaucracy developed by the German sociologist Max Weber, who viewed bureaucracies as rational, hierarchical organizations in which decisions are based on logical reasoning.

Whig Party A major party in the United States during the first half of the nineteenth century, formally established in 1836. The Whig Party was anti-Jackson and represented a variety of regional interests.

Whip A member of Congress who aids the majority or minority leader of the House or the Senate.

Whistleblower Someone who brings to public attention gross governmental inefficiency or an illegal action.

White House Office The personal office of the president, which tends to presidential political needs and manages the media.

White Primary A state primary election that restricts voting to whites only; outlawed by the Supreme Court in 1944.

Winter Garden An area of South Texas known for its vegetable production.

Writ of *Certiorari* An order issued by a higher court to a lower court to send up the record of a case for review.

Writ of *Habeas Corpus* *Habeas corpus* means, literally, "you have the body." A writ of *habeas corpus* is an order that requires jailers to bring a prisoner before a court or a judge and explain why the person is being held.

Z

Zero-based Budgeting A budgeting practice in which existing programs are evaluated as if they were new programs rather than on the basis of past levels of funding.

INDEX

G

J

M

N

Q

R

T